TWELFTH EDITION

Our Sexuality

Robert Crooks | Karla Baur

WADSWORTH
CENGAGE Learning

Australia • Brazil • Canada • Mexico • Singapore • Spain • United Kingdom • United States

WADSWORTH
CENGAGE Learning·

Our Sexuality, **Twelfth Edition**
Robert Crooks and Karla Baur

Publisher: Jon-David Hague

Executive Editor: Jaime Perkins

Developmental Editors: Tangelique Williams
    and Thomas Finn

Assistant Editor: Audrey Espey

Editorial Assistant: Audrey Espey

Media Editor: Jasmin Tokatlian

Senior Brand Manager: Elisabeth Rhoden

Market Development Manager: Christine Sosa

Content Project Manager: Pat Waldo

Art Director: Vernon Boes

Manufacturing Planner: Karen Hunt

Rights Acquisitions Specialist: Dean Dauphinais

Production Service: Lachina Publishing Services

Photo Researcher: Wendy Granger, BSG

Text Researcher: Pablo D'Stair

Copy Editor: Lachina Publishing Services

Art Editor: Lachina Publishing Services

Illustrator: Lachina Publishing Services

Text Designer: Lisa Buckley

Cover Image Credit: Paul D. Van Hoy II/Getty
    Images

Cover designer: Irene Morris

Compositor: Lachina Publishing Services

For product information and technology assistance, contact us at
Cengage Learning Customer & Sales Support, 1-800-354-9706

For permission to use material from this text or product, submit all requests online at **www.cengage.com/permissions**
Further permissions questions can be emailed to
permissionrequest@cengage.com

Library of Congress Control Number: 2012943396

Student Edition:
ISBN-13: 978-1-133-94336-5
ISBN-10: 1-133-94336-5

Paper Edition:
ISBN-13: 978-1-133-94341-9
ISBN-10: 1-133-94341-1

Loose-leaf Edition:
ISBN-13: 978-1-133-94338-9
ISBN-10: 1-133-94338-1

Wadsworth Cengage Learning
20 Davis Drive
Belmont, CA 94002-3098
USA

Cengage Learning is a leading provider of customized learning solutions with office locations around the globe, including Singapore, the United Kingdom, Australia, Mexico, Brazil, and Japan. Locate your local office at **www.cengage.com/global**.

Cengage Learning products are represented in Canada by Nelson Education, Ltd.

To learn more about Wadsworth, visit **www.cengage.com/wadsworth**

Purchase any of our products at your local college store or at our preferred online store **www.cengagebrain.com**

Printed in Canada
2 3 4 5 16 15 14 13

For our loving spouses, Sami Tucker and Jim Hicks, and the staff of IT HELPS Kenya. IT HELPS is a tax exempt public charity that has previously conducted an HIV/AIDS intervention program in the southeastern interior of Kenya and is now implementing a new project in the Ukunda south coast region of Kenya.

Photos courtesy of Robert Crooks

IT HELPS peer educators conducting HIV/AIDS prevention workshops for groups comprised of either students or members of the adult community.

About the Authors

The integration of psychological, social, and biological components of human sexuality in this text is facilitated by the blending of the authors' academic and professional backgrounds.

ROBERT CROOKS has a Ph.D. in psychology. His graduate training stressed clinical and physiological psychology. In addition, he has considerable background in sociology, which served as his minor throughout his graduate training. His involvement with teaching human sexuality classes at the university, college, and medical school levels spans over two decades. Recently Bob and his wife, Sami Tucker, have been involved in the establishment and implementation of another HIV/AIDS intervention program in coastal Kenya. Over the previous 10 years, their work with this project includes designing a research strategy for assessing behavior change, developing a peer educator-based educational strategy, and conducting training sessions for Kenyan peer educator staff. In the fall of 2009, Bob and Sami initiated another HIV/AIDS intervention program on the coast of Kenya. Over the previous seven years they have traveled extensively in Africa and have devoted many months to their evolving HIV/AIDS prevention projects.

KARLA BAUR has a master's degree in social work; her advanced academic work stressed clinical training. She is a licensed clinical social worker in private practice, specializing in couples and sex therapy. Karla has been certified as a sex educator, therapist, and sex therapy supervisor by the American Association of Sex Educators, Counselors, and Therapists. She has instructed sexuality classes at a medical school and several colleges and universities and has provided clinical training for other mental health professionals. Karla has also found a way to combine her clinical skills with her love of horses by providing performance enhancement training for equestrians. Furthermore, Karla has been involved in the HIV/AIDS program in Kenya, and in 2004 she joined Bob and Sami to train peer educators.

The authors have a combined total of over 70 years of teaching, counseling, and research in the field of sexology. Together they taught college sexuality courses for a number of years. They present workshops and guest lectures to a wide variety of professional and community groups, and they counsel individuals, couples, and families on sexual concerns. Their combined teaching, clinical, and research experiences, together with their graduate training, have provided them with an appreciation and sensitive understanding of the highly complex and personal nature of human sexuality.

It is the authors' belief that a truly sensitive understanding of our sexuality must be grounded in both the female and the male perspectives and experiences. In this sense, their courses, their students, and this text have benefited from a well-balanced perception and a deep appreciation of human sexual behavior.

Brief Contents

Contents

LWA/Stephen Welstead/Blend Images/age fotostock

3 Female Sexual Anatomy and Physiology 49

Jack Dagley Photography/Shutterstock.com

Stefano Oppo/The Image Bank/Getty Images

Marin/PhotoAlto Agency RF/Jupiterimages

8 Sexual Behaviors 225

© Ron Royals/Corbis

9 Sexual Orientations 248

10 Contraception 278

11 Conceiving Children: Process and Choice 310

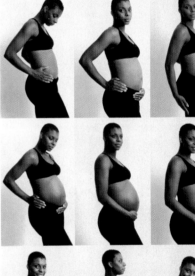

Michael Krasowitz/Getty Images

© Paul Steel

12 Sexuality During Childhood and Adolescence 342

13 Sexuality and the Adult Years 373

Robert Nicholas/OJO Images/Getty Images

14 Sexual Difficulties and Solutions 397

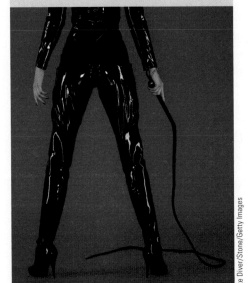

Mike Diver/Stone/Getty Images

AP Photo/Michael Manning

Special Interest Features

SEX AND POLITICS Boxes

This feature, added in the 10th edition, is designed to illustrate the significant influence of politics on sexual issues. We utilize this feature to broaden understanding of the influence on sexuality by advocacy groups and government bodies—local, state, federal, and international. We present a range of topics, where sex and politics meet, including:

- Sex Research Under Siege
- "Intactivists" Attempt to Criminalize Infant Circumcision in San Francisco
- Goals of the Gay Rights Movement
- The Power of Pro-Life Anti-Contraception Politics
- Opposition to Emergency Contraception
- Abortion Restrictions at the State Level
- Antigay Harassment/Bullying of Teenagers
- U.S. Congress Considering Measures to Reduce Teen Pregnancy Prevention Programs
- Abstinence-Only Sex Education
- Marriage in Crises
- Legal Marriage for Same-Sex Couples?
- Arguments Against and for Mandatory HPV Vaccination
- U.S. Policy During the Bush Administration Reduced Condom Promotion in Africa
- Pornography as Social Criticism
- Contemporary Censorship and Free Speech Controversies

LET'S TALK ABOUT IT Boxes

These boxes, integrated throughout the text, provide practical advice on how to communicate effectively about sensitive sexual and relationship issues. Content includes:

- Respectful Communication With a Transsexual or Transgendered Individual
- A Child/Parent Sex Talk
- Coping With the Green-Eyed Monster
- The Benefits of Affectionate Communication
- Guidelines for Coming Out to Friends
- Don't Go Inside Without Your Rubbers On
- Telling a Partner (about possible transmission of an STI)
- Helping a Partner or Friend Recover From Rape

SPOTLIGHT ON RESEARCH Boxes

These boxes highlight recent important research studies. Examples of this feature include:

- Cross-Cultural Sex Differences in Personality Traits
- Monitoring Brain Function During Sexual Arousal With Functional Magnetic Resonance Imaging
- Monitoring Genital Changes During Sexual Arousal With Functional Magnetic Resonance Imaging
- Sex Differences in Sex Drive
- Differences in Men's and Women's Desire for Sexual Variety
- Normative Sexual Behavior in Children: A Contemporary Sample
- Circumcision as a Strategy for Preventing HIV Infection

YOUR SEXUAL HEALTH Boxes and Marginal Icons

This feature highlights and emphasizes important sexual health matters. Boxes include:

- Genital Self-Exam for Women
- Kegel Exercises
- How to Examine Your Breasts
- Male Genital Self-Examination
- Which Contraception Method Is Best for You?
- Folic Acid and Fetal Development
- Know Your Partner
- Index of Sexual Satisfaction
- Dealing With Rape and Attempted Rape

Theme Index

Coverage of Cultural Diversity

Preface

Our Sexuality, now in its twelfth edition, provides students with an engaging, personally relevant, politically astute, and academically sound introduction to human sexuality. The text's comprehensive integration of biological, psychological, behavioral, cultural, and political aspects of sexuality has been consistently well received in each previous edition.

New in This Edition

- More than 1,000 new citations, reflecting the most recent research in sexology, have been added. Most of these citations are current, drawn from data published in 2011 and 2012.
- A wealth of new and significantly updated information in every chapter, highlights of which are described below:

Chapter 1: Perspectives on Sexuality

- Increase in interracial dating.
- Increasing controversy about the laws and meaning of Muslim women wearing headscarves.
- New research about correlation between gender equality and similarity of male/female sexual attitudes and behaviors.
- Updates on the media and its various impacts on sexual attitudes and behaviors.

Chapter 2: Sex Research: Methods and Problems

- Updates pertaining to the Sex and Politics box, "Sex Research Under Siege."
- Discussion of one of the largest nationally representative sexual health and behavior surveys to date, the National Survey of Sexual Health and Behavior (NSSHB).

Chapter 3: Female Sexual Anatomy and Physiology

- New resources for the appreciation of vulva diversity.
- New section on genital alteration.
- New figure of the complexity of the clitoral complex.
- Expanded information on the G-spot.
- Updated information on female genital cutting.
- Expanded information about ovulation and sexual response.
- Research updates on hormone replacement after menopause.

Chapter 4: Male Sexual Anatomy and Physiology

- Updated discussion of circumcision including a new Sex and Politics box detailing efforts to ban circumcision in San Francisco.
- Major revision and updates of material dealing with prostate cancer with integration of recent research findings.
- Discussion of new diagnostic tools that may aid in assessing the aggressiveness of prostate cancer.

Chapter 5: Gender Issues

- Inclusion of data from a new national study pertaining to the performance of males and females on mathematics tests and inclination to enter a math intensive professional occupation
- New information about the relationship between endorsing traditional gender roles and attitudes about what constitutes and ideal partner of the other sex.
- New Sex and Politics box discussing how the religious right has influenced American politics.
- New information regarding parental influence on the development of gender roles, especially as related to the gendered division of household labor.

- Updated discussion of the impact of children's books on the development of gender roles.

Chapter 6: Sexual Arousal and Response

- Expanded discussion of aphrodisiacs and anaphrodisiacs.
- Updated discussion of hormones and sexual behavior.
- Discussion of findings from the NSSHB survey pertaining to human sexual response, especially female orgasm.
- New information about the use of MRI technology in Grafenberg Spot research.
- Latest information about genital cosmetic surgery.
- NSSHB findings regarding multiple orgasms.

Chapter 7: Love and Communication in Intimate Relationships

- New research on the link between feelings of being in love and the release of neurotransmitters and other brain chemicals.
- Recent research on the relationship between use of hormonal contraceptives and women's attractiveness to potential love/sex partners.
- Latest research on partner choice and race.
- Expanded discussion of adult intimate relationships as an attachment process.
- Latest research findings on friends with benefits relationships (FWBRs).
- Revised and updated information pertaining to Internet relationships.

Chapter 8: Sexual Behaviors

- New research on religiosity and sexual fantasy.
- Updated data on attitudes toward and patterns of masturbation.
- Detailed information about G-spot stimulation during self and manual stimulation and intercourse, including a new drawing of the "tailgate" position.
- New research on how people define "real sex."
- New data on incidence of anal sex.

Chapter 9: Sexual Orientations

- Expanded definition of sexual orientation.
- Increased emphasis on sexual orientation as a multidimensional phenomenon.
- Inclusion of new terms, "heteroflexibility" and "homoflexibility."
- New table on self-identified sexual orientation.
- New research about asexuality.
- Information about the unique arousal pattern of bisexual men.
- New research about differences in beliefs about the underlying sexual orientation of bisexual men versus women.

- New section on "performative bisexuality."
- New Spotlight on Research box about the inconsistent parameters that research studies use to define homosexuality.
- Current data on belief whether or not homosexuality is innate.
- New section on the separation of same-sex behavior and self-identification as homosexual among men in the Pastun tribe of Afganistan.
- Updates on global trends in persecution or acceptance of homosexuality.
- Updates and controversies on "conversion therapy."
- Updates on continuing increases of acceptance of homosexuality in the United States.
- Reversal of "Don't ask, don't tell."
- Detailed discussion on gay marriage and its ever-increasing support from the general public.
- Updated information about greater inclusion of gay, lesbian, and bisexual characters on television.
- Many examples of the detrimental effect of antigay prejudice.
- Updated information on the increase in adoption by same-sex couples.

Chapter 10: Contraception

- New data about teen use of contraceptives.
- Increased political activism to reduce access to contraception.
- New regulations requiring private health insurance to cover contraceptives.
- Updated data on need for increased worldwide contraceptive use.
- Updated information on all methods of contraception.
- Compensation for victims of forced sterilizations.

Chapter 11: Conceiving Children: Process and Choice

- Increasing rates of women choosing not to have children.
- Updated information about sex selection abortions and infanticide of females.
- Increase in twin births from assisted reproductive technologies and women having children later in life.
- New statistics on rates of unplanned pregnancy and abortion in United States and across the globe.
- New data on the characteristics and context of women who are more likely to have abortions after 13 weeks of pregnancy.
- Updated information on anti-abortion political activism.
- Updated statistics on worldwide maternal mortality.
- Increase in rate of caesarean section in the United States.
- More data about benefits of breastfeeding.

Chapter 12: Sexuality During Childhood and Adolescence

- Findings from the NSSHB survey regarding adolescent sexual behavior.
- Recent research findings on the predictive relationship between oral and vaginal sex.
- Addition of a new section dealing with the emerging social phenomenon of adolescent sexting.
- Inclusion of the latest research findings on adolescent coitus.
- Significantly updated and expanded discussion of adolescents online.
- A new unit on adolescent multi-person sex (MPS).
- A new Sex and Politics box on antigay harassment/bullying of teenagers.
- Expanded and updated section dealing with adolescent pregnancy.
- A new Sex and Politics box focusing on steps by the U.S. Congress to reduce teen pregnancy.
- Expanded discussion of the use of contraceptives by teenagers, includlng adolescents' access to emergency contraception (EC).
- Discussion of factors that have influenced a reduction in school-based abstinence-only sex education.

Chapter 13: Sexuality and the Adult Years

- Latest data on the increase in number of single adults.
- Male/female similarities and differences in reactions to non-committed sexual relationships.
- Characteristics of individuals who cohabit.
- Update on decrease in percentage of U.S. households of married couples.
- New information about forced marriage.
- New section on child marriage.
- Current statistics on the increase of the rates of and the public approval for interracial marriage.
- New data on extramarital relationships.
- Differences in reasons for extramarital affairs between men and women.
- The relationship between power and likelihood of affairs.
- New data about women's sex lives improving later in life.
- Gender differences in likelihood of orgasm with relationship and non-relationship partners.
- New data about the importance of tenderness for men compared to women.

Chapter 14: Sexual Difficulties and Solutions

- Expanded information about faking orgasm.
- New DSM5 name for vaginal pain with intercourse.
- Impact of sexual guilt on sexual function.
- Differences in body image concerns between groups of women.
- Male sexual functioning with on-going as compared to non-relationship partners.

Chapter 15: Sexually Transmitted Infections

- Major updating throughout the chapter.
- Latest data pertaining to the incidence and treatment of sexually transmitted infections.
- Discussion of oral sex, HPV transmission, and throat cancer.
- Updated Sex and Politics box dealing with HPV vaccination.
- New information on the treatment of hepatitis C infections.
- Latest incidence data on HIV/AIDS in the United States and worldwide.
- Discussion of the impact of the economic downturn on the treatment of HIV/AIDS.
- Discussion of immunosenescence, a form of premature aging, as a result of HAART treatment of HIV/AIDS.
- Discussion of recent evidence indicating that treating HIV-infected people with antiretroviral medications at an early stage of the disease can reduce the likelihood of transmitting HIV to an uninfected partner.
- Significantly revised and updated section on the search for an HIV/AIDS vaccine.
- New information about the role of pre-exposure prophylaxis (PrEP) in reducing the transmission of HIV.
- New findings about the search for effective microbicides.

Chapter 16: Atypical Sexual Behavior

- Updating throughout chapter.
- Expanded and updated discussion of video voyeurism.

Chapter 17: Sexual Coercion

- Inclusion of latest rape incidence statistics and updated discussion of this topic.
- Detailed discussion of the FBI's revised definition of rape and its impact on our understanding of this coercive behavior.
- Major expansion of the impact of rape on survivors, with emphasis on the tendency for college survivors of rape to be victimized again due in large part to a lack of institutional response to allegations of sexual assault.
- Addition of information about the rape and sexual assault of Jewish women during the Holocaust.
- Updated section on rape and sexual assault of males.

- Expanded discussion of factors that lead to the underreporting of child sexual abuse.
- Addition of a discussion of sexual abuse by members of the clergy with emphasis on a report by the Catholic Church on abuse by priests and reactions to same.
- Revised and expanded discussion of pedophiles in cyberspace.
- Significantly updated discussion of sexual harassment on the job and in academic settings.
- A new section dealing with cyberstalking.

Chapter 18: Sex for Sale

- Legal dilemmas dealing with sexting.
- Peter Lenk's "Global Players" included in pornography as social criticism.
- Updates on revenues from pornography.
- New table of countries that spend the most on pornography.
- Expanded section of ways pornography can be harmful to individuals and couples.
- Emphasis on pornography as poor sex education.
- Updated information about call girls.
- Increase in sex workers advertising on the Internet and Facebook.
- Increased information on recruitment and trafficking of teenagers into sex work in the United States.
- New research about customers of sex workers.
- New section about the glorification of pimps in the United States.
- Updated information about legal status of sex work and prosecution of customers.

Other Continuing Features

- **A personal approach.** Users of the text have responded favorably to our attempts to make the subject human and personal, and in this twelfth edition we have retained and strengthened the elements that contributed to this approach and expanded coverage of the impact that political decisions and policies have on individuals and groups.
- **Authors' files.** One of the most popular features of *Our Sexuality* has been the incorporation of voices of real people through the use of authors' files. These quotations—taken from the experiences and observations of students, clients, and colleagues—are woven into the text but set apart in conversation bubbles. Each chapter opens with an authors' file quotation illustrating an important concept pertinent to that chapter.
- **Nonjudgmental perspective.** Consistent with our personal focus, we have avoided a prescriptive stance on most issues introduced in the text. We have attempted to provide information in a sensitive, nonsexist, inclusive, nonjudgemental manner that assumes the reader is best qualified to determine what is most valid and applicable in her or his life.

- **Psychosocial orientation.** We focus on the roles of psychological and social factors in human expression, reflecting our belief that human sexuality is governed more by psychological factors than by biological determinants. At the same time, we provide the reader with a solid basis in the anatomy and physiology of human sexuality and explore new research pertaining to the interplay of biology, psychology, and social learning.
- **Critical Thinking questions**, some of which are new to this edition, appear in the margin. These questions are designed to help students apply their knowledge and experience while developing their own outlook. Each question encourages students to stop and think about what they are reading, in an attempt to facilitate higher-order processing of information and learning.
- **Sexuality and Diversity discussions**, integrated throughout the text, deal with topics such as ethnic variations in gender roles, female genital cutting, cultural variations in sexual arousal, ethnic variations in intimate communication, cross-cultural issues in preselecting a baby's sex, the clash between sex therapy practices and cultural values, AIDS in Africa, and cultural values that punish women who have been raped. Many of these Sexuality and Diversity discussions have been revised, expanded, and updated for the twelfth edition.
- **At a Glance tables** designed to present important information in summary form. Examples of this feature include tables that summarize sex research methods, factors involved in typical and atypical prenatal differentiation, major physiological changes during the sexual response cycle, information to consider when choosing a birth control method, and features of common sexually transmitted infections.
- **Pedagogy.** Individuals learn in different ways. We therefore provide a variety of pedagogical aids to be used as the student chooses. Each chapter opens with an outline of the major topic headings, complete with **chapter opening questions** that focus attention on important topics. **Key words** are boldfaced within the text, and a pronunciation guide follows selected key words. A **running glossary** in the text margin provides a helpful learning tool. Each chapter concludes with a **Summary** in outline form for student reference, annotated **Suggested Readings**, and annotated **Web Resources**. A complete **Glossary** as well as a complete **Bibliography** are provided at the end of the book.

Integrated Teaching and Learning Aids

For Students

CourseMate

Cengage Learning's Psychology CourseMate brings course concepts to life with interactive learning, study, and exam preparation tools that support the printed textbook. Access an integrated eBook, learning tools including glossaries, flashcards, quizzes, videos, weblinks, and more in your Psychology CourseMate. Go to CengageBrain.com to register or purchase access.

For Instructors

The Safer Sex and Contraception Kit
(1-285-17722-9)

The kit is available to qualified adopters in the United States only. This kit is intended for classroom demonstrations of various forms of contraceptives. It includes the new O-ring, the patch, the diaphragm, contraceptive jelly, birth control pills, and more. A Virtual Safer Sex and Contraception Kit includes photos of all these devices and is available to all adopters on the Instructor's Resource CD-ROM in PowerPoint.

CourseMate

Cengage Learning's Psychology CourseMate brings course concepts to life with interactive learning, study, and exam preparation tools that support the printed textbook. CourseMate includes an integrated eBook, glossaries, flashcards, quizzes, videos, weblinks, and more—as well as EngagementTracker, a first-of-its-kind tool that monitors student engagement in the course. The accompanying instructor website, available through login.cengage.com, offers access to password-protected resources such as *an electronic version of the instructor's manual, test bank files, and PowerPoint® slides*. CourseMate can be bundled with the student text. Contact your Cengage sales representative for information on getting access to CourseMate.

WebTutor

Jumpstart your course with customizable, rich, text-specific content within your Course Management System. Whether you want to Web-enable your class or put an entire course online, WebTutor™ delivers. WebTutor™ offers a wide array of resources including access to the eBook, glossaries, flashcards, quizzes, videos, weblinks, and more.

PowerLecture™ With ExamView®
(1-285-17500-3)

PowerLecture instructor resources are a collection of book-specific lecture and class tools on CD or DVD. The fastest and easiest way to build powerful, customized media-rich lectures, PowerLecture assets include chapter-specific PowerPoint® presentations authored by Lindsy M. Jorgensen of University of Utah, images, animations and video, instructor manuals, test banks, useful web links, and more. PowerLecture media-teaching tools are an effective way to enhance the educational experience. ExamView offers a Quick Test Wizard and Online Test Wizard that guide you step by step through the process of creating tests, while its "what you see is what you get" interface allows you to see the test you are creating on the screen exactly as it will print or display online. JoinIn content (for use with most "clicker" systems) delivers instant classroom assessment and active learning. Take polls and attendance, quiz, and invite students to actively participate while they learn.

Instructor's Manual With Test Bank
(1-285-17499-0)

The Instructor's Manual and Test Bank (IMTB) contains a variety of resources to aid instructors in preparing and presenting text material in a manner that meets their personal preferences and course needs. It presents chapter-by-chapter suggestions and resources to enhance and facilitate learning. Helpful instructional materials, such as a sample syllabus and teaching techniques, will be included in an appendix. The test bank has been extensively revised and includes more than 100 questions per chapter, each indicating their level in Bloom's Taxonomy.

Acknowledgments

Upon completion of the twelfth edition of *Our Sexuality* we reflect on the enormous contributions of others to the quality and success of this textbook. We are indebted to the dedication and skills of the reviewers and professionals who have had a hand in this edition. We also remain indebted to our students who inspired our first edition.

Professors and specialty reviewers who lent their expertise at various stages in revising this and previous editions are listed on the following pages. Of all the members of the highly professional, competent, and supportive staff of Wadsworth who contributed to this and previous editions, Tangelique Williams-Grayer, whose superb organizational oversight and attention to detail effectively kept the revision process moving ahead through each of its many stages, and Thomas Finn, freelance developmental editor, was a pleasure to work with and he contributing many insights, some gleaned from his experiences in the classroom, that contributed positively to the twelfth revision. Our acquisitions editor, Jaime Perkins, effectively established the focus of the twelfth edition and supported the authors in their efforts. Editorial Assistant, Audrey Espey, competently took care of a myriad of details. Pat Waldo and Samen Iqbal, content production editors, efficiently managed the often complicated and hectic production schedule. Senior art director Vernon Boes, together with Lisa Buckley, managed the demanding job of developing the new design elements of this edition—which has turned out to be the authors' favorite design of any edition. Audrey Espey, assistant editor, adeptly managed the development of the excellent print supplements and Jasmin Tokatlian, media editor, lent her valuable expertise to make the media products meaningful assets to students and professors.

Several freelance professionals made indispensable contributions to the excellence of this edition. Chris Black and Dana Richards of Lachina Publishing Services provided production services in a highly accomplished and professional manner. We greatly appreciate Carolyn Crabtree for the exceptionally competent and stellar work she performed as copy editor on this edition. Research assistant Sami Tucker's broad knowledge of the research needs of this edition and her tenacious commitment to finding relevant information in the recent journal literature from a wide range of academic disciplines was a key component in the academic excellence of *Our Sexuality*. Karla would like to thank Jim Hicks for his patient and generous ongoing computer assistance, which greatly expedited this revision.

We also appreciate the outstanding marketing team at Wadsworth that developed creative and effective promotional material for this edition. We offer special thanks to Chris Sosa, our marketing manager, and Angeline Low, marketing associate.

We would like to extend our thanks to the many reviewers who provided guidance, support, and insight for the current edition:

Kenneth Walters
SUNY, Oneonta

Rosemary Cogan
Texas Tech University

Sorah Dubitsky
Florida International University

Andrea Zabel
Midland College

Kathy Erickson
Pima Community College

Chuck Tate
San Francisco State University

Jana Tiefenwerth
Stephen F. Austin State University

We also extend our continued thanks to reviewers of the previous eleven editions:

Suzy Horton
Mesa Community College

Pat Lefler
Bluegrass Community and Technical School

Dianne Kerr
Kent State University

Peggy Skinner
South Plains College

David Yarbrough
University of Louisiana at Lafayette

Marilyn Myerson
University of South Florida

Cheris Current
Walla Walla University

Jacob Pastoetter
President, German Society for Social Scientific Sexuality Research

Elizabeth Calamidas
Richard Stockton College

Mary Devitt
Jamestown College

Ann Stidham
Presbyterian College

Theodore Wagenaar
Miami University

Linda Zaitchik
Newbury College

Daniel Adame
Emory University

Sylvester Allred
Northern Arizona University

Malinde Althaus
University of Minnesota

Linda Anderson,
University of North Carolina

Veanne Anderson,
Indiana State University

Wayne Anderson
University of Missouri, Columbia

Ann Auleb
San Francisco State University

Janice Baldwin
University of California–Santa Barbara

Tommy Begay
University of Arizona

Jim Belcher
Valencia Community College

Betty Sue Benison
Texas Christian University

M. Betsy Bergen
Kansas State University

Thomas E. Billimek
San Antonio College

Linda Bilsborough
California State University–Chico

Jane Blackwell
Washington State University

John Blakemore
Monterey Peninsula College

Marvin J. Branstrom
Cañada College

Tom Britton, M.D.
Planned Parenthood, Portland, Oregon

Elizabeth Calamidas
Richard Stockton College

Anthony Cantrell
University of Colorado

Charles Carroll
Ball State University

Nick Chittester
Washington State University

Joan Cirone
California Polytechnic State University

Bruce Clear
The First Unitarian Church, Portland

David R. Cleveland
Honolulu Community College

Gretchen Clum
University of Missouri, St. Louis

Rosemary Cogan
Texas Tech University

Ellen Cole
Alaska Pacific University

Jeff Cornelius
New Mexico State University

Laurel Cox
Ventura College

John Creech
Collin Community College, Preston Ridge Campus

Susan Dalterio
University of Texas, San Antonio

Joseph Darden
Kean College

Deborah Davis
University of Nevada, Reno

Brenda M. DeVellis
University of North Carolina

Lewis Diana
Virginia Commonwealth University

Richard Dienstbier
University of Nebraska–Lincoln

Mary Doyle
Arizona State University

Beverly Drinnin
Des Moines Area Community College

Judy Drolet
Southern Illinois University, Carbondale

Andrea Parrot Eggleston
Cornell University

John P. Elia
San Francisco State University

Carol Ellison
Clinical Psychologist

Karen Eso
Bakers field College

Peter Fabian
Edgewood College

April Few
Virginia Poly and State University

Catherine Fitchen
Dawson College

Karen Lee Fontaine
Purdue University, Calumet

Rod Fowers
Highline Community College

Lin S. Fox
Kean College of New Jersey

Gene Fulton
University of Toledo

David W. Gallagher
Pima Community College

Carol Galletly
Ohio State University

Kenneth George
University of Pennsylvania

David A. Gershaw
Arizona Western College

Glen G. Gilbert
Portland State University

Brian A. Gladue
University of Cincinnati

Mike Godsey
College of Marin

Gordon Hammerle
Adrian College

Debra Hansen
College of the Sequoias

Stephen Harmon
University of Utah

Claudette Hastie-Beahrs
Clinical Social Worker

Pearl A. Hawe
New Mexico State University

Bob Hensley
Iowa State University

Graham Higgs
Columbia College

Timothy Hulsey
Southwest Texas State University

Rosemary Iconis
York College

Barbara Ilardi
University of Rochester

Thomas Johns
American River College

David Johnson
Portland State University

James A. Johnson
Sam Houston State University

Kathleen Kendall-Tackett
University of New Hampshire

Al Kielwasser
San Francisco State

Sally Klein
Dutchess Community College

Peggy Kleinplatz
University of Ottawa

Patricia B. Koch
Pennsylvania State University

Kris Koehne
University of Tennessee

Robin Kowalski
Western Carolina University

Virginia Kreisworth
San Diego State University

Eric Krenz
California State University–Fresno

Vickie Krenz
California State University–Fresno

Lauren Kuhn
Portland Community College

Luciana Lagana
California State University–Northridge

Miriam LeGare
California State University–Sacramento

Sandra Leiblum
University of Medicine and Dentistry/Robert Wood Johnson

Sanford Lopater
Christopher Newport University

Joseph LoPiccolo
University of Missouri

Laura Madson
New Mexico State University

Peter Maneno
Normandale College

Milton Mankoff
Queens College

Christel J. Manning
Hollins College

Jerald J. Marshall
University of Central Florida

Rhonda Martin
University of Tulsa

Donald Matlosz
California State University–Fresno

Leslie McBride
Portland State University

Deborah McDonald
New Mexico State University

Sue McKenzie
Dawson College

Brian McNaught
Gloucester, Massachusetts

Gilbert Meyer
Illinois Valley Community College

Deborah Miller
College of Charleston

John Money
Johns Hopkins University

Denis Moore
Honolulu Metropolitan Community Church

Charlene Muehlenhard
University of Kansas

Louis Munch
Ithaca College

Ronald Murdoff
San Joaquin Delta College

Kay Murphy
Oklahoma State University

James Nash
California Polytechnic State University

Jean L. Nash
Family Nurse Practitioner, Portland, Oregon

Teri Nicoll-Johnson
Modesto Junior College

William O'Donohue
University of Nevada, Reno

Roberta Ogletree
Southern Illinois University, Carbondale

Shirley Ogletree
Texas State University–San Marcos

Al Ono, M.D.
Obstetrician/Gynecologist

D. Kim Openshaw
Utah State University

Bruce Palmer
Washington State University

Monroe Pasternak
Diablo Valley College

Calvin D. Payne
University of Arizona

J. Mark Perrin
University of Wisconsin, River Falls

John W. Petras
Central Michigan University

Valerie Pinhas
Nassau Community College

Ollie Pocs
Illinois State University

Robert Pollack
University of Georgia

Benjamin G. Rader
University of Nebraska, Lincoln

Patty Reagan

University of Utah

Deborah Richardson

University of Georgia

Barbara Rienzo

University of Florida

Barbara Safriet

Lewis and Clark Law School

Nancy Salisbury, M.D.

Portland, Oregon

Sadie Sanders

University of Florida

Marga Sarriugarte

Portland Rape Victim Advocate Project

Dan Schrinsky, M.D.

Portland, Oregon

Cynthia Schuetz

San Francisco State University

Lois Shofer

Essex Community College

Jennifer Siciliani

University of Missouri–St. Louis

Sherman K. Sowby

California State University–Fresno

Lee Spencer

Arizona State University

Susan Sprecher

Illinois State University

Howard Starr

Austin College

Wendy Stock

Texas A&M University

Diana Taylor

Oregon Health Sciences University

Veronica Tonay

University of California–Santa Cruz

Perry Treadwell

Decatur, Georgia

Thomas Tutko

San Jose State University

James E. Urban

Kansas State University

Robert Valois

University of South Carolina

Jaye F. Van Kirk

San Diego Mesa College

Peter Vennewitz

Portland Planned Parenthood

Margaret Vernallis

California State University, Northridge

John P. Vincent

University of Houston

Laurie Volm

Lake Grove Women's Clinic, Tualatin, Oregon

David Ward

Arkansas Tech

Mary Ann Watson

Metropolitan State College of Denver

Paul Weikert

Grand Valley State University

Marianne Whatley

University of Wisconsin–Madison

Josephine Wilson

Wittenberg University

David Winchester, M.D.

Urologist

Deborah R. Winters

New Mexico State University

Michelle Wolf

San Francisco State

William Yarber

Indiana University

Prologue

Throughout this textbook we discuss sexual attitudes, ideals, and behaviors of the past and present. We highlight similarities and differences in the Western world and beyond and emphasize the controversies inherent in sexual issues.

Finding one's way through the complex and conflicting perspectives related to human sexuality is both a personal and a societal challenge. We would like to open *Our Sexuality* with the Declaration of Sexual Rights, adopted by the World Association of Sexology,* as possible unifying guidelines:

Sexuality is an integral part of the personality of every human being. Its full development depends upon the satisfaction of basic human needs such as the desire for contact, intimacy, emotional expression, pleasure, tenderness, and love.

Sexuality is constructed through the interaction between the individual and social structures. Full development of sexuality is essential for individual, interpersonal, and societal well-being.

Sexual rights are universal human rights based on the inherent freedom, dignity, and equality of all human beings. Since health is a fundamental human right, so must sexual health be a basic human right. In order to assure that human beings and societies develop healthy sexuality, the following sexual rights must be recognized, promoted, respected, and defended by all societies through all means. Sexual health is the result of an environment that recognizes, respects, and exercises these sexual rights:

1. **The right to sexual freedom.** Sexual freedom encompasses the possibility for individuals to express their full sexual potential. However, this excludes all forms of sexual coercion, exploitation, and abuse at any time and situations in life.

2. **The right to sexual autonomy, sexual integrity, and safety of the sexual body.** This right involves the ability to make autonomous decisions about one's sexual life within a context of one's own personal and social ethics. It also encompasses control and enjoyment of our own bodies free from torture, mutilation, and violence of any sort.

3. **The right to sexual privacy.** This involves the right for individual decisions and behaviors about intimacy as long as they do not intrude on the sexual rights of others.

4. **The right to sexual equity.** This refers to freedom from all forms of discrimination regardless of sex, gender, sexual orientation, age, race, social class, religion, or physical and emotional disability.

5. **The right to sexual pleasure.** Sexual pleasure, including autoeroticism, is a source of physical, psychological, intellectual, and spiritual well-being.

6. **The right to emotional sexual expression.** Sexual expression is more than erotic pleasure or sexual acts. Individuals have a right to express their sexuality through communication, touch, emotional expression, and love.

7. **The right to sexually associate freely.** This means the possibility to marry or not, to divorce, and to establish other types of responsible sexual associations.

8. **The right to make free and responsible reproductive choices.** This encompasses the right to decide whether or not to have children, the number and spacing of children, and the right to full access to the means of fertility regulation.

9. **The right to sexual information based upon scientific inquiry.** This right implies that sexual information should be generated through the process of unencumbered and yet scientifically ethical inquiry, and disseminated in appropriate ways at all societal levels.

10. **The right to comprehensive sexuality education.** This is a lifelong process from birth throughout the life cycle and should involve all social institutions.

11. **The right to sexual health care.** Sexual health care should be available for prevention and treatment of all sexual concerns, problems, and disorders.

*Originally declared at the 13th World Congress of Sexology, 1997, Valencia, Spain. Revised and approved by the General Assembly of the World Association for Sexology (WAS) on August 26, 1999, during the 14th World Congress of Sexology, Hong Kong, and People's Republic of China. Reprinted with permission.

Perspectives on Sexuality

Sexual Intelligence

The multiple dimensions of sexuality affect us throughout our lives, and most students take this course, at least in part, to enhance their understanding of themselves sexually and their ability to relate well in a sexual relationship. Understanding oneself sexually and having interpersonal sexual skills and integrity are two characteristics we consider to be part of **sexual intelligence**, and these abilities help us make responsible decisions about our sexual behavior based on our personal values.

sexual intelligence
Sexual intelligence involves self-understanding, interpersonal sexual skills, scientific knowledge, and consideration of the cultural context of sexuality.

Sexual intelligence also depends on having accurate scientific knowledge about sexuality. Sexual science is a relatively young field. However, great leaps in research-based knowledge over the last century allow us to know, for example, about what happens to our bodies during sexual arousal and how to enhance pleasure, about biological components to sexual orientation, and about how to best protect ourselves and others from sexually transmitted infections.

The fourth component of sexual intelligence is the critical consideration of the broader cultural and political contexts of sexual issues. As the authors of *Sexuality, Health, and Human Rights* state, "Sexuality cannot be understood in isolation from the social, political, and economic structures with which it is embedded—or without reference to cultural and ideological discourses that give it meaning" (Correa et al., 2008, p. 3). The website by Marty Klein, PhD, www.SexualIntelligence.org, is an excellent source for provocative articles that examine the sexual implications of current political and cultural issues.

When it comes to sexuality, the phrase "the personal is political" is apropos. For example, a woman's access to emergency contraception depends on her state's "conscience clause" law. Many states have laws that make it legal for pharmacists to refuse to fill a woman's prescription for emergency contraception if the pharmacists' personal beliefs oppose the use of such medication. Other states have laws that make the pharmacists' refusals illegal (Guttmacher Institute, 2011c; National Conference of State Legislatures, 2011a).

State laws that make abortion more difficult to obtain are perhaps the most volatile issue in which the personal is political in the United States. In 2011, states enacted significantly more provisions to restrict abortion than in any previous year, as shown in ▌ Figure 1.1 (Gold & Nash, 2012). We will discuss the specific restrictions further in Chapter 11. The most controversial laws require women to undergo an ultrasound or receive information on having an ultrasound prior to abortion. The ultrasound device

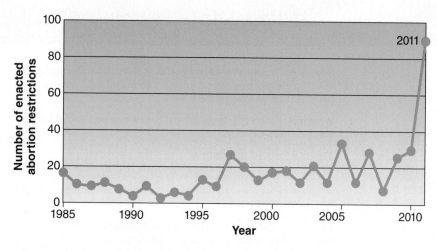

▌ **Figure 1.1** Enacted abortion restrictions by year.

SOURCE: Gold & Nash (2012) "Troubling Trend: More States Hostile to Middle Ground as Middle Ground Shrinks", *Guttmacher Policy Review*, 15, 14-20. Copyright © 2010 Guttmacher Institute. Reprinted by permission.

creates a blurry picture of the fetus and makes the sound of the fetal heartbeat audible when placed on the woman's belly or inserted inside her vagina. An ultrasound is not medically necessary for a safe abortion and increases its cost. The most extreme law came into effect in February 2012 when Texas began requiring women in that state to have a vaginal ultrasound 24 hours before the abortion procedure (Kristof, 2012; Nash, 2012). Republican Governor Rick Perry signed the bill into law and became the subject of *Doonesbury* comic strips that mocked Perry's support of the law (Stanford, 2012).

Throughout this text, we strive to provide opportunities to support and develop the four aspects of sexual intelligence for our readers, understanding that the final expert on your sexuality is *you*. We welcome you to this book and to your human sexuality class.

A Psychosocial Orientation

To assist you on your journey to greater sexual intelligence, this book takes a **psychosocial** approach, reflecting our view that psychological factors (emotions, attitudes, motivations) and social conditioning (the process by which we learn our social groups' expectations and norms) have a crucial impact on sexual attitudes, values, and behaviors. *Our Sexuality* also covers the crucial biological foundations of human sexuality, including the roles of hormones and the nervous system, the biological components of sexual orientation, theories about the role of genetic selection through thousands of years of human evolution, and the impact of specific genetic variables on an individual. The term *biopsychosocial* describes the integration of the three dimensions.

We may not always be aware of the extent to which our sexual attitudes and behaviors are strongly shaped by our society in general and by the particular social and cultural groups to which we belong (Laumann et al., 1994). The subtle ways we learn society's expectations regarding sexuality often lead us to assume that our behaviors or feelings are biologically innate, or natural. However, an examination of sexuality in other periods of Western history or in other societies (or even in different ethnic, socioeconomic, and age groups within our own society) reveals a broad range of acceptable behavior. What we regard as natural is clearly relative. For example, Margaret Mead's studies of Pacific Islanders from 1928 to 1949 found that Islander parents encouraged adolescents to be sexually active, demonstrating that expectations in the United States for adolescents to be chaste were by no means universal (Correa et al., 2008).

psychosocial
Refers to a combination of psychological and social factors.

The diversity of sexual expression throughout the world tends to mask a fundamental generalization that can be applied without exception to all social orders: All societies have rules regulating the conduct of sexual behavior. "Every society shapes, structures, and constrains the development and expression of sexuality in all of its members" (Beach, 1978, p. 116). Knowledge about the impact of culture and individual experience can make it easier to understand and make decisions about our own sexuality. Therefore, the major emphasis in *Our Sexuality* will be on the psychosocial aspects of human sexuality. We hope this approach serves as an asset to you throughout this course and throughout your lives.

Controversy and Diversity in Human Sexuality

Few topics generate as much attention and evoke as much pleasure and distress as the expression and control of human sexuality. In a sexuality class, students represent a diversity of ages, ethnic and religious backgrounds, life experiences, and liberal and conservative attitudes. Students' sexual experiences vary; most students who have had sexual experiences relate sexually only with the other sex,* while some seek sexual relationships with members of the same sex, and still others seek sexual contact with both sexes. Some students have had no sexual partners; others have had many partners; still others have had one partner; and some have had long-term partnerships and marriages.

Students' sexual choices and experiences also vary greatly in the degree of pleasure or distress that accompanies each situation. There are virtually no universals in sexual attitudes and experiences. With this in mind, we have attempted to bring an inclusive philosophy to our book. We begin this chapter with an overview of sexual practices and beliefs within the United States, the Islamic Middle East, and in China.

The United States

Our Sexuality explores the sexual attitudes and behaviors of people in many places around the globe, including the United States. Individuals of many ethnic and religious groups have made their homes in the United States, resulting in a wide range of sexual values and behaviors here. An ethnic group typically shares a common historical ancestry, religion, and language. We must also note that there is fluidity within the same ethnic group. Educational level and socioeconomic status are crucial in influencing sexual attitudes and behaviors. For instance, people with more education masturbate more often than less-educated people do (Kinsey et al., 1948; Michael et al., 1994). Another group-related difference has to do with oral–genital sex, which tends to be most common among young, college-educated Whites and least common among African Americans and individuals with less education (Michael et al., 1994).

It should be stressed that differences between groups are generalities, not universal truths; even within groups, great diversity exists (Agbayani-Siewert, 2004). For example, Asian Americans include the descendants of Chinese laborers brought to the United States in the 19th century to build railroads, refugees from the Vietnam and Korean wars, and individuals

The Museum of Sex opened its doors in New York City in September 2002 with an exhibit about the history of sex in that city. The museum's mission is to preserve and present the history and cultural significance of human sexuality.

*We use the term *other sex* instead of *opposite sex* to emphasize that men and women are more alike than opposite.

To expand your understanding of your attitudes and experiences related to sexuality, you might consider interviewing your parents about their experiences and beliefs if you have not already had this type of conversation.

"WHAT?!? Talk to *my* parents about *sex*?!?"

The following ideas and suggestions may make this endeavor seem less daunting.

"But my mom and dad would *never* answer any questions about sex."

You might be quite surprised by how open your parents are to your interest. The tell-the-children-when-they-ask parenting approach is common. Plus, you can test the waters first: Start with a low-key question, and if they respond with a direct or an indirect "I don't want to talk about it," stop the interview and change the subject.

The first step is to pick your interviewee.* You may feel most comfortable beginning with a grandparent or another relative instead of a parent. Find a time when you will not be rushed and a place that will be private. (Alternatively, you can use e-mail, a phone call, or a letter; you might also find that several shorter conversations work best for you.) A possible way to begin is, "I'm taking a human sexuality class this term, and it made me wonder if you had any sex education in school."

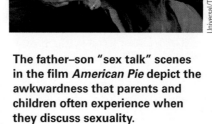

The father–son "sex talk" scenes in the film *American Pie* depict the awkwardness that parents and children often experience when they discuss sexuality.

Now you have broken the ice, and if you have had a good reception, you can ask specifics about your interviewee's sexual education. Be sure to encourage elaboration after each question, and don't rush to the next one: "What types of things did you learn about sex in school? What did you learn outside of school—from friends, your parents, books? What did your religion teach you? What sorts of bad information did you get about sex? What do you wish someone had told you?"

If things are rolling along, you might take a more personal bent: "How did you feel about your body changing from a child to a teenager? How quickly did you mature compared with your classmates? Did you know about menstruation/ejaculation before you experienced it? Who was your first crush? What do you wish you knew as a child or young adult that you know now? What do you think was easier, and what was more difficult, about sexuality for your generation than for mine?"

If your interview has come this far, you probably have a greater understanding and appreciation for the important aspects of your interviewee's life and, hopefully, of your own. So, who's next?

*Do not choose someone to interview unless there is a lot of goodwill in the relationship.

from Hong Kong, Japan, the Pacific islands, and many other Asian places (Brotto et al., 2005). Similarly, Muslims in the United States originate from more than 60 countries, and the Hispanic population comes from 22 different countries. Many of these subgroups within the Muslim, Asian American, and Hispanic populations consider themselves culturally distinct from one another. However, in spite of the intragroup differences, when research looks at patterns, some inter-group differences emerge. For example, Asian Americans, *on the whole*, have more conservative sexual attitudes and are less likely to engage in premarital intercourse than are Hispanic Americans, African Americans, or Americans of European descent (Benuto & Meana, 2008; Woo et al., 2011). Again, Hispanic culture, *on the whole*, often endorses sexual exploration for males but places a high value on chastity before marriage for women (Deardorff et al., 2010).

The degree of *acculturation*—that is, replacing traditional beliefs and behavior patterns with those of the dominant culture—also creates differences within subcultures. Recent immigrants tend to be close to the traditional values of their places of origin, but most individuals whose families have lived in North America for several generations are well assimilated. Films such as *My Big Fat Greek Wedding, American Desi*, and *Monsoon Wedding* depict the conflicts that can arise in immigrant families when the younger generation becomes more Americanized.

Stand-up comic and second-generation Korean American Margaret Cho shatters stereotypes of the submissive, reticent Asian female in her act. She takes provocative topics—such as bisexuality, what it would be like if men menstruated, and needing foreplay to have an orgasm—over the top.

A factor that blurs differences between ethnic groups is that a significant, and ever-increasing, proportion of the U.S. population is *multiracial*; that is, some people have descended from two or more racial groups. President Barack Obama is biracial, having an African father and a Caucasian mother.

Race and ethnicity are rarely simple, nonoverlapping classifications. "People all over the world have engaged in various degrees of mixing, particularly in the United States. . . . There is no way to look at every person and determine their exact racial background" (Wyatt, 1997, p. xv). The merging of ethnicity will likely increase over time in the United States because attitudes in each younger generation have become more accepting of interracial dating. About 50% of the general population has dated someone from a different racial group (Poulin & Rutter, 2011).

Sexual attitudes, behaviors, and beliefs about sexuality and gender often vary widely even within the same religious group. For example, although the traditional Roman Catholic view condemns all sexual activity that does not potentially lead to procreation, the views and behaviors of American Catholics vary greatly on issues such as contraception, abortion, and homosexuality, often disagreeing with the long-standing tenets of the Church. For example, 98% of sexually experienced Catholic women have used contraception (Jones & Drewke, 2011). Furthermore, fundamentalist Christians, who claim to interpret the Bible literally, differ greatly in their views about sexuality from Christians who do not ascribe to literal biblical interpretation (Ostling, 2000). For example, fundamentalist Christianity typically holds that sexual intercourse before marriage is sinful, and it may oppose the use of birth control, whereas liberal Christianity emphasizes caring in a relationship and appreciates how contraception can enhance sexual intimacy. Similarly, Orthodox Jews have much more conservative views regarding sexuality and gender roles than do Reform Jews. For example, Orthodox Judaism forbids sexual intercourse during menstruation, whereas Reform Judaism allows for individual preferences.

Barack Obama and his maternal grandparents lived together in Hawaii during most of his high school years. He is one of the many individuals in the United States who have multiracial and multiethnic families.

Fundamentalists—whether Christian, Muslim, or Jewish—are far more restrictive of sexual behavior and roles for men and women than are their more-liberal counterparts. Researchers have found that from "Afghanistan to Arkansas . . . the subordination of women is often a significant . . . objective" (Phillips, 2006, p. 370). A key desire of fundamentalists is to impose their own concept of truth on a diverse and plural world. Over the last decade, extreme fundamentalism in these religions has increased and has engaged in political activism in conflicts over sexual and gender-role issues, often following cultural traditions rather than religious teachings (Artyk, 2008; Correa et al., 2008).

These similarities and differences in sexual beliefs, values, and behaviors are part of the *psychosocial* orientation of this textbook.

The Islamic Middle East

Islam is the world's fastest-growing religion, and its followers are called Muslims. Islam predominates in the Middle East, yet it is present in many other parts of the world: One fifth of the world's population is Muslim, and about 2.6 million Muslims live in the United States (Hodge & Nadir, 2008; Pew Forum on Religion and Public Life, 2011). Muslim Americans are more affluent and integrated than are Muslim communities in other countries in the Western world. Their average education and income are on par with those of other groups in the United States, whereas in Europe their standard of living is lower than that of many Europeans (Miller, 2007).

Muslims adhere to the teachings of the prophet Muhammad (ca. 570–632 CE), which are recorded in the Qur'an. Muhammad opposed intercourse before marriage but valued intercourse within marriage as the highest good in human life, to be enjoyed by men and women alike; he encouraged husbands to be "slow and delaying" (Abbott, 2000). Women are considered inherently sexual. Muhammad's son-in-law proclaimed, "Almighty God created sexual desire in ten parts: then he gave nine parts to women and one to men." The Qur'an requires both men and women to show modesty in public by wearing loose-fitting, body-covering clothing. A woman in Islamic dress is said to be like "a pearl in a shell" (Jehl, 1998), too precious to be seen by men other than family members (Kotb, 2008).

Before Islam's development, *polygamy* (one man having multiple wives at the same time) was a common practice. When war led to a disproportionately higher number of women than men, polygamy provided husbands for widows and fathers for orphans. The Qur'an did not subsequently prohibit polygamy. It allows a man to have up to four wives, provided that the husband is fair to each of them (Khan et al., 2007).

The Qur'an contains many passages that reconcile Islam with women's rights, religious pluralism, and homosexuality, and moderate Muslims do not share the prejudices of radical fundamentalists who stray from the Qur'an's teachings (Manji, 2006). Oppression of women and many of the extreme sexually related restrictions and punishments in Islamic countries do not stem from religion and the Qur'an but from Middle Eastern patriarchal cultural traditions and the emergence of fundamentalist sects. For example, Muslim fundamentalists are following patriarchal traditions, not the Qur'an, when they require girls to be genitally cut, insist that women be completely covered by clothing in public, or sanction "honor killing" (murdering a woman who has "dishonored" her husband and family by having been raped or having sex outside of marriage) (Fang, 2007).

A media campaign based on Christian values hopes to break down antihomosexual prejudice.

Courtesy of Dr. Heba Kotb

Dr. Heba Kotb, the first licensed sexologist in Egypt, is host of a sexual advice show in Egypt, *The Very Big Talk*. She bases her teachings on the Qur'an, encouraging a strong sexual relationship between husband and wife. She does not discuss topics that are prohibited by Islam, including sex outside of marriage, anal sex, or sex during menstruation.

Controversy occurs between Muslims over many traditions, for example, women wearing headscarves (Salam, 2012). In an attempt to support secularism, the Muslim country of Turkey has for decades banned women from wearing headscarves in universities. In early 2008 Turkey's Parliament lifted the ban, allowing university women to wear headscarves. However, the issue remained controversial: People opposed to women wearing headscarves protested at some campuses, while some university leaders continued to enforce the ban that Parliament had removed (Naili, 2011).

Conflicts about Muslim traditions also occur in countries where Muslims are a minority of the population. In 2001 the French government banned the wearing of veils in public, basing the policy on the country's principles of secularism and gender equality (Mevel, 2011). Women who violate the ban can be fined $215.00 or be sent to prison. Protests against the ban are ongoing and are based on freedom of expression and religion (Colchester, 2011).

China

China's ancient history is rich in erotic literature and art. Indeed, the earliest known sex manuals, produced in China sometime around 2500 BCE, portrayed sexual techniques and a great variety of intercourse positions. In ancient China, Taoism (dating from around the second century BCE) actively promoted sexual activity—oral sex, sensual touching, and intercourse—for spiritual growth and harmony in addition to procreation (Brotto et al., 2005). The sexual connection of man and woman during intercourse was believed to join the opposing energies of yin (female) and yang (male), thereby balancing the essences of the two in each individual. Men were encouraged to ejaculate infrequently to conserve yang energy; orgasm for women helped create more yin energy and was sought after.

These liberal Taoist attitudes were replaced by a much stricter sexual propriety that emerged during a renaissance of Confucianism around 1000 CE. Sexual conservatism

CLARO CORTES IV/Reuters/Landov

Liu Dalin, sexologist and curator of the China Sex Museum in Shanghai, shows snuff bottles with erotic designs dating back to the late Qing Dynasty (late 19th century). Shanghai is rediscovering its uninhibited past thanks to more than a decade of growth and liberalization.

increased further after the Communist victory in 1949, and the government attempted to eliminate "decadent" Western sexual behaviors of pornography and prostitution. Under Communist rule, romantic gestures—even holding hands in public—put people at risk of persecution (Fan, 2006). Sex outside marriage was considered a bourgeois transgression, and sex within marriage more than once a week was deemed a counterproductive diversion of energy. A positive result of these measures and attitudes was that China all but eradicated sexually transmitted infections (Wehrfritz, 1996).

Since China's economic reform and the Open Door policy of the 1980s, China's government has eased its control over individual lifestyle choices (Yuxin et al., 2007). As the government has grown more permissive toward sexuality, people's attitudes and behaviors have changed, including a slightly more open attitude toward homosexuality (Lowenthal, 2010). Sexual behaviors, including masturbation, use of pornography, and premarital intercourse, have increased significantly, particularly among men and women in their 20s and 30s (Wong, 2010). In 2005, 70% of residents in Beijing reported having had sexual relations before marriage, in contrast to 15.5% in 1989 (Beech, 2005). However, virginity before age 20 has remained the norm in rural China, and in all of China, for both men and women, the median interval between first sexual intercourse and marriage is a year or less (Parish et al., 2007).

John Stanmeyer/VII Photo Agency

Younger Chinese in larger cities have embraced Western styles. Punk rock guitarist Li Li, age 20, talks with his girlfriend outside the Zai Hui club in west Beijing, China.

Unfortunately, sexual knowledge and safe-sex skills have not kept up with the loosening of restrictions on sexual behavior, as shown by an increase in the number of single women obtaining abortions and by the rapidly growing rates of HIV infection, especially among Chinese 15 to 24 years old (Beech, 2005). Young men, both single and recently married, have significantly increased their contacts with sex workers. Combined with minimal condom use, this trend places young men—and the women they date and marry—at high risk for HIV (Parish et al., 2007).

Our Cultural Legacy: Sex for Procreation and Rigid Gender Roles

In the discussion of the Islamic Middle East and China, we saw that sexual pleasure for both men and women was more highly valued in earlier times than in the contemporary era. In the Western world the opposite is generally true, due to cultural changes regarding the purpose of sexual behavior and societal expectations for male and female sexuality. The patterns, conflicts, and changes stem from two themes: the belief that procreation is the only legitimate reason for sexual expression and the value of rigid distinctions between male and female roles. We will review these themes in the following two sections.

Sex for Procreation

Historically in North America the idea that procreation was the only legitimate reason for sexual activity was prevalent. Contemporary Roman Catholic doctrine and some pro-life organizations continue to hold the belief that the only moral sexual expression occurs within marriage for purposes of procreation. For example, the American Life League maintains that people should not use contraception because "birth control leads to a state of mind that treats sexual activity as if it has nothing to do with procreation. Sexual activity becomes a recreational activity, birth control becomes a recreational drug and babies become 'accidents' or burdens to be eliminated" (American Life League, 2011a, p. 1). In this view, when a couple has sexual intercourse, they have committed themselves to any resultant pregnancy. An opposing view maintains, "Attacks on reproductive rights are attacks on sexuality. Frankly, I'm tired of a small anti-sex, anti-pleasure, anti-life minority imposing their outrageous sex-negative views on the rest of us" (Goddard, 2011).

Sexual behaviors that provide pleasure without the possibility of procreation—such as masturbation, oral sex, anal intercourse, and sex between same-sex partners—have been viewed at various times as immoral, sinful, perverted, or illegal (Roffman, 2005). In fact, oral sex and anal sex remained illegal in 10 states until 2003, when the Supreme Court overturned the laws forbidding those behaviors. The Court determined that the constitutional right to privacy protects private sexual contact between consenting adults.

Although most North Americans today do not believe that sexual activity is only for procreation, a residual effect of this belief is that many in our society often think of *sex* and *intercourse* as synonymous. Therefore, anything other than a penis in a vagina is not "sex." In the scandal involving President Bill Clinton and Monica Lewinsky, which began in 1998, Clinton's initial declaration that he did not have "sex with that woman" was true if "sex" is restricted to mean "intercourse," excluding kissing, oral sex, and genital petting. This perspective remains commonplace: In a study published in 2010, 80% of college students did not think that they "had sex" if they experienced only oral sex (Hans et al., 2010).

Certainly penile–vaginal intercourse can be a fulfilling part of heterosexual sexual expression, but excessive emphasis on intercourse can have negative consequences, as the following situation that brought a young couple to sex therapy illustrates:

> When we started going out, we decided to wait a while before having intercourse, but we had lots of hot sex together—orgasms and all. After we started having intercourse, all the other great stuff went by the wayside and sex became very routine and not much fun. (Authors' files)

Thinking of intercourse as the only "real sex" perpetuates the notions that a man's penis is the primary source of satisfaction for his partner and that her sexual response and orgasm are supposed to occur during penetration. Such a narrow focus places tremendous performance pressures on both women and men and can create unrealistic expectations of coitus itself. This view can also result in devaluing nonintercourse sexual intimacy, which is often relegated to the secondary status of *foreplay* (usually considered any activity before intercourse), implying that such activity is not important in and of itself and is to be followed by the "real sex" of intercourse. In addition, sexual activity between members of the same sex does not fit the model of sex for procreation, causing people unfamiliar with gay and lesbian sexual practices, knowing that they do not involve penile–vaginal intercourse, to wonder, "What do they actually do during sex?"

Male and Female Gender Roles in Sexuality

The second theme and legacy of great significance is a rigid distinction between male and female roles. The gender-role legacy is based on far more than the physiological differences between the sexes. Although physiological differences between males and females create gender characteristics and inclinations in each sex, socialization limits, shapes, and exaggerates our biological tendencies. Rigid gender-role conditioning can limit each person's potential and can harm his or her sexuality (Petersen & Hyde, 2011). A report from researchers who analyzed data about sexual behavior from 59 countries identified gender inequality as a key factor negatively affecting individual sexual health (Wellings et al., 2006). For example, gender-role expectations of "appropriate" behavior for men and women might contribute to the notion that the man must always initiate sexual activity while the woman must either set limits or comply. These patterns can place tremendous responsibility on a man and severely limit a woman's likelihood of discovering her own needs (Berman & Berman, 2001).

Across most cultures, women face more restrictions on, and experience greater sanctions against, their sexuality than men. In the United States, for example, the word *slut* remains predominantly an indictment of females (Abraham, 2011). A survey found this idea to be prevalent among teens: 90% of boys and 92% of girls stated that girls get bad reputations for having sex (Kaiser Family Foundation, 2003). It appears that when overall gender equality is greater, individuals of both sexes see male and female sexuality more similarly. A recent meta-analysis of research on sexual attitudes and behaviors found that in countries with greater gender equality, men and women's sexual attitudes and behaviors were more similar than in societies with less gender equality (Petersen & Hyde, 2010).

To better understand the influence of contemporary social beliefs on sexuality in the Western world, we must examine their historical roots, particularly those that pertain to the legacies of sex for procreation and rigid gender roles. Where did these ideas come from, and how relevant are they to us today?

The first "SlutWalk" in April 2011 in Toronto, Canada, was a protest against a police officer's comment that women should avoid dressing like sluts to avoid rape. It became a movement of rallies around the world.

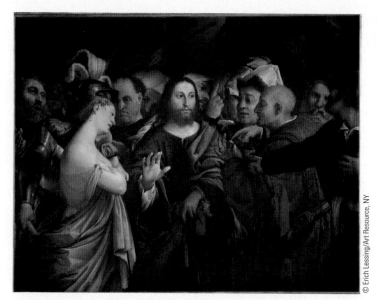

The teachings of Jesus Christ emphasized love, compassion, and forgiveness. Death by stoning was the prescribed punishment for a woman who committed adultery, but Jesus admonished the men who had brought her to him for judgment: "He that is without sin among you, let him first cast a stone at her" (John 8:7). After all the men left without throwing any stones, Jesus told the woman, "Neither do I condemn thee: go, and sin no more" (John 8:11).

Sexuality in the Western World: A Historical Perspective

Judaic and Christian Traditions

By the time Hebraic culture was established, gender roles were highly specialized. The book of Proverbs, in the Hebrew Bible, lists the duties of a good wife: She must instruct servants, care for her family, keep household accounts, and obey her husband. Procreation (the bearing of children, especially sons) was essential; the Hebrews' history of being subjugated, persecuted, and enslaved made them determined to preserve their people—to "be fruitful, and multiply, and replenish the earth" (Genesis 1:28).

Yet sex within marriage was believed to be more than a reproductive necessity. To "know" a partner sexually, within marriage, was recognized in the Old Testament of the Bible and in tradition as a blessing of profound physical and emotional experience (Kunst, 2011; Walker, 2008). The Song of Songs in the Bible (also known as the Song of Solomon) contains sensuous love poetry. In this small excerpt, the bridegroom speaks:

> How fair is thy love, . . . my bride!
> How much better is thy love than wine!
> And the smell of thine ointments than all manner of spices!
> Thy lips, oh my bride, drop honey—honey and milk are under thy tongue.
>   (Song of Songs 4:10–11)

And the bride:

> I am my beloved's and his desire is toward me.
> Come, my beloved, let us go forth into the field; Let us lodge in the villages. . . .
> There will I give thee my love.
>   (Song of Songs 7:10–12)

The joyful appreciation of sexuality displayed in these lines is part of the Judaic tradition. This view was overshadowed, however, by teachings of Christianity. To understand why this happened, we have to remember that Christianity developed during the later years of the Roman Empire, a period of social instability. Many exotic cults had been imported from Greece, Persia, and other parts of the empire to provide sexual entertainment and amusement. Early Christians separated themselves from these practices by associating sex with sin.

We know little about Jesus' specific views on sexuality, but the principles of love and tolerance were the foundation of his teachings. However, Paul of Tarsus, a follower of Christianity, had a crucial influence on the early church. (He died in 66 CE, and many of his writings were incorporated into the Christian Bible, in the New Testament.) Paul believed that all things of the flesh were bad, and only things of the spirit were good—or "godly" (Walker, 2008). He emphasized the importance of overcoming "desires of the flesh"—including anger, selfishness, hatred, and nonmarital sex—in order to inherit the Kingdom of God. He associated spirituality with sexual abstinence and saw **celibacy** (SEH-luh-buh-see), the state of being unmarried and therefore abstaining from sexual

Critical Thinking Question

How do your religious views influence your decision making with regard to sexuality?

celibacy
Historically defined as the state of being unmarried; currently defined as abstention from sexual behavior.

intercourse, as superior to marriage. Hence, sex, which is essential for reproduction, was a necessary but religiously denigrated act.

Sex as Sinful

Later church fathers expanded on the theme of sex as sin. The bishop Augustine (354–430) declared that lust was the original sin of Adam and Eve; his writings formalized the notion that intercourse could rightly take place only within marriage, for the purpose of procreation (Bullough, 2001). Augustine also believed that female subordination was intrinsic to God's creation, which led to the idea that any intercourse position other than the one with the man on top was "unnatural" (Wiesner-Hanks, 2000).

During the Middle Ages (the period of European history from the fall of the Western Roman Empire in 476 to the beginning of the Renaissance in about 1400), attitudes toward sex varied from era to era and place to place, but the belief that sex was sinful persisted throughout. Theologian Thomas Aquinas (1224–1274) further refined this idea in a small section of his *Summa Theologica*. Aquinas maintained that human sexual organs were designed for procreation and that any other use—as in homosexual acts, oral–genital sex, anal intercourse, or sex with animals—was against God's will, heretical, and a "crime against nature." Local priests relied on handbooks called *Penitentials*, catalogs of sins with corresponding penances, to guide them in responding to confessions. Using withdrawal to avoid pregnancy was the most serious sin and could require a penance of fasting on bread and water for years. "Unnatural acts" of oral or anal sex were also viewed as gravely sinful and drew more severe penances than murder (Fox, 1995). Of course, homosexual relations precluded the possibility of reproduction and consisted of many "unnatural acts." From Aquinas's time on, homosexuals were to find neither refuge nor tolerance anywhere in the Western world (Boswell, 1980).

Antagonism toward women reached a climax during the witch hunts of the 15th century.

Eve Versus Mary

During the Middle Ages two contradictory images of women crystallized, and each image had its own impact on society's view of female sexuality and on women's place in society. The first image is the Virgin Mary; the second image is Eve as an evil temptress.

Initially, Mary was a figure of secondary importance in the Western church. Her status was elevated and she became more prominent when the Crusaders returned from Constantinople, the seat of the Eastern church. They brought to the West a view of Mary as a gracious, compassionate protector and an exalted focus of religious devotion.

The practice of *courtly love*, which evolved at about this time, reflected a compatible image of woman as pure and above reproach. Ideally, a young knight would fall in love with a married woman of higher rank. After a lengthy pursuit, he would find favor, but his love would remain unconsummated because her marriage vows ultimately proved inviolable. This paradigm caught the medieval imagination, and troubadours performed ballads of courtly love in courts throughout Europe.

The medieval image of Eve as the temptress in the Garden of Eden provided a counterpoint to the unattainable, compassionate Virgin Mary. This image, promoted by the church, reflected an increasing emphasis on Eve's sin and ultimately resulted in heightened antagonism toward women. This antagonism reached its climax in the witch hunts led by the Catholic Church in continental Europe and the British Isles. They began in the late 15th century—after the Renaissance was well under way—and lasted for close to 200 years. Witchcraft was blamed on carnal lust, and most "witches" were accused of engaging in sexual orgies with the devil (Wiesner-Hanks, 2000). Ironically, while Queen Elizabeth I (1533–1603) brought England to new heights, an estimated 100,000 women were executed as witches in Europe between the 15th and 18th centuries (Pinker, 2011).

Interpretations of Adam and Eve's transgressions in the Garden of Eden have influenced values about sexuality.

A Sex-Positive Shift

The prevailing view of nonreproductive sex as sinful was modified by Protestant reformers of the 16th century. Both Martin Luther (1483–1546) and John Calvin (1509–1564) recognized the value of sex in marriage (Berman & Berman, 2001). According to Calvin, marital sex was permissible if it stemmed "from a desire for children, or to avoid fornication, or to lighten and ease the cares and sadnesses of household affairs, or to endear each other" (Taylor, 1971, p. 62). The Puritans, often maligned for having rigid views about sex, also shared an appreciation of sexual expression within marriage (D'Emilio & Freedman, 1988; Wiesner-Hanks, 2000).

The 18th-century Enlightenment was partly an outgrowth of the new scientific rationalism: Ideas reflected facts that could be objectively observed, rather than subjective beliefs and superstition. Women were to enjoy increased respect, at least for a short time. Some women, such as Mary Wollstonecraft of England, were acknowledged for their intelligence, wit, and vivacity. Wollstonecraft's book *A Vindication of the Rights of Woman* (1792) attacked the limited gender roles for females, such as the prevailing practice of giving young girls dolls rather than schoolbooks. Wollstonecraft also asserted that sexual satisfaction was as important to women as to men and that premarital and extramarital sex was not sinful.

In the Victorian era the marriageable woman possessed morals that were as tightly laced as her corset. Ironically, prostitution flourished at this time.

The Victorian Era

Unfortunately, these progressive views did not prevail. The Victorian era, which took its name from the queen who ascended the British throne in 1837 and ruled for over 60 years, brought a sharp turnaround. The sexes had highly defined roles. Women's sexuality was polarized between the images of Madonna and Eve (which evolved in the vernacular into the "Madonna–whore" dichotomy). Upper- and middle-class Victorian women in Europe and the United States were valued for their delicacy and ladylike manners—and consequently were constrained by such restrictive devices as corsets, hoops, and bustles. The idealization of their presumed fragility put them on a pedestal that limited women's roles both at home and in the outside world (Glick & Fiske, 2001; Real, 2002). Popular opinion of female sexuality was reflected by the widely quoted physician William Acton, who wrote, "The majority of women are not very much troubled with sexual feelings of any kind" (Degler, 1980, p. 250). Women's duties centered on fulfilling their families' spiritual needs and providing a comfortable home for their husbands to retreat to after working all day. The world of women was clearly separated from that of men. Consequently, intensely passionate friendships sometimes developed between women, providing the support and comfort that were often absent in marriage.

In general, Victorians encouraged self-restraint in all aspects of their lives, and Victorian men were expected to conform to the strict propriety of the age. However, prostitution flourished during this period because Victorian men often set morality aside in the pursuit of sexual companionship. The gender-role separation between the worlds of husbands and wives created a sexual and emotional distance in many Victorian marriages. Victorian men could smoke, drink, joke, and find sexual companionship with the women who had turned to prostitution out of economic necessity, whereas their wives were caught in the constraints of propriety and sexual repression.

Critical Thinking Question

How does the Madonna–whore dichotomy affect your sexuality today?

Despite the prevailing notions about the asexual Victorian woman, Celia Mosher, a physician born in 1863, conducted the only known research about the sexuality of women of that era. Over a span of 30 years, 47 married women completed her questionnaire. The information gathered from the research revealed a picture of female sexuality different from the one commonly described (perhaps even prescribed) by "experts" of the time. Mosher found that most of the women experienced sexual desire, enjoyed intercourse, and experienced orgasm (Ellison, 2000).

Nineteenth-century U.S. culture was full of sexual contradictions. Women's sexuality was polarized between the opposing images of Madonna and whore, and men were trapped between the ideal of purity and the frank pleasures of sexual expression. Gender-role beliefs about sexuality were taken to even greater extremes in the cases of African American men and women under slavery. Furthermore, the oppressive myths about African American men and women were used to justify slavery, as examined in the following Sexuality and Diversity discussion. Unfortunately, shades of these myths have persisted and play a role in contemporary racial tensions.

SEXUALITY and DIVERSITY
Slavery's Assault on Sexuality and Gender Roles

An extreme manifestation of gender roles and sexuality was imposed on Black slaves in the United States; stereotypes of Black sexuality provided a justification for the institution of slavery and White power.* Europeans' ethnocentric reactions in their first encounters with black Africans set the stage for the denigration of Black sexuality during slavery. Europeans reacted to African customs with disgust and fear, comparing the sexual habits of Africans to those of apes. Dehumanizing Blacks as animalistic, oversexed "heathens" gave many White slave owners a rationale for exploitation and domination (Moran, 2001).

The Madonna–whore dichotomy was drastically exaggerated in the case of female slaves. The dominant image of Black womanhood was the Jezebel—a treacherous seductress with an insatiable sexual appetite. White men (including some Union soldiers who raped slave women as they plundered towns and plantations) used these prejudices to exempt their sexual abuse and exploitation of Black women from questions of their own

Slaves had no rights to physical privacy, protection from bodily harm, or reproductive autonomy.

*Adapted from Douglas (1999) and Wyatt (1997).

immorality (Guy-Sheftall, 2003). Enslaved women lacked clothing to cover their bodies "properly," and their work in the fields and the house often required them to raise their dresses above their knees—nothing a "decent" woman would do. Slaves had no rights to their own bodies (Block, 2006). During slave sales they were stripped naked so that prospective buyers could closely examine their bodies, including their genitals, as if they were cattle. The irrational logic that no self-respecting woman would allow herself to be put on such display was used by Whites to confirm Black women's wanton nature. Slave owners publicly discussed female slaves' reproductive capacity and managed their "breeding" (often by the slave owner and his sons), forcing promiscuity on them (Solinger, 2005). The economic benefit of rapid births of slave children was clearly expressed by Thomas Jefferson: "I consider a woman who brings a child every two years as more profitable than the best man on the farm; what she produces is an addition to capital" (Davis, 2002, p. 109).

The stereotype of "Mammy" provided slave owners with a counterbalance to the Jezebel and represented the slave owners' successful civilizing of Black women, including their sexuality. Mammy was supposed to be loyal, obedient, and asexual. She cooked, cleaned, and cared for White children, often even nursing infants. Her labors enabled many White women to maintain their delicate, ladylike images.

The male complement to the Jezebel was the stereotype of the highly sexual, potentially violent "buck." Whites considered him a powerful animal and exploited his ability to work and to produce offspring with his mythical, larger-than-White-sized penis. On the one hand, slave owners depended economically on Black men's physical strength and sexual virility. On the other hand, they feared those same qualities. The fabricated threat of sexual seduction of White women and racist logic sanctioned the tools necessary to control Black men and to assuage the slave owners' insecurities that their own stereotypes created. During the slavery era, Black men were beaten, whipped, castrated, and lynched with impunity. After emancipation, people freed from slavery had greater opportunities to shape their own lives, but the lynching of Black men and raping of Black women continued as a means of maintaining social control over those who challenged the norms of White supremacy (Douglas, 1999; Wyatt, 1997).

The historical events and their surrounding controversies discussed in the previous sections show that the sex-for-procreation and gender-role issues are legacies of the Hebrew and Christian Bibles, of Augustine and Thomas Aquinas, of the Victorian era, and of slavery. These legacies are with us still, found in the complex conflicts between the values of personal pleasure, practicality, and tradition in 20th-century Western life (Jakobsen & Pellegrini, 2003).

The Beginning of the 20th Century*

Sigmund Freud (1856–1939) led in changing perspectives about sexuality in the 20th century with the first of several books, *The Interpretation of Dreams* (1900). Freud's belief that sexuality was innate in women as well as in men helped expand Victorian concepts about sexuality. The physician Havelock Ellis (1859–1939), in his book *On Life and Sex* (1920), emphasized "the love-rights of women," and his seven-volume *Studies in the Psychology of Sex* regarded any sexual practice—including masturbation and homosexuality, previously considered "perversions"—as healthy so long as no one was harmed. Theodore Van de Velde (1873–1937) stressed the importance of sexual pleasure in his popular marriage manuals.

© CORBIS

Many women in the 1920s broke out of traditional "at home" roles and enjoyed the independence the automobile provided. The clothing styles of the "flapper" expressed women's rejection of Victorian moral standards.

*Our primary sources for this material are Czuczka (2000) and Glennon (1999).

While ideas about the "proper" role of female sexuality were changing, the woman suffrage movement began in the late 19th century. Its goal of giving women the right to vote grew out of several related developments, such as the abolition of slavery and the demand that women be permitted to attend universities and hold property. The passage in 1920 of the 19th Amendment to the U.S. Constitution guaranteed women the right to vote but did not usher in a new era of equality.

However, subsequent historical events and technology brought new sexual perspectives and possibilities. U.S. involvement in World War I created an environment for increased equality and flexibility of gender roles, as thousands of women left the traditional homemaker role and took paying jobs for the first time. American men serving as soldiers in Europe were introduced to the more open sexuality there. Soon after the soldiers returned home from the war, Henry Ford's mass-produced automobiles of the 1920s provided increased independence and privacy for young

During World Wars I and II, U.S. soldiers who socialized with European women were influenced by more cosmopolitan sexual mores.

people's sexual explorations. The advent of movies presented romance and sex symbols for public entertainment. The "flappers"—young, urban, single, middle-class women—rejected the ideals of Victorian restraint for short, slinky dresses and the exuberant, close-contact dancing of the Roaring Twenties. The changes in sexual mores consisted mainly of the prevalence of kissing and "petting" (sex play short of intercourse) among young unmarried people that went beyond acceptable Victorian standards, but women usually avoided premarital intercourse to prevent pregnancy and jeopardizing their reputations.

A return to more restrained behavior came with the Great Depression in the 1930s. Conversely, the hardships of the time also led to new laws mandating the right of women to have access to contraceptive information and devices. Before the development of penicillin in the 1940s, no effective treatment existed for life-threatening sexually transmitted infections. Once penicillin became available, another feared consequence of sex became less harmful. During World War II, housewives once again filled the gaps in the workplace left by men who were fighting overseas and encountering more open European sexuality.

After World War II

After World War II, living in the suburbs became the ideal and goal of middle-class families, financed by the father as breadwinner. Women returned the workplace to men and devoted themselves to their homes, children, and husbands. Popular media portrayed the postwar housewives as happy and content (Coontz, 2011). Psychology of the era claimed that women who worked outside the home were neurotic and suffered from "penis envy." The fashion industry "refeminized" women with clothing that emphasized the bustline and small waist and featured full skirts.

During the postwar retreat into traditional gender roles, Alfred Kinsey and associates' *Sexual Behavior in the Human Male* (1948) and *Sexual Behavior in the Human Female* (1953) were best sellers in spite of (or possibly because of) denunciations of their work by medical professionals, clergy, politicians, and the press (Brown & Fee, 2003). Kinsey's data pertaining to the prevalence of women's sexual interest and response were particularly shocking to both professionals and the public. The surprising statistics on same-sex behavior, masturbation, and novel acts in the bedroom contributed to the growing acceptance of a variety of sexual behaviors.

As the television series *Mad Men* shows, the ultrafeminine clothing of the 1950s and '60s reflected the cultural emphasis on distinct female gender roles.

In the 1950s, television, which emphasized suburban social conformity and featured sitcoms portraying married couples in separate beds, entered American homes at the same time as the first issue of *Playboy*, which emphasized sex as recreation. Together, these media represented a dichotomy that played out through the 1950s.

The Times They Are a-Changin'

It was not until the 1960s—after the flurry of post–World War II marriages, the baby boom, and widespread disappointment in the resulting domesticity of women—that a new movement for gender-role equality began. In *The Feminine Mystique*, author Betty Friedan's descriptions of feelings of depression, guilt, and a lack of meaning resonated with many women whose lives were limited to the housewife role. In the 1960s and throughout the 1970s, feminism and the "sexual revolution" confronted the norms of previous decades. The oral contraceptive pill, introduced in the 1960s, and later the intrauterine device (IUD), morning-after pills, and spermicides gave women newfound security in pursuing sexual pleasure with greatly reduced fear of pregnancy (Ofman, 2000).

By 1965 the Supreme Court had made contraceptive use by married couples legal, and by 1972 contraceptive use by unmarried individuals was legal. The widespread acceptance of contraceptives and the subsequent availability of legal abortion by Supreme Court mandate in 1973 permitted sexuality to be separated from procreation as never before in Western cultures. The world had changed, too, so that many people were concerned with the ecological and economic costs of bearing children—costs that were not as relevant in the preindustrial world.

Masters and Johnson's *Human Sexual Response* (1966) and *Human Sexual Inadequacy* (1970) illuminated women's capacity for orgasm and propelled sex therapy into a legitimate endeavor. Sexual self-help books appeared, such as *Our Bodies, Ourselves* (Boston Women's Health Book Collective, 1971) and *For Yourself: The Fulfillment of Female Sexuality* (Barbach, 1975). These books emphasized women's sexual self-awareness, whereas *The Joy of Sex* (Comfort, 1972) highlighted varied, experimental sexual behavior for couples.

In the increasingly tolerant atmosphere of the late 1960s and the 1970s, attitudes began to change toward a long-standing taboo, homosexuality. Gays and lesbians began to openly declare their sexual orientation and to argue that such a personal matter should not affect their rights and responsibilities as citizens. In 1973 the American Psychiatric Association removed homosexuality from its diagnostic categories of mental disorders. Then, the early 1980s brought the first AIDS diagnosis. The so-called gay plague dramatically increased the visibility of homosexual individuals and amplified both negative and positive public sentiments toward homosexuality.

Current efforts taking place in election campaigns and in federal and state legislatures, both supporting and opposing civil unions or marriage for same-sex couples, exemplify the continuing disagreement in the United States about homosexuality. Almost every election results in both gains and losses on each side of the issue. Notably, Barack Obama's 2009 inauguration speech was the first by a president-elect to include "gays and straights" in his description of Americans, and in 2011 a CNN Poll reported that support for marriage equality broke the 50% barrier for the first time (CNN, 2011).

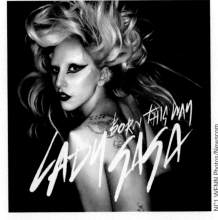

The lyrics of Lady Gaga's single "Born This Way" emphasize acceptance and empowerment for those outside the mainstream "norm."

Mainly as a result of gay activism, by the mid-1990s, television began to incorporate gays and lesbians into programming. Gay and lesbian characters appeared on shows such as *ER, Sex and the City, Roseanne,* and *Friends.* Ellen DeGeneres's coming-out show on *Ellen* was an event of the 1997 season. She currently has a daily TV talk show and in 2009 became CoverGirl's spokesperson. In the footsteps of *Ellen's* trailblazing lesbian lead character, *Will and Grace* had gay and lesbian story lines for eight seasons, with main characters who were likable, although at times they received some criticism for reinforcing stereotypes (Colucci, 2006). In 2010 more gay and lesbian characters appeared on television than in prior years, including in *Modern Family, Glee, Weeds, Friday Night Lights, Desperate Housewives, Brothers & Sisters, Project Runway,* and *The Amazing Race* (Alston, 2010).

Changes in the media's portrayal of homosexuality illustrate how the media simultaneously reflect and influence sexual information, attitudes, and behaviors (Gross, 2001). What do the media say to us about sexuality? The following sections explore that very question.

Well-known individuals, including Wanda Sykes, Don Lemon, Suze Orman, and Rachel Maddow, who have made their homosexuality public also affect public attitudes.

The Media and Sexuality

The phenomenon that we know as mass media began less than 600 years ago. The invention of typesetting in 1450 meant that books, instead of being laboriously handwritten, could be mechanically printed, which made them available to the common woman and man. Black-and-white silent movies first played for a paying audience in 1895, and in 1896, *The Kiss,* the first film in cinematic history of a couple kissing, was criticized as scandalous and brought demands for censorship (Dirks, 2006). The first black-and-white television sets arrived in the 1940s (initially so fascinating that families would sit in the living room watching test patterns on the screen). By 1972 the number of color television sets in U.S. homes finally exceeded the number of black-and-white TVs. The explosion of media technology since then has flooded us with exposure to sexual words and images. Increased amounts and explicitness of sexual content have accompanied the huge technological advances (see ▌ Figure 1.2).

Television

Television has likely had a significant effect on sexual attitudes and behaviors, given the amount of time people spend watching it. By the time we are 18 years old, each of us has watched TV for an average of 20,000 hours—certainly enough time for it to have some influence on our perspectives about sexuality (Manganello et al., 2008; Media Project, 2008). Despite all the new technologies, television remains dominant (Foehr, 2006). Young people's computer, video game, e-mail, and instant messaging use does not displace time spent with television—it simply adds to the total time spent using media. On average, 8- to 18-year-olds spend 58 hours a week using some type of entertainment media—an increase of almost 9 hours a week since 2004 (Rideout et al., 2010).

The number of sexual scenes on standard network programs has nearly doubled since 1998, and Figure 1.2 shows when various types of sexual content first appeared on television. Among the 20 shows most watched by teens, 70% include sexual content (talking about sex, sexual innuendo) and 45% include sexual behavior. However, compared to 10 years ago, fewer young people are shown engaging in sexual activity: One in ten depictions of sexual intercourse involves teens and young adults, compared with one in four in 1998 (Kaiser Family Foundation, 2006).

The Federal Communications Commission imposes standards on public network television, but not on cable stations. Cable TV programs contain far more sexual explicitness than do network programs—as shown by *Sex and the City*, in which four New York City women talk with one another about faking orgasm, disappointment with penis size and rapid ejaculation, "funky spunk" (bad-tasting ejaculate), and an uncircumcised penis. *The L Word* and *Queer as Folk* were the first cable programs portraying the lives—and highlighting the sex lives—of lesbian and gay individuals. Reality TV programs—*Big Brother*, *Real World*, *The Bachelor*, and the like—are fueled by sexual intrigue and expression.

Many critics are concerned that such material presents a far too cavalier approach to sex, encouraging youth to be sexually active too early, but most studies on the subject have been inconclusive (Escobar-Chaves et al., 2005). One study established a sexual media diet (SMD) by weighing the amount of sexual content in the TV shows, movies, music, and magazines teens consumed regularly, along with the amount of time teens spent using the four forms of media. The study found that White teens whose SMD was in the top 20% were 2.2 times more likely to have had sexual intercourse by age 16 than were those whose SMD was in the lowest 20% (Brown & L'Engle, 2008).

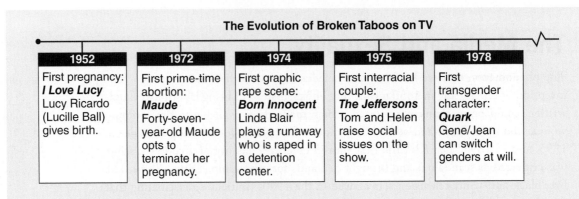

The Evolution of Broken Taboos on TV

1952	1972	1974	1975	1978
First pregnancy: *I Love Lucy* Lucy Ricardo (Lucille Ball) gives birth.	First prime-time abortion: *Maude* Forty-seven-year-old Maude opts to terminate her pregnancy.	First graphic rape scene: *Born Innocent* Linda Blair plays a runaway who is raped in a detention center.	First interracial couple: *The Jeffersons* Tom and Helen raise social issues on the show.	First transgender character: *Quark* Gene/Jean can switch genders at will.

▌ Figure 1.2 The evolution of broken taboos on TV.

SOURCE: Adapted from *TV Guide*, August 2, 2003.

However, as with most research, these findings indicate a correlation, not causation, and it may be that teens who are more sexually experienced seek out more sexual content in media. However, many depictions of sexuality in the media may trivialize the complexity of sexuality and create unrealistic expectations regarding sexual experiences.

At times, the ways sexual issues are presented on television have beneficial effects—promoting greater knowledge, tolerance, and positive social change. *The Oprah Winfrey Show* (which began airing in 1986) provided a forum for people to learn about and discuss many aspects of human sexuality. Network and cable programs on child abuse, rape, and transgender concerns have helped to increase knowledge and to reduce the stigma associated with such topics (American Academy of Pediatrics, 2001). Television advice and educational programs can offer constructive guidance. For example, *Loveline* host Drew Pinsky discusses young people's concerns about relationships and sex and gives advice. Various studies have found that shows that portrayed negative consequences of sexual activity led to more negative attitudes toward intercourse before marriage, and portrayals of safe sex on television shows increased positive attitudes about condom use (Eyal & Kunkel, 2008). In addition, information about the potentially harmful physical and emotional consequences of sex has increased in programming. In 2005, 27% of television shows depicting or discussing intercourse referred to the risks and responsibilities of sex—twice the rate of 1998. Shows popular with teens have had an even greater increase in safe-sex content (Kaiser Family Foundation, 2006).

One study found a significant increase in viewers' knowledge about mother-to-child HIV transmission after viewing a *Grey's Anatomy* episode on the topic. ▌Figure 1.3 shows the increase in the viewers' knowledge about an HIV-positive woman's chance of having a healthy baby (Rideout, 2008). Television programs that model communication about sex may help some viewers talk to their sexual partners. For example, researchers showed three groups of students different edited versions of *Sex and the City* episodes: In one, the characters Samantha and Miranda discussed sexually transmitted infections with friends, doctors, and sexual partners. The second version included content about STIs, but none of the characters discussed this topic with each other. The third episode had no reference to STIs. Two weeks later, the study participants completed a questionnaire asking whether they had talked to anyone about sexual infections. Forty-six percent of college students who watched the episode in which characters discussed STIs said they had discussed sexual health issues with their partners since viewing the show. Twenty-one percent of those who saw the second version and 15% of those who watched the third version reported discussing the topic with their sexual partners (Moyer-Guse et al., 2011).

The media can play a significant role in countries where sexual information has been taboo. For example, in the last decade Egypt and China have allowed the first sex education programs to be presented via public media. In 2006, an Egyptian sex therapist began the country's first televised sex education program. Without discussing

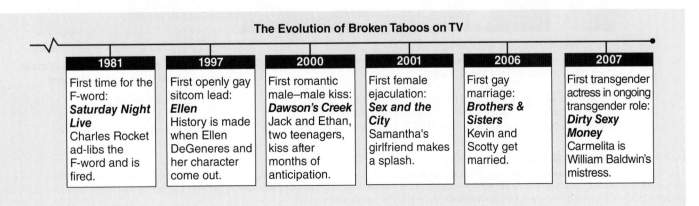

The Evolution of Broken Taboos on TV

1981	1997	2000	2001	2006	2007
First time for the F-word: **Saturday Night Live** Charles Rocket ad-libs the F-word and is fired.	First openly gay sitcom lead: **Ellen** History is made when Ellen DeGeneres and her character come out.	First romantic male–male kiss: **Dawson's Creek** Jack and Ethan, two teenagers, kiss after months of anticipation.	First female ejaculation: **Sex and the City** Samantha's girlfriend makes a splash.	First gay marriage: **Brothers & Sisters** Kevin and Scotty get married.	First transgender actress in ongoing transgender role: **Dirty Sexy Money** Carmelita is William Baldwin's mistress.

topics that are prohibited by Islam—sex outside of marriage, anal sex, or sex during menstruation—*The Very Big Talk* attempts to correct widespread sexual misinformation in a culturally acceptable manner by melding Islam with modern sexual knowledge (El-Noshokaty, 2006). In China, the *Tonight's Whisperings* radio program began in 1998 to address the gap between the sexual ignorance created by the repression of sexual information during the Cultural Revolution and the increase in teen sexual behavior. The show's hosts respond to questions viewers send via e-mail and text message, many of which reveal a lack of knowledge of basic sexual facts (Fan, 2006).

Music Videos

Since 1981, televised music video programs have bridged television and the music industry. Up to 75% of music videos (depending on the type of music) have sexual content. They usually portray men as sexually aggressive and women as sexually submissive objects (Conrad et al., 2009). Research finds that exposure to more sexually explicit music videos is associated with stronger endorsement of the double standard (Zhang et al., 2008). Further studies found that adolescents who listened to music with degrading sexual lyrics were twice as likely to have had sexual intercourse and engaged in a greater variety of sexual activities compared with adolescents who had the least exposure to songs with lyrics that were not degrading (Martino et al., 2006; Primack et al., 2009). Another study found that college students' exposure to more sexually explicit music videos was associated with a stronger endorsement of the double standard. A United Kingdom government report recommended that sexually provocative music videos should not be shown until after 9 p.m. to reduce children's exposure to hypersexualized images (Turner, 2010).

Critical Thinking Question

Can you think of an advertisement that helped reshape sexual stereotypes? How did the advertisement achieve that result?

ABC-TV/THE KOBAL COLLECTION/GARFIELD, SCOTT

Grey's Anatomy viewers were asked the following question before, one week after, and six weeks after viewing an episode about mother-to-child HIV transmission:

"If a woman who is HIV positive becomes pregnant and receives the proper treatment, what is the chance that she will give birth to a healthy baby—that is, a baby who is NOT infected with HIV?"

15%
61%
45%

0% 10% 20% 30% 40% 50% 60% 70% 80%
Percentage of viewers who gave the correct answer (more than a 90% chance)

■ Before *Grey's* episode
■ One week after *Grey's* episode
■ Six weeks after *Grey's* episode

❚ **Figure 1.3** Health knowledge gain and retention from a *Grey's Anatomy* episode.

SOURCE: Rideout, V. (2008). Television as Health Educator: A Case Study of *Grey's Anatomy*, p. 3. Kaiser Family Foundation. Reprinted with permission from the Henry J. Kaiser Family Foundation. The Kaiser Family Foundation is a non-profit private operating foundation, based in Menlo Park, California, dedicated to producing and communicating the best possible analysis and information on health issues.

Advertising

Advertising either is present in most forms of media or stands alone, as on the ubiquitous billboard. Sexual images, often blatant but sometimes subtle, are designed to help attract attention to and sell products. An ad that has high sexual appeal can be a powerful marketing tool. For example, jeans sales doubled following the 1980s ad in which a young Brooke Shields promised that nothing came between her and her Calvin Klein jeans (Kuriansky, 1996). Advertising relies on the false promises that love or sex or both will come with the acquisition of a certain beauty product, brand of liquor, brand of clothing, sound system, or car. Most sexual content in advertising trivializes sex and reinforces the idea that only young, hard male and female bodies merit attraction. The exception to this rule is advertising aimed at the large consumer group of aging baby boomers. Occasionally, advertising helps to break down taboos. For example, presidential candidate Bob Dole's advertisements for Viagra helped bring erectile dysfunction into public discourse.

Magazines

Popular magazines contain a range of sexually related articles—from excellent information about self-help and relationship skills to articles that promote stereotypical gender roles, body-image insecurity, superficiality, and manipulation in relationships (Markle, 2008; Menard & Kleinplatz, 2008). On the positive side, a study of sexual health behaviors and magazine reading among college students found that more frequent reading of mainstream magazines was associated with more

Advertisers increasingly use group sex scenes to market their products.

consistent use of contraceptives and with greater sexual health knowledge and safe-sex behaviors (Walsh & Ward, 2010). Further, articles about sexual interaction may provide positive support for sexual exploration and assertiveness; such an article in *Cosmopolitan* encouraged its readers to stimulate their clitoris during intercourse to enhance arousal and help them experience orgasm.

Conversely, articles like "Do You Make Men M-E-L-T?" may reinforce gender-role stereotypes and performance pressure and overemphasize techniques (Menard & Kleinplatz, 2008). Ubiquitous information telling readers how to make themselves prettier, skinnier, and sexier ("Boy Magnet Beauty" and "Untamed Va-jay-jays") may contribute to body-image insecurity (Moore, 2010). Magazines designed for young men often emphasize two themes: information about "what women want" and how to promote "kinky" sexual variety with partners (Taylor, 2005).

Critical Thinking Question

Do you think that most young women's main interest in sex is having "kinky" sexual variety?

Cyberspace and Sexuality

The comprehensive research study about sexuality in the United States, the National Health and Social Life Survey (NHSLS), concluded that our attitudes and behaviors are dramatically influenced by the people in our social groups (Laumann et al., 1994). This research was conducted before the explosion in online communication in the 1990s. By 2010 there were almost 2 billion Internet users worldwide. China has 477 million Internet users—more than any other country in the world. The United States is second, with 221 million people using the Internet. Of considerable significance is that the current worldwide usage rate consists of only 30.2% of the population, leaving enormous growth potential (Internet World Stats, 2011). See ▮ Figure 1.4 for more statistics about Internet use around the globe.

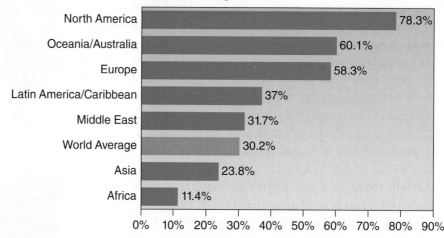

(a) Percentage of Population That Uses the Internet by Geographic Region

Region	Percentage
North America	78.3%
Oceania/Australia	60.1%
Europe	58.3%
Latin America/Caribbean	37%
Middle East	31.7%
World Average	30.2%
Asia	23.8%
Africa	11.4%

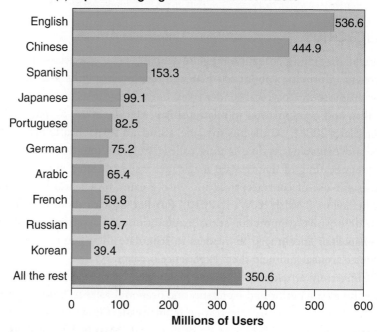

(b) Top Ten Languages in the Internet in 2010

Language	Millions of Users
English	536.6
Chinese	444.9
Spanish	153.3
Japanese	99.1
Portuguese	82.5
German	75.2
Arabic	65.4
French	59.8
Russian	59.7
Korean	39.4
All the rest	350.6

■ Figure 1.4 Worldwide Internet users.

SOURCE: Internet World Stats, www.internetworldstats.com. Copyright © Miniwatts Marketing Group. Reprinted by permission.

The impact of this communication revolution on sexual attitudes and behaviors is potentially epic. Now people in disparate social groups—different age groups, races, religions, ethnic groups, and economic groups—can communicate more easily than ever before. Distance and cultural barriers are becoming smaller and smaller, which presents "[t]he possibility for the kinds of quantum leaps that human minds can make when they share ideas" (Shernoff, 2006, p. 20). The number of social networking sites has increased dramatically in a very short time. For example, Facebook was set up in 2004 and had 519 million users by 2011 (Internet World Stats, 2011).

Communicating and obtaining information via the Internet have become very significant to individuals who previously felt very alienated and alone with regard to their sexuality, as the following explains:

> The first time I found someone else on the Internet who experienced sexual arousal the same way I did was a profound relief. Even before I was a teenager, I was strongly aroused by seeing girls and women swimming. I'm in my 40s now and have to be in a pool with my wife to be able to become aroused enough to have sex when we get home. The "pornography" that I use is of women in water. Finding out how many other people are like me has helped me and my wife to work better with the challenges my means of arousal bring instead of only being upset about it. (Authors' files)

Up to 80% of people obtain health information from the Internet (Fine, 2008), and it can provide quick access to useful information related to sexuality. "Dear Abby"–type sex columnists answer online questions, and the abundance of self-help information ranges from websites for breast and prostate cancer to message boards posting wig-care tips for transsexuals. An exploratory study found that teens may be judicious consumers of sexuality information on the Internet. Most did not trust the Internet for accurate online information, concerned that it is often user-generated and incorrect (Jones & Biddlecom, 2011).

The Internet has also become a huge dating service, an interactive personal-ad opportunity that people can use for online conversations to see if they want to meet in person. Although it has risks, Internet dating can have the advantages of clarifying one's agenda for a relationship up front, whether one is seeking casual sex or a life partner. For some, the level of self-disclosure online may actually establish more intimacy before they initiate a physical relationship than meeting face-to-face without prior online communication.

The Internet and cell phones have also become sources of sexual self-expression. About 80% of 13- to 17-year-olds and 93% of 18- to 24-year-olds use cell phones in the United States—a number that is surely rising as you read this. Using the built-in cameras, 30% of young adults ages 20 to 26 report that they have sent or posted naked or partially naked photos or videos of themselves to flirt with someone or just for fun. "Sexting" is the term for sending nude photos on cell phones (Lithwick, 2009). Even more have sent sexually suggestive text messages (National Campaign to Prevent Teen and Unplanned Pregnancy, 2008a). (See Chapter 12 for a discussion of sexting.)

Online sexual activity (OSA) extends far beyond sending nude photos by cell phone. In contrast to social networking, self-help, and general sexuality education, the approximately 72 million people who visit adult sites each month in the United States are looking for something else in the consumer-driven interactive sexual supermarket. Many users seek sexually explicit images or webcam live-action "cyberstrippers" to arouse themselves during masturbation. Sexually explicit self-expression occurs when individuals, couples, or groups make homemade sexual videos of themselves and post them to Internet websites for others to view. Some use chat rooms to talk about their wildest fantasies or participate in multiplayer interactive adult games, often experimenting by assuming different personae and sexes (Ross, 2005). Others engage in real-time chat via instant messaging and use audio devices and video cameras for online interaction. Remote interactive technology, dubbed "teledildonics," provides interactive, rather than solo, stimulation. Teledildonics allows one person to control another's sex toy over the Internet. Users manipulate a control panel that varies the intensity of motion of the other person's sleeve-style vibrator or dildo with an attached vibrating bunny for clitoral stimulation.

Most of the Internet's technological developments have been advanced by the sex industry, and adult programming continues to be a significant revenue source for recent developments in cell phones, iPod "pod porn," PDAs, PSP game handhelds, and broadband video streaming platforms (Alexander, 2006).

Research has found that most people use adult websites for benign recreational activity. However, almost 9% of one study's participants spent *at least* 11 hours a week online viewing adult sites, an investment of time that created problems in their lives. They became so involved with sex online that their personal sexual relationships and other life responsibilities suffered (Cooper et al., 1999). Also a significant problem is that some sexual predators use the Internet to sexually exploit others, and a site like MySpace.com is a sexual predator's dream come true (Romano, 2006). Further, the easily available extreme sexual material on the Internet is not developmentally appropriate for young people, but it can be difficult for them to avoid.

The constructive and problematic possibilities of cyberspace sexuality appear unlimited, and we will discuss various elements of this topic throughout the text.

Sexuality: Where the Personal Is Political

The personal and political (laws, policies, and norms) are truly merged when it comes to sexuality. The historical, cross-cultural, and intra-cultural perspectives that we have examined in this chapter clearly show the impact of social norms on sexuality and may help us to appreciate the unique position in which we currently find ourselves. We can define our own sexuality on the basis of personal choices to a far greater degree than was possible for the ancient Hebrews, the early Christians, the Europeans of the Middle Ages, the Victorian Europeans, and North Americans of the 19th century—and to a far greater degree than is possible for many contemporary non-Western societies. With the increased understanding and acceptance of diversity in human sexuality that developed during the 20th century, we have greater freedoms and responsibilities today.

Yet, the exponential changes in the last century have left us with many unresolved questions. Consequently, in the 21st century we face controversies about social policies, laws, and ethics in almost every area related to human sexuality—many of which are decided by voters, the executive branch of the government, state and federal courts, the U.S. Supreme Court, and school boards (Bernstein & Schaffner, 2005). We have seen throughout this chapter that social norms, sometimes codified into law, can support or interfere with the individual's right to privacy and personal choice (Kaiser, 2004; Wildman, 2001).

Critical Thinking Question

How did local, state, and federal governments determine the content of your high school sex education class?

For example, for many decades the United States Agency for International Development (USAID) has provided funding for family planning and maternal–child health services organizations in the developing world where lack of access to contraceptive services results in millions of unintended pregnancies each year. The unintended pregnancies often result in increased hardship for poverty-stricken families or in abortion—many of them unsafe. Across the globe, eight women die every hour from unsafe abortion (Center for Health and Gender Equality, 2009).

These funds and the women and children who benefit from or suffer without the services they provide have had a long history of vulnerability to politics. USAID funding can be restricted by the president of the United States. In 1984 the Reagan administration established a policy, commonly known as the Global Gag Rule (GGR), which prohibited providing money and contraceptives to any family planning organizations that used their own non-U.S. funds to offer information, referrals, and services related to abortion. Further, the policy defunded overseas organizations if they engaged in advocacy for safe abortion in their own countries (Ipas, 2007).

The 1984 Reagan funding restriction remained in place until Bill Clinton overturned the restriction after his 1993 election as U.S. president. In spite of evidence documenting the Global Gag Rule's impact of increasing abortion rates, in 2001 President George W. Bush's first act as president was to reinstate the Global Gag Rule. It remained in place until Barack Obama assumed the presidency in 2008 and freed USAID funding from GGR restrictions.

The change in presidential administrations will, however, not end controversy and political conflict in international and domestic issues pertaining to sexuality (Cohen, 2012a). "Abstinence only" sex education in public schools, federal and state laws regarding gay civil rights and marriage, restrictions on abortion, public funding for sex research, promotion of condoms for HIV/AIDS prevention in Africa—these are only a few of the contentious subjects that we will discuss throughout the text.

We hope that your experience grappling with today's challenges related to sexuality contributes to your sexual intelligence and your personal ability to navigate all the different topics that make up our sexuality.

Critical Thinking Question

How does the Global Gag Rule controversy relate to our sex-for-procreation and rigid gender-role legacies?

Summary

Sexual Intelligence

- Understanding oneself sexually and having interpersonal sexual skills and integrity are two characteristics we consider to be part of sexual intelligence, and these abilities help us make responsible decisions about our sexual behavior based on our personal values.

A Psychosocial Orientation

- This book stresses the role of psychological factors and social conditioning in shaping human sexuality.

Controversy and Diversity in Human Sexuality

- To better appreciate the importance of social conditioning, we can compare sexual attitudes and behaviors in other cultures.

- Variations in acculturation, religious belief, and socioeconomic status create sexual diversity within ethnic groups of the United States.
- Followers of Islam, or Muslims, believe enjoyment of sex in marriage is important for men and women. Female sexuality is seen as powerful, and some Muslim fundamentalists, following patriarchal traditions, consider veils, female genital cutting, and segregation of the sexes until marriage necessary to contain women's sexuality.
- In ancient China sexual activity was a means to spiritual growth. Communist China's government attempted to isolate its people from Western sexual attitudes and practices, and its sexual norms were conservative until recent loosening of government restrictions.

Our Cultural Legacy: Sex for Procreation and Rigid Gender Roles

■ This book critically explores the effects of two pervasive themes related to sexuality: sex limited to reproduction (procreation) and inflexible gender roles.

Sexuality in the Western World: A Historical Perspective

■ The ancient Hebrews stressed the importance of childbearing and had an appreciation of sexuality within marriage.

■ Gender-role differences between men and women were well established in ancient Hebraic culture. Women's most important roles were to manage the household and bear children, especially sons.

■ Christian writers such as Paul of Tarsus, Augustine, and Thomas Aquinas contributed to the view of sex as sinful, justifiable only in marriage for the purpose of procreation.

■ Two contradictory images of women developed in the Middle Ages: the pure and unattainable woman on a pedestal, manifested in the cult of the Virgin Mary and in courtly love; and the evil temptress, represented by Eve and by women persecuted as witches.

■ Leaders of the Reformation of the 16th century challenged the requirement that clergy remain celibate and recognized sexual expression as an important aspect of marriage.

■ Women were viewed as asexual in the Victorian era, and the lives of "proper" Victorian men and women were largely separate. Men often visited prostitutes for companionship as well as sexual relations.

■ The theories of Freud, research findings, and feminism changed the Victorian notion of women being asexual.

■ U.S. involvement in World Wars I and II exposed American men to the more open sexuality of Europe and placed American women in the workforce (temporarily).

■ Technical advances in contraception in the 20th century permitted people to separate sexuality from procreation to a degree not previously possible.

■ Dramatic changes in understanding and acceptance of homosexuality began in the 1960s.

The Media and Sexuality

■ Mass media as we know it has existed a short time relative to the greater human experience.

■ The explosion of mass media—radio, movies, television, VCRs and DVDs, and the Internet—presents a vast array of sexual information and misinformation that at least highlights the diversity in human sexuality.

■ Sexual explicitness in all popular media continues to increase.

■ The impact of the Internet on sexual attitudes, knowledge, and behavior has both constructive and problematic possibilities.

Sexuality: Where the Personal Is Political

■ The scientific, psychological, and social changes in the 20th century led to the contemporary individual's increased ability to make personal decisions regarding sexuality.

■ Laws, social policies, and norms related to sexuality merge this personal subject with "politics."

Media Resources

Log in to CengageBrain.com to access the resources your instructor requires.

Go to CengageBrain.com to access Psychology CourseMate, where you will find an interactive eBook, glossaries, flashcards, quizzes, videos, and more.

Also access links to chapter-related websites, including **It's Your Sex Life,** the **Sexuality Information and Education Council of the United States (SIECUS),** and **Ask NOAH About Sexuality.**

Sex Research:
Methods and Problems

2

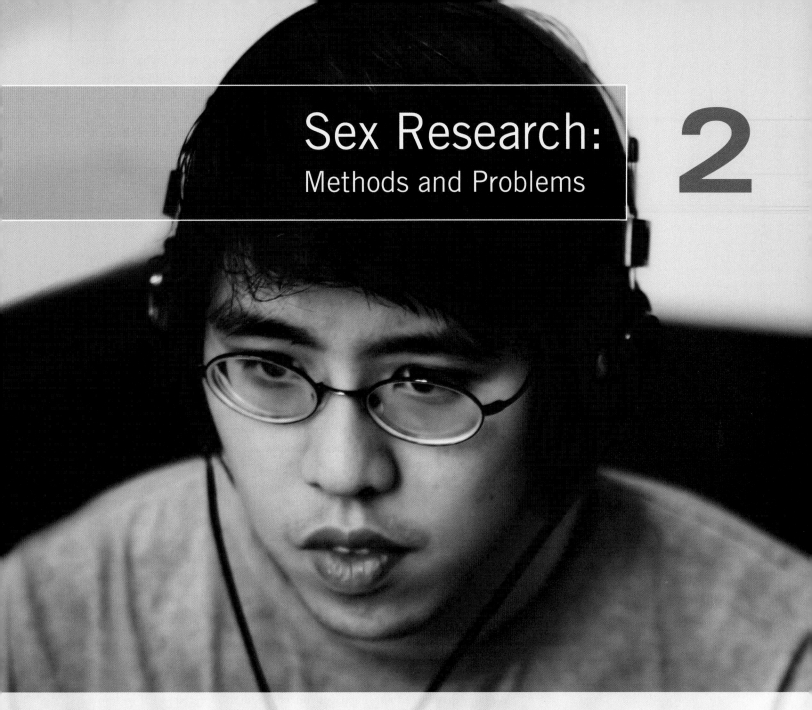

The Goals of Sexology
What are the major goals of sexology?

Is applying research findings to control or modify behavior a legitimate aim of sex research?

Nonexperimental Research Methods
What are the advantages and disadvantages of each of the three nonexperimental research methods used to study sexuality?

Which of the nonexperimental research methods has provided the most data about human sexuality?

The Experimental Method
How do researchers study sexual behavior in laboratory investigations of human sexuality?

What are the advantages and limitations of experimental studies of human sexuality?

Technologies in Sex Research
How do researchers measure sexual arousal electronically?

Can computers and the Internet aid in gathering sensitive information?

Ethical Guidelines for Human Sex Research
What ethical issues do sex researchers face, and how are they addressed?

Is it ethical to conduct sex research in cyberspace?

Evaluating Research: Some Questions to Ask
To what degree can we rely on the findings of sex research?

What important questions should be asked when evaluating a particular example of sex research?

- A number of social observers have suggested that men who are active consumers of sexually violent films, magazines, and other pornography are likely to adopt abusive attitudes toward women. As a result, they show an increased tendency to commit rape and other abusive acts toward women.
- Many people believe that a few drinks make sex more enjoyable. After imbibing a little alcohol, they say that their inhibitions relax; they feel more sensual and more friendly toward the person they are with.
- Early in the last century, Sigmund Freud asserted that women's orgasms resulting from vaginal penetration are more "mature" than those resulting from clitoral stimulation alone. A common assumption today is that "vaginal" orgasms are superior to clitoral orgasms.

You have probably heard these three assertions before, and you may agree with one or even all of them. But if you were called on to prove that they were true or untrue, how would you go about compiling evidence? Or, as the quotation at the top of this page asks, How do you study sex?

sexology
The study of sexuality.

The role of **sexology**, the study of sexuality, is to test such assumptions in a scientific way, to find out whether they are true or false and to document what underlying relationships, if any, they reveal. This task is not easy. Although intrinsically interesting to most of us, human sexual behavior is also inherently difficult to study because it occupies an intensely private area in our lives. People often feel embarrassed or even threatened when asked to disclose details about their sexual attitudes or behavior to another person, especially to a sex researcher who is a stranger to them. In addition, the subject matter of sexology abounds with myth, exaggeration, secrecy, and value judgments.

Despite these problems, sex researchers are accumulating a growing body of knowledge about human sexual behaviors and attitudes—including the three assumptions with which we began this chapter: Does violent pornography lead to abusive behaviors such as rape? Does alcohol increase sexual pleasure? What are the differences between vaginal and clitoral orgasms? We will revisit these and other questions in this chapter as we discuss the methods used to study sexuality, the kinds of questions appropriate to each method, and the problems inherent in each method. In the process, we will also learn something about evaluating published research.

We hope that in the following pages you will begin to appreciate what we know and what we do not know and how confident we can be about the available knowledge. You may also begin to sense the steps we can take to further expand our scientific knowledge of sexual behavior. Perhaps you will contribute to our understanding of this important area of human experience. We invite you to do so.

The Goals of Sexology

People who study human sexuality share certain goals with scientists in other disciplines. These goals include *understanding*, *predicting*, and *controlling* or influencing the events that are the subject matter of their respective fields.

The first two scientific goals—understanding and predicting behavior—are not difficult to comprehend. For example, a pharmacologist who knows how blood pressure medications interfere with sexual functioning can use this knowledge to predict what dosage of a drug could be tolerated by a patient with a particular health condition without experiencing impaired sexual functioning. Similarly, a psychologist who knows something about the way certain behavior patterns influence the quality of couples' interactions can help a couple predict whether they will have a happy marriage.

The third goal, using scientifically acquired knowledge to control behavior, is a more difficult concept to comprehend. Understandably, many people express concern about the legitimacy of applying scientific knowledge to control people's behavior. A certain amount of skepticism in this area is probably healthy, and it would be inaccurate to suggest that all knowledge acquired through research leads directly to behavior control. Nevertheless, sexologists have been able to influence, to some degree, a large body of phenomena. For example, understanding how adolescents make decisions about contraceptive use has resulted in the development of school-based sex-education programs, many of which are linked to family planning clinic services. These innovative programs have often resulted in positive behavioral changes, such as increased contraceptive use among sexually active teenagers. Similarly, knowledge about the psychobiological causes of certain sexual problems, such as premature ejaculation and lack of vaginal lubrication, has enabled specialists to develop therapies aimed at controlling such disruptive symptoms, as we will see in Chapter 14.

Most of us would not object to the goal of controlling or influencing events in the examples just described. However, sexologists, like other scientists, must also contend with situations in which the application of this goal raises important questions. For instance, is it appropriate for fertility specialists to use their knowledge to help a couple conceive a child of a desired biological sex? Is it appropriate for a sex therapist to subject imprisoned sex offenders to aversive stimuli (such as putrid odors) in an effort to control deviant sexual urges? Clearly, the goal of controlling or influencing human behavior should be carefully evaluated within a framework of ethical consideration.

Compared with many other disciplines, sexology is an infant science, having originated largely in the 20th century. The pioneering work of Alfred Kinsey, the first researcher to conduct an extensive general survey of American sexual behaviors, took place only in the late 1940s and early 1950s. Many questions remain unanswered, although a considerable body of knowledge is accumulating. In the remainder of this chapter, we examine some of the research methods that have been used to explore human sexuality.

Nonexperimental Research Methods

We began this chapter with three common notions about human sexual behavior: that exposure to violent pornography can increase a man's tolerance of, and willingness to commit, sexually violent acts, such as rape; that alcohol can enhance sexual responsiveness; and that vaginal orgasms are superior to clitoral orgasms. How do researchers go about investigating hypotheses such as these? In this section, we will look at three nonexperimental methods: (1) the case study, (2) the survey, and (3) direct observation. Later in the chapter, we will learn about a fourth method, experimental research. ■ Table 2.1 summarizes these four major methods of studying sexual behavior. As we will see, not every research method is appropriate to every type of research question.

Case Studies

A **case study** examines either a single subject or a small group of subjects, each of whom is studied individually and in depth. Data are gathered using a variety of means, including direct observation, questionnaires, testing, and even experimentation.

case study
A nonexperimental research method that examines either a single subject or a small group of subjects individually and in depth.

People often become subjects for case studies because they behave in an atypical way or have a physical or emotional disorder. For example, much of what is known about sex offenders, incest victims, transsexuals, sex workers, and the like has been learned from case studies. Also, a large portion of our information about difficulties in sexual response (such as erectile disorders in men and lack of orgasmic response in women) or atypical sexual response patterns comes from case studies of people seeking better understanding of, or treatment for, these problems. An interesting contemporary example of this research is the phenomenon of *spontaneous orgasms*, documented by a series of recent case studies that revealed an association between taking various antidepressant medications and experiencing orgasm without sexual sensory stimulation (Campbell & Schubert, 2007; Silverberg, 2008a). We discuss this unusual side effect of psychiatric medications in Chapter 6.

Not surprisingly, a number of case studies have investigated the relationship between sexually violent media and rape. In many of these studies, rapists report high levels of exposure to sexually violent films, magazines, and books. However, it is unclear whether violent attitudes toward women and behaviors such as rape result directly from exposure to sexually violent media. The mere fact that rapists seem more inclined than nonrapists to consume pornography does not necessarily imply a cause-and-effect relationship. Perhaps there are other plausible explanations. For example, the types of environments that tend to socialize men to be violent toward women might also be characterized by accessibility to violent pornography. Alternatively, men who have abusive proclivities directed toward women may be inclined to consume sexually violent pornography. Thus, although the case-study method shows that this media exposure is often associated with rape, it cannot tell us the exact nature of the relationship.

The case-study method has also been used to investigate the common assertion that alcohol enhances sexual responsiveness and pleasure. In fact, evidence from some case studies suggests just the reverse, at least among chronic alcoholics. Case studies

At a Glance

■ TABLE 2.1 A Summary of Research Methods

Method	Brief Description	Advantages	Disadvantages
Case study	Examines a single subject or a small group of subjects, each of whom is studied individually and in depth.	Flexibility in data-gathering procedures. In-depth explorations of behaviors, thoughts, and feelings.	Limited generalizability of findings. Accuracy of data limited by fallibility of human memory. Not suitable for many kinds of research questions.
Survey	Data pertaining to sexual attitudes and behaviors derived from relatively large groups of people by means of questionnaires or interviews.	Relatively cheap and quick method for obtaining large amounts of data. Can obtain data from more people than is practical to study in the laboratory or through case studies.	Problems of: Nonresponse Demographic bias Inaccurate information
Direct observation	Researchers observe and record responses of participating subjects.	Virtually eliminates the possibility of data falsification. Behavioral record can be kept indefinitely on videotapes or films.	Subjects' behavior can be influenced by presence of observer(s) or the artificial nature of the environment where observations are made.
Experimental method	Researcher manipulates a set of conditions, or variables, and observes the effect of this manipulation on subjects' behavior.	Provides a controlled environment for managing relevant variables. Suited to discovering causal relationships between variables.	Artificiality of laboratory settings can adversely influence or bias subjects' responses.

of alcoholic subjects have shown decreased arousability and lowered sexual interest, although it is possible that this effect is due to the general physical deterioration that accompanies heavy, long-term alcohol use.

The case-study approach offers some advantages to researchers. One advantage is the flexibility of data-gathering procedures. Although the open-ended format of the case study offers little opportunity for investigative control, it often provides opportunities to acquire insight into specific behaviors. The highly personal, subjective information about what individuals actually think and feel about their behavior is an important step beyond simply recording activities. The case-study method sacrifices some control, but it offers opportunities to explore specific behaviors, thoughts, and feelings in depth and can add considerable dimension to our information.

The case-study method does have some limitations, however. Because case studies typically focus on individuals or small samples of especially interesting or atypical cases, it is often difficult to generalize findings accurately to broader populations. A second limitation of case studies is that a person's past history, especially the person's childhood and adolescence, usually does not become a target of research until the individual manifests some unusual behavior later in life, as an adult. People often have trouble accurately remembering events from years ago. Furthermore, memory is also subject to intentional efforts to distort or repress facts.

A third limitation of the case study is that it is not suitable for many kinds of research questions. For instance, a case study might not be the best method for testing the third assumption on this chapter's opening page—that vaginal orgasms are superior to clitoral orgasms. And because personal accounts can be influenced by factors such as emotions, values, and the vagaries of memory, the reliability of the case-study method can also be in doubt.

Surveys

Most of our information about human sexuality has been obtained from a second important research method, the **survey**, in which people are asked about their sexual experiences or attitudes. The survey method enables researchers to collect data from a large number of people, usually more than can be studied in a clinical setting or in the laboratory. Surveys can be conducted orally, through face-to-face or telephone interviews, or through paper-and-pencil questionnaires. Computerized interviews are also used to gather information about sexual behaviors and other sensitive topics. We will discuss this technological aid to sex research later in this chapter.

Although the methods of conducting written and oral surveys are somewhat different, their intent is the same. Each tries to use a relatively small group, called the *survey sample*, to draw inferences or conclusions about a much larger group with a particular characteristic (called a *target population*). Examples of target populations are married adults and high school adolescents.

Choosing the Sample

The questions asked by sexologists often apply to populations that are too large to study in their entirety. For example, if you wanted to obtain information about the sexual practices of American married couples in their later years, your population would include all married couples in the United States over a given age, say, 65. Clearly, it would be impossible

survey
A research method in which a sample of people are questioned about their behaviors and/or attitudes.

© David Young-Wolff/Photo Edit

Most information about human sexual behavior has been obtained through questionnaire or interview surveys.

representative sample
A type of limited research sample that provides an accurate representation of a larger target population of interest.

to question everyone in this group. Sex researchers resolve this problem by obtaining data from a relatively small sample of the target population. The confidence with which conclusions about the larger population can be drawn depends on the technique used to select this sample.

Typically, researchers strive to select a **representative sample** (sometimes called a *probability sample*)—that is, a sample in which various subgroups are represented proportionately to their incidence in the target population. Target populations can be subdivided into smaller subgroups by such criteria as age, economic status, geographic locale, and religious affiliation. In a representative sample, every individual in the larger target population has a chance of being included.

What procedures would you use to select a representative sample that could be surveyed to assess the sexual practices of older American married couples? How would you ensure the representativeness of your selected sample? A good beginning would be to obtain U.S. Census Bureau statistics on the number of married couples whose partners are age 65 and older who reside in major geographic regions of the United States (East, South, and so on). Next, you would select subgroups of your sample according to the actual distribution of the larger population. Thus, if 25% of older married couples live in the East, 25% of your sample would be drawn from this region. Similarly, if 15% of older married couples in the East fall into an upper socioeconomic status category, 15% of those subjects selected from the East would be drawn from this group.

Once you had systematically compiled your lists of potential subjects, your final step would be to select your actual subjects from these lists. To ensure that all members of each subgroup had an equal chance of being included, you might use a table of random numbers to generate random selections from your lists. If these procedures were correctly applied, and if your final sample was large enough, you could be reasonably confident that your findings could be generalized to all married American couples age 65 or older.

random sample
A randomly chosen subset of a population.

Another kind of sample, the **random sample**, is selected from a larger population, using randomization procedures. A random sample may or may not be the same as a representative sample. For example, assume that you are a social scientist on the faculty of a rural university in the Midwest whose students are inclined to hold relatively conservative social views. You wish to conduct a survey to assess American university students' experience with "hook-ups" (short-term or one-time loveless sexual encounters between strangers or casual acquaintances). Since it is convenient to draw your subjects from the student population enrolled at your university, you randomly select your survey sample from a roster of all enrolled students.

A substantial majority of your sample respond to your well-designed, anonymously administered questionnaire. Can you now be relatively confident that your results reflect the propensity of students to engage in hook-ups—if not in the greater United States, at least in your geographic region? Unfortunately, you cannot, because you have selected subjects from a sample that is not necessarily representative of the broader community of university students. Students at your university tend to have conservative social views, a trait that may both influence their likelihood of engaging in hook-ups and render them atypical of large segments of American university students, especially those enrolled in urban universities on the East and West Coasts, whose student populations tend to hold more-liberal social views.

Critical Thinking Question

What procedures would you use to select a representative sample of American college students ages 18 to 22, to assess the effect of alcohol consumption on sexual functioning?

Thus, even though randomization is often a valid selection tool, a study sample cannot be truly representative unless it reflects all the important subgroups in the target population. All things considered, representative samples generally allow for more-accurate generalizations to the entire target population than do random samples. However, random samples are often quite adequate and thus are used widely.

Questionnaires and Interviews

Once selected, subjects in a sample can be surveyed through a paper-and-pencil or computerized questionnaire or a face-to-face interview. These procedures involve asking the participants a set of questions, which might range from a few to over 1,000. These questions can be multiple-choice, true-or-false, or discussion questions; subjects can respond alone, in the privacy of their homes, or in the presence of a researcher.

Each survey method has advantages and disadvantages. Questionnaires tend to be quicker and cheaper to administer than interview surveys. In addition, because filling out a form affords greater anonymity than facing an interviewer, subjects might be considerably more likely to answer questions honestly, with minimal distortion. Sexual behavior is highly personal, and in interviews subjects might be tempted to describe their behaviors or attitudes in a more favorable light. Finally, because most written questionnaires can be evaluated objectively, their data are less subject to researcher bias than are data from interviews.

On the other hand, interviews have some advantages that questionnaires do not have. First, the format of an interview is more flexible. If a particular question is confusing to the subject, the interviewer can clarify it. In addition, interviewers have the option of varying the sequence of questions if it seems appropriate for a particular respondent. And, finally, skillful interviewers can establish excellent rapport with subjects, and the resulting sense of trust may produce more revealing responses than is possible with paper-and-pencil or computerized questionnaires.

Problems of Sex Survey Research: Nonresponse, Inaccuracy, and Demographic Bias

Regardless of the survey strategy used, sex researchers find that it is difficult to secure a representative sample. This occurs because many people do not want to participate in sex studies. For instance, assuming that you used proper sampling procedures to choose your sample of older married couples in the example discussed earlier, what proportion of your representative sample would actually be willing to answer your questions? **Nonresponse**, the refusal to participate in a research study, is a common problem that consistently plagues sex survey research (Turner, 1999; Wiederman, 2001).

No one has ever conducted a major sex survey in which 100% of the selected subjects voluntarily participated. In fact, some studies include results obtained from samples in which only a small minority responded. This situation raises an important question: Are people who agree to take part in sex surveys any different from those who refuse?

Perhaps volunteer subjects in sex research are a representative cross section of the population, but we have no theoretical or statistical basis for that conclusion. As a matter of fact, the opposite might well be true. People who volunteer to participate may be the ones who are the most eager to share their experiences, who have explored a wide range of activities, or who feel most comfortable with their sexuality. (Or it may be that the most experienced people are those who are least willing to respond because they feel that their behaviors are atypical or extreme.) A preponderance of experienced, inexperienced, liberal, or conservative individuals can bias any sample.

Research suggests that **self-selection**, or volunteer bias, is an important concern for sex researchers (Plaud et al., 1999; Wiederman, 2001). Studies strongly suggest that volunteers for sex research are more sexually experienced and hold more positive attitudes toward sexuality and sex research than do nonvolunteers (Boynton, 2003; Plaud et al., 1999). In addition, research indicates that women are less likely than men to volunteer for sex research (Boynton, 2003; Plaud et al., 1999), a finding that suggests female sex research samples may be more influenced by volunteer bias than male samples.

nonresponse
The refusal to participate in a research study.

self-selection
The bias introduced into research study results because of participants' willingness to respond.

Another problem inherent in sex survey research has to do with the accuracy of subjects' responses. Most data about human sexual behavior are obtained from respondents' own reports of their experiences, and people's actual behavior can be quite different from what they report (Catania, 1999; Ochs & Binik, 1999). How many people accurately remember when they first masturbated, and with what frequency, or at what age they first experienced orgasm? Some people may also distort or falsify their self-disclosures to maintain or even enhance their social image (Catania, 1999). This tendency to provide *socially desirable* responses can involve people who consciously or unconsciously conceal certain facts about their sexual histories because they view them as abnormal, foolish, or painful to remember. People can also feel pressure to deny or minimize their experiences regarding behaviors for which strong taboos exist, such as incest, homosexuality, and masturbation. In other cases, people can purposely inflate their experience, perhaps out of a desire to appear more liberal, experienced, or proficient.

A third type of problem that affects sex surveys is **demographic bias**. Most of the data available from sex research in the United States have come from samples weighted heavily toward White, middle-class volunteers. Typically, college students and educated white-collar workers are overrepresented. Ethnic and racial minorities and less-educated individuals are underrepresented.

How much of an effect do nonresponse and demographic bias have on sex research findings? We cannot say for sure. But as long as elements of society, including the less educated and ethnic and racial minorities, are underrepresented, we must be cautious in generalizing findings to the population at large. The informational deficit pertaining to sexual behaviors of American racial and ethnic minorities is lessening with the emergence of several studies that included members of various ethnic minority groups in the United States. These studies demonstrate that ethnicity often exerts considerable influence on sexual attitudes and behaviors (Okazaki, 2002). Throughout this textbook, we describe results from several studies as we discuss ethnicity in relation to a variety of topics.

The Kinsey Reports

The studies of Alfred Kinsey are perhaps the best known and most widely cited example of survey research. With his associates Kinsey published two large volumes in the decade following World War II: One, on male sexuality, was published in 1948; the follow-up report on female sexuality was published in 1953. These volumes contain the results of extensive survey interviews, the aim of which was to determine patterns of sexual behavior in American males and females.

The Kinsey sample consisted of 5,300 White males and 5,940 White females. Respondents came from both rural and urban areas in each state and represented a range of ages, marital statuses, occupations, educational levels, and religions. However, the sample had a disproportionately greater number of better-educated, city-dwelling Protestants, whereas older people, rural dwellers, and those with less education were underrepresented. African Americans and other racial minorities were completely omitted from the sample. And, finally, all subjects were volunteers. Thus in no way can Kinsey's study population be viewed as a representative sample of the American population.

Although published over 50 years ago, many of Kinsey's data are relevant today. The passage of time has not altered the validity of certain findings—for example, that sexual behavior is influenced by educational level and that heterosexuality or homosexuality is often not an all-or-none proposition. However, certain other areas—such as coital rates among unmarried people—are more influenced by changing societal norms. Therefore we might expect the Kinsey data to be less predictive of contemporary practices in these areas. Nevertheless, even here the data are still relevant; they provide one possible basis for estimating the degree of behavioral change over the years.

---

demographic bias
A kind of sampling bias in which certain segments of society (such as White, middle-class, white-collar workers) are disproportionately represented in a study population.

The National Health and Social Life Survey

The outbreak of the devastating AIDS epidemic in the 1980s occurred at a time when the U.S. public health community was ill informed about the contemporary sexual practices of the citizenry. To fill this informational void with data that could be used to predict and prevent the spread of AIDS, in 1987 an agency within the U.S. Department of Health and Human Services called for proposals to study the sexual attitudes and practices of American adults. A team of distinguished researchers at the University of Chicago answered this call with a plan for a national survey to assess the prevalence of a broad array of sexual practices and attitudes and to place them in their social contexts within the U.S. population. The research team—Edward Laumann and his colleagues John Gagnon, Robert Michael, and Stuart Michaels—were initially heartened by the acceptance of their proposal in 1988 and by the provision of government funds adequate to support a survey of 20,000 people.

A sample size this large would have allowed the investigators to draw reliable conclusions about various subpopulations in America, such as diverse ethnic minorities and homosexuals. However, after more than two years of extensive planning, the research team's efforts were dealt a crushing blow when federal funding for their study was withdrawn. In 1991, conservative members of Congress, offended by the prospect of government funding of sex research, introduced legislation that effectively eliminated federal funding for such studies. Unfortunately, legitimate sexuality research remains under fire, largely from conservative organizations and politicians who continue to feel threatened by this type of research (see the Sex and Politics box, "Sex Research Under Siege").

Alfred Kinsey, a pioneer sex researcher, conducted one of the most comprehensive surveys on human sexuality.

Undaunted by this setback, Laumann and his colleagues secured funding from several private foundations that enabled them to proceed with their project, albeit with a much smaller sample. The research team, working with the National Opinion Research Center at the University of Chicago, used sophisticated sampling techniques to select a representative sample of 4,369 Americans ages 18 to 59. An amazing 79% of the sample subjects agreed to participate, yielding a final study group of 3,432 respondents. This high response rate dramatically demonstrates that a broad array of people will participate in a highly personal sex survey when they are assured that the societal benefits of the research are important and that the confidentiality of their responses is guaranteed. Furthermore, this unusually high participation rate, together with the fact that the study population closely approximated many known demographic characteristics of the general U.S. population, yielded data that most social scientists believe reliably indicate the sexual practices of most American adults ages 18 to 59.

Forced to limit their sample size, Laumann and his associates had to forgo sampling a broad range of subpopulations and instead oversampled African Americans and Hispanic Americans to secure valid information about these two largest ethnic minorities in America. Thus, although the study population was representative of White Americans, African Americans, and Hispanic Americans, too few members of other racial and ethnic minorities (such as Jews, Asian Americans, and Native Americans) were included to provide useful information about these groups.

Laumann and his colleagues trained 220 professionals with prior interviewing experience to interview all 3,432 respondents face-to-face. They designed the questionnaire to be easily understood and to flow naturally across various topics. Using trained,

Critical Thinking Question

Should the federal government fund sex research? Are there potential benefits for the American people that justify such expenditures?

Conservative organizations and politicians have made a concerted effort to pressure federal agencies (a major funding source) to withdraw or minimize financial support for sexuality research. At present it is exceedingly difficult to obtain funding for sex research (Flam, 2008). Christian fundamentalist groups, such as the Traditional Values Coalition, have zealously lobbied Congress to block funding for a variety of sex research projects, especially research aimed at study populations deemed inappropriate, such as gay men and prostitutes (Kaiser, 2003).

Fortunately, some members of Congress, most notably Representative Henry Waxman (Democrat from California), have defended federal funding for sex research while decrying efforts by the Traditional Values Coalition and similar organizations to block valuable scientific investigations.

This "rattling of the sabers" by conservative forces has had a chilling impact on sexuality research in America. A prime example of fallout from such pressure was the closing of the Boston University Sexuality Research and Treatment Program in 2004, which ended a 20-year-old program and valuable research into human sexual arousal and response (Clark, 2005). The threat of funding cuts has caused some sex researchers to seek financial support from drug companies whose primary interest is in developing pharmaceutical treatments for sexual difficulties. A direct consequence of this shift in funding sources has been a de-emphasis on the psychosocial aspects of human sexual functioning and a diversion of sex research "from

its original mission—deepening our understanding of this critical aspect of human behavior in a way that benefits all of society" (Clark, 2005, p. 18).

In recent years conservative politicians, such as Senate Republican Leader Mitch McConnell, have continued to demean legitimate social and sex research. In February 2010 McConnell issued a news release claiming that money from the economic stimulus was being used to study the sex lives of college women. The research he referred to, the Women's Health Project conducted at Syracuse University by Michael Carey, is a wide-ranging study designed to improve women's health, including areas such as alcohol use, physical activity, anxiety and depression, eating disorders, the impact of sexual hook-ups on mental and physical health, intimate partner coercion, and sexually transmitted infections. Even though the overall focus of this research was to provide information about how to more effectively promote health for women, McConnell chose to emphasize only the sexual behavior aspect of this study in his attack on legitimate research (PolitiFact, 2010).

The scientific community is united in the belief that allowing the political clout of organized extremist groups to influence or control research funding would set a very dangerous precedent. It is hoped that opposition to political meddling in scientific research will sustain the integrity of scientific peer review and thus leave decisions on what constitutes legitimate research in the hands of competent professionals, not elected officials.

experienced interviewers ensured that respondents understood all the questions posed. In addition, to validate the overall responses, the questionnaire contained internal checks to measure the consistency of answers.

This study, titled the National Health and Social Life Survey (NHSLS), provided the most comprehensive information about adult sexual behavior in America since Kinsey's research. In fact, because Laumann and his associates used far better sampling techniques than did the Kinsey group, the NHSLS study is a representative U.S. sex survey that reliably reflects the sexual practices of the general U.S. adult population in the 1990s. An analysis of the NHSLS findings was published in two books. The first book is a detailed and scholarly text titled *The Social Organization of Sexuality: Sexual Practices in the United States* (Laumann et al., 1994). Michael, Gagnon, Laumann, and Gina Kolata—a respected *New York Times* science author—wrote a less technical companion volume for the public titled *Sex in America: A Definitive Study*. This book, also published in 1994, emerged as a popular trade book.

The NHSLS findings contradicted conventional wisdom—promulgated by magazine surveys and mass media images—that envisioned a "sex crazy" American populace madly pursuing excessive indulgence in all kinds of conventional and unconventional sexual practices. In reality, the results of the NHSLS reflect an American people who are more content with their erotic lives, less sexually active, and more sexually conservative than was widely believed. These findings are especially ironic in view of the judgmental opposition to the Laumann study by conservative legislators who feared it would provide a mandate for excessive sexual expression.

As previously mentioned, our understanding of the impact of ethnic diversity on sexual behavior has been improving as a result of several research studies. The NHSLS is a good example of this expanding knowledge base.

The NHSLS research team, *left to right*: Robert Michael, John Gagnon, Stuart Michaels, and Edward Laumann.

The National Survey of Sexual Health and Behavior (NSSHB)

In 2010 one of the largest nationally representative investigations of sexual health and behaviors to date was released by Indiana University's Center for Sexual Health Promotion. This study, titled the National Survey of Sexual Health and Behavior (NSSHB), was conducted by Michael Reece, Debby Herbenick, J. Dennis Fortenberry, Brian Dodge, Stephanie Sanders, and Vanessa Schick (2010a). These investigators reported on data reflecting the sexual experiences of 5,865 adolescents and adults ages 14 to 94. The researchers used a probability sampling of a frame of residential addresses in the U.S. Postal Service's file that includes approximately 98% of all U.S. households (Reece et al., 2010a). Data were collected, via the Internet, from participants randomly selected from this probability sample. The survey included more than 40 combinations of sexual acts engaged in during sexual events, patterns of condom use, and the percentage of subjects who participated in same-sex encounters.

The NSSHB survey is the first broadly comprehensive study of sexual and sexual health–related behaviors in the almost two decades since publication of the NHSLS study. Many sexologists and related scientists believe that this important research will play a significant role in guiding future research and education in the field of sexology (Barclay, 2010).

The primary findings obtained via the NSSHB survey were presented in nine articles published in an October 1, 2010, special issue of the *Journal of Sexual Medicine*. Major findings from the NSSHB survey will be presented in various chapters of this textbook.

Survey Findings Regarding Two Issues: Violent Pornography and Alcohol Use

How might the survey method be used to clarify the three assertions with which we began this chapter? The first assertion, concerning violent media and men's likelihood to develop abusive attitudes and behaviors toward women, has been the subject of a number of surveys.

One of the most notable studies involved 222 male nonoffender college students who were administered a questionnaire regarding their use of pornography and their self-reported likelihood of committing rape or using sexual force. Of these men, 81% had used nonviolent pornography during the previous year, whereas 35% had used sexually violent pornography. Of the subjects who had used sexually violent pornography, many more indicated a likelihood of raping or using sexual force against a woman than did subjects who used only nonviolent pornography (Démare et al., 1988). Other surveys of different populations of men (including some imprisoned rapists) have provided further indications that exposure to sexually violent media can lead to increased tolerance for sexually aggressive behavior, greater acceptance of the myth that women want to be raped, reduced sensitivity to rape victims, desensitization to violence against women, and, in some cases, an increased probability of committing a rape (Donnerstein & Linz, 1984; Rosen & Beck, 1988).

The second assertion, concerning the effect of alcohol on sexual responsiveness, has also been the subject of survey research. One study conducted in 1970 asked 20,000 middle- and upper-middle-class Americans whether drinking enhanced their sexual pleasure (Athanasiou et al., 1970). Most respondents answered yes—60% stated that alcohol helped put them "in the mood" for sex, with a significantly higher proportion of women providing this response. This finding should be interpreted with some caution, however, because people's memories of events can differ considerably from their actual behaviors. For the third assertion, regarding the superiority of vaginal orgasms, any survey results would also need to be interpreted with caution, for the same reasons. A more appropriate method for studying this question is direct observation, to which we turn next.

Direct Observation

A third method for studying human sexual behavior is **direct observation**. In this method, researchers observe and record responses of participating subjects. Although observational research is quite common in the social sciences, such as anthropology, sociology, and psychology, little research of this nature occurs in sexology because of the highly personal and private nature of human sexual expression.

The most famous example of direct observational research is the widely acclaimed work of William Masters and Virginia Johnson, cited frequently in this textbook. Masters and Johnson used direct observation in a laboratory setting to learn about physiological changes during sexual arousal. The result, *Human Sexual Response* (1966), was based on laboratory observations of 10,000 completed sexual response cycles. Their research sample consisted of sexually responsive volunteers (382 women and 312 men), drawn largely from an academic community of above-average intelligence and socioeconomic background—obviously not a representative sample of the entire U.S. population. However, the physical signs of sexual arousal, the subject of their study, appear to be rather stable across a wide range of people with diverse backgrounds.

Masters and Johnson used a number of techniques to record physiological sexual responses. These included the use of photographic equipment and instruments to measure and record muscular and vascular changes throughout the body. They also used direct observation as well as ingenious measurement devices to record changes in sex organs. (Electronic devices for measuring sexual arousal will be described later in this chapter.) Masters and Johnson recorded responses to a variety of stimulus situations in their laboratory: masturbation, coitus with a partner, and stimulation of the breasts alone. As a follow-up to all recorded observations, each participant was extensively interviewed.

Masters and Johnson's observational approach provided a wealth of information about the manner in which women and men respond physiologically to sexual stimulation. Among other findings, they observed no biological difference between clitoral and vaginal orgasms. This finding and other observations by Masters and Johnson will be discussed at greater length in Chapter 6.

A more contemporary example of the direct observation method is provided by recent cutting-edge research that employs a technological tool called *functional magnetic resonance imaging* (fMRI) to observe, record, and map areas of the human brain that are activated when individuals are exposed to visual erotica. Magnetic resonance imaging has also been used to provide precise measurements of genital changes during sexual arousal. Two Spotlight on Research boxes in Chapter 6 highlight fascinating findings associated with the use of this powerful technology.

Direct observation has clear advantages as a research method. For studying sexual response patterns, seeing and measuring sexual behavior firsthand is clearly superior to relying on subjective reports of past experiences. Direct observation virtually eliminates the possibility of data falsification through memory deficits, boastful inflation, or guilt-induced repression. Furthermore, records of such behaviors can be kept indefinitely on videotape or film. But this approach also has disadvantages. A major problem lies in the often unanswerable question of just how much a subject's behavior is influenced by the presence of even the most discreet observer. This question has been asked often since the publication of Masters and Johnson's research. Researchers using direct observation attempt to minimize this potential complication by being as unobtrusive as possible, remaining in a fringe location, observing through one-way glass, or perhaps using technological tools such as remotely activated video cameras or fMRI devices. But the subject is still aware that he or she is being observed.

Although there is merit to criticisms of the direct-observation method, Masters and Johnson's research has demonstrated that it can withstand the test of time. Their findings are still applied in many areas—including infertility counseling, conception control, sex therapy, and sex education—with beneficial results.

William Masters and Virginia Johnson used direct observation to study the physiological sexual responses of women and men.

The Experimental Method

A fourth method, **experimental research**, is being used with increasing frequency to investigate human sexual behavior. Studies using this method, typically conducted in a laboratory environment, have a major advantage over other methods because they provide a controlled environment in which all possible influences on subjects' responses, other than the factors that are being investigated, can be ruled out. A researcher using the experimental method manipulates a particular set of conditions, or variables, and observes the effect of this manipulation on subjects' behavior or their physical or mental status. The experimental method is particularly suited to discovering *causal* relationships between variables.

There are two types of *variables* (behaviors or conditions that can have varied values) in any experimental research design: independent and dependent. An **independent variable** is a condition or component of the experiment that is under the control of the researcher, who manipulates or determines its value. Conversely, a **dependent variable** is an outcome or resulting behavior that the experimenter observes and records but does not control.

With this brief summary of the experimental method in mind, let us consider how this technique might clarify the relationship between sexually violent media and rape attitudes and behavior. A number of experimental research studies have provided compelling evidence that sexually violent media can cause attitudes to shift toward greater tolerance of sexually aggressive behavior and can contribute to some rapists' assaultive behaviors. We consider three experiments, the first involving college men and the other two using convicted rapists as subjects.

The first study was conducted with 271 college men who were assigned to two groups. Subjects in the first group were exposed to movies with nonviolent sexual themes, whereas subjects in the second group saw R-rated films in which men were shown committing sexual violence against women who eventually experienced a transformation from victim to willing partner. A few days after viewing the movies, all subjects completed an attitude questionnaire. The results demonstrated that the men who viewed the violent films were generally much more accepting of sexual violence toward

experimental research
Research conducted in precisely controlled laboratory conditions so that subjects' reactions can be reliably measured.

independent variable
In an experimental research design, a condition or component that is under the control of the researcher, who manipulates or determines its value.

dependent variable
In an experimental research design, an outcome or resulting behavior that the experimenter observes and records but does not control.

Critical Thinking Question

What are the independent and dependent variables in this study? (See p. 48 for the answer.)

Critical Thinking Question

Of the four research techniques discussed (case study, survey, direct observation, and experimental study), which method do you think would be most helpful for investigating the effect of chronic pain on sexual functioning? Why?

Critical Thinking Question

What are the independent and dependent variables in this study? (See p. 48 for the answer.)

women than were those subjects who were exposed to movies with consensual, nonviolent erotic themes (Malamuth & Check, 1981).

Two other research studies, with comparable research designs, compared the erectile responses (dependent variable) of matched groups of rapists and nonrapists to two different taped descriptions of sexual activity (independent variable)—one involving rape and the other, mutually consenting sexual activity (Abel et al., 1977; Barbaree et al., 1979). While subjects listened to the tapes, penile tumescence (engorgement) was measured with a penile strain gauge, which is described in the next section of this chapter. In both experiments rapists experienced erections while listening to violent descriptions of rape, whereas their nonrapist counterparts did not. Descriptions of consenting sexual activity produced similar levels of arousal in both groups of men. These findings suggest that exposure to sexually violent media not only encourages attitudes of violence toward women but also influences at least some men who rape to "sexualize" violence.

The experimental method has also been used to study the relationship between alcohol use and sexual responsiveness (although it has not been used to study vaginal orgasms). In one study of 48 male college students, a penile strain gauge was used to measure engorgement as subjects watched a sexually explicit film, first while not under the influence of alcohol and then several days later, after the subjects had consumed controlled amounts of alcohol. Findings showed that sexual arousal was reduced by drinking alcohol and that the more alcohol consumed, the greater the reduction (Briddell & Wilson, 1976). A similar experiment tested the relationship between arousal and alcohol intake in women, with consistent results (Wilson & Lawson, 1976).

These studies illustrate one of the primary advantages of the experimental method. Because researchers can control variables precisely, they are able to draw conclusions about causal relationships to a degree not possible with other research methods. However, this method also has disadvantages. One of the most important limitations has to do with the artificiality of laboratory settings, which can adversely influence or bias subjects' responses. As in direct-observation research, the fact that people know they are in an experiment can alter their responses from those that might occur outside the laboratory.

Not all experimental research in sexology is conducted within the relative artificiality of a laboratory setting. A landmark experimental study designed to test the hypothesis that circumcision may be an effective strategy for preventing HIV infection was conducted in South Africa. Investigators recruited over 3,000 uncircumcised and uninfected men and randomly assigned them to two groups: 50% who were circumcised at the onset of the clinical trial and the other 50% who were scheduled for circumcision at the end of a planned 21-month study. Participants were frequently tested for HIV infection during the course of the study. The investigation was halted after 18 months when it became clear that circumcision significantly reduced the risk of HIV infection (Auvert et al., 2005). This and other recent experimental studies, discussed in Chapter 15, have provided evidence that circumcision is one of many effective strategies for reducing the spread of HIV/AIDS.

Before concluding this chapter, we turn our attention to several additional areas of concern regarding how we acquire information about sexual practices. First, we examine three technologies used in sex research. Next, we discuss ethical guidelines for conducting human sex research. Finally, we end this chapter by describing a process for evaluating research.

Technologies in Sex Research

Sex researchers have benefited from the development of three distinct technologies for collecting data. The first technology we will discuss—electronic devices for measuring sexual arousal—has been around for several decades. The other technologies—computerized assessment of sexual behavior and sex research in cyber-space—are both relatively new.

Electronic Devices for Measuring Sexual Arousal

Experimental research and direct-observation studies of human sexual responses often use measures of sexual arousal. In the early years of sex research, investigators had to rely largely on subjective reports of these responses. However, advances in technology over the last few decades have produced several devices for electronically measuring arousal (see ▌ Figure 2.1).

The penile strain gauge is a flexible loop that looks something like a rubber band with a wire attached. It is actually a thin rubber tube filled with a fine strand of mercury. A tiny electrical current from the attached wire flows through the mercury continuously. The gauge is placed around the base of the penis. As an erection occurs, the rubber tube stretches, and the strand of mercury becomes thinner, changing the flow of the current. These changes are registered by a recording device. The penile strain gauge can measure even the slightest changes in penis size and is so sensitive that it can even record every pulse of blood into the penis. In the interests of privacy a subject can attach the gauge to his own penis. Researchers can also measure male sexual arousal with a penile plethys-mograph or a metal-band gauge, devices that also fit around the penis and reflect small changes in its circumference.

When a woman is sexually aroused, her vaginal walls fill with blood in a manner comparable to the engorgement of a man's penis. The vaginal photoplethysmograph is a device designed to measure this increased vaginal blood volume. It consists of an acrylic cylinder, about the size and shape of a tampon, that is inserted into the vagina. The cylinder contains a light that is reflected off the vaginal walls and a photocell that is sensitive to the reflected light. When the vaginal walls fill with blood during sexual arousal, less light is reflected to the photocell. These changes in light intensity, continuously recorded by an electronic device, provide a measure of sexual arousal comparable to that provided by the penile strain gauge. Like the male device, the vaginal photoplethys-mograph can be inserted in privacy by the research subject. Another electronic device, the clitoral photoplethysmograph, assesses clitoral blood volume and has recently been shown to be a sensitive tool for measuring genital arousal in women (Gerritsen et al., 2009). In addition, two other devices are used to measure sexual response: The vaginal myograph and the rectal myograph are implements inserted into the vagina or rectum that measure muscular activity in the pelvic area.

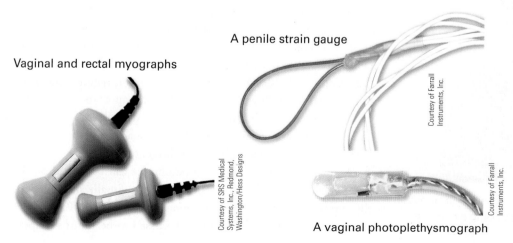

Vaginal and rectal myographs

A penile strain gauge

A vaginal photoplethysmograph

Courtesy of SRS Medical Systems, Inc., Redmond, Washington/Hess Designs

Courtesy of Farrall Instruments, Inc.

Courtesy of Farrall Instruments, Inc.

▌ **Figure 2.1** Devices for electronically measuring sexual arousal.

Computerized Assessment of Sexual Behavior

When an interviewer-administered questionnaire (IAQ) is used in sex research, the human element involved in a face-to-face encounter can influence the respondent to underreport certain sensitive behaviors and to overreport more normative or socially acceptable behaviors (Dolezal et al., 2011; Potdar & Koenig, 2005). A written or self-administered questionnaire (SAQ) provides an alternative survey method that can overcome some of the difficulties of an IAQ by providing a more private and potentially less threatening means of reporting sensitive behavior. However, SAQs can also be limited by the reading ability or literacy of respondents. Failure to understand written survey questions can be a significant limiting factor when people with relatively low literacy are surveyed.

The recent advent of computer-assisted self-interview (CASI) technology for surveying children, adolescents, and adults has provided an excellent tool for overcoming these barriers to successful sex research. With CASI technologies literacy problems and the potentially negative effect of a human interviewer are minimized. Furthermore, researchers can be confident that key elements of questions' presentation and measurement are standardized for all respondents.

Two varieties of CASI technology are currently used. In video CASI technology, respondents view questions on a monitor and enter their answers by pressing labeled keys on the keyboard. Audio CASI offers a somewhat more advanced technology in which respondents listen through headphones to questions (which may also be simultaneously displayed in print on-screen) and enter their answers by keystrokes. The audio component has voice-quality sound. Unlike video CASI and more traditional survey methods, audio CASI does not require respondents to be literate. Furthermore, because questions are prerecorded, this technology allows multilingual administration without requiring researchers to be multilingual.

The application of CASI technology is becoming more widespread, and numerous studies have demonstrated that this method is effective for collecting sensitive information on a variety of topics (Dolezal et al., 2011; Hollander, 2008a; Midanik & Greenfield, 2008). For example, a recent investigation used two data collection methods—CASI and a traditional telephone survey—to obtain sensitive information about sexually transmitted infection (STI) incidence from a sample of more than 2,000 men and women. Subjects were randomly assigned to one of these survey methods. Respondents who participated via CASI were significantly more likely than those who spoke with a telephone interviewer to acknowledge having contracted a variety of STIs (Hollander, 2008a).

Teenagers are more willing to share sensitive information about sexual behavior when they are using a computer.

Sex Research in Cyberspace

As the Internet has rapidly evolved into a common household technology, opportunities have emerged to conduct sex research using this technology (Mustanski, 2001; Parks et al., 2006; Rhodes et al., 2003). Traditionally, the Internet has been used by scientists to distribute research information rather than to collect data. Today, the Internet provides access to a diverse and growing population of potential research participants and is an important medium for conducting research. In this section we will describe the advantages and disadvantages of sex research in cyberspace and examine some of the ethical issues posed by this technology.

Almost any kind of survey questionnaire can be posted on the Internet, and these survey instruments can be visually and functionally similar or identical to conventional questionnaires. The nationally representative NSSHB survey, discussed earlier in this chapter, is a contemporary example of an excellent study conducted via the Internet. So what are the advantages of Internet-based surveys over conventional instruments? Cyberspace questionnaires are considerably cheaper than traditional paper-and-pencil questionnaires because they eliminate printing costs, decrease the need for data collection staff, and do not require distribution and collection costs, such as for postage and envelopes. In comparison with mailed, self-administered questionnaires, Internet-based surveys save time. Research also indicates that people responding to electronic surveys are less influenced by social desirability and more inclined to share information that they might not disclose through traditional written questionnaires or interviews. Perhaps this is because they believe that their responses are more anonymous and secure (Bowen, 2005; Parks et al., 2006).

The collection and management of data are also typically more efficient with Internet-based surveys. For example, survey data can be automatically inserted via e-mail into a corresponding database. Furthermore, researchers can make adjustments to Internet-based surveys as unforeseen problems related to item comprehension are discovered. In addition to the ease of revising items, new follow-up queries, based on preliminary data analysis, can be added as desired.

With hundreds of millions of people worldwide accessing the Internet daily, the Web provides an almost limitless pool of potential study respondents across geographical and cultural boundaries. Researchers conducting sex research on the Internet can also recruit hidden populations of geographically isolated participants or those who might otherwise be difficult to find locally (Bowen, 2005).

A significant disadvantage of Internet-based sex surveys is their association with considerable sample-selection bias (Wallis et al., 2003). At present, a "digital divide" exists, meaning that Internet users are still not representative of the general U.S. population. Internet users tend to be younger, better educated, and more affluent than nonusers. Because of this demographic bias, findings from Internet surveys must be cautiously interpreted. This divide will likely diminish over time as access to the Internet continues to become cheaper and more widespread.

Other challenges and disadvantages of this approach to sex research include low response rates for Internet-based surveys and multiple survey submissions (Coutts & Jann, 2011; Rhodes et al., 2003). Thus, the problem of nonresponse or volunteer bias that plagues all sex survey research is a concern for online investigators as well.

Privacy issues are especially acute when doing sex research in cyberspace. Unfortunately, promises of anonymity on the Internet can rarely, if ever, be given with 100% certainty. Risks of exposure are small, but a few incidents have been reported. To minimize participants' risks, Internet researchers are increasingly using special techniques to provide anonymity (Coutts & Jann, 2011).

Critical Thinking Question

In light of widespread media reports of unauthorized access to personal files by Internet hackers, is it ethical for sexologists to conduct sex research online? Why or why not?

Ethical Guidelines for Human Sex Research

Researchers in a range of investigative fields, including sexology, share a common commitment to maintaining the welfare, dignity, rights, well-being, and safety of their human subjects. Detailed lists of ethical guidelines have been prepared by a number of professional organizations, including the American Psychological Association (APA), the American Medical Association (AMA), and the Society for the Scientific Study of Sexuality (SSSS).

The ethical guidelines require, among other things, that no pressure or coercion be applied to ensure the participation of volunteers in research and that researchers avoid procedures that might cause physical or psychological harm to human subjects. Researchers need to obtain informed consent from participants before conducting an experiment. Obtaining informed consent involves explaining the general purpose of the study and each participant's rights as a subject, including the voluntary nature of participation and the potential costs and benefits of participation (Kuyper et al., 2011; Seal et al., 2000). Researchers must also respect a subject's right to refuse to participate at any time during the course of a study. In addition, special steps must be taken to protect the confidentiality of the data and to maintain participants' anonymity unless they agree to be identified (Margolis, 2000).

The issue of deception in research remains controversial. Some studies would lose their effectiveness if participating subjects knew in advance exactly what the experimenter was studying. The ethical guideline generally applied to this issue is that if deception must be used, a postexperiment debriefing must thoroughly explain to participants why the deception was necessary. At that time, subjects must be allowed to request that their data be removed from the study and destroyed.

An extreme example of violating ethical guidelines occurred in the 1940s when U.S. researchers deliberately injected thousands of Guatemalans with sexually transmitted infections (STIs) such as gonorrhea and syphilis (Walter, 2012). These injections, which occurred without accompanying warnings, were integral to research designed to provide ways to prevent STIs. Between 1946 and 1948, U.S. government researchers experimented without consent on more than 5,000 Guatemalan soldiers, prisoners, prostitutes, orphans, and people with psychiatric disorders. Many of these unwitting participants suffered from severe symptoms of STIs, some for a lifetime. These experiments, ethically unconscionable, were uncovered in 2010 and subsequently condemned by U.S. health officials as being "repugnant and abhorrent."

Sometimes it is hard for researchers to weigh objectively the potential benefits of a study against the possibility of harming subjects. In recognition of this difficulty, virtually every institution conducting research in the United States has established an ethics committee that reviews all proposed studies. If committee members perceive that the subjects' welfare is insufficiently safeguarded, the proposal must be modified or the research cannot be conducted. In addition, federal funding for research is denied to any institution that fails to conduct an adequate ethics committee review before data collection begins.

Evaluating Research: Some Questions to Ask

We hope that the material presented here and elsewhere in our book will help differentiate legitimate scientific sex research from the many frivolous nonscientific polls and opinion surveys that are widespread in the contemporary media. Even when you are exposed to the results of serious investigations, it is wise to maintain a critical eye and to avoid the understandable tendency to accept something as factual just because it is presented as being "scientific." The following list of questions may prove useful as you evaluate the legitimacy of any research, sex or otherwise, that you are exposed to.

1. What are the researchers' credentials? Are the investigators professionally trained? Are they affiliated with reputable institutions (research centers, academic institutions, or the like)? Are they associated with any special-interest groups that may favor a particular research finding or conclusion?
2. Through what type of media were the results published: reputable scientific journals, scholarly textbooks, popular magazines, newspapers, the Internet?
3. What approach or type of research method was used, and were proper scientific procedures adhered to?
4. Were a sufficient number of subjects used, and is there any reason to suspect bias in the selection method?

5. Is it reasonable to apply the research findings to a larger population beyond the sample group? To what extent can legitimate generalizations be made?
6. Is there any reason to believe that the research methods could have biased the findings? (Did the presence of an interviewer encourage false responses? Did cameras place limitations on the response potentials?)
7. Are there any other published research findings that support or refute the study in question?

Summary

The Goals of Sexology

■ The goals of sexology include understanding, predicting, and controlling behavior.
■ Pursuit of the goal of controlling behavior is often modified or tempered by ethical issues.

Nonexperimental Research Methods

■ Nonexperimental methods for studying sexuality include case studies, surveys, and direct observation.
■ Case studies typically produce a great deal of information about one or a few individuals. They have two advantages: flexibility and the opportunity to explore specific behaviors and feelings in depth. Disadvantages include lack of investigative control, possible subjective bias on the researcher's part, and poor sampling techniques, which often limit the possibility of making generalizations to broad populations.
■ Most information about human sexual behavior has been obtained through questionnaire or interview surveys of relatively large populations of respondents. Questionnaires have the advantage of being anonymous, inexpensive, and quickly administered. Interviews are more flexible and allow for more rapport between researcher and subject.
■ Sex researchers who use surveys face certain common problems. These include the following:
  ➤ The virtual impossibility of getting 100% participation of randomly selected subjects, making it difficult to obtain a representative sample. Self-selection of samples, or volunteer bias, is a common problem.
  ➤ Biases created by nonresponse: Do volunteer participants have attitudes and behaviors significantly different from those of nonparticipants?
  ➤ The problem of accuracy: Respondents' self-reports may be less than accurate because of limitations of memory, boastfulness, guilt, or simple misunderstandings.
  ➤ Demographic biases: Most samples are heavily weighted toward White, middle-class, better-educated participants.

■ Research has demonstrated that ethnicity often exerts considerable influence on sexual attitudes and behaviors.
■ The Kinsey surveys were broad-scale studies of human sexual behavior that were somewhat limited by sampling techniques that overrepresented young, educated city dwellers.
■ The National Health and Social Life Survey (NHSLS) has provided a reliable view of the sexual practices of the general U.S. adult population in the 1990s.
■ The NSSHB survey conducted in 2010 provided one of the most expansive, nationally representative studies of sexual behavior and condom use to date.
■ There is little direct-observation sex research because of the highly personal nature of sexual expression. When direct observation can be used, the possibility of data falsification is significantly reduced. However, subjects' behavior might be altered by the presence of an observer. Furthermore, the reliability of recorded observations can sometimes be compromised by preexisting researcher biases.

The Experimental Method

■ A researcher using the experimental method manipulates a particular set of conditions, or variables, and observes the effect of this manipulation on subjects' behavior or their physical or mental status.
■ The purpose of the experimental method is to discover causal relationships between independent and dependent variables.
■ An independent variable is a condition or component of an experiment that is controlled or manipulated by the experimenter.
■ A dependent variable is an outcome or resulting behavior that the experimenter observes and records but does not control.
■ Experimental research offers two advantages: control over the relevant variables and direct analysis of possible causal factors. However, the artificiality of the experimental laboratory setting can alter subject responses from those that might occur in a natural setting.

Technologies in Sex Research

- The penile strain gauge, vaginal photoplethysmograph, clitoral photoplethysmograph, vaginal myograph, and rectal myograph are devices used for electronically measuring human sexual response.
- Video CASI and audio CASI are two versions of computer-assisted self-interview technology that are increasingly being effectively used to collect sensitive information from children, adolescents, and adults.
- The Internet has become an important medium for conducting sex research. The collection and management of data are more efficient with Internet-based surveys, which are cheaper, faster, and more error free than traditional survey methods.
- Disadvantages of Internet-based sex surveys include sample-selection bias, low response rates, and multiple survey submissions.

Ethical Guidelines for Human Sex Research

- Sexologists and other researchers operate under ethical guidelines that seek to ensure the welfare, dignity, rights, well-being, and safety of their human subjects.
- These ethical guidelines require that researchers obtain informed consent from participants, avoid procedures that might cause physical or psychological harm to subjects, and maintain confidentiality of both data and participants.

Evaluating Research: Some Questions to Ask

- In evaluating any study of sexual behavior, it is helpful to consider who conducted the research, examine the methods and sampling techniques, and compare the results with those of other reputable studies.

Answer to Question on p. 42

The independent variable in this experiment was the degree of violence in the movies observed by the participants. The dependent variable was the subjects' responses to the questionnaire.

Answer to Question on p. 42

The independent variable in this experiment was circumcision status (circumcised or uncircumcised). The dependent variable was HIV status (infected or uninfected).

Media Resources

Log in to CengageBrain.com to access the resources your instructor requires.

Go to CengageBrain.com to access Psychology CourseMate, where you will find an interactive eBook, glossaries, flashcards, quizzes, videos, and more.

Also access links to chapter-related websites, including the **Kinsey Institute, The Continuum Complete International Encyclopedia of Sexuality (CCIES), The Society for the Scientific Study of Sexuality (SSSS), Centers for Disease Control and Prevention, The U.S. Census Bureau, The National Health and Social Life Survey (NHSLS), Society for the Psychological Study of Lesbian, Gay, and Bisexual Issues,** and the **Electronic Journal of Human Sexuality.**

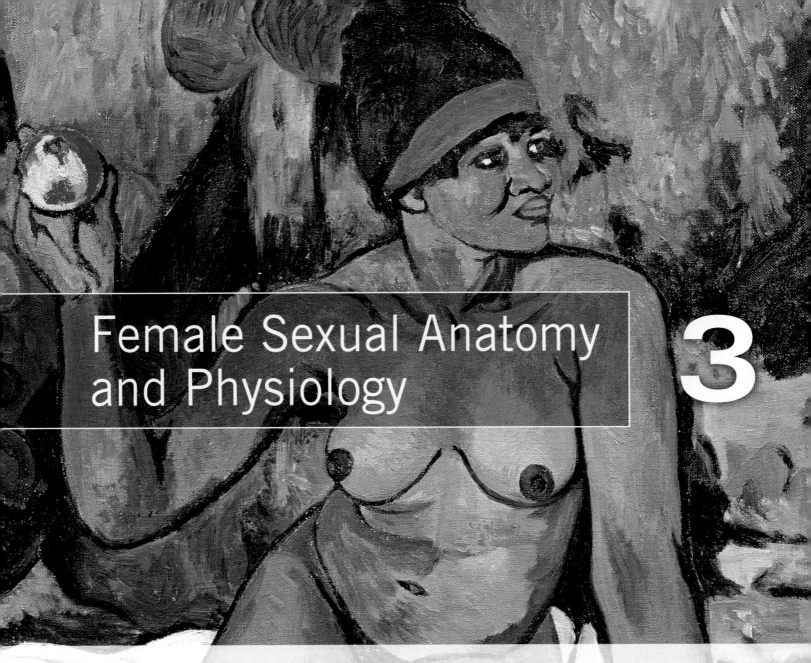

Female Sexual Anatomy and Physiology

3

The Vulva
What factors motivate women to alter the appearance of their vulvas?

What are two reasons to do a genital self-exam?

Does the clitoris serve any purpose other than sexual pleasure?

What are some myths about the hymen?

Underlying Structures
What is the function of the bulbs and glands that underlie the vulval tissue?

What are Kegel exercises, and how can they affect a woman's sexual responsiveness?

Internal Structures
How (and why) does vaginal lubrication occur?

Which internal structure produces the most hormones?

Menstruation
Are there physiological signs that a woman is ovulating and therefore at the most fertile point in her menstrual cycle?

What are the symptoms of premenstrual syndrome and dysmenorrhea?

What can a woman do to minimize these symptoms?

Menopause
What are some positive effects of menopause?

What are the potential benefits and risks of hormone replacement therapy?

Gynecological Health Concerns
Why do vaginal infections and urinary tract problems occur?

How effective is the Pap smear in detecting cervical cancer?

The Breasts
What are the steps for a breast exam?

What percentage of breast cancers is attributed to a genetic flaw?

I had three children and was 45 years old before I ever really looked at my genitals. I was amazed at the delicate shapes and subtle colors. I'm sorry it took me so long to do this because I now feel more sure of myself sexually after becoming more acquainted with me. (Authors' files)

Women today are usually more familiar with their genitals than in previous decades. However, gaining even more knowledge and understanding can be an important aspect of a woman's sexual well-being and her sexual intelligence. In this chapter we present a detailed description of all female genital structures, external and internal. The discussion is intended to be easy to use for reference, and we encourage women readers to do a self-exam as part of reading it (see the Your Sexual Health box on p. 52). We begin with a discussion of the external structures, then discuss the underlying structures and the internal organs. The chapter continues with information about menstruation, menopause, and breasts and then closes with women's health information.

The Vulva

vulva
The external genitals of the female, including the pubic hair, mons veneris, labia majora, labia minora, clitoris, and urinary and vaginal openings.

The **vulva** encompasses all female external genital structures: the hair, the folds of skin, and the urinary and vaginal openings. *Vulva* is the term we use most frequently in this textbook to refer to the external genitals of the female. The vulva is sometimes mistakenly referred to as the vagina, an internal structure with only the opening a part of the vulva. For reference, see ▌ Figure 3.1. A new term for the vulva and vagina leapt into common usage in 2006. The ABC series *Grey's Anatomy* introduced the term *vajayjay*, and Oprah Winfrey began using it on her show, which legitimized its use for some 46 million U.S. viewers each week. Perspectives vary on the meaning behind the term: Does *vajayjay* fill a cultural void for a word for female genitals that is neither clinical nor used in a demeaning manner toward women? Or, is it a euphemism that encourages a woman's childlike relationship to her vulva and vagina and perpetuates anxiety, shame, and negativity toward female genitals (Rosenbloom, 2007)?

Critical Thinking Question

What do you believe the meaning and impact of the term *vajayjay* are?

The appearance of the vulva, which varies from person to person, has been likened to that of certain flowers, seashells, and other forms found in nature. Transformed vulva-like shapes have been used in artwork, including *The Dinner Party* by Judy Chicago, on permanent exhibit at the Brooklyn Museum. This work consists of 39 ceramic plates symbolizing significant women in history.

Most women are not aware of the true diversity of vulva shapes and colors. In recent years several books have been published to help women appreciate the range of normal vulva diversity. For example, Wrenna Robertson's book, *I'll Show You Mine*, has personal stories about the 60 women and the life-size, close-up, color photos of their vulvas. *Petals*, by Nick Karras, contains 48 black-and-white photographs of vulvas, "the primal source of sexual magic" (Karras, 2003, p. 5). The accompanying photograph of cast molds of women's vulvas is an example of artwork designed with the same intention of appreciating individual variations in vulva shapes.

The Mons Veneris

mons veneris
A triangular mound over the pubic bone above the vulva.

Translated from Latin, **mons veneris** means "the mound of Venus." Venus was the Roman goddess of love and beauty. The mons veneris, or mons, is the area covering the pubic bone. It consists of pads of fatty tissue between the pubic bone and the skin. Touch and pressure on the mons can be sexually pleasurable because of the presence of

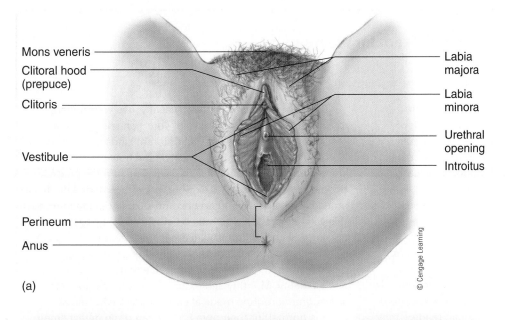

Mons veneris

Clitoral hood (prepuce)

Clitoris

Vestibule

Perineum

Anus

Labia majora

Labia minora

Urethral opening

Introitus

© Cengage Learning

(a)

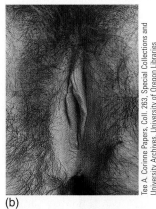

Tee A. Corinne Papers, Coll. 263, Special Collections and University Archives, University of Oregon Libraries

(b)

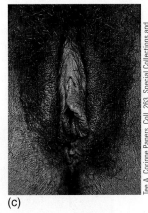

Tee A. Corinne Papers, Coll. 263, Special Collections and University Archives, University of Oregon Libraries

(c)

Tee A. Corinne Papers, Coll. 263, Special Collections and University Archives, University of Oregon Libraries

(d)

❚ Figure 3.1 The structures and variations of the vulva: (a) external structures and (b–d) different colors and shapes. External female genitals have many common variations.

numerous nerve endings. At puberty the mons becomes covered with hair that varies in color, texture, and thickness from woman to woman.

During sexual arousal the scent that accompanies vaginal secretions is held by the pubic hair and can add to sensory erotic pleasure. Pubic hair also prevents uncomfortable friction and provides cushioning during intercourse. Many women and their partners enjoy the lush sensuality of their pubic hair.

Prior to the 1990s, removing pubic hair was primarily the practice of porn stars and exotic dancers, but it has become a grooming trend some mainstream women practice (Fetters, 2011). Women remove their pubic hair by trimming, shaving, waxing, or using a depilatory; some remove it permanently by laser. Some keep only a "landing strip"—a triangle or small strip on the mons—while a few remove all pubic hair and go "bald" (Merkin, 2006).

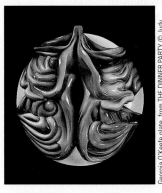

Georgia O'Keefe plate, from THE DINNER PARTY © Judy Chicago, 1979. China paint on porcelain, 14" diameter. Photo © Through the Flower Archives.

© Charles Marden Fitch/SuperStock

Vulva shapes in art and nature: one of the plates in Judy Chicago's *Dinner Party*, a permanent exhibit symbolizing women in history at the Brooklyn Museum; the vulvalike beauty of a flower.

Female Sexual Anatomy and Physiology   **51**

Women are born with curiosity about their bodies. In fact, physical self-awareness and exploration are important steps in a child's development. Unfortunately, many women receive negative conditioning about the sexual parts of their bodies from earliest childhood. They learn to think of their genitals as "privates" or "down there"—parts of their body not to be looked at, touched, or enjoyed. It is common for women to react with discomfort to the suggestion of examining their genitals.

This self-exploration exercise provides an opportunity to learn about yourself—your body and your feelings. As with many other exercises and information throughout this textbook that are aimed at helping students improve their self-knowledge or sexual health, some female readers may choose to read about this exercise but not do it, or do only a few steps.

To begin the self-exam, use a hand mirror, perhaps in combination with a full-length mirror, to look at your genitals from different angles and postures—standing, sitting, lying down. You may find it helpful to draw a picture of your genitals and label the parts (identified in Figure 3.1). All women have the same parts, but the shades of color, the shapes, and the textures vary from woman to woman. As you are looking, try to become aware of whatever feelings you have about your genital anatomy. Women have different kinds of reactions to looking at their genitals:

> I don't find it to be an attractive part of my body. I wouldn't go as far as to call it ugly. I think it would be easier to accept if it was something you weren't taught to hide and think was dirty, but I've never been able to understand why men find the vulva so intriguing. (Authors' files)
>
> I think it looks very sensuous; the tissues look soft and tender. (Authors' files)
>
> I was told by a previous partner that my vulva was very beautiful. His comment made me feel good about my body. (Authors' files)

Besides examining yourself visually, use your fingers to explore the various surfaces of your genitals. Focus on the sensations produced by the different kinds of touching. Note which areas are most sensitive and how the nature of stimulation varies from place to place. The primary purpose of doing this exercise is to explore, not to become sexually aroused. However, if you do become sexually excited during this self-exploration, you may be able to notice changes in the sensitivity of different skin areas that occur with arousal.

The genital self-exam serves another purpose besides helping women feel more comfortable with their anatomy and sexuality. Monthly self-examinations of the genitals can augment routine medical care. Women who know what is normal for their own bodies can often detect small changes and seek medical attention promptly. Problems usually require less extensive treatment when they are detected early. If you discover any changes, consult a health practitioner immediately. **Gynecology (guy-nuh-KOL-uh-jee)** is the medical specialty for female sexual and reproductive anatomy.

Routine self-examination is an aspect of preventive health care.

gynecology
The medical practice specializing in women's health and in diseases of the female reproductive and sexual organs.

labia majora
The outer lips of the vulva.

The Labia Majora

The **labia majora** (LAY-bee-uh muh-JOR-uh), or outer lips, extend downward from the mons on each side of the vulva. They begin next to the thigh and extend inward, surrounding the labia minora and the urethral and vaginal openings. Next to the thigh the outer lips are covered with pubic hair; their inner parts, next to the labia minora, are hairless. The skin of the labia majora is usually darker than the skin of the thighs. The nerve endings and underlying fatty tissue are similar to those in the mons.

The Labia Minora

The **labia minora** (LAY-bee-uh muh-NOR-uh), or inner lips, are located within the outer lips and usually protrude between them. The inner lips are hairless folds of skin that join at the **prepuce** (PREE-pyoos), or clitoral hood, and extend downward past the urinary and vaginal openings. They contain extensive nerve endings and blood vessels and sweat and oil glands. They vary considerably in size, shape, length, and color from woman to woman, as Figure 3.1 shows. During and after pregnancy the inner lips may become darker in color.

labia minora
The inner lips of the vulva, one on each side of the vaginal opening.

prepuce
The foreskin or fold of skin over the clitoris.

Genital Alteration

Piercing and wearing jewelry on vulva tissues is one way some women alter the appearance of their genitals. Prior to the 1990s, in the Western world, body piercing was associated with exotic, faraway peoples seen in *National Geographic*. Now some men and women in the West have extended this form of "body art" to their genitals. The most common sites for female genital piercings are the clitoral hood and the labia minora or majora. Rings and/or barbells are placed through the piercings.

It is unknown to what extent vulva jewelry genuinely improves erotic stimulation. Risks from the piercing procedure include contracting HIV, hepatitis B, and bacterial infections. After the piercing, local and systemic infections, abscess formation, allergic reactions, torn flesh, and problematic scarring can result. The rings and barbells can also damage the genital tissue of the sexual partner (Kreahling, 2005; Meltzer, 2005).

In recent years some women have had cosmetic surgery to alter the size or shape of their labia minora (Deans et al., 2011). Women typically ask surgeons who do this procedure, called *labiaplasty*, to make their labia smaller or more symmetrical. Increased exposure to Internet, magazine, and film pornography in which the inner labia are frequently small or nonexistent may contribute to women's belief that their labia should look different than they do naturally (Drysdale, 2010; W. Robertson, 2011). Many porn magazines airbrush or digitally remove the inner labia. This "digital labiaplasty" results in a vulva whose appearance, especially when pubic hair is removed, is more similar to that of prepubescent girls than to sexually mature females (Salber, 2010).

The motivation for undergoing the procedure comes more often from the women themselves than from their male partners. A 2008 survey of 24,000 men and women in Germany found that women contemplated labiaplasty in order to make their vulvas look like those of porn stars. Women were more concerned about the appearance of their vulvas than their male partners were (Drey et al., 2009). However, some women sought labiaplasty because of disparaging comments by sexual partners (Deans et al., 2011). Men who persuade their partners to have labiaplasty typically want their partners' labia to conform to the vulva appearance that appeals to them most when watching pornography (Douglas et al., 2005).

The idea that there is one aesthetic ideal for the vulva can contribute to a woman's negative feelings about her vulva, which can impact her sexuality. One research study found that the more women were dissatisfied with the appearance of their genitals, the more genital self-consciousness and the less sexual satisfaction they experienced during sexual intimacy (Schick et al., 2010). Another study found benefits of positive genital self-image: Women

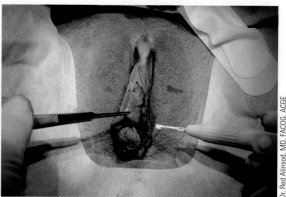

A surgeon is surgically removing portions of the labia minora in a cosmetic labiaplasty.

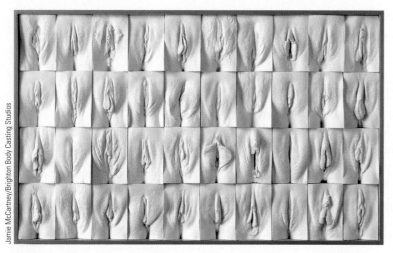

To counter the trend of young women having their labia altered by plastic surgery, sculptor Jamie McCartney's work, *The Great Wall of Vagina*, celebrates the endless variety of fascinating vulva shapes. The 30-foot long sculpture consists of 400 casts of vulvas made from real women, ages 18 to 64. The sculptor hopes to help women take pride in their uniqueness instead of believing they should match some standard of sameness. Shown here is panel 1 of 10.

who felt positively about their genitals were more likely to have masturbated more often, have used a vibrator for self-stimulation, have had a gynecological exam in the last year, and have recently done a genital self-exam (Herbenick et al., 2011b).

Currently, plastic surgeons extensively advertise vaginal plastic surgery, and it's now the third fastest growing cosmetic procedure in the United States (M. Lee, 2011). A great deal of controversy exists about whether surgeons should perform surgery of the vulva solely for cosmetic reasons. Some maintain that labiaplasty is essentially the same as the female genital cutting that occurs in third world countries, a premise that will be discussed further in the Sexuality and Diversity box.

At the very least, labiaplasty removes erotically sensitive tissue. Risks associated with cosmetic labia surgery include a reduction in pleasurable sensations, nerve damage that results in unpleasant hypersensitivity and decreased sexual function, infection, and scarring (L. Liao et al., 2010).

clitoris
A highly sensitive structure of the female external genitals, the only function of which is sexual pleasure.

glans
The head of the clitoris, which is richly endowed with nerve endings.

shaft
The length of the clitoris between the glans and the body.

crura
The innermost tips of the cavernous bodies that connect to the pubic bones.

The Clitoris

The **clitoris** (KLIT-uh-rus) comprises the external **glans** and **shaft** and the internal **crura** (KROO-ra; Latin for "legs") that project inward from each side of the clitoral shaft. The shaft and glans are located just below the mons area, where the inner lips converge. They are covered by the clitoral hood, or prepuce. The shaft itself cannot be seen, but it can be felt, and its shape can be seen through the hood. The glans is usually not visible under the clitoral hood, but it can be seen if a woman gently lifts the clitoral hood and parts the labia minora, as seen in ▌ Figure 3.2. The glans looks smooth, rounded, and slightly translucent. The size, shape, and position of the clitoris vary from woman to woman. These normal differences have no known relation to sexual arousal and functioning. The clitoris increases in size during the several days prior to ovulation (Battaglia et al., 2008).

Initially, it may be easier for a woman to locate her clitoris by touch rather than sight because of its sensitive nerve endings. The external part of the clitoris, although tiny, has about the same number of nerve endings as the head of the penis. The clitoral glans in particular is highly sensitive, and women usually stimulate this area with the hood covering it to avoid direct stimulation, which may be too intense. Research into female masturbation patterns has found that clitoral stimulation, rather than vaginal insertion, is more often how women achieve arousal and orgasm when masturbating. Although all other sexual organs, male and female, have additional functions in

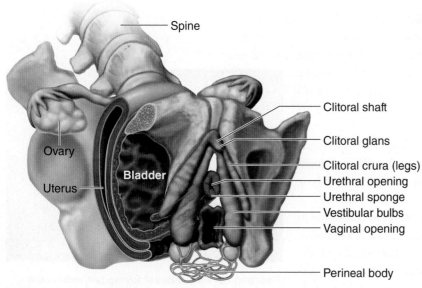

Spine
Clitoral shaft
Clitoral glans
Clitoral crura (legs)
Urethral opening
Urethral sponge
Vestibular bulbs
Vaginal opening
Perineal body
Ovary
Bladder
Uterus

▌ **Figure 3.2** The underlying structures of the clitoral complex.

reproduction or waste elimination, the only purpose of the clitoris is sexual pleasure and arousal.

A good deal of controversy has surrounded the role of the clitoris in sexual arousal and orgasm. Despite long-existing scientific knowledge about the highly concentrated nerve endings in the clitoris, the erroneous belief has persisted that vaginal rather than clitoral stimulation is—or should be—exclusively responsible for female sexual arousal and orgasm. However, the clitoris is far more sensitive to touch than the vagina, and most women are more likely to experience orgasm not only from self-stimulation but also from partner manual and oral stimulation of the clitoris than from vaginal penetration (Brewer & Hendrie, 2011).

The interior of the vagina does contain nerve endings, but not the type that respond to light touch (Pauls et al., 2006). (This is why women do not feel tampons or diaphragms when they are correctly in place.) Nevertheless, many women find internal pressure and stretching sensations inside the vagina during manual stimulation or intercourse highly pleasurable. Some women experience more intense arousal from vaginal stimulation than from clitoral stimulation, especially after they are aroused and the vaginal tissues are fully engorged. Research using brain-imaging technology has found that women (with and without spinal cord injury) can experience orgasm using cervical self-stimulation (Whipple & Komisaruk, 2006). As more and more scientific research is done, a wider range of individual variation becomes apparent (Ellison, 2000).

In some parts of the world, the sexual role of the clitoris is so troubling that the structure is removed during female genital cutting, as described in the following Sexuality and Diversity discussion.

Critical Thinking Question

What should parents tell their daughters about their clitorises?

SEXUALITY and DIVERSITY

Female Genital Cutting: Torture or Tradition?

Each year approximately 2 million girls and women in more than 40 countries in Africa, the Middle East, and Asia undergo one of several types of genital cutting, usually as part of an initiation during childhood in order to become eligible for marriage (Leye et al., 2006). In many countries, most of the female population has undergone female genital cutting (FGC). It is estimated that between 100 million and 140 million women and girls now living have experienced genital cutting (Alo & Babatunde, 2011).

The village midwife or a health worker performs the procedures, which are usually arranged by the girl's mother (Rosenberg, 2008). Razor blades or broken glass are used to cut the tissue, and the procedure is usually done without anesthetics, disinfectants, or sterile instruments (Rosenthal, 2006). The simplest procedure, circumcision, consists of cutting off the clitoral hood. Most types involve removal of the clitoris itself, called *clitoridectomy*. In the most extreme practice, genital infibulation, the clitoris and the labia are cut off. Then both sides of the vulva are scraped raw and stitched up (sometimes with thorns) while the girl is held down. The girl's legs are bound closed around the ankles and thighs for about a week (Nour, 2000). The tissue then grows together, leaving only a small opening for urine and menstrual flow to pass through.

The most serious gynecological and obstetric complications often arise from genital infibulation. These include bleeding and pain that lead to shock and death, prolonged bleeding that leads to anemia, and infection that causes delayed healing, tetanus, and gangrene. Long-term consequences include urinary obstruction, blockage of menstrual flow, and recurrent reproductive tract infections. Infertility rates are higher among women whose labia were removed

A baby girl is about to undergo female genital cutting in Ethiopia, where both Muslims and Christians continue this practice despite a constitutional ban.

(Ball, 2005). Extensive vaginal scarring can cause serious difficulties during childbirth; 50% more women who have undergone genital cutting die from delivery complications (along with their babies) than women who have not been cut (Eke & Nkanginieme, 2006).

The main objective of genital cutting is to ensure virginity before marriage. Young girls are considered unmarriageable if they do not have the prescribed excision. Because marriage is usually the only role for a woman in these cultures, her future and her family's pride depend on upholding this tradition. The social stigma for remaining uncircumcised is severe. For example, in Sudan, one of the most vile invectives a man can be called is "the son of an uncircumcised mother" (Al-Krenawi & Wiesel-Lev, 1999). Some groups also believe that the clitoris must be removed because contact with the clitoris is dangerous for a man or for a baby being born (Einstein, 2008).

Also, many women who have undergone genital cutting believe that their genitals are made more appealing. In fact, many men and women in countries where FGC occurs consider uncut female genitals ugly and too closely resembling male genitals (Einstein, 2008). The strength of cultural tradition in many societies remains difficult to overcome, and even where the practice is illegal, the laws are difficult to enforce (Alo & Babatunde, 2011).

Concerns about the appearance of the vulva are also, as previously discussed, the main motivation for women in the Western world to have their genitals surgically modified. Although female genital cutting in Africa and the Middle East is done to young girls, and some of the procedures are much more severe than labiaplasty in the Western world, most of the procedures are done due to societal pressures that lead women to believe that their normal vulvas are unacceptable. Female circumcision in Africa and labiaplasty in the West are done for the same reasons—to conform to a cultural ideal of appearance, to transcend shameful feelings about their genitals, and to feel acceptably feminine and to be desirable to sexual partners. One could even argue that Western women who consent to and pay to have their genitals altered are more strongly oppressed by cultural gender expectations than are females who undergo genital cutting as children (Olujobi, 2009).

The outcry over female genital cutting has pushed the United Nations to suspend its policy of nonintervention in the cultural practices of individual nations. The World Health Organization has called for a ban of the procedures and defines cutting of the labia or clitoris as female genital mutilation (Johnsdotter & Essén, 2010). The practice of FGC has decreased in some countries. For example, in Egypt, 97% of married women have experienced FGC, but the percentage of schoolgirls in Egypt who have undergone FGC is less: Approximately 62% of schoolgirls in rural schools, 46% in government urban schools, and 9% in private urban schools have undergone FGC. The higher the educational level of the mother and father, the less likely their daughters are to undergo FGC (Alo & Babatunde, 2011; Tag-Eldin et al., 2008). Educational programs in villages have also been shown to change attitudes and reduce the practice of female genital cutting (Marshall, 2009; Shell-Duncan et al., 2011).

In spite of damage to the clitoris and vulva from genital cutting, some women remain able to experience sexual arousal and orgasm. For others, groundbreaking specialized reconstructive surgery can help them regain increased pleasure and their ability to climax. Also, surgery to correct the narrowed vaginal opening caused by infibulation can allow the woman to experience intercourse without pain (Baldaro-Verde et al., 2007; Foldes & Silvestre, 2007; Ogodo, 2009). Surgeons from around the world volunteer their services in Africa to provide free clitoral reconstruction and defibulation (Schwarz, 2007).

The Vestibule

The **vestibule** (VES-ti-byool) is the area of the vulva inside the labia minora. It is rich in blood vessels and nerve endings, and its tissues are sensitive to touch. (In

Critical Thinking Question

How are the genital piercing and cosmetic labiaplasty done for women in the Western world similar to and different from the genital cutting done to women in Africa, the Middle East, and Asia?

vestibule
The area of the vulva inside the labia minora.

architectural terminology the word *vestibule* refers to the entryway of a house.) Both the urinary and the vaginal openings are located within the vestibule.

The Urethral Opening

Urine collected in the bladder passes out of a woman's body through the urethral opening. The **urethra** (yoo-REE-thruh) is the short tube connecting the bladder to the urinary opening, located between the clitoris and the vaginal opening.

urethra
The tube through which urine passes from the bladder.

The Introitus and the Hymen

The opening of the vagina, called the **introitus** (in-TROH-i-tus), is located between the urinary opening and the anus. Partially covering the introitus is a fold of tissue called the **hymen** (HIGH-men), which is typically present at birth and usually remains intact until initial intercourse. The hymen opening is usually large enough to insert tampons. Occasionally, this tissue is too thick to break easily during intercourse; a medical practitioner might then be needed to make a minor incision. In rare cases an *imperforate hymen*, tissue that completely seals the vaginal opening, causes menstrual flow to collect inside the vagina. When this condition is discovered, a medical practitioner can open the hymen with an incision. Although it is rare, it is possible for a woman to become pregnant even if her hymen is still intact and she has not experienced penile penetration. If semen is placed on the labia minora, the sperm can swim into the vagina. Unless pregnancy is desired, sexual play involving rubbing the penis and vulva together without contraception should be avoided.

introitus
The opening to the vagina.

hymen
Tissue that partially covers the vaginal opening.

Although the hymen can protect the vaginal tissues early in life, it has no other known function. Nevertheless, many societies, including our own, have placed great significance on its presence or absence (Blank, 2007). Euphemisms such as *cherry* or *maidenhead* have been used to describe the hymen. In our society and many others, people have long believed that a woman's virginity can be proved by the pain and bleeding that can occur with initial coitus, or "deflowering." At different times in various cultures, bloodstained wedding-night bedsheets were seen as proof that the groom had wed "intact goods" and that the marriage had been consummated. Currently, some Muslim families or future husbands insist on a pelvic exam to prove the woman's virginity prior to marriage (Manier, 2008; Sciolino & Mekhennet, 2008b). Some women, particularly women from the Middle East who have immigrated to Europe and North America and later marry men from the Middle East, undergo *hymenalplasty*, surgical reconstruction of the hymen, to conceal the loss of their virginity (Essen et al., 2010; Sciolino & Mekhennet, 2008a).

Although pain or bleeding sometimes occurs during initial coitus, the hymen can be partial, flexible, or thin enough for no discomfort or bleeding to occur; it may even remain intact after intercourse. If a woman manually stretches her hymen before initial intercourse, she may be able to minimize the discomfort that sometimes occurs. To do this, first insert a lubricated finger (using saliva or a water-soluble sterile lubricant) into the vaginal opening and press downward toward the anus until you feel some stretching. After a few seconds, release the pressure and relax. Repeat this step several times. Next, insert two fingers into the vagina and stretch the sides of the vagina by opening the fingers. Repeat the downward stretching with two fingers as well. ●

The Perineum

The **perineum** (per-uh-NEE-um) is the area of smooth skin between the vaginal opening and the anus (the sphincter through which bowel movements pass). The perineal tissue is endowed with nerve endings and is sensitive to touch. During childbirth, an incision called an *episiotomy* is sometimes made in the perineum to prevent the ragged

perineum
The area between the vagina and anus of the female and the scrotum and anus of the male.

tearing of tissues that can occur when the newborn passes through the birth canal. We will discuss this in more detail in Chapter 11.

Underlying Structures

If the hair, skin, and fatty pads were removed from the vulva, several underlying structures could be seen. If you look at Figure 3.2, which shows the structures underneath the labia and clitoris beneath the hood, you are looking at a complex of structures with erectile tissue that engorges with blood during sexual arousal, causing the vulva to swell and creating increased erotic sensations. You can see that the glans is connected to the shaft. The shaft contains two small spongy structures called the **cavernous bodies**. The clitoral shaft expands into the large spongy erectile tissue of the crura that connect to the pubic bones in the pelvic cavity. The **vestibular** (veh-STIB-yoo-ler) **bulbs** lie under the inner labia and extend from below the clitoris to surround the urethral and vaginal openings (O'Connell, 2007). The urethra is also surrounded by erectile tissue, called the *urethral sponge*. Underneath the skin between the opening of the vagina and the anus, a dense network of blood vessels, the *perineal sponge*, fills with blood and also becomes more sensitive to touch and pressure (Chalker, 2002). Compression of the engorged complex of erectile tissues by insertion of fingers, sex toys, or the penis into the vagina causes internal sensations that some women find pleasurable (Ellison, 2000).

Bartholin's glands, one on each side of the vaginal opening, typically produce a drop or two of fluid just before orgasm. The glands are usually not noticeable, but sometimes the duct from a Bartholin's gland becomes clogged, and the fluid that is normally secreted remains inside and causes enlargement. If this occurs and the swelling does not subside within a few days, it is best to see a health-care practitioner.

Besides the glands and network of vessels, a complex musculature underlies the genital area, as seen in ▌Figure 3.3. The *pelvic floor muscles* have a multidirectional design that allows the vaginal opening to expand greatly during childbirth and to contract afterward.

Internal Structures

Internal female sexual anatomy consists of the vagina, cervix, uterus, and ovaries. These are discussed in the following sections. Refer to ▌Figure 3.4 for cross-section and front views of the female pelvis.

cavernous bodies
The structures in the shaft of the clitoris that engorge with blood during sexual arousal.

vestibular bulbs
Two bulbs, one on each side of the vaginal opening, that engorge with blood during sexual arousal.

Bartholin's glands
Two small glands slightly inside the vaginal opening that secrete a few drops of fluid during sexual arousal.

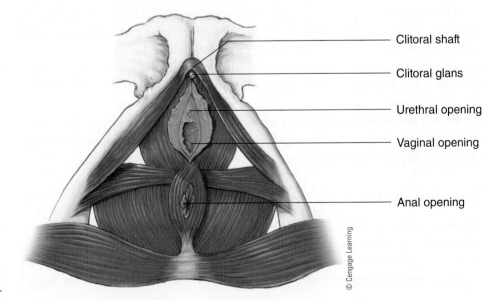

▌**Figure 3.3** The underlying muscles of the vulva. These muscles can be strengthened by using the Kegel exercises described in the Your Sexual Health box.

Clitoral shaft
Clitoral glans
Urethral opening
Vaginal opening
Anal opening

© Cengage Learning

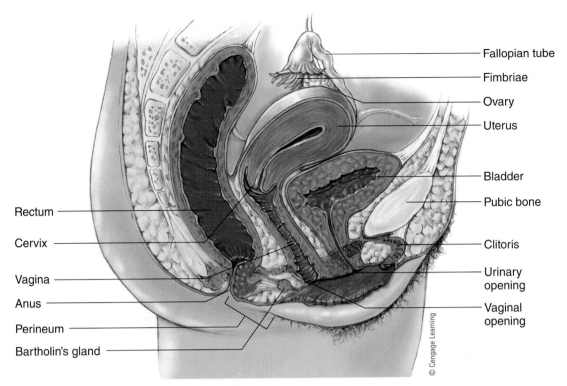

(a) **Side view**

Fallopian tube
Fimbriae
Ovary
Uterus
Bladder
Pubic bone
Clitoris
Urinary opening
Vaginal opening

Rectum
Cervix
Vagina
Anus
Perineum
Bartholin's gland

© Cengage Learning

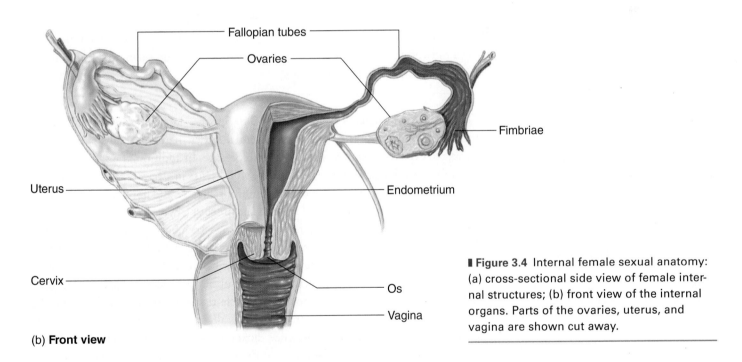

Fallopian tubes
Ovaries
Fimbriae
Uterus
Endometrium
Cervix
Os
Vagina

(b) **Front view**

▌**Figure 3.4** Internal female sexual anatomy: (a) cross-sectional side view of female internal structures; (b) front view of the internal organs. Parts of the ovaries, uterus, and vagina are shown cut away.

The Vagina

The **vagina** is a canal that opens between the labia minora and extends into the body, angling upward toward the small of the back, to the cervix and uterus. Most women have never seen inside their own vaginas, but it is possible to do so during their regular pelvic exams. The health-care practitioner can use a mirror to show a woman her vagina while the **speculum** is holding the vaginal walls open. Women who are unfamiliar with their anatomy can have a difficult time when they first try inserting a tampon into the vagina:

vagina
A stretchable canal in the female that opens at the vulva and extends about 3 to 5 inches into the pelvis.

speculum
An instrument used to open the vaginal walls during a gynecological exam.

The pelvic floor muscles squeeze involuntarily at orgasm; they can also be trained to contract voluntarily through a series of exercises known as **Kegel (KAY-gul) exercises**. These exercises were developed by Arnold Kegel in 1952 to help women regain urinary control after childbirth. (Because of excessive stretching and tearing of perineal muscles during childbirth, women who have recently given birth commonly lose urine when they cough or sneeze) (Ray, 2011). Kegel exercises have been shown to have other effects besides restoring muscle tone (Beji, 2003). After about six weeks of regular exercise, many women report increased sensation during intercourse and a general increase in genital sensitivity. These results seem to be associated with women's increased awareness of their sex organs and their improved muscle tone.

The steps for the Kegel exercises are as follows:

1. Locate the muscles surrounding the vagina. This can be done by stopping the flow of urine to feel which muscles contract. An even more effective way of contracting the pelvic floor muscles is to contract the anal sphincter as if to hold back gas.
2. Insert a finger into the opening of your vagina and contract the muscles you located in Step 1. Feel the muscles squeeze your finger.
3. Squeeze the same muscles for 10 seconds. Relax. Repeat 10 times.
4. Squeeze and release as rapidly as possible, 10 to 25 times. Repeat.
5. Imagine trying to suck something into your vagina. Hold for 3 seconds.

This exercise series should be done three times a day.

> No matter how hard I tried, I couldn't get a tampon in until I inserted a finger and realized that my vagina slanted backward. I had been pushing straight up onto the upper wall. (Authors' files)

Kegel exercises
A series of exercises that strengthen the muscles underlying the external female or male genitals.

mucosa
Collective term for the mucous membranes; moist tissue that lines certain body areas such as the penile urethra, vagina, and mouth.

rugae
The folds of tissue in the vagina.

The unaroused vagina is approximately 3 to 5 inches long. The analogy of a glove is often used to illustrate the vagina as a potential rather than an actual space, with its walls able to expand enough to serve as a birth passage. In addition, the vagina changes in size and shape during sexual arousal, as we will discuss in Chapter 6.

The vagina contains three layers of tissue: mucous, muscle, and fibrous tissue. All these layers are richly endowed with blood vessels. The **mucosa** (myoo-KOH-suh) is the layer of mucous membrane that a woman feels when she inserts a finger inside her vagina. The folded walls, or **rugae** (ROO-jee), feel soft, moist, and warm, resembling the inside of one's mouth. The walls normally produce secretions that help maintain the chemical balance of the vagina. During sexual arousal, a lubricating substance exudes through the mucosa.

Most of the second layer, composed of muscle tissue, is concentrated around the vaginal opening. These muscles contract rhythmically at orgasm and contribute to the pleasurable sensations women experience during orgasm. One research study found that women are more likely to be aware of the vaginal contractions at orgasm during manual clitoral stimulation than during intercourse (Carrobles & Gamez, 2007).

Because of the concentration of musculature in the outer third and the expansive ability of the inner two thirds of the vagina, a situation often develops that can be at best funny and at worst embarrassing. During headstands and certain yoga or intercourse positions with the pelvis elevated, gravity causes the inner two thirds to expand and draw air into the vagina. The outer muscles tighten, and the trapped air is forced back out through the tightened muscles, creating a sound we usually associate with a different orifice. The occurrence is popularly known as "queef," although one student has suggested calling this phenomenon "varting," because the sound is similar to that of a fart (fortunately, there is no unpleasant smell). Surrounding the muscular layer is the innermost vaginal layer, composed of fibrous tissue. This layer aids in vaginal contraction and expansion and acts as connective tissue to other structures in the pelvic cavity.

The Grafenberg Spot (G-Spot)

The **Grafenberg spot**, better known as the *G-spot*, is an area within the anterior (or front) wall of the vagina, about 1 centimeter from the skin's surface and one third to one half the distance from the vaginal opening to the back of the vagina. It consists of a system of glands (Skene's glands) and ducts that surround the urethra. This area is believed to be the female counterpart to the male prostate gland, developed from the same embryonic tissue.

The G-spot has generated considerable interest because of reports that some women experience sexual arousal, orgasm, and an ejaculation of fluid when stimulated there (Darling et al., 1990), although many women do not have such an area of increased sensation. We will discuss the role of the G-spot in female sexual response more fully in Chapter 6.

Arousal and Vaginal Lubrication

So far in this chapter, we have described the parts of the female sexual anatomy, but we have said relatively little about how these structures function. Because lubrication is a unique feature of the vagina, the process is explained here. Other physiological aspects of female arousal will be discussed in Chapter 6.

During sexual arousal, a clear, slippery fluid begins to appear on the vaginal mucosa within 10 to 30 seconds after effective physical or psychological stimulation begins. This lubrication is a result of **vasocongestion**, caused by the extensive network of blood vessels in the tissues surrounding the vagina engorging with blood. Clear fluid seeps from the congested tissues to the inside of the vaginal walls to form the characteristic slippery coating of the sexually aroused vagina.

Vaginal lubrication serves two functions. First, it enhances the possibility of conception by helping to alkalinize the normally acidic vaginal chemical balance. Vaginal pH level changes from 4.5 to 6.0–6.5 with sexual arousal (Meston, 2000). Sperm travel faster and survive longer in an alkaline environment than in an acidic one. (The seminal fluid of the male also helps alkalinize the vagina.) Second, vaginal lubrication can increase sexual enjoyment. During manual genital stimulation, the slippery wetness can increase the sensuousness and pleasure of touching. During oral–genital sex, some women's partners enjoy the erotic scent and taste of the vaginal lubrication. During intercourse, vaginal lubrication makes the walls of the vagina slippery, which facilitates entry of the penis into the vagina. Lubrication also helps make the thrusting of intercourse pleasurable. Without adequate lubrication, entry of the penis and subsequent thrusting can be uncomfortable for the woman—and often for the man. Irritation and small tears of the vaginal tissue can result.

Insufficient vaginal lubrication can be remedied in several ways, depending on the source of the difficulty. Changing any anxiety-producing circumstances and engaging in effective stimulation are important. Saliva, lubricated condoms, or a nonirritating water-soluble jelly can be used to provide additional lubrication. Occasionally, hormone treatment is necessary. ●

Vaginal Secretions and Chemical Balance of the Vagina

Both the vaginal walls and the cervix (discussed on p. 62) produce white or yellowish secretions. These secretions are normal and are a sign of vaginal health. They vary in appearance according to hormone level changes during the menstrual cycle. (Keeping

Grafenberg spot (G-spot)
Glands and ducts in the anterior wall of the vagina. Some women experience sexual pleasure, arousal, orgasm, and an ejaculation of fluids from stimulation of the Grafenberg spot.

vasocongestion
The engorgement of blood vessels in particular body parts in response to sexual arousal.

SEXUALHEALTH

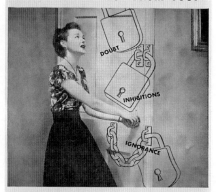
This Lysol ad from 1948 misled women about their vaginal health. The Lysol actually eliminated the healthy vaginal chemical and bacterial balance, allowing problematic organisms to multiply.

douching
Rinsing out the vagina with plain water or a variety of solutions. It is usually unnecessary for hygiene, and douching too often can result in vaginal irritation.

cervix
The small end of the uterus, located at the back of the vagina.

os
The opening in the cervix that leads to the interior of the uterus.

uterus
A pear-shaped organ inside the female pelvis, within which the fetus develops.

track of these variations is the basis for one method of birth control, discussed in Chapter 10.) The taste and scent of vaginal secretions can also vary with the time of a woman's cycle and her level of arousal.

The vagina's natural chemical and bacterial balance helps promote healthy mucosa. The chemical balance is normally rather acidic (pH 4.5*—the same as in red wine) (Angier, 1999). Regular bathing with a mild soap and washing between the folds of the vulva are all that are necessary for proper hygiene. A variety of factors can alter this balance, resulting in vaginal problems. Among these are **douching** (rinsing out the inside of the vagina) and using feminine-hygiene sprays. Douching is definitely *not* necessary for routine hygiene. Although most women mistakenly believe douching is healthy, it can alter the natural chemical balance of the vagina and increase a woman's susceptibility to vaginal infections and sexually transmitted diseases (Hutchinson et al., 2007; Tsai et al., 2009). Various studies have found that douching increases the risk of pelvic inflammatory disease, endometriosis (discussed on p. 70), transmission of HIV, ectopic pregnancy (discussed on p. 63), and decreased fertility. Moreover, douching during pregnancy increases the likelihood of preterm births (Cottrell, 2003). Feminine-hygiene sprays can cause irritation, allergic reactions, burns, infections, dermatitis of the thighs, and numerous other problems. In fact, genital deodorant sprays and body powders have been associated with an increased risk of ovarian cancer (Cook et al., 1997). Furthermore, deodorant tampons are unnecessary: Menstrual fluid has virtually no odor until it is outside the body.

For most of the past hundred years, advertising has turned our cultural negativity about female sexual organs into an extremely profitable business. Consequently, women in the United States spend millions of dollars each year on over-the-counter douches. Minorities and educationally and economically disadvantaged women appear more vulnerable to this misinformation: Twice as many African American women douche than White women, and regardless of race, the prevalence of douching is higher in women who have less education and income (Cottrell, 2003).

The Cervix

The **cervix** (SER-viks), located at the back of the vagina, is the small end of the pear-shaped uterus (see Figure 3.4). The cervix contains mucus-secreting glands. Sperm pass through the vagina into the uterus through the **os**, the opening in the center of the cervix.

A woman can see her own cervix if she learns to insert a speculum into her vagina. She can also ask for a mirror when she has her pelvic exam. A woman can feel her own cervix by inserting one or two fingers into the vagina and reaching to the end of the canal. (Sometimes squatting and bearing down brings the cervix closer to the vaginal entrance.) The cervix feels somewhat like the end of a nose, firm and round in contrast to the soft vaginal walls.

The Uterus

The **uterus** (YOO-tuh-rus), or womb, is a hollow, thick, pear-shaped organ, approximately 3 inches long and 2 inches wide in a woman who has never had a child. (It is somewhat larger after pregnancy.) The uterus is suspended in the pelvic cavity by ligaments; in different women its position can vary from *anteflexed* (tipped forward toward the abdomen) to *retroflexed* (tipped back toward the spine). Women with retroflexed uteri are more likely to experience menstrual discomfort or have difficulty inserting

---

*pH is a measure of acidity or alkalinity. A neutral substance (neither acidic nor alkaline) has a pH of 7. A lower number means a substance is more acidic; a higher number means it is more alkaline.

a diaphragm. Although it was once thought that a retroflexed uterus interfered with conception, it does not impair fertility.

The walls of the uterus consist of three layers. The external layer is a thin membrane called the **perimetrium** (pear-ee-MEE-tree-um). The middle layer, or **myometrium** (my-oh-MEE-tree-um), is made of longitudinal and circular muscle fibers that interweave like the fibers of a basket; this enables the uterus to stretch during pregnancy and contract during labor and orgasm. At the top of the uterus, an area called the *fundus*, the uterine walls are especially thick. The inner lining of the uterus is called the **endometrium** (en-doh-MEE-tree-um). Rich in blood vessels, the endometrium nourishes the *zygote* (united sperm and egg), which travels down to the uterus from the fallopian tubes after fertilization. In preparation for this event, the endometrium thickens in response to hormone changes during the monthly menstrual cycle, discussed later in this chapter. The endometrium is also a source of hormone production.

perimetrium
The thin membrane covering the outside of the uterus.

myometrium
The smooth muscle layer of the uterine wall.

endometrium
The tissue that lines the inside of the uterine wall.

The Fallopian Tubes

Each of the two 4-inch **fallopian** (fuh-LOH-pee-un) **tubes** extends from the uterus toward an ovary, at the left or the right side of the pelvic cavity (see Figure 3.4). The outside end of each tube is shaped like a funnel, with fringelike projections called **fimbriae** (FIM-bree-eye) that hover over the ovary. When the egg leaves the ovary, it is drawn into the tube by the fimbriae.

Once the egg is inside the fallopian tube, the movements of tiny hairlike cilia and the contractions of the tube walls move it along at a rate of approximately 1 inch every 24 hours. The egg remains viable for fertilization for about 24 to 48 hours. Therefore, fertilization occurs while the egg is still close to the ovary. After fertilization the zygote begins developing as it continues traveling down the tube to the uterus.

An **ectopic pregnancy** occurs when a fertilized ovum implants in tissue outside the uterus, most commonly in the fallopian tube (Ramakrishnan & Scheid, 2006). This implantation can rupture the tube and cause uncontrolled bleeding, which is a serious medical emergency. The most common symptoms of ectopic pregnancy are abdominal pain and spotting that occur 6 to 8 weeks after the last menstrual period. Diagnostic tests can establish the presence of an ectopic pregnancy, and medical and surgical procedures are used to treat it (Scott, 2006).

fallopian tubes
Two tubes, extending from the sides of the uterus, in which the egg and sperm travel.

fimbriae
Fringelike ends of the fallopian tubes, into which the released ovum enters.

ectopic pregnancy
A pregnancy that occurs when a fertilized ovum implants outside the uterus, most commonly in a fallopian tube.

The Ovaries

The two **ovaries**, which are about the size and shape of almonds, are at the ends of the fallopian tubes, one on each side of the uterus. They are connected to the pelvic wall and the uterus by ligaments. The ovaries are endocrine glands that produce three classes of sex hormones. The estrogens, as mentioned in Chapter 5, influence development of female physical sex characteristics and help regulate the menstrual cycle. The progestational compounds also help regulate the menstrual cycle and promote maturity of the uterine lining in preparation for pregnancy. Around the onset of puberty the female sex hormones play a critical role in initiating maturation of the uterus, ovaries, and vagina and in developing the secondary sex characteristics, such as pubic hair and breasts.

The ovaries contain about 1 million immature ova at birth and between 400,000 and 500,000 at menarche (Federman, 2006). During the years between puberty and menopause, one or the other ovary typically releases an egg during each cycle. Only 400 ova are destined for full maturation during a woman's reproductive years (Macklon & Fauser, 1999). **Ovulation** (ahv-yoo-LAY-shun), or egg maturation and release, occurs as the result of the complex chain of events we know as the menstrual cycle, discussed in the next section.

ovaries
Female gonads that produce ova and sex hormones.

ovulation
The release of a mature ovum from the ovary.

Menstruation

menstruation
The sloughing off of the built-up uterine lining that takes place if conception has not occurred.

Menstruation (men-stroo-A-shun), the sloughing off of uterine lining that takes place if conception has not occurred, is a sign of normal physical functioning. Negative attitudes about it persist in contemporary American society; however, young women typically have more positive attitudes about menstruation than do women in older generations (Marvan et al., 2005).

Attitudes About Menstruation

American folklore reveals many interesting ideas about menstruation and raises a question about whether negative beliefs about menstruation are meant to constrain women and reinforce their lower social status (Forbes et al., 2003). Negative myths surrounding menstruation date back to the Old Testament: "And if a woman have an issue and her issue in her flesh be blood, she shall be apart seven days: and whosoever toucheth her shall be unclean until the even" (Leviticus 15:19). Some Orthodox Jews still conform to this belief, and in practice, an Orthodox Jewish woman avoids sexual activity until after a ceremonial cleansing bath following the end of her period (Rothbaum & Jackson, 1990). Myths of past American folklore include the belief that it is harmful for a woman to be physically active during menstruation, that a corsage worn by a menstruating woman will wilt, and that a tooth filling done during menstruation will fall out (Milow, 1983).

The meanings of menstrual rituals in other cultures are often ambiguous, and little is actually known about the significance of menstrual taboos. In some societies a menstruating woman goes to a "menstrual house" for the duration of her menstruation. Researchers have rarely asked about the meaning of and experiences in the menstrual huts. Do women feel stigmatized or honored and relieved by the break from normal labor? Scattered reports suggest considerable variability, with positive meanings being fairly common. Menstrual customs can provide women with a means of solidarity, influence, and autonomy. For example, in some Native American traditions, women were believed to be at their most powerful during menstruation. They would retreat to a "moon lodge" to be free of mundane daily chores. Blood flow was believed to purify women and to enable them to gather spiritual wisdom to benefit the entire tribe. Most Native American tribes also had celebrations for a girl's first menstruation (Angier, 1999; Owen, 1993). For the Inca Indians in South America, shedding blood symbolized the transformation into adulthood; boys bled when elders pierced the boys' ears and inserted large ear spools as part of their coming-of-age ceremony (Wiesner-Hanks, 2000).

In a few cultures, menstruation is described in lyrical words and positive images. The Japanese expression for a girl's first menstruation is "the year of the cleavage of the melon," and one East Indian description of menstruation is the "flower growing in the house of the god of love" (Delaney et al., 1976). In some contemporary Hindu and Muslim Indian families, a religious ceremony is held after a girl begins menstruation (Marvan et al., 2006).

Courtesy of Dr. Wolfgang Lauber

Distinctive relief sculptures of stylized and oversized male and female genitals adorn the menstrual house of the Dogon Tribe in present-day Mali, Africa. During menstruation, married women retreat to this house, completely separated from their families and relieved of their daily work of caring for children, cooking, carrying water, and going to market. The only contact they have is with older women who supply their daily needs.

Despite negative myths and societal attitudes toward menstruation, most women associate regular menstrual cycles with healthy functioning and femininity. Further, research has found that women who have positive attitudes toward, and are comfortable with, menstruation are less likely to take sexual risks and more likely to be more comfortable with their bodies and with being sexually assertive than are women who have negative attitudes toward menstruation (Schooler et al., 2005). In addition, women who had been sexual with their partner during their periods were particularly comfortable with menstruation and were more aroused by sexual activities (Rempel & Baumgartner, 2003).

Some women and families are redefining menstruation from a more positive perspective. For example, some may have a celebration or give a gift to a young woman when she has her first menstrual period (Kissling, 2002). One aspect of the menstrual cycle that people often see as positive is its cyclic pattern, typical of many natural phenomena.

Menarche

The menstrual cycle usually begins in the early teens, between the ages of 11 and 15, although some girls begin earlier or later. The first menstrual bleeding is called **menarche** (MEH-nar-kee). The timing of menarche appears to be related to heredity, general health, and altitude (average menarche is earlier in lower altitudes) and occurs during a time of other changes in body size and development. The age of menarche for girls in the United States is almost a year earlier for girls born after 1980 (12.4 years of age) compared to girls born before 1920 (13.3 years of age). Researchers attribute the decrease in age of first menses to the increase in the number of girls who are overweight—16% of girls who are currently 6 to 11 years old are overweight, compared to 4% prior to the 1970s. Fat cells produce a hormone, leptin, which supports reproductive functions and is likely the primary cause of earlier menstruation. Exposure to chemicals in the environment that have estrogenic effects in the body may also be a significant factor (Ginty, 2007).

Differences in the age of menarche are often a concern for young women, especially those who begin earlier or later than the norm. Many young women, and most young men, are still not fully informed about the developments and changes that accompany the onset of menstruation, and that lack of knowledge can result in confusion and apprehension. Menstrual cycles end at menopause, which in most women occurs between the ages of 45 and 55.

Menstrual Physiology

During the menstrual cycle the uterine lining is prepared for the implantation of a fertilized ovum. If conception does not occur, the lining sloughs off and is discharged as menstrual flow. The length of the menstrual cycle is usually measured from the beginning of the first day of flow to the day before the next flow begins. The menstrual period itself typically lasts 2 to 6 days. It is normal for the volume of the menstrual flow (usually 6 to 8 ounces) to vary. The cycle length varies from woman to woman; it can be anywhere from 24 to 42 days.

Regardless of the total cycle length, the interval between ovulation and the onset of menstruation is 14 days, plus or minus 2 days, even when there is several weeks' difference in the total length of the cycle, as shown in ▌ Figure 3.5. Some women experience a twinge, cramp, or pressure in the lower abdomen, called *Mittelschmerz* (German for "middle pain"), at ovulation. Mittelschmerz is caused by the swelling and bursting of

Critical Thinking Question

What messages about menstruation do you observe in advertising and television programs?

menarche
The initial onset of menstrual periods in a young woman.

the follicle or by a little fluid or blood from the ruptured follicle that irritates the sensitive abdominal lining. The released ovum then travels to the fallopian tube. Occasionally, more than one ovum is released. If two ova are fertilized, nonidentical twins will develop. When one egg is fertilized and then divides into two separate zygotes, identical twins result.

Around the time of ovulation, secretions of cervical mucus increase because of increased levels of estrogen. The mucus also changes, becoming clear, slippery, and stretchy. The pH of this mucus is more alkaline; as noted earlier, a more alkaline vaginal environment contributes to sperm motility and longevity. This is the time in the cycle when a woman can most easily become pregnant.

The Menstrual Cycle

The menstrual cycle is regulated by intricate relationships between the hypothalamus and various endocrine glands, including the pituitary gland, the adrenal glands, and the ovaries and uterus. The hypothalamus monitors hormone levels in the bloodstream throughout the cycle, releasing chemicals that stimulate the pituitary to produce two hormones that affect the ovaries: **follicle-stimulating hormone (FSH)** and **luteinizing** (LOO-te-uh-ny-zing) **hormone (LH)**. FSH stimulates the ovaries to produce estrogen and causes ova to mature in follicles (small sacs) within the ovaries. LH causes the ovary to release a mature ovum. LH also stimulates the development of the **corpus luteum** (the portion of the follicle that remains after the matured egg has been released), which produces the hormone progesterone.

The menstrual cycle is a self-regulating and dynamic process. Each hormone is secreted until the organ it acts on is stimulated; at that point the organ releases a substance that circulates back through the system to reduce hormonal activity in the initiating gland. This *negative-feedback mechanism* provides an internal control that regulates hormone fluctuation during the three phases of the menstrual cycle. These phases, described in the following paragraphs, are illustrated in ▌Figure 3.6.

Menstrual Phase

During the **menstrual phase** the uterus sheds the thickened inner layer of the endometrium, which is discharged through the cervix and vagina as menstrual flow. Menstrual flow typically consists of blood, mucus, and endometrial tissue.

follicle-stimulating hormone (FSH)
A pituitary hormone secreted by a female during the secretory phase of the menstrual cycle. FSH stimulates the development of ovarian follicles. In males it stimulates sperm production.

luteinizing hormone (LH)
The hormone secreted by the pituitary gland that stimulates ovulation in the female. In males it is called the interstitial cell hormone (ISCH) and stimulates production of androgens by the testes.

corpus luteum
A yellowish body that forms on the ovary at the site of the ruptured follicle and secretes progesterone.

menstrual phase
The phase of the menstrual cycle during which menstruation occurs.

▌**Figure 3.5** Ovulation timing and cycle length. Regardless of the length of the cycle, ovulation occurs 14 days before menstruation.

O = Ovulation

M = 1st day of menstruation

© Cengage Learning

(a) Brain

The hypothalamus in the brain measures levels of hormones and releases GnRH (gonadotropin-releasing hormone) to stimulate the pituitary to secrete FSH and LH into the bloodstream.

(b) Blood Levels of FSH and LH

The levels of FSH (red line) and LH (purple line) vary during the complete cycle.

(c) Ovary

Ovarian changes during the phases of the cycle.

(d) Blood Levels of Estrogen and Progesterone

Fluctuations in blood levels of estrogen and progesterone produced by the ovaries.

(e) Endometrium of Uterus

Effects of estrogen and progesterone on the lining of the uterus. After ovulation, the glands and ducts inside the endometrium (drawn as vertical tubes and spirals) develop and secrete nutrients that, if the woman became pregnant, would support the embryo.

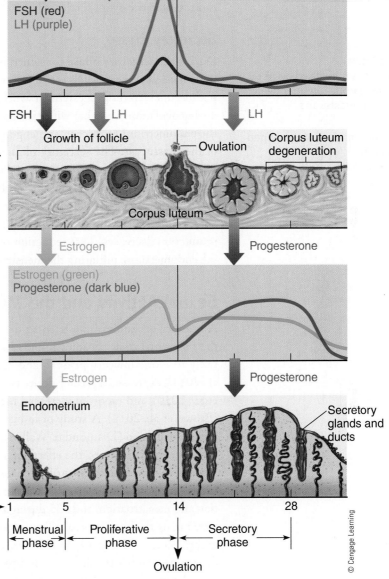

Figure 3.6 Changes during the menstrual cycle.

The shedding of the endometrium is triggered by reduced progesterone and estrogen levels in the bloodstream. As these hormone levels fall, the hypothalamus stimulates the pituitary gland to release FSH. This action initiates the second, or *proliferative*, phase of the menstrual cycle.

Proliferative Phase

During the **proliferative phase** the pituitary gland increases production of FSH, which stimulates the developing follicles to mature and to produce several types of estrogen. Estrogen in turn causes the endometrium to thicken. Although several follicles begin to mature, usually only one reaches maturity; the other follicles degenerate. When the level of ovarian estrogen circulating in the bloodstream reaches a peak, the pituitary gland depresses the release of FSH and stimulates LH production.

Regardless of cycle length, ovulation occurs 14 days prior to the onset of menstruation. In response to the spurt of LH secreted by the pituitary gland, the mature follicle ruptures and the ovum is released.

Secretory Phase

During the **secretory phase** continued pituitary secretions of LH cause the cells of the ruptured follicle to develop into a yellowish bump called the corpus luteum. The corpus luteum secretes progesterone, which inhibits the production of the cervical mucus during ovulation. Together with estrogen produced by the ovaries, progesterone causes the endometrium to thicken and engorge with blood in preparation for implantation of the **blastocyst**. The secretory phase is so named because glands and ducts in the endometrium produce and secrete nutrients to ensure development of the blastocyst. If implantation does not occur, the pituitary gland responds to high estrogen and progesterone levels in the bloodstream by shutting down production of LH and FSH. This action causes the corpus luteum to degenerate, and estrogen and progesterone production decreases. This reduction of hormone levels triggers the sloughing off of the endometrium, initiating the menstrual phase once again.

Sexual Activity and the Menstrual Cycle

A number of studies have tried to determine whether sexual interest is affected by the menstrual cycle. Studies found that women responded emotionally more positively to erotic imagery prior to and during ovulation (Mass et al., 2009; Rudski et al., 2011), expressed a greater desire to engage in sexual activity with men (Gangestad et al., 2010), and reported increased masturbation and sexual behavior with partners (Brown et al., 2011). A study of lesbians also found an increase in sexual motivation around ovulation (Diamond & Wallen, 2011).

One study examined the effects of stages of the menstrual cycle by measuring the amount of tips received by professional lap dancers working in strip clubs. The results showed that lap dancers averaged $70 per hour during ovulation, $50 between ovulation and menstruation, and $35 during menstruation. Of further interest, dancers who were taking the birth control pill averaged $37 per hour with no peak in tips compared to the average of $53 per hour for women not taking the pill. The researchers could not determine whether the difference in tips was based on subtle differences that ovulation caused in the women's behavior or from fluctuations in body odor or other subtle alterations in physical features that the customers responded to appreciatively (Miller et al., 2007). Evidence from other studies suggested that heterosexual men experience heightened sexual interest when women are in the fertile phase of their cycles (Gildersleeve et al., 2012; Haselton & Gildersleeve, 2011; Miller & Maner, 2011).

Couples sometimes avoid sexual activity and intercourse during menstruation (Barnhart et al., 1995), although from a medical point of view there are no health reasons to avoid intercourse during menstruation (except in the case of excessive bleeding or other menstrual problems). Reasons for avoiding sex during a woman's period vary.

Some women and men avoid sexual activity because of culturally induced shame about menstruation. Religious beliefs can also be a factor. Uncomfortable physical symptoms of breast tenderness and pelvic discomfort can reduce sexual desire or pleasure, and the messiness can inhibit sexual playfulness. If people do prefer to abstain from coitus during menstruation, the remaining repertoire of sexual activities is still available:

> When I'm on my period, I leave my tampon inside and push the string in, too. My husband and I have manual and oral stimulation, and a great time! (Authors' files)

Some women use a diaphragm or cervical cap to hold back the menstrual flow during coitus. Orgasm by any means of stimulation can be beneficial to a menstruating woman. The uterine contractions and release of vasocongestion often reduce backache, feelings of pelvic fullness, and cramping.

Menstrual Cycle Problems

Popular culture, as reflected by the media, tends to put forth negative and distorted perspectives about the menstrual cycle, particularly about premenstrual syndrome (PMS). An analysis of 78 magazine articles showed the perpetuation of the stereotype of the maladjusted woman, listing 131 different symptoms of PMS. Titles included "The Taming of the Shrew Inside of You" and "Premenstrual Frenzy" (Chrisler & Levy, 1990).

Most scientific research about menstruation has focused on negative effects. However, one study compared women's responses to the Menstrual Joy Questionnaire (MJQ) with those of a commonly used research tool, the Menstrual Distress Questionnaire. The MJQ's questions about such positive qualities as increased sexual desire, high spirits, feelings of affection, and self-confidence did result in subjects later reporting more-positive attitudes and fewer negative symptoms about menstruation. The researchers concluded that the way menstruation is portrayed by research and popular culture affects how women think about their menstrual cycles (Chrisler et al., 1994).

Premenstrual Syndrome

Most women undergo some physical or mood changes, or both, during their menstrual cycles. In many cases any negative changes are minor; for others the symptoms interfere with their daily lives (Waldman, 2012). **Premenstrual syndrome (PMS)** is a catchall term used to identify myriad physical and psychological symptoms that can occur before each menstrual period. As many as 200 premenstrual symptoms are listed in medical and research literature (O'Brien et al., 2000). Typical symptoms include bloating, breast swelling, and pain. (Fat layers in the waist and thighs become slightly thicker before menstruation—hence the period-related tight-jeans syndrome) (Pearson, 2000.) PMS also can increase food cravings, particularly for foods with high fat, sugar, and salt. Psychological symptoms include more negative self-image, irritability, tension, depression, mood swings, and a feeling of a lack of emotional control. Some of these PMS symptoms can be disruptive to close relationships and result in increased conflict and withdrawal (Fritz & Speroff, 2010; Stanicic & Jokic-Bergic, 2010).

Approximately 80–95% of women experience mild discomfort premenstrually, and only 5% have no PMS symptoms before menstruation. Five percent of women have symptoms severe enough for a diagnosis of **premenstrual dysphoric disorder (PMDD)**, with symptoms significantly affecting their normal functioning (Steiner et al., 2006).

premenstrual syndrome (PMS)
Symptoms of physical discomfort and emotional irritability that occur 2 to 12 days before menstruation.

premenstrual dysphoric disorder (PMDD)
Premenstrual symptoms severe enough to significantly disrupt a woman's functioning.

Not all of the causes of PMS and PMDD are known, but the drop in estrogen levels in the week prior to menstruation has a significant effect (Girman et al., 2003). Placebo-controlled studies have shown that medications used for depression, called SSRIs, can alleviate physical and psychological symptoms and improve quality of life and interpersonal functioning for some women (Vargas-Cooper, 2012). Oral contraceptives may also help alleviate symptoms (Marr et al., 2011).

Dysmenorrhea

dysmenorrhea
Pain or discomfort before or during menstruation.

prostaglandins
Hormones that induce uterine contractions.

Painful menstruation is called **dysmenorrhea** (dis-meh-nuh-REE-uh). *Primary dysmenorrhea* occurs during menstruation and is usually caused by the overproduction of **prostaglandins**, chemicals that cause the muscles of the uterus to contract. Problems with primary dysmenorrhea usually appear with the onset of menstruation at adolescence. One study found that 67% of adolescents experienced some degree of dysmenorrhea (Scharma et al., 2008). The symptoms are generally most noticeable during the first few days of a woman's period and include abdominal aching and/or cramping. Some women also experience nausea, vomiting, diarrhea, headache, dizziness, fatigue, irritability, or nervousness.

Secondary dysmenorrhea occurs before or during menstruation and is characterized by constant and often spasmodic lower abdominal pain that typically extends to the back and thighs. The symptoms are often similar to those of primary dysmenorrhea and are caused by factors other than prostaglandin production; possible causes include the presence of an intrauterine device (IUD), pelvic inflammatory disease (chronic infection of the reproductive organs), benign uterine tumors, obstruction of the cervical opening, and **endometriosis** (en-doh-mee-tree-OH-sis). Endometriosis, which affects up to 10% of premenopausal women in the United States (including adolescents), occurs when endometrial-like tissue implants in the abdominal cavity (Bulun, 2009). The implanted tissue often adheres to other tissue in the pelvic cavity, reducing mobility of the internal structures while engorging with blood during the proliferative phase. The engorged tissues and adhesions can cause painful menstruation, lower backache, and pain from pressure and movement during intercourse. Once the cause of secondary dysmenorrhea has been diagnosed, appropriate treatment can begin (Propst & Laufer, 1999).

endometriosis
A condition in which uterine tissue grows on various parts of the abdominal cavity.

Amenorrhea

amenorrhea
The absence of menstruation.

Besides discomfort or pain, another fairly common menstrual difficulty is **amenorrhea** (ay-meh-nuh-REE-uh), the absence of menstruation. Two types of amenorrhea exist: primary and secondary. *Primary amenorrhea* is the failure to begin to menstruate at puberty. It can be caused by problems with the reproductive organs, hormonal imbalances, poor health, or an imperforate hymen. *Secondary amenorrhea* involves the disruption of an established menstrual cycle, with the absence of menstruation for 3 months or more (Hormone Foundation, 2011). This is a normal condition during pregnancy and breast-feeding. It is also common in women who have just begun menstruating and in women approaching menopause. Women who discontinue birth control pills occasionally do not menstruate for several months, but this situation is usually temporary and resolves spontaneously.

Amenorrhea is more common among athletes than among the general population (Colino, 2006). Women who experience athletic amenorrhea also have decreased estrogen levels. This reduction in estrogen can place them at increased risk for developing serious health problems, such as decreased bone mineral density, with a resultant increased incidence of bone fractures and atrophy of the genital tissues. Athletic amenorrhea can be reversed by improving diet, gaining weight, or, in some cases, decreasing training intensity (Epp, 1997). Anabolic steroid use to attempt to enhance athletic performance will, among more dangerous side effects, cause amenorrhea (Kuipers, 1998). Medical or hormonal problems can produce amenorrhea (Hagan & Knott, 1998; Stener-Victorin et al., 2000). Women with *anorexia nervosa*, an eating disorder that often results in extreme weight loss, frequently stop menstruating because of hormonal changes that accompany emaciation.

Planned amenorrhea can be desirable at times; most women would prefer not to be menstruating on their honeymoons, while camping, at a swim competition, or in many other situations. Since the standard oral contraceptive pill was introduced, many women have skipped the last seven dummy pills and begun a new pack to avoid a period (L. Miller, 2001). An oral contraceptive pill called Seasonale, designed so that women have only four periods a year, became available in 2003 (Kalb, 2003).

Self-Help for Menstrual Problems

Women may be able to alleviate some of the unpleasant symptoms before and during menstruation by their own actions. Moderate to vigorous exercise throughout the month as well as proper diet can contribute to improvement of menstrual difficulties (Mackeen, 2007). For example, increasing fluids and fiber helps with the constipation that sometimes occurs before and during menstruation. Decreasing salt intake and avoiding foods high in salt (salad dressing, potato chips, bacon, pickles, to name a few) can help reduce swelling and bloating caused by water retention. Food supplements such as calcium, magnesium, B vitamins, and 200 IU of vitamin E twice a day can also help relieve cramps and bloating (Gaby, 2005). Oral contraceptives usually decrease menstrual cramps and the amount of flow, and some women use them for those reasons alone (Nelson, 2006). Continuous-use birth control pills may eliminate premenstrual symptoms (Humphrey, 2011).

A woman who experiences menstrual pain may find it useful to keep a diary to track symptoms, stresses, and daily habits, such as exercise, diet, and sleep. She may be able to note a relationship between symptoms and habits and modify her activities accordingly. The information can also be helpful for specific diagnosis if she consults a health-care practitioner. If a woman notices changes in her cycle that last for three months, she should consult her health-care provider (Colino, 2006). ●

Toxic Shock Syndrome

In May 1980 the Centers for Disease Control (CDC) published the first report of **toxic shock syndrome (TSS)** in menstruating women who used tampons. Symptoms of TSS, which is caused by toxins produced by the bacterium *Staphylococcus aureus*, include fever, sore throat, nausea, vomiting, diarrhea, red skin flush, dizziness, and low blood pressure (Hanrahan, 1994). Because TSS progresses rapidly and can cause death, a person with several of the symptoms of TSS should consult a physician immediately.

TSS is rare, and the number of reported TSS cases has fallen sharply since the peak in 1980, most likely as a result of removing highly absorbent tampons from the market (Petitti & Reingold, 1988). Some guidelines have been developed that can help to prevent toxic shock. One suggestion has been to use sanitary napkins instead of tampons. For women who want to continue using tampons, it is advisable to use regular instead of super-absorbent tampons, to change tampons three to four times during the day, and to use napkins for some time during each 24 hours of menstrual flow.

toxic shock syndrome (TSS)
A disease that occurs most commonly in menstruating women and that can cause a person to go into shock.

Menopause

The term **climacteric** (kli-MAK-tuh-rik) refers to the physiological changes that occur during the transition period from fertility to infertility in both sexes. In women

climacteric
Physiological changes that occur during the transition period from fertility to infertility in both sexes.

around 40 years of age, the ovaries begin to slow the production of estrogen. This period before complete cessation of menstruation is called **perimenopause**, and it can last for up to 10 years. Menstruation continues but cycles can become irregular, with erratic or heavy bleeding as menopause approaches (Bastian et al., 2003). Up to 90% of women experience a change in menstrual patterns and sexual response during perimenopause. Also, by age 40 a woman's level of circulating testosterone is half what it was when she was 20 years old (S. Davis, 2000). Some women in perimenopause experience symptoms similar to those described in the following menopause section (Torpy, 2003). Low-dose birth control pills are sometimes prescribed to alleviate the perimenopausal symptoms and to prevent bone loss (Seibert et al., 2003).

Menopause, one of the events of the female climacteric, is the permanent cessation of menstruation. Menopause occurs as a result of certain physiological changes and takes place at a mean age of 51 but can occur in the 30s or as late as the 60s (Andrews, 2006). About 10% of women reach menopause by age 45 (Speroff & Fritz, 2005). Research indicates that women who experience earlier menopause smoke tobacco, began their periods by age 11, had shorter cycles, had fewer pregnancies, had used oral contraceptives, had a history of endometriosis, and had higher blood levels of perfluorocarbons (man-made chemicals used in many household products) (Knox et al., 2011; Palmer et al., 2003; Pokoradi et al., 2011).

The experience of menopause varies greatly from woman to woman. Some women experience few physical symptoms other than cessation of menstruation. For these women menopause is surprisingly uneventful:

> After hearing comments for years about how menopause was so traumatic, I was ready for the worst. I was sure surprised when I realized I had hardly noticed it happening. (Authors' files)

A recent research study found that women who reported fewer symptoms of menopause had more positive views of the effects of menopause on their health and attractiveness (Strauss, 2011). In addition, most women feel relieved that they no longer need to be concerned about pregnancy, contraception, and menstruation. They may experience an increased sense of freedom in sexual intimacy as a result (Andrews, 2006).

However, for many women, menopause brings a range of symptoms that can vary from mild to severe (Pinkerton & Zion, 2006). The most acute menopausal symptoms occur in the two years before and the two years following the last menstrual period. Hot flashes and night sweats are common difficulties. Hot flashes can range from a mild feeling of warmth to a feeling of intense heat and profuse perspiration, especially around the chest, neck, and face. A severe hot flash can soak clothing or sheets in perspiration. The flashes usually last for one to five minutes. Hot flashes can occur several times a day and during sleep. About 75% of women experience hot flashes, and women smokers experience hot flashes more frequently than nonsmokers (Staropoli et al., 1997). For unknown reasons, African American women experience more hot flashes and women of Asian descent have fewer hot flashes than other racial and ethnic groups (Avis et al., 2001). Researchers have studied the physiology of hot flashes for over 30 years and still do not know how hot flashes occur (Schatz & Robb-Nicholson, 2006).

Other menopausal symptoms can significantly affect a woman's daily life and, indirectly, her sexuality. Research has found that sleep disturbance, night sweats, and symptoms of depression are associated with a decrease in sexual interest (Reed et al., 2007). Thinning of the vaginal walls and less lubrication as a result of the decline in estrogen can make intercourse uncomfortable or painful (Krychman, 2011). A woman may take longer to become sexually aroused. Sleep disturbance can easily contribute to fatigue, irritability, short-term memory loss, and difficulty concentrating during the day (Maki et al., 2008).

Hormone Therapy

Hormone therapy (HT)* for women involves using supplemental hormones—estrogen, progesterone, and/or testosterone—to alleviate problems that can arise from the decrease in natural hormone production that occurs during the female climacteric. Also, younger women with hormone deficiencies following removal of their ovaries often use HT. ■ Table 3.1 summarizes some of the benefits and risks of each of these hormones.

hormone therapy (HT)
The use of supplemental hormones during and after menopause or following surgical removal of the ovaries.

Hormones used in HT come from three main sources. Estrogen and progesterone are made from synthetic chemicals or can be derived from plants, some of which are bioidentical to human estrogen (i.e., they have the same chemical structure). Testosterone is made from synthetic chemicals. The most widely used estrogen in the United States, conjugated equine estrogen (CEE), is made from pregnant mares' urine. (Some oppose this practice because of the treatment the mares and foals endure in order for the urine to be harvested.) The CEE used in the HT products Premarin (estrogen only) and Prempro (estrogen and progesterone) is not bioidentical to human estrogen, and it contains impurities with unknown medical properties (Food and Drug Administration, 1997; Rosenshein, 2007). However, most of the hormone therapy research in the United States has involved women using conjugated equine estrogen (Love & Rochman, 2006).

Unfortunately, data are currently insufficient to support the effectiveness of complementary and alternative therapies such as soy, herbs, acupuncture, and naturopathy for treating menopausal symptoms (Hall, 2007; Nedrow et al., 2006).

At a Glance

■ TABLE 3.1 Benefits and Risks of Hormone Therapy

Hormone	Benefits	Problems
Estrogen	Reduces risk of breast cancer when used without progestin.	Increases risk of breast cancer when used in conjunction with progestin.
	Maintains thickness and vascularity of vaginal and urethral tissue for comfort and lubrication during sexual interaction.	Increases the incidence of endometrial and ovarian cancer when used without progesterone.
	Increases sexual interest and enjoyment.	Increases risk of blood clots.
	Helps prevent urinary tract problems.	
	Reduces hot flashes and sleep disturbance from night sweats.	
	Protects against osteoporosis (abnormal bone loss) and resultant fractures, particularly of the hip.	
	No increased risk of coronary heart disease when started at menopause.	
	Reduces risk of colon cancer and Alzheimer's.	
Progesterone	Eliminates the estrogen-caused increase in endometrial and ovarian cancer.	Alters the type of fats in the bloodstream and increases the risk of cardiovascular disease.
		Increases the incidence of breast cancer.
Testosterone*	Helps maintain or restore sexual interest and arousal. Increases overall energy.	Side effects can include increase in hair growth and acne.

*Testosterone is not approved by the FDA for treatment for sexual interest and arousal in women, but many physicians prescribe it "off label" for that purpose. Clinical trials on testosterone therapy for women are ongoing (Davis et al., 2008).

SOURCES: Allen (2011); Chen et al. (2012); Hampton (2012); Davis et al. (2008); Fritz & Speroff (2010); LaCroix et al. (2011); National Cancer Institute (2011b); Pines et al. (2008).

---

*Another abbreviation commonly seen for hormone therapy is HRT, or hormone replacement therapy. In the past, treatment with hormones was intended to return the hormone levels after menopause to premenopause levels. Currently, the smallest dose of hormone therapies that alleviates symptoms associated with menopause is the usual treatment approach.

Bioidentical Hormones

Bioidentical hormones have the same molecular structure as hormones produced by the human body. Both pharmaceutical companies and compounding pharmacies (pharmacies that mix hormones for individual patients) make bioidentical hormones, but compounding pharmacies can vary amounts and ratios of hormones for each individual based on the physician's prescription (Vogel, 2006). Opponents voice concern about the quality, purity, and potency of the ingredients of bioidentical hormones from compounding pharmacies due to less stringent FDA oversight (Benda, 2008).

Women in other countries, particularly European countries and China, have used bioidentical hormones for many years (Moskowitz, 2006). Unfortunately, few studies have examined the health consequences for women using bioidentical compared to synthetic hormones (Baber, 2011). However, there are indications that bioidentical estrogen and micronized progesterone may be safer in regard to breast cancer and heart disease compared to synthetic hormones (Oz & Roizen, 2010). A 12-year French study of almost 100,000 women found that those who used estrogen and a bioidentical progesterone that is unavailable in the United States experienced no significant increase in breast cancer compared to women who never took any menopausal hormones (Fugh-Berman, 2008).

Controversy in Hormone Therapy Research

Choosing whether or not to use menopausal hormone therapy is one of the most complicated health decisions women must make. Few medical topics are in such a state of flux and controversy as hormone therapy for menopause. The most contradictory and confusing concerns about HT relate to heart disease and breast cancer.

Regarding heart disease, the timing relative to the onset of menopause appears to make a key difference. Most studies have found that women who began HT at the onset of menopause had a significantly lower risk of cardiovascular disease than women who did not use HT. In contrast, women who began HT when they were 20 or more years past menopause had an increased risk of heart disease (Fritz & Speroff, 2010). This variation is likely due to the effects of aging on the cardiovascular system. Prior to menopause, estrogen has a protective effect, and if a woman begins taking estrogen at menopause, it helps maintain the health of her cardiovascular tissue. When a woman waits many years after menopause before taking estrogen, the estrogen can cause the plaque that has formed in the intervening years on the walls of the veins and arteries of the heart to separate from the tissue, form clots, and cause heart attacks (National Cancer Institute, 2011b; Taylor & Manson, 2011).

Whether a woman takes estrogen or a combination of estrogen and progesterone makes a difference in breast cancer risk. Women who do not have a uterus can take estrogen only, whereas women with a uterus use both estrogen and progestin. Research currently indicates the following: Women who took only estrogen for hormone therapy had a 23% lower risk for breast cancer compared with those who had taken a placebo (LaCroix et al., 2011). Compared to the placebo group, women ages 50 to 79 who used estrogen and progestin HT had a greater incidence of breast cancer and a higher number of deaths from breast cancer—2.6 deaths per 100,000 compared to the placebo group's rate of 1.3 deaths per 100,000 (Chlebowski et al., 2010). To keep the increase in perspective, it is important to note that the 1.3 per 100,000 death rate is less than is associated with the risk factors of a positive family history, being overweight after menopause, or alcohol intake (Fritz & Speroff, 2010).

A Challenging Decision

A menopausal woman should weigh the potential benefits and risks of HT against the symptoms of hormone deficiency. For many women the benefits far outweigh the risks, and for other women the opposite is true. New research results emerge continually, and although these results can be contradictory, women and their health-care providers have this information available when deciding whether to use HT (Oz & Roizen, 2010). We recommend that women thoroughly discuss the available evidence and their individual health history and lifestyle with a health-care practitioner specializing in menopause and HT. ●

Gynecological Health Concerns

Gynecological health problems range from minor infections to cancer. In this section, we provide information and self-help suggestions on several topics.

Urinary Tract Infections

Women often develop infections of the urinary tract, the organ system that includes the urethra, bladder, and kidneys. If the infection progresses all the way to the kidneys, severe illness can result (Pace, 2000). The symptoms of urinary tract infections include a frequent need to urinate, a burning sensation when urinating, blood or pus in the urine, and sometimes lower pelvic pain. A conclusive diagnosis of a urinary tract infection requires laboratory analysis of a urine sample. Such an infection generally responds to short-term antibiotic treatment.

Bacteria that enter the urethral opening typically are the cause of urinary tract infections (Raz et al., 2000). Observing a few routine precautions can help prevent urinary tract infections. Penile–vaginal intercourse is the most frequent means by which bacteria enter the urinary tract; the bacteria are massaged into the urethra by the thrusting motions of intercourse. For those who have frequent problems with such infections, it is important that both partners wash their hands and genitals before and after intercourse. Using intercourse positions that cause less friction against the urethra can also help. In addition, women can use water-soluble lubricants (not petroleum jelly) when vaginal lubrication is insufficient, because irritated tissue is more susceptible to infection. Urinating immediately after intercourse helps wash out bacteria. Careful wiping from front to back after both urination and bowel movements helps keep bacteria away from the urethra. Urinating as soon as you feel the urge also reduces the likelihood of infection. It can also be helpful to drink plenty of liquids, especially cranberry juice (Kiel & Nashelsky, 2003), and to avoid substances such as coffee, tea, and alcohol, which have an irritating effect on the bladder. ●

Vaginal Infections

When the natural balance of the vagina is disturbed or when a nonnative organism is introduced, a vaginal infection, or **vaginitis** (va-juh-NYE-tus), can result. Usually the woman herself first notices symptoms of vaginitis: irritation or itching of the vagina and vulva, redness of the introitus and labia, unusual discharge, and sometimes a disagreeable odor. (An unpleasant odor can also be due to a forgotten tampon or diaphragm.) Types of vaginal infections include yeast infections, bacterial infections, and trichomoniasis, discussed in detail in Chapter 15.

vaginitis
Inflammation of the vaginal walls caused by a variety of vaginal infections.

It is important for vaginitis to be treated and cured. Chronic irritation from long-term infections can play a part in predisposing a woman to cervical cell changes that can lead to cancer. The following suggestions may help prevent vaginitis from occurring in the first place (Solomini, 1991):

1. Eat a well-balanced diet low in sugar and refined carbohydrates.
2. Maintain general good health with adequate sleep, exercise, and emotional release.
3. Use good hygiene, including (a) bathing regularly with mild soap; (b) wiping from front to back, vulva to anus, after urinating and having bowel movements; (c) wearing clean cotton underpants (nylon holds in heat and moisture that encourage bacterial growth); (d) avoiding the use of feminine-hygiene sprays and douching, colored toilet paper, bubble bath, and other people's washcloths or towels to wash or wipe your genitals; and (e) ensuring that your sexual partner's hands and genitals are clean before beginning sexual activity.
4. Be sure that you have adequate lubrication before coitus, either natural lubrication or a water-soluble lubricant. Do not use petroleum-based lubricants (such as Vaseline), because they are not water soluble and are likely to remain in the vagina and harbor bacteria. Petroleum-based lubricants can also weaken, and will eventually degrade, latex condoms or diaphragms.
5. Use condoms if you, or your partner, are nonmonogamous. ●

The Pap Smear

Pap smear
A screening test for cancer of the cervix.

The **Pap smear** is an essential part of routine preventive health care for all women, including sexually active adolescents and postmenopausal women. During this screening test for cervical cancer, cells are taken from the cervix. The vaginal walls are held open with a speculum, and a few cells are removed with a cervical brush or a small wooden spatula; these cells are put on a glass slide and sent to a laboratory to be examined. The cells for a Pap smear are taken from the *transition zone*, the part of the cervix where long, column-shaped cells called *columnar cells* meet flat-shaped cells called *squamous cells*. A Pap smear is not painful, because there are so few nerve endings on the cervix. A vaginal Pap smear is done when the woman's cervix has been removed, although the incidence of vaginal cancer is low.

Since the development of Pap smears in 1941, early detection and follow-up treatments have decreased the death rate from cervical cancer by 75% in the United States (Dolgoff, 2008). Women throughout the world who are economically disadvantaged and do not participate in screening programs are far more likely to die from cervical cancer than are other women. For example, an average of only 41% of women across the developing world survive cervical cancer (Parry, 2006). Each year about 250,000 women in the developing world die of cervical cancer (Kalb & Springen, 2006).

Several factors increase the risk of developing cervical cancer. These include having sexual intercourse at an early age, having multiple sexual partners, smoking tobacco, inhaling secondary smoke, and having had certain sexually transmitted infections (Wyand & Arrindell, 2005).

The U.S. Preventive Services Task Force currently recommends that women have their first Pap smear at age 21 and have subsequent screenings every 3 years until age 30 and every 5 years between the ages of 30 and 65, depending on their health-care provider's recommendations (Conley, 2012). Research has found that a different type of test for human papilloma virus (HPV), a sexually transmitted infection, is more effective than the Pap test in detecting cervical cancer, and in 2009 the test was approved by the FDA to screen for HPV and cervical cancer (Mechcatie, 2009). ●

Surgical Removal of the Uterus and Ovaries

Some medical problems may require a woman to undergo a **hysterectomy** (his-tuh-REK-tuh-mee), surgical removal of the uterus, or an **oophorectomy** (oh-uh-fuh-REK-tuh-mee), surgical removal of the ovaries, or both. Such problems include bleeding disorders, severe pelvic infections, and the presence of benign (noncancerous) tumors (Kilbourn & Richards, 2001). Cancer of the cervix, uterus, or ovaries is also cause for hysterectomy or oophorectomy.

Of these three cancers, ovarian cancer is by far the deadliest (Torpy et al., 2011). In about 80% of women with ovarian cancer, the disease is advanced when diagnosed (Kaelin et al., 2006). The cancer is difficult to detect in its early stages because the symptoms are often similar to those caused by other problems (Eheman et al., 2006). The following symptoms may indicate ovarian cancer if they appear daily for three weeks: Abdominal pain or bloating, pelvic pain, difficulty eating or feeling full quickly, and frequent or urgent urination (American Cancer Society, 2009).

In the United States, approximately 600,000 women have hysterectomies each year (Tucker, 2010). An estimated 33% of women have a hysterectomy by age 65, making it the second most frequently performed major operation for women in the United States (Gretz et al., 2008). Hysterectomy rates are higher among low-income women, women with less than a high-school education, and women who live in the South. Researchers suspect that a lack of preventive health care in these groups allows problems to advance to the point where other treatments are not viable (Palmer et al., 1999). Before consenting to undergo a hysterectomy or similar surgery, it is important for a woman to obtain a second opinion; to fully inform herself of the benefits, risks, and alternatives to surgery; and to arrange for thorough preoperative and postoperative information and counseling (Pearson, 2011).

The effects of hysterectomy on a woman's sexuality vary. Hysterectomy does not affect the sensitivity of the clitoris. Some women find that the elimination of medical problems and painful intercourse, assured protection from unwanted pregnancy, and lack of menstruation enhance their quality of life in general and their sexual functioning and enjoyment (Flory et al., 2006). An important variable in postsurgical sexual adjustment is the degree of satisfaction with the sexual relationship prior to surgery: If a woman had low sexual satisfaction prior to surgery, the surgery is much less likely to have a positive impact on her sexuality (Lonee-Hoffman & Schei, 2007).

However, other women experience an alteration or decrease in their sexual response after removal of the uterus. Sensations from uterine vasocongestion and elevation during arousal as well as uterine contractions during orgasm are absent and can change the physical experience of sexual response. Some changes can result from damage to the nerves in the pelvis. The exact locations of nerves vital to female sexual function have not been identified, and no nerve-sparing procedures are done during pelvic surgeries in women (Berman & Berman, 2005). Scar tissue or alterations to the vagina can also have an effect. When ovaries are removed, symptoms common to menopause will occur unless hormone therapy is undertaken.

hysterectomy
Surgical removal of the uterus.

oophorectomy
Surgical removal of the ovaries.

The Breasts

Breasts are not part of the internal or external female genitalia. Instead, they are **secondary sex characteristics** (physical characteristics other than genitals that distinguish males from females). In a physically mature woman, the breasts consist internally of fatty tissue and **mammary** (MAM-uh-ree), or milk, **glands** (❙ Figure 3.7). The glandular tissue in the breasts responds to sex hormones. During adolescence, both the fatty and the glandular tissues develop markedly. The amount of glandular tissue

secondary sex characteristics
The physical characteristics other than genitals that indicate sexual maturity, such as body hair, breasts, and deepened voice.

mammary glands
Glands in the female breast that produce milk.

in the breasts varies little from woman to woman, despite differences in overall size. Consequently, the amount of milk produced after childbirth does not correlate with the size of the breasts. Variation in breast size is due primarily to the amount of fatty tissue distributed around the glands. It is common for one breast to be slightly larger than the other. Breasts show some size and texture variations at different phases of the menstrual cycle and when influenced by pregnancy, nursing, or birth control pills.

The *nipple* is in the center of the *areola* (ah-REE-oh-luh), the darker area of the external breast. The areola contains sebaceous (oil-producing) glands that help lubricate the nipples during breast-feeding. The openings of the mammary glands are in the nipples. Some nipples point outward from the breast, others are flush with the breast, and still others sink into the breast. The nipples become erect when small muscles at their base contract in response to touch, sexual arousal, or cold. For many women breast and nipple stimulation is an important source of pleasure and arousal during masturbation or sexual interaction. Some find that such stimulation helps build the sexual intensity that leads to orgasm; others enjoy it for its own sake. Other women find breast and nipple touching a neutral or unpleasant experience.

Breasts come in a multitude of sizes and shapes. One writer explained, "On real women, I've seen breasts as varied as faces: breasts shaped like tubes, breasts shaped like tears, breasts that flop down, breasts that point up, breasts that are dominated by thick, dark nipples and areola, breasts with nipples so small and pale they look airbrushed" (Angier, 1999, p. 128).

Breast size is a source of considerable preoccupation for many women and men in our society:

> In talking with my friends about how we feel about our breasts, I discovered that not one of us feels really comfortable about how she looks. I've always been envious of women with large breasts because mine are small. But my friends with large breasts talk about feeling self-conscious about their breasts too. (Authors' files)

Critical Thinking Question

Should adolescents be allowed to have breast enlargement surgery? Why or why not?

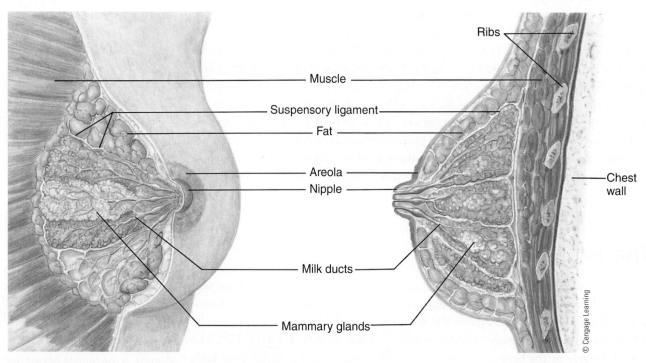

Figure 3.7 Cross-section front and side views of the female breast.

Labels: Ribs, Muscle, Suspensory ligament, Fat, Areola, Nipple, Chest wall, Milk ducts, Mammary glands

© Cengage Learning

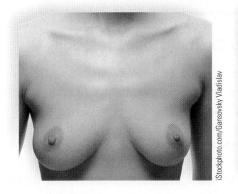

Breast size and shape vary from woman to woman.

Surgeries to enlarge or reduce breasts reflect the dissatisfaction many women feel because their breasts do not fit the cultural ideal. In 2008 over 355,600 women in the United States had cosmetic breast implant surgery (American Society for Aesthetic Plastic Surgery, 2009). Since the late 1980s, increasing numbers of young women have been receiving breast augmentation (Farr, 2000). Many women who have cosmetic breast augmentation are pleased with the results. Others experience painful or disfiguring complications and poor results, such as loss of breast sensation, asymmetric breasts, and capsular contraction (scar tissue develops around the implant, which turns the soft capsule into a hard disk). One study found that 73% of women with breast implants experienced side effects, and 27% of women had their implants removed within 3 years because of infection, painful scar tissue, or a broken or leaking implant (about 15% rupture by 10 years) (Springen, 2003).

Breast Self-Exam

A breast self-examination (BSE) is an important part of self–health care for women, especially for women at high risk for breast cancer (Doheny, 2009). This exam can help a woman know what is normal for her own breasts. She can do the breast exam herself and can also teach her partner to do it. Ninety percent of breast lumps, most of which are benign, are found by women themselves. Women find most cancerous tumors accidentally, by routine touching in the shower or while dressing, or when their partners notice a lump. One method of doing a breast exam is illustrated in the Your Sexual Health box, "How to Examine Your Breasts." It is helpful to fill out a chart, such as the one shown in ▌ Figure 3.8, to keep track of lumps in the breasts. Many breasts

SEXUALHEALTH

Fill out a chart, like the one shown here, when you examine your breasts. For any lump you find, mark

1. its location
2. its size (BB, pea, raisin, grape)
3. its shape (rounded or elongated)

Compare each record with the last one, and consult your health practitioner regarding any changes. A new or changing lump should be checked as soon as possible. Most such lumps will prove to be benign.

Today's date _____

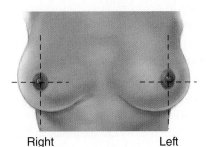

Right   Left

▌ **Figure 3.8** It is helpful to use a chart similar to this one to keep track of lumps in the breasts.

SOURCE: Reprinted with permission from Kaiser Foundation Health Plan of Oregon.

1. In the shower: Examine your breasts during a bath or shower; hands glide more easily over wet skin. With fingers flat, move your hands gently over every part of each breast. Use your right hand to examine your left breast and your left hand to examine your right breast. Check for any lump, hard knot, or thickening.

2. Before a mirror: Inspect your breasts with your arms at your sides. Next, raise your arms high overhead. Look for any changes in the contour of each breast: a swelling, a dimpling of the skin, or changes in the nipple. Then rest your palms on your hips and press down firmly to flex your chest muscles. Left and right breasts will not match exactly—few women's breasts do.

3. Lying down: To examine your right breast, put a pillow or folded towel under your right shoulder. Place your right hand behind your head (this distributes breast tissue more evenly on the chest). With your left hand, fingers flat, press gently in small circular motions around an imaginary clock face. Begin at the outermost top of your right breast for 12 o'clock, then move to 1 o'clock, and so on around the circle back to 12. A ridge of firm tissue in the lower curve of each breast is normal. Then move in an inch, toward the nipple, and keep circling to examine every part of your breast, including the nipple. This requires at least three more circles. Now slowly repeat this procedure on your left breast.

Finally, squeeze the nipple of each breast gently between thumb and index finger. Any discharge, clear or bloody, should be reported to your doctor immediately—as should the discovery of any unusual lump, swelling, or thickening anywhere in the breast.

  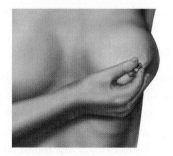

Breast self-exam.

normally feel lumpy. Once a woman becomes familiar with her own breasts, she can notice any changes. If there is a change, she should consult a health-care practitioner, who might recommend further diagnostic testing.

Symptoms of inflammatory breast cancer, a rare but aggressive kind of breast cancer, include redness, swelling, and warmth in the breast. The skin on the breast may also appear pitted, like the skin of an orange. A lump is usually not present. The symptoms usually develop over a period of weeks or months (National Cancer Institute, 2006). ●

Breast Cancer Screening

Breast self-examination and routine clinical breast exams by your health-care provider are important screening tools. Another such tool is **mammography** (ma-MAWG-ruh-fee), a highly sensitive X-ray screening test to help detect cancerous breast cells and lumps. Mammography uses low levels of radiation to create an image of the breast, called a *mammogram*, on film or paper. Mammography can often detect a breast lump up to several years before it can be felt manually; it can also sometimes find cancerous cell changes that occur even before a lump develops (Aldridge et al., 2006). With earlier detection of breast cancer, a decrease in mortality and an increase in breast-conserving treatments are possible. The American Medical Association, the American Cancer Society, and the National Cancer

mammography
A highly sensitive X-ray test for the detection of breast cancer.

Institute recommend yearly mammograms for women age 40 and older, including those who have previously had breast cancer (Houssami et al., 2011; Kaelin et al., 2006).

Besides mammograms, additional testing methods are used, and others are under development. Magnetic resonance imaging (MRI) uses magnetic fields to create images of body tissue and blood flow and can produce a more detailed image of breast tissue to clarify inconclusive findings (Hudepohl, 2011; Kingsbury, 2007a). Pregnant or lactating women, women at high risk, and those with dense breast tissue can use ultrasonography as a supplemental test (Singh et al., 2008). Researchers are evaluating and testing additional screening and diagnostic methods, including genetic tests (Laino, 2008). Currently, the best method for early detection of breast cancer is a combination of monthly manual self-exams, routine exams by a health-care practitioner, and mammography as recommended.

It is especially important for lesbians to be conscientious about scheduling regular exams and mammograms; they tend to be screened less often than heterosexual women because they do not have birth control medical appointments. Lesbians may also avoid health-care services rather than confront the insensitivity and ignorance of some medical practitioners (Hammond, 2006; Heck et al., 2006). Many lesbians report that past negative experiences have made them less likely to seek services when they have a problem (Makadon, 2006).

In 5–10% of women, breast cancer can develop from flaws in a gene that is now detectable. Women with this gene flaw have up to an 85% chance of developing breast cancer and may have an increased risk for ovarian cancer (Pluta & Golub, 2011; Metcalfe et al., 2008). Women now have the opportunity to decide whether to use drugs for cancer prevention or to have a preventive mastectomy.

Breast Lumps

Three types of lumps can occur in the breasts. The two most common are *cysts*, which are fluid-filled sacs, and *fibroadenomas*, which are solid, rounded tumors. Both are benign (not cancerous or harmful) tumors, and together they account for approximately 80% of breast lumps. In some women the lumps create breast tenderness that ranges from mild to severe discomfort, which is called *fibrocystic disease* (Deckers & Ricci, 1992). The causes of fibrocystic disease are unknown but may be hormonally related. Caffeine in coffee, tea, cola drinks, and chocolate might contribute to the development of benign breast lumps. Dietary changes that have helped some women reduce their symptoms include eating more fish, chicken, and grains and less red meat, salt, and fats.

The third kind of breast lump is a *malignant tumor* (a tumor made up of cancer cells). Breast cancer affects approximately 1 in 8 women in the United States. In one year breast cancer kills about 40,000 U.S. women and 500,000 women worldwide (American Cancer Society, 2010; Leitzmann et al., 2008). The risk of breast cancer rises with age; half of all breast cancers are diagnosed in women age 65 and older. Although breast cancer is less common in women in their 20s and 30s, cancers that occur in young women are often more aggressive and result in a higher mortality rate (Fraunfelder, 2000). Breast cancer in men is relatively rare, accounting for 1% of all cases—in 2010 about 2,000 men had breast cancer, which was fatal for 390 (Fentiman et al., 2006; National Cancer Institute, 2011b).

The good news is that overall mortality from breast cancer in the United States is at its lowest since 1950, most likely because of earlier detection. Unfortunately, the survival rate for Black women (78%) is lower than that for White women (90%) (National Cancer Institute, 2010). African American women are more likely to have aggressive cancers, and socioeconomic characteristics of lower income, lack of health-care coverage, and apprehension about using health and medical services lead to differences in preventive health care (such as breast exams and mammograms). As a result, African American women tend to have more-advanced breast cancer prior to detection (Aldridge et al., 2006; Brinton et al., 2008).

Breast cancer is no longer a disease that primarily affects women in North America and Western Europe. The incidence in Asia, Africa, Latin America, and Eastern Europe is increasing steadily, partially because women in these regions are living longer, having fewer children, and adopting Western lifestyle patterns (e.g., eating fatty foods and not exercising) (Porter, 2008). For example, a study of Chinese women found that those who ate a Western diet were 60% more likely to develop breast cancer than were those who ate a traditional diet of vegetables, beans, tofu, soy milk, and fish. In addition, breast cancer detection and treatment in poorer countries is inadequate. For example, in South Africa 5% of breast cancers are detected in the early stage, compared to 50% in the United States (Kingsbury, 2007b).

Breast Cancer

Certain risk factors that increase or decrease a woman's chances of developing breast cancer are outlined in ■ Table 3.2. Some researchers believe that 40% of breast cancers in postmenopausal women may be prevented by lifestyle factors. Hormone use, alcohol consumption, high coffee consumption, weight gain, and lack of physical activity contribute significantly to the risk of breast cancer after menopause (Sprague et al., 2008; Tang et al., 2009). Several studies have found a correlation between breast cancer and greater exposure to artificial light at night (Spivey, 2010). Scientific evidence also indicates that environmental exposure to toxic chemicals may contribute to as much as 50% of breast cancers (Evans, 2006). Exposure to environmental pollution, pesticides, radiation, and synthetic chemicals found in plastics, detergents, and pharmaceutical drugs can mimic estrogen's effects on the body and can cause cells to grow out of control and form tumors

At a Glance

■ TABLE 3.2 Risk Factors for Breast Cancer

Higher Risk	Lower Risk
Inherited breast cancer gene	No inherited breast cancer gene
Higher lifetime cumulative estrogen exposure	Lower lifetime estrogen exposure
Menstruation onset before age 12	Menstruation onset after age 12
No pregnancies	One or more pregnancies
First child after age 30 and subsequent children later in life	First child before age 30 and subsequent children early in life
Never breast-fed a child	Breast-fed a child
Menopause after age 55	Menopause prior to age 54
Obesity	Slenderness
Intact ovaries	Both ovaries removed early in life
Two or more first-degree relatives with breast cancer	No family history of breast cancer
Over age 65	Below age 65
Sedentary lifestyle	Regular strenuous exercise
One or more alcoholic drinks (beer, wine, or spirits) a day	Less than one alcoholic drink a day
Diet high in meats and saturated fats	Diet of fruits, vegetables, low-fat dairy products, fish, soy products, vitamin D, calcium, and unsaturated fats
Normal dose of aspirin or ibuprofen (Advil) fewer than 3 times per week	Normal dose of aspirin or ibuprofen (Advil) 3 times per week

SOURCES: Bingham et al. (2003), Bissonauth et al. (2008), Cain (2000), Cardenas & Frisch (2003), Higa (2000), Leitzmann et al. (2008), Li et al. (2007), Nelson (2008), Verloop et al. (2000).

(Cohn et al., 2007; Sung et al., 2007). Some breast cancer scientists and activist groups are attempting to have a greater percentage of cancer research funds allocated to investigations into environmental causes of cancer to assist advances in prevention (Lyman, 2006).

Once breast cancer has been diagnosed, several forms of treatment can be used, and others are being developed. Radiation therapy, chemotherapy, hormone therapy, immunotherapy, *lumpectomy* (surgical removal of the lump and small amounts of surrounding tissue only), **mastectomy** (surgical removal of all or part of the breast), or a combination of these procedures can be performed. If the cancer is small, localized, and in an early stage, lumpectomy with chemotherapy or radiation can provide as good a chance of a cure as a mastectomy (National Cancer Institute, 2010). Breakthroughs in treatment are improving survival rates (Kaelin et al., 2006).

Breast cancer and its treatments can adversely affect a woman's sexuality (Reitsamer et al., 2007). Research indicates that approximately 50% of women who have had breast cancer experience sexual problems resulting from the physical effects of chemotherapy, radiation, and hormone therapy (Fleming & Kleinbart, 2001). The loss of one or both breasts is usually significant to women. Breasts symbolize many aspects of femininity and can be an important aspect of self-image (Potter & Ship, 2001). The stimulation of a woman's breasts during lovemaking, by massaging, licking, or sucking—and the stimulation her partner receives from doing these things and from simply looking at her breasts—is often an important component of sexual arousal for both the woman and her partner. Consequently, surgical removal of one or both breasts can create challenges of sexual adjustment for the couple (Polinsky, 1995).

Reconstructive breast surgery can enhance a woman's emotional and sexual adjustment following a mastectomy. In many cases a new breast can be made with a silicone pouch containing silicone gel or saline water that is placed under the woman's own skin and chest muscle. In 2002 about 70,000 women in the United States had implants following mastectomy (Healy, 2003).

In 1974 Betty Ford and Happy Rockefeller were the first public figures to openly discuss their breast cancer and mastectomies. Before their courageous actions most women kept their breast cancer and its treatment as private as possible. In the ensuing years extensive resources have arisen to help women and their loved ones better manage a diagnosis of breast cancer. Political activism has also increased the previous disproportionately small percentage of government funding for breast cancer research. An organization known as Susan G. Komen for the Cure was formed in the mid-1980s and has developed a global grassroots network of cancer survivors and activists (Brinker, 2009). The organization raises funds for cancer research and treatment, provides education, and is well known for sponsoring Race for the Cure running events.

The American Cancer Society's Reach to Recovery program provides an important service to women with breast cancer. Volunteers in the program, who have all had surgery and other treatments, meet with women who have recently been diagnosed or had treatment and offer them emotional support and encouragement. They also provide

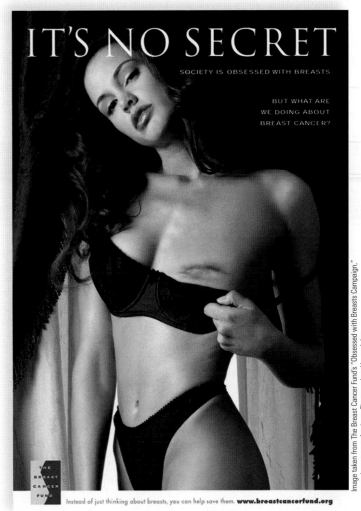

Image taken from The Breast Cancer Fund's "Obsessed with Breasts Campaign." www.breastcancerfund.org. Photographer: Heward Jue.

The Breast Cancer Fund's "Obsessed with Breasts" campaign used this attention-getting image to promote breast cancer education.

mastectomy
Surgical removal of the breast(s).

positive models of women who have successfully adjusted to dealing with breast cancer. In fact, a growing body of evidence suggests that many breast cancer survivors, like many survivors of other cancers, report positive changes in personal relationships, appreciation of life, and their life priorities (Bellizzi & Blank, 2006).

Summary

The Vulva

- Pornography has influenced some women to surgically alter their vulvas rather than understanding and appreciating all the normal variations of shapes.
- Genital self-exploration is a good way for a woman to learn about her own body and to notice any changes that may require medical attention.
- The female external genitals, also called the vulva, comprise the mons veneris, labia majora, labia minora, clitoris, and urethral and vaginal openings. Each woman's vulva is unique in shape, color, and texture.
- The mons veneris and labia majora have underlying pads of fatty tissue and are covered by pubic hair beginning at adolescence.
- The labia minora are folds of sensitive skin that begin at the hood over the clitoris and extend downward to below the vaginal opening, or introitus. The area between them is called the vestibule.
- The clitoris is composed of the external glans and shaft and the internal crura. The glans contains densely concentrated nerve endings. The only function of the clitoris is sexual pleasure.
- The urethral opening is located between the clitoris and the vaginal introitus.
- Many cultures have placed great importance on the hymen as proof of virginity. However, there are various sizes, shapes, and thicknesses of hymens, and many women can have initial intercourse without pain or bleeding. Also, women who have decided to have coitus can learn how to stretch their hymens to help make their first experience comfortable.

Underlying Structures

- Below the surface of the vulva are the vestibular bulbs and the pelvic floor muscles.

Internal Structures

- The vagina, with its three layers of tissue, extends about 3 to 5 inches into the pelvic cavity. It is a potential rather than an actual space and increases in size during sexual arousal, coitus, and childbirth. The other internal reproductive structures are the cervix, uterus, fallopian tubes, and ovaries.
- Kegel exercises are voluntary contractions of the vaginal muscles.
- Vaginal lubrication, the secretion of alkaline fluid through the vaginal walls during arousal, is important both in enhancing the longevity and motility of sperm cells and in increasing the pleasure and comfort of intercourse.
- The Grafenberg spot occupies about 1 centimeter along the surface of the top wall of the vagina. Many women report erotic sensitivity to pressure in some area of their vaginas.
- The vaginal walls and cervix produce normal secretions.

Menstruation

- The menstrual cycle results from a complex interplay of hormones. Although negative social attitudes have historically been attached to menstruation, some people are redefining it in a more positive fashion.
- There are usually no medical reasons to abstain from intercourse during menstruation. However, many people do limit their sexual activity during this time.
- Some women have difficulties with PMS (premenstrual syndrome), PMDD (premenstrual dysphoric disorder), or primary or secondary dysmenorrhea. Knowledge about the physiological factors that contribute to these problems is increasing, and some of the problems can be treated.
- Amenorrhea occurs normally during pregnancy, while breast-feeding, and after menopause. It can also be due to medical problems or poor health. A pill that prevents menstruation for 3 months has been developed.

- Toxic shock syndrome (TSS) is a rare condition that occurs most often in menstruating women. Its symptoms include fever, sore throat, nausea, red skin flush, dizziness, and low blood pressure. If untreated, it can be fatal.

Menopause

- Menopause is the cessation of menstruation, and it signals the end of female fertility. The average age of menopause is 51. Because of increases in life expectancy, women can expect to live half their adult lives following menopause.
- Most women experience few uncomfortable symptoms during the aging process and maintain sexual interest and response. Others experience symptoms such as hot flashes, sleep disturbance, depression or anxiety, headaches, and sensitivity to touch as a result of declining estrogen levels.
- Hormone therapy (HT) is a medical treatment for menopausal symptoms that has potential benefits and risks that should be carefully considered before it is used.

Gynecological Health Concerns

- Occasionally, a vaginal infection occurs that results in irritation, unusual discharge, or a disagreeable odor.
- The Pap smear has significantly reduced deaths from cervical cancer. A woman can use her own speculum to examine her cervix.
- There is considerable medical controversy about the appropriate use of hysterectomy. Hysterectomy or oophorectomy can affect—either positively or negatively—a woman's sexuality.

The Breasts

- The breasts are composed of fatty tissue and milk-producing glands. Self-examination of the breasts is an important part of health care.
- Three types of lumps can appear in the breasts: cysts, fibroadenomas, and malignant tumors. Careful diagnosis of a breast lump is important. Mammography and other tests can help detect and diagnose breast cancer. A lumpectomy is often as effective as more-severe procedures.

Media Resources

Log in to CengageBrain.com to access the resources your instructor requires.

Go to CengageBrain.com to access Psychology CourseMate, where you will find an interactive eBook, glossaries, flashcards, quizzes, videos, and more.

Also access links to chapter-related websites, including **GYN101, OBGYN.net, National Women's Information Center,** and the **North American Menopause Society.**

Male Sexual Anatomy and Physiology

Sexual Anatomy

What are the major external and internal male sex structures, and what functions do they serve?

Why is it important to conduct regular genital self-exams, and what should a man look for?

Male Sexual Functions

What physiological processes cause an erection?

How do psychological and physiological factors interact to influence erections?

How does ejaculation occur?

Concerns About Sexual Functioning

How does penis size affect sexual interaction?

Why are most males circumcised shortly after birth? What is the current medical evidence regarding the value and risks of circumcision?

Male Genital Health Concerns

What kinds of diseases and injuries affect the male genital and reproductive structures, and how are these conditions treated?

Why is it important for men to be aware of the issues and controversies associated with prostate cancer diagnosis and treatment?

Musee Rodin, Paris, France/Photo © Boltin Picture Library/The Bridgeman Art Library

This statement, from a student in a sexuality class, illustrates two common assumptions. The first is that male sexual anatomy is simple. All you need to know is "hanging out there." The second, perhaps more subtle implication is that female genital structures are considerably more complicated and mysterious than men's.

These assumptions call for some rethinking, for a few reasons. One is that there is more than meets the eye. The sexual anatomy of men and women is complex and varies widely from one individual to another. Another reason is that knowing about our own sexual anatomy and functioning, although it does not guarantee sexual satisfaction, at least provides a degree of comfort with our bodies and perhaps a greater ability to communicate with a partner. Equally important, an understanding of our own bodies provides a crucial basis for detecting potential health problems. In this chapter, we provide information that every man should know regarding self-exams and health care. Expanding knowledge and understanding of his genital anatomy and physiology can be an important aspect of a man's sexual well-being and his sexual intelligence. As in Chapter 3, we encourage readers to use the pages that follow as a reference for their own self-knowledge and improved health.

Sexual Anatomy

We begin with discussions of the various structures of the male sexual anatomy. Descriptive accounts are organized according to parts of the genital system for easy reference. Later in this chapter (and in Chapter 6) we will look more closely at the way the entire system functions during sexual arousal.

The Penis

The **penis** consists of nerves, blood vessels, fibrous tissue, and three parallel cylinders of spongy tissue. It does not contain a bone or an abundance of muscular tissue, contrary to some people's beliefs. However, an extensive network of muscles is present at the base of the penis. These muscles help eject both semen and urine through the urethra.

A portion of the penis extends internally into the pelvic cavity. This part, including its attachment to the pubic bones, is referred to as the **root**. When a man's penis is erect, he can feel this inward projection by pressing a finger upward between his anus and scrotum. The external, pendulous portion of the penis, excluding the head, is known as the **shaft**. The smooth, acorn-shaped head is called the **glans**.

Running the entire length of the penis are the three cylinders referred to earlier. The two larger ones, the **cavernous bodies** (*corpora cavernosa*), lie side by side above the smaller, third cylinder, the **spongy body** (*corpus spongiosum*). At the root of the penis the innermost tips of the cavernous bodies, or *crura*, are connected to the pubic bones. At the head of the penis the spongy body expands to form the glans. These structures are shown in ▌Figure 4.1.

All these cylinders are similar in structure. As the terms *cavernous* and *spongy* imply, the cylinders are made of spongelike irregular spaces and cavities. Each cylinder is also richly supplied with blood vessels. When a male is sexually excited, the cylinders become engorged with blood, resulting in penile erection. During sexual arousal the spongy body may stand out as a distinct ridge along the underside of the penis.

penis
A male sexual organ consisting of the internal root and the external shaft and glans.

root
The portion of the penis that extends internally into the pelvic cavity.

shaft
The length of the penis between the glans and the body.

glans
The head of the penis; it is richly endowed with nerve endings.

cavernous bodies
The structures in the shaft of the penis that engorge with blood during sexual arousal.

spongy body
A cylinder that forms a bulb at the base of the penis, extends up into the penile shaft, and forms the penile glans.

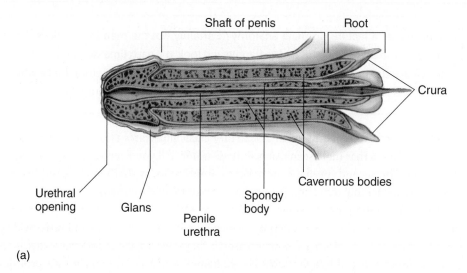

Shaft of penis   **Root**

Crura

Urethral opening   Glans   Penile urethra   Spongy body   Cavernous bodies

(a)

Top of penis

Cavernous bodies

Skin

Penile urethra

Spongy body

© Cengage Learning

Underside of penis

(b)

❚ Figure 4.1 Interior structure of the penis: (a) view from above and (b) cross section of the penis.

foreskin
A covering of skin over the penile glans.

The skin covering the penile shaft is usually hairless and quite loose, which allows for expansion when the penis becomes erect. Although the skin is connected to the shaft at the neck (the portion just behind the glans), some of it folds over and forms a cuff, or hood, over the glans. This loose covering is called the **foreskin**, or *prepuce*. In some males the foreskin covers the entire glans, whereas in other males only a portion of the glans is covered. Typically, the foreskin can be retracted (drawn back from the glans) quite easily. *Circumcision* involves the surgical removal of this sleeve of skin. Although familiar in our culture, circumcision is only one of many procedures for altering male genitalia that are practiced around the world, as described in the following Sexuality and Diversity discussion on male genital modification and mutilation.

SEXUALITY and DIVERSITY
Male Genital Modification: Cultural Beliefs and Practices

Throughout the world, people hold strong beliefs about the importance and implications of altering male genitals through a variety of procedures. These rituals and customs have been chronicled through the ages (Aggleton, 2007). (Female genital modification is also widespread, as discussed in Chapter 3.)

The most common genital alteration is *circumcision*, the surgical removal of the foreskin. Circumcision is practiced in many societies for religious, ritual, or hygienic reasons. Circumcision is an old practice (Glick, 2005). Examinations of ancient Egyptian mummies have revealed evidence of circumcision as far back as 6000 BCE, and Egyptian records at least 5,000 years old depict circumcised men. Australian aborigines, Muslims, and some African tribes have also used male circumcision to mark a rite of passage or to signify a covenant with God (Melby, 2002b).

For thousands of years Jews have practiced circumcision according to scripture (Genesis 17:9–27) as a religious rite (Haught, 2008). The ceremony, called a *bris*, takes place on the eighth day after birth. Similarly, the followers of Islam have a long-standing tradition of circumcision. Although circumcision is widespread among Middle Eastern and African societies, it is relatively uncommon in Europe today.

A variation of circumcision, called *superincision* (in which the foreskin, instead of being removed, is split lengthwise along its top portion), is practiced among certain South Pacific cultures as a kind of rite of passage or initiation ritual into sexual maturity (Janssen, 2008). Mangaia and the Marquesas Islands are home to two societies that perform this procedure when a boy reaches adolescence (Janssen, 2008).

Castration, removal of the testes, is a more extreme male genital mutilation that also has its roots in antiquity. This practice has been justified for a variety of reasons: to prevent sexual activity between harem guards (eunuchs) and their charges, to render war captives docile, to preserve the soprano voices of European choirboys during the Middle Ages, and as part of religious ceremonies (in ancient Egypt hundreds of young boys were castrated in a single ceremony). In the United States in the mid-19th century, castration was sometimes performed as a purported cure for the evils of masturbation (Melby, 2002b). During this same period American medical journals also reported that castration was often a successful treatment for "insanity."

In more modern times castrations have occasionally been performed for legal reasons, either as a method of eugenic selection (e.g., to prevent a person with mental disabilities from having offspring) or as an alleged deterrent to sex offenders (see Chapter 6). The ethical basis of these operations is highly controversial. Finally, castration is sometimes performed as medical treatment for diseases, such as prostate cancer and genital tuberculosis (Wassersug & Johnson, 2007).

The entire penis is sensitive to touch, but the greatest concentration of nerve endings is found in the glans. Although the entire glans area is extremely sensitive, many men find that two specific locations are particularly responsive to stimulation. One is the rim, or crown, which marks the area where the glans rises abruptly from the shaft. This distinct ridge is called the **corona** (kuh-ROH-nuh). The other is the **frenulum** (FREN-yoo-lum), a thin strip of skin connecting the glans to the shaft on the underside of the penis. The location of these two areas is shown in ❚ Figure 4.2.

corona
The rim of the penile glans.

frenulum
A highly sensitive thin strip of skin that connects the glans to the shaft on the underside of the penis.

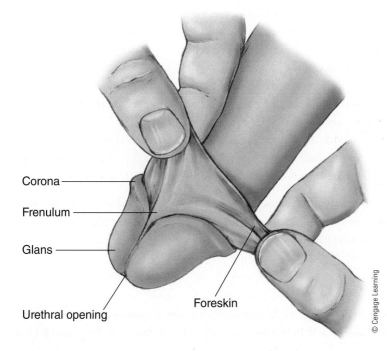

Corona

Frenulum

Glans

Urethral opening

Foreskin

© Cengage Learning

❚ **Figure 4.2** The underside of the uncircumcised penis, showing the location of the corona and frenulum—two areas on the penis that harbor a high concentration of sensitive nerve endings.

Most men enjoy having the glans stimulated, particularly the two areas just mentioned, but individuals vary in their preferences. Some men occasionally or routinely prefer being stimulated in genital areas other than the glans of the penis. The mode of stimulation, either manual (by self or partner) or oral, can influence the choice of preferred sites. Some of these variations and individual preferences are noted in the following accounts:

> When I masturbate I frequently avoid the head of my penis, concentrating instead on stroking the shaft. The stimulation is not so intense, which allows a longer time for buildup to orgasm. The result is that the climax is generally more intense than if I focus only on the glans. (Authors' files)

> During oral sex with my girlfriend, I sometimes have to put my hand around my penis, leaving just the head sticking out, so she will get the idea what part feels best. Otherwise, she spends a lot of time running her tongue up and down the shaft, which just doesn't do it for me. (Authors' files)

Strengthening Musculature Around the Penis

SEXUALHEALTH

As previously mentioned, the internal extension of the penis is surrounded by an elaborate network of muscles. This musculature is comparable to that in the female body, and strengthening these muscles by doing Kegel exercises can produce benefits for men similar to those experienced by women. In most men these muscles are quite weak because they are usually only contracted during ejaculation. The following description, adapted from *Male Sexuality* (Zilbergeld, 1978, p. 109), is a brief outline of how these muscles can be located and strengthened:

1. Locate the muscles by stopping the flow of urine several times while urinating. The muscles you squeeze to accomplish this are the ones on which you will concentrate. If you do a correct Kegel while not urinating, you will notice your penis move slightly. Kegels done when you have an erection will cause your penis to move up and down.
2. Begin the exercise program by squeezing and relaxing the muscles 15 times, twice daily. Do not hold the contraction at this stage. (These are called "short Kegels.")
3. Gradually increase the number of Kegels until you can comfortably do 60 at a time, twice daily.
4. Now practice "long Kegels" by holding each contraction for a count of 3.
5. Combine the short and long Kegels in each daily exercise routine, doing a set of 60 of each, once or twice a day.
6. Continue with the Kegel exercises for at least several weeks. You may not notice results until a month or more has passed. By this time the exercises will probably have become automatic, requiring no particular effort.

Some of the positive changes men have reported after doing the male Kegel exercises include stronger and more pleasurable orgasms, better ejaculatory control, and increased pelvic sensation during sexual arousal. ●

The Scrotum

scrotum
The pouch of skin of the external male genitals that encloses the testes.

The **scrotum** (SKROH-tum), or scrotal sac, is a loose pouch of skin that is an outpocketing of the abdominal wall in the groin area directly underneath the penis (❚ Figure 4.3).

Normally, it hangs loosely from the body wall, although cold temperatures or sexual stimulation can cause it to move closer to the body.

The scrotal sac consists of two layers. The outermost layer is a covering of thin skin that is darker in color than other body skin. It typically becomes sparsely covered with hair at adolescence. The second layer, known as the *tunica dartos*, is composed of smooth muscle fibers and fibrous connective tissue.

Within the scrotal sac are two separate compartments, each of which houses a single **testis** (plural *testes*), or *testicle*. (For a diagram of the testes within the scrotal sac, see ▌Figure 4.4.) Each testis is suspended in its compartment by the **spermatic** (spur-MAT-ik) **cord**. The spermatic cord contains the sperm-carrying tube, or *vas deferens*, and blood vessels, nerves, and *cremasteric muscle* fibers, which influence the position of the testis in the scrotal sac. These muscles can be voluntarily contracted, causing the testes to move upward. Most males find that they can produce this effect with practice; this exercise is one way for a man to become more familiar with his body. As shown in Figure 4.3, the spermatic cord can be located by palpating the scrotal sac above either testis with the thumb and forefinger. The cord is a firm, rubbery tube that is generally quite pronounced.

The scrotum is sensitive to any temperature change, and numerous sensory receptors in its skin provide information that prevents the testes from becoming either too warm or too cold. When the scrotum is cooled, the tunica dartos contracts, wrinkling the outer skin layer and pulling the testes up closer to the warmth of the body. This process is involuntary, and the reaction sometimes has amusing ramifications:

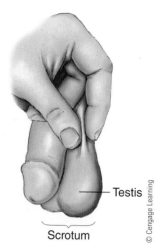

▌**Figure 4.3** The scrotum and the testes. The spermatic cord can be located by palpating the scrotal sac above either testis with the thumb and forefinger.

testis
Male gonad inside the scrotum that produces sperm and sex hormones.
spermatic cord
A cord attached to the testis that contains the vas deferens, blood vessels, nerves, and cremasteric muscle fibers.

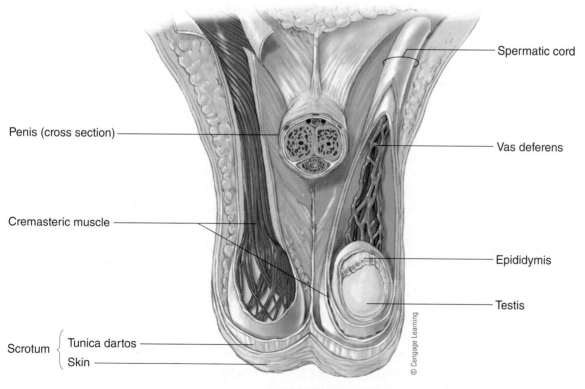

▌**Figure 4.4** Underlying structures of the scrotum. This illustration shows portions of the scrotum cut away to reveal the cremasteric muscle, spermatic cord, vas deferens, and a testis within the scrotal sac.

> When I took swimming classes in high school, the trip back to the locker room was always a bit traumatic. After peeling off my swimsuit, it seemed like I had to search around for my balls. The other guys seemed to have the same problem, since they were also frantically tugging and pulling to get everything back in place. (Authors' files)

Another kind of stimulation that causes the scrotum to draw closer to the body is sexual arousal. One of the clearest external indications of impending male orgasm is the drawing up of the testes to a position of maximum elevation. The major scrotal muscle involved in this response is the cremasteric muscle. Sudden fear can also cause strong contractions of this muscle, and it is also possible to initiate contractions by stroking the inner thighs. This response is known as the *cremasteric reflex*.

The Testes

The testes, or testicles, have two major functions: the secretion of sex hormones and the production of sperm. The testes form inside the abdominal cavity, and late in fetal development they migrate through the *inguinal canal* from the abdomen to the scrotum (Kaftanovskaya et al., 2011).

At birth the testes are normally in the scrotum, but in some cases one or both fail to descend. This condition, known as **cryptorchidism** (krip-TOR-kuh-di-zum), meaning "hidden testis," affects 3–5% of male infants (Kollin et al., 2006). Undescended testes often move into place spontaneously sometime after birth. However, if they have not descended by age 6 months, the likelihood of spontaneous descent is small (Kelsberg et al., 2006). Recent research indicates that parental exposure to pesticides in the environment may contribute to cryptorchidism (Gaspari et al., 2011).

Parents should watch out for cryptorchidism, especially when both testes are affected. Sperm production is affected by temperature. Average scrotal temperature is several degrees lower than body temperature, and sperm production appears to be optimal at this lower temperature. Undescended testes remain at internal body temperature, which is too high for normal sperm production, and infertility could result (Dalgaard, 2012; Thorup et al., 2011). Cryptorchidism is also associated with an increased risk for developing testicular cancer (Dalgaard, 2012; Shaw, 2008). Surgical or hormonal treatment is sometimes necessary to correct this condition (Thorup et al., 2011).

In most men the testes are asymmetric. Note in Figure 4.3 that the left testis hangs lower than the right testis. This is usually the case because the left spermatic cord is generally longer than the right. It is no more unusual than a woman having one breast that is larger than the other. Our bodies simply are not perfectly symmetric.

It is important for men to become familiar with their testes and to examine them regularly. The testes can be affected by a variety of diseases, including cancer, sexually transmitted infections, and an assortment of other infections. (Diseases of the male sex organs are discussed at the end of this chapter and in Chapter 15.) Most of these conditions have observable symptoms, and early detection allows for rapid treatment; early detection can also prevent far more serious complications. ●

Unfortunately, most men do not regularly examine their testes. Yet this simple, painless, and potentially lifesaving process, which takes only a few minutes, is an excellent method for detecting early signs of disease. This procedure is described and illustrated in the Your Sexual Health box, "Male Genital Self-Examination" on page 94.

cryptorchidism
A condition in which the testes fail to descend from the abdominal cavity to the scrotal sac.

SEXUALHEALTH

The Seminiferous Tubules

Within the testes are two separate areas involved in the production and storage of sperm. The first of these, the **seminiferous** (seh-muh-NI-fuh-rus) **tubules** (sperm-bearing tubules), are thin, highly coiled structures located in the approximately 250 cone-shaped lobes that make up the interior of each testis (▌ Figure 4.5). Sperm production takes place in these tubules, usually beginning sometime after the onset of puberty. Men continue to produce viable sperm well into their old age, often until death, although the production rate diminishes with aging. The **interstitial** (in-ter-STI-shul) **cells**, or *Leydig's cells*, are located between the seminiferous tubules. These cells are the major source of androgen, and their proximity to blood vessels allows direct secretion of their hormone products into the bloodstream. (We will discuss the role of hormones in sexual behavior in Chapter 6.)

seminiferous tubules
Thin, coiled structures in the testes in which sperm are produced.

The Epididymis

The second important area for sperm processing is the **epididymis** (eh-puh-DID-uh-mus; literally, "over the testes"). Sperm produced in the seminiferous tubules moves through a maze of tiny ducts into this C-shaped structure that adheres to the back and upper surface of each testis (see Figure 4.5). Evidence suggests that the epididymis serves primarily as a storage chamber where sperm cells undergo additional maturing, or ripening, for a period of several weeks. During this time they are completely inactive. Researchers theorize that a selection process also occurs in the epididymis, in which abnormal sperm cells are eliminated by the body's waste removal system.

interstitial cells
Cells located between the seminiferous tubules that are the major source of androgen in males.

epididymis
The structure along the back of each testis in which sperm maturation occurs.

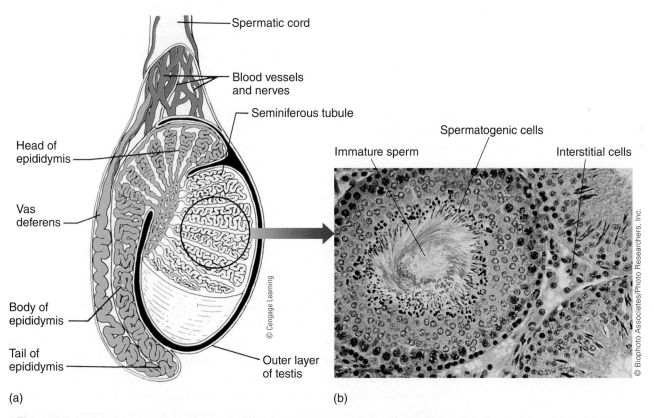

(a)   (b)

▌ **Figure 4.5** (a) Internal structure of a testis. Sperm are produced in the seminiferous tubules and transported to the epididymis, which serves as a storage chamber. (b) The cross-section enlargement view of the seminiferous tubules shows spermatogenic (sperm-making) cells and the interstitial cells.

Our male readers can conduct a self-examination of their genitals standing, reclining against a backrest, or in a sitting position (see photo). A good time to do this is after a hot shower or bath, because heat causes the scrotal skin to relax and the testes to descend. This relaxed, accessible state of the testes can make detecting any unusual condition easier.

First, notice the cremasteric cycle of contraction and relaxation, and experiment with initiating the cremasteric reflex. Then explore the testes one at a time. Place the thumbs of both hands on top of a testis and the index and middle fingers on the underside. Then apply a small amount of pressure and roll the testis between your fingertips. The surface should be fairly smooth and firm in consistency. The contour and texture of male testes varies from individual to individual, and it is important to know your own anatomy so that you can note changes. Having two testes allows for direct comparison, which is helpful in spotting abnormalities (although it is common for the two testes to vary slightly in size). Areas that appear swollen or feel painful to the touch can indicate the presence of an infection. The epididymis, which lies along the back of each testis, occasionally becomes infected, sometimes causing an irregular area to become tender to the touch. Also, be aware of any mass within the testis that feels hard or irregular to the fingertips but that can be painless to touch. This mass, which may be no larger than a BB shot or small pea, could be an indication of early-stage testicular cancer. This cancer, although relatively rare, can progress rapidly. Early detection and prompt treatment are essential to successful recovery. Testicular cancer is discussed further at the end of this chapter.

While examining your genitals, also be aware of any unusual changes in your penis. A sore or an unusual growth anywhere on its surface can be a symptom of an infection, a sexually transmitted infection, or, in rare cases, penile cancer. Although cancer of the penis is among the rarest of cancers, it is also one of the

© Joel Gordon

Self-examination can increase a man's familiarity with his genitals. Any irregularity, such as a lump or tender area in the scrotum, should be examined immediately by a physician.

most traumatic and, unless diagnosed and treated early, deadly (Zhu et. al., 2011). Penile cancer usually begins as a small, painless sore on the glans or, in the case of uncircumcised men, the foreskin. The sore can remain the same for weeks, months, or even years until it changes into a cauliflower-like mass that is chronically inflamed and tender. Clearly, the time to first seek medical attention is immediately after first noticing the sore, when the prospect for a cure remains good.

The Vas Deferens

vas deferens
A sperm-carrying tube that begins at the testis and ends at the urethra.

vasectomy
Male sterilization procedure that involves removing a section from each vas deferens.

ejaculatory ducts
Two short ducts located within the prostate gland.

Sperm held in the epididymis eventually drain into the **vas deferens** (vas DEH-fuh-renz), a long, thin duct that travels up through the scrotum inside the spermatic cord. The vas deferens is close to the surface of the scrotum along this route, which makes the common male sterilization procedure, **vasectomy** (vuh-SEK-tuh-mee), relatively simple. (Vasectomy is described in Chapter 10.)

The spermatic cord exits the scrotal sac through the inguinal canal, an opening that leads directly into the abdominal cavity. From this point the vas deferens continues its upward journey along the top of the bladder and loops around the ureter, as shown in ▌ Figure 4.6. (This pathway is essentially the reverse of the route taken by the testis during its prenatal descent.) Turning downward, the vas deferens reaches the base of the bladder, where it is joined by the excretory duct of the *seminal vesicle*, forming the **ejaculatory duct**.

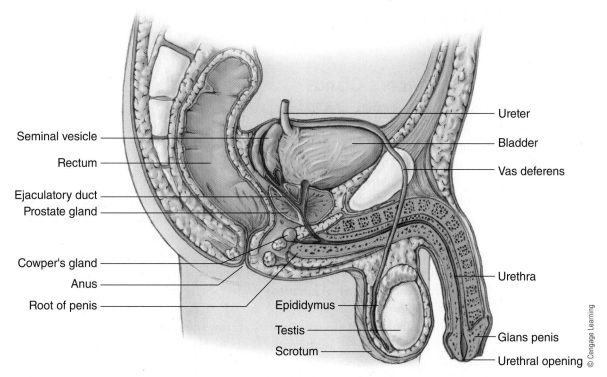

Seminal vesicle

Rectum

Ejaculatory duct

Prostate gland

Cowper's gland

Anus

Root of penis

Epididymus

Testis

Scrotum

Ureter

Bladder

Vas deferens

Urethra

Glans penis

Urethral opening

© Cengage Learning

❚ Figure 4.6 Male sexual anatomy: A cross-section side view of the male reproductive organs.

The two ejaculatory ducts (one from each side) are very short, running their entire course within the prostate gland. At their ends they open into the prostatic portion of the **urethra** (yoo-REE-thruh), the tube through which urine passes from the bladder.

The Seminal Vesicles

The **seminal vesicles** (SEH-muh-nul VEH-si-kuls) are two small glands adjacent to the terminals of the vas deferens (see Figure 4.6). The seminal vesicles play an important role in male fertility by contributing to the formation of healthy semen and functional sperm (Zhang & Jin, 2007). These glands secrete an alkaline fluid that is rich in fructose. This secretion constitutes a major portion of the seminal fluid, perhaps as much as 70%, and its sugar component seems to contribute to sperm nutrition and motility (Gonzales, 2001). Up to this point in its journey from the testis, a sperm cell is transmitted through the elaborate system of ducts by the continuous movement of *cilia*, tiny hairlike structures that line the inner walls of these tubes. Once stimulated by energy-giving secretions of the seminal vesicles, however, sperm propel themselves by the whiplike action of their own tails.

The Prostate Gland

The **prostate** (PROS-tayt) **gland** is a structure about the size and shape of a walnut, located at the base of the bladder (see Figure 4.6). As described earlier, both ejaculatory ducts and the urethra pass through this gland. The prostate is made up of smooth muscle fibers and glandular tissue, whose secretions account for about 30% of the seminal fluid released during ejaculation.

Although the prostate is continually active in a mature male, it accelerates its output during sexual arousal. Its secretions flow into the urethra through a system of sievelike ducts, and here the secretions combine with sperm and the seminal vesicle secretions to form the seminal fluid. The prostatic secretions are thin, milky, and alkaline. This alkalinity helps counteract the unfavorable acidity of the male urethra and the female

urethra
The tube through which urine passes from the bladder to the outside of the body.

seminal vesicles
Small glands adjacent to the terminals of the vas deferens that secrete an alkaline fluid (conducive to sperm motility) that constitutes the greatest portion of the volume of seminal fluid released during ejaculation.

prostate gland
A gland located at the base of the bladder that produces about 30% of the seminal fluid released during ejaculation.

vaginal tract, making a more hospitable environment for sperm. We will discuss some prostate gland health concerns at the end of this chapter.

The Cowper's Glands

Cowper's glands
Two pea-sized glands located alongside the base of the urethra in the male that secrete an alkaline fluid during sexual arousal.

The **Cowper's glands**, or *bulbourethral glands*, are two small structures, each about the size of a pea, located one on each side of the urethra just below where the urethra emerges from the prostate gland (see Figure 4.6). Tiny ducts connect both glands directly to the urethra. When a man is sexually aroused, these organs often secrete a slippery, mucuslike substance that appears as a droplet at the tip of the penis. Like the prostate's secretions, this fluid is alkaline and helps buffer the acidity of the urethra; it is also thought to lubricate the flow of seminal fluid through the urethra. In many men this secretion does not appear until well after the beginning of arousal, often just before orgasm. Other men report that the droplet appears immediately after they get an erection, and still others rarely or never produce these preejaculatory droplets. All these experiences are normal variations of male sexual functioning.

The fluid from the Cowper's glands should not be confused with semen; however, it does occasionally contain active, healthy sperm. This is one reason among many why the withdrawal method of birth control is not highly effective. (Withdrawal and other methods of birth control are discussed in Chapter 10.)

Semen

semen or seminal fluid
A viscous fluid ejaculated through the penis that contains sperm and fluids from the prostate, seminal vesicles, and Cowper's glands.

As we have seen, the **semen** or **seminal fluid** ejaculated through the opening of the penis comes from a variety of sources. Fluids are supplied by the seminal vesicles, the prostate gland, and the Cowper's glands, with the seminal vesicles providing the greatest portion (DeMoranville, 2008). The amount of seminal fluid that a man ejaculates—roughly 1 teaspoon on average—is influenced by a number of factors, including the length of time since the last ejaculation, the duration of arousal before ejaculation, and age (older men tend to produce less fluid). The semen of a single ejaculation typically contains between 200 million and 500 million sperm, which account for only about 1% of the fluid's total volume. Chemical analysis shows that semen is also made up of ascorbic and citric acids, water, enzymes, fructose, bases (phosphate and bicarbonate buffers), and a variety of other substances. None of these materials is harmful if swallowed during oral sex. However, semen of an HIV-infected man can transmit the virus to the man's partner if the recipient has open sores or bleeding gums in his or her mouth (see Chapter 15).

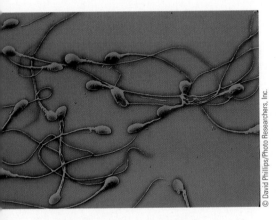

© David Phillips/Photo Researchers, Inc.

Sperm, as seen under a microscope.

Male Sexual Functions

Up to this point in the chapter, we have looked at the various *parts* of the male sexual system, but we have not described their *functioning* in much detail. In the following pages, we examine two of these functions: erection and ejaculation.

Erection

erection
The process by which the penis or clitoris engorges with blood and increases in size.

An **erection** is a process coordinated by the parasympathetic division of the autonomic nervous system (Ryan-Berg, 2011). When a male becomes sexually excited, the nervous system sends out messages that cause expansion of the arteries leading to the three erectile cylinders in the penis. As a result, the rate of blood flow into these parallel cylinders increases rapidly. Because blood flowing out of the penis through veins cannot keep up with the inflow, it accumulates in the spongelike tissues of the three erectile cylinders, causing erection. The penis remains erect until the messages from the nervous system stop and the inflow of blood returns to normal.

The capacity for erection is present at birth. It is common and quite natural for infant boys to experience erections during sleep or diapering, from stimulation by clothing, and later by touching themselves. Nighttime erections occur during the rapid eye movement (REM), or dreaming, stage of sleep (Silverberg, 2008b). Erotic dreams can play a role, but the primary mechanism seems to be physiological, and erections often occur even when the dream content is clearly not sexual. Often a man awakens in the morning just after completing a REM cycle. This explains the phenomenon of morning erections, which were once erroneously attributed to a full bladder.

Although an erection is basically a physiological response, it also involves psychological components. In fact, some writers distinguish between psychogenic (from the mind) and physiogenic (from the body) erections, although in most cases of sexual arousal, inputs come simultaneously from both thoughts and physical stimulation.

How great an influence does the mind have on erections? We know that it can inhibit the response: When a man becomes troubled by erection difficulties, the problem might be psychological, as we will discuss in Chapter 14. Also, extensive evidence shows that men can enhance their erection (as reflected in increased penile tumescence) by forming vivid mental images or fantasies of sexual activity (Smith & Over, 1987).

Ejaculation

The second basic male sexual function is **ejaculation**—the process by which semen is expelled through the penis to the outside of the body. Many people equate male orgasm with ejaculation. However, these two processes do not always take place simultaneously. Before puberty a boy might experience hundreds of "dry orgasms"—orgasms without any ejaculation of fluid. Occasionally, a man may have more than one orgasm in a given sexual encounter, with the second or third orgasm producing little or no expelled semen. Thus, although male orgasm is generally associated with ejaculation, these two processes do not necessarily occur together.

ejaculation
The process by which semen is expelled from the body through the penis.

From a neurophysiological point of view, ejaculation—like erection—is basically a spinal reflex (Truitt & Coolen, 2002). Effective sexual stimulation of the penis (manual, oral, or coital) results in the buildup of neural excitation to a critical level. When a threshold is reached, several internal physical events are triggered.

The actual ejaculation occurs in two stages (❚ Figure 4.7, page 98). During the first stage, sometimes called the **emission phase**, the prostate, seminal vesicles, and *ampulla* (upper portions of the vas deferens) undergo contractions. These contractions force various secretions into the ejaculatory ducts and prostatic urethra. At the same time, both internal and external *urethral sphincters* (two muscles, one located where the urethra exits the bladder and the other below the prostate) close, trapping seminal fluid in the *urethral bulb* (the prostatic portion of the urethra, between these two muscles). The urethral bulb expands like a balloon. A man typically experiences this first stage as a subjective sense that orgasm is inevitable, the "point of no return" or "ejaculatory inevitability."

emission phase
The first stage of male orgasm, in which the seminal fluid is gathered in the urethral bulb.

In the second stage, sometimes called the **expulsion phase**, the collected semen is expelled out of the penis by strong, rhythmic contractions of muscles that surround the urethral bulb and root of the penis. In addition, contractions occur along the entire urethral route. The external urethral sphincter relaxes, allowing fluid to pass through, while the internal sphincter remains contracted to prevent the escape of urine. The first two or three muscle contractions around the base of the penis are quite strong and occur

expulsion phase
The second stage of male orgasm, during which the semen is expelled from the penis by muscular contractions.

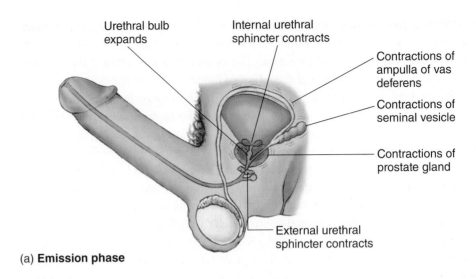

(a) **Emission phase**

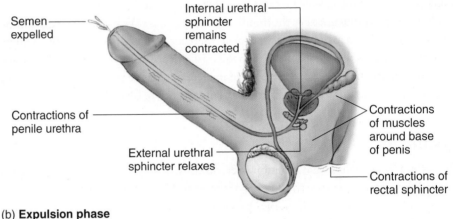

(b) **Expulsion phase**

■ **Figure 4.7** Male sexual anatomy during ejaculation: (a) the emission phase and (b) the expulsion phase.

© Cengage Learning

SEXUALHEALTH

retrograde ejaculation
The process by which semen is expelled into the bladder instead of out of the penis.

nocturnal emission
Involuntary ejaculation during sleep; also known as a wet dream.

at close intervals. Most of the seminal fluid is expelled in spurts corresponding to these contractions. Several more muscle responses typically occur, with a gradual diminishing of intensity and lengthening of time intervals between contractions. The entire expulsion stage usually occurs in 3 to 10 seconds.

Some men have an experience known as **retrograde ejaculation**, in which semen is expelled into the bladder rather than through the penis. This results from a reversed functioning of the two urethral sphincters (the internal sphincter relaxes while the external sphincter contracts). The condition sometimes occurs in men who have undergone prostate surgery (Kassabian, 2003). In addition, illness, congenital anomaly, and certain drugs (most notably, tranquilizers and medications for high blood pressure) can induce this reaction (Mayo Clinic, 2008). Retrograde ejaculation itself is not harmful (the seminal fluid is later eliminated with the urine). However, a man who consistently experiences this response would be wise to seek medical attention, not only because the effective result is sterility but also because retrograde ejaculation could be a sign of an underlying health problem. ●

Sometimes a man experiences orgasm without direct genital stimulation. The most familiar of these occurrences are **nocturnal emissions**, which are commonly known as wet dreams. The exact mechanism that produces this response is not fully understood. (Women can also experience orgasm during sleep.) The possibility of a man using fantasy alone to reach orgasm in a waking state is exceedingly remote. Kinsey and his associates (1948) stated that only 3 or 4 of the males in their sample of over 5,000 reported this experience. In contrast, significantly greater numbers of women in Kinsey's sample (roughly 2%) reported orgasms from fantasy alone (Kinsey et al., 1953). Another kind of nongenitally induced ejaculation that men sometimes report is reaching orgasm during sex play (activities such as mutual kissing or manual or oral stimulation of his partner) when there is no penile stimulation.

Concerns About Sexual Functioning

Men frequently voice a variety of concerns about sexual functioning. Several of these are addressed throughout this textbook. At this point we want to discuss two areas that receive considerable attention: the significance of penis size and the necessity and impact of circumcision. Claims are frequently made that one or both of these physical characteristics can influence the sexual pleasure of a man or his partner. In the following sections we examine the available evidence.

Penis Size

> When I was a kid, my friends were unmerciful in their comments about my small size. They would say things like, "I have a penis, John has a penis, but you have a pee-pee." Needless to say, I grew up with a very poor self-image in this area. Later it was translated into anxiety-ridden sexual encounters where I would insist that the room be completely dark before I would undress. Even now, when I realize that size is irrelevant in giving sexual pleasure, I still worry that new partners will comment unfavorably about my natural endowment. (Authors' files)

> All my life I have been distressed about the size of my penis. I have always avoided places such as community showers where I would be exposed to others. When my penis is hard it is about five inches long; but when it is flaccid, it is rarely longer than an inch or inch and a half, and thin as well. I don't like to be nude in front of the girls I sleep with, and that feeling of uneasiness is often reflected during sex. (Authors' files)

These men are not alone in their discomfort. Their feelings are echoed in more accounts than we can remember. Penis size has occupied the attention of most men and many women at one time or another. In general, it is more than idle curiosity that stimulates interest in this topic. For many it is a matter of real concern, perhaps even cause for apprehension or anguish.

It does not take much imagination to understand why penis size often seems so important. As a society, we tend to be overly impressed with size and quantity; bigger cars are better than compacts, the bigger the house the better it is, and by implication, big penises provide more pleasure than smaller ones. Certainly, the various art forms, such as literature, painting, sculpture, and movies, do much to perpetuate this obsession with big penises. The concern some men feel over perceived size inadequacy has contributed to a surge in cosmetic surgery to enlarge this body part.

Introduced in the United States over a decade ago, *phalloplasty*, or *penis augmentation*, involves lengthening the penis, increasing its girth, or a combination of both. To increase length, a surgeon makes an incision at the base of the penis and severs the

Preoccupation with penis size is evident in a variety of cultures and art forms.

ligaments that attach the penile root to the pelvic bone. This allows the portion of the penis normally inside the body cavity to drop down to the exterior, increasing its visible length by an inch or more (Li et al., 2006). Additional thickness or girth can be added by tissue grafts or by injections of fat taken by liposuction from other body areas, usually the abdomen (Austoni & Guarneri, 1999; J. Taylor, 1995).

There have been no controlled clinical studies of penile augmentation to date, and no reputable scientific research validates any method of penile augmentation (CNN HEALTH Library, 2008). A number of anecdotal reports suggest that the results of these procedures are rarely impressive and can be disconcerting, disfiguring, and even dangerous (Collins, 2002; Fraser, 1999). Ligament-cutting surgery can result in some loss of sensation, scarring, and a changed angle of erection (the erect penis may point down instead of up). Many men who have undergone these procedures have reported being dissatisfied, embarrassed, and embittered by the results (Hitti, 2006; Li et al., 2006; Wessells et al., 1996). Anyone contemplating this potentially dangerous or disfiguring procedure should be extremely cautious. Both the American Urological Association and the American Society of Plastic and Reconstructive Surgeons have issued policy statements against penile surgical augmentation procedures that have not been shown to be either safe or effective (CNN HEALTH Library, 2008).

The result of all this attention to penis size is that men often come to view size in and of itself as an important attribute in defining their masculinity or their worth as lovers. Such a concept of virility can contribute to a poor self-image. Furthermore, if either a man or his partner views his penis as being smaller than it should be, this evaluation can decrease sexual satisfaction for one or both of them—not because of physical limitations but rather as a self-fulfilling prophecy.

As we learned in Chapter 3, the greatest sensitivity in the vaginal canal is concentrated in its outer portion. (We focus here on heterosexual penile–vaginal intercourse because concerns about penis size often relate to this kind of sexual activity.) Although some women do find pressure and stretching deep within the vagina to be pleasurable, this sensation is not usually required for female sexual gratification. In fact, some women find deep penetration painful, particularly if it is quite vigorous:

> You asked if size was important to my pleasure. Yes, but not in the way you might imagine. If a man is quite large, I worry that he might hurt me. Actually, I prefer that he be average or even to the smaller side. (Authors' files)

Critical Thinking Question

Assume that you are assigned to debate whether a cause and effect relationship exists between penis size and sexual satisfaction of women during penile–vaginal intercourse. Which position would you argue? What evidence would you use to support your position?

A physiological explanation exists for the pain or discomfort some women feel during deep penetration. Because the female ovaries and male testes originate from the same embryonic tissue source, they share some of the same sensitivity. If the penis bangs into the cervix and causes the uterus to be slightly displaced, this action can in turn jar an ovary. The resulting sensation is somewhat like a male's experience of getting hit in the testes. Fast stretching of the uterine ligaments has also been implicated in deep-penetration pain. However, some women find slow stretching of these same ligaments pleasurable.

These observations indicate the importance of being gentle and considerate during intercourse. If one or both partners want deeper or more vigorous thrusting, they can experiment by gradually adding these components to their coital movements. It might also be helpful for the woman to be in an intercourse position other than underneath her partner, so that she has more control over the depth and vigor of penetration.

▌ Figure 4.8 shows several flaccid (nonerect) penises. Penis size is not related to body shape, height, length of fingers, race, or anything else (Money et al., 1984). Small flaccid penises tend to increase more in size during erection than do penises that are larger in the flaccid state (Masters & Johnson, 1966). Even though physiological evidence

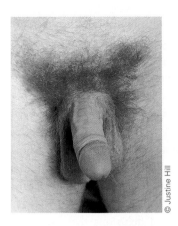

Figure 4.8 Many variations exist in the shape and size of the male genitals. The penis in the right-hand photo is uncircumcised.

indicates that large penises are not necessary for female sexual pleasure during coitus, some women do have subjective preferences regarding penis size and shape, just as some men have such preferences about breasts. Research indicates, however, that women are no more sexually aroused by depictions of large penises than by portrayals of medium or small penises (Fisher et al., 1983).

Finally, as we close this section, we take a look at another interesting cultural phenomenon that reflects a rather unusual, even bizarre, concern about penises that some men in other cultures experience in epidemic proportions: koro.

SEXUALITY and DIVERSITY
Koro: The Genital Retraction Syndrome

Genital retraction syndrome (GRS) is an unusual, culture-bound phenomenon that has attracted considerable attention in many areas of the world community, especially Asia and Africa (Schroer, 2008). GRS, known under a variety of local names or phrases that mean "shrinking penis," is most widely referred to as **koro**. A man afflicted with koro typically believes that he is the victim of a contagious disease that causes his penis to shrink and retract into his body, an alarming prospect made worse by local tradition or folklore that adds the warning that this condition is usually fatal (Kovacs & Osvath, 2006; Vaughn, 2003). The belief in koro is thousands of years old, and numerous accounts of its existence have surfaced in Malaysia, Indonesia, China, India, and several countries in West Africa. The term koro is believed to derive from the Malaysian word for "tortoise," the association being the capacity of the tortoise to retract its head and legs into its body (carapace). In Malaysia the word for "tortoise" is often used as a local slang word for "penis" (Vaughn, 2003).

Although koro sometimes manifests as an isolated anomaly in a single individual (Ritts, 2003), it is most commonly expressed as a fast-spreading social belief that affects hundreds or even thousands of males, causing widespread panic and hysteria. One such instance took place in Singapore in 1967 (Vaughn, 2003). A rapidly spread rumor that contaminated pork was causing penis shrinkage resulted in Singapore hospitals being swamped with thousands of men who were convinced that their penises were shrinking and retracting. Many of these men had used mechanical means—clamps made from chopsticks, weights hung from their penises, and even relatives or friends grabbing firmly on to their "disappearing" anatomy—to keep their penises from slipping away. A coordinated public education program initiated by local physicians resulted in the eventual dissipation of this mass hysteria with no fatalities or lost penises, although many bruised private parts were undoubtedly left in its wake.

The mass-hysteria nature of GRS was also reflected in an epidemic of koro in northeastern India in 1982. It was caused by a fast-moving rumor that the penises of boys were shrinking. Thousands of panicked parents brought their sons to hospitals, usually with their penises bound up or otherwise restrained to prevent further shrinkage. This epidemic

genital retraction syndrome (GRS)
Unusual, culture-bound phenomenon in which a male believes his penis is shrinking and retracting into his body.

koro
A widely used term for the genital retraction syndrome.

was quelled by medical authorities, who toured the region with loudspeakers to reassure anxious citizens. The authorities also conducted large-scale public measuring of penises at regular intervals to demonstrate that no shrinking was taking place (Nixin, 2003).

In countries along the west coast of Africa, from Cameroon to Nigeria, koro is commonly associated with black magic and sorcerers and typically involves penis theft rather than retraction (Schroer, 2008; Vaughn, 2003). Outbreaks of "penis thievery" have been reported in Nigeria, Cameroon, Ghana, and Ivory Coast. These episodes usually involve public accusations of penis theft, usually as the result of an unexpected or unwelcome touch from a stranger (Dzokoto & Adams, 2005; Mather, 2005). Accused perpetrators of penis snatching are often physically assaulted and sometimes killed by angry victims and other concerned citizens (Abidde, 2008).

Epidemics of koro are best explained as anxiety-based delusions that are modeled and communicated among vulnerable men (Mather, 2005; Schroer, 2008). GRS appears to have much in common with the Western phenomenon of panic attacks, with the added dimension of sexual overlay. In some Asian and African cultures where sexual anxiety is high and stories of genital retraction are common, it is not surprising that a man might panic in response to widespread rumors of genital retraction or thievery, especially when such rumors are reinforced by his own observations of the natural process of genital shrinking in response to cold or anxiety (McLaren & Ringe, 2006). Furthermore, when a man's guilt and/or anxiety arise out of real or imagined sexual excesses, he can be easily transformed into a prime candidate for irrational beliefs and receptivity to the seemingly bizarre syndrome of koro (Ritts, 2003).

Circumcision

circumcision
Surgical removal of the foreskin of the penis.

Circumcision (ser-kum-SI-zhun), the surgical removal of the foreskin (❚ Figure 4.9), is widely practiced throughout the world for religious, ritual, or health reasons. About 80% of men in the United States are circumcised (Rabin, 2010). The prevalence of circumcision in the United States, the only nation where nonreligious circumcisions occur in large numbers, has declined steadily over the last four decades (Ahmed & Ellsworth, 2012; Rabin, 2010). However, it is still a relatively common procedure experienced by a slight majority of U.S. newborn males. A recent nationwide survey of American hospitals revealed that 54.7% of male newborns were circumcised (Zhang et al., 2011).

Male circumcision is legal in the vast majority of the world's nations, although mutilation of female genitals is banned in most Western countries. One noteworthy exception is Finland, which bans male circumcision but does allow exceptions for religious reasons (Evans et al., 2011). A recent vote on a Massachusetts ballot measure to outlaw circumcision in this state failed (Evans et al., 2011). However, efforts to outlaw male circumcision within areas of the United States continue. A recent example of this legal

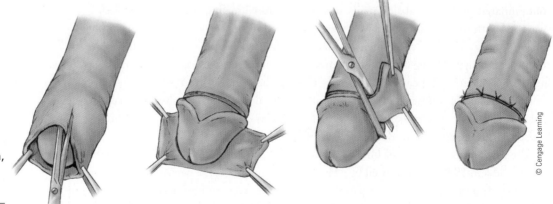

❚ Figure 4.9 Circumcision, the surgical removal of the foreskin.

© Cengage Learning

"Intactivists" Attempt to Criminalize Infant Circumcision in San Francisco

In 2011 a community of anticircumcision "intactivists" launched a bid to criminalize infant circumcision in the city of San Francisco, claiming that this procedure "is essentially culturally accepted genital mutilation" (Dreier, 2011, p. 1). Jewish and Muslim groups formed a coalition to block this effort to outlaw circumcision via a measure that was to appear on a November 2011 ballot (Dreier, 2011). Governor Jerry Brown vetoed this measure in July 2011, and a San Francisco Superior Court judge ordered removal of this controversial measure from the November election (Gordon, 2011).

Opponents of this ballot measure argued that these efforts, especially the images used in ads supporting the measure, were blatantly anti-Semitic (Vekshin, 2011). When the Intactivist initiative ultimately failed, opponents felt vindicated, claiming that residents of the politically liberal city of San Francisco would not support establishing an anticircumcision law that would adversely impact religious traditions and the right of parental choice.

push occurred in San Francisco as discussed in the Sex and Politics feature entitled "'Intactivists' Attempt to Criminalize Infant Circumcision in San Francisco."

Proponents of routine circumcision have maintained that the procedure has significant health benefits. The area under the foreskin, if not routinely cleaned, can harbor a variety of infection-causing organisms. Numerous studies indicate that circumcision decreases the incidence of childhood urinary tract infections, adult penile cancer, and genital wart infections (Klausner & Morris, 2012; Tobian & Gray, 2012). There is also strong evidence that circumcision provides increased protection against HIV, the virus that causes AIDS. (See Chapter 15 for a discussion of the relationship between circumcision status and vulnerability to HIV infection.)

Opponents of routine circumcision have, with increasing frequency, leveled several arguments against it. First, the foreskin could serve some important function yet to be determined. Second, some investigators have expressed concern that sexual function may be altered by excising the foreskin; we consider this question shortly. Finally, some health professionals think that performing this procedure on a newborn is unnecessarily traumatic and invites possible surgical complications.

Despite recommendations for the use of pain relief analgesia for circumcision issued by the American Academy of Pediatrics and the American Society of Anesthesiologists, less than half the number of infant boys undergoing this procedure receive any analgesia at all (Boschert, 2004; Horton, 2005). However, infants undergoing circumcision without analgesia feel and respond to pain (Boschert, 2004; Van Howe & Svoboda, 2008). Some health risks of circumcision include hemorrhage, infections, mutilation, shock, and psychological trauma (Ahmed & Ellsworth, 2012; Meldrum & Rink, 2005).

Because the circumcision issue has so many pros and cons, it is not surprising that the medical profession in the United States has been somewhat indecisive in its position regarding circumcision. In 1989 the American Academy of Pediatrics (AAP) assumed a neutral stance by suggesting that circumcision has both medical advantages and some risks (Schoen et al., 1989). In 1999 the AAP modified its position on circumcision by shifting from neutrality to a position of moderate opposition to this medical procedure (Task Force on Circumcision, 1999), a stance it reaffirmed in 2000 and 2005. In its most recent statement, the AAP concluded that while there are potential medical benefits associated with circumcision, the clinical data are not sufficient to recommend routine circumcision of newborns (Ahmed & Ellsworth, 2012; Dickerman, 2007).

Clearly, the debate about the potential health benefits of infant circumcision will continue, and future editions of this textbook may present still other modifications of

Critical Thinking Question

Which of the research methods described in Chapter 2 might effectively demonstrate whether being circumcised affects a man's sexual response and pleasure? What kind of research design would you use in such a study?

the AAP position on the issue. However, to put this continuing debate and current medical evidence into proper perspective, we note that in most cases good personal genital hygiene practices allow uncircumcised boys to grow into adulthood without encountering health problems (Gange, 1999; Van Howe, 1998).

Beyond the issue of hygiene, another question has often come up about circumcision: Do circumcised men enjoy any erotic or functional advantages over uncircumcised men (or vice versa)?

Some people assume that circumcised men respond more quickly during penile–vaginal intercourse because of the fully exposed glans. However, except when a condition known as **phimosis** (an extremely tight foreskin) exists, there is no difference in contact during intercourse. The foreskin of an uncircumcised man is retracted during coitus, so the glans is fully exposed. It might be assumed, in fact, that the glans of a circumcised man is less sensitive, because of the toughening effect of constant exposure to chafing surfaces.

Masters and Johnson (1966) reported finding no difference in the sensitivity of the glans of circumcised and uncircumcised men. However, a more recent study reported that the glans of the circumcised penis is less sensitive to touch than the glans of the uncircumcised penis (Sorrells et al., 2007). Neither of these studies included the all-important dimension of subjective assessment by men who have experienced both conditions after achieving sexual maturity. Anecdotal reports in the medical literature testify that some men experience less sexual satisfaction after undergoing adult circumcision (Gange, 1999; Melby, 2002b; Task Force on Circumcision, 1999). One study of men who were circumcised as adults to alleviate medical conditions such as phimosis found that many reported experiencing improved sexual satisfaction subsequent to the surgical procedure (Carson, 2003). It would seem that questions about the relationship between circumcision and male sexual arousal remain to be answered, and "little consensus exists regarding the role of the foreskin in sexual performance and satisfaction" (Laumann et al., 1997, p. 1052).

Male Genital Health Concerns

The male genital and internal reproductive structures can be adversely affected by a variety of injuries and diseases. We describe some of these health concerns in the following pages. Should any of our male readers become affected by one of these conditions, we urge immediate consultation with a urologist. **Urology** (yoo-ROL-oh-jee) is the medical specialty that focuses on the male reproductive structures.

The Penis: Health-Care Issues

Caring for the penis is an important aspect of sexual self-health. Washing the penis at least once a day is an excellent self-health practice. (There is also evidence, discussed in Chapter 15, that washing the genitals before and after sex can reduce the chances of exchanging infectious organisms with one's partner.) Uncircumcised males should pay particular attention to drawing the foreskin back from the glans and washing all surfaces, especially the underside of the foreskin. A number of small glands located in the foreskin secrete an oily, lubricating substance. If these secretions are allowed to accumulate under the foreskin, they combine with sloughed-off dead skin cells to form a cheesy substance called **smegma**. When smegma builds up over time, it generally develops an unpleasant odor, becomes grainy and irritating, and can serve as a breeding ground for infection-causing organisms.

Men can protect their penises by using a condom during all sexual encounters with individuals whose health status is unknown to them. This practice affords improved

phimosis
A condition characterized by an extremely tight penile foreskin.

Critical Thinking Question

If you had a newborn son, would you have him circumcised? Why or why not?

urology
The medical specialty dealing with reproductive health and genital diseases of the male and urinary tract diseases in both sexes.

SEXUALHEALTH ▶

smegma
A cheesy substance of glandular secretions and skin cells that sometimes accumulates under the foreskin of the penis or hood of the clitoris.

protection against the transmission of sexually transmitted infections for both partners. Other strategies for preventing transmission of infections are described in Chapter 15.

Some sexual gadgets can also be hazardous to penile health. For example, a "cock ring" (a tight-fitting ring that encircles the base of the penis) may accomplish its intended purpose of sustaining erections, but it can also destroy penile tissue by cutting off the blood supply. In the past, sexually oriented magazines published testimonials attesting to the pleasure of masturbating with a vacuum cleaner. This is not a good idea! Research suggests that severe penile injuries (including decapitation of the glans) resulting from masturbating with vacuum cleaners and electric brooms are much more common than reported (Benson, 1985; Grisell, 1988).

On rare occasions, the penis can be fractured (Morey, 2012). This injury involves a rupture of the cavernous bodies when the penis is erect. This injury most commonly occurs during coitus. A student reported his encounter with this painful injury:

> I was having intercourse with my girlfriend in a sitting position. She was strad-
> dling my legs using the arms of the chair and her legs to move her body up and
> down on my penis. In the heat of passion, she raised up a little too far, and I
> slipped out. She sat back down hard, expecting me to repenetrate her. Unfortu-
> nately, I was off target and all of her weight came down on my penis. I heard a
> cracking sound and experienced excruciating pain. I bled quite a bit inside my
> penis, and I was real sore for quite a long time. (Authors' files)

This account suggests that taking precautions during coitus is wise. This injury usually happens in the heat of passion and often involves putting too much weight on the penis when attempting to gain or regain vaginal penetration. When the woman is on top, the risk increases. Communicating the need to go slow at these times can avert a painful injury. Treatment of penile fractures varies from splinting and ice packs to surgery. Most men injured in this fashion regain normal sexual function. ●

Penile Cancer

As stated earlier in this chapter, men can be afflicted with penile cancer, a rare malignancy that can be deadly if not diagnosed and treated in its earliest stages. Of the approximately 1,300 men in the United States who develop penile cancer in a given year, only half will be alive 5 years later. However, early detection yields a much improved survival rate, a fact that emphasizes the critical importance of seeking medical attention for any sore on the penis (Zhu et al., 2011) (see also the Your Sexual Health box, "Male Genital Self-Examination," earlier in this chapter for a description of the early symptoms of penile cancer). Risk factors associated with penile cancer include being over age 50; having a history of multiple sexual partners and sexually transmitted infections, especially genital warts; maintaining poor genital hygiene; being uncircumcised (see earlier discussion of circumcision); experiencing phimosis; and having a long history of tobacco use (Brossman, 2008; Pettaway, 2008). Penile cancer, left untreated, will ultimately destroy the entire penis and spread to lymph nodes and beyond.

Testicular Cancer

Testicular cancer accounts for 1–2% of all cancers that occur in males, with an annual incidence of 4 per 100,000 men (Richie, 2011). It is the most common malignancy that occurs in young men ages 20 to 35 (NHS Choices, 2009). Risk factors for testicular cancer include smoking, family history, White race, and cryptorchidism (Shaw, 2008; Wood & Elder, 2009). During the early stages of testicular cancer, there are usually no symptoms beyond a mass within the testis. The mass feels hard or irregular to the fingertips and is distinguishable from surrounding healthy tissue. It may be painless to touch, but some men do report tenderness in the area of the growth. Occasionally, other symptoms are reported; these include fever, a dull ache in the groin area, sensation of dragging or heaviness in a testis, tender breasts and nipples, and painful accumulation of fluid or swelling in the scrotum. Some types of testicular cancers tend to grow more rapidly than any other tumors that have been studied. Therefore, for successful treatment, it is important to detect the mass as soon as possible and to seek medical attention immediately. Improved therapeutic procedures have consistently yielded a survival rate better than 90% among men treated for early-detected testicular cancer (Shaw, 2008).

Diseases of the Prostate

As you will recall from our earlier discussion, the prostate gland is a walnut-sized structure at the base of the bladder that contributes secretions to the seminal fluid. The prostate is a focal point of some of the more common "male problems," which range from inflammation and enlargement to cancer.

Prostatitis

One of the most frequent disorders of the prostate gland, *prostatitis*, occurs when the prostate becomes enlarged and inflamed, often as a result of an infectious agent, such as the gonococcus bacterium (responsible for gonorrhea) or the protozoan *Trichomonas*. (These agents are discussed in Chapter 15.) Prostatitis affects about 10% of men of all ages and most often occurs in men in their 40s (Pluta et al., 2012). Prostatitis symptoms include pain in the pelvic area or base of the penis, lower abdominal ache, backache, aching testes, the urgent need to urinate frequently, a burning sensation while urinating, a cloudy discharge from the penis, and difficulties with sexual functions, such as painful erections or ejaculations and reduced sexual interest. Prostatitis can be effectively treated with a variety of prescription drugs—most commonly, antibiotics. Other medications, such as anti-inflammatory agents and alpha-blockers, have also proved to be beneficial in some instances (Luzzi & Schaeffer, 2007; Thunyarat et al., 2011). Cranberry powder (1,500 mg per day) has also proved to be beneficial in men with chronic nonbacterial prostatitis (Gaby, 2011).

Benign Prostatic Hyperplasia

As men grow older, the prostate gland tends to increase in size, a condition known as *benign prostatic hyperplasia* (BPH). About 50% of men over age 60 and 90% of men over age 85 experience this problem (Davidson & Chutka, 2008; Pisco, 2011). The enlarged gland tends to put pressure on the urethra, thus decreasing urine flow. If this problem is severe, surgery or medications can help (Edwards, 2008; Keister & Neal, 2008). Recently, a minimally invasive procedure that reduces blood flow to the prostate has been shown to be an effective treatment for BPH (Pisco, 2011).

Prostate Cancer

Among U.S. males, cancer of the prostate is the second most frequently diagnosed cancer (skin cancer is more common) and is currently the second leading cause of cancer death after lung cancer (R. Hoffman, 2011). An estimated 240,000 men in the United States are diagnosed with prostate cancer each year, and about 34,000 die from the

© Doug Pensinger/Getty Images

American cyclist Lance Armstrong won the 1999, 2000, 2001, 2002, 2003, 2004, and 2005 Tour de France cycling races after undergoing successful treatment for testicular cancer.

disease each year (R. Hoffman, 2011). Frequent sexual activity has been reported to reduce the risk of prostrate cancer (Allameh et al., 2011).

Factors known to be associated with the development of prostate cancer include old age, family history of prostate cancer, African American ethnicity, smoking, high fat consumption, and daily intake of 400 or more IUs of vitamin E (Dall'Era et al., 2009; R. Hoffman, 2011; Hoskote et al., 2012). The incidence of prostate cancer is 70% higher among Black men than among White men, and Black men have a lower survival rate than White men for comparable stages of prostate cancer (U.S. Preventive Services Task Force, 2008). The reasons for the increased risk and lower survival rate among Black men are not known, but genetic, hormonal, and nutritional factors have been implicated.

Symptoms of prostate cancer include many of those previously listed for prostatitis, especially pain in the pelvis and lower back and urinary complications. However, prostate cancer often lacks easily detectable symptoms in its early stages. A physical examination and a blood test may be performed in an effort to make an early diagnosis. In the physical examination, a physician inserts a finger into the rectum, a procedure called a digital rectal examination (DRE). Under normal conditions, this exam is only mildly uncomfortable. The discovery of a marker for prostate cancer—*prostate-specific antigen* (PSA)—detectable by a blood test has added another tool for physicians to use in diagnosing early prostate cancer. A normal PSA level is less than 4 nanograms (ng) PSA per milliliter (mL) of blood (Garnick & Rose, 2008). Efforts to detect prostate cancer using the DRE and PSA level as screening tools are far from precise. Many tumors are not detected by DRE. Both benign and malignant tumors can cause elevations in PSA levels (Garnick & Rose, 2008). Furthermore, even a mildly elevated PSA may lead to a cascade of events (laboratory tests and medical procedures) with "considerable cost implications for the majority of men who will not have a diagnosis of cancer" (Zeliadt et al., 2011, p. e126).

The U.S. government sponsors a task force of medical experts who regularly issue statements that address preventive health services for use in primary care clinical settings, including screening tests, counseling of patients, and treatment strategies. This task force, called the U.S. Preventive Services Task Force (USPSTF), released its latest recommendations for prostate cancer screening in May 2012. The Task Force advised healthy men not to get a PSA test for diagnosis of prostate cancer. This recommendation was based on an exhaustive review of the latest scientific evidence indicating that PSA tests do not save lives and often result in unnecessary patient anxiety, medical tests and biopsies, and serious complications including incontinence and impotence (Colliver, 2011; Stein, 2011).

An evaluation of several large prostate cancer screening trials concluded that more years of harmful side effects (such as erectile dysfunction and urinary incontinence) "will be experienced as a result of treatment than years of life saved by screening and treatment" (Chu and Benoit, 2011, p. e20). Furthermore, no conclusive evidence has emerged that PSA screening reduces the mortality associated with prostate cancer (Slatkoff et al., 2011; Susman, 2011).

Once prostate cancer has been diagnosed, it can be treated in a number of ways, including simply monitoring the cancer to determine whether its rate of progression poses a serious health threat. Among treatment options are radical prostatectomy (removal of the entire prostate gland); cryotherapy, in which the cancerous cells are destroyed by freezing; and two forms of radiation—external-beam radiotherapy and internal radiotherapy by means of implanted radioactive iodine or palladium seeds (O'Shaughnessy et al., 2011). Because growth of prostatic cancer tumors is stimulated by androgen, another treatment option is either orchidectomy (surgical removal of the testes) or the use of androgen-blocking drugs or hormones (Antonarakis & Eisenberger, 2011). Finally, because the dangers or complications of surgery, radiation therapy, or hormone therapy can outweigh potential benefits, especially for older men, an approach called active surveillance, which involves "watchful waiting" with deferred treatment, is sometimes most appropriate (Eggener et al., 2009; Freedland et al., 2011).

Considerable controversy exists about the optimal approach to treating early-detected prostate cancer. Furthermore, a debate rages over whether the benefits outweigh the health risks of treatment. Medical experts differ widely as to whether treatment should be immediate or deferred. Arguments for immediate treatment, especially for young men, include longer survival time, significantly less pain, and prevention of metastatic disease (the spread of cancer to other areas). Support for active surveillance comes from studies indicating that most men die from unrelated causes before experiencing serious complications from untreated prostate cancer; furthermore, surgical, radiation, or hormonal treatments can result in a variety of complications, including incontinence, bowel problems, erection difficulties, and inability to experience orgasm (Elliott, 2012; Symons et al., 2011; Penson, 2011). Furthermore, active surveillance can lead to a significant cost savings both to the individual and the U.S. health-care system (Corcoran & Benoit, 2011; Keegan et al., 2011).

Prostate cancer specialists are actively seeking biological markers that might distinguish between cancer likely to remain confined to the prostate versus a more aggressive variety likely to progress to metastatic disease. A recent study discovered that sarcosine, an amino acid that can be detected in the urine, increases significantly during prostate cancer progression to metastasis (Sreekumar et al., 2009). Another potentially useful biological marker for aggressive prostate cancer, a protein labeled Cry61, has also been identified (Terada et al., 2011). Two possible genetic markers for aggressive prostate cancer—PCA3 and TMPRSS2:ERG—were indicated by recent research (Salagierski & Schalken, 2012). It is hoped that further research will confirm and clarify the role of viable biological and/or genetic markers for aggressive prostate cancer.

Until well-controlled, long-term studies of treatment outcomes provide clear evidence supporting a specific prostate cancer treatment, both clinicians and patients will continue to struggle with the dilemma of treatment choice. For now, good medical management of prostate cancer involves extensive counseling about treatment options and active involvement of the patient in decisions about treatment. We hope that by the time our young male readers reach middle age, better treatment options and more powerful diagnostic tools will be available.

Summary

Sexual Anatomy

- The penis consists of an internal root within the body cavity; an external, pendulous portion known as its body, or shaft; and the smooth, acorn-shaped head, called the glans. Running the length of the penis are three internal cylinders filled with spongelike tissue that becomes engorged with blood during sexual arousal.
- The scrotum is a loose outpocketing of the lower abdominal wall, consisting of an outer skin layer and an inner muscle layer. Housed within the scrotum are the two testes, or testicles, each suspended within its respective compartment by the spermatic cord.

- Human testes have two major functions: sperm production and secretion of sex hormones.
- Sperm development requires a scrotal temperature slightly lower than normal body temperature.
- The interior of each testis is divided into a large number of chambers that contain the thin, highly coiled seminiferous tubules, in which sperm production occurs.
- Adhering to the back and upper surface of each testis is a C-shaped structure, the epididymis, within which sperm cells mature.
- Sperm travel from the epididymis of each testis through a long, thin tube, the vas deferens, which eventually

terminates at the base of the bladder, where it is joined by the ejaculatory duct of the seminal vesicle.

- The seminal vesicles are two small glands, each near the terminal of a vas deferens. They secrete an alkaline fluid that makes up about 70% of semen and appears to nourish and stimulate sperm cells.
- The prostate gland, located at the base of the bladder and traversed by the urethra, provides about 30% of the seminal fluid released during ejaculation.
- Two pea-sized structures, the Cowper's glands, are connected by tiny ducts to the urethra just below the prostate gland. During sexual arousal, the Cowper's glands often produce a few drops of slippery alkaline fluid, which appear at the tip of the penis.
- Semen consists of sperm cells and secretions from the prostate, seminal vesicles, and Cowper's glands. The sperm component is only a tiny portion of the total fluid expelled during ejaculation.

Male Sexual Functions

- Penile erection is an involuntary process that results from adequate sexual stimulation—physiological, psychological, or both.
- Ejaculation is the process by which semen is transported out through the penis. It occurs in two stages: the emission phase, when seminal fluid is collected in the urethral bulb, and the expulsion phase, when strong muscle contractions expel the semen. In retrograde ejaculation, semen is expelled into the bladder.

Concerns About Sexual Functioning

- Penis size does not significantly influence the ability to give or receive pleasure during penile–vaginal intercourse. Nor is it correlated with other physical variables, such as body shape or height.
- Phalloplasty, or penis augmentation, which involves lengthening the penis, increasing its girth, or a combination of both, can be disfiguring and/or dangerous.

- Circumcision, the surgical removal of the foreskin, is widely practiced in the United States. The potential medical benefits of circumcision include reduced risks of penile cancer, HIV infection, and urinary tract infection. Data concerning the effect of circumcision on erotic function are limited and inconclusive.

Male Genital Health Concerns

- The male genital and internal reproductive structures can be adversely affected by a variety of diseases and injuries.
- Injuries to the penis can be avoided by not using various sexual gadgets and by taking precautions during coitus.
- Penile cancer is a rare malignancy that can be deadly if not diagnosed and treated in its earliest stage. Testicular cancer is more common than penile cancer, especially in young men. If detected in its early stages, testicular cancer is also highly curable.
- The prostate gland is a focal point of some of the more common male problems, including prostatitis, benign prostatic hyperplasia, and prostate cancer. A variety of drugs and surgical procedures are used to treat these conditions. Considerable controversy exists about what constitutes the best treatment strategy for prostate cancer.

Media Resources

Log in to CengageBrain.com to access the resources your instructor requires.

Go to CengageBrain.com to access Psychology CourseMate, where you will find an interactive eBook, glossaries, flashcards, quizzes, videos, and more.

Also access links to chapter-related websites, including the **Male Health Center, Circumcision Information and Resource Pages,** *The Journal of Urology,* **Prostate Cancer Research and Education Foundation, Testicular Cancer and Resource Center,** and the **Lance Armstrong Foundation.**

5 Gender Issues

Male and Female, Masculine and Feminine

What is the difference between sex and gender?

What is the relationship between gender identity and gender role?

Gender-Identity Formation

Is our sense of being male or female based more on biological factors or on social learning?

What is the best treatment strategy for intersexed children who are born with an ambiguous mixture of male and female external genitals?

Transsexualism and Transgenderism

What causes transsexualism, and how is this condition distinguishable from transgenderism?

What is the relationship between variant gender identity and sexual orientation?

Gender Role

What are the relative influences of parents, peers, schools, textbooks, television, and religion on the socialization of gender roles?

How do gender-role expectations affect our sexuality?

Transcending Gender Roles: Androgyny

What behavioral traits are expressed by androgynous men and women?

Is androgyny an ideal state, free of potential problems?

How does androgyny influence sexuality?

AP Photo/Lennox McLendon

> I was taught early on what appropriate gender behavior was. I remember thinking how unfair it was that I had to do weekly cleaning duties while all my brother had to do was take out the garbage. When I asked my mom why, she said, "Because he is a boy and that is man's work, and you are a girl and you do woman's work." (Authors' files)

Among the residents of a small island near New Guinea, awareness of gender-appropriate behavior, as described in the preceding anecdote, is virtually nonexistent. Research by anthropologist Maria Lepowsky (1994) revealed that inhabitants of Vanatinai Island, known locally as "the motherland," behave in a truly gender-egalitarian manner. Men and women are considered equal, and there are no separate gender ideologies in this culture. Women have the same access as men to power and prestige. Both sexes are involved in important decision making, and both appear to enjoy the same freedom to explore their sexuality. Furthermore, the Vanatinai language contains no feminine or masculine pronouns. This pronounced difference between egalitarian roles for men and women in Vanatinai society and gender-based behavior expectations that predominate in American culture raises certain fundamental questions: What constitutes maleness and femaleness? How can the expectations and assumptions for each sex differ so greatly from one society to another? If some gender-related behaviors are learned, do any of the behavioral differences between men and women have a biological basis? How do gender-role expectations affect sexual interactions? These are questions that we will address in this chapter.

Male and Female, Masculine and Feminine

Through the ages people have held to the belief that we are born males or females and just naturally grow up doing what men or women do. The only explanation required has been a reference to "nature taking its course." This viewpoint has a simplicity that helps make the world seem like an orderly place. However, closer examination reveals a much greater complexity in the way our maleness or femaleness is determined and in the way our behavior, sexual and otherwise, is influenced by this aspect of our identity. This fascinating complexity is our focus in the pages that follow. But first it will be helpful to clarify a few important terms.

Sex and Gender

Many writers use the terms *sex* and *gender* interchangeably. However, each word has a specific meaning. **Sex** refers to our biological femaleness or maleness. There are two aspects of biological sex: *genetic sex*, which is determined by our sex chromosomes, and *anatomical sex*, the obvious physical differences between males and females. **Gender** is a term or concept that encompasses the behaviors, socially constructed roles, and psychological attributes commonly associated with being male or female. Thus, although our sex is linked to various physical attributes (chromosomes, penis, vulva, and so forth), our gender refers to the psychological and sociocultural characteristics associated with our sex—in other words, our femininity or masculinity. In this chapter we use the terms *masculine* and *feminine* to characterize the behaviors that are typically attributed to males and females. One undesirable aspect of these labels is that they can limit the range of behaviors that people are comfortable expressing. For example, a man might hesitate to be nurturing lest he be labeled feminine, and a woman might be reticent to act assertively for fear of being considered masculine. It is not our intention

sex
Biological maleness and femaleness.

gender
The psychological and sociocultural characteristics associated with our sex.

Do you believe that traditional American interpretations of femininity and masculinity have benefited American culture? Have both sexes benefited equally? In what behavioral area(s) do you see the most noteworthy changes?

gender assumptions
Assumptions about how people are likely to behave based on their maleness or femaleness.

gender identity
How one psychologically perceives oneself as either male or female.

gender role
A collection of attitudes and behaviors that a specific culture considers normal and appropriate for people of a particular biological sex.

to perpetuate the stereotypes often associated with these labels. However, we find it necessary to use these terms when discussing gender issues.

When we meet people for the first time, most of us quickly note their sex and make assumptions about how they are likely to behave based on their maleness or femaleness. These are **gender assumptions**. For most people gender assumptions are an important part of routine social interaction. We identify people as being either the same sex as we are or the other sex. (We have avoided using the term *opposite sex* because we believe it overstates the differences between males and females.) In fact, many of us find it hard to interact with a person whose gender is ambiguous. When we are unsure of our identification of someone's gender, we may become confused and uncomfortable.

Gender Identity and Gender Role

Gender identity refers to each individual's personal, subjective sense of being male or female. Most of us realize in the first few years of life that we are either male or female. However, there is no guarantee that a person's gender identity will be consistent with his or her biological sex, and some people experience considerable confusion in their efforts to identify their own maleness or femaleness. We will look into this area in more detail later in this chapter.

Gender role (sometimes called *sex role*) refers to a collection of attitudes and behaviors that are considered normal and appropriate in a specific culture for people of a particular sex. Gender roles establish sex-related behavioral expectations that people are expected to fulfill. Behavior thought to be socially appropriate for a male is called masculine; for a female, feminine. When we use the terms *masculine* and *feminine* in subsequent discussions, we are referring to these socialized notions.

Gender-role expectations are culturally defined and vary from society to society. For example, a kiss on the cheek is considered a feminine act and therefore inappropriate between men in American society. In contrast, such behavior is consistent with masculine role expectations in many European and Middle Eastern societies.

Gender role expectations may vary widely in other cultures as evidenced by this photo of two Arab men greeting each other with a kiss.

Gender-Identity Formation

Like the knowledge that we have a particular color hair or eyes, gender is an aspect of our identity that most people take for granted. Certainly, gender identity usually—but not always—comes with the territory of having certain biological parts. But there is more to it than simply looking like a female or a male. As we will see in the following paragraphs, the question of how we come to think of ourselves as either male or female has two answers. The first explanation centers on biological processes that begin shortly after conception and are completed before birth. But a second important explanation has to do with social-learning theory, which looks to cultural influences during early childhood to explain both the nuances of gender identity and the personal significance of being either male or female. We explore first the biological processes involved in gender-identity formation, summarized in ■ Table 5.1.

■ **TABLE 5.1 Gender Identity as a Biological Process—Typical Prenatal Differentiation**

Characteristic	Female	Male
Chromosomal sex	XX	XY
Gonadal sex	Ovaries	Testes
Hormonal sex	Estrogens	Androgens
	Progestational compounds	
Internal reproductive structures	Fallopian tubes	Vas deferens
	Uterus	Seminal vesicles
	Inner portions of vagina	Ejaculatory ducts
External genitals	Clitoris	Penis
	Inner vaginal lips	Scrotum
	Outer vaginal lips	
Sex differentiation of the brain	Hypothalamus becomes estrogen sensitive, influencing cyclic release of hormones.	Estrogen-insensitive male hypothalamus directs steady production of hormones.
	Two hypothalamic areas are smaller in the female brain	Two hypothalamic areas are larger in the male brain.
	Cerebral cortex of right hemisphere is thinner in the female brain.	Cerebral cortex of right hemisphere is thicker in the male brain.
	Corpus callosum is thicker in the female brain.	Corpus callosum is thinner in the male brain.
	Less lateralization of function in the female brain compared to the male brain.	More lateralization of function in the male brain compared to the female brain.

Gender Identity as a Biological Process: Typical Prenatal Differentiation

From the moment of conception many biological factors contribute to the differentiation of male or female sex. In the following paragraphs, we explore how biological sex differentiation occurs during prenatal development. Our discussion follows a chronological sequence. We begin at conception, looking at chromosomal differences between male and female, and then continue with the development of gonads, the production of hormones, the development of internal and external reproductive structures, and, finally, sex differentiation of the brain.

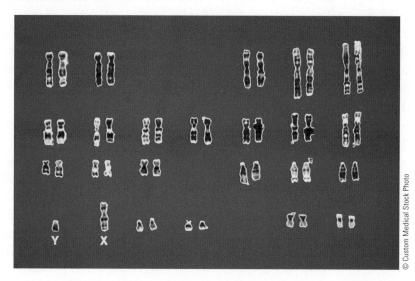

© Custom Medical Stock Photo

■ **Figure 5.1** Human cells contain 22 pairs of matched autosomes and 1 pair of sex chromosomes. A normal female has two X chromosomes, and a normal male has an X and a Y chromosome.

Chromosomal Sex

Our biological sex is determined at conception by the chromosomal makeup of the **sperm** (male reproductive cell) that fertilizes an **ovum**, or egg (female reproductive cell). Except for the reproductive cells, human body cells contain 46 chromosomes, arranged in 23 pairs (see ▮ Figure 5.1). Twenty-two of these pairs are matched; that is, the two chromosomes of each pair look almost identical. These matched sets, called **autosomes** (AW-tuh-sohmes), are the same in males and females and do not significantly influence sex differentiation. One chromosome pair, however—the **sex chromosomes**—differs in females from that in males. Females have two similar chromosomes, labeled XX, whereas males have dissimilar chromosomes, labeled XY.

As noted, the reproductive cells are an exception to the 23-pair rule. As a result of a biological process known as *meiosis*, mature reproductive cells contain only half the usual complement of chromosomes—one member of each pair. (This process is necessary to avoid doubling the chromosome total when sex cells merge at conception.) A normal female ovum (or egg) contains 22 autosomes plus an X chromosome. A normal male sperm cell contains 22 autosomes plus either an X or a Y chromosome. If the ovum is fertilized by a sperm carrying a Y chromosome, the resulting XY combination will produce a male child. In contrast, if an X-chromosome–bearing sperm fertilizes the ovum, the result will be an XX combination and a female child. Two X chromosomes are necessary for internal and external female structures to develop completely. But if one Y chromosome is present, male sexual and reproductive organs will develop (Harley et al., 1992).

Researchers have located a single gene on the short arm of the human Y chromosome that seems to play a crucial role in initiating the sequence of events that leads to the development of the male gonads, or **testes**. This maleness-determining gene is called *SRY* (Marchina et al., 2009; Nishi et al., 2011).

Findings from a study conducted by scientists from Italy and the United States suggest that a gene or genes for femaleness also exist. These researchers studied four cases of chromosomal males with feminized external genitals. All these individuals were found to have XY chromosomes and a working *SRY* (maleness) gene. Three of the four individuals exhibited clearly identifiable female external genitals; the fourth had ambiguous genitals. If the maleness gene was the dominant determinant of biological sex, the external genitals of these individuals would have developed in a typical male pattern. What, then, triggered this variation from the expected developmental sequence? Examination of these individuals' DNA revealed that a tiny bit of genetic material on the short arm of the X chromosome had been duplicated. As a result, each of the subjects had a double dose of a gene designated as *DSS*. This condition resulted in feminization of an otherwise chromosomally normal male fetus (Bardoni et al., 1994).

These findings suggest that a gene (or genes) on the X chromosome helps to push the undifferentiated gonads in a female direction just as the *SRY* gene helps to start construction of male sex structures. Such observations contradict the long-held belief that the human fetus is inherently female and that, unlike male prenatal differentiation, no gene triggers are necessary for female differentiation.

Gonadal Sex

In the first weeks after conception the structures that will become the reproductive organs, or **gonads**, are the same in males and females (see ▮ Figure 5.2a). Differentiation begins about 6 weeks after conception. Genetic signals determine whether the mass of undifferentiated sexual tissue develops into male or female gonads (Dragowski et al., 2011; Wilhelm et al., 2007). At this time an *SRY* gene product (or products) in a male fetus triggers the transformation of embryonic gonads into testes. In the absence of *SRY*,

---

sperm
The male reproductive cell.

ovum
The female reproductive cell.

autosomes
The 22 pairs of human chromosomes that do not significantly influence sex differentiation.

sex chromosomes
A single set of chromosomes that influences biological sex determination.

testes
Male gonads inside the scrotum that produce sperm and sex hormones.

gonads
The male and female sex glands: ovaries and testes.

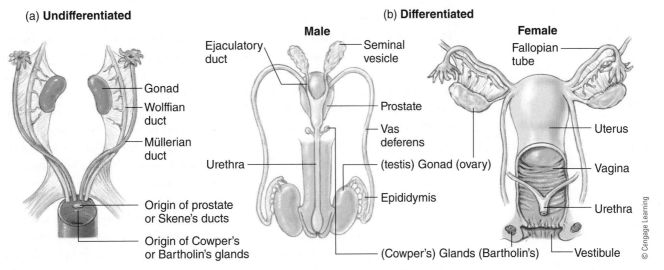

(a) Undifferentiated

Gonad
Wolffian duct
Müllerian duct
Origin of prostate or Skene's ducts
Origin of Cowper's or Bartholin's glands

(b) Differentiated

Male

Ejaculatory duct
Seminal vesicle
Prostate
Vas deferens
Urethra
(testis) Gonad (ovary)
Epididymis
(Cowper's) Glands (Bartholin's)

Female

Fallopian tube
Uterus
Vagina
Urethra
Vestibule

© Cengage Learning

▌**Figure 5.2** Prenatal development of male and female internal duct systems from (a) undifferentiated (before 6th week) to (b) differentiated.

and perhaps under the influence of the *DSS* or other femaleness gene, the undifferentiated gonadal tissue develops into **ovaries** (see ▌ Figure 5.2b; Dragowski et al., 2011).

Once the testes or ovaries develop, these gonads begin releasing their own sex hormones. As we will see next, these hormones become the critical factor in further sex differentiation, and genetic influence ceases.

Hormonal Sex

The gonads produce hormones and secrete them directly into the bloodstream. Ovaries produce two classes of hormones: **estrogens** (ES-troh-jens) and **progestational compounds**. Estrogens, the most important of which is *estradiol*, influence the development of female physical sex characteristics and help regulate the menstrual cycle. Of the progestational compounds, only *progesterone* is known to be physiologically important. It helps to regulate the menstrual cycle and to stimulate development of the uterine lining in preparation for pregnancy. The primary hormone products of the testes are **androgens** (AN-droh-jens). The most important androgen is *testosterone*, which influences the development of male physical sex characteristics and sexual motivation in both sexes. In both sexes the adrenal glands also secrete sex hormones, including small amounts of estrogen and greater quantities of androgen.

Sex of the Internal Reproductive Structures

By about 8 weeks after conception the sex hormones begin to play an important role in sex differentiation. The two duct systems shown in Figure 5.2a—the *Wolffian ducts* and the *Müllerian ducts*—begin to differentiate into those internal structures shown in Figure 5.2b. In a male fetus, androgens secreted by the testes stimulate the Wolffian ducts to develop into the vas deferens, seminal vesicles, and ejaculatory ducts. Another substance released by the testes is known as *Müllerian-inhibiting substance* (MIS). MIS causes the Müllerian duct system to shrink and disappear in males (Wilhelm et al., 2007). In the absence of androgens the fetus develops female structures (Clarnette et al., 1997). The Müllerian ducts develop into the fallopian tubes, the uterus, and the inner third of the vagina, and the Wolffian duct system degenerates.

ovaries
Female gonads that produce ova and sex hormones.

estrogens
A class of hormones that produce female secondary sex characteristics and affect the menstrual cycle.

progestational compounds
A class of hormones, including progesterone, that are produced by the ovaries.

androgens
A class of hormones that promote the development of male genitals and secondary sex characteristics and influence sexual motivation in both sexes. These hormones are produced by the adrenal glands in males and females and by the testes in males.

Sex of the External Genitals

The external genitals develop according to a similar pattern. Until the gonads begin releasing hormones during the 6th week, the external genital tissues of male and female fetuses are undifferentiated (▋ Figure 5.3). These tissues will develop into either male or female external genitals, depending on the presence or absence of a testosterone product known as *dihydrotestosterone* (DHT) (Hotchkiss et al., 2008). DHT stimulates the *labioscrotal swelling* to become the scrotum and the *genital tubercle* and *genital folds* to differentiate into the glans and shaft of the penis, respectively. The genital folds fuse around the urethra to form the shaft of the penis, and the two sides of the labioscrotal swelling fuse to form the scrotum; these fusions do not occur in females. In the absence of testosterone (and possibly under the influence of a substance or substances triggered by the *DSS*, or femaleness gene), the genital tubercle becomes the clitoris, the genital folds become the inner vaginal lips (labia minora), and the two sides of the labioscrotal swelling differentiate into the outer vaginal lips (labia majora). By the 12th week the differentiation process is complete: The penis and scrotum are recognizable in males; the clitoris and labia can be identified in females.

Because the external genitals, gonads, and some internal structures of males and females originate from the same embryonic tissues, it is not surprising that they have corresponding, or homologous, parts. ▋ Table 5.2 summarizes these female and male counterparts.

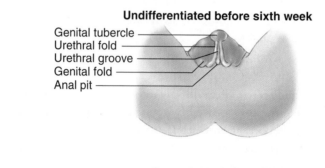

Undifferentiated before sixth week

Genital tubercle
Urethral fold
Urethral groove
Genital fold
Anal pit

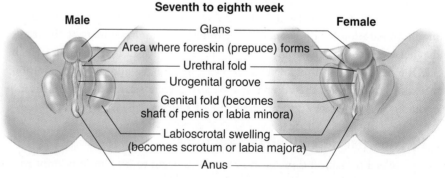

Seventh to eighth week

Male   Female

Glans
Area where foreskin (prepuce) forms
Urethral fold
Urogenital groove
Genital fold (becomes
shaft of penis or labia minora)
Labioscrotal swelling
(becomes scrotum or labia majora)
Anus

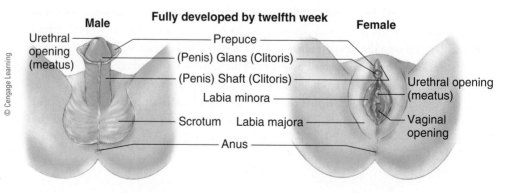

Fully developed by twelfth week

Male   Female

Urethral opening (meatus)
Prepuce
(Penis) Glans (Clitoris)
(Penis) Shaft (Clitoris)
Labia minora
Urethral opening (meatus)
Scrotum   Labia majora
Vaginal opening
Anus

© Cengage Learning

▋ **Figure 5.3** Prenatal development of male and female external genitals from undifferentiated to fully differentiated.

Sex Differentiation of the Brain

Important structural and functional differences in the brains of human females and males are in part a result of prenatal sex-differentiation processes (Becker et al., 2008; Hines, 2004; Mccarthy et al., 2011). Many areas of the developing prenatal brain are significantly affected by circulating hormones (both testosterone and estrogen), which contribute to the development of these sex differences (Hines, 2004; Zuloaga et al., 2008).

At the broadest level, there is a significant sex difference in overall brain size. By age 6, when human brains reach full adult size, male brains are approximately 15% larger than female brains (Gibbons, 1991). Researchers believe that this size difference results from the influence of androgens, which stimulate faster growth in boys' brains (Wilson, 2003). Other specific human brain sex differences involve at least three major areas: the *hypothalamus* (hy-poh-THAL-uh-mus), the left and right *cerebral hemispheres*, and the *corpus callosum* (❚ Figure 5.4).

A number of studies link marked differences between the male and female **hypothalamus** to the presence or absence of circulating testosterone during prenatal differentiation (McEwen, 2001; Reiner, 1997a, 1997b). In the absence of circulating testosterone, the female hypothalamus develops specialized receptor cells that are sensitive to estrogen in the bloodstream. In fetal males the presence of testosterone prevents these cells from developing sensitivity to estrogen. This prenatal differentiation is critical for events that take place later. During puberty the estrogen-sensitive female hypothalamus directs the pituitary gland to release hormones in cyclic fashion, initiating the menstrual cycle. In males the estrogen-insensitive hypothalamus directs a relatively steady production of sex hormones.

Research has uncovered several intriguing findings pertaining to sex differences in one tiny hypothalamic region called the *bed nucleus of the stria terminalis* (BST) (Chung et al., 2002; Gu et al., 2003). The BST contains androgen and estrogen receptors and appears to exert a significant influence on human sex differences and human sexual functioning. One central area of the BST is much larger in men than in women (Zhou et al., 1995), and a posterior region of the BST is more than twice as large in men as in women

❚ TABLE 5.2 Homologous Sex Organs

Female	Male
Clitoris	Glans of penis
Hood of clitoris	Foreskin of penis
Labia minora	Shaft of penis
Labia majora	Scrotal sac
Ovaries	Testes
Skene's ducts	Prostate gland
Bartholin's glands	Cowper's glands

hypothalamus
A small structure in the central core of the brain that controls the pituitary gland and regulates motivated behavior and emotional expression.

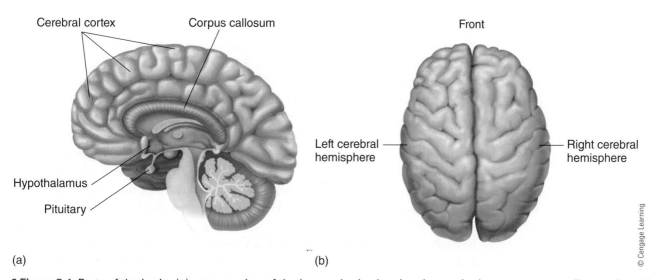

(a)　　　(b)

❚ **Figure 5.4** Parts of the brain: (a) cross section of the human brain showing the cerebral cortex, corpus callosum, hypothalamus, and pituitary gland; (b) top view showing the left and right cerebral hemispheres. Only the cerebral cortex covering of the two hemispheres is visible.

(Allen & Gorski, 1990). Researchers have also reported sex differences in an anterior region of the hypothalamus, called the *preoptic area* (POA). One specific site in the POA is significantly larger in adult men than in adult women (Swaab et al., 1995). Evidence from these and other studies has led some theorists to hypothesize that sex differences in both human sexual behavior and gender-based behavior in children and adults result, in part, from a generalized sex-hormone–induced masculinization or feminization of the brain during prenatal development (Cohen-Kettenis, 2005; Mathews et al., 2009).

Other key differences between male and female brains have been demonstrated in the function and structure of the cerebral hemispheres and the corpus callosum. The **cerebrum**, consisting of two **cerebral hemispheres** and the interconnection between them, is the largest part of the human brain. The two hemispheres, although not precisely identical, are almost mirror images of each other (see Figure 5.4b). Both cerebral hemispheres are covered by an outer layer, called the **cerebral cortex**, which is a major brain structure responsible for higher mental processes, such as memory, perception, and thinking. Without a cortex we would cease to exist as unique, functioning individuals.

As Figure 5.4b illustrates, the two hemispheres are approximately symmetric, with areas on the left side roughly matched by areas on the right side. A variety of functions, such as speech, hearing, vision, and body movement, are localized in various regions of the cortical hemispheres. Furthermore, each hemisphere tends to be specialized for certain functions. For example, in most people verbal abilities, such as the expression and understanding of speech, are governed more by the left hemisphere than by the right. In contrast, the right hemisphere seems to be more specialized for spatial orientation, including the ability to recognize objects and shapes and to perceive relationships between them.

The term *lateralization of function* is used to describe the degree to which a particular function is controlled by one rather than both hemispheres. If, for example, a person's ability to deal with spatial tasks is controlled exclusively by the right hemisphere, we could say that this ability in this person is highly lateralized. In contrast, if both hemispheres contribute equally to this function, the person would be considered bilateral for spatial ability.

Even though each cerebral hemisphere tends to be specialized to handle different functions, the hemispheres are not entirely separate systems. Rather, our brain functions mostly as an integrated whole. The two hemispheres constantly communicate with each other through a broad band of millions of connecting nerve fibers, called the **corpus callosum** (see Figure 5.4a) (Smith et al., 2005). In most people a complex function such as language is controlled primarily by regions in the left hemisphere, but interaction and communication with the right hemisphere also play a role. Furthermore, if a hemisphere primarily responsible for a particular function is damaged, the remaining intact hemisphere might take over the function.

Keeping in mind this general overview of brain lateralization, we note that research has revealed some important differences between male and female brains in the structure of the cerebrum. First, studies of the fetal brains of both humans and rats have found that the cerebral cortex in the right hemisphere tends to be thicker in male brains than in female brains (De Lacoste et al., 1990; Diamond, 1991). Perhaps of even greater significance is the finding of differences between male and female brains in the overall size of the corpus callosum. Several studies have demonstrated that this structure is significantly thicker in women's brains than in men's brains (Smith et al., 2005). This greater thickness of the corpus callosum allows for more intercommunication between the two hemispheres, which could account for why female brains are less lateralized for function and male brains have larger asymmetries in function (Savic & Lindstrom, 2008).

Research has clearly demonstrated differences between male and female brains in the degree of hemispheric specialization for a variety of cognitive tasks. One recent study found significant sex-linked differences in neural activity among men and women as they judged the aesthetic quality of artistic and natural visual stimuli. Brain activity was bilateral or

cerebrum
The largest part of the brain, consisting of two cerebral hemispheres.

cerebral hemispheres
The two sides (right and left) of the cerebrum.

cerebral cortex
Outer layer of the cerebral hemispheres that is responsible for higher mental processes.

corpus callosum
The broad band of nerve fibers that connects the left and right cerebral hemispheres.

symmetrical in the hemispheres of women exposed to stimuli they described as beautiful, whereas in men aesthetically pleasing stimuli instigated neural activity lateralized in their right hemispheres (Cela-Conde et al., 2009). Other research has demonstrated sex differences in the degree of hemispheric specialization for verbal and spatial cognitive skills. Women tend to use both brain hemispheres when performing verbal and spatial tasks, whereas men are more likely to exhibit patterns of hemispheric asymmetry by using only one hemisphere for each of these functions (Savic & Lindstrom, 2008; Wisniewski et al., 2005). The stronger communication network between the two halves of a female's brain might explain why women typically exhibit less impairment of brain function than men do after comparable neurological damage to one hemisphere (Majewska, 1996).

Researchers and theorists are debating whether these structural differences between male and female cerebrums can explain differences between the sexes in cognitive functioning. Females often score higher than males on tests of verbal skills, whereas the reverse is often true for mathematics and spatial tests (Halpern & LaMay, 2000; Hetzner, 2010; Nowak et al., 2011). Some researchers suggest that differences between male and female hemispheric and corpus callosum structures indicate a possible biological basis for such differences between the sexes in cognition (Geer & Manguno-Mire, 1997; Leibenluft, 1996). However, many theorists argue that reported differences between males and females in cognitive skills are largely due to psychosocial factors (Hyde, 2007; Kurtz-Costes et al., 2008). This viewpoint is supported by substantial evidence that such differences have declined sharply or disappeared in recent years. Several major national studies have reported few differences in the science and mathematics skills of male and female children and adolescents over the last three decades (Kurtz-Costes et al., 2008). A recent National Science Foundation study found that girls had achieved parity with boys on standardized math tests in every grade from 2 through 11 (Hyde, 2006). Another national study found that girls perform as well as boys on state math tests (Hetzner, 2010). Nevertheless, females are markedly less likely than males to enter math-intensive professional occupations (e.g., engineering, computer sciences, and physics), a discrepancy that may have more to do with factors related to parental child-rearing practices than to differences in cognitive skills (Barnett & Rivers, 2012; Ceci & Williams, 2011; Zakaib, 2011).

Finally, to put the question of sex differences in proper perspective, we acknowledge the informed observation of eminent psychologist Carol Tavris (2005), who stated that "the similarities between the sexes in behavior and aptitude are far greater than the differences" (p. 12).

Atypical Prenatal Differentiation

Thus far we have considered only typical prenatal differentiation. However, much of what is known about the impact of biological sex differentiation on the development of gender identities comes from studies of atypical differentiation.

We have seen that the differentiation of internal and external sex structures occurs under the influence of biological cues. When these signals deviate from normal patterns, the result can be ambiguous biological sex. A person with ambiguous or contradictory sex characteristics is sometimes called a *hermaphrodite* (her-MAF-roh-dite), a term derived from the mythical Greek deity Hermaphroditus, who was thought to possess biological attributes of both sexes. It is becoming more common to refer to such people as **intersexed** rather than as hermaphroditic (Gurney, 2007).

When discussing the condition of being intersexed, it is important to distinguish between *true hermaphrodites* and *pseudohermaphrodites*. True hermaphrodites, who have both ovarian and testicular tissue in their bodies, are exceedingly rare (Gurney, 2007). Their external genitals are often a mixture of female and male structures. Pseudohermaphrodites are much more common, occurring with an approximate frequency of 1 in

intersexed
A term applied to people who possess biological attributes of both sexes.

every 2,000 births (Colapinto, 2000). These individuals also possess ambiguous internal and external reproductive anatomy, but unlike true hermaphrodites, pseudohermaphrodites are born with gonads that match their chromosomal sex. Studies of pseudohermaphrodites have helped to clarify the relative roles of biology and social learning in the formation of gender identity. This intersex condition can occur because of an atypical combination of sex chromosomes or as a result of prenatal hormonal irregularities. In this section, we consider evidence from five varieties of pseudohermaphrodites, summarized in ■ Table 5.3.

Sex-Chromosome Disorders

Errors occasionally occur at the first level of biological sex determination, and individuals are born with one or more extra sex chromosomes or missing one sex chromosome. More than 70 atypical conditions of the sex chromosomes have been identified. These irregularities are associated with various physical, health, and behavioral effects. We consider two of the most widely researched of these conditions: Turner's syndrome and Klinefelter's syndrome.

Turner's syndrome
A rare condition, characterized by the presence of one unmatched X chromosome (XO), in which affected individuals have normal female external genitals but their internal reproductive structures do not develop fully.

Turner's Syndrome **Turner's syndrome** is a relatively rare condition characterized by the presence of only one sex chromosome, an X (Knickmeyer et al., 2011; Rivkees et al., 2011). This condition is estimated to occur in about 1 in every 2,500–3,000 live female births (Morgan, 2007). The number of chromosomes in the fertilized egg is 45 rather than the typical 46; the sex-chromosome combination is designated XO. People with this combination develop normal external female genitals and consequently are classified as females. However, their internal reproductive structures do not develop fully; ovaries are absent or represented only by fibrous streaks of tissue. Females with Turner's syndrome do not develop breasts at puberty (unless given hormone treatment), do not menstruate, and are sterile. As adults, women with this condition tend to be unusually short (Ross et al., 2011; Zeger et al., 2011).

Because the gonads are absent or poorly developed, and because the hormones are consequently deficient, Turner's syndrome permits gender identity to be formed in the absence of gonadal and hormonal influences (the second and third levels of biological sex determination). Individuals with Turner's syndrome identify themselves as female, and as a group they are not distinguishable from biologically normal females in their interests and behavior (Kagan-Krieger, 1998). This characteristic strongly suggests that a feminine gender identity can be established in the absence of ovaries and their products.

Klinefelter's syndrome
A condition characterized by the presence of two X chromosomes and one Y chromosome (XXY) in which affected individuals have undersized external male genitals.

Klinefelter's Syndrome A more common sex-chromosome error in humans is **Klinefelter's syndrome**. This condition, estimated to occur once in about every 1,000 live male births (Intersex Society of North America, 2006), results when an atypical ovum containing 22 autosomes and 2 X chromosomes is fertilized by a Y-chromosome–bearing sperm, creating an XXY individual. Despite the presence of both the XY combination characteristic of normal males and the XX pattern of normal females, individuals with Klinefelter's syndrome are anatomically male. This condition supports the view that the presence of a Y chromosome triggers the formation of male structures. However, the presence of an extra female sex chromosome impedes the continued development of these structures, and males with Klinefelter's syndrome typically are sterile and have undersized penises and testes. Furthermore, these individuals often have little or no interest in sexual activity (Money, 1968; Rabock et al., 1979). Presumably, this low sex drive is related, at least in part, to deficient production of hormones from the testes.

■ TABLE 5.3 Examples of Atypical Prenatal Sex Differentiation

Syndrome	Chromosomal Sex	Gonadal Sex	Reproductive Internal Structures	External Genitals	Fertility	Secondary Sex Characteristics	Gender Identity
Turner's Syndrome	45, XO	Fibrous streaks of ovarian tissue	Uterus and fallopian tubes	Normal female	Sterile	Undeveloped; no breasts	Female
Klinefelter's syndrome	47, XXY	Small testes	Normal male	Undersized penis and testes	Sterile	Some feminization of secondary sex characteristics; may have breast development and rounded body contours.	Usually male, although higher than usual incidence of gender identity confusion
Androgen insensitivity syndrome	46, XY	Undescended testes	Lacks a normal set of either male or female internal structures	Normal female genitals and a shallow vagina	Sterile	At puberty, breast development and other signs of normal female sexual maturation appear, but menstruation does not occur.	Female
Fetally androgenized females	46, XX	Ovaries	Normal female	Ambiguous (typically more male than female)	Fertile	Normal female (individuals with adrenal malfunction must be treated with cortisone to avoid masculinization).	Usually female, but significant level of dissatisfaction with female gender identity; oriented toward traditional male activities.
DHTdeficient males	46, XY	Undescended testes at birth; testes descend at puberty	Vas deferens, seminal vesicles, and ejaculatory ducts but no prostate; partially formed vagina	Ambiguous at birth (more female than male); at puberty, genitals are masculinized.	Sterile	Female before puberty; become masculinized at puberty.	Female prior to puberty; majority assume traditional male identity at puberty.

Males with Klinefelter's syndrome tend to be tall and somewhat feminized in their physical characteristics; they might exhibit breast development and rounded body contours (Looy & Bouma, 2005). Testosterone treatments during adolescence and adulthood can enhance the development of male secondary sexual characteristics and can increase sexual interest (Rogol et al., 2010; Wikstrom et al., 2011). These individuals usually identify themselves as male; however, they often manifest some degree of gender-identity confusion (Mandoki et al., 1991).

Disorders Affecting Prenatal Hormonal Processes

The ambiguous sex characteristics associated with pseudohermaphroditism can also result from genetically induced biological errors that produce variations in prenatal hormonal processes. We consider three examples of disorders caused by hormonal errors: androgen insensitivity syndrome, fetally androgenized females, and DHT-deficient males.

Androgen Insensitivity Syndrome A rare genetic defect causes a condition known as **androgen insensitivity syndrome (AIS)**, wherein the body cells of a chromosomally normal male fetus are insensitive to androgens (Zuloaga et al., 2008; Bertelloni et al., 2011). The result is feminization of prenatal development, so that the baby is born with normal-looking female genitals and a shallow vagina. Not surprisingly, babies with AIS are identified as female and reared accordingly. The anomaly is often discovered only in late adolescence, when a physician is consulted to find out why menstruation has not started (Gurney, 2007). Recent reviews of many AIS studies reveal that these individuals acquire a clear female gender identity and behave accordingly (Mazur, 2005; T'Sjoen et al., 2010). In one study, investigators compared psychological outcomes and gender development in a group of 22 women with AIS and a control group of 22 women without AIS. No significant differences were found between the women with AIS and the matched control subjects for any psychological outcome measures, including gender identity, sexual orientation, gender-role behaviors, and overall quality of life (Hines et al., 2003).

At first glance these observations seem to support the importance of social learning in shaping gender-identity formation. However, a case can also be made that these findings indicate the strong impact of biological factors in gender-identity formation. The lack of receptivity to androgen in individuals with AIS might prevent the masculinization of their brains necessary to develop a male identity, just as it results in failure to develop male genitals.

Fetally Androgenized Females In a second type of rare atypical sex differentiation, chromosomally normal females are prenatally masculinized by exposure to excessive androgens—the excess usually caused by a genetically induced malfunctioning of their own adrenal glands (*adrenogenital syndrome*) (Achermann et al., 2011). As a result, such babies are born with masculine-looking external genitals: An enlarged clitoris can look like a penis, and fused labia can resemble a scrotum. These babies are usually identified as female by medical tests, treated with minor surgery or hormone therapy to eliminate their genital ambiguity, and reared as girls.

Numerous studies have revealed that even though a substantial majority of **fetally androgenized females** develop a female gender identity, many engage in traditionally male activities and reject behavior and attitudes commonly associated with a female gender identity (Dessens et al., 2005; Rosario, 2011). A small number of these individuals experience such discomfort with the female sex of assignment that they eventually assume a male gender identity with commensurate male gender-role behaviors (Meyer-Bahlburg et al., 1996; Slijper et al., 1998). These various studies of fetally androgenized females appear to reflect the significant impact of biological factors in gender-identity formation.

DHT-Deficient Males A third variety of atypical prenatal differentiation is caused by a genetic defect that prevents conversion of testosterone into the hormone dihydrotestosterone (DHT), which is essential for normal development of external genitals in a male fetus. The testes of males with this disorder do not descend before birth, the penis and scrotum remain undeveloped so that they resemble a clitoris and labia, and a shallow

androgen insensitivity syndrome (AIS)
A condition resulting from a genetic defect that causes chromosomally normal males to be insensitive to the action of testosterone and other androgens. These individuals develop female external genitals of normal appearance.

fetally androgenized female
A chromosomally normal (XX) female who, as a result of excessive exposure to androgens during prenatal sex differentiation, develops external genitalia resembling those of a male.

vagina is partially formed. Because their genitals look more female than male, **DHT-deficient males** are typically identified as female and reared as girls. However, because their testes are still functional, an amazing change occurs at puberty as accelerated testosterone production reverses the DHT deficiency. This causes the testes to descend and the clitoris-like organs to enlarge into penises. In short, these DHT-deficient males undergo rapid transformation, from apparently female to male! How do they respond?

Research has shown that a majority of DHT-deficient males make a switch from a female gender identity to a male gender identity, usually in adolescence or early adulthood (Cohen-Kettenis, 2005; Imperato-McGinley et al., 1979). These findings challenge the widely held belief that once gender identity is formed in the first few years of life, it cannot be changed.

These examples of atypical sex differentiation appear to provide contradictory evidence. In the first example of males with AIS, chromosomal males insensitive to their own androgens acquire a female gender identity consistent with the way they are reared. In the second example, prenatally masculinized chromosomal females tend to behave in a typically masculine manner even though they are reared female. Finally, in the third example, chromosomal males whose biological maleness is not apparent until puberty are able to switch their gender identity to male, despite early socialization as girls. Are these results at odds with one another, or is there a plausible explanation for their seeming inconsistencies?

As described earlier, some data suggest that prenatal androgens influence sex differentiation of the brain just as they trigger masculinization of the sex structures. The same gene defect that prevents masculinization of the genitals of males with AIS might also block masculinization of their brains, thus influencing the development of a female gender identity. Similarly, the masculinizing influence of prenatal androgens on the brain might also account for the tomboyish behaviors of fetally androgenized females. But what about DHT-deficient males who appear to make a relatively smooth transition from a female to a male gender identity? Perhaps these boys' brains were prenatally programmed along male lines. Presumably, they had normal levels of androgens and, except for genital development, could respond appropriately to these hormones at critical stages of prenatal development. We cannot state with certainty that prenatal androgens masculinize the brain. However, this interpretation offers a plausible explanation for how DHT-deficient individuals, already hormonally predisposed toward a male gender identity despite being identified as female, can change to a male identity at adolescence in response to changes in their bodies.

These fascinating studies underscore the complexity of biological sex determination. We have seen that many steps, each susceptible to errors, are involved in sex differentiation before birth. There is substantial research evidence that biological factors, especially prenatal brain exposure to androgens, contribute to gender-identity formation. But there is more to the question, Just what makes us female or male? To help answer this question, we now turn to the role of social-learning factors in influencing gender-identity formation *after* birth.

Social-Learning Influences on Gender Identity

Thus far we have considered only the biological factors involved in the determination of gender identity. Our sense of femaleness or maleness is not based exclusively on biological conditions, however. Social-learning theory suggests that our identification with either masculine or feminine roles or a combination thereof (androgyny) results primarily from the social and cultural models and influences that we are exposed to during our early development (Lips, 1997; Lorber, 1995).

DHT-deficient male
A chromosomally normal (XY) male who develops external genitalia resembling those of a female as a result of a genetic defect that prevents the prenatal conversion of testosterone into dihydrotestosterone (DHT).

Even before their baby is born, parents (and other adults involved in child rearing) have preconceived notions about how boys and girls differ. And through a multitude of subtle and not so subtle means, they communicate these ideas to their children. Gender-role expectations influence the environments in which children are raised, from the choice of room color to the selection of toys. They also influence the way parents think of their children. For example, in one study parents were asked to describe their newborn infants. Parents of boys described them as "strong," "active," and "robust," whereas parents of girls used words such as "soft" and "delicate"—even though all their babies were of similar size and muscle tone (Rubin et al., 1974). Not surprisingly, gender-role expectations also influence the way parents respond to their children: A boy might be encouraged to suppress his tears if he scrapes a knee and to show other "manly" qualities, such as independence and aggressiveness, whereas girls might be encouraged to be nurturing and cooperative (Hyde, 2006; Mosher & Tomkins, 1988).

By age 3, most children have developed a firm gender identity (DeLamater & Friedrich, 2002). From this point, gender-identity reinforcement typically becomes somewhat self-perpetuating, as most children actively seek to behave in ways that they are taught are appropriate to their own sex (DeLamater & Friedrich, 2002). It is not unusual for little girls to go through a period of insisting that they wear fancy dresses or practice baking in the kitchen—sometimes to the dismay of their own mothers, who have themselves adopted more-practical wardrobes and have abandoned the kitchen for a career. Likewise, young boys may develop a fascination for superheroes, policemen, and other cultural role models and try to adopt behaviors appropriate to these roles.

Anthropological studies of other cultures also lend support to the social-learning interpretation of gender-identity formation. In several societies the differences between males and females that we often assume to be innate are simply not evident. In fact, Margaret Mead's classic book *Sex and Temperament in Three Primitive Societies* (1963) reveals that other societies may have different views about what is considered feminine or masculine. In this widely quoted report of her fieldwork in New Guinea, Mead discusses two societies that minimize differences between the sexes. She notes that among the Mundugumor both sexes exhibit aggressive, insensitive, uncooperative, and non-nurturing behaviors that would be considered masculine by our society's norms. In contrast, among the Arapesh both males and females exhibit gentleness, sensitivity, cooperation, nurturing, and nonaggressive behaviors that would be judged feminine in our society. And, in a third society studied by Mead, the Tchambuli, masculine and feminine gender roles are actually the reverse of what Americans view as typical. Because there is no evidence that people in these societies are biologically different from Americans, their often diametrically different interpretations of what is masculine and what is feminine seem to result from different processes of social learning.

Although parents are becoming more sensitive to the kinds of toys children play with, many still choose one set of toys and play activities for boys and another set for girls.

Studies of intersexed children also provide support for the social-learning interpretation of gender-identity formation as described in the following section.

Intersex Children and Social-Learning Theory

Proponents of the social-learning interpretation of gender-identity formation refer to various studies of intersexed children born with ambiguous external genitals who are assigned a particular sex and reared accordingly. Much of the early work in this area was performed at Johns Hopkins University Hospital by a team headed by John Money. When these treatment approaches were being implemented, Money and his colleagues believed that a person is psychosexually neutral or undifferentiated at birth and that social-learning experiences are the essential determinants of gender identity and gender-role behavior (Money, 1963; Money & Ehrhardt, 1972). Therefore, little attention was paid to matching external genitals with sex chromosomes. Rather, because the guiding principle was how natural the genitals could be made to look, many of these intersexed infants were assigned to the female sex, because surgical reconstruction of ambiguous genitalia to those of a female form is mechanically easier and aesthetically and functionally superior to constructing a penis (Nussbaum, 2000; Rosario, 2011).

Money and his colleagues followed these surgically altered children over a period of years and reported that in most cases children whose assigned sex did not match their chromosomal sex developed a gender identity consistent with the way they were reared (Money, 1965; Money & Ehrhardt, 1972). Additional evidence supporting these findings was recently published. Researchers surveyed 39 adult participants who had undergone surgical alteration as infants at Johns Hopkins. All of these individuals are genetic males who were born with a micropenis with a urethral opening on its underside. Some of the individuals were altered to be anatomical females and others to be anatomical males, with gender assigned accordingly. Most of these respondents (78% of women and

76% of men) reported being satisfied with the gender chosen for them and with their body image, sexual functioning, and sexual orientation. However, 2 of the 39 switched gender as adults (Migeon et al., 2002).

Research has revealed that at least some intersexed children may not be as psychosexually neutral at birth as originally believed. Long-term follow-ups of several intersexed children treated under the Johns Hopkins protocol revealed that some of these individuals have had serious problems adjusting to the gender assigned to them (Diamond, 1997; Diamond & Sigmundson, 1997). One especially compelling account involved two identical twin boys, one of whom experienced a circumcision accident that destroyed most of his penile tissue. Because no amount of plastic surgery could adequately reconstruct the severely damaged penis, it was recommended that the child be raised as a female and receive appropriate sex-change surgery. A few months later the parents decided to begin raising him as a girl. Shortly thereafter, castration and initial genital surgery were performed to facilitate feminization. Follow-up analyses of these twins during their early childhood years revealed that, despite possessing identical genetic materials, they responded to their separate social-learning experiences by developing opposite gender identities. Furthermore, the child reassigned to the female gender was described as developing into a normally functioning female child.

If the story of these twins ended here, we would have strong evidence of the dominant role of social learning in gender-identity formation. However, a later follow-up (Diamond & Sigmundson, 1997) found that, beginning at age 14, still unaware of the XY chromosome status and against the recommendations of family and treating clinicians, this person decided to stop living as a female. This adamant rejection of living as a female, together with a much improved emotional state when living as a male, convinced therapists of the appropriateness of sex reassignment. His postsurgical adjustment was excellent and, aided by testosterone treatments, he "emerged" as an attractive young man. At the age of 25 he married a woman, adopted her children, and comfortably assumed his role as father and husband. This remarkable story is told in a book by John Colapinto (2000) titled *As Nature Made Him: The Boy Who Was Raised as a Girl*.

This case study illustrates the critical importance of long-term longitudinal studies of children whose sex has been reassigned. The early tracking during the childhood phase of this person was widely reported in the press and the academic and medical communities as providing clear evidence that gender identity is psychologically neutral at birth, as yet uninfluenced by social-learning experiences. Now, after many years during which this viewpoint predominated, we have learned in subsequent follow-ups how wrong this interpretation may be. Even John Money, formerly a major proponent of this perspective, moderated his position in later years (see Money, 1994b).

As a footnote to this famous case of apparent misapplication of the Johns Hopkins protocol, we mention another, underreported case with a different outcome. It concerns a boy whose penis was burned off during a circumcision procedure. This individual, also raised as a girl from infancy, was interviewed by professionals at ages 16 and 26. Although tomboyish as a child and bisexual as an adult, this person has maintained a female gender identity, unlike the more famous example of the twin who assumed a male gender identity as an adult (Bradley et al., 1998).

Another study has raised questions about the common practice of surgically assigning a sex to a child with ambiguous external genitals. This investigation reported on the development of 27 children born without penises (a condition known as *cloacal exstrophy*) but who were otherwise males with normal testes, chromosomes, and hormones. Twenty-five of the 27 underwent sex reassignment shortly after birth, by means of castration, and their parents raised them as females. All 25 exhibited play activities typical of males, and 14 eventually declared themselves boys. The two boys who were not reassigned and thus were raised as boys seemed to be better adjusted than their reassigned counterparts. These results led William Reiner, lead researcher on this investigation, to conclude that "with time and age, children may well know what their gender is, regardless of any and all information and child rearing to the contrary" (Reiner, 2000, p. 1).

Several prominent researchers now argue that prevailing assumptions about gender neutrality at birth and the efficacy of sex reassignment of children may be wrong. In fact, more and more evidence has shown that, despite great care in rearing chromosomal males sex-reassigned as females, some—perhaps many—of them manifest strong male tendencies in their developmental years and may even change their assigned sex after they reach puberty (Colapinto, 2000; Diamond & Sigmundson, 1997; Reiner, 1997b). Concerns about the benefits and ethics of standard treatment practices used with intersexed individuals have provoked lively debate among intersexed individuals, researchers, and practitioners as discussed in the following section.

Treatment Strategies for Intersexed People: Debate and Controversy

People born with ambiguous external genitals are often viewed as biological accidents that need to be fixed. John Money and his colleagues at Johns Hopkins were the primary architects of a treatment protocol for intersexed individuals that became standard practice by the early 1960s and persists to the present. According to this protocol, a team of professionals, in consultation with the parents, choose which gender to assign an intersexed child. To reduce the possibility of future adjustment problems or gender confusion, the physicians usually provide surgical and/or hormonal treatments.

Questions have emerged about both the long-term benefits and the ethical appropriateness of this standard treatment protocol (Dreger, 2003; Fausto-Sterling, 2000; Gurney, 2007). Milton Diamond, an outspoken critic of John Money's treatment strategies, has conducted long-term follow-ups of a number of intersexed individuals treated under this standard protocol. His research has revealed that some of these individuals experience significant adjustment problems that they attribute to the biosocial "management" of their intersexed conditions (Diamond, 1998; Diamond & Sigmundson, 1997).

The research of Diamond and others, and the testimony of people who have been harmed by treatment they have received via the standard protocol, has triggered an intense debate among intersexed people, researchers, and health-care professionals about what constitutes proper treatment of intersexed infants (Meyer-Bahlburg, 2005). Many specialists still support Money's protocol and argue that intersexed infants should be unambiguously assigned a gender at the earliest possible age, certainly before the emergence of gender identity in the second year of life. This position endorses surgical and/or hormonal intervention to minimize gender confusion. An alternative viewpoint, championed by Diamond and others, suggests a threefold approach to treating intersexed people. First, health-care professionals should make an informed best guess about the intersexed infant's eventual gender identity and then counsel parents to rear the child in this identity. Second, genital-altering surgeries (which later might need to be reversed) should be avoided during the early years of development. And third, quality counseling and accurate information should be provided to both the child and his or her parents during the developmental years to ensure that the child is eventually able to make an informed decision about any additional treatment steps, such as surgery and/or hormone treatments. A distinguished group of intersex researchers has strongly advocated delaying medical intervention until a child is old enough to have developed a male or female gender identity (Caldwell, 2005).

Both Diamond's treatment strategy and the standard protocol raise important questions. Does genital-altering surgery performed on mere babies violate their rights as humans to give informed consent? Would intersexed children left with ambiguous genitals have problems functioning in schools or other settings where their condition might become known to others? Might society eventually evolve beyond the two-sex model

Critical Thinking Question

Assume that you are the leader of a team of health professionals who must decide the best treatment for an intersexed infant. Would you assign a gender identity and perform the surgical and/or hormonal treatments consistent with the assigned gender? If so, what gender would you select? Why? If you would decide not to assign a gender, what kind of follow-up or management strategy would you suggest during the child's developmental years?

and embrace the legitimacy of a third, intersexed condition located somewhere on the spectrum between male and female?

A number of case studies have reported instances of people who comfortably adjusted to their untreated intersexed condition (Fausto-Sterling, 1993, 2000; Laurent, 1995). Furthermore, in recent years a number of intersexed people treated under the standard protocol have expressed strong resentment over being subjected to medical intervention as infants (Looy & Bouma, 2005; Rosario, 2011).

Intersex activists, who have established organizations such as the Intersex Society of North America (ISNA) and Advocates for Informed Choice (AIC), argue that inter-sexed people are cases of genital variability, not genital abnormality. The ISNA advo-cates a noninterventionist, child-centered approach in which an intersexed child is not subjected to genital-altering surgery; he or she may choose such procedures later in life (Caldwell, 2005; Tamar-Mattis, 2011).

More questions than answers exist about the most appropriate treatment strategy for intersexed infants. This uncertainty is due largely to a scarcity of long-term out-come studies on intersexed individuals (Meyer-Bahlburg, 2005). We hope that time and research will eventually resolve this dilemma.

The Interactional Model

Scientists have argued for decades about the relative importance of nature (biological determinants) versus nurture (social learning and the environment) in shaping human development. Today it seems clear that gender identity is a product of both biological fac-tors and social learning. The evidence is simply too overwhelming to conclude that nor-mal infants are psychosexually neutral at birth. We have seen that human infants possess a complex and yet to be fully understood biological substrate that predisposes them to interact with their social environment in either a masculine or a feminine mode. However, few researchers believe that human gender identity has an exclusively biological basis. There is simply too much evidence supporting the important role of life experiences in shaping the way we think about ourselves—not only as masculine or feminine but in all aspects of how we relate to those around us. Consequently, most theorists and research-ers support an *interactional model*, which acknowledges both biology and experience in the development of gender identity (Dragowski et al., 2011; Looy & Bouma, 2005). Let us hope that as we acquire more data from further research, especially from long-term longitudinal analyses, we will gain a clearer understanding of the relative impact of these two powerful forces on gender-identity formation and gender-role behavior.

Transsexualism and Transgenderism

We have learned that gender-identity formation is a complex process influenced by many factors, with congruity between biological sex and gender identity by no means guaran-teed. We have become increasingly aware of the rich diversity in gender identities and roles. Many people fall somewhere within a range of variant gender identities. The com-munity of gender-variant people, composed of *transsexual* and *transgendered* individuals, has acquired considerable voice in both the professional literature and the popular media.

A **transsexual** is a person whose gender identity is opposite to his or her biological sex. Such people feel trapped in a body of the "wrong" sex, a condition known as **gender dysphoria**. Thus an anatomically male transsexual feels that *she* is a woman who, by some quirk of fate, has been provided with male genitals but who wishes to be socially identified as female. Some theorists, based largely on their clinical experiences treating transsexuals, maintain that the "trapped in the body of the wrong sex" conceptualization

transsexual
A person whose gender identity is opposite to his or her biological sex.

gender dysphoria
Unhappiness with one's biological sex or gender role.

of transsexualism is incomplete or inaccurate, especially as applied to some male-to-female transsexuals (Bailey & Triea, 2007; Lawrence, 2007). Prominent among them is psychologist Roy Blanchard (1991, 1995), who maintains that there are two distinct sub-types of male-to-female transsexuals: (1) those with a homosexual orientation, who are exclusively attracted to men, and (2) individuals with a paraphilia labeled *autogynephilia*, which is a propensity to be sexually aroused by the thought or image of oneself as female. (See Chapter 16 for a discussion of paraphilias.) This interpretation, while controversial within the transsexual community, continues to generate research and discussion among professionals who study and treat transsexualism. For example, physician and researcher Anne Lawrence (2007), who herself is a male-to-female transsexual, has recently argued that it is a misconception to view autogynephilia as a purely erotic phenomenon. She suggests that autogynephilia can be more accurately conceptualized as a variety of romantic love embraced by men who "love women and want to become what they love" (p. 516).

Many transsexuals undergo sex-reassignment procedures involving extensive screening, hormone therapy, and genital-altering surgery. However, not all gender-dysphoric people want complete sex reassignment. Instead, they may want only the physical body, gender role, or sexuality of the other sex. Many gender-dysphoric individuals, including most transsexuals, want all three of these aspects of the other sex, but some are content to take on only one or two (Carroll, 1999). Furthermore, some transgendered people who manifest variant gender-role behaviors experience little or no gender dysphoria.

The term **transgendered** is generally applied to individuals whose appearance and/or behaviors do not conform to traditional gender roles (Dragowski et al., 2011; Olson et al., 2011). In other words, transgendered people, "to varying degrees, 'transgress' cultural norms as to what a man or woman 'should be'" (Goodrum, 2000, p. 1). These "transgressions" often involve cross-dressing, either occasionally or full time. Variations of transgendered behaviors include:

transgendered
A term applied to people whose appearance and/or behaviors do not conform to traditional gender roles.

- androphilic (attracted to males) *men* who cross-dress and assume a female role either to attract men (often heterosexual men) or, less commonly, to entertain (i.e., female impersonators).
- *gynephilic* (attracted to females) *men* who may have urges to become female but are reasonably content to live in a male role that may include being married to a woman and frequently cross-dressing and/or socializing as a woman.
- *gynephilic* (attracted to females) *women* who manifest masculine qualities (sometimes a complete male identity) but never seek sex reassignment (Carroll, 1999).

Nontranssexual cross-dressers used to be labeled *transvestites*. This term is now generally applied only to people who cross-dress to achieve sexual arousal (see the discussion of *transvestic fetishism* in Chapter 16). Transgendered people who cross-dress typically do so to obtain psychosocial rather than sexual gratification.

Some intersexed people, who were born exhibiting a mixture of male and female external genitals, also consider themselves members of the transgendered community. This group can include intersexed individuals who have undergone surgical and/or hormonal treatments to establish congruence between their anatomical sex structures and their gender identity (Goodrum, 2000).

The primary difference between a transsexual and a transgenderist is that the transgenderist does not want to change his or her physical body to create a better fit with personal or societal role expectations. Transsexuals often undergo major surgeries to make their physical bodies congruent with their gender identity. In contrast, most transgendered people have no wish to undergo anatomical alterations but do occasionally or frequently dress like and take on the mannerisms of the other sex. Some transgenderists live full time manifesting gender-role behaviors opposite to those ascribed by society to someone of their biological sex (Bolin, 1997).

Variant Gender Identity and Sexual Orientation

Many people are confused about the difference between gender identity (especially variant gender identity) and sexual orientation. Simply stated, gender identity is who we are—our own subjective sense of being male, female, or some combination of the two. Sexual orientation refers to which of the sexes we are emotionally and sexually attracted to (see Chapter 9).

Before sex reassignment, most transsexuals are attracted to people who match them anatomically but not in gender identity. Thus a transsexual with a female gender identity who feels trapped in a man's body (and is probably identified as a male by society) is likely to be attracted to men. In other words, she has a heterosexual orientation based on her own self-identification as female. If she acts on her sexual desires before undergoing sex reassignment, she may be falsely labeled as homosexual. In terms of postsurgical sexual orientation, almost all female-to-male transsexuals desire female sexual partners, whereas male-to-female transsexuals can be sexually oriented to either sex, with most preferring male sex partners (Zhou et al., 1995). It is important to note that most transsexuals who pursue sex reassignment are motivated primarily by a desire to alleviate a gender-identity conflict rather than to increase their sexual attractiveness to desired partners (Bockting, 2005).

Although transsexuals are predominantly heterosexual, the transgendered community is more eclectic, consisting of gay men, lesbians, bisexuals, and heterosexuals (Burdge, 2007; Goodrum, 2000).

Transsexualism: Etiology, Sex-Reassignment Procedures, and Outcomes

In the 1960s and early 1970s, when medical procedures for altering sex were first being developed in the United States, approximately three out of every four people requesting a sex change were biological males who wished to be females (Green, 1974). Although most health professionals believe that males seeking sex reassignment still outnumber females, evidence indicates that the ratio has narrowed appreciably (Olsson & Moller, 2003). Male-to-female transsexualism has become increasingly common in developed nations, with an estimated prevalence of about 1 in 12,000 people having undergone male-to-female sex-reassignment procedures (Lawrence, 2007).

A vast accumulation of clinical literature has focused on the characteristics, causes (etiology), and treatment of transsexualism. Certain factors are well established. We know that most transsexuals are biologically normal individuals with healthy sex organs, intact internal reproductive structures, and the usual complement of XX or XY chromosomes (Meyer-Bahlburg, 2005). Furthermore, transsexualism is usually an isolated condition, not part of any general psychopathology, such as schizophrenia or major depression (Cohen-Kettenis & Gooren, 1999). What is less understood is why these individuals reject their anatomies.

Many transsexuals develop a sense of being at odds with their genital anatomy in early childhood; some recall identifying strongly with characteristics of the other sex at as early as 5, 6, or 7 years of age. In some cases these children's discomfort is partially relieved by imagining themselves to be members of the other sex, but many of them eventually progress beyond mere imagining to actual cross-dressing. Less commonly, a strong identity with the other sex may not emerge until adolescence or adulthood.

The etiology of transsexualism is not clearly understood. Moreover, considerable controversy exists regarding the most appropriate clinical strategies for dealing with

Respectful Communication With a Transsexual or Transgendered Individual

Alexander John Goodrum (2000) wrote an informative article on transsexualism and transgenderism in which he discussed how people should communicate or interact with individuals with variant gender identities and/or behaviors. We summarize his suggestions as follows:

- It is important to refer to transsexual or transgendered individuals appropriately. If someone identifies himself as male, refer to him as *he*; if she identifies herself as female, refer to her as *she*. If you are not sure, it is all right to ask what this person prefers or expects. Once you know, try to be consistent. If you occasionally forget and use the wrong pronoun, make the correction. Most transsexual or transgendered people will understand slipups and appreciate your efforts.

- Never "out" someone by telling others, without permission, that he or she is transsexual or transgendered. Furthermore, do not assume that other people know about a person's variant gender identity. Many transgendered and transsexual individuals pass very well, and the only way others would know about their variant gender status would be by being told. Clearly, the decision whether to communicate gender status should be made only by the individual, and failure to honor this right would be highly disrespectful.

- Common sense and good taste mandate that we never ask transsexual or transgendered people what their genital anatomy looks like or how they relate sexually to others.

- Finally, make no assumptions about whether a person has a homosexual, bisexual, or heterosexual orientation. A person who believes that it is appropriate to reveal information about sexual orientation may elect to communicate this to you.

this condition. Keeping this debate in mind, we will summarize the tenuous state of knowledge about this highly unusual variant gender identity.

Etiology

Many theories have tried to explain transsexualism, but the evidence is inconclusive (Cole et al., 2000; Money, 1994a). Some writers maintain that biological factors play a decisive role. One theory suggests that prenatal exposure to inappropriate amounts of hormones of the other sex causes improper brain differentiation (Dessens et al., 1999; Zhou et al., 1995). Some evidence indicates that in transsexuals, sexual differentiation of the brain and the genitals occurs discordantly (Krujiver et al., 2000; Meyer-Bahlburg, 2005). Support for this interpretation was recently provided by an Australian study that reported evidence of a possible genetic link with transsexualism (Hare et al., 2009). The investigators conducted a DNA analysis of 112 male-to-female transsexuals with a longer-than-normal version of the androgen receptor gene. Longer versions of this gene are associated with less efficient prenatal production of testosterone. Reduction in the action of this hormone may have an effect on gender development in the womb by under-masculinizing the brain during prenatal development, thereby contributing to the female gender identity of male-to-female transsexuals. Other research has found evidence of genetic factors in transsexuals (Bentz et al., 2008; Hare et al., 2009).

It has also been suggested that transsexualism can be induced by abnormal levels of adult sex hormones. However, this explanation is contradicted by numerous indications that sex hormone levels are normal in adult transsexuals (Zhou et al., 1995).

Another theory, which has some supporting evidence, holds that social-learning experiences contribute significantly to the development of transsexualism. A child may be exposed to a variety of conditioning experiences that support behaving in a manner traditionally attributed to the other sex (Bradley & Zucker, 1997; Cohen-Kettenis & Gooren, 1999). Such cross-gender behaviors may be so exclusively rewarded that it may be difficult or impossible for the individual to develop the appropriate gender identity.

Options for Transsexuals

The mental health field has traditionally considered only two possible solutions for overcoming the gender dysphoria of transsexuals: changing gender identity to match the physical body or changing the body to match gender identity (Carroll, 1999). Other options exist, however, and clinical evidence has indicated that some preoperative transsexuals have discovered that it may be psychologically sufficient to express themselves through such activities as cross-dressing (Carroll, 1999). Nevertheless, in most cases, psychotherapy, without accompanying biological alterations, has generally been inadequate to help transsexuals adjust to their bodies and gender identities. For such individuals the best course of action might be to change their bodies to match their minds, through surgical and hormonal alteration of genital anatomy and body physiology. However, medical alteration is not a simple solution, because it is both time-consuming and costly.

A recent study revealed that 33% of major American employers offer transgender-inclusive benefits including sex-reassignment surgery (Gillespie, 2012). This fivefold benefits increase from the previous year reflects a major push from guidelines provided by the Human Rights Campaign. In future years we can expect an increase in research data pertaining to sex-reassignment as a direct result of the increased affordability of these procedures now often covered under employer benefits policies.

Sex-Reassignment Procedures

The initial step of a sex change involves extensive screening interviews, during which a person's motivations for undergoing the change are thoroughly evaluated. Individuals with real conflicts and confusion about their gender identity are not considered for surgical alteration. Individuals with an apparently genuine incongruence between their gender identity and their biological sex are then instructed to adopt a lifestyle consistent with their gender identity (i.e., dress style and behavior patterns). If, after several months to a year or longer, it appears that the individual has successfully adjusted to that lifestyle, the next step is hormone therapy, a process designed to accentuate latent traits of the desired sex. Thus males wishing to be females are given drugs that inhibit testosterone production together with doses of estrogen that induce some breast growth, soften the skin, reduce facial and body hair, and help to feminize body contours. Muscle strength diminishes, as does sexual interest, but there is no alteration of vocal pitch. Women who want to become men are treated with testosterone, which helps to increase growth of body and facial hair and produces a deepening of the voice and a slight reduction in breast size. Testosterone also suppresses menstruation. Most health professionals who provide sex-change procedures require a candidate to live for at least 1 year as a member of the other sex while undergoing hormone therapy, before surgery (Bockting et al., 2011). At any time during this phase, the process can be reversed, although few transsexuals choose this option.

The final step of a sex change is surgery (▌ Figure 5.6). Surgical procedures are most effective for men wishing to be women. The scrotum and penis are removed, and a vagina is created through reconstruction of pelvic tissue (see Figure 5.6a). During this surgical procedure, great care is taken to maintain the sensory nerves that serve the skin of the penis, and this sensitive skin tissue is relocated to the inside of the newly fashioned vagina. Intercourse is possible, although use of a lubricant may be necessary, and many male-to-female transsexuals report postsurgical capacity to experience sexual arousal and orgasm (Lawrence, 2005; Schroder & Carroll, 1999). Hormone treatments can produce sufficient breast development, but some individuals also receive implants. Body and facial hair, which were reduced by hormone treatments, can be further removed by electrolysis. Finally, if desired, an additional surgical procedure can be performed to raise the pitch of the voice in male-to-female transsexuals (Brown et al., 2000).

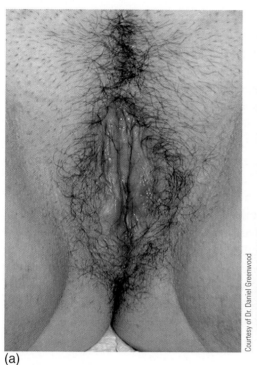
(a)

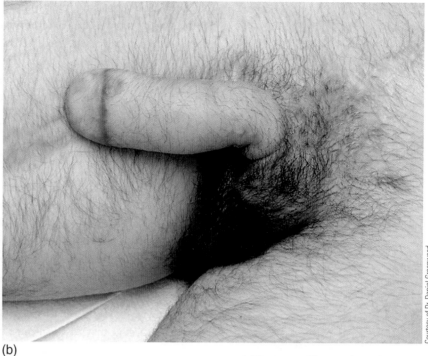
(b)

Courtesy of Dr. Daniel Greenwood

❚ Figure 5.6 The genitals following sex-change surgery: (a) Male-to-female sex-change surgery is generally more effective than (b) female-to-male sex-change surgery.

A biological female who desires to be male generally undergoes surgical procedures in which the breasts, uterus, and ovaries are removed and the vagina is sealed off. Constructing a penis is much more difficult than constructing a vagina. In general, the penis is fashioned from abdominal skin or from tissue from the labia and perineum (see Figure 5.6b). This constructed organ cannot achieve a natural erection in response to sexual arousal. However, several options are available that can provide a rigid penis for intercourse. One involves fashioning a small, hollow skin tube on the underside of the penile shaft into which a rigid silicone rod can be inserted. Another option is an implanted inflatable device, which will be described in Chapter 14. If erotically sensitive tissue from the clitoris is left embedded at the base of the surgically constructed penis, erotic feelings and orgasm are sometimes possible (Lief & Hubschman, 1993).

Outcomes of Sex Reassignment

Numerous studies of the psychosocial outcome of gender reassignment provide a basis for optimism about the success of sex-reassignment procedures. The single most consistent finding of these investigations is that most people who have undergone these procedures experience significant improvement in their overall adjustment to life (De Cuypere et al., 2005; Khoosal et al., 2011; Lawrence, 2003).

Gender Roles

We have seen that social learning is an important influence on the formation of gender identity early in life, so that even by the age of 2 or 3 years, most children have no doubt about whether they are boys or girls. This influence continues throughout our lives, because we are influenced by *gender roles*—that is, behaviors that are considered appropriate and normal for men and women in a society.

The ascribing of gender roles leads naturally to certain assumptions about how people will behave. For example, men in North American society have traditionally been expected to be independent and aggressive, whereas women were supposed to be

stereotype
A generalized notion of what a person is like based only on that person's sex, race, religion, ethnic background, or similar criteria.

dependent and submissive. Once these expectations are widely accepted, they may begin to function as stereotypes. A **stereotype** is a generalized notion of what a person is like based only on that person's sex, race, religion, ethnic background, or similar category. Stereotypes do not take individuality into account. Stereotypes pertaining to sex differences in personality traits were recently examined in a major cross-cultural study, described in the Spotlight on Research box.

Many traditional gender-based stereotypes are widely accepted in our society. Some of the prevailing notions about men maintain that they are aggressive (or at least assertive), logical, unemotional, independent, dominant, competitive, objective, athletic, active, and, above all, competent. Conversely, women are frequently viewed as nonassertive, illogical, emotional, subordinate, warm, and nurturing. These common gender-role stereotypes also tend to be found in many different cultures (Jandt & Hundley, 2007). For example, one study found remarkable consistency in how these traditional role stereotypes are ascribed to women and men in 30 different cultures (Williams & Best, 1990).

A recent study of college women found that women who endorse traditional gender roles view an ideal male partner as one who conforms to traditional masculine roles involving power over women, self-reliance, emotional control, and risk taking. In contrast, women who identified themselves as feminists not supportive of traditional gender roles indicated that an ideal male partner would be one who did not conform to

SPOTLIGHT ON RESEARCH ▶ Cross-Cultural Sex Differences in Personality Traits

Social scientists generally agree that sex differences in traditional gender roles tend to appear early in life and often persist across the life cycle. However, the origin of these differences remains controversial. On the one hand, *evolutionary psychologists* maintain that many of our behaviors and personality attributes are innate traits inherited from ancient hunter-and-gatherer ancestors. Alternatively, psychologists in the *social-learning* camp assert that the personalities and behaviors of both sexes have been largely shaped by traditional social roles. Evolutionary psychologists might hypothesize that sex differences in personality traits would be somewhat consistent across divergent cultures. If a long period of biological evolution favors selection of genes that contribute to the survival of the species, there should be a predictable consistency across various subcategories (cultures) of the human species. Conversely, social-learning advocates would likely hypothesize that sex differences in personality traits will diminish as women spend more time outside the home in the competitive workplace and less time in the traditional female roles of homemaker and nurturer of children.

These two hypotheses were recently put to a worldwide test in which 17,637 people drawn from 55 nations were administered the Big Five Inventory (BFI; translated from English into 28 languages), a self-report questionnaire designed to assess the traits of extraversion, agreeableness, conscientiousness, neuroticism, and openness. The survey's findings stand in marked contrast to likely predictions based on the two psychological perspectives

just described. First, the extent of sex differences in personality traits was found to vary considerably among the 55 cultures surveyed, a result that is inconsistent with the evolutionary psychology viewpoint. Perhaps even more startling was the finding that personality differences between men and women were smaller in traditional cultures like those of Botswana or India than in more egalitarian nations like the United States or France. Thus, contrary to the social-learning hypothesis, a working husband and stay-at-home wife in the patriarchal Botswana culture are more similar in personality traits than a working couple in Denmark. Or, stated another way, the more men and women in a given culture are egalitarian in jobs and rights, the more their personality traits seem to diverge (Schmitt et al., 2008).

These findings are so counterintuitive and inconsistent with predictions derived from either the social-learning or the evolutionary psychology perspective that some researchers have suggested that they result from culturally based problems with the BFI (Tierney, 2008). However, lead author David Schmitt and his colleagues conclude that their study revealed general trends that are valid albeit controversial in the context of widely held theories. Can we expect that the personality gap between men and women will widen further as the sexes become more equal in affluent societies that increasingly embrace egalitarian values and reduce barriers between women and men? Hopefully future research will provide additional insights and help to clarify this question.

The religious right in America has long labored to reinforce traditional gender roles through its efforts to shape American politics. However, as described in Clyde Wilcox and Carin Robinson's book *Onward Christian Soldiers? The Religious Right in American Politics* (2011), this movement has had relatively few political successes.

traditional masculine norms of aggression and violence, power over women, and self-reliance (Backus & Mahalik, 2011).

The religious right in America has consistently espoused traditional gender roles as described in the box, "The Religious Right Embraces Traditional Gender Roles."

In recent years there has been a trend away from strict adherence to gender-typed behavior, especially among younger people (Ben-David & Schneider, 2005; Lindberg et al., 2008). Research suggests that women are less entrenched than men in rigid gender-role stereotypes and are more inclined to embrace positions of equality with men (Ben-David & Schneider, 2005). In spite of these positive changes in American culture, stereotypical gender roles still pervade our society. Indeed, many individuals are comfortable fulfilling a traditional masculine or feminine role, and we do not wish to demean or question the validity of their lifestyles. Rather, we are concerned with finding out why gender roles are so prevalent in society. We turn to this question next.

How Do We Learn Gender Roles?

You have probably heard the argument that behavioral differences between men and women are biologically determined, at least to some degree. Men cannot bear or nurse children. Likewise, biological differences in hormones, muscle mass, and brain structure and function can influence some aspects of behavior. However, most theorists explain gender roles as largely a product of **socialization**—that is, the process by which individuals learn, and adopt, society's expectations for behavior. In the following Sexuality and Diversity discussion, we see how cultural and ethnic groups within a society have varying expectations of men's and women's behavior.

socialization
The process by which our society conveys behavioral expectations to the individual.

SEXUALITY and DIVERSITY
Ethnic Variations in Gender Roles

Throughout this textbook we have focused primarily on gender assumptions that prevail in the traditional mainstream—White Americans of European origin. Here we look briefly at gender roles among three different ethnic groups: Hispanic Americans, African Americans, and Asian Americans.

Traditional Hispanic American gender roles are epitomized by the cultural stereotypes of *marianismo* and *machismo*. Marianismo derives from the Roman Catholic notion that women should be pure and self-giving—like the Virgin Mary. It ascribes to women the primary role of mothers who are faithful, virtuous, passive, and subordinate to their husbands and who act as the primary preserver of the family and tradition (Bourdeau et al., 2008; Estrada et al., 2011). The concept of machismo projects an image of the Hispanic American male as strong, independent, virile, and dominant—the head of the household and major decision maker in the family (Bourdeau et al., 2008; Estrada et al., 2011). Machismo also embodies the notion that it is acceptable to be sexually aggressive and to seek conquests outside the marriage. Thus Hispanic culture often expresses a double standard in which wives are to remain faithful to one man and husbands can have outside affairs (McNeill et al., 2001). This double standard has it origins in the early socialization of Hispanic youth, which encourages boys to be sexually adventurous and girls to be virtuous and virginal (Bourdeau et al., 2008; Estrada et al., 2011).

Of course, marianismo and machismo are just stereotypes, and many Hispanic Americans do not embrace these gender-role assumptions (Vasquez, 1994). Furthermore, assimilation, urbanization, and upward mobility of Hispanic Americans are combining to diminish the impact of these cultural stereotypes as they reduce gender-role inequities (McNeill et al., 2001). This is especially true of young Hispanic Americans, who often do not embrace their parents' traditional gender-role beliefs (Cespedes & Huey, 2008).

In a second ethnic group, African Americans, women play a central role in families that tends to differ from the traditional nuclear family model of mother, father, and children (Bulcroft et al., 1996; Reid & Bing, 2000). African American women have traditionally been a bulwark of strength in their communities since the days of slavery. Because women could not depend economically on men under the system of slavery, African American men did not typically assume the dominant role in the family. This accounts, in part, for why relationships between African American women and men have tended more toward egalitarianism and economic parity than has been true of other cultural groups, including the dominant White culture (Blee & Tickamyer, 1995; Bulcroft et al., 1996). The historical absence of economic dependence also helps explain why so many African American households are headed by women who define their own status.

Another factor is the high unemployment rate among African American males— more than double the rate for Whites (Bureau of Labor Statistics, 2012). The realities of high unemployment among African American males and their frequent absence from the family home often result in African American women assuming gender-role behaviors that reflect a reversal of the gender patterns traditional among White Americans.

A third minority group, Asian Americans, represents great diversity both in heritage and country of origin (China, the Philippines, Japan, India, Korea, Vietnam, Cambodia, Thailand, and others). Asian Americans tend to place more value on family, group solidarity, and interdependence than do White Americans (Okazaki, 2002; Yoshida & Busby, 2012). Like her Hispanic counterparts, the Asian American woman expects her family obligations to take higher priority than her own individual aspirations (Pyke & Johnson, 2003). Thus, although more Asian American women work outside the home than do women in any other American ethnic group, many spend their lives supporting others and subordinating their needs to the family (Bradshaw, 1994; Cole, 1992). As a result, achievement-oriented Asian women are often caught in a double bind, torn between contemporary American values of individuality and independence and the traditional gender roles of Asian culture.

Although no typical pattern exists, the diverse Asian cultures still tend to allow greater sexual freedom for men than for women while perpetuating the gender-role assumption of male dominance (Ishii-Kuntz, 1997a, 1997b; Pyke & Johnson, 2003). Asian culture also tends to promote a higher level of sexual conservatism in both sexes than is typical of other U.S. ethnic groups, including Whites (Benuto & Meana, 2008; Okazaki, 2002). However, culturally based gender-role stereotypes are less likely to be embraced by Asian American youth, who increasingly adhere to broader American cultural values (Ying & Han, 2008).

As these accounts illustrate, social learning and cultural traditions influence gender-role behaviors within American society. How does society convey these expectations? In the following sections we look at five agents of socialization: parents, peers, schools and books, television, and religion.

Parents as Shapers of Gender Roles

Many social scientists view parents as influential agents of gender-role socialization (Dragowski et al., 2011; Iervolino et al., 2005; Kane, 2006). A child's earliest exposure to what it means to be female or male is typically provided by parents. As we saw earlier, in the discussion of gender-identity formation, parents often have different expectations for girls and boys, and they demonstrate these expectations in their interactions (Eliot, 2009). In general, parents tend to be more protective and restrictive of girl babies and provide less intervention and more freedom for boys (Skolnick, 1992). Furthermore, research has found that sons are more likely than daughters to receive parental encouragement for self-assertion behaviors and for controlling or limiting their emotional expression, whereas girls receive more encouragement for expressing social-engagement behavior (Leaper et al., 1998). Recent research has also revealed that having a daughter, versus having a son, causes fathers to reduce their support for traditional gender roles (Shafer & Malhotra, 2011).

Although an increasing number of parents are becoming sensitive to the gender-role implications of a child's playthings, many others encourage their children to play with toys that help prepare them for specific adult gender roles (Jadva, 2010). Girls are often given dolls, tea sets, and miniature ovens. Boys frequently receive trucks, cars, balls, and toy weapons. Children who play with toys thought appropriate only for the other sex are often rebuked by their parents. Because children are sensitive to these expressions of displeasure, they usually develop toy preferences consistent with their parents' gender-role expectations.

Although more and more parents try to avoid teaching their children gender stereotypes, many still encourage their children to engage in gender-typed play activities and household chores (Menvielle, 2004). "The gendered division of household labor begins early in life with girls doing more household work than boys from childhood on" (Berridge & Romich, 2011, p. 157).

The establishment of stereotypical masculine or feminine roles can be influenced by traditional child-rearing practices.

The Peer Group

A second important influence in the socialization of gender roles is the peer group (Arnon et al., 2008). One element of peer-group influence that begins early in life is a voluntary segregation of the sexes. This separation begins during the preschool years, and by first grade, children select members of their own sex as playmates about 95% of the time (Maccoby, 1998). Segregation of the sexes, which continues into the school years, contributes to sex typing in play activities that helps prepare children for adult gender roles (Moller et al., 1992). Girls often play together with dolls and tea sets, and boys frequently engage in athletic competitions and play with toy guns. Such peer influences contribute to the socialization of women who are inclined to be nurturing and nonassertive and of men who are comfortable being competitive and assertive.

By late childhood and adolescence, the influence of peers becomes even stronger (Doyle & Paludi, 1991; Hyde, 2006). Children of this age tend to view conformity as important,

One aspect of peer-group structure among American children that helps to perpetuate traditional gender roles is the tendency to select same-sex playmates most of the time.

and adhering to traditional gender roles promotes social acceptance by their peers (Absi-Semaan et al., 1993). Most individuals who do not behave in ways appropriate to their own sex are subjected to pressure in the form of ostracism or ridicule.

Schools, Books, and Gender Roles

Studies indicate that girls and boys often receive quite different treatment in the classroom, a process that strongly influences gender-role socialization. Among the findings of these studies are that teachers call on and encourage boys more than girls; that teachers are more likely to tolerate inappropriate behavior of boys than girls; and that boys are more likely than girls to receive attention, remedial help, and praise from their teachers (Duffy et al., 2001; Eccles et al., 1999; Keller, 2002).

School textbooks and children's books have also perpetuated gender-role stereotypes. In the early 1970s, two major studies of children's textbooks found that girls were typically portrayed as dependent, unambitious, and not very successful or clever, whereas boys were shown to have just the opposite characteristics (Saario et al., 1973; Women on Words and Images, 1972). In the early 1980s, men played the dominant roles in about two out of every three stories in American reading texts—an improvement from four out of every five stories in the early 1970s (Britton & Lumpkin, 1984). A recent review of children's books also demonstrated a male bias and a message that women and girls are less important than men and boys (McCabe et al., 2011).

Fortunately, schools in the United States are now acting to reduce classroom perpetuation of stereotypical gender roles (Meyerhoff, 2004). An influx of younger teachers who are products of a more gender-aware generation has aided in this gradual transformation of classroom environments. One of the most striking examples of this change has been a concerted effort by American schools to ensure equal educational opportunities for both sexes in math and science and to create educational environments in which girls as well as boys are encouraged to participate in these subjects. However, like the culture they represent, textbooks and children's books are still not completely free of stereotyped gender roles.

A recent review of illustrations in award-winning children's books in the period 1990–2009 found that "larger proportions of female characters in the books used household artifacts, whereas larger proportions of male characters used production artifacts outside the home" (Crabb & Marciano, 2011, p. 390).

Television and Gender-Role Stereotypes

Another powerful agent of gender-role socialization is television. Depictions of men and women in TV dramas are often blatantly stereotypical (Lauzen et al., 2008). Men are more likely than women to appear as active, intelligent, and adventurous, and to take positions of leadership. Men are also often featured in work-related roles while female characters are more likely to be portrayed in interpersonal roles involved with romance, family, and friends (Lauzen et al., 2008). Furthermore, an analysis of the sexual content of five prime-time programs found that male characters are commonly portrayed as actively and aggressively pursuing sex whereas female characters are more often depicted as willingly objectifying themselves (e.g., exploiting their bodies), thus conforming to stereotypical conceptions of femininity (e.g., behaving seductively), and being judged by their sexual conduct (Kim et al., 2007). However, these stereotypes are in the process of breaking down. A number of TV dramas, such as *The Good Wife*, *Cold Case*, *Fringe*, and *Body of Proof* feature multidimensional and competent female characters. Nevertheless, prime-time television remains largely a male-dominated medium. In television news and political talk programs, men also continue to be disproportionately represented as the authoritative sources on most topics.

Television commercials also tend to further gender stereotypes. In commercials for nonhousehold products aimed at adult consumers, men are more likely than women to appear as the authoritative source of information. However, changes in gender stereotypes in advertising are beginning to diminish as women are now more commonly portrayed as powerful and in control rather than as passive sex objects (Halliwell et al., 2011).

It is safe to assume that the sexist stereotypes depicted by television programming have some impact as agents of socialization, considering that most American children spend hours in front of the TV each day. Fortunately, the television industry is gradually reducing gender biases in its programming, partly because of the influence of media advocacy groups who have worked tirelessly to reduce the portrayal of traditional stereotypes of male and female roles.

Religion and Gender Roles

Organized religion plays an important role in the lives of many Americans. Despite differences in doctrines, most religions exhibit a common trend in their views about gender roles (Eitzen & Zinn, 2000). Children who receive religious instruction are likely to be socialized to accept certain gender stereotypes, and people who are religious are inclined to endorse gender stereotypes (Robinson et al., 2004). In Jewish, Christian, and Islamic traditions these stereotypes commonly embrace an emphasis on male supremacy, with God presented as male through language such as *Father*, *He*, or *King*. The biblical conceptualization of Eve as created from Adam's rib provides a clear endorsement of the gender assumption that females are meant to be secondary to males.

The number of women ordained as clergy has increased dramatically.

The composition of the leadership of most religious organizations in the United States provides additional evidence of male dominance and of the circumscription of female gender roles. Until 1970 no women were ordained as clergy in any American Protestant denomination. No female rabbis existed until 1972, and the Roman Catholic Church still does not allow female priests.

Movements are afoot to change the traditional patriarchal nature of organized religion in America, as evidenced by several recent trends. Data from the Bureau of Labor Statistics indicate that from 1994 to 2009, the numbers of women clergy in the United States doubled to 73,000 (Lee, 2011). In 2006 Katherine Jefferts Schori was elected presiding bishop of the Episcopal Church in America—the first woman to lead a church in the history of the worldwide Anglican Communion (Banerjee, 2006). Female enrollment in seminaries and divinity schools has increased dramatically. Efforts are also under way to reduce sexist language in church proceedings and religious writings (Grossman, 2011; Haught, 2009).

We see, then, that family, friends, schools, books, television (and other media, such as movies, magazines, and popular music), and religion frequently help to develop and reinforce traditional gender-role assumptions and behaviors in our lives. We are all affected by gender-role conditioning to some degree, and we could discuss at great length how this process discourages development of each person's full potential. However, this textbook deals with our sexuality, so it is the impact of gender-role conditioning on this aspect of our lives that we examine in the next section.

Gender-Role Expectations: Their Impact on Our Sexuality

Gender-role expectations exert a profound impact on our sexuality. Our beliefs about males and females, together with our assumptions about what constitutes appropriate behaviors for each, can affect many aspects of sexual experience. Our assessment of ourselves as sexual beings, the expectations we have for intimate relationships, our perception of the quality of such experiences, and the responses of others to our sexuality are all significantly influenced by our identification as male or female.

In the following pages we examine some of our gender-role assumptions and their potential effects on relations between the sexes. We do not mean to imply that only heterosexual couples are limited by these assumptions. Gender-role stereotypes can influence people regardless of their sexual orientation, although homosexual couples might be affected somewhat differently by them.

Women as Undersexed, Men as Oversexed

A long-standing, mistaken assumption in many Western societies is that women are inherently less sexually inclined than men. Such gender stereotypes can result in women being subjected to years of negative socialization during which they are taught to suppress or deny their natural sexual feelings. Although these stereotypes are beginning to fade as people strive to throw off some of the behavior constraints of generations of socialization, many women are still influenced by such views. Some women, believing that it is not appropriate to be easily aroused sexually, direct their energies to blocking or hiding these normal responses.

Males can be harmed by being stereotyped as supersexual. A man who is not immediately aroused by a person he perceives as attractive and/or available can feel somehow inadequate. After all, are not all men supposed to be instantly eager when confronted with a sexual opportunity? We believe that such an assumption is demeaning and reduces men to insensitive machines that respond automatically when the correct button is pushed. Male students in our classes frequently express their frustration and ambivalence over this issue. The following account is typical of these observations:

> When I take a woman out for the first time, I am often confused over how the sex issue should be handled. I feel pressured to make a move, even when I am not all that inclined to hop into the sack. Isn't this what women expect? If I don't even try, they may think there is something wrong with me. I almost feel like I would have to explain myself if I acted uninterested in having sex. Usually it's just easier to make the move and let them decide what they want to do with it. (Authors' files)

Clearly, this man believes that he is expected to pursue sex, even when he does not want to, as part of his masculine role. This stereotypical view of men as the initiators of sex in developing relationships can be distressing for both sexes, as we see in the next section.

Men as Initiators, Women as Recipients

In our society traditional gender roles establish the expectation that men will initiate intimate relationships (from the opening invitation for an evening out to the first overture toward sexual activity) and that women will respond with permission or denial (Dworkin & O'Sullivan, 2005). As the following comment reveals, this expectation can make men feel burdened and pressured:

> Women should experience how anxiety-provoking it can be. I get tired of always being the one to make the suggestion, since there's always the potential of being turned down. (Authors' files)

A woman who feels compelled to accept a passive female role can have a difficult time initiating sex. It could be even harder for her to assume an active role during sexual activity. Many women are frustrated, regretful, and understandably angry that such cultural expectations are so deeply ingrained in our society. The following comments, expressed by women talking together, reflect some of these thoughts:

> I like to ask men out and have often done so. But it's frustrating when many of the men I ask out automatically assume that I want to jump in bed with them just because I take the initiative to make a date. (Authors' files)

> It is hard for me to let my man know what I like during lovemaking. After all, he is supposed to know, isn't he? If I tell him, it's like I am usurping his role as the all-knowing one. (Authors' files)

Women as Controllers, Men as Movers

Many women grow up believing that men always have sex on their minds. For such a woman, it may be a logical next step to become the controller of what takes place during sexual interaction. By this we do not mean actively initiating certain activities, which she sees as the prerogative of men, the movers. Rather, a woman may see her role as controlling her male partner's rampant lust by making certain he does not coerce her into unacceptable activities. Thus, instead of enjoying how good it feels to have her breasts caressed, she may concentrate on how to keep his hand off her genitals. This concern with control can be particularly pronounced during the adolescent dating years. It is not surprising that a woman who spends a great deal of time and energy regulating sexual intimacy might have difficulty experiencing sexual feelings when she finally allows herself to relinquish her controlling role.

Conversely, men are often conditioned to see women as sexual challenges and to go as far as they can during sexual encounters. They too may have difficulty appreciating the good feelings of being close to and touching someone when all they are thinking about is what they will do next. Men who routinely experience this pattern can have a hard time relinquishing the mover role and being receptive rather than active during sexual interaction. They might be confused or even threatened by a woman who switches roles from controller to active initiator.

Men as Unemotional and Strong, Women as Nurturing and Supportive

Perhaps one of the most undesirable of all gender-role stereotypes is the notion that being emotionally expressive, tender, and nurturing is appropriate only for women. Men are often socialized to be unemotional. A man who is trying to appear strong might find it difficult to express vulnerability, deep feelings, and doubts. This conditioning can make it exceedingly difficult for a man to develop emotionally satisfying intimate relationships.

For example, a man who accepts the assumption of nonemotionality might approach sex as a purely physical act, during which expressions of feelings have no place. This behavior results in a limited kind of experience that can leave both parties feeling dissatisfied. Women often have a negative reaction when they encounter this characteristic in men, because women tend to place great importance on openness and willingness to express feelings in a relationship. However, we need to remember that many men must struggle against a lifetime of "macho" conditioning when they try to express long-suppressed emotions. Women, on the other hand, can grow tired of their role as nurturers, particularly when their efforts are greeted with little or no reciprocity.

We have discussed how strict adherence to traditional gender roles can limit and restrict the ways we express our sexuality. These cultural legacies are often expressed more subtly today than in the past, but rigid gender-role expectations linger on, inhibiting our growth as multidimensional people and our capacity to be fully ourselves with others. Although many people are breaking away from stereotyped gender roles and are learning to accept and express themselves more fully, we cannot underestimate the extent of gender-role learning that still occurs in our society.

Many people are now striving to integrate both masculine and feminine behaviors into their lifestyles. This trend, often referred to as *androgyny*, is the focus of the final section of this chapter.

Transcending Gender Roles: Androgyny

androgyny
A blending of typical male and female behaviors in one individual.

The word **androgyny** (an-DRAW-ji-nee), meaning "having characteristics of both sexes," is derived from the Greek roots *andr-*, meaning "man," and *gyne-*, meaning "woman." The term is used to describe flexibility in gender role. Androgynous individuals have integrated aspects of masculinity and femininity into their personalities and behavior. Androgyny offers the option of expressing whatever behavior seems appropriate in a given situation instead of limiting responses to those considered gender appropriate. Thus androgynous men and women might be assertive on the job but nurturing with friends, family members, and lovers. Many men and women possess characteristics consistent with traditional gender assumptions but also have interests and behavioral tendencies typically ascribed to the other sex. Actually, people can range from being very masculine or feminine to being *both* masculine and feminine—that is, androgynous.

Social psychologist Sandra Bem (1975, 1993) developed a paper-and-pencil inventory for measuring the degree to which individuals are identified with masculine or feminine behaviors or a combination thereof. Similar devices have been developed since Bem's pioneering work. Armed with these devices for measuring androgyny, a number of researchers have investigated how androgynous individuals compare with strongly gender-typed people.

A number of studies indicate that androgynous people are more flexible in their behaviors, are less limited by rigid gender-role assumptions, have higher levels of self-esteem, make better decisions in group settings, have better communication skills, and exhibit more social competence and motivation to achieve than do people who are strongly gender typed or those who score low in both areas (Hirokawa et al., 2004; Kirchmeyer, 1996; Shimonaka et al., 1997). Research also demonstrates that masculine and androgynous people of both sexes are more independent and less likely to have their opinions swayed than are individuals who are strongly identified with the feminine role (Bem, 1975). In fact, both androgyny and high masculinity appear to be adaptive for both sexes at all ages (Sinnott, 1986). However, feminine and androgynous people of both sexes appear to be significantly more nurturing than those who adhere to the masculine role (Bem, 1993; Ray & Gold, 1996).

We need to be cautious about concluding that androgyny is an ideal state, free of potential problems. One study found that masculine-typed males demonstrated better overall emotional adjustment than did androgynous males (Jones et al., 1978). Another study, of college professors in their early careers, found that androgynous individuals exhibited greater personal satisfaction but more job-related stress than those who were strongly gender typed (Rotheram & Weiner, 1983). In a large sample of college students, masculine personality characteristics were also more closely associated with being versatile and adaptable than was the trait of androgyny (Lee & Scheurer, 1983). Other studies have also indicated that it may be masculinity, not femininity or androgyny, that is most closely associated with successful adjustment and positive self-esteem

(Ungar & Crawford, 1992; D. Williams & D'Alessandro, 1994). This may be "because masculine attributes are viewed more positively and consequently lead to greater social rewards" (Burn et al., 1996, p. 420). Thus, although androgyny is often associated with emotional, social, and behavioral competence, more information is necessary for a complete picture of its effect on personal adjustment and satisfaction.

Androgynous individuals, both male and female, seem to have more positive attitudes toward sexuality and are more aware of and expressive of feelings of love than are individuals who are traditionally gender typed (Ganong & Coleman, 1987; Walfish & Myerson, 1980). Androgynous people also appear to be more tolerant and less likely to judge or criticize the sexual behaviors of others (Garcia, 1982). Studies have found that androgynous women are more orgasmic and experience more sexual satisfaction than do feminine-typed women (Kimlicka et al., 1983; Radlove, 1983). However, two separate investigations have revealed that masculine males are significantly more comfortable with sex than are androgynous females, indicating that biological sex may still exert a stronger effect than gender typing (Allgeier, 1981; Walfish & Myerson, 1980).

Our own guess is that androgynous people tend to be flexible and comfortable in their sexuality. We would expect such people, whether men or women, to have great capacity to enjoy both the emotional and the physical aspects of sexual intimacy. Androgynous lovers are probably comfortable both initiating and responding to invitations for sexual sharing, and they are probably not significantly limited by preconceived notions of who must do what—and how—during their lovemaking. These observations are supported by research indicating that androgynous couples experience more emotional and sexual satisfaction and personal commitment in their relationships than do gender-typed couples (Rosenzweig & Daily, 1989; Stephen & Harrison, 1985).

Research on androgyny continues, and we certainly have good reasons to be cautious about an unequivocally enthusiastic endorsement of this behavioral style. Nevertheless, evidence collected thus far suggests that people who can transcend traditional gender roles are able to function more comfortably and effectively in a wider range of situations. Androgynous individuals can select from a broad repertoire of feminine and masculine behaviors. They can choose to be independent, assertive, nurturing, or tender, based not on gender-role norms but rather on what provides them and others with optimum personal satisfaction in a given situation.

Summary

Male and Female, Masculine and Feminine

- The processes by which our maleness and femaleness are determined and the manner in which they influence our behavior, sexual and otherwise, are highly complex.
- Sex refers to our biological maleness or femaleness, as reflected in various physical attributes (chromosomes, reproductive organs, genitals, and so forth).
- Gender is a term or concept that encompasses the behaviors, socially constructed roles, and psychological attributes commonly associated with being male or female. Our ideas of masculinity and femininity involve gender assumptions about behavior based on a person's sex.

- Gender identity refers to each person's subjective sense of being male or female.
- Gender role refers to a collection of attitudes and behaviors a specific culture considers normal and appropriate for people of a particular sex.
- Gender roles establish sex-related behavioral expectations, which are culturally defined and therefore vary from society to society and from era to era.

Gender-Identity Formation

- Research efforts to isolate the many biological factors that influence a person's gender identity have resulted in the identification of six biological categories, or levels: chromosomal sex, gonadal sex, hormonal sex, sex of the internal reproductive structures, sex of the external genitals, and sex differentiation of the brain.

- Under normal conditions these six biological variables interact harmoniously to determine our biological sex. However, errors can occur at any of the six levels. The resulting irregularities in the development of a person's biological sex can seriously complicate acquisition of a gender identity.
- The social-learning interpretation of gender-identity formation suggests that our identification with either masculine or feminine roles results primarily from the social and cultural models and influences to which we are exposed.
- Most theorists embrace an interactional model in which gender identity is seen as a result of a complex interplay of biological and social-learning factors.

Transsexualism and Transgenderism

- A transsexual is a person whose gender identity is opposite to his or her biological sex.
- The term *transgendered* is generally applied to individuals whose appearance and behaviors do not conform to the gender roles society ascribes to people of a particular sex.
- Most transsexuals are heterosexually oriented. The transgendered community has a more eclectic composition of gay men, lesbians, bisexuals, and heterosexuals.
- The scientific community has not reached a consensus about the causes and best treatment for transsexualism. Some transsexuals have successfully undergone sex-reassignment procedures in which their bodies are altered to match their gender identities.

Gender Roles

- Widely accepted gender-role assumptions can begin to function as stereotypes, which are notions about what people are like based not on their individuality but on their inclusion in a general category, such as age or sex.
- Many common gender-based stereotypes in our society encourage us to prejudge others and restrict our opportunities.

- Socialization is the process by which society conveys its behavioral expectations to us.
- Ethnic variations in gender roles are observed among Hispanic Americans, African Americans, and Asian Americans.
- Parents, peers, schools, books, television, and religion all act as agents in the socialization of gender roles.
- Gender-role expectations can have a profound effect on our sexuality. Our assessment of ourselves as sexual beings, the expectations we have for intimate relationships, our perception of the quality of such experiences, and the responses of others to our sexuality are all significantly influenced by our own perceptions of our gender roles.

Transcending Gender Roles: Androgyny

- Androgynous individuals are people who have moved beyond traditional gender roles by integrating aspects associated with both masculinity and femininity into their lifestyles.

Media Resources

Log in to CengageBrain.com to access the resources your instructor requires.

Go to CengageBrain.com to access Psychology CourseMate, where you will find an interactive eBook, glossaries, flashcards, quizzes, videos, and more.

Also access links to chapter-related websites, including **Gender Talk, Intersex Society of North America (ISNA), Ingersoll Gender Center, Bodies Like Ours, International Foundation for Gender Education, Gender Inn,** and **World Professional Association for Transgender Health.**

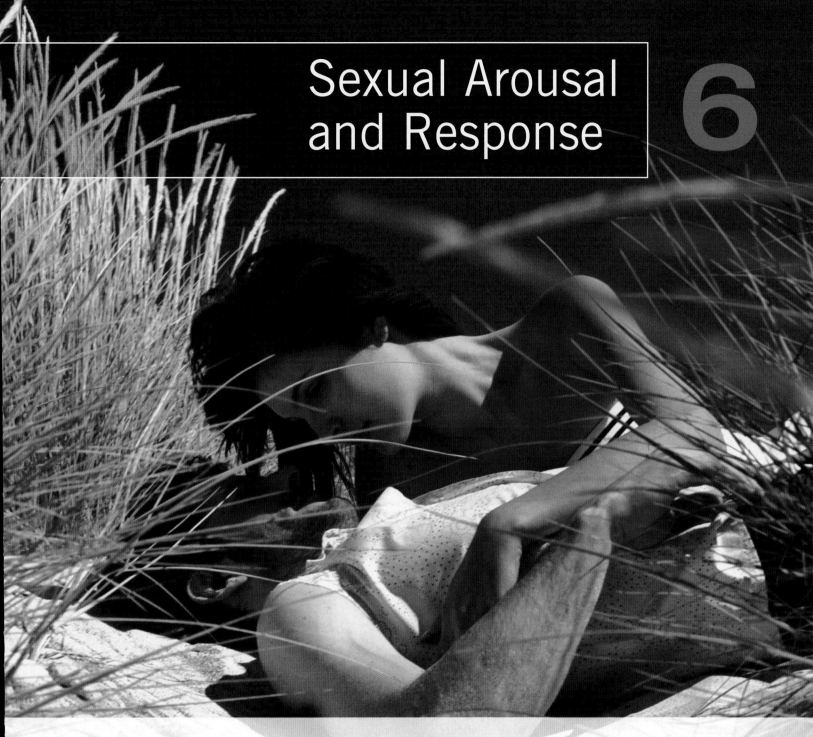

Sexual Arousal and Response

6

The Brain and Sexual Arousal
In what ways does the brain influence sexual arousal?

The Senses and Sexual Arousal
How do the senses of touch, vision, smell, taste, and hearing contribute to erotic arousal?

Aphrodisiacs and Anaphrodisiacs in Sexual Arousal
What substances have been shown to either heighten or reduce sexual arousal?

The Role of Hormones in Sexual Behavior
What is the role of hormones in human sexual arousal?

Sexual Response
What common physiological changes accompany each stage of the sexual response cycles?

Aging and the Sexual Response Cycle
What common variations occur in the sexual response cycles of older women and men?

Differences Between the Sexes in Sexual Response
What are some of the significant differences between the sexes in response patterns?

Stephen Orsillo/Shutterstock.com

There was never any heat or passion in my five-year relationship with Doug. He was a nice man, but I could never bridge the gap between us, which was due, in large part, to his unwillingness or inability to let go and express his feelings and vulnerability. Our lovemaking was like that too—kind of mechanical, as though he was there physically but not emotionally. I seldom felt any sexual desire for Doug, and sometimes my body barely responded during sex. How different it is with Matt, my current and, hopefully, lifetime partner. There was an almost instant closeness and intimacy at the beginning of our relationship. The first time we made love I felt like I was on fire. It was like we were melded together, both physically and emotionally. Sometimes just hearing his voice or the slightest touch arouses me intensely. (Authors' files)

Sexual arousal and sexual response in humans are influenced by many factors: our brain's capacity to create images and fantasies, our emotions, various sensory processes, hormones, the level of intimacy between two people, and a host of other influences. We begin this chapter by discussing some of the things that influence sexual arousal. We then turn our attention to ways our bodies respond to sexual stimulation. We concentrate primarily on biological factors and events associated with human sexual arousal and response, but by focusing on physiology we do not mean to minimize the importance of psychological and cultural influences. In fact, psychosocial factors probably play a greater role than biological factors do in the extremely varied patterns of human sexual response, as we will discover in later chapters. However, it is always difficult, if not impossible, to differentiate between the complementary roles of psychological and biological factors as they influence our sexuality. How do you separate the rich diversity of psychological influences from where they are collected, interpreted, and stored in the human nervous system? Clearly, the expression of our sexuality is determined by a complex interplay or interaction among social, emotional, and cognitive factors; hormones; brain neurons; and spinal reflexes. Furthermore, an improved understanding of the various influences that help to shape our individual patterns of sexual arousal and response can add an important dimension to our expanding sexual intelligence.

The Brain and Sexual Arousal

The brain plays an important role in our sexuality. Our thoughts, emotions, and memories are all mediated through the brain's complex mechanisms. Sexual arousal can occur without any sensory stimulation; it can result from *fantasy* (for example, thinking of erotic images or sexual interludes). Some individuals can even reach orgasm during a fantasy experience without any physical stimulation (Komisaruk et al., 2006; Whipple & Komisaruk, 1999).

We know that specific events can cause us to become aroused. Less apparent is the role of individual experience and cultural influence, both of which are mediated by our brains. Clearly, we do not all respond similarly to the same stimuli. Some people can become highly aroused if their partners use explicit sexual language; others find such words threatening or a sexual turnoff. Cultural influences also play an important role. For example, the smell of genital secretions may be more arousing to many Europeans than to members of our own deodorant-conscious society. Before turning to a more detailed discussion of the brain and sexual arousal, we take a brief look at cultural influences on sexual arousal in the following Sexuality and Diversity discussion.

Although the biological mechanisms underlying human sexual arousal and response are essentially universal, the particular sexual stimuli and/or behaviors that people find arousing are greatly influenced by cultural conditioning. For example, in Western societies, in which the emphasis during sexual activity tends to be heavily weighted toward achieving orgasm, genitally focused activities are frequently defined as optimally arousing. In contrast, in some Asian societies sexual practices are interwoven with spiritual traditions of Hinduism, Buddhism, and Taoism, in which the *primary* goal of sexual interaction is not the mere achievement of orgasm but an extension of sexual arousal for long periods of time, often several hours (Stubbs, 1992). Devotees of Eastern Tantric traditions often achieve optimal pleasure by emphasizing the sensual and spiritual aspects of shared intimacy rather than orgasmic release (Michaels & Johnson, 2006; Richard, 2002).

In many non-Western societies, especially some African cultures, female orgasm is either rare or completely unknown (Ecker, 1993). Furthermore, in some of these societies, vaginal lubrication is negatively evaluated, and male partners may complain about it (Ecker, 1993).

Even in American society, ethnicity influences sexual response, and its effect is evident in female orgasm rates reported in the National Health and Social Life Survey (NHSLS). In this study 38% of African American women reported that they always have an orgasm during sexual interaction with their primary partner, compared with 26% of White American women and 34% of Hispanic women (Laumann et al., 1994). In the following paragraphs, we provide brief examples of some other facets of cultural diversity in human sexual arousal.

Kissing on the mouth, a universal source of sexual arousal in Western society, is rare or absent in many other parts of the world. Certain North American Inuit people and inhabitants of the Trobriand Islands would rather rub noses than lips, and among the Thonga of South Africa kissing is viewed as odious behavior. Hindu people of India are also disinclined to kiss because they believe that such contact symbolically contaminates the act of sexual intercourse. In their survey of 190 societies, Clellan Ford and Frank Beach (1951) found that mouth kissing was acknowledged in only 21 societies and was practiced as a prelude or accompaniment to coitus in only 13.

Oral sex (both cunnilingus and fellatio) is a common source of sexual arousal among island societies of the South Pacific, in industrialized nations of Asia, and in much of the Western world. In contrast, in Africa (with the exception of northern regions), such practices are likely to be viewed as unnatural or disgusting.

Foreplay in general, whether it be oral sex, sensual touching, or passionate kissing, is subject to wide cultural variation. In some societies, most notably those with Eastern traditions, couples strive to prolong intense states of sexual arousal for several hours (Devi, 1977). Although varied patterns of foreplay are common in Western cultures, these activities are often of short duration, as lovers move rapidly toward the "main event" of coitus. In still other societies foreplay is either sharply curtailed or absent altogether. For example, the Lepcha farmers of the southeastern Himalayas limit foreplay to men briefly caressing their partners' breasts, and among the Irish inhabitants of Inis Beag, precoital sexual activity is reported to be limited to mouth kissing and rough fondling of the woman's lower body by her partner (Messenger, 1971).

Another indicator of cultural diversity is the wide variety in standards of attractiveness. Although physical qualities exert a profound influence on human sexual arousal in virtually every culture, standards of attractiveness vary widely, as can be seen in the accompanying photos of women and men from around the world who are considered attractive in their own cultures. What may be attractive or a source of erotic arousal in

Our standards of physical attractiveness vary widely, as can be seen in these six photos of women and men from around the world who are considered attractive in their cultures.

one culture may seem strange or unattractive in others. For instance, although some island societies attach erotic significance to the shape and textures of female genitals, most Western societies do not. To cite a final example, in many societies, bare female breasts are not generally viewed as erotic stimuli, as they are in the United States.

The brain is the storehouse of our memories and cultural values, and consequently its influence over our sexual arousability is profound. Strictly mental events, such as fantasies, are the product of the **cerebral cortex**, the outer layer of the cerebral hemispheres that is responsible for higher mental processes. The cerebral cortex represents only one level of functioning at which the brain influences human sexual arousal and response. At a subcortical level the **limbic system** seems to play an important part in determining sexual behavior, both in humans and in other animals.

▌Figure 6.1 shows some key structures in the limbic system. These include the *cingulate gyrus*, the *amygdala*, the *hippocampus*, and parts of the *hypothalamus*, which plays a regulating role. Research links various sites in the limbic system with sexual behavior (Arnow et al., 2002; Karama et al., 2002; Stark, 2005). Investigators have begun to use functional magnetic resonance imaging (fMRI) technology to record brain activity during sexual arousal. This research, described in the Spotlight on Research box, has provided further evidence of the involvement of the limbic system in sexual responding.

Evidence indicates that electrical stimulation of the hypothalamus in human subjects produces sexual arousal, sometimes culminating in orgasm. Medical researcher

cerebral cortex
The outer layer of the brain's cerebrum that controls higher mental processes

limbic system
A subcortical brain system composed of several interrelated structures that influences the sexual behavior of humans and other animals.

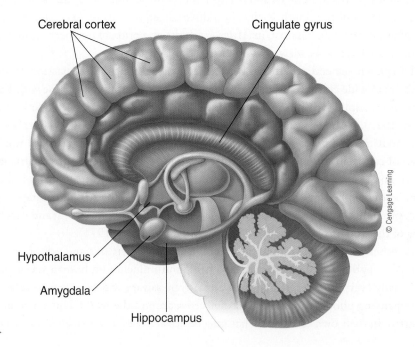

▌**Figure 6.1** The limbic system, a region of the brain associated with emotion and motivation, is important in human sexual function. Key structures, shaded in color, include the cingulate gyrus, portions of the hypothalamus, the amygdala, and the hippocampus.

Monitoring Brain Function During Sexual Arousal With Functional Magnetic Resonance Imaging

Cutting-edge research has demonstrated the benefits of using a powerful technology to map or record brain activity during sexual arousal. *Functional magnetic resonance imaging (fMRI)* is a research and diagnostic device that provides images of the soft tissues of the brain, blood flow in various brain regions, and indications of which regions of the brain activate or "light up" (via accelerated neuron firing) during various mental processes, such as thinking or emoting. Researchers have demonstrated that fMRI can be used to record brain activity during sexual arousal of either sex (Arnow et al., 2002; Holstege et al., 2003; Karama et al., 2002; Whipple & Komisaruk, 2006).

In one study, male and female subjects viewed erotic video clips while undergoing fMRI scanning (Karama et al., 2002). Brain activation in regions of the limbic system, especially pronounced in the amygdala, was observed in both sexes. In another experiment, men viewed erotic video clips while being scanned in an MRI machine. Brain activation during sexual arousal was observed in these research subjects, especially in the hypothalamus and cingulate gyrus, both limbic system structures (Arnow et al., 2002). Another study used fMRI scanning to record brain activity during women's orgasmic responses. Heightened levels of brain activation were observed in several areas of the limbic system, including the hypothalamus, amygdala, hippocampus, and cingulate gyrus (Komisaruk et al., 2006; Whipple & Komisaruk, 2006).

The results of these and similar studies demonstrate that fMRI technology offers an excellent tool for monitoring the brain during sexual arousal and response. Clearly this technology holds great promise for advancing our understanding of the role of the brain in our sexuality.

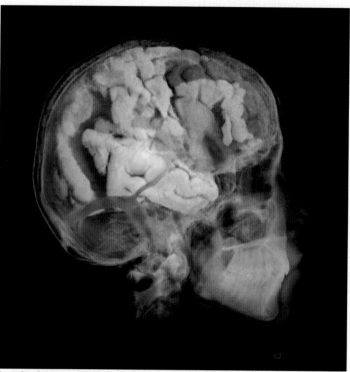

Source: Barry R. Komisaruk, Ph.D., Rutgers University Psychology Department. Imaging by TheVisualMD.com

Robert Heath (1972) experimented with limbic system stimulation in patients suffering from various disorders. He theorized that stimulation-induced pleasure would prove to have some therapeutic value. One patient, a man with an emotional disorder, was provided with a self-stimulation device that he used up to 1,500 times per hour to administer stimulation to an area in his limbic system. He described the stimulation as producing intense sexual pleasure, protesting each time the unit was taken away from him. Another patient, a woman with an epileptic disorder, reported intense sexual pleasure and experienced multiple orgasmic responses as a direct result of brain stimulation.

Several studies have implicated the hypothalamus in sexual functioning. When certain parts of the hypothalamus are surgically destroyed, the sexual behavior of both males and females of several species can be dramatically reduced (Paredes & Baum, 1997). One region in the preoptic area of the hypothalamus, the *medial preoptic area (MPOA)*, has been implicated in sexual arousal and sexual behavior. Electrical stimulation of the MPOA increases sexual behavior, and damage to this area reduces or eliminates sexual activity in males of a wide variety of species (Stark, 2005). Opiate drugs, such as heroin and morphine, have a suppressive effect on the MPOA and are known to inhibit sexual performance in both sexes (Argiolas, 1999).

dopamine
A neurotransmitter that facilitates sexual arousal and activity.

serotonin
A neurotransmitter that inhibits sexual arousal and activity.

Certain naturally occurring brain substances, called *neurotransmitters* (chemicals that transmit messages in the nervous system), are also known to influence sexual arousal and response by their effect on the MPOA. One of these transmitter substances, **dopamine**, induces neural activity in the MPOA that has a facilitatory effect on sexual arousal and response in males of many species (Giargiari et al., 2005; Wilson, 2003). Furthermore, testosterone is known to stimulate the release of dopamine in the MPOA in both males and females (Wilson, 2003). This finding indicates one possible mechanism by which testosterone stimulates libido in both sexes.

In contrast to the facilitatory impact of dopamine on sexual behavior, the neurotransmitter **serotonin** appears to inhibit sexual activity. Male ejaculation causes a release of serotonin in both the MPOA and the *lateral hypothalamus*, an area on the sides of the hypothalamus. This released serotonin temporarily reduces sex drive and behavior by inhibiting the release of dopamine (Hull et al., 1999). Serotonin also suppresses sexual arousal by blocking the action of oxytocin (Wilson, 2003). Humans who suffer from depression are often provided antidepressant medications called *selective serotonin reuptake inhibitors* (SSRIs). These drugs, whose effect is to increase serotonin levels in the brain, often interfere with libido and sexual response. Research has shown that SSRIs diminish genital sensitivity and reduce orgasmic capacity in both sexes (Bahrick, 2008).

Collectively these various findings provide strong evidence that dopamine facilitates sexual arousal and activity in women and men, whereas serotonin appears to provide an inhibitory effect on both sexes.

It is doubtful that researchers will ever find one specific "sex center" in the brain. However, it is clear that both the cerebral cortex and the limbic system play important roles in initiating, organizing, and controlling human sexual arousal and response. In addition, the brain interprets a variety of sensory inputs that often exert a profound influence on sexual arousal. We examine this topic in the next section.

The Senses and Sexual Arousal

It has been said that the brain is the most important sense organ for human sexual arousal. This observation implies that any sensory event, if so interpreted by the brain, can serve as an effective sexual stimulus. The resulting variety in the sources of erotic stimulation helps explain the tremendous sexual complexity of humans.

Of the major senses, touch tends to predominate during sexual intimacy. However, all the senses have the potential to become involved; sights, smells, sounds, and tastes can all be important contributors to erotic arousal. There are no blueprints for the *what* and *how* of sensory stimulation. Each of us is unique; we have our own individual triggers of arousal.

Touch

Stimulation of the various skin surfaces is probably a more frequent source of human sexual arousal than any other type of sensory stimulus. The nerve endings that respond to touch are distributed unevenly throughout the body, which explains why certain areas are more sensitive than others. Those locations that are most responsive to tactile pleasuring are commonly referred to as the **erogenous zones**. A distinction is often made between primary erogenous zones and secondary erogenous zones.

Primary erogenous zones are those areas that contain dense concentrations of nerve endings. A list of primary erogenous zones generally includes the genitals, buttocks, anus, perineum, breasts (particularly the nipples), inner surfaces of the thighs, armpits, navel, neck, ears (especially the lobes), and the mouth (lips, tongue, and the

erogenous zones
Areas of the body that are particularly responsive to sexual stimulation.

primary erogenous zones
Areas of the body that contain dense concentrations of nerve endings.

entire oral cavity). It is important to remember, however, that just because a given area qualifies as a primary erogenous zone does not guarantee that stimulating it will produce arousal in a sexual partner. What is intensely arousing for one person may produce no reaction—or even irritation—in another.

Secondary erogenous zones are other areas of the body that have taken on erotic significance through sexual conditioning. Secondary erogenous zones include virtually all other regions of the body aside from the primary erogenous zones named earlier. For example, if your lover tenderly kissed and stroked your upper back during each sexual interlude, this area could be transformed into an erogenous zone. Such secondary locations become eroticized because they are touched within the context of sexual intimacies. A man and a woman describe how touch enhances their sexual experiences:

PhotoAlto/Katarina Sundelin/Getty Images

Sensual touching is one of the most frequent sources of erotic stimulation.

> I love being touched all over, particularly on my back. Each touch helps to develop trust and a sense of security. (Authors' files)

secondary erogenous zones
Areas of the body that have become erotically sensitive through learning and experience.

> Soft touches, not necessarily genital, arouse me most. When he lightly traces my neck and back with his fingers, my nerves become highly sensitive, and my entire body starts tingling with arousal. (Authors' files)

Vision

In our society visual stimuli appear to be of great importance. Prime evidence is the emphasis we often place on physical appearance, including such activities as personal grooming, wearing the right clothes, and the extensive use of cosmetics. Therefore it is not surprising that vision is second only to touch in the hierarchy of stimuli that most people view as sexually arousing.

The popularity of sexually explicit men's magazines in our society suggests that the human male is more aroused by visual stimuli than is the female. Early research seemed to support this conclusion. Kinsey found that more men than women reported being sexually excited by visual stimuli, such as pinup erotica and stag shows (Kinsey et al., 1948, 1953). However, this finding reflects several social influences, including the greater cultural inhibitions attached to such behavior in women at the time of his research and the simple fact that men had been provided with far more opportunities to develop an appetite for such stimuli. Furthermore, many women found the old-style porn films and videos, which were made to appeal exclusively to men, to be offensive and insensitive and thus not something they would acknowledge as a source of sexual arousal (Striar & Bartlik, 2000). This interpretation is supported by later research that used physiological recording devices (see Chapter 2) to measure sexual arousal under controlled laboratory conditions. These studies have demonstrated strong similarities in the physical responses of males and females to visual erotica (Murnen & Stockton, 1997; Rubinsky et al., 1987). Most women display physiologically measurable arousal while watching erotic films, even those who report no feelings of being aroused (Laan & Everaerd, 1996). Research findings suggest that when sexual arousal is measured by self-reports rather than by physiological devices, women are less inclined than men to report being sexually aroused by visual erotica (Chivers et al., 2010; Koukounas & McCabe, 1997). This finding could reflect the persistence of cultural influences that make women reluctant to acknowledge being aroused by filmed erotica, or it could indicate that females have greater difficulty than males identifying signs of sexual arousal in their bodies, or it could be a combination of these factors.

Critical Thinking Question

It has been said that women enjoy hugging and touching more than genital sex, whereas men have little interest in the "preliminaries," preferring to "get down to the real thing." Do you believe this statement reflects a genuine difference between the sexes? If so, is it learned or biologically determined?

Smell

A person's sexual history and cultural conditioning often influence what smells he or she finds arousing. We typically learn through experience to view certain odors as erotic and others as offensive. From this perspective there may be nothing intrinsic to the fragrance of genital secretions that causes them to be perceived as either arousing or distasteful. We might also argue the contrary—that the smell of genital secretions would be universally exciting to humans were it not for conditioning that taught some people to view it as offensive. This latter interpretation is supported by the fact that some societies openly recognize the value of genital smells as a sexual stimulant. For example, in areas of Europe where the deodorant industry is less pervasive, some women use the natural bouquet of their genital secretions, strategically placed behind an ear or in the nape of the neck, to arouse their sexual partners.

Two people describe the impact of smell on their sexuality:

> Sometimes my partner exudes a sex smell that makes me instantly aroused. (Authors' files)

> There is really something stimulating about the scent of a woman, and I enjoy both the smell and taste of a woman's skin. (Authors' files)

The near obsession many people in our society have with masking natural body odors makes it difficult to study the effects of these smells. Any natural odors that might trigger arousal tend to be well disguised by frequent bathing, perfumes, deodorants, and antiperspirants. Nevertheless, each person's unique experiences allow certain smells to acquire erotic significance, as the following anecdote reveals:

> I love the smells after making love. They trigger little flashes of erotic memories and often keep my arousal level in high gear, inducing me to go on to additional sexual activities. (Authors' files)

In a society that is often concerned about natural odors, it is nice to see that some people appreciate scents associated with sexual intimacy and their lovers' bodies.

pheromones
Certain odors produced by the body that relate to reproductive functions.

The females of many species secrete certain substances, called **pheromones** (FARE-oh-mones), during their fertile periods (Rako & Friebely, 2004; Wyatt, 2003). Two anatomically distinct sites in the human nose may be involved in pheromonal receptivity (Shah & Breedlove, 2007). These two sites are the *vomeronasal organ* (VNO) and the *olfactory epithelium* (OE). Both of these areas transmit neural messages to the brain. A number of studies indicate that these sites in human noses can detect and respond to pheromones (Rako & Friebely, 2004; Savic et al., 2005; Touhara & Vosshall, 2009). In one study, Swedish researchers isolated two substances suspected of being human pheromones: *Estratetraenol* (EST), an estrogenlike chemical found in female urine, and *androstadienone* (AND), a derivative of testosterone found in men's sweat. Using fMRI and PET (positron emission tomography) brain scans, these scientists found that exposure to EST activated ("lit up") the hypothalamuses of heterosexual men but not heterosexual women, whereas smelling AND activated this brain structure in women but not men. (As described earlier in this chapter, the hypothalamus is implicated in sexual functioning.) One additional finding of interest in this study is that when the brains of gay men were scanned, their hypothalamuses responded to AND and EST in a similar way to those of the heterosexual female subjects (Savic et al., 2005).

Although mounting evidence suggests that humans do indeed secrete pheromones, there is insufficient evidence to determine whether these substances act as sexual attractants. Undaunted by the inconclusive nature of the available data, a number of American and international corporations have invested in the commercial development and marketing of perfumes and colognes allegedly containing substances that possess human pheromone properties (Cutler, 1999; Kohl, 2002). However, the jury is still out on whether these products contain genuine sexual-attractant pheromones.

Taste

Taste, which has yet to be fully investigated, seems to play a relatively minor role in human sexual arousal. This is no doubt at least partly influenced by industry advertisements that promote breath mints and flavored vaginal douches. Besides making many individuals extremely self-conscious about how they taste or smell, such commercial products can mask any natural tastes that relate to sexual activity. Nevertheless, some people can still detect and appreciate certain tastes that they learn to associate with sexual intimacy, such as the taste of vaginal secretions or semen.

Hearing

Whether people make sounds during sexual activity is highly variable, as is a partner's response. Some people find words, intimate or erotic conversation, moans, and orgasmic cries to be highly arousing; others prefer that their lovers keep silent during sex play. Some people, out of fear or embarrassment, make a conscious effort to suppress spontaneous noises during sexual interaction. Because of the silent, stoic image accepted by many males, it may be exceedingly difficult for men in particular to talk, cry out, or groan during arousal. Female reluctance to emit sounds during sex play might be influenced by the notion that "nice" women are not supposed to be so passionate that they make noises.

Besides being sexually arousing, talking to each other during a sexual interlude can be informative and helpful ("I like it when you touch me that way," "A little softer," and so on). If you happen to be a person who enjoys noisemaking and verbalizations during sex, your partner may respond this way if you discuss the matter beforehand. We will discuss talking about sexual preferences in Chapter 7.

Two people describe how sounds affect their lovemaking:

> It is very important for me to hear that my partner is enjoying the experience. A woman who doesn't mind moaning is a pleasure to be with. It is good to be with someone who does not mind opening up and letting you know she is enjoying you. If my partner doesn't provide enough voice communication with sex, forget it. (Authors' files)

> I like to hear our bodies slapping together as we make love and to hear him moan and groan for more. I also like to hear my name being called, and I like to say his. (Authors' files)

Critical Thinking Question

In your opinion, which of the senses has the greatest impact on sexual arousal and sexual interaction? Why? Do men and women differ in terms of which senses predominate during sexual intimacy?

Aphrodisiacs and Anaphrodisiacs in Sexual Arousal

Up to this point, we have considered the impact of brain processes and sensory input on human sexual arousal. Several other factors can also affect a person's arousability in a particular situation. Some of these directly affect the physiology of arousal; others can have a strong impact on a person's sexuality through the power of belief. In the pages that follow we examine the effects of a number of products that people use to attempt to heighten or reduce sexual arousal.

Aphrodisiacs: Do They Work?

aphrodisiac
A substance that allegedly arouses sexual desire and increases the capacity for sexual activity.

An **aphrodisiac** (a-fruh-DEE-zee-ak; named after Aphrodite, the Greek goddess of love and beauty) is a substance that supposedly arouses sexual desire or increases a person's capacity for sexual activities. Almost from the beginning of time, people have searched for magic potions and other agents to revive flagging erotic interest or to produce Olympian sexual performances. That many have reported finding such sexual stimulants bears testimony, once again, to the powerful role of the mind in human sexual activity. We first consider a variety of foods that have been held to possess aphrodisiac qualities, and then we turn our attention to other alleged sexual stimulants, including alcohol and an assortment of chemical substances.

Almost any food that resembles the male external genitals has at one time or another been viewed as an aphrodisiac (Foley, 2006; Nordenberg, 2008). Many of us have heard the jokes about oysters, although for some a belief in the special properties of this particular shellfish is no joking matter. One wonders to what extent the oyster industry profits from this pervasive myth. Other foods sometimes considered aphrodisiacs include bananas, asparagus, cucumbers, tomatoes, ginseng root, and potatoes (Castleman, 1997; Nordenberg, 2008). Particularly in Asian countries, a widespread belief persists that the ground-up horns of animals such as rhinoceros and reindeer are powerful sexual stimulants (Foley, 2006). (Have you ever used the term *horny* to describe a sexual state? Now you know its origin.) Unfortunately, the rhinoceros population in Africa has dwindled to the point of near extinction, largely as a result of the erroneous belief that rhinoceros horn is an effective aphrodisiac.

A number of drugs are also commonly thought to have aphrodisiac properties. Of these drugs, perhaps more has been written about the supposed stimulant properties of alcohol than about any other presumed aphrodisiac substance. In our culture the belief in the erotic enhancement properties of alcoholic beverages is widespread:

> I am a great believer in the sexual benefits of drinking wine. After a couple glasses I become a real "hound in bed." I can always tell my partner is in the mood when she brings out a bottle of chilled rosé. (Authors' files)

Far from being a stimulant, alcohol has a depressing effect on higher brain centers and thus reduces cortical inhibitions, such as fear and guilt, that often block sexual expression (McKay, 2005; Prause et al., 2011). Alcohol can also impair our ability to cognitively process information (e.g., values and expectations for behavioral consequences) that might otherwise put the brakes on sexual impulses. In addition, alcohol can facilitate sexual activity by providing a convenient rationalization for behavior that might normally conflict with one's values ("I just couldn't help myself, with my mind fogged by booze"), and by reducing anxiety that may accompany sexual activity (Ryan-Berg, 2011).

Consumption of significant amounts of alcohol, however, can have serious negative effects on sexual functioning. Research has demonstrated that with increasing levels of intoxication both men and women experience reduced sexual arousal (as measured physiologically), decreased pleasurability and intensity of orgasm, and increased difficulty in attaining orgasm (McKay, 2005; Rosen & Ashton, 1993). Heavy alcohol use can also result in general physical deterioration, which commonly reduces a person's interest in and capacity for sexual activity.

Alcohol use can have even more serious potential consequences in conjunction with sexual activity. Research has demonstrated a strong association between alcohol use and an inclination to participate in sexual practices that have a high risk for contracting a life-threatening disease, such as AIDS. (Other mind-altering drugs, such as marijuana and cocaine, have also been implicated in high-risk sexual behavior.) ●

In addition to alcohol, several other drugs have been ascribed aphrodisiac qualities. Some of the substances included in this category are amphetamines, such as methylene-dioxymethamphetamine (MDMA), commonly known as ecstasy; methamphetamine, often referred to as crystal meth; barbiturates; cantharides, also known as Spanish fly; cocaine; LSD and other psychedelic drugs; marijuana; amyl nitrite (a drug used to treat heart pain), also known as poppers; and L-dopa (a medication used in the treatment of Parkinson's disease). As you can see in the summary provided in ■ Table 6.1, not one of these drugs possesses attributes that qualify it as a true sexual stimulant.

Researchers are investigating one drug that may eventually be shown to have aphrodisiac qualities for at least some people. Since the 1920s, reports have touted the aphrodisiac properties of yohimbine hydrochloride, or yohimbine, a crystalline alkaloid derived from the sap of the yohimbe tree, which grows in West Africa. Several recent studies with male humans suggest that yohimbine treatment has the capacity to positively affect sexual desire and response (Adeniyi et al., 2007; Riley, 2010; Stein et al., 2008). Another study also demonstrated that yohimbine increases physiologically measured sexual arousal in postmenopausal women who report below-normal levels of sexual desire (Meston & Worcel, 2002).

Three prescription drugs used to treat male erectile dysfunction—Viagra, Levitra, and Cialis—may technically be classified as aphrodisiacs in that they increase capacity for sexual activity by facilitating genital vasocongestion and erection (see Chapter 14). None of these drugs increases sexual desire.

In view of the widespread inclination of humans to seek out substances with aphrodisiac qualities, and in light of escalating advances in the realm of sexual medicine, it seems likely that a variety of genuine aphrodisiacs will be available in the future. At present, people continue to use various substances despite clear-cut evidence that they lack true aphrodisiac qualities. Why do so many people around the world swear by the effects of a little powdered rhino horn, that special meal of oysters and banana salad, or the marijuana cigarette before an evening's dalliance? The answer lies in faith and suggestion; these are the ingredients frequently present when aphrodisiac claims are made. If a person believes that something will improve his or her sex life, this faith is often translated into the subjective enhancement of sexual pleasure. From this perspective, literally anything has the potential of serving as a sexual stimulant. Consistent with this perspective is Theresa Crenshaw's (1996) cogent observation that "love, however you define it, seems to be the best aphrodisiac of all" (p. 89).

Anaphrodisiacs

Several drugs are known to inhibit sexual behavior. Substances that have this effect are called **anaphrodisiacs** (an-a-fruh-DEE-zee-aks). Common drugs with anaphrodisiac potential include antiandrogens, opiates, tranquilizers, anticoagulants, antihypertensives (blood pressure medicine), antidepressants, antipsychotics, nicotine, birth control

Critical Thinking Question

Assume that research eventually reveals that yohimbine or some other substance has genuine aphrodisiac qualities. What possible benefits might be associated with its use? What possible abuses might arise? Would you consider using an aphrodisiac? If so, under what conditions?

anaphrodisiac
A substance that inhibits sexual desire and behavior.

■ TABLE 6.1 Some Alleged Aphrodisiacs and Their Effects

Name (and Street Name)	Reputed Effect	Actual Effect
Alcohol	Enhances arousal; stimulates sexual activity.	Can reduce inhibitions to make sexual behaviors less stressful. Alcohol is actually a depressant and in quantity can impair erectile ability, arousal, and orgasm.
Amphetamines ("speed," "uppers")	Elevate mood; enhance sexual experience and abilities.	Central nervous system stimulants; amphetamines reduce inhibitions. High doses or long-term use can cause erectile disorder, delayed ejaculation, and inhibition of orgasm in both sexes and can reduce vaginal lubrication in women.
Amyl nitrite ("snappers," "poppers")	Intensifies orgasms and arousal.	Dilates arteries to brain and also to genital area; produces time distortion and warmth in pelvic area. Can decrease sexual arousal, delay orgasm, and inhibit or block erection.
Barbiturates ("barbs," "downers")	Enhance arousal; stimulate sexual activity.	Reduce inhibitions in similar fashion to alcohol and may decrease sexual desire, impair erection, and inhibit ejaculation.
Cantharides ("Spanish fly")	Stimulates genital area, causing person to desire coitus.	Not effective as a sexual stimulant. Cantharides acts as a powerful irritant that can cause inflammation to the lining of the bladder and urethra.
Cocaine ("coke")	Increases frequency and intensity of orgasm; heightens arousal.	Central nervous system stimulant; cocaine loosens inhibitions and enhances sense of well-being. May impair ability to enjoy sex, reduce sexual desire, inhibit erection, or cause spontaneous or delayed ejaculation.
LSD and other psychedelic drugs (including mescaline, psilocybin)	Enhance sexual response.	No direct physiological enhancement of sexual response. Can produce altered perception of sexual activity; frequently associated with unsatisfactory erotic experiences.
L-dopa	Sexually rejuvenates older males.	No documented benefits to sexual ability. L-dopa occasionally produces a painful condition known as priapism (constant, unwanted erection).
Marijuana	Elevates mood and arousal; stimulates sexual activity.	Enhances mood and reduces inhibitions in a way similar to alcohol. Can inhibit sexual response and may distort the time sense, with the resulting illusion of prolonged arousal and orgasm.
Yohimbine	Induces sexual arousal and enhances sexual performance.	Appears to have genuine aphrodisiac effect on rats. Recent evidence suggests it may enhance sexual desire or performance in some humans.

SOURCES: Crenshaw (1996), Crenshaw & Goldberg (1996), Eisner et al. (1990), Finger et al. (1997), McKay (2005), Rosen & Ashton (1993), Shamloul & Bella (2011), and Yates & Wolman (1991).

pills, sedatives, ulcer drugs, appetite suppressants, steroids, anticonvulsants used for treating epilepsy, cardiovascular medications, cholesterol reducers, over-the-counter allergy medicines that cause drowsiness, and drugs for treating cancer, heart disease, fluid retention, and fungus infections (Bahrick, 2008; DeLamater & Sill, 2005).

A great deal of evidence indicates that regular use of opiates, such as heroin, morphine, and methadone, often produces a significant—and sometimes dramatic—decrease in sexual interest and activity in both sexes (Ackerman et al., 1994; Finger et al., 1997). Serious impairment of sexual functioning associated with opiate use can include erectile problems and inhibited ejaculation in males, and reduced capacity to experience orgasm in females.

Tranquilizers, used widely in the treatment of a variety of emotional disorders, have been shown sometimes to reduce sexual motivation, impair erection, and delay or inhibit orgasm in both sexes (Graedon & Graedon, 2008).

Many antihypertensives, drugs used for treating high blood pressure, have been experimentally demonstrated to seriously inhibit erection and ejaculation, reduce the intensity of orgasm in male subjects, and reduce sexual interest in both sexes (DeLamater & Sill, 2005).

Another class of commonly prescribed psychiatric medications, antidepressants, almost without exception cause adverse changes in sexual response. These changes include decreased desire in both sexes, erectile disorder in men, and delayed or absent orgasmic response in both sexes (Bahrick, 2008; Balon & Segraves, 2008). A rare side effect, *spontaneous orgasm*, has been documented in both women and men who are taking antidepressant medications. A number of case studies of this unusual phenomenon have revealed that spontaneous orgasms can occur without sexual sensory stimulation or as a result of nonsexual stimulation (e.g., vibrations from riding a subway or sensations from a bowel movement) (Silverberg, 2008a). While studies have not identified the etiology of spontaneous orgasms, researchers think the cause has something to do with the neurotransmitter serotonin (Silverberg, 2008a).

Antipsychotic drugs are also likely to disrupt sexual response. Potential adverse reactions include erectile disorder and delay of ejaculation in men and orgasm difficulties and reduced sexual desire in both sexes (Finger et al., 1997).

Recent research indicates that men who take the drug finasteride (commonly known as Propecia and Proscar) to treat male pattern hair loss may report a reduction in sexual motivation and erectile dysfunction (Traish et al., 2011). These adverse sexual side effects of finasteride suggest that this drug has anaphrodisiac properties.

Many people are surprised to hear that birth control pills are also commonly associated with reduced sexual desire (Lee et al., 2011). A study of the effects of four different oral contraceptives on various sex hormones found that all four produced a marked reduction in the blood levels of free testosterone (Wiegratz et al., 2003). As discussed in the next section, free testosterone influences both female and male libido. Perhaps the most widely used and least recognized anaphrodisiac is nicotine. There is evidence that smoking can significantly retard sexual motivation and function by constricting the blood vessels (thereby retarding vasocongestive response of the body to sexual stimulation) and perhaps by reducing testosterone levels in the blood (McKay, 2005; Ryan-Berg, 2011).

The Role of Hormones in Sexual Behavior

A number of hormones influence sexuality, sensuality, and interpersonal attraction in humans. Among the most widely discussed are androgens and estrogens, commonly referred to as sex hormones. These substances belong to the general class of **steroid hormones** that are secreted by the gonadal glands (testes and ovaries) and the adrenal glands.

steroid hormones
The sex hormones and the hormones of the adrenal cortex.

No doubt you have heard the common descriptive expressions *male sex hormones* and *female sex hormones*. As we will see, linking specific hormones to one or the other sex is somewhat misleading—*both* sexes produce male and female sex hormones. As discussed in Chapter 5, the general term for male sex hormones is *androgens*. In males about 95% of total androgens are produced by the testes. Most of the remaining 5% are produced by the outer portions of the adrenal glands (called the adrenal cortex). A woman's ovaries and adrenal glands also produce androgens in approximately equal amounts (Davis, 1999; Rako, 1996). The dominant androgen in both males and females is testosterone. Men's bodies typically produce 20 to 40 times more testosterone than women's bodies do (Worthman, 1999). Female sex hormones, estrogens, are produced predominantly by the ovaries in females. Male testes also produce estrogens, but in quantities much smaller than what occurs in female bodies.

neuropeptide hormones
Chemicals produced in the brain that influence sexuality and other behavioral functions.

oxytocin
A neuropeptide produced in the hypothalamus that influences sexual response and interpersonal attraction.

The arousal, attraction, and response components of human sexuality are also influenced by **neuropeptide hormones**, which are produced in the brain. One of the most important neuropeptide hormones, **oxytocin**, is sometimes referred to as a "love hormone"; it appears to influence our erotic and emotional attraction to one another. In the following sections, we discuss research findings that link oxytocin to human sexual attraction, arousal, and behavior. But first we consider the evidence linking testosterone to sexual functioning in both sexes and examine the role of estrogens in female sexuality.

Sex Hormones in Male Sexual Behavior

A number of research studies have linked testosterone with male sexuality (Leprout & Van Cauter, 2011; O'Conner et al., 2011; Shah & Montoya, 2007). This research indicates that testosterone generally has a greater effect on male sexual desire (libido) than on sexual functioning (Crenshaw, 1996). Thus a man with a low testosterone level might have little interest in sexual activity but nevertheless be fully capable of erection and orgasms.

castration
Surgical removal of the testes.

orchidectomy
The surgical procedure for removing the testes.

One source of information about testosterone's effect on male sexual function is studies of men who have undergone **castration**. This operation, called **orchidectomy** in medical language, involves removal of the testes, and it is sometimes performed as medical treatment for such diseases as genital tuberculosis and prostate cancer (Parker & Dearnaley, 2003; Wassersug & Johnson, 2007). Two European studies reported that surgically castrated men experience significantly reduced sexual interest and activity within the first year after undergoing this operation (Bremer, 1959; Heim, 1981). Other researchers have recorded incidences of continued sexual desire and functioning for as long as 30 years following castration, without supplementary testosterone treatment (Greenstein et al., 1995). However, even when sexual behavior persists following castration, the levels of sexual interest and activity generally diminish, often markedly (Bradford, 1998; Rosler & Witztum, 1998). That this reduction occurs so frequently indicates that testosterone is an important biological instigator of sexual desire.

A second line of research investigating links between hormones and male sexual functioning involves androgen-blocking drugs. A class of drugs known as *antiandrogens* has been used in Europe and America to treat sex offenders as well as certain medical conditions, such as prostate cancer (Kafka, 2009; Kelly, 2008). Antiandrogens drastically reduce the amount of testosterone circulating in the bloodstream. One of these drugs, medroxyprogesterone acetate (MPA; also known by its trade name, Depo-Provera), has received a great deal of media attention in the United States. A number of studies have found that MPA and other antiandrogens are often effective in reducing both sexual interest and sexual activity in human males (and females) (Kafka, 2009). However, altering testosterone levels is not a completely effective treatment for sex offenders, especially in cases where sexual assaults stem from nonsexual motives, such as anger or the wish to exert power and control over another person (Kelly, 2008).

hypogonadism
Impaired hormone production in the testes that results in testosterone deficiency.

A third source of evidence linking testosterone to sexual motivation in males is research on **hypogonadism**, a state of testosterone deficiency that results from certain diseases of the endocrine system. Hypogonadism is also associated with the aging process in some older men (Page et al., 2011). If this condition occurs before puberty, maturation of the primary and secondary sex characteristics is retarded, and the individual may never develop an active sexual interest. The results are more variable if testosterone deficiency occurs in adulthood. Extensive studies of hypogonadal men provide strong evidence that testosterone plays an important role in male sexual desire (Corona et al., 2011; Jones et al., 2011; Kaminetsky et al., 2011). For example, hypogonadal men who receive hormone treatments to replace testosterone often experience increased sexual interest and activity (Kaminetsky et al., 2011; Dandona & Dhindsa, 2011; Seftel, 2012).

Sex Hormones in Female Sexual Behavior

Although we know that estrogens contribute to a general sense of well-being, help maintain the thickness and elasticity of the vaginal lining, and contribute to vaginal lubrication (Frank et al., 2008; Kingsberg, 2002), the role of estrogens in female sexual behavior is still unclear. Some researchers have reported that when postmenopausal women (menopause is associated with marked reduction in estrogen production) or women who have had their ovaries removed for medical reasons receive estrogen therapy (ET), they experience not only heightened vaginal lubrication but also somewhat increased sexual desire, pleasure, and orgasmic capacity (Dow et al., 1983; Kingsberg, 2002). The sexual benefits that often result from ET occur because estrogen provides "mood-mellowing" benefits and thus creates an emotional atmosphere receptive to sexual involvement (Crenshaw, 1996; Wilson, 2003). See Chapter 3 for a more detailed discussion of ET, including the link between ET and breast cancer.

Other investigators have found that ET has no discernible impact on sexual desire, and, when estrogen is administered in relatively high doses, it can even decrease libido (Frank et al., 2008; Levin, 2002). In view of these contradictory findings, the role of estrogens in female sexual motivation and functioning remains unclear.

There is less ambiguity about the role of testosterone in female sexuality. Considerable evidence indicates that testosterone plays an important role as a libido facilitating hormone in females (Davis et al., 2008; Tucker, 2004). Clear evidence exists that there is "a testosterone dependent component of women's sexuality . . ." (Bancroft & Graham, 2011, p. 717). Numerous experimental evaluations of the effects of testosterone on female sexuality provide evidence of a causal relationship between levels of circulating testosterone and sexual desire, genital sensitivity, and frequency of sexual activity. For instance, many studies have shown that testosterone replacement therapy enhances sexual desire and arousal in postmenopausal women (Frank et al., 2008; Shah & Montoya, 2007).

Other investigations have found that women who received testosterone or estrogen-testosterone therapy after natural menopause or surgical removal of their ovaries (ovariectomy) experienced remarkably greater levels of sexual desire, sexual arousal, and sexual fantasies than women who received estrogen alone or no hormone therapy after surgery (Nusbaum et al., 2005; Tucker, 2004).

Most of the evidence indicating the importance of testosterone in female sexual functioning has come from studies of women with low levels of this hormone because of ovariectomy, adrenalectomy, or natural menopause. One study of considerable interest sought to determine the effects of supplemental testosterone on the physiological and subjective sexual arousal in a group of sexually functional women with normal hormone levels. The investigators found that sublingually administered testosterone (under-the-tongue tablets) caused a significant increase in genital responsiveness within a few hours and that there was a strong and significant association between the increase in genital arousal and subjective reports of "genital sensation" and "sexual lust" (Tuiten et al., 2000).

Other studies have found that when testosterone is administered to women with a history of low sex drive and inhibited sexual arousal, the reported frequencies of sexual fantasies, masturbation, and satisfying sexual interaction with a partner typically increase (Davis, 2008; Nappi et al., 2011). Furthermore, when researchers compared testosterone levels in a group of healthy, sexually functional women with levels in a group of women with a reported lifetime history of low sex drive, they found evidence linking low libido with reduced testosterone levels. Women in the low-libido group were found to have significantly lower levels of testosterone than those in the sexually functional group (Riley & Riley, 2000).

How Much Testosterone Is Necessary for Normal Sexual Functioning?

Now that we have learned that testosterone plays an important role in maintaining sexual desire in both sexes, we might ask, How much testosterone is necessary to ensure normal sexual arousability? The answer to this question is complex and is influenced by several factors.

Testosterone in the bodies of both sexes comes in two forms: attached (bound) and unattached (free). About 95% of the testosterone circulating in a man's blood is bound on a protein molecule (either albumin or globulin), where it is inactive or metabolically ineffective. The remaining 5% is the unattached version of testosterone, which is metabolically active and influences male libido (Crenshaw, 1996; Donnelly & White, 2000). Comparable figures for women are 97 to 99% bound testosterone and only 1 to 3% free testosterone to produce effects on bodily tissues (Rako, 1996). The sum of free and bound testosterone in each man or woman is total testosterone. The normal range of total testosterone in the blood of a man is 300–1,200 ng/dL (nanograms per deciliter; a nanogram is one-billionth of a gram). In women the normal range of total testosterone is 20–50 ng/dL (Rako, 1996; Winters, 1999). The essential amount, or critical mass, of testosterone necessary for adequate functioning varies from person to person in both sexes. That women normally have much smaller amounts of testosterone than men do does not mean that women have lower or weaker sex drives than men. Rather, women's body cells seem more sensitive to testosterone than men's body cells. Therefore only a little testosterone is necessary to stimulate female libido (Bancroft, 2002; Crenshaw, 1996).

Too much testosterone can have adverse effects on both sexes. Excess testosterone supplements in men can cause a variety of problems, including disruption of natural hormone cycles, salt retention, fluid retention, and hair loss. Furthermore, although no evidence suggests that testosterone causes prostate cancer, excess testosterone can stimulate growth of preexisting prostate cancer (Jannini et al., 2011). In women excess testosterone can stimulate significant growth of facial and body hair, increase muscle mass, reduce breast size, and enlarge the clitoris (Kingsberg, 2002; Shah & Montoya, 2007). However, in most instances only the use of irresponsibly high doses of testosterone over a sustained period of time results in the development of adverse side effects in either sex (Rako, 1999). Furthermore, as we have seen, supplementary testosterone can help restore sexual desire to men and women with deficient levels of this libido hormone.

A normal level of total testosterone in either sex does not necessarily rule out a biological basis for a flagging sex drive, because the key hormonal component in libido—free testosterone—can be abnormally low even though the total testosterone level is within normal limits. Consequently, should you find yourself experiencing testosterone deficiency (see the next section), it is important that, as an informed consumer of health care, you have your free testosterone levels assessed in addition to your total testosterone level. ●

Finally, the rate at which testosterone production diminishes with aging differs markedly in men and women. As commonly happens, when a woman's ovaries begin to shut down at menopause, her total testosterone may fall quickly in just a matter of months. For other women the onset of testosterone deficiency is more gradual, taking place over a period of several years (Kingsberg, 2002). (Women who have their ovaries surgically removed are more likely to experience an abrupt or precipitous loss of testosterone.) When a woman's ovaries are no longer producing normal levels of testosterone, even though her adrenal glands continue to produce testosterone, their output also diminishes (Rako, 1999).

SEXUALHEALTH ▶

In contrast, in men the decline in testosterone with aging is usually much less precipitous. Testosterone production remains stable in most men until around age 40, after which it declines by 1 to 2% each year (Makinen et al., 2011).

The general signs of testosterone deficiency are similar in both sexes, even though they have a more rapid onset in women than in men. The most obvious symptoms of testosterone deficiency are listed in ■ Table 6.2.

Testosterone Replacement Therapy

If you find yourself experiencing some of the symptoms listed in Table 6.2, you might want to seek medical advice regarding possible testosterone replacement therapy (TRT). At present, men generally find it much easier than women to secure medical advice about TRT. The use of testosterone supplements to treat male sexual difficulties is relatively common. In marked contrast, the medical community is often reluctant to prescribe supplementary testosterone for women who manifest symptoms of deficiency. However, a gradual awakening to the benefits of testosterone supplement therapy is under way. In fact, several leading authorities on gynecology and menopause stress the need for educating medical practitioners as well as health-care consumers, especially postmenopausal women, about the use of supplementary testosterone (Gelfand, 2000; Johnson, 2002).

Because of the highly individualized way that both men and women respond to hormones, there is no clear-cut right or wrong approach to TRT. Furthermore, TRT is not necessary for every person whose testosterone levels are lower than normal. Ideally, a person will seek the counsel of an informed physician who will both determine the appropriateness of TRT and work with him or her to find the best dosage and method of administration to effectively alleviate the symptoms of testosterone deficiency.

Testosterone supplements can be administered to men or women orally (swallowing), sublingually (under-the-tongue tablets), by injection, by implantation of a pellet, or by direct application to the skin, using either a testosterone gel formulation or a transdermal skin patch (Morales, 2003; Sinclair & Kligman, 2005). Testosterone can also be applied to women by means of vaginal creams and gels. Experts on TRT caution against taking too much testosterone. Taking a dose greater than necessary to eliminate deprivation symptoms is not likely to improve libido and general energy level and could result in adverse side effects.

At a Glance

■ TABLE 6.2 Common Signs of Testosterone Deficiency in Both Sexes

- Decrease in one's customary level of sexual desire.
- Reduced sensitivity of the genitals and the nipples to sexual stimulation.
- Overall reduction in general levels of sexual arousability, possibly accompanied by decreased orgasmic capacity and/or less intense orgasms.
- Diminished energy levels and possibly depressed mood.
- Increased fat mass.
- Decreased bone mineral density, which can result in osteoporosis in both sexes.
- Reduced body hair.
- Decreased muscle mass and strength.

SOURCES: Cunningham & Toma (2011), McNicholas et al. (2003), Nusbaum et al. (2005), and Sadovsky (2005).

Oxytocin in Male and Female Sexual Behavior

The neuropeptide hormone *oxytocin*, which is produced in the hypothalamus, exerts significant influence on sexual response, sensuality, and interpersonal erotic and emotional attraction (Wade, 2011; Young, 2009). Some refer to oxytocin as the snuggle chemical because its release during breast-feeding facilitates mother–child bonding (Galbally et al., 2011). The release of oxytocin during sexual arousal and response may have a similar bonding effect on sexual partners (Young, 2009).

Oxytocin is secreted during cuddling and physical intimacy, and touch is an especially powerful triggering mechanism for its release (Ishak et al., 2011). Increased levels of circulating oxytocin have been shown to stimulate sexual activity in a variety of animals, including humans (Anderson-Hunt & Dennerstein, 1994; Wilson, 2003). This hormone increases skin sensitivity to touch and thus encourages or facilitates affectionate behavior (Love, 2001; McEwen, 1997). In humans oxytocin levels increase as a person moves through a sexual response cycle from initial excitement to orgasm, and high levels of oxytocin are associated with orgasmic release in both sexes (Anderson-Hunt & Dennerstein, 1994; Wilson, 2003).

The significant escalation of oxytocin release at the point of orgasm, together with the elevated levels of this hormone that remain in the blood for a time afterward, could contribute to the emotional and erotic bonding of sexual partners and to a sense of shared attraction (Young, 2009). Research with human subjects indicates that oxytocin plays an important role in facilitating social attachment with others and in the development and fostering of feelings of being in love (Donaldson & Young, 2008; Tabak et al., 2011). Autistic children, who commonly exhibit a reduced ability to form social attachments and express love, often have significantly reduced levels of oxytocin (Green et al., 2001; Ishak et al., 2011). This finding provides further evidence of the association between oxytocin levels and the capacity to form attachments and loving interactions.

Cuddling and physical intimacy are powerful triggering mechanisms for the release of oxytocin.

Sexual Response

Human sexual response is a highly individual physical, emotional, and mental process. Nevertheless, there are a number of common physiological changes that allow us to outline some general patterns of the sexual response cycle. Masters and Johnson (1966) and Helen Singer Kaplan (1979), a noted sex therapist and author, have described these patterns. We briefly outline Kaplan's ideas before turning to a detailed analysis of Masters and Johnson's work.

Kaplan's Three-Stage Model

Kaplan's model of sexual response, an outgrowth of her extensive experience as a sex therapist, contains three stages: *desire*, *excitement*, and *orgasm* (see ▮ Figure 6.2). Kaplan suggested that sexual difficulties tend to fall into one of these three categories and that it is possible for a person to have difficulty in one while continuing to function normally in the other two.

One of the most distinctive features of Kaplan's model is that it includes desire as a distinct stage of the sexual response cycle. Many other writers, including Masters and Johnson, do not discuss aspects of sexual response that are separate from genital changes. Kaplan's description of desire as a prelude to physical sexual response stands as a welcome addition to the literature. Kaplan's model was initially widely embraced as one that rectified a perceived deficiency in the Masters and Johnson model. However, it is now realized that simply adding a desire phase does not necessarily provide a complete model of human sexual arousal and response. One problem with assuming that desire belongs in such a model is that perhaps as much as 30% of sexually experienced, orgasmic women rarely or never experience spontaneous sexual desire (Levin, 2002). Fewer men appear to be included in this category. For example, in the NHSLS, 33% of women reported being uninterested in sex compared with 16.5% of men (Laumann et al., 1994).

It is clear, then, that not all sexual expression is preceded by desire. For example, a couple might agree to engage in sexual activity even though they are not feeling sexually inclined at the time. Frequently, they may find that their bodies begin to respond sexually to the ensuing activity, despite their lack of initial desire.

Masters and Johnson's Four-Phase Model

Masters and Johnson distinguish four phases in the sexual response patterns of both men and women: *excitement*, *plateau*, *orgasm*, and *resolution*. ▌ Figures 6.3 and 6.4 illustrate these four phases of sexual response. These charts provide basic maps of common patterns characterized by strong similarities in the responses of men and women to sexual stimuli. Masters and Johnson did, however, note one significant difference between the sexes: the presence of a *refractory period* (a recovery stage in which there is a temporary inability to reach orgasm) in the male resolution phase.

The simplified nature of these diagrams can easily obscure the richness of individual variation that does occur. Masters and Johnson were charting only the physiological responses to sexual stimulation. Biological reactions might follow a relatively predictable course, but the variability in individual responses to sexual arousal is considerable. These variations are suggested in the several individual reports of arousal, orgasm, and resolution included later in this chapter.

Two fundamental physiological responses to effective sexual stimulation occur in both women and men. These are *vasocongestion* and *myotonia*. These two basic reactions are the primary underlying sources for almost all biological responses that take place during sexual arousal.

Vasocongestion is the engorgement with blood of body tissues that respond to sexual excitation. Usually the blood flow into organs and tissues through the arteries

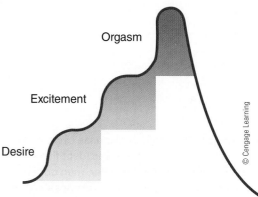

▌ **Figure 6.2** Kaplan's three-stage model of the sexual response cycle. This model is distinguished by its identification of desire as a prelude to sexual response.

Source: Kaplan (1979).

vasocongestion
The engorgement of blood vessels in particular body parts in response to sexual arousal.

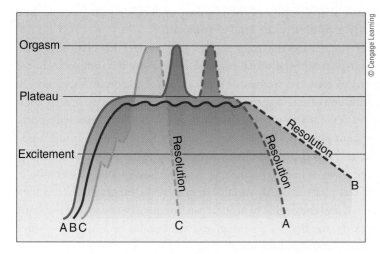

▌ **Figure 6.3** Female sexual response cycle. Masters and Johnson identified three basic patterns in female sexual response. Pattern A most closely resembles the male pattern, except that a woman can have one or more orgasms without dropping below the plateau level of sexual arousal. Variations of this response include an extended plateau with no orgasm (pattern B) and a rapid rise to orgasm with no definitive plateau and a quick resolution (pattern C).

SOURCE: *Human Sexual Response*, by W.H. Masters and V.E. Johnson. Copyright © 1966

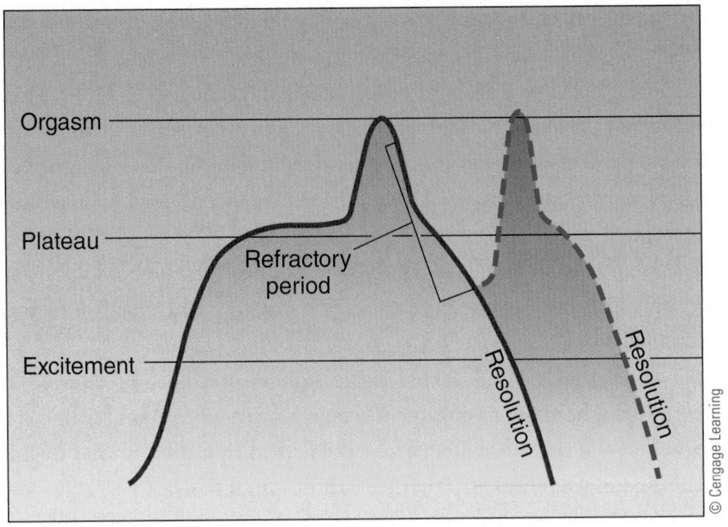

Figure 6.4 Male sexual response cycle. Only one male response pattern was identified by Masters and Johnson. However, men do report considerable variation in their response pattern. Note the refractory period; males do not have a second orgasm immediately after the first.

SOURCE: *Human Sexual Response*, by W.H. Masters and V.E. Johnson. Copyright © 1966

myotonia
Muscle tension.

excitement phase
Masters and Johnson's term for the first phase of the sexual response cycle, in which engorgement of the sexual organs and increases in muscle tension, heart rate, and blood pressure occur.

sex flush
A pink or red rash that can appear on the chest or breasts during sexual arousal.

is balanced by an equal outflow through the veins. During sexual arousal, however, the arteries dilate, increasing the inflow beyond the capacity of the veins to carry blood away. This results in widespread vasocongestion in both superficial and deep tissues. The visible congested areas might feel warm and appear swollen and red as a result of increased blood content. The most obvious manifestations of this vasocongestive response are the erection of the penis in men and blood engorgement of the clitoris and lubrication of the vagina in women. In addition, other body areas can become engorged—the labia, testes, clitoris, nipples, and even the earlobes.

As described in Chapter 2, Masters and Johnson and other researchers have used devices such as the vaginal photoplethysmograph and the penile strain gauge to electronically measure vasocongestion during sexual arousal. Investigators have also used functional magnetic resonance imaging (fMRI) technology to study sexual response. This approach to assessing the physiology of sexual arousal is described in the Spotlight on Research box.

The second basic physiological response is **myotonia** (my-uh-TOH-nee-uh), the increased muscle tension that occurs throughout the body during sexual arousal. Myotonia is evident in both voluntary flexing and involuntary contractions. Its most dramatic manifestations are facial grimaces, spasmodic contractions of the hands and feet, and the muscular spasms that occur during orgasm.

The phases of the response cycle follow the same general patterns, regardless of the method of stimulation. Masturbation, manual stimulation by one's partner, oral pleasuring, penile–vaginal intercourse, dreaming, fantasy, and, in some women, breast stimulation can all result in completion of the response cycle. Often the intensity and rapidity of response vary according to the kind of stimulation.

■ Table 6.3 on p. 166 summarizes the major physiological changes that occur in women and men during the four phases of the sexual response cycle. Note the similarities in the sexual response patterns of men and women. We discuss some important differences in greater detail at the conclusion of this chapter. In the following paragraphs we provide a few observations regarding each of the four phases of sexual response and some personal reports.

During the **excitement phase** both sexes experience an increase in myotonia, vasocongestion, heart rate, and blood pressure. Although the appearance of a **sex flush** (a pink or red rash on the chest or breasts) can occur in either sex, it is more common in females. The length of this phase is highly variable in both sexes, ranging from less than a minute to several hours, and the degree of arousal can fluctuate between low and high. The following two reports, the first by a woman and the second by a man, give some indication of subjective variations in how people describe their sexual arousal.

Earlier in this chapter we discussed the use of functional magnetic resonance imaging (fMRI) to monitor the brain during sexual arousal. This fMRI technology can also provide images of the soft tissues of the genitals. These images can be used to monitor changes in blood engorgement of the genital tissues as demonstrated in several studies of female sexual arousal (Deliganis et al., 2000; Maravilla et al., 2000, 2003).

An excellent example of this technological advance is research conducted by Kenneth Maravilla and his colleagues (2003). These investigators recruited a number of sexually functional women to participate in a series of three studies in which genital tissues were monitored using fMRI while the women viewed videos of erotic content and video segments of nonerotic, neutral images. Participants also rated their subjective levels of sexual arousal by completing questionnaires. All three investigations yielded similar results. All subjects reported sexual arousal on the subjective questionnaires that was closely associated with increased clitoral

blood volume and size. Maravilla and his colleagues found that the magnetic resonance images provided excellent visualization of the genital anatomic structures of the participants, including major blood vessels involved in vasocongestion. In addition, the images allowed precise calculation of changes in clitoral size and in blood volume of the genital tissues during sexual arousal. Among the findings was an increase in both the degree of blood engorgement and overall size of the clitoris during the erotic video segment compared with its state during the neutral segment. On average, clitoral size more than doubled from the unaroused state to the aroused state for all subjects.

These investigations and similar studies demonstrate that fMRI is an excellent method for observing and quantitatively measuring genital changes during sexual arousal. Application of this technology offers an advanced alternative to the use of electronic devices for measuring sexual arousal, such as the vaginal photoplethysmograph and the penile strain gauge, described in Chapter 2.

> When I am aroused, I get warm all over, and I like a lot of holding and massaging of other areas of my body besides my genitals. After time passes with that particular stimulation, I prefer more direct manual stroking if I want orgasm. (Authors' files)

> When I am sexually aroused, my whole body feels energized. Sometimes my mouth gets dry, and I may feel a little light-headed. I want to have all of my body touched and stroked, not just my genitals. I particularly like the sensation of feeling that orgasm is just around the corner, waiting and tantalizing me to begin the final journey. Sometimes a quick rush to climax is nice, but usually I prefer making the arousal period last as long as I can stand it, until my penis feels like it is dying for the final strokes of ecstasy. (Authors' files)

The term **plateau phase** is somewhat of a misnomer in that in the behavioral sciences the term *plateau* is typically used to describe a leveling-off period during which no observable changes in behavior can be detected. For example, it might refer to a flat spot in a learning curve where no new behaviors occur for a certain period of time. The plateau stage has been diagrammed in just this manner in the male chart (Figure 6.4) and in pattern A of the female chart (Figure 6.3). In actuality, the plateau level of sexual arousal involves a powerful surge of sexual tension in both sexes (e.g., increase in blood pressure and heart and breathing rates) that continues to mount until it reaches the peak that leads to orgasm.

The plateau phase is often brief, typically lasting a few seconds to several minutes. However, many people find that prolonging sexual tensions at this high level produces greater arousal and ultimately more-intense orgasms. This is reported in the following subjective accounts:

plateau phase
Masters and Johnson's term for the second phase of the sexual response cycle, in which muscle tension, heart rate, blood pressure, and vasocongestion increase.

When I get up there, almost on the verge of coming, I try to hang in as long as possible. If my partner cooperates, stopping or slowing when necessary, I can stay right on the edge for several minutes, sometimes even longer. I know that all it would take is one more stroke and I'm over the top. Sometimes my whole body gets to shaking and quivering, and I can feel incredible sensations shooting through me like electric charges. The longer I can make this supercharged period last, the better the orgasm. (Authors' files)

When I masturbate, I like to take myself almost to the point of climaxing and then back off. I can tell when orgasm is about to happen because my vagina tightens up around the opening, and sometimes I can feel the muscles contract. I love the sensations of balancing myself on the brink, part of me wanting to come and the other part holding out for more. The longer I maintain this delicate balance, the more shattering the climax. Sometimes the pleasure is almost beyond bearing. (Authors' files)

■ **TABLE 6.3 Major Physiological Changes During Each of the Four Phases of the Sexual Response Cycle**

Phase	Reactions Common to Both Sexes	Female Responses	Male Responses
Excitement	■ Increase in myotonia, heart rate, and blood pressure. ■ Sex flush and nipple erections occur (more common in females).	■ Clitoris swells. ■ Labia majora separate away from vaginal opening. ■ Labia minora swell and darken in color. ■ Lubrication begins. ■ Uterus elevates. ■ Breasts enlarge.	■ Penis becomes erect. ■ Testes elevate and engorge. ■ Scrotal skin thickens and tenses.
Plateau	■ Myotonia becomes pronounced, and involuntary muscular contractions may occur in hands and feet. ■ Heart rate, blood pressure, and breathing increase.	■ Orgasmic platform (engorgement of outer third of the vagina) forms. ■ Clitoris withdraws under its hood. ■ Uterus becomes fully elevated. ■ Areola becomes more swollen.	■ Engorgement and elevation of testes becomes more pronounced. ■ Cowper's gland secretions may occur.
Orgasm	■ Involuntary muscle spasms throughout body. ■ Blood pressure, breathing, and heart rates at maximum levels. ■ Involuntary contractions of rectal sphincter.	■ Orgasmic platform contracts rhythmically 3 to 15 times. ■ Uterine contractions occur. ■ Clitoris remains retracted under its hood. ■ No further changes in breasts or nipples.	■ During emission phase, internal sex structures undergo contractions, causing pooling of seminal fluid in urethral bulb. ■ During expulsion phase, semen expelled by contractions of muscles around base of penis.
Resolution	■ Myotonia subsides, and heart rate, blood pressure, and breathing rates return to normal immediately after orgasm. ■ Sex flush disappears rapidly. ■ Nipple erection subsides slowly.	■ Clitoris descends and engorgement slowly subsides. ■ Labia return to unaroused size. ■ Uterus descends to normal position. ■ Lack of orgasm after period of high arousal may dramatically slow resolution.	■ Erection subsides over a period of a few minutes. ■ Testes descend and return to their normal size. Scrotum resumes wrinkled appearance. ■ Resolution quite rapid in most men.

As effective stimulation continues, many people move from plateau to **orgasm**. Orgasm is the shortest phase of the sexual response cycle, typically lasting only a few seconds. Men almost always experience orgasm after reaching the plateau level of sexual response. In contrast to men, women sometimes obtain plateau levels of arousal without the release of sexual climax (Wallen et al., 2011). This is often the case during penile–vaginal intercourse when the man reaches orgasm first or when effective manual or oral stimulation is replaced with penetration as the female approaches orgasm.

The NSSHB (National Survey of Sexual Health and Behavior) found that 64% of adult females experienced orgasm during their most recent sexual experience with another person (most commonly a sex partner of the other sex). The comparable figure for adult males was 85% (Reece et al., 2010a). Adult females were most likely to have an orgasm when they engaged in a variety of sex acts, such as oral sex, partnered masturbation, and vaginal intercourse. Another study reported that women typically experience orgasm during partnered sex via manipulation of the clitoris or oral sex, and much less frequently during vaginal penetration (Brewer & Hendrie, 2010).

For both sexes the experience of orgasm can be an intense mixture of highly pleasurable sensations, but whether that experience differs from male to female has been the subject of considerable debate. This question was evaluated in two separate experimental analyses of orgasm descriptions provided by college students (Wiest, 1977; Wiest et al., 1995). When compared using a standard psychological rating scale, women's and men's subjective descriptions of orgasm were indistinguishable in both investigations. Similar results were obtained in an earlier study, in which 70 expert judges were unable to distinguish reliably between the written orgasm reports of men and women (Proctor et al., 1974). Another investigation found that when men and women were asked to use adjectives to describe their subjective experience of orgasm, similarities in description significantly outweighed differences (Mah & Binik, 2002).

Beyond the question of sex differences in orgasmic experiences, it is clear that great individual variation exists in how people, both men and women, describe orgasms. The following Sexuality and Diversity discussion provides some indication of the varied ways people experience and describe their orgasmic experiences.

SEXUALITY and DIVERSITY
Subjective Descriptions of Orgasm

The following accounts, selected from our files, illustrate the diversity of orgasmic descriptions. The first account is by a woman and the second by a man. The final three descriptions—labeled Reports A, B, and C—contain no specific references that identify the sex of the describers. Perhaps you would like to try to determine whether they were reported by a man or a woman. The answers follow the summary at the end of the chapter.

> Female: When I'm about to reach orgasm, my face feels very hot. I close my eyes and open my mouth. It centers in my clitoris, and it feels like electric wires igniting from there and radiating up my torso and down my legs to my feet. I sometimes feel like I need to urinate. My vagina contracts anywhere from 5 to 12 times. My vulva area feels heavy and swollen. There isn't another feeling like it—it's fantastic!

> Male: Orgasm for me draws all my energy in toward a core in my body. Then, all of a sudden, there is a release of this energy out through my penis. My body becomes warm and numb before orgasm; after, it gradually relaxes and I feel extremely serene.

orgasm
A series of muscular contractions of the pelvic floor muscles occurring at the peak of sexual arousal.

Critical Thinking Question

Do you believe that men and women differ in the importance they attach to experiencing orgasm during sexual sharing? Why or why not?

Report A: It's like an Almond Joy, "indescribably delicious." The feeling runs from the top of my head to the tips of my toes as I feel a powerful surge of pleasure. It raises me beyond my physical self into another level of consciousness, and yet the feeling seems purely physical. What a paradox! It strokes all over, inside and out. I love it simply because it's mine and mine alone.

Report B: An orgasm to me is like heaven. All my tensions and anxieties are released. You get to the point of no return, and it's like an uncontrollable desire that makes things start happening. I think that sex and orgasm are one of the greatest phenomena that we have today. It's a great sharing experience for me.

Report C: Having an orgasm is like the ultimate time I have for myself. I am not excluding my partner, but it's like I can't hear anything, and all I feel is a spectacular release accompanied with more pleasure than I've ever felt doing anything else. (Authors' files)

Although the physiology of female orgasmic response is relatively well understood, misinformation about its nature has prevailed in our culture. Sigmund Freud (1905/2000) developed a theory of the vaginal versus clitoral orgasm that has adversely affected people's thinking about female sexual response. Freud viewed the vaginal orgasm as more mature than the clitoral orgasm and thus preferable. The physiological basis for this theory was the assumption that the clitoris is a stunted penis. This led to the conclusion that erotic sensations, arousal, and orgasm resulting from direct stimulation of the clitoris were expressions of "masculine" rather than "feminine" sexuality (Sherfey, 1972). Unfortunately, this theory led many women to believe, incorrectly, that they were sexually maladjusted. Our knowledge of embryology has established the falseness of the theory that the clitoris is a masculine organ, as we have seen in our discussion of the genital differentiation process in Chapter 5.

Contrary to Freud's theory, the research of Masters and Johnson suggests that there is one kind of orgasm in females, physiologically speaking, regardless of the method of stimulation. Most female orgasms result from direct or indirect stimulation of the clitoris. However, as we note elsewhere, females can experience orgasm from fantasy alone, during sleep (nocturnal orgasms), or by stimulation of other body areas such as the nipples or the *Grafenberg spot*, or *G-spot*.

The Grafenberg Spot

A number of studies have reported that some women are capable of experiencing orgasm, and perhaps an ejaculation of fluid, when an area along the anterior (front) wall of the vagina is vigorously stimulated (Levin, 2003a; Whipple & Komisaruk, 1999). This area of erotic sensitivity, mentioned in Chapter 3, has been named the *Grafenberg spot* (or *G-spot*) in honor of Ernest Grafenberg (1950), a gynecologist who first noted the erotic significance of this location in the vagina almost 60 years ago. It has been suggested that the G-spot is not a point that can be touched by the tip of one finger but rather is a fairly large area composed of the front wall of the vagina and the underlying urethra and surrounding glands (Skene's glands; Song et al., 2009). Recent research utilizing MRI technology identified a G-spot in six of seven women in the study group (Wimpissinger et al., 2009).

The G-spot can be located by systematic palpation of the entire front wall of the vagina. Two fingers are usually used, and it is often necessary to press deeply into the tissue to reach

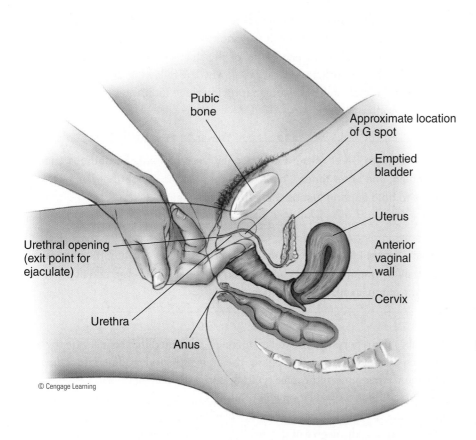

© Cengage Learning

Figure 6.5 Locating the Grafenberg spot. Usually two fingers are used, and it is often necessary to press deeply into the anterior wall of the vagina to reach the spot.

the spot. This exploration can be conducted by a woman's partner, as shown in ▌Figure 6.5. Some women are able to locate their G-spot through self-exploration.

G-spot orgasms are sometimes accompanied by the ejaculation of fluid from the urethral opening (Schubach, 1996; Whipple, 2000). Research indicates that the source of this fluid may be the "female prostate," discussed in Chapter 3. The ducts from this system empty directly into the urethra. In some women, G-spot orgasms result in fluid being forced through these ducts and out the urethra. In view of the homologous nature of G-spot tissue and the male prostate, we can speculate that the female ejaculate is similar to the prostatic component of male seminal fluid (Zaviacic & Whipple, 1993). This notion has been supported by research in which specimens of female ejaculate were chemically analyzed and found to contain high levels of an enzyme, prostatic acid phosphatase (PAP), characteristic of the prostatic component of semen (Addiego et al., 1981; Belzer et al., 1984).

One final point regarding the G-spot should be noted. Some medical practitioners are now providing *G-spot amplification*, which involves injecting the G-spot with collagen to allegedly produce a temporary enhancement of sexual arousal and response (Wendling, 2007). We caution readers to avoid this procedure in light of inconclusive supporting data and the potential for serious complications, including infections, scarring, altered sensation, and painful coitus (Campos, 2008; Wendling, 2007).

From a broader perspective, we encourage our readers to think critically about the many unsubstantiated claims made by surgeons touting genital cosmetic surgery and the increasing number of websites that misinform women about what is considered normal female genital anatomy. Dr. Leonore Tiefer (2011), noted sexologist, is an outspoken critic of these phony claims for procedures that border on female genital mutilation. ●

SEXUALHEALTH

resolution phase
The fourth phase of the sexual response cycle, as outlined by Masters and Johnson, in which the sexual systems return to their nonexcited state.

During the final phase of the sexual response cycle, **resolution**, the sexual systems return to their nonexcited state. If no additional stimulation occurs, the resolution begins immediately after orgasm. Some of the changes back to a nonexcited state take place rapidly, whereas others occur more slowly. The following two self-reports, the first by a man and the second by a woman, provide some indication of how people vary in their feelings after orgasm:

> After orgasm I feel relaxed and usually very content. Sometimes I feel like sleeping, and other times I feel like I want to touch my partner if she is willing. I like to hold her and just be there. (Authors' files)

> After orgasm I feel very relaxed. My moods do vary—sometimes I'm ready to start all over; other times I can jump up and really get busy; and at other times I just want to sleep. (Authors' files)

These subjective reports sound similar. But one significant difference exists in the responses of women and men during this phase: their physiological readiness for further sexual stimulation. After orgasm the male typically enters a **refractory period**—a time when no amount of additional stimulation will result in orgasm. The length of this period ranges from minutes to days, depending on a variety of factors, such as age, frequency of previous sexual activity, and the degree of the man's emotional closeness to and sexual desire for his partner. In contrast to men, women generally experience no comparable refractory period. They are physiologically capable of returning to another orgasmic peak from anywhere in the resolution phase. However, a woman may or may not want to do so. In the last two sections of this chapter, we discuss the effects of aging on sexual arousal and response and then consider some differences between men's and women's patterns of sexual response.

refractory period
The period of time following orgasm in the male, during which he cannot experience another orgasm.

Aging and the Sexual Response Cycle

As people grow older, they will notice changes in sexual arousal and response patterns. In this section we briefly summarize some of the more common variations that occur in the sexual response cycles of women and men.

The Sexual Response Cycle of Older Women

In general, all phases of the response cycle continue to occur for older women but with somewhat decreased intensity (Masters & Johnson, 1966; Segraves & Segraves, 1995). A recent study of almost 2,000 women ages 45 to 80 reported that 60% were sexually active (Harvard Women's Health Watch, 2012). Another study of 806 sexually active older women found that sexual satisfaction actually increased with age for many of the women in this survey (Trompeter et al., 2012). Still another study found that sexual desire decreases among older women in long-term relationships with sexually dysfunctional partners (McCabe & Goldhammer, 2012).

Excitement Phase

SEXUALHEALTH

The first physiological response to sexual arousal, vaginal lubrication, typically begins more slowly in an older woman. Instead of taking 10 to 30 seconds, it may take several minutes or longer before vaginal lubrication is observed. In most cases the amount of lubrication is reduced (Nusbaum et al., 2005). When lubrication and vaginal expansion during sexual response are considerably diminished, uncomfortable or painful intercourse can result (Mansfield et al., 1995). In addition, some women report decreased sexual desire and sensitivity of the clitoris, both of which interfere with sexual excitement. Hormone therapy, estrogen creams applied to the vagina, and vaginal lubricants can often help these symptoms (Kingsberg, 2002). ●

Plateau Phase

During the plateau phase, the vaginal orgasmic platform develops, and the uterus elevates. In a postmenopausal woman these changes occur to a somewhat lesser degree than before menopause (Masters & Johnson, 1966).

Orgasm Phase

Contractions of the orgasmic platform and the uterus continue to occur at orgasm, although the number of these contractions is typically reduced in older women. Older women remain capable of multiple orgasms and may continue to experience them (Nusbaum et al., 2005). However, many older women require a longer period of stimulation to reach orgasm, and some experience a reduced capacity to have an orgasm (Nusbaum et al., 2005).

Orgasm appears to be an important aspect of sexual activity to older women. One survey found that 69% of women ages 60 to 91 listed "orgasm" first in response to the question "What do you consider a good sexual experience?" (Starr & Weiner, 1981). Only 17% of the women answered "intercourse" to the same question. In addition, "orgasm" was the most frequent response to the question "What in the sex act is most important to you?" Sixty-five percent of the women reported that their frequency of orgasm was the same as when they were younger.

Resolution Phase

The resolution phase typically occurs more rapidly in postmenopausal women (Nusbaum et al., 2005). Labia color change, vaginal expansion, orgasmic platform formation, and clitoral retraction all disappear soon after orgasm. This is most likely due to the overall reduced amount of pelvic vasocongestion during arousal.

In summary, the effects of aging on female sexuality vary considerably. Most women experience minor changes, and some find their sexual interest, excitement, and orgasmic capacity seriously affected. An active sex life helps maintain vaginal health, and a functional and interested partner, as well as good couple communication, contributes to gratifying sexual relations for the older woman. Hormone therapy can also resolve many of the problems that interfere with enjoyable sexual response.

The Sexual Response Cycle of Older Men

Most changes in the sexual response cycle of older men involve alterations in the intensity and duration of response (Masters & Johnson, 1966; Segraves & Segraves, 1995).

Excitement Phase

During youth, many males can experience an erection in a few seconds. This ability is typically altered with the aging process. Instead of requiring 8 to 10 seconds, a man might require several minutes of effective stimulation to develop an erect penis. Furthermore, an older man's erection may be less firm than was typical of his younger days. More direct physical stimulation, such as hand caressing or oral stimulation, may also be desirable or necessary.

Most men retain their erectile capacities throughout their lifetimes. When a man and his partner understand that a slowed rate of obtaining an erection is normal, the altered pattern has little or no effect on their enjoyment of sexual expression.

Plateau Phase

Older men do not typically experience as much myotonia (muscle tension) during the plateau phase as when they were younger. Complete penile erection is frequently not obtained until late in the plateau phase, just before orgasm. One result of these changes is that an older man is often able to sustain the plateau phase much longer than he did when he was younger, which can significantly enhance his pleasure. Many men and their partners appreciate this prolonged opportunity to enjoy other sensations of sexual response besides ejaculation. When a man engages in intercourse, his partner also may appreciate his greater ejaculatory control.

Orgasm Phase

Most aging males continue to experience considerable pleasure from their orgasmic responses. In fact, 73% of older men in one study reported that orgasm was "very important" in their sexual experiences (Starr & Weiner, 1981). However, they may note a decline in intensity. Frequently absent are the sensations of ejaculatory inevitability that correspond with the emission phase of ejaculation. The number of muscular contractions occurring during the expulsion phase is typically reduced and so is the force of ejaculation (Nusbaum et al., 2005).

Resolution Phase

Resolution typically occurs more rapidly in older men (Nusbaum et al., 2005). Loss of erection is usually quite rapid, especially compared with that of younger men. Resolution becomes faster with aging, and the refractory period between orgasm and the next excitement phase gradually lengthens (DeLamater & Friedrich, 2002). Men may begin to notice this as early as their 30s or 40s. Often, by age 60 the refractory period lasts for several hours, even days in some cases.

■ Table 6.4 summarizes the common changes in the sexual response cycles of older women and men.

At a Glance

■ TABLE 6.4 Typical Age-Related Changes in the Sexual Response Cycles of Older Men and Women

Phase	Typical Changes in Women	Typical Changes in Men
Excitement	■ Vaginal lubrication is somewhat delayed and occurs with less volume. ■ Vaginal mucosa thins, and length and width of vagina decrease.	■ Longer time required to obtain an erection. ■ Erection may be less firm.
Plateau	■ Orgasmic platform less pronounced. ■ Less elevation of uterus.	■ Less overall muscle tension. ■ Less elevation of testes. ■ This phase is often elongated in time.
Orgasm	■ Fewer orgasmic contractions. ■ Occasionally uterine contractions may be painful.	■ Number of muscular contractions decrease, and force of ejaculation is lessened. ■ Sensations of ejaculatory inevitability may be absent.
Resolution	■ Typically occurs more rapidly as vaginal expansion, orgasmic platform, and clitoral retraction disappears soon after orgasm.	■ Occurs more quickly with rapid loss of erection. ■ Refractory period between orgasm and the next excitement phase gradually lengthens.

Differences Between the Sexes in Sexual Response

More and more, writers are emphasizing the basic similarities of sexual response in men and women. We see this as a positive trend away from the once-popular notion that great differences exist between the sexes—an opinion that undoubtedly helped create a big market for many "love manuals" designed to inform readers about the mysteries and complexities of the "opposite sex." Now we know that much can be learned about our partners by carefully observing our own sexual patterns. Nevertheless, there are some real and important primary differences. In the following pages we outline and discuss some of them. Readers may also find the Spotlight on Research box, which describes a cross-cultural survey of sex differences in sex drive, to be of interest.

Greater Variability in Female Response

One major difference between the sexes is the range of variations in the sexual response cycle. Although the graphs in Figures 6.3 and 6.4 do not reflect individual differences, they do demonstrate a wider range in the female response. One pattern is outlined for the male, and three patterns are drawn for the female.

In the female chart the sexual response pattern represented by line A is most similar to the male pattern (see Figure 6.3). It differs in an important way, however, in its potential for additional orgasms without dropping below the plateau level. Line B represents quite a different female pattern: a smooth advance through excitement to the level of plateau, where the responding woman may remain for some time without experiencing orgasm. The consequent resolution phase is more drawn out. Line C portrays a rapid rise in excitement, followed by one intense orgasm and a quick resolution.

Although it appears that women often have more variable sexual response patterns than men have, this does not imply that all males experience the response cycle in exactly the same way. Men report considerable variation from the Masters and Johnson standard, including several mild orgasmic peaks followed by ejaculation, prolonged pelvic contractions after the expulsion of semen, and extended periods of intense excitement before ejaculation that feel like one long orgasm (Zilbergeld, 1978). In other words, there is no single pattern of sexual response, nor is there one "correct way." All patterns and variations—including one person's different reactions to sexual stimuli at different times or in different situations—are completely normal.

Are the sexual behaviors and attitudes of women more variable (erotically plastic) than those of men and thus more susceptible to the influence of sociocultural factors? A study of college women and men that addressed this question did not find evidence supporting the view that women are more erotically plastic than men (Benuto & Meana, 2008).

The Male Refractory Period

The refractory period in the male cycle is certainly one of the most significant differences in sexual responses between the sexes. Men typically find that a certain minimum time must elapse after an orgasm before they can experience another climax. Most women have no such physiologically imposed shutdown phase.

Speculation about why only men have a refractory period is considerable. It seems plausible that some kind of short-term neurological inhibitory mechanism is triggered

A British Broadcasting Corporation (BBC) Internet survey of more than 200,000 participants from around the world provided strong evidence of a consistent difference in strength of sex drive between male and female respondents (Lippa, 2008). Participants were residents of 53 different nations, with the largest numbers from the United Kingdom (45%), the United States (29%), Canada (4%), and Australia (4%). The BBC data set included samples of 90 or more respondents from each of the countries included in the survey, with men and women represented in approximately equal numbers. Sex drive was measured by two items ("I have a strong sex drive" and "It doesn't take much to get me sexually excited"). Participants responded to these two items using a 7-point scale that ranged from "disagree" to "agree." In the sample sets from all 53 nations, men reported having stronger sex drives than did women. These sex differences in reported sex drive were consistent across all countries, and "they were not moderated by gender equality or associated with economic development" (p. 18).

A second finding of interest in this study is that women in all the nations surveyed indicated having more variable sex drives than their male counterparts. Richard Lippa, who wrote the article reporting the results of this survey, interpreted this finding in terms of what he labeled *sexual selection* and *parental investment*. From these perspectives, women may be viewed as the "choosier" sex in that they often provide sexual privileges to men whom they consider to be good providers of financial resources, protection, and commitment. Since they are motivated by a desire to find a *good partner*, "it seems reasonable to hypothesize that sexual selection would endow women, on average, with less urgent sex drives that are more subject to rational control" (p. 19). For women, then, the main concern is not so much finding men to impregnate them but rather inducing these men to stay around after impregnation. In contrast, male parental success, defined as transmitting their genes to future generations, is enhanced by sexual activity with multiple partners, which has led men, Lippa theorizes, "to have stronger and more consistently 'turned on' sex drives than women" (p. 19).

Caution should be exercised in drawing broad conclusions from this study, however. While the sample size is certainly impressive, it definitely is not a representative sample of participants in any of the 53 nations included in the survey. Rather, respondents tended to be young, well educated, relatively affluent, and Internet savvy and thus more representative of a nation's educated elite as compared with a broader slice of a specific national population. As pointed out in Chapter 2, sample selection bias is a significant disadvantage of Internet-based sex surveys. On the other hand, this survey has significant strengths, as reflected in the size and diversity of the BBC sample. To have access to self-report data on sex drive from an international sample comprising more than 200,000 participants is both impressive and unprecedented.

by ejaculation. This notion is supported by research conducted by British scientists (Barfield et al., 1975). These researchers speculated that certain chemical pathways between the midbrain and the hypothalamus—pathways known to be involved in regulating sleep—might have something to do with post-orgasm inhibition in males. To test their hypothesis, the researchers destroyed a specific site, the *ventral medial lemniscus*, along these pathways in rats. For comparison they surgically eliminated three other areas in hypothalamic and midbrain locations in different rats. Later observations of sexual behavior revealed that the elimination of the ventral medial lemniscus had a dramatic effect on refractory periods, cutting their duration in half.

Some people believe that the answer to the riddle of refractory periods is somehow connected with the loss of seminal fluid during orgasm. Most researchers have been skeptical of this idea because there is no known substance in the expelled semen to account for an energy drain, marked hormone reduction, or any of the other implied biochemical explanations.

Still another explanation suggests that *prolactin*, a pituitary hormone secreted copiously following orgasm in both sexes, may be the biological "off switch" that induces the male refractory period (Kruger et al., 2002; Levin, 2003b). This interpretation, while provocative, fails to account for the absence of a female refractory period. Whatever the reason for it, the refractory period is common not just to human males but to males of virtually all other species for which data exist, including rats, dogs, and chimpanzees.

Multiple Orgasms

Differences between the sexes occur in still a third area of sexual response patterns: the ability to experience **multiple orgasms**. Technically speaking, the term *multiple orgasms* refers to having more than one orgasmic experience within a short time interval.

Although researchers differ in their views of what constitutes a multiple orgasmic experience, for our own purposes we can say that if a man or woman has two or more sexual climaxes within a short period (a few minutes or less), that person has experienced multiple orgasms. There is, however, a distinction between males and females that is often obscured by such a definition. It is not uncommon for a woman to have several sequential orgasms, separated in time by the briefest of intervals (perhaps only seconds). In contrast, the spacing of male orgasms is typically more protracted. The research of Masters and Johnson demonstrated differences in the capacity of females and males to experience multiple orgasms:

> If a female who is capable of having regular orgasms is properly stimulated within a short period after her first climax, she will in most instances be capable of having a second, third, fourth, and even a fifth and a sixth orgasm before she is fully satiated. As contrasted with the male's usual inability to have more than one orgasm in a short period, many females, especially when clitorally stimulated, can regularly have five or six full orgasms within a matter of minutes. (Masters & Johnson, 1961, p. 792)

Thus, while most women have the capacity for multiple orgasms, research indicates that many women do not routinely experience them. As indicated elsewhere in this book, penile–vaginal intercourse often does not produce sexual stimulation optimal for female orgasm. Furthermore, because of the male's tendency to stop after his orgasm, women are not likely to continue beyond their initial orgasm. In sharp contrast, several researchers have demonstrated that women who masturbate and those who relate sexually to other women are considerably more likely both to reach initial orgasm and to continue to additional orgasms (Athanasiou et al., 1970; Masters & Johnson, 1966). Finally, the NSSHB survey also revealed that women who engage in a variety of sexual behaviors during partnered sex are more likely to experience multiple orgasms (Herbenick et al., 2010b).

We do not mean to imply that all women should be experiencing multiple orgasms. On the contrary, many women prefer sexual experiences during which they have a single orgasm or perhaps no orgasm at all. The data on multiple orgasmic capacities of women are not meant to be interpreted as the way women "should" respond. This approach could lead to a new kind of arbitrary sexual standard. The following quotation illustrates the tendency to set such standards:

> When I was growing up, people considered any young, unmarried woman who enjoyed and sought active sexual involvements to be disturbed or promiscuous. Now I am told that I must have several orgasms each time I make love in order to be considered "normal." What a switch in our definitions of normal or healthy—from the straightlaced, noninvolved person to this incredible creature who is supposed to get it off multiple times at the drop of a hat. (Authors' files)

multiple orgasms
More than one orgasm experienced within a short time period.

Critical Thinking Question
Women collectively appear to have a greater capacity for orgasm, to experience orgasm from a wider range of stimulation, and to have more problems experiencing orgasm than men. To what factors do you attribute this greater variation in female orgasmic response patterns?

As suggested earlier, multiple orgasms are considerably less common among males. They are most often reported by very young men, and their frequency declines with age. It is unusual to find men, even those of college age, who routinely experience more than one orgasm during a single sexual encounter. However, we agree with Alex Comfort (1972), who asserted that most men are probably more capable of multiple orgasms than they realize. Many have been conditioned by years of masturbation to get it over with as quickly as possible to avoid detection. Such a mental set hardly encourages an adolescent to continue experimenting after the initial orgasm. Through later experimentation, though, many men make discoveries similar to the one described in the following personal reflection of a middle-aged man:

> Somehow it never occurred to me that I might continue making love after experiencing orgasm. For 30 years of my life, this always signaled endpoint for me. I guess I responded this way for all the reasons you stated in class and a few more you didn't cover. My wife was with me the night you discussed refractory periods. We talked about it all the way home, and the next day gave it a try. Man, am I mad at myself now for missing out on something really nice all of these years. I discovered that I could have more than one orgasm in one session, and while it may take me a long time to come again, the getting there is a very nice part. My wife likes it, too! (Authors' files)

One research study provided information about male multiple orgasmic capacity. In this investigation, 21 men (ages 25 to 69) were interviewed, and all of them stated that they were usually but not always multiply orgasmic. The researchers who conducted this study defined male multiple orgasms as "two or more orgasms with or without ejaculation and without, or with only very limited, detumescence [loss of erection] during one and the same sexual encounter" (Dunn & Trost, 1989, p. 379). The men's patterns varied, with some men experiencing ejaculation with the first orgasm, followed by more "dry" orgasms. Other men reported having several orgasms without ejaculation followed by a final ejaculatory orgasm. Still others reported variations on these two themes.

It is not necessary for lovemaking always to end with ejaculation. Many men find it pleasurable to continue sexual activity after a climax:

> One of the best parts of sex for me is having intercourse again shortly after my first orgasm. I find it is relatively easy to get another erection, even though I seldom experience another climax during the same session. The second time round I can concentrate fully on my partner's reactions without being distracted by my own building excitement. The pace is generally mellow and relaxed, and it is a real high for me psychologically. (Authors' files)

Thus, multiple orgasms can be seen not as an ultimate goal to be sought above all else but rather as a possible area to explore. A relaxed approach to this possibility can give interested women and men an opportunity to experience more of the full range of their sexual potentials.

Summary

The Brain and Sexual Arousal

- The brain plays an important role in human sexual arousal by mediating our thoughts, emotions, memories, and fantasies.
- Evidence links stimulation and surgical alteration of various brain sites with sexual arousal in humans and other animals.
- The limbic system, particularly the hypothalamus, plays an important part in sexual function.
- Certain neurotransmitter substances in the brain are known to influence sexual arousal and response. Dopamine facilitates sexual arousal and activity in women and men, and serotonin provides an inhibitory effect on both sexes.

The Senses and Sexual Arousal

- Touch tends to predominate among the senses that stimulate human sexual arousal. Locations on the body that are highly responsive to tactile pleasuring are called erogenous zones. Primary erogenous zones are areas with dense concentrations of nerve endings; secondary erogenous zones are other areas of the body that take on erotic significance through sexual conditioning.
- Vision is second only to touch in providing stimuli that most people find sexually arousing. Recent evidence suggests that women respond to visual erotica as much as men do.
- Research has yet to clearly demonstrate whether smell and taste play a biologically determined role in human sexual arousal, but our own unique individual experiences may allow certain smells and tastes to acquire erotic significance. However, our culture's obsession with personal hygiene tends to mask natural smells and tastes that relate to sexual activity.
- Research on nonhuman animals has isolated a variety of pheromones (sexual odors) that are strongly associated with reproductive sexual activities.
- Studies have provided tentative evidence that humans also produce pheromones that act as sexual attractants.
- Some individuals find sounds during lovemaking to be highly arousing, whereas others prefer that their lovers be silent during love play. Communication during a sexual interlude, besides being sexually stimulating to some, can also be informative.

Aphrodisiacs and Anaphrodisiacs in Sexual Arousal

- No clear evidence indicates that any substance we eat, drink, smoke, or inject has genuine aphrodisiac qualities. Faith and suggestion account for the apparent successes of a variety of alleged aphrodisiacs.
- Certain substances are known to have an inhibitory effect on sexual behavior. These anaphrodisiacs include drugs such as opiates, tranquilizers, antihypertensives, antidepressants, antipsychotics, nicotine, birth control pills, and sedatives.

The Role of Hormones in Sexual Behavior

- Both sexes produce so-called male sex hormones and female sex hormones. In men the testes produce about 95% of total androgens and some estrogens. A woman's ovaries and adrenal glands produce androgens in roughly equal amounts, and estrogens are produced predominantly by her ovaries.
- The dominant androgen in both sexes is testosterone. Men's bodies typically produce 20 to 40 times as much testosterone as women's bodies, but women's body cells are more sensitive to testosterone than men's are.
- Although it is difficult to distinguish the effects of sex hormones from those of psychological processes on sexual arousal, research strongly indicates that testosterone plays a critical role in maintaining sexual desire in both sexes.
- A major symptom of testosterone deficiency in both sexes— a decrease in one's customary level of sexual desire—can be eliminated by testosterone replacement therapy. However, raising the level of testosterone above a normal range can have adverse effects on both sexes.
- The neuropeptide hormone oxytocin, produced in the hypothalamus, exerts significant influence on sexual responses, sensuality, and interpersonal erotic and emotional attraction.

Sexual Response

- Kaplan's model of sexual response contains three stages: desire, excitement, and orgasm. This model is distinguished by its inclusion of desire as a distinct stage of the sexual response cycle separate from genital changes.
- Masters and Johnson describe four phases in the sexual response patterns of both women and men: excitement, plateau, orgasm, and resolution.

- During the excitement phase, both sexes experience increased myotonia (muscle tension), heart rate, and blood pressure. Sex flush and nipple erection often occur, especially among women. Female responses include engorgement of the clitoris, the labia, and the vagina (with vaginal lubrication), elevation and enlargement of the uterus, and breast enlargement. Males experience penile erection, enlargement and elevation of the testes, and sometimes Cowper's gland secretions.
- The plateau phase is marked by dramatic accelerations of myotonia, hyperventilation, heart rate, and blood pressure. In females the clitoris withdraws under its hood, the labia minora deepen in color, the orgasmic platform forms in the vagina, the uterus is fully elevated, and the areolas become swollen. In males the corona becomes fully engorged, the testes continue both elevation and enlargement, and Cowper's glands are active.
- Orgasm is marked by involuntary muscle spasms throughout the body. Blood pressure, heart rate, and respiration rate peak. Orgasm lasts slightly longer in females. Male orgasm typically occurs in two stages: emission and expulsion. It is difficult to distinguish subjective descriptions of female and male orgasms.
- Masters and Johnson suggest that one kind of physiological orgasm occurs in females, regardless of the method of stimulation.
- Some women can experience orgasm and perhaps ejaculation when the Grafenberg spot, an area along the anterior wall of the vagina, is vigorously stimulated.
- During the resolution phase, sexual systems return to their nonexcited state, a process that can take several hours, depending on a number of factors. Erection loss occurs in two stages, the first rapid and the second more protracted.

Aging and the Sexual Response Cycle

- As women and men grow older, they notice changes in their sexual arousal and response patterns. For both sexes all phases of the response cycle generally continue to occur but with somewhat decreased intensity.
- An older woman typically requires more time to achieve vaginal lubrication. The sexual response cycle of the older woman is also characterized by less vaginal expansion, diminished orgasmic intensity, and a more rapid resolution.
- Less commonly, women can experience a decrease in sexual desire, clitoral sensitivity, and/or the capacity for orgasm.
- Older men typically require longer periods of time to achieve erection and reach orgasm. Greater ejaculatory control may enhance sexual pleasure for both their partners and themselves.
- The sexual response cycle of the aging male is also characterized by less myotonia, reduced orgasmic intensity, more rapid resolution, and longer refractory periods.

Differences Between the Sexes in Sexual Response

- Many writers now emphasize the fundamental similarities in the sexual responses of men and women. However, certain important primary differences exist between the sexes.
- As a group, females demonstrate a wider variability in their sexual response patterns than do men.
- The presence of a refractory period in the male is one of the most significant differences in the response cycles of the two sexes. No cause for this period has been clearly demonstrated, but evidence suggests that ejaculation activates neurological inhibitory mechanisms.
- Multiple orgasms occur more often in females than in males.
- Women are more likely to experience multiple orgasms while masturbating than during coitus. Evidence suggests that some men can also experience a series of orgasms in a short time period.

Answer to Sexuality and Diversity Quiz on p. 168

Report A: Male; Report B: Female; Report C: Female

Media Resources

Log in to CengageBrain.com to access the resources your instructor requires.

Go to CengageBrain.com to access Psychology CourseMate, where you will find an interactive eBook, glossaries, flashcards, quizzes, videos, and more.

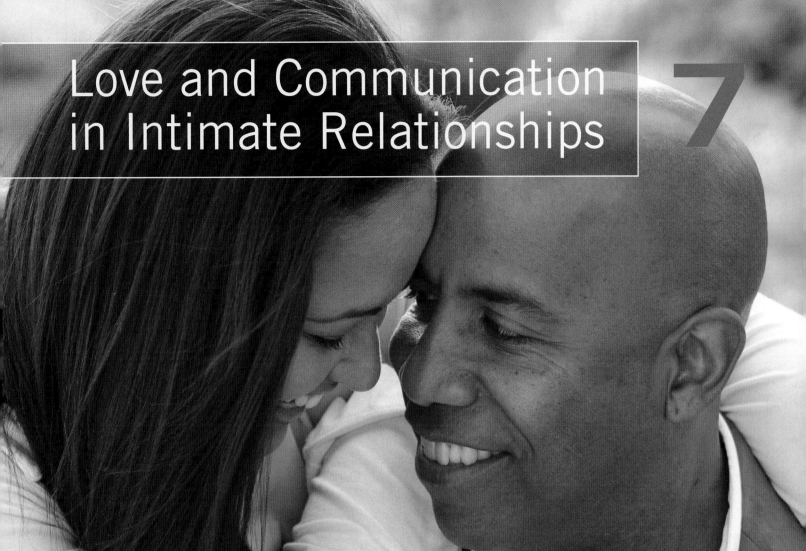

Love and Communication in Intimate Relationships

7

What Is Love?
Can love be defined? Can it be meaningfully measured?

Types of Love
What characterizes passionate love and companionate love?

Falling in Love: Why and With Whom?
What factors influence our choice of a mate?

Love and Styles of Attachment
How do various styles of attachment form, and how do they influence how we relate to others?

Issues in Loving Relationships
Does sexual intimacy deepen a relationship?

Maintaining Relationship Satisfaction
What ingredients do most lasting, satisfying love relationships have in common?

The Importance of Sexual Communication
What is the basis for effective sexual communication?

Talking: Getting Started
What kinds of strategies can make it easier to begin communication about sex?

Listening and Feedback
What are key traits of good listeners?

Discovering Your Partner's Needs
What are effective ways of learning about your partner's wants and needs?

Learning to Make Requests
How can we effectively express our sexual needs?

Expressing and Receiving Complaints
What strategies can help us constructively register a complaint with a partner and respond to complaints?

Saying No
What are potentially useful ways to say no to intimate involvements?

Nonverbal Sexual Communication
What aspects of nonverbal communication have particular significance for our sexuality?

Communication Patterns in Successful and Unsuccessful Relationships
What patterns of couple communication characterize successful and unsuccessful relationships?

iStockphoto.com/digitalskillet

179

For me, the potential for falling in love begins with a physical attraction. But looks only count for so much. I need an intimate friendship and closeness in order to possibly fall in love. Trust is another important part of a relationship that can lead to love. A prospective partner would also need to share some of my interests, and I would need to share some of his. Finally, and perhaps most important, good communication in a relationship is essential for me to be truly in love. (Authors' files)

Love, attraction, attachment, and sexual communication in intimate relationships are important and complex aspects of people's lives. In this chapter, we look at these interactions from various perspectives and examine some of the research dealing with them. We consider a number of questions: What is love? What kinds of love are there? What determines why we fall in love with one person and not another? How do various styles of attraction influence our relationships with others? How does sex fit into relationships? How does love relate to jealousy? What qualities or behaviors help to maintain relationship satisfaction over many years? And finally, how does sexual communication contribute to the satisfaction of intimate relationships?

What Is Love?

> O Love is the crooked thing,
> There is nobody wise enough
> To find out all that is in it
> For he would be thinking of love
> Till the stars had run away
> And the shadows eaten the moon.
>> William Butler Yeats, "Brown Penny"

Love has intrigued people throughout history. Its joys and sorrows have inspired artists and poets, novelists, filmmakers, and other students of human interaction. Indeed, love is one of the most pervasive themes in the art and literature of many cultures. Each of our own lives has been influenced in significant ways by love, beginning with the love we received as infants and children. Our best and worst moments in life can be tied to a love relationship.

But what is love? How do we define it?

Love is a special kind of attitude, with strong emotional and behavioral components. It is also a phenomenon that eludes easy definition or explanation. As the following definitions suggest, love can mean different things to different people:

Love is patient and kind; love is not jealous or boastful; it is not arrogant or rude. Love does not insist on its own way; it is not irritable or resentful; it does not rejoice at wrong, but rejoices in the right. Love bears all things, believes all things, hopes all things, endures all things. (I Corinthians 13:4–7)

Love is a temporary insanity curable by marriage or by removal of the patient from the influences under which he incurred the disorder. (Bierce, 1943, p. 202)

Love is that condition in which the happiness of another person is essential to your own. (Heinlein, 1961, p. 345)

As difficult as love is to define, can it be meaningfully measured? Some social scientists have attempted to do so, with varied results (Davis & Latty-Mann, 1987; Graham, 2011;

Love has been the inspiration for some of our greatest works of literature, art, and music.

© Rolf Konow/Sygma/Corbis

Hatfield & Sprecher, 1986). In the last 60 years, over 30 different measures of love have been developed (Hatfield et al., 2012). Perhaps the most ambitious attempt to measure love was undertaken years ago by psychologist Zick Rubin (1970, 1973), who developed a 13-item questionnaire (the Love Scale) designed to assess a person's desire for intimacy with, and caring and attachment for, another. Some evidence supporting the validity of the Love Scale was obtained in an investigation of the popular belief that lovers spend a great deal of time looking into one another's eyes (Rubin, 1970). Couples were observed through a one-way mirror while they waited to participate in a psychological experiment. The findings revealed that weak lovers (couples who scored below average on the Love Scale) made significantly less eye contact than did strong lovers (those with above-average scores).

Perhaps in the years ahead we will have access to a variety of new perspectives on the question of what love is, largely because of a marked increase in the number of scientists, especially social psychologists, who have begun to study love.

Types of Love

Love takes many forms. Love exists between parent and child and between family members. Love between friends, known to the ancient Greeks as *philia*, involves concern for the other's well-being. Lovers may experience two additional types of love: passionate love and companionate love. In this section we look more closely at these two widely discussed types of love and then present two contemporary models, or theories, of love.

Passionate Love

Passionate love, also known as romantic love or infatuation, is a state of extreme absorption with and desire for another. It is characterized by intense feelings of tenderness, elation, anxiety, sexual desire, and ecstasy. Generalized physiological arousal, including increased heartbeat, perspiration, blushing, and stomach churning along with a feeling of great excitement, often accompanies this form of love.

passionate love
State of extreme absorption in another person; also known as romantic love.

Intense passionate love typically occurs early in a relationship. It sometimes seems as though the less one knows the other person, the more intense the passionate love is. In passionate love, people often overlook faults and avoid conflicts. Logic and reasoned consideration are swept away by the excitement. One perceives the object of one's passionate love as providing complete personal fulfillment.

Not surprisingly, passionate love is often short-lived, typically measured in months rather than years. Love that is based on ignorance of a person's full character is likely to change with increased familiarity. However, this temporary aspect of passionate love is often overlooked, especially by young people who lack experience with long-term love relationships. Many couples, convinced of the permanence of their passionate feelings, choose to make some kind of commitment to each other (becoming engaged, moving in together, getting married, etc.) while still fired by the fuel of passionate love—only to become disillusioned later. When ecstasy gives way to routine, and the annoyances and conflicts typical of ongoing relationships surface, lovers may begin to have some doubts about their partners.

> The first weeks and months of my relationship with Bob were incredible. I felt like I had found the perfect partner, someone who filled all that was missing in my life. Then, suddenly, he started to get on my nerves, and we started fighting every time we saw each other. It took a while to realize that we were finally seeing each other as real people instead of dream companions. (Authors' files)

Some couples can work through this period to ultimately find a solid basis on which to build a lasting relationship of mutual love. Others discover, often to their dismay, that the only thing they ever really shared was passion. Unfortunately, many people who experience diminishing passion believe that this is the end of love rather than a possible transition to a different kind of love.

A recent study of 274 married couples revealed that passionate love may be surprisingly enduring. Of the couples in the sample married for longer than 10 years, 40% reported being "very intensely in love." Correlates of long-term intense love included positive thoughts about the partner, affectionate behavior, shared activities, frequent sexual activity, and general life happiness (O'Leary et al., 2012).

Companionate Love

companionate love
A type of love characterized by friendly affection and deep attachment based on extensive familiarity with the loved one.

Companionate love is a less intense emotion than passionate love. It is characterized by friendly affection and a deep attachment that is based on extensive familiarity with the loved one. It involves a thoughtful appreciation of one's partner. Companionate love often encompasses a tolerance for another's shortcomings along with a desire to overcome difficulties and conflicts in a relationship. This kind of love is committed to ongoing nurturing of a partnership. In short, companionate love is often enduring, whereas passionate love is frequently transitory.

Sex in a companionate relationship typically reflects feelings associated with familiarity, especially the security of knowing what pleases the other. This foundation of knowledge and sexual trust can encourage experimentation and subtle communication. As companionate love grows and the relationship develops over time, verbal communication about sexual issues and concerns becomes more comfortable and increasingly frequent (Humphreys & Newby, 2007). Sexual pleasure, enhanced by communication, strengthens the overall bond of a companionate relationship. Although sex may be less exciting than in passionate love, it is often experienced as richer, more meaningful, and more deeply satisfying, as the following statement reveals:

Critical Thinking Question

What do you think are the key differences between passionate love and companionate love? How do these characteristics fit into a list of things that you believe are essential to a successful, lasting love relationship?

Sternberg's Triangular Theory of Love

The distinction between passionate and companionate love has been further refined by psychologist Robert Sternberg (1986, 1988), who has proposed an interesting theoretical framework for conceptualizing what people experience when they report being in love. According to Sternberg, love has three dimensions or components: passion, intimacy, and commitment (▌ Figure 7.1):

passion
The motivational component of Sternberg's triangular love theory.

- **Passion** is the motivational component that fuels romantic feelings, physical attraction, and desire for sexual interaction. Passion instills a deep desire to be united with the loved one. In a sense, passion is like an addiction, because its capacity to provide intense stimulation and pleasure can exert a powerful craving in a person.

intimacy
The emotional component of Sternberg's triangular love theory.

- **Intimacy** is the emotional component of love that encompasses the sense of being bonded with another person. It includes feelings of warmth, sharing, and

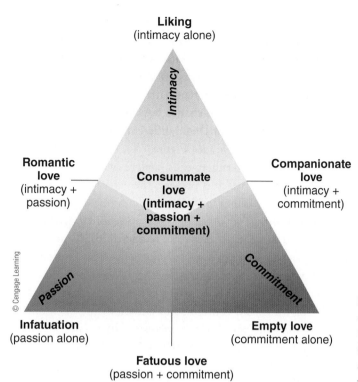

Liking
(intimacy alone)

Intimacy

Romantic love
(intimacy + passion)

**Consummate love
(intimacy + passion + commitment)**

Companionate love
(intimacy + commitment)

Passion

Commitment

© Cengage Learning

Infatuation
(passion alone)

Empty love
(commitment alone)

Fatuous love
(passion + commitment)

❚ Figure 7.1 In Sternberg's love triangle, various combinations of the three components of love (passion, intimacy, and commitment) make up the different kinds of love. Note that nonlove is the absence of all three components.

emotional closeness. Intimacy also embraces a willingness to help the other and openness to sharing private thoughts and feelings with the beloved.

- **Commitment** is the thinking or cognitive aspect of love. It refers to the conscious decision to love another and to maintain a relationship over time despite difficulties that may arise.

Sternberg maintains that passion tends to develop rapidly and intensely in the early stages of a love relationship and then declines as the relationship progresses. In contrast, intimacy and commitment continue to build gradually over time, although at different rates (❚ Figure 7.2). Thus Sternberg's theory provides a conceptual basis for the transition from passionate to companionate love. Passionate love, consisting mainly of romantic feelings and physical attraction, peaks early and quickly subsides. However, as passion weakens, many couples experience a growth in both intimacy and commitment as their relationship evolves into one of companionate love (Sprecher & Regan, 1998). If intimacy does not flourish and if a couple does not make a mutual decision to commit to

commitment
The thinking component of Sternberg's triangular love theory.

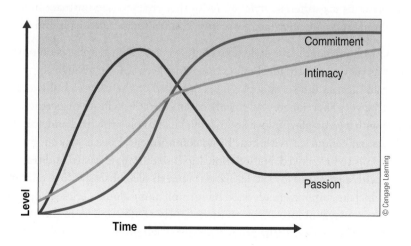

Commitment

Intimacy

Passion

Level

Time

© Cengage Learning

❚ Figure 7.2 Sternberg theorizes that the passion component of love peaks early in a relationship and then declines, whereas the other two components, intimacy and commitment, continue to build gradually over time.

each other, their relationship will be on shaky ground when passion fades and conflicts surface. In contrast, commitment and a sense of bondedness and mutual concern can sustain a relationship during periods of dissatisfaction and conflict.

All three of Sternberg's love components are important dimensions of a loving relationship, but they typically exist in different patterns and to varying degrees in different relationships. Moreover, they often change over time within the same relationship. Sternberg suggests that such variations yield different kinds of love—or at least differences in how people experience love (see Figure 7.1). For instance, the absence of all three components yields what Sternberg calls *nonlove* (what most of us feel for casual acquaintances). When only intimacy is present, the experience is one of *friendship* or liking. If only passion exists, without intimacy or commitment, one experiences *infatuation*. The presence of commitment without passion and intimacy yields *empty love* (such as might be experienced in a long-term, static relationship). If intimacy and commitment exist without passion, one experiences *companionate love* (often characteristic of happy couples who have shared many years together). When passion and commitment are present but without intimacy, the experience is *fatuous love*, a kind of foolish involvement characteristic of whirlwind courtships or situations in which one worships and longs for another person from afar. Love characterized by passion and intimacy but no commitment is described by Sternberg as *romantic love*. Finally, when all three components are present, the experience is *consummate love*, the fullest kind of love, which people often strive for but find difficult to achieve and sustain.

Empirical research has provided some support for Sternberg's love model. One study of dating couples reported that the presence of two of Sternberg's love components—intimacy and commitment—was predictive of relationship stability and longevity (Hendrick et al., 1988). Another investigation found that married people demonstrated higher levels of commitment to their relationships than unmarried people did, a finding consistent with Sternberg's model (Acker & Davis, 1992). This same study found that, although intimacy continued to rise in longer relationships, passion declined for both sexes but more sharply for women than for men. Further investigations of Sternberg's triangular theory found that lovers' definition and communication of the three components of love remained relatively stable over time (Reeder, 1996) and that compatibility of a couple is enhanced if both partners possess similar levels of passion, intimacy, and commitment (Drigotas et al., 1999).

Lee's Styles of Loving

Instead of attempting to describe different patterns or *types* of love, John Allan Lee (1974, 1988, 1998) proposed a theory that uses terms derived from ancient Greek words to describe six different *styles of loving* that characterize intimate human relationships: romantic, game playing, possessive, companionate, altruistic, and pragmatic.

- People with a *romantic* love style (*eros*) tend to place their emphasis on physical beauty as they search for ideal mates. Romantic, erotic lovers delight in the visual beauty and tactile and sensual pleasures provided by their lover's body, and they tend to be very affectionate and openly communicative with their partner.
- People with a *game-playing* love style (*ludus*) like to play the field and acquire many sexual "conquests" with little or no commitment. Love is for fun, the act of seduction is to be enjoyed, and relationships are to remain casual and transitory.
- People with a *possessive* love style (*mania*) tend to seek obsessive love relationships, which are often characterized by turmoil and jealousy. These people live a roller-coaster style of love, in which each display of affection from the lover brings ecstasy and the mildest slight produces painful agitation.

- People with a *companionate* love style (*storge* [STOR-gay]) are slow to develop affection and commitment but tend to experience relationships that endure. This style is love without fever or turmoil, a peaceful and quiet kind of relating that usually begins as friendship and develops over time into affection and love.
- People with an *altruistic* love style (*agape*) are characterized by selflessness and a caring, compassionate desire to give to another without expectation of reciprocity. Such love is patient and never demanding or jealous.
- People with a *pragmatic* love style (*pragma*) tend to select lovers based on rational, practical criteria (such as shared interests) that are likely to lead to mutual satisfaction. These individuals approach love in a businesslike fashion, trying to get the best "romantic deal" by seeking partners with social, educational, religious, and interest patterns that are compatible with their own.

What happens when two different people in a relationship naturally tend toward different styles of loving? For Lee this is a critical question. He suggests that loving relationships frequently fail to thrive over time because "too often people are speaking different languages when they speak of love" (Lee, 1974, p. 44). Even though both partners try to build a lasting involvement, their efforts can be undermined by a losing struggle to integrate incompatible loving styles. In contrast, satisfaction and success in loving relationships often depend on finding a mate who "shares the same approach to loving, the same definition of love" (Lee, 1974, p. 44).

An inventory called the Love Attitude Scale has been developed to measure Lee's six loving styles (Hendrick & Hendrick, 1986, 2003), and this research tool has generated some empirical studies of his theory. Studies that have used this scale provide some support for Lee's hypothesis that relationship success is influenced by compatibility in styles of loving (Davis & Latty-Mann, 1987; Hendrick & Hendrick, 2003). College students prefer to date people with love styles similar to their own (Hahn & Blass, 1997; Hendrick & Hendrick, 2003). Evidence also exists of sex differences in college students' styles of love. One investigation revealed that college women are more likely than men to embrace companionate, pragmatic, and possessive love styles, whereas college men are more likely to manifest romantic or game-playing love styles (Hendrick & Hendrick, 2003). Another study also found sex differences in love styles among college students, with women more likely to manifest companionate, pragmatic, and romantic styles, and men more likely to embrace game-playing and altruistic styles (Lacey et al., 2004).

Falling in Love: Why and With Whom?

What determines why people fall in love and with whom they fall in love? These questions are exceedingly complex. Some writers believe that people fall in love to overcome a sense of aloneness and separateness. Psychoanalyst Erich Fromm (1965) suggested that union with another person is the deepest need of humans. Another psychoanalyst and writer, Rollo May, author of *Love and Will* (1969), also believed that as people experience their own solitariness, they long for the refuge of union with another through love. Other observers see loneliness as a by-product of our individualistic and highly mobile society rather than as an inherent part of the human condition (Seepersad et al., 2008). This view emphasizes the connectedness that we all have with the people around us—through all our social relationships, language, and culture. According to this view, love relationships are one aspect of a person's social network rather than a cure for the "disease" of loneliness.

We have seen that love is a complex human emotion that can be explained, at least in part, by various psychosocial interpretations of its origins. However, the answer to why we fall in love also encompasses, to some degree, complex neurochemical processes that occur in our brains when we are attracted to another person. We discuss findings about the chemistry of love in the next section.

The Chemistry of Love

People caught up in the intense passion of blooming love often report feeling swept away or feeling a kind of natural high. Such reactions might have a basis, at least in part, in brain chemistry, according to researchers Michael Liebowitz, author of *The Chemistry of Love* (1983), and Anthony Walsh, author of *The Science of Love* (1991). These investigators contend that the initial elation and the energizing "high" of excitement, giddiness, and euphoria characteristic of passionate love result from surging levels of three key brain chemicals: norepinephrine, dopamine, and especially phenylethylamine (PEA). These chemicals, called *neurotransmitters*, allow brain cells to communicate with each other, and they are chemically similar to amphetamine drugs; thus they produce amphetamine-like effects, such as euphoria, giddiness, and elation.

The amphetamine-like highs and elevated sexual arousal associated with new love typically do not last—perhaps in part because the body eventually develops a tolerance to PEA and related neurotransmitters, just as it does to amphetamines. With time, our brains simply become unable to keep up with the demand for more and more PEA to produce love's special kick. Thus the highs that we feel at the beginning of a relationship eventually diminish. This observation provides a plausible biological explanation for why passionate or romantic love is short-lived.

Liebowitz points out another parallel to amphetamine use. He notes that the anxiety, despair, and pain that follow the loss—or even potential loss—of a romantic love relationship are similar to what a person addicted to amphetamines experiences during drug withdrawal. In both cases the loss of mood-lifting chemicals results in a sometimes protracted period of emotional pain.

Other brain chemicals exist that help to explain why some relationships endure beyond the initial highs of passionate love. The continued progression from infatuation to the deep attachment characteristic of long-term loving relationships results, at least in part, from the brain gradually stepping up production of another set of neurotransmitters called *endorphins*. These morphinelike, pain-blunting chemicals are soothing substances that help produce a sense of euphoria, security, tranquility, and peace. Thus they can cause us to feel good when we are with a loved partner. This could be another reason why abandoned lovers feel so terrible after their loss: They are deprived of their daily dose of feel-good chemicals. Perhaps in the near future medical intervention may be able to boost the level of these chemicals to counter a dangerous depression sometimes associated with the "heartbreak" of lost love (Fischetti, 2011a).

As we learned in Chapter 6, dopamine and oxytocin are brain chemicals that also contribute to sexual arousal and feelings of being in love. Results of a study provide evidence of the role of dopamine in the chemistry of love. In this investigation, researchers used functional magnetic resonance imaging (fMRI) to scan the brains of men and women while they viewed photos of a loved romantic partner and of a close friend. It was the photos of lovers, not friends, that caused areas of the brain rich in dopamine to "light up" (Bartels & Zeki, 2004). Other research utilizing fMRI has provided additional evidence of a strong link between feelings of being in love and the release of neurotransmitters and other brain chemicals such as dopamine, serotonin, oxytocin, and vasopression (Fischetti, 2011b).

Recent research suggests that the use of hormonal contraceptives may reduce women's attractiveness to potential love/sex partners, a condition that may be based on altered chemistry (Wang, 2011). Women appear to emit chemical signals when they are fertile and/or ovulating, and these chemical cues appear to be altered or eliminated by hormonal-based birth control methods. Thus, it appears that birth control pills or injections may mask the chemistry of attraction that plays a role in bringing romantic partners together (Wang, 2011). This possibility opens up an area for new research, which may or may not confirm that hormonal birth control methods are linked to the chemistry of attraction and love.

Just as we know little about why people fall in love, we have no simple explanation for why they fall in love with one person instead of another. A number of factors are often important: proximity, similarity, reciprocity, and physical attractiveness.

Proximity

Although people often overlook **proximity**, or geographic nearness, in listing factors that attracted them to a particular person, proximity is one of the most important variables. We often develop close relationships with people whom we see frequently in our neighborhood, in school, at work, or at our place of worship.

Why is proximity such a powerful factor in interpersonal attraction? Social psychologists have offered a number of plausible explanations. One is simply that familiarity breeds liking or loving. Research has shown that when we are repeatedly exposed to novel stimuli—unfamiliar musical selections, works of art, human faces, and so on—our liking for such stimuli increases (Bornstein, 1989; Brooks & Watkins, 1989). This phenomenon, called the **mere exposure effect**, explains in part why we are attracted to people in proximity to us.

Proximity also influences whom we are attracted to because people often meet each other in locations where they are engaging in activities that reflect common interests. This observation is supported by the National Health and Social Life Survey (NHSLS; see Chapter 2), which included questions about where people are most likely to meet their intimate partners. Laumann and his associates (1994) sorted their data into high- and low-preselection locales. High preselection meant that people were together in locations where they shared common interests, such as physical health and fitness (working out at the local fitness center) or topics of study (taking the same classes at school). Low-preselection locales included places that bring a diverse group of people together, such as bars and vacation sites. Predictably, Laumann and his colleagues found that places with high levels of preselection were more likely to yield sex-partner connections than locales with low-preselection values.

proximity
The geographic nearness of one person to another, which is an important factor in interpersonal attraction.

mere exposure effect
A phenomenon in which repeated exposure to novel stimuli tends to increase an individual's liking for such stimuli.

similarity
The similarity of beliefs, interests, and values, which is a factor in attracting people to one another.

Similarity

Similarity is also influential in determining whom we fall in love with. Contrary to the old adage that opposites attract, people who fall in love often share common beliefs, values, attitudes, interests, and intellectual abilities (Graf & Schwartz, 2011; Morry et al., 2011). We also are inclined to pair romantically with people whose level of physical attractiveness is similar to our own (Garcia & Markey, 2007; Taylor et al., 2011; van Straaten et al., 2009).

We also tend to be attracted to people who are similar to us in age, educational status, and religious affiliation. Similarity in personal characteristics is referred to as *homophily*, or the tendency to form relationships with people of similar or equal status in various social and personal attributes. Data from the NHSLS reflecting homophily in age, educational status, and religion for various types of relationships appear in ■ Table 7.1.

People who fall in love often share common interests.

■ **TABLE 7.1 Percentage of Couples in Various Types of Relationships That Are Homophilous for Age, Educational Status, and Religion**

	Type of Relationship			
Type of Homophily	**Marriage (%)**	**Cohabitation (%)**	**Long-Term Partnership (%)**	**Short-Term Partnership (%)**
Age (defined as difference of no more than 5 years in partners' ages)	78	75	76	83
Educational status (defined as difference of no more than one educational category[a])	82	87	83	87
Religion (defined as having same affiliation)	72	53	56	60

[a]Categories: Less than high school, high school graduate, vocational training, 4-year college degree, postgraduate
SOURCE: Adapted from Laumann et al. (1994).

The NHSLS also revealed that people generally tend to form partnerships with people of similar race and ethnicity. The following Sexuality and Diversity discussion describes this dimension of attraction.

SEXUALITY and DIVERSITY
Partner Choice and Race

The NHSLS provided data about the extent to which people form intimate relationships with members of the same race. As described in Chapter 2, a lack of funds forced Edward Laumann and his associates (1994) to include adequate numbers of only the two largest ethnic minorities in America. Consequently, ■ Table 7.2 contains data pertaining only to White Americans, African Americans, and Hispanic Americans. These data summarize a sample of almost 2,000 nonmarital, noncohabitational heterosexual partnerships.

As you can see by examining the values in Table 7.2, the percentages of same-race noncohabitational partnerships are very high for both sexes among Whites and African Americans. In contrast, the percentage of same-race noncohabitational partnerships is considerably lower among Hispanic respondents. Thus it would appear that "Hispanics as a group are less exclusive with respect to sexual partnering than are whites or blacks" (Laumann et al., 1994, p. 246).

A more recent investigation of heterosexual dating profiles of over 6,000 U.S. citizens found that Whites are least open to out-dating and "are far more likely than minorities to prefer to date only within their race" (Robnett & Feliciano, 2011, p. 32). Hispanic Americans, African Americans, and Asian Americans are more likely to consider Whites as possible dating partners than Whites are to include them as prospective partners. Blacks are far more exclusionary of Whites than is the case with Hispanics and Asians. All men, with the exception of African American men, are the most exclusionary of African American women.

■ **TABLE 7.2 Noncohabitational Sexual Partnerships by Race and Sex**

	Percentage of Same-Race Partnerships	
Race	**Men (%)**	**Women (%)**
White	92	87
African American	82	97
Hispanic American	54	65

SOURCE: Laumann et al. (1994).

Why are we drawn to people who are like us? For one thing, people with similar attitudes and interests are often inclined to participate in the same kinds of leisure activities. Even more important, we are more likely to communicate well with people whose ideas and opinions are similar to ours, and communication is an important aspect of enduring relationships. It is also reassuring to be with similar people, because they confirm our view of the world, validate our own experiences, and support our opinions and beliefs (Amodio & Showers, 2005).

Perceived similarity in others could be especially attractive to us because we have strong expectations of being accepted and appreciated by people who are like us (Sprecher & McKinney, 1993). That these expectations are often fulfilled is reflected in research findings indicating that people who are similar in a variety of social and personal traits are more likely to stay together than are people who are less similar (Weber, 1998).

Reciprocity

Still another factor drawing us to a particular individual is our perception that that person is interested in us. People tend to react positively to flattery, compliments, and other expressions of liking and affection. In the study of interpersonal attraction, this concept is reflected in the principle of **reciprocity**, which holds that when we receive expressions of liking or loving, we tend to respond in kind (Sprecher, 1998; Whitchurch et al., 2011). In turn, reciprocal responses can set in motion a further escalation of the relationship: By responding warmly to people who we believe feel positively toward us, we often induce them to like us even more. Furthermore, our sense of self-esteem is affected by the extent to which we feel attached to and liked by others. Knowing that someone likes us increases our sense of belonging or being socially integrated in a relationship and hence bolsters our self-esteem (Baumeister & Leary, 1995).

reciprocity
The principle that when we are recipients of expressions of liking or loving, we tend to respond in kind.

Physical Attractiveness

As you might expect, **physical attractiveness** often plays a dominant role in drawing lovers together (Baredis et al., 2011; Swami & Furnham, 2008). Despite the saying that beauty is only skin deep, experiments have shown that physically attractive people are more likely to be sought as friends and lovers and to be perceived as more likable, interesting, sensitive, poised, happy, sexy, competent, and socially skilled than are people of average or unattractive appearance (Baron et al., 2006; Jaeger, 2011; Marcus & Miller, 2003).

physical attractiveness
Physical beauty, which is a powerful factor in attracting lovers to each other.

Why is physical beauty such a powerful factor in attracting us to others? One answer has to do with aesthetics. We all enjoy looking at something or someone whom we consider beautiful. Another factor is that many people apparently believe that beautiful people have more to offer in terms of desirable personal qualities than those who are less attractive. We might also be attracted to beautiful people because they offer us the possibility of status by association. And perhaps beautiful people, by virtue of having been treated well by others over the course of their lives, are secure and comfortable with themselves, a fact that can translate into especially satisfying relationships with others. Finally, evidence shows that people consider physical beauty an indicator of health and that, other things being equal, we are attracted to healthy people (Marcus & Miller, 2003; Swami & Furnham, 2008).

Researchers have sought to determine whether both sexes are equally influenced by physical attractiveness in forming impressions of people they meet. Several studies have found that male college students place significantly greater emphasis on physical appearance in selecting a partner for a sexual or long-term relationship than do college women, who tend to place greater emphasis on such traits as ambition, status, earning potential, interpersonal warmth, and personality characteristics (Eastwick et al., 2008; McGee & Shevlin, 2009). Other studies have found that American men place a greater emphasis on physical attractiveness than do American women (Coutino, 2007; Fisher et al., 2008). Is this difference typical of men and women in other cultures as well?

A cross-cultural study of sex differences in heterosexual mate preferences provided strong evidence that men worldwide place greater value than do women on mates who are both young and physically attractive. In this study, conducted by psychologist David Buss (1994), subjects from 37 samples drawn from Africa, Asia, Europe, North and South America, Australia, and New Zealand were asked to rate the importance of a wide range of personal attributes in potential mates. These attributes included dependability, attractiveness, age, good financial prospects, intelligence, sociability, and chastity.

Without exception, men in all the surveyed cultures placed greater emphasis on a potential mate's youth and attractiveness than women did (Buss, 1994). In contrast, women placed greater value on potential mates who were somewhat older, had good financial prospects, and were dependable and industrious. This is not to say that physical attractiveness was unimportant to women of these varied cultures. In fact, many women considered physical attractiveness important—although less so than financial responsibility and dependability.

What accounts for the apparent consistency across so many cultures in what appeals to men and to women in a potential mate? And what accounts for the differences between men and women? Buss provides a *sociobiological* explanation—that is, he explains a species' behavior in terms of its evolutionary needs. According to Buss (1994), evolution has biased mate preferences in humans, as it has in other animals. Males are attracted to young, physically attractive females because these characteristics are good predictors of reproductive success. Simply put, a young woman has more reproductive years remaining than does an older woman. Furthermore, smooth, unblemished skin, good muscle tone, lustrous hair, and similar features of physical attractiveness are indicators of good health—and thus are strong signs of reproductive value. On the other hand, women tend to find older, established men more attractive because characteristics such as wealth and high social rank are predictors of security for their offspring. Youth and physical attractiveness are less important to females, because fertility is less related to age for males than it is for females.

Studies have also revealed that American women typically consider traits such as ambition and being a good provider more important in mate selection than do their male counterparts (Eastwick et al., 2008; Janssens et al., 2011; McGee & Shevlin, 2009). Differences between American men and women in other aspects of mate selection are described in the following Sexuality and Diversity discussion.

SEXUALITY and DIVERSITY

Differences Between American Men and Women in Mate Selection Preferences

Researchers Susan Sprecher, Quintin Sullivan, and Elaine Hatfield (1994) surveyed a national representative sample of more than 13,000 English- or Spanish-speaking people in the United States, age 19 or older. ▌ Figure 7.3 shows the average response rating of men and women to several items on a questionnaire used in the survey. One part of the questionnaire contained several items that asked respondents how willing they would be to marry someone who had more or less education, was older or younger, was not likely to hold a steady job, and so on. Subjects indicated their level of agreement with each item on a scale from 1 ("not at all") to 7 ("very willing").

How Willing Would You Be to Marry Someone Who . . .

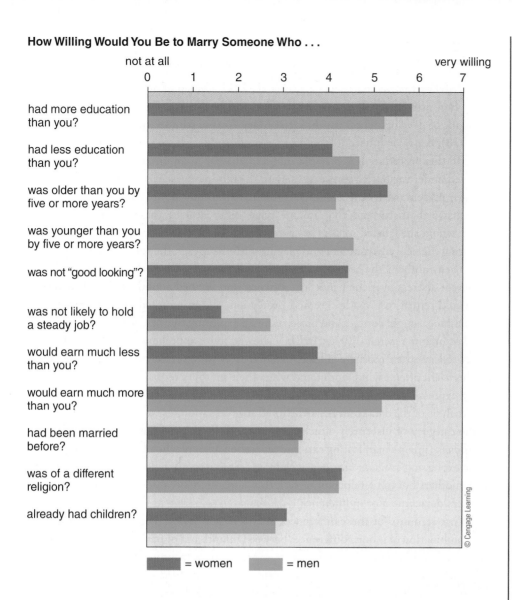

Figure 7.3 Differences between American men and women in aspects of mate selection.

The results indicate that women respondents were significantly more willing than men to marry someone who was better educated, was older, would earn more, and was not good looking. Conversely, women were significantly less willing than men to marry someone who had less education, was younger, was not likely to hold a steady job, and would earn less. There were only minor differences between the sexes on items related to prior marriages, religion, and already having children.

Love and Styles of Attachment

Attachment is a term for the intense emotional tie that develops between two individuals, such as the tie between an infant and a parent or between adult lovers (Rholes et al., 2006). It is possible to experience attachment without love, but it is unlikely that love of one person for another can exist in the absence of attachment. Although love itself is difficult to measure and study, researchers have had considerable success in investigating various aspects of attachment, including how it forms, effects of attachment deprivation, and styles of attachment. The last of these dimensions, styles of attachment, is of particular interest to social scientists. In the following pages, we examine key research findings pertaining to attachment and human relationships.

attachment
Intense emotional tie between two individuals, such as an infant and a parent or adult lovers.

Attachment Styles

The way we form attachments, which has its roots in infancy, has a great impact on how we relate to loved partners (Zayas et al., 2011). Much of our scientific knowledge about how attachment styles are established and how they later affect us comes from the work of developmental psychologist Mary Ainsworth (1979, 1989; Ainsworth et al., 1978). Ainsworth used a laboratory procedure that she labeled the "strange situation." In this procedure a 1-year-old infant's behavior in an unfamiliar environment is assessed under various circumstances: with the mother present, with the mother and a stranger present, with only a stranger present, and totally alone.

Ainsworth discovered that infants react differently to these strange situations. Some, whom she labeled *securely attached*, used their mothers as a safe base for happily exploring the new environment and playing with the toys in the room. When separated from their mothers, the securely attached infants appeared to feel safe, expressed only moderate distress over their mothers' absence, and seemed confident that their mothers would return to provide care and protection. When reunited with their mothers, these infants sought contact and often resumed exploring their environments. *Insecurely attached* infants reacted differently. They showed more apprehension and less of a tendency to leave their mothers' sides to explore. They were severely distressed when their mothers left, often crying loudly, and when their mothers returned, they often seemed angry, expressing hostility or indifference.

Analysis of the data from Ainsworth's strange-situation research allowed subdivision of the category of insecurely attached infants into those expressing *anxious-ambivalent attachment* (infants manifesting extreme separation anxiety when their mothers left) and those expressing *avoidant attachment* (infants seeming to want close bodily contact with their mothers but to be reluctant to seek this, apparently because they could sense their mothers' detachment or indifference).

What accounts for these differences in attachment styles? The answer probably lies in a combination of inborn differences between infants and of parenting practices. Some infants are innately predisposed to form more secure attachments than others, just as some newborns seem to respond more positively to being held and cuddled than others (Picardi et al., 2011). A second factor contributing to differences in babies' reactions to the strange situation was the way their mothers responded to them at home. Mothers of securely attached infants were inclined to be sensitive and responsive to their infants. For example, some mothers fed their babies when they were hungry rather than following a set schedule. They also tended to cuddle their babies at times other than during feeding or diapering. In contrast, mothers of infants classified in one of the two insecurely attached categories tended to be less sensitive and responsive and were inconsistent in their reactions to their babies. For example, they fed their infants when they felt like it and sometimes ignored their babies' cries of hunger at other times. These mothers also tended to avoid close physical contact with their babies.

The establishment of a trusting, secure attachment between a child and a parent appears to have demonstrable effects on a child's later development. Several studies have shown that securely attached children, who learn that parents are a source of security and trustworthiness, are likely to demonstrate much greater social competence than children in either category of insecure attachment (Aspelmeier & Kerns, 2003). Anxious-ambivalent children, who have learned that parents respond inconsistently to their needs, are often plagued with uncertainty in new situations, and they frequently exhibit negative reactions to life situations, such as angry outbursts, an obsessive need to be near their parents, and an inconsistency in responses to others that reflects ambivalence about how to respond. Avoidant children, whose parents often neglect them, develop negative views of others and are reluctant to let others get close to them.

According to research on attachment, the quality of cuddling and snuggling behaviors that occur between babies and parents influences comparable interactions between adult lovers.

© Jeff Greenberg/PhotoEdit

These various attachment styles, developed during infancy, tend to continue throughout our lives and to exert considerable influence on both our capacity to form loving attachments and the way we relate to significant others.

Adult Intimate Relationships as an Attachment Process

A number of social scientists have conceptualized adults' close or romantic relationships as an attachment process (e.g., Aspelmeier & Kerns, 2003; Feeney & Noller, 1996; Sprecher & Fehr, 2011). From this perspective, individuals transfer attachment styles and patterns acquired from parent–child relationships to peers with whom they become emotionally and sexually involved. In this sense, romantic partners come to serve as attachment figures (Collins et al., 2006; Riggs et al., 2011; Van Ecke, 2007).

Adult attachments between lovers or partners can be one of the three varieties we described. Securely attached adults seem to be best equipped to establish stable, satisfying relationships. These individuals find it relatively easy to get close to others and feel comfortable with others being close to them. They feel secure in relationships and do not fear being abandoned. In contrast, adults with an anxious-ambivalent attachment style often have a poor self-image and feel insecure and dissatisfied with their romantic relationships (Samantha et al., 2011). Reflecting the third attachment style, avoidant adults feel uncomfortable with any degree of closeness to a partner (Mashek et al., 2011). Avoidantly attached individuals "may be less resistant to temptations for infidelity due to lower levels of commitment in romantic relationships" (DeWall et al., 2011, p. 1302). These individuals often have difficulty trusting or depending on a partner. They frequently view others negatively and thus find it hard to let others get close to them and share intimacy. This trait is reflected in the findings of a study of Canadian married couples indicating that subjects with an avoidant attachment style tended to report low levels of sexual satisfaction in their relationship (Butzer & Campbell, 2008). Avoidant adults desire a great deal of independence. Research reveals that slightly more than half of U.S. adults are securely attached, about one fourth are avoidant, and one fifth are anxious-ambivalent (Hazan & Shaver, 1987). ■ Table 7.3 outlines some of the common ways the three attachment styles influence interpersonal relationships.

At a Glance

■ TABLE 7.3 Impact of Attachment Styles on Intimate Relationships

Securely Attached Adults	Anxious-Ambivalent Adults	Avoidant Adults
Find it relatively easy to get close to others. Comfortable having others close to them.	Want to be close to others but believe that others may not want to be close to them.	Very uncomfortable with being close to others.
Feel secure in relationships and do not fear abandonment.	Worry that partners do not really love them and thus may leave them.	Believe that love is only transitory and that their partner will inevitably leave at some point in time.
Comfortable with both depending on partner and being depended upon.	May want to merge completely and be engulfed by partner.	Worry about becoming dependent on another and distrustful of someone depending on them.
Love relationships typically characterized by happiness, satisfaction, trust, and reciprocal emotional support.	Relationships characterized by roller-coaster emotional shifts and obsessive sexual attraction and jealousy.	Generally want less closeness than their partners seem to desire. Fear intimacy and experience emotional shifts from highs to lows.
Relationship duration averages 10 years.	Relationship duration averages 5 years.	Relationship duration averages 6 years.

SOURCES: Adapted from Ainsworth (1989), Ainsworth et al. (1978), and Shaver et al. (1988).

Research indicates that people who form couples commonly have the same style of attachment—further evidence of how influential similarity is in determining whom we fall in love with (Gallo & Smith, 2001; Latty-Mann & Davis, 1996). The most common pairing was composed of people who both had a secure attachment style (Chappell & Davis, 1998). This is not surprising, because secure people tend to respond positively to others and feel comfortable with closeness; their attachment style thus makes them more desirable as love partners than people with any other attachment style. In one study of 354 couples, over half comprised people who both had a secure attachment style. Predictably, there were no pairings of people who both had an anxious-ambivalent or an avoidant attachment style—no doubt because such people would be quite incompatible with each other. People with a secure attachment style reported the highest level of relationship satisfaction, especially if their partner also had that style (Kirkpatrick & Davis, 1994).

Issues in Loving Relationships

In the following paragraphs, we explore dynamics that cause complications in intimate relationships, focusing on two questions in particular. First we discuss the relationship between love and sex. Next we explore how jealousy affects relationships and what, if anything, can be done to keep it under control.

What Is the Relationship Between Love and Sex?

Although we tend to associate sex with love, the connection is not always clear. It is certainly true that some people engage in sexual relations without being in love. One example of sex without love is the relatively common practice of **hook-ups** (or "hooking up"), which are short-term, loveless, sexual liaisons that occur during a brief interval (e.g., spring break, an ocean cruise, or a "one-nighter") (Lambert et al., 2003). Another example of loveless sex is the phenomenon of **"friends with benefits" relationships (FWBRs)**, which encompass sexual interaction between people who consider each other friends but not partners in a romantic relationship (Furman & Shaffer, 2011; Lehmiller et al., 2011; Owen et al., 2011). Researchers find it intriguing that such involvements combine the dual benefits of friendship and sexual gratification while avoiding the responsibilities and commitment associated with romantic love relationships (Hughes et al., 2005). However, partners in some FWBRs do desire a transition into a more stable, romantic relationship (Vanderdrift et al., 2012). Evidence suggests that FWBRs are quite common on college campuses (Lehmiller et al., 2011; Owen & Fincham, 2011). On four separate campuses the percentages of students reporting their involvement in FWBRs were 51%, 54%, 60%, and 61.7% (Afifi & Faulkner, 2000; McGinty et al., 2007; Mongeau et al., 2003; Puentes et al., 2008).

Recent research reveals that women and men differ in how they view FWBRs. Women participants tended to view such relationships as being more emotionally involved, with the emphasis on friendship, whereas men were inclined to view the relationship as more casual, with an emphasis on sexual benefits (Lehmiller et al., 2011; McGinty et al., 2007).

Love can also exist independently of any sexual attraction or expression. However, the ideal intimate relationship for most of us is one replete with feelings of both mutual love and mutual sexual gratification.

Feelings of being in love with and sexually attracted to another person are frequently intertwined, and these feelings are especially pronounced in the early stages of a relationship. Research on college students indicates that both women and men consider

hook-ups
Short-term, loveless sexual liaisons that occur during a brief interval.

"friends with benefits" relationships (FWBRs)
Sexual interaction between friends who do not define their relationship as romantic.

sexual desire and attraction an important ingredient of romantic love (Regan, 1998). The complex interplay between love and sex gives rise to many questions: Does sexual intimacy deepen a love relationship? Do men and women have different views of the relationship between sex and love? And is sex without love appropriate? Here, we attempt to shed light on these and related questions.

Does Sexual Intimacy Deepen a Love Relationship?

> I had known Chris for some time and thought I was ready to be sexual with him. So, after an evening out together, I asked him if I could stay at his place, and he said yes. I felt really aroused as we got in bed. I really enjoyed exploring the shapes and textures of his body. As we started to touch each other's genitals, though, I felt uncomfortable. If we proceeded in the direction we were headed, we would be going beyond the level of emotional intimacy I felt. It seemed that I would have to shut out the closeness I felt in order to go further. I had to choose between intimacy and genital contact. Our closeness was more important to me, and I told him that I wanted us to know each other more before going further sexually. (Authors' files)

The woman just quoted made the decision to postpone further sexual involvement until she became more comfortable in her relationship. Many individuals take a different course, moving quickly to sexual intimacy. In some cases this can deepen a relationship. However, this result is certainly not assured. In fact, when a relationship becomes sexual before a couple has established a more generalized bond of intimacy—fostered by a growing awareness, understanding, and appreciation of each other—the individuals involved can actually feel farther apart emotionally.

It is reasonable to suspect that people sometimes attempt to justify their sexual behavior by deciding they are in love. Indeed, it is likely that some couples enter into premature commitments (such as going steady, moving in together, becoming engaged, or even getting married) to convince themselves of the depth of their love and thus of the legitimacy of their sexual involvement.

Do Men and Women View Sex and Love Differently?

In general, men and women tend to view the relationship between sex and love somewhat differently (Hendrick & Hendrick, 1995; Regan & Berscheid, 1995). For instance, men are more likely than women to define being in love, and to assess the quality of the romantic involvement, in terms of sexual satisfaction (Fischer & Heesacker, 1995; McCabe, 1999). Studies also indicate that it is easier for men than for women to have sexual intercourse for pleasure and physical release without an emotional commitment (Buss, 1999; Conley, 2011). This difference is probably a reflection, at least in part, of cultural factors that socialize women to link love and sexual desire more closely than men do (Kaestle & Halpern, 2007). However, this difference between men and women diminishes somewhat with age; older women are more likely than younger women to list desire for physical pleasure as an important motivation for sex (Murstein & Tuerkheim, 1998). Furthermore, as suggested by the results of a recent study, the likelihood of a woman accepting an offer of casual sex is increased when she anticipates experiencing sexual pleasure (Conley, 2011).

Despite differences in how men and women view the association between love and sex, both sexes are similar in what they consider important ingredients of successful and rewarding loving relationships (Regan, 1998; Sprecher et al., 1995). Among attributes ranked as very important by both men and women are good communication, commitment, and a high quality of emotional and physical intimacy (Byers & Demmons, 1999; Fischer & Heesacker, 1995; McCabe, 1999).

Do Heterosexuals, Gay Men, and Lesbians View Love and Sex Differently?

> I would not consider myself to be biased against homosexuals. However, I do feel some degree of disapproval of the gay lifestyle, which often seems to involve casual affairs based more on sex than genuine caring. Some gay men I know have had more partners in the last couple of years than I have had in a lifetime. (Authors' files)

This opinion reflects a belief widespread among heterosexuals that homosexuals, especially gay men, form liaisons with same-sex partners that are based primarily on sexual interaction and that are often devoid of genuine attachment, love, commitment, and overall satisfaction. A number of researchers have revealed the essential fallacy of this thinking by demonstrating that homosexuals, like heterosexuals, generally seek out loving, trusting, caring relationships that embrace many dimensions of sharing in addition to sexual intimacy (Kurdek, 1995b; Zak & McDonald, 1997). Lesbians and gay men differ in the degree to which they associate emotional closeness or love with sex, consistent with overall differences between men and women in their views of sex and love. Whereas men in general are more likely than women to separate sex and love, gay men have shown a particularly strong inclination to make this separation. Some gay men have engaged in frequent casual sexual encounters without love or caring attachment; such activity was especially common before the AIDS epidemic (Bell & Weinberg, 1978; M. Gross, 2003). Rather than indicating that gay men do not value love, this finding merely reveals that some gay men value sex as an end in itself. In contrast, most lesbians postpone sexual involvement until they have developed emotional intimacy with a partner (Zak & McDonald, 1997). A number of researchers have suggested that such differences between gay men and lesbians result from patterns of gender-role socialization that make casual sex more permissible for males than for females.

Finally, love plays a prominent role in the lives of homosexual people as a nexus for establishing a self-imposed identity as either a lesbian or a gay man. Many heterosexually oriented people have had sexual contact with same-sex partners. This is especially true during late childhood and during adolescence, when same-sex contact can be either experimental and transitory or an expression of a lifelong orientation (see Chapter 12). These same-sex sexual activities are not sufficient in and of themselves to establish an identity as a homosexually oriented person. Rather, it is falling in love with a person of the same sex that often supplies the key element necessary to establish a gay or lesbian identity (Troiden, 1988).

Jealousy in Relationships

Jealousy has been defined as an aversive emotional reaction evoked by a real or imagined relationship involving one's partner and a third person (Bringle & Buunk, 1991). Many people think that jealousy is a measure of devotion and that the absence of jealous feelings implies a lack of love (Buss, 2000; Knox et al., 2007). People commonly have ambivalent attitudes toward jealousy, "seeing it sometimes as a sign of insecurity, sometimes as a sign of love, and sometimes as both simultaneously" (Puente & Cohen, 2003, p. 458). Jealousy is related more to injured pride, or to people's fear of losing what they want to control or possess, than to love. For example, a person who finds that a spouse enjoys someone else's company might feel inadequate and therefore jealous. As described in our discussion of reciprocity, we often enter into and remain in relationships because they provide a sense of belongingness and bolster our self-esteem. We often rely on our partner to validate our positive sense of self. Consequently, we can feel threatened and sense a potential loss of both reciprocity and a positive self-image if we perceive that our partner is considering a replacement for us (Boekhout et al., 1999).

Some people are more prone to feeling jealousy than others. Individuals who have a low opinion of themselves, reflected in feelings of insecurity and inadequacy, are more likely to feel jealousy in a relationship (Brehm et al., 2002; Buss, 1999). This relates to a point we have already made—that a healthy self-esteem is the foundation for building intimate relationships. In addition, people who see a large discrepancy between who they are and who they would like to be are also prone to jealousy. Not surprisingly, such individuals also are likely to have low self-esteem. And finally, people who place a high value on traits such as wealth, fame, popularity, and physical attractiveness might be more likely to feel jealousy in a relationship (Salovey & Rodin, 1985).

Jealousy is frequently a factor in precipitating violence in marriages and dating relationships (Knox et al., 2007; Puente & Cohen, 2003; Vandello & Cohen, 2003). Research demonstrates that jealousy-precipitated violence is more commonly directed toward one's partner or lover than toward a third-party rival (Mathes & Verstrate, 1993; Paul & Galloway, 1994).

Although it is clear that jealousy has many negative effects, it is not always clear how jealous feelings should be handled when they occur in a relationship. The Let's Talk About It box, "Coping With Jealousy, the Green-Eyed Monster," offers suggestions to people who want to decrease feelings of jealousy, either in themselves or in their partners.

The Sexes' Differing Experiences of Jealousy

Not everyone responds to jealousy in the same way, and a number of studies have found differences in the ways women and men respond. In general, women are more likely than men to acknowledge feeling jealous (Barker, 1987; Clanton & Smith, 1977). Furthermore, several studies have suggested that a woman's jealousy tends to focus on her partner's emotional involvement with another person, whereas a man's jealousy tends to focus on his partner's sexual involvement with another (Cramer et al., 2008; Treger & Sprecher, 2011).

Another difference between women's and men's jealousy patterns is that women often blame themselves when a conflict over jealousy arises, whereas men typically attribute their jealousy to a third party or to their partner's behavior (Barker, 1987; Daly et al., 1982). Women have also been shown to be more inclined than men to deliberately provoke jealousy in their partners (Sheets et al., 1997; White & Helbick, 1988). This difference in the sexes' jealousy patterns might stem from the fact that women experiencing jealousy often suffer simultaneously from feelings of inadequacy and worthlessness. Consequently, a woman's efforts to arouse jealousy in a partner can actually be an attempt to bolster self-worth by eliciting increased attention from a partner concerned about her actions. Men also often attach feelings of inadequacy to jealousy. However, the relationship is frequently reversed in men, with awareness of jealousy occurring first, followed by feeling inadequate (White & Helbick, 1988).

Critical Thinking Question

Research indicates that women are more likely than men to acknowledge feeling jealous. What do you think accounts for this difference between the sexes?

It is common for the green-eyed monster, jealousy, to raise its ugly head at least sometime during a relationship. Dealing with jealousy can be difficult, because such feelings often stem from a deep sense of inadequacy within the jealous individual rather than within the relationship. A person threatened by insecurity-induced feelings of jealousy often withdraws from his or her partner or goes on the attack with accusations or threats. These ineffective coping behaviors often provoke a similar reaction in the nonjealous partner: withdrawal or counterattack. A more effective approach for the jealous person is to acknowledge his or her own feelings of jealousy and to clarify their source. Thus a jealous person might initiate discussion by saying, "Ashley, I am afraid for us and a little bit crazy over all the time you spend working late with your coworkers, especially with that guy Jason!" Such an open acknowledgment of feelings without threats or accusations might prompt Ashley to respond with reassurances, and a positive dialogue might ensue.

In many situations, a jealous person will not acknowledge that a problem exists and will not express a desire to work on it. If so, the essential first step to resolving the problem is to motivate that person to begin working to eliminate the painful jealousy feelings and the destructive behaviors that such feelings often induce. Robert Barker (1987), a marital therapist, provides valuable guidelines for accomplishing this in his book *The Green-Eyed Marriage: Surviving Jealous Relationships*. Barker maintains that a jealous person is most likely to become motivated to work on the problem and to permit help from others when he or she is

Jealousy is an uncomfortable feeling that often harms a relationship and stifles the pleasure of being together.

- *confident that there is no danger of losing the valued partner.* Direct reassurance that the relationship is not in danger is often ineffective and sometimes can even be counterproductive. A more effective strategy is to refer, at various times, to being together in the future. Consequently, a nonjealous partner planning to initiate a discussion about jealousy might first pick a few opportune times to say such things as "It will be great when the children are all grown and we have more time just for us."
- *assured that the problem comes from the relationship rather than from defects in his or her character.* A jealous person is much more likely to begin dealing with the jealousy when both partners acknowledge that it is a shared problem. The nonjealous partner can move thinking in this direction by stating, "This is a problem we share, and we both have to work equally to overcome it."
- *confident about being genuinely loved and respected.* Because jealousy often stems from feelings of inadequacy and insecurity, the nonjealous partner can help minimize these negative emotions and bolster self-esteem and confidence by "regularly reaffirming affection for the jealous person verbally, emotionally, and physically" (Barker, 1987, p. 100).
- *not provoked into feeling shame or guilt.* Understandably, many people who are undeservedly targets of jealousy become angry and inclined to strike back with sarcasm, ridicule, or put-downs to shame their jealous partners into abandoning their unfounded accusations. Unfortunately, such negative counterattacks are likely to have the opposite effect, promoting more anger and defensiveness. Worse yet, the jealous person might be even less willing to acknowledge a need for change.
- *able to empathize with the person who has been hurt by the jealous behavior.* When jealous people can understand and empathize with the pain their behavior has caused their partner, the incentive to change may increase. The challenge for the nonjealous partner is to foster empathy rather than guilt. This can be accomplished by verbalizing the pain but not blaming the jealous partner. Thus, Ashley might say to her jealous partner, "I love you, Mike, and I feel really bad when I have to work late and I know you are at home wishing we could be together. It is really painful to think that my work situation sometimes seems more important than our relationship."

Once the motivation for change is established, and once a couple begins a dialogue to deal with jealousy, several of the communication strategies outlined in this chapter can help them work on the problem. Suggestions for self-disclosure, listening, feedback, and asking questions can help to clearly establish what each partner wants and expects of the relationship. For example, after disclosing his fears, Mike might tell Ashley that he would worry less if she would spend less time working with Jason after hours or maybe just include others from the office when working late.

Maintaining Relationship Satisfaction

Human relationships present many challenges. One challenge involves building positive feelings about ourselves. Another involves establishing satisfying and enjoyable relationships with family, peers, teachers, coworkers, employers, and other people in our social network. A third challenge involves developing special intimate relationships with friends and, when we want them, sexual relationships. Finally, many people confront the challenge of maintaining satisfaction and love within an ongoing committed relationship. In this section, we present factors that contribute to ongoing satisfaction in relationships. We also discuss the value of sexual variety within a relationship.

Ingredients in a Lasting Love Relationship

Ingredients commonly present in a lasting love relationship include self-acceptance, acceptance by one's partner, appreciation of one another, commitment, good communication, realistic expectations, shared interests, equality in decision making, and the ability to face conflict effectively. These characteristics are not static; they evolve and change and influence one another over time. Often they need to be deliberately cultivated.

One review of the research on marital satisfaction reported that successful marriages that remain strong over the long haul often exhibit certain other characteristics (Karney & Bradbury, 1995):

- Parents of both spouses had successful, happy marriages.
- Spouses have similar attitudes, interests, and personality styles.
- Both spouses are satisfied with their sexual sharing.
- The couple has an adequate and steady income.
- The woman was not pregnant when the couple married.

In another study, researchers asked a sample of 560 women and men to judge the importance of a number of different elements to the success of a marriage or a long-term committed relationship. Elements judged to be important for high-quality relationships included the following (Sprecher et al., 1995):

- Supportive communication: Open and honest communication and a willingness to talk about difficult issues and concerns.
- Companionship: Sharing mutual interests and enjoying many activities together.
- Sexual expression: Spontaneity and variety in sexual sharing, and feeling sexually attractive to one's partner.

In still another study of 300 happily married couples, the most frequently named reason for an enduring and happy marriage was seeing one's partner as one's best friend. Qualities that individuals especially appreciated in a partner were caring, giving, having integrity, and having a sense of humor. These couples were aware of flaws in their mates, but they believed that the likable qualities were more important. Many said that their mates had become more interesting to them over time. They preferred shared rather than separate activities, which appeared to reflect the richness in the relationship. Most couples were generally satisfied with their sex lives, and for some the sexual passion had become more intense over time (Lauer & Lauer, 1985). One recent study of over 1,000 middle-aged and older couples, together for a median of 25 years, found that satisfaction with their sexual functioning was a major predictor of relationship happiness for both men and women (Heiman et al., 2011).

Maintaining frequent positive interactions is crucial to continued satisfaction in a relationship. The saying "It's the little things that count" is especially meaningful here.

© Dennis MacDonald/Alamy

An older couple's intimacy and affection develop from years of shared experiences.

When one partner says to the other, "You do not love me anymore," that often means, "You are not doing as many of the things as you used to do that show me you love me." These behaviors are often so small that the partners may not really notice them. However, when couples do fewer things to make one another feel loved (or when they stop doing them entirely), the deficit is often experienced as a lack of love. Continuing affectionate and considerate interaction helps maintain a feeling of love:

> The kinds of things that enhance my feeling that my partner still loves me may seem quite inconsequential, but to me they aren't. When he gets up to greet me when I come home, when he takes my arm crossing the street, when he asks, "Can I help you with that," when he tells me I look great, when he holds me in the middle of the night, when he thanks me for doing a routine chore—I feel loved by him. Those little things—all added up—make a tremendous difference to me. (Authors' files)

It is also useful to talk with our partners, to communicate what is especially enjoyable, or to suggest new ideas. The golden rule ("Do unto others as you would have them do unto you") does not always apply in relationships, because people's preferences are often quite different. One partner may not know what the other partner wants unless that person expresses it. Enjoyment with and appreciation of one another in nonsexual areas typically enhance sexual interest and interactions. Often couples report a lack of desire for sexual intimacy when they are not feeling emotionally intimate.

Sexual Variety: An Important Ingredient

Many people have a strong desire to seek variety in life's experiences. They might acquire an assortment of friends, each of whom provides a unique enrichment to their lives. Likewise, they might read different kinds of books, pursue a variety of recreational activities, eat different kinds of foods, and take a variety of classes. Yet many of these same people settle for routine in their sex lives.

Unfortunately, many people enter into a committed relationship thinking that intense sexual excitement will always follow naturally when two people are in love. But, as we have seen in this chapter, the initial excitement must eventually be replaced by realistic and committed efforts to maintain the vitality and rewards of a working relationship. Once a person is committed to a primary partner, the variety offered by a succession of relationships is no longer available. Some individuals may need to seek variety in other ways.

Not every couple feels the need for sexual variety. Many people are quite comfortable with established routines and have no desire to change them. However, if you prefer to develop more variety in your sexual relationship, the following paragraphs may be helpful.

Communication is critical. Talk to your partner about your needs and feelings. Share with him or her your desire to try something different. Perhaps some of the guidelines for sexual communication discussed in the following sections will help you make requests and exchange information.

Even though time inevitably erodes the novelty of a relationship, the resulting decline of passion can be countered by introducing novelty into patterns of sexual sharing. This can be accomplished by avoiding routine times and places. Make love in places other than the bed (on the laundry room floor, in the shower, alongside a mountain trail) and at various times ("birdsong in the morning," a "nooner," or in the middle of the night when you wake up feeling sexually aroused).

Some of the most exciting sexual experiences take place on the spur of the moment, with little or no planning. It is easy to see how such experiences might occur frequently during courtship. It is equally apparent how they can become distant memories after a couple settles into the demanding daily schedule of living together. Nevertheless, you may find that striving to maintain this spontaneity will stand you in good stead as your relationship is nurtured over months or years together.

On the other hand, planning for intimate time—sexual and nonsexual—can also help maintain closeness. Make dates with one another and consciously continue the romantic gestures that came naturally early in the relationship. Commit your energy and time to your sexual relationship.

Do not let questions of what is "normal" get in the way of an enriched and varied erotic life. Too often, people refrain from experiencing something new because they believe that different activities are "abnormal." In reality, only you can judge what is normal for you. Sexologists concur that any sexual activity is normal so long as it gives pleasure and does not cause emotional or physical discomfort or harm to either partner. Emotional comfort is important because "discomfort and conflict rather than intimacy and satisfaction can result if behaviors are tried which are too divergent from personal values and attitudes" (Barbach, 1982, p. 282).

We do not mean to imply that all people must have active, varied sex lives to be truly happy; this is not the case. As we have already seen, some partners find comfort and contentment in repeating familiar patterns of sexual interaction. Others consider sex relatively unimportant compared with other aspects of their lives and choose not to exert special efforts in pursuing its pleasures. However, if your sexuality is an important source of pleasure in your life, perhaps these suggestions and others in this textbook will be important to you. ●

Do men and women differ in their desire for sexual variety? The cross-cultural research described in the Spotlight on Research box provides strong evidence that the sexes do differ in the desire for sexual variety.

In the remainder of this chapter, we discuss sexual communication: the ways people express their feelings and convey their needs and desires to sexual partners. We consider the reasons that such attempts are sometimes unsuccessful; we also explore ways to enhance this important aspect of our sexual lives.

The Importance of Sexual Communication

Sexual communication can contribute greatly to the satisfaction of an intimate relationship. Good communication about sexual desires and concerns has frequently been identified as a valuable asset to the development and maintenance of a satisfying and enduring sexual relationship (Byers, 2011; Montesi et al., 2011; Timm & Kelley, 2011). We do not mean that extensive verbal dialogue is essential to all sexual sharing; there are times when spoken communication is more disruptive than constructive. Nevertheless, partners who never talk about the sexual aspects of their relationship are denying themselves an opportunity to increase their closeness and pleasure through learning about each other's needs and desires.

Central to this discussion is our belief that the basis for effective sexual communication is **mutual empathy**—the underlying knowledge that each partner in a relationship cares for the other and knows that the care is reciprocated. Receiving and providing expressions of love and appreciation are important ingredients in the maintenance of mutual empathy, as discussed in the Let's Talk About It box, "The Benefits of Affectionate Communication."

mutual empathy
The underlying knowledge that each partner in a relationship cares for the other and knows that the care is reciprocated.

A study of American college students indicated that men are inclined to desire multiple sex partners, whereas women are more likely to seek only one sex partner (Fenigstein & Preston, 2007). A number of evolutionary psychologists have hypothesized that this and other differences between the mating strategies of men and women have evolved differentially. An especially pronounced difference can be seen in the motivations underlying the pursuit of short-term sexual relationships. According to this perspective, men seeking short-term mates are often motivated by a desire for sexual variety, which is reflected in their inclinations both to pursue numerous sex partners and to consent to sex relatively quickly. In contrast, women's underlying motivations for seeking short-term relationships seem to be focused on selectively obtaining men of higher status and/or excellent genetic quality (Schmitt, 2003; Schmitt et al., 2001).

Support for this interpretation was provided by a cross-cultural survey of 16,288 people selected from 10 major world regions: North America, South America, western Europe, eastern Europe, southern Europe, the Middle East, Africa, Oceania, South and Southeast Asia, and eastern Asia. This investigation was conducted by evolutionary psychologist David Schmitt (2003). Schmitt used an anonymous nine-page survey questionnaire, translated into local languages, to assess three primary variables: (1) the number of sexual partners desired at differing time intervals ("Number of Partners" measure), (2) relationship duration before experiencing sexual intercourse ("Time Known" measure), and (3) the extent to which participants were actively seeking short-term mating partners ("Short-Term Seeking" measure).

The results of this comprehensive investigation provided strong evidence that men and women differ fundamentally in their short-term mating psychology, especially in the desire for sexual variety, and that these differences appear to be culturally universal throughout the sampled world regions. Schmitt's findings revealed that "men not only possess a greater desire than women do for a variety of sexual partners, men also require less time to elapse than women do before consenting to sexual intercourse, and men tend to more actively seek short-term mateships than women do" (Schmitt, 2003, p. 101). Schmitt concluded that his investigation strongly supported the evolutionary psychology viewpoint that men's evolved short-term mating strategies are rooted in a desire for sexual variety.

In the rest of this chapter we discuss various approaches to sexual communication that have proved helpful in the lives of many people. We do not claim to have the final word on the many nuances of human communication, nor do we suggest that the ideas offered here will work for everyone. Communication strategies often need to be individually modified, and sometimes the differences between two people are so profound that even the best communication cannot ensure a mutually satisfying relationship. We hope, though, that some of these shared experiences and suggestions can be helpful in your own life.

Talking: Getting Started

How does one begin communicating about sex? In this section we explore a few of the many ways of breaking the ice. These suggestions may be useful not just at the beginning of a relationship but throughout its course.

Talking About Talking

When people feel uneasy about a topic, often the best place to start is to talk about talking. Discussing *why* it is hard to talk about sex can be a good place to begin. Each of us has our own reasons for finding this difficult, and understanding those reasons can help set a relationship on a solid foundation. Perhaps you can share experiences about earlier efforts to discuss sexual topics with parents, teachers, physicians, friends,

Research has consistently demonstrated that receiving expressions of love and appreciation (affectionate communication) from a loved one fulfills a profound human need while providing a broad array of psychological, biological, and relational benefits (Floyd, 2006; Floyd et al., 2007). Various studies have revealed that, compared to those who do not receive such communication, people who are consistent recipients of affectionate communication are at less risk for illness, psychological stress, depression, loneliness, and alcohol abuse; are less likely to be involved in interpersonal violence; and are prone to exhibit enhanced ability to heal from the effects of illness or injuries (Downs & Javidi, 1990; Floyd et al., 2007; Schwartz & Russek, 1998; Shuntich et al., 1998).

Affectionate communication, displayed by both verbal and nonverbal means (touches, hugs, etc.), appears to provide the benefits just described in a variety of ways. For one, the free exchange of affection is a common characteristic among couples who experience high levels of emotional closeness and interpersonal satisfaction. Partners in such relationships may be especially vigilant or watchful of each other's physical health and emotional well-being (Floyd & Morman, 2000). Moreover, people who are frequent recipients and providers of expressions of love and appreciation tend to have relatively high levels of self-esteem, confidence, and happiness, all personal traits that act to enhance their capacity for dealing effectively with their emotional and physical needs (Floyd et al., 2007).

Finally, research also demonstrates that affectionate communication can help the body protect itself against the negative consequences of stress. This can be accomplished in a number of ways, including a reduction in both heart rate and the production of stress hormones, both of which often become elevated in response to stressful events. One leading investigator of the benefits of affectionate communication, Kory Floyd, concluded that "affectionate behavior in close relationships is beneficial to health and well-being" (Floyd et al., 2007, p. 156).

or lovers. It might be helpful to move gradually into the arena of sexual communication by directing your initial discussions to nonthreatening, less personal topics (such as new birth control methods, pornography laws, etc.). Later, as your mutual comfort increases, you may be able to talk about more personal feelings and concerns.

Reading and Discussing

Because many people find it easier to read about sex than to talk about it, articles and books dealing with the subject can provide the stimulus for personal conversations. Partners can read the material separately, then discuss it together, or a couple can read it jointly and discuss their individual reactions. Often it is easier to make the transition from a book or article to personal feelings than to begin by talking about highly personal concerns.

Sharing Sexual Histories

Another way to start talking is to share sexual histories. There may be many questions that you would feel comfortable discussing with your partner. For instance, how was sex education handled in your home or at school? How did your parents relate to each other—were you aware of any sexuality in their relationship? When did you first learn about sex, and what were your reactions? Many other items could be added to this brief list; the questions depend on the feelings and needs of each individual.

Mike Kemp/RubberBall/age fotostock

Reading together about sensitive matters can foster discussion.

Listening and Feedback

Communication, sexual or otherwise, is most successful when it is two-sided, involving both an effective communicator and an active listener. In this section, we focus on the listening side of this process.

Have you ever wondered why certain people seem to draw others to themselves like iron to a magnet? With some thought, you will probably conclude that, among other things, these individuals are often good listeners. What special skills do they possess that make us feel that they really care about what we have to say? The next time you are with such a person, observe closely. Make a study of his or her listening habits. Perhaps your list of good listening traits will include several of the following: being an active listener, maintaining eye contact, providing feedback, supporting one's partner's communication efforts, and expressing unconditional positive regard.

Be an Active Listener

Some people are *passive* listeners. They stare blankly into space as their companion talks, perhaps grunting "uh-huh" now and then. Such responses make us, the talker, think that the listener is indifferent, even when this is not the case, and we may soon grow tired of trying to share important thoughts with someone who does not seem to be receptive:

> When I talk to my husband about anything really important, he just stares at me with a blank expression. It is like I am talking to a piece of stone. I think he hears the message, at least sometimes, but he rarely shows any response. Sometimes I feel like shaking him and screaming, "Are you still alive?" Needless to say, I don't try communicating with him very much anymore. (Authors' files)

Being an *active* listener means actively communicating that you are both listening to and genuinely interested in what your partner is saying (Cole & Cole, 1999; Gottman et al., 1998). You can communicate this interest through using attentive body language, making appropriate and sympathetic facial expressions, nodding your head, asking questions ("Could you give me an example?"), or making brief comments ("I see your point"). Sometimes it is helpful to reciprocate in the conversation. For example, as your partner relates a feeling or incident, you may be reminded of a similar point in your own life. Making such associations and candidly expressing them—provided that you do not sidetrack the conversation to your own needs—can encourage your partner to continue voicing important concerns.

Maintain Eye Contact

Maintaining eye contact is one of the most vital aspects of good face-to-face communication. Our eyes are wondrously expressive of feelings. When our partners maintain eye contact with us while we are sharing important thoughts or feelings with them, the message is clear: They care about what we have to say. When we fail to maintain eye contact, we deny our partners valuable feedback about how we are perceiving their messages.

Provide Feedback

The purpose of communication is to provide a message that has some effect on the listener. However, a message's impact is not always the same as its intent, because communications can be (and often are) misunderstood. This is particularly true with a topic such as sexuality, where language is often roundabout or awkward. Therefore, giving our partners *feedback*, or reaction to their message, *in words* can be helpful. Besides clarifying how we have perceived our partners' comments, such verbal feedback reinforces that we are actively listening.

We can also benefit by asking our partners to respond to a message we think is important. A question such as "What do you think about what I have just said?" can encourage feedback that can help us determine the impact of our message on our partners.

Support Your Partner's Communication Efforts

Many of us can feel vulnerable when communicating important messages to our partners. Support for our efforts can help alleviate our fears and anxieties and can encourage us to continue building the communication skills so important for a viable relationship. Think how good it can feel, after struggling to voice an important concern, to have a partner say, "I'm glad you told me how you really feel," or "Thanks for caring enough to tell me what was on your mind." Such supportive comments can help foster mutual empathy while ensuring that we will continue to communicate our thoughts and feelings candidly.

Express Unconditional Positive Regard

The concept of unconditional positive regard is borrowed from the immensely popular *Client-Centered Therapy*, by Carl Rogers (1951). In personal relationships unconditional positive regard means conveying to our partners the sense that we will continue to value and care for them regardless of what they do or say. Unconditional positive regard encourages a person to talk about even the most embarrassing or painful concerns. The following anecdote reveals one person's response to this valued attribute:

> I know that my wife will continue to love me no matter what I say or reveal. In an earlier marriage, I could never express any serious concerns without my wife getting defensive or just plain mean. As a consequence, I quit talking about the things that really mattered. What a relief it is to be with someone who I can tell what is on my mind without worrying about the consequences. (Authors' files)

Discovering Your Partner's Needs

Discovering what is pleasurable to your partner is an important part of sexual intimacy. Many couples want to know each other's preferences but are uncertain how to find out. In this section, we look at some effective ways of learning about our partners' wants and needs.

Asking Questions

One of the best ways to discover your partner's needs is simply to ask. However, there are several ways of asking: Some can be helpful, whereas others may be ineffective or even counterproductive. We review a few of the most common ways of asking questions and the effect each is likely to have.

Yes/No Questions

Imagine being asked one or more of the following questions in the context of a sexual interlude with your partner:

1. Was it good for you?
2. Do you like oral sex?
3. Do you like it when I touch you this way?

At first glance these questions seem reasonably worded. However, they all share one characteristic that reduces their effectiveness: They are **yes/no questions**. Each asks for a one-word answer, even though people's thoughts and feelings are rarely so simple.

For example, consider question 2, "Do you like oral sex?" Either answer—"Yes, I do," or "No, I don't"—gives the couple little opportunity to discuss the issue. Certainly, the potential for discussion exists. Nevertheless, in a world where sexual communication is often difficult under the best of circumstances, the asker may get no more than the specific information requested. In some situations, of course, a brief yes or no is all that is necessary. But the person responding might have mixed feelings about oral sex (for example), and the phrasing of the question leads to oversimplification. **Open-ended questions**, or questions that allow the respondent to state a preference, can make it easier for your partner to give accurate replies.

Open-Ended Questions

Some people find that asking open-ended questions is a particularly helpful way to discover their partners' desires. The following list gives some examples of open-ended questions:

1. What gives you the most pleasure when we make love?
2. What things about our sexual relationship would you most like us to change?
3. What are your feelings about oral sex?

A primary advantage of open-ended questions is that they allow your partner freedom to share any feelings or information she or he thinks is relevant. With no limitations or restrictions attached, you can learn much more than a simple yes/no answer could provide.

One possible drawback of the open-ended approach is that your partner may not know where to begin when asked such general questions. Consider being asked "What do you like best about our lovemaking?" Some people might welcome the unstructuredness of this question, but others might have difficulty responding to such a broad query, particularly if they are not accustomed to openly discussing sex. If this is the case, a more structured approach may have a better chance of encouraging talk. There are several ways of structuring your approach; one is the use of either/or questions.

Either/Or Questions

The following list gives examples of **either/or questions**:

1. Would you like the light on when we make love, or should we turn it off?
2. Is this the way you want to be touched, or should we experiment with a different kind of caress?
3. Do you want to talk now or later?

Either/or questions offer more structure than do open-ended questions, and they encourage more participation than simple yes/no queries. People often appreciate the opportunity to consider a few alternatives.

yes/no question
A question that asks for a one-word answer (yes or no) and thus provides little opportunity for discussing an issue.

open-ended question
A question that allows a respondent to share any feelings or information she or he thinks is relevant.

either/or question
A question that allows statement of a preference.

Besides asking questions, we can discover the sexual needs of our partners in other ways. Here, we discuss three other communication techniques: self-disclosure, discussing sexual preferences, and giving permission.

Self-Disclosure

Direct questions often put people on the spot. Whether you have been asked "Do you enjoy oral sex?" or "How do you feel about oral sex?" it may be difficult to respond candidly, simply because you do not know your partner's feelings on the subject. If the topic has strong emotional overtones, it may be difficult to reply—no matter how thoughtfully the question has been phrased. It is the content, not the communication technique, that causes the problem.

One way to broach potentially loaded topics is to start with a self-disclosure:

> For the longest time, I avoided the topic of oral sex with my lover. I didn't have the slightest idea what she felt about it. I was afraid to bring it up for fear she would think I was some kind of pervert. Eventually I could no longer tolerate not knowing her feelings. I brought it up by first talking about my mixed emotions, like feeling that maybe it wasn't natural but at the same time really wanting to try it out. As it turned out, she had similar feelings but was afraid to bring them up. Afterward we laughed about how we had both been afraid to break the ice. Once we could talk freely, it was easy to add this form of stimulation to our sex life. (Authors' files)

Personal disclosures require give and take. It is much easier to share feelings about strongly emotional topics when a partner is willing to make similar disclosures (Maisel et al., 2008). Admittedly, such an approach has risks, and occasionally one can feel vulnerable sharing personal thoughts and feelings. Nevertheless, the increased possibility for open, honest dialogue may be worth the discomfort a person may feel about making the first disclosure. Research clearly reveals that self-disclosure in general enhances intimacy in relationships and that self-disclosure of sexual desires and needs is positively associated with obtaining sexual satisfaction in intimate relationships (Bauminger et al., 2008; Greene & Faulkner, 2005; Oattles & Offman, 2007). Research also indicates that when one partner openly discusses his or her own feelings, the other partner is likely to do the same (Derlego et al., 1993; Hendrick & Hendrick, 1992).

It is becoming more and more common for people to engage in intimate communication online. The lack of face-to-face monitoring may increase both the rapidity and emotional intensity of self-disclosures (Ben-Ze'ev, 2003). Thus a potential drawback of online sex talk is that it may induce premature and perhaps ill-advised disclosures. However, the relative anonymity of cyberspace may empower people to disclose personal feelings about sexual issues. This may be especially true for men, who often find it difficult to discuss their feelings (Basow & Rubenfeld, 2003; Bowman, 2008; Levant, 1997). We consider relating on the Web in more detail in the following section.

Internet Relationships

The Internet has created a virtual community that has radically expanded options for meeting potential intimate partners and for communicating about sex (Albright, 2008; A. Brown, 2011; Parker-Pope, 2011). Facilitating and managing relationships online has become a billion-dollar industry in

© Bruce Ayres/Getty Images

Discovering what is pleasurable to your partner is an important part of sexual intimacy.

the United States (A. Brown, 2011). Earlier in this chapter, we described how proximity, or geographical nearness, influences whom we are attracted to. Cyberspace has created a world of virtual proximity, in which people can be electronically close while being separated by hundreds or thousands of miles.

People may be drawn to various relationship-oriented websites because of a perceived commonality of interest with others who visit the site. Some may be surfing the Web looking for meaningful romantic connections. Others may be motivated by a desire to discuss sexual fantasies or to share online sexual activity (OSA) (Grov et al., 2011; Shaughnessy et al., 2010). The absence of relationship constraints posed by face-to-face (FTF) interaction may help explain the growing popularity of computer-mediated relating (CMR). For people who have difficulty relating to others FTF, the anonymity of online relationships may allow them to express themselves more easily, which can lead to an improved sense of social connectedness and the formation of strong online attachments (Fleming & Rickwood, 2004; Ross et al., 2007). Online interaction also provides avenues for refusing requests for romantic involvements that may be less stressful than in FTF communication (Tom Tong & Walther, 2011).

Online communication may contribute to the development of romantic relationships by eliminating the role that physical attractiveness plays in the development of attraction. In the absence of this dimension of interpersonal attraction, formed impressions of another may be strongly influenced by imagination, which can create a powerful attraction to another (Ben-Ze'ev, 2004; Ross et al., 2007). Freed from the influence of visual cues, romantic or erotic connections may evolve from emotional intimacy rather than from physical attraction. CMR may also be less constrained by the gender-role assumptions that frequently influence FTF interactions between the sexes.

These relative advantages of CMR are counterbalanced by potential drawbacks of relating on the Internet. For example, erotic or intimate connections may develop with such rapidity that the tempering influence of good judgment may not be applied (Benotsch et al., 2002; Genuis & Genuis, 2005). This rapid escalation of relationship intensity may be triggered by a reduction in feelings of vulnerability when disclosing personal information in the relative anonymity of cyberspace and by the psychological comfort of revealing private thoughts while in a safe, cozy home environment.

Another potential disadvantage of communicating online is that people may be untruthful when disclosing such topics as personal interests, occupation, marital status, and age (Rosenblum, 2011). In addition, FTF meetings with online partners carry considerable risk. The media is replete with accounts of Web relationships that result in abuse, violence, stalking, or harassment. Furthermore, research indicates that the chances of engaging in risky, condomless sex during an initial FTF meeting with an online partner are quite high (Genuis & Genuis, 2005; Horvath et al., 2008).

The phenomenon of Internet relationships is rapidly evolving, and future research will no doubt provide a better understanding of the impact of the Web on people's intimate lives. Perhaps the best advice we can offer readers who are exploring relationships via the Internet is to take it slow, communicate honestly and encourage your partner to do the same, disclose carefully, and by all means, if you choose to meet FTF, do so in a safe, public place and without expectations of a sexual encounter.

Discussing Sexual Preferences

While planning an evening out, many couples consider it natural to discuss each other's preferences: "Would you like to go to a concert, or would you rather go to the movies?" "How close do you like to sit?" "Do you prefer vegetarian, Italian, or meat and potatoes?" Afterward they may candidly evaluate the evening's events: "The drummer was great." "I think we should sit farther from the speakers next time." "Boy, I wouldn't order the scampi again." Yet many of the same couples never think of sharing thoughts about mutual sexual enjoyment.

Admittedly, discussing sexual preferences and evaluating specific sexual encounters are a big step up from discussing an evening out. Nevertheless, people do engage in this type of sexual dialogue. Some people feel comfortable discussing sexual preferences with a new lover before progressing to lovemaking. They might talk about what areas of their bodies are most responsive, how they like to be touched, what intercourse positions are particularly desirable, the easiest or most satisfying way to reach orgasm, time and location preferences, special turn-ons and turn-offs, and a variety of other likes and dislikes.

The appeal of this open, frank approach is that it allows a couple to focus on particularly pleasurable activities rather than discovering them by slow trial and error. However, some people feel that such dialogues are far too clinical, perhaps even robbing the sexual experience of the excitement of experimentation and mutual discovery. Furthermore, what a person finds desirable might differ with different partners, so it might be difficult to assess one's own preferences in advance.

Couples might also find it helpful to discuss their feelings after having sex. They can offer reactions about what was good and what could be better. They can use this time to reinforce the things they found particularly satisfying in their partner's lovemaking ("I loved the way you touched me on the insides of my thighs"). A mutual feedback session can be extremely informative; it can also contribute to a deeper intimacy between two people.

Giving Permission

Discovering your partner's needs can be made immeasurably easier by the practice we call **giving permission**. Basically, giving permission means providing encouragement and reassurance. One partner tells the other that it is okay to talk about specific feelings or needs—indeed, that he or she wants very much to know how the other feels about the subject.

giving permission
Providing reassurance to one's partner that it is okay to talk about specific feelings or needs.

> **He:** I'm not sure how you like me to touch you when we make love.
>
> **She:** Any way you want to is good.
>
> **He:** Well, I want to know what you like best, and you can help me by saying what feels good while I touch you.

Many of us have felt rebuffed in our efforts to communicate our needs to others. It is no wonder that people often remain silent even when they want to share personal feelings. Giving and receiving permission to express needs freely can contribute to the exchange of valuable information and mutual trust.

Learning to Make Requests

People are not mind readers. Nevertheless, many lovers seem to assume that their partners know (perhaps by intuition?) just what they need. People who approach sex with this attitude are not taking full responsibility for their own pleasure. If sexual encounters are unsatisfactory, it is often more convenient to blame a partner—"You don't care about my needs"—than to admit that one's own reluctance to express needs may be the problem. Expecting partners to somehow know what is wanted without telling them places a heavy burden on them. Many people think that they shouldn't have to ask. But in fact, asking a partner to do something can be an affirmative, responsible action that helps both people.

Taking Responsibility for Our Own Pleasure

> When two people are really in harmony with each other, you don't have to talk about your sexual wants. You each sense and respond to the other's desires. Talking just tends to spoil these magical moments. (Authors' files)

The situation this person describes seems to exist more in the fantasyland of idealized sex than in the real world. As we just noted, people are not mind readers, and intuition leaves much to be desired as a substitute for genuine communication. A person who expects another to know his or her needs by intuition is saying, "It's not my business to let you know my needs, but it is yours to know what they are," and by inference, "If my needs are not fulfilled, it is your fault, not mine." Needless to say, this is a potentially destructive approach that can lead to blaming, misunderstandings, and unsatisfying sex.

The best way to get our needs met is to speak up. Two individuals willing to communicate their desires and take responsibility for their own pleasure create an excellent framework for effective, fulfilling sexual intimacy. Deciding to assume responsibility for our own satisfaction is an important step. Just as important are the methods we select for expressing our needs. The way a request is made has a decided effect on the reaction it draws. Suggestions are listed in the next two sections.

Making Requests Specific

The more specific a request is, the more likely it is to be understood and heeded. Lovers often ask for changes in the sexual aspects of their relationships in the vaguest language. It can be uncomfortable, even anxiety provoking, to be on the receiving end of an ill-defined request. Just how does one respond? Probably by doing little, if anything.

The key to preventing unnecessary stress for both partners is delivering requests as clearly and concisely as possible. Thus an alternative to the vague request "I'd like you to try touching me differently" might be "I would like you to touch me gently around my clitoris but not directly on it." Other examples of specific requests follow:

1. I would like you to spend more time touching and caressing me all over before we have intercourse.
2. I really enjoy it when you keep on kissing and caressing me after you're inside me.
3. I would like you to stroke my penis with your hand.

Using "I" Language

Counselors encourage their clients to use "I" language when stating their needs to others (Worden & Worden, 1998). This forthright approach brings the desired response more often than does a general statement. For example, saying "I would like to be on top" is considerably more likely to produce that result than "What would you think about changing positions?"

Expressing requests directly may not always be effective. Some people want to make all the decisions, and they may not take kindly to requests from their partners during lovemaking. A partner's assertiveness might offend them. You might want to determine whether this is your partner's attitude before a sexual encounter, because doing so can help you avoid an awkward situation. One way to determine this is to ask the open-ended question "How do you feel about asking for things during lovemaking?" Or you might choose to wait and find out during sex play. At any rate, if a person appears closed to direct requests, you may wish to reevaluate your strategy. Perhaps making your needs known at some time other than during sexual interaction will give your partner a more relaxed opportunity to consider your desires. Nevertheless, we strongly encourage you to use "I" language in whatever context you make your requests.

Expressing and Receiving Complaints

Contrary to the popular romantic image, no two people can fill all of each other's needs all the time. It seems inevitable that people in an intimate relationship will sometimes need to register complaints and request changes. Accomplishing this may not be easy for caring individuals whose relationship is characterized by mutual empathy. The most effective way to voice a concern is to complain rather than to criticize (Gottman, 1994).

Complaining involves constructively expressing relationship concerns rather than criticizing (and is by no means synonymous with whining). Occasional constructive complaining actually benefits a relationship because it helps partners identify problems that need to be discussed and resolved. Complaining involves several of the strategies outlined in the following sections, such as being sensitive about when to express a complaint, using "I" language, and tempering complaints with praise. Complaints are voiced in the expectation that constructive change beneficial to both partners will occur.

In contrast, criticisms are often leveled to hurt, downgrade, express contempt, get even, or gain dominant status over a partner. Criticism almost always feels hostile (Wright, 2011), and it often involves "attacking someone's personality or character—rather than a specific behavior—usually with blame" (Gottman, 1994, p. 73). Couple communication patterns tainted by expressions of denigration, criticism, and contempt can deeply harm a relationship. We discuss the effects of such negative communication tactics in more detail later in this chapter. When complaints pertain to the emotionally intense area of sexual intimacy, they can be doubly difficult to express and receive. Partners will want to think carefully about appropriate strategies for, and potential obstacles to, accomplishing these delicate tasks.

Constructive Strategies for Expressing Complaints

One important consideration for effectively verbalizing a complaint to your partner is to pick the right time and place.

Choose the Right Time and Place

> Whenever my lover brings up something that is bothering her about our sex life, it inevitably is just after we have made love. Here I am, relaxed, holding her in my arms, thinking good thoughts, and she destroys the mood with some criticism. It's not that I don't want her to express her concerns, but her timing is terrible. The last thing I want to hear after lovemaking is that it could have been better. (Authors' files)

This man's dismay is obvious. His partner's decision to voice her concerns during the afterglow of lovemaking works against her purpose. He may feel vulnerable, and he clearly resents having his good mood following sex broken by the prospect of a potentially difficult conversation. Of course, other couples find this time, when they are exceedingly close to each other, a good occasion to air their concerns.

*"If something is bothering you about our relationship,
Lorraine, why don't you just spell it out."*

Many people, like the woman in the example, do not choose the best time to confront their lovers. Rather, the time chooses them: They jump right in when the problem is uppermost in their mind. Although dealing with an issue immediately can have benefits, it is not always the best strategy. Negative emotions, such as disappointment, resentment, or anger, when running at full tide, can easily hinder constructive interaction. We should avoid expressing complaints when anger is at its peak. Although we may have every intention of making our complaint constructive, anger has a way of disrupting a search for solutions. Sometimes, however, it is necessary to express anger; at the end of this section we consider how to do so appropriately.

In most cases it is unwise to tackle a problem when either you or your partner has limited time or is tired, stressed, preoccupied, or under the influence of drugs or alcohol. Rather, try to select an interval when both of you have plenty of time and feel relaxed and close to each other.

A pragmatic approach to timing is simply to tell your lover, "I really value our sexual relationship, but there are some concerns I would like to talk over with you. Is this a good time, or would you rather we talked later?" Be prepared for some anxiety-induced stalling. If your partner is hesitant to talk now, support his or her right to pick another time or place. However, it is important to agree on a time, particularly if you sense that your partner might prefer to let the matter go.

Choosing the right place for expressing sexual concerns can be as important as timing. Some people find sitting at the kitchen table while sharing a pot of coffee a more comfortable setting than the place where they make love; others might prefer the familiarity of their bed. A walk through a park or a quiet drive in the country, far removed from the potential interferences of a busy lifestyle, may prove best for you. Try to sense your partner's needs. When and where is she or he most likely to be receptive to your requests for change?

Picking the right time and place to deliver a complaint does not ensure a harmonious outcome, but it certainly improves the prospects of your partner's responding favorably to your message. Using other constructive strategies can also increase the likelihood of beneficial interaction. One of these is to combine a complaint with praise.

Temper Complaints With Praise

The strategy of tempering complaints with praise is based largely on common sense. All of us tend to respond well to a compliment, but we tend to find a harsh complaint or criticism difficult to accept, especially by itself. The gentler approach of combining compliment and complaint is a good way to reduce the negative impact of the complaint. It also gives your partner a broader perspective from which to evaluate the complaint, reducing the likelihood that he or she will respond defensively or angrily. Consider how you might react differently to the following complaints, depending on whether they are accompanied by praise:

Choosing the right time and place to express sexual concerns can facilitate communication.

Complaint Alone

1. When we make love, I feel that you are inhibited.

2. I am really getting tired of your turning off the lights every time we make love.

3. I think our lovemaking is far too infrequent. It almost seems like sex is not as important to you as it is to me.

Complaint With Praise

1. I like it when you respond to me while we make love. I think it could be even better if you would take the initiative sometimes. Does this seem like a reasonable request?

2. I enjoy hearing and feeling you react when we make love. I also want to watch you respond. How would you feel about leaving the lights on sometimes?

3. I love having sex with you, and it has been bothering me that we don't seem to have much time for it recently. What do you think about this?

Sadly, just about all of us have been on the receiving end of complaints like those in the left column. Common reactions are anger, humiliation, anxiety, and resentment. Although some people respond to such harsh complaints by resolving to make things better, that response is unlikely. On the other hand, affirmative complaints, such as the examples in the right-hand column, are more likely to encourage efforts to change. A good deal of wisdom lies in the saying "People are usually more motivated to make a good thing better than to make a bad thing good." This applies as much to sexual activity as to any other area of human interaction.

When delivering complaints, it is also a good idea to ask for feedback. Regardless of how much warmth and goodwill we put into this difficult process, the possibility always exists that our partners will become silent or change the subject. Asking them how they feel about our requests for change helps reduce this possibility. (Note that all the preceding "Complaint With Praise" examples end with a request for feedback.)

Avoid "Why" Questions

People frequently use "why" questions as thinly veiled efforts to criticize or attack their partners while avoiding full responsibility for what is said. Have you ever asked or been asked any of the following questions?

1. Why don't you make love to me more frequently?
2. Why don't you show more interest in me?
3. Why don't you get turned on by me anymore?

Such questions have no place in a loving relationship; they are hurtful and destructive. Rather than conveying simple requests for information, they typically convey hidden messages of anger that the speaker is unwilling to communicate honestly. These are hit-and-run tactics that cause defensiveness and seldom induce positive changes.

Critical Thinking Question

Some people think that combining praise with a complaint is a manipulative technique designed to coerce behavior changes by tempering requests with insincere praise. Do you agree with this point of view? Why or why not?

Express Negative Emotions Appropriately

Earlier we noted that it is wise to avoid confronting our partners when resentment or anger is riding high. However, there probably will be times when we feel compelled to express negative feelings. If so, certain guiding principles can help defuse a potentially explosive situation.

Avoid focusing your anger on the character of your partner ("You are an insensitive person"). Instead, try directing your dissatisfaction toward his or her behaviors ("When you don't listen to my concerns, I think they are unimportant to you and I feel sad"). At the same time, express appreciation for your partner as a person ("You are very important to me, and I don't like feeling this way"). This acknowledges that we can feel distressed by our partners' behaviors yet still feel loving toward them—an often overlooked but important truth.

Negative feelings are probably best expressed with clear, honest "I" statements rather than with accusatory and potentially inflammatory "you" statements. Consider the following:

"You" Statements	*"I" Statements*
1. You don't give a damn about me.	1. Sometimes I feel ignored, and this makes me afraid for us.
2. You always blame me for our problems.	2. I don't like being blamed.
3. You don't love me.	3. I feel unloved.

"I" statements are self-revelations, expressing how we feel without placing blame or attacking our partners' character. In contrast, "you" statements frequently come across as attacks on our partners' character or as attempts to fix blame. When we express a concern with a statement that begins with *I* instead of *you*, our partners are less likely to feel criticized and thus to become defensive. Furthermore, using "I" statements to express emotions such as sadness, hurt, or fear conveys a sense of our vulnerability to our partners. They may find it easier to respond to these "softer" emotional expressions than to accusations expressing resentment, anger, or disgust.

Limit Complaints to One per Discussion

Many of us tend to avoid confrontations with our partners. This understandable reluctance to deal with negative issues can result in an accumulation of unspoken complaints. Consequently, when we finally reach the point where we need to say something, it may be difficult to avoid unleashing a barrage of complaints that includes everything on our current list of grievances. Such a response, although understandable, only serves to magnify rather than resolve conflicts between lovers, as reflected in the following account:

> My wife lets things eat on her without letting me know when I do something that she disapproves of. She remembers every imagined shortcoming and blows it way out of proportion. But I never learn about it until she has accumulated a long list of complaints. Then she hits me with all of them at once, dredging them up like weapons in her arsenal, all designed to make me feel like an insensitive creep. I sometimes hear about things that happened years ago. She wonders why I don't have anything to say when she is done haranguing me. But what do you say when somebody has just given you 10 or 20 reasons why your relationship with her is lousy? Which one do you respond to? And how can you avoid being angry when somebody rubs your face in all your shortcomings, real or imagined? (Authors' files)

You can reduce the likelihood of creating such a counterproductive situation in your own relationships by limiting your complaints to one per discussion. Even if you have half a dozen complaints you want to talk about, it will probably serve your relationship better to pick one and relegate the rest to later conversations.

Most of us find a complaint that goes on and on hard to listen to, even when it is about just one thing. When delivering a complaint, be concise. Just briefly describe the concern, limit examples to one or two, and then stop.

Receiving Complaints

Delivering complaints to a partner is difficult; likewise, receiving complaints from someone you love can be an emotionally rending experience. However, people involved in an intimate, loving relationship inevitably need to register complaints on occasion. How you respond to a complaint can significantly affect not only your partner's inclination to openly share concerns in the future but also the probability of resolving the complaint in a manner that strengthens rather than weakens the relationship.

When your partner delivers a complaint, take a few moments to gather your thoughts. A few deep breaths are probably a much better initial response than blurting out, "Yeah, well, what about the time that you . . . !" Ask yourself, Is this person trying to give me information that may be helpful? In a loving relationship where mutual empathy prevails, perhaps you will be able to see the potential for positive consequences, even though you have just received a painful message. You can respond to such a communication in several ways. We hope one or more of the following suggestions will help in such circumstances.

Responding appropriately to a complaint can help strengthen a relationship.

Acknowledge a Complaint and Find Something to Agree With

Perhaps if you allow yourself to be open to a complaint, you will see a basis for it. Suppose that your partner feels angry about your busy schedule and complains that you are not devoting enough time to the relationship. Maybe you think he or she is overreacting or forgetting all the time you have spent together. However, you also know that this concern has some basis. It can be helpful to acknowledge that basis by saying something like "I can understand how you might feel neglected because I have been so preoccupied with my new job." Such constructive acknowledgment can occur even if you think the complaint is largely unjustified. By reacting in an accepting and supportive manner, you are conveying the message that you hear, understand, and appreciate the basis for your partner's concern.

Ask Clarifying Questions

Your partner may deliver a complaint so vaguely that you need clarification. If this happens, ask questions. Suppose your partner complains that you do not take enough time in your lovemaking. You might respond by asking, "Do you mean that we should spend more time touching before we have intercourse, or that I should wait longer before coming, or that you want me to hold you for a longer time after we have sex?"

Express Your Feelings

It can be helpful to talk about your feelings in response to a complaint rather than letting those feelings dictate your response. Your partner's complaint may cause you to feel angry, hurt, or dejected. Putting your feelings into words is probably more effective than acting them out. Responses such as yelling, stomping out of the room, crying, or retreating into a shell of despair are unlikely to lead to productive dialogue. Instead, it may be helpful to tell your partner, "That was really hard to hear, and I feel hurt" or

"Right now I feel angry, so I need to stop and take a few breaths and figure out what I am thinking and feeling."

Focus on Future Changes You Can Make

An excellent way to close discussion of a complaint is to focus on what the two of you can do to make things better. Perhaps this is the time to say, "My new job is really important to me, but our relationship is much more important. Maybe we can set aside special times each week when we will keep outside concerns from intruding on our time together."

Sometimes people agree to make things better but neglect to discuss concrete changes that will resolve what triggered the complaint. Taking the time to identify and agree on specific changes is crucial.

Saying No

Many of us have difficulty saying no to others. Our discomfort in communicating this direct message is perhaps most pronounced when it applies to intimate areas of relationships. This is reflected in the following anecdotes:

> Sometimes my partner wants to be sexual when I only want to be close. The trouble is, I can't say no. I am afraid she would be hurt or angry. Unfortunately, I am the one who ends up angry at myself for not being able to express my true feelings. Under these circumstances, sex isn't very good. (Authors' files)
>
> It is so hard to say no to a man who suggests having sex at the end of a date. This is especially true if we have had a good time together. You never know if they are going to get that hangdog hurt look or become belligerent and angry. (Authors' files)

These accounts reveal common concerns that inhibit us from saying no. We might believe that a rejection will hurt the other person or make him or her angry or even combative. Laboring under such fears, we might decide that it is less stressful simply to comply. Unfortunately, this reluctant acquiescence can create such negative feelings that the resulting shared activity may be less than pleasurable for both parties.

Many of us have not learned that it is okay to say no. Perhaps more importantly, we may not have learned strategies for saying this. In the following section we consider some potentially useful ways to say no.

A Three-Step Approach to Saying No

Many people have found it helpful to have a definite plan or strategy in mind for saying no to invitations for intimate involvements. Having such a strategy can help you prevent being caught off guard, not knowing how to handle a potentially unpleasant interaction with tact. One approach you may find helpful involves three distinct steps, or phases:

1. Express appreciation for the invitation (e.g., "Thanks for thinking of me" or "It's nice to know that you like me enough to invite me"). You may also wish to validate the other person ("You are a good person").
2. Say no in a clear, unequivocal fashion ("I would prefer not to make love/go dancing/ get involved in a dating relationship").
3. Offer an alternative, if applicable ("However, I would like to have lunch sometime/ give you a back rub").

The positive aspects of this approach are readily apparent. We first indicate our appreciation for the expressed interest in us. At the same time, we clearly state our wish not to comply with the request. Finally, we end the exchange on a positive note by offering an alternative. Of course, this last step will not always be an option (e.g., when turning down a request from someone with whom we wish to have no further contact). Between lovers, however, a mutually acceptable alternative often exists.

Avoid Sending Mixed Messages

Saying no in clear, unmistakable language is essential to the success of the strategy just outlined. Nevertheless, when it comes to sexual intimacy, many of us sometimes send mixed messages about what we do and do not want. Consider, for example, someone who responds positively to a partner's request for sexual intimacy but then spends an inordinate amount of time soaking in the bathtub while the patiently waiting partner falls asleep. Or consider a person who expresses a desire to have sex but instead becomes engrossed in a late-night talk show. Both of these people are sending mixed messages that may reflect their own ambivalence about engaging in sexual relations.

As described in the next section, many of the messages we send about our sexual desires are conveyed nonverbally. When our nonverbal messages seem to contradict our verbal messages, our partners can have difficulty grasping our true intention. For example, we might say we are not interested in being sexual but then touch our partner in an intimate manner, or we might express willingness to engage in intercourse but then not be very responsive. In such circumstances, when our verbal and nonverbal messages seem discordant, our partners are likely to have difficulty determining what we are actually communicating. Furthermore, when the verbal and nonverbal components of communication are inconsistent with each other, the nonverbal component usually prevails (Preston, 2005).

The effect of such mixed messages is usually less than desirable. The recipient is often confused about the other person's intent. He or she may feel uncertain or even inadequate ("Why can't I figure out what you really want?"), and such feelings may turn to anger ("Why do I have to guess?") or withdrawal. These reactions are understandable under the circumstances. Faced with contradictory messages, most of us are unsure what to do: act on the first message or on the second one? Consider the following:

> It really bothers me when my partner says we will make love when I get home from night school and then she is too busy studying to take a break. Even though it was her suggestion, sometimes I wonder if she had any intention to make love. (Authors' files)

All of us can benefit from occasionally considering whether we are sending mixed messages. Try looking for inconsistencies between your verbal messages and your subsequent actions. Does your partner seem confused or uncertain when interacting with you? If you do spot yourself sending a double message, decide which one you really mean, then state it in unmistakable language. It can also be helpful to consider why you sent contradictory messages.

If you are on the receiving end of such messages, it may be helpful to discuss your confusion and ask your partner which of the two messages you should act on. Perhaps your partner will recognize your dilemma and act to resolve it. If she or he seems unwilling to acknowledge the inconsistency, it may be helpful to express your feelings of discomfort and confusion as the recipient of the conflicting messages.

Nonverbal Sexual Communication

Sexual communication is not confined to words. Sometimes a touch or a smile can convey a great deal of information. Tone of voice, gestures, facial expressions, and changes in breathing are also important elements of such communication:

> Sometimes when I want my lover to touch me in a certain place, I move that portion of my body closer to his hands or just shift my position to make the area more accessible. Occasionally, I will guide his hand with mine to show him just what kind of stimulation I want. (Authors' files)

These examples reveal some of the varieties of nonverbal communication that have particular significance for our sexuality. One recent study of young couples in committed relationships found that nonverbal initiation of sexual activity was more common than verbal initiations (Vannier & O'Sullivan, 2010). In this section we direct our attention to four important components of nonverbal sexual communication: facial expressions, interpersonal distance, touching, and sounds.

Facial Expressions

Facial expressions often communicate the feelings a person is experiencing. Although people's expressions certainly vary, most of us have learned to accurately identify particular emotions from facial expressions. The rapport and intimacy between lovers can further increase the reliability of this skill.

Facial expressions of emotion are often a powerful component of nonverbal communication.

Looking at our lovers' faces during sexual activity often gives us a quick reading of their level of pleasure. If we see a look of complete rapture, we are likely to continue providing the same type of stimulation. However, if the look conveys something less than ecstasy, we may decide to try something different or ask our partners for verbal direction.

Facial expressions can also provide helpful cues when talking over sexual concerns with a partner. If a lover's face reflects anger, anxiety, or some other disruptive emotion, it might be wise to deal with this emotion immediately ("I can tell you are angry. Can we talk about it?"). Conversely, a face that shows interest, enthusiasm, or appreciation can encourage us to continue expressing a particular feeling or concern. It is also a good idea to be aware of the nonverbal messages you are giving when your partner is sharing thoughts or feelings with you. Sometimes we inadvertently shut down potentially helpful dialogue by tightening our jaws or frowning at an inappropriate time.

Interpersonal Distance

Social psychologists and communication specialists have much to say about *personal space*. The essence of this idea is that we tend to maintain different distances between ourselves and the people with whom we have contact, depending on our relationship (actual or desired) to them. The intimate space to which we admit close friends and lovers restricts contact much less than the distance we maintain between ourselves and people we do not know or like.

When someone attempts to decrease interpersonal distance, it is generally interpreted as a nonverbal sign that she or he is attracted to the other person or would like more intimate contact. Conversely, if someone withdraws when another person moves close, this action can usually be interpreted as a lack of interest or a gentle kind of rejection.

Lovers, whose interpersonal distance is generally at a minimum, can use such spatial cues to signal desire for intimacy. When your lover moves in close, making his or her body available for your touches or caresses, the message of wanting physical intimacy (not necessarily sex) is apparent. Similarly, when he or she curls up on the other side of the bed, it may be a way of saying, "Please don't come too close tonight."

Touching

Touch is a powerful vehicle for nonverbal sexual communication between lovers. Hands can convey special messages. For example, reaching out and drawing your partner closer can indicate your readiness for more intimate contact. In the early stages of a relationship, touch can also be used to express a desire to become closer.

> When I meet a man and find myself attracted to him, I use touch to convey my feelings. Touching him on the arm to emphasize a point or letting my fingers lightly graze across his hand on the table generally lets my feelings be known. (Authors' files)

Decreased interpersonal space often indicates attraction and perhaps a desire for more intimate contact.

Touch can also defuse anger and heal rifts between temporarily alienated lovers. As one man stated:

> I have found that a gentle touch, lovingly administered to my partner, does wonders in bringing us back together after we have exchanged angry words. Touching her is my way of reestablishing connection. (Authors' files)

Sounds

Many people like making and hearing sounds during sexual activity. Some individuals find increased breathing, moans, groans, and orgasmic cries extremely arousing. Also, such sounds can be helpful indicators of how a partner is responding to lovemaking. Some people find the absence of sounds frustrating:

> My man rarely makes any sounds when we make love. I find this to be very disturbing. In fact, it is a real turn-off. Sometimes I can't even tell if he has come or not. If he wasn't moving, I'd think I was making love to a corpse. (Authors' files)

Some people make a conscious effort to suppress spontaneous noises during sex play. In doing so, they deprive themselves of a potentially powerful and enjoyable form of nonverbal sexual communication. Not uncommonly, their deliberate silence also hinders their partners' sexual arousal, as the foregoing example illustrated.

In this section on nonverbal sexual communication, we have acknowledged that not everything has to be spoken between lovers. However, facial expressions, interpersonal distance, touching, and sounds cannot convey all our complex needs and emotions in a close relationship; words are needed, too. Furthermore, nonverbal cues are open to interpretation, which in some situations can lead to misinterpretation and potential conflict (Humphreys & Newby, 2007). One writer observed, "As a supplement to verbal communication, acts and gestures are fine. As a substitute, they don't quite make it" (Zilbergeld, 1978, p. 158).

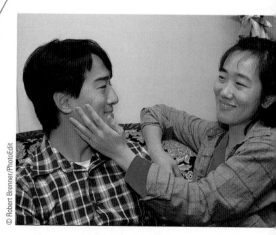

Touch is a powerful vehicle for nonverbal sexual communication.

Communication Patterns in Successful and Unsuccessful Relationships

What does research reveal about the communication patterns in successful, satisfying, long-lasting relationships versus the communication patterns in unhappy relationships that usually fail in the long run? The most informative research on communication patterns in relationships has been conducted by psychologist John Gottman and his colleagues (Gottman, 1994; Gottman & Silver, 2000; Gottman et al., 1998, 1999, 2003). They used a multimethod research model for building an extensive database drawn from many studies of married couples (see Chapter 13 for a description of Gottman's research methods). Gottman identified a number of communication patterns that are predictive of marital happiness or unhappiness. Happily married couples resolve conflicts by using a variety of *constructive* communication tactics, which are described in the following section.

Gottman's Constructive Communication Tactics

Gottman identified a number of constructive communication tactics. These tactics include leveling and editing, validating, and volatile dialogue.

Leveling and Editing

Leveling involves stating our thoughts and feelings clearly, simply, and honestly—preferably while using "I" language. For example, Tyler is distressed because his partner, Emily, seldom initiates sex. Tyler might say, "I love having sex with you, and I am concerned that most of the time it seems to be my idea that we make love. I am not sure what this means." When we begin to level with our partners, we might also need to do some editing of what we say. *Editing* means that we do not say things that we know would be hurtful to our partners and that we limit our comments to information relevant to the issue at hand. Even though Tyler might feel anger toward Emily, it would be counterproductive for him to say, "Your seeming indifference to having sex with me ticks me off and makes me wonder what your problem is." It would also be unhelpful to add comments irrelevant to the issues, such as "And I get real tired having to be the one who does all the shopping and making all the decisions about what we are going to eat."

Validating

Validating involves telling our partners that, given their point of view, we can understand why they think or feel the way they do. Validating a partner's viewpoint does not mean that we invalidate our own position regarding the issue at hand. Rather, we are simply facilitating constructive dialogue by acknowledging the reasonableness of our partner's concern. For example, Emily might respond to Tyler by saying, "I really enjoy our lovemaking, and I can see why you might think differently since I usually let you take the lead."

Volatile Dialogue

Even happily paired couples occasionally butt heads on certain issues, and Gottman's research suggests that some degree of conflict is actually essential to the long-term happiness of a relationship. While studying couples' interaction patterns and reported levels of satisfaction over time, Gottman and his colleagues made a rather startling discovery. Couples in the early stages of a relationship who experienced some conflicts and arguments reported less satisfaction than early-stage couples who rarely or never argued. However, after 3 years the situation reversed itself, and couples who occasionally argued reported significantly more relationship satisfaction than those who avoided arguments.

What accounts for this seemingly paradoxical finding? Gottman suggests that couples who do not argue are likely ignoring important issues that should be addressed rather than left to fester and erode happiness. When problems are never discussed and resolved, both partners can harbor feelings of resentment and frustration that, when allowed to build over time, can drive a wedge between them. In contrast, conflict in a relationship fulfills the crucial role of identifying issues that need to be discussed for the relationship to thrive. Gottman found that some of his long-term happy couples actually used rather passionate or volatile dialogue to resolve conflicts.

Gottman's Destructive Communication Tactics

From his observations of hundreds of couples, Gottman also identified destructive communication tactics. These tactics include criticism, contempt, defensiveness, stonewalling, and belligerence.

Criticism

As described earlier, *criticism* is different from complaining. Criticism that involves expression of contempt and denigration can harm a relationship. In contrast, complaining can be healthy because it allows expression of frustration and identifies issues that need to be discussed and resolved. Complaints are effectively registered with "I" language that focuses on the issue, whereas criticisms usually involve attacking someone's character with "you" statements. Receiving a complaint stated as "I feel frustrated that our lovemaking has become somewhat predictable and routine" can feel very different from receiving a criticism stated as "You always want to make love in the same old way." The latter statement is likely to be taken as a personal attack, which puts the recipient in a defensive position that clearly does not encourage constructive dialogue.

Contempt

Contempt is similar to criticism, but it degrades communication to an even more intense level of negativity by adding insults, sarcasm, and even name-calling to the critical commentary. For example, someone might say, "You are so narrow and limited in your approach to lovemaking and life in general. How did I ever connect with such a stilted, boring person?" Contempt can also be expressed nonverbally by sneering, rolling one's eyes, or ignoring a partner's messages. This negative communication tactic causes emotional pain, does nothing to remedy or resolve issues, creates new problems in the form of defensiveness, anger, and resentment, and thereby erodes the quality of a relationship.

Defensiveness

A person who feels personally attacked or victimized by a partner's criticism or contempt is likely to respond with *defensiveness*. This involves constructing a defense rather than attempting to discuss and resolve an issue. Defensiveness can take the form of self-protective responses, such as making excuses, denying responsibility, or replying with a criticism of one's own. Thus the recipient of the contemptuous criticism described earlier might respond by saying, "You think I'm a boring lover? Take a long look at yourself. All you ever care about is your own pleasure, and you never give me a chance to say what I want!" In this situation one partner attacks and the other defends and counterattacks. Will a relationship that involves such tactics survive? Not likely.

Stonewalling

Stonewalling occurs when a person concludes that any response to a partner's criticism or complaint will not be helpful or productive and therefore decides not to respond at all. The stonewaller simply puts up a wall and refuses to communicate, responding instead with silence, by walking out of the room, by turning on the TV, by picking up a book, or the like. This silent-treatment tactic communicates disapproval, distancing, and the belief that nothing one can do will improve the situation, so one might as well say nothing. A person who stonewalls a partner may have found that previous efforts to defuse the partner's critical attacks have been ineffective and that it is therefore no longer productive to engage in seemingly futile dialogue.

Belligerence

The fifth destructive communication tactic involves a confrontational, "in your face" type of interaction that is likely to emerge as a relationship suffers from prolonged patterns of poor communication. *Belligerence* often entails a purposely provoking style of interaction intended to diminish or challenge a partner's right to influence patterns of interaction in the relationship. For example, a belligerent person might say to his or her partner, "So what if I always want to be on top when we have intercourse. What are you going to do about it?"

Clearly, all five of these destructive tactics erode and interfere with rather than improve a couple's communication. Such styles of communication are likely to increase conflict and negativity, diminish positive exchanges between partners, and cause an escalation of hostility rather than solve problems. People in a relationship characterized by these negative, harmful exchanges may eventually decide that they would be better off ending the relationship—a conclusion supported by Gottman's research finding that long-term relationship survival rates are low for such couples.

We can conclude from the research on couple communication that partners who have satisfying, long-lasting relationships communicate in ways that differ markedly from those used by partners who have unhappy, often short-lived relationships. Positive communication strategies are not limited to those discussed in this section. Many of the strategies outlined in this chapter, when incorporated into a couple's communication about sex and other relationship issues, are predictive of satisfying and enduring partnerships.

Summary

What Is Love?

- Zick Rubin developed a 13-item questionnaire for measuring love.

Types of Love

- Passionate love is characterized by intense, vibrant feelings that tend to be relatively short-lived.
- Companionate love is characterized by deep affection and attachment.
- Robert Sternberg's triangular theory maintains that love has three components: passion (the motivational component), intimacy (the emotional component), and commitment (the cognitive component). Various combinations of these three components yield eight different kinds of love.

- John Allan Lee proposed a theory that describes six different styles of loving: romantic, game playing, possessive, companionate, altruistic, and pragmatic.

Falling in Love: Why and With Whom?

- Falling in love has been explained as resulting from the need to overcome a sense of aloneness, the desire to justify sexual involvement, or sexual attraction.
- The intense feelings of being passionately in love might have a basis in surging levels of the brain chemicals norepinephrine, dopamine, and especially phenylethylamine (PEA). The progression from passion to deep attraction might result from the gradual increase of endorphins in the brain.

- Factors known to contribute strongly to interpersonal attraction and falling in love include proximity, similarity, reciprocity, and physical attractiveness. We often develop loving relationships with people whom we see frequently, who share similar beliefs, who seem to like us, and whom we perceive as physically attractive.

Love and Styles of Attachment

- The way we form attachments, which has its roots in infancy, greatly affects how we relate to loved partners.
- Securely attached children, who learn that parents are a source of security and trust, demonstrate much greater social competence than insecurely attached children, who are classified as either anxious-ambivalent or avoidant.
- Attachment styles developed during infancy continue throughout life to considerably influence a person's capacity to form loving attachments and the way the person relates to significant others.
- Securely attached adults are best equipped to establish stable, satisfying relationships. They are comfortable being close to others, feel secure in relationships, and do not fear being abandoned.
- Anxious-ambivalent adults often have a poor self-image, are insecure in relationships, and struggle with ambivalence about achieving closeness with others.
- Avoidant adults are uncomfortable with any degree of closeness, have problems trusting or depending on a partner, and often view others negatively.
- People who become couples often have similar styles of attachment. The most common pairing comprises partners who both have a secure attachment style.
- People with a secure attachment style report the highest levels of relationship satisfaction, especially if both partners in a relationship have a secure attachment style.

Issues in Loving Relationships

- Various perspectives exist on the connections between love and sex. For most people the ideal intimate relationship is one replete with feelings of both mutual love and mutual sexual gratification.
- Women consistently link love with sexual behavior more than men do, but research indicates that men and women are becoming more similar on this issue.
- Gay men and lesbians, like heterosexuals, generally seek out loving, trusting, caring relationships that embrace many dimensions of sharing in addition to sexual intimacy.
- Some people consider jealousy a sign of love, but it might actually reflect fear of losing possession or control of another.

- Jealousy is frequently a factor in precipitating violence in marriages and dating relationships.
- Research indicates that men and women react differently to jealousy.

Maintaining Relationship Satisfaction

- Ingredients often present in a lasting love relationship include self-acceptance, acceptance of one's partner, appreciation of one another, commitment, good communication, realistic expectations, shared interests, equality in decision making, and the ability to face conflict effectively.
- Variety is often an important ingredient of enjoyable sex in a long-term relationship. For some couples, however, the security of routine is more satisfying.

The Importance of Sexual Communication

- Sexual communication often contributes to the contentment and enjoyment of a sexual relationship; infrequent or ineffective sexual communication is a common reason that people feel dissatisfied with their sex lives.
- An excellent basis for effective sexual communication is mutual empathy—the underlying knowledge that each partner in a relationship cares for the other and knows that care is reciprocated.

Talking: Getting Started

- It is often difficult to start talking about sex. Suggestions for getting started include talking about talking, reading about sex and discussing the material, and sharing sexual histories.

Listening and Feedback

- Communication is most successful between an active listener and an effective speaker.
- The listener can facilitate communication by maintaining eye contact with the speaker, providing feedback, expressing appreciation for communication efforts, and maintaining an attitude of unconditional positive regard.

Discovering Your Partner's Needs

- Efforts to communicate with sexual partners are often hindered by yes/no questions, which encourage limited replies. Effective alternatives include open-ended and either/or questions.
- Self-disclosure can make it easier for a partner to communicate her or his own needs. Sharing fantasies, beginning with mild desires, can be a particularly valuable kind of exchange.
- Discussing sexual preferences either before or after a sexual encounter can be beneficial.

- The Internet has contributed to the development of romantic relationships by eliminating the role of physical attractiveness and gender-role assumptions and increasing the influence of imagination. Potential drawbacks of communication on the Web include a reduction of good judgment, a rapid increase in relationship intensity, a lack of truthfulness, and potentially risky FTF meetings.
- Giving permission encourages partners to share feelings freely.

Learning to Make Requests

- Making requests is facilitated by (1) taking responsibility for one's own pleasure, (2) making sure requests are specific, and (3) using "I" language.

Expressing and Receiving Complaints

- It is important to select the right time and place for expressing sexual concerns. Avoid registering complaints when anger is at its peak.
- Complaints are generally most effective when tempered with praise. People are usually more motivated to make changes when they are praised for their strengths as well as made aware of things that need improvement.
- "Why" questions that blame a partner do not further the registering of constructive complaints.
- It is wise to direct anger toward behavior rather than toward a person's character. Anger is probably best expressed with clear, honest "I" statements rather than with accusatory "you" statements.
- Relationships are better served when complaints are limited to one per discussion.
- Acknowledging an understanding of the basis for a partner's complaint can help establish a sense of empathy and lead to constructive dialogue.
- It can be helpful to ask clarifying questions when complaints are vague. Calmly verbalizing the feelings aroused when one receives a complaint often avoids nonproductive, heated exchanges.
- An excellent closure to receiving a complaint is to focus on what can be done to rectify the problem in a relationship.

Saying No

- A three-step strategy for saying no to invitations for intimate involvements is expressing appreciation for the invitation, saying no clearly and unequivocally, and offering an alternative, if applicable.
- To avoid sending mixed messages, occasionally check for inconsistencies between verbal messages and subsequent actions. Recipients of mixed messages might find it helpful to express their confusion and to ask which of the conflicting messages they are expected to act on.

Nonverbal Sexual Communication

- Sexual communication is not confined to words alone. Facial expressions, interpersonal distance, touching, and sounds also convey a great deal of information.
- The value of nonverbal communication lies primarily in its ability to supplement, not replace, verbal communication.

Communication Patterns in Successful and Unsuccessful Relationships

- Constructive communication tactics that contribute to relationship satisfaction and longevity include leveling and editing, validating, and volatile dialogue.
- Destructive communication tactics include criticism, contempt, defensiveness, stonewalling, and belligerence. Such tactics lead to increased conflict and negativity, cause an escalation of hostility, and frequently result in relationship failure.

Media Resources

Log in to CengageBrain.com to access the resources your instructor requires.

Go to CengageBrain.com to access Psychology CourseMate, where you will find an interactive eBook, glossaries, flashcards, quizzes, videos, and more.

Also access links to chapter-related websites, including **Relationship Issues, Sexual Communication, Communicating About Sex, The Human Awareness Institute, The Couples Place,** and the **American Association for Marriage and Family Therapy.**

Sexual Behaviors 8

Celibacy
What are some of the benefits and disadvantages of celibacy?

Erotic Dreams and Fantasy
What are some of the functions of sexual fantasy?

How do male and female sexual fantasies differ?

Masturbation
How have attitudes about masturbation changed since the 1800s?

Sexual Expression: The Importance of Context
What characteristics of sexual behavior lead it in positive or negative directions?

Kissing and Touching
Why is touching important?

Oral–Genital Stimulation
What are the technical terms for oral stimulation of a woman and of a man?

How have attitudes about oral sex changed over time?

Anal Stimulation
How common is anal intercourse? What are important precautions regarding its practice?

Coitus and Coital Positions
What are some different intercourse positions?

What is an important element of Tantric sex?

Marin/PhotoAlto Agency RF/Jupiterimages

225

> My sexuality has had many different dimensions during my life. My childhood masturbation was a secret desire and guilt that I never did admit to the priest in the confessional. "Playing doctor" was intriguing and exciting in its "naughtiness." The hours of hot kissing and petting of my teenage and early college years developed my sexual awareness. My first intercourse experience was with a loved and trusted boyfriend. It was a profound physical and emotional experience; years later the memory still brings me deep pleasure. As a young adult my sexual expression alternated between periods of recreational sex and celibacy. Within marriage the comforts and challenges of commitment; combining sex with an intense desire to become pregnant; the primal experience of pregnancy, childbirth, and nursing greatly expanded the parameters of my sexuality. Now, balancing family, career, personal interests, my sexuality is a quiet hum in the background. I'm looking forward to retirement and time and energy for more than coffee and a kiss in the morning. (Authors' files)

People express their sexuality in many ways. Sexual expression can vary greatly from person to person, within the contexts of different relationships, and over the course of one's lifespan. The emotions and meanings that people attach to sexual behavior also vary widely. In this chapter, we discuss the importance of context in sexual expression and describe a variety of sexual behaviors. We consider individuals first and later look at couples' sexual behavior. We begin with a discussion of celibacy.

Celibacy

complete celibacy
An expression of sexuality in which an individual does not engage in either masturbation or interpersonal sexual contact.

partial celibacy
An expression of sexuality in which an individual does not engage in interpersonal sexual contact but continues to engage in masturbation.

A physically mature person who does not engage in sexual behavior is said to be *celibate*. In **complete celibacy** a person neither masturbates nor has sexual contact with another person. In **partial celibacy** an individual masturbates but does not have interpersonal sexual contact. Celibacy is not commonly thought of as a form of sexual expression. However, when it represents a conscious decision not to engage in sexual behavior, this decision in itself is an expression of one's sexuality, and it may manifest a person's sexual intelligence. Celibacy, or abstinence, can be a viable option until the context for a sexual relationship is appropriate and positive for a given individual (Zafar, 2010).

Celibacy is most commonly associated with religious devotion; joining a religious order or becoming a priest or nun often includes a vow of celibacy. The ideal of religious celibacy is to transform sexual energy into service to humanity (Abbott, 2000). Mother Teresa of Calcutta and Mahatma Gandhi of India exemplified this ideal, and they are admired for their moral leadership (Sipe, 1990).

Historically, some women embraced celibacy to free themselves from the limitations of the expected gender roles of marriage and motherhood. In the Middle Ages a woman could obtain an education if she became a nun. In a convent, nuns had access to libraries and could correspond with learned theologians. Laywomen were prohibited such privileges. Elizabeth I, England's Virgin Queen, avoided marriage to maintain her political power, but she had several unconsummated love affairs during her rule. She entertained proposals from numerous well-connected suitors for her own political purposes, subjecting herself to repeated court inspections to confirm her virginity (Abbott, 2000).

Today many factors can lead a person to be celibate. Some people choose to be celibate until marriage because of religious or moral beliefs. Others maintain celibacy until their personal criteria for a good sexual relationship have been met. Some choose celibacy because they have experienced confusion or disappointment in past sexual relationships, and they want to spend some time establishing new relationships without the complicating factor of sexual interaction (Terry, 2007). A 28-year-old man explained:

> There was a period not too long ago in my life where I had been abstinent for about four years. I had been on both sides of the cheating fence and began to realize that sex wasn't just something that I wanted to take, or could take, lightly. The feelings that can be created out of a physical relationship are simply too powerful to toy around with. I was terribly afraid of being hurt again, or of perhaps hurting someone else, so I chose not to get sexual with anyone. (Authors' files)

At times a person can be so caught up in other aspects of life that sex is simply not a priority. Health considerations, such as concerns about pregnancy or sexually transmitted infections, can also prompt a decision not to have sexual intercourse.

Some people find that a period of celibacy can be rewarding. They can often refocus on themselves during such a period—exploring self-pleasuring; learning to value their aloneness, autonomy, and privacy; or giving priority to work and nonsexual relationship commitments. Friendships can gain new dimensions and fulfillment. Of the many options for sexual expression, celibacy is one that people sometimes have considerable trouble understanding. However, celibacy can be a personally valuable choice.

Erotic Dreams and Fantasy

Some forms of sexual experience occur within a person's mind, with or without sexual behavior. These are erotic dreams and fantasy—mental experiences that arise from our imagination or life experience or that are stimulated by the Internet, books, drawings, photographs, or movies.

Erotic Dreams

Erotic dreams, and occasionally orgasm, can occur during sleep without a person's conscious direction. One study found that 93% of men and 86% of women reported having erotic dreams (Schredl et al., 2004). A person might waken during such a dream and notice signs of sexual arousal: erection, vaginal lubrication, or pelvic movements. Orgasm can also occur during sleep; this is called **nocturnal orgasm**. When orgasm occurs, males usually notice the ejaculate—hence the term *wet dream* or *nocturnal emission*. Women also experience orgasm during sleep, but female orgasm may be more difficult to determine because of the absence of visible evidence.

nocturnal orgasm
Involuntary orgasm during sleep.

Erotic Fantasy

Erotic waking fantasies commonly occur during daydreams, masturbation, or sexual encounters with a partner. A review of research about fantasy found that about 95% of men and women reported having experienced sexual fantasies. Comparing the content of homosexuals' and heterosexuals' fantasies revealed more similarities than differences, leaving aside the sex of the imagined partner (Leitenberg & Henning, 1995). How strongly religious individuals are appears to impact frequency and variety of erotic fantasies. Men and women who are *less* religious fantasize about sex *more* frequently than those who are more religious. Further, women who are agnostic or atheist have a much greater variety of fantasies than women with religious beliefs (Ahrold et al., 2011).

Sexual fantasies can take you to times and places that are impractical or impossible in real life.

Vasko Miokovic/Vetta/Getty Images

Functions of Fantasy

Erotic fantasies serve many functions. First, they can be a source of pleasure and arousal. Erotic thoughts typically serve to enhance sexual arousal during masturbation and partners' sexual activities. Fantasies can be a way to mentally rehearse and anticipate new sexual experiences. Imagining seductive glances, that first kiss, or a novel intercourse position may help a person implement such activities more comfortably.

Sexual fantasies can allow tolerable expression of "forbidden wishes." That a sexual activity in a fantasy is forbidden can make it more exciting. People in sexually exclusive relationships can fantasize about past lovers or others to whom they feel attracted, even though they are committed to a single sexual partner. In a fantasy, a person can experience lustful group sex, cross-orientation sexual liaisons, brief sexual encounters with strangers, erotic relations with friends and acquaintances, incestuous experiences, sex with animals, or any other sexual activity imaginable—all without actually engaging in it.

Another function of erotic fantasy can be to provide relief from gender-role expectations. Women's fantasies of being the sexual aggressor and men's fantasies of being forced to have sex can offer alternatives to stereotypical roles. In her first book about male sexual fantasy, Nancy Friday reported that one of the major themes is men's releasing control in favor of passivity:

> It may seem lusty and dashing always to be the one who chooses the woman, who decides when, where, and how the bedroom scene will be played. But isn't her role safer? The man is like someone who has suggested a new restaurant to friends. What if it doesn't live up to expectations he has aroused? The macho stance makes the male the star performer. (Friday, 1980, p. 274)

The notion of control, aggression, and sex can play out in different ways for women and men. Although the fantasy of being forced to have sex provides an alternative to gender-role expectations for men, the same type of fantasy has other meanings for women. For women, who often learn to have mixed feelings about being sexual, this type of fantasy offers sexual adventures free from the responsibility and guilt of personal choice (Critelli & Bivona, 2008). Research indicates that almost twice as many women as men fantasize about being forced to have sex (Maltz & Boss, 1997). One study found that 62% of women have had one or more fantasies about rape (Bivona & Critelli, 2009). Another study found that women who reported having fantasies of being forced to have sex had more positive feelings about sex in general than women who did not have such fantasies. The research also showed that forced-sex fantasies are not usually an indication of having had past abusive experiences (Critelli & Bivona, 2008). It is important to emphasize that enjoyment of forced-sex fantasies does not mean women really want to be raped. A woman is in charge of her fantasies, but as a victim of sexual aggression she is not in control.

Male/Female Similarities and Differences in Sexual Fantasy

Men's and women's fantasy lives have some aspects in common. First, the frequency of fantasy is similar for both sexes during sexual activity with a partner. Second, both men and women indicate a wide range of fantasy content. A research summary of heterosexual male/female content of sexual fantasy (Leitenberg & Henning, 1995) found notable differences:

- Men's fantasies are more active and focus more on a woman's body and on what they want to do to it, whereas women's fantasies are more passive and focus more on men's interest in their bodies.
- Men's sexual fantasies focus more on explicit sexual acts, nude bodies, and physical gratification, whereas women use more emotional context and romance in their sexual fantasies. Similarly, a more recent study of reactions to types of erotic stories found that women reported arousal to both suggestive and explicit erotic stories, whereas men experienced a significant increase in arousal only to explicit erotic stories (Scott & Cortez, 2011).
- Men are more likely to fantasize about multiple partners and group sex than are women.
- Men are more likely to have dominance fantasies, whereas women are more likely to have submission fantasies.

Fantasies: Help or Hindrance?

Erotic fantasies are generally considered a healthy and helpful aspect of sexuality (Goleman, 2006). Many sex therapists encourage their clients to use sexual fantasies as a source of stimulation to help them increase interest and arousal. Research found that people who felt less guilty about sexual fantasies during intercourse reported higher levels of sexual satisfaction and functioning than did others who felt more guilty about having sexual fantasies (Cado & Leitenberg, 1990). Sexual fantasies help some men and women experience arousal and orgasm during sexual activity. Conversely, a lack of erotic fantasy and a focus on nonerotic thoughts can contribute to problems of low sexual desire and arousal (Boss & Maltz, 2001; Purdon & Watson, 2011).

Some people decide to incorporate a particular fantasy into their actual sexual behavior with a partner. Acting out a fantasy can be pleasurable; however, if it is uncomfortable for a partner, is counter to one's value system, or has possible negative consequences, one should consider the advantages and disadvantages of acting it out. For some people, fantasies are more exciting when they remain imaginary and are disappointing when acted out.

Several Internet activities and technologies present an intermediate step between private fantasy and actual behavior. Sharing and developing one's sexual fantasies online—in chat rooms, during online multiplayer erotic games, and with webcam technology—involve revealing the fantasies, usually to strangers. Interestingly, talking about fantasies online with strangers does help some individuals take the step of expressing their previously private sexual imaginings and interests to their actual partners.

Individuals who have experienced sexual abuse as children are sometimes troubled by intrusive, unwanted sexual fantasies. Developing new fantasies based on self-acceptance and loving relationships can be a part of healing for these individuals (Boss & Maltz, 2001). As with most other aspects of sexuality, what determines whether fantasizing is helpful or disturbing to a relationship is its meaning and purpose for the individuals concerned.

Although most of the available research supports sexual fantasy as helpful, in some situations sexual fantasies can be problematic. For example, some men have difficulty experiencing orgasm during intercourse because the idiosyncratic sexual fantasies they require for intense arousal are discordant with their partner's sexual behavior (Perelman, 2001). Fantasizing privately during sex with a partner can erode intimacy in the

People use webcam technology to act out fantasies with other individuals.

relationship. One study found that college students had a double standard about their own sexual fantasies versus their partner's. Study participants of both sexes thought that fantasizing about someone other than their partner was normal and did not jeopardize the exclusivity of the relationship. However, the idea that their partner fantasized about someone else made the participants feel jealous and threatened, as though the fantasy was a kind of unfaithfulness. The most threatening fantasy a partner could have was about a mutual friend or classmate rather than a fantasy about someone who in reality was an unlikely rival, such as a movie star (Yarab & Allgeier, 1998).

In some cases fantasy can influence a person to act in a way that harms others. This outcome is of particular concern in the case of people who sexually assault children or adults. A person who thinks that he or she is in danger of committing such an act should seek professional psychological assistance. ●

Masturbation

masturbation
Stimulation of one's own genitals to create sexual pleasure.

In this textbook the word **masturbation** is used to describe self-stimulation of one's genitals for sexual pleasure. *Autoeroticism* is another term used for masturbation. We discuss some perspectives on and purposes of masturbation and specific techniques used in masturbation.

Perspectives on Masturbation

Masturbation has been a source of social concern and censure throughout Judeo-Christian history. This state of affairs has resulted in both misinformation and considerable personal shame and fear. Many of the negative attitudes toward masturbation are rooted in early Jewish and Christian views that procreation was the only legitimate purpose of sexual behavior. Because masturbation obviously could not result in conception, it was condemned (Wiesner-Hanks, 2000). During the mid-18th century, the "evils" of masturbation received a great deal of publicity in the name of science, largely because of the writings of a European physician named Samuel Tissot. He believed that semen was made from blood and that the loss of semen was debilitating to health, and he wrote vividly about the mind- and body-damaging effects of "self-abuse." This view of masturbation influenced social and medical attitudes in Europe and North America for generations, as reflected by an "encyclopedia" of health published in 1918, which describes the following "symptoms" of masturbation:

> The health soon becomes noticeably impaired; there will be general debility. . . . Next come sore eyes, blindness, stupidity, consumption, spinal affliction, emaciation, involuntary seminal emissions, loss of all energy or spirit, insanity and idiocy—the hopeless ruin of both body and mind. (Wood & Ruddock, 1918, p. 812)

In the 1800s, sexual abstinence, simple foods, and fitness were lauded as crucial to health. The Reverend Sylvester Graham, who promoted the use of whole-grain flours and whose name is still attached to graham crackers, wrote that ejaculation reduced precious "vital fluids." He beseeched men to abstain from masturbation and even marital intercourse to avoid moral and physical degeneracy. John Harvey Kellogg, a physician, carried Graham's work further and developed the cornflake to help prevent masturbation and sexual desire. (Kellogg believed that bland food dampened sexual desires.) Other techniques to control masturbation included bandaging the genitals, tying one's hands at

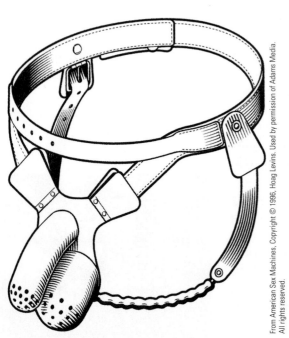

This lockable metal genital pouch with leather straps, patented in 1910, was designed to prevent masturbation by patients in mental hospitals.

night, performing a clitoridectomy, applying carbolic acid to the clitoris, and suturing foreskins shut, as well as employing mechanical devices (Planned Parenthood Federation of America, 2003).

Freud and most other early psychoanalysts recognized that masturbation does not harm physical health, and they saw it as normal during childhood. However, they believed that masturbation in adulthood could be a sign of "immature" sexual development and the inability to form good sexual relationships.

Views today reflect conflicting beliefs about masturbation; some of the traditional condemnation still exists. For example, in 1976 the Vatican issued a "Declaration on Certain Questions Concerning Sexual Ethics," which described masturbation as an "intrinsically and seriously disordered act." This perspective was maintained in 1993 by Pope John Paul II's condemnation of masturbation as morally unacceptable. Many religious fundamentalists have negative attitudes about masturbation (Ahrold et al., 2011). Indeed, some individuals abstain from masturbation because of their religious beliefs.

> I don't masturbate, because I've learned from my church and my parents that sexual love in marriage is an expression of God's love. Any other kind of sex diminishes the meaning I will find with my wife. (Authors' files)

In contrast to negativity about masturbation, beginning in the 1970s, feminists countered religious condemnation by promoting masturbation as a legitimate form of women's self-loving and sexual self-discovery, as well as a component of partner lovemaking (Chalker, 2002). For example, Betty Dodson, author of *Liberating Masturbation*, writes:

> Masturbation, of course, is our first natural sexual activity. It's the way we discover our eroticism, the way we learn to respond sexually, the way we learn to love ourselves and build self-esteem. (Dodson, 1974, p. 13)

Purposes of Masturbation

People masturbate for a variety of reasons, not the least of which is the pleasure of arousal and orgasm. The most commonly reported reason is to relieve sexual tension (Michael et al., 1994). Masturbation is also valuable as a means of self-exploration. Sex educator Eleanor Hamilton recommends masturbation to adolescents as a way to release tension and to become "pleasantly at home with your own sexual organs" (1978, p. 33). Indeed, people can learn a great deal about their sexual responses from masturbation. Self-stimulation is often helpful for women learning to experience orgasms and for men experimenting with their response patterns to increase ejaculatory control. (We discuss masturbation as a tool for increasing sexual satisfaction in Chapter 14.) Finally, some people find that masturbation helps them get to sleep at night, because the same generalized feelings of relaxation that often follow a sexual encounter can also accompany self-pleasuring.

At times the satisfaction from an autoerotic session can be more rewarding than an interpersonal sexual encounter, as the following quotation illustrates:

SEXUALHEALTH

> I had always assumed that masturbation was a second-best sexual expression. One time, after reflecting back on the previous day's activities of a really enjoyable morning masturbatory experience and an unsatisfying experience that evening with a partner, I realized that first- and second-rate were very relative. (Authors' files)

Some people find that the independent sexual release available through masturbation can help them make better decisions about relating sexually with other people and can also be a safe-sex alternative (Shelton, 2010). Furthermore, within a relationship masturbation can help to even out the effects of dissimilar sexual interest. Masturbation can also be a shared experience:

> When I am feeling sexual and my partner is not, he holds me and kisses me while I masturbate. Also, sometimes after making love I like to touch myself while he embraces me. It is so much better than sneaking off to the bathroom alone. (Authors' files)

The National Survey of Sexual Health and Behavior (NSSHB) found that 48% of teenage girls and 73% of teenage boys between the ages of 14 and 17 had masturbated (Robbins et al., 2011). The difference between the percentages of females and males who masturbate lessens for people in their 20s. Almost 85% of women and over 94% of men between ages 25 and 29 had masturbated (Herbenick et al., 2010b). ■ Table 8.1 shows the range in frequency of masturbation among college students. A current meta-analysis of research found that although males masturbate more frequently, men's and women's attitudes toward masturbation are very similar. This same analysis found that in countries with more equality between the sexes, men and women had smaller differences in attitudes and behaviors pertaining to masturbation than in less egalitarian countries. This pattern strongly suggests that there is a sociocultural component to gender similarities and differences regarding masturbation (Petersen & Hyde, 2011).

A common concern about masturbation is "doing it too much." Even in writings where masturbation is said to be normal, masturbating "to excess" is often presented as unhealthy. A definition of excess rarely follows. If a person were masturbating so much that it significantly interfered with any aspect of his or her life, there might be cause for concern. However, in that case masturbation would be a symptom or manifestation of some underlying problem rather than the problem itself. For example, someone who is experiencing intense emotional anxiety might use masturbation as a way to relieve anxiety or as a form of self-comforting. The problem in this case is the intense emotional anxiety, not the masturbation. ●

Masturbation is often considered inappropriate when a person has a sexual partner or is married. Some people believe that they should not engage in a sexual activity that excludes their partners or that experiencing sexual pleasure by masturbation deprives their partners of pleasure. Others mistakenly interpret their partner's desire to masturbate as a sign that something is wrong with their relationship. But unless it interferes with mutually enjoyable sexual intimacy in the relationship, masturbation can be considered a normal part of each partner's sexual repertoire. It is common for people to continue masturbation after they marry (Reece et al., 2010a; Herbenick et al., 2010a). In fact, individuals who masturbate more often also engage in sexual activity

■ TABLE 8.1 Two Thousand College Students Answer the Question "How Often Do You Masturbate?"

	Men (%)	Women (%)
Two or more times a week	50	16
Less than two times a week but more than never	38	44
Never	12	40

SOURCE: Elliott & Brantley (1997).

with their partners more frequently than other individuals who masturbate less often (Laumann et al., 1994). Moreover, one study found that married women who masturbated to orgasm had greater marital and sexual satisfaction than women who did not masturbate (Hurlbert & Whittaker, 1991).

Although masturbating is valuable for many people in various situations, not everyone wants to do it. Sometimes, in our attempts to help people who would like to eradicate their negative feelings about self-stimulation, it may sound as if the message is that people *should* masturbate. This is not the case. Masturbation is an option for sexual expression, not a mandate.

Ethnicity and Masturbation

Adults who are most likely to masturbate, and most likely to masturbate more frequently than others, have several characteristics in common—indicating that even this private sexual behavior is strongly influenced by a person's social group (Laumann et al., 1994). They have liberal views, are college educated, and are living with a sexual partner. White men and women masturbate more than African American men and women. Among White, African, and Hispanic Americans, Hispanic women have the lowest rate of masturbation.

Self-Pleasuring Techniques

In this section we offer descriptions of self-pleasuring techniques. Specific techniques for masturbation vary. Males commonly grasp the penile shaft with one hand, as shown in ❚ Figure 8.1. Some men prefer to use lotion; others like the natural friction of a dry hand. Up-and-down motions of differing pressures and tempos provide stimulation. A man can also stroke the glans and frenulum or caress or tug the scrotum. Or, rather than using his hands, a man can rub his penis against a mattress or pillow.

❚ **Figure 8.1** Male masturbation.

Women enjoy a variety of stimulation techniques. Typically, the hand provides circular, back-and-forth, or up-and-down movements against the mons and clitoral area (see ❚ Figure 8.2). The glans of the clitoris is rarely stimulated directly, although it can be stimulated indirectly when covered by the hood. Some women thrust the clitoral area against an object such as bedding or a pillow. Others masturbate by pressing their thighs together and tensing the pelvic floor muscles that underlie the vulva. Some women insert their fingers or sex toys into their vaginas during masturbation, especially for G-spot stimulation. Dildos and vibrators that have a curve at the end are particularly good for G-spot stimulation (Blue, 2007).

Sex Toys

Some individuals also use vibrators and other sex toys for added enjoyment or variation in self-stimulation. Research has found that about 53% of women and 45% of men have used vibrators in solo or partnered sexual activities and that vibrator use among women and men is associated with positive sexual function (Herbenick et al., 2011a; Reece et al., 2009). Sex toy use appears to be more common among gay and bisexual men than among heterosexual men. Almost 79% of gay and bisexual-identified

❚ **Figure 8.2** Female masturbation.

© Cengage Learning

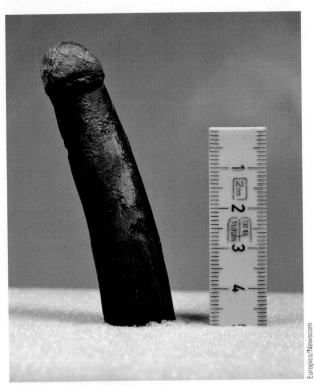

This phallic shape was found at a Stone Age settlement in Sweden. It is carved from a deer antler and is believed to be a 6,000 to 8,000 year old dildo.

men have used at least one sex toy for self-stimulation or with a partner (Rosenberger et al., 2012).

Ninety percent of women who masturbate with a vibrator are comfortable talking to their partner about it, and many couples incorporate vibrators into their sex play (Berman, 2004). Sociologist Pepper Schwartz encourages men not to feel threatened by including a vibrator with their partners: "Gentlemen, this is not your competition, it's your colleague" (Schwartz, 2006). Several different types of vibrators are available, and people's preferences vary.

The vibrator is only one kind of sex toy for self-pleasuring and enhancing sexual interaction with one's partner. The *dildo*, or artificial penis, has been used to enhance sexual arousal throughout history, and dildos have been found at archeological sites dating from 4000 BCE (Chalker, 2002). Dildos are also used for anal stimulation. Men can use latex or rubber simulations of female genitals for masturbation. More elaborate sex toys that stimulate several genital sites at once are also available, and new variations are always being developed (Davies, 2011).

Sexual Expression: The Importance of Context

Up to this point in the chapter, we have been looking primarily at ways that people express themselves sexually as individuals. However, many of the sexual behaviors with which we are concerned take place as interactions between people. In the sections that follow we discuss some of the more common forms of shared sexual behavior.

The ring fits at the base of the penis, and the ball stimulates the clitoris.

Vibrators come in many forms. The TV show *Sex and the City* brought the rabbit to the public's attention.

Ann Summers's sex toy.

The Context of Sexual Expression

Although the following sections include discussions of sexual techniques, a sexual interaction cannot stand on its own; it exists within the context of motivation and meanings of the individuals involved and the relationship as a whole (M. Cooper et al., 2011). One writer explained:

> Sex can be motivated by excitement or boredom, physical need or affection, desire or duty, loneliness or complacency. It can be a bid for power or an egalitarian exchange, a purely mechanical release of tension or a highly emotional fusion, a way to wear oneself out for sleep or a way to revitalize oneself. Sex can be granted as a reward or inducement, an altruistic offering or a favor; it can also be an act of selfishness, insecurity, or narcissism. Sex can express almost anything and mean almost anything. (Fillion, 1996, p. 41)

■ Table 8.2 shows the top 15 out of 237 reasons college men and women gave for being sexual with a partner. Notably, 20 of the top 25 reasons were identical for men and women (Meston & Buss, 2007).

■ TABLE 8.2 Top 15 Reasons College Women and Men Give for Having Sex

	Women	Men
1.	I was attracted to the person.	I was attracted to the person.
2.	I wanted to experience the physical pleasure.	It feels good.
3.	It feels good.	I wanted to experience the physical pleasure.
4.	I wanted to show my affection to the person.	It's fun.
5.	I wanted to express my love for the person.	I wanted to show my affection to the person.
6.	I was sexually aroused and wanted the release.	I was sexually aroused and wanted the release.
7.	I was horny.	I was horny.
8.	It's fun.	I wanted to express my love for the person.
9.	I realized I was in love.	I wanted to achieve an orgasm.
10.	I was "in the heat of the moment."	I wanted to please my partner.
11.	I wanted to please my partner.	The person's physical appearance turned me on.
12.	I desired emotional closeness (i.e., intimacy).	I wanted the pure pleasure.
13.	I wanted the pure pleasure.	I was "in the heat of the moment."
14.	I wanted to achieve an orgasm.	I desired emotional closeness (i.e., intimacy).
15.	It's exciting, adventurous.	It's exciting, adventurous.

The Maltz Hierarchy

The context within which sexual experiences occur is critically important in determining whether they are positive for individuals and relationships. Author and sex therapist Wendy Maltz developed a model of sexual expression that describes levels of constructive and destructive sexual experiences (Maltz, 2001). Maltz sees sexual energy as a neutral force; however, the intent and consequences of sexual behavior can lead in negative or positive directions. For example, marital intercourse may be intensely passionate; alternatively, it may be spousal rape.

The three positive levels of sexual interaction are built on mutual choice, caring, respect, and safety. As shown in ■ Figure 8.3, Level +1 (Positive Role Fulfillment) reflects well-defined gender roles, established by social or religious custom, in which (in heterosexual relationships) the man is the initiator and the woman is the receiver. Sexual interactions at this level are characterized by mutual respect, a lack of coercion and resentment, and a strong sense of safety and predictability. Pregnancy and reduction of sexual tension are common goals for sex.

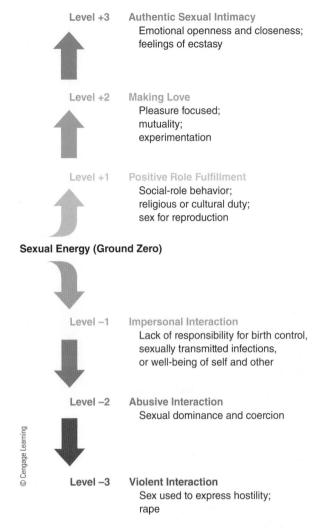

Level +3 **Authentic Sexual Intimacy**
Emotional openness and closeness;
feelings of ecstasy

Level +2 **Making Love**
Pleasure focused;
mutuality;
experimentation

Level +1 **Positive Role Fulfillment**
Social-role behavior;
religious or cultural duty;
sex for reproduction

Sexual Energy (Ground Zero)

Level −1 **Impersonal Interaction**
Lack of responsibility for birth control,
sexually transmitted infections,
or well-being of self and other

Level −2 **Abusive Interaction**
Sexual dominance and coercion

Level −3 **Violent Interaction**
Sex used to express hostility;
rape

Figure 8.3 The Maltz hierarchy of sexual interactions.
SOURCE: Maltz (2001).

Level +2 (Making Love) emphasizes mutual pleasure through individual sexual creativity and experimentation. Traditional gender-role behavior is set aside, and sex expands to an erotic recreational experience. Partners reveal themselves more deeply through sexual self-expression and communication that create greater intimacy.

Level +3 (Authentic Sexual Intimacy) brings a shared sense of deep connection both to oneself and to one's partner, with reverence toward the body in the erotic experience. The enjoyment of sensual pleasure includes a profound expression of love for one another. Emotional honesty and openness are of paramount importance, and each partner gains a deeper sense of wholeness. Authentic sexual intimacy can be a momentary peak experience, or it can characterize an entire lovemaking experience.

Maltz points out that sexual interactions can also be upsetting or traumatic ordeals, often imposed on one person by another. On the negative side of her hierarchy, each level becomes increasingly destructive and abusive.

Level −1 (Impersonal Interaction) is marked by a lack of respect and responsibility toward oneself and the other person. Here, individuals disregard possible negative consequences for themselves and their partners, including unwanted pregnancy and exposure to sexually transmitted infections, including HIV. Enduring unpleasant sex and being dishonest about issues relevant to the partner (health status or meaning of the sexual experience) occur at this level. These experiences result in uncomfortable, uneasy feelings. An example of such a result can be how a person feels about himself or herself after "hooking up." One study found that college women were more likely than college men to have negative reactions after a one-time sexual encounter (Owen & Fincham, 2011). Alcohol and drug use is often an element in sexual experiences that individuals later regret (Kaiser Family Foundation, 2003).

Level −2 (Abusive Interaction) involves one person's conscious domination of another by psychological coercion. This can include coercion for a particular sexual activity. For example, one study found that about 50% of young women had felt pressured to engage in oral sex on one or more occasions (Hammond et al., 2011). Other examples include nonviolent acquaintance rape and incest, and degrading coercive communication. Distorted thinking allows the exploitative person to rationalize or deny the harm he or she is inflicting on the other person. The experience usually damages the exploited person's self-esteem.

Level −3 (Violent Interaction) occurs when sexual energy is used purposefully to express hostility. Sex organs are weapons and targets. Rape is the most extreme example.

Frequency of Partner Sexual Activity

The 2005 Global Sex Survey of 317,000 people in 41 countries found that, on average, individuals have sex 103 times a year. ■ Table 8.3 shows the range of frequency in several countries.

The following discussions of shared sexual behaviors, except for coitus and gay and lesbian sexual expression, are directed toward all individuals, regardless of their sexual orientation. In fact, because sex between same-sex partners does not duplicate the pervasive heterosexual model's emphasis on penile–vaginal intercourse, gays' and lesbians' sexual repertoire is often more expansive and creative than heterosexuals' (Nichols, 2000; Sanders, 2000). In lesbian sexual relationships the mutual desire for an appreciation of touching can result in increased sexual arousal and orgasm compared to women in heterosexual relationships (Laumann et al., 1994). When a heterosexual sexual

© Cengage Learning

■ TABLE 8.3 Frequency of Sex in Selected Countries

Country	Frequency of Sex per Year
Greece	138
Croatia	134
Bulgaria	127
United States	113
South Africa	109
Canada	108
Germany	104
China	96
India	75
Japan	45

SOURCE: Global Sex Survey, 2005.

experience has a greater variety of sexual behaviors, research finds that it is more likely for the woman to experience orgasm (Herbenick et al., 2010a). ■ Table 8.4 compares sexual behaviors and responses of lesbians and heterosexual women.

■ TABLE 8.4 Comparison of Lesbians' and Heterosexual Women's Last Sexual Experience

Experience During Last Sexual Contact	Lesbians (%)	Heterosexual Women (%)
Had more than one orgasm	32	19
Received oral sex	48	20
Lasted 15 minutes or less	4	14
Lasted more than 1 hour	39	15

SOURCES: Lesbian statistics from *Advocate* magazine survey (Lever, 1994); heterosexual statistics from the National Health and Social Life Survey (Laumann et al., 1994).

The sequence in which the following sexual behaviors are presented does not mean that such a progression is best in a particular sexual relationship or encounter; for example, a heterosexual couple may desire oral–genital stimulation *after* coitus rather than before. Nor is any one of these activities necessary in a given relationship or encounter: Complete sexual experience can consist of any or all of them, with or without orgasm. A sex therapist explained: "Once you've begun to think of sex as creating mutual erotic pleasure rather than as manufacturing orgasms, sex is a continuum of possibilities. You may find, for example, that low-key genital—or even non-genital—stimulation can be surprisingly erotic and relaxing" (Ellison, 2000, p. 317). In addition, because sexuality is influenced by the relationship as a whole, it may be best to think of foreplay as how partners have treated each other since their last sexual experience together (Joannides, 1996).

Kissing and Touching

i like my body when it is with your
body. It is so quite new a thing.
Muscles better and nerves more.
i like your body. i like what it does,
i like its hows. i like to feel the spine
of your body and its bones, and the trembling
-firm-smoothness and which i will

again and again and again
kiss, i like kissing this and that of you,
i like, slowly stroking the, shocking fuzz
of your electric fur, and what-is-it comes
over parting flesh. . . . And eyes big love crumbs,
and possibly i like the thrill
of under me you so quite new

e. e. cummings*

*"i like my body when it is with your . . ." Copyright 1923, 1925, 1951, 1953 © 1991 by the Trustees for the E. E. Cummings Trust. Copyright © 1976 by George James Firmage, from *Complete Poems: 1904–1962* by E. E. Cummings, edited by George J. Firmage. Used by permission of Liveright Publishing Corporation.

The marble sculpture *Le Retour* by Auguste Seysses, 1898, in The Musee des Augustins, Toulouse, France.

Auguste Seysses, "Le Retour", Toulouse, Musée des Augustins, Photo: Daniel Martin

Kissing

Many of us can remember our first romantic kiss; most likely it was combined with feelings of awkwardness. Kissing can be an intense, erotic, profound experience. The lips and mouth are generously endowed with sensitive, pleasure-producing nerve endings that make it feel good to kiss and to be kissed in infinite variations. The classical Indian text on eroticism, the *Kama Sutra*, describes 17 kinds of kisses (Ards, 2000). Kissing with closed mouths tends to be more tender and affectionate, whereas open-mouth or deep or French kissing is usually more sexually intense. Kissing can also run the gamut of oral activities, such as licking, sucking, and mild biting. All places on the body are possibilities for kissing.

Western practices and attitudes about kissing are by no means universal. Mouth-to-mouth kissing is completely absent in the highly explicit erotic art of ancient Chinese and Japanese civilizations. In Japan in the 1920s mouth kissing was viewed so negatively that Rodin's famous sculpture *The Kiss* was concealed from public view when it was displayed there as part of an exhibit of European art. Other cultures—the Lepcha of Eurasia, the Chewa and Thonga of Africa, and the Siriono of South America—consider kissing unhealthy and disgusting (Tiefer, 1995).

Touching

Touch is one of the first and most important senses that we experience when we emerge in this world. Infants who have been fed but deprived of this basic stimulation have died for lack of it. A classic animal study showed that when baby monkeys' and other primates' physical needs were met but they were denied their mothers' touch, they grew up to be extremely maladjusted (Harlow & Harlow, 1962). Touch forms the cornerstone of human sexuality shared with another (Kluger, 2004). In Masters and Johnson's evaluation:

Touch is an end in itself. It is a primary form of communication, a silent voice that avoids the pitfall of words while expressing the feelings of the moment. It bridges the physical separateness from which no human being is spared, literally establishing a sense of solidarity between two individuals. Touching is sensual pleasure, exploring the textures of skin, the suppleness of muscle, the contours of the body, with no further goal than enjoyment of tactile perceptions. (1976, p. 253)

The body's erogenous zones are especially responsive to touch. For example, about 81% of women and 51% of men reported that stimulation of their breasts and nipples caused and/or enhanced their arousal (Levin & Meston, 2006). However, touch does not need to be directed to an erogenous area to be sexual. The entire body surface is a sensory organ, and touching—almost anywhere—can enhance intimacy and sexual arousal. Different people like different types and intensities of touch, and the same person can find a certain touch highly arousing one time and unpleasant the next. It is helpful for couples to communicate openly about touching.

Contrary to the stereotype that sexual experiences of gay men are completely genitally focused, extragenital eroticism and affection are important aspects of sexual contact for many male couples. "Compared to other men, gay men are often able to have more diversity, self-expression, and personal enjoyment in their sexual contact" (Sanders, 2000, p. 253). Hugging, kissing, snuggling, and total-body caressing are important. A survey of gay men found that 85% liked such interactions more than any other category of sexual behavior (Lever, 1994).

Rubbing genitals together or against other parts of a partner's body can be included in any couple's sexual interaction and is common in lesbian lovemaking. Rubbing one's genitals against someone else's body or genital area is called **tribadism**. Many lesbians like this form of sexual play because it involves all-over body contact and a generalized sensuality. Some women find the thrusting exciting; others straddle a partner's leg and rub gently. Some rub the clitoris on the partner's pubic bone (Loulan, 1984).

Manual Stimulation of the Female Genitals

The kinds of genital touches that induce arousal vary from one woman to another. Even the same woman might vary in her preference from one moment to the next. Women can prefer gentle or firm movements on different areas of the vulva. Direct stimulation of the clitoris is uncomfortable for some women; touches

Figure 8.4 Manual stimulation can be a highly pleasurable way for partners to explore each other's sensations.

above or along the sides are sometimes preferable. Insertion of one or more fingers into the vagina can enhance arousal. One technique for G-spot stimulation is for the partner to insert two fingers and firmly stroke the urethral sponge with a "come here" motion (Taormino, 2011). Most women approaching orgasm commonly need steady, consistent rhythm and pressure of touch through orgasm (Ellison, 2000).

The vulval tissues are delicate and sensitive. If not enough lubrication exists to make the vulva slippery, it can easily become irritated. A lubricant such as Astroglide, a lotion without alcohol or perfume, or saliva can be used to moisten the fingers and vulva to make the touch more pleasurable.

Manual Stimulation of the Male Genitals

Men also have individual preferences for manual stimulation, and, like women, they might desire a firmer or softer touch—and faster or slower strokes—as their arousal increases. Gentle or firm stroking of the penile shaft and glans and light touches or tugging on the scrotum may be desired, as shown in ▌ Figure 8.4. Some men find that lubrication with an oil, lotion, or saliva increases pleasure. (For heterosexual couples, if intercourse might follow, lotion should be nonirritating to the woman's genital tissues.) Immediately following orgasm the glans of the penis may be too sensitive to stimulate.

Oral–Genital Stimulation

Both the mouth and the genitals are primary biological erogenous zones, areas of the body generously endowed with sensory nerve endings. Thus couples that are psychologically comfortable with oral–genital stimulation often find both giving and receiving it to be highly pleasurable. Oral–genital contact can produce pleasure, arousal, or orgasm. As one woman stated:

> I think that men put too much emphasis on a woman coming from "regular sex." A lot of women I know, including myself, have only experienced orgasm (aside from masturbation) through oral sex. I thoroughly enjoy getting and giving oral sex. I love the sounds, sights, smells, and tastes. (Authors' files)

tribadism
Rubbing one's genitals against another's body or genitals.

Figure 8.5 During oral sex one partner can devote full attention to the experience of giving while the other can enjoy receiving.

cunnilingus
Oral stimulation of the vulva.

fellatio
Oral stimulation of the penis.

SEXUALHEALTH ▶

Oral–genital stimulation can be done individually (by one partner to the other) or simultaneously. Some people prefer oral sex individually, because they can focus on either giving or receiving, as in ▌ Figure 8.5. Others especially enjoy the mutuality of simultaneous oral–genital sex. Simultaneous stimulation is sometimes referred to as 69 because of the body positions suggested by that number (▌ Figure 8.6). Besides the position illustrated in the figure, a variety of other positions can be used, such as lying side by side and using a thigh for a pillow. Because arousal becomes intense during mutual oral–genital stimulation, partners need to be careful not to suck or bite too hard.

Different terminology is used to describe oral–genital stimulation of women and oral–genital stimulation of men. **Cunnilingus** (kuh-ni-LIN-gus) is oral stimulation of the vulva: the clitoris, labia minora, vestibule, and vaginal opening. Many women find the warmth, softness, and moistness of the partner's lips and tongue highly pleasurable and effective in producing sexual arousal or orgasm. In fact, there is research evidence that women are most likely to experience orgasm in sexual encounters that include cunnilingus (Richters et al., 2006). Variations of stimulation include rapid or slow circular or back-and-forth tongue movement on the clitoral area, sucking the clitoris or labia minora, and thrusting the tongue into the vaginal opening. Some women are especially aroused by simultaneous manual or dildo stimulation of the vagina and oral stimulation of the clitoral area. According to the NSSHB study, over half of women ages 18 to 49 had received oral sex from a male partner in the previous year (Herbenick et al., 2010b).

Fellatio (fuh-LAY-shee-oh) is oral stimulation of the penis and scrotum. Options for oral stimulation of the male genitals include gently or vigorously licking and sucking the glans, the frenulum, and the penile shaft, and licking or enclosing a testicle in the mouth. Some men enjoy combined oral stimulation of the glans and manual stroking of the penile shaft, testes, or anus. Among homosexual men fellatio is the most common mode of sexual expression—more so than anal sex (Lever, 1994).

It is usually best for the partner performing fellatio to control the other's movements by grasping the penis manually below her or his lips to prevent it from going farther into the mouth than is comfortable. This helps avoid a gag reflex. Also, too vigorous thrusting could result in lacerations of the partner's lips as he or she attempts to protect the penis from his or her teeth. ●

Figure 8.6 Simultaneous oral–genital stimulation in the 69 position.

Couples differ in their preference for including ejaculation into the mouth as a part of male oral–genital stimulation. Many find it acceptable, and some find it exciting. For those who do not want oral sex to include ejaculation into the mouth, a couple can agree beforehand that the one being stimulated will indicate when he is close to orgasm and withdraw from his partner's mouth. For couples who are comfortable with ejaculating into the mouth, the ejaculate can be swallowed or not, according to one's preference. The flavor of ejaculate varies from person to person and is influenced by the factors described in ■ Table 8.5.

■ **TABLE 8.5 Factors Affecting Taste of Ejaculate**

Sources of Unpleasant Bitter or Salty-Tasting Ejaculate	Sources of Milder-Tasting Ejaculate
Coffee, alcohol, cigarettes, junk food, and recreational drugs	Water—1 to 2 liters a day
Red meats and dairy products	Fruit, especially pineapple juice
Garlic, onions, cabbage, broccoli, cauliflower, and asparagus	Veggies with high chlorophyll content, such as parsley and celery
	Cinnamon, cardamom, peppermint, and lemon

SOURCE: Tarkovsky, 2006.

In the United States, differences in oral sex experience and attitudes exist among population segments, as shown in the following Sexuality and Diversity discussion.

SEXUALITY and DIVERSITY

Oral Sex Experiences Among American Men and Women

The National Health and Social Life Survey (Laumann et al., 1994) questioned men and women of different ethnic, educational, and religious backgrounds to compare their experiences of oral sex. The findings are summarized in ■ Table 8.6. In general, White Americans (both men and women) have the highest level of experience with oral sex, followed by Hispanic Americans; African Americans have the lowest rate of oral sex. However, socioeconomic level is more important than race. A study comparing African American and White American men of matched socioeconomic status found similar rates of oral sex experience (Samuels, 1997).

■ **TABLE 8.6 Oral Sex Experiences From the National Health and Social Life Survey**

	Performed Oral Sex (%) Men	Women	Received Oral Sex (%)[a] Men	Women
Race				
White	81	75	81	78
African American	51	34	66	49
Hispanic American	71	60	73	64
Education				
Less Than High School	59	41	61	50
High School Graduate	75	60	77	67
Any College	81	78	84	82
Religion				
Conservative Protestant	67	56	70	65
Other Protestant	82	74	83	77
Catholic	82	74	82	77
Other or None	79	78	83	83

[a]Rounded to nearest percentage point.

SOURCE: Laumann et al. (1994, p. 141).

Some people have qualms about oral–genital stimulation. They may believe that their own or the partner's genitals are unattractive. Although routine, thorough washing of the genitals with soap and water is adequate for cleanliness, some people think the genitals are unsanitary because they are close to the urinary opening and anus. Despite these negative attitudes, oral–genital contact is quite common and has become even more so in the last 15 years (Herbenick et al., 2010b). The meaning and role of oral–genital sex have also changed greatly over time. For example, women born before 1950 almost never experienced oral sex in high school or before marriage, and oral sex occurred after the couple had been having intercourse for some time. Currently, most adults believe that oral sex is more intimate than intercourse, whereas most teens and young adults believe the opposite (Chambers, 2007; Gelperin, 2005). Furthermore, research indicates that young people who have had sexual intercourse are as likely to have had oral sex (De Rosa et al., 2010). A study of 15- to 19-year-olds found that about 55% of teenagers have had oral sex—5% more than have had sexual intercourse (Duberstein et al., 2008). Some research even indicates that young people do not consider oral sex to be "sex." A survey that asked, "Would you say you 'had sex' with someone if you engaged in ____" found that only 20% believed this was true if they had oral sex. However, 98% agreed that they had sex if they had penile–vaginal intercourse, and 78% agreed they had sex if they had anal intercourse (Hans et al., 2010). Does this mean that "sex" only happens if a penis is put inside another's body?

SEXUALHEALTH ▶

Some individuals may engage in oral sex instead of intercourse because they believe they cannot contract HIV (the virus that causes AIDS) through oral sex. Although the risk of transmitting HIV through oral–genital contact is low, only monogamous partners who are both free of the virus are completely safe when engaging in such behavior. Because oral–genital contact involves an exchange of bodily fluids, it does pose the risk of transmitting or contracting HIV. This virus can enter the bloodstream through small breaks in the skin of the mouth or genitals. In addition, oral cancers can be caused by the human papillomavirus (HPV), also a sexually transmitted infection. The risk increases with the more oral sex partners an individual has (Girshman, 2011). (We discuss HIV and HPV extensively in Chapter 15). ●

Anal Stimulation

Anal sex among heterosexuals has become more common in the United States. The NSSHB study found that 20% of men ages 25 to 49 and women ages 20 to 39 reported anal sex in the last year. The percentages of people who have had anal sex at least once in their lifetimes have doubled—40% of men ages 25 to 59 and women ages 20 to 39 (Herbenick et al., 2010a).

The anus has dense groups of nerve endings that can respond erotically. Individuals and couples may use anal stimulation for arousal and variety. Manually stroking the outside of the anal opening, inserting one or more fingers into the anus, or licking the anus can be pleasurable for some people during masturbation or partner sex. Some women report orgasmic response from anal intercourse (Masters & Johnson, 1970), and heterosexual and homosexual men often experience orgasm from stimulation during penetration. For others, anal sex is unappealing, uncomfortable, or painful (Carter et al., 2010). In fact, one study found that almost half of young heterosexual women had to discontinue their first anal intercourse because of pain or discomfort. These findings highlight the importance of information, education, and partner communication about anal intercourse (Stulhofer & Ajduković, 2011).

Because the anus contains delicate tissues, special care needs to be taken during anal stimulation. A nonirritating lubricant and gentle penetration are necessary to avoid discomfort or injury. It is helpful to use lubrication on both the anus and the penis or whatever object is being inserted. The partner inserting needs to go slowly and gently, keeping the penis or other object tilted to follow the direction of the colon (Morin, 1981). It is essential for sex toys or other objects used for anal stimulation to have a larger base than tip; otherwise an object can slip past the anal opening and become trapped by the anal sphincter, requiring a trip to the emergency room to remove the object.

Important health risks are associated with anal intercourse (McBride & Fortenberry, 2010). Heterosexual couples should never have vaginal intercourse directly following anal intercourse, because bacteria in the anus can cause vaginal infections. Oral stimulation of the anus, known as **analingus** (or, in slang, "rimming"), is extremely risky; various intestinal infections, hepatitis, and sexually transmitted infections can be contracted or spread through oral–anal contact, even with precautions of thorough washing. Careful use of a dental dam helps prevent transmission of bacteria and viruses.

analingus
Oral stimulation of the anus.

Anal intercourse is one of the riskiest of all sexual behaviors associated with transmission of HIV, particularly for the receptive partner because tissue in the anus is relatively fragile and can tear easily. For women the risk of contracting this virus through unprotected anal intercourse is greater than the risk of contraction through unprotected vaginal intercourse (Maynard et al., 2009). Heterosexual and gay male couples who wish to reduce their risk of transmitting or contracting this deadly virus should use a condom or refrain from anal intercourse. In Chapter 15 we more fully discuss precautions to avoid transmission of HIV. ●

Coitus and Coital Positions

A heterosexual couple can choose a wide range of positions for penile–vaginal intercourse, or coitus. ■ Table 8.7 shows college students' three favorite positions. Many people have a favorite position yet enjoy others, as shown in ❚ Figures 8.7 through 8.11. A 30-year-old man stated:

> Different intercourse positions usually express and evoke particular emotions for me. Being on top, I enjoy feeling aggressive; when on the bottom, I experience a special kind of receptive sensuality. In the side-by-side position, I easily feel gentle and intimate. I like sharing all these dimensions of myself with my lover. (Authors' files)

■ **TABLE 8.7 College Students Answer the Question "What Is Your Favorite Intercourse Position?"**

	Men (%)	Women (%)
Man on top	25	48
Woman on top	45	33
Doggie style	25	15

SOURCE: Elliott & Brantley (1997).

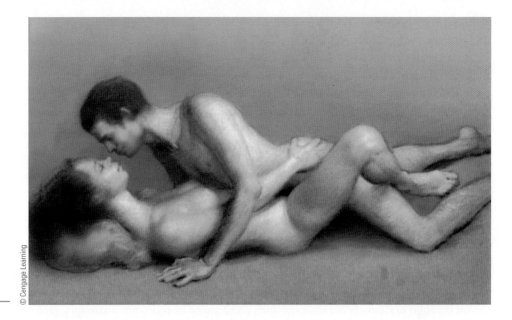

Figure 8.7 Man-above, face-to-face intercourse position.

Each position provides various opportunities for physical and emotional expression. Changes in health, age, weight, pregnancy, or partners can create different preferences. In some positions, one person has greater freedom to initiate and control the tempo, angle, and style of movement to create arousing stimulation. In other positions, mutual control of the rhythm of thrusting works well. Some positions—such as the woman above, sitting upright—lend themselves to manual stimulation of the clitoris during intercourse. Many couples like a position that allows partners to make eye contact and see each other's bodies. The face-to-face, side-lying position can provide a particularly relaxed connection, with each partner having one hand free to caress the other's body. Rear entry can be a good position during pregnancy, when pressure against the woman's abdomen is uncomfortable. The "tailgate" position is a rear-entry position where the woman is lying flat on her stomach, and the man enters from behind (Taormino, 2011). This position is

Figure 8.8 The woman-above intercourse position.

Figure 8.9 Tailgate position.

particularly good for G-spot stimulation. Beyond options for position, cooperation and consideration are important, particularly at **intromission** (entry of the penis into the vagina). Often the woman can best guide her partner's penis into her vagina by moving her body or using her hand. If the penis slips out of the vagina, which can occur fairly easily in some positions, it is usually easiest for the woman to lend a helping hand to guide the penis back into the vagina.

intromission
Insertion of the penis into the vagina.

Intercourse the Tantric Way

The concept of male orgasm as the ultimate point of heterosexual intercourse is alien to the concepts and practices of Tantric sex (Yarian & Anders, 2006). Margo Anand, in her book *The Art of Sexual Ecstasy* (1991), explains that Tantra was an ancient Eastern path of spiritual enlightenment, begun in India around 5000 BCE. Tantric thought holds that an erotic act of love between a god and a goddess created the world. According to this viewpoint, sexual expression can become a form of spiritual meditation and a path of deep connection (Kuriansky & Simonson, 2005).

Figure 8.10 Face-to-face, side-lying intercourse position.

Figure 8.11 The rear-entry intercourse position can be a comfortable option during pregnancy.

In Tantric sex the male learns to control and delay his own orgasm and to redirect the sexual energy throughout his and his partner's body. Before intercourse, lovers usually slowly and erotically stimulate each other. When both partners are ready for intercourse, the woman guides gentle, relaxed penetration. The couple initially keeps thrusting to a minimum, generating energy by subtle inner movements, such as contractions of the muscles surrounding the opening of the vagina. The couple harmonizes their breathing, finding a common rhythm of inhaling and exhaling, while visualizing the warmth, arousal, and energy in the genitals moving upward in their bodies. Movements can become active and playful, always slowing or stopping to relax before the man experiences orgasm. The partners welcome feelings of profound intimacy and ecstasy, often looking into each other's eyes, creating a "deep relaxation of the heart" (Anand, 1991). Research indicates that studying Tantra Yoga improves the physical and psychological aspects of sexual experience (Yekenkurul, 2007).

Summary

Celibacy

- Celibacy means not engaging in sexual activities. Celibacy can be complete (avoiding masturbation and interpersonal sexual contact) or partial (including masturbation). In many circumstances celibacy is a positive way of expressing one's sexuality.

Erotic Dreams and Fantasy

- Erotic dreams often accompany sexual arousal and orgasm during sleep. Erotic fantasies serve many functions: They can enhance sexual arousal, help overcome anxiety or compensate for a negative situation, allow rehearsal of new sexual experiences, permit tolerable expression of forbidden wishes, and provide relief from gender-role expectations.

Masturbation

- Masturbation is self-stimulation of the genitals, intended to produce sexual pleasure.
- Past attitudes toward masturbation have been highly condemnatory. However, the meaning and purposes of masturbation are currently being more positively reevaluated.
- Masturbation is a behavior that tends to continue throughout adulthood, although its frequency varies with age and sex.

Sexual Expression: The Importance of Context

- The meaning of sexual expression can vary from a profound sense of love for self and other to exploitation and abuse. The Maltz hierarchy delineates six levels.

Kissing and Touching

- The body's entire surface is a sensory organ, and kissing and touching are basic forms of communication and shared intimacy.
- Preferences as to the tempo, pressure, and location of manual genital stimulation vary from person to person. A lubricant, a nonirritating lotion, or saliva on the genitals can enhance pleasure.

Oral–Genital Stimulation

- Oral–genital contact has become more common in recent years. Qualms about oral–genital stimulation usually stem from false ideas that it is unsanitary or solely a homosexual act or from religious beliefs that it is immoral.
- Cunnilingus is oral stimulation of the vulva; fellatio is oral stimulation of the male genitals.

Anal Stimulation

- Couples engage in anal stimulation for arousal, orgasm, and variety. Careful hygiene is necessary to avoid introducing anal bacteria into the vagina. To reduce the chances of transmitting the AIDS virus, couples should avoid anal intercourse or use condoms and practice withdrawal before ejaculation.

Coitus and Coital Positions

- The diversity of coital positions offers potential variety during intercourse. The man-above, woman-above, side-by-side, and rear-entry positions are common.
- Tantric sex emphasizes intense, prolonged sexual intimacy.

Media Resources

Log in to CengageBrain.com to access the resources your instructor requires.

Go to CengageBrain.com to access Psychology CourseMate, where you will find an interactive eBook, glossaries, flashcards, quizzes, videos, and more.

Also access links to chapter-related websites, including **Healthy Sex, Good Vibrations,** and **Go Ask Alice.**

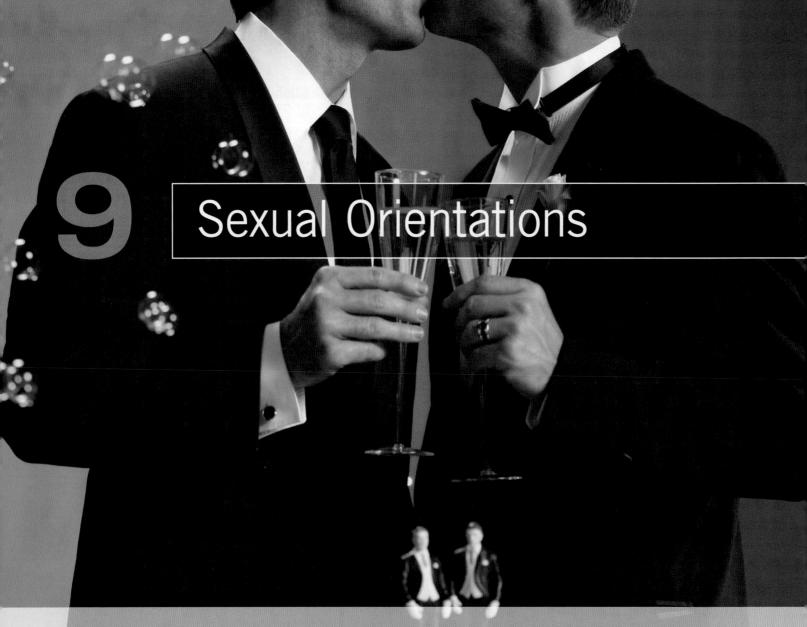

9 Sexual Orientations

© Ron Royals/Corbis

My life as a young lesbian was very different from the lesbian youth I see today. No one I knew talked about homosexuality, and I dated boys because my friends did. I was in my early thirties before my first sexual experience with a woman, but even that blissful experience didn't make me think of myself as a lesbian. It was several more years before I identified myself as a lesbian and had gay friends other than my partner. Today young lesbians have lots of positive information and images to help them understand and accept themselves. But they also face intense negativity from conservative reactions to gay rights. In my era the fact that homosexuality was so "hush-hush" gave us considerable privacy and protection by being overlooked. We never confronted the harassment, violence, or antigay activism that is now part of the picture. (Authors' files)

A Continuum of Sexual Orientations

We begin this chapter with a discussion of the continuum and characteristics of sexual orientations. *Homosexuality*, **bisexuality**, *heterosexuality*, and **asexuality** are words that identify various **sexual orientations**. Multidimensional components indicate a specific sexual orientation and can include whether an individual:

1. Engages in sexual behavior with men, women, both, or neither.
2. Feels sexual desire for men, women, both, or neither.
3. Falls in love with men, women, both, or neither.
4. Identifies himself or herself with a specific sexual orientation.

The complexity and ambiguity of defining sexual orientation result from the varying combinations and degrees of these four components. For example, how much sexual attraction to and experience with the same sex can someone have and still be heterosexual? And, vice versa, how much sexual attraction to and behavior with the other sex can someone have and still be homosexual? Or, is everyone who does not consistently and completely meet these four components bisexual? Further, can someone who self-identifies as heterosexual but is sexual exclusively with same-sex partners really be heterosexual? Even scientists who do research about sexual orientation do not use consistent criteria in categorizing subjects according to sexual orientation. In some studies, subjects are included in the bisexual/homosexual category if they have had any element of same-sex attraction, behavior, or self-identity. In other studies, subjects are not considered homosexual unless their sexual behavior, attraction, and self-identity have been consistently with the same sex since puberty.

Thinking of sexual orientation as a multidimensional phenomenon likely provides the most valid conceptualization of this complex human dimension (Jordan-Young, 2010; Laumann et al., 1994). However, in the most simplistic definitions, exclusive and consistent attraction to and sexual involvement with same-sex partners is a homosexual orientation: *Gay* is a common term for homosexual men, as *lesbian* is for women. Exclusive and consistent attraction to and sexual behavior with other-sex partners is a heterosexual orientation, also referred to as *straight*. Bisexuality refers to degrees of attraction to both sexes. Asexuality is a lack of sexual attraction to either sex. Because sexual orientation is only one aspect of a person's life, we use these four terms as descriptive adjectives rather than as nouns that label one's total identity.

▌ Figure 9.1 shows the seven-point continuum that Alfred Kinsey devised in his analysis of sexual orientations in American society (Kinsey et al., 1948). The Kinsey scale did not include asexuality. The scale ranges from 0 (consistent and exclusive contact with and

bisexuality
Sexual attraction to both men and women.

asexuality
A lack of sexual attraction to either sex.

sexual orientation
Sexual attraction to one's own sex (homosexual), to the other sex (heterosexual), or to both sexes (bisexual), or lack of sexual interest in either sex (asexual).

0	1	2	3	4	5	6
Exclusively heterosexual with no homosexual	Predominantly heterosexual, only incidentally homosexual	Predominantly heterosexual but more than incidentally homosexual	Equally homosexual and heterosexual	Predominantly homosexual but more than incidentally heterosexual	Predominantly homosexual but incidentally heterosexual	Exclusively homosexual with no heterosexual

▌**Figure 9.1** Kinsey's continuum of sexual orientation, based on both feelings of attraction and sexual behavior.

heteroflexibility
Individuals who are primarily heterosexual and have some degree of sexual interest in and/or experience with the same sex.

homoflexibility
Individuals who are primarily homosexual and have some degree of sexual interest in and/or experience with the other sex.

sexual fluidity
Variability in same-sex and other-sex attraction and involvement at different times and in different situations throughout the life span.

erotic attraction to the other sex) to 6 (consistent and exclusive contact with and attraction to the same sex). Category 3 represents equal same- and other-sex attraction and experience. In between 0 and 3 and 3 and 6 are various combinations of same- and other-sex attraction. The terms **heteroflexibility** and **homoflexibility** are new terms that may be useful to describe individuals who are primarily heterosexual or homosexual, yet have some degree of sexual interest in and/or experience with both sexes. A recent research study found that almost 13% of women and over 5% of men in the United States had experienced sexual contact with both same- and other-sex partners (Chandra et al., 2011).

Self-identity with a particular sexual orientation is one of the variables of sexual orientation. ▌Table 9.1 shows what percentages of 15- to 44-year-olds in the United States defined themselves as having a specific sexual orientation. The totals do not add up to 100% because some respondents were not certain how to define their sexual orientation.

Sexual Fluidity

The Kinsey scale may be interpreted incorrectly to indicate that all people have a fixed, stable sexual orientation. In fact, sexual orientation is more accurately determined by patterns over time rather than at any given point in time (Baumgardner, 2007). Psychologist and researcher Lisa Diamond (2008a) uses the term **sexual fluidity** to describe variability in same-sex and other-sex attraction and/or involvement at various times and situations throughout the life span. Her research indicates that, for some women, sexual self-identity and the biological sex of preferred sexual partners can vary over time and experience unexpected transitions.

Lisa Diamond's research on sexual fluidity followed almost 80 women ages 18 to 25 over a 10-year period. At the beginning of the study, all the subjects were involved with other women and labeled themselves variably as lesbian, bisexual, or unlabeled. At the end of the study, about one third of the women were consistent in their self-identification as lesbian and in their attraction to and sexual involvement with women. However, the remaining women—initially self-identified as lesbian, bisexual, or unlabeled—had changed their self-identification at least once during the 10 years. Notably, these changes were variable: Lesbian changed to bisexual or unlabeled, bisexual changed to lesbian or unlabeled, unlabeled changed to bisexual or lesbian, and some previously self-identified lesbian, bisexual, and unlabeled changed to heterosexual. Some of the changes in self-labeling were due to sexual and/or romantic attraction to or involvement with men. However, the women who became involved with men continued to feel the same amount of attraction toward other women as they had at the beginning of the study 10 years earlier (Diamond, 2008b).

Conversely, women who have identified themselves as lesbians well into adulthood sometimes develop relationships with men. Feminist folksinger Holly Near and JoAnn Loulan, a longtime lesbian activist and the author of *Lesbian Sex*, were prominent in the gay community for many years prior to establishing relationships with men. This shift occurs often enough that a woman who becomes involved with a man

▌**TABLE 9.1 Self-Identified Sexual Orientation**

	WOMEN	MEN
Self-identify as homosexual	1.1%	1.7%
Self-identify as bisexual	3.5%	1.1%
Self-identify as heterosexual	94%	96%

SOURCE: Chandra et al., 2011.

after being known as a lesbian may be labeled a "hasbian" (Diamond, 2008a; White, 2003).

For men, unless they identify themselves as bisexual, sexual fluidity between same-sex and other-sex attraction and relationships is less common than it is for women (Mock & Eiback, 2011). Scientists tend to agree that the male–female differences in sexual fluidity may be due to variations in biological developmental pathways (Diamond, 2008a). The extent to which the greater social stigma directed toward male homosexuality than toward female homosexuality restricts sexual fluidity in men is unknown, but it may also be an even more significant variable. As stigma toward male homosexuality continues to lessen, greater sexual fluidity in men may become apparent in younger men who tend to be more accepting of homosexuality. For example, in a large study of young people ages 12 to 25, males and females who identified as a sexual minority were equally likely to change their sexual orientation identity during the 13 years of the study (Ott et al., 2011).

Let's now take a closer look at the four categories of sexual orientation—asexuality, bisexuality, homosexuality, and heterosexuality—keeping in mind the understanding that these are not static categories but are merely a way to orient ourselves when discussing the fluid and complex nature of our sexuality.

Asexuality

According to the Asexual Visibility and Education Network, "An asexual is someone who does not experience sexual attraction. Unlike celibacy, which a person can choose, 'asexuality is an intrinsic part of who we are'" (Asexual Visibility and Education Network, 2009, p. 1). The Asexual Visibility and Education Network, founded in 2001, has 35,000 members worldwide, about 60% of whom are women in their teens through 30s. A national probability study of 18,000 people in Britain found that 1% of those surveyed said they were asexual (Bogaert, 2004).

Most asexual men and women have been asexual throughout their lives. Although they lack sexual attraction toward others, they vary in their interests in friendships, affection, romance, and partnerships, including marriage (DeLuzio, 2011; L. Harris, 2010). Another study found that the majority of the respondents did not feel distressed about their asexuality. Seventy-three percent of individuals who identified themselves as asexual had never engaged in sexual intercourse and felt no interest in partnered sexual expression. However, most respondents (80% of males and 77% of females) did masturbate (Knudson et al., 2007). Further evidence that asexuality is usually not related to a lack of sexual response was found in a small study involving women who self-identified as asexual, bisexual, lesbian, and heterosexual. While watching erotic audiovisual material, the asexual women experienced subjective and physiological sexual arousal similar to that of the other groups of women (Brotto & Yule, 2011).

Bisexuality

The parameters for bisexuality can be difficult to establish. At present "no scientific or popular consensus exists on the precise cluster of experiences that qualify

When sexually fluid relationships involve prominent women in the entertainment industry, they are widely publicized. For example, prior to 2004, actress Cynthia Nixon (Miranda on the TV show *Sex and the City*) had been with a man for 15 years and had two children with him. She then became involved with a woman whom she married in 2011 after marriage was legalized in New York.

Critical Thinking Question

Where would you place yourself on the Kinsey scale?

A recent study found that heterosexual and homosexual women experienced genital arousal in response to video clips of mating bonobos, but the women subjects reported arousal only while viewing sexual activities that were compatible with their self-identified sexual orientation.

Critical Thinking Question

How do you account for the discrepancies between subjective reports and physical arousal in women? Do you think women aren't aware of their vaginal arousal because it is internal and not as obvious as an erection? Are they too uncomfortable acknowledging that bonobo sex and gay sex scenes turn them on? Or . . . ?

an individual as lesbian, gay, or bisexual [or heterosexual] instead of just curious, confused, or experimenting" (Diamond, 2008a, pp. 26–27). As seen in Table 9.1, 3.5% of women and 1.1% of men identify themselves as bisexual (Chandra et al., 2011). Even when people consider themselves bisexual, their bisexuality is often unknown to others because of the common assumption that people are either straight or gay, based on the sex of their current partner (Plato, 2008).

Research about bisexuality is quite limited, but what does the available research tell us? One study of men indicated that sexual arousal in self-identified bisexual men is associated with a unique and specific pattern. The researchers measured the subjective—how aroused they felt—and erectile responses of bisexual, homosexual, and heterosexual men while they watched various sexual videos—male–male, male–female, and a man having sex with both a woman and another man. As anticipated, homosexual and heterosexual men demonstrated arousal, respectively, to male–male videos and male–female videos. Bisexual men were aroused by both gay and straight videos, but their arousal by the video of a man engaging in sex with both a man and a woman was significantly higher than gay and straight men's arousal by the same video (Cerny & Janssen, 2011).

Several research studies have found that more women than men feel sexual attraction to both sexes (Lippa, 2006). Further, women who identify themselves as straight or lesbian may actually experience a greater range of sexual attraction and arousal than they are aware of. Laboratory research examined heterosexual and homosexual men's and women's physical and subjective arousal patterns by having the subjects watch movie clips of heterosexual, gay, and lesbian sexual encounters; a man masturbating; a woman masturbating; and bonobo apes mating. While watching each clip, subjects rated their subjective arousal on a keypad. Simultaneously, researchers measured women participants' physical arousal with a tampon-sized device that monitored increases in vaginal blood flow and resultant lubrication. Men wore an apparatus that fit on the penis and measured the degree of erection. The study found that women—regardless of their self-identified sexual orientation—experienced varying degrees of genital arousal in response to all of the video clips, including the mating bonobos. However, the women said that they were aroused only while viewing sexual activity that was compatible with their self-identified sexual orientation: Heterosexual women said that they were aroused only by heterosexual clips, and lesbians only by clips of women being sexual together or masturbating. In contrast, gay and straight men were physically aroused by the clips that they said they found arousing. Further, what turned men on was consistent with their sexual orientation. Gay men were aroused only by male–male sexual interaction and straight men by male–female and female–female material (Chivers et al., 2005).

Research with people who have high sex drives suggests further variability in the way sexual orientation expresses itself. Data from more than 3,600 research subjects showed that high sex drive in women who identified themselves as heterosexual was associated with increased sexual attraction to both men and women. The higher a woman's sex drive, the more likely she was to feel sexual desire for both sexes. In contrast, high sex drive in straight men, gay men, and lesbians was associated with increased sexual attraction only to one sex or the other. These findings are consistent across age groups and have been replicated in many regions of the world, including Latin America, Australia, India, and Western Europe (Lippa, 2006).

It's Not Always Easy Being Bisexual

Both heterosexual and homosexual individuals are sometimes judgmental toward those who identify themselves as bisexual and would feel more comfortable if bisexuals adhered to a single orientation (Baumgardner, 2008). In addition, gay men and lesbians sometimes view a bisexual person as someone who is really homosexual but lacks the courage to identify himself or herself as such. These views can be difficult for bisexual individuals. A bisexual woman says,

> "I don't feel like I fit anywhere. I don't feel 'straight' enough in the straight world, and I don't feel 'gay' enough in the gay world. I can't be all of who I am anywhere." (Levy, 2010, p. 66)

One study compared male and female heterosexuals' attitudes toward bisexuality. The researchers found that straight women equally accepted bisexual men and women, but straight men were less accepting of bisexual men than of bisexual women. Heterosexuals of both sexes doubted the validity of bisexuality. However, their beliefs about bisexual men were the opposite of their beliefs about bisexual women. They maintained that the male bisexual individuals were "really gay," but the female bisexuals were "really heterosexual" (Yost & Thomas, 2012).

"Performative Bisexuality"

Professor Breanne Fahs, author of *Performing Sex: The Making and Unmaking of Women's Erotic Lives*, characterizes heterosexual-identified women who interact sexually with other women for the purpose of pleasing and arousing men as engaging in "performative bisexuality." In performative bisexuality, women are not being sexual with other women from feelings of inherent desire and intrinsic pleasure. Women are motivated to perform as bisexual in order to appear sexy and desirable to men and to accommodate men's fantasies of two women together. Performative bisexuality has become common enough that some men feel entitled to use considerable pressure to persuade their female partners to interact sexually with other women. Younger women, in particular, can feel that being sexual with other women is part of the contemporary expectation for "good femininity." Some examples of performative bisexuality include the middle-class college women in *Girls Gone Wild* DVDs who kiss, fondle, and perform oral sex with each other as requested by the director of the DVD. Performative bisexuality also occurs publicly at fraternity parties, bars, and clubs or privately in the context of a threesome with two women and one man or during group sex (Fahs, 2011, p. 102).

Homosexuality

Numerous studies over the years have attempted to establish the percentage of men and women who are homosexual, and the percentages vary from study to study. As noted earlier in the chapter, the 2011 National Survey of Family Growth (NSFG), based on in-person interviews of 13,495 individuals ages 15 to 44, found that 1.1% of women and 1.7% of men identified themselves as lesbian or gay. A greater percentage of respondents had experienced at least one same-sex contact in their lifetime—13% of women and 5.2% of men (Chandra et al., 2011).

The common synonym for homosexual is **gay**. The term has moved into popular use to describe homosexual men and women as well as the social and political concerns related to homosexual orientation. It has also come to be used, mainly by teens, as a negative label, as in "That is so gay!" (Caldwell, 2003). Pejorative words such as *faggot*, *fairy*, *homo*, *queer*, *lezzie*, and *dyke* have traditionally been used to demean homosexuality.

Critical Thinking Question

Is performative bisexuality sexually liberating or exploitative for women? Does it create new possibilities for women to explore same-sex experiences? Or does it take women farther away from their own genuine sexual self-expression to accommodate the sexual interests of men?

gay
A homosexual person, typically a homosexual male.

However, in certain gay and lesbian subcultures, some people use these terms with each other in positive or humorous ways (Bryant & Demian, 1998).

Many men and women born after 1970 call themselves *queer* and refer to *queer culture* to defuse the negativity of the word and blur the boundaries between subgroups of gay men, lesbians, bisexuals, and all variations of transgendered people belonging to the "queer nation." The inclusive acronym LGBTQ—lesbian, gay, bisexual, transgendered, and questioning—is often used in discussions of civil rights for nonheterosexual people (Vary, 2006).

What Determines Sexual Orientation?

Psychosocial explanations of the development of a homosexual orientation versus a heterosexual orientation relate to life incidents, parenting patterns, or psychological attributes of the individual.

Psychosocial Theories

Bell and his colleagues (1981) conducted a comprehensive study about the development of sexual orientation. They used a sample of 979 homosexual men and women matched to a control group of 477 heterosexual people. All research subjects were asked questions about their childhood, adolescence, and sexual practices during 4-hour, face-to-face interviews. Bell then used sophisticated statistical techniques to analyze possible causal factors in the development of homosexuality or heterosexuality. We cite this research frequently throughout this section because of its excellent methodology.

The "By Default" Myth

Some people believe that unhappy heterosexual experiences cause a person to become homosexual. Statements such as "All a lesbian needs is a good lay" or "He just needs to find the right woman" reflect the notion that homosexuality is a default choice for people who have not had satisfactory heterosexual experiences and relationships. Contrary to this myth, Bell's analysis of the data indicated that homosexual orientation reflects neither a lack of heterosexual experience nor a history of negative heterosexual experiences (Bell et al., 1981). Bell and his colleagues found that homosexual and heterosexual groups did not differ in their frequency of dating during high school, but fewer homosexual subjects reported that they enjoyed heterosexual dating.

The Seduction Myth

Some people believe that young women and men become homosexual because they have been seduced by older homosexual people or because they have been "turned" by someone else—particularly a well-liked and respected teacher who is homosexual. Contrary to these myths, research indicates that sexual orientation is most often established before school age and that most homosexual people have their first sexual experiences with someone close to their own age (Bell et al., 1981). In addition, most gays and lesbians have identified themselves as homosexual prior to their first same-sex contact (Calzo et al., 2011).

Freud's Theory

Another prevalent theory has to do with certain patterns in a person's family background. Psychoanalytic theory implicated both childhood experiences and relationships with parents. Sigmund Freud (1905/2000) maintained that one's relationship with one's father and mother was crucial. He believed that in "normal" development, we all pass through a "homoerotic" phase. Boys, he argued, could become fixated at this homosexual phase if they had a poor relationship with their father and an overly close relationship with their mother; the same thing might happen to a woman if she developed envy for the penis (Black, 1994). However, this particular family dynamic is occasionally present in the family backgrounds of both gay and straight individuals and is absent in the family life of many homosexual individuals. Bell and his colleagues (1981) concluded that no particular phenomenon of family life could be singled out as "especially consequential for either homosexual or heterosexual development" (p. 190)—a conclusion supported by subsequent research (Epstein, 2006).

In the next section we discuss the most relevant and current research that attempts to understand the biological factors that may influence sexual orientation.

Research Into Biological Factors

Although considerable research exploring biological factors contributing to homosexuality has been done over the years, many of the findings are contradictory, and still no definitive scientific answers exist. The lack of clear-cut, consistent research findings is likely due in large part to the unique physiological and environmental factors underlying each individual's development of sexual orientation. A behavior pattern as complex and variable as homosexuality is unlikely to be due to a single, simple biological cause. In fact, as we mentioned earlier, researchers do not appear to agree on what characteristics define where one sexual orientation begins and another ends. Some examples of these differences are detailed in the Spotlight on Research box.

Researchers often use twin studies to better understand the relative influences of social environment (nurture) and genetic makeup (nature). Identical twins originate from a single fertilized ovum that divides into two separate fetuses with identical genetic codes. Therefore, any differences between the twins must be due to environmental influences. In contrast, fraternal twins occur when a woman's ovaries release two ova and each ovum is fertilized by a different sperm cell. Because fraternal twins result from the fertilization of two separate eggs, their genetic makeup is no more alike than that of any other siblings. Physical and behavioral differences between fraternal twins may be due to genetic factors, environmental influences, or a combination of the two. When identical twins are more alike (*concordant*) than same-sex fraternal twins in a particular trait, we can assume that the trait has a strong genetic basis. Conversely, when a trait shows a comparable degree of concordance in both types of twins, we can reasonably assume that environment is exerting the greater influence.

The most recent twin study recruited subjects from a twin registry in Australia. Over 1,500 same-sex identical and fraternal male and female twin pairs were included in this study. Each participant completed an anonymous questionnaire that addressed broad areas of sexuality, including items pertaining to sexual orientation. Using a strict criterion for determining homosexual orientation, the researchers found a concordance rate (the percentage of pairs in which both twins are homosexual) of 20% among identical male twins and 0% among pairs of male fraternal twins. The corresponding concordance rates for female identical and fraternal pairs were 24% and 10.5%, respectively (Bailey et al., 2000). The higher concordance rates for identical twin pairs than for fraternal twin pairs provide strong evidence of a genetic component to sexual orientation in some individuals. Two other studies that used broader criteria for inclusion as homosexual reported much higher concordance rates for a homosexual orientation among male and female identical twins (52% and 48%, respectively) compared to same-sex male and female fraternal twin concordance rates of 22% and 16% (Bailey et al., 1991; Bailey et al., 1993).

Research about sexual orientation would ideally use the same criteria for categorizing subjects as homosexual, bisexual, or heterosexual. If identical criteria were used, study results could build upon and be compared with one another. In practice, however, great variations exist in studies of the characteristics of individuals included in a specific sexual orientation (Jordan-Young, 2010). ▌ Figure 9.2 uses the Kinsey scale to show how differently researchers group subjects into sexual orientations.

As seen in the figure, individuals considered heterosexual can range from exclusive and lifelong to almost equal other- and same-sex sexual attraction, behavior, and self-identity. The range of parameters for including individuals in the bisexual/homosexual category is broader—including, in the Gastaud study, all individuals who did not have an exclusive and lifelong heterosexual orientation. Another variable not evident in the figure is that some studies exclude individuals who identify themselves as gay or lesbian from the homosexual category if they were not consistent in sexual fantasies and sexual behavior since puberty—which actually excludes "the *majority* of self-described lesbians and many gay men from studies on sexual orientation" (Jordan-Young, 2010, p. 172).

When reading about research in this text and the media, it is important to keep in mind that research findings about sexual orientation are not based on the same uniform criteria for inclusion in a gay, bisexual, or straight research group. The most important implication of these variations in sexual orientation categories is that they are often based on groupings that will show the strongest differences between the characteristics the researchers are studying. Consequently, differences reported between groups tend to be exaggerated (Jordan-Young, 2010).

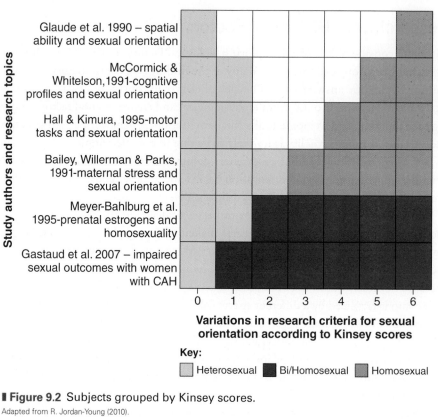

Variations in research criteria for sexual orientation according to Kinsey scores

Key:
☐ Heterosexual ■ Bi/Homosexual ▨ Homosexual

▌ **Figure 9.2** Subjects grouped by Kinsey scores.
Adapted from R. Jordan-Young (2010).

gender nonconformity
A lack of conformity to stereotypical masculine and feminine behaviors.

Gender nonconformity is the extent to which an individual differs from stereotypical characteristics of masculinity or femininity during childhood. A biological predisposition toward homosexuality in some individuals is indicated by the strong link between adult homosexuality and gender nonconformity as a child (Bailey et al., 2000; Ellis et al., 2005). In a recent study, the researchers viewed home videos of children from infancy to 15 years of age. Without knowing the sexual orientation of the adults whose childhood videos they saw, the researchers rated the children on gender conforming and nonconforming characteristics. The results indicated that homosexual male and female adults exhibited significantly more gender nonconformity as children than did heterosexual adults (Rieger et al., 2008).

Research using brain scanning technology, magnetic resonance imaging (MRI), and positron emission tomography (PET) has typically found male–female differences in brain areas related to emotional expression and verbal skills. A 2008 Swedish study used brain scanning technology to compare these areas of the brains of homosexual and heterosexual subjects. These researchers found sex-atypical brain characteristics in the homosexual research subjects. The brain structures related to language and emotional expression were similar for gay men and heterosexual women. To a lesser extent, these areas in lesbians' brains had similarities to those in straight men's brains. These findings demonstrated differences in adult brain structure and function based on sexual orientation. The researchers concluded that "the results cannot be primarily ascribed to learned effects, and they suggest a linkage to neurobiological entities" (Savic & Lindstrom, 2008, p. 9403).

Left- or right-handedness appears to be established before birth; when observed by ultrasound, a fetus indicates right- or left-handedness by thumb-sucking choice and greater movement of one arm. In a meta-analysis of studies with a combined total of almost 25,000 subjects, homosexual participants had 39% greater odds of being left-handed than did heterosexuals (Lalumiere et al., 2000). Later research found that gay men had far greater odds of being left-handed than did lesbians (Lippa, 2003). These types of studies typically create comparison groups that are limited to individuals at the ends of the Kinsey scale in order to increase the chance of finding differences (Jordan-Young, 2010).

Two male whales rub their penises together as one example of homosexual behavior in animals. The world's first museum exhibition about homosexuality among animals opened in 2006 at the Oslo Natural History Museum in Norway. Male and female homosexuality has been observed in more than 1,500 animal species and is well documented for 500 animals. Giraffes, parrots, penguins, beetles, and hyenas exhibit some of the bisexual behaviors of the bonobo, a type of chimpanzee, which has sexual interactions with both males and females as a means of social bonding (Doyle, 2006).

Patterns of finger length tend to differ in males and females. Heterosexual women's index fingers tend to be about the same length as their ring fingers, but heterosexual men's ring fingers are often considerably longer than their index fingers. Researchers have compared these finger length patterns to lesbians' and gay men's finger length ratios. The various studies have produced widely mixed findings—some reported that gay men had finger length ratios more similar to those of straight women and that lesbians had ratios more similar to those of straight men, but several studies found no differences between finger length ratios between homosexual and heterosexual subjects. On balance, research does not compellingly suggest that gay men and lesbians differ in finger length patterns from heterosexual men and women (Jordan-Young, 2010).

Variation in Research Findings Between Homosexual Men and Women

In some research, gay men are more likely than lesbians to have characteristics that are not typical of heterosexuals. This finding indicates that biological influences may affect men and women somewhat differently. The timing of the onset of puberty is one example. The onset of puberty in the general population is typically 12 months later for boys than for girls. However, numerous studies have found that gay and bisexual men begin puberty earlier than heterosexual men, but the timing of puberty for lesbians is the same as for straight women (Bogaert et al., 2002).

Some research has found a correlation between being homosexual and having older siblings for men but not for women. These studies reported that men with older brothers have a statistically significant increase in their chance of being homosexual, and each older brother increases the odds. No such relationship with older siblings of either sex has been found for lesbians. Researchers speculate that a maternal immune response to male fetuses occurs and increases with each pregnancy of a male fetus, and that this response influences prenatal sexual differentiation of the brain (Bogaert, 2005; Schagen et al., 2011). However, most of the studies excluded volunteer subjects who, although they identified themselves as gay or straight, did not meet the studies' criteria of consistent sexual fantasies and behavior. One study excluded 33% of the subjects (Jordan-Young, 2010). Further, other research that used a nationally representative sample of men and women five times larger than the sample size of other studies did not find a statistically significant correlation between male homosexuality and older brothers, calling into question those findings (Francis, 2008).

In conclusion, research suggests that a biological predisposition to homosexuality and bisexuality may exist for some individuals. However, in general, the causes of sexual orientation remain a matter of speculation. Rather than thinking in terms of a single cause for sexual orientation, it seems more appropriate to consider the continuum of sexual orientation as being influenced by dynamic interactions among various biological, environmental, and cultural factors, which are unique to each person and can vary over the life span. As researcher Lisa Diamond states, "Sexual and emotional feelings—like all complex patterns of human experience—develop as a result of dynamic interchanges among innate, environmental, and cultural factors" (2008a, p. 250).

Implications if Biology Is Destiny

The evidence for biological causation of homosexuality raises important issues: Would people be more accepting of homosexuality if a clear biological basis for it were established? Recent research indicates that people who do believe that homosexuality is biologically based—that people are born gay—have more positive feelings toward homosexuals and are more supportive of gay civil rights, including marriage, than are people who believe that homosexuality is learned or an individual choice (Jones, 2011). How common is the belief that homosexuality is innate? Approximately 40% of the population thinks a person is born gay, and 42% believe it is due to upbringing and environment (Jones, 2011).

If homosexuality were labeled as biologically "defective," would that promote medical treatments during pregnancy or after birth to eliminate factors that contribute to its development? In 2010 a controversy developed that emphasized this question. CAH (congenital adrenal hyperplasia) is a genetic disorder in girls that creates unusually high levels of exposure to androgens during prenatal development and childhood. These girls engage less in typical female gender-role behaviors, they develop large clitorises, facial hair, and deep voices, and they are more likely to have lesbian and bisexual orientations. When the steroid desamethasone is given during pregnancy and during childhood, it counters the masculinizing effects of the genetic disorder. The controversy centered on whether the treatments were motivated too strongly by social pressure for gender-role conformity and heterosexuality (Begley, 2010; Dreger et al., 2010).

Societal Attitudes Regarding Homosexuality

Around the world societal attitudes toward homosexuality vary considerably, as we learn in the following Sexuality and Diversity discussion.

SEXUALITY and DIVERSITY
Homosexuality in Cross-Cultural Perspective

Attitudes toward homosexuality vary considerably across cultures. A number of studies of other cultures, including ancient ones, have revealed widespread acceptance of homosexual behaviors. For example, over 50% of 225 Native American tribes accepted male homosexuality, and 17% accepted female homosexuality. In ancient Greece homosexual relationships between men, especially between men and boys, were considered a superior intellectual and spiritual expression of love, whereas heterosexuality provided the more pragmatic benefits of children and a family unit (Pomeroy, 1965).

Some societies *require* their members to engage in homosexual activities. For example, all male members of the Sambia society in the mountains of New Guinea engage in exclusively homosexual behaviors from approximately 7 years of age until the late teens or early 20s, when men marry. Sambian men believe that a prepubertal boy becomes a strong warrior and hunter by drinking as much semen as possible from postpubertal boys' penises. Once a boy reaches puberty, he must no longer fellate other boys but can experience erotic pleasure from fellatio by boys who cannot yet ejaculate. From the start of their erotic lives and during the years of peak orgasmic capacity, young men engage in frequent obligatory and gratifying homoeroticism. During the same period, looking at or touching females is taboo. Yet as they approach marriage, these youths create powerful erotic daydreams about women. During the first weeks of marriage, they experience only fellatio with their wives; thereafter they make intercourse part of their heterosexual activity. After marriage they stop homosexual activity, experience great sexual desire for women, and engage exclusively in heterosexual activity for the rest of their lives (Stoller & Herdt, 1985).

We previously discussed self-identification as asexual, homosexual, bisexual, or heterosexual as one component of sexual orientation. In the Pashtun tribe in Afghanistan, self-definition is almost completely unrelated to actual sexual behavior. A United States and British Forces research team recently reported on the long-standing cultural tradition of Pashtun men in which they predominantly have sex with prepubertal boys and other adult men. However, even men who have had sex only with other men do not label themselves or their partners as homosexual. Homosexuality is defined narrowly in this Muslim culture as the love of another man, not as the use of another male for sexual gratification. Homosexuality is an enormous sin in Islam, and self-definition as homosexual could be a life-and-death matter (Cardinalli, 2010).

In contrast to accepting same-sex behavior or not defining it as homosexuality, extreme violation of basic human rights for gays and lesbians is common in many places around the globe. Homosexuality is illegal in 76 countries and punishable by death in five countries—Iran, Mauritania, Saudi Arabia, Sudan, and Yemen—and in sections of Nigeria and Somalia (Bruce-Jones & Itaborahy, 2011).

Since the Islamic Revolution in Iran in 1979, the government has executed 4,000 people charged with homosexual acts (Shah, 2011). Extreme abuses occur in countries without the death penalty, including "social cleansing" death squads in Colombia, illegal clinics in Ecuador that use physical and mental abuse to attempt to "cure" homosexuality, and persecution of gay and AIDS activists in many countries (Luongo, 2007; Romo, 2012; Samuels, 2008). In the United States since 1990, the Immigration and Naturalization Service has granted political asylum to people fleeing persecution based on sexual orientation (Burr, 1996). Currently, most LBGT asylum seekers come from Jamaica, Russia, Grenada, Peru, and Uzbekistan. Few asylum seekers come from the Middle East because it is much more difficult for them to get visas to the United States.

A trend toward increased approval of homosexuality is occurring in most nations around the world (T. Smith, 2011). Events in Cuba demonstrate how a society can make rapid positive changes regarding homosexuality. During the first 35 years of the Communist revolution, lesbians and gay men were seen as deviant antirevolutionaries and were expelled from the Communist Party and from state and university jobs. Some were sent to labor camps. In 1992 Cuban leader Fidel Castro blamed the previous homophobia on ingrained attitudes of *machismo*. He expressed support for gay rights and described homosexuality as a natural human tendency that must be respected. Castro's niece, Mariela Castro, has been instrumental in working through a government-funded organization to promote acceptance of lesbians, gay men, and transgendered individuals. As a consequence of this and other efforts, in 2008 Cuba passed a resolution allowing transgender individuals to undergo sex-reassignment surgeries free of charge (Rowe, 2009).

In other places, equal rights have increased. Countries that are most supportive of homosexual rights tend to have high levels of economic development, advanced levels of education, and lower levels of religiousness (T. Smith, 2011). Fourteen countries, mostly European, have established national laws that protect gay men, lesbians, and bisexuals from discrimination. (The United States is not included with these countries because it has yet to pass a federal law against discrimination based on sexual orientation.) Domestic partnerships have legal status in Argentina, Belgium, Canada, Denmark, Iceland, Norway, the Netherlands, Portugal, South Africa, Spain, and Sweden. Twenty countries have eliminated bans on gays in the military (Quindlen, 2009a). Notably, in 2011 the United Nations Human Rights Council passed a resolution affirming human rights based on sexual orientation and gender identity.

Judeo-Christian Attitudes Toward Homosexuality

According to the Judeo-Christian tradition that predominates in our own American culture, homosexuality has been viewed negatively. Many religious scholars believe that the condemnation of homosexuality increased during a Jewish reform movement beginning in the 7th century BCE, through which Jewish religious leaders wanted to develop a distinct closed community. Homosexual activities were a part of the religious practices of many peoples in that era, and rejecting such practices was one way of keeping the Jewish religion unique (Fone, 2000; Kosnik et al., 1977). The Old Testament included strong prohibitive statements: "You shall not lie with a man as one lies with a female; it is an abomination" (Lev. 18:22; Leviticus also deems the eating of shellfish [Lev. 11:10] and the cutting of men's hair [Lev. 19:27] abominations). Today Jewish people are divided over their religious stance toward homosexuality. In Israel in 2002 the first openly gay man was appointed to the Knesset, or parliament, drawing dissent from Orthodox Jews (Landsberg, 2002). Reform Judaism sanctioned same-sex marriages in 2000, and conservative Jewish leaders are reexamining their ban on same-sex marriages and the ordination of openly gay and lesbian clergy (Friess, 2003).

Laws against homosexual behaviors, which stem from biblical injunctions against same-sex contact, have historically been exceedingly punitive. People with homosexual orientations have been tortured and put to death throughout Western history. In the American colonies homosexual people were condemned to death by drowning and burning. In the late 1770s, Thomas Jefferson was among the political leaders who suggested reducing the punishment from death to castration for men who committed homosexual acts (Fone, 2000; Katz, 1976).

Current Christian theological positions toward homosexuality express a great range of convictions. Different denominations, and different groups within the same denomination, have taken different stances. In many mainstream denominations, groups such as Affirmation (United Methodist Church), Dignity USA (Catholic Church), and Integrity (Episcopal Church) are working to open their congregations to gay and lesbian parishioners and clergy, while fundamentalists in the same denominations oppose such inclusion. Conflicts between these two positions are likely to increase as denominations attempt to establish clear positions and policies about homosexuality, particularly as younger church members become more accepting of homosexuality. For example, one poll found that 44% of young (ages 18–29), White evangelicals support gay marriage, compared to around 20% of evangelicals ages 65 and over (Nolan, 2011).

The Unitarian Universalist Association, the United Church of Christ, and the Evangelical Lutheran Church in America are the only Christian denominations that officially

Critical Thinking Question

How do your religious beliefs, or absence of beliefs, influence your attitudes toward homosexuality?

sanction the blessing of gay and lesbian unions. Although many churches' official policies do not allow church bonding ceremonies for gays and lesbians, some clergy support and perform these ceremonies for homosexual couples.

In 2003 the Right Reverend V. Gene Robinson was consecrated as a bishop in the Episcopal Church, becoming the first openly gay bishop in any mainstream denomination. Many members left the Episcopal Church to form the Anglican Church of North America in a protest against Robinson's position as bishop (Martin, 2009). In 2010 Mary Glasspool became the Episcopal Church's first openly lesbian bishop, resulting in further controversy within the church (Harmon, 2010). In 2011 the Presbyterian Church (U.S.A.) approved ordination of gay people in same-sex relationships as ministers, elders, and deacons (Goodstein, 2011).

From Sin to Sickness

In the early to mid-1900s, societal attitudes toward homosexuality shifted. The belief that homosexual people were sinners was replaced to some degree by the belief that they were mentally ill. The medical and psychological professions have used drastic treatments in attempting to cure the "illness" of homosexuality. Surgical procedures such as castration were performed in the 1800s. As late as 1951, lobotomy (surgery that severs nerve fibers in the frontal lobe of the brain) was performed as a cure for homosexuality. Psychotherapy, drugs, hormones, hypnosis, shock treatments, and aversion therapy (pairing nausea-inducing drugs or electrical shock with homosexual stimuli) have all been used to the same end (Murphy, 2008).

In 1973, after great internal conflict, the American Psychiatric Association removed homosexuality from its diagnostic categories of mental disorders. In light of contemporary research on homosexuality—and the fact that both the American Psychiatric Association and the American Psychological Association no longer categorize homosexuality as a mental illness—most therapists and counselors have changed the focus of therapy. Rather than attempting to "cure" homosexual clients by changing their sexual orientation, therapists provide **gay-affirmative therapy** to help them overcome any internalized negative feelings about their sexual orientation and to cope with a society that harbors considerable hostility toward them (American Psychological Association, 2012; Bolton & Sareen, 2011; Kuyper & Fokkema, 2011b).

gay-affirmative therapy
Therapy to help homosexual clients cope with negative societal attitudes.

Some religious groups and mental health practitioners who believe that homosexuality is symptomatic of developmental defects or spiritual and moral failings advocate therapy to help dissatisfied homosexual individuals control, lessen, or eliminate their homosexual feelings and behavior through **conversion therapy** or **sexual reorientation therapy**. Ministry groups such as Exodus International, a nondenominational Christian organization, blend religious teachings with group counseling to focus on childhood traumas believed to have caused the participants' homosexuality: abandonment by fathers, absent mothers, sexual abuse, or violent parents. Individuals who belong to a fundamentalist religion and whose families react negatively to homosexuality appear to be most likely to participate in sexual reorientation therapy (Maccio, 2010).

conversion therapy/sexual reorientation therapy
Therapy to help homosexual men and women change their sexual orientation.

The American Psychological Association maintains that conversion therapy is, at best, ineffective (American Psychological Association, 2009). For many people who cannot make the changes they wish for, the belief that one can only "be with God or be gay" presents irreconcilable choices, and such a dilemma can contribute to depression and suicide (Crary, 2009; Reitan, 2011). However, a recent longitudinal study of religiously based support groups found that some degree of change in sexual identity, attraction, and functioning were possible for some individuals (Jones & Yarhouse, 2011). Ninety-eight subjects (72 men and 26 women) began the 7-year study, and a total of 65 participants completed it. At the beginning of the study, most participants indicated some degree of heterosexual attraction along with their predominant homosexual attraction. The 23% who reported increased heterosexual self-identity, attraction, and behavior still maintained varying degrees of homosexual attraction. These subjects appear to have shifted from the homosexual to the heterosexual direction on a bisexual continuum, rather than from exclusive homosexuality to exclusive heterosexuality (Throckmorton, 2011).

Homophobia

homophobia
Irrational fears of homosexuality, the fear of the possibility of homosexuality in oneself, or loathing toward one's own homosexuality.

The term **homophobia** describes antihomosexual attitudes that stigmatize and denigrate any behaviors, identities, relationships, and communities that are not heterosexual (Van Voorhis & Wagner, 2002). Irrational fears of homosexual people or fear and loathing of homosexual feelings in oneself are also characteristics. Homophobia can be best thought of as a prejudice similar to racism, anti-Semitism, or sexism. *Heterosexism* is the belief that heterosexuality is superior to homosexuality; such a belief can often lead to discrimination and the stigmatization of gay, lesbian, bisexual, and transgender people. The recognition of homophobia and heterosexism as the problem represents a significant shift from the view that homosexuality itself was the problem.

The degree of homophobia has lessened greatly in the United States (Ahmad & Bhugra, 2010). For example, a study found that gay athletes who came out between 2008 and 2010 obtained better support from their teammates compared with those who came out between 2000 and 2002 (Anderson, 2011). Unfortunately, homophobia is still common and often plays a big role in the lives of many gay men, lesbians, and bisexuals. Its most extreme form is revealed in hate crimes. Hate crimes include assault, robbery, and murder committed because the victim belongs to a certain race, religion, or ethnic group or has a certain sexual orientation (Ghent, 2003; Herek et al., 1999).

Hate Crimes

Hate crimes are subject to severer sentences than other crimes. In 2009 the U.S. Congress passed the Hate Crimes Prevention Act, which included attacks motivated by sex, sexual orientation, gender identity, and disability. Previously, federal hate crime law pertained only to attacks motivated by race, color, national origin, or religion. Prior to the federal legislation, about 33 states had established hate crime laws.

Causes of Homophobia and Hate Crimes

Voting to allow discrimination against homosexual people in employment and the right to marry, calling a lesbian a dyke to insult her, and murdering a gay man may seem unrelated, but they have some key elements in common. First, they reflect at the most fundamental level humankind's poor record of accepting and valuing differences among people. The lack of acceptance of racial, religious, and ethnic differences has fueled vicious, inhuman events such as ethnic cleansing, the Holocaust, and the Inquisition. The many religions that define homosexuality negatively also predispose groups and individuals to assume the same view (Negy & Eisenman, 2005).

Second, homophobia and hate crimes are usually related to traditional gender-role identification: Individuals who hold traditional gender-role stereotypes tend to have more negative feelings about homosexuality than do others (Merek & Gonzalez-Rivera, 2006; Morrison & Morrison, 2011). Furthermore, men typically have more negative attitudes toward homosexuality than do women—reflecting, perhaps, the more rigid gender-role parameters for boys and men compared with girls and women in our culture (Herek & Capitanio, 1999; Kite & Whitley, 1998b). Lesbians do not evoke as negative feelings in heterosexual men as gay men do (Mahaffey et al., 2005). This may be, in part,

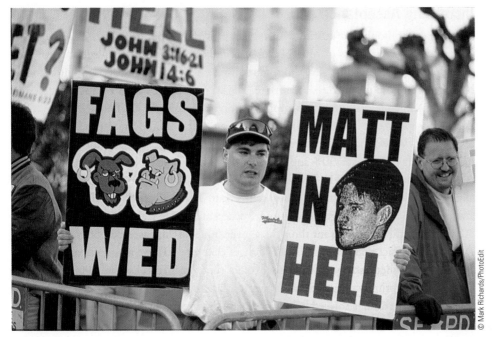

Public awareness of hate crimes against gays rose sharply after the 1998 death of Matthew Shepard. Shepard was an openly gay, 21-year-old University of Wyoming student who hoped for a career in diplomacy and human rights. After two 21-year-old high school dropouts pistol-whipped Shepard, crushing his skull, they tied him to a fence outside town and left him to die. Most people were horrified by this crime; 700 mourners came to his funeral. But outside the church, other people carried signs with such messages as "No tears for queers" and "No fags in heaven."

because heterosexual men do not feel uncomfortable about their sexual feelings toward women in general.

Homophobia can have an especially significant effect on the depth of intimacy in male friendships. Men's fear of same-sex attraction often keeps them from allowing themselves the emotional vulnerability required for deep friendship, thus limiting their relationships largely to competition and "buddyship." Conformity to stereotypic masculine norms and disdain for homosexuality are even correlated with reduced academic motivation in males (Kahn et al., 2011).

Researchers have found that most perpetrators of antigay hate crimes—only males, to date—claim that homosexuality's violation of male gender norms is the primary motivation for their violence. Perpetrators, often acting in pairs or in larger groups, try to reassure themselves and their friends of their "masculinity" by assaulting a man who has stepped outside the rigid boundaries of male gender roles. The same motivation makes transgendered individuals frequent targets of violence. Increased collaboration for social change between transgendered individuals and groups and gay rights organizations evolved, in part, from understanding the importance of gender diversity (Coleman, 1999).

Another element involved in homophobia and hate crimes may be an attempt to deny or suppress homosexual feelings in oneself. Uncomfortable with his or her own sexuality, the homophobic person focuses on what is "wrong" with the sexuality of other people. However, research studies on the correlation between antigay bias and hidden attraction to men have yielded inconsistent findings (Mahaffey et al., 2011).

Some of the most virulent antigay rhetoric has come from deeply closeted men in positions of religious leadership. For example, the Reverend Ted Haggard promoted antigay sentiments and policy as president of the 30-million-member National Association of Evangelicals and senior pastor of the 14,000-member New Life Church in Colorado Springs, Colorado. A regular consultant to former President George W. Bush, the married father of five children admitted in 2006 to participating in "sexually immoral conduct" and left both leadership positions after a man claimed that Haggard had paid him for sex nearly every month for 3 years (Dokoupil, 2009; Signorile, 2009a). The Reverend Steven Baines, an elder in the Christian Church (Disciples of Christ), explains this dynamic: "[W]hen religion is used to bring repression and darkness rather than liberation and light, it is toxic to both leaders and followers" (Baines, 2006, p. 2).

Homophobia is infrequently directed toward lesbians. Female same-sex sexual behavior is sexually arousing to many people, and ads suggesting lesbian sex are common in advertising.

Increasing Acceptance

Individuals' homophobic attitudes can change with deliberate effort, experience, or education. Individual acts of courage can also make an impact; the college student who invites people regardless of sexual orientation to his party, the gay accountant who has his partner's photo on his desk at work, or the straight doctor with a lesbian sister who confronts someone making a derogatory gay joke all help make a difference (Solmonese, 2005). Acceptance of homosexuality is increasing in the United States: In 2011, 56% of respondents viewed homosexual relations as "morally acceptable," and for the first time national polls found over 50% support for marriage equality (Jones, 2011; Movement Advancement Project, 2011). People who personally know someone who is gay are usually more accepting of homosexuality (Fingerhut, 2011; Span & Vidal, 2003). Young adults (ages 18–29) are significantly more accepting of gay rights than are people over 30, who are still more tolerant than those over 50. The increased acceptance may have to do with the fact that 65% of people younger than age 50 have a homosexual friend or acquaintance, whereas only 45% of people older than age 50 do (Leland, 2000b). Women have more accepting attitudes toward gay men than men in general do, but women's and men's attitudes toward lesbians are similar (Petersen & Hyde, 2011).

The gay rights movement, which began in the 1960s, has provided support for many homosexual men and women and promoted greater knowledge and acceptance in the general community. In the following section, we describe some of the movement's activities.

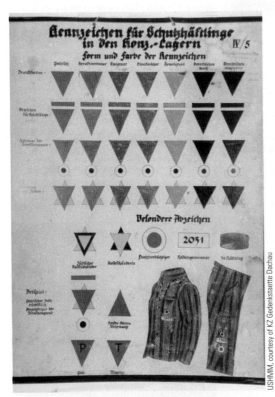

The Nazis linked homosexuality to a Jewish plot to weaken the masculinity of Aryan men. Nazi Germany decimated the base of the world's gay rights movement in Berlin. Forced to wear a pink triangle symbol on their sleeves, more than 100,000 gay men were arrested and about 50,000 were sent to death camps. The U.S. Holocaust Memorial Museum's exhibit The Nazi Persecution of Homosexuals, 1933–1945, illustrates this persecution of gay men (Karlin, 2003). In 2006, Berlin added a monument to gay victims of Nazi persecution to the city's Holocaust memorial.

The Gay Rights Movement

Forty years before World War II, the first organization promoting education about homosexuality and the abolition of laws against homosexuality was founded in Germany. However, the Nazis' rise to power ended the homosexual rights movement in Germany, and about 50,000 gay men were sent to death camps (Schoofs, 1997).

Not until the 1950s did people in the United States found organizations for homosexual men and women, despite the conservative atmosphere of the time. The Mattachine Society had chapters in many cities and provided a national network for support and communication. The Daughters of Bilitis, an organization of lesbians, published a journal called *The Ladder*, which contained fiction, poetry, and political articles. The goals of both organizations were to educate homosexual and heterosexual people about homosexuality, increase understanding of homosexuality, and eliminate laws discriminatory to homosexual individuals (Katz, 1976).

The Stonewall Incident and Beyond

During the 1960s many people began to question traditional attitudes in American society in all areas, including the sexual. In this atmosphere, more and more homosexual people began to challenge the social problems they faced. The symbolic birth of homosexual activism occurred in 1969 in New York City when police raided a gay bar, the Stonewall Inn. Police raids on gay bars were common, but this time the bar's patrons fought back. A riot ensued and did not end until the following day. The Stonewall incident served as a catalyst for the formation of gay rights groups, and activities such as Gay Pride Week and parades are held yearly to commemorate the Stonewall riot. In 1999 the Stonewall Inn was added to the National Register of Historic Places (Ring, 2012).

Since the early 1970s various groups and individuals have worked to promote civil rights for lesbians, gays, and bisexual and transgendered people while others have worked against these goals. Homosexual civil rights efforts fall into three general areas: decriminalization of private sexual behavior, antidiscrimination, and positive rights (Stein, 1999).

Decriminalization of Private Sexual Behavior

The United States had a long history of laws declaring sodomy illegal. Sodomy was legally defined as oral and/or anal sex between adults of any sexual orientation, but these laws were selectively enforced against homosexual individuals and couples. In 2003 the U.S. Supreme Court, basing its decision on the constitutional right to privacy, overturned a Texas sodomy law that made private same-sex sexual contact illegal. The *Lawrence et al. v. Texas* ruling also overturned laws in four other states that banned same-sex sex and in another nine states that banned sodomy between partners of any sexual orientation. Supporters of gay rights applauded the ruling, as did the majority of U.S. citizens, who believe that government should stay out of the bedrooms of consenting adults.

Antidiscrimination

The National Gay and Lesbian Task Force was founded in 1973 to help meet the second goal of the gay rights movement: ending various kinds of discrimination against homosexuals. Enormous progress has been made in nondiscrimination in employment: Ninety-nine percent of major U.S. companies now have nondiscrimination policies (Movement Advancement Project, 2011). ■ Table 9.2 shows the states that have established laws and policies prohibiting antigay discrimination. The District of Columbia and many city governments have also done so (National Gay and Lesbian Task Force, 2012).

Gay civil rights supporters hope to see the U.S. Congress pass the Employment Non-Discrimination Act (ENDA), which would prevent employers from discriminating on the basis of sexual orientation and gender identity. Another major legislative goal of gay civil rights advocates is to amend the 1964 Civil Rights Act to include "affectional or sexual orientation" along with race, creed, color, and sex (Wildman, 2001). This amendment would make it illegal to discriminate in housing, employment, insurance, and public accommodations on grounds of sexual orientation. With regard to global issues, in 2009, the Obama administration endorsed the United Nations statement calling for worldwide decriminalization of homosexuality, which former president George W. Bush had previously refused to endorse (Lee, 2009).

In September 2011 the U.S. military's "Don't ask, don't tell" policy was repealed. Implemented in 1992 by Congress and signed by President Bill Clinton, the policy allowed homosexual individuals to serve in the military—even though the military considered them unfit for service—provided that they kept their orientation secret. An estimated 13,000 gays and lesbians were expelled from the military during the years this policy was in effect (Miklaszewski & Kube, 2011).

This policy compromised U.S. military efforts by needlessly removing capable service members. It also resulted in unnecessary

© Christopher Lane

Two linguists in the Army—one fluent in Korean, the other fluent in three languages and training to be an interrogator—were among the 322 linguists discharged from the military under the "Don't ask, don't tell" policy (Curtis, 2005).

■ TABLE 9.2 States With Nondiscrimination Laws for Sexual Orientation

California	Colorado	Connecticut
Delaware	Hawaii	Illinois
Iowa	Maine	Maryland
Massachusetts	Minnesota	New Hampshire
New Jersey	New Mexico	New York
Nevada	Oregon	Rhode Island
Vermont	Washington	Wisconsin

SOURCE: National Gay and Lesbian Task Force (2012).

hardships for the gays and lesbians who served in the military. For example, during the Iraq occupation, partners at home had no access to support services that the military provides families; consequently, they were unlikely to be informed if their loved ones were wounded, captured, or killed (Biederman, 2003). Ironically, closeted gay and lesbian U.S. troops served alongside openly homosexual troops from Great Britain and Australia (Neff, 2004).

Legal Civil Marriage for Same-Sex Couples

Many gay–civil rights advocates are currently striving to have the United States join Argentina, Belgium, Canada, Denmark, Iceland, Norway, the Netherlands, Portugal, South Africa, Spain, and Sweden in recognizing the legal right of homosexual people to marry. Why is securing this right important?

First, it would end discrimination in marriage and provide equality under governmental laws (Olson, 2010). In good conscience, how can a democratic country withhold the civil right of marriage from law-abiding, taxpaying same-sex partners? As a graduate student clarified this view, "I feel about marriage the same way I do about the military: It isn't an institution I wish to join, but if it exists, it ought to be open to everyone" (Gaboury, 2005, p. 29).

The U.S. government has changed marriage laws based on equal rights many times in its history. It ended the legal subordination of women in marriage by eliminating laws that prohibited married women from owning property and entering into contracts. It made marital rape illegal. Federal law established the right of people of different races to marry. Laws also changed to give couples, not the government, the right to decide to divorce. Such changes have helped evolve marriage into a union of equals who are together because of love and a desire to make a commitment to build a life with one another (Coontz, 2005).

Each time in the past when a law was changed to establish greater equality and privacy in marriage, opponents fought the change, many claiming that it went against God's will and would ruin the institution of marriage. A large portion of the funds for current legislative campaigns against gay marriage come from religious groups (Kirchick, 2009b). However, U.S. democracy is based on the principle of separation of church and state, and religion should not dictate to government which couples can obtain civil marriage licenses (Sullivan, 2011). Freedom of religion guarantees the right of every church not to marry any specific couple for any reason, but religion is a common basis for opposition to same-sex civil marriage, as expressed by William Bennett, editor of *The Book of Virtues* and codirector of Empower America:

> The legal union of same-sex couples would shatter the conventional definition of marriage, change the rules which govern behavior, endorse practices which are completely antithetical to the tenets of all of the world's religions, send conflicting

signals about marriage and sexuality, particularly to the young, and obscure marriage's enormous consequential function—procreation and child-rearing. (Bennett, 1996, p. 27)

In contrast, a proponent of gay marriage, Andrew Sullivan (formerly a senior editor of *The New Republic* and author of *Virtually Normal: An Argument About Homosexuality*), stated:

> What we seek is not some special place in America but merely to be a full and equal part of America. . . . Some of us are lucky enough to meet the person we truly love. And we want to commit to that person in front of our family and country for the rest of our lives. . . . Why indeed would any conservative seek to oppose those very family values for gay people that he or she supports for everybody else? (Sullivan, 1996, p. 26)

A significant setback to civil rights in marriage for sexual minorities occurred in 1996 when the U.S. Congress passed, and President Clinton signed, the Defense of Marriage Act (DOMA). This act denied federal recognition of same-sex marriages that were made legal in individual states, and it gave states the right not to recognize such marriages performed in other states. With DOMA in place, gay and lesbian families and their children in the United States lack the 1,000-plus federal benefits that married heterosexual couples have, including benefits regarding inheritance; Social Security; child custody; immigration rights; joint insurance policies for health, home, or auto; and status as next of kin for hospital visits or even for making funeral arrangements for a partner (Movement Advancement Project, 2011; Murphy, 2011). Ironically, although the ban on gay men and lesbians serving in the military no longer exists, DOMA prohibits active-military same-sex couples from receiving standard service benefits such as housing, health insurance, death benefits, and shopping privileges at the base commissary (Dao, 2011). In 2011 President Obama directed the Justice Department to stop defending DOMA in court on the grounds that it is unconstitutional. However, at the time of this writing the law remains in effect, and it is unknown whether the current Congress and the Obama administration will revoke the Defense of Marriage Act (Savage & Stolberg, 2011).

Many are perplexed by the name "Defense of Marriage Act," wondering how preventing same-sex marriages "defends" heterosexual marriages. As conservative Republican Bob Hall states, "The anti-same-sex-marriage amendment isn't going to help my marriage by so much as a red whisker. If you think it will protect your marriage, that marriage is already shot" (Hall, 2006, p. 1). Ironically, in 2003, Massachusetts, where same-sex marriage is legal, had the lowest divorce rate in the United States: 5.7 divorces per 1,000 married people. In contrast, some of the states where strong opposition to same-sex marriage predominates have the highest rates: 10.8 divorces per 1,000 married people in Kentucky and 12.7 in Arkansas (Goldberg, 2006).

At the state level, in 2011, 37 states had discriminatory laws defining marriage as a union between a man and a woman (National Conference of State Legislatures, 2011b). In contrast, in 2004 Massachusetts affirmed a constitutional right to same-sex marriage, making it the first state to issue fully legal marriage licenses to gay and lesbian couples. Connecticut, the District of Columbia, Iowa, Maine, Maryland, New Hampshire, New York, Vermont, and Washington subsequently legalized same-sex marriage (National Gay and Lesbian Task Force, 2011). Some states that have not established gay marriage have approved civil unions or domestic partnership laws that provide some or all of the 300 rights, benefits, and responsibilities that states provide to married heterosexual couples. These

Cindy McCain, wife of U.S. Senator John McCain, and Laura Bush, wife of former president George W. Bush, came out in support of gay marriage in 2010.

include California, Colorado, Delaware, Hawaii, Illinois, Nevada, New Jersey, Oregon, Rhode Island, and Wisconsin.

About 22% of all same-sex couples in the United States have formalized their relationships under state laws of various types (Badgett & Herman, 2011). Some same-sex couples consider the increased legitimacy and benefits of civil union to be highly important, while others do not consider civil union to be significant in comparison to marriage (Rothblum et al., 2011). The percentage of same-sex couples who marry is significantly higher than the percentage of couples who establish civil unions and domestic partnerships, indicating that the meaning of marriage goes beyond the practical aspects of a legally recognized relationship (Gates et al., 2008). Being married may provide psychological as well as practical benefits for gays and lesbians (Buffie, 2011; Shulman et al., 2012). Research does indicate that discriminatory laws and antigay political initiatives against same-sex marriage create psychological stress for sexual minorities and their families (Fingerhut et al., 2011; Frost, 2011; Herek, 2011).

In 2011, for the first time several national polls of the general population found over 50% support for same-sex marriage. Younger people, women, liberal Democrats, and people who were not affiliated with a religion tended to view same-sex marriage more favorably (Sherkat et al., 2011). Support for same-sex marriage has increased and is expected to continue to do so because of younger people's more accepting attitudes. In addition, in May 2012, President Obama announced his personal support of same-sex marriage.

Controversy over legal civil marriage for gays and lesbians will play out at the state and national levels for years to come. The conflict is about much more than two same-sex people marrying; it is also about what kind of country the United States will be: "Is America indeed to be a nation where we *all*, minorities as well as majorities, popular as well as unpopular, get to make important choices in our lives, or is it to be a land of liberty and justice for some?" (Wolfson, 2005, p. 18).

Homosexuality and the Media

The media have both reflected the changing attitudes toward homosexuality and influenced public awareness and attitudes. Making gays more commonly known in the mainstream media provides an opportunity for greater familiarity with and understanding of homosexuality. Since the mid-1960s, daytime talk shows have brought previously unknown visibility to gays, lesbians, and bisexual people. Talk shows' focus on controversial topics gave homosexual guests unprecedented opportunities to represent their own lives and issues. Homosexuality also became more visible—and was portrayed in a more positive light—in films during the 1990s. For example, the 1993 film *Philadelphia*, starring Tom Hanks, was the first major Hollywood feature to confront homophobia and AIDS and was a box-office success. In the later 1990s, movies such as *My Best Friend's Wedding* began to portray homosexuals in more ordinary roles. The movie *Brokeback Mountain*, a love story of two Wyoming cowboys, won numerous awards and was the first same-sex romance to be number one at the box office (Vary, 2006).

Gay, lesbian, and bisexual characters now appear in many TV shows. Some that are particularly popular with critics and viewers include *Glee*, *True Blood*, *The Good Wife*, *Grey's Anatomy*, and *Modern Family*. For the 2011–2012 television season, the five broadcast networks—ABC, NBC, CBS, Fox, and The CW—had 19 gay, lesbian, and bisexual characters, and mainstream cable had approximately 28 gay, lesbian, and bisexual characters on regular series programs (GLAAD, 2011).

In 2009 Ellen DeGeneres became the celebrity spokesperson for CoverGirl and Olay Simply Ageless makeup.

Coming Out

We look now at how gay people must deal with the conflict of being gay in a predominantly heterosexual society, and the potentially hostile social environment that is posed to them as a result. The decision to be secretive or open about their sexual orientation affects the lives of all gay men and lesbians.

The extent to which homosexual individuals decide to be secretive or open about their sexual orientation significantly impacts their lives in profound ways. There are various degrees of being "in the closet," and several steps are involved in **coming out**—acknowledging, accepting, and openly expressing one's homosexuality (Patterson, 1995). Gays, lesbians, and bisexual people base decisions about coming out on issues of safety and acceptance for themselves and others. Individuals come out at all ages, including at advanced ages, as portrayed in the 2011 film *Beginners*. Being openly lesbian, gay, or bisexual can be personally liberating but may not be adaptive in every situation (Legate et al., 2012). Passing as heterosexual can help an individual avoid negative social consequences but exacts its toll in the stresses of maintaining secrecy (Malcolm, 2008). Individual circumstances significantly affect decisions about coming out.

Historical context also influences coming out, as indicated in a study of three different generations of lesbians:

1. Lesbians who became adults before the gay rights era began in the 1970s
2. Lesbians who became adults during the gay rights era, between 1970 and 1985
3. Lesbians who became adults after 1985

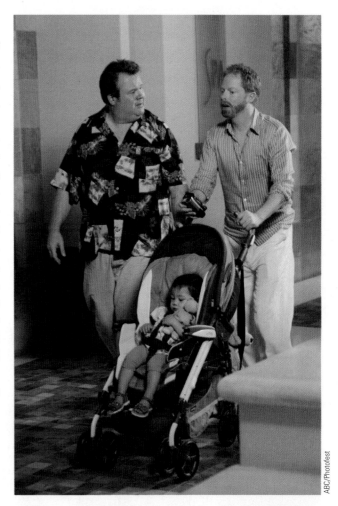

Modern Family began its first season in 2009 on ABC and has won numerous awards as well as receiving criticism for reinforcing sexist stereotypes. The sitcom features three families, one of which is a gay couple with an adopted Vietnamese baby girl.

ABC/Photofest

With each consecutive age group, women's awareness of their sexual orientation, initial same-sex sexual experience, labeling of themselves as lesbian, and disclosing to others occurred earlier in life. For example, women in the youngest group were, on average, 20 years old when they identified themselves as lesbian, whereas women in the oldest group were 32 years old. The most significant change over time was that more and more women had sexual experiences with other women before having such experiences with men. This was true for most women in the youngest group, whereas the opposite was true for most women in both older groups (Parks, 1999).

Although coming-out decisions are unique to each individual and situation, many have common elements: self-acknowledgment, self-acceptance, and disclosure. We look at each of these in the following sections.

Self-Acknowledgment

The initial step in coming out is usually a person's realization that she or he feels different from the mainstream heterosexual model (Meyer & Schwitzer, 1999). Some people report knowing that they were attracted to the same sex when they were small children. Many realize during adolescence that something is missing in their heterosexual involvements and that they find same-sex peers sexually attractive (Cloud, 2005). Some may feel uncertain of their sexual orientation: One study found that 2% of youth ages 12 to 25 reported being "unsure" of their sexual orientation (Ott et al., 2011).

coming out
The process of becoming aware of and disclosing one's homosexual identity.

In the 2005 film *Brokeback Mountain*, two ranch hands fall in love with each other and struggle with their lives and a community that has no space or tolerance for their relationship. The movie won three Academy Awards.

The president of a high school Gay Straight Alliance holds a badge she wears at a White House LBGT Conference on Safe Schools and Communities in 2012.

Once individuals recognize homosexual feelings, they must usually confront their own internalized homophobia as they deal with the reality that they belong to a stigmatized minority group (Herek et al., 2009). Some lesbian, gay, and bisexual individuals attempt to conceal or suppress their sexual orientation, even from their own awareness. These people actively seek sexual encounters with members of the other sex, and it has not been uncommon for them to marry in an attempt to convince themselves of their "normalcy" and avoid openly confronting their sexual orientation (Hudson et al., 2007; Malcolm, 2008). Marrying in spite of same-sex orientation is more likely the more stigmatized and taboo homosexuality is. For example, although prejudice against homosexuality has lessened slightly in China, nearly 80% of men who identify themselves as homosexual either are married or intend to marry (Cui, 2006).

Self-Acceptance

Accepting one's homosexuality is the next important step after realizing it. Self-acceptance is often difficult, because it involves overcoming the internalized negative and homophobic societal view of homosexuality. When individuals belong to a socially stigmatized group, self-acceptance becomes a difficult but essential challenge (Ryan & Futterman, 2001).

Coming out can be especially problematic for teenagers. Most gay and lesbian teens experience confusion about their feelings and have few places to go for support and guidance. At a stage of development when a sense of belonging to their peer group is especially important, almost half of gay and lesbian teens lost at least one friend after they came out (Ryan & Futterman, 1997). Especially if they exhibit gender nonconformity, they may encounter considerable hostility, bullying, and rejection that can negatively affect psychological well-being (Rieger & Savin-Williams, 2011). Prompted by media reports of teen suicides from bullying, sex columnist Dan Savage launched the "It Gets Better" project on YouTube in 2010. The project shows LGBT adults telling their personal stories about overcoming stigma during their lives.

Judgment from their own families is another source of stress for people who come out. Some parents throw their gay children out of the house or stop providing support for their education. A study of 60,000 high school students in Massachusetts found that 25% of gay and lesbian students were homeless, compared to 3% of heterosexual students (Lazar, 2011). In addition, lesbian, gay, and bisexual young adults who experienced family rejection during their adolescence due to their sexual orientation were over eight times more likely to have attempted suicide, almost six times more likely to report high levels of depression, and over three times more likely to have used illegal drugs and to have engaged in unprotected intercourse compared to peers who experienced little or no family rejection (Ryan et al., 2009). Conversely, research has found that a positive reaction from the mother to the youth's coming out serves as a significant protective factor (Padilla et al., 2010).

Despite the discrimination that homosexual adolescents face, many of them can cope effectively and develop an integrated and positive identity (Savin-Williams, 2005). Sexual orientation itself is not correlated to poor psychological well-being of high school students (Rieger & Savin-Williams, 2011). It is helpful for gay and lesbian adolescents to find at least one supportive, nonjudgmental adult with whom to talk. The Internet provides teens with sexual health education and connections to others to help reduce their isolation (Mustanski et al., 2011). Support groups and gay teen organizations are emerging to help teens deal with the difficulties they face. More than 3,600 high schools sponsor gay–straight alliances to foster acceptance of sexual minority students (Setoodeh, 2008). The first accredited public high school for gay students, Harvey Milk School, in New York City, opened its doors in fall 2003 to provide students with a safe and supportive learning environment (Henneman, 2003).

Disclosure

Following acknowledgment and self-acceptance is the decision to be secretive or open. Occasionally, a gay man, lesbian, or bisexual individual will find others abruptly opening the closet door for him or her. *Outing* is the term for the public disclosure of someone's secret homosexual orientation by someone else. Otherwise, being homosexual usually requires ongoing decisions about whether to be in or out of the closet as new relationships and situations unfold. **Passing** is a term sometimes used for maintaining the false image of heterosexuality. Passing as heterosexual is usually easy because most people assume that everyone is heterosexual. Heterosexual people sometimes do not understand disclosure issues, as exemplified by the following comment:

passing
Presenting a false image of being heterosexual.

> I don't see any reason why they have to tell anyone. They can just lead their lives without making such a big deal out of it. (Authors' files)

In some daily interactions, sexual orientation is irrelevant, but sexual orientation is a strong undercurrent that touches many parts of life. Imagine being a closeted homosexual person and hearing a friend make a derogatory reference to "fags" or "dykes"; being asked, "When are you going to settle down and get married?"; being invited to bring a date to an office party where acceptance is uncertain; or not ever being able to hang out with your significant other with friends, family, or in public at all.

With some exceptions, the more within "the system" one is or desires to be, the more risk there is in being open about one's sexual orientation. Jobs, social position, and friendships can all be placed in jeopardy. The conservativeness of the surrounding community or time in history can further affect one's decisions about whether to come out and to whom. Urban settings often increase the likelihood that individuals will express their gay or lesbian sexual orientation (Chiang, 2009). In the Let's Talk About It box, "Guidelines for Coming Out to Friends," we offer some suggestions for coming out.

Courtesy of Representative Jason Bartlett

Jason Bartlett won reelection as a state representative in Connecticut after coming out to his constituents during his first term, becoming the first openly gay African American state legislator in the United States.

If you are a gay man or lesbian, the unexpected is to be expected when you come out to a friend. A friend who is "liberal" may have more difficulty than a more "conservative" person. It is essential to remember that your friend's reactions say more about his or her own strengths and weaknesses than about you. The following guidelines are meant to help you begin devising your own plan of disclosure. They are adapted from the book *Outing Yourself*, by Michelangelo Signorile (1995).

1. *Form a support network.* You should have a support network of gays in place, especially those who have come out to lots of different people in their lives. Their experiences and support will give you a solid base from which to act.

2. *Choose the first person to tell.* Try to make your first disclosure to a heterosexual person an easy one. You might not choose your best straight friend, because the stakes are high. Pick someone whom you would expect to be accepting. The person also needs to be trustworthy and capable of keeping your news private for a while as you come out to others.

3. *Practice mentally.* Practice imagining yourself coming out in realistic detail. Picture yourself in a familiar setting where both you and your friend will be comfortable. Envision feeling pleased with yourself for sharing something you feel good about (not something you have to apologize for). Practice saying, "There's something I want to tell you about myself, because our friendship is important to me. I trust you, and you're close to me. I am a lesbian/I am gay."

4. *Plan in advance.* Plan the time: Be sure to allow enough time to talk at length if things go well. Plan the place: Be sure it is somewhere both of you will be comfortable. Arrange to have at least one of your gay friends available for support afterward and for debriefing. Be prepared to calmly answer such questions as, "How do you know you're gay?" "How long have you known?" "What caused it?" "Can you change?" "Do you have AIDS?"

5. *Rely on patience.* Remember that you are telling your friend something he or she has not had a chance to prepare for, whereas you have had a lot of time to prepare. Many people are surprised, shocked, and confused and need some time to think or ask questions. An initial negative reaction does not necessarily mean the friend will not accept it. If a friend reacts negatively but shows respect, stay and talk things over. Sympathize with his or her shock and confusion: "I can see this news upsets you."

6. *Control your anger.* If the person becomes hostile or insulting, politely end the meeting: "I'm sorry you aren't accepting my news well, and it's best for me to go now." Don't give your friend a real reason to be mad at you by being mean or rude or flying off the handle. As you come out to people, you will find that some are not able or willing to maintain their friendship with you. With others, letting them know you more fully will allow the meaning and closeness in the relationship to grow. Over time you will create a network of friends with whom you can enjoy the freedom of being your full self.

Telling the Family

Disclosing one's homosexuality to family can be more difficult than disclosing it to others. Coming out to one's family is a particularly significant step, as the following account by a 35-year-old man illustrates:

> Most of my vacation at home went well, but the ending was indeed difficult. Gay people kept cropping up in conversation. My mother was very down on them (us), and I of course was disagreeing with her. Finally she asked me if I was "one of them." I said yes. It was very difficult for her to deal with. She asked a lot of questions, which I answered as calmly, honestly, and rationally as I could. We spent a rather strained day together. It was so painful for me to see her suffering so much heartache over this and not even having a clue that the issue is the oppression of gay people. I just wish my mother didn't have to suffer so much from all this. (Authors' files)

Parents may react with anger or guilt about what they "did wrong." Research does indicate that as societal attitudes become more positive about homosexuality, parents react more receptively to disclosure (Pearlman, 2005). Families that are less rigid and authoritarian and more cohesive are more likely to react with less stress to disclosure of homosexuality (Willoughby et al., 2006). The organization Parents, Families, and Friends of Lesbians and Gays (PFLAG), which has over 350 chapters nationwide, helps parents and others develop understanding, acceptance, and support. Potentially more problematic than coming out to one's parents is coming out to one's spouse and children. A gay man or lesbian closeted in a heterosexual marriage may have grave concerns about the reactions of his or her spouse and children, who indeed tend to struggle with the disclosure (Sanders, 2000).

To a greater extent than White homosexual people, gay, lesbian, and bisexual people from other racial and ethnic groups are more likely to stay in the closet with their families and community than to be open and face alienation, not only from their families but also from their heritage (Span & Vidal, 2003). For example, traditional Asian cultures place greater significance on loyalty and conformity to one's family than on individual needs and desires. Being openly homosexual is seen as shaming the family, and not marrying and creating heirs to carry on the family name is a failure for the whole extended family. In addition, lesbianism is an affront to the traditions of an ethnic group that expects virginity for unmarried women and views "good women" as primarily nonsexual.

The emphasis on masculinity as the ideal gender norm in the lower socioeconomic segment of the African American community—and the emphasis on *machismo* for Hispanic men—creates particular difficulty for gender-nonconforming individuals. In one study, more Latino gays reported negative family reactions to their sexual orientation as adolescents than did any other group of lesbian, gay, or bisexual teens (Ryan et al., 2009). Another study found that suicide risk among young African American and Hispanic lesbians, gay men, and bisexuals may be greater than for Caucasian LGB youth (O'Donnell et al., 2011).

In general, the African American community has stronger negative views of homosexuals than does White society. Consequently, African American lesbians and gay men have a greater incidence of psychological distress than do White homosexual people as a result of racism and homophobia (Szymanski & Gupta, 2009). Although leaders such as the Reverend Al Sharpton, Coretta Scott King, and the Reverend Jesse Jackson have supported gay civil rights, the influence of strong fundamentalist Christian beliefs contributes to the higher degree of intolerance in the Black community. Many African American lesbians and gay men who were affiliated with the Black church as children find continued participation untenable as adults due to church-sanctioned antigay prejudice (R. Miller, 2008). Unfortunately, antigay prejudice has gravely hindered African American communities from proactively addressing the AIDS crisis (Bond, 2006).

Involvement in the Gay Community

The need to belong is a deeply felt human trait. For many, the sexual minority community helps provide a feeling of belonging and the affirmation and acceptance that are missing in the larger culture (Russell & Richards, 2003). Social and political involvement with other homosexual people is another step in coming out. Homosexual people have helped found service organizations, educational centers, and professional organizations, such as the Gay and Lesbian Medical Association and Gay and Lesbian Criminal Justice Professionals. Gay fraternities have formed on college campuses across the United States. Homosexual retirement communities provide alternatives to traditional retirement communities, in which older gays and lesbians may have to be on their guard against negative attitudes of other residents (Rosenberg, 2001). Religious organizations for homosexual people have been established, including the 43,000-member Metropolitan Community Church, with 300 congregations in 22 countries, and denominational groups such as Dignity for Roman Catholics and Integrity for Episcopalians. In addition, the Internet has provided a gay virtual community in ways never before possible.

The AIDS crisis precipitated increased community involvement and coherence. The gay and lesbian communities mobilized educational efforts, developed innovative programs for caring for AIDS patients, created an impressive network of volunteers to provide needed support for persons with AIDS, and lobbied—often quite visibly—for increased AIDS awareness and medical research funding.

Homosexual Relationships in Context

We sometimes hear references to the "gay lifestyle" in popular vernacular. What is the gay lifestyle exactly? The term does not imply that all gays engage in the same work, recreation, and spiritual activities. The word *lifestyle* seems to be a euphemism for sexual conduct between same-sex partners (Howey & Samuels, 2000). There is no "gay lifestyle" just as there is no "straight lifestyle." Homosexuals live as varied a life as heterosexuals. All social classes, occupations, races, religions, and political persuasions are represented among homosexual people. The only characteristics that homosexual people necessarily have in common are their desire for emotional and sexual fulfillment with someone of the same sex and their experiences of oppression from a hostile social environment.

Some people mistakenly think that homosexual partners always enact the stereotypically active "male" and passive "female" roles. However, more egalitarian relationships are being followed by both heterosexual and homosexual couples today. In regard to gender roles, a homosexual relationship may well be more flexible than a heterosexual one in our society.

Gay and lesbian couples face challenges similar to those heterosexual couples face in creating and maintaining satisfying relationships. In addition, they have distinctive concerns as members of a stigmatized minority (Mohr & Daly, 2008). Developing self-acceptance can be important because research finds that internalized homophobia is associated with increased relationship problems (Frost & Meyer, 2009). In the absence of social acceptance, couples face challenges regarding disclosing their relationship in their personal and work lives and coping with the stress from antigay discrimination and prejudice (Otis et al., 2006), such as we discussed in the previous section on coming out.

Comparison of Gay and Straight Relationships

The Gottman Institute conducted a 12-year study of gay and lesbian couples to examine what makes same-sex relationships succeed or fail (Gottman et al., 2004). When the researchers compared the findings to results of their investigations with heterosexual couples, they discovered that overall relationship satisfaction and quality were similar for lesbian, gay, and straight couples. However, most of the differences between gay/lesbian and straight couples revealed more strengths in the same-sex relationships. Compared to straight couples, gay and lesbian couples:

1. Used more affection and humor in the face of conflict and disagreement.
2. Were more likely to remain positive after a disagreement.
3. Displayed less belligerence, fear, and domineering behavior with each other.

However, gay men were less skilled at making up after a disagreement than were straight and lesbian couples.

Additional studies have found greater relationship quality, compatibility, and intimacy and lower levels of conflict in gay and lesbian relationships; lesbians were especially effective at working harmoniously together (Balsam et al., 2008; Roisman et al., 2008). Researchers speculate that the greater strengths of same-sex couples may be due to the lack of the gender-role conflicts that are inherent in heterosexual relationships.

With regard to sexual interactions, lesbian sexual patterns tend to have more of the characteristics often associated with greater sexual enjoyment for women. A review of the research comparing lesbians' and heterosexual women's sexual experiences found that lesbian couples had more nongenital sexual interaction before genital contact, took more time in a sexual encounter, felt more comfortable using erotic language with each other, were more assertive sexually, and had lower rates of problems with orgasm than did straight women (Iasenza, 2000). Further research that compared the subjective sexual experiences of partners in heterosexual relationships to those of partners in same-sex relationships found that heterosexual men derived somewhat less satisfaction from tender, sensual, and erotic sexual activities than did heterosexual women and gay and lesbian couples (Holmberg & Blair, 2008).

Differences Between Gays and Lesbians in Sexual Attitude and Behavior

Homosexual men and women differ in the average number of their sexual partners. Lesbians are likely to have had far fewer sexual partners, and lesbian couples are much more likely than male couples to have monogamous relationships (Dubé, 2000; Rothblum, 2000). Lesbians associate emotional closeness with sex more than do gay men, a finding consistent with the male/female heterosexual patterns discussed in Chapter 7. One study found that most lesbians waited to have sex with a partner until they had developed emotional intimacy. Although 46% of gay men had become friends with their partners before having sex, as a group they were more likely than lesbians to have had sexual experiences with casual acquaintances or people they had just met (Sanders, 2000).

Beginning in the 1980s a lesbian "radical sex" subculture began to develop that was unparalleled among heterosexual women. Involvement in recreational sex, anonymous sex, "kinky" sex, group sex, sadomasochistic sex, and role-polarized sex play went beyond the typical boundaries of female sexuality. Organizations sprang up for lesbians who pursue these sexual expressions, and this subculture continues to grow (Bonet et al., 2006; Nichols, 2000).

Before the AIDS epidemic some homosexual men had frequent casual sexual encounters (Bell & Weinberg, 1978; Kinsey et al., 1948). These encounters were sometimes exceedingly brief, occurring in bathhouses, in public restrooms, or in film booths in pornography shops. This type of brief recreational sexual contact is on the rise again, as AIDS has become less of a death sentence (Jefferson, 2005). However, sexual involvement with many partners is not universal among homosexual men (Kurdek, 1995a). Some men want to have a strong emotional relationship before becoming sexually involved. And for some men, being involved in an ongoing relationship eliminates sexual interest in other men.

Family Life

Traditionally, a family has been considered to consist of a heterosexual couple and their children, but many forms of family life exist in contemporary society. Surveys indicate that between 45% and 80% of lesbians and between 40% and 60% of gay men are currently in a steady relationship, and many have long-term cohabiting relationships (National Gay and Lesbian Task Force, 2003). Homosexual people also form family units, either as single parents or as couples, with children, who are included in the family through a variety of circumstances. Census data show that 17% of lesbian and gay couples are raising children (Gates & Cooke, 2011). Many have children who were born in previous heterosexual marriages. Others become parents with foster or adopted children: In the last 10 years the number of same-sex couples who adopt has tripled to almost 22,000 (Seager, 2011). A gay man or couple may enlist the help of a surrogate to have a baby. In 2010 CNN presented a documentary titled *In America: Gary and Tony Have a Baby*, which followed the gay couple through their decision to become parents, their surrogacy process, and the first 6 months of their son's life.

Most laws about adoption by homosexual parents are ambiguous, and in many cases homosexual people have to adopt as individuals rather than as couples. In 1998 New Jersey became the first state to allow partners in gay and lesbian couples to jointly adopt children, and California, Colorado, Connecticut, the District of Columbia, Florida, Illinois, Massachusetts, New York, Pennsylvania, and Vermont have since established laws to permit such adoptions (Human Rights Campaign, 2011).

People have questioned the ability of homosexual parents to provide a positive family environment for children. However, research has found that concern to be unfounded. The U.S. National Longitudinal Lesbian Family Study (NLLFS) has followed lesbian mothers and their children since 1980, and the study's results show that children of lesbian mothers are essentially no different from other children in terms of general development, self-esteem, gender-related problems, gender roles, and sexual orientation (Bos & van Balen, 2008; Bos et al., 2008). After analyzing scientific research on gay and lesbian parenthood, the American Academy of Pediatrics decided to endorse adoption by gay and lesbian couples to provide children with the security of two legally recognized parents (Contemporary Sexuality, 2002). The American Psychiatric Association also supports the rights of gay and lesbian parents (Gartell et al., 2011).

Unfortunately, children with gay or lesbian parents often face various expressions of homophobia, such as bullying, name-calling in school, or being forbidden by friends' parents to visit those friends at home (Signorile, 2011; van Gelderen et al., 2012). Research has found that attending schools with curricula that include discussions of homosexuality and socializing with other lesbian families helped to lessen the impact of the homophobic stigma the children encountered (Bos, van Balen et al., 2008). A comparison between children of lesbian mothers in the United States and the Netherlands found that the Dutch children were more open with their peers about having lesbian parents, reflecting the differing levels of acceptance in the two countries. For example, 49% of people in the United States compared to 66% of people in the Netherlands said that they believe homosexual couples should have the legal right to adopt a child (Bos, van Balen et al., 2008). As acceptance of homosexuality increases, the well-being of gay and lesbian parents will benefit from a favorable legal climate, gay-friendliness of the neighborhood, and support in the workplace and from friends and families (Goldberg & Smith, 2011).

Summary

A Continuum of Sexual Orientations

- Asexuality is a lack of sexual attraction to either sex.
- Kinsey's seven-point continuum ranges from exclusive heterosexuality to exclusive homosexuality. Kinsey based his ratings on a combination of erotic attraction and overt sexual behaviors.
- Bisexuality can be characterized by overt behaviors and/or erotic responses to both males and females. It is difficult to establish a clear-cut definition of bisexuality.

- Sexual fluidity appears much more often in women than in men.
- According to estimates from the National Health and Social Life Survey, approximately 1.7% of men and 1.3% of women identify themselves as homosexual.

What Determines Sexual Orientation?

- A number of psychosocial and biological theories have attempted to explain the development of homosexuality.

- Psychosocial theories relate to parenting patterns, life experiences, or psychological attributes of a person.
- Theories of biological causation look to prenatal and genetic factors. A biological predisposition toward homosexuality for some gays and lesbians is suggested by research on the brain, twin studies, and evidence regarding finger length, handedness, and gender nonconformity.
- Sexual orientation, regardless of where it falls on the continuum, seems to form through a composite of factors unique to each person.

Societal Attitudes Regarding Homosexuality

- Cross-cultural attitudes toward homosexuality range from condemnation to acceptance. Acceptance continues to increase in the United States.
- Current Judeo-Christian positions toward homosexuality vary greatly.
- Homophobia is the irrational fear of homosexuality, the fear of homosexual feelings within oneself, or self-loathing because of one's own homosexuality. Young males often exhibit the most extreme homophobia, especially in perpetrating hate crimes.
- Since the early 1990s, the media have increasingly portrayed homosexuality in a positive light—a development that may help lead to increasing familiarity with and acceptance of homosexuality.

The Gay Rights Movement

- Homosexual activism arose in the late 1960s. Its major current goals are antidiscrimination in employment, housing, and the military, and positive rights, such as marriage and adoption. These goals are opposed by various individuals and groups.

Coming Out

- The choice of coming out or being "in the closet" often has a significant effect on a homosexual person's lifestyle. The steps of coming out involve recognizing one's homosexual orientation, deciding how to view oneself, and being open about one's homosexuality.

Homosexual Relationships in Context

- Overall research finds relationship satisfaction and quality similar for lesbian, gay, and straight couples. However, most of the differences between gay/lesbian and straight couples revealed more strengths in the same-sex relationships.
- Gay, lesbian, and straight couples have many similarities. However, homosexual couples tend to manage conflict more effectively than do heterosexual couples.
- Gay men tend to have more sexual partners than lesbians do. Differences between homosexual men and homosexual women with regard to casual versus committed sex follow general gender-role patterns. Lesbian "sex radicals" are moving past the typical boundaries of female sexuality.
- People have questioned the ability of homosexual parents to provide a positive family environment for children. However, research has found that concern to be unfounded.

Media Resources

Log in to CengageBrain.com to access the resources your instructor requires.

Go to CengageBrain.com to access Psychology CourseMate, where you will find an interactive eBook, glossaries, flashcards, quizzes, videos, and more.

Also access links to chapter-related websites, including **An Encyclopedia of Gay, Lesbian, Bisexual, and Queer Culture; Bisexual Resource Center; Sexual Orientation: Science, Education, and Policy; Parents, Family and Friends of Lesbians and Gays (PFLAG); Youth Talkline; Human Rights Campaign; *The Advocate* Online; and Lesbian Mothers Support Society.**

10 Contraception

Historical and Social Perspectives
In what ways can contraception contribute to personal and societal well-being in the United States and in developing countries?

Sharing Responsibility and Choosing a Birth Control Method
What do both men and women have to gain by sharing responsibility for birth control?

What should an individual or a couple consider in choosing a method of birth control?

Hormone-Based Contraceptives
How do hormone-based contraceptives work? What are some risks associated with their use?

Barrier and Spermicide Methods
What is the only method that provides protection from transmission of sexually transmitted infections (STIs)?

What are some of the advantages of male and female condoms, vaginal spermicides, and cervical barrier methods compared with hormone-based contraceptives?

Intrauterine Devices
Why might a woman choose to use an intrauterine device (IUD)?

Emergency Contraception
What are the types of emergency contraception?

Fertility Awareness Methods
What are the four fertility awareness methods?

How do they work, and which one is most reliable?

Sterilization
What are the benefits of vasectomy compared to female sterilization?

Unreliable Methods
How reliable are breast-feeding, withdrawal, and douching as methods of contraception?

New Directions in Contraception
What new contraceptive methods are being developed for men and women?

GlowImages/age footstock

It's a good thing that there are lots of birth control options, because I've used different ones at one time or another. I did have the good sense to use the sponge the first time I had intercourse, and I insist on condoms when I'm with a new partner. I tried the combination pill and the minipill, then used an IUD when I had a long-term boyfriend. I haven't had any particular problems with any of the methods, and I'm very grateful not to have had an unwanted pregnancy. But I do wonder if there will ever be a method I don't have to remember every day or use at the last minute and is 100% effective and reversible. (Authors' files)

Historical and Social Perspectives

People's concern with controlling conception goes back at least to the beginning of recorded history. In ancient Egypt women placed dried crocodile dung next to the cervix to prevent conception. In 6th-century Greece, eating the uterus, testis, or hoof paring of a mule was recommended. In more recent historical times, the 18th-century Italian adventurer Giovanni Casanova was noted for his animal-membrane condoms tied with a ribbon at the base of the penis. In 17th-century western Europe, vaginal sponges soaked in a variety of solutions were used for contraception (McLaren, 1990).

Contraception in the United States

Although we may take for granted the variety of contraceptive, or birth control, methods available in the United States today, this situation is quite recent. Throughout American history both the methods available for contraception and the laws concerning their use have been restrictive. In the 1870s, Anthony Comstock, then secretary of the New York Society for the Suppression of Vice, succeeded in enacting national laws that prohibited the dissemination of contraceptive information through the U.S. mail on the grounds that such information was obscene; these laws were known as the Comstock Laws. At that time, the only legitimate form of birth control was abstinence, and reproduction was viewed as the only acceptable reason for sexual intercourse.

Margaret Sanger was the person most instrumental in promoting changes in birth control legislation and availability in the United States. Sanger was horrified at the misery of women who had virtually no control over their fertility and bore child after child in desperate poverty. In 1915 she opened an illegal clinic where women could obtain and learn to use the diaphragms she had shipped from Europe. She also published birth control information in her newspaper, *The Woman Rebel*. As a result, Sanger was arraigned for violating the Comstock Laws. She fled to Europe to avoid prosecution but later returned to promote research on birth control hormones, a project financed by her wealthy friend Katherine Dexter McCormack.

Sanger and McCormack wanted to develop a reliable method by which women could control their own fertility (Tone, 2002). However, it was not until 1960 that the first birth control pills came on the U.S. market, after limited testing and research in Puerto Rico. Fertility control through contraception rather than abstinence was a profound shift that implied an acceptance of female sexual expression and broadened the roles that women might choose (D'Emilio & Freedman, 1988; Rubin, 2010).

Prior to the 1965 U.S. Supreme Court ruling in *Griswold v. Connecticut*, states could prohibit the use of contraceptives by married people (381 U.S. 479). The Court based

Critical Thinking Question

How does the belief that abstinence is the only moral form of birth control play out today?

Margaret Sanger dedicated herself to helping women and families have every child be a wanted child.

its decision to overrule states' prohibitions on the right to privacy of married couples. In 1972 the Supreme Court case *Eisenstadt v. Baird* extended the right to privacy to unmarried individuals by decriminalizing the use of contraception by single people (405 U.S. 438). A 9% overall drop in the birth rate of 15- to 20-year-old women occurred after access to the birth control pill became legal (Thomas, 2009).

In the ensuing years other laws governing contraceptive availability have continued to change. In most states, laws now allow the dispensing of contraceptives to adolescents without parental consent and permit pharmacies to display condoms, spermicidal foam, and contraceptive sponges on shelves in the main store rather than behind the counter. However, anti-contraception forces continue to engage in political battles on various fronts to reduce access to contraception, as discussed in the Sex and Politics box, "The Power of Pro-Life Anti-Contraception Politics."

Contraception as a Contemporary Issue

In the United States, 99% of the approximately 62 million women of reproductive age have used contraception at one time or another (Jones & Dreweke, 2011). Furthermore, the typical heterosexual woman may need some form of contraception for 30 or more years because she is only trying to become pregnant, or is pregnant, for a small percentage of her reproductive life (Gold & Sonfield, 2011). The increase in teenagers' contraceptive use in the United States is very positive news. A significantly larger proportion of teens are using contraceptives than did 20 years ago, even the first time they have sexual intercourse. Of sexually experienced teens ages 15 to 19, 78% of females and 85% of males used contraception the first time they had sexual intercourse (Martinez et al., 2011). However, the United States continues to have among the highest rates of teen pregnancy, birth, and abortion in the developed world (Kaiser Family Foundation, 2011). In Europe where teen pregnancy rates are much lower, governments support mass media public health messages to encourage the use of contraception, emphasizing both safety and pleasure (Alford & Hauser, 2011).

The availability and use of reliable birth control is desirable for a variety of reasons. First and foremost, with contraception heterosexual couples can enjoy sexual intimacy with minimal risk of unwanted pregnancies (May, 2010). Children are more likely to be born to parents who are prepared for the responsibility of rearing them, and the ability to space children at least 18 months apart increases newborn health (Conde-Agudelo et al., 2006). Far fewer women than ever before have to decide to have an abortion. Effective birth control methods have also allowed women in the United States to become equal partners with men in modern society. As a result of the increased earning power of women, men have had opportunities unknown to their own fathers to expand their involvement with their children.

Insurance coverage for contraceptive costs is an important variable in accessibility in the United States. As of 2011, 28 states required insurers that cover prescription drugs to provide coverage for contraceptive drugs and devices (Guttmacher Institute, 2011b). In addition, following recommendations from the National Academy of Sciences, the Obama administration required private health insurance plans written after August 1, 2012, to cover all FDA-approved contraceptives for women without co-payments. Despite the fact that 71% of U.S. voters support having health plans cover prescription birth control at no cost, conservative Republican politicians and leaders of the Catholic Church quickly advocated the elimination of the required coverage (Condon, 2012; Jervis, 2012; Pear, 2012).

Objections to contraception often stem from religious beliefs, and a few individuals and couples do not use a birth control device because of their religion. Fully 88% of voters in the United States support women's access to contraception, and most contemporary religious groups approve of and even favor the use of birth control (National

Campaign to Prevent Teen and Unplanned Pregnancy, 2011). Despite the fact that 98% of Catholic women in the United States have used a contraceptive method, the official doctrine of the Church continues to maintain that all birth control methods other than abstinence and methods based on the menstrual cycle are immoral (Jones & Dreweke, 2011). Many far-right Christians, self-described as "pro-life," also oppose contraceptive use, explained further in the Sex and Politics box, "The Power of Pro-Life Anti-Contraception Politics."

Contraception as a Global Issue

Worldwide contraceptive use has increased dramatically in the last several decades: An estimated 63% of partnered women of reproductive age practice contraception. Unfortunately, the use of modern contraceptives by the poorest of the world's poor in developing countries remains low. For example, only 6% of married women in Nigeria, compared to more than 70% in the United States and China, use birth control. About 215 million women across the globe are not using effective contraception (Reading, 2012). Tragically, millions of women and couples around the world are unable to exercise their right to decide freely and responsibly whether and when to have children. Each year in sub-Saharan Africa, South Central Asia, and Southeast Asia, 49 million married and unmarried women have unintended pregnancies (Darroch et al., 2011). Further, in these countries, a woman's chance of dying from complications of pregnancy, childbirth, and abortion averages 1 in 65. Africa's poorest nation, Sierra Leone, has the worst rate: 1 in 8 mothers there dies in childbirth. In contrast, women in the United States have a 1 in 4,800 chance of suffering the same fate (Anghelescu, 2008b).

For many years, the United States has contributed less of its gross national income than European countries to help fund international contraceptive and reproductive health services (Barot, 2009). However, following President Obama's election in 2008, his administration expanded funding and the scope of services supported by the United States by 40% from the level a year earlier at the end of the Bush administration (Cohen, 2010). Services expanded to include comprehensive contraceptive and sex education instead of abstinence-only programs, including a crucial shift to a broader view encompassing the impact of poverty, the rights of individuals, and gender equality, with an emphasis on the interaction between these issues (Fritz & Speroff, 2010).

Making contraceptives available to the men and women throughout the world who desire to use them will enhance the quality of their lives and help alleviate overpopulation. At the end of the 20th century, worldwide population stood at 6.5 billion, compared with less than half that number—2.3 billion—in 1950. The United Nations projects an increase to 8.9 billion by 2050. Of that growth, 95% is expected to occur in poorer, developing countries whose populations already exceed the availability of bare necessities: housing, food, and fuel. When impoverished families have many children, they cannot secure adequate food, health care, and education for each child. Moreover, overpopulation (and overconsumption of the world's resources by developed countries) poses a dire threat to the earth's environment. An essential factor in controlling population levels is to expand women's access to education and economic opportunity (Douglas, 2006). Throughout the world, women with higher levels of education have fewer children and are more likely to use contraception (Saleem & Pasha, 2008).

Critical Thinking Question

What role, if any, did religion play in your parents' contraceptive use? In your birth control decisions?

Critical Thinking Question

How are the limits to contraception access gained by pro-life religious groups compatible or incompatible with freedom of religion?

Nirmala Palsamy was named Heroine of the Planet in honor of her work to educate women about family planning and birth control.

Although the vast majority of U.S. citizens have a favorable view of modern birth control methods, much of the pro-life religious right opposes all contraceptive methods. Anti-contraception religious groups do not see contraceptives as a means of preventing abortion. Rather, they believe that birth control itself is abortion or a gateway to abortion. "Abortion will never end as long as society accepts the use of contraception" (American Life League, 2011a, p. 1). Far-right politicians and groups have attempted to establish "personhood" amendments in the state constitutions of Colorado and Mississippi. These amendments define a "person" as every human being from the moment of fertilization. Under such amendments it could be possible to make some contraceptives illegal (Khan, 2011; Sheppard, 2011).

False claims about how methods work appear to be a thin veneer on pro-lifers' overall opposition to birth control. Even methods like condoms, spermicides, and diaphragms that prevent the egg and sperm from reaching one another are believed to offend God because they prevent the conception of a human being: "[A]ny act of sexual intercourse must occur within marriage and be open to . . . procreative purposes" (American Life League, 2004, p. 3). In spite of the enormous personal and public health benefits of condoms, anti-contraception abstinence-only groups—including Pro-Life America, United for Life, Physicians for Life, American Life League, and the Vatican—have been engaged in a well-financed anti-contraception campaign. Many individuals and groups who oppose contraceptive use embrace the traditional role of women staying at home and raising children as an ideal. Therefore, they view access to contraception, with its potential to help women expand their roles beyond obligatory reproduction into traditional male realms of work and politics, as a threat that they must combat (Quindlen, 2005; Scheidler, 2006).

The political influence of anti-contraception groups increased during the administration of George W. Bush. Bush

J.P. Moczulski/Reuters/CORBIS

UCLA's Fowler Museum exhibit, "Dress Up Against AIDS," hoped to destigmatize condoms and inspire their use to prevent AIDS. It featured 14 garments designed by Brazilian artist Adriana Bertini, made entirely of condoms rejected by industry quality tests.

appointed anti-birth control individuals to key reproductive health, judicial, and scientific positions in the government, and in attempting to achieve the goals of his far-right supporters, his administration implemented many restrictive policies and laws concerning reproductive health (Tummino, 2006). For example, anti-contraception forces succeeded in reducing federal and state funding for contraceptive services (Stevens, 2008). By 2006, funding for community clinics that provide free or affordable birth control had declined significantly, leaving several million low-income women without access to contraception, in spite of the fact that 73% of Americans believe that access to birth control should not be limited by inability to pay for it (Harris Poll, 2006).

During the recent economic downturn, federally funded family planning and Planned Parenthood clinics have experienced an increased demand for services due to the increase in uninsured clients and a decrease in clients who are able to pay the full fee (National Campaign, 2011). Beginning in 2009, funding for public family planning services increased under the Obama administration as part of its "abortion reduction" strategy (Gold et al., 2009). Increased federal funding for contraceptive services did decrease rates of unplanned pregnancies (Kost et al., 2012). However, since then antichoice activists and politicians have attempted to block federal funding for contraceptive services. This effort failed on the federal level, but several state legislatures passed laws that severely limited or completely eliminated funding for family planning and Planned Parenthood clinics, which has resulted in increased rates of unintended pregnancies (Ertelt, 2011; Gibbons, 2011; Kost et al., 2012; Simon, 2012). The sex-negative motivation behind these kinds of activism was expressed by Rick Santorum during his bid to become the 2012 Republican presidential candidate (Bettelheim, 2012; Volsky, 2011). He pledged to repeal all federal funding for contraception, claiming that birth control devalues sexual union: "It's a license to do things in a sexual realm that is counter to how things are supposed to be" (Begala, 2012).

Sharing Responsibility and Choosing a Birth Control Method

Each birth control method has its advantages and disadvantages. An individual or a couple might find that one method suits a certain situation best (Gordon & Pitts, 2012). Sharing the responsibility enhances a particular method's use.

It Takes Two

Research shows that more couples share contraceptive decision making now than in the past (Grady et al., 2000). Sharing the responsibility of contraception can enhance a relationship and can be a good way to initiate discussing personal and sexual topics. Couples who do talk openly about sex and birth control are more likely to use contraception (Durex, 2008; Manlove et al., 2007). Failing to talk about birth control can cause women to resent men for putting the entire responsibility on them. Furthermore, it is foolish for a man to assume that a woman has "taken care of herself." As one male student asked,

> If you have sex with a girl and she tells you she's on the pill, how do you know if she's telling the truth? (Authors' files)

Many women do not regularly practice birth control, and some use methods inconsistently or incorrectly (Wilson & Koo, 2008). Not using contraception can negatively affect both partners' sexual experience and general feelings of well-being, and dealing with an unwanted pregnancy is difficult. It is in the best interests of both partners to be actively involved in choosing and using contraception (Montgomery et al., 2008).

The first step in sharing contraceptive responsibility may be for one partner to ask the other about birth control before having intercourse for the first time. Both male and female college students need to develop skills to discuss contraception. Women need to become effective in obtaining contraceptives, and men need to learn to be assertive about refusing to engage in intercourse without effective contraception. Openness to using condoms or to engaging in noncoital sexual activities, whether as the contraceptive method of choice or as a backup or temporary method, is another way for partners to share responsibility for birth control.

Choosing a Birth Control Method

Many forms of birth control are available to couples. However, an ideal method—one that is 100% effective, completely safe, with no side effects, reversible, separate from sexual activity, inexpensive, easy to obtain, usable by either sex, and not dependent on the user's memory—is unavailable now and in the foreseeable future. Each current method has advantages and disadvantages with regard to effectiveness, side effects, cost, and convenience (as summarized in ■ Tables 10.1 and 10.2). It is a good idea to be familiar with the various methods available because most people will use several of them during their active sex lives. In addition, a woman who is satisfied with her contraceptive method is more likely to use it consistently and, hence, improve its effectiveness (Frost & Darroch, 2008).

Would you be more careful if it was you that got pregnant?

See your pharmacist for free information on family planning, venereal disease and other communicable diseases.

For the Clinic nearest you call your local Health Department or (800) 952-5250

Sponsored by PPS Pharmacists Planning Service, Inc in conjunction with La Clinica De La Raza, Oakland, California

Photography by DALE ALISON BARON

© PPSI 1986

■ TABLE 10.1 Factors to Consider When Choosing a Birth Control Method

Method	Cost per Year for 100 Occurrences of Intercourse	Advantages	Disadvantages
Outercourse	0	No medical side effects; helps develop non-intercourse sexual intimacy.	Risk of unplanned intercourse; no protection from STIs.
Hormone-based methods			
Estrogen-progestin pills, including Seasonale	$384–$516 ($32–$43 per cycle)	Very effective. No interruption of sexual experience. Reduces PMS and premenstrual dysphoric disorder, menstrual cramps, and flow. Improves acne. May reduce migraine headaches associated with menstrual cycle fluctuations. Reduced risk of ovarian, endometrial, and colon cancer. No increased risk of stroke in healthy, non-smoking women under age 35.	No protection from STIs. Slightly increased risk of blood clot, especially in first 2 years of use. Increased risk of cervical cancer. May increase migraine headaches. May suppress some degree of normal bone mineral development when used during adolescence. Possible side effects of nausea, fluid retention, irregular bleeding, decreased sexual interest.
Progestin-only pills	$384–$456 ($32–$38 per cycle)	Very effective. No interruption of sexual experience. No estrogen-related side effects. Can be used during breast-feeding.	No protection from STIs. Breakthrough bleeding. May worsen acne. Must be taken same time each day to be effective.
Vaginal ring (NuvaRing)	$580	Do not have to remember to take daily pill. Consistent, low-dose release of hormone. No interruption of sexual experience.	No protection from STIs. Increased vaginal discharge. Expulsion of ring. Not effective for women over 198 pounds.
Skin patch (Ortho Evra)	$580	Same as vaginal ring.	Higher incidence of blood clots than with pill or ring. Slightly higher breakthrough bleeding than with oral contraceptives. Skin irritation. No protection from STIs.
Depo-Provera injection	$132–$300 for 4 injections each year	Very effective. No interruption of sexual experience. Do not have to remember to take on daily basis. No estrogen-related side effects. Good choice during breast-feeding.	No protection from STIs. Breakthrough bleeding. Weight gain. Headaches. Mood change. Clinic visit and injection every 3 months.
Lunelle	$420 for 12 injections per year	Same as for Depo-Provera. May have estrogen-related side effects. No breakthrough bleeding.	Same as for Depo-Provera, but clinic visit and injection required monthly.
Implanon	$130–$270 (initial cost $400–$800, but lasts for 3 years)	Offers longer protection than any other hormonal contraceptive. Highly effective. No need to remember to use daily or monthly method. No estrogen-related side effects. No increased cardiovascular risks.	No protection from STIs. May cause amenorrhea, irregular bleeding, spotting, and headaches. Risks of progestin-related side effects.
Progestin IUD			
Mirena	$35–$100 per each of 5 years (initial cost $175–$500)	Very effective. No interruption of sexual activity. Don't have to remember to use. Can be used during breast-feeding.	No protection from STIs. Increased risk of pelvic inflammatory disease for women with multiple partners. Cramps. May be expelled. Rare incidence of perforating the uterine wall.
Barrier and spermicide methods			
Male condoms	$100 ($1.00 each)	Some protection from STIs. Available without a prescription.	Interruption of sexual experience. Reduces sensation.
Female condoms	$400 ($4.00 each); 2nd generation $200 ($2.00 each)	Same as male condoms.	Same as male condoms. Higher cost than male condoms. Difficulty inserting.
Vaginal spermicides	$85 (85¢ per application)	No prescription necessary.	Interruption of sexual experience. Skin irritation. No protection from STIs. Not effective enough to be used without a condom.

■ **TABLE 10.1 Factors to Consider When Choosing a Birth Control Method (*continued*)**

Method	Cost per Year for 100 Occurrences of Intercourse	Advantages	Disadvantages
Cervical barrier methods with spermicide			
Diaphragm	$15–$75 ($7.50–$38.00 if used for 2 years); $85 for spermicide	Some protection from bacterial STIs. Can be put in before sexual experience. No side effects. Decreased incidence of cervical cancer.	Limited protection from STIs. Increased urinary tract infections. Requires practice to use correctly. Can cause vaginal or cervical irritation.
Cervical cap	Same as diaphragm	Same as diaphragm. No increase in urinary tract infections.	Same as diaphragm.
Sponge	$400 ($4 each)	Same as diaphragm. No increase in urinary tract infections.	Same as diaphragm.
FemCap	$65 ($32.50 if used for 2 years); $85 for spermicide	Same as diaphragm. Does not need to be fitted by health-care practitioner. Has a loop to assist removal.	Same as diaphragm.
Lea's Shield	$145 ($60 each, replaced every year); $85 for spermicide	Same as diaphragm. Does not need to be fitted by health-care practitioner. Has a loop to assist removal.	Same as diaphragm.
Nonhormonal IUD			
Copper-T (ParaGard)	$15–$42 per each of 12 years; initial cost $175–$500	Can be kept for 12 years. Don't have to remember to use. Also used for emergency contraception. Can be used during breast-feeding.	No protection from STIs. Increased menstrual flow and cramps. May be expelled. Increased risk of pelvic inflammatory disease for women with multiple partners. Rare incidence of perforating the uterine wall.
Sterilization			
Tubal sterilization	$1,500 – $6,000	Highly effective and permanent. Reduces risk of ovarian cancer. Transcervical sterilization is safest and least expensive of female sterilization procedures.	No protection from STIs. Not easy to reverse for fertility. Discomfort after procedure.
Vasectomy	$350–$1,000	Easier procedure, less expensive, and lower failure rate than female sterilization.	No protection from STIs. Not easy to reverse for fertility. Discomfort after procedure.
Fertility awareness			
Standard days method	0	Most effective of fertility awareness methods. Acceptable to Catholic Church.	No protection from STIs. Uncertainty of safe times. Periods of abstinence from intercourse or use of other methods. Requires careful observation and tracking.
Rhythm, calendar, basal temperature, and cervical mucus methods	0	Acceptable to Catholic Church. No medical side effects.	No protection from STIs. Uncertainty of safe times. Periods of abstinence from intercourse or use of other methods.
Withdrawal	0	No medical side effects.	No protection from STIs. Interruption of intercourse.
No method	0	Acceptable only if pregnancy desired.	No protection from STIs.

SOURCES: Berenson et al. (2008), Berenson & Rahman (2009), Blumenthal et al. (2008), Halbreich et al. (2012), Hannaford et al. (2007), International Collaboration of Epidemiological Studies of Cervical Cancer (2007), Jensen et al. (2008), Lurie et al. (2008), Mansour (2008), Merki-Feld et al. (2008), Nanda et al. (2011), Panzer et al. (2006), Pikkarainen et al. (2008), Pitts & Emans (2008), Planned Parenthood Federation of America (2008), and Speroff & Fritz (2005).

■TABLE 10.2 Effectiveness of Various Birth Control Methods

Method	Failure Rate[a] if Used Correctly and Consistently	Typical Number[a] Who Become Pregnant Accidentally
Outercourse	0	0
Hormone-based methods		
Estrogen-progestin pills, including Seasonale	0.3	8
Progestin-only pills	0.5	3
Vaginal ring (NuvaRing)	0.3	8
Skin patch (Ortho Evra)	0.3	8
Depo-Provera injection	0.3	0.7
Lunelle	0.05	0.2
Implanon	0.05	0.1
Progestin IUD	0.1	0.1
Mirena	0.5	0.1
Barrier and spermicide methods		
Male condoms	2	17.4
Female condoms	5	27
Vaginal spermicides	18	29
Cervical barrier methods with spermicide		
Diaphragm with spermicide	6	16
Cervical cap		
Woman has been pregnant	20	40
Woman has never been pregnant	9	20
Sponge		
Woman has been pregnant	26	32
Woman has never been pregnant	9	16
FemCap	4	15
Lea's Shield	6	18
Nonhormonal IUD		
ParaGard	0.5	0.8
Sterilization		
Tubal sterilization	0.5	0.7
Vasectomy	0.1	0.2
Fertility awareness		
Standard days method	5	12
Rhythm, calendar, basal temperature, and cervical mucus methods	9	20
Withdrawal	4	27
No method	85	85

[a]Number of women out of 100 who become pregnant by the end of the first year of using a particular method.

SOURCES: Graesslin & Korver (2008), Guttmacher Institute (2008a), Hutti (2003), Planned Parenthood Federation of America (2008), and Speroff & Fritz (2005).

Effectiveness

failure rate

The number of women out of 100 who become pregnant by the end of 1 year of using a particular contraceptive.

Contraceptive effectiveness is best evaluated by looking at the **failure rate** (the number of women out of 100 who become pregnant by the end of the first year of using a particular method). Table 10.2 shows the failure rate when contraceptive methods are used correctly and consistently; it also shows the rate of accidental pregnancies resulting from improper or inconsistent use. The most important variable of method effectiveness is human error. Ignorance of the correct use of a method, negative beliefs about using a method, lack of partner involvement, forgetfulness, or deciding that "this one time won't matter" all greatly reduce effectiveness and increase the chances of pregnancy. Some individuals eroticize or romanticize the risk of pregnancy (Higgins et al., 2008). In addition, people who feel guilty about sex may be less likely to use contraception effectively. Men and women who are uncomfortable with their sexuality are likely to take a passive role in contraceptive decision making, leaving themselves vulnerable to whatever their partners do, or do not do, about birth control. A woman may also be concerned about whether her partner sees her as a "nice girl" or as "easy." A simple way to appear as a "nice girl" is to be unprepared with birth control (Angier, 1999). Unfortunately, that's also a simple way to have an unwanted pregnancy or contract an unwanted STI.

Using Backup Methods to Increase Contraceptive Effectiveness

About half of all unintended pregnancies occur among women using contraceptives (Frost & Darroch, 2008). Unmarried women younger than 30 years old are most likely to have a contraceptive failure, and married women older than 30 are least likely to do so. In addition, low-income women experience greater failure rates than more-affluent women, possibly because of limited availability of health care (Fu et al., 1999).

Under various circumstances, a couple may need or want to use **backup methods**—that is, more than one method of contraception used simultaneously. Condoms, contraceptive foam, and the diaphragm are possible backup methods that can be combined in many ways with other birth control methods for extra contraceptive protection (Peipert et al., 2011). Circumstances in which a couple might use a backup method include the following:

backup methods
Contraceptive methods used simultaneously with another method to support it.

- During the first cycle of the pill.
- For the remainder of the cycle, after forgetting to take two or more birth control pills or after several days of diarrhea or vomiting while on the pill.
- The first month after changing to a new brand of pills.
- When taking medications, such as antibiotics, that reduce the effectiveness of the pill.
- During the initial 1 to 3 months after IUD insertion.
- When first learning to use a new method of birth control.
- When the couple wants to increase the effectiveness of contraception (for instance, using foam and a condom together offers effective protection).

Which Contraceptive Method Is Right for You?

Effectiveness is not the only important factor in choosing a method of birth control. Many additional factors—including cost, ease of use, and potential side effects—influence individuals' and couples' decisions about whether to use or to continue a particular birth control method (Westhoff et al., 2007). Table 10.1 summarizes some of the most important factors: comparative expenses, advantages versus disadvantages, and possible side effects of the most commonly used methods. The costs in the table are estimates because the price of contraceptives can vary greatly; prices at Planned Parenthood and campus and government health clinics can be considerably lower than standard pharmacy prices. The IUD is the lowest-cost reversible method if a woman continues to use it for the allowed time period (Trussell et al., 2009). Coverage of contraception by health insurance companies also helps reduce costs, and some states have required that prescription benefits include birth control. Further prescription benefits became available nationwide in August 2012. Regulations established by the Obama administration required private health insurance plans written after that date to cover all FDA-approved contraceptives for women without co-payments.

Another means of contraceptive backup is to be prepared and have emergency contraception on hand— pills taken after unprotected sex.

Answer yes or no to each statement as it applies to you and, if appropriate, your partner.

1. You have high blood pressure or cardiovascular disease.
2. You smoke cigarettes.
3. You have a new sexual partner.
4. An unwanted pregnancy would be devastating to you.
5. You have a good memory.
6. You or your partner has multiple sexual partners.
7. You prefer a method with little or no bother.
8. You have heavy, crampy periods.
9. You need protection against sexually transmitted infections.
10. You are concerned about endometrial and ovarian cancer.
11. You are forgetful.
12. You need a method right away.
13. You are comfortable touching your genitals and your partner's.
14. You have a cooperative partner.
15. You like a little extra vaginal lubrication.
16. You have sex at unpredictable times and places.
17. You are in a monogamous relationship and have at least one child.

Scoring

Recommendations are based on *yes* answers to the following numbered statements:

- Combination pill and Lunelle: 4, 5, 6, 8, 16
- Progestin-only pill: 1, 2, 5, 7, 16
- Condoms: 1, 2, 3, 6, 9, 12, 13, 14
- Depo-Provera: 1, 2, 4, 7, 11, 16
- Cervical barrier methods: 1, 2, 13, 14
- IUD: 1, 2, 7, 11, 13, 16, 17
- Spermicides and the sponge: 1, 2, 12, 13, 14, 15

Beyond the variables listed in Table 10.1, the decision about which birth control method to use must take into account one more important factor: the individuals who will be using it (Ranjit et al., 2001). The statements presented in the Your Sexual Health box titled "Which Contraceptive Method Is Best for You?" are designed to help you take into account your own concerns, circumstances, physical condition, and personal qualities as you make this very individual decision. We discuss a number of commonly used contraceptive methods in the paragraphs that follow, and this more specific information may help you make your choice.

"Outercourse"

outercourse
Noncoital forms of sexual intimacy.

This important method deserves special mention because it involves the decision to be sexual without engaging in penile–vaginal intercourse. Noncoital forms of sexual intimacy, which have been called **outercourse**, can be a viable form of birth control. Outercourse includes all avenues of sexual intimacy other than penile–vaginal intercourse, including kissing, touching, mutual masturbation, and oral and anal sex. The voluntary avoidance of coitus offers effective protection from pregnancy, provided that the male does not ejaculate near the vaginal opening. Outercourse can be used as a primary or temporary means of preventing pregnancy, and it can also be used when it is advisable not to have intercourse for other reasons—for example, following childbirth or abortion or during a herpes outbreak. This method has no undesirable contraceptive side effects. However, it does not eliminate the chances of spreading sexually transmitted infections, especially if it involves oral or anal sex.

Hormone-Based Contraceptives

In this section, we look at the most popular hormone-based birth control methods: oral contraceptives, the vaginal ring, the transdermal patch, injected contraception, and contraceptive implant.

Oral Contraceptives

Oral contraceptives have evolved during 40 years of developing variations in the chemical structure and dosage of hormones, resulting in a wide range of choices. Oral contraceptives are the most commonly used reversible method of birth control by women younger than 35 in the United States, and 80 % of women have used the pill during their lifetime (Dempsey et al., 2011; Guttmacher Institute, 2008a). More than 100 million women worldwide use the pill (Blackburn et al., 2000). Four basic types of oral contraceptives are currently on the market: the constant-dose combination pill, the triphasic pill, the extended-cycle pill, and the progestin-only pill.

Placebo-controlled studies of oral contraceptives have found no significant difference in side effects such as headache, nausea, breast pain, or weight gain. Bleeding irregularity was correlated with the low-estrogen dose pills (Grimes & Schultz, 2011). Taking the pill does not interfere with subsequent ability to become pregnant (Mansour et al., 2011). For most women who use them, oral contraceptives improve overall health (Speroff & Fritz, 2005). However, for about 16% of women, oral contraceptive use is not advisable (Shortridge & Miller, 2007): This percentage includes women with a history of blood clots, strokes, circulation problems, heart problems, jaundice, cancer of the breast or uterus, and undiagnosed genital bleeding. In addition, a woman who has a liver disease or who suspects or knows that she is pregnant should not take the pill. ● Women who smoke cigarettes or have migraine headaches, depression, high blood pressure, epilepsy, diabetes or prediabetes symptoms, asthma, or varicose veins should weigh the potential risks most carefully and use the pill only under close medical supervision. ■ Table 10.3 describes rare but serious side effects of the birth control pill.

The Pill: Four Basic Types

The **constant-dose combination pill** has been available since the early 1960s and is the most commonly used oral contraceptive in the United States. It contains two hormones, synthetic estrogen and progestin (a progesterone-like substance). The dosage of these hormones remains constant throughout the menstrual cycle. There are more than 32 different varieties of combination pills, and each variety contains various amounts and ratios of the two hormones. The amount of estrogen in pills has decreased from as much as 175 micrograms in 1960 to an average of 25 micrograms (Ritter, 2003).

constant-dose combination pill
Birth control pill that contains a constant daily dose of estrogen.

At a Glance

■ TABLE 10.3 Remember "ACHES" for the Pill: Symptoms of Possible Serious Problems With the Birth Control Pill

Initial	Symptoms	Possible Problem
A	Abdominal pain (severe)	Gallbladder disease, liver tumor, or blood clot*
C	Chest pain (severe) or shortness of breath	Blood clot in lungs or heart attack
H	Headaches (severe)	Stroke, high blood pressure, or migraine headache
E	Eye problems: blurred vision, flashing lights, or blindness	Stroke, high blood pressure, or temporary vascular problems at many possible sites
S	Severe leg pain (calf or thigh)	Blood clot in legs

*The risk of nonfatal blood clots among users of birth control pills containing drospireone is greater than that of pills containing levonorgestrel (FDA, 2011).

SOURCE: Adapted from Hatcher & Guillebaud (1998).

triphasic pill
Birth control pill that varies the dosages of estrogen and progestin during the menstrual cycle.

Seasonale
Birth control pill that reduces menstrual periods to four times a year.

progestin-only pill
Contraceptive pill that contains a small dose of progestin and no estrogen.

The **triphasic pill**, which has been on the market since 1984, is another type of oral contraceptive. Unlike the constant-dose combination pill, the triphasic pill provides fluctuations of estrogen and progestin levels during the menstrual cycle. The triphasic pill is designed to reduce the total hormone dosage and any side effects while maintaining contraceptive effectiveness.

Another constant-dose pill on the market is called an *extended-cycle* contraceptive because it is taken continuously for 3 months without placebo pills. The only brand on the market, **Seasonale**, has a lower dose of estrogen and progestin than most other constant-dose or triphasic pills. Seasonale reduces the number of menstrual periods to 4 instead of 13 per year, which significantly benefits women who have uncomfortable menstrual symptoms during the placebo phase of using the combination pill (Kripke, 2006).

The **progestin-only pill**, which has been on the market since 1973, contains only 0.35 milligrams of progestin—about one third the amount in an average-strength combination pill. Like the combination pill, the progestin-only pill has a constant-dose formula. The progestin-only pill contains no estrogen and is a good option for women who prefer or require a non-estrogen pill (Burkett & Hewitt, 2005).

How Oral Contraceptives Work

The estrogen in the combination, triphasic, and extended-release pills prevents conception primarily by inhibiting ovulation. The progestin in these pills provides secondary contraceptive protection by thickening and chemically altering the cervical mucus so that the passage of sperm into the uterus is hampered. Progestin also causes changes in the lining of the uterus, making it less receptive to implantation by a fertilized egg (Larimore & Stanford, 2000). In addition, progestin can inhibit ovulation. The progestin-only pill works somewhat differently. Most women who take the progestin-only pill probably continue to ovulate at least occasionally. The primary effect of this pill is to alter the cervical mucus to a thick and tacky consistency that effectively blocks sperm from entering the uterus. As with the combination pill, secondary contraceptive effects are provided by alterations in the uterine lining that make it unreceptive to implantation.

How to Use Oral Contraceptives

Several ways exist to begin taking oral contraceptives; a woman who does so should carefully follow the instructions of her health-care practitioner. Unlike other oral contraceptives that are taken in 28-day cycles, Seasonale is taken daily for 3 months, followed by 7 days of inactive tablets before taking it for another 3 months. Some medications reduce the effectiveness of oral contraceptives; these are listed in ■ Table 10.4.

Forgetting to take one or more pills sharply reduces the effectiveness of oral contraceptives, as does taking the pill at a different time each day. Missing one or more pills can lower hormone levels and allow ovulation to occur. A significant number of women do forget to take the pill each day. However, women underestimate how often they forget their pills. A study that relied on electronic tracking of the time and date women took pills from the container, rather than on user self-report, found that up to 50% of users missed three or more pills per cycle, greatly reducing the contraceptive effectiveness of the method (Potter et al., 1996). To help prevent missing pills, a woman can use a pill case with a built-in clock and alarm to alert her at the same time each day if she has not taken her pill.

If you are using oral contraceptives and you miss a pill, you should take the missed pill as soon as you remember and then take your next pill at the regular time. If you forget more than one pill, it is best to consult your health-care practitioner. You should also use a backup method, such as contraceptive foam or condoms, for the remainder of your cycle. ●

SEXUALHEALTH

■ **TABLE 10.4** Medications That Reduce Oral Contraceptive Effectiveness

■ **TABLE 10.4** Medications That Reduce Oral Contraceptive Effectiveness

Some medications can reduce the effectiveness of birth control pills. Tell every physician who gives you medication that you are taking oral contraceptives. Use a backup method, such as foam or condoms, when you use any of the following medications or herbal remedies.	
Barbiturates	Dilantin
Ampicillin	Rifampin (for tuberculosis)
Tetracycline	Phenylbutazone (for arthritis)
Tegretol	St. John's Wort

SOURCES: Markowitz et al. (2003) and Zlidar (2000).

Deciding to discontinue using the pill requires thoughtful planning to prevent pregnancy. About 61% of unintended pregnancies are attributable to women discontinuing the pill and adopting a less effective method or using no method (Dempsey et al., 2011).

The Vaginal Ring and the Transdermal Patch

NuvaRing and Ortho Evra are two hormone-based contraceptive methods that do not require taking a pill each day. Both synthetic estrogen and progestin are embedded in either a 2-inch-diameter soft and transparent vaginal ring (NuvaRing) or a beige matchbook-size transdermal patch (Ortho Evra), as shown in ▮ Figure 10.1.

How the Ring and Patch Work

Both NuvaRing and Ortho Evra release the hormones embedded in them through the vaginal lining or skin into the bloodstream. The hormones then work in the same way as the pill to prevent pregnancy. Women using the ring report fewer side effects than do oral contraceptive users (Kerns & Darney, 2011).

How to Use the Ring and Patch

The ring is inserted into the vagina between day 1 and day 5 of a menstrual period. It is worn inside the vagina for 3 weeks, then removed for 1 week and replaced with a new ring. The ring can remain in place during intercourse, or it can be removed for up to 3 hours at a time without reducing its contraceptive effectiveness (Long, 2002).

In using the patch, a woman chooses a specific day of the week after a menstrual period starts and identifies that day as "patch change day." She replaces the old patch with a new patch on that same day each week for 3 weeks, followed by a patch-free 7-day interval. The patch can be placed on the buttock, abdomen, upper outer arm, or upper torso.

© J. Darin Derstine

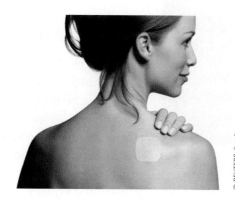

© REUTERS /Landov

▮ **Figure 10.1** The ring, *left,* and patch, *right,* eliminate the need to remember a birth control pill each day.

Injected Contraceptives

Depo-Provera is an injectable hormone-based contraceptive. It was approved by the U.S. Food and Drug Administration (FDA) in 1992. Lunelle, another injected contraceptive, was approved in 2000.

How Injected Contraceptives Work

The active ingredient in Depo-Provera is progestin, which inhibits the secretion of gonadotropins and prevents follicular maturation and ovulation. These actions also cause the endometrial lining of the uterus to thin, preventing implantation of a fertilized egg. Progestin also alters the cervical mucus. Lunelle combines progestin and estrogen, as do combination pills.

How to Use Injected Contraceptives

A health-care provider gives the Depo-Provera shot once every 12 weeks, ideally within 5 days of the beginning of menstruation. It usually takes 10 months after stopping Depo-Provera for a woman to get pregnant (Galewitz, 2000). Lunelle requires a monthly injection, and fertility returns immediately after stopping injections.

Contraceptive Implant

Implanon is a matchstick-size slender rod 1½ inches long. It is inserted under the skin of the upper arm and releases contraceptive hormones. Implanon had been sold in more than 30 countries since 1998 before it was approved by the FDA in 2006 for use in the United States (Bridges, 2006). In developing countries, long-acting methods play a critical role in providing effective contraception, and efforts to reduce its cost and expand awareness of the method are essential for more widespread use (Neukom et al., 2011; Tumlinson et al., 2011).

How the Implant Works

Implanon releases a slow, steady dose of progestin, and it prevents pregnancy in the same ways as the progestin-only minipill. It may not be effective for women more than 30% heavier than their medically ideal weight.

How to Use the Implant

A medical practitioner inserts the rod in a quick surgical procedure that requires only a local anesthetic. It is effective for up to 3 years, and fertility usually returns quickly after removal of the device (Graesslin & Korver, 2008).

Couples can include the use of barrier contraceptives in their sex play.

3660 Group Inc./CMSP

Barrier and Spermicide Methods

Hormone-based methods cause changes in a woman's body that inhibit ovulation and implantation. Another group of contraceptive devices works in a different way—by preventing sperm from reaching an ovum. In this section, we look at condoms and four cervical barrier devices. In addition, we include vaginal spermicides in this section because their effect is also to prevent sperm from reaching an egg. Other than the condom, barrier methods do not protect against STIs, including AIDS and genital warts (Winer et al., 2006).

Couples who use barrier methods can incorporate their use into sex play instead of viewing them as an "interruption." Either partner—or both—can put a condom on or insert a female condom, cervical barrier device, or spermicide. Using a barrier method can be an extension of erotic touching.

Condoms

A **condom** is a sheath that fits over the erect penis. It has a long history. An illustration of a man wearing a condom was painted on a wall in a cave in France 12,000 to 15,000 years ago (Planned Parenthood Federation of America, 2002). In 1564 an Italian anatomist, Fallopius, described a penile sheath made of linen. Mass production of inexpensive modern condoms began after the development of vulcanized rubber in the 1840s.

Condoms, also called prophylactics and rubbers, are the only temporary method of birth control available for men and the only form of contraception that effectively reduces transmission of sexually transmitted infections, including AIDS (Reece et al., 2010b). A study of 15-year-old students from 24 countries found that condoms were the most frequently used method of contraception (Godeau et al., 2008). In the United States, 80% of male and 69% of female sexually active adolescents reported using a condom at last penile–vaginal sex (Fortenberry et al., 2010). Significantly, teens who use condoms at their first sexual intercourse are more likely to continue their use and consequently have fewer sexually transmitted infections than are teens who do not use condoms at their sexual debut (Shafii et al., 2007). Condoms are used twice as often with casual sexual partners as with partners in established relationships (Reece et al., 2010b).

Condoms are made of thin surgical latex, polyurethane, or natural membrane (from sheep intestines). However, natural-membrane condoms contain small pores that can permit the passage of viruses associated with several STIs, including AIDS, genital herpes, and hepatitis. Some condoms have special features, such as being colored or flavored, having "ribs" to supposedly increase sensation, or incorporating a desensitizing agent on the inside to help delay ejaculation. Some condoms have a small nipple at the end, called a reservoir tip, and others have a contoured shape or textured surface. Most condoms come rolled up and wrapped in foil or plastic, and they are lubricated or nonlubricated (❚ Figure 10.2). Lubricated condoms are less likely to break than nonlubricated ones.

Condoms are available without prescription at pharmacies and grocery stores, from family planning clinics, by mail order, in vending machines, and in school-based condom programs. They have an average shelf life of about 5 years (not all packages are dated). Condoms should not be stored in hot places, such as the glove compartment of a car or a back pocket, because heat can cause the condom to deteriorate.

How the Condom Works

When a man uses a condom properly, both the ejaculate and the fluid from Cowper's gland secretions (sometimes called "precum" or "prejack" in slang) are contained in the tip. The condom thus serves as a mechanical barrier, effectively preventing any sperm from entering the vagina.

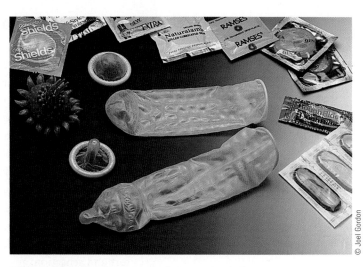

© Joel Gordon

❚ **Figure 10.2** Condoms come in many varieties.

Europics/Newscom

A new condom called Sensis has two pull tabs that make putting on a condom quicker and easier.

condom
A sheath that fits over the penis and is used for protection against unwanted pregnancy and sexually transmitted infections.

How to Use the Condom

Correct and consistent use of the condom is essential for its effectiveness, but studies of college students have found that user error is common. Putting a condom on after vaginal penetration but before ejaculation is a common error that increases the risk of pregnancy and STI transmission (Barclay, 2010). The Let's Talk About It box discusses the importance of condom use and provides some suggestions for communicating more effectively about their use.

Condoms are available in different sizes. A man may benefit from trying different sizes to find what fits him best, because poor fit increases the likelihood of the condom's breaking or slipping off (Hollander, 2008b). Most condoms are packaged rolled up. Correct use includes unrolling the condom over the erect penis before any contact between the penis and the vulva occurs. Sperm in the Cowper's gland secretions (the prejack) or in the ejaculate can travel from the labia into the vagina. For maximum comfort and sensation, an uncircumcised man can retract the foreskin before unrolling the condom over the penis (Bolus, 1994). When using a plain-end condom (without the reservoir tip), the end needs to be twisted before unrolling the condom over the penis, as shown in ❙ Figure 10.3. Doing this leaves some room at the end for the ejaculate and reduces the chances of the condom breaking. In the unusual case that a condom breaks or slips off during intercourse, contraceptive foam, cream, or jelly should be inserted into the vagina *immediately* (Walsh et al., 2004).

A condom breaks more easily without lubrication than with it, so if the condom is nonlubricated, put some saliva or water-based lubricant on the vulva and on the outside of the condom before inserting the penis into the vagina. Do *not* use oil-based lubricants, because they reduce the condom's integrity and increase the chances of breakage (Spruyt et al., 1998). See ■ Table 10.5 for a detailed list of safe and unsafe lubricants to use with condoms.

Because the penis begins to decrease in size and hardness soon after ejaculation, it is important to hold the condom at the base of the penis before withdrawing from the vagina. Otherwise the condom can slip off and spill semen inside the vagina. Condoms are best disposed of in the garbage rather than the toilet, because they can clog plumbing. ●

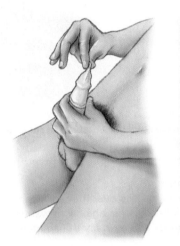

Courtesy of San Francisco AIDS Foundation

❙ **Figure 10.3** (a) The end of a plain-end condom needs to be twisted, leaving space at the tip, before it is unrolled over the penis. (b) A condom with a reservoir tip does not need to be twisted.

The Female Condom

The female condom (❙ Figure 10.4) is made of polyurethane or latex and was approved by the U.S. Food and Drug Administration in 1993 (Beksinska et al., 2011). It resembles a male condom but is worn internally by the woman. In 2009 the FDA approved the FC2 female condom, which is made of softer material for quieter use and is about one-third less expensive than the original female condom, and since then other female condoms have become available or are in development (Beksinska et al., 2011; Heavy, 2009). A flexible plastic ring at the closed end of the sheath fits loosely against the cervix, rather like a diaphragm (discussed in the following section). Another ring encircles the labial area. Although the female condom fits the contours of the vagina, the penis moves freely inside the sheath, which is coated with a silicone-based lubricant. Used correctly, female condoms can substantially reduce the risk of transmission of some STIs and are of particular benefit for women in countries with high HIV rates (Center for Health and Gender Equity, 2011).

The writers of a sex education book expressed their strong distaste for anyone who still whines about using a condom:

> If we hear any more whining about how condoms are annoying, uncomfortable deal breakers, we are going to *puke*. Could it be you've been using nonlubricated, inch-thick, five-cent prophylactics from a vending machine all your life? So condoms don't figure in your full-on, flesh-to-flesh fantasy world—we get it. We're also sure that oozing genital ulcers and child support payments don't pop up in that utopia either. (Taylor & Sharkey, 2003, pp. 182–183)

Women purchase 50% of condoms sold today. One study found that refusing to have sex unless a partner used a condom was the most common approach used by college women to encourage condom use (De Bro et al., 1994). These facts represent good condom sense because, along with unwanted pregnancy, women have much more to lose than men when a couple does not use a condom. A woman is much more likely to get an STI (including HIV/AIDS) from one act of intercourse than is a man, and bacterial STIs do much more damage to a woman's reproductive tract than to a man's and can eliminate her subsequent ability to have a baby.

The book *Before You Hit the Pillow, Talk* (Foley & Nechas, 1995) offers suggestions for communicating about condoms. Basically, be clear and assertive and do not get drawn into an argument. Deciding beforehand that you will not have intercourse without using a condom will give your position the strength it needs. Some examples of specific conversations follow.

Partner's Statement	Your Response
"I'm on the pill. You don't need to use a rubber."	"I'd like to use one anyway, then we'll be doubly protected."
"It doesn't feel as good with a condom."	"It will still feel better than nothing."
"It's not very romantic."	"Neither is pregnancy or disease."
"I wouldn't do anything to hurt you."	"Great. Let me help you put it on."
"I'd rather not have sex if we have to use a condom."	"Okay. What would you like to do instead?"

■ **TABLE 10.5 Which Lubricants Are Safe and Unsafe to Use With Condoms?**

Safe	Unsafe
Water-based or silicone lubricants	Aldara cream
Aqualube	Baby oil or cold creams
Astroglide	Bag Balm
Cornhuskers Lotion	Edible oils (e.g., vegetable, olive, peanut, corn, sunflower)
Water and saliva	Body lotions
Glycerin	Massage oils
All ID lubricants (except ID Cream)	Mineral oil
Aloe-9	Petroleum jelly
H-R Lubricating Jelly	Rubbing alcohol
K-Y Lubricating Jelly	Shortening
Prepair	Suntan oils and lotions
Probe	Whipped cream
ForPlay	Vaginal yeast infection creams and suppositories
Gynol II	
Wet (except Wet Oil)	
Silicone lubricant	
DeLube	
Vaginal spermicides	

SOURCE: Adapted from Hatcher (2003).

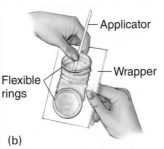

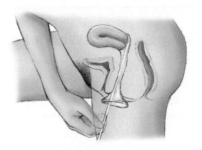

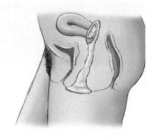

Applicator

Wrapper

Flexible rings

(b)

J. Darin Derstine

(a)

■ **Figure 10.4** (a) The female condom. (b) A female condom consists of two flexible polyurethane rings and a soft, loose-fitting polyurethane sheath.

Vaginal Spermicides

vaginal spermicides
Foam, cream, jelly, suppositories, and film that contain a chemical that kills sperm.

Several types of **vaginal spermicides** are available without a prescription: foam, suppositories, the sponge, creams and jellies, and contraceptive film (■ Figure 10.5). *Foam* is a white substance that resembles shaving cream. It comes in a pressurized can and has a plastic applicator. *Vaginal suppositories* have an oval shape, and the *sponge* is a

(a) Vaginal contraceptive foam

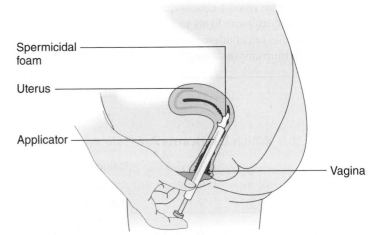

Spermicidal foam

Uterus

Applicator

Vagina

(b) An applicator filled with foam is inserted into the vagina, and the foam is deposited in the back of the vaginal canal

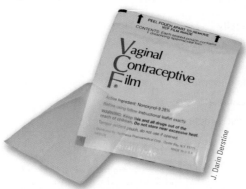

(c) Vaginal contraceptive film

(d) The contraceptive sponge

■ **Figure 10.5** Vaginal spermicides are available in pharmacies without a prescription.

doughnut-shaped spermicide-containing device that absorbs and subsequently kills sperm. *VCF*, a vaginal contraceptive film, is a paper-thin, 2-by-2-inch sheet that is laced with spermicide. It is packaged in a matchbook-like container holding 10 to 12 sheets.

How Spermicidal Methods Work

Foam, suppositories, the sponge, creams and jellies, and VCF all contain a *spermicide*, a chemical that kills sperm. When foam is inserted with the applicator, it rapidly covers the vaginal walls and the cervical os, or opening to the uterus (see Figure 10.5). Contraceptive vaginal suppositories take about 20 minutes to dissolve and cover the walls. One brand of suppository, Encare, effervesces and creates foam inside the vagina; other brands melt. Once VCF is inserted into the vagina, next to the cervix, it dissolves into a stay-in-place gel.

How to Use Vaginal Spermicides

Spermicides are less effective in preventing pregnancy than are most other methods, so they need to be used with condoms. Complete instructions for use come with each package of vaginal spermicide. For maximum protection, it is important to use the product as directed. Another application of spermicide is necessary before each additional act of intercourse. In contrast, the sponge is effective for repeated acts of intercourse and can be inserted up to 24 hours before intercourse. It is probably better to shower rather than take a bath after sex when using a spermicide, to prevent the spermicide from being rinsed out of the vagina.

Cervical Barrier Devices

The practice of covering the cervix to provide protection from pregnancy has existed for centuries. In 18th-century Europe, Casanova promoted the idea of using a squeezed-out lemon half to cover the cervix, and European women shaped beeswax to cover the cervix. In 1838 a German gynecologist took wax impressions of each patient's cervix to make custom caps out of rubber (Seaman & Seaman, 1978).

As shown in ▮ Figure 10.6, the diaphragm, cervical cap, FemCap, and Lea's Shield are four methods combining a physical barrier that covers the cervix with vaginal spermicide to protect the cervix from contact with viable sperm. These devices are dome shaped, with a rim around the open side. The diaphragm covers the upper vaginal wall from behind the cervix to underneath the pubic bone. The cervical cap fits over the cervix only. The FemCap and the Lea's Shield have rims that rest on the vaginal wall surrounding the cervix and have removal straps. Unlike the other devices, the Lea's Shield allows a one-way flow of fluid from the cervix to the vagina but prevents semen from contact with the cervix.

How to Use Cervical Barrier Devices

The diaphragm and cervical cap are individually fitted by a skilled health-care practitioner. The practitioner should also teach women how to insert it properly so that they are confident about using it on their own (Hollander, 2006). In contrast, the FemCap and Lea's Shield do not have to be fitted. However, unlike the case in several other countries, where they are available over the counter, they require a prescription in the United States. All barrier devices are used with spermicidal cream or jelly placed inside the dome of the cup and on the rim. Do *not* use oil-based lubricants with a diaphragm or cervical cap because these devices are made of latex and will deteriorate when used with oil-based lubricants. (The FemCap and Lea's Shield are made from silicone.)

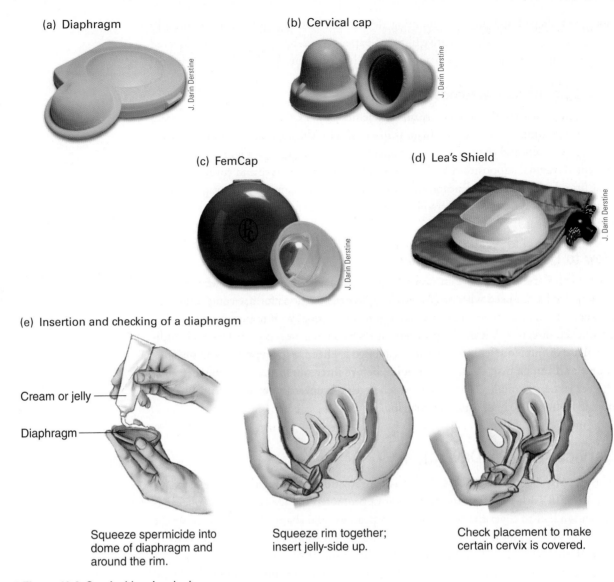

(a) Diaphragm

(b) Cervical cap

(c) FemCap

(d) Lea's Shield

(e) Insertion and checking of a diaphragm

Cream or jelly

Diaphragm

Squeeze spermicide into dome of diaphragm and around the rim.

Squeeze rim together; insert jelly-side up.

Check placement to make certain cervix is covered.

Figure 10.6 Cervical barrier devices.

To insert any of these barrier devices, squeeze the sides of the rim together with one hand, and use your other hand to open the lips of the vulva, as shown in Figure 10.6e. With the spermicide side up, push the device into the vagina. After you have inserted it, you or your partner need to feel inside the vagina to make sure the dome covers the cervix. Some women prefer to insert the dome ahead of time, in privacy, whereas others share the insertion with their partners.

All cervical barrier devices should remain in the vagina for at least 8 hours to provide time for the spermicide to kill sperm in the folds of the vagina. If intercourse occurs again before 8 hours elapse, leave the device in place and apply additional spermicide inside the vagina. Recommendations vary by method for the length of time before intercourse for insertion and after intercourse for removal:

	Hours Before Intercourse	Hours After Intercourse
Diaphragm	Up to 6	At least 8, no more than 24
Cervical cap	Up to 6	At least 8, no more than 24
FemCap	Up to 8	At least 8, no more than 48
Lea's Shield	Up to 8	At least 8, no more than 48

To remove the diaphragm or cervical cap, put a finger under the front rim to break the air seal, then pull the device out of the vagina. The FemCap and Lea's Shield have flexible loops for removal. After removal, wash the device with a mild soap and warm water and then dry it. The diaphragm and cervical cap can last for several years, but the FemCap and Lea's Shield are usable for only one year. Take the device with you to your annual exam and Pap smear so that your health-care practitioner can evaluate its fit and condition. A pregnancy (including a miscarriage or an abortion) or a weight change of more than 10 pounds may require a different diaphragm.

Intrauterine Devices

Intrauterine devices, commonly referred to as IUDs, are small, plastic objects that are inserted into the uterus. The two IUDs are the ParaGard and Mirena (▌ Figure 10.7). The ParaGard is a plastic T with a copper wire wrapped around its stem and copper sleeves on the side arms. Mirena is a polyethylene T with a cylinder containing progestin (Akert, 2003). The IUDs have fine plastic threads attached; the threads are designed to hang slightly out of the cervix into the vagina.

intrauterine device (IUD)
A small, plastic device that is inserted into the uterus for contraception.

The IUD is the most common reversible contraceptive used by women in the developing world (Salem, 2006). About 6% of women in the United States use the IUD, and those who do use this method are usually very pleased with it, as indicated by its 80% continuation rate (how many women who start using a method are still using it one year later; Nordqvist, 2011). This is a higher continuation rate than for pills, patches, rings, condoms, or Depo-Provera (Hatcher, 2006). The IUD and implant are the only long-acting reversible contraceptives (Thompson et al., 2011). In addition, serious complications are rare with the modern IUD (Campbell et al., 2007) and are described in ▪ Table 10.6.

How the IUD Works

Both the copper and the progestin in IUDs are effective in preventing fertilization. The ParaGard with copper seems to alter the tubal and uterine fluids, which affects the sperm and egg so fertilization does not occur. Mirena has effects similar to those of hormonal contraceptive methods such as the pill and Depo-Provera. It disrupts ovulatory patterns, thickens cervical mucus, alters endometrial lining, and impairs tubal motility (G. Stewart, 1998).

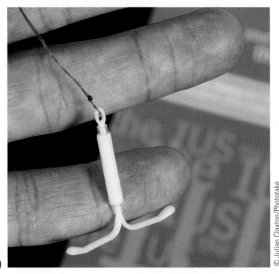

(a)

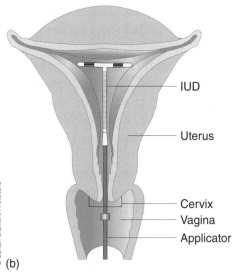

(b)

IUD

Uterus

Cervix

Vagina

Applicator

▌ **Figure 10.7**

(a) The Mirena IUD.
(b) Position of the IUD after insertion by a health-care practitioner.

■ TABLE 10.6 Remember "PAINS" for the IUD: Symptoms of Possible Serious Problems With the IUD

Initial	Symptoms
P	Period late, no period
A	Abdominal pain
I	Increased temperature, fever, chills
N	Nasty discharge, foul discharge
S	Spotting, bleeding, heavy periods, clots

SOURCE: Adapted from G. Stewart (1998).

How to Use the IUD

The IUD is inserted by a health-care professional using sterile instruments. The inserter and IUD are introduced through the cervical os into the uterus; the inserter is then withdrawn, leaving the IUD in place. The ParaGard can be in place for 12 years, and the progestin IUD Mirena for 5 years (Planned Parenthood Federation of America, 2008). A woman should be screened for gonorrhea and chlamydia before IUD insertion because the procedure can carry bacteria associated with these STIs into the uterus. The use of the IUD is best limited to women who are in monogamous relationships and do not have other risk factors for sexually transmitted infections (Speroff & Fritz, 2005).

SEXUALHEALTH ▶

While a woman is using an IUD, she or her partner needs to check each month after her menstrual period to see that the thread is the same length as when the device was inserted. To do this, one reaches into the vagina with a finger and finds the cervix. The thread should be felt in the middle of the cervix, protruding out of the small indentation in the center. Occasionally it curls up in the os and cannot be felt, but any time a woman or her partner cannot find it, she needs to check with her health-care specialist. She should also seek attention if the thread seems longer or if the plastic protrudes from the os; this probably means that her body is expelling the IUD. ●

Emergency Contraception

What if a condom slips off, or a divorced couple is unexpectedly intimate (for "old time's sake") without birth control, or a couple runs out of condoms and uses only foam, or a woman is raped while trying to walk to her car after a night class, or a woman is two days late starting a new pack of pills, or a woman drinks too much at a party and has unprotected sex, or a woman leaves her NuvaRing in longer than 5 weeks, or a couple with a new baby have intercourse before they restart birth control? What if a woman is one of the 54% of single, nonmonogamous women who do not use birth control every time (Beil, 2009)? Studies indicate that each night more than one million women in the United States who do not want to get pregnant have unprotected sex (G. Harris, 2010).

emergency contraception
Hormone pills or an IUD that can be used after unprotected intercourse to prevent pregnancy.

Fortunately, in these and numerous other situations, a possible pregnancy can be prevented by using **emergency contraception** (**EC**). After unprotected intercourse, a hormone pill, packaged as Plan B or Next Choice (❙ Figure 10.8); a nonhormonal pill, Ella; or insertion of a ParaGard IUD are options for emergency contraception. The IUD is the most effective in preventing pregnancy and can be inserted up to 7 days after unprotected intercourse. If the ParaGard IUD is inserted up to 5 days after unprotected intercourse, it is over 99% effective in preventing pregnancy (Golden et al., 2001). It is appropriate for women who plan to use the IUD as an ongoing method of

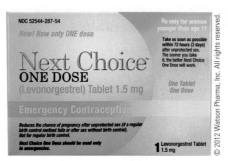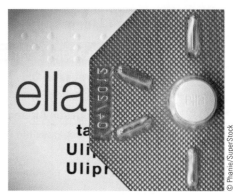

∎ **Figure 10.8** Emergency contraception pills.

contraception, but its use is limited to women who are at low risk of sexually transmitted infections and pelvic inflammatory disease (Long, 2002).

Plan B or Next Choice is the most commonly used method and is most effective taken within the first 24 hours after intercourse, typically 95% effective in preventing pregnancy. Within 72 hours both are 75% effective, and even within 120 hours, they can provide a small degree of protection from pregnancy (G. Harris, 2010; Piaggio et al., 2011). Any woman or man, 17 years of age or older, can get Plan B or Next Choice by asking a pharmacist (Wood et al., 2012). However, a pharmacist is not required by law to dispense emergency contraception, and one study found that one in five pharmacists may refuse to give emergency contraception to young women (Szalavitz, 2012). Search the website http://ec.princeton.edu for a pharmacy in your area that dispenses EC, or call the telephone hotline at 1-888-668-2528.

In 2010 the FDA approved another emergency contraceptive, Ella, that works up to 5 days after unprotected sex. Ella, available only by prescription, is a nonhormonal pill and contains ulipristal, a drug that blocks the effects of key hormones necessary for conception.

As shown in ∎ Table 10.7, two or more oral contraceptives can be substituted if the emergency contraceptive treatment is not available. These hormone treatments work primarily by inhibiting ovulation (Population Council, 2005). They may also provide secondary protection by altering cervical mucus and the lining of the uterus. When a woman uses EC, she should also be aware of and watch for side effects similar to those related to birth control pills. ●

Increased knowledge and use of EC could prevent an estimated 2.3 million unintended pregnancies each year in the United States. A study of college students found that only 16% knew EC was available at their college health center (Miller, 2011). Most women are not aware that an IUD is a possibility for emergency contraception (Wright et al., 2012). Studies at abortion clinics indicate that 50 to 60% of the patients would have been treatable with and would have wanted to use emergency contraception rather than have an abortion if they had known about it and had had access to it (Speroff & Fritz, 2005). Women in London, England, can order emergency contraception over the Internet, and a courier will deliver it within two hours (Hope, 2012).

SEXUALHEALTH

Fertility Awareness Methods

The birth control methods that we have discussed so far require the use of pills or devices. Some of these methods have side effects in some users, and there can be health risks associated with using oral contraceptives and the IUD. The barrier methods we have looked at—condoms, vaginal spermicides, and the diaphragm—have fewer side

■ TABLE 10.7 Oral Contraceptive Pills for Emergency Contraception

Instead of Progestin-Only Plan B

Ovrette: 20 pills as soon as possible within 120 hours and 20 pills 12 hours later after unprotected intercourse

Estrogen-Progestin Alternatives[a]

2 pills as soon as possible within 120 hours after unprotected intercourse and 2 more 12 hours later:

Ogestrel	Ovral

4 pills as soon as possible within 120 hours after unprotected intercourse and 4 more 12 hours later:

Cryselle	Levlen
Levora	Lo/Ovral
Low-Ogestrel	Nordette
Portia	Seasonale
Seasonique	

5 pills as soon as possible within 120 hours after unprotected intercourse and 5 more 12 hours later:

Alesse	Aviane
Lessina	Levlite
Lutera	

[a]In 28-day packs, only the first 21 pills can be used. The last 7 contain *no* hormones.

SOURCE: Adapted from Princeton University, Office of Population Research & Association of Reproductive Health Professionals (2006), *Answers to Frequently Asked Questions About Emergency Contraception in the United States of America*. Retrieved 2006 from the Emergency Contraception website: http://ec.princeton.edu/.

fertility awareness methods
Birth control methods that use the signs of cyclic fertility to prevent or plan conception.

effects, but they require that the couple use them each time they have intercourse. In the next paragraphs, we look at methods of birth control based on changes during the menstrual cycle. These methods, which may answer some couples' needs, are sometimes referred to as *natural family planning* or **fertility awareness methods**. They are based on the fact that a fertile woman's body reveals subtle and overt signs of cyclic fertility that can be used both to help prevent and to plan conception.

There are four different fertility awareness methods: the standard days method, the mucus method, the calendar method, and the basal body temperature method. Any of these can be used in combination to increase effectiveness (Frank-Hermann et al., 2007). About 3% of Catholic women in the United States use natural family planning (Jones & Dreweke, 2011). During the fertile period, couples using fertility awareness methods can abstain from intercourse and engage in other forms of sexual intimacy or can continue having intercourse and use other methods of birth control during the fertile time (Gribble et al., 2008). Unfortunately, present research indicates that, other than the standard days method, fertility awareness methods are considerably less effective than most other birth control methods (Jennings et al., 1998).

Standard Days Method

standard days method
A birth control method that requires couples to avoid unprotected intercourse for a 12-day period in the middle of the menstrual cycle.

The **standard days method** is the newest approach to natural family planning. It is appropriate for women who have menstrual cycles between 26 and 32 days long. Couples avoid unprotected intercourse on days 8 through 19 of each menstrual cycle. This "fertile window" is 12 days long to take into account both the days around ovulation and the possible variations in timing of ovulation from one cycle to another. The standard days method has been clinically tested and shows the highest rate of effectiveness for natural family planning methods (Arevalo et al., 2002). A woman can keep track on a calendar or use the CycleBeads shown in ■ Figure 10.9 to help track the days.

Figure 10.9 CycleBeads, based on the standard days method, help a woman track her menstrual cycle and know when she can and cannot get pregnant. To use the CycleBeads, a woman moves a black ring each day onto the next of 32 color-coded beads, which represent fertile and low-fertility days.

J. Darin Derstine

Mucus Method

The **mucus method**, also called the *ovulation method*, is based on the cyclic changes of cervical mucus that reveal periods of fertility in a woman's cycle. To use this method, a woman learns to "read" the amounts and textures of vaginal secretions and to maintain a daily chart of the changes. A woman reads her mucus by putting her fingers inside her vagina and noting the consistency of the secretions:

- After menstruation some "dry days" pass when no vaginal discharge appears on the vulva.
- When a yellow or white sticky discharge appears, unprotected coitus should be avoided.
- Several days later, the ovulatory mucus appears. It is clear, stringy, and stretchy in consistency, similar to egg white. A drop of this mucus will stretch between an open thumb and forefinger for at least 1 1/2 inches before breaking. A vaginal feeling of wetness and lubrication accompanies this discharge, which has a chemical balance and texture that help sperm enter the uterus.
- Approximately 4 days after the ovulatory mucus begins and 24 hours after a cloudy discharge resumes, it is considered safe to resume unprotected intercourse.

The fertile period usually totals 9 to 15 days out of each cycle. In many cities classes in the mucus method are offered at a hospital or clinic. Each woman's mucus patterns vary, and taking a class is the best way to learn how to interpret the changes.

mucus method
A birth control method based on determining the time of ovulation by means of the cyclical changes of the cervical mucus.

Calendar Method

Using the **calendar method**, also called the *rhythm method*, a woman estimates the calendar time during her cycle when she is ovulating and fertile. To use this method, a woman keeps a chart, preferably for 1 year, of the length of her cycles. (She cannot be using oral contraceptives during this time because they impose a cycle that may not be the same as her own.)

- The first day of menstruation is counted as day 1. The woman counts the number of days of her cycle, the last day being the one before the onset of menstruation.
- To determine high-risk days, on which she should avoid unprotected coitus, the woman subtracts 18 from the number of days of her shortest cycle. For example, if her shortest cycle was 26 days, day 8 would be the first high-risk day.
- To estimate when unprotected coitus can resume, the woman subtracts 10 from the number of days in her longest cycle. For example, if her longest cycle is 32 days, she would be able to resume intercourse on day 22.

calendar method
A birth control method based on abstinence from intercourse during calendar-estimated fertile days.

Basal Body Temperature Method

basal body temperature method
A birth control method based on body temperature changes before and after ovulation.

Another way of estimating high-fertility days is through temperature, using the **basal body temperature method**. Immediately before ovulation the basal body temperature (BBT, the body temperature in the resting state on waking in the morning) drops slightly. After ovulation the corpus luteum releases more progesterone, which causes the body temperature to rise slightly (0.2°F). Because these temperature changes are slight, a thermometer with easy-to-read gradations must be used. Special electronic thermometers have been developed for measuring BBT and are effective in indicating fertile times in the cycle.

Sterilization

Sterilization is the most effective method of birth control except abstinence from sexual intercourse, and its safety and permanence appeal to many who want no more children or who prefer to remain childless. Sterilization is the leading method of birth control in the United States and around the world (Peterson, 2008). Although medical procedures to reverse sterilization in both men and women can be performed, current reversal procedures involve complicated surgery, and a subsequent pregnancy is uncertain (Hsiao et al., 2012). Therefore, sterilization is recommended only to those who desire a permanent method of birth control (Lawrence et al., 2011b).

Needless to say, sterilization should always be the decision of each individual or couple. Unfortunately, that has not always been the policy in the United States. In 1924 a Supreme Court decision, *Buck v. Bell*, legalized forced sterilization as part of the eugenics (good breeding) program in the United States. Continuing into the 1970s, more than 30 states participated in the forced or coerced sterilization of 70,000 U.S. citizens. Most victims were women, and more than 60% were African Americans. Some women were sterilized without their knowledge after giving birth. Others were forced to choose sterilization or termination of family welfare benefits. The state ordered some sterilizations for women it defined as lazy or promiscuous. To date, North Carolina is the only state to issue a formal apology and to establish a commission to make amends to the victims (Schoen, 2006; Sinderbrand, 2005). Since 2003 a North Carolina task force has identified 48 of the estimated 2,000 victims still living and is working toward providing monetary compensation for them and establishing a museum exhibit about the state's eugenics program (Goldschmidt, 2012; Kessel & Hopper, 2011).

Female Sterilization

tubal sterilization
Female sterilization accomplished by severing or tying the fallopian tubes.

Female sterilization has become a relatively safe, simple, and inexpensive procedure. Approximately 25% of married women of childbearing age in the United States rely on female sterilization as their method of contraception (Mosher & Jones, 2010). **Tubal sterilization** can be accomplished by a variety of techniques that use small incisions and either local or general anesthesia. A *laparoscopy* is shown in ▌ Figure 10.10. One or two small incisions are made in the abdomen, usually at the navel and slightly below the pubic hairline. A narrow, lighted viewing instrument called a laparoscope is inserted into the abdomen to locate the fallopian tubes. The tubes are then tied off, cut, clipped, or cauterized to block passage of sperm and eggs. The incisions are generally so small that adhesive tape rather than stitches is used to close them after surgery. Sometimes, in a procedure called a *culpotomy*, the incision is made through the back of the vaginal wall.

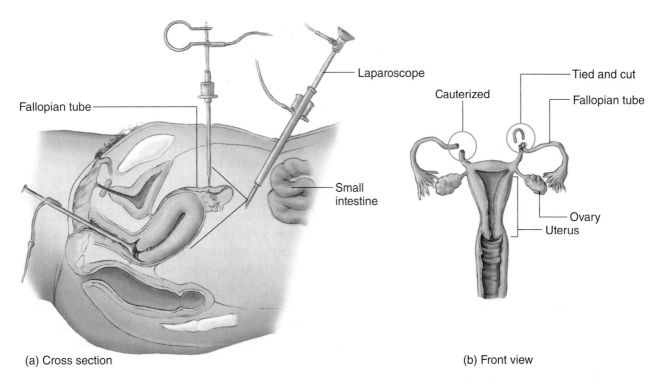

(a) Cross section

(b) Front view

▍ Figure 10.10 Female sterilization by laparoscopic ligation. Front view shows tubes after ligation.

Newer techniques do not require an operating room, general anesthesia, or much recovery time (Lee-St. John & Gallatin, 2008). The procedure takes half an hour and is performed using local anesthesia. During a **transcervical sterilization**, a physician inserts a tiny coil, called Essure (shown in ▍ Figure 10.11), made of polyester fibers and nickel-titanium alloy (the same material that is used to make artificial heart valves), or a silicone implant, called Adiana, into the vagina, through the cervix, and into the opening of each fallopian tube in the uterus. Essure and Adiana promote tissue growth that, after 3 months, blocks the fallopian tubes and prevents the ovum and sperm from meeting. Women and/or their partners should use another form of birth control during those 3 months (Hollander, 2008c). The most common side effect is cramping; in rare cases the device is expelled or perforates the fallopian tube.

Sterilization does not affect a woman's reproductive and sexual systems. Until menopause her ovaries continue to release their eggs. The released eggs simply degenerate, as do millions of other cells daily. The woman's hormone levels and the timing of menopause remain unchanged. Her sexuality is not physiologically changed, but she may find that her interest and arousal increase because she is no longer concerned about pregnancy or birth control methods.

Male Sterilization

Male sterilization is as effective as female sterilization and has the advantages of being safer and less expensive and having fewer complications following surgery. However, of people who

transcervical sterilization
A method of female sterilization using a tiny coil that is inserted through the vagina, cervix, and uterus into the fallopian tubes.

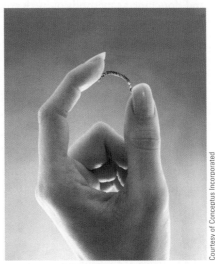

Courtesy of Conceptus Incorporated

▍ Figure 10.11 Essure, a tiny coil that is used in female sterilization.

have sterilizations, less than half are men (Shih et al., 2011). Worldwide, 3% of women of reproductive age rely on their partner's vasectomy for contraception (Kols & Lande, 2008).

Vasectomy is a 20-minute minor surgical procedure, usually done in a physician's office, that involves cutting and closing each vas deferens, the sperm-carrying duct, so that sperm are blocked from passing out the penis during sexual arousal and ejaculation (❙ Figure 10.12). Under a local anesthetic, a small incision or puncture is made in the scrotal sac, well above the testis. The vas is lifted out, and a small segment is removed. The free ends are tied off, clipped, or cauterized to prevent rejoining. A man can expect swelling, inflammation, or bruising in the region of the surgery—an effect that lasts from 1 day to 2 weeks. In one study, about 25% of men reported some brief pain following vasectomy; a few from that group continued to experience discomfort for more than 3 months and required analgesics or medical attention (Rasheed et al., 1997).

A significant number of sperm are stored beyond the site of the incision, and a man remains fertile for some time after the operation. Therefore, effective alternative methods of birth control should be used until semen analysis reveals no sperm in the seminal fluid. Many physicians recommend that a vasectomized man have a test for sperm 3 months after the vasectomy (Shah & Fisch, 2006). In 2008 the FDA approved Sperm-Check, a test that can be used at home to determine infertility following vasectomy (Kates, 2008). In rare cases the two free ends of the severed vas grow back together (this is called *recanalization*; Stewart & Carignan, 1998).

Vasectomy does not alter production of male sex hormones. In addition, a vasectomized man continues to produce sperm, which are absorbed and eliminated by his body. The consistency and odor of his semen remain the same, and his ejaculations contain almost as much volume as before, because sperm constitute less than 1% of the total ejaculate. Some men avoid vasectomy because they fear that it will negatively affect their sexual functioning (Kols & Lande, 2008), but many experience greater spontaneity and pleasure when they are free from concern about impregnating their partners.

Unreliable Methods

Besides the contraceptive methods we have been discussing, others exist that are far less effective and less commonly used. We mention some of them here because people may have misconceptions about their effectiveness. We discuss nursing, withdrawal, and douching as methods of birth control.

Nursing

Nursing a baby delays a woman's return to fertility after childbirth when the baby is only breast-fed. However, breast-feeding is not a fully reliable method of birth control because there is no way of knowing when ovulation will resume. Amenorrhea (lack of menstruation) usually occurs during nursing, but it is not a reliable indication of inability to conceive. Nearly 80% of breast-feeding women ovulate before their first menstrual period. The longer a woman breast-feeds, the more likely it is that ovulation will occur (Kennedy & Trussell, 1998).

Withdrawal

The practice of the man removing his penis from the vagina just before he ejaculates is known as *withdrawal*. It is ineffective because the preejaculatory Cowper's gland secretions can carry sperm that can fertilize an egg. Also, it may be difficult for the man to

(1) The vas deferens is located.

(2) A small incision in the scrotum exposes the vas.

(3) A small section of the vas is removed, and the ends are cut and/or cauterized.

(4) The incision is closed.

(5) Steps 1–4 are repeated on the other side.

❙ **Figure 10.12** Male sterilization by vasectomy.

judge exactly when he must withdraw, and his tendency is to remain inside the vagina as long as possible, which may be too long. Any sperm deposited on the labia while the man withdraws his penis can swim into the vagina. Both partners may experience pleasure-reducing anxiety about whether he will withdraw in time (Whittaker et al., 2010). One study found that almost 12% of sexually active 15-year-olds from 24 countries used withdrawal as their primary means of contraception (Godeau et al., 2008).

Douching

Although some women use *douching* after intercourse as a method of birth control, it is ineffective. After ejaculation some sperm reach the inside of the uterus in a matter of 1 or 2 minutes. In addition, the movement of the water from douching may actually help sperm reach the opening of the cervix. Furthermore, frequent douching is not recommended because it can irritate vaginal tissues.

New Directions in Contraception

As we have seen in this chapter, potential health hazards and inconveniences are associated with available contraceptive methods. Unwanted pregnancies occur each year because of contraceptive and user failure. We look at future possibilities for both men and women.

New Directions for Men

Current research has focused on methods designed to inhibit sperm production, motility, or maturation or the sperm's ability to join with the ovum—without causing significant side effects or impairing sexual interest and function. The most promising possibility is using various formulations of testosterone or a combination of progestin and testosterone, which appears to work in 95% of men. Researchers are also attempting to develop nonhormonal contraception for men, including the use of medications for other purposes that result in infertility (Belluck, 2011).

Research has shown that most men would use a male contraceptive pill if it were available. Most women say they would trust their partners to use such a pill; only 2% said they would not trust their partners to do so. In addition, men and women think that a male pill is a good idea because the responsibility for contraception tends to fall too much to women (Nieschlag & Henke, 2005). The "male pill" will most likely, however, be administered by injection or implant, patches, or cream (Belluck, 2011).

Additional sterilization methods in clinical trials with human subjects in India, China, and the United States may be more easily reversible than vasectomy. One involves injecting a blocking gel into the vas deferens; to reverse the procedure, the gel can be dissolved. The second method uses the Intra Vas Device, which consists of two plugs inserted into each vas deferens; the plugs can be removed later. Implantation and removal of these devices can be done in 20 minutes each (International Male Contraception Coalition, 2011).

New Directions for Women

Other new directions for women consist of variations on methods of delivery and formulations of hormones in existing methods. A spray-on contraceptive may be added to the choices of transdermal contraceptives, and a vaginal contraceptive ring used continuously for one year is under development (Harrison-Hohner, 2010). Some of the research on new contraceptive methods for women is focusing on nonhormonal means of birth control, including a contraceptive vaccine, a vaginal ring, and vaginal spermicide with nonhormonal substances that block sperm motility (Brown, 2008; Z. Williams et al., 2006). Possible new designs for IUDs include a reversible plug in the oviduct that has been shown to be effective in preventing pregnancy in rabbits and has a high rate of pregnancy subsequent to removal (Wang et al., 2011).

Hoping to provide women with STI and HIV protection that is under their own control, researchers are studying spermicides that contain microbicides (substances that stop STI transmission; Kerns & Darney, 2011). Research with these gels also includes feedback from women about the consistency of gel that best enhances sexual pleasure (Littlefield, 2011). (See Chapter 15 for a discussion of microbicides.)

Since the advent of the pill, contraceptive options have greatly increased. However, the ideal of 100% effective, reversible contraceptives for men and women—methods that also have no side effects and protect against sexually transmitted infections—will, unfortunately, not be available anytime in the foreseeable future.

Summary

Historical and Social Perspectives

- From the beginning of recorded history, humankind has been concerned about birth control.
- Margaret Sanger opened the first birth control clinics in the United States at a time when it was illegal to provide birth control information and devices.
- Objections to contraception stem from Roman Catholic doctrine and far-right anti-contraception beliefs. However, most church members in the United States approve of and use some kind of artificial contraception.

Sharing Responsibility and Choosing a Birth Control Method

- A man can share contraceptive responsibility with his female partner by getting informed, asking a new partner about birth control, accompanying his partner to her exam, using condoms and/or coital abstinence if the couple chooses, and sharing the expense of the exam and contraceptive method.
- Comparison of convenience, safety, cost, and effectiveness may influence the choice of contraception.
- People who feel guilty, have negative attitudes about sexuality, and do not talk with their partners about contraception are less likely to use contraception effectively than are people who have positive attitudes about sexuality.

Hormone-Based Contraceptives

- Four types of oral contraceptives are available. The constant-dose combination pill contains steady doses of estrogen and

progestin. The triphasic pill provides fluctuations of estrogen and progestin levels throughout the menstrual cycle. The extended-cycle pill reduces menstrual cycles to four per year. The progestin-only pill consists of low-dose progestin.

- Advantages of oral contraceptives include high effectiveness and lack of interference with sexual activity. Birth control pills are also associated with lower incidences of uterine, ovarian, and colon cancer. An additional advantage is reduction of menstrual flow and cramps. The advantage of the progestin-only pill is the reduced chance of side effects from estrogen. The vaginal ring (NuvaRing), the transdermal patch (Ortho Evra), and the injectable Depo-Provera are hormone-based contraceptives that do not require remembering to take a pill each day.
- Disadvantages of hormone-based contraceptives include possible side effects such as a slight increase in the likelihood of blood clots, an increase in migraine headaches, nausea, fluid retention, irregular bleeding, and reduced sexual interest. Disadvantages of the progestin-only pill include irregular bleeding and the possibility of additional side effects. In general, the health risks of oral contraceptives are far lower than those from pregnancy and birth.
- Depo-Provera is an injectable contraceptive that lasts for 3 months.

Barrier and Spermicide Methods

- Condoms are available in a variety of styles. Advantages include protection from sexually transmitted infections and availability as a backup method. Disadvantages include interruption of sexual activity if the couple do not incorporate its use into their sex play. A female condom has also been developed.

- Vaginal spermicides (including contraceptive foam, the sponge, vaginal suppositories, creams and jellies, and contraceptive film) are available without a prescription. Advantages of vaginal spermicides include lack of serious side effects and added lubrication. Disadvantages include low level of effectiveness unless used with a condom, possible irritation of genital tissues, and interruption of sexual activity.

- Advantages of cervical barrier methods include lack of side effects, high effectiveness with knowledgeable and consistent use, and possible promotion of vaginal health. Disadvantages include interruption of sexual activity, potential irritation from the spermicidal cream or jelly, and possible misplacement during insertion or intercourse.

Intrauterine Devices

- ParaGard and Mirena are the only intrauterine devices (IUDs) on the U.S. market. Advantages of the IUD include uninterrupted sexual interaction and simplicity of use. Disadvantages include the possibilities of increased cramping and spontaneous expulsion. Uterine perforation is rare. The IUD increases risk of pelvic inflammatory disease for women with multiple partners.

Emergency Contraception

- Plan B, oral contraceptives, and the ParaGard IUD can be used for emergency contraception when a woman has had unprotected intercourse.

- The FDA denied over-the-counter status to emergency contraception, against its committee's recommendation.

Fertility Awareness Methods

- Contraceptive methods based on the menstrual cycle—including the standard days, mucus, calendar, and basal body temperature methods—help in planning coital activity to avoid a woman's fertile period.

Sterilization

- At this time sterilization should be considered permanent. A decision to be sterilized should be carefully evaluated.

- Tubal ligation is the sterilization procedure most commonly performed for women. It does not alter a woman's hormone levels or menstrual cycle or the timing of menopause.

- Vasectomy, the sterilization procedure for men, is not effective for birth control immediately after surgery because sperm remain in the vas deferens above the incision.

Unreliable Methods

- Breast-feeding, douching, and the withdrawal method are not reliable methods of contraception.

New Directions in Contraception

- Possible contraceptive methods for men in the future include the use of hormones and nonhormonal methods to reduce the production and motility of sperm or to create a "dry orgasm."

- Possible future contraceptive methods for women include nonhormonal contraception, variations of the IUD, and new methods for delivering hormones.

Media Resources

Log in to CengageBrain.com to access the resources your instructor requires.

Go to CengageBrain.com to access Psychology CourseMate, where you will find an interactive eBook, glossaries, flashcards, quizzes, videos, and more.

Also access links to chapter-related websites, including **Margaret Sanger Papers Project, Successful Contraception, International Planned Parenthood Federation, Birth Control: How Hormones Work to Prevent Pregnancy, The National Woman's Health Information Center, New Male Contraceptives, When Timing Is Everything, and Condomania.**

11
Conceiving Children:
Process and Choice

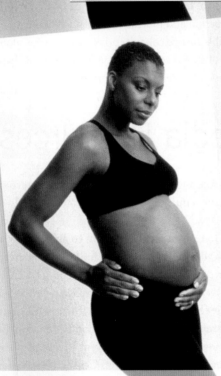

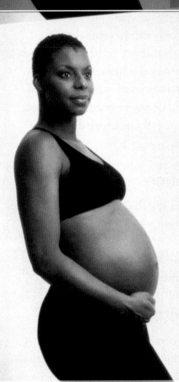

Parenthood as an Option
What are the pros and cons of being parents or remaining child-free?

Becoming Pregnant
What are some of the causes of male and female infertility?

What are the current artificial reproductive technologies? How do they work?

Spontaneous and Elective Abortion
How can a miscarriage affect a woman and couple emotionally?

What factors most influence a country's abortion rate?

What procedures are used for abortion?

How have laws regarding abortion changed since *Roe v. Wade*?

The Experience of Pregnancy
How does pregnancy affect sexuality?

A Healthy Pregnancy
How does the fetus change in each trimester of pregnancy?

What factors can harm the fetus during pregnancy?

Childbirth
What occurs in each of the three stages of childbirth?

After Childbirth
What are advantages and disadvantages of breast-feeding?

What criteria should a couple use to decide when to resume intercourse?

Michael Krasowitz/Getty Images

I've been an "expectant" father twice, but my role was drastically different the second time because of changes in obstetrical practices. During my first child's birth, it was the classic scene of Dad pacing the waiting room floor while my wife was in the delivery room. In my second marriage, the pregnancy was "our pregnancy" from the beginning. I went to doctor's appointments and saw our baby's ultrasound pictures. Seeing his heart beat so early in the pregnancy gave me a feeling of connection right from the start. We attended prepared childbirth classes together, and I was there from start to finish during labor and when she delivered our baby. I went with him to the nursery for all the weighing, measuring, and cleaning, then brought him back to his mother in the birthing suite. I wish I'd had those experiences with my first child's birth. (Authors' files)

One of the most important decisions we will probably make in our lifetime is whether to become a parent. In this chapter we address the pros and cons of parenthood. We also discuss the processes of conception, pregnancy, and birth and some of the emotions that accompany them from the viewpoints of the parents. We encourage people who desire further information to seek more extensive references or to consult a health-care practitioner. As a starting point, we look at the option of parenthood and some of the alternatives that are available for people who want to become parents.

Parenthood as an Option

More couples and individuals than in the past are choosing to be "kid-free." In 1975 about 9% of 40- to 44-year-old women did not have children; in 2010 almost 19% were childless (U.S. Census Bureau, 2010). Remaining childless has many potential advantages. Individuals and couples have much more time for themselves, more financial resources, and more spontaneity with regard to their recreational, social, and work patterns. The personal importance placed on leisure time may be especially important, as one study found that women who valued leisure time more put less importance on motherhood than did women who rated motherhood as more important (Mcquillan et al., 2008). Nonparents can more fully pursue careers, creating more opportunity for fulfillment in their professional lives. At the same time, there is usually more time and energy for companionship and intimacy in an adult relationship.

In general, childless marriages are less stressful, and some studies show that they are happier and more satisfying than marriages with children, especially in the years following a first child's birth (Doss et al., 2009). Not having to worry about providing for the physical and psychological needs of children can make a difference, because conflict about *who* does *what* for the children is a major source of disenchantment for many couples (Vejar et al., 2006). Note, however, that the reduced marital satisfaction after children may be because many unhappily married couples remain together because they have young children.

Becoming parents of adopted or biological children also has many potential advantages. A national representative sample found that 98% of fathers and 97% of mothers agreed with the statement, "The rewards of being a parent are worth it, despite the costs and work it takes" (Martinez et al., 2006, p. 28). Children give as well as receive love, and their presence can enhance the love between couples as they share in the experiences of raising their offspring. Successfully managing the challenges of parenthood can also build self-esteem and provide a sense of accomplishment. Parenthood is often an opportunity for discovering new and untapped dimensions of oneself that can give one's life greater meaning and satisfaction.

The potential rewards of either becoming parents or remaining childless can be romanticized or unrealistic for a given person or couple, and some people experience considerable ambivalence (Eibach & Mock, 2011). As one writer put it, having children changes your life—but so does not having them (Cole, 1987).

Becoming Pregnant

In the remainder of this chapter, we look at some of the developments, experiences, and feelings involved in the physiological process of becoming parents, starting with becoming pregnant. This first step can be difficult for some couples.

Enhancing the Possibility of Conception

Choosing the right time for intercourse is important in increasing the probability of conception. Conception is most likely to occur within the 6-day period ending on the day of ovulation. It is difficult to predict the exact time of ovulation, but several methods permit a reasonable approximation. Ovulation predictor tests, which measure the rise in luteinizing hormone (LH) in urine before ovulation, can accurately identify the best time for conception and can be purchased over the counter. Otherwise, the mucus method, body temperature, and the principles of the calendar method can also be used to estimate ovulation time, as discussed in Chapter 10. ●

Some individuals and couples are interested in enhancing the possibility of conceiving a child of a specific sex, as discussed in the following Sexuality and Diversity section.

SEXUALITY and DIVERSITY

Preselecting a Baby's Sex: Technology and Cross-Cultural Issues

The desire to have a child of a certain sex has existed since ancient times. Superstitions about determining the sex of a child during intercourse are part of Western folk tradition—for example, the belief that if a man wore a hat during intercourse, he would father a male child or that if a man hung his trousers on the left bedpost, he would sire a girl.

Couples sometimes try "low-tech" methods to conceive a boy or girl. Timing intercourse closer to ovulation (to conceive a boy) or further from ovulation (to conceive a girl), making the vaginal environment more acidic or alkaline by douching with water and vinegar (girl) or water and baking soda (boy), or using different intercourse positions such as man on top (girl) or rear-entry (boy) are among the techniques that couples may try. However, there is no scientific consensus as to whether any of these methods are effective.

An effective technique for sex selection, pre-implantation genetic diagnosis (PGD), creates embryos in the laboratory. The sex of the embryos is tested, and a physician subsequently inserts the embryos of the desired sex into the woman's uterus. The approximately $20,000 procedure offers almost 100% certainty of the baby's sex (Dayal & Zarek, 2008). Less certain results occur with more commonly used laboratory techniques that can separate X-chromosome–bearing sperm from Y-chromosome–bearing sperm. Once the laboratory separation process is complete, the desired X or Y portion is introduced into the vagina by artificial insemination. Success rates are about 90% for female babies and 70% for male babies. However, the rather "unromantic" nature of semen collection and artificial insemination will probably limit the use of sex selection techniques unless parents have compelling reasons to conceive a child of a particular sex.

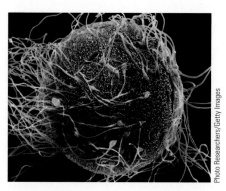

The first stage of pregnancy: Only one of the sperm surrounding this ovum will fertilize it.

SEXUALHEALTH ▸

Sex preselection offers benefits to couples at risk for passing on X-chromosome–linked diseases to their children, and research indicates that the public strongly favors its use for that purpose (Kalfoglou et al., 2008).

In China, India, and South Korea, the preference for a son is particularly strong, and selective abortion of female fetuses and the killing of infant girls are common. In India a woman can obtain an ultrasound for about $12 to determine the sex of the fetus, and if it is a girl have an abortion for about $35 (Power, 2006). Consequently, an imbalance in the numbers of boys and girls has occurred: For every 100 girls there are 120 boys in China and 109 in India. The imbalance is most severe in wealthier regions where couples can afford the ultrasound tests (Halarnkar, 2011; Hvisten-dahl, 2011). Overall, there are currently 100 million more males than females in Asia (Ferguson, 2011).

Economic and cultural factors contribute to the importance of sons in many Asian cultures. Sons provide for parents through their old age, offering security in the absence of governmental social support. In Hindu and Confucian religious traditions in Asia, only sons can light their parents' funeral pyres and pray to release the souls of dead parents. Sons will bring future earnings to their parents, but daughters are a financial liability to their families when they require the expense of a dowry. Women's work will also contribute to the family into which they marry instead of to their birth family (Garlough, 2008). These traditions are so strong that even Asian couples who have immigrated to the United States are using medical technology to have sons instead of daughters. Interviews with immigrant Indian women who pursued fetal sex selection found that 40% of the women had terminated prior pregnancies with female fetuses and that 89% of women carrying female fetuses in their current pregnancy pursued an abortion (Puri et al., 2011).

Infertility

Sixty percent of couples become pregnant within 3 months, but if attempts at impregnation are unsuccessful after 6 months, a couple should consult a physician. It has been estimated that about 12% of U.S. couples attempting pregnancy experience fertility problems, defined as not conceiving after at least 1 year (Bell et al., 2012; Hannon, 2009). Because approximately 40% of infertility cases involve male factors (20% involve both male and female factors), it is important that both partners be evaluated (Rabin, 2007a). We usually think of infertility as the inability to conceive any children, but secondary infertility—the inability to conceive a second child—occurs in 10% of couples (Diamond et al., 1999).

Infertility is a complex and distressing problem (Greil et al., 2011). It can have a demoralizing effect on the infertile individual's sense of self and on the couple's sense of their integrity as a healthy unit (Galhardo et al., 2011; Wischmann et al., 2009). Its causes are sometimes difficult to determine and remain unidentified in many cases. However, between 85% and 90% of infertility cases can be treated with drug therapy or surgical procedures (Hannon, 2009).

Infertility's Impact on Sexual Relationships

Most people grow up believing that they can conceive children when they decide to begin a family. Experiencing infertility is an unanticipated shock and crisis (Wilkes, 2006). As their infertility becomes more evident and undeniable, a couple may feel a great sense of isolation from others during social discussions of pregnancy, childbirth, and child rearing. As one woman who has been unable to conceive stated,

Problems with infertility can have profoundly negative effects on a couple's relationship and sexual functioning (Keskin et al., 2011). Partners can also become isolated from each other and believe that the other does not really understand. Each partner might feel inadequate about his or her masculinity or femininity because of problems with conceiving. Each may feel anger and guilt and wonder, "Why me?" Finally, both may feel grief over life experiences they can never have—namely, pregnancy, birth, and conceiving and rearing their own biological children (Steuber & Solomon, 2008).

Intercourse itself can evoke these uncomfortable feelings and can become an emotionally painful rather than pleasurable experience, fraught with anxiety and sadness about failing to conceive. Studies have found that most infertile couples experience some sexual dissatisfaction or dysfunction at one point or another (Mahoney, 2007). In addition, the medical procedures used in fertility diagnosis and treatment are disruptive to the couple's sexual spontaneity and privacy. Sex can become stressful and mechanical, resulting in performance anxiety that interferes with sexual arousal and emotional closeness.

In contrast, 20% of men and 25% of women report that infertility helped their marriage. The determining characteristics were whether men actively communicated their feelings instead of avoiding conversations about pregnancy and burying themselves in work. In addition to increasing closeness in the relationship, couples who communicated with each other about the infertility also reduced their overall individual stress by doing so (Aaronson, 2006).

Female Infertility

A woman can have difficulty conceiving or be unable to conceive for a number of reasons. Problems with ovulation account for approximately 20% of infertility (Urman & Yakin, 2006). Increasing age reduces fertility significantly (Brandes et al., 2011; Schmidt et al., 2012): A woman's fertility peaks between ages 20 and 24 and begins to decrease rapidly after age 30. Fertility rates in women ages 35 to 39 are up to 46% lower, and in ages 40 to 45 are 95% lower than women at their peak fertility (Fritz & Speroff, 2010). Women over age 35 are twice as likely to have unexplained infertility than are younger women (Maheshwari et al., 2008).

Hormone imbalances, severe vitamin deficiencies, metabolic disturbances, poor nutrition, genetic factors, emotional stress, or medical conditions can contribute to ovulatory problems. Ovulation, and thus pregnancy, can also be inhibited by a below-normal percentage of body fat, which results from excessive dieting or exercise. Being even 10–15% below normal weight is sufficient to inhibit ovulation. Women who smoke cigarettes are less fertile and take longer to become pregnant than nonsmokers, and alcohol and drug abuse reduces fertility in women. Environmental toxins—including

Some fertility specialists think that celebrity moms who have babies later in life, such as Tina Fey, give the false impression that conception at any age is easy.

HRC WENN Photos/Newscom

chemicals in carpets, food packaging, nonstick cookware, and pesticides—may also impair female fertility (Fei et al., 2009; Hannon, 2009). Ovulation problems can sometimes be treated with a variety of medications that stimulate ovulation. Although often successful and generally safe, these drugs can produce certain complications, including a greatly increased chance of multiple births.

If tests indicate that the woman is ovulating and that her partner's semen quality is satisfactory, the next step often is a postcoital test to see whether the sperm remain viable and motile in the cervical mucus. A woman's cervical mucus can contain antibodies that attack her partner's sperm, or it can form a plug that blocks their passage (Ginsburg et al., 1997). Intrauterine insemination (placing semen directly into the uterus) can be helpful in some cases.

Infections and abnormalities of the cervix, vagina, uterus, fallopian tubes, or ovaries can destroy sperm or prevent them from reaching the egg. Scar tissue from old infections—in the fallopian tubes or in or around the ovaries—can block the passage of sperm and eggs. Sexually transmitted infections (STIs) are a common cause of these problems. Tubal problems can sometimes be resolved by surgically removing the scar tissue around the fallopian tubes and ovaries.

Male Infertility

Most causes of male infertility are related to the presence of too few sperm to fertilize an egg or to abnormal sperm shape or motility (the vigor with which sperm cells propel themselves) (American Society for Reproductive Medicine, 2008). A major cause of infertility in men is a damaged or enlarged vein in the testis or vas deferens, called a **varicocele** (Abdel-Meguid, 2012; Zohdy et al., 2011). The varicocele causes blood to pool in the scrotum, which elevates temperature in the area, impairing sperm production (Mishail et al., 2009). Infectious diseases of the male reproductive tract can alter sperm production, viability, and transport. For instance, mumps, when it occurs in adulthood, can affect the testes, lowering sperm output, and infection of the vas deferens can block the passage of sperm. Infections caused by STIs are another major cause of infertility. Smoking, alcohol, and drug use and abuse reduce fertility as well (Springen, 2008). Cocaine use decreases spermatogenesis, and marijuana impedes sperm motility. Environmental toxins, such as chemicals, pollutants, and radiation, can also produce low sperm counts and abnormal sperm cells. Sperm absorb and metabolize environmental toxins more easily than do other body cells, which can also result in birth defects. Environmental factors are the likely cause for the worldwide drop in sperm counts in the last 50 years (Joensen et al., 2009).

To improve the quality of sperm, research indicates that ejaculating daily is helpful (Henderson, 2007). In contrast, when the sperm count is low, to increase the concentration of sperm, the optimal frequency of ejaculation during intercourse is usually every other day, beginning 6 days before ovulation and during the week that the woman is ovulating. A man with a low sperm count might also want to avoid taking hot baths, wearing tight clothing and undershorts, and riding bicycles long distances, because these and similar environments subject the testes to higher than normal temperatures. ●

For poor semen quality or quantity, **intracytoplasmic sperm injection (ICSI)** can result in pregnancy. ICSI involves injecting each harvested egg with a single sperm and is one of the advances in reproductive technology we discuss in the next section.

Reproductive Alternatives

Various alternatives have been developed to help couples overcome the problem of infertility. **Artificial insemination** is one option to be considered in certain instances. In this procedure, semen is mechanically introduced into the woman's vagina or cervix

varicocele
A damaged or enlarged vein in the testis or vas deferens.

SEXUALHEALTH

intracytoplasmic sperm injection (ICSI)
Procedure in which a single sperm is injected into an egg.

artificial insemination
A medical procedure in which semen is placed in a woman's vagina, cervix, or uterus.

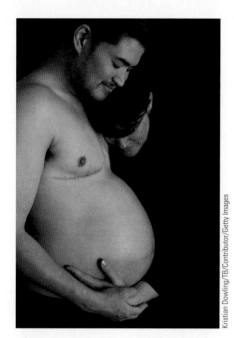

Thomas and Nancy Beatie at home in May 2008 prior to the birth of their first child.

surrogate mother
A woman who is artificially inseminated by the male partner in a childless couple, carries the pregnancy to term, delivers the child, and gives it to the couple for adoption.

assisted reproductive technology (ART)
The techniques of extrauterine conception.

in vitro fertilization (IVF)
Procedure in which mature eggs are removed from a woman's ovary and fertilized by sperm in a laboratory dish.

After a two-year, bicoastal search of fertility clinics and egg donors, Doug Okun, 38, and Eric Ethington, 37, became parents to twins Elizabeth and Sophia thanks to a surrogate mother.

or, in some cases, directly into her uterus, a procedure called *intrauterine insemination*. If the man is not producing adequate viable sperm or if a woman does not have a male partner, artificial insemination with a donor's semen is another option. More than a million people who are alive today in the United States were conceived by donor insemination (Egan, 2012).

Perhaps the most unique pregnancy by artificial insemination is that of the "pregnant man," Thomas Beatie. Thomas was born female but had sex reassignment procedures including testosterone supplementation and chest reconstructive surgery. He is legally recognized as a male. However, he did not alter his female genitals and reproductive organs. When his wife, Nancy, was unable to conceive, the couple decided that he would try to become pregnant. He stopped his testosterone supplementation, used semen purchased via the Internet for artificial insemination, and conceived on the second insemination. Their healthy baby girl, Susan, was born in July 2008. They wanted more children so Thomas became pregnant two more times, and they now have three children.

A **surrogate mother** is a woman who is willing to be artificially inseminated by the male partner of a childless heterosexual, lesbian, or gay couple or to undergo in vitro fertilization using eggs and sperm from a couple. She carries the pregnancy to term, delivers the child, and gives it to the couple for adoption. In the last 30 years, surrogate mothers in the United States have given birth to approximately 25,000 children, and surrogate births rose to 1,000 in 2007, compared to 260 in 2006 (Ginty, 2008b).

Surrogacy can be done anonymously through an attorney or privately by arrangement between the woman and the couple. Some states have made surrogacy illegal, while others permit it but allow only nominal payment to cover medical and incidental expenses (Apel, 2011). In the few states that allow surrogate mothers to be compensated, they typically receive a fee between $20,000 and $30,000. Individuals and couples from European and Middle Eastern countries where surrogacy is illegal travel to the United States and India for surrogates. Surrogacy in India costs 10% of what it costs in the United States and generates $445 million in yearly revenues (Bates, 2010).

The techniques of extrauterine conception are referred to as **assisted reproductive technology (ART)**. The world's first test-tube baby was born in England in 1978. More than 2 million women and couples worldwide have children conceived through IVF, and in the United States about 48,000 women each year deliver babies that were conceived in a laboratory of one of 430 reproductive technology centers (Evans, 2009). In **in vitro fertilization (IVF)** the ovaries are stimulated by hormonal fertility drugs to produce multiple ova. The mature eggs are removed from the woman's ovary and are fertilized in a laboratory dish by her partner's sperm. After 2 or 3 days several fertilized eggs are then introduced into the woman's uterus. Excess embryos are often frozen so that if the first implantation does not take place, the procedure can be repeated. If this procedure is successful, at least one egg will implant and develop. Research had found that couples initially seeking medical help for infertility tend to overestimate the success rates of treatment (van den Boogaard et al., 2011). The success rate of live births from IVF is between 50% and 72%. Live births are twice as likely when the mother is under age 35 (Boyd, 2009). Research on ways to increase the pregnancy rate from IVF is ongoing (Devroey et al., 2009).

Variations on IVF involve transferring fertilized ova to a fallopian tube rather than to the uterus, a procedure known as zygote intrafallopian transfer (ZIFT). In **gamete intrafallopian transfer (GIFT)**, the sperm and ova are placed directly in the fallopian tube, where fertilization normally occurs.

Donated ova can be used for IVF when the woman does not have ovaries, does not produce her own ova, or has a heritable genetic disease. Donation of ova is analogous to donor artificial insemination. Donors are usually women in their 20s, a sister or friend of the infertile woman, or another woman undergoing IVF who donates her ova to another woman wanting the IVF procedure. In cases in which both partners are infertile, IVF can be done with both donated sperm and donated ova.

Financial and Health Costs of Assisted Reproductive Technologies

Assisted reproductive technologies are expensive. One IVF procedure costs an average of $12,000 and up to $15,000, and more than one attempt is often needed. Donor eggs or sperm, ICSI, and any other additional procedures add to the cost (Gurevich, 2011).

Preliminary research on single births has found a twofold increase in heart problems, cleft lip and palate, and abnormalities in the esophagus or rectum in infants conceived with IVF compared to infants conceived naturally. However, since these birth defects are rare to begin with, this increase is small. For example, in the United States cleft lip typically occurs in one out of 950 births, whereas the risk for infants conceived with IVF is one in 425 (Reefhuis et al., 2008).

Multiple embryos are usually implanted during IVF to increase the chances of conception (Roberts et al., 2011). Consequently, the twin birth rate rose by 76% from 1980 to 2009. In 1980, one in every 53 babies was a twin, compared to one in every 30 in 2009. One third of the increase is attributed to more women having babies later in life instead of IVF (Martin et al., 2012). The triplet-or-more birth rate increased by 380% during a similar period (Martin et al., 2009). Any multiple pregnancy increases the danger to babies, with greater incidence of prenatal and postnatal death, prematurity, low birth weight, and birth defects (Wadhawan et al., 2011). For mothers the risks of cesarean deliveries, high blood pressure, and other birth complications, including death, increase with multiple births (MacKay et al., 2006). In some cases one or more fetuses are removed during the pregnancy to increase the likelihood that at least one or two others will survive and be healthy (Stone et al., 2008).

The rate of multiple births following IVF decreased in the late 1990s after the American Society for Reproductive Medicine published guidelines for reducing the number of multiple births (Martin et al., 2009). Other countries have strict regulations: Some European countries have laws instead of guidelines limiting IVF to one or two embryos (Gibbs, 2008).

Legal, Ethical, and Personal Dilemmas Associated With Assisted Reproductive Technologies

Assisted reproductive technologies have given rise to unprecedented ethical and legal dilemmas. Extra embryos often result from the assisted reproductive process, and some couples generously put their surplus embryos up for adoption, to be implanted in another woman. Other women and couples donate the embryos for stem-cell research. One study found that 60% of couples were willing to donate their surplus embryos to research, 22% were willing to donate to another couple, and 24% would discard them (Kliff, 2007). Other situations result in controversy, as when a divorcing couple disagrees about what to do with the embryos they froze before they ended their marriage. By 2000, more than 20,000 frozen embryos were the subjects of such disputes (Silvertsen, 2000).

zygote intrafallopian transfer (ZIFT) Procedure in which an egg is fertilized in the laboratory and then placed in a fallopian tube.

gamete intrafallopian transfer (GIFT) Procedure in which the sperm and ovum are placed directly in a fallopian tube.

Critical Thinking Question

Do you think children conceived by donor sperm and/or egg insemination should be told about this? Why or why not?

Janise Wulf, who is 62 years old, holds her 4-day-old baby boy, Adam, born in February 2006. The newborn is her 12th child.

Further ethical questions arise regarding selling embryos and paying women for their ova and men for their sperm. Unlike the United States, Canada and China prohibit paying women for ova, resulting in a shortage of eggs and embryos for IVF. Women with sufficient financial resources resort to "international reproductive travel"—going to other countries to purchase ova or embryos for IVF (Heng, 2009).

Pre-implantation genetic diagnosis of embryos is currently available and is used to screen for serious genetic problems. Genetic alteration prior to implantation might be implemented in the near future (Geary & Moon, 2006). Genetic alteration could give parents with a known genetic defect—predisposing them to developing Alzheimer's, breast cancer, cystic fibrosis, or another illness—the ability to have their eggs and sperm genetically altered to remove the illness-causing genetic material prior to in vitro fertilization and implantation (Begley, 2001). Nine months later the couple's baby will be born without the legacy of family genetic problems. Many bioethicists support this development, which can shield children from disabling and life-threatening genetic problems. Others oppose this technology because it could be used to genetically engineer "designer babies," selecting for characteristics such as hair, eye, and skin color (Moses, 2009).

Reproductive technology has made it possible for women past the age of menopause to become pregnant, carry the pregnancy, and deliver their babies. The postmenopausal woman's own ova are not viable, so ova from a younger woman are fertilized in vitro, usually with the sperm from the older woman's husband. With hormonal assistance, the woman's uterus can maintain a pregnancy. Women as old as 70 have had babies by means of ART (Caplan, 2008). In the future, younger women may have their ova preserved by freezing to offer them some protection against the decline in fertility with aging (Stoop et al., 2011).

Should elderly parents who may die before their children reach adulthood be denied the use of reproductive technology? Some believe that the welfare of current and future children should be taken into account, but others maintain that it is unethical to deny women the opportunity to conceive on the basis of age alone (Murray, 2009). Current guidelines from the American Society for Reproductive Medicine state that fertility programs can withhold services only if they have well-substantiated judgments that the woman or couple cannot provide adequate child rearing (Rubin, 2009).

Fifty years ago assisted reproductive techniques were found in science fiction stories instead of at the numerous assisted reproductive centers in the United States. Assisted reproduction is currently a $3 billion a year industry (Coeytaux et al., 2011). Financial incentive and technological advancements will continue to expand the options for reproductive technologies as well as the legal, ethical, and personal quandaries that invariably accompany them. The director of the Project on Biotechnology in the Public Interest at the Center for Genetics and Society summarizes:

> Responsible federal oversight of the fertility industry, in ways that protect reproductive rights and actually improve appropriate access to fertility, is not only possible but long overdue. Comprehensive policies have been adopted in Canada, the United Kingdom, and elsewhere. It's time for the United States to catch up and move beyond its reputation as the "Wild West" of assisted reproduction. (Reynolds, 2009, p. 3)

Pregnancy Detection

The initial signs of pregnancy can provoke feelings from joy to dread, depending on the woman's desire to be pregnant, her partner's feelings, and a variety of surrounding circumstances. Although some women have either a light blood flow or spotting (irregular bleeding) after conception, usually the first indication of pregnancy is the absence of the menstrual period at the expected time. Breast tenderness, nausea, vomiting, or other nonspecific symptoms (such as extreme fatigue or change in appetite) can also accompany pregnancy in the first weeks or months.

Any of these clues might cause a woman to suspect that she is pregnant. Medical techniques such as blood or urine tests and pelvic exams can make the determination with greater certainty. The blood and urine of a pregnant woman contain the hormone **human chorionic gonadotropin** (cohr-ee-AH-nik goh-na-duh-TROH-pun) **(HCG)**, which is secreted by the placenta. Sensitive blood tests for HCG have been developed that can detect pregnancy as early as 7 days after conception. Commercially available at-home pregnancy urine or saliva tests can detect pregnancy shortly after a missed menstrual period. Because elective home pregnancy tests can yield both false-positive and false-negative results, a health-care practitioner should confirm the results.

human chorionic gonadotropin (HCG)
A hormone that is detectable in the urine of a pregnant woman within 1 month of conception.

Spontaneous and Elective Abortion

Not every pregnancy results in a birth. Many pregnancies end in spontaneous or elective abortion.

Miscarriage and Stillbirth

Even when pregnancy has been confirmed, complications can prevent full-term development of the fetus. A **miscarriage** is a **spontaneous abortion** that occurs in the first 20 weeks of pregnancy; many occur before the woman finds out that she is pregnant. At least one in seven known pregnancies ends in miscarriage (Springen, 2005). ■ Table 11.1 gives the most common causes of miscarriage, but in many cases doctors are unable to determine the specific cause (Kaare, 2009).

spontaneous abortion (miscarriage)
The spontaneous expulsion of the fetus from the uterus early in pregnancy, before it can survive on its own.

Early miscarriages can appear as a heavier than usual menstrual flow; later miscarriages might involve uncomfortable cramping and heavy bleeding. Fortunately for women who desire a child, one miscarriage rarely means that a later pregnancy will be unsuccessful, although many women and couples worry about the possibility of having another miscarriage in a subsequent pregnancy.

When a fetus dies after 20 weeks of pregnancy, it is sometimes referred to as a *stillbirth*. About 26,000 fetal deaths occur each year in the United States, and rates of fetal death are higher for teenagers and women age 35 and older, and for twin and other multiple births (MacDorman & Kirmeyer, 2009). As with miscarriage, the causes of stillbirth are often unknown. Problems with the placenta or umbilical cord, the baby's health or development, and maternal health problems such as diabetes or high blood pressure are some of the known factors.

Miscarriage and stillbirth can be a significant loss for the woman or couple. Couples may need to grieve the loss of this pregnancy and baby for several months

At a Glance
■ **TABLE 11.1 Prime Suspects: Possible Causes of Miscarriage**
Maternal age greater than 35 years
More than 5 alcoholic drinks per week
Smoking tobacco
More than 375 mg of caffeine per day (2–3 cups of coffee)
Rejection of abnormal fetus
Cocaine use
Damaged cervix
Chronic kidney inflammation
Abnormal uterus
Infection
Underactive thyroid gland
Autoimmune reaction
Diabetes
Emotional shock
Aspirin and nonsteroidal anti-inflammatory drugs early in pregnancy
Obesity

SOURCES: Baba et al. (2011), Lash & Armstrong (2009), and Speroff & Fritz (2005).

before pursuing another pregnancy. Some parents who lose an unborn child find it meaningful to create a memory book of the pregnancy and baby and hold a memorial ceremony of some kind. With a stillbirth, parents may find it important to have photos and footprints of the baby (Price, 2008).

Elective Abortion

elective abortion
Medical procedure performed to terminate pregnancy.

In contrast to a spontaneous abortion, an **elective abortion** involves a decision to terminate a pregnancy by using medical procedures. Each year, nearly half of all pregnancies of women in the United States are unplanned. Women who are 18 to 24 years old, poor, and cohabiting have two to three times the national rate (Finer & Zolna, 2011). Many of the unplanned pregnancies become welcome and wanted. However, about 4 in 10 of these unplanned pregnancies are terminated by abortion. In 2008, 1.2 million women had an abortion, and an estimated 33% of women in the United States will have had an abortion by age 45 (Guttmacher Institute, 2011a).

Recent statistics find that women in their 20s have more than half of all abortions, and teenagers have 18% of abortions. About 61% of women having abortions each year have one or more children. Among women having an abortion, 37% identify themselves as Protestant and 28% as Catholic (Guttmacher Institute, 2011a).

How Women Decide

After a woman confirms that she is pregnant (assuming that she was not trying to conceive), she must then decide whether to carry the pregnancy and keep the child, give the child up for adoption, or have an abortion. Abortion is a last resort for women who are faced with pregnancies they did not want. Research indicates that women rely on practical and emotional matters to make their decisions about their dilemma (Wind, 2006). Concern and responsibility for others is a frequent reason for choosing to terminate the pregnancy. Women without children often say they are unprepared for motherhood, and women who already have one or more children cite their desire to be a good parent and the difficulties in meeting their current responsibilities as a mother as their primary reason for needing an abortion (Guttmacher Institute, 2011a; R. Jones et al., 2008).

In the United States two thirds of women who have abortions say their primary reason is that they cannot afford a child, and 60% of abortions occur among those with an annual income below $28,000 for a family of three (Boonstra et al., 2006). Unfortunately, in part because of the erosion of government-funded contraceptive services between 1994 and 2008, low-income women were considerably more likely to have an unplanned pregnancy than are higher-income women (Wind, 2006). After President Obama's election in 2008, his administration increased government-funded family planning services to help reduce rates of unplanned pregnancy and abortion (Slaetan, 2009). However, by 2012 tens of thousands of teenagers and low-income women lost access to subsidized contraception as many states with Republican-led legislatures cut or reduced funding for family planning services (Simon, 2012).

Shared Responsibility

SEXUALHEALTH ▶ A couple can share responsibility for the decision about whether to have an abortion and for the abortion itself, if that choice is made, in several ways. First, the man can help his partner clarify her feelings and can express his own regarding the unwanted pregnancy and how best to deal with it. Important topics for a couple to discuss include each person's life situation at the time, their feelings about the pregnancy and each other, the pros and cons of the possible choices, and their future plans as individuals and as a couple. If the man and woman disagree on what to do, the final decision rests with the woman: Male partners do not have a legal right to demand or deny abortion for the woman. Research has found that most partners of single and married women who have abortions know about and are supportive of the decision. However, women were unlikely to disclose the pregnancy and abortion to partners who had been physically abusive to them prior to the pregnancy (Jones et al., 2010). ●

Psychological Reactions to Abortion

Choosing to have an abortion is usually a difficult decision for a woman and her partner. It means weighing and examining highly personal values and circumstances. Even when the pregnancy is unwanted, one or both partners may feel loss and sadness. Research found that women who felt that the abortion was not primarily their decision and did not feel clear emotional support after the abortion had some emotional distress following abortion (Kimport et al., 2011). However, well-designed studies of psychological reactions following abortion have consistently found that the risk of mental health problems is no greater than for women who continue their pregnancies. Ongoing feelings of sadness, guilt, regret, and depression after an abortion are uncommon (American Psychological Association, 2008; Munk-Olsen, 2011; Steinberg & Finer, 2011).

Pregnancy Risk Taking and Abortion

In many cases an unwanted pregnancy is clearly a matter of contraceptive failure. About 54% of women who have had an abortion were using contraception when they became pregnant (Guttmacher Institute, 2011a). For other women or couples seeking abortions, the pregnancy can be traced to contraceptive risk taking—that is, not using contraceptives consistently or reliably, sometimes because of inconvenience, side effects of certain methods, or perceived low risk of pregnancy (Perlman & McKee, 2009). Being under the influence of alcohol or drugs reduces judgment and greatly increases contraceptive risk taking, unless the woman is using a method such as the pill or IUD. Women who feel guilty about sex may not proactively use contraception because doing so acknowledges their intent to engage in intercourse. Women may also not be assertive about contraception if they fear alienating a partner by asking for his cooperation in planning and using birth control.

Rates of Abortion

The United States has one of the highest abortion rates in the developed world. Each year, 21 out of every 1,000 women of reproductive age have an abortion (Guttmacher Institute, 2012a). In contrast, abortion rates in western Europe of 12 per 1,000 women are the lowest in the world. Differences in many social policies contribute to the lower abortion rates in other developed countries, including comprehensive sex education in schools and easy access to inexpensive or free birth control and emergency contraceptives. In addition, these countries assist mothers by providing maternity leave, health care, education and training, an adequate minimum wage, and other social services. In contrast, from 2001 to 2009 the Bush administration strongly opposed and restricted funding for these policies despite the fact that they result in lower abortion rates. However, to the extent possible given Republican opposition, the Obama administration reestablished these kinds of programs that have helped reduce abortion rates in other developed nations (Bendavid et al., 2011).

Worldwide, about one in five pregnancies ends in abortion (Guttmacher Institute, 2012a). The very highest abortion rates are in countries that severely restrict abortion but do not provide the social services, sex education, and access to contraception that Western European governments do. For example, each year, 56 out of 1,000 women in Peru have abortions, compared to 8 out of 1,000 in the Netherlands (Boonstra et al., 2006). In the developing world, abortion rates are lowest in subregions where contraceptive use is high (Barot, 2011).

Procedures for Abortion

Several different abortion procedures are used at different stages of pregnancy. In the United States, 62% of legal abortions occur within the first 8 weeks of pregnancy, and 92% of abortions are done in the first 12 weeks (Mugge, 2011). Early abortion is very safe. The risk of dying from a surgical abortion is 0.1 per 100,000 women, while the risk of pregnancy fatality is 11.8 per 100,000 (Zielinski, 2006). The most common procedures are *medical abortion, suction curettage, D and E,* and *prostaglandin induction.*

Medical abortion uses pills instead of surgery to end a pregnancy (Templeton & Grimes, 2011). A woman can have a medical abortion within days of a missed period and up to 9 weeks into a pregnancy. The medication mifepristone, commonly known as RU 486, became available in 2000 to women in the United States. Medical abortion has been available in European countries since 1980—20 years earlier than in the United States. Decades of anti-abortion political action against the U.S. manufacture and distribution of medications for abortion caused the delay (Jones & Henshaw, 2002). Medical abortions account for about 13% of all elective abortions in the United States (Ginty, 2008b). Women with 12 years or more of education are more likely than women with less than a high school education to have medical abortions (Yunzal-Butler et al., 2011).

A medical abortion is 99% effective in ending pregnancies of less than 7 weeks and 91% effective in the 8th week of pregnancy (Speroff & Fritz, 2005). It is safer than the abortion procedures done later in pregnancy and safer than childbirth itself. In addition, a woman who opts for a medical abortion can see her family doctor at an office instead of going to another facility (Quindlen, 2009b).

Medical abortion works by blocking the hormone progesterone, which causes the cervix to soften, the lining of the uterus to break down, and bleeding to begin. A few days later the woman takes a second medicine that makes the uterus contract and expel the grape-size embryonic sac. ▌ Figure 11.1 shows how a medical abortion works. Side effects can include cramping, headaches, nausea, or vomiting, but many women experience no physical side effects (Hausknecht, 2003).

Suction curettage is a surgical technique used 7 to 13 weeks past the last menstrual period. A suction curettage is performed by physicians at clinics or hospitals and takes about 10 minutes. During the procedure local anesthetic is used and a small plastic tube is inserted through the cervical os into the uterus. The tube is attached to a vacuum aspirator, which draws the placenta, built-up uterine lining, and fetal tissue out of the uterus. Rare complications include uterine infection or perforation, hemorrhage, or incomplete removal of the uterine contents. Research data indicate that a first-trimester abortion does not have a significant effect on subsequent fertility, pregnancy or health of the newborn (Guttmacher Institute, 2011a).

If a pregnancy progresses past approximately 12 weeks, the suction curettage procedure is no longer as safe, because the uterine walls have become thinner, making perforation and bleeding more likely. For pregnancy termination between 13 and 21 weeks, a **D and E**, or **dilation and evacuation**, is the safest and most widely used technique. A combination of suction equipment, special forceps, and a curette (a metal instrument

medical abortion
The use of medications to end a pregnancy of 7 weeks or less.

suction curettage
A procedure in which the cervical os is dilated by using graduated metal dilators or a laminaria; then a small plastic tube, attached to a vacuum aspirator, is inserted into the uterus, drawing the fetal tissue, placenta, and built-up uterine lining out of the uterus.

dilation and evacuation (D and E)
An abortion procedure in which a curette and suction equipment are used.

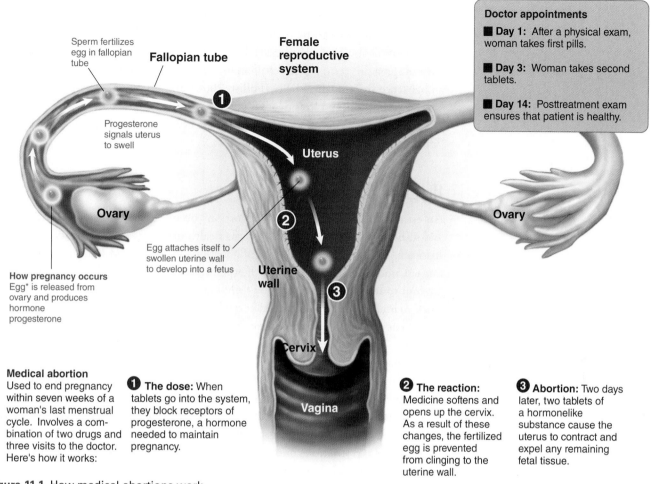

Sperm fertilizes egg in fallopian tube

Fallopian tube

Female reproductive system

Progesterone signals uterus to swell

① Uterus

Ovary

Ovary

Egg attaches itself to swollen uterine wall to develop into a fetus

② Uterine wall

How pregnancy occurs
Egg* is released from ovary and produces hormone progesterone

③ Cervix

Vagina

Medical abortion
Used to end pregnancy within seven weeks of a woman's last menstrual cycle. Involves a combination of two drugs and three visits to the doctor. Here's how it works:

① The dose: When tablets go into the system, they block receptors of progesterone, a hormone needed to maintain pregnancy.

② The reaction: Medicine softens and opens up the cervix. As a result of these changes, the fertilized egg is prevented from clinging to the uterine wall.

③ Abortion: Two days later, two tablets of a hormonelike substance cause the uterus to contract and expel any remaining fetal tissue.

▌**Figure 11.1** How medical abortions work.

---

used to scrape the walls of the uterus) is used. General anesthesia is usually required, and the procedure is riskier. About 8.9 women out of 100,000 will die from an abortion after 20 weeks of pregnancy—still less than the rate of 11.8 out of 100,000 who die from a full-term pregnancy (Zielinski, 2006). Women who are more likely to have abortions at 13 weeks or later have some characteristics in common. They have less education and are more likely to be African American than are women who have first-trimester abortions. They have also experienced three or more disruptive life events in the past year, such as being a victim of a crime, becoming unemployed, having a medical problem, or experiencing the death of a friend or family member (Jones & Finer, 2011). Teens are more likely than older women to delay having an abortion until after 15 weeks of pregnancy (Guttmacher Institute, 2011a).

Second-trimester pregnancies can also be terminated by using compounds such as **prostaglandins**, hormones that cause uterine contractions. The prostaglandin is introduced into the vagina as a suppository or into the amniotic sac by inserting a needle through the abdominal wall; the fetus and placenta are usually expelled from the vagina within 24 hours. Complications from procedures that induce labor contractions include nausea, vomiting, and diarrhea; tearing of the cervix; excessive bleeding; and the possibility of shock and death.

Late-term abortion, or **intact dilation and evacuation**, is done after 20 weeks and before viability at 24 weeks' gestation. It is reserved for situations when serious health risks to the woman, or severe fetal abnormalities, exist. In this procedure the cervix is dilated, the fetus emerges feet first out of the uterus, and the fetal skull is collapsed to

prostaglandins
Hormones that are used to induce uterine contractions and fetal expulsion for second-trimester abortions.

late-term abortion (intact dilation and evacuation)
An abortion done between 20 and 24 weeks when serious health risks to the woman or severe fetal abnormalities exist.

permit passage of the head through the cervix and vagina. Although late-term abortions after 21 weeks of pregnancy are rare, comprising 1.3% of all abortions in the United States, they continue to be the focus of intense political controversy (Mugge, 2011). Opponents of abortion rights call this procedure "partial-birth abortion," and the media have adopted this term instead of dilation and evacuation despite its imprecise meaning and absence from medical texts (Pollitt, 2006). In 2003 Congress approved a ban on late-term abortion, and President George W. Bush signed the bill. In 2007 the Supreme Court upheld the legislation, creating the first-ever federal ban on a medical procedure (Guttmacher Institute, 2009b).

Illegal Abortions

An estimated 21.6 million unsafe abortions occur yearly, resulting in 47,000 deaths and millions of women left with serious health problems and infertility (Guttmacher Institute, 2012a). More than 95% of abortions in Africa and Latin America are performed under unsafe conditions. Desperate to end unwanted pregnancies, women attempt to self-induce abortions by drinking turpentine, bleach, or tea made with livestock manure. They insert herbal preparations into the vagina or cervix and push a stick, coat hanger, or chicken bone through the cervix into the uterus (Guttmacher Institute, 2008c). Illegal abortionists typically insert a sharp instrument or object into the uterus to induce contractions.

Laws that make abortion illegal do not decrease the incidence of abortion. In fact, higher rates of abortion are found in countries where abortion is illegal, primarily because of the unavailability of contraception. There is a worldwide trend toward legalization of abortion. Since 1997 only three countries—El Salvador, Nicaragua, and Russia—have increased legal restrictions on abortion, and 17 countries have legalized or broadened the grounds for legal abortion during the same period (Guttmacher Institute, 2012a).

Abortion supporters and opponents usually believe very strongly in their positions.

The Abortion Controversy

Elective abortion continues to be a highly controversial political issue in the United States and many other countries (Kulczycki, 2011). Beliefs regarding the beginning of life, women's right to reproductive choice, and the role of government influence the stand individuals take regarding elective termination of pregnancy.

Abortion: Historical Overview

Laws regulating abortion have changed over time. In ancient China and Europe, abortion early in pregnancy was legal. In the 13th century, St. Thomas Aquinas delineated the Catholic Church's view that the fetus developed a soul after conception—after 40 days for males and 90 days for females. Centuries later, in the late 1860s, Pope Pius IX declared that human life begins at conception and is at any stage just as important as the mother's. The Roman Catholic Church still maintains this position, although 58% of American Catholics believe one can be a "good Catholic" and disregard the church's teachings on abortion (L. Miller, 2008).

Early American law, based on English common law, allowed abortion until the pregnant woman felt quickening, or movement of the fetus. During the 1860s, abortion became illegal in the United States, except when necessary to save the woman's life. Reasons for this change included the belief that population growth was important to the country's developing economy and, perhaps, the male-dominated political system's unease about the emerging movement of middle-class White women seeking independence and equality (Sheeran, 1987). Consequently, women who had enough money would travel to a country where abortion was legal or persuade an American physician to perform a safe, illegal abortion. Women without the money to pursue such options may have been fortunate enough to find one of the skilled underground abortion providers working for free or for little compensation. Otherwise, they resorted to desperate measures: "back alley" abortions using unsafe, unskilled, and unsanitary procedures, or self-induced abortions, sometimes using a wire coat hanger, douching with bleach, or swallowing turpentine (Solinger, 2005). The momentum for legalizing abortion arose from these circumstances.

Roe v. Wade and Beyond

By the 1960s, advocacy groups were lobbying for change and had begun to win a few battles on the state level. In 1973, based on the constitutional right to privacy, the U.S. Supreme Court in *Roe v. Wade* legalized a woman's right to terminate her pregnancy before the fetus has reached the age of viability. *Viability* is defined as the fetus's ability to survive independently of the woman's body—an ability that develops by the 6th or 7th month of pregnancy. *Roe v. Wade* voided the remaining state laws that treated abortion as a criminal act for both the doctor performing the abortion and the woman undergoing the procedure. ▌ Figure 11.2 shows the decline in deaths from abortion following the repeal or reform of laws against abortion in 15 states and the Court's ruling in *Roe v. Wade* that made abortion legal in all states.

However, the legalization of abortion in 1973 did not end the controversy. In 1977 Congress passed the Hyde Amendment, which restricted the use of federal Medicaid funds for abortions, leaving millions of low-income women of reproductive age, who obtain their health care through Medicaid, without this resource (Boonstra & Sonfield, 2000). States may use their own funds for this purpose, but only 17 states pay for abortions for low-income women. Consequently, many poor women either sacrifice their rent, food, and clothing money for themselves and their children to pay for an abortion, or bring another child into already difficult circumstances (Boonstra et al., 2006). The abortion rate among poor women (those living below the federal poverty level) rose 18% between 2000 and 2008 (Jones & Kavanaugh, 2011). Availability of low-cost contraceptive services and methods is essential in reducing these rates (Thompson et al., 2011).

Since the Hyde Amendment, the Supreme Court has made additional rulings that allow states to place restrictions on abortion. These regulations impede, and often eliminate, women's access to abortion. The Sex and Politics box discusses current state restrictions on abortion and their impact.

The Current Debate

The abortion controversy centers on the debate between the pro-choice and the anti-choice, or right-to-life, positions. Recent polls have found that equal numbers (47%) of people in the United States identify themselves as pro-choice or right-to-life (Saad, 2011). Pro-choice advocates maintain that safe and legal abortion is a necessary last resort and oppose government control over a woman's right to make her own reproductive decisions. They want women faced with the dilemma of an unwanted pregnancy to be free to decide that terminating it is their best alternative (National Abortion Rights

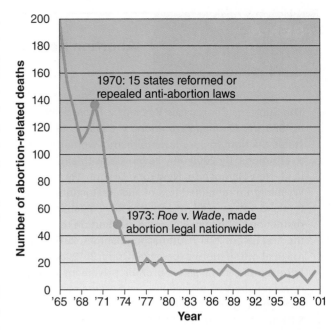

▌ **Figure 11.2** Deaths from abortion declined dramatically after legalization.

The Supreme Court cases *Webster v. Reproductive Rights* in 1989 and *Planned Parenthood v. Casey* in 1992 gave states the right to pass laws to restrict women's access to abortions. By 2009 only seven states (Maine, Maryland, New Hampshire, New York, Oregon, Vermont, and Washington) remained free of such restrictions. Legislators and voters in all other states have established myriad restrictions, and states enacted 80 abortion restrictions in the first half of 2011 (Guttmacher Institute, 2011d). Some make abortion more expensive (Crary, 2012; Joyce, 2011). For example, some states prohibit private insurance from covering abortion procedures, and others restrict insurance coverage of abortion for public employees. About 20 states that require counseling also mandate a waiting period of up to 24 hours between receiving counseling and undergoing abortion, adding to child-care and travel costs and loss of income due to time taken from work (G. Robertson, 2011). In 2012 the legislature in Utah established a waiting period of 72 hours for women seeking an abortion (Gryboski, 2012).

Thirty-five states require a minor to notify and/or obtain the consent of one or both parents before she can have an abortion, or to obtain a judge's permission to do so without parental consent. Parental consent laws can delay teens' access to abortion: Research has found that increased rates of second-term abortions occur after states have established parental notification laws (Joyce et al., 2006). Although most adolescents do discuss their pregnancy options with their parents, laws that require parental notification and consent assume that all parents have their daughters' best interests at heart. Sadly, this is not the case for abusive and neglectful parents. It is ironic that parental consent is not required for a pregnant young woman to have the baby and take on the responsibilities of parenthood, but it is required if she decides *not* to become a mother (Stotland, 1998). For these and other reasons, many leading medical groups oppose mandatory parental consent requirements—groups such as the American Medical

Association, the American Academy of Pediatrics, and the American Academy of Family Physicians.

Mandatory counseling sessions are an especially controversial issue because of the faulty information that some of the 34 states require abortion providers to present to women prior to an abortion. This misinformation can include the claim that abortion endangers future pregnancies and poses significant risks of death, breast cancer, long-lasting psychological problems, or suicide. In South Dakota, an abortion provider is required to tell any woman seeking an abortion that abortion ends a human life (Ewing, 2011). The goal of these requirements is to dissuade women from having abortions rather than provide accurate medical information to help the woman make a well-informed decision. Further, this type of "counseling" forces health-care professionals to either disregard the ethics of informed consent and medical practice or break the state law (H. Hall, 2009; Lazzarini, 2008).

Although an ultrasound is not routinely medically necessary for a first-trimester abortion, laws and legislative bills in more than 27 states require health-care providers to offer women seeking abortions the opportunity to have an ultrasound of the fetus and listen to its heartbeat: Seven states require the provider to conduct an ultrasound and offer the woman the opportunity to see the image (Guttmacher Institute, 2012b).

It would seem logical to assume that states that restrict abortion would provide increased resources for the children who are born into difficult circumstances because abortion was not an option. However, states with the most legal restrictions on abortion also provide the fewest resources to facilitate adoption, the least assistance to children in low-income families, and the lowest funds to educate children (C. Cooper, 2008). Former president Jimmy Carter, a devout Baptist, states, "Many fervent pro-life activists do not extend their concern to the baby who is born, and are the least likely to support benevolent programs that they consider 'socialistic'" (2005, p. 94).

Action League, 2009). One columnist has stated, "Mothering is so critical and so challenging that to force anyone into its service is immoral" (Quindlen, 2003, p. 26). Many prestigious organizations, including many associated with religious institutions, have made public statements opposing anti-abortion legislation: Catholics for Choice, the National Academy of Sciences, the American Public Health Association, the American Medical Association, and the American College of Obstetricians and Gynecologists. Of the American public, 64% want *Roe v. Wade* to remain in place (Marcus, 2009).

Antichoice advocates believe that once an ovum has been fertilized, it is a human being whose right to life supersedes the woman's right to choose whether to continue her pregnancy. Consequently, advocates believe that abortion is immoral and constitutes murder of a "pre-born" child. Anti-abortion organizations and advocates want to see *Roe v. Wade* overturned and want Congress to pass the Life at Conception Act or to amend the U.S. Constitution with the Paramount Human Life Amendment, both of which establish the fertilized egg as an independent being entitled to equal protection under the law (National Pro-Life Alliance, 2009). Another anti-abortion group continues to attempt to pass "personhood" amendments in several states that define a fertilized egg as having legal rights (Cohen, 2012b; Raasch, 2012). All of the 2012 Republican candidates for the U.S. presidency ran on platforms to overturn *Roe v. Wade* and to eliminate federal funding for abortion (White, 2012).

Extreme anti-abortion activists have gone beyond legal means to restrict abortion—blocking clinic entrances; harassing patients, physicians, and staff; and burning or bombing clinics. In 2008, about 57% of non-hospital facilities that provide abortion experienced some kind of harassment. Levels of harassment are highest in the Midwest and the South (Jones & Kooistra, 2011). Pro-life extremists have resorted to killing physicians and staff who work in abortion clinics, believing that these murders are justified to save unborn babies. In May 2009 a pro-life extremist shot and killed Dr. George Tiller as he entered his church for Sunday services. He had previously escaped death in 1993 when an anti-abortion extremist shot him in both arms and claimed at her trial that she had done nothing wrong in her attempt to kill a physician who performed abortions (Kissling, 2009). Doctors and clinics that provide abortions must implement stringent security measures: metal detectors, alarms, and bulletproof glass and vests (Joffe, 2009; National Abortion Rights Action League, 2009). The abortion debate will remain passionate and bitter because of fundamental differences in beliefs and worldviews of people with strong commitments to one side or the other. However, most people experience considerable ambivalence about abortion (Kliff, 2010). Many people who believe abortion is wrong also believe that any woman who wants an abortion should be able to obtain it legally.

The Experience of Pregnancy

Pregnancy is a unique and significant experience for both a woman and her partner. In the following pages, we look at the experience and the effect it has on the individuals and the couple. Many of the experiences are encountered by heterosexual and lesbian couples alike. In this section the heterosexual couple is used as a frame of reference.

The Woman's Experience

Each woman has different emotional and physical reactions to pregnancy, and the same woman may react differently to different pregnancies. Here are two reactions at the opposite ends of the continuum:

> I loved being pregnant. My face glowed for nine months. I felt like a kindred spirit to all female mammals and discovered a new respect for my body and its ability to create life. The bigger I got, the better I liked it. (Authors' files)

> If I could have babies without the pregnancy part, I'd do it. Looking fat and slowed down is a huge drag. (Authors' files)

Factors influencing a woman's emotional reactions can include how the decision for pregnancy was made, current and impending lifestyle changes, her relationship with others, her financial resources, her self-image, and hormonal changes. The woman's acquired attitudes and knowledge about childbearing and her hopes and fears about parenthood also contribute to her experience. Positive support and attention from her partner are helpful in creating a happy pregnancy.

Women sometimes feel that they should experience only positive emotions when they are pregnant. However, pregnancy often elicits an array of contradictory emotions. One study of 1,000 women found a wide range of feelings about pregnancy: 35% loved being pregnant, 40% had mixed feelings about it, 8% hated it, and the remainder had different experiences with each of their pregnancies. The researchers concluded that the degree of physical discomfort a woman experiences during the 9 months of pregnancy greatly influences her feelings about being pregnant (Genevie & Margolies, 1987). For some women pregnancy is a very difficult period; about 12% of women experience significant depression during pregnancy (Stewart, 2011).

The Man's Experience

An expectant father obviously does not experience the same physical sensations that a pregnant woman does (although occasionally a "pregnant father" reports psychosympathetic symptoms, such as the nausea or tiredness his partner is experiencing). However, the experiences of pregnancy and birth are often profound for the father. What exactly does the "male pregnancy" involve?

Like the woman, he often reacts with a great deal of ambivalence. He may feel ecstatic but also fearful about the woman's and the baby's well-being. It is common for a man to feel frightened about the impending birth and about whether he will be able to "keep it together." He may feel especially tender toward his partner and become more solicitous. At the same time, he may feel a sense of separateness from the woman because of the physical changes that only she is experiencing. However, prenatal ultrasonography allows fathers to see the fetus growing in the uterus and can create greater feelings of involvement (Sandelowski, 1994). Most men feel concern over the impending increase in financial responsibility. In all, the expectant father has special needs, as does his partner, and it is important that the woman be aware of these needs and be willing to respond to them.

Sexual Interaction During Pregnancy

In pregnancies with no risk factors, the woman and couple can continue sexual activity and orgasm as desired until the onset of labor (C. Jones et al., 2011). A woman's sexual interest and responsiveness will likely change throughout the course of her pregnancy. Nausea, breast tenderness, and fatigue can inhibit sexual interest during the first 3 months. A resurgence of sexual desire and arousal occurs for some women in the second trimester, with increased vasocongestion of the genitals during pregnancy heightening sexual desire and response. However, most research shows a progressive decline in sexual interest and activity over the 9 months of pregnancy (Bogren, 1991). Some of the most common reasons women give for decreasing sexual activity during pregnancy include physical discomfort, feelings of physical unattractiveness, and fear of injuring the unborn child (Colino, 1991).

The partner's feelings also affect the sexual relationship during pregnancy. Reactions to the woman's changing body and to the need for adjustment in the couple's sexual repertoire can vary from increased excitement to inhibition for the partner.

During pregnancy a couple will need to modify intercourse positions. The side-by-side, woman-above, and rear-entry positions are generally more comfortable than the man-above position as pregnancy progresses. Oral and manual genital stimulation as well as total body touching and holding can continue as usual. In fact, pregnancy is a time when a couple can explore and develop these dimensions of lovemaking more fully; even if intercourse is not desired, intimacy, eroticism, and sexual satisfaction can continue. Open communication, accurate information, mutual support, and flexibility in sexual frequency and activities can help maintain and strengthen the bond between the partners. ●

A Healthy Pregnancy

Once a woman becomes pregnant, her previous lifestyle and her health habits and medical care during pregnancy play an important part in the development of a healthy fetus (Melhado, 2011).

Fetal Development

The 9-month (40-week) span of pregnancy is customarily divided into three 13-week segments, called *trimesters*. Characteristic changes occur in each trimester.

First-Trimester Development

As with all mammals, a human begins as a **zygote** (ZYE-goht), a united sperm cell and ovum. The sperm and egg unite in one of the fallopian tubes, where the egg's fingerlike microvilli draw the sperm to it. The zygote then develops into the multicelled **blastocyst** (BLAS-tuh-sist) that implants on the wall of the uterus about 1 week after fertilization (❙ Figure 11.3). Growth progresses steadily. By 9–10 weeks after a woman's last menstrual period, the fetal heartbeat can be heard with a special ultrasound stethoscope known as the Doppler. By the beginning of the 2nd month from the time of conception, the fetus is 0.5 to 1 inch long, grayish, and crescent shaped. During the 2nd month, the spinal canal and rudimentary arms and legs form, as do the beginnings of recognizable eyes, fingers, and toes. During the 3rd month, internal organs, such as the liver, kidneys, intestines, and lungs, begin limited functioning in the 3-inch fetus.

zygote
The single cell resulting from the union of sperm and egg cells.

blastocyst
Multicellular descendant of the united sperm and ovum that implants on the wall of the uterus.

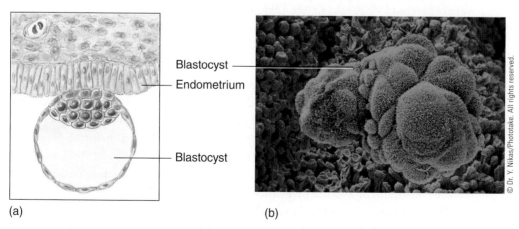

(a)   (b)

❙ **Figure 11.3** The blastocyst implanted on the uterine wall, shown (a) in diagram and (b) in photo taken by a scanning electron microscope.

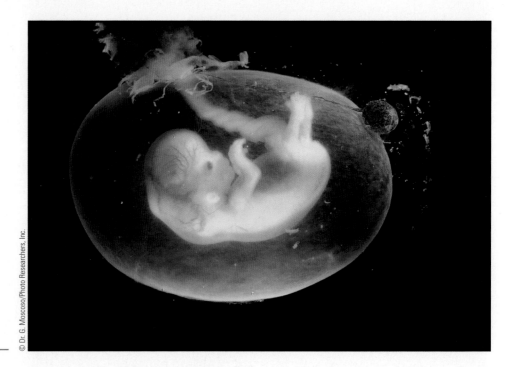

Fetal development at 9 weeks. The fetus is connected to the placenta by the umbilical cord.

Second-Trimester Development

The second trimester begins with the 4th month of pregnancy. By now the sex of the fetus can often be distinguished. External body parts, including fingernails, eyebrows, and eyelashes, are clearly formed. The fetus's skin is covered by fine, downlike hair. Future development consists primarily of growth and refinement of the features that already exist. Fetal movements, or quickening, can be felt by the end of the 4th month. By the end of the 5th month the fetus's weight has increased to 1 pound. Head hair can appear at this time, and subcutaneous fat develops. By the end of the second trimester, the fetus has opened its eyes.

Third-Trimester Development

In the third trimester, the fetus continues to grow, developing the size and strength it will need to live on its own (❙ Figure 11.4). It increases in weight from 4 pounds in the 7th month to an average of over 7 pounds at birth. The downlike hair covering its body disappears, and head hair continues growing. The skin becomes smooth rather than wrinkled. The fetus is covered with a protective creamy, waxy substance called the **vernix caseosa** (VER-niks ka-see-OH-suh).

vernix caseosa
A waxy, protective substance on the fetus's skin.

Prenatal Care

Some of the problems with fetal development are genetic and unpreventable, but the mother's own general good health, good nutrition, adequate rest and exercise, and abstinence from alcohol and recreational drugs are crucial to providing the best environment for fetal development and for her own physical well-being during pregnancy and childbirth (Hannon, 2009). The Your Sexual Health box, "Folic Acid and Fetal Development," describes what every woman of childbearing age needs to be doing right now for the health of a future pregnancy.

Thorough prenatal care also involves health care and childbirth education. It is important for a woman to have a complete physical examination and health assessment before becoming pregnant, or as soon as she knows she is pregnant. She should also have a test to determine her immunity to rubella (German measles), a disease that can cause severe

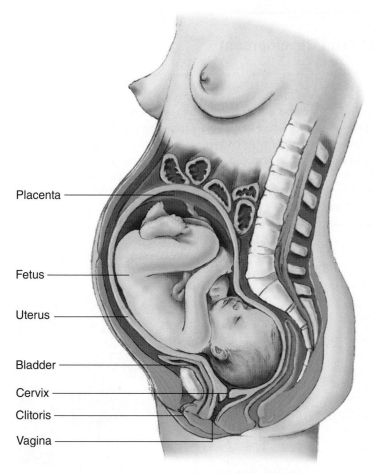

Placenta

Fetus

Uterus

Bladder

Cervix

Clitoris

Vagina

▌Figure 11.4 Pregnancy in the 9th month. The uterus and abdomen have increased in size to accommodate the fetus.

fetal defects if the mother contracts it while she is pregnant. An HIV test should also be done before or during pregnancy, because HIV can be transmitted to the developing fetus during pregnancy, and therapies are available to prevent mother-to-child transmission of HIV and to improve maternal and infant health (Lalleman et al., 2011).

Unfortunately, in the United States many babies are born without adequate prenatal care, a situation that increases the chance that problems will occur, including low birth weight, lung disorders, brain damage, and abnormal growth patterns. These problems can have lifelong effects (Lundgren et al., 2011). Women most likely to delay obtaining adequate prenatal care are unmarried African American or Hispanic American individuals under age 20 who have not graduated from high school and are uninsured or on Medicaid. They typically live in low-income neighborhoods with crowded clinics and a shortage of doctors' offices (Bloche, 2004).

Furthermore, statistics indicate that three to four times as many African American women as Hispanic American or White women die from childbirth complications (S. Johnson, 2011). Because of the poor access to health care for people without health insurance or adequate government-funded clinics, the United States compares unfavorably with other countries in maternal and infant mortality rates. Forty-nine countries have lower maternal mortality rates and 41 have lower infant mortality rates than does the United States (Larsen, 2007).

The fate of pregnant women in developing countries is severe: A total of 99% of all maternal deaths occur in developing countries, mainly in sub-Saharan Africa and South

Women can prevent several devastating birth defects by taking folic acid, a B vitamin, throughout their childbearing years. Folic acid assists the body in making new cells and helping the fetus's neural tube develop into the brain and spinal cord. A lack of folic acid can cause conditions in which the brain is partly missing or improperly formed, resulting in fetal death or severe permanent disability. Folic acid also helps prevent cleft lip and palate and several serious pregnancy complications, including premature birth (Boulet et al., 2008).

A woman must be taking folic acid before becoming pregnant for the baby to benefit fully from it. The baby's brain and spinal cord develop in the first 3 to 4 weeks of pregnancy—before women know they are pregnant—so enough folic acid must be in the body before conception. Folic acid also provides health benefits to men and non-pregnant women. Studies show that folic acid may lower the risks of heart disease, stroke, Alzheimer's disease, and some kinds of cancer (Centers for Disease Control, 2009b).

Where do I get folic acid and how much do I need?

Many cereals, breads, pastas, and grain products are fortified with folic acid; about 30 breakfast cereals have 100% of the daily amount a person needs when not pregnant. (The nutrition label on the side of the box will tell you whether the product contains folic acid and how much of the daily recommended value it contains.) Other foods that are high in folic acid are asparagus, green vegetables, nuts

and dried beans, oranges, and bananas. Taking a supplement or a multiple vitamin with 100% of the daily requirement will ensure you are getting an adequate amount of folic acid. Government guidelines recommend that during the childbearing years—whether or not a woman is intending to become pregnant—she needs at least 400 micrograms (mcg) of folic acid each day. When a woman is trying to get pregnant and for the first 3 months of pregnancy, she should take 1,200 mcg daily. For the remainder of the pregnancy, she should take 600 mcg, and during breast-feeding, 500 mcg each day (Centers for Disease Control, 2009b).

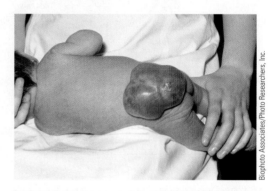

Biophoto Associates/Photo Researchers, Inc.

Folic acid helps prevent spina bifida, a birth defect in the development of the vertebrae that leaves a portion of the spinal cord exposed.

Asia. For every 1,000 births, 74 women in developing countries die, compared to 7 in developed countries (World Health Organization, 2009). Afghanistan has the world's highest rate of maternal mortality, and more than 85% of women give birth with no medical help; 1 in 19 babies dies in the first month of life (Streib, 2011). Substandard health-care services, poverty, lack of education, women's underlying poor health, and gender-related factors resulting in women's lack of decision-making power in their families all contribute to these high mortality rates (UN Department of Public Information, 2010).

Risks to Fetal Development

The rapidly developing fetus depends on the mother for nutrients, oxygen, and waste elimination as substances pass through the **placenta** (a disk-shaped organ attached to the wall of the uterus, shown in ▮ Figure 11.5). The fetus is joined to the placenta by the umbilical cord. The fetal blood circulates independently within the closed system of the fetus and the inner part of the placenta. Maternal blood flows in the uterine walls and through the outer part of the placenta. Fetal blood and maternal blood do not normally intermingle. All exchanges between the fetal and maternal circulatory systems

placenta

A disk-shaped organ attached to the uterine wall and connected to the fetus by the umbilical cord. Nutrients, oxygen, and waste products pass between mother and fetus through the cell walls of the placenta.

occur by passage of substances through the walls of the blood vessels. Nutrients and oxygen from the maternal blood pass into the fetal blood vessels; carbon dioxide and waste products from the fetus pass into the maternal blood vessels, to be removed by maternal circulation.

The placenta prevents some kinds of bacteria and viruses—but not all—from passing into the fetal circulatory system. Many bacteria and viruses, including HIV, do cross through the placenta. Certain prescription medications, legal drugs such as tobacco and alcohol, and illegal drugs are dangerous to the developing fetus. Tobacco and alcohol affect a far greater number of babies each year, with more significant health consequences, than do illegal drugs (Yuan et al., 2001).

Approximately 13% of U.S. women continue to smoke throughout their pregnancies; smoking reduces the amount of oxygen in the bloodstream and thereby increases the chances of miscarriage, low fetal birth weight, and other pregnancy complications that can result in fetal or infant death (Fifer et al., 2009). Children of mothers who smoked during pregnancy have more respiratory diseases, have a 50–70% greater chance of having a cleft lip or palate, and have significantly lower developmental scores and an increased incidence of reading disorders compared with matched children of nonsmokers (Williams, 2000). Research in Denmark found that prenatal tobacco exposure was correlated with hormonal changes in adolescence and adulthood. Males had smaller testicles, lower total sperm counts, impairment in testicular function, lower adult height, and a higher adult fat to body size ratio (Ravnborg et al., 2011). Daughters of women who smoked 10 or more cigarettes a day began menstruating almost three months earlier than daughters of nonsmoking mothers (Shrestha et al., 2011).

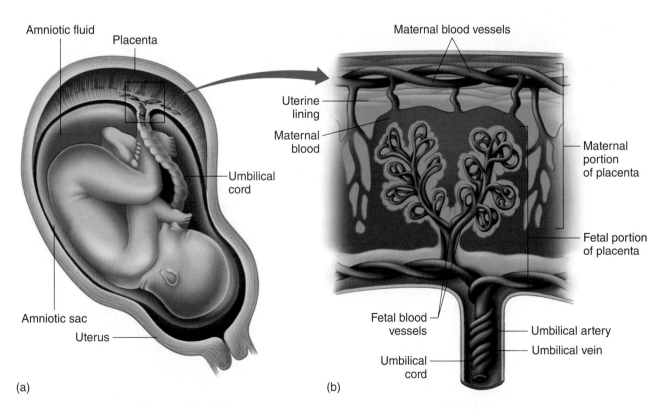

(a) (b)

❙ Figure 11.5 The placenta exchanges nutrients, oxygen, and waste products between the maternal and fetal circulatory systems. (a) The placenta attached to the uterine wall. (b) Close-up detail of the placenta.

fetal alcohol syndrome (FAS)
Syndrome in infants caused by heavy maternal prenatal alcohol use; characterized by congenital heart defects, damage to the brain and nervous system, numerous physical malformations of the fetus, and below-normal IQ.

Moderate exercise usually contributes to a healthy pregnancy and delivery. A pregnant woman should consult her health-care provider for guidelines specific to her situation.

Alcohol easily crosses the placental membranes into all fetal tissues, especially brain tissue. **Fetal alcohol syndrome (FAS)** is the leading cause of birth defects and developmental disabilities in the United States. Because a safe level of alcohol consumption is unknown, the Food and Drug Administration has advised women to abstain *completely* from alcohol use during pregnancy to avoid the risk of damage to their babies. One drink per day has been associated with adverse birth effects, and binge drinking (five or more drinks per occasion) is extremely toxic to the fetus. Alcohol use can cause intrauterine death and spontaneous abortion, premature birth, congenital heart defects, damage to the brain and nervous system, and numerous physical malformations of the fetus. The effects of FAS persist through childhood; children with FAS continue to be smaller than normal and developmentally delayed and to have behavior problems (Willford et al., 2006). Perhaps as a result of public health educational efforts, fewer women drink alcohol during pregnancy: In 2004, 12% of pregnant women drank alcohol, compared to 30% in 1989 (Grant et al., 2009).

The babies of mothers who regularly used illegal addictive drugs, such as amphetamines and opiates, during pregnancy are often born premature and have low birth weight. In addition, after birth these babies experience withdrawal from the drug: They have tremors, disturbed feeding and sleep patterns, and abnormal muscle tension, and they often require hospitalization in neonatal intensive care units. These children can experience permanent birth defects and damage to sensory, motor, and cognitive abilities that continue past infancy (Zambrana & Scrimshaw, 1997).

In a number of tragic situations, children have been damaged by prescription and over-the-counter medications taken by their mothers during pregnancy. For example, the drug thalidomide, prescribed as a sedative to pregnant women in the early 1960s, caused severe deformities to the extremities. Some grown children of women who were given diethylstilbestrol (DES) while pregnant have developed genital tract abnormalities, including cancer (Koren, 2009). Antibiotics need to be prescribed selectively during pregnancy because tetracycline, a frequently used antibiotic, can damage an infant's teeth and cause stunted bone growth if it is taken after the 14th week of pregnancy. Many over-the-counter medications, such as ibuprofen, aspirin, and histamines, can be detrimental to the fetus, and effects are unknown for many other nonprescription drugs and herbs. A woman and her health-care provider should carefully evaluate medications used during pregnancy (Mitchell et al., 2011).

Pregnancy After Age 35

An increasing number of women delay having children until after 35 years of age: Almost twice as many women between the ages of 35 and 44 become pregnant now than was the case in 1980. Women who have their first baby when older appear to have some psychological advantages. They are more resilient, report their partners are less controlling, and report lower symptoms of depression and anxiety during pregnancy than their younger counterparts (McMahon et al., 2011).

The greatest risk women and their partners face when they postpone having a child until the woman is in her mid-30s or older is that her fertility decreases with age. Women who have the financial resources to do so can have their eggs retrieved and frozen (a procedure called *oocyte cryopreservation*) when they are younger and more fertile, to increase their chances of becoming pregnant after their fertility declines with age (Stoop et al., 2011). The approximate cost is $15,000 plus a yearly storage fee of $400 (Lehmann-Haupt, 2009).

Healthy older women have no higher risk than younger women of having a child with birth defects *not* related to abnormal chromosomes. However, the rate of fetal defects resulting from chromosomal abnormalities (such as Down syndrome) rises with maternal age. For example, Down syndrome rates for children of mothers ages 40 to 54 are about 14 times higher than those for women younger than age 30 (Martin et al., 2009). For women between the ages of 35 and 44, prenatal testing for chromosomal birth defects and elective abortion reduce the risk of bearing an infant with a severe birth defect to a level comparable to that for younger women (Yuan et al., 2000).

Pregnancy in women over age 35 poses additional increased risks to the mother and fetus. Slightly higher rates of maternal death, premature delivery, cesarean sections, and low birth-weight babies occur (Hoffman et al., 2007). Most physicians find that pregnancy for a healthy woman over age 35 is safe and not difficult to manage medically because chronic illnesses such as diabetes and high blood pressure play a greater role than age itself in problems with labor, delivery, and infant health (Yuan et al., 2000).

Fatherhood After Age 45

Although men maintain their fertility much longer than women do, increasing evidence is showing that later-in-life fatherhood may carry some increased risk of birth defects for their children. Scientists have found changes in the DNA of older men's sperm. Some studies suggest that single-gene mutations may be four to five times higher in men age 45 and older compared to men in their 20s. Increases in rare birth defects, autism disorders, and schizophrenia have been associated with higher paternal age (Rabin, 2007b).

Childbirth

The full term of pregnancy usually lasts about 40 weeks from the last menstrual period, although there is some variation in length. Some women have longer pregnancies; others give birth to fully developed infants up to a few weeks before the 9-month term is over. The experience of childbirth also varies a good deal, depending on many factors: the woman's physiology, her emotional state, the baby's size and position, the kind of childbirth practices used, and the kind of support she receives.

Contemporary Childbirth

Before the 1970s, fathers were not allowed in the delivery room while their babies were being born (Larsen, 2007). Today's parents-to-be can expect to work as part of a team with their health-care provider in preparing and planning for the physical and emotional aspects of childbirth. *Obstetricians* are medical doctors and *midwives* are nurses who specialize in pregnancy and childbirth care. In the United States during the last 20 years, the number of hospital births attended by midwives has increased to about 10% of births. Midwives typically work with women who have low-risk pregnancies and uncomplicated births, and often help coach the woman throughout her labor (Cantor, 2012; North American Registry of Midwives, 2008). Physicians have additional training in managing medical complications during labor and childbirth, and women who work with midwives need to have this care readily available.

Parents-to-be often participate in **prepared childbirth** classes that provide thorough information about medical interventions and the process of labor and birth. The classes also provide training for the pregnant woman and her labor coach (either her partner, family member, or a friend) in breathing and relaxation exercises designed to

prepared childbirth
Birth following an education process that can involve information, exercises, breathing, and working with a labor coach.

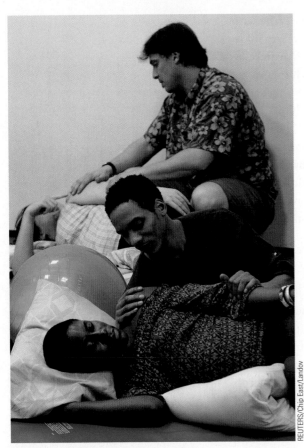

Prepared childbirth classes help prepare expectant mothers and fathers for childbirth.

first-stage labor
The initial stage of childbirth in which regular contractions begin and the cervix dilates.

effacement
Flattening and thinning of the cervix that occurs before and during childbirth.

second-stage labor
The middle stage of labor, in which the infant descends through the vaginal canal.

third-stage labor
The last stage of childbirth, in which the placenta separates from the uterine wall and comes out of the vagina.

afterbirth
The placenta and amniotic sac following their expulsion through the vagina after childbirth.

cesarean section (C-section)
A childbirth procedure in which the infant is removed through an incision in the abdomen and uterus.

cope with the pain of childbirth. Research has found that women assisted by a birth attendant during labor had fewer cesarean sections, less pain medication, shorter length of labor, and greater satisfaction with the birth experience (Campbell et al., 2006).

Approaches to contemporary childbirth began to develop when Grantly Dick-Read and Fernand Lamaze began presenting their ideas about childbirth in the late 1930s and early 1940s. They believed that most of the pain during childbirth stemmed from the muscle tension caused by fear. To reduce anxiety, they advocated education about the birth process; relaxation and calm, consistent support during a woman's labor; breathing exercises; and voluntarily relaxing abdominal and perineal muscles.

Stages of Childbirth

Despite variations in childbirth, there are three generally recognizable stages in the process (see ▌Figure 11.6). A woman can often tell that labor has begun when regular contractions of the uterus begin. Another indication of beginning **first-stage labor**, the gradual dilation of the cervix to 10 centimeters, is the "bloody show" (discharge of the mucus plug from the cervix). The amniotic sac can rupture in the first stage of labor, an occurrence sometimes called "breaking the bag of waters." Before the first stage begins, **effacement** (flattening and thinning) of the cervix has usually already occurred, and the cervix has dilated slightly. The cervix continues to dilate throughout the first stage. The first stage is the longest of the three stages, usually lasting 10 to 16 hours for the first childbirth and 4 to 8 hours in subsequent births.

Second-stage labor begins when the cervix is fully dilated and the infant descends farther into the vaginal birth canal. Usually the descent is headfirst, as shown in Figure 11.6b. The second stage often lasts from half an hour to 2 hours—although it can be shorter or longer. During this time the woman can actively push to help the baby out, and many women report their active pushing to be the best part of labor:

> I knew what "labor" meant when I was finally ready to push. I have never worked so hard, so willingly. (Authors' files)

The second stage ends when the infant is born.

Third-stage labor lasts from the time of birth until the delivery of the placenta, shown in Figure 11.6c. With one or two more uterine contractions, the placenta usually separates from the uterine wall and comes out of the vagina, generally within half an hour of the birth. The placenta is also called the **afterbirth**.

Delivery by Cesarean Section

A **cesarean** (sih-ZEHR-ee-un) **section**, or **C-section**, in which the baby is removed through an incision made in the abdominal wall and uterus, can be a lifesaving surgery for the mother and child (Ananth & Vintzileos, 2011). Cesarean birth is recommended in a variety of situations, including when the fetal head is too large to pass through the mother's pelvic structure, when the mother is ill, or when there are indications of fetal distress during labor or birth complications, such as a breech

(a) First stage
Dilation of cervix, followed by transition phase, when baby's head can start to pass through the cervix

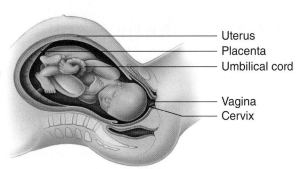

Uterus
Placenta
Umbilical cord

Vagina
Cervix

(b) Second stage
Passage of the baby through the birth canal, or vagina, and delivery into the world

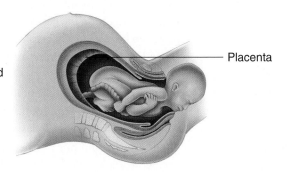

Placenta

(c) Third stage
Expulsion of the placenta, blood, and fluid ("afterbirth")

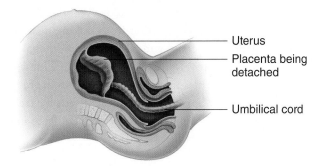

Uterus
Placenta being detached

Umbilical cord

❚ **Figure 11.6** The three stages of childbirth: (a) first-stage labor, (b) second-stage labor, and (c) third-stage labor.

presentation (feet or bottom coming out of the uterus first). Mothers who experience a C-section often have anesthesia that allows them to be awake to greet their baby when he or she is born. In many hospitals fathers remain with the mothers during cesarean births.

A decade ago, one in five babies was delivered by C-section: Currently one out of three babies is delivered by C-section (Hunter, 2011). Some maintain that high rates reflect better use of medical technology. Others believe that cesarean sections are used too readily. An analysis of birth data found that 11% of C-sections for a first pregnancy and 65% of repeat C-sections may not have been necessary (Kabir, 2005). Intensive fetal monitoring, aggressive malpractice lawsuits if serious problems follow a vaginal birth, and maternal and physician preference are three reasons for the increase (Hunter, 2011).

Second-stage labor is usually the highlight of the birth process.

After Childbirth

postpartum period
The first several weeks after childbirth.

The first several weeks following birth are referred to as the **postpartum period**. This is a time of both physical and psychological adjustment for each family member, and it is likely to be a time of intensified emotional highs and lows. The new baby affects the roles and interactions of all family members. The parents can experience an increased closeness to each other as well as some troublesome feelings. Both partners may want extra emotional support from each other, but each may have less than usual to give. The time and energy demands of caring for an infant can contribute to weariness and stress. Conflict about the division of household and child-care labor can become problematic in the early months and years of the child's life (Cowan & Cowan, 1992). A good support system for the new parents can be immensely helpful. Understanding that these feelings are a common response to adjustments to the new baby may help new parents cope with the stresses involved.

postpartum depression (PPD)
Symptoms of depression and possibly obsessive thoughts of hurting the baby.

Postpartum depression (PPD) affects 15% of mothers (Routh, 2000). Unlike the more common "baby blues"—tearfulness and mood swings lasting up to 10 days that about 75% of new mothers feel—PPD involves classic symptoms of depression, including insomnia, anxiety, panic attacks, and hopelessness (Knudson-Martin & Silverstein, 2009). At its most extreme, women suffering from PPD lose interest in their babies or develop obsessive thoughts about harming themselves or their babies. Such reactions may be partly due to the sudden emotional, physical, and hormonal changes following birth. Sleep deprivation from waking many times in the night to care for the newborn also is stressful and diminishes emotional and physical reserves. Fortunately, PPD can be effectively treated (Beck, 2006). However, evidence demonstrates racial and ethnic disparities in rates of postpartum depression treatment. In a study of low-income women who received Medicaid funds for treatment, African American women and Latinas were less likely than White women to initiate treatment and continue care for PPD (Kozhimannil et al., 2011).

Breast-Feeding

colostrum
A thin fluid secreted by the breasts during later stages of pregnancy and the first few days after delivery.

After childbirth the mother's breasts first produce a yellowish liquid, called **colostrum**, which contains antibodies and protein. Lactation, or milk production, begins about one to three days after birth. Pituitary hormones stimulate milk production in the breasts in response to the stimulation of the infant suckling the nipples. If a new mother does not begin or continue to nurse, milk production subsides within a matter of days.

Breast-feeding has many practical and emotional advantages. For the infant, breast milk provides a digestible food filled with antibodies and other immunity-producing substances (J. Hall, 2009). Research has revealed that babies who are breast-fed are less distressed than other infants when experiencing pain or stress (Shah et al., 2006). Breast-feeding through the 6th month also reduces the risk of sudden infant death syndrome by about 50% (Vennemann et al., 2009). A study in Ireland found that breast-feeding was associated with higher reading and writing scores among 9-year-olds, even after controlling for variables in child, maternal, socioeconomic, and socio-environmental characteristics (McCrory & Layte, 2011). For the mother, breast-feeding can be a positive emotional and sensual experience and an opportunity for close physical contact with the baby. Nursing also induces uterine contractions that help speed the return of the uterus to its pre-pregnancy size. Research indicates that breast-feeding may also reduce maternal stress levels (Hahn-Holbrook et al., 2011).

> I love seeing the contentment spread over my baby's face as she fills her tummy with milk from my breasts. It's an awe-inspiring continuation of our physical connection during pregnancy to see her growing chubby-cheeked from nourishment my body provides her. (Authors' files)

Nursing can temporarily inhibit ovulation, particularly for women who feed their babies only breast milk. However, as we saw in Chapter 10, nursing is not a reliable method of birth control. Estrogen-containing birth control pills should not be used during nursing because the hormones reduce the amount of milk and affect milk quality. Nonhormonal contraception, including the IUD, is an option for postpartum contraception (Glazer et al., 2011).

Nursing also has some short-term disadvantages. For one, nursing causes reduced levels of estrogen, which conditions and maintains vulvar tissue and promotes vaginal lubrication. As a result, the nursing mother may be less interested in sexual activity, and her genitals may become sore from intercourse (Barrett et al., 2000). The woman's breasts may also be tender and sore. Milk may be ejected involuntarily from her nipples during sexual stimulation—a source of potential amusement or embarrassment. It is often easier to share child-care responsibilities by bottle-feeding than by nursing; the father can have a greater role in holding and feeding the infant. However, a nursing mother can use a breast pump to extract her milk so that it is available to her partner or another caregiver for bottle-feeding the baby (Rasmussen & Geraghty, 2011).

For a woman who decides to nurse, breast-feeding is another opportunity for close physical contact with her baby.

The Centers for Disease Control and Prevention has set a goal for 75% of mothers in the United States to nurse their babies, and the American Academy of Pediatrics and the World Health Organization recommend exclusive breast-feeding for the first 6 months (Norton, 2009). In the United States, 80% of women begin breast-feeding after birth. Six months later, only 15% of women continue breast-feeding exclusively, while 45% continue some degree of breast-feeding (Allers, 2011; Rochman, 2012). Women most likely to have breast-fed were college graduates in the highest income level, and women least likely to have breast-fed were at the lowest education and income levels, residents of the South, teenage mothers, African American mothers, and smokers (Ruowei, 2002). Most common reasons for not nursing are medical issues, returning to work, difficulty with nursing, and concern that the baby is not getting enough food (Springen, 2007). Social bias and negative attitudes against women who breast-feed may also be factors (J. Smith et al., 2011). Breast-feeding rates in Sweden are significantly higher than in the United States, due in large part to generous parental leave of 16 months at 80% of their wages for each parent (Streib, 2011). Of all the industrialized countries, only the United States and Australia lack laws that require paid parental leave with a guaranteed return to work (Jeffery, 2006).

Sexual Interaction After Childbirth

Couples are commonly advised that intercourse can resume after the flow of the reddish uterine discharge, called **lochia** (LOH-kee-uh), has stopped and after **episiotomy** incisions or vaginal tears have healed, usually in about 3–4 weeks. However, the most important factor to consider is when intercourse is physically comfortable for the woman. This depends on the type of birth, the size and presentation of the baby,

lochia
A reddish uterine discharge that occurs after childbirth.

episiotomy
An incision in the perineum that is sometimes made during childbirth.

the extent of episiotomy or lacerations, and the individual woman's rate of healing. The postpartum decrease in hormones, especially pronounced with breast-feeding, can cause discomfort during intercourse. After a cesarean birth the couple needs to wait until the incision has healed enough for intercourse to occur without discomfort. Other sexual and affectionate relations can be shared while waiting.

A new baby brings significant changes in daily life that can affect sexual intimacy (Botros et al., 2006). Research has found high levels of sexual difficulties after childbirth. Before pregnancy, 38% of the study participants reported experiencing sexual problems, but 80% experienced one or more sexual problems in the first 3 months after delivery. At 6 months, 64% were still having difficulty. The most common concerns were decreased sexual interest, vaginal dryness, and painful intercourse. As would be expected, women who experience postpartum depression often have less sexual arousal, orgasm, and satisfaction than nondepressed women (Chivers et al., 2011). A researcher, who has written books about pregnancy and the first year of motherhood, warns women and their partners to be prepared for their sex lives to be "downright crummy" for up to a year: "Mother Nature is using her entire arsenal of tricks, from hormones to humility, to keep you focused on your baby and not on getting pregnant again" (Iovine, 1997, p. 158). Women and their partners, whose sexual activity has been disrupted by pregnancy and birth, may feel out of practice in their sexual relationship. It is often helpful to resume sexual activity in an unhurried, exploratory manner. ●

Summary

Parenthood as an Option

- An increasing number of couples are choosing not to be parents.
- The realities of parenthood or child-free living are difficult to predict.

Becoming Pregnant

- Timing intercourse to correspond to ovulation enhances the likelihood of conception.
- About 12% of couples in the United States have problems with infertility, and a cause is not found in many infertile couples.
- Failure to ovulate and blockage of the fallopian tubes are typical causes of female infertility. Low sperm count is the most common cause of male infertility.
- Alcohol, illegal drug use, cigarette smoking, and sexually transmitted infections reduce fertility in both women and men.
- The emotional stress and the disruption of a couple's sexual relationship from infertility can result in sexual problems.
- The legal and social issues related to artificial insemination, surrogate motherhood, and assisted reproductive technologies are complex and will continue to create controversy.

- The first sign of a pregnancy is usually a missed menstrual period. Urine and blood tests and pelvic examinations are used to determine pregnancy.

Spontaneous and Elective Abortion

- Spontaneous abortion, or miscarriage, occurs in approximately one in seven known pregnancies. Most miscarriages occur within the first 3 months of pregnancy.
- Elective abortion is a highly controversial social and political issue in the United States today. Medications, suction curettage, D and E, and prostaglandin induction are the medical techniques used to induce abortion.
- Contraceptive method failure is a major contributor to women's having repeat abortions.
- Contraceptive failure or contraceptive risk taking often precede an unplanned pregnancy and consequent abortion.
- In 1973 the U.S. Supreme Court legalized a woman's right to decide to terminate her pregnancy before the fetus reaches the age of viability. In 1977 the Hyde Amendment restricted the use of federal Medicaid funds for abortion and limited low-income women's access to abortion. Since then, many state legislatures have imposed further limitations on the availability of abortion.

The Experience of Pregnancy

- Women have a wide range of psychological reactions to pregnancy, including 20% who experience significant depression.
- Men have become increasingly involved in the prenatal, childbirth, and child-rearing processes.
- Although changes of position may be necessary, sensual and sexual interaction can continue as desired during pregnancy, except in occasional cases of medical complications.

A Healthy Pregnancy

- Pregnancy is divided into three trimesters, each of which is marked by fetal changes.
- Nutrient, oxygen, and waste exchange between the woman and her fetus occurs through the placenta. Substances harmful to the fetus can pass through the placenta from the mother's blood.
- Smoking, alcohol, illegal drugs, and certain medications can severely damage the developing fetus.
- More women are deciding to have children after age 35. These women have decreased fertility and a higher risk of conceiving a fetus with chromosomal abnormalities.

Childbirth

- Prepared childbirth, popularized by Fernand Lamaze and Grantly Dick-Read, has changed childbirth practices. Most hospitals now support participation of the woman's partner and a team approach to decision making about the birth process.
- Second-stage labor is the descent of the infant into the birth canal, ending with birth. The placenta is delivered in the third stage.

- The rate of cesarean sections has increased significantly in the United States, with continuing debate about the procedure.

After Childbirth

- Many physical, emotional, and family adjustments must be made following the birth of a baby. Postpartum depression affects up to 15% of new mothers.
- Both breast- and bottle-feeding have advantages and disadvantages.
- Intercourse after childbirth can usually resume once the flow of lochia has stopped and any vaginal tearing or the episiotomy incision has healed. However, it may take longer for sexual interest and arousal to return to normal.

Media Resources

Log in to CengageBrain.com to access the resources your instructor requires.

Go to CengageBrain.com to access Psychology CourseMate, where you will find an interactive eBook, glossaries, flashcards, quizzes, videos, and more.

Also access links to chapter-related websites, including **InterNational Council on Infertility Information Dissemination (INCIID), Guttmacher Institute, NARAL Pro-Choice America,** and **Lamaze International.**

12

Sexuality During Childhood and Adolescence

Sexual Behavior During Infancy and Childhood

What common patterns characterize emerging sexuality during childhood?

What is the nature and meaning of sex play with friends during childhood?

The Physical Changes of Adolescence

What major physical changes accompany the onset of puberty in boys and girls?

How do the physical changes of adolescence affect sexuality?

Sexual Behavior During Adolescence

What behavior patterns are characteristic of teenage sexuality?

What trends have been evident in adolescent coital activity over the last several decades?

Adolescent Pregnancy

What are the major trends in and causes and implications of teenage pregnancy in the United States?

What strategies might be effective in reducing teenage pregnancy?

Sex Education

How can parents provide valuable and effective sex education for their children?

How does sex education influence young people's sexual experimentation?

© Paul Steel

My earliest recollection of an experience that could be labeled as sexual in nature involved thrusting against the pillow in my crib and experiencing something that felt really good, which I now believe must have been an orgasm (actually, I remember doing this many times). I was probably around 2 at the time, give or take a few months. What is odd about these early experiences is that I distinctly remember sleeping in my parents' bedroom but never being reprimanded for this "self-abuse" behavior. Either my parents were very heavy sleepers, or they were very avant-garde in their view of sex. Knowing my parents, I presume the former is true. (Authors' files)

In many Western societies, including the United States, it was once common to view the period between birth and puberty as a time when sexuality remains unexpressed. However, as many of you can no doubt attest from your own experiences, the early years of life are by no means a period of sexual dormancy. Perhaps you can even recall sensual or sexual experiences similar to the quoted account that date from the early years of your life. In this chapter, we outline many of the common sexual experiences and behaviors that take place during the formative years from infancy through adolescence.

Sexual Behavior During Infancy and Childhood

Research over the last several decades has clearly demonstrated that a variety of behaviors and body functions, including sexual eroticism, develop during infancy and childhood. In some ways sexuality is especially important during this period, because many experiences during these formative years have a great effect on the future expression of adult sexuality.

In this section we briefly outline some typical sexual and sensual behaviors that occur during infancy and childhood.

Infant Sexuality

For most people the capacity for sexual response is present from birth (Newman, 2008; Thanasiu, 2004). In the first 2 years of life, a period generally referred to as infancy, many girls and boys discover the pleasures of genital stimulation (Yang et al., 2005). As reflected in the quotation from our files that opened this chapter, this activity often involves thrusting or rubbing the genital area against an object, such as a doll or a pillow. Pelvic thrusting and other signs of sexual arousal in infants, such as vaginal lubrication and penile erection, are often misinterpreted or unacknowledged. However, careful observers have noted these indicators of sexuality in the very young (Ryan, 2000; Thanasiu, 2004). In some cases both male and female infants have been observed experiencing what appears to be an orgasm (Newman, 2008). The infant, of course, cannot offer spoken confirmation of the sexual nature of such reactions, but the behavior is so remarkably similar to that exhibited by sexually responding adults that little doubt exists about its nature. Alfred Kinsey and his associates, in their book on female sexuality, detailed the observations of a mother who had frequently seen her 3-year-old daughter engaging in unmistakably masturbatory activity:

Lying face down on the bed, with her knees drawn up, she started rhythmic pelvic thrusts, about one second or less apart. The thrusts were primarily pelvic, with the legs tensed in a fixed position. The forward components of the thrusts were in a smooth and perfect rhythm, which was unbroken except for momentary pauses during which the genitalia were readjusted against the doll on which they were pressed; the return from each thrust was convulsive, jerky. There were 44 thrusts in unbroken rhythm, a slight momentary pause, 87 thrusts followed by a slight momentary pause, concentration and intense breathing with abrupt jerks as orgasm approached. She was completely oblivious to everything during these later stages of the activity. Her eyes were glassy and fixed in a vacant stare. There was noticeable relief and relaxation after orgasm. (Kinsey et al., 1953, pp. 104–105)

Kinsey also detailed references to male infant sexuality:

The orgasm in an infant or other young male is, except for lacking of ejaculation, a striking duplicate of orgasm in an older adult. The behavior involves a series of gradual physiologic changes, the development of rhythmic body movements with distinct penis throbs and pelvic thrusts, an obvious change in sensory capacities, a final tension of muscles, especially of the abdomen, hips, and back, a sudden release with convulsions, including rhythmic anal contractions—followed by the disappearance of all symptoms. A fretful baby quiets down under the initial sexual stimulation, is distracted from other activities, begins rhythmic pelvic thrusts, becomes tense as climax approaches, is thrown into convulsive action, often with violent arm and leg movements, sometimes with weeping at the moment of climax. (Kinsey et al., 1948, p. 177)

It is impossible to determine what such early sexual experiences mean to infants, but it is reasonably certain that these activities are gratifying. Many infants of both sexes engage quite naturally in self-pleasuring unless such behavior produces strong negative responses from parents or other caregivers.

Clearly, an infant is unable to differentiate sexual pleasure from other forms of sensual enjoyment. Many of the natural everyday activities involved in caring for an infant, such as breast-feeding and bathing, involve pleasurable tactile stimulation that, although essentially sensual in nature, produces a genital or sexual response (Frayser, 1994; Martinson, 1994).

Childhood Sexuality

What constitutes normal and healthy sexual behavior in children? This is a difficult question for which we have no definitive answer; the data on childhood sexuality are scarce. Research in this area is limited by a number of factors, not the least of which is the difficulty of obtaining financial support for basic research on childhood sexuality, and federal guidelines in the United States either prohibit such studies or make them considerably difficult to conduct. Some years ago, a team of researchers surmounted some of these obstacles to research in the United States by interviewing a large sample of primary caregivers (all mothers) of children, ages 2 to 12. The results of this informative study are described in the Spotlight on Research box, "Normative Sexual Behavior in Children: A Contemporary Sample."

People show considerable variation in their sexual development during childhood, and diverse influences are involved (Bancroft, 2003). Despite these differences, however, certain common features in the developmental sequence tend to emerge. As we outline our somewhat limited knowledge of some of these typical behaviors, keep in mind that each person's unique sexual history can differ in some respects from the described behaviors. It is also important to realize that, other than reports from primary caregivers, most of what we know about childhood sexual behavior is based on recollections of adults who are asked to recall their childhood experiences. As we noted in Chapter 2, accurately remembering experiences that occurred many years earlier is quite difficult.

A child can learn to express her or his affectionate and sensual feelings through activities such as kissing and hugging. The responses the child receives to these expressions of intimacy can have a strong influence on the manner in which he or she expresses sexuality in later years. The inclinations we have as adults toward giving and receiving affection seem to be related to our early opportunities for warm, pleasurable contact with significant others, particularly parents (DeLamater & Friedrich, 2002; Newman, 2008). A number of researchers believe that children who are deprived of "contact comfort" (being touched and held) during the first months and years of life can have difficulty establishing intimate relationships later in their lives (Harlow & Harlow, 1962; Prescott, 1989). Furthermore, other research suggests that affection and physical violence are, to some extent, mutually exclusive. For example, a study of 49 separate societies found that in cultures where children are nurtured with physical affection, instances of adult violence are few. Conversely, high levels of adult violence are manifested in those cultures in which children are deprived of physical affection (Prescott, 1975).

Enjoying sexual intimacy as an adult may be related to childhood experiences of warm, pleasurable contact, particularly with parents.

Childhood Masturbation

Infants fondle their genitals and masturbate by rubbing or thrusting their genital area against an object, such as a pillow or a doll, but the rhythmic manipulation of the genitals associated with adult masturbation generally does not occur until a child reaches the age of 2½ or 3 years old (DeLamater & Friedrich, 2002; Kaestle & Allen, 2011).

Masturbation is one of the most common and natural forms of sexual expression during the childhood years (Thanasiu, 2004). The study described in the Spotlight on Research box reported that approximately 16% of mothers observed their 2- to 5-year-old children masturbating with their hands (Friedrich et al., 1998). Various other studies indicate that approximately one third of female respondents and two thirds of males reported having masturbated before adolescence (Elias & Gebhard, 1969; Friedrich et al., 1991). In one study of college students, a slightly larger percentage of women respondents (40%) than men respondents (38%) reported masturbating before reaching puberty (Bancroft et al., 2003). A review of numerous studies of childhood sexuality revealed that a "substantial proportion" of people of both sexes experience first orgasm before puberty, often via masturbation (Janssen, 2007).

Parental reactions to self-pleasuring can be an important influence on developing sexuality. Most parents and other primary caregivers in American society tend to discourage or prohibit such activities and may even describe them to other adults as unusual or problematic. Comments about masturbation that pass from parent to child are typically either nonexistent or often negative. Think back to your youth. Did your parents ever express to you that they accepted this activity? Or did you have an intuitive sense that your parents were comfortable with self-pleasuring in their children? Probably not. Most often, a verbal message to "stop doing that," a disapproving look, or a slap on the hand is the response children receive to masturbation. These gestures may be noted even by a very young child who has not yet developed language capabilities.

Psychologist William Friedrich and his colleagues (1998) at the Mayo Clinic interviewed a large sample of mothers regarding sexual behaviors they had observed in their children. Sexual behaviors were reported for 834 children, ages 2 to 12, who were screened for the absence of sexual abuse. The mother informants were asked how often they had seen their children displaying 38 different sexual behaviors over the past 6 months. When 20 or more mothers reported observing a specific behavior, Friedrich and his associates considered it a developmentally normal form of childhood sexual expression. We outline some of the key findings of this important study in the following paragraphs.

A wide range of sexual behaviors were observed at varying levels of frequency throughout the entire age range of children. As shown in ■ Table 12.1, the most frequently observed sexual behaviors were self-stimulation, exhibitionism (often exposure of private body parts to another child or adult), and behavior related to personal boundaries, such as touching their mother's or other women's breasts. Sexually intrusive behaviors—such as a child putting his or her hand on another child's genitals—were observed less frequently.

The frequency of observed sexual behaviors was inversely related to age, with overall frequency peaking at age 5 for both sexes and then declining over the next 7 years. The observed decline in sexual behaviors after age 5 does not necessarily suggest that children actually engage in fewer sexual behaviors as they grow older. Rather, Friedrich and his colleagues suggested that it is likely that children become more private about sexual expression as they mature. Furthermore, older children spend more time with their peers, and thus there are fewer opportunities for parental observation.

Ethnicity was not significantly related to the reported childhood sexual behaviors. There was, however, a positive association between maternal attitudes toward sexuality and frequency of observed sexual behaviors. Mothers who described themselves as having a "relaxed" approach to such things as family nudity and sleeping and/or bathing with their children reported higher levels of sexual activity in their children.

Friedrich and his colleagues concluded that overt sexual behavior, particularly in young children, appears to be a normal part of development.

■TABLE 12.1 Percentage of Mothers Who Reported Observing Sexual Behavior in Their Children at Least Once in the Preceding 6-Month Period

Observed Behavior	Males, Age (in Years)			Females, Age (in Years)		
	2–5	6–9	10–12	2–5	6–9	10–12
Touches sex parts in public	26.5	13.8	1.2	15.1	6.5	2.2
Touches sex parts at home	60.2	39.8	8.7	43.8	20.7	11.6
Touches other child's sex parts	4.6	8.0	1.2	8.8	1.2	1.1
Touches adult's sex parts	7.8	1.6	0.0	4.2	1.2	0.0
Touches breasts	42.4	14.3	1.2	43.7	15.9	1.1
Shows sex parts to children	9.3	4.8	0.0	6.4	2.4	1.1
Shows sex parts to adults	15.4	6.4	2.5	13.8	5.4	2.2
Masturbates with hand	16.7	12.8	3.7	15.8	5.3	7.4
Masturbates with toy/object	3.5	2.7	1.2	6.0	2.9	4.3
Talks about sex acts	2.1	8.5	8.9	3.2	7.2	8.5
Puts mouth on breasts	5.7	0.5	0.0	4.3	2.4	0.0
Knows more about sex	5.3	13.3	11.4	5.3	15.5	17.9

SOURCE: Adapted with permission from "Normative Sexual Behavior in Children: A Contemporary Sample," by W. Friedrich et al., *Pediatrics*, Vol. 101, p. e9, Copyright 1998.

SEXUALHEALTH ▶ How can adults convey their acceptance of this natural and normal form of self-exploration? One way to begin is by not reacting negatively to the genital fondling that is typical of infants and young children. Later, as we respond to children's questions about their bodies, it may be desirable to mention the potential for pleasure that exists in their genital anatomy ("It feels good when you touch it"). Respecting privacy—for example, knocking before entering a child's room—is another way to foster comfort with this very personal activity. Perhaps you may feel comfortable with making specific accepting responses to self-pleasuring activity in your children, as did the parent in the following account:

> One day my seven-year-old son joined me on the couch to watch a football game. He was still in the process of toweling off from a shower. While he appeared to be engrossed in the activity on the screen, I noticed one hand was busy stroking his penis. Suddenly his eyes caught mine observing him. An uneasy grin crossed his face. I wasn't sure how to respond, so I simply stated, "It feels good, doesn't it?" He didn't say anything, nor did he continue touching himself, but his smile grew a little wider. I must admit I had some initial hesitancy in openly indicating my approval for such behavior. I was afraid he might begin openly masturbating in the presence of others. However, my fears were demonstrated to be groundless in that he continues to be quite private about such activity. It is gratifying to know that he can experience the pleasures of his body without the unpleasant guilt feelings that his father grew up with. (Authors' files)

Another concern, voiced in the previous anecdote, is that children will begin masturbating openly in front of others if they are aware that their parents accept such behavior. This also is a reasonable concern. Few of us would be enthusiastic about needing to deal with Johnny or Suzy masturbating in front of Grandma. However, children are generally aware enough of social expectations to maintain a high degree of privacy in something as emotionally laden and personal as self-pleasuring. Most of them are much more capable of making important discriminations than parents sometimes acknowledge. In the event that children do masturbate in the presence of others, it would seem reasonable for parents to voice their concerns, taking care to label the choice of location and not the activity as inappropriate. An example of how this situation can be handled with sensitivity and tact is to say to the child, "I know that feels good, but it is a private way to feel good. Let's find a place where you will have the privacy you need" (Planned Parenthood Federation of America, 2002, p. 12).

Many children masturbate. Telling them to stop this behavior rarely eliminates it, even if such requests are backed with threats of punishment or claims that masturbation causes mental or physical deterioration. Rather, these negative responses most likely succeed only in greatly magnifying the guilt and anxiety associated with this behavior (Singer, 2002). ●

Childhood Sex Play

Besides self-stimulation, prepubertal children often engage in play that can be viewed as sexual (Sandnabba et al., 2003; Thanasiu, 2004). Such play takes place with friends or siblings of the same sex or other sex who are about the same age (Thanasiu, 2004). It can occur as early as the age of 2 or 3 years, but is more likely to take place between the ages of 4 and 7 (DeLamater & Friedrich, 2002). Alfred Kinsey and colleagues (1948, 1953) noted that 45% of the females and 57% of the males in their sample reported having these experiences by age 12. In other research, 61% of a sample of American college students reported engaging in one or more forms of sex play with another child before age 13 (Greenwald & Leitenberg, 1989), 83% of Swedish high school seniors (81% of males, 84% of females) acknowledged engaging in childhood sex play prior to age 13 (Larsson & Svedin, 2002), and 56% of a group of adult professionals remembered engaging in activities perceived as sexual with other children before age 12 (Ryan et al., 1988). The activities ranged from exhibition and inspection of the genitals, often under the guise of playing doctor, to simulating intercourse by rubbing genital regions together. Although most adults, particularly parents, tend to react to the apparent sexual nature of this play, for many children the play aspects of the interaction are far more significant than any sexual overtones.

Curiosity about what is forbidden probably plays an important role in encouraging early sexual exploration. Curiosity about the sexual equipment of others, particularly the other sex, is quite normal (DeLamater & Friedrich, 2002; Thanasiu, 2004). Many day-care centers and nursery schools now have bathrooms open to both sexes so that children can learn about sex differences in a natural, everyday way.

Besides showing interest in sexual behaviors, many children in the 5–7 age range begin to act in ways that mirror the predominant heterosexual marriage script in our society. This is apparent in the practice of playing house, which is typical of children of this age. Some of the sex play described earlier occurs within the context of this activity.

By the time children reach the age of 8 or 9, there is a pronounced tendency for boys and girls to begin to play separately, although romantic interest in the other sex may exist at the same time (DeLamater & Friedrich, 2002; O'Sullivan et al., 2007). Furthermore, despite an apparent decline in sex play with others, curiosity about sexual matters remains high. This is an age when many questions about reproduction and sexuality are asked (Gordon & Gordon, 1989; Parsons, 1983).

Most 10- and 11-year-olds are keenly interested in body changes, particularly those involving the genitals and secondary sex characteristics, such as underarm hair and breast development. They often wait in eager anticipation for these signs of approaching adolescence. Many prepubescent children become extremely self-conscious about their bodies and may be reticent about exposing them to the view of others. Separation from the other sex is still the general rule, and children of this age often strongly protest any suggestions of romantic interest in the other sex (Goldman & Goldman, 1982).

Sex play with friends of the same sex is common during the childhood years (DeLamater & Friedrich, 2002; Sandnabba et al., 2003). In fact, during this time, when the separation of the sexes is particularly strong, same-sex activity is probably more common than heterosexual encounters (DeLamater & Friedrich, 2002). In most instances these childhood same-sex encounters are transitory, soon replaced by the heterosexual relationships of adolescence (Reinisch & Beasley, 1990). Nevertheless, for some of these children, sex play with friends of the same sex can reflect a homosexual or bisexual orientation that will develop more fully during adolescence and adulthood. However, youthful same-sex experiences in and of themselves rarely play a determinant role in establishing a homosexual orientation (Bell et al., 1981; Van Wyk, 1984). We encourage parents who become aware of these behaviors to avoid responding in a negative fashion or labeling such activity as homosexual in the adult sense.

It is clear that self-discovery and peer interactions are important during childhood development of sexuality. These factors continue to be influential during the adolescent years, as we will discover later in this chapter. But first we turn our attention to the physical changes that accompany the onset of adolescence.

The physical changes of adolescence are rapid and often eagerly anticipated.

Rob Melnychuk/Taxi/Getty Images

The Physical Changes of Adolescence

Adolescence is a time of dramatic physiological changes and social-role development. In Western societies it is the transition between childhood and adulthood that typically spans the period between ages 12 and 20. Most of the major physical changes of adolescence take place during the first few years of this period. However, important and often profound changes in behavior and role expectations occur throughout this phase of life. By cross-cultural standards, adolescence in our society is rather extended.

In many cultures (and in Western society in preindustrial times), adult roles are assumed at a much earlier age. Rather than undergoing a protracted period of child-adult status, the child is often initiated into adulthood upon reaching puberty.

Puberty (from the Latin *pubescere*, "to be covered with hair") is a term frequently used to describe the period of rapid physical changes in early adolescence. The mechanisms that trigger the chain of developments are not fully understood. However, we do know that the brain coordinates the physical changes that occur during puberty and that the hypothalamus plays an especially important role in this process (Westwood, 2007). In general, when a child is between 8 and 14 years old, the hypothalamus increases secretions that cause the pituitary gland to release larger amounts of hormones known as **gonadotropins** into the bloodstream (Westwood, 2007). These hormones stimulate activity in the gonads, and they are chemically identical in boys and girls. However, in males they cause the testes to increase testosterone production, whereas in females they act on the ovaries to produce elevated estrogen levels. From the age of 9 or 10 years, the levels of these gonadal steroid hormones begin to increase as the child approaches puberty (Bancroft, 2003). Girls typically enter puberty at age 10 or 11, whereas boys experience puberty a little later, at an average age of 12 years (Westwood, 2007). In the United States, 15% of girls begin puberty by age 7 (Newman, 2011). Research has demonstrated that overweight girls tend to enter puberty at an earlier age than the norm for girls (Diaz et al., 2008).

In response to higher levels of male and female hormones, external signs of characteristic male and female sexual maturation begin to appear. The resulting developments—breasts; deepened voice; and facial, body, and pubic hair—are called **secondary sex characteristics**. Growth of pubic hair in both sexes and breast budding (slight protuberance under the nipple) in girls are usually the earliest signs of puberty. A growth spurt also follows, stimulated by an increase in sex hormones, growth hormone, and a third substance called insulin-like growth factor 1 (Caufriez, 1997). A deficiency in growth hormone levels is associated with short stature in youth, a condition that can be remedied by the administration of growth hormone during puberty (Collett-Solberg, 2011; Root et al., 2011). The growth spurt eventually terminates, again under the influence of sex hormones, which send signals to close the ends of the long bones. External genitals also undergo enlargement; the penis and testes increase in size in the male, and the labia become enlarged in the female (Figure 12.1).

The only event of puberty that is clearly different in boys and girls is growth. Because estrogen is a much better facilitator of growth hormone secretion by the pituitary gland than is testosterone, as soon as a girl starts to show pubertal development, she starts to grow more quickly. Even though the magnitude of the pubertal growth spurt is roughly equal in both sexes, it begins about 2 years earlier in girls (Westwood, 2007). This is why the average 12-year-old girl is considerably taller than her male counterpart.

Under the influence of hormone stimulation, the internal organs of both sexes undergo further development during puberty. In girls the vaginal walls become thicker, and the uterus becomes larger and more muscular. Vaginal pH changes from alkaline to acidic as vaginal and cervical secretions increase in response to the changing hormone status. Eventually, menstruation begins; the first menstrual period is called *menarche* (discussed in Chapter 3). Initial menstrual periods can be irregular and can occur without ovulation. Some adolescent girls experience irregular menstrual cycles for several years before their periods become regular and predictable. Consequently, methods of birth control based on the menstrual cycle can be particularly unreliable for females in this age group. Most girls begin menstruating around the age of 12 or 13, but there is widespread variation in the age at menarche (Chumlea et al., 2003).

Many children find the play aspects of interactions such as this one more important than any sexual overtones.

puberty
A period of rapid physical changes in early adolescence during which the reproductive organs mature.

gonadotropins
Pituitary hormones that stimulate activity in the gonads (testes and ovaries).

secondary sex characteristics
The physical characteristics other than genital development that indicate sexual maturity, such as body hair, breasts, and deepened voice.

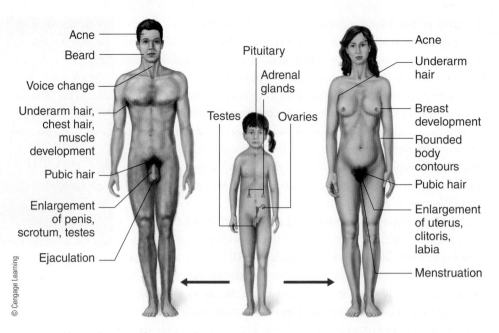

Figure 12.1 Hormonal changes during puberty, triggered by the influence of the hypothalamus over the pituitary gland, stimulate rapid growth and the development of secondary sex characteristics.

© Cengage Learning

The median age at menarche for all girls in the United States and other developed nations, 12.43 years, has remained stable for the last 50 years (Segal & Stohs, 2007). Only 10% of U.S. girls are menstruating by age 11.1 years, but by age 13.75 years, 90% are menstruating (Chumlea et al., 2003). There are, however, significant differences in the ages at menarche for different racial and ethnic groups in the United States, as described in the following Sexuality and Diversity discussion.

SEXUALITY and DIVERSITY
American Ethnic Diversity in Age at Menarche

An analysis of menstrual status data obtained from a nationally representative sample of 2,510 girls, ages 8 to 20 years, found significant ethnic differences in age at menarche (Chumlea et al., 2003). This analysis provided estimates of the median ages at which 10%, 25%, 50%, 75%, and 90% of the population had attained menarche for each of three ethnic samples: White Americans, African Americans, and Hispanic Americans. The data, summarized in ■ Table 12.2, reveal that African American girls start to menstruate earlier than girls in the other two ethnic groups. This difference is significant when compared with White girls at the age levels at which 10%, 25%, and 50% of the girls had started menstruating. In terms of statistical significance, Hispanic American girls began menstruating earlier than White girls only at the 25% level.

■**TABLE 12.2 Age at Menarche (in Years) for Selected Percentiles of U.S. Girls**

	Percentile				
	10%	**25%**	**50%**	**75%**	**90%**
Ages by race					
White	11.32	11.90	12.55	13.20	13.78
African American	10.52	11.25	12.06	12.87	13.60
Hispanic American	10.81	11.49	12.25	13.01	13.69
Overall median age	11.11	11.73	12.43	13.13	13.75

SOURCE: Adapted with permission from "Age at Menarche and Racial Comparisons in U.S. Girls," W. Chumlea et al., *Pediatrics*, Vol. 111, pp.110–113, Copyright 2003.

In boys the prostate gland and seminal vesicles increase noticeably in size during puberty. Although boys can experience orgasms throughout childhood, ejaculation is not possible until the prostate and seminal vesicles begin functioning under the influence of increasing testosterone levels. Typically, the first ejaculation occurs a year after the growth spurt has begun, usually around age 13, but as with menstruation, the timing is highly variable (Janssen, 2007). The initial appearance of sperm in the ejaculate typically occurs at about age 14 (Wheeler, 1991). There appears to be a period of early adolescent infertility in many girls and boys following initial menstruation or ejaculation. However, this should not be depended on for birth control. In some males sperm production occurs in the early stages of puberty, and even the first ejaculation can contain viable sperm.

Voice changes caused by growth of the voice box (larynx) occur in both sexes, but they are more dramatic in boys, who often experience an awkward time when their voice alternates between low and high pitches. Facial hair in boys and axillary (underarm) hair in both sexes usually appear approximately 2 years after pubic hair does. Increased activity of oil-secreting glands in the skin can cause facial blemishes, or acne.

Many of these physical developments are sources of concern or pride to the adolescent and his or her family and friends. Feeling self-conscious is a common reaction, and individuals who mature early or late often feel particularly self-conscious. Recent research indicates that early maturing girls experience significantly higher levels of social anxiety than girls who mature within a normative time frame (Blumenthal et al., 2011).

Social changes also take place. Boy–girl friendships often change, and adolescents are likely to become—at least temporarily—more homosocial, relating socially primarily with members of the same sex. This phase does not last very long, however. The period of adolescence is marked not only by physical changes but also by important behavioral changes. In the following pages, we look at some important areas of adolescent sexual behavior.

Sexual Behavior During Adolescence

Adolescence is a period of exploration, when sexual behavior—both self-stimulation and partner-shared stimulation—generally increases. However, the results of the NSSHB Survey, which included adolescents in its national probability sample, indicate that teenage sexual behavior is somewhat less pervasive than it is often portrayed by the media. In fact, "At any given time point, most adolescents are not engaging in any sexual behavior, with the possible exception of masturbation" (Fortenberry et al., 2010, p. 314). Although much of teenage sexuality is a progression from childhood behaviors, a new significance is attached to sexual expression. We will look at some areas in which important developments occur during adolescence, including the sexual double standard, masturbation, noncoital sex, development of ongoing relationships, intercourse, and homosexuality.

The Sexual Double Standard

Although children have been learning gender-role stereotypes since infancy, the emphasis on gender-role differentiation often increases during adolescence. One way that gender-role expectations for males and females are revealed is through the existence of a sexual double standard: different standards of sexual permissiveness for women and men, with more restrictive standards almost always applied to women (Abbey, 2011; England, 2010; Lyons et al., 2011). As we will see in Chapter 14, the double standard can influence both male and female sexuality throughout our lives. Sexually emerging teenagers often receive the full brunt of this polarizing societal belief. However, evidence gathered in recent years indicates that the sexual double standard is diminishing among adolescents and adults in North America, especially among women (Coontz, 2012; Davidson et al., 2008; Lyons et al., 2011).

Because the double standard continues to affect adolescent sexual behavior, let us briefly consider some of its potential influences. For males the focus of sexuality may be sexual conquest. Young men who are nonaggressive or sexually inexperienced are often labeled with highly negative terms such as *sissy*. On the other hand, peers often provide social reinforcement for stereotypically masculine attitudes and behaviors; for example, approval is given to aggressive and independent behaviors. For some young men, telling their peers about their sexual encounters is more important than the sexual act itself:

> My own self-image was at stake. There I was—good-looking, humorous, athletic, liked to party—but still a virgin. Everybody just assumed that I was an expert at making love. I played this role and, without a doubt, always implied, "Yes, we did, and boy, was it fun." (Authors' files)

For females the message and the expectations are often very different. The following account illustrates one woman's view of both sides of the double standard:

> It always seemed so strange, how society encouraged virginity in girls but it was okay for boys to lose theirs. I came from a large family, with my brother being the oldest child. I remember when word got around how much of a playboy my brother was (he was about 18). My parents were not upset, but rather seemed kind of proud. But when my sisters and I were ready to go out, our parents became suspicious. I can always remember how I felt and how if I ever became a parent I wouldn't allow such an inequality and emphasis on female virginity. (Authors' files)

Many girls face a dilemma. They may learn to appear sexy to attract males, yet they often experience ambivalence about overt sexual behavior. If a young woman refuses to have sex, she may worry that boyfriends will lose interest and stop dating her. But if she engages in sex, she may fear that she has gained a reputation for being "easy."

Masturbation

Although a significant number of teenagers do not experience sexual intercourse by the age of 19, many masturbate. As we saw earlier in this chapter, masturbation is a common sexual expression during childhood. The NSSHB Survey found that masturbation was considerably more common than partnered sexual activities during adolescence (Herbenick et al., 2010a). During adolescence the behavior tends to increase in frequency. Masturbation frequency rates among females are notably lower than among males for all age groups, including adolescents. The NSSHB Survey reported that about 26% of females, ages 16–19 years, reported solo masturbation during the previous month. A comparable figure for males in the same age range was approximately 60%. By age 19 about 66% of females and 86% of males had engaged in solo masturbation (Herbenick et al., 2010a).

Masturbation can serve as an important avenue for sexual expression during adolescence (Kaestle & Allen, 2011). Besides providing an always available outlet for sexual tension, self-stimulation is an excellent way to learn about one's body and its sexual potential. Teenagers can experiment with different ways of pleasuring themselves, thereby increasing their self-knowledge. This information may later prove helpful during sexual interaction with a partner.

Noncoital Sexual Expression

Noncoital sexual expression provides an important way for many couples to relate to one another, often as an alternative to intercourse. **Noncoital sex** refers to erotic physical contact that can include kissing, holding, touching, manual stimulation, or oral–genital stimulation—but not coitus. Perhaps one of the most noteworthy changes in the pattern of noncoital sexual adolescent behaviors involves oral sex. A number of recent surveys have shown that the incidence of oral–genital stimulation among teenagers has risen significantly (Brady & Halpern-Felsher, 2007; Halpern-Felsher et al., 2006). The NSSHB Survey found that while oral sex was relatively uncommon among young teens ages 14 and 15, by age 19 over 62% of females and 59% of males had been on the receiving end of oral sex with a partner of the other sex (Herbenick et al., 2010a).

A recent survey of more than 600 high school students in California found evidence of a predictive relationship between oral and vaginal sex. Teenage participants who had experienced oral sex by the end of the 9th grade were three times more likely to have engaged in penile–vaginal sex by the end of the 11th grade as compared to youth who delayed their experience with oral sex until the end of the 11th grade (Song & Halpern-Felsher, 2011).

Many teenagers consider oral sex to be more acceptable in dating situations and significantly less risky than coitus in reference to health, social, and emotional consequences (Brady & Halpern-Felsher, 2007; Knox et al., 2008). Unfortunately, many teens seem to be unaware of the potential health risks associated with oral sex, including transmission of infections like genital herpes, gonorrhea, and HIV (see Chapter 15).

For some young people noncoital sex is highly valued because it provides perceived opportunities to experience sexual intimacy while technically maintaining virginity. However, the very notion of virginity is problematic for a number of reasons. Most important, defining virginity as the absence of a single act (coitus) perpetuates the twin beliefs that "real sex" equals penile–vaginal intercourse and that virginity involves only heterosexual coitus. What about lesbians, gay men, and heterosexuals who have not experienced coitus but who engage in other forms of sexual behavior, such as mutual masturbation, oral–genital, oral–anal, penile–anal, and genital–genital contact? Are these individuals all "technically virgins"? What about women whose only experience with penile intromission occurred during an act of rape? Are they no longer virgins despite their lack of consent?

The very idea that people can engage in virtually every conceivable form of sexual interaction but one and still remain virgins seems to be a questionable (antiquated?) concept. Perhaps it is time to begin de-emphasizing the term *virgin*, which is both value laden and exclusive.

Ongoing Sexual Relationships

Despite the lingering double standard, data indicate that early sexual experiences, both coital and noncoital, are now more likely to be shared within the context of an ongoing relationship than they were in Kinsey's time. Studies conducted in the United States have shown that from early to late adolescence the percentage of teens involved in romantic relationships approximately doubles from about 30% in early adolescence to

noncoital sex
Physical contact, including kissing, touching, and manual or oral–genital stimulation—but excluding coitus.

Critical Thinking Question

From your point of view, what constitutes the definition of a "virgin"?

Many adolescents form caring relationships with each other.

approximately 70% in late adolescence (Overbeck et al., 2003). Furthermore, contemporary adolescents are most likely to be sexually intimate with someone they love or to whom they feel emotionally attached (Cheng & Landale, 2011; Overbeck et al., 2003).

A recent study of several hundred college freshmen found that 80% of female and 66% of male respondents indicated that a primary motivation for engaging in sexual relations was having a boyfriend/girlfriend they loved (Patrick et al., 2007). Another recent national study of more than 8,000 adolescents found that most youth established an ongoing romantic relationship by late adolescence and that romantic events, such as holding hands, kissing, and publicly acknowledging themselves and their partner as being a couple, generally occur before sexual interaction takes place. This investigation also reported that this tendency to establish a secure base through romantic interactions prior to sexual sharing was consistent across several ethnic groups, including Asian, White, Hispanic, and Black adolescents (O'Sullivan et al., 2007).

Recent changes in the attitudes and behaviors of both sexes appear to show a merging of attitudes regarding sexual activity. Teenage women seem to be more comfortable with having sex with someone for whom they feel affection rather than believing they must "save themselves" for a love relationship. At the same time, adolescent males are increasingly inclined to have sex within an affectionate or loving relationship rather than engaging in sex with a casual acquaintance or stranger, which was once typical for adolescent males (Laumann et al., 1994; O'Sullivan et al., 2007). Nevertheless, casual sexual relationships via "hook-ups" (see Chapter 7) are also relatively common among adolescents (George et al., 2006; Puentes et al., 2008).

An emerging social phenomenon, adolescent sexting, is receiving considerable attention from legal scholars and legislature officials. We discuss this rapidly evolving social trend in the next section.

Adolescent Sexting

sexting
Sending sexually suggestive photos or text messages via the Internet, cell phones, or other electronic devices.

Recently many states in America have struggled to cope with sexting (Melby, 2011). **Sexting**—sending sexually suggestive photos or text messages via the Internet, cell phones, or other electronic devices—is often associated with teenagers. However, it is probably more common among young adults as revealed by a recent report from the PEW Research Center's Internet and American Life Project that reported sexting to be most common among people ages 18 to 29 (Parker-Pope, 2011). Nevertheless, to date legal scholars have focused primarily on sexting by minors. Some observers of this trend describe the racy photos exchanged during youthful sexting as self-produced child pornography. Other commentators are adamantly opposed to establishing sexting as a crime out of concerns about First Amendment rights and fear that defining sexting as an offense will sweep reckless but not criminal youth into the court system (Hoffman, 2011).

Some states have sought to define sexting as a criminal offense and other states have allowed charging youthful practitioners of sexting with a misdemeanor, which provides the option of diversion programs and subsequent purging of their legal records. For example, New Jersey is debating a legislative bill that would route all first-offense juveniles charged with sexting to an educational diversion program. Other states take different approaches to sexting by juveniles. In Nebraska, youths who forward a risqué image may be punished while the creator of the image is not charged. Some states advocate charging minors who produce the image as well as those who forward it. North Dakota supports legal sanctions for anyone shown to have circulated a sexually suggestive photo with the intention of humiliating the teenager depicted in the photo (Hoffman, 2011). Several states (such as Florida, Texas, and New Jersey) have decriminalized sexting, instead opting to levy small fines or require several hours of community service (Melby, 2011).

States disagree not only about who should be prosecuted but also about how to define the images sent via sexting (Duncan, 2011). Some legal scholars argue that prosecution should occur in the case of "lewd and lascivious" images while other legal experts consider any nude images to be a violation. As we shall see in Chapter 18, legal experts have struggled for decades trying to define pornography, which no doubt encompasses "lewd and lascivious" in the minds of some politicians and legal experts. The viewpoint that all nude images are lewd or pornographic is especially susceptible to First Amendment challenges.

Sexting sometimes involves images or messages sent between an adult and a minor. For example, a 32-year-old female high school teacher in Arizona was recently arrested for sending sexual photos of herself to a 16-year-old male student (Younger, 2011).

Officials in many American states continue to discuss and debate the nature of legal transgressions that involve sexting—who should be punished and what factors may influence how criminal charges are levied. We will watch closely as the practice of sexting evolves along with the response of legal scholars and state officials to this aspect of technology.

Teenagers often engage in sexting with a cell phone.

Sexual Intercourse

A frequently quoted statistic in sex research is the number of people in a given category who have engaged in "premarital sex." As a statistic in sex surveys, premarital sex is defined as penile–vaginal intercourse that takes place between partners before they are married. However, the term *premarital sex* is misleading for two reasons. First, as a measure that is frequently used to indicate the changing sexual or moral values of American youth, it excludes a broad array of noncoital heterosexual and homosexual activities. For some people, abstaining from coitus before marriage might not reflect a lack of sexual activity. Second, the term *premarital* has connotations that may seem highly inappropriate to some people:

> I really hate those survey questions that ask, "Have you engaged in premarital sex?" What about those of us who plan to remain single? Does this mean we will be engaging in "premarital sex" all of our lives? I object to the connotation that marriage is the ultimate state that all are supposed to evolve into. (Authors' files)

Because of these limitations, we avoid using the term *premarital sex* in subsequent discussions. We now turn to some of the available data on sexual intercourse during adolescence; then we look at two related areas—adolescent pregnancy and the use of contraceptives.

Incidence of Adolescent Coitus

Even though many contemporary teenagers have not experienced sexual intercourse, the results of 13 nationwide surveys reveal a strong upward trend in adolescent coitus from the 1950s through the 1970s (■ Table 12.3). Results of the more recent of these surveys (and other surveys) suggest that this upward trend has leveled off and even decreased somewhat over the last two decades (National Center for Health Statistics, 2011). Data from the National Youth Risk Behavior Surveys (YRBSs) for the years 1995, 1999, 2001, 2005, 2007, and 2009, presented in ■ Table 12.4, indicate that from 1995 to 2009 the overall percentage of high school students in the United States who had ever had sexual intercourse declined somewhat for all grade levels. The prevalence of condom use during last sexual intercourse among sexually active high school students increased somewhat during this 14-year period.

■TABLE 12.3 Percentage of Adolescents Who Reported Experiencing Coitus by Age 19

Study	Females (%)	Males (%)
Kinsey et al. (1948, 1953)	20	45
Sorenson (1973)	45	59
Zelnick & Kantner (1977)	55	No males in survey
Zelnick & Kantner (1980)	69	77
Mott & Haurin (1988)	68	78
Forrest & Singh (1990)	74	No males in survey
Sonenstein et al. (1991)	No females in survey	79
Centers for Disease Control (1996)	66[a]	67[a]
Centers for Disease Control (2000b)	66[a]	64[a]
Centers for Disease Control (2002)	60[a]	61[a]
Centers for Disease Control (2006a)	62[a]	64[a]
Centers for Disease Control (2008a)	66[a]	63[a]
Centers for Disease Control (2010i)	65[a]	60[a]

[a]Percentages reporting having had intercourse by their senior year (usually age 17 or 18).

■TABLE 12.4 Percentage of U.S. High School Students Who Reported Sexually Risky Behaviors, 1991–2009

Grade	Survey Year	Ever Had Sexual Intercourse (%)	Four or More Sexual Partners During Lifetime (%)	Currently Sexually Active (%)	Condom Use During Last Sexual Intercourse (%)
9	1995	36.9	12.9	23.6	62.9
	1999	38.6	11.8	26.6	66.6
	2001	34.4	9.6	22.7	67.5
	2005	34.3	9.4	21.9	74.5
	2007	32.8	8.7	20.1	69.3
	2009	31.6	8.8	21.4	64.0
10	1995	48.0	15.6	33.7	59.7
	1999	46.8	15.6	33.0	62.6
	2001	40.8	12.6	29.7	60.1
	2005	42.8	11.5	29.2	65.3
	2007	43.8	13.4	30.6	66.1
	2009	40.9	11.7	29.1	67.8
11	1995	58.6	19.0	42.4	52.3
	1999	52.5	17.3	37.5	59.2
	2001	51.9	15.2	38.1	58.9
	2005	51.4	16.2	39.4	61.7
	2007	55.5	17.0	41.8	62.0
	2009	53.0	15.2	40.3	61.4
12	1995	66.4	22.9	49.7	49.5
	1999	64.9	20.6	50.6	47.9
	2001	60.5	21.6	47.9	49.3
	2005	63.1	21.4	49.4	55.4
	2007	64.6	22.4	52.6	54.2
	2009	62.3	20.9	49.1	55.0

SOURCE: Adapted from Centers for Disease Control (1998, 2000b, 2002, 2006a, 2008a, 2010i).

Evidence indicates that the leveling off in adolescent coital rates has not been as pronounced among young teenagers. Data from a number of studies indicate that over the last several decades there has been a trend toward experiencing first coitus at an earlier age in both sexes, and this trend is consistent across a diverse range of ethnic groups (Allen & Forcier, 2011; Centers for Disease Control, 2010i). However, different American ethnic groups vary in their experiences with adolescent sex. These differences are described in the following Sexuality and Diversity discussion.

SEXUALITY and DIVERSITY
American Ethnic Diversity in Adolescent Sexual Experiences

A variety of studies have consistently reported that African American teenagers are more likely to engage in adolescent coitus than either White or Hispanic American teenagers (Cavazos-Rehg et al., 2011; Centers for Disease Control, 2010i). For example, a nationwide study reported that African American high school seniors were significantly more likely than Hispanic American seniors and White American seniors to have experienced sexual intercourse (Centers for Disease Control, 2010i). The results of this study, summarized in ■ Table 12.5, also revealed that African American youth tend to have their initial experiences with intercourse at an earlier age than either Hispanic American or White youth.

■TABLE 12.5 Ethnicity and Percentage of Adolescents Reporting Having Had Sexual Intercourse

	Males			Females			Males and Females Combined		
	White (%)	Black (%)	Hispanic (%)	White (%)	Black (%)	Hispanic (%)	White (%)	Black (%)	Hispanic (%)
By 12th grade	39.6	72.1	52.8	44.7	58.3	45.4	42.0	65.2	49.1
Before age 13	4.4	24.9	9.8	2.2	5.6	3.7	3.4	15.2	6.7

SOURCE: Centers for Disease Control (2010i).

These ethnic differences in adolescent sexual experiences could be related more to economic status than to race or ethnicity. Poverty is a strong predictor of sexual activity among adolescents (Kissinger et al., 1997; Singh & Darroch, 2000). Teenagers from the least affluent segments of American society are more likely to engage in sexual activity than are those from more affluent classes, and African Americans and Hispanic Americans are often less affluent than White Americans. Furthermore, studies indicate that African American adolescents raised in more affluent homes are significantly more likely to abstain from sexual intercourse than are their poorer counterparts (Leadbeater & Way, 1995; Murry, 1996).

The trend in both sexes toward having intercourse at an earlier age is a source of considerable concern for many social scientists and health practitioners. Numerous studies have linked early sexual intercourse with increased risk for adverse health outcomes, including unintended pregnancy, delinquency, reduced educational attainment, increased probability of exposure to HIV and other sexually transmitted infections (STIs), and increased number of lifetime sexual partners (Andruff & Wentland, 2012; Cheng & Landale, 2011; Pearson et al. 2012).

Reasons for Engaging in Adolescent Coitus

A number of conditions motivate teenagers to engage in sexual intercourse. An accelerated output of sex hormones, especially testosterone, increases sexual desire and arousability in both sexes. Some adolescents are motivated by curiosity and a sense of readiness to experience intercourse. About half the men and one fourth of the women in the NHSLS reported that their primary reason for engaging in their initial coital experience was curiosity and feeling ready for sex (Laumann et al., 1994). Many teenagers consider sexual intercourse a natural expression of affection or love (O'Sullivan et al., 2007). Almost half the women and one fourth of the men who responded in the NHSLS reported that affection for their partner was the primary reason for engaging in first intercourse (Laumann et al., 1994). A push toward "adult" behaviors, peer pressure, pressure from dating partners, and a sense of obligation to a loyal partner are other reasons that adolescents engage in coitus (Lammers et al., 2000; Rosenthal et al., 1999).

Factors That Predispose Teenagers to Early or Late Onset of Coitus

Researchers have identified several factors that appear to predispose young adolescents to engage in sexual intercourse while very young or to delay coitus until they are older. Various psychosocial factors have been shown to be potentially powerful predisposing conditions for early onset of coitus. These include poverty, family conflict or marital disruption, teens living in single-parent or reconstituted families, parents' lack of education, lack of parental supervision, substance abuse (especially alcohol), low self-esteem, and a sense of hopelessness (Cavazos-Rehg et al., 2011; O'Donnell et al., 2006; Regnerus & Luchies, 2006). Other predisposing factors that have been identified include poor academic performance and low educational expectations (Lammers et al., 2000; Steele, 1999), tolerance for antisocial behavior and association with delinquent peers (French & Dishion, 2003), exposure to a diet of television high in sexual content (Ashby et al., 2006; Chandra et al., 2008), and having been sexually victimized (molested or raped) (Lammers et al., 2000). Adolescent females who are involved with a partner who is several years older are much more likely to experience coitus than females with same-age partners (Kaestle et al., 2002; Ryan et al., 2008).

Critical Thinking Question

Assume that you are a parent of a teenager who asks, "How do I know when I should have sex?" What would you answer, and why?

Research has also provided insights into the characteristics and experiences of adolescents who choose to delay onset of sexual intercourse. A few studies suggest that strong religious beliefs, regular religious service attendance, and spiritual interconnectedness with friends lessen the likelihood of early sexual intercourse (Cheng & Landale, 2011; Davidson et al., 2008; Pearson et al., 2012). A survey of 26,000 students in grades 7–12 found that factors significantly associated with postponing coitus included higher socioeconomic status, good school performance, high parental expectations, and adolescents' belief that they had one or more adults in their lives who cared about them (Lammers et al., 2000). Several other studies have also found a positive link between delayed onset of teenage sexual activity and high-quality parent–child relationships and communication (Akers et al., 2011; Hutchinson & Cederbaum, 2011; Parkes et al., 2011). However, the growing role of the Internet in the lives of adolescents may be adversely affecting parent–child relationships, as described in the next section.

Adolescents Online: Social Networking and Communication

Currently most American adolescents have access to the Internet at home, many via personal computers located in their bedrooms. Teenagers also use all kinds of mobile devices, such as cell phones and iPads, to surf the Internet (Feldman, 2011). Accessing social media sites such as MySpace and Facebook is one of the most common activities of American youth (O'Keeffe & Clarke-Pearson, 2011). The emergence of varied kinds of Web-based social media sources and methods of gaining access to these sources has "meant that exposure to sexuality, to sexual information, and to sexual images has substantially affected sexual attitudes and behaviors for this contemporary generation of adolescents (Fortenberry et al., 2010, p. 306).

Teenagers engage in a broad range of online behaviors, including blogging (creating and maintaining personal Internet sites that allow their authors and others to post content, thus creating a personal network), interacting and social networking with peers in chat rooms, seeking health information, accessing pornography, researching topics related to school assignments, posting personal profiles on sites such as MySpace and Facebook, and countless other online activities (Bleakley et al., 2011; Mitchell & Ybarra, 2009; O'Keeffe & Clarke-Pearson, 2011; Versteeg et al., 2009).

A number of social scientists have suggested that while adolescents often access valuable information and support on various websites, "electronic communication may also be reinforcing peer communication at the expense of communication with parents" (Subrahmanyam & Greenfield, 2008, p. 119). However, the "Internet can also strengthen family ties because it provides a continuously connected presence" (Brown, 2011, p. 32). Family members can communicate with each other via cyberspace, and young people away at college can maintain more contact with their parents by Skyping and web-texting. A recent survey found that adolescents today feel closer to their parents than did their older siblings (Brown, 2011).

Such online activities, in addition to having a potentially adverse impact on family relations, often result in a decline in face-to-face communication with peers. Therefore, a possible consequence of the rise of online networking and communicating may be a reduction in real-world interpersonal competence. In addition, troubled teens who frequently access online sites such as Facebook and MySpace may experience depression, especially if they are already dealing with low self-esteem (O'Keeffe & Clarke-Pearson, 2011). Cyberbullying and exposure to inappropriate online content are additional dangers that confront adolescents online (O'Keeffe & Clarke-Pearson, 2011). Finally, contacts made in cyberspace can potentially endanger adolescents, as described in Chapter 17.

On a positive note, social networking and interaction with strangers online may alleviate some of the negative effects teenagers experience as a result of social rejection in the real world (Subrahmanyam & Greenfield, 2008).

Adolescent Multi-Person Sex

Recent evidence indicates that adolescent sexual interaction involving multiple simultaneous partners is an emerging public health concern (Rothman et al., 2011). **Multi-person sex (MPS)**, which may be either consensual or forced, increases health risks of participants, who often engage in unsafe, condomless sex and who may be injection drug users. (See Chapter 15 for a discussion of risks associated with injection drug use and having sexual intercourse without the protection of condoms.)

National surveys that ask questions about adolescent sexual behavior do not collect data about MPS, which appears to be an emerging phenomenon. One recent anonymous survey of 328 females, ages 14–20, reported that over 7% of the participants had experienced MPS and that almost half of these incidents were accomplished by threats or force (Rothman et al., 2011). In this study MPS was found to be associated with several variables including sexual experience prior to age 15, having an STI, dating violence victimization, child sexual abuse victimization, and recent exposure to pornography. About a quarter of the participants in this survey reported that a current or former boyfriend was involved in the MPS encounter.

Clearly more research needs to be directed toward this risky and/or exploitive form of adolescent sexual behavior in an effort to better understand multi-person sex among teens.

multi-person sex (MPS)
Adolescent sexual interaction involving multiple simultaneous partners that may be either consensual or forced.

Homosexuality

Various studies indicate that 6–11% of girls and 11–14% of boys report having experienced same-sex contact during their adolescent years (Haffner, 1993; Hass, 1979). A recent survey of more than 17,000 adolescents found that about 1 in 10 teenagers report having experienced sexual contact with same-sex partners (Pathela, 2011). Most of these contacts took place not with older adults but between peers. These data, or the behaviors they describe, do not entirely reflect later orientation. Same-sex contact with the intent of sexual arousal can be either experimental and transitory or an expression of a lifelong sexual orientation. Many gay and lesbian adolescents do not act on their sexual feelings until adulthood, and many people with heterosexual orientations have one or more early homosexual experiences.

Gay, lesbian, and bisexual teenagers frequently encounter adverse societal reactions to their sexual orientation (Savage & Miller, 2011). Consequently, they may find it especially difficult to become comfortable with their developing sexuality. Unlike many other cultures in the world community, American society is not noted for embracing the fact of adolescent sexuality, even the often assumed heterosexuality of its young people. American teenagers who are at variance with the dominant heterosexual script can therefore experience a double societal rebuke of both their sexual orientation and the fact that they are sexually active.

For most gay, lesbian, and bisexual adolescents the process of reconciling their sexuality with the expectations of their peers and parents can be a difficult and often painful process that can create severe problems, including unusually high incidences of depression, loneliness, hostility toward others, substance abuse, and suicide attempts (DiFulvio, 2011; Hatzenbuehler, 2011; Pathela, 2011; Russell & Toomey, 2012). Not being "part of the crowd" can be emotionally painful for teenagers, who often find themselves scorned by their peers (Poteat, 2008; see the Sex and Politics box, "Antigay Harassment/Bullying of Teenagers"). Adolescents who are suspected of being homosexual are sometimes verbally abused, bullied, sexually harassed, or physically assaulted (Poteat, 2011; Rivers & Noret, 2008). Many lesbian and gay adolescents are unable to talk openly with their parents about their sexual orientation. "Coming out," as discussed in Chapter 9, is often a complex and difficult process. Those who do reveal their same-sex orientation are sometimes emotionally (if not physically) forsaken by their families (Dempsey, 1994; Frankowski, 2004), and they may eventually leave home, voluntarily or otherwise, because their parents cannot accept their sexuality. Some gay, lesbian, and bisexual teenagers even experience antigay violence at the hands of family members (Saewyc et al., 2008; Safren & Heimberg, 1999). Even though parents often react with disapproval and anger when they first learn that their child is homosexual, many parents "eventually recover to the extent that they are able to maintain supportive relationships with their children" (LaSala, 2007, p. 50). Young people with a homosexual orientation often find it difficult to find confidants with whom they can share their concerns or find guidance (Espelage et al., 2008). Parents, ministers, physicians, and teachers often are unable to offer constructive help or support. In addition, a society that generally fears and rebukes same-sex orientations has traditionally provided few positive role models for gay, lesbian, or bisexual teenagers, though that has been changing in recent years with more prominent and positive gay and lesbian representation in the mass media.

It is apparent from this brief discussion that American gay, lesbian, and bisexual adolescents often must achieve self-acceptance of their sexual orientation within the context of powerful societal pressures not to accept and/or act on that orientation—not an enviable task. Fortunately, people in the United States have gradually become more accepting of behaviors that vary from the dominant scripts for sexual and gender behaviors. Information about homosexuality is becoming increasingly available, as

During 2010 there were four known cases of teenagers committing suicide after becoming targets of antigay harassment/bullying (Crary, 2010). This deplorable situation has become even more pronounced with the advent of cyber attacks on gay teens. This problem was tragically exemplified by the September 2010 death of Tyler Clementi, an 18-year-old Rutgers University freshman who jumped to his death from a bridge after his roommate used a secret webcam to record and post on the Internet his sexual encounter with another man. Clementi's suicide focused national attention on victimization of gays. In March 2012 Clementi's roommate, Dharun Ravi, was convicted on all counts of hate-crime charges. In May 2012, he was sentenced to 30 days of jail time, 3 years of probation, 300 hours of community service, and he was ordered to undergo counseling (DiBlasio, 2012).

Currently most high schools, colleges, and universities do not have effective programs in place to address antigay harassment and bullying. According to a 2009 survey by the Gay, Lesbian and Straight Education Network, an organization that strives to improve the school environment for gay students nationwide, over 80% of schools lack comprehensive programs for addressing and countering antigay bullying. This deficiency is unfortunate because such programs have been shown to reduce victimization of gay teens (Crary, 2010).

This issue has become something of a political football with gay-rights supporters insisting on the implementation of anti-bullying programs while conservative religious organizations and politicians oppose these measures, suggesting that introducing such programs would be an unnecessary tactic designed to manipulate teenagers' beliefs about homosexuality. We can only hope that school officials will recognize antigay harassment and bullying as a human rather than a political issue that needs to be addressed via effective programs that counter negative treatment of gay teens.

is support for people with same-sex orientations. Some colleges and high schools in the United States now provide a more accepting environment for the establishment of support groups for gay and lesbian students. Nationwide, there are more than 3,000 Gay-Straight Alliances (GSAs) on middle school, high school, and college campuses (Warbelow, 2008). GSAs are clubs composed of both homosexual and heterosexual students who meet to exchange information, provide support to one another, and devise strategies for changing antihomosexual attitudes in their schools. While the establishment of these support groups is a welcome development, research indicates that public

Teenagers march in the sixth annual Gay/Straight Youth Pride March in Boston. Several thousand young people took part in the rally, demanding respect and declaring that their sexuality is their own business.

school districts across the United States are still largely remiss in addressing the needs of gay, lesbian, and bisexual students (Crary, 2010; Rienzo et al., 2006).

Internet chat rooms and message boards can be especially helpful sources of support and constructive information for gay, lesbian, and bisexual teenagers. In addition, in recent years homosexuality has become more visible and has been portrayed in a more positive light in the media. Several prominent entertainment and sports celebrities who have openly acknowledged their homosexuality are now available as potential role models. (See Chapter 9 for more detailed information about homosexuality and the media and the gay Internet community.) We hope that increasing societal acceptance of homosexuality, together with more positive role models and media portrayals, will help make this time of life easier for adolescents with homosexual orientations.

The Effect of AIDS on Teenage Sexual Behavior

Many health professionals are concerned that American teens are particularly at risk for becoming infected with HIV, the virus that causes AIDS (Trepka et al., 2008). Various surveys have shown that most adolescents in the United States are familiar with the basic facts about AIDS and are aware that high-risk activities can lead to transmission of HIV. Unfortunately, even though most teens know the basic facts about HIV/AIDS, this knowledge has not resulted in behavior changes in many teenagers. Several studies of high-school–age and college-age youths suggest that because most teenagers do not believe that they are at risk for contracting HIV, most do not significantly alter their sexual behavior to avoid infection (Feroli & Burstein, 2003; Trepka et al., 2008).

The notion of the "personal fable" (Elkind, 1967) is relevant to a consideration of adolescent risk taking and sexual behavior. Adolescents are particularly susceptible to a kind of cognitive egocentrism, an illusionary belief pattern in which they view themselves as somehow invulnerable and immune to the consequences of dangerous and risky behavior (Feroli & Burstein, 2003). Thus many adolescents continue to engage in high-risk sexual behaviors, not because they are ignorant about HIV/AIDS and other STIs but because they falsely view themselves as being at very low (or no) risk of suffering negative consequences (Feroli & Burstein, 2003). Also, research suggests that having a friend who engages in unprotected sexual intercourse increases the likelihood that a teenager will also engage in unprotected intercourse (Kim et al., 2011).

SEXUALHEALTH

Behaviors that put young people at risk for HIV infection include engaging in intercourse without condoms; using alcohol, cocaine, and other drugs that impair judgment, reduce impulse control, and thus increase the likelihood of hazardous sexual activity; sharing needles with other intravenous drug users; exposing themselves to multiple sexual partners; and choosing sexual partners indiscriminately (Dariotis et al., 2011; Grossbard et al., 2007; Trepka et al., 2008). The continuing trend toward a younger age of first intercourse is disturbing because people who begin sexual activity by age 15 tend to have significantly more lifetime sexual partners than those who begin having sexual intercourse at an older age (Cheng & Landale, 2011). (Exposure to multiple sexual partners is a high-risk sexual behavior, as discussed in Chapter 15.) Furthermore, young adolescent females who have their initial sexual experiences with older male partners are more likely to engage in unprotected, risky sexual behavior in adulthood (Senn et al., 2011). ●

With the growing awareness that teenage women are at risk for HIV infection (and other STIs), most family clinic counselors now encourage clients, even those on birth control pills, to regularly use condoms to protect themselves against STIs. Unfortunately, this advice is often unheeded, for a variety of reasons. Many young women and their partners are unwilling to deal with the minor inconvenience of condoms when they believe that they are already adequately protected from an unwanted pregnancy (Ott et al., 2002;

On February 11, 2011, the Appropriations Committee of the U.S. House of Representatives proposed severely cutting or completely eliminating funding for several programs designed to reduce adolescent pregnancy. This position is clearly antithetical to efforts to prevent teen pregnancy and stands in marked contrast to President Obama's 2012 budget proposal released on February 14, 2011. The Obama proposal provides hundreds of millions of dollars for evidence-based teen pregnancy prevention programs.

Hopefully, these efforts by the Republican-controlled House to undermine the Obama administration's efforts to fund science-based approaches to preventing teen pregnancy will not succeed and thereby put the ongoing American success story of reduced adolescent pregnancy at risk.

Zimmerman et al., 2007). A study of 436 sexually active adolescents found that condom use among teenagers who used birth control pills was much lower than condom use among adolescents who did not use oral contraceptives (Ott et al., 2002).

Adolescent Pregnancy

The incidence of births to teenagers in the United States has declined steadily from its peak in 1991. In 2009 the birthrate for U.S. teens was 39.1 births per 1,000 females, a 37% decrease from 61.8 births per 1,000 teenage females in 1991 and the lowest rate of teen births ever recorded (Centers for Disease Control, 2011g). Even though adolescent birthrates in the United States have declined, the still alarmingly high rate of teenage pregnancies and births, especially among African American and Hispanic teens, continues to be an urgent social concern. Among Western industrialized nations, the United States has the highest rate of teen pregnancy (Allen & Forcier, 2011; Akers et al., 2011). Approximately 750,000 unmarried American adolescents become pregnant each year, and 80% of these pregnancies are unintended. This adolescent pregnancy rate is as much as nine times higher than in other developed countries and two to four times higher than in several Western European nations whose age-specific levels of teenage sexual activity are comparable to those in the United States (Splete, 2011; Winik, 2008). This finding raises the obvious question of whether contraception is significantly underused or misused by adolescents in the United States. We address this issue in a later section of this chapter.

At the time of this writing, efforts are under way in Congress to reduce or eliminate federal funding for programs that focus on reducing teen pregnancy. These efforts are described in the Sex and Politics box, "U.S. Congress Considering Measures to Reduce Teen Pregnancy Prevention Programs."

As described in Chapter 10, females ages 16 and younger are currently required to obtain a prescription for EC, whereas older women can access this medication over the counter without a prescription. In November 2010 the Center for Reproductive Rights filed a legal brief charging the U.S. Food and Drug Administration (FDA) with being in contempt for not complying with a March 2009 court order to end age restrictions on EC. In passing this order the court supported evidence that there are no valid medical contraindications for EC use in female adolescents (Brakman, 2011). In 2011 the FDA recommended lifting the restrictions on access to EC by teenagers 16 and younger. Unfortunately, the Obama administration overruled the FDA and elected to continue requiring EC prescriptions for teenage females 16 and younger.

Negative Consequences of Teenage Pregnancy

The cited statistics on teenage pregnancy represent a great deal of human suffering. A pregnant teenager is more likely to have physical complications than a woman in her 20s. These complications include anemia, toxemia, hypertension, hemorrhage, miscarriage, and even death (American Academy of Pediatrics, 2006). Adolescent pregnancy is also associated with prenatal and infant mortality rates that are markedly higher than the rates among older pregnant women (American Academy of Pediatrics, 2006; Centers for Disease Control, 2011g).

Pregnant teenagers are also at especially high risk for STIs because of a likely reduction in the use of condoms, which are no longer needed to prevent pregnancy. Research indicates that less than 30% and perhaps as few as 8% of sexually active pregnant adolescent women use condoms consistently during intercourse (Byrd et al., 1998; Niccolai et al., 2003). These findings are disturbing because the resultant increase in susceptibility to STIs during pregnancy can have negative health consequences for both the youthful mother and her baby.

A teenager's unintended pregnancy and the decision to keep her child often have a serious negative effect on her education and on her financial resources (American Academy of Pediatrics, 2006; Cavazos-Rehg et al., 2011). Although it is now illegal to bar pregnant teenagers and teen mothers from public school, a large number of these young women drop out of school, and many do not return (Centers for Disease Control, 2011g; Harrison et al., 2012). Faced with the burden of child-care duties and the limitations of inadequate education, teenage mothers are often underemployed or unemployed and dependent on social services agencies (Paukku et al., 2003; Shearer et al., 2002). Furthermore, low education levels and limited employment skills often thwart the efforts of these young mothers to obtain economic independence as they move beyond their teenage years.

The negative effect of adolescent pregnancy is further exhibited in the lives of the resulting children. Teenage mothers often provide parenting of a lower quality than adult mothers do (Coley & Chase-Lansdale, 1998; Stier et al., 1993). In addition, the children of teenage mothers are at greater risk of having physical, cognitive, and emotional problems than are the children of adult mothers (Cavazos-Rehg et al., 2011; Centers for Disease Control, 2011g). These children of young mothers are also more likely to demonstrate deficits in intellectual ability and school performance than are children of older mothers (Cavazos-Rehg et al., 2011; Harrison et al., 2012).

Use of Contraceptives

Despite the physical, economic, lifestyle, and emotional stress of pregnancy and parenthood—and despite the availability of birth control today—many sexually active American teenagers do not use contraceptives consistently or effectively (Barclay, 2010; Reece et al., 2010b; Scott et al., 2011). Furthermore, many adolescents do not use any contraception at all the first few times they have sexual intercourse (Centers for Disease Control, 2012b).

A recent national survey revealed that in 2009, 60% of sexually active male teens and 44% of sexually active female teens used condoms during their last intercourse experience (Centers for Disease Control, 2011g). The NSSHB found that adolescent men used condoms during 79% of their last 10 vaginal intercourse experiences whereas only 58% of teen women reported using condoms during their previous 10 involvements in vaginal intercourse (Reece et al., 2010b). Findings from the NSSHB do support a consensus among sexologists that there is a definite trend among adolescents to increasingly use condoms during penile–vaginal intercourse (Fortenberry et al., 2010; Reece et al., 2010b).

Approximately 750,000 unmarried American teenage women become pregnant each year. Many experience considerable hardship as a result of their pregnancy.

© David Young-Wolff/PhotoEdit

For many sexually active teenagers the use of hormonal contraceptive methods (pills or injectables) alone or in combination with condoms remains low (Centers for Disease Control, 2011g). However, recent research provided encouraging evidence that the percentage of male teens who use condoms during their initial experience with intercourse is on the rise—71% in 2006 and 85% in 2010 (National Center for Health Statistics, 2011).

Many teenagers wait months after becoming sexually active to seek birth control advice, and some never seek counsel. Misconceptions about possible health risks associated with some contraceptive methods, fear of the pelvic exam, embarrassment associated with seeking out and/or purchasing contraceptive devices, and concerns about confidentiality keep many teenagers from seeking birth control advice (Guttmacher Institute, 2006; Iuliano et al., 2006). In reality, most American obstetrician-gynecologists are willing to provide contraceptives to adolescents without notifying their parents (Lawrence et al., 2011a).

Several factors or personal attributes have been found to be associated with adolescents' use or nonuse of birth control. Teenage women who experience infrequent intercourse are likely to be ineffective contraception users (Glei, 1999; Klein, 2005). Furthermore, teenage women whose partners are several years older are significantly less likely to use birth control than are their peers who have partners closer in age (Ryan et al., 2008; Senn et al., 2011). Being involved with an older partner may result in "reduced power in a sexual relationship and reduced control over contraceptive decision-making" (Manlove et al., 2004, p. 265). Adolescents who experience intercourse at an early age are less likely to use contraception than are their peers who delay intercourse onset (Manlove & Terry-Humen, 2007; Ryan et al., 2007).

Research also indicates that sexually active adolescents in close, loving relationships are less likely to use condoms to prevent pregnancies and STIs than those in casual relationships (Reece et al., 2010b). This finding suggests that teens in close relationships may prioritize trust, romance, and love over concerns about unwanted pregnancies and STIs and thus engage in risky sexual behaviors (Zimmerman et al., 2007). Inequities in power within intimate relationships often reduce a teenage woman's ability to effectively negotiate condom use (Silverman et al., 2011). Many sexually active young women believe that they lack the right to communicate about and/or control aspects of their sexual interaction with men, and thus lack of sexual assertiveness is often associated with inconsistent contraceptive use (Manlove & Terry-Humen, 2007; Rickert et al., 2002).

Strong parent–child relationships that embrace healthy patterns of communication about everyday life, including sex and contraception, have been positively linked to adolescent contraceptive use (Halpern-Felsher et al., 2004; Manlove & Terry-Humen, 2007). Experiencing academic success in school and having well-educated parents are also associated with effective use of contraception (Klein, 2005; Manlove & Terry-Humen, 2007). Research also indicates that adolescents raised in families that stress personal responsibility for behavior tend to be effective users of birth control (Whitaker et al., 1999; Wilson et al., 1994). Finally and perhaps most obviously, adolescents who are the most knowledgeable about contraceptives are the most likely to use them consistently and effectively (Lagana, 1999).

Strategies for Reducing Teenage Pregnancy

Many authorities on adolescent sexuality agree that educational efforts designed to increase teenagers' awareness of contraception and other aspects of sexuality would be much more effective if they treated sexuality as a positive aspect of our humanity rather than something that is wrong or shameful. In many Western European countries, where teenage birthrates are dramatically lower than in the United States even though levels of

Critical Thinking Question

Should parents provide birth control devices to their teenage children who are actively dating or going steady? Why or why not?

adolescent sexual activity are equal to or greater than those in America, sex is viewed as natural and healthy, and teenage sexual activity is widely accepted. This stands in sharp contrast to the United States, where sex is often romanticized and flaunted but also frequently portrayed as something sinful or dirty that should be hidden.

We offer a list of suggestions for reducing teenage pregnancy rates in the United States. These suggestions were gleaned from a large body of research on adolescent sexuality.

1. The American family planning clinic system and school-based health clinics need to be upgraded and expanded to provide free or low-cost contraceptive services to all adolescents who want them. Of equal importance is the need to publicize that clinics maintain the confidentiality of their clients.

2. The United States should follow the lead of several European nations in establishing a compulsory national sex education curriculum that is extended to all grade levels. Safe expression of adolescent sexuality should be treated as a health issue rather than as a political or religious issue. Research indicates that teenagers who have been exposed to comprehensive sex education are considerably less likely to become pregnant than those who have had no such education, especially if exposure to sex education occurs before the young people become sexually active (Masters et al., 2008; Zimmerman et al., 2008).

3. Adolescent boys must share responsibility for birth control measures. Efforts to educate teenagers to prevent unwanted pregnancies must recognize that male attitudes are important for the practice and effectiveness of birth control. Adolescent boys often consider birth control to be their partners' responsibility. Sex education programs should stress that responsibility for contraception is shared.

4. Condoms should be made readily available in middle schools and high schools. The results of several studies confirm that distributing condoms in schools is not associated with an increase in sexual frequency or younger age of sexual debut (Vamos et al., 2008). This research indicates that school-based condom availability can reduce teenage pregnancy and lower the risk of contracting STIs, including HIV/AIDS. Educational efforts should be directed toward encouraging teens to use condoms correctly during every intercourse experience. This is especially important because even when teens do use condoms, they often use them incorrectly (for example, starting intercourse without a condom; Barclay, 2010).

5. Adolescent–parent communication about sex must be increased. A nationwide survey found that almost half (47%) of American youths ages 12–14 reported that their parents exerted more influence than others on their decisions about sexual activity (Albert, 2004). A huge majority (87%) of these participants indicated that they would be better prepared to postpone sexual activity and avoid unplanned pregnancies if they could talk more freely and openly with their parents about sex, especially the use of contraception to prevent pregnancy. Unfortunately "many teens do not talk with their parents about ways to prevent pregnancy" (Centers for Disease Control, 2011g, p. 419). This finding, together with comparable results of other studies, strongly indicates that a key strategy for reducing teen pregnancy is the development and implementation of programs designed to enhance adolescent–parent communication about sex. One such program, introduced as an after-school educational activity at middle schools in southeast Texas, demonstrated that parents who are willing to openly discuss sex with their children may be especially effective agents in efforts to reduce the rate of teenage pregnancies (Lederman et al., 2008).

Sex Education

Many parents today want to contribute to the sex education of their children. Societal values about sex are rapidly changing, and we all are exposed to contrasting opinions. How much should children see, or how much should they be told? Many parents—even some who are comfortable with their own sexuality—have difficulty judging the "best" way to react to their children's sexuality.

Perhaps the information that we offer in the following paragraphs will help modify some of this uncertainty. We do not profess to have the last word on raising sexually healthy children, so we advise you to read this material with a critical eye. Along the way, however, you may acquire some new insights that will aid you in your efforts to provide meaningful sex education for your children, either now or in the future.

Answering Children's Questions About Sex

Parents often ask us when they should start telling their children about sex. One answer is, when the child begins to ask questions. It seems typical for children to inquire about sex along with myriad other questions they ask about the world around them. Research has indicated that by about age 4, most children begin asking questions about how babies are made (Martinson, 1994). What is more natural than to ask where you came from? Yet this curiosity is often stopped short by parental response. A flushed face and a few stammering words, a cursory "Wait till your mother (or father) comes home to ask that question," or "You're not old enough to learn about such things" are a few of the common ways that communication in this vital area is blocked before it has a chance to begin. Putting off questions at this early age means that you may be confronted with the potentially awkward task of starting a dialogue on sexual matters at a later point in your children's development.

It can be helpful for parents to include information about sex (when appropriate) in everyday conversations that their children either observe or participate in. Accomplishing this with a sense of ease and naturalness can increase the comfort with which the children introduce their own questions or observations about sex.

If a child's questions either do not arise spontaneously or get sidetracked at an early age, there might be a point when you as a parent will feel it is important to begin to talk about sex. Perhaps a good starting point is to share your true feelings with your child—that possibly you are a bit uneasy about discussing sex or that maybe you are confused about some of your own feelings or beliefs. By expressing your own indecision or vulnerability, you may actually make yourself more accessible. During this initial effort, simply indicating your feelings and leaving the door open to future discussions may be all that is needed. An incubation period is often valuable, allowing a child to interpret your willingness to talk about sexuality. If no questions follow this first effort, it might be wise to select a specific area for discussion. Some suggested open-ended questions for a low-key beginning include the following:

- What do you think sex is?
- What do you know about how babies are made?
- What are some of the things that your friends tell you about sex?
- How do you feel about the changes in your body? (for older children or early adolescents)

Understandably, parents sometimes tend to overload a child who expects a relatively brief, straightforward answer to his or her question. For example, 5-year-olds who inquire, "Where did I come from?" probably are not asking for a detailed treatise on the physiology of sexual intercourse and conception. It is probably more helpful to just briefly discuss the basics of sexual intercourse, perhaps including the idea of potential pleasure in such sharing. It is also a good idea to check to see whether your child has understood your answer to his or her question. In addition, you might wish to ask if you have provided the information that was desired and also to let the child know that you are open to more questions. When young children want more information, they will probably ask for it, provided that an adult has been responsive to their initial questions.

Some parents believe that it is inappropriate to tell their children that sexual interaction is pleasurable. Others conclude that there is value in discussing the joy of sex with their children, as revealed in the following account:

> One evening, while I was sitting on my daughter's bed talking about the day's events, she expressed some concern over her next-door playmate's announcement that her father was going to purchase a stud horse. Apparently, she had been told to have me build a higher fence to protect her mare. Even though she knew all about horses mating, she asked why this was necessary. I explained the facts to her, and then she asked the real question on her mind: "Do you and Mom do that?" to which I replied, "Yes." "Do my uncle and aunt do that?" Again, "Yes," which produced the final pronouncement, "I don't think I'll get married." Clearly, she felt some strong ambivalence about what this sexual behavior meant to her. It seemed very important that I make one more statement—namely that not only did we do this but that it is a beautiful and pleasurable kind of sharing and lots of fun! (Authors' files)

Reluctance to express the message that sex can be enjoyable can stem from parents' concern that their children will rush right out to find out what kind of good times they have been missing. There is little evidence to support such apprehension. There are, however, many unhappy lovers striving to overcome early messages about the dirtiness and immorality of sex.

Initiating Conversations When Children Do Not Ask Questions

Some topics never get discussed, at least not at the proper time, unless parents are willing to take the initiative. We are referring to certain aspects of sexual maturation that a child may not consider until he or she experiences them. These include menstruation, first ejaculation, and nocturnal (nighttime) orgasms. Experience with first menstruation or ejaculation can come as quite a shock to the unprepared, as revealed in the following two anecdotes:

> I hadn't even heard of menstruation when I first started bleeding. No one was home. I was so frightened I called an ambulance. (Authors' files)

> I remember the first time I ejaculated during masturbation. At first I couldn't believe it when something shot out of my penis. The only thing I could figure is that I had whipped up my urine. However, considering earlier lectures from my mother about the evils of "playing with yourself," I was afraid that God was punishing me for my sinful behavior. (Authors' files)

It is important that youngsters be aware of these physiological changes before they actually happen. Children's natural curiosity about sex might cause them to discuss these topics with friends, who are usually not the most reliable sources of information. It is certainly better for parents to provide a more accurate description of these natural events.

Most young people prefer that their parents be the primary source of sex information and that their mothers and fathers share equally in this responsibility (Brewster, 2012; Kreinin et al., 2001; Somers & Surmann, 2004). A recent national survey revealed that about half of teen respondents had spoken with their parents about how to say no to sex or about methods of birth control. Fewer teens (males, 27%; females, 44%) had discussed both topics with their parents, and 38% of males and 24% of females had not spoken about either topic with their parents (Centers for Disease Control, 2011g). These data indicate that teenagers often have difficulty communicating with their parents about sex, for a number of reasons. These include embarrassment, concern that their parents will assume that they are sexually active, and thinking that their parents will not understand them (Lederman et al., 2008). Research indicates that parents also often feel uncomfortable and experience difficulty talking with their children about sex (Byers, 2011; Shtarkshall et al., 2007). This dual discomfort of both children and parents is unfortunate in that youth can benefit greatly from candid discussions with their parents about sex, as exemplified by the following anecdote provided by a young woman enrolled in a sexuality class:

> First my mother, and later my father, talked to me at separate times about sex. I was enlightened by these conversations, and they created a closer bond and increased confidentiality and trust among all of us. I was very thankful that both of my parents talked with me about sex. I realized that they really cared about my well-being, and I appreciated their efforts to say to me what their parents did not say to them. (Authors' files)

To the extent that parents do take an active role in the sex education of their children, mothers are far more likely than fathers to fulfill this function and girls are more likely than boys to be recipients of parent communication about sex (Hutchinson & Cederbaum, 2011; Tobey et al., 2011). Unfortunately, most American parents do not provide adequate sex education to their children (Kreinin et al., 2001; Meschke et al., 2000). Even where there is close and open communication between parents and children, sex often is not discussed. Several studies have shown that friends, and to a lesser extent the media, are the principal source of information about sex for young people in the United States (Sprecher et al., 2008). Thus the gap created by lack of information in the home is likely to be filled with incorrect information from peers and other sources (Newman, 2008; Whitaker & Miller, 2000). This can have serious consequences; for example, an adolescent may hear from friends that a girl will not get pregnant if she has intercourse only now and then. Peers may also encourage traditional gender-role behavior, and they often put pressure on each other to become sexually active. Thus the challenge for parents is whether they want to become actively involved in their children's sex education, minimizing some of the pitfalls faced by children and adolescents who turn to their peers for sex (mis)information.

Positive parent–adolescent communication about sex has been linked to decreased risk of contracting STIs, more effective and consistent use of birth control, and decreased incidence of teenage pregnancies (Halpern-Felsher et al., 2004; Lehr et al., 2005; Stone & Ingham, 2002).

Critical Thinking Question

Many people believe that sex education can itself cause problems, because they think that the more children learn about sex, the more likely they are to experiment sexually. Do you think this assumption is valid? If so, do you believe that it is a good reason not to teach children about sex?

School-Based Sex Education

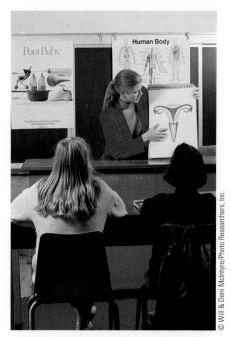

Although opposition to sex education in the schools continues, a huge majority of parents support the idea.

In response to the frequent lack (or insufficiency) of information from the home and the inaccuracy of much of what children hear from peers, other social institutions in the United States, especially schools, are attempting to provide sex education. However, the quality and extent of school-based sex education programs vary considerably. Most efforts to provide sex education in schools have utilized one of two principal approaches: comprehensive sex education and abstinence-only programs. Comprehensive sex education treats abstinence as merely one option for youths in a curriculum that provides broad-based information about such topics as sexual maturation; contraception; abortion; strategies for effective decision making and for saying no to unwanted sex; STIs; relationship issues; and sexual orientation. In abstinence-only programs, youths are instructed to abstain from sex until marriage, and discussions of contraception are either prohibited entirely or permitted only to emphasize the alleged shortcomings of birth control methods.

Various surveys reveal that while an overwhelming majority of parents and other adults support including comprehensive sex education in schools, only a minority of U.S. schools offer comprehensive sex education courses (Constantine et al., 2007; Trevor, 2002).

Public school sex education programs are often hampered by pressures from well-organized and highly vocal minorities opposed to such education. In response to these pressures, some school systems completely omit sex education from their curricula, and others attempt to avert controversy by allowing only discussion of "safe" topics, such as reproduction and anatomy. A recent national survey revealed that, in spite of limitations often placed on school-based sex education, most teens indicated they had received "formal sex education before age 18 years that either covered saying no to sex (females, 87%; males, 81%) or provided information on methods of birth control (females, 70%, males, 62%); 65% of females and 53% of males received education on both topics" (Centers for Disease Control, 2011g, p. 417). Unfortunately, the interpersonal aspects of sexuality were often omitted from sex education programs. We discuss the adverse impact of abstinence-based sex education in American public schools in the Sex and Politics box, "Abstinence-Only Sex Education."

In contrast to the dismal record of abstinence-only sex education, as outlined in the Sex and Politics box, numerous studies provide strong evidence that comprehensive sex education programs that stress safer sex and provide accurate information about various contraceptive methods actually increase the use of birth control, reduce teenage pregnancies, reduce high-risk sexual behavior, do not hasten the onset of intercourse (and in some cases actually delay onset), do not increase the frequency of intercourse, and do not increase the number of an adolescent's sexual partners (in some cases they reduce number) (Cavazos-Rehg et al., 2012; Kirby, 2002; Masters et al., 2008; Schaalma et al., 2004; Smith, 2005). Leading researchers in the field of sex education recently concluded that "comprehensive sex education has demonstrated its effectiveness in reducing negative sexual outcomes such as teenage pregnancy and STIs, whereas abstinence-only programs have not" (Masters et al., 2008, p. 90).

SEX & POLITICS ▶ Abstinence-Only Sex Education

In 1996 the U.S. Congress allocated $250 million to fund abstinence-only programs at a rate of $50 million per year for the period 1998–2002 (Goodson et al., 2003). Federal funding for abstinence-only programs grew steadily, from $9 million to $176 million annually, between 1997 and 2007 (Masters et al., 2008). To date over $1.5 billion federal taxpayer dollars have been spent on such programs (Herbenick, 2010a). What does research reveal about the efficacy of abstinence-only programs, largely funded by taxpayers?

A number of comprehensive investigations of abstinence-only programs have provided no substantial evidence that such programs either delay the onset of sexual intercourse (or other sexual behaviors) or significantly change adolescents' attitudes about engaging in sexual relations (Kirby, 2008a; Masters et al., 2008; Marx & Hopper, 2005; Smith, 2005). A recent comprehensive analysis of scientifically sound studies of abstinence-only programs revealed that children exposed to this form of sex education were no more likely to abstain from sex than those in a control group not exposed to abstinence-only instruction. Furthermore, youth assigned to either the abstinence-only or control group conditions had similar numbers of sexual partners (Kirby, 2008a). In one recent study, widely reported by the media, several hundred youths who took a virginity pledge, indicating their support of abstinence, reported a comparable level of sexual intercourse before marriage to that of a group of closely matched non-pledging youth in a longitudinal study that assessed sexual experiences five years after pledging (Rosenbaum, 2009).

Programs that teach abstinence without also providing essential information about sexual health, contraception, and safer-sex strategies do little to reduce adolescent pregnancy and the spread of STIs (Franklin & Dotger, 2011). It is now exceedingly clear that a sex education curriculum based on abstinence only "does not educate American adolescents about safer sex practices and leaves a knowledge gap in these adolescents that follows them into college" (Franklin & Dotger, 2011, p. 199). Studies of adolescents in Texas—a state that has aggressively promoted an abstinence-only approach in its schools, pronouncements, and policies—reveal that the pregnancy rate among Texas 15- to 19-year-olds is the highest of all 50 states, and STI rates among adolescents are well above national averages (Zenilman, 2006). In Texas, where parental consent is necessary, it is very difficult for teenagers to get contraceptives (Collins, 2011).

Lack of effective comprehensive sex education contributes to a variety of other negative outcomes, including sexual abuse, dysfunctional relationships, and inability to achieve a satisfying sex life (Newman, 2008). Various reviews reveal that a majority of the federally funded abstinence-only programs are replete with inaccurate and misleading information and often inject ideology into sex education while failing to maintain a separation of science and religion (Santelli, 2008; Tauber et al., 2005).

Thankfully, due largely to the efforts of President Obama and key players in his administration, "abstinence-only sex education seems to have had—for the time being at least—its moment in the sun" (Hess, 2011, p. 1080). In 2010 the federal funding for abstinence-only school sex education programs was eliminated (Tucker, 2011). How and why the abstinence-only approach to sex education came to dominate school-based sex education for more than a decade is the subject of an informative book, *The Politics of Virginity: Abstinence in Sex Education*, written by Alesha Doan and Jean Williams (2008).

Summary

Sexual Behavior During Infancy and Childhood

- The traditional view of infancy and childhood as a time when sexuality remains unexpressed is not supported by research findings.
- Infants of both sexes are born with the capacity for sexual pleasure and response, and some experience observable orgasm.
- Self-administered genital stimulation is common among both boys and girls during the first two years of life.
- The inclinations we have as adults toward giving and receiving affection seem to be related to our early opportunities for pleasurable contact with others, especially parents.

- Masturbation is one of the most common sexual expressions during the childhood years. Parental reactions can be an important influence on developing sexuality.
- Sex play with other children, which can occur as early as age 2 or 3, increases in frequency during the 5- to 7-year-old age range.
- Separation of the sexes tends to become pronounced by the age of 8 or 9. However, romantic interest in the other sex and curiosity about sexual matters are typically high during this stage of development.
- The ages of 10 and 11 are marked by keen interest in body changes, continued separation of the sexes, and a substantial incidence of homosexual encounters.

The Physical Changes of Adolescence

- Puberty encompasses the physical changes that occur in response to increased hormone levels. These physical developments include maturation of the reproductive organs and consequent menstruation in girls and ejaculation in boys.

Sexual Behavior During Adolescence

- The sexual double standard often pressures males to view sex as a conquest and places females in a double bind about saying yes or no.
- The percentage of adolescents who masturbate increases between the ages of 13 and 19.
- An emerging social phenomenon, adolescent sexting, involves sending sexually suggestive photos or text messages via the Internet, cell phones, or other electronic devices.
- Noncoital sexual expression is a common sexual behavior among adolescents. Noncoital sex refers to erotic contact that might include kissing, touching, manual stimulation, or oral–genital stimulation—but not coitus.
- Adolescent sexual expression is now more likely to take place within the context of an ongoing relationship than it was during Kinsey's time.
- A significant increase in the number of both young men and young women who experience intercourse by age 19 has occurred over the last five decades. This increase has been considerably more pronounced among females.
- Teenagers engage in blogging, social networking with peers, seeking health information, accessing pornography, researching school topics, and posting personal profiles.
- Adolescent participation in forced or consensual multi-person sex (MPS) is an emerging public health concern. MPS is associated with a variety of variables including experiencing sex prior to age 15, having an STI, dating and/or child sexual abuse victimization, and recent exposure to pornography.
- During the 1990s and early 2000s, adolescent coital rates leveled off and even decreased appreciably for all but young teenagers.
- Same-sex experiences during adolescence can be experiments or an expression of permanent sexual orientation.

Adolescent Pregnancy

- The United States has the highest rate of adolescent pregnancy in the industrialized West. In recent years the incidence of adolescent pregnancy in the United States has fallen.
- Approximately 750,000 unmarried U.S. adolescent females become pregnant each year. Adolescent pregnancy is often associated with social, medical, educational, and financial difficulties.
- Many adolescents who have intercourse do not use contraceptives consistently or effectively.

- The low rate of contraceptive use among U.S. adolescents is related to a number of factors, including ignorance, false beliefs, inadequate home- or school-based sex education, misconceptions about health risks associated with some contraception methods, embarrassment over acquiring contraceptive devices, concerns about confidentiality, and lack of communication with partners about birth control.
- Strategies for reducing the teenage pregnancy rate in the United States include upgrading the family planning clinic system, establishing a compulsory national sex education curriculum, educating males about their contraceptive responsibility, providing access to condoms in middle schools and high schools, and increasing dialogue between parents and children about sex.

Sex Education

- One answer to the question of when to start discussing sex with our children is when they start asking questions. If communication does not spontaneously occur, it may be helpful for parents to initiate dialogue, perhaps by simply sharing their feelings or asking nonstressful, open-ended questions.
- Some important topics—particularly menstruation, first ejaculation, and nocturnal orgasms—are rarely discussed unless parents take the initiative.
- Although most adolescents prefer their parents to be the primary source of sex information, evidence indicates that peers are considerably more likely than parents to provide this information, often in a biased and inaccurate manner.
- Even though an overwhelming majority of parents and other adults support school sex education, only a minority of American schools offer comprehensive sex education programs.
- Research indicates that comprehensive school-based sex education programs increase the use of birth control, reduce teenage pregnancies, reduce high-risk sexual behavior, do not hasten the onset or frequency of coitus, and do not increase the number of an adolescent's sexual partners.

Media Resources

Log in to CengageBrain.com to access the resources your instructor requires.

Go to CengageBrain.com to access Psychology CourseMate, where you will find an interactive eBook, glossaries, flashcards, quizzes, videos, and more.

Also access links to chapter-related websites, including **I Wanna Know: Sexuality Information for Teens, Coalition for Positive Sexuality, A Web Page by Teens for Teens, Guttmacher Institute, Hetrick-Martin Institute (HMI), Sex, etc., Teenwire, two websites sponsored by the American Social Health Association,** and **Advocates for Youth.**

Sexuality and the Adult Years

13

Single Living
How have adult single-living patterns changed in the United States?

In what ways do levels of sexual activity differ between single people and married couples?

Cohabitation
What explains the significant increase in the number of cohabiting couples in America?

Marriage
What are the essential differences between marriage in collectivist and individualist cultures?

How are various governments around the globe attempting to influence marriage?

What is unique about adult sexual relationships in Mosuo society?

What are the crucial components of successfully predicting marital satisfaction?

Nonmonogamy
What are some of the different forms of nonmonogamy that people engage in?

What are the unique variables of polyamory?

What are the possible consequences of extramarital relationships for the marriage and for the individual?

Divorce
How have divorce rates changed since the late 1970s?

What are some of the causes of the increase in rates of divorce since the 1950s?

Sexuality and Aging
What does research find about sexuality and older adults?

What are some psychological and lifestyle changes that occur in older individuals that can enhance their sexual lives?

How is the postmarital adjustment of widowhood different from that of divorce?

> After 44 years of marriage, with our kids in homes of their own, we can really enjoy ourselves. We often go out to dinner, come back home, talk, kiss, massage each other, and then maybe even have sexual intercourse. Our lovemaking can take several hours, and we're both completely satisfied. (Authors' files)

Intimate relationships of several forms occupy a position of considerable significance in many adults' lives. One's adult relationship status—single, married, or living with someone—is an important element of one's identity, both to oneself and to others. In this chapter, we examine several forms of adult relationships and the influences of aging on intimate relationships.

Single Living

Remaining single instead of marrying or living together, or following divorce, has become an increasingly prominent lifestyle in the United States. In contrast to 1970, four times the percentage of men and women between 30 and 34 years old have never been married—33%

of men and 25% of women (Straus, 2006). Single adults comprise 45% of the population in the United States (DePaulo, 2012). The increased number of single adults is partly due to men and women marrying later (Jayson, 2012). The median age at first marriage has risen since 1970—from age 23 to 28 for men and from age 21 to 26 for women (Wolfers, 2010). However, the main reason for the increase may be that more people prefer to be single. A recent survey found that 55% of unmarried individuals said they were not looking for a committed relationship (DePaulo, 2012).

Not long ago, women who pursued higher education were more likely to remain single. However, today they are more likely to marry than are women with lower levels of education, although they marry later than the average woman due to their desire to establish themselves professionally before marriage (Romano, 2009).

Single living encompasses a range of sexual patterns and differing degrees of personal satisfaction. Some people who live alone remain celibate by choice or because of lack of available partners. Others are involved in a long-term, sexually exclusive relationship with one partner. Some practice *serial monogamy*, moving through a succession of sexually exclusive relationships. Some single people develop a primary relationship with one partner and have occasional sex with others. "Friends with benefits" (FWB) are relationships with a blend of friendship and physical intimacy outside a committed romantic relationship. Researchers found that most women and men had more positive than negative emotional reactions to their FWB relationships, although men were even more positive about FWB relationships than women were (Owen & Fincham, 2011). Still other single adults prefer concurrent sexual and emotional involvements with a number of different partners. Regarding one-night stands and single life, a study found differences between men and women. Eighty-one percent of men, compared to 54% of women, said that they enjoyed the experience, and women were much more likely than men to say that they regretted having had the one-night stand (Campbell, 2008).

Most single people are happy with their nonmarried status, whether temporary or permanent (McGinn, 2006). In terms of how happy singles are about their sex lives, research suggests that married people experience higher levels of sexual activity and satisfaction than singles, but many singles claim that their sex lives are more exciting (Laumann et al., 1994; Schachner et al., 2008).

Singles and the Internet

The more than 1,000 Internet sites in the United States designed for singles to connect with one another have greatly altered the "singles scene." Each month, over 40% of single adults in the United States visit dating sites (Howes, 2011). The largest demographic group using these sites consists of higher-income, college-educated individuals, but the fastest-growing segment of Internet dating traffic is the 50-and-older population (Juarez, 2006; Straus, 2006). Match.com was the first large singles dating site, started in 1995. By 2012 it had expanded its dating sites to 25 countries (Match.com, 2012). Neil Warren, founder of the site eHarmony, claims to be responsible for 5% of marriages in the United States (Howes, 2011). On the other end of the continuum, seeking sexual partners with "no strings attached" is ubiquitous on the Internet (Sevcikova & Daneback, 2011).

Although being single has become more acceptable in our society, most people still choose to live with a partner or marry, and we examine these options next.

Cohabitation

In the past few decades both the number of people choosing **cohabitation** (living together in a sexual relationship without being married) and societal acceptance of what was once an unconventional practice have increased significantly (Kreider, 2010; Tavernise, 2011a). Census figures reveal that by 2010 about 7.5 million unmarried heterosexual couples were living together in the United States (Kreider, 2010). About 28% of men and women ages 15 to 44 cohabited before their first marriage, and almost half of the individuals who cohabit transition to marriage within three years (Goodwin et al., 2010).

The most common reasons people give for deciding to cohabit are to spend more time together, for convenience, to evaluate compatibility, and to share expenses (Huang et al., 2011; Rhoades et al., 2009). Sharing living expenses has become more important during the current economic downturn in the United States and may be a significant factor in the increase in cohabitation. Men and women with low incomes have the greatest percentages of increases in cohabitation, and those without a high school diploma or GED are more likely to cohabit than individuals with more education, as shown in ▮ Figure 13.1.

Domestic partnership is a term applied to the relationship of straight, lesbian, and gay couples who live with a partner in the same household in a committed relationship but who are not legally married. Many local, state, and national governments and private businesses have provided established benefits such as health insurance for couples in domestic partnerships. In Sweden the 30% of couples who share a household and are not married have all the rights and obligations of married couples, unlike the legal vulnerabilities inherent in cohabitation in the United States (Mezin, 2006). In contrast, older heterosexual couples may cohabit rather than marry because remarriage can mean higher income tax rates, the end of alimony payments, and the loss of spousal pension, military, and Social Security benefits.

cohabitation
Living together and having a sexual relationship without being married.

domestic partnership
An unmarried couple living in the same household in a committed relationship.

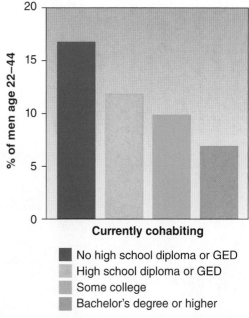

▮ **Figure 13.1** Percentage of men ages 22 to 44 who are currently cohabiting, by level of education.
SOURCE: Martinez et al. (2006).

Research shows that marriage involves a higher degree of commitment and stability than does cohabitation: Seventy-eight percent of marriages last 5 years or more, compared with less than 30% of cohabiting relationships (Goodwin et al., 2010), which may be one reason that marriage continues to enjoy widespread appeal. About 96% of adults in the United States have married at some point, and many marry more than once (U.S. Census Bureau, 2006). However, in 2010, for the first time in the United States, married couples represented a minority of all American households. The percentage of married couples has declined over time, from 78% in 1950 to 48% in 2010 (Tavernise, 2011a). A closer look at the institution of marriage might provide some insights into both its continuing allure and decreasing prevalence.

Marriage

Marriage is an ever-changing institution found in virtually every society. It has traditionally served several functions for society and individuals. It typically provides stable family units, in which children acquire knowledge about their society's rules and mores through the teachings of their married parents or kinship groups. Marriage functions as an economic partnership that integrates child rearing, performance of household tasks, and earning an income into one family unit. Marriage also defines inheritance rights to family property. For thousands of years, marriage has been about property and politics instead of personal happiness and love (Nordlund, 2009). Arranged marriage prevailed in Europe before the 19th century. Parents in elite classes arranged their children's marriages to develop alliances between families, consolidate wealth and political power, and even maintain peace between countries. Marriage in lower classes was also an economic arrangement; building a labor pool of children and combining skills, resources, and helpful in-laws were primary considerations (Coontz, 2005).

Marriage in Current Collectivist and Individualist Cultures

Scientists who study cultures have identified two opposing characteristics that differentiate cultures from each other: collectivism and individualism. Whether a culture is collectivist or individualist influences its views regarding the purpose of marriage. *Collectivist cultures*—such as those of contemporary India, Pakistan, Thailand, the Philippines, the Middle East, and other parts of Asia and Africa—emphasize group, or collective, goals over individual aspirations. In such cultures the primary purpose of marriage is to unite families rather than just two people. Parents in collectivist cultures often arrange the marriages of their children. For example, in contemporary India 90% of marriages are arranged (Cullen & Masters, 2008). Individuals are expected not to put their own feelings for someone above the more important commitments to the needs of family, community, or religion.

On their wedding day, a groom in Kenya lifts the veil of his bride, whose face he may never have seen before.

As more families from collectivist cultures have immigrated to Western countries, tradition-bound parents may coerce young women into unwanted arranged marriages. One study found 3,000 known or suspected cases of forced marriage in the United States over a two-year period (Goldberg, 2011a). In some parts of the world, consequences for those, especially women, who deviate from the expected norms can be fatal. A senior official in the Human Rights Commission of Pakistan said that in the first nine months of 2010, there were 129 known killings of women by male family members for marrying without permission (Agence France-Presse, 2011).

In contrast to collectivist cultures, *individualist cultures*, such as those of Canada, Europe, Australia, "European" Brazil, and the United States, stress individual desires and goals over family interests. People in individualist cultures place considerably more emphasis on feelings of love as a basis for marriage than do people in collectivist cultures (Levine et al., 1995). The importance of love in deciding to marry is a recent innovation in the long history of human existence. It was not until the end of the 1700s that personal choice based on love replaced family interests as the ideal basis of marriage in the Western world (Coontz, 2006). When collectivist cultures become more individualist, people are less likely to remain in marriages, as we see in China. The easing of government control over individual choices and an increase in Western influence contributed to a 21% increase in divorces in one year's time in 2004 (Beech, 2005).

Many societies today are concerned about how marriage affects the social order and attempt to modify its impact, as discussed in the Sex and Politics box, "Marriage in Crisis" on page 378.

Polygamy

Collectivist cultures are likely to practice polygamy—a marriage between one man and several women. Although it is unfamiliar to much of the Western world, polygamy has been the most common form of marriage across the ages, and it remains prevalent today in the Middle East and other parts of Africa. The religion of Islam allows a man to have up to four wives; the man's personal wealth and his ability to provide for numerous wives usually determine how many he marries (Arusha, 2008).

In countries where polygamy is the norm, some people do oppose its practice (al-Mograbi, 2011; Amnesty International, 2011). For example, in the African country of Swaziland, a man's right to polygamy is part of the new constitution. However, despite the fact that the king has 13 wives, his 18-year-old daughter, Princess Sikhanyiso, is leading opposition to the tradition. The opponents—including women in both urban and rural areas—view polygamy as a cover for having extramarital affairs. Men make their girlfriends into short-term wives and soon discard them for new girlfriend-wives. Women's desire to have love and sexual satisfaction without sharing a man with other women is the primary motivation for the opposition and reflects a trend toward individualism in collectivist cultures. A study comparing Bedouin Arab wives in monogamous and polygamous

HBO's *Big Love* portrayed the tribulations and joys of a family with one husband, three wives, and their children. Viagra helped the devoutly religious and hardworking husband keep "up" with his marital duties. Typical family tensions were multiplied by the dynamics of one man and three women, and their attempt to keep their marital arrangement secret from their suburban neighbors.

Many countries around the world consider the status and role of marriage to be in crisis, but the specific concerns vary greatly. For example, economic planners in Spain would like the 50% of women between ages 25 and 29 who are single to stimulate the country's economic growth by marrying earlier and having more children. The German, Austrian, French, Japanese, Russian, and Korean governments want to increase the number of births, and some even provide financial incentives and preferential access to housing and child care for people who have children, regardless of marital status. For example, for a couple having a second child, the Russian government offers payment of $9,200, longer paid maternity leave, and financial assistance for child care (Niedowski, 2006).

Several countries are concerned about various kinds of obstacles to marriage for men. Leaders in Saudi Arabia and the United Arab Emirates want families to lower high bride prices so young men can afford to marry. In Italy commentators criticize the 33% of single men between ages 30 and 35 who still live at home, enjoying their mothers' cooking and housekeeping. The governments and people of India and China are worried about the millions of men who by 2020 will be without women to marry as a result of the imbalanced ratio of boys to girls (Hesketh & Xing, 2006). The Bill and Melinda Gates Foundation funded a study in a rural area of India that found that, among children under 6 years of age, there are 628 girls for every 1,000 boys. The greater number of boys than girls has occurred because female fetuses are often aborted and female infants are killed due to the strong cultural preference for boys (Chung, 2006; Power, 2006). In India, according to Hindu tradition, sons have the important role of lighting their parents' funeral pyres. Sons will earn future wealth for the family, but the dowries daughters require in order to marry are a financial loss to their families. The Indian government has begun to offer families scholarships for girls' education to attempt to encourage births of female children. However, the many-centuries-old tradition of higher status for having male children will be very difficult to change (Power, 2006).

marriages found that polygamy tended to negatively affect women: Women in polygamous marriages reported more depression, anxiety, and problems in family functioning and less self-esteem and marital satisfaction than did women in monogamous marriages (Al-Krenawi & Slonim-Nevo, 2008). Furthermore, the spread of HIV throughout the family of wives in a polygamous marriage is of great concern.

In the United States' early history, Mormons practiced polygamy, but the Mormon Church disavowed the practice in 1890 (Hertzberg, 2008). However, fundamentalist sects that broke away from the Mormon Church continue to practice polygamy—despite the fact that it is against the law in all 50 states (Kovach & Murr, 2008). Experts believe that 30,000 to 50,000 polygamists live in the United States, including a growing number of Muslims and evangelical Christians (Peyser, 2006). Polygamy activist groups are lobbying for decriminalization of the practice. They maintain that individuals should have the right to engage in the private conduct of polygamy without government interference.

Child Marriage

Around the world, about 60 million girls under age 18—some as young as 8 years old—are married. In Niger, 82% of girls marry before age 18; in a region of Ethiopia, 50% of girls are married before age 15; and 7% of girls in Nepal marry before age 10. These child wives face forced sex, denial of education, and special health risks (Tamimi, 2011). They face few, if any, life options after marriage. Most have to leave school when they marry, thus severely limiting their future economic opportunities (International Center for Research on Women, 2009).

Health risks for child brides are numerous, and damage can be lifelong (Santhya et al., 2010). Young wives whose bodies have not fully matured often experience traumatic childbirth: They can be in labor for days, which can result in a dead baby and a permanently damaged birth canal (Pathfinder International, 2006). In Yemen, complications from pregnancy are the leading cause of death for young women between ages 15 and 19 (Khalife, 2011). Further, child and teen wives typically have much older husbands, who are often polygamous: The husbands' age and polygamy increase the chances that they are already infected with HIV and will transmit it to their wives soon after marriage (Ali, 2006).

Poverty is a major factor promoting child marriage. The financial burden of girls in poor families is eliminated when they are married, and families may receive a bride dowry payment. Girls who live in refugee camps are especially likely to become child brides. The United Nations, UNICEF, and other organizations are campaigning in the Middle East and other parts of Africa and Asia to prevent girls ages 13 and younger from being married and to obtain for them the right to full and free consent to marriage (Veneman, 2009). However, in countries where child marriage has been a traditional custom, it continues to occur even after laws against it have been established (Hedayat, 2011). In 2009 the U.S. Congress passed a bill to provide funding for educational and economic opportunities for girls so that they and their families have viable alternatives to early marriage (Hedayat, 2011).

In Afghanistan this 11-year-old girl had to quit school when she became engaged to her 40-year-old husband-to-be.

Few cultures recognize unions between one woman and several men (polyandry), and even fewer approve of sexual activity outside marriage. However, a matriarchal culture in China turns common concepts of marriage upside down, as discussed in the following Sexuality and Diversity feature.

SEXUALITY and DIVERSITY

Where Women Choose

In a remote part of China, on the shore of a lake at a high altitude, surrounded by towering mountains, the Mosuo society has one of the most unusual marriage arrangements in the world. This ancient **matriarchal society** of about 50,000 people has lasted nearly 2,000 years and thrives today. Because of their isolated location, the Mosuo people have been successful in resisting the imposition of patriarchal family traditions common in other parts of China. Since the society is a matriarchy, women carry the family name and govern the economic and social affairs of the extended family. All of the sons and daughters of each woman live their entire lives together in their mother's house.

After an initiation ceremony into adulthood at age 13, each girl is given her own room in the family house. There she can welcome lovers of her choice to come in the evening and stay overnight with her. Each dawn, her lover returns to his own mother's home, where he lives. This tradition is called "walking marriage" because men walk to women's houses to be with them overnight. A woman initiates a walking marriage by a glance or a special touch on the palm of her chosen's hand. Men never initiate, but they can decline an invitation.

When a Mosuo woman becomes pregnant and bears a child, the child stays in the family house of the woman's mother. The woman's brothers help raise their sister's children. The biological father assumes no fathering role except for his sisters' children. The only reasons men and women get together are for love and sexual intimacy, not for

matriarchal society
A society in which women carry the family name through the generations, and women govern the economic and social affairs of the community.

Dressed for an annual festival, this Mosuo woman invites men of her choosing to spend the night with her in her room at her mother's home.

Each Mosuo house is usually a home for two to three generations of women and their sons and daughters.

child rearing. Therefore, walking marriages are easily begun and ended. Once love dies for either partner, the walking marriage is over: The woman might find that her lover's nightly visits stop, or her lover might arrive to find her door locked (Bennion, 2005; Ryan & Jetha, 2010).

Marriage in the Western World

Marriage based on love promises regular companionship, sexual gratification, a loving and enduring involvement, and parenting options—all within the security of a legitimized social institution. And on the whole, married people are happier and healthier, both physically and psychologically, than unmarried people (Pew Research Center, 2009a). Married men move up the career ladder faster and earn more money than single men (Elder, 2005). However, such benefits hold only for certain marriages. Individuals in distressed marriages are in poorer health than those in nondistressed marriages, as found by a national longitudinal survey. In fact, they have greater health risks than divorced individuals. Furthermore, the adverse health effects of a distressed marriage have a cumulative effect, increasing with time in the marriage and therefore greater at older ages (Umberson et al., 2006).

Changing Expectations and Marital Patterns

A large discrepancy exists between the American marriage ideal and actual marriage practices. Although cohabitation, high divorce rates, and extramarital sexual involvement are all antithetical to the traditional ideal, they are widespread. In fact, the most politically conservative area of the country—the so-called Bible Belt—has some of the highest rates of divorce and numbers of unwed mothers, which may be partially correlated to younger ages at marriage and higher poverty rates (Coontz, 2005; Stockdale et al., 2011). Some reasons for the contradictions between ideal marriage and actual marriage practices have to do with changes in both the expectations for marriage and the social framework of marriage.

Contemporary couples usually marry for love and enter marriage with expectations for fulfilling their sexual, emotional, spiritual, social, financial, and perhaps coparenting needs (Li & Fung, 2011). One survey found that three times as many respondents believed the main purpose of marriage was mutual happiness and fulfillment rather than bearing and raising children (Crary, 2007). Ironically, as people's expectations for marriage have risen, our society's support networks for marriage have declined. Extended families and small communities have become less close-knit and supportive, placing increased demands on marriage to meet a variety of needs. Couples are often hard-pressed to find outside resources for help with household tasks, child-care assistance, financial aid, and emotional support. Although the challenges of sharing everyday life in marriage can enrich and fulfill some couples, such challenges can disillusion others (Patz, 2000). Furthermore, people now live much longer—life expectancy is in the high 70s—than they did in the past, requiring marriages to keep pace with the ever-changing needs of each partner over many more years (Bennett & Ellison, 2010).

The arrival of children poses significant challenges to marital happiness for couples (Ali, 2008). An analysis of 90 studies found a 42% drop in marital satisfaction following the birth of a first child, and a slightly smaller drop with each additional child. Up to 50% of new-parent couples experience as much marital distress as couples who are in marital therapy to address their problems, and men and women report similar amounts of deterioration in relationship functioning (Doss et al., 2009; Picker, 2005). In marriages most likely to remain happy in parenthood, research has found that the husband understands his wife's inner life, admires her, and actively keeps romance alive (Gottman & Silver, 2000).

Interracial Marriage

As recently as 1967, interracial marriage was banned in more than a dozen states. *Miscegenation*—sex between members of different races, whether or not the people involved were married—was also illegal until the U.S. Supreme Court invalidated those laws in 1967. Since the elimination of those discriminatory and racist laws, interracial marriage has increased dramatically—from less than 3.2% of all marriages in 1980 to over 8.4% in 2010. Further, in 2010 about 15% of all new marriages in the U.S. were of mixed race and ethnicity (Wang, 2012). Public approval of interracial marriage has also risen significantly, from 54% in 1995 to 80% in 2009 (Meacham, 2009). Younger people are, in general, more accepting of interracial marriage than are older adults (Herman & Campbell, 2012; Poulin & Rutter, 2011). In addition, 1 in 19 children born today—compared with 1 in 100 in 1970—is of mixed race (Pew Research Center, 2006).

One of the few studies on relationship quality in interracial couples found that interracial and same-race couples were similar in conflict and attachment styles. However, interracial couples reported significantly higher relationship satisfaction than same-race couples. The researchers concluded that either interracial relationships are less burdened with problems than same-race relationships, or individuals in interracial relationships are more effective in coping with problems (Troy et al., 2006).

Predicting Marital Satisfaction

Studies conducted by psychologist John Gottman and his colleagues have revealed surprisingly accurate criteria for predicting marital success. Gottman did not study long-term cohabiting gay and lesbian couples. Some of his findings would apply to same-sex couples, but the patterns based on male–female relationships do not. Gottman and his associates identified a number of patterns that predict marital discord, unhappiness, and separation. Identifying such patterns has provided the basis for predicting with better than 90% accuracy whether a couple will separate within the first few years of marriage. These patterns included the following:

The Obamas' marriage—a union of self-sufficient and devoted equals—embodies the post-1960s marriage ideal (Romano, 2009).

- A ratio of at least five positive interactions to each negative interaction
- Facial expressions of disgust, fear, or misery
- High levels of heart rate
- Defensive behaviors, such as making excuses and denying responsibility for disagreement
- Verbal expressions of contempt by the wife
- Stonewalling by the husband (showing no response when his wife expresses her concerns)

For successful marriages, the ratio of five positive interactions to one negative interaction is key. Gottman summarized, "It is the balance between positive and negative emotional interactions in a marriage that determines its well-being—whether the good moments of mutual pleasure, passion, humor, support, kindness, and generosity outweigh the bad moments of complaining, criticism, anger, disgust, contempt, defensiveness, and coldness" (1994, p. 44). The 5:1 ratio is even more important than how much a couple fights or how compatible they are socially, financially, and sexually. When couples maintain or improve this ratio, they can have long-lasting, satisfying marriages regardless of their particular relationship style. Gottman's research found that both men and women say that the quality of the friendship with their spouse is the most important factor in marital satisfaction (Gottman & Silver, 2000). Another study found that people in marriages where individuals believed in shared decision making and husbands shared a greater proportion of housework had greater satisfaction and less conflict (Dush & Taylor, 2012).

Gottman found other critical patterns in newlyweds who wind up in stable and happy marriages (Gottman et al., 1998). These successful patterns are distinct for women and men. Women typically initiate discussions about concerns and problems in the marriage. To the extent that women use a "softened start-up"—a calm, kind, diplomatic beginning to the discussion—they have stable and happy marriages. Conversely, men who accept influence from their wives end up in long-term good marriages. Husbands who reject their wives' requests and concerns—in essence, husbands who refuse to share their power with their wives—find themselves in unstable, unhappy marriages that are more likely to lead to divorce. A husband's ability to accept his wife's influence is unrelated to his age, income, occupation, or educational level. The following Your Sexual Health box on the next page contains a quiz devised by Gottman.

Although these patterns are unique for each sex, the positive interaction between them is evident: A wife will be more inclined to use a softened start-up if she knows her husband will be responsive to her, and a husband will be more likely to accept the influence of a wife who begins a conflict discussion in a diplomatic fashion.

Sexual Behavior and Satisfaction in Marriage

Compared with Kinsey's research groups, married women and men in the United States today appear to be engaging in a wider repertoire of sexual behaviors and enjoying sexual interaction more. The frequency and duration of sexual play before intercourse have increased, with more people focusing on such play itself rather than viewing it as preparation for coitus. Oral stimulation of the breasts and manual stimulation of the genitals have increased; so has oral–genital contact, both fellatio and cunnilingus (Clements, 1994; Herbenick et al., 2010b; Laumann et al., 1994).

Sexual satisfaction and relationship quality in marriage are often found together—as in relationships other than marriage, in which sexual satisfaction is associated with relationship satisfaction, love commitment, and stability (Aponte & Machado, 2006; Sprecher, 2002). Data indicate slightly greater sexual satisfaction for married people than for single people, as shown in ■ Table 13.1. In an extensive analysis of the National Health and Social Life Survey (NHSLS) data, couples reported that the quality of sex in marriage became slightly less with greater duration of marriage (Liu, 2003). However, a recent

Test the strength of your relationship in this quiz prepared by John Gottman.

True or False

1. I can name my partner's best friends.
2. I can tell you what stresses my partner is currently facing.
3. I know the names of some of the people who have been irritating my partner lately.
4. I can tell you some of my partner's life dreams.
5. I can tell you about my partner's basic philosophy of life.
6. I can list the relatives my partner likes the least.
7. I feel that my partner knows me pretty well.
8. When we are apart, I often think fondly of my partner.
9. I often touch or kiss my partner affectionately.
10. My partner really respects me.
11. There is fire and passion in this relationship.
12. Romance is definitely still a part of our relationship.
13. My partner appreciates the things I do in this relationship.
14. My partner generally likes my personality.
15. Our sex life is mostly satisfying.
16. At the end of the day, my partner is glad to see me.
17. My partner is one of my best friends.
18. We just love talking to each other.
19. There is lots of give-and-take in our discussions (both partners have influence).
20. My partner listens respectfully, even when we disagree.
21. My partner is usually a great help as a problem solver.
22. We generally mesh well on basic values and goals in life.

Scoring

Give yourself 1 point for each true answer.

Above 12: You have a lot of strength in your relationship. Congratulations.

Below 12: Your relationship could stand some improvement and could probably benefit from some work on the basics, such as improving communication.

Copyright © 2012 The Gottman Institute. Used with permission.
http://www.gottman.com/qz1/HowWellDoYouKnowYourPartner.html

---

study found that some couples sustain romantic love—defined as intensity, engagement, and sexual interest—in long-term relationships. As might be expected, the more intense the romantic love, the more satisfaction with their relationships and the greater sense of individual well-being and high self-esteem they reported (Acevedo & Aron, 2009).

Men and women in marriages are not equally satisfied with their sexual lives. Research indicates that married women report lower levels of sexual satisfaction than do their husbands (Liu, 2003). This difference is a complicated issue, and the causes for it are unknown. Liu speculated that the lower satisfaction wives express stems from two factors. First, wives experience orgasm in fewer sexual experiences than their husbands do. Second, because women typically invest more time and energy in the general relationship than men, women may have greater expectations for the quality of the sexual relationship than men do.

Sexless unions are not uncommon in marriage. A psychologist who interviewed married people between the ages of 25 and 55 stated, "I was astonished at how many married couples said they hadn't had sex in years" (Murray, 1992, p. 64). Former U.S. labor secretary Robert Reich made a point about the pressures faced by overworked couples when he applied this acronym to them: DINS—dual income, no sex (Deveny, 2003). Demands of employment, doing laundry, fixing the lawn mower, socializing with two sets of relatives and friends, and countless other activities can reduce the time and energy a couple has for intimate sharing. It is important to note, however, that a lack of sexual interaction does

© Mark Hanauer/CORBIS

Married couples are engaging in a wider variety of sexual behaviors and enjoying sexual interaction more often than in previous eras.

■ TABLE 13.1 Relationship Status and Orgasm Experience

	Always or Usually Have an Orgasm with Partner	
	Men (%)	Women (%)
Dating	94	62
Living together	95	68
Married	95	75

SOURCE: Laumann et al. (1994).

"No, but I do think there should be a law against no-sex marriage."

nonmonogamy
Sexual interaction outside a couple relationship.

Critical Thinking Question

Why do you think married women tend to be less satisfied with their sex lives than married men are?

not necessarily mean the marriage is bad. For some, sex is not, and perhaps never was, a high priority. And, as the psychologist previously mentioned observed, "There are many forms of human connection. These couples are not willing to sacrifice a marriage that is working on other levels" (Murray, 1992, p. 64).

Nonmonogamy

The term **nonmonogamy** refers to sexual interaction outside a couple relationship, whether the couple is married, is living together, or identifies themselves as a couple. Nonmonogamy is a general term that makes no distinction between the many ways in which extramarital sexual activity occurs. Such activity can be secret or based on an agreement between the married partners. The outside relationship may be casual or may involve deep emotional attachment; it may last for a brief time or an extended one. *Extramarital relationship* is a term used only for married couples.

Most societies have restrictive norms pertaining to extramarital sex, norms typically more restrictive for women than for men. For example, historically women in Pakistan who were convicted of adultery were sentenced to death or given mandatory prison sentences. In 2006 Pakistani president Pervez Musharraf amended the law so the more than 6,000 women in prison on adultery charges could be released on bail (UN Office for the Coordination of Humanitarian Affairs, 2006). However, the Human Rights Commission of Pakistan reported at least 675 "honor killings" by male relatives of Pakistani women and girls in the first nine months of 2011, and many were murdered after being accused of having "illicit relations" (Agence France-Presse, 2011).

In contrast, some societies have allowed extramarital sex for both men and women, as described in the following Sexuality and Diversity discussion.

SEXUALITY and DIVERSITY

Extramarital Sexuality in Other Cultures

The Aborigines of Western Australia's Arnhem Land openly accept extramarital sexual relationships for both wives and husbands. They welcome the variety in experience and the break in monotony offered by extramarital involvements. Many report increased appreciation of, and attachment to, their spouse as a result of such experiences.

The Polynesian Marquesans, although not open advocates of extramarital affairs, nevertheless tacitly accept such activity. A Marquesan wife often takes young boys or her husband's friends or relatives as lovers. Conversely, her husband may have sexual relations with young unmarried girls or with his sisters-in-law. Marquesan culture openly endorses the practices of partner swapping and sexual hospitality, in which unaccompanied visitors are offered sexual access to the host of the other sex. Some Inuit groups also practiced sexual hospitality, in which a married female host had intercourse with a male visitor (Gebhard, 1971).

The Turu of central Tanzania regard marriage primarily as a cooperative economic and social bond. Affection between husband and wife is generally thought to be out of place; most members of this society believe that the marital relationship is endangered by the instability of love and affection. The Turu have evolved a system of romantic love, called *Mbuya*, which allows them to seek affection outside the home without threatening the stability of the primary marriage. Both husband and wife actively pursue these outside relationships (Gebhard, 1971).

Consensual Extramarital Relationships

Consensual extramarital relationships occur in marriages where both partners know about and agree to sexual involvements outside the marriage. A variety of arrangements fall under the category of consensual extramarital involvements. We briefly examine three arrangements: swinging, open marriage, and polyamory.

Swinging

Swinging refers to a form of consensual extramarital sex that a married couple shares (de Visser & McDonald, 2007). The emphasis is on recreational, nonemotionally intimate encounters (Megan, 2008). Couples do not have individual contact with outside partners but participate together at the same location—usually in suburban homes, at clubs, or sometimes at "conventions" for "adventures into sensual living" with other couples (Nelson, 2010). In an online survey of about 1,400 swingers, the most common reasons given for engaging in swinging activities were sexual variety and fantasy fulfillment. Both men and women scored at the high end of marital and sexual satisfaction scales, but men were more likely than women to have initially suggested swinging, and over half the women involved in swinging considered themselves bisexual (Fernandes, 2008). A documentary released in 2000 titled *The Lifestyle: Group Sex in the Suburbs*, features interviews of typical swingers: middle-class, middle-aged, suburban married couples who look to the recreational sex of swinging for enhancement of the sex in their long-term marriage.

A variation on swinging, called *hotwifing* by Cody Alston, author of a book by that name, is where a couple enjoys the woman having sexual contact with one or more men, even though the male partner is sexually exclusive to his partner. The boyfriend or husband usually initiates hotwifing because he finds it highly sexually arousing to share his partner with other men. Couples prefer various contexts for the sexual encounters—some women are sexual with the other men while their partners are present to watch, and other women meet alone for their liaisons (Alston, 2012).

Open Marriage and Polyamory

The 1972 book *Open Marriage*, by George and Nena O'Neill, brought widespread public attention to the concept of **open marriage**, in which wife and husband agree to have intimate and sexual relationships outside their marriage. A more current term, the *new monogamy*, involves a primary attachment of the couple, while allowing outside involvements of varying types (Nelson, 2010; Perel, 2006). Writer Dan Savage has coined the word *monogamish*, for couples who have a primary bond yet allow one another various parameters for sexual relationships with others (Karpel, 2011).

Polyamory is a term many people use to describe multiple consensual sexual relationships. Polyamorists distinguish their relationships from other nonmonogamous relationships by their emphasis on emotional commitment in multiple sexual relationships (Megan, 2008). Polyamorist literature emphasizes honest, ethical relationships that consist of trios, groups of couples, and intentionally created families (Wise, 2006). All parties in polyamorous relationships are expected to communicate fully about whom they are involved with and what they do together (Williams, 2008). In 2005 the Dutch government recognized a three-person cohabitation contract between a married couple and another individual, who formed the first government-recognized polyamorous union (Hanus, 2006a).

Nonconsensual Extramarital Relationships

In **nonconsensual extramarital sex** a married person engages in a sexual relationship outside the marriage, without the consent (or, presumably, the knowledge) of his or her

consensual extramarital relationship
A sexual relationship that occurs outside the marriage bond with the consent of one's spouse.

swinging
The exchange of marital partners for sexual interaction.

open marriage
A marriage in which spouses, with each other's permission, have intimate relationships with other people as well as with the marital partner.

polyamory
Multiple consensual sexual relationships of trios, groups of couples, and intentionally created families that emphasize emotional commitment.

nonconsensual extramarital sex
Sexual interaction in which a married person engages in an outside sexual relationship without the consent (or, presumably, the knowledge) of his or her spouse.

spouse. Affairs vary from one-night stands to deep emotional involvements (Allen & Rhoades, 2008). Nonconsensual extramarital sex has been given many labels, including *cheating, adultery, infidelity, having an affair,* and *fooling around.* These negative labels reflect the fact that more than 90% of the general U.S. public says that extramarital sex is "always" or "almost always" wrong (Treas & Giesen, 2000).

How Common Are Extramarital Affairs?

It is difficult to determine accurately how many people have affairs because people may be reluctant to admit to an affair, even for research. For example, a study of almost 5,000 married women found that in face-to-face interviews, 1% of the women said that they had been unfaithful to their husbands in the last year, but with the anonymity of a computer questionnaire, 6% of the same group of women answered yes to this question (Whisman & Snyder, 2007). The NHSLS, with its sample of 3,432 Americans ages 18 to 59, found reported rates of extramarital involvement at some time during marriage of 25% of married men and 15% of married women (Laumann et al., 1994). A more recent study in 2011 found that over 23% of men and 19% of women said that they had "cheated" during their current relationship (Mark et al., 2011). ■ Table 13.2 shows a global comparison of the percentage of adults who say they have had an extramarital affair.

Why Do People Have Affairs?

Various complex theories abound on the reasons for nonconsensual extramarital sex. In part, intrinsic conflicts in human nature contribute. As author Erica Jong explained, "We are pair-bonding creatures—like swans or geese. We can also be as promiscuous as baboons or bonobos. Those are the two extremes of human sexuality, and there are all gradations of chastity and sensuality in between" (2003, p. 48). Sometimes nonconsensual extramarital relationships are motivated simply by a desire for excitement and variety, even when an individual has no particular complaints about his or her marriage and even says the marriage is happy (Nelson, 2010; Straus, 2006). A recent study found that men who had a higher propensity for sexual excitement were more likely to have sex outside their relationships. This correlation was not found for women (Mark et al., 2011).

Often, the reason for outside involvements is the unavailability of sex within the marriage. A lengthy separation or a debilitating illness of one partner can leave one vulnerable to an affair. A partner's disinterest or unwillingness to relate sexually can influence a person to look elsewhere for sexual fulfillment. A recent study found that sexual incompatibility was a stronger predictor of sexual affairs for women than for men (Mark et al., 2011).

In other cases, people are highly dissatisfied with their marriages. If emotional and sexual needs are not being met within the marriage, having an affair may seem particularly inviting. Affairs in which emotional involvement is strong have been shown to be related to dissatisfaction with the primary relationship prior to the affair to a greater degree than have affairs with low emotional involvement. Affairs with strong emotional involvement are also more likely to lead to divorce (Allen & Rhoades, 2008). Recent research has found that women are more likely to have affairs when they are unhappy in their relationship, whereas this correlation was not found with men (Mark et al., 2011). In some situations, affairs also provide the impetus to end a marriage that is no longer satisfying.

■ TABLE 13.2 **Percentage of Population in 2005 Global Sex Survey That Say They Have Had at Least One Extramarital Affair**

	Extramarital Affair (%)
Israel	7
Poland	10
Spain	10
Germany	11
Hong Kong	11
Ireland	12
United Kingdom	14
China	15
Greece	15
India	15
Australia	16
Thailand	16
United States	17
Canada	18
Japan	21
Global percentage	**22**
Czech Republic	24
Portugal	24
France	25
Italy	26
South Africa	26
Sweden	26
Chile	30
Netherlands	31
Finland	36
Vietnam	36
Iceland	39
Norway	41
Denmark	46
Turkey	58

SOURCE: Durex (2006).

A study of couples in marital therapy found several differences between couples in which infidelity was occurring and couples in which it was not. Couples in which it was occurring had more marital instability, dishonesty, arguments about trust, self-centeredness, and time spent apart (Atkins et al., 2005). The important question to ask about these negative marital characteristics is which came first—the dissatisfaction or the infidelity? It is just as possible for the dissatisfaction to have increased because of the infidelity as for the dissatisfaction to have motivated the infidelity. The person having the affair may treat his or her spouse differently due to feelings of guilt or to comparing the marriage with the excitement of the new relationship.

Living circumstances can play a role in regard to sexual exclusivity. When individuals have weak ties to their spouse's friends, family, and activities and are not involved in a religious community, the chances are greater of having affairs (Ali & Miller, 2004). People are more likely to be unfaithful if they have greater access to potential partners at work, through out-of-town travel, or simply by living among many people in the relative anonymity of a large city. The increased number of women in the workforce may account in large part for the increased number of women having affairs (Carollo, 2011).

In the United States, we are accustomed to media headlines about prominent men being discovered having affairs. The lack of women in the same predicament creates the impression that many more men than women are unfaithful in their marriages. However, recent research findings suggest that power may be a stronger predictor of infidelity than gender. An anonymous online survey of over 1,500 people by a prestigious business magazine found that men and women who were in top positions of power in their professions were equally likely to have had affairs and to be considering them in the future. These men and women were also much more likely to have had affairs, and to have had more affairs, than people who had less power in their professional lives. The gender imbalance in media headlines may be due to the fact that fewer women than men are in positions of power (Lammers et al., 2011).

The Internet's Role in Affairs

With access to the Internet and websites designed specifically for those interested in extramarital affairs, the opportunity for an individual to develop intimate, secret relationships outside his or her committed relationship has taken on new dimensions (Hymowitz, 2011; Wysocki & Childers, 2011). Even a secret e-mail relationship can become emotionally charged and easily cross the line from friendship to loving someone romantically (Teich, 2006). More women than men believe that cybersex is cheating (Knox et al., 2008). While the Internet makes it very easy to reconnect with past loves and to find people for extramarital sexual relationships, this means of communication makes it almost as easy for a spouse (or an employer) to discover such relationships.

Media headlines in the United States have a parade of prominent men who have been discovered to have affairs, including Tiger Woods, Arnold Schwarzenegger, and Jesse James.

Most marital therapists have seen a significant increase in couples coming to therapy in crisis following a spouse's discovery of an Internet-initiated affair (Cooper, 2004). Also, online contact is increasingly part of the cause of divorce (Hovde, 2011).

The Impact of Extramarital Sex on Individuals and Marriage

Involvement in an extramarital affair can have serious consequences for the participants, including loss of self-respect, severe guilt, stress associated with leading a secret life, damage to reputation, loss of love, and complications of sexually transmitted infections. The dynamics of the secrecy typically have damaging effects on the quality of the couple's relationship. The secrecy and lying (even by omission) erode the connection between spouses and amplify emotional intensity and the illusion of closeness to the affair partner. Frank Pittman, author of *Private Lies: Infidelity and the Betrayal of Intimacy*, maintains that a person becomes more distant from whomever he or she lies to, and closer to whomever he or she tells the truth to (Pittman, 1990). Researchers examined secrecy in relationships and found that subjects spent more time thinking about former lovers who were kept secret than about those whom their current partner knew about (Wegner et al., 1994). The researchers also set up a laboratory experiment involving male and female university students. Subjects were seated in mixed-sex pairs for card games, and couples were asked to touch feet under the table while playing cards with another couple. Sometimes this game of footsie was secret; at other times it was not. Couples in the "secret footsie" group reported greater attraction to each other after the game than did couples whose foot touching was not secret.

Research finds that marriages usually fare better when an unfaithful spouse proactively discloses an affair to the other spouse than when the other spouse discovers it on his or her own (Aaronson, 2005). Regardless of how a betrayed spouse finds out about infidelity, he or she often feels devastated. The betrayed spouse can experience a variety of emotions, including feelings of inadequacy and rejection, extreme anger, resentment, shame, and jealousy.

Research has found that in heterosexual couples, men are more likely to believe their female partners would have an emotional affair, and women believe their male partners are more likely to have an affair for the sake of the sex. Psychological distress for both men and women was greater if their partners had affairs that violated their expectations. More women were distressed by imagining a partner falling in love with someone else; in contrast, imagining a partner having sex distresses more men than women (Cramer et al., 2008).

Divorced individuals often mention extramarital relationships as a cause of their breakup. However, the discovery of infidelity does not necessarily end a marriage or ultimately erode the quality of a marriage. In some cases such a crisis is beneficial, in that it motivates a couple to search for, and attempt to resolve, sources of discord in the relationship—a process that can ultimately lead to an improved marriage (Kalb, 2006).

Divorce

Almost 96% of adults in the United States today have married during their lifetime, and more than 50% of couples in the United States remain in their first marriage (Heiman et al., 2011). Research confirms that the proportion of all marriages—first, second, or more—ending in divorce increased dramatically since the 1950s, when one in four marriages ended in divorce. By 1977 the ratio was one divorce to every two marriages. Since 1977 the ratio of divorces to marriages has tended to level off and has held relatively steady, with the exception of one age group. The divorce rate has doubled in the past 2 decades for people ages 50 and older (Thomas, 2012). Most divorced people remarry: Approximately 26% of men and women ages 40 to 44 have been married two or more times (Goodwin et al., 2010).

Explaining the High Divorce Rate

A number of investigators have speculated on the causes of the high divorce rate in the United States. One cause is the comparative ease of obtaining no-fault divorces since the liberalization of divorce laws in the 1970s. Obtaining a divorce has become a simpler, less expensive legal process, and as divorces have occurred more often, the social stigma of divorce has lessened. A frequently mentioned cause is increased expectations for marital and sexual fulfillment, which have caused people to be less willing to persist in unsatisfying marriages.

The increased economic independence of women (one third of married women earn more than their husbands) increases the importance of relationship satisfaction over financial dependence in women's decisions to divorce (Goad, 2006). There also appears to be an inverse relationship between level of education and divorce rate; that is, the lower the educational level, the higher the divorce rate (Schoen & Cheng, 2006). The one exception is a disproportionately high divorce rate among women who have achieved graduate degrees. Perhaps the increased economic and social independence of professional women with advanced degrees contributes to this exception in divorce rate patterns (Amato & Previti, 2003).

Research has revealed another variable associated with marriages ending in divorce: age at marriage. People who marry in their teen years are more than twice as likely to divorce as those who wed in their 20s. Individuals who marry after age 30 have even lower divorce rates. The correlation between age at marriage and divorce rate is of particular interest in light of a clear upward trend in the median age at first marriage. Before 1900 most couples in the United States married while they were still in their teens. In 1950 the median marriage age was 22 for men and 20 for women (Bergman, 2006). The median age at first marriage has continued to rise, to age 28 for men and age 26 for women (Wolfers, 2010). Later age at marriage may contribute positively to the stability of marriage: The likelihood of divorce is reduced for every year older a person is when she or he marries (Bennett & Ellison, 2010). The leveling off and even slight decline in the U.S. divorce rate reflects, in part, the influence of older age at first marriage.

Because divorce has become more common, more children have been raised by divorced parents. Research shows that people raised by divorced parents have more negative attitudes about marriage and are themselves more likely to divorce than are people raised by parents who remained married (Amato, 2001; Riggio & Weiser, 2008). However, parents who stay together in unhappy marriages may not help prevent their children from divorcing a future spouse. Young adults who believe that their parents should end their marriage are more likely to have positive views of divorce, even when their parents have negative views (Kapinus, 2005).

Reasons People Give for Divorce

A study has provided some much-needed empirical evidence of what divorced people say is the cause of their divorce (Amato & Previti, 2003). The researchers readily admit that the study cannot identify whether people's perceptions of their divorces represent actual causes or are after-the-fact reconstructions. In the randomly selected national sample of divorced individuals, the respondents gave infidelity as the most commonly reported cause of divorce. Poor general quality of the relationship—lack of communication, incompatibility, personality clashes, and growing apart—are other factors people reported. Serious problems, such as drinking, drug use, and mental and physical abuse, were further reasons for divorce. Men and women tended to give different reasons for divorce. Women were more likely to report that their husbands' problematic behavior led to divorce, whereas men were more likely to say that they did not know what caused the divorce.

Socioeconomic status (SES) was another variable resulting in differences. High-SES divorced individuals were more likely to attribute their divorces to lack of love and communication, incompatibility, and their spouses' self-centeredness, but low-SES divorced individuals described financial problems, abuse, and drinking as major factors. In terms of positive emotional adjustment following a divorce, people who perceived that they initiated the divorce did better than those who said their partner initiated the divorce (Amato & Previti, 2003).

Adjusting to Divorce or Breakup of Long-Term Relationships

Although the chain of events leading to marriage is unique for each individual, most people marry with the hope that the relationship will last. Divorce often represents loss of this hope as well as loss of one's spouse, lifestyle, the security of familiarity, and part of one's identity and self-worth (Park et al., 2011). Divorce also often represents stressful changes in parenting time and circumstances (Schrodt, 2011). In the following discussion, we refer to a breakup as divorce, but people who end nonmarital intimate relationships also can experience these losses (Sbarra, 2006).

The loss a person feels during a divorce or a breakup of a meaningful relationship is often comparable to the loss experienced when a loved one dies (Napolitane, 1997). In both cases one undergoes a grieving process, but no recognized grief rituals are provided by society to help one ending a relationship. Initially, a person may experience shock: "This cannot be happening to me." What might follow is a feeling of disorientation— a sense that one's entire world has turned upside down. Volatile emotions may unexpectedly surface. Feelings of guilt may become strong. Loneliness is common. Learning to reach out to others for emotional support can help diminish feelings of aloneness. Finally (usually not for several months or a year), a sense of relief and acceptance may come. After several months of separation, a person who is not developing a sense of acceptance may benefit from professional help.

Although many of the feelings that accompany ending a relationship are uncomfortable and painful, a potential exists for personal growth in the adjustment process. Many people come to experience an exciting sense of autonomy. Others find that being single presents opportunities to experience more fully dimensions of themselves that had been submerged in the marriage. The end of an important relationship or marriage can offer an opportunity to reassess oneself and one's past, a process that may lead to a new life.

Sexuality and Aging

In general, people are living longer and being sexually active for a greater portion of their lives (Elders, 2010). In the later years of life, most people begin to note certain physical changes taking place in their sexual response patterns (Herbenick et al., 2010b), as described in Chapter 6. Some women and men who understand the nature of these changes accept them in stride. Others observe them with concern.

An important source of the confusion and frustration that many aging people feel is the prevailing notion that old age is a sexless time (Kellett, 2000). Why has aging in our society and in other societies often been associated with sexlessness? (See ▮ Figure 13.2

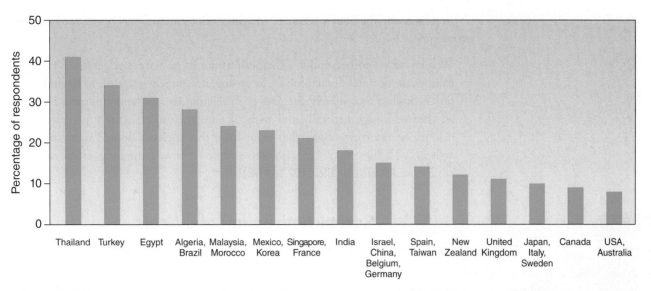

Figure 13.2 The percentage of respondents in each country who agreed with the statement "Older people no longer have sex."

SOURCE: Adapted from Global Study of Sexual Attitudes and Behaviors (2002).

for a global comparison.) Part of the answer is that U.S. culture is still influenced by a philosophy that equates sexuality with procreation and makes it seem not quite acceptable for older people to have and express sexual needs. Moreover, the media usually link love, sex, and romance to the young. However, as the percentage of seniors in the population continues to increase, the consumer goods market more frequently presents vibrant, sensual ads featuring older women and men (Jarrell, 2000). In addition, as the generation that reached adulthood during the so-called sexual revolution era moves into senior citizenship, the notion of a sexless old age may become obsolete, and the view of sexuality as a potential for a lifetime of pleasure will become more common (Elders, 2010).

The Double Standard and Aging

In previous chapters we have discussed the double standard as it relates to male and female sexual expression during adolescence and adulthood. The assumptions and prejudices implicit in the sexual double standard continue into old age, imposing a particular burden on women. Although a woman's sexual capabilities can continue throughout her lifetime, the cultural image of an erotically appealing woman is commonly one of youth.

In contrast, the sexual attractiveness of men is often considered enhanced by aging. Gray hair and facial wrinkles are often thought to look distinguished on men—signs of accumulated life experience and wisdom. Likewise, it is relatively common for a man's achievements and social status—both of which usually increase with age—to be closely associated with his sexual appeal. However, the professional achievements of women may be perceived as threatening to some potential male partners.

The pairing of powerful older men and young beautiful women reflects this double standard of aging. The marriage of a 55-year-old man and a 25-year-old woman generates a much smaller reaction than that of a 55-year-old woman and a 25-year-old man. And as you might expect, pairings of older men and young women occur much more commonly than the reverse. However, a survey found that 34% of women over age 40 were dating younger men, and more women marry younger men now than in the past (Coontz, 2006; Mahoney, 2003).

Older women are appearing more often in advertising as the baby boomer generation ages.

In response to the double standard of aging, writer Susan Sontag presented an alternative view:

> Women have another option. They can aspire to be wise, not merely nice; to be competent, not merely helpful; to be strong, not merely graceful; to be ambitious for themselves, not merely themselves in relation to men and children. They can let themselves age naturally and without embarrassment, actively protesting and disobeying the conventions that stem from this society's double standard about aging. . . . [T]hey can . . . remain active adults, enjoying the long, erotic career of which women are capable. (1972, p. 38)

The need for affection and intimacy extends into the older years, which can be a time of erotic sharing and closeness.

© Bruce Ayres/Getty Images

Sexual Activity in Later Years

We have seen that our society tends to perceive the older years as a time when sexuality no longer has a place in people's lives. What does research show about the reality of sexuality among older people in our own society? For many older adults sexuality is part of what makes their lives full and rich. In fact, research indicates that sexual interest and activity continue as a natural part of aging. For some, sexuality can actually improve in later life. Of a representative sample of adults over age 60, 61% of those who were sexually active said that their sex life today was either the same as or more physically satisfying than in their 40s (Dunn & Cutler, 2000).

A research study that asked older adults the questions, "Has sex gotten better or worse over your life course?" and "When did improvements occur and why?" found it was common for women to say that their later-life sexuality was more fulfilling than their early-in-life experiences. As young women, ignorance of their own bodies and a gender-role sexual passivity led them to defer sexual interaction to often ill-informed male partners. Many reached middle age before they had enough experience to discover their own sexual desires and be confident enough to initiate them, which enhanced their sexual lives considerably (Gullette, 2011).

How sexually active are older adults? A nationally representative survey of men and women age 60 and older found that about half are sexually active. "Sexually active" was defined as engaging in vaginal intercourse, oral sex, anal intercourse, or masturbation at least once a month (Dunn & Cutler, 2000). Frequency of sexual activity for people who continue to be sexually active does not decrease significantly until after age 74 (Lindau et al., 2007). New sexual relationships may also develop in later adulthood (Cheever, 2011; Vasconcellos et al., 2006). A 67-year-old woman explained:

> Eight years after my husband died, I met a widower on a tour of New Orleans. The physical attraction was intense for both of us. Neither of us had had sex for many years, but two days after discovering each other we were in bed with clothes strewn all over the floor. The sex (which neither of us was sure we'd be able to achieve) was sensational. We're very much in love but have decided not to marry because we both love our homes, need "space," and are financially independent. Our children accept our lifestyle and are very happy with our respective "significant other." (Authors' files)

Many older adults are dating and many use dating websites, and it is not unusual for individuals to have a new sexual partner later in life. Several studies have reported that

women were most likely to experience orgasm with someone they were sexual with who was not a relationship partner. Eighty-one percent of women reported having an orgasm in their last sexual encounter if their partner was a non-relationship partner, compared to 58% who experienced orgasm with a relationship partner. Perhaps women find a new partner more arousing, or women who seek out new partners are inherently more sexually motivated. In contrast, men were more likely to experience orgasm with a relationship partner (Schick et al., 2010).

Sexual activity of older adults is, unfortunately, evidenced by the rising incidence of HIV/AIDS in this group (Harvard Women's Health Watch, 2012). Only about 20% of sexually active older men and 24% of women who are not in an ongoing exclusive relationship say they used a condom during their last sexual experience (Schick et al., 2010). Many health-care professionals do not routinely screen for sexually transmitted infections in seniors, but some public health agencies offer safe-sex seminars to seniors (Levy, 2001; McGinn & Skipp, 2002).

Factors in Maintaining Sexual Activity

Aging does affect the number of people who engage in sexual activity, and the percentage of sexually active adults does decline with each decade (Doskoch, 2011), as shown in ■ Table 13.3.

What factors contribute to remaining sexually active in later years? Research has consistently revealed a close correlation between the level of a person's sexual activity in early adulthood and his or her sexual activity in later years (Kinsey et al., 1948; Kinsey et al., 1953; Leiblum & Bachmann, 1988). Lifelong consistent sexual activity may reflect an overall higher sex drive and positive attitudes toward sexuality, since both are significant influences on sexual desire and response (DeLamater & Sill, 2005).

Typically the most crucial factor influencing sexual activity in older adulthood is health. Poor health and illness have a greater effect on sexual functioning than does age itself. In long-term relationships, the poor health and loss of sexual interest by one person limits the partner's sexual expression as well (Fisher, 2010). Besides contributing to general and sexual health, regular physical exercise, a healthy diet and weight, and light or no alcohol use help maintain sexual desire and response (Harvard Health Publications, 2006).

Older adults often find new techniques for maintaining or enhancing their enjoyment of sex despite progressive physiological changes. Oral sex, viewing sexually explicit materials, fantasy, manual stimulation, and use of a vibrator are some of the variations older couples may integrate into their sexual experiences. Openness to experimenting with and developing new sexual strategies with a supportive

Critical Thinking Question

What factors might be involved in the difference between men and women with regard to experiencing orgasm with a relationship partner versus a non-relationship partner?

■ TABLE 13.3 Percentage of Sexually Active Adults

	Men (%)	Women (%)
Sexually active in their 60s	71	51
Sexually active in their 70s	57	30
Sexually active in their 80s	25	20

SOURCE: Dunn & Cutler (2000).

partner is instrumental in continuing sexual satisfaction (Trudel et al., 2008). When genital contact becomes less frequent, interest and pleasure in and frequency of nongenital activities, such as kissing, caressing, and embracing, may remain stable or increase (Kellett, 2000). In fact, a study of 1,000 couples (in the United States, Brazil, Germany, Japan, and Spain) who had been together an average of 25 years found that cuddling and caressing are important for long-term relationship satisfaction. Contrary to gender stereotypes, tenderness was rated as more important to men than to women (Heiman et al., 2011).

Homosexual Relationships in Later Years

Although most of the challenges and rewards of aging are experienced by adults regardless of sexual orientation, gay men and lesbians experience some unique aspects. Some gay men and lesbians are better prepared for coping with the adjustments of aging than are many heterosexual men and women. Facing the adversities of belonging to a stigmatized group throughout their lives may help prepare them to deal with the losses that come with aging (Altman, 1999). Many have created a more extensive network of supportive friends than have most heterosexual individuals (Alonzo, 2003). Retirement centers oriented to gay men and lesbians have been developed (Lisotta, 2007), and New York City opened the nation's first full-time senior center for sexual minorities (Tucker, 2012). As acceptance of homosexuality and gay and lesbian relationships continues to increase in the United States, stigma from antihomosexual attitudes will become a less stressful factor in the lives of older gay men and lesbians (Kuyper & Fokkema, 2011a; Jones, 2011). Further, as laws establishing same-sex marriage expand, more gay and lesbian couples will be able to experience an increased sense of security and recognition (Lannutti, 2011).

Overall, studies find that older gay men and lesbians match or exceed comparable groups in the general population on a measure of life satisfaction (Woolf, 2001). A study of gay men revealed a change over time toward fewer sexual partners, but frequency of sexual activity remained quite stable, and 75% were satisfied with their current sex lives. Most of these men reported that they socialized primarily with same-age peers. Socializing and partnering with same-age peers is likely an important aspect of life satisfaction for older gay men, because the sexual marketplace setting of bars and bathhouses, where youth and physical appearance define desirability, is often inhospitable to older gay men (Berger, 1996).

As a group, older lesbians have some advantages over older heterosexual women. Research shows that most older lesbians prefer women of similar age as partners (Daniluk, 1998). Therefore, an older lesbian is less likely to be widowed than is a heterosexual woman, because women tend to live longer than men. If her partner does die, she does not face the limited pool of potentially eligible male partners. Furthermore, women are less likely than men to base attraction on a physical ideal, so the double standard of aging is less of an issue for lesbians than for straight women (Berger, 1996).

The 2011 film *Beginners* is about the son's experience of his 75-year-old father coming out as gay after his wife's death.

Focus Features/Photofest

Last Love

People who continue to grow in age can develop a wholeness of self that transcends the limited roles and life experience of youth. Intimacy can then involve a sharing of that integrated multidimensional self (Friedan,

1994; Wales & Todd, 2001). A sex and marital therapist further explains:

> The essence of sexual intimacy lies not in mastering specific sexual skills . . . but in the ability to allow oneself to deeply know and to be deeply known by one's partner. So simple to articulate, so difficult to achieve, this ability of couples to really see each other, to see inside each other during sex, requires the courage, integrity, and maturity to face oneself and, even more frightening, convey that self—all that one is capable of feeling and expressing—to the partner. . . . Adult eroticism is more a function of emotional maturation than of physiological responsiveness. (Schnarch, 1993, p. 43)

As a Turkish proverb observes, "Young love is from the earth, and late love is from heaven" (Koch-Straube, 1982).

A network of close friends and connection with the gay community can add quality to the lives of older individuals and couples.

Widowhood

Although a spouse can die during the early- or middle-adult years, widowhood usually occurs later in life. In most heterosexual couples the man dies first, a tendency that became more pronounced during the 20th century. There are more than four widows for every widower (U.S. Census Bureau, 2002). Older men without partners often seek young female companions, which reduces the pool of potential partners for older heterosexual women.

The postmarital adjustment of widowhood is different in some ways from that of divorce. Widowed people typically do not have the sense of having failed at marriage. The grief may be more intense, and the quality of the emotional bond to the deceased mate is often quite high. For some people this emotional tie remains so strong that other potential relationships appear dim by comparison. However, many people who have lost a spouse through death do remarry—about half of widowed men and one fourth of widowed women (Lown & Dolan, 1988).

Summary

Single Living

- The increase in numbers of single adults is partly due to men and women marrying at later ages than in the 1970s.

Cohabitation

- Almost 7.5 million couples were cohabiting (living together without marriage) in 2010.
- Increases in cohabitation rates may be partly due to an increased need to share expenses because of the economic downturn.

Marriage

- In 2010 married households represented less than 50% of all households in the United States.
- Many governments across the globe see marriage in crisis and are attempting to influence its role in shaping society.
- In a unique matriarchal culture in China, women and men live their entire lives in their mothers' homes. A woman chooses the man she is interested in, and he comes to her room in the evening and leaves in the morning for as long as they both feel love and attraction.

- The expectations of marriage to fulfill many needs and the reduced support networks for couples and their children are part of what makes marriage a challenge.
- As recently as 1967, interracial marriage was banned in more than a dozen states. Young adults are most accepting of interracial dating and marriage.
- Research can predict with a high degree of success the probability that a couple will experience marital happiness and remain married.
- Married couples are engaging in a wider variety of sexual behaviors than in the past.

Nonmonogamy

- Consensual extramarital relationships occur with a spouse's knowledge and agreement.
- Swinging is a practice in which couples have sexual relations with other couples simultaneously and in the same location.
- The sexually open marriage and polyamory can include emotional, social, and sexual components in an extramarital relationship.
- Nonconsensual extramarital relationships occur without the partner's consent.
- The NHSLS found that 25% of married men and 15% of married women have had an extramarital involvement at some time during their marriages.
- It is not clear to what extent problems in a marriage are a cause or a result of a nonconsensual extramarital affair.
- The Internet has made it easier for people to get involved in extramarital affairs and for spouses to discover the affairs.

Divorce

- Divorces increased dramatically from the 1950s to the late 1970s. Since the 1970s there has been about one divorce for every two marriages.
- Some of the causes of the high divorce rate are the liberalization of divorce laws, a reduction in the social stigma attached to divorce, high expectations for marital and sexual fulfillment, and increased economic independence of women.

- Women tend to report that their husband's problematic behavior led to divorce, and men are more likely to say that they do not know what caused the divorce.
- Divorce typically involves many emotional, sexual, interpersonal, and lifestyle changes and adjustments.

Sexuality and Aging

- The options for sexual expression change in the older years, and many individuals continue to enjoy their sexual relationships.
- Good physical health and an available partner are often the most important variables in maintaining sexual functioning and satisfaction.
- Gay men and lesbians may be better prepared to cope with aging, given the adversity they have already learned to face and the extensive network of friendships they have often established.
- Since men tend to die earlier, there are more than four widows for every widower.

Media Resources

Log in to CengageBrain.com to access the resources your instructor requires.

Go to CengageBrain.com to access Psychology CourseMate, where you will find an interactive eBook, glossaries, flashcards, quizzes, videos, and more.

Also access links to chapter-related websites, including **The Couples Place, Divorce Source, Aging and Human Sexuality Resource Guide,** and **WebMD.**

Sexual Difficulties and Solutions

14

Specific Sexual Difficulties

What is the most common problem that brings people to sex therapists?

What are the symptoms of sexual aversion?

What is the definition of male erectile disorder?

What percentage of women has never experienced orgasm?

How common is the problem of premature ejaculation?

What conditions can cause painful intercourse in men and in women?

Origins of Sexual Difficulties

What kinds of medical problems and medications can interfere with sexual function?

What relationship factors can create sexual problems?

Basics of Sexual Enhancement and Sex Therapy

How can individuals increase their sexual self-awareness?

What are the guidelines for sensate focus?

What are the steps for a woman who wants to learn to experience orgasm?

What is the process for resolving vaginismus?

How can a man learn to prolong his arousal before ejaculating?

What is the typical course of therapy for a man having difficulty with erections?

What medications are available for women with hypoactive sexual desire disorder?

How might someone select a sex therapist?

BananaStock/Jupiterimages

> I wish my first time had been better. I would have had sex with someone I at least liked, instead of just with someone who would do it with me. We were both pretty drunk, but not drunk enough to forget how fast I came. Word got around about it, and I avoided sex for a long time. My first girlfriend after that was cool about it, and after a while I could relax and last longer. (Authors' files)

Sexual health, "a state of physical, emotional, mental, and sexual well-being related to sexuality," goes beyond identifying and treating sexual problems (Sadovsky & Nusbaum, 2006, p. 3). This definition of sexual health by the World Health Organization is what guides us in this chapter's discussion about a number of relatively common sexual problems, the factors that frequently contribute to them, and self-help and sex therapy approaches to help resolve sexual difficulties.

As you read this chapter, it is important to remember that sexual satisfaction is a subjective perception (McClelland, 2010). A person or couple could experience a specific sexual problem and yet be satisfied with their sex lives, or they could experience no problem in physical sexual functioning and be very dissatisfied with their sexual experiences (Balon, 2008; Basson et al., 2003). ▌ Figure 14.1 shows how men and women around the world rate the pleasure of sexual interaction.

Research indicates that sexual problems as typically identified by medical, clinical, and research literature are quite common. For example, in the National Health and Social Life Survey (NHSLS), 43% of women stated that they experienced some type of sexual dysfunction, according to the study's criterion of having experienced the sexual problem for 3 or more of the last 12 months. The prevalence of sexual problems in the NHSLS sample is shown in ▪ Table 14.1.

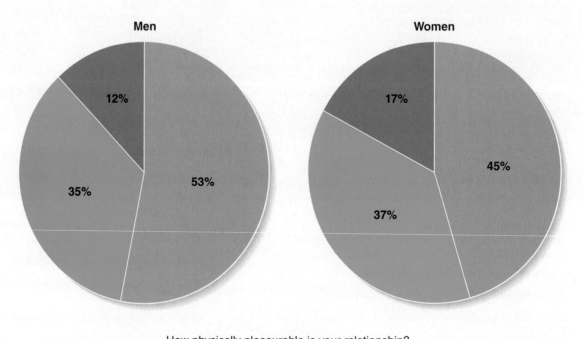

How physically pleasurable is your relationship?

■ Extremely or very   ■ Moderately   ■ Slightly or not at all

▌ Figure 14.1 Men and women worldwide were asked, "How physically pleasurable is your relationship?" The Pfizer Global Study of Sexual Attitudes and Behaviors, the first worldwide study of its kind, surveyed more than 26,000 men and women in 29 countries around the globe.

SOURCE: From Global Study of Sexual Attitudes and Behaviors funded by Pfizer Inc. Copyright 2002 Pfizer Inc.

■ TABLE 14.1 Prevalence of Sexual Problems by Selected Demographic Characteristics

	Lack Interest in Sex		Cannot Achieve Orgasm		Erectile Dysfunction	Pain During Sex	Climax Too Early
	Women (%)	Men (%)	Women (%)	Men (%)	Men (%)	Women (%)	Men (%)
Age[a]							
18–29	32	14	26	7	7	21	
30–39	32	13	28	7	9	15	
40–49	30	15	22	9	11	13	
50–59	27	17	23	9	18	8	
Education							
Less than high school	42	19	34	11	13	18	38
High-school graduate	33	12	29	7	9	17	35
College graduate	24	14	18	7	10	10	27

[a]Sexual problems are most common among younger women and older men.
SOURCE: Laumann et al. (1999).

However, individuals who have what researchers or clinicians consider sexual problems may not feel distressed and sexually dissatisfied. A subsequent random phone survey (less rigorous than the NHSLS) by the Kinsey Institute also asked women subjects whether they considered their lack of interest, arousal, or orgasm to be a problem. Slightly over 24% of the subjects reported distress about their sexual dysfunction (Bancroft et al., 2003). A more current study found that of women who had sexual problems, 36.5% reported feeling distress about their sexual functioning. In the same study, 16.5% of women without sexual problems reported feeling distress (Burri et al., 2011). For readers currently in a sexual relationship, the self-assessment inventory in the Your Sexual Health box on page 401 will give you an indication of your level of satisfaction.

Studies have found that women were most likely to report distress about sex in the context of other factors. For example, they were more likely to report distress about sex when also reporting poor personal emotional well-being, feelings of general anxiety, or a negative emotional relationship with their partners (Bancroft et al., 2003; Burri et al., 2011). Research does indicate that sexual problems can be associated with overall well-being. People with sexual problems report lower satisfaction with overall life than do those without sexual difficulties (Hellstrom et al., 2006; Mallis et al., 2006).

To be accurately considered a sexual disorder, the problem happens in spite of the person having adequate physical and psychological sexual stimulation. For example, in one study, "too little foreplay" was reported by 42% of women who reported sexual distress and problems (Witting, Santtila, & Varjonen, 2008). On the other side of the coin, research has found a correlation between greater physical stimulation and increased sexual response: Women who routinely experience orgasm engage in a relatively greater repertoire of sexual techniques than do women who do not reliably experience orgasm (Fugl-Meyer et al., 2006). Further, with a longer duration of stimulation prior to orgasm, women's orgasms tend to be more intense than after shorter lengths of time of stimulation (Laan, 2009).

Adequate psychological stimulation is also essential. For example, a man who ejaculates quickly after his partner demands, "Hurry up and get it over with!" is not receiving adequate physical and psychological stimulation and cannot be considered to have a problem with premature ejaculation from that situation alone. In another example, a diagnosis of lack of sexual desire would be inappropriate for a woman whose partner continually pressures her to be sexual in ways that he likes but that she does not enjoy or find arousing.

Critical Thinking Question

The NHSLS used the criterion of an individual having experienced the sexual problem for 3 or more of the last 12 months. Do you think this period is long enough to identify someone as having a sexual problem? Under what life circumstances might 3 months of lack of sexual desire and/or response be "normal" instead of appropriately defined as a sexual problem?

Specific Sexual Difficulties

In this section, we consider some of the specific problems that people encounter with desire, excitement, orgasm, and pain during intercourse. In reality, the line between "normal" and a "disorder" is not clearly defined in clinical practice (Althof et al., 2005). For example, how many times would a man need to have difficulty with his erections to have erectile disorder? In what context would not being able to become erect be normal instead of an indication of a problem? In addition, there is often considerable overlap: Problems with desire and arousal also affect orgasm, and orgasm difficulties can easily affect a person's interest and ability to become aroused. For example, about 44% of men who have problems with experiencing erections also frequently ejaculate rapidly (Fisher et al., 2006).

The sexual problems that we will discuss also vary in duration and focus from one person to another. A specific difficulty can occur throughout life (*lifelong sexual disorder*) or be acquired at a specific time (*acquired sexual disorder*). A person can experience the problem in all situations with all partners (*generalized type*) or only in specific situations or with specific partners (*situational type*) (American Psychiatric Association, 2000). The categories and labels for the problems that we discuss come from the *Second International Consultation on Sexual Medicine: Sexual Dysfunctions in Men and Women* (Lue, Basson, et al., 2004), *A New View of Women's Sexual Problems* (Kaschak & Tiefer, 2002), and from the International Society of Sexual Medicine, and the American Psychiatric Association's *Diagnostic and Statistical Manual* (DSM-IV and DSM-5); we have added a few categories and labels of our own.

Desire-Phase Difficulties

In this section, we discuss inhibited sexual desire, desire discrepancy, and sexual aversion.

Hypoactive Sexual Desire Disorder

Hypoactive sexual desire disorder (HSDD) is the absence or minimal experience of sexual thoughts, fantasies, and interest *prior to* sexual activity, as well as a lack of sexual desire *during* the sexual experience (Basson et al., 2004). Until recently, HSDD was defined exclusively by lack of sexual interest, thoughts, and fantasies outside sexual activity. However, many women and some men who do not experience a "sexual appetite" do enjoy and become aroused by and desirous of a sexual experience after it has begun (Elton, 2010). Therefore, the pattern of sexual desire following, rather than preceding, sexual excitement is not considered hypoactive sexual desire disorder (Laan, 2008). Although desire difficulties are the most common sexual difficulty experienced by women (see Table 14.1), significant numbers of men also experience low sexual desire and seek help for it in counseling (McCarthy & McDonald, 2009).

Desire Discrepancy

Sexual partners usually have discrepancies in their preferences for frequency, type, and timing of sexual activities, often referred to clinically as *desire discrepancy* (Willoughby & Vitas, 2011). A couple's incompatibility in terms of these preferences can contribute to sexual dissatisfaction, even when either of their preferences is, in itself, not a sexual problem (A. Smith et al., 2011). Male–female differences stand out when it comes to the frequency with which they desire sex: The 2005 Global Sex Survey found that 41% of men and 29% of women want sex more frequently (Durex, 2006). Sometimes the relationship can accommodate these individual differences. However, when sexual differences are a source

hypoactive sexual desire disorder (HSDD)
Lack of interest prior to and during sexual activity.

Hypoactive sexual desire disorder frequently reflects relationship problems.

Tomasz Trojanowski, 2009. Used under license from Shutterstock.com.

For readers who are sexually involved, this questionnaire is designed to measure the degree of satisfaction you have in the sexual relationship with your partner. It is not a test, so there are no right or wrong answers. Answer each item as carefully and accurately as you can by placing a number beside each one according to the following scale:

1. Rarely or none of the time
2. A little of the time
3. Some of the time
4. A good part of the time
5. Most or all of the time

1. I feel that my partner enjoys our sex life. ___
2. My sex life is very exciting. ___
3. Sex is fun for my partner and me. ___
4. I feel that my partner sees little in me except for the sex I can give. ___
5. I feel that sex is dirty and disgusting. ___
6. My sex life is monotonous. ___
7. When we have sex, it is too rushed and hurriedly completed. ___
8. I feel that my sex life is lacking in quality. ___
9. My partner is sexually very exciting. ___
10. I enjoy the sex techniques that my partner likes or uses. ___
11. I feel that my partner wants too much sex from me. ___
12. I think sex is wonderful. ___
13. My partner dwells on sex too much. ___
14. I try to avoid sexual contact with my partner. ___
15. My partner is too rough or brutal when we have sex. ___

16. My partner is a wonderful sex mate. ___
17. I feel that sex is a normal function of our relationship. ___
18. My partner does not want sex when I do. ___
19. I feel that our sex life really adds a lot to our relationship. ___
20. My partner seems to avoid sexual contact with me. ___
21. It is easy for me to get sexually excited by my partner. ___
22. I feel that my partner is sexually pleased with me. ___
23. My partner is very sensitive to my sexual needs and desires. ___
24. My partner does not satisfy me sexually. ___
25. I feel that my sex life is boring. ___

Scoring

Items 1, 2, 3, 9, 10, 12, 16, 17, 19, 21, 22, and 23 must be reverse-scored. (For example, if you answered 5 on one of these items, you would change that score to 1.) After these positively worded items have been reverse-scored, if there are no omitted items, the score is computed by summing the individual item scores and subtracting 25. This assessment has been shown to be valid and reliable.

Interpretation

Scores can range from 0 to 100, with a high score indicative of sexual dissatisfaction. A score of 30 or above is indicative of dissatisfaction in one's sexual relationship.

SOURCE: Adapted from Hudson (1992).

of significant conflict or dissatisfaction, a couple can experience considerable distress. Instead of moving toward some compromise, the couple polarizes, and each individual believes that his or her partner either "never" or "always" wants to be sexual.

Sexual Aversion Disorder

A fear of sex and a compelling desire to avoid sexual situations are considered a **sexual aversion disorder.** Sexual aversion can range from feelings of discomfort, repulsion, and disgust to an extreme irrational fear of sexual activity. Even the thought of sexual contact can result in intense anxiety and panic. A person who experiences sexual aversion exhibits physiological symptoms such as sweating, increased heart rate, nausea, dizziness, trembling, or diarrhea as a consequence of fear.

sexual aversion disorder
Extreme and irrational fear of sexual activity.

Excitement-Phase Difficulties

Inhibited sexual excitement occurs when physiological arousal, erotic sensation, or the subjective feeling of being turned on is chronically diminished or absent. Excitement-phase disorders among women take the form of lack of vaginal lubrication or lack of subjective awareness of physical arousal (Basson, 2002), whereas in men an inability to achieve or maintain erection is typical.

Female Sexual Arousal Disorder

As we saw in Chapters 3 and 6, vaginal lubrication is a woman's first physiological response to sexual arousal. The persistent inability to attain or maintain the lubrication-swelling response indicates **female genital sexual arousal disorder**. In contrast, **female subjective sexual arousal disorder** is indicated when physical signs of arousal are present but feelings of sexual excitement and pleasure are absent or markedly diminished. **Combined genital and subjective sexual arousal disorder** is a combination of both disorders (Basson et al., 2004).

Persistent Genital Arousal Disorder

Persistent genital arousal disorder (PGAD) is spontaneous, intrusive, and unwanted genital arousal—tingling, throbbing, pulsating—in the absence of sexual interest (Leiblum & Goldmeier, 2008). One or more orgasms do not relieve the uncomfortable feelings of arousal, and the arousal can persist for hours or days (Basson, 2009). It is an uncommon disorder, first identified in 2001. Most of the women who are evaluated for this disorder have normal findings from laboratory tests and psychiatric evaluations, although using or stopping the use of SSRI antidepressants has been related to developing PGAD (Leiblum & Goldmeier, 2008). Preliminary research has found that some of the women also have problems with restless leg syndrome and overactive bladder syndrome, which indicates a possible common cause for the three problems (Waldinger & Schweitzer, 2009). Tests using MRI and transvaginal ultrasonography have found pelvic varicose veins (abnormally dilated veins) in women with PGAD (Waldinger et al., 2009).

Male Erectile Disorder

Erectile disorder (ED) is defined as the consistent or recurrent inability over at least 3 months to have or maintain an erection sufficient for sexual activity (Ryan-Berg, 2011). An estimated one in five men older than 20 years experiences ED, and ED is a frequent reason that men seek sex therapy (Saigal et al., 2006). The incidence of ED increases with age, as shown in ▮ Figure 14.2. A man in his 50s is over two times more likely to experience erection problems than a man in his 20s.

Special procedures have been developed to evaluate physical factors in erection problems. Some techniques involve recording erection patterns during sleep, because erections normally occur during this time. Other instruments measure penile blood pressure and flow to determine whether erectile difficulties are caused by vascular problems. Injections of medications that produce erections can also be used to detect possible difficulties: If no erection occurs following an injection, then vascular impairment is likely (Lue, Giuliano et al., 2004).

Orgasm-Phase Difficulties

Other sexual difficulties specifically affect orgasmic response, and both men and women report a variety of such difficulties. Some of these difficulties involve total absence or infrequency of orgasms. Others involve reaching orgasm too rapidly or too slowly. We also consider faking orgasm to be problematic.

Female Orgasmic Disorder

Female orgasmic disorder means the absence, marked delay, or diminished intensity of orgasm, despite high subjective arousal from any type of stimulation

female genital sexual arousal disorder
Persistent inability to attain or maintain the lubrication-swelling response.

female subjective sexual arousal disorder
Absent or diminished awareness of physical arousal.

combined genital and subjective sexual arousal disorder
Absent or diminished subjective and physical sexual arousal.

persistent genital arousal disorder (PGAD)
Spontaneous, intrusive, and unwanted genital arousal.

erectile disorder (ED)
Consistent or recurring lack of an erection sufficiently rigid for penetrative sex, for a period of at least 3 months.

female orgasmic disorder
The absence, marked delay, or diminished intensity of orgasm.

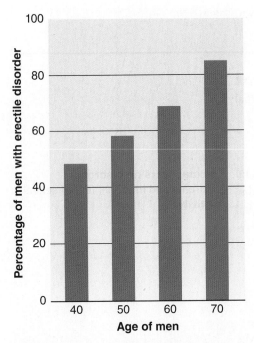

▮ **Figure 14.2** The incidence of erectile disorder related to age (Kim & Lipshultz, 1997).

(Basson et al., 2004). About 5–10% of adult women in the United States have never experienced orgasm by any means of self or partner stimulation, but data indicate that the number of women who have never experienced orgasm has decreased since the 1960s (LoPiccolo, 2000). This apparent decrease may be due to a cultural shift to acceptance of women being more sexually expressive and to the excellent self-help books and DVDs that were not previously available for women who want to learn to experience orgasm.

A woman who has *situational female orgasmic disorder* is orgasmic when masturbating but not when stimulated by a partner. Women who have experienced orgasm sometimes have difficulty doing so: About 25% of women reported having problems with orgasm within the last year (Laumann et al., 1994). Women most likely to experience difficulty with orgasm are unmarried and younger and have less education than women without problems with orgasm (Laumann et al., 1999). For many women, experiencing orgasm is something they learn to do: One survey found that almost 62% of women were 18 years old or older when they first experienced orgasm (Ellison, 2000). ■ Table 14.2 shows the incidence of orgasm in college students.

■ **TABLE 14.2 College Students Answer the Question "Have You Ever Had an Orgasm?"**

	Female (%)	Male (%)
Yes	87	94
No	13	6

SOURCE: Elliott & Brantley (1997).

Female Orgasm During Intercourse

Most sex therapists believe that women who enjoy intercourse and experience orgasm in some way other than during coitus do not have a sexual problem (Hamilton, 2002; LoPiccolo, 2000). Many more women experience orgasm from masturbation, manual stimulation by a partner, and oral sex than women who experience it during intercourse (Fugl-Meyer et al., 2006). For many women the stimulation that occurs during coitus is simply less effective than direct manual or oral stimulation of the clitoral area. As sex therapist pioneer Helen Kaplan stated, "There are millions of women who are sexually responsive, and often multiply orgasmic, but who cannot have an orgasm during intercourse unless they receive simultaneous clitoral stimulation" (1974, p. 397). Unfortunately, women and men may not always understand this: A Canadian study found that 23% of the women participants identified infrequent orgasm during intercourse as a problem (Gruszecki et al., 2005).

Male Orgasmic Disorder

The term **male orgasmic disorder**, also referred to as *inhibited ejaculation*, generally refers to the inability of a man to ejaculate during sexual activity with a partner (Sandstrom & Fugl-Meyer, 2007). Masturbation is most often the preferred method for men with male orgasmic disorder to experience orgasm (Robbins-Cherry et al., 2011). Eight percent of men experience this difficulty (Laumann et al., 1994). The terms *male coital anorgasmia* (difficulty with orgasm only during intercourse) and *partner anorgasmia* (difficulty with orgasm by partner manual and oral stimulation) are more descriptive than the general term *male orgasmic disorder* (Apfelbaum, 2000).

male orgasmic disorder
The inability of a man to ejaculate during sexual stimulation from his partner.

Premature Ejaculation

The most common male sexual difficulty is **premature ejaculation (PE)** (Strassberg, 2007). Almost all men ejaculate quickly during their first intercourse, which may be disappointing but should not be seen as a sexual problem unless it persists after more experiences. The International Society for Sexual Medicine defines premature ejaculation as a pattern of quick ejaculations (under one minute) combined with a man's inability to delay ejaculation during vaginal penetration and with distress about or avoidance of sexual intimacy because of his rapid orgasm (McMahon, 2008). In general, approximately

premature ejaculation (PE)
A pattern of ejaculations within 1 minute and an inability to delay ejaculation, resulting in a man's impairing his or his partner's pleasure.

22% of sexually active men experience PE (Steggall et al., 2008), and about 30% of those men ejaculate early without a full erection (Lue, Giuliano et al., 2004). Research indicates that men with PE underestimate the intensity of their physical arousal, experience rapid high arousal to penile stimulation, ejaculate before reaching full sexual arousal, and report less enjoyment of orgasm than men who do not have problems with rapid ejaculation (Rowland et al., 2000). Some men with PE may also have penile hypersensitivity that contributes to their rapid ejaculation (Wylie & Hellstrom, 2011).

Faking Orgasms

A final orgasmic difficulty we discuss is faking orgasms—pretending to experience orgasm without actually doing so. Some men fake orgasm, and a growing number of young, healthy men whose compulsive viewing of pornography make arousal with a partner difficult are faking orgasm (Robinson, 2011; Rothbart, 2011). However, faking orgasm is typically discussed in reference to women. ■ Table 14.3 shows rates of faking orgasm. Women report faking orgasm most often during intercourse, but also during oral sex, manual stimulation, and phone sex (Muehlenhard & Shippee, 2010). The most common reasons given by women for pretending orgasm is to avoid disappointing or hurting their partners, a desire to get sex over with (sometimes due to discomfort or pain), or poor communication about or limited knowledge of sexual techniques (Ellison, 2000; Muehlenhard & Shippee, 2010).

Can heterosexual men tell if their women partners experience orgasm? One study found a 20% discrepancy in how many men believed that their partners climaxed compared to the women who said that they did. About 85% of men reported that their partner had an orgasm at their most recent sexual event. However, 64% of women said that they experienced an orgasm at their most recent sexual event (Reece et al., 2010).

Men are also more likely than women to believe that men can tell if a woman is faking orgasm (Knox et al., 2008).

Faking orgasm often leads to a vicious cycle. The person's partner is likely not to know that his or her partner has pretended to climax. Consequently, the deceived partner continues to do what he or she has been led to believe is effective, and the other partner continues to fake to prevent discovery of the deception. Once established, a pattern of deception can be difficult to break. Although some women and men find faking orgasm to be an acceptable solution in their individual situations, others find that faking itself becomes troublesome. At the least, faking orgasms creates emotional distance at a time of potential closeness and satisfaction (Masters & Johnson, 1976; Sytsma & Taylor, 2008).

Is this woman faking it, or not? How could you tell?

B2M Productions/Photodisc/Jupiterimages

Critical Thinking Question

Do you think it's okay for a partner to fake orgasm to spare your feelings? Why or why not?

■ **TABLE 14.3 College Students Answer the Question "Have You Ever Faked an Orgasm?"**

	Female Heterosexual (%)	Lesbian or Bisexual Female (%)	Male Heterosexual (%)	Gay or Bisexual Male (%)
Yes	60	71	17	27
No	40	29	83	73

SOURCE: Elliott & Brantley (1997).

Dyspareunia

The medical term for painful intercourse is **dyspareunia** (dis-puh-ROO-nee-uh). Both men and women can experience pelvic and coital pain, although it is more common for women to have this problem.

dyspareunia
Pain or physical discomfort during sexual intercourse.

Dyspareunia in Men

Painful intercourse in men is unusual but does occur. If the foreskin of an uncircumcised male is too tight, he can experience pain during an erection. Under such circumstances minor surgery may be indicated. Inadequate hygiene of an uncircumcised penis can result in the accumulation of smegma beneath the foreskin, causing irritation of the glans during sexual stimulation. This problem can be prevented by routinely pulling back the foreskin and washing the glans area with soap and water. Infections of the urethra, bladder, prostate gland, or seminal vesicles can induce burning, itching, or pain during or after ejaculation (Davis et al., 2009; Davis & Noble, 1991). Proper medical attention can generally alleviate these sources of discomfort during coitus.

Another possible source of pain or discomfort for men is **Peyronie's** (PAY-run-eez) **disease**, in which fibrous tissue and calcium deposits develop in the space above and between the cavernous bodies of the penis. This fibrosis results in pain and curvature of the penis upon erection that can interfere with erection and even intercourse (Casabe et al., 2011). Peyronie's disease is usually caused by traumatic bending of the penis during intercourse or by medical procedures involving the urethra (Rees, 2008). Surgical procedures can sometimes be effective in addressing this condition (Djinovic, 2011; Shaeer, 2011).

Peyronie's disease
Abnormal fibrous tissue and calcium deposits in the penis.

Dyspareunia in Women

The new *Diagnostic and Statistical Manual* of the American Psychiatric Association has relabeled pain with partial vaginal entry, during intercourse, and after intercourse as **Genito-Pelvic Pain/Penetration Disorder**. It is common among women, and many who experience pain have done so since their first intercourse experience (Coady & Fish, 2011; Donaldson & Meana, 2011). When it is severe and ongoing, it is likely to create severe distress in a woman's sexual experiences (Smith & Pukall, 2011).

Genito-Pelvic Pain/Penetration Disorder
Pain with partial vaginal entry, during intercourse, and after intercourse.

A variety of factors can cause vaginal discomfort and pain related to penetration. Discomfort at the vaginal entrance or inside the vaginal walls is commonly caused by inadequate arousal and lubrication. Physiological conditions such as insufficient hormones can reduce lubrication. Using a lubricating jelly can provide a temporary solution so that intercourse can take place comfortably, but this may bring only short-term relief. Yeast, bacterial, and trichomoniasis infections cause inflammations of the vaginal walls and can result in painful intercourse. Foam, contraceptive cream or jelly, condoms, and diaphragms can irritate the vaginas of some women. Pain at the opening of the vagina can also be attributed to an intact or inadequately ruptured hymen, a Bartholin's gland infection, or scar tissue at the opening (Kellog-Spadt, 2006). If smegma collects under the clitoral hood, it can irritate the clitoris when the hood is moved during sexual stimulation. Gentle washing of the clitoris and hood can help prevent this.

About 10% of women experience severe pain at the entrance of the vagina known as **vestibulodynia**, and this may be the most common cause of painful intercourse (Bergeron, 2009). Typically, a small reddened area is painfully sensitive, even to light pressure, but the area may be so small that it is difficult for even a health-care practitioner to see. Treatment options include topical medicines and surgery to excise the hypersensitive area (Goldstein et al., 2006).

vestibulodynia
A small area at the entrance of the vagina that causes severe pain.

Pain deep in the pelvis during coital thrusting can be due to jarring of the ovaries or stretching of the uterine ligaments. A woman may experience this type of discomfort only in certain positions or at certain times in her menstrual cycle, usually during ovulation or menstruation. If the woman controls positions and pelvic movements during coitus, she can avoid what is painful. Another source of deep pelvic pain is endometriosis, a condition in which tissue that normally grows on the walls of the uterus implants on various parts of the abdominal cavity (Tripoli et al., 2011). This extra tissue can prevent internal organs from moving freely, resulting in pain during coitus. Birth control pills are sometimes prescribed to control the buildup of tissue during the monthly cycle (Reiter & Milburn, 1994).

Gynecological surgeries for uterine and ovarian cancer and infections in the uterus, such as those from gonorrhea, can also result in painful intercourse. In fact, pelvic pain is often the first physical symptom noticed by a woman who has gonorrhea. If the infection has caused considerable scar tissue to develop, surgery may be necessary.

Vaginismus

vaginismus
Involuntary spasmodic contractions of the muscles of the outer third of the vagina.

Vaginismus (vah-juh-NIZ-mus) is characterized by strong involuntary contractions of the muscles in the outer third of the vagina. These contractions make attempts to insert a penis into the vagina extremely uncomfortable or painful for a woman. The painful contractions of vaginismus are a conditioned, involuntary response, usually preceded by a history of painful intercourse (Van Lankveld et al., 2006). A woman with vaginismus usually experiences the same contracting spasms during a pelvic exam (Weiss, 2001). Even the insertion of a finger into her vagina can cause great discomfort. It is important for women and their partners to know that intercourse, tampon use, and pelvic exams should not be uncomfortable. If they are uncomfortable, it is essential to investigate the cause of the discomfort.

Although a woman who experiences vaginismus can learn to prevent the contractions, she does not consciously will them to occur. In fact, the deliberate effort to overcome the problem by having intercourse despite the pain can have just the opposite effect, contributing to a vicious cycle that makes the vaginismus worse. Sexual coercion in marriage can contribute to this problem. For example, a study of sexual problems in traditional Islamic cultures found that 58% of women who had been married without their consent had vaginismus (Aziz & Gurgen, 2009).

Some women who experience vaginismus are sexually responsive and orgasmic with manual and oral stimulation, but others are uncomfortable with most sexual activity and do not experience desire and arousal (Borg et al., 2011; Leiblum, 2000). Because many heterosexual couples regard coitus as a highly important component of their sexual relationship, vaginismus typically causes great concern, even if the couple is sexually involved in other ways.

Unfortunately, the aerobic and strength-building benefits of bicycle riding can come at a cost to sexual functioning. Pressure on the genitals from the seat can damage nerves and impair blood flow, resulting in sexual problems. Active cyclists can get genital-friendly bike seats to prevent problems (Carr, 2006).

© Image Source/Alamy

Courtesy of Wilderness Trail Bikes, Inc.

Origins of Sexual Difficulties

In the following paragraphs, we examine some of the physiological, cultural, individual, and relational factors that can contribute to sexual difficulties. Significant interaction among these factors also occurs. For example, any degree of physiological impairment can make a person's sexual response and functioning more vulnerable to disruption by negative emotions or situations. Thus a man with moderate diabetes may have no difficulty achieving an erection when he is rested and feeling comfortable with his partner, but he may be unable to do so when he is under stress—after a hard day at work or after an argument with his partner. It is also important to keep in mind that it is usually difficult to identify a consistent cause of a specific sexual difficulty because the same type of sexual problem will be caused by different factors in different individuals (Vardi et al., 2008; Waldinger, 2008).

Physiological Factors

Physiological factors often play a role in sexual problems, so it is often wise to have a general physical and a gynecological or urological exam to help rule out such causes. Hormonal, vascular, and neurological problems can contribute to sexual disorders (Beckman et al., 2006). Unfortunately, research has shown that only about one third of individuals with sexual problems talk to their physicians about it.

As more research about physiological contributions to sexual problems has been conducted, some difficulties that in the past were believed to be primarily due to psychological causes have been shown to have physical components as well. For example, premature ejaculation is sometimes associated with hyperthyroidism and improves when thyroid levels have returned to normal following treatment (Cihan et al., 2009). A genetic component may even play a role for some men. Compared to men without life-long premature ejaculation, men with this condition are more likely to have a genotype that is associated with less activity of the neurotransmitter serotonin in the section of the brain that is involved in ejaculation (Janssen et al., 2009).

Recent research suggests that individual variations, such as sensitivity to touch, can contribute to sexual disorders. For example, some men with a rapid ejaculation problem may have an innate biological hypersensitivity that causes them to ejaculate quickly (Waldinger & Schweitzer, 2006). Evidence also suggests that some women with difficulty becoming sexually aroused have lower levels of general sensitivity to touch (Frohlich & Meston, 2005). Research on sexual function continues to increase knowledge about the physiological aspects of sexual problems. At this time, more is known about the effects of illnesses, medications, and disabilities on male sexuality than on female sexuality because of the greater amount of research that has been conducted on male sexual function (Heiman, 2009).

Good Health Habits = Good Sexual Functioning

Good health is closely tied to sexual health. A healthy diet and exercise that result in a normal weight form the foundation of sex drive and functioning (Frisch et al., 2011). For example, obese men and women tend to report low sexual quality of life (Østbye, 2011). Body fat, especially around the abdomen, reduces testosterone levels in men. A high waist circumference and low levels of physical activity are associated with increased likelihood of having erectile disorder (Janiszewski et al., 2009). A study of more than 22,000 healthy men over 14 years found that men who were obese were 90% more likely to develop erectile disorder. In contrast, men with the highest exercise levels were 30% less likely than other men to develop ED (Bacon et al., 2006).

Avoiding the use of tobacco and recreational drugs is another health habit that can contribute to sexual functioning. For example, women who do not smoke, who have a history of moderate or less alcohol use, and who are a healthy weight are much less likely to have sexual dissatisfaction and disorders than those with the opposite characteristics (Addis et al., 2006). Tobacco use can have a dramatic negative effect on male sexual functioning: Men who smoke are twice as likely to have erectile difficulties than men who do not smoke (Harte & Meston, 2008a). In one study, even nonsmoking women who used nicotine gum experienced decreased sexual arousal (Harte & Meston, 2008b). ■ Table 14.4 lists other recreational drugs that can impair sexual functioning. ●

Chronic Illness

Many of us will confront chronic illness in ourselves or our partners at some point in our lives. The illness may impair the nerves, hormones, or blood flow essential to sexual functioning. Some medications and side effects of treatments for the illness can also negatively affect sexual interest and response. Any accompanying pain and fatigue can

A limp cigarette makes a graphic statement about the detrimental effects of smoking on sexual functioning.

■ TABLE 14.4 Sexual Effects of Some Abused and Illicit Drugs

Drug	Effects
Alcohol	Chronic alcohol abuse causes hormonal alterations (reduces size of testes and suppresses hormonal function) and permanently damages the circulatory and nervous systems.
Marijuana	Reduces testosterone levels in men and decreases sexual desire in both sexes.
Tobacco	Adversely affects small blood vessels in the penis and decreases the frequency and duration of erections (Mannino et al., 1994).
Cocaine	Causes erectile disorder and inhibits orgasm in both sexes.
Amphetamines	High doses and chronic use result in inhibition of orgasm and decrease in erection and lubrication.
Barbiturates	Cause decreased desire, erectile disorders, and delayed orgasm.

SOURCE: Finger et al. (1997).

distract from erotic thoughts and sensations or limit specific sexual activities (Schover, 2000). For example, erectile dysfunction is often associated with diabetes, high blood pressure, and cardiovascular problems. In fact, when men are unable to experience erections, health-care practitioners often see the sexual problem as a predictor of these serious medical problems, particularly cardiovascular disease. In contrast, research indicates that men who experience erections but have difficulty maintaining them are more likely to have a psychological cause behind the problem (Corona et al., 2006).

The following paragraphs describe the sexual effects of specific illnesses.

Diabetes Diabetes is a disease of the endocrine system that results when the pancreas fails to secrete adequate amounts of insulin or when cells in the body are insulin resistant. Nerve damage and circulatory problems from diabetes cause about 50% of diabetic men to have a reduction in or loss of capacity for erection. Some diabetic men experience retrograde ejaculation (ejaculating into the bladder). Heavy alcohol use and poor blood sugar control increase the chances of erectile problems in diabetic men. Women with diabetes are likely to have problems with sexual desire, lubrication, and orgasm (Diabetes Care, 2009; Wessells et al., 2011).

Cancer Cancer and its treatments can be particularly devastating to sexuality because they can impair hormonal, vascular, and neurological functions necessary for normal sexual interest and response. Chemotherapy and radiation therapy can cause hair loss, skin changes, nausea, fatigue, and permanent hormonal changes—all of which can negatively affect sexual feelings (Hill et al., 2011; Incrocci, 2006). Some cancer surgeries result in permanent scars, loss of body parts, or an ostomy (a surgically created opening for evacuation of body wastes after removal of the colon or bladder)—all of which can result in a negative body image (Hill et al., 2011; Ogden & Lindridge, 2008). Pain from the cancer or its treatments can also greatly interfere with sexual interest and arousal (Fleming & Pace, 2001).

Although all forms of cancer can affect sexual functioning, cancers of the reproductive organs often have the worst impact. For example, men who have had prostate cancer often experience the absence or significant reduction of ejaculation and are 10 to 15 times more likely to experience sexual problems because of treatment (Glina, 2006; Harvard Health Publications, 2006).

Multiple Sclerosis Multiple sclerosis (MS) is a neurological disease of the brain and spinal cord in which damage occurs to the myelin sheath that covers nerve fibers. Vision, sensation, and voluntary movement are affected. Studies have found that most MS patients experience changes in their sexual functioning and that at least half have sexual problems. A person with MS can experience either a reduction in or a loss of sexual interest, genital sensation, arousal, or orgasm; he or she can also experience uncomfortable hypersensitivity to genital stimulation (Smeltzer & Kelley, 1997).

Strokes   Strokes, or cerebrovascular accidents, occur when brain tissue is destroyed as a result of either blockage of the blood supply to the brain or hemorrhage (breakage of a vessel, causing internal bleeding). Strokes often result in limited mobility, altered or lost sensation, impairment of verbal communication, and depression. Stroke survivors frequently report a decline in their frequency of sexual interest, arousal, and activity (Giaquinto et al., 2003; Rees et al., 2007).

Medication Effects on Sexual Functioning

At least 200 prescription and nonprescription medications have negative effects on sexual desire and/or functioning (Finger et al., 2000). Research indicates that even use of nonsteroidal anti-inflammatory drugs may contribute to erectile dysfunction (Gleason et al., 2011). As much as 25% of cases of ED are related to medication side effects (Miller, 2000). Health-care practitioners do not always discuss potential sexual side effects of medications, so you may need to ask about the possible effects of any prescribed medicines on sexuality. Often another medication can be substituted that will have fewer or milder negative effects on sexual interest, arousal, and orgasm.

Psychiatric Medications   Antidepressants called SSRIs cause reduced sexual interest and arousal and delayed or absent orgasm in up to 60% of users (Apantaku-Olajide et al., 2011; Corona et al., 2009; Simon, 2010). The use of the antidepressant Wellbutrin (bupropion), Viagra, or ginkgo biloba (240–900 mg a day) can sometimes reverse the sexual side effects from SSRI antidepressants (Balon & Segraves, 2008; Heiman, 2008). Antipsychotic medications frequently cause lack of desire and erection and delay or absence of ejaculation and orgasm, and tranquilizers such as Valium and Xanax can interfere with orgasmic response.

Antihypertensive Medications   Medications prescribed for high blood pressure can cause problems with desire, arousal, and orgasm. Some hypertension medications are more likely than others to have negative sexual effects.

Miscellaneous Medications   Prescription gastrointestinal and antihistamine medications can interfere with desire and arousal function. Methadone (a synthetic opioid) can cause decreased desire, arousal disorder, lack of orgasm, and delayed ejaculation. Some over-the-counter antihistamines, motion sickness remedies, and gastrointestinal medications have been associated with desire and erection problems. Research also indicates that women who use hormonal forms of contraception report less arousal, less frequent sex, and fewer orgasms than women using nonhormonal methods of birth control. However, both groups report similar levels of sexual satisfaction (M. Smith, 2011).

Disabilities

Major disabilities, such as spinal cord injury, cerebral palsy, blindness, and deafness, have widely varying effects on sexual responsiveness. Some people with these disabilities can maintain or restore satisfying sex lives; others find that their sexual expression is permanently reduced or impaired by their difficulties. In the following sections, we look at some of these problems and discuss sexual adjustments that people with disabilities can make.

Spinal Cord Injury   People with spinal cord injuries (SCIs) have reduced motor control and sensation because the damage to the spinal cord obstructs the neural pathways

Good communication and creative exploration can help individuals and couples minimize the sexual effects of disabilities and illnesses.

between body and brain. Although the SCI does not necessarily impair sexual desire and psychological arousal, a person with an SCI may have impaired physical ability for arousal and orgasm; this impairment varies greatly according to the specific injury (Alexander & Rosen, 2008). Research indicates that 86% of men and women with SCIs feel sexual desire, more than half experience arousal from physical stimulation, about 30% become aroused from psychological stimulation, and 33% experience orgasm or ejaculation (Mathieu et al., 2006). Research has found that Viagra can increase arousal and erection for some men with SCIs (DeForge & Blackmer, 2005).

Cutting-edge research on women with complete spinal cord injuries has found that vaginal/cervical self-stimulation can cause orgasm. Brain imaging techniques that have identified brain activity occurring during orgasm in uninjured women have identified similar activity from vaginal/cervical self-stimulation in women with complete spinal injuries (Pappas, 2012). The physiological data indicate that the vagus nerve provides an alternate pathway from the vagina/cervix to the brain, bypassing the spinal cord (Whipple & Komisaruk, 2006).

Much of the sex counseling for individuals and couples faced with SCIs consists of redefining and expanding sexual expression. Thus, *sensory amplification*—developing heightened sexual responsiveness in the inner arm, breasts, neck, or some other area that has retained some feeling—can enhance pleasure and arousal (Rosengarten, 2007).

Cerebral Palsy Cerebral palsy (CP) is caused by damage to the brain that can occur before or during birth or during early childhood. It is characterized by mild to severe lack of muscular control. Involuntary muscle movements can disrupt speech, facial expressions, balance, and body movement. Severe involuntary muscle contractions can cause limbs to jerk or assume awkward positions. A person's intelligence may or may not be affected. Unfortunately, it is often mistakenly assumed that people with CP have low intelligence because of their physical difficulty in communicating.

Genital sensation is unaffected by CP. However, spasticity and deformity of arms and hands can make masturbation difficult or impossible without assistance, and the same problems in the hips and knees can make certain intercourse positions painful or difficult. For women with CP, chronic contraction of the muscles surrounding the vaginal opening can create pain during intercourse. Options that can help individuals with CP include trying different positions, propping legs up on pillows to ease spasms, and exploring nongenital lovemaking. Partners can help with positions, and focusing on genital pleasure can help to distract from pain. The sexual adjustment of a person with CP depends not only on what is physically possible but also on environmental support for social contacts and privacy. People with CP and SCIs may require the help of someone who can assist in preparation and positioning for sexual relations (Joseph, 1991; Renshaw, 1987).

Blindness and Deafness The sensory losses of blindness and deafness can affect a person's sexuality primarily when the visual or hearing deficits interfere with learning the subtleties of social interaction skills and with a person's independence (Mona & Gardos, 2000). Sexually, other senses can play an expanded role, as a man who was born blind explained:

> During lovemaking, my other senses—touch, smell, hearing, and taste—serve as the primary way I become aroused. The caress of my partner, and the way she touches me, is tremendously exciting, perhaps even more so than for a sighted person. The feel of her breasts on my face, the hardness of her nipples pressing into my palms, the brush of her hair across my chest . . . these are just some of the ways I experience the incredible pleasures of sex. (Kroll & Klein, 1992, p. 136)

Enhancement Strategies for People With Chronic Illnesses and Disabilities

Individuals and couples can best cope with the sexual limitations of illness or disability by accepting those limitations and developing the options that remain. For example, couples can minimize the effects of pain by planning sexual activity at optimal times of the day, using methods of pain control such as moist heat or pain medication, finding comfortable positions, and focusing on genital pleasure or arousing erotic images to distract from pain (Schover & Jensen, 1988). As we emphasize in the "Basics of Sexual Enhancement and Sex Therapy" section of this chapter, expanding the definition of sexuality beyond genital arousal and intercourse to include dimensions such as erotic thoughts and sensual touch, and developing flexibility in sexual roles and innovation in sexual technique can be helpful.

Cultural Influences

Culture strongly influences both the way we feel about our sexuality and the way we express it. In this section, we examine some influences in Western society—particularly in the United States—that affect our sexuality and can contribute to sexual problems.

Negative Childhood Learning

We learn many of our basic, important attitudes about sexuality during childhood. While growing up, we observe and integrate the models of human relationships from our families. We notice how our parents use touch and how they feel about one another. For example, one research study found that women with low sexual desire perceived their parents' attitudes toward sex and their affectionate interaction with each other to be significantly more negative than did women with higher sexual desire (Stuart et al., 1998).

A variety of therapist researchers have reported that religious orthodoxy that creates guilt about sex by equating it with reproduction or labeling it as sinful is common to the backgrounds of many sexually troubled people (Fox et al., 2006; Hunt & Jung, 2009). One study found that women who reported more guilt about sex had lower sexual desire than women with little or no guilt (Woo et al., 2011). Further, research indicates that people who leave their religion report dramatic improvement in their sexual lives. The more sexually conservative the religion was, the greater the improvement reported (Ray, 2012).

The way others react to childhood genital exploration can affect how children learn to feel about their sexual anatomy.

The Sexual Double Standard

Global research on sexuality indicates that equality of gender roles is associated with men's and women's sexual satisfaction. In the male-dominated cultures in Asia, Africa, and the Middle East, significantly fewer people report that they have satisfying sexual lives than people in the Western world (Laumann et al., 2006). As greater equality between men and women has developed over time, the sexual double standard has diminished in the United States. However, opposing sexual expectations for women and men are still prevalent in U.S. society and can negatively affect sexuality (Fugere et al., 2008). Women may learn to be sexually restrained to avoid acquiring the reputation of being a "slut," while men frequently learn that sexual conquest is a measure of "manliness" and that men "should always be capable of responding sexually, regardless of the time and place, our feelings about ourselves and our partners, or any other factors" (Zilbergeld, 1978, p. 41) As a result of these expectations, men tend to see sexual interaction as a performance, in which their highest priority is to "act like a man" to confirm their male gender role in every sexual experience. "Acting like a man" for many men makes it difficult to express "feminine" characteristics, such as tenderness or receptivity. The requirements of masculine self-reliance and dominance can make asking for guidance from a sexual partner more difficult. The restrictions of gender-role expectations can lead to anxiety, frustration, and resentment for both women and men (Bonierbale et al., 2006).

In contrast, sexual intimacy that transcends gender-role stereotypes—when both individuals are active and receptive, wild and tender, playful and serious—moves beyond caricatures of men and women and expresses the richness of humanness (Kasl, 1999; McCarthy, 2001). Same-sex couples may not have to struggle with opposing gender-role expectations in their sexual expression. They tend to have a more varied sexual repertoire than heterosexuals, in part because of the lack of rigid gender-role scripts and of a concept of how sex "should" happen (Nichols, 2000).

A Narrow Definition of Sexuality

As we have seen repeatedly in this textbook, the notion that sex equals penile–vaginal intercourse can contribute to inadequate stimulation for women and place burdensome and anxiety-provoking expectations on intercourse. For example, research indicates that women are more likely to orgasm when they engage in a variety of sexual behaviors and when oral sex or vaginal intercourse is included (Reece et al., 2010). Sex therapist Leonore Tiefer observes that the current emphasis on medical treatments that enhance erection, such as Viagra, reinforces the overemphasis on intercourse. "For every dollar devoted to perfecting the phallus, I would like to insist that a dollar be devoted to assisting women with their complaints about partner impairments in kissing, tenderness, talk, hygiene, and general eroticism. Too many men still can't dance, write love poems, erotically massage the clitoris, or diaper the baby and let Mom get some rest" (Tiefer, 1995, p. 170).

Performance Anxiety

Performance anxiety can block natural sexual arousal by diminishing the pleasurable sensations that would produce them. Marty Klein, sex therapist and author of *Sexual Intelligence: What We Really Want from Sex and How to Get It*, describes this experience. "Many people are *watching* themselves during sex more than they are *experiencing* sex, which typically undermines sexual enjoyment" (Klein, 2012a, p. 16). For example, a woman monitoring how aroused she is because she believes that she should have an orgasm during a sexual experience—and she should hurry up about it—can interfere with her experiencing the physical and emotional feelings that could arouse her

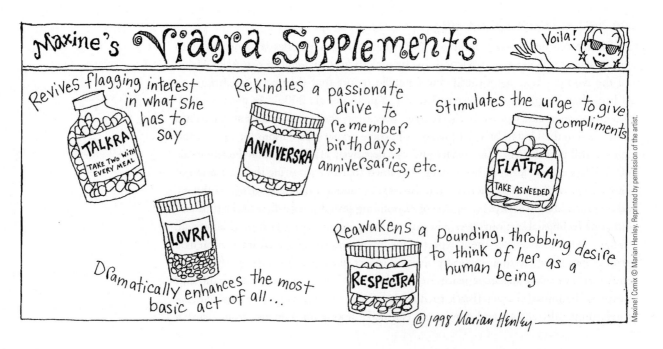

Maxine! Comix © Marian Henley. Reprinted by permission of the artist.

(Lavie-Ajayi & Joffe, 2009). Studies found that men were more likely than women to be distracted by performance concerns during sexual experiences (Meana & Nunnink, 2006; Nelson & Purdon, 2011) A transitory sexual problem, such as an inability to achieve an orgasm or erection because of fatigue or just not being in the mood, can produce enough anxiety for the problem to occur in the next sexual encounter as well (Benson, 2003). Problems with erectile dysfunction frequently begin with the worry that follows a first-time incident. Inhibited orgasm in both men and women can result from extreme performance pressure and an inability to be "selfish" and pursue one's own heightened arousal instead of focusing on the partner's pleasure (Apfelbaum, 2000).

Individual Factors

Beyond the cultural influences on sexual feelings and expression, sexual difficulties can stem from psychological factors that are usually unique to each individual.

Sexual Knowledge and Attitudes

Our knowledge and attitudes about sex have a direct influence on our sexual expression. When difficulties are based on ignorance or misunderstanding, accurate information can sometimes alleviate sexual dissatisfaction. For example, if a woman knows about the function of her clitoris in sexual arousal, she will most likely have experiences different from those of a woman who lacks this knowledge. The fact that women have fewer sexual problems as they get older and have more self-knowledge supports the idea that sexuality develops throughout our lives (Leland, 2000a).

Self-Concept

The term *self-concept* refers to the feelings and beliefs we have about ourselves. Our self-concept can influence our relationships and sexuality (Coleman, 2007; Foley, 2003). Research has found that self-esteem and self-confidence correlate with higher sexual satisfaction and lack of sexual problems (Galinsky & Sonenstein, 2011; Higgins et al., 2011). For example, a woman who feels comfortable with her body, believes she is entitled to sexual pleasure, and takes an active role in attaining sexual fulfillment is likely to have a more satisfying sexual relationship than a woman who lacks those feelings about herself (Nobre & Pinto-Gouveia, 2006; Sanchez et al., 2006). Conversely, a sexual problem can negatively affect self-concept (Althof et al., 2006). For example, in a study about Viagra use, prior to treatment, men with erectile disorder had lower scores on self-esteem tests than men without ED. After 10 weeks of taking Viagra, the men's scores increased to equal the scores of the men without ED (Capellen et al., 2006).

Body image is an aspect of self-concept that can strongly affect sexuality. The more one is distracted by negative thoughts about one's body, the less one will be able to go with physical and emotional pleasures during sexual activity (Seal & Meston, 2007). In Western cultures women's bodies are looked at, evaluated, and sexualized more than men's bodies, and thinness and beauty are often equated with sexual desirability. Women's concerns about weight begin earlier than men's do. Even when boys and girls have the same percentage of body fat, girls express greater dissatisfaction with their body weight and body image than boys do (Rierdan et al., 1998; Wood et al., 1996). Eve Ensler, author of *The Vagina Monologues*, clarifies: "We Americans like to tell ourselves we are free, but we are imprisoned. We are controlled by a corporate media that decrees what we should look like and then determines what we have to buy in order to get and keep that look" (2006, p. 47).

Studies have found that comparing oneself to thin models can result in body image problems (Bergstrom et al., 2009). In the last decades, media images of women have become less and less representative of the average size of women and have contributed

China Photos/Getty Images

Body weight for today's supermodels is super-skinny compared with the typical model of 30 years ago.

to the perceived importance of thinness (Gazzar, 2008). In the early 1980s the average model weighed 8% less than the average American woman; she now weighs 23% less (Jeffery, 2006). In an unprecedented action in 2006, the internationally prominent Madrid Fashion Week imposed minimum weight criteria on models. The show banned too-thin models who did not meet the World Health Organization's guidelines for healthy height-to-weight ratios. Over 30% of the models who had participated in the previous year's show were disqualified, including top models such as Britain's Kate Moss.

A woman's self-consciousness about her nude body during physical intimacy with a male partner is quite common, and the more concerned women are about being nude with a partner, the less sexual satisfaction they report (Penhollow & Young, 2008; Pujois et al., 2010). A research study of college women in the Midwest found that 35% reported physical self-consciousness during physical intimacy with a male partner, agreeing to statements such as "If a partner were to put a hand on my buttocks, I would think, 'My partner can feel my fat'" and "I would prefer having sex with my partner on top so that my partner is less likely to see my body." Women who were less self-conscious about their bodies viewed themselves as good sexual partners, were more assertive with partners, and had more heterosexual experience than women who were more self-conscious—even when their bodies were similar in size (Wiederman, 2000). Familiarity and attachment with a partner may make a difference: Women who were in exclusive relationships reported less self-consciousness during sexual activity than did women who were not in exclusive relationships (Steer & Tiggemann, 2008).

Problematic concerns about body image may be greater among White heterosexual women than among women in some minority groups. Research indicates that African American women rate themselves more sexually attractive than White women do (Bancroft et al., 2011). Further, other studies find that women in sexual relationships with other women feel more comfortable with their bodies than do women involved with men (Huxley et al., 2011).

Men are less likely to report body image concerns during sexual activity than women are (Nelson & Purdon, 2011). However, recent trends suggest that media images of men contribute to men's insecurity about their bodies as well, and consequently men compromise their sex lives by concerns about their appearance. For example, college men who spend more time reading men's magazines and watching music videos and prime-time TV are much less comfortable with their body hair and sweat than men who have less exposure to mass media (Schooler & Ward, 2006). Men in magazines and on television usually have no visible body hair. Male body hair is often a subject for jokes, as in the movie *The 40-Year-Old Virgin*, in which the protagonist tries to have his chest hair waxed off to be more appealing to his partners. Furthermore, men's dissatisfaction with their own bodies was indicated by a study of body preference; most men preferred photos of bodies with 30 pounds more muscle than their own (O'Neill, 2000). One study found that men who were more satisfied with their strength, build, and exercise frequency and were more comfortable with being nude were also more sexually satisfied than men who felt less satisfied about these variables (Penhollow & Young, 2008).

Even though many partners do not put a priority on penis size, a man's concern about the size of his penis can interfere with his arousal and enjoyment. In a survey of over 52,000 heterosexual men and women, only 55% of men were satisfied with their penis size, but 85% of women were satisfied with their sexual partners' penis size (Lever et al., 2006). Unlike viewing typical-sized penises in classic artwork, such as Michelangelo's nude sculpture *David*, watching pornography can contribute to a man's distorted sense of what is "normal," because male porn stars are selected for their oversized genitals.

A study of over 27,000 men ages 20 to 75 in eight countries (the United States, Britain, Germany, France, Italy, Spain, Mexico, and Brazil) provided a positive sign that

Hair removal by waxing was once the province of women only.

AP Photo/Lucas Jackson

men perceive their masculinity differently from the way popular media typically portray it. Men were found to value many qualities more than their physical attractiveness and sexual prowess. Being honorable, self-reliant, and respected by friends and having good health and a positive relationship with their wives were deemed most important to them (Sand et al., 2005).

The Western world is not unique in its concerns about cultural definitions of beauty, as the following Sexuality and Diversity discussion explains.

SEXUALITY and DIVERSITY

Suffering for Beauty

Brazil's 4,700 miles of coastline and Brazilian men's preference for women with large, curvy bottoms have made butt-enhancing cosmetic surgery common in Brazil's cities. One of two methods is used: taking fat from the thighs and injecting it into the buttocks or inserting implants to create a fuller rear. In Asia, the most frequently performed cosmetic surgery, called the "hitch and stitch," creates a fold above each eye to make a woman's eyes look rounder and more "Western." Women in South Africa who consider lighter skin to be the ideal of beauty use bleaching creams and soaps containing a substance that has been banned for causing skin damage and disfigurement (Jones, 2003).

Courtesy of Charles S. Lee, MD/Enhance Plastic Surgery

Eyes before and after surgery to make them appear more Caucasian.

Personal ads in China often specify height—the taller the better. Hundreds of women each year undergo surgeries to increase their leg length so they will be 2 to 4 inches taller. A team of five surgeons spends 3 hours sawing, drilling, and hammering; then a frame is secured around the leg with screws drilled through the leg and into the bone. The frame forces the leg to lengthen while the bone regenerates—a process that takes at least 1 year.

Emotional Difficulties

The NHSLS found that unhappiness with life correlated with sexual problems. The data did not clarify whether one causes the other, but women and men who were experiencing sexual problems were considerably more likely to be unhappy with their lives in general than were respondents without sexual difficulties (Laumann et al., 1999). *Emotional intelligence*—the ability to identify, feel comfortable with, and manage one's emotions—appears to have significant effects on sexuality. One study found that women who were better able to identify and manage their emotions had more frequent orgasms during intercourse and masturbation than did women with less ability to do so (Burri et al., 2009). Research has found that men with orgasmic inhibition have difficulty relaxing, being playful, and releasing the sense of being in control. They also have difficulty feeling emotionally dependent with a partner (Sandstrom & Fugl-Meyer, 2007).

Lack of sexual interest and response is a common symptom of depression (Quinta & Nobre, 2011). Moreover, stressful life problems such as a death in the family, divorce, or extreme family or work difficulties can interfere with a person's ability to focus on the pleasure of the sexual experience (De Jong, 2009). Severe stress and trauma, as experienced by combat veterans, can also interfere with emotional intimacy and sexual functioning (Helfing, 2008; Letourneau et al., 1997).

Sexual Abuse and Assault

The essential conditions for positive sexual interaction—consent, equality, respect, trust, and safety—are absent in sexual abuse. Boys and girls who are sexually abused are robbed of the opportunity to explore and develop their sexuality at their own age-appropriate pace (Maltz, 2003). According to the NHSLS, 12% of men and 17% of women were sexually abused before adolescence (Laumann et al., 1999). It is important to note that not all sexual abuse results in sexual problems in adulthood. Research shows that women with a history of childhood sexual abuse have more negative feelings about sex, report less sexual satisfaction, and are two to four times more likely than other women to have chronic pelvic pain and to experience depression, anxiety, and low self-esteem (Meston et al., 2006; Rellini & Meston, 2011; Rellini et al., 2011). Research on male survivors is very limited, but male survivors often have deep-seated concerns about their masculinity from having been a sexual victim (Lew, 2004). In addition, survivors of sexual abuse often experience aversion reactions to sexual behaviors that are similar to what was done to them during the abuse. They may have flashbacks—sudden unwanted memories of the smells, sounds, sights, feelings, or other sensations of past sexual abuse—that dramatically interrupt any positive feelings and sexual pleasure (Courtois, 2000a, 2000b; Koehler et al., 2000).

Even teenage girls who engage in unwanted sex because they fear their boyfriends will be angry if they say no experience subsequent anxiety and depression. One study found that almost 41% of girls between 14 and 17 had been sexual when they did not want to be, and 10% said their boyfriends forced them to have sex. In addition, the teen girls who experienced unwanted sex were also more likely to have sexually transmitted infections and unwanted pregnancies, and their partners were less likely to use condoms (Blythe et al., 2006).

The film *The Reader* portrays the intense sexual involvement between a teenage boy and an older woman (Kate Winslet) and the impact it has on the boy's adult life (Ralph Fiennes).

Research has also indicated serious sexual consequences for survivors of sexual assault during adulthood (Lutfey et al., 2006). One study of 372 female survivors of sexual assault found that almost 59% experienced sexual problems after the assault—with about 70% of this group linking these problems to the assault. Fear of sex and lack of desire or arousal were the most frequently mentioned problems (Becker et al., 1986). In addition, the effects of sexual assault can be long-lasting; 60% of rape victims had sexual problems for more than three years after the assault (Becker & Kaplan, 1991).

The problems following childhood sexual abuse and adult sexual assault are often difficult for partners of survivors to understand and to cope with effectively (Haansbaek, 2006). Wendy Maltz, a sex therapist, developed *The Sexual Healing Journey* and the DVD or video *Partners in Healing* specifically to help survivors of sexual abuse and their partners resolve problems originating from that abuse.

Relationship Factors

Besides personal feelings and attitudes, relationship factors strongly influence the satisfaction and quality of a sexual relationship. One research study indicated that familiarity and security support men's sexual function because men reported fewer problems with erectile function during sex with an ongoing partner than with a nonrelationship partner (Herbenick et al., 2010). Other studies have shown that greater satisfaction with the overall relationship was related to higher sexual satisfaction and fewer sexual problems (Witting et al., 2008). People in satisfying relationships may even experience benefits from sex that individuals in unsatisfying relationships do not. A study that explored the link between stress and sexual activity found that sexual intercourse relieved stress for men and women in satisfying relationships, but did not relieve stress for those in unsatisfying relationships (Ein-Dor & Hirschberger, 2012).

*"Don't be too upset. If we were meant to have good sex,
we probably would have married other people."*

Unresolved resentments, lack of trust or respect, or dislike of a partner can easily lead to sexual disinterest and problems with arousal and orgasm. One partner can even use his or her lack of sexual interest, consciously or subconsciously, to hurt or punish the other. A person who is frequently pressured to engage in sex or who feels guilty about saying no can feel less and less desire. In addition, someone who experiences a lack of power and control in the relationship can lose her or his sexual desire or responsiveness (Hall, 2008; LoPiccolo, 2000). Sexual difficulties can also occur when partners are too dependent on each other; partners need a balance of togetherness and separateness (DeVita-Raeburn, 2006; Perel, 2006). Even without specific relationship conflicts, lack of emotional intimacy can interfere with sexual interest and response (S. Levine, 2007).

Lack of sexual desire may reflect unresolved relationship problems and negative interaction patterns (Dennerstein et al., 2009; Hayes et al., 2008). One study found that women with HSDD reported more dissatisfaction with relationship issues than did women with other sexual problems, such as difficulty reaching orgasm (Stuart et al., 1998). In this study, diminished desire was associated with a few specific relationship characteristics:

- The woman's partner did not behave affectionately except before intercourse.
- Communication and conflict resolution were unsatisfactory.
- The couple did not maintain love, romance, and emotional closeness.

Ineffective Communication

Without effective verbal and nonverbal communication, couples must base their sexual encounters on assumptions, past experiences, and wishful thinking—all of which can make a sexual experience feel routine and unsatisfying. Research has found that sexual satisfaction is correlated with the use of sexual terms and a greater degree of self-disclosure about sexual preferences (Hess & Coffelt, 2011; MacNeil & Byers, 2009). A frequent source of communication problems is stereotyped gender roles—in particular, the myth that sex is primarily the man's responsibility and that sexual assertiveness in a woman is "unfeminine." For example, women who do not experience orgasm have more difficulty communicating their desire for direct clitoral stimulation to a partner than women who do experience orgasm (Kelly et al., 1990).

"Over all, I liked it, but I have a couple of notes."

Fears About Pregnancy or Sexually Transmitted Infections

The fear of an unwanted pregnancy can interfere with coital enjoyment in a heterosexual relationship, especially when couples do not use an effective method of contraception (Sanders et al., 2003). On the other hand, many couples who want to conceive and have difficulties doing so often find that their sexual relationship becomes anxiety ridden, especially if they have to modify and regulate the timing and pattern of sexual interaction to enhance the possibility of conception.

Anxiety about contracting a sexually transmitted infection, particularly HIV, can interfere with sexual arousal in both homosexual and heterosexual relationships. For people who are not in a monogamous, infection-free relationship, some risk exists. Guidelines for safer sex are outlined in Chapter 15.

Sexual Orientation

Another reason that a woman or man experiences sexual dissatisfaction or has sexual problems in a heterosexual relationship can be a desire to be involved with individuals of the same sex (Althof, 2000). Although much progress has been made in establishing gay rights, following one's homosexual orientation still involves facing significant societal disapproval, if not outright discrimination. To avoid these repercussions, some homosexual people attempt to live in heterosexual relationships despite their lack of sexual desire in such relationships.

Sexual difficulties can also occur in homosexual men or women who are in same-sex relationships but have not yet been able to rid themselves of internalized negative beliefs about homosexuality (Nichols, 1989), as this woman explained:

> It had been a 10-year struggle for me to accept myself as a lesbian. I tried dating men, but always found that a special, meaningful feeling was missing. I had several relationships with women that didn't work out. Then I met Carol. I liked her, respected her, and was very attracted to her. I was looking for a long-term relationship, and the compatibilities and feelings were right. Sex was great until she told me she loved me. A switch went off, and I stopped feeling interested. In therapy, I was able to realize that the lingering feelings of my mother's disapproval had stopped me cold from allowing myself to be fully happy and complete in a "queer" relationship. I worked through those feelings and am now enjoying my sexuality in a loving, committed relationship for the first time in my life. (Authors' files)

Basics of Sexual Enhancement and Sex Therapy

The various self-help and sex therapy suggestions offered in the following sections have proved helpful to many people in enhancing sexual relationships or resolving sexual problems (Van Lankveld, 2009). However, the same techniques do not work for everyone, and exercises often need to be individually modified. Furthermore, professional help may be called for when individual efforts, couple efforts, or both do not produce the desired results. Recognizing that therapy is sometimes necessary to promote change, we have included guidelines for seeking sex therapy in the last section of this chapter.

Increased self-knowledge is often an important step in sexual enhancement. With this in mind, we briefly outline procedures for improving awareness and acceptance of your body and present activities that provide the most pleasurable stimulation.

Self-Awareness

Physical and emotional self-awareness and self-expression are crucial elements in satisfying sexual experiences (Morehouse, 2001; Schwartz, 2003). A good way to increase self-awareness and comfort with our sexuality is to become well acquainted with our sexual anatomy, as described in Chapters 3 and 4. Experimenting with masturbation is also an effective way for both men and women to learn about and expand sexual response, as we explained in Chapter 8. Self-stimulation and exploration are frequently an important part of women's learning how to experience orgasm and men's learning to delay ejaculation.

People may have a style of masturbation that interferes with their ability to be aroused by a partner. For example, 65% of men who sought help for ejaculatory inhibition had patterns of intensity, pressure, and speed of self-stimulation that were impossible to reproduce during intercourse. Some of the men rubbed against specific surfaces or used very heavy manual pressure or exceptionally fast strokes (Helien et al., 2005). Women can also have patterns of masturbation, such as crossing their legs and rocking, which a partner is unable to replicate. Modifying masturbation techniques to resemble partner stimulation and intercourse more closely is one step toward experiencing orgasm from partner stimulation.

Communication

One of the primary benefits of sex therapy—whether the immediate goal is learning to have orgasms with partners, overcoming premature ejaculation, or solving almost any other problem—is that partners participating together in the treatment often develop more effective communication skills. This quotation from our files illustrates how important communication can be in solving sexual difficulties:

> He would say he was sorry he was so fast, and that maybe it would get better with time. Finally, I asked him to come to class with me the day you showed the film demonstrating the technique. Once we really talked openly things began to work well. He showed me how he liked to be stimulated, things he had never told me before. He became much more aware of my needs and what I needed to be satisfied. We really started getting into a lot of variety in our lovemaking, instead of just kissing and intercourse. By the way, the technique did work in slowing him down, but I think the biggest benefit has been breaking down the communication barriers. (Authors' files)

We encourage you to review the communication strategies in Chapter 7 to help improve your communication.

It can be particularly valuable for partners to communicate with each other about what kind of touching they find arousing by showing each other how they masturbate. This activity is often a part of sex therapy for women learning to experience orgasm with a partner and for resolving premature ejaculation and erectile difficulties. Masturbation is also a way to accommodate a potentially problematic difference in sex drive in a couple. The partner who wants sexual release more often than the other can masturbate while the other partner kisses and caresses him or her without needing to become aroused or experience orgasm.

Sensate Focus

sensate focus
A process of touching and communication used to enhance sexual pleasure and to reduce performance pressure.

One of the most useful couple-oriented activities for enhancing mutual sexual enjoyment is a series of touching exercises called **sensate focus** (❚ Figure 14.3). Masters and Johnson developed the technique of sensate focus to use as a basic step in treating sexual problems. Sensate focus can help to reduce anxiety caused by goal orientation and to increase communication, pleasure, and closeness (De Villers & Turgeon, 2005). This technique is also useful for any couple wanting to enhance their sexual relationship.

In the sensate focus touching exercises, partners take turns touching each other while following some essential guidelines. Both homosexual and heterosexual couples can benefit from sensate focus. In the following descriptions, we assume that the one doing the touching is a woman and the one being touched is a man. To start, the person who will be doing the touching takes some time to "set the scene" so that the environment will be comfortable and pleasant for her; for example, she might turn off any phones and arrange a warm, cozy place with relaxing music and lighting. The two people then undress, and the toucher begins to explore her partner's body, following this important guideline: She is to touch not to please or arouse her partner but to please herself. The goal is for the toucher to focus on her perception of textures, shapes, and temperatures. The person being touched notices how the touching feels, and he remains quiet except when any touch is uncomfortable. In that case, he describes the uncomfortable feeling and what the toucher could do to make it more comfortable. For example: "That tickles. Please touch the other side of my arm." This guideline helps the toucher attend fully to her own sensations without worrying about whether something she is doing is unpleasant for her partner. The nondemanding quality

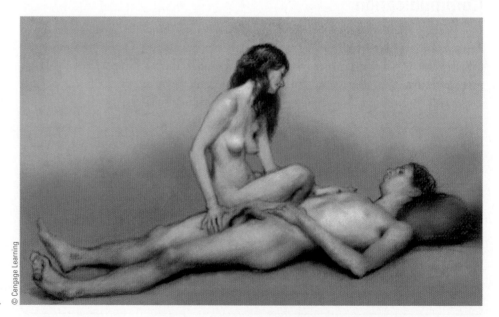

❚ **Figure 14.3** The process of sensate focus, in which partners sensually explore each other's body, can contribute to the mutual enhancement of a couple's sexual enjoyment.

© Cengage Learning

of this kind of touching helps reduce or eliminate performance anxiety and allows the couple to expand touch beyond goal-directed stimulation.

In the next sensate focus exercise, the two people switch roles, following the same guidelines as before. In these initial sensate focus experiences, intercourse and touching the breasts and genitals are prohibited. Only after the partners have focused on touch and on communicating uncomfortable feelings do they include breasts and genitals as part of the exercise. Again, the toucher focuses on his or her own interest and pleasure, not the partner's. After the inclusion of breasts and genitals, the partners progress to a simultaneous sensate focus experience. Now they touch one another at the same time and experience feelings from both touching and being touched.

Modern Western sex therapy is based on the assumption that the values of open communication, emotional intimacy, and physical pleasure for both partners guide treatment and are its goals. However, these principles are antithetical to many cultures' norms (Goodman, 2001), as we explain in the following Sexuality and Diversity discussion.

SEXUALITY and DIVERSITY
How Modern Sex Therapy Can Clash With Cultural Values

Cultural beliefs influence sexual practices, the perception of sexual problems, and modes of treatment. For example, in much of the Middle East the marital sexual relationship is based primarily on the two dimensions of male sexual potency and couple fertility. For both men and women, only when intercourse itself is impaired—not interest or pleasure—do couples seek treatment. Unconsummated marriage is a common complaint in conservative societies of the Middle East (Ghanem, 2011).

A study conducted in Saudi Arabia found that the most common problem leading a couple to sex therapy was erectile disorder. Women in Saudi Arabia, who are raised to inhibit their sexual desires, came to sex therapy only with problems of painful intercourse. Unlike their counterparts in Western countries, the women did not seek help for lack of desire, arousal, or orgasm (Osman & Al-Sawaf, 1995). A study of Islamic sex therapy centers found that 80% of female clients came for treatment of vaginismus (Aziz & Gurgen, 2009).

Many cultural traditions allow for little or no education or communication about sexual matters. Asians may consider it shameful to discuss sex, especially with someone outside the family. Muslims are often taught to avoid talking about sexuality with people of the other sex (including their spouses). Taking a sex history can be distressing for clients with these beliefs, especially when the husband and wife are interviewed together. In cultures in which women are expected to be innocent about sex, the sex-education component of therapy conflicts with the prevailing values. In Pakistan the lack of formal sex education leads to misinformation. For example, men who experience premature ejaculation usually believe that masturbation and ejaculation during sleep have damaged muscles and blood vessels in the penis, causing their sexual problem (Bhatti, 2005).

Western sex therapy techniques often contradict cultural values. For example, masturbation exercises to treat anorgasmia, erectile difficulties, or premature ejaculation conflict with religious prohibitions of Orthodox Jews and some fundamentalist Christians and Muslims (Sungur, 2007). The gender equality inherent in sensate focus exercises and the avoidance of intercourse in such exercises are also often objectionable to many religious and ethnic groups.

Sex therapy needs to take into account the clients' cultural values and the implications they have for intimate behavior (Nasserzadeh, 2009). Therapists should attempt to adjust therapy to their clients' well-integrated ethnic and religious perspectives (Richardson et al., 2006; Shtarkshall, 2005). This is likely to be more helpful than attempting to impose the cultural norms inherent in Western sex therapy (Ribner, 2009).

In the remainder of this chapter, we look at some strategies and sex therapy approaches that are used to deal with female and male sexual problems and sexual desire disorder.

Specific Suggestions for Women

In this section, we describe procedures that may help women learn to increase sexual arousal and reach orgasm by themselves or with a partner. We also include suggestions for dealing with vaginismus.

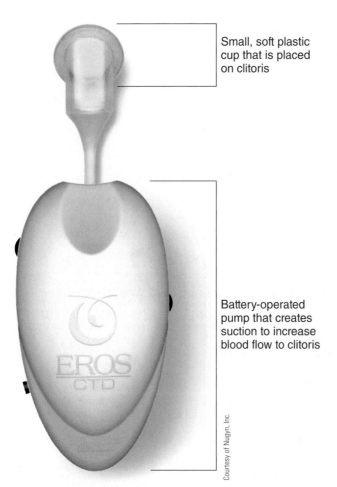

Small, soft plastic cup that is placed on clitoris

Battery-operated pump that creates suction to increase blood flow to clitoris

Courtesy of Nugyn, Inc.

▌**Figure 14.4** The EROS Clitoral Therapy Device, approved by the FDA in 2000, works by increasing vasocongestion of the clitoris.

Becoming Orgasmic

Therapy programs for learning to experience orgasm are based on progressive self-awareness activities that a woman does at home between therapy sessions. At the beginning of treatment, body exploration, genital self-exam, and Kegel exercises (see Chapter 3) are emphasized; then therapy and home exercises move progressively to self-stimulation exercises similar to those described in Chapter 8 (see "Self-Pleasuring Techniques"). One advantage of self-stimulation is that a woman who does not have a partner can learn to become orgasmic.

A vibrator is sometimes used to help a woman experience orgasm for the first time so she knows that she can have this response. (A vibrator is often less tiring to use than the fingers and supplies more intense stimulation.) After she has experienced a few orgasms with the vibrator, it is helpful for her to return to manual stimulation. This step is important because it is easier for a partner to replicate a woman's own touch than the stimulation of a vibrator. Another method, involving the EROS Clitoral Therapy Device (shown in ▌Figure 14.4), is designed to increase blood flow to, and thereby arousal of, the clitoris (Munarriz et al., 2003). The hormones and products discussed in the section on treating low sexual desire may also be useful for increasing arousal.

Experiencing Orgasm With a Partner

Once a woman has learned to experience orgasm through self-stimulation, sharing her discoveries with her partner can help her partner know what forms of stimulation are most pleasing to her. Each partner takes turns visually exploring the other's genitals, locating all the parts discussed in Chapters 3 and 4. After looking thoroughly, they experiment with touch, noticing and sharing what different areas feel like. The next step is for the woman to stimulate herself in her partner's presence, and her partner can be holding and kissing her or lying beside her, as shown in ▌Figure 14.5. This step is often a difficult one. One woman described how she dealt with her discomfort:

> When I wanted to share with my partner what I had learned about myself through masturbation, I felt anxious about how to do it. Finally, we decided that to begin with, I would be in the bedroom, and he would be in the living room, knowing I was masturbating. Then he would sit on the bed, not looking at me. The next step was for him to hold and kiss me while I was touching myself. Then I could be comfortable showing him how I touch myself. (Authors' files)

∎ **Figure 14.5** Masturbating in the presence of a partner can be an effective way for an individual to indicate what kind of touching she or he finds arousing.

Next the partner begins nondemanding manual genital pleasuring. The couple can do this in any position that suits them. The woman places her hand over her partner's hand on her genitals to guide the partner's touch. They can use lubricants to increase pleasure of the sensations. The purpose of the initial sessions is for the woman to teach her partner what feels good rather than to produce orgasm. Once the woman thinks she is ready to experience orgasm, she indicates to her partner to continue the stimulation until she experiences climax. Orgasm will probably not occur until the couple has had several sessions.

Couples can use several specific techniques to increase a woman's arousal and the possibility of orgasm during intercourse. The first has to do with when to begin intercourse. Rather than beginning intercourse after a certain number of minutes of foreplay or when there is sufficient lubrication, a woman can be guided by her feeling of what might be called "readiness." Readiness is a vaginal sensation of wanting intercourse. Not all women experience this feeling of readiness, but for those who do, beginning intercourse at this time (and not before) can enhance the ensuing erotic sensations. Of course, the woman's partner will have to cooperate by waiting for her to indicate when she is ready and by not attempting to begin intercourse before then.

A woman who wants increased stimulation during coitus might benefit from initiating the kinds of movements and pressure she finds most arousing. A woman can also stimulate her clitoris manually or with a vibrator during intercourse, as shown in ∎ Figure 14.6 on page 424. Her partner's manual stimulation of her clitoris during intercourse will likely also enhance arousal. ∎ Table 14.5 highlights how women who are routinely orgasmic during intercourse facilitate experiencing orgasm (Ellison, 2000).

Dealing With Vaginismus

Treatment for vaginismus usually begins during a pelvic exam, in which the health-care practitioner demonstrates the vaginal spasm reaction to the woman or couple. Subsequent therapy starts with relaxation and self-awareness exercises, including a

At a Glance

∎ TABLE 14.5 Facilitating Orgasm

In this study, 2,371 women completed the sentence "In addition to getting specific physical stimulation, I often have done the following to help me reach orgasm during sex with a partner."

Activity	Percentage
Positioned my body to get the stimulation I needed	90
Paid attention to my physical sensations	83
Tightened and released my pelvic muscles	75
Synchronized the rhythm of my movements to my partner's	75
Asked or encouraged my partner to do what I needed	74
Got myself in a sexy mood beforehand	71
Focused on my partner's pleasure	68
Felt/thought how much I love my partner	65

SOURCE: Ellison (2000, p. 244).

Figure 14.6 The use of a vibrator for clitoral stimulation during coitus.

© Cengage Learning

soothing bath, general body exploration, and manual external genital pleasuring. Next the woman learns to insert first a fingertip, then a finger, and eventually three fingers into her vagina without experiencing muscle contractions. At each stage the woman practices relaxing and contracting the vaginal muscles, as with Kegel exercises (see Chapter 3). Dilators, which are cylindrical rods of graduated sizes, are also sometimes used to accustom the vaginal walls to relaxing (Leiblum, 2000). Biofeedback and physical therapy treatments to lessen muscle tension in the pelvic floor can also be helpful for vaginismus and other forms of dyspareunia (Goldfinger et al., 2009; Rosenbaum, 2011).

Once the woman has completed the preceding steps, her partner can begin to participate by following the same steps that she completed by herself. After the man can insert three fingers without inducing a muscle spasm, the woman controls a slow insertion of her partner's penis, with many motionless pauses that allow the woman to become familiar with vaginal containment of the penis. Pelvic movements and pleasure focusing are added later, only when both partners are comfortable with penetration.

Specific Suggestions for Men

In the following paragraphs, we outline methods for dealing with the common difficulties of premature ejaculation and erectile disorder. We also discuss a way to treat the less common condition of orgasmic disorder.

Lasting Longer

Some self-help and sex therapy approaches to learning ejaculatory control are easy to implement—in many cases, without professional guidance.

SEXUALHEALTH ▶ **Strategies for Delaying Ejaculation** In some cases, men can gain considerable control over ejaculation by practicing a few simple strategies. Men for whom premature ejaculation is not a problem and women readers may find the following discussion valuable simply because they would sometimes like sexual intercourse to last longer.

- *Ejaculate more frequently.* Men with premature ejaculation problems sometimes find that they can delay ejaculation when they are having more frequent orgasms, by masturbation or partner sex.
- *Come again!* A couple can experiment with continuing sexual interaction after the man's first ejaculation, then resume intercourse when his erection returns. This

strategy is most useful for younger men, who experience erections again soon after ejaculation.

- *Change positions.* If a man wants to delay ejaculation, he may gain some control by lying on his back and increasing physical relaxation. (See page 244 for a variation of the woman-above position.) However, if a man attempts energetic pelvic movements in this position, it will be counterproductive because he will be increasing muscle tension by moving both his own weight and his partner's.
- *Talk with each other.* To delay climax, the man often finds it essential to slow down or completely cease movements. He needs to tell his partner when to reduce or stop stimulation.
- *Consider alternatives.* To minimize performance anxiety about rapid ejaculation (and most of the other problems discussed here), it is often useful to think of intercourse as just one of several options for sexual sharing. ●

The Stop-Start Technique James Semans, a urologist, developed the **stop-start technique**, which enables the man to become acquainted with and ultimately control his ejaculatory reflex. The partner is instructed to stimulate the man's penis, either manually or orally, to the point of impending orgasm—at which time stimulation is stopped until the preejaculatory sensations subside (Semans, 1956). (A man can also practice this technique on himself during solo masturbation sessions [Zilbergeld, 1992].) These sessions generally last 15 to 30 minutes and occur as often as once a day for several days or weeks. During each session, the couple repeats the stimulation and the stop-start procedure several times and then allows ejaculation to occur on the last cycle. The couple should reach an agreement about sexual stimulation and orgasm for the man's partner. If the partner desires these, the couple can engage in nonintercourse sexual activity.

As the man's ejaculatory control improves, the couple progresses to intercourse. For heterosexual couples, the best position is the woman above, sitting up. The first step is for the man to guide his penis in the woman's vagina and lie quietly for several moments before beginning slow movements. When he begins to feel close to orgasm, they lie quietly again. This stop-start intercourse technique is continued as the man experiences progressively better ejaculatory control.

Medical Treatments A combination of sex therapy and medical treatments can be more helpful than either alone in helping men extend their arousal prior to ejaculation (Steggall et al., 2008). Small doses of selective serotonin reuptake inhibitors (SSRIs), medication usually prescribed for depression, can help men to delay ejaculation. One of the side effects of these medications is suppressed orgasm in men and women, which is often helpful in treating rapid ejaculation. Other medications for treating premature ejaculation are under study, including dapoxetine, which has been developed specifically for such treatment and has shown positive results in research studies (Douglass & Lin, 2010; McMahon et al., 2011b; Serefoglu et al., 2011).

Reducing the sensitivity of the penis is another approach to reducing rapid ejaculation (Carson & Wyllie, 2010). In a placebo-controlled study, using an anesthetic spray five minutes before intercourse helped men extend the length of time of intercourse before they ejaculated from an average of 36 seconds to nearly 4 minutes. Their experience of orgasm improved as well: About 62% said that their orgasm was good or very good, whereas only 20% had said so prior to treatment (Hellstrom, 2010).

Dealing With Erectile Dysfunction

Besides physically caused erection difficulties, performance anxiety is a major source of erectile dysfunction. Therefore, most sex therapy concentrates on reducing or

stop-start technique
A treatment technique for premature ejaculation, consisting of stimulating the penis to the point of impending orgasm and then stopping until the preejaculatory sensations subside.

eliminating anxiety. Initially, a couple uses the sensate focus exercises, understanding that at this point the touching is intended not to result in erection, ejaculation, or intercourse, but to focus on and enjoy the touch without a further goal. The following account shows a common reaction to the exercise:

> When the therapist told us that intercourse was off limits, at least for the time being, I couldn't believe how relieved I felt. If I couldn't get hard, so what? After all, I was told not to use it even if I did. Those first few times touching and getting touched by my wife were the first really worry-free pleasurable times I had experienced in years. (Authors' files)

If a couple wants to, they can agree in advance for the partner to have an orgasm at the close of a session by whatever mode of stimulation other than intercourse seems comfortable to both (self-stimulation, being touched by the partner, oral stimulation, etc.). When the couple has progressed to a point where both partners feel comfortable with sensate focus, the couple explores what kinds of genital stimulation other than intercourse are particularly pleasurable for the man. When the man experiences a full erection, his partner should stop doing what has aroused him. It is crucial that they allow his erection to subside at this point to alter the man's belief that once his erection is lost it will not return. The couple spends this time holding each other close or exchanging nongenital caresses. Once the penis is completely flaccid, the man's partner resumes genital pleasuring.

The final phase of treatment for heterosexual couples who desire intercourse involves penetration and coitus. With the man on his back and the woman astride, the couple begins with sensate focus and then moves to genital stimulation. When the man has an erection, his partner lowers herself onto his penis, maintaining stimulation with gentle pelvic movements. It is important to allow the man to be "selfish," concentrating exclusively on his own pleasure (Kaplan, 1974). Occasionally a man loses his erection after penetration. If this happens, his partner returns to the oral or manual stimulation that originally produced his erection. If his response continues to be blocked, it is wise to stop genital contact and return to the original nondemand pleasuring of sensate focus before moving forward again.

Medical Treatments Some men who have impaired erectile functioning as the result of physiological problems make a satisfactory sexual adjustment to the absence of erection by emphasizing and enjoying other ways of sexual sharing. For other men with erection difficulties, several types of medical treatments are available. Viagra, a pill for erectile problems, became available in 1998. Originally developed for cardiovascular disease, it became the fastest-selling prescription drug in history. Almost 40,000 prescriptions were dispensed in the first 2 weeks on the market (Holmes, 2003). In 2003 and 2004 the FDA approved two additional Viagra-like drugs, Levitra and Cialis. These medications work by prolonging the vasodilator effects of nitric oxide in the body. Blood vessels in the penis expand, and erections result from the increase in blood flow (Hoffman, 2009). Research has consistently shown that a combination of ED medication and couple sex therapy is more effective in helping this problem than medication alone (Aubin et al., 2009).

Viagra, Levitra, and Cialis have similar side effects; the most common are flushing, headaches, upset stomach, and nasal congestion (Gotthardt, 2003; Hazell et al., 2009). Erectile dysfunction drugs can also cause priapism, in which an erection does not subside and can result in permanent damage to penile tissue unless medical treatment is obtained (Adams, 2003). Hydrogen

© Bill Aron/PhotoEdit

Viagra ads initially focused on older men with erectile dysfunction. Ads now tend to appeal to a wider variety of ages, including younger men and even women who use Viagra for sexual enhancement rather than treatment.

sulfide is a vasodilator found in small amounts in the human body, and researchers are studying it as another potential treatment for ED (Conner, 2009).

For many couples, erection-enhancing drugs can be wonder drugs that restore the intimacy of intercourse (Verheyden et al., 2007). Many studies have shown significant improvement in the partner's feelings of sexual desirability and satisfaction as well as her own sexual functioning when the man uses erection-enhancing medications (Eardley et al., 2006; M. McCabe et al., 2011). However, some men have found that firm erections are secondary to a good relationship (Metz & McCarthy, 2008). In a troubled relationship the use of such a medication can clarify for the couple that they have other relationship problems, which may lead the couple to work toward resolving them (Cooper, 2006).

Viagra has greatly increased general conversation and awareness about erectile problems. In fact, men who do not have erectile dysfunction are using erection-enhancing drugs for firmer and longer-lasting erections. The appeal to men to be able to extend intercourse beyond one or more ejaculations contributes to the recreational use of such drugs. Reports also indicate that Viagra has emerged among college students and others as a party drug for recreational and casual sex (Apodaca & Moser, 2011; Harte & Meston, 2011). Unfortunately, mixing Viagra and recreational drugs combines enduring erections with the poor judgment of an altered mental state in which men engage in high-risk sexual behaviors that they otherwise would avoid (Adams, 2003).

Mechanical Devices Devices that suction blood into the penis and hold it there during intercourse have been available since the mid-1980s (Korenman & Viosca, 1992). External vacuum constriction devices, which are available by prescription, consist of a vacuum chamber, pump, and penile constriction bands. The vacuum chamber is placed over the flaccid penis. The pump creates a negative pressure inside the chamber and draws blood into the penis. The elastic band is then placed around the base of the penis to trap the blood, and the chamber is removed (Levy et al., 2000). Another mechanical device recently approved by the FDA to help men experience erections is the VIBERECT device. It provides vibrations to two surfaces of the penis, stimulating reflexive reactions that initiate blood flow for an erection to occur (Ostrovsky, 2011).

Surgical Treatments A surgically implanted penile prosthesis is an option for men who are not helped by Viagra or other methods. The main reason for implants is radical prostatectomy. The surgery is expensive and involves risks, including infection, and men should evaluate this option carefully and include their partner in pre- and postsurgical counseling. There are two basic types of penile implants. One type consists of a pair of semi-rigid rods made of metal wires or coils inside a silicone covering; the rods are placed inside the cavernous bodies of the penis. Although this type is easier to implant than the second type, a potential disadvantage is that the penis is always semierect. The second type of prosthesis is an inflatable device that enables the penis to change from flaccid to erect (▮ Figure 14.7). Two inflatable cylinders are implanted into the cavernous bodies of the penile shaft. They are connected to a fluid-filled reservoir located near the bladder and to a pump in the scrotal sac. To become erect, a man squeezes the pump several times, and the fluid fills the collapsed cylinders, producing an erection. When an erection is no longer desired, a release valve causes the fluid to go back into the reservoir (Shaw & Garber, 2011).

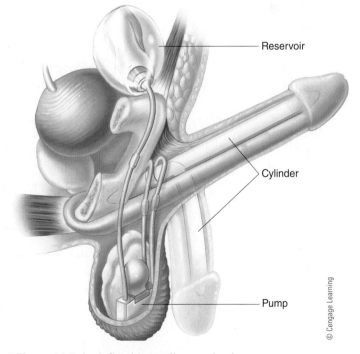

Reservoir

Cylinder

Pump

© Cengage Learning

▮ **Figure 14.7** An inflatable penile prosthesis.

Neither of these devices can restore sensation or the ability to ejaculate if it has been lost as a result of medical problems. Furthermore, the surgery to implant the devices may diminish sensation. They do, however, provide an alternative for men who want to mechanically restore their ability to have erections. Most men who have them report improved sexual activity, and about 85% are satisfied with the results of the surgery (Cortez-Gonzales & Glina, 2009; Richter et al., 2006).

Reducing Male Orgasmic Disorder

Sex therapy usually begins with a few days of sensate focus, when the man should not have an ejaculation by masturbation or partner interaction. If his partner desires orgasm, this can be accomplished in whatever fashion is comfortable for both partners. The next step is for the man to stimulate himself to orgasm with his partner present. Once both partners feel comfortable with the man masturbating, the couple can move on to the next phase, where the partner attempts to bring him to orgasm with whatever stimulation is most arousing. It may take several sessions before the partner's stimulation produces an ejaculation, and it is important for the man not to ejaculate by masturbation during this period. Most therapists agree that once he can reach orgasm by his partner's touch, an important step has been accomplished.

When the man is ejaculating consistently in response to partner stimulation, the couple can move on to the final phase of treatment, in which ejaculation takes place during penetration. After building arousal by other means, the couple tries penetration. If he does not ejaculate shortly after penetration, he should withdraw and resume other stimulation until he is about to ejaculate, at which point the couple resumes penetration. Once the man experiences a few ejaculations during penetration, the mental block that is usually associated with ejaculatory disorder often disappears. In addition, psychotherapy to understand and resolve deeper personal or couple problems may be necessary to resolve male orgasmic disorder.

Treating Hypoactive Sexual Desire Disorder

Many aspects of the treatment for hypoactive sexual desire disorder are similar to specific suggestions for resolving other sexual problems. These include

- Encouraging erotic responses through self-stimulation and arousing fantasies
- Reducing anxiety with appropriate information and sensate focus exercises
- Enhancing sexual experiences through improved communication and increased skills— both in initiating desired sexual activity and in refusing undesired sexual activity
- Expanding the repertoire of affectionate and sexual activities

Most therapists combine suggestions for specific activities with insight therapy, which can help a person understand and resolve any subconscious conflicts about sexual pleasure and intimacy. When low sexual desire is a symptom of unresolved relationship problems, therapy focuses on the interactions between partners that contribute to the lack of sexual desire (Alperstein, 2001).

Medical Treatments

Men with low levels of testosterone often use testosterone supplementation—usually a transdermal gel—to increase their sex drive (Tomlinson et al., 2006). The number of testosterone prescriptions has tripled in recent years as a growing number of men are taking testosterone to offset the normal age-related decline of the hormone (Harvard Health Publications, 2006).

A review of controlled studies on estrogen and testosterone and postmenopausal women's sexual functioning found that both estrogen and testosterone therapies are associated with increased sexual interest, arousal, and satisfaction with masturbation and partner sexual activity (Davis, 2007; Leventhal-Alexander, 2005). Testosterone can also increase sexual interest for premenopausal women with below-normal levels of testosterone (Berga & McCord, 2005; Reinberg, 2006). In 2004 the FDA turned down an application for Intrinsa, a testosterone patch for women, in spite of studies showing improvement in desire and pleasure for postmenopausal women (Dennerstein & Goldstein, 2005; Herper, 2011). Therefore, testosterone is available to women only by prescription for off-label use. Physicians wrote over 2 million such prescriptions for women in 2006 and 2007, a rate that indicates a need for FDA-approved testosterone products for women (Snabes & Simes, 2009). Research about side effects, especially cancer and heart disease, from testosterone therapy for both men and women continues in order to clarify risks and benefits (Reinberg, 2006). The testosterone patch has been available in several European countries since 2007 (Whittelsey, 2007).

The search for the "female Viagra" remains elusive, and several medications have not met FDA approval. Research into other medical possibilities for improving sexual interest and arousal in women is under way (Jordan et al., 2011; Nappi et al., 2010). Two nonprescription products that have been researched in accordance with FDA standards and published in peer-reviewed journals are Zestra, an oil applied to the clitoris and vulva, and ArginMax, a nutritional supplement. Zestra was found to increase sexual response (Ferguson et al., 2010), and study participants using ArginMax reported increased clitoral sensation, sexual desire, vaginal lubrication, frequency of orgasm, and sexual satisfaction (Ferguson et al., 2003; Ito et al., 2001).

Seeking Professional Assistance

Although some people with sexual problems improve over time without professional help, sometimes therapy is necessary. In fact, sometimes alleviation of sexual problems is a side effect of successful psychotherapy for general psychological problems (Hoyer et al., 2009). However, seeking therapy is often a difficult step. A community medical practice found that, when asked, many men reported various sexual problems, but none had previously sought professional help (Rosenberg et al., 2006).

What Happens in Therapy?

Many people are apprehensive about going to see a sex therapist, so it can be helpful to have some idea about what to expect. Each therapist works differently, but most therapists follow certain steps. During the first appointment, the therapist will help the client (or clients, if a couple) clarify the problem and his or her feelings about it and identify the client's goals for the therapy. The therapist will usually ask questions about when the problem began, how it has developed over time, what the client thinks caused it, and how she or he has already tried to resolve it. Sometimes the therapist may only need to provide specific information that the client lacks or to reassure the client that his or her thoughts, feelings, fantasies, desires, and behaviors that enhance personal satisfaction are normal. On the other hand, some people may benefit from permission not to engage in certain sexual activities they dislike.

Over the next few sessions (most therapy occurs in 1-hour weekly sessions), the therapist may gather more extensive sexual, personal, and relationship histories. The therapist will likely obtain information about medical history and current physical functioning to make any necessary referrals for further physical screenings. During these

The Gottman Institute, founded by John and Julie Gottman (pictured here), is a well-known center for research-based couple's therapy. It has a web-based sexual enhancement program at www.gottsex.com. It is designed to help couples in long-term relationships develop and maintain loving, intimate sex.

sessions, the therapist will also explore whether the client has a lifestyle conducive to a good emotional and sexual relationship and determine whether she or he has problems with substance abuse or domestic violence.

Once the therapist and the individual (or couple) more fully realize the nature of the difficulty and have defined the therapy goals, the therapist helps the client understand and overcome obstacles to meeting the goals as the sessions continue. The therapist often provides psychoeducational information and gives assignments, such as masturbation or sensate focus exercises, for the client to do between therapy sessions (Althof, 2006). Successes and difficulties with the assignments are discussed at subsequent meetings. In some cases personal emotional difficulties or relationship problems are causing the sexual issue, and various forms of intensive therapy are necessary.

Therapy is terminated when the client reaches his or her goals. The therapist and client may also plan one or more follow-up sessions. It is often helpful for a client to leave with a plan for continuing and maintaining progress.

Selecting a Therapist

SEXUALHEALTH ▶

To select a therapist, you might ask your sexuality course instructor or health-care practitioner for referrals or contact either the American Association of Sex Educators, Therapists, and Counselors or the American Board of Sexology. After consulting some of these sources, you should have several potential therapists from which to choose. A professional who has specialized in sex therapy should have a minimum of a master's degree and credentials as a licensed psychiatrist, psychologist, social worker, or counselor. To do sex therapy, he or she should also have participated in sex therapy training, supervision, and workshops. It is very appropriate for you to inquire about the specific training and certification of a prospective therapist.

To help determine whether a specific therapist will meet your needs, pay attention to how you feel about talking with the therapist. Therapy is not intended to be a light social interaction, and it can be quite uncomfortable to discuss personal sexual concerns. However, for therapy to be useful, you need to have the sense that the therapist is open and willing to understand you.

After the initial interview, you can decide to continue with that particular therapist or ask for a referral to another therapist more appropriate to your personality or needs. If you become dissatisfied once you begin therapy, discuss your concerns with your therapist. Decide jointly, if possible, whether to continue therapy or to seek another therapist. It is usually best to continue for several sessions before making a decision to change. Occasionally, clients expect magic cures rather than the difficult but rewarding work that therapy often demands. ●

Unethical Relationships: Sex Between Therapist and Client

SEXUALHEALTH ▶

It is highly unethical for professional therapists to engage in sexual relationships with clients they treat—both during therapy and after it has ended (Lamb et al., 2003; Reamer, 2003). It is the professional's responsibility to set boundaries that ensure the integrity of the therapeutic relationship. Psychiatry, psychology, social work, and counseling professional associations have codes of ethics against sexual relations between psychotherapists and their clients. In addition, some states have criminalized sexual behavior with patients. However, research has found that up to 3% of female therapists and 12% of male therapists admit to having sexual contact with a current client (Berkman et al., 2000).

Sexual involvement between client and therapist can have negative effects on the client. Research has indicated that women who experienced sexual contact with their therapists (including psychotherapists in general, not just sex therapists) felt greater mistrust of and anger toward men and therapists than did a control group of women. They also experienced more psychological and psychosomatic symptoms, including anger, shame, anxiety, and depression (Finger, 2000; Regehr & Glancy, 1995). If at any time a therapist makes verbal or physical sexual advances toward you, you have every right to leave immediately and terminate therapy. Furthermore, it will be helpful to others who might become victims of this abuse of professional power if you report the incident to the state licensing board for the therapist's profession. ●

Summary

- Sexual health is a state of physical, emotional, mental, and sexual well-being.
- The National Health and Social Life Survey (NHSLS) found that many people reported problems in their sex lives.
- Sexual problems can contribute to lower satisfaction with overall life.

Specific Sexual Difficulties

- A sexual problem must occur within the context of adequate physical and psychological stimulation to be considered a disorder.
- Hypoactive sexual desire disorder (HSDD) is characterized by the absence or minimal experience of sexual interest prior to and during the sexual experience.
- Dissatisfaction with frequency of sexual activity occurs when individual differences in sexual interest result in relationship distress.
- Sexual aversion disorder is an extreme irrational fear or dislike of sexual activity.
- Female genital sexual arousal disorder is an inhibition of the vasocongestive response; female subjective sexual arousal disorder is a lack of subjective feelings of arousal when physical signs of arousal are present; combined genital and subjective sexual arousal disorder involves both.
- Persistent sexual arousal disorder is spontaneous and unwanted genital arousal that is not relieved by orgasm.
- Male erectile dysfunction is the consistent or recurring inability over at least 3 months to have or maintain an erection.
- Female orgasmic disorder is the absence, marked delay, or diminished intensity of orgasm despite high subjective arousal.
- Situational female orgasmic disorder occurs when a woman can experience orgasm during masturbation but not with a partner.
- Coitus provides mostly indirect clitoral stimulation, and for many women it does not provide sufficient stimulation to result in orgasm.
- Male orgasmic disorder is the inability of a man to ejaculate during sexual activity with a partner.

- Premature ejaculation occurs when a man consistently ejaculates quickly and is unable to control the timing of his ejaculation.
- Both men and women fake orgasm, although women do so more often. Pretending usually perpetuates ineffective patterns of relating and reduces the intimacy of the sexual experience.
- Dyspareunia, or pain during coitus, is disruptive to sexual interest and arousal in both women and men. Numerous physical problems can cause painful intercourse. Vestibulodynia may be the most common cause of painful intercourse for women.
- Peyronie's disease, in which fibrous tissue and calcium deposits develop in the penis, can cause pain and curvature of the penis during erection.
- Vaginismus is an involuntary contraction of the outer vaginal muscles that makes penetration of the vagina difficult and painful. Many women who have vaginismus are interested in and enjoy sexual activity.

Origins of Sexual Difficulties

- Physiological conditions can be the primary causes of sexual problems or can combine with psychological factors to result in sexual dysfunction. It is important to identify or rule out physiological causes of sexual problems through medical examinations.
- Good sexual functioning correlates with good health habits, including a healthy diet, exercise, moderate or no alcohol use, and not smoking.
- Chronic illnesses and their treatments can greatly affect sexuality. Diseases of the neurological, vascular, and endocrine systems can impair sexual functioning.
- Diabetes causes damage to nerves and the circulatory system, impairing sexual arousal.
- Cancer and its therapies can impair the hormonal, vascular, and neurological functions necessary for normal sexual activity. Cancer of the reproductive organs often has the worst impact.

- Multiple sclerosis is a neurological disease of the brain and spinal cord that can affect sexual interest, genital sensation, arousal, or capacity for orgasm.
- Cerebrovascular accidents, or strokes, can reduce a person's frequency of interest, arousal, and sexual activity.
- Most people with spinal cord injuries remain interested in sex, and more than half experience some degree of sexual arousal.
- People with cerebral palsy, which is characterized by mild to severe lack of muscular control, may need help with preparation and positioning for sexual relations.
- Blind and deaf individuals can enhance sexual interaction by developing increased sensitivity with their other senses.
- Medications that can impair sexual functioning include drugs used to treat high blood pressure, psychiatric disorders, depression, and cancer. Use of recreational drugs (including barbiturates, narcotics, and marijuana), alcohol, and tobacco can interfere with sexual interest, arousal, and orgasm.
- Equality of gender roles is associated with greater sexual satisfaction for men and women.
- An emphasis on intercourse can increase performance anxiety and reduce pleasurable options in lovemaking.
- Sexual difficulties can be related to personal factors such as limited or inaccurate sexual knowledge, problems of self-concept and body image, or emotional difficulties.
- Experiencing sexual abuse as a child or sexual assault as an adult often leads to sexual problems. As a result of the abuse experiences, a survivor often associates sexual activity with negative, traumatic feelings.
- Relationship problems, ineffective communication, and fear of pregnancy or sexually transmitted infections can often inhibit sexual satisfaction.
- A woman or man whose sexual orientation is homosexual will often have difficulty with sexual interest, arousal, and orgasm in a heterosexual sexual relationship.

Basics of Sexual Enhancement and Sex Therapy

- Exploring one's own body, sharing knowledge with a partner, and establishing good communication between partners are important elements of therapy.
- Sensate focus is a part of therapy for many different sexual problems.
- Masturbating in each other's presence can be an excellent way for partners to indicate to each other what kind of touching they find arousing.
- Therapy programs for women to learn to experience orgasm are based on progressive self-awareness activities.
- Women who wish to become orgasmic with a partner can benefit from programs that start with sensate focus, mutual genital exploration, and nondemand genital pleasuring by the partner.

- Treatment for vaginismus generally involves promoting increased self-awareness and relaxation. Insertion of a lubricated finger (first one's own and later the partner's) into the vagina is an important next step in overcoming this condition. Penile insertion is the final phase of treatment for vaginismus.
- A variety of approaches can help a man learn to delay his ejaculation, and a couple can use the stop-start technique. Certain antidepressant medications can also help delay ejaculation.
- A behavioral approach designed to reduce performance anxiety is used to treat psychologically based erectile disorder.
- Medications to stimulate blood flow to the penis are in widespread use, and vascular surgery, surgically implanted penile prostheses, external vacuum constriction, and vasoactive injections are available if medication does not help.
- A behavioral approach to male orgasmic disorder combines self-stimulation, sensate focus, and partner manual stimulation, ultimately leading to ejaculation by the partner's stimulation.
- Many of the basic sex therapy techniques are used to help with hypoactive sexual desire disorder, and therapists also often include insight therapy and couples counseling.
- Testosterone can be helpful for men and women with low sexual desire, but because of its possible links to cancer and heart disease, its safety is not well established.
- Two nonprescription products have been shown in research to be helpful with low desire and arousal in women, and other products are being studied.
- Professional counseling is often helpful and sometimes necessary in overcoming sexual difficulties, but few people with problems seek help.
- A skilled therapist can provide useful information, problem-solving strategies, and sex therapy techniques.
- It is unethical for a therapist to have sexual relations with a client, either during or after treatment.

Media Resources

Log in to CengageBrain.com to access the resources your instructor requires.

Go to CengageBrain.com to access Psychology CourseMate, where you will find an interactive eBook, glossaries, flashcards, quizzes, videos, and more.

Also access links to chapter-related websites, including **American Association of Sex Educators, Therapists, and Counselors, and the American Board of Sexology.**

Sexually Transmitted Infections

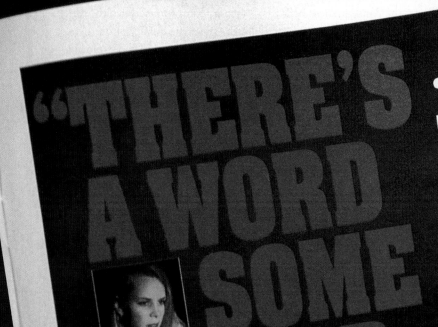

"THERE'S A WORD SOME FIND

Mary Chapin Carpenter COUNTRY AIDS

Using latex condoms does help prevent the spread of HIV, the virus that causes AIDS. But you have to use them properly... and that means every time you have sex, from start to finish. So even if you find it hard to say "condoms," you'll find they are easy to use. They could save your life.

Bacterial Infections

Why do health authorities now consider chlamydia infections a major health problem?

What kinds of complications can accompany gonorrhea?

Why are health authorities concerned about syphilis in the United States?

Viral Infections

Can the herpes virus be transmitted if an open sore is not present?

Why do health practitioners consider genital warts a serious problem?

Can both hepatitis A and hepatitis B be transmitted sexually? What symptoms are associated with hepatitis?

Common Vaginal Infections

What is a male partner's role in transmitting bacterial vaginosis?

What factors are associated with the development of candidiasis, and how is this infection treated?

How common is trichomoniasis, and what possible complications are associated with this infection?

Ectoparasitic Infections

Can pubic lice be transmitted by ways other than sexual interaction?

How contagious is scabies, what are its symptoms, and how is it treated?

Acquired Immunodeficiency Syndrome (AIDS)

How is HIV transmitted, and what behaviors put one at risk for becoming infected with HIV?

Among what portions of the population is AIDS increasing most rapidly?

Has there been significant progress in the search for either an effective treatment or a cure for this disease?

Preventing Sexually Transmitted Infections

What are some effective methods of preventing STIs or reducing the likelihood of contracting one?

For more information, call your local AIDS service organization or the CDC National AIDS Hotline at 800 - 342 - AID

> The possibility of getting a sexually transmitted infection has caused me to be extremely cautious and selective about whom I choose to be sexual with. It also makes every decision in a sexual relationship so critical and has made me much more careful in the choices I make. (Authors' files)

sexually transmitted infections (STIs)
Infections that are transmitted by sexual contact.

In this chapter, we discuss a variety of **sexually transmitted infections (STIs)***—that is, infections that can be transmitted through sexual interaction. ■ Table 15.1 summarizes the STIs described in this chapter. Some of these infections are curable; others are not. As we will see, the consequences of STIs—such as compromised health, pain and discomfort, infertility, and even death—can adversely affect the quality of our lives.

Our purpose in including a chapter on STIs is not to discourage you from exploring the joys of sexuality. Rather, we wish to help you make good decisions by presenting a realistic picture of what STIs are, how to recognize them, what should be done to treat them, and what measures can be taken to avoid contracting or transmitting them. We believe that this information is especially relevant to our college-age readers. The transmission of STIs on American college campuses continues to pose significant health concerns (Williams et al., 2008). Moreover, it is estimated that about half the STIs diagnosed annually in the United States occur among 15- to 24-year-olds, although that population constitutes only one quarter of the overall sexually active population in the United States (Dariotis et al., 2011). Furthermore, most HIV infections in America occur among young people under the age of 30 (Barnard, 2011; Crosby & Danner, 2008).

You may wonder why we postpone our discussion of HIV/AIDS until later in this chapter. Certainly AIDS has received far more attention in the media than any of the other infections discussed in this chapter. This emphasis on AIDS, although understandable in view of the continuing worldwide spread of this deadly ailment, tends to obscure the fact that many other STIs are substantially more prevalent. Furthermore, many of these commonly occurring STIs, such as chlamydia and genital warts, pose major health risks that are escalating in proportion to the increasing incidence of these infections.

Many factors contribute to the epidemic of STIs in the United States. Engaging in risky sexual behavior, such as having multiple sexual partners and unprotected (condomless) sex, is a prime reason for the high incidence of STIs. Such behavior is especially prevalent during adolescence and early adulthood, when the incidence of STIs is the highest (Workowski et al., 2010). It is also believed that increased use of oral contraceptives has contributed to the epidemic of STIs—both by increasing susceptibility of women to some STIs and by reducing the use of condoms, a contraceptive method known to offer protection against many infections. Lack of adequate public health measures and limited access to effective systems for prevention and treatment of STIs also contribute to this ongoing epidemic. In addition, many health-care providers in the United States are reluctant to ask questions about their patients' sexual behaviors, thus missing opportunities for STI-related counseling, diagnosis, and treatment. Moreover, a number of studies indicate that many college students do not receive adequate STI-related information from their college or university health service (Williams et al., 2008).

The spread of STIs is facilitated by the unfortunate fact that many of these infections do not produce obvious symptoms. In some cases, particularly among women, there may be no outward signs at all. Under these circumstances, people may unknowingly infect others. In addition, feelings of guilt and embarrassment that often accompany having an STI may prevent people from seeking adequate treatment or from informing their sexual partners. In the Let's Talk About It box, "Telling a Partner," we explore why informing sexual partners is important and suggest ways to do so more easily.

---

*Some health professionals prefer to call these conditions sexually transmitted diseases, or STDs.

In the following sections, we focus on the most common STIs. We also provide an expanded discussion of AIDS and the progress being made in treating this dreadful malady. The Centers for Disease Control and Prevention (CDC) periodically provides updated guidelines for treating STIs. The most recent guidelines, published at the end of 2010 (Workowski et al., 2010), are the basis for most of the treatment information provided for the infections discussed in this chapter.

At a Glance

■ TABLE 15.1 Common Sexually Transmitted Infections: Transmission, Symptoms, and Treatment

STI	Transmission	Symptoms	Treatment(s)
Chlamydia	The *Chlamydia trachomatis* bacterium is passed through sexual contact. Infection can spread from one body site to another via fingers.	**Women**: Pelvic inflammatory disease, disrupted menstruation, pelvic pain, raised temperature, nausea, vomiting, headache, infertility, and ectopic pregnancy. **Men**: Urethra infection; discharge and burning during urination; with epididymitis, heaviness in and painful swelling at bottom of affected testis, inflammation of scrotum.	Doxycycline by mouth for several days, or one dose of azithromycin.
Gonorrhea	The *Neisseria gonorrhoeae* bacterium is passed through penile–vaginal, oral–genital, oral–anal, or genital–anal contact.	**Women**: Green or yellowish discharge (usually remains undetected); pelvic inflammatory disease may develop. **Men**: Cloudy discharge from penis and burning during urination; complications include painful swelling at bottom of affected testis and inflammation of scrotum.	Dual therapy of one dose of a cephalosporin medication (e.g., ceftriaxone), plus one dose of azithromycin (or doxycycline for 7 days).
Nongonococcal urethritis (NGU)	Primarily caused by various bacteria transmitted through coitus. Some NGU results from allergic reactions or from *Trichomonas* infection.	**Women**: Mild discharge of pus from vagina (often remains undetected). **Men**: Discharge from penis and irritation during urination.	One dose of azithromycin, or doxycycline for 7 days.
Syphilis	The *Treponema pallidum* bacterium is passed from open lesions during penile–vaginal, oral–genital, oral–anal, or genital–anal contact.	**Primary Stage**: Painless chancre at site where bacterium entered body. **Secondary Stage**: Chancre disappears, and generalized skin rash appears. **Latent Stage**: There may be no visible symptoms. **Tertiary Stage**: Heart failure, blindness, mental disturbance, and more; death may result.	Benzathine penicillin G, doxycycline, tetracycline, or ceftriaxone.
Herpes	HSV-2 (genital herpes virus) passed primarily through penile–vaginal, oral–genital, oral–anal, or genital–anal contact. HSV-1 (oral herpes) passed by kissing or oral–genital contact.	Small, painful, red bumps appear in the genital region or mouth. Bumps become painful blisters and eventually rupture to form wet, open sores.	No known cure. A variety of treatments can reduce symptoms. Oral acyclovir, valacyclovir, or famciclovir promote healing and suppress recurrent outbreaks.
Genital warts	Human papillomavirus (HPV) is passed primarily through penile–vaginal, oral–genital, oral–anal, or genital–anal contact.	Hard and yellow-gray growths on dry skin areas. Soft, pinkish-red, and cauliflower-like growths on moist areas.	Freezing, application of topical agents, cauterization, surgical removal, or vaporization by carbon dioxide laser.

STI	Transmission	Symptoms	Treatment(s)
Viral hepatitis	Hepatitis B virus can be passed through blood, semen, vaginal secretions, and saliva. Manual, oral, or penile stimulation of anus is strongly associated with spread of hepatitis B. Hepatitis A is spread by means of oral–anal contact, especially when the mouth encounters fecal matter. Hepatitis C is spread through intravenous drug use and less frequently through contaminated blood products, sexual contact, or mother-to-fetus or mother-to-infant contact.	Varies from no symptoms to mild, flulike symptoms to an incapacitating illness characterized by high fever, vomiting, and severe abdominal pain.	No specific treatment for hepatitis A and B. Bed rest and adequate fluid intake. Combination therapy with antiviral drugs may be effective against hepatitis C.
Bacterial vaginosis	Different types of bacterial microorganisms are passed through coitus.	**Women:** Fishy- or musty-smelling, light-gray, thin discharge (consistency of flour paste). **Men:** Usually asymptomatic.	Metronidazole (Flagyl) by mouth. Intravaginal applications of topical metronidazole gel or clindamycin cream.
Candidiasis (yeast infection)	The fungus *Candida albicans* accelerates growth when normal chemical balance of the vagina is disturbed. Can be passed through sexual interaction.	**Women:** White, "cheesy" discharge, irritation of vaginal and vulval tissues. **Men:** Usually asymptomatic but may have itching or reddening of the penis and burning during urination.	Vaginal suppositories or topical cream, such as clotrimazole and miconazole. Oral fluoconazole or itraconazole.
Trichomoniasis	The protozoan parasite *Trichomonas vaginalis* is usually passed through sexual contact.	**Women:** White or yellow vaginal discharge with unpleasant odor; vulva is sore and irritated. **Men:** Usually asymptomatic but may have urethral discharge, urge to urinate frequently, or painful urination.	One dose of metronidazole (Flagyl or tinidazole) for women and men.
Pubic lice ("crabs")	Pubic louse is spread through body contact or through shared clothing or bedding.	Persistent itching. Lice are visible and can be located in pubic or other body hair.	Prescription or over-the-counter medications (lotions or creams) applied to all affected areas.
Scabies	Highly contagious. Can be passed by close physical contact (sexual and nonsexual).	Small bumps and a red rash that itch intensely (especially at night).	Topical scabicide applied from neck down to toes.
Acquired immunodeficiency syndrome (AIDS)	Blood, semen, and vaginal fluids are the major vehicles for transmitting HIV (which attacks the immune system). Passed primarily through penile–vaginal, oral–genital, oral–anal, or genital–anal contact or by needle sharing among injection drug users.	Varies with the types of opportunistic infections or cancers that can afflict an infected person. Common symptoms include fever, night sweats, weight loss, chronic fatigue, swollen lymph nodes, diarrhea and/or bloody stool, atypical bruising or bleeding, skin rashes, headache, chronic cough, and a whitish coating on the tongue or throat.	Commence treatment with a combination of three or more antiretroviral drugs (HAART) when CD4 count is significantly low. Specific treatments may be necessary to treat opportunistic infections and tumors.

Most of us would find it difficult to discuss with our lover(s) the possibility that we have transmitted an infection to her or him during sexual activity. Because of the stigma often associated with STIs, it can be bad enough admitting to yourself that you have one of these infections. The need to tell others that they might have "caught" something from you may seem like a formidable task. You might fear that such a revelation will jeopardize a valued relationship, or you might worry that you will be considered "dirty." In relationships presumed to be monogamous, you might fear that telling your partner about an STI will threaten mutual trust. At the same time, however, concealing a sex-related illness places a good deal more at risk in the long run. Moreover, a recent study found that people who had disclosed their STI to their partners "had significantly more positive feelings about aspects of their sexual self-concept than those who had not disclosed their STI to their partners" (Newton & McCabe, 2008, p. 187).

Most important, not disclosing the existence of an STI risks the health of your partner(s). Many people may not have symptoms and thus may not become aware that they have contracted an infection until they discover it for themselves, perhaps only after they have developed serious complications. Furthermore, if a lover remains untreated, she or he may reinfect you even after you have been cured. Unlike some diseases (such as measles and chicken pox), STIs do not provide immunity against future infections. You can get one, give it to your lover, be cured, and then get it back again if he or she remains untreated.

The following suggestions provide some guidelines for telling a partner about your STI. Remember, these are only suggestions that have worked for some people; they may need to be modified to fit your particular circumstances. This sensitive issue requires thoughtful consideration and planning.

1. Be honest. There is nothing to be gained by downplaying the potential risks associated with STIs. If you tell a partner, "I have this little drip, but it probably means nothing," you may regret it. Be sure your partner understands the importance of obtaining a medical evaluation.

2. Even if you suspect that your partner may have been the source of your infection, there is little to be gained by blaming him or her. Instead, you may wish simply to acknowledge that you have an infection and are concerned that your partner gets proper medical attention.

3. Your attitude may have a considerable effect on how your partner receives the news. If you display high levels of anxiety, guilt, fear, or disgust, your partner may reflect these feelings in her or his response. Try to present the facts in as clear and calm a fashion as you can manage.

4. Be sensitive to your partner's feelings. Be prepared for reactions of anger or resentment. These are understandable initial responses. Being supportive and demonstrating a willingness to listen without becoming defensive may be the best tactics for diffusing negative responses.

5. Engaging in sexual intimacies after you become aware of your condition and before you obtain medical assurances that you are no longer contagious is clearly inappropriate. Discuss with your partner that abstinence from sexual intercourse is crucial for persons who are being treated for an STI or whose partners are undergoing treatment.

6. Medical examinations and treatments for STIs, when necessary, can be a financial burden. Offering to pay for some or all of these expenses may help to maintain (or reestablish) goodwill in your relationship.

If you want more information, we recommend that you contact your county health service, an STI/STD clinic, or a Planned Parenthood clinic, or that you call the National STI Resource Center.* These services can answer questions, send free literature, and, most important, give you the name and phone number of a local physician or public clinic that will treat STIs for free or at minimal cost. ●

Bacterial Infections

A variety of STIs are caused by bacterial agents. We begin this section with a discussion of chlamydia, one of the most prevalent and damaging of all STIs. The other bacterial infections we describe are gonorrhea, nongonococcal urethritis, and syphilis. We discuss bacterial vaginosis, a common vaginal infection, in a later section of this chapter.

---

*The American Social Health Association's STI Resource Center can be dialed toll-free from 8:00 a.m. to 8:00 p.m. on weekdays and from 10:00 a.m. to 6:00 p.m. on weekends, Pacific time. The number is (800) 227-8922.

Chlamydia Infection

Chlamydia (cluh-MID-ee-uh) is caused by *Chlamydia trachomatis*, a bacterial microorganism that grows in body cells. This organism is now recognized as the cause of a diverse group of genital infections and is a common cause of preventable blindness.

Incidence and Transmission

Chlamydia is the most frequently reported infectious disease in the United States (Powers et al., 2011; Workowski et al., 2010). Sexually active teenagers, especially females, have higher infection rates than any other age group (Powers et al., 2011). It appears that teenage girls and young women in their early 20s are especially susceptible to chlamydia infection, largely because their cervixes have not fully matured (Centers for Disease Control, 2009b).

Chlamydia infection is transmitted primarily through vaginal, anal, or oral sexual contact. It can also be spread by fingers from one body site to another, such as from the genitals to the eyes.

Symptoms and Complications

Two general types of genital chlamydia infections affect females. The first of these, infection of the mucosa of the lower reproductive tract, commonly takes the form of an inflammation of the urethral tube or an infection of the cervix. In both cases women experience few or no symptoms (Centers for Disease Control, 2009b). When symptoms do occur, they include a mild irritation or itching of the genital tissues, a burning sensation during urination, and a slight vaginal discharge.

The second type of genital chlamydia infection in women is invasive infection of the upper reproductive tract, expressed as **pelvic inflammatory disease (PID)**. PID typically occurs when bacteria that cause chlamydia or gonorrhea spread from the cervix upward, infecting the lining of the uterus (*endometritis*), the fallopian tubes (*salpingitis*), and possibly the ovaries and other adjacent abdominal structures (Gottlieb et al., 2011; Wendling, 2011). An estimated 40% of women with untreated chlamydia will develop PID (Centers for Disease Control, 2009b).

PID resulting from chlamydia infection often produces a variety of symptoms, which can include disrupted menstrual periods, chronic pelvic pain, lower back pain, fever, nausea, vomiting, and headache. Salpingitis caused by chlamydia infection is the primary preventable cause of female infertility and ectopic pregnancy (Gottlieb et al., 2011). Even after PID has been effectively treated, residual scar tissue in the fallopian tubes can leave some women sterile.

A woman who has had PID should be cautioned about the use of the IUD as a method of contraception. An IUD does not prevent fertilization (see Chapter 10 for an explanation of how the IUD prevents pregnancy); thus a tiny sperm cell could negotiate a partially blocked area of a scarred fallopian tube and fertilize an ovum that, because of its larger size, subsequently becomes lodged in the scarred tube. The result is an *ectopic pregnancy*, a serious hazard to the woman. The incidence of ectopic pregnancies in the United States has increased dramatically in the last two decades, largely because of an escalation in the occurrence of chlamydia infections. Chlamydia also often reduces fertility in women without detectable fallopian tube damage (Coppus et al., 2011).

In men, untreated chlamydia may result in a variety of symptoms, including a discharge from the penis and/or a burning sensation during urination, itching around the opening of the penis, and, less commonly, pain and swelling in the testicles (Centers for Disease Control, 2009b).

One of the most disheartening aspects of chlamydia is that symptoms are either minimal or nonexistent in a majority of infected women and about half of infected men

chlamydia
Urogenital infection caused by the bacterium *Chlamydia trachomatis*.

pelvic inflammatory disease (PID)
An infection in the uterus and pelvic cavity.

(Centers for Disease Control, 2009b). Most women and men with rectal chlamydia infections also manifest few or no symptoms (Kent et al., 2005).

Another complication associated with *Chlamydia trachomatis* is **trachoma** (truh-KOH-muh), a chronic, contagious form of **conjunctivitis** (kun-junk-ti-VIE-tus) (inflammation of the mucous membrane that lines the inner surface of the eyelid and the exposed surface of the eyeball) (Kari et al., 2011). Trachoma is the world's leading cause of preventable blindness; it is particularly prevalent in Asia and Africa (Karpecki & Shechtman, 2008). *Chlamydia trachomatis* is a common cause of eye infections (conjunctivitis) in newborns, who can become infected as they pass through the birth canal (Workowski et al., 2010). In addition, many babies of infected mothers will develop pneumonia caused by chlamydia infection (Workowski et al., 2010). Chlamydia infection in pregnant women can also lead to premature delivery (Ball, 2011; H. Johnson et al., 2011). The CDC recommends that pregnant women be tested for chlamydia during their first prenatal visit.

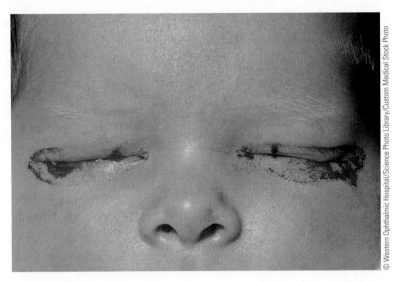

Chlamydia conjunctivitis in a newborn, acquired from an infected mother during birth.

The Centers for Disease Control (2009b) estimates that women infected with chlamydia are up to five times more likely to become infected with HIV (the virus that causes AIDS) if exposed to it.

Treatment

CDC guidelines suggest treating uncomplicated chlamydia infections with a 7-day regimen of doxycycline taken by mouth or a single 1-gram dose of azithromycin. All sexual partners exposed to chlamydia should be examined for STIs and treated if necessary.

Gonorrhea

Gonorrhea (gah-nuh-REE-uh), known in street language as "the clap," is an STI caused by the bacterium *Neisseria gonorrhoeae* (also called *gonococcus*).

Incidence and Transmission

Gonorrhea is the second most reported infectious condition in the United States, trailing only chlamydia (Workowski et al., 2010). The CDC estimates that there are more than 700,000 new cases of gonorrhea each year (Bolan et al., 2012). Unfortunately, after declining or remaining stable for many years, national rates of gonorrhea increased slightly in recent years, and the incidence of gonorrhea remains exceptionally high among teenagers and young adults, especially in lower-socioeconomic ethnic-minority communities (Bolan et al., 2012; Bradley et al., 2012).

The *gonococcus* bacterium thrives in the warm mucous membrane tissues of the genitals, anus, and throat. Its mode of transmission is by sexual contact—penile–vaginal, oral–genital, oral–anal, or genital–anal.

Symptoms and Complications

Early symptoms of gonorrhea infection are more likely to be evident in men than in women (Centers for Disease Control, 2009c). Most men who experience gonococcal urethritis have some symptoms, ranging from mild to pronounced. However, it is not uncommon for men with this type of infection to have no symptoms and yet be potentially infectious.

trachoma
A chronic, contagious form of conjunctivitis caused by chlamydia infections.

conjunctivitis
Inflammation of the mucous membrane that lines the inner surface of the eyelid and the exposed surface of the eyeball.

gonorrhea
A sexually transmitted infection that initially causes inflammation of mucous membranes.

Early Symptoms in the Male In men early symptoms typically appear 2–5 days after sexual contact with an infected person. However, symptoms can show up as late as 30 days after contact or, in a small number of cases, may not appear at all. The two most common signs of infection are a bad-smelling, cloudy discharge from the penis (see ▌ Figure 15.1) and a burning sensation during urination. Some infected men also have swollen and tender lymph glands in the groin. These early symptoms sometimes clear up on their own without treatment. However, this is no guarantee that the infection has been eradicated by the body's immune system. The bacteria may still be present, and a man may still be able to infect a partner.

Complications in the Male If the infection continues without treatment for 2 to 3 weeks, it can spread up the genitourinary tract. Here, it can involve the prostate, bladder, kidneys, and testes. Most men who continue to harbor *gonococcus* have only periodic flare-ups of the minor symptoms of discharge and a burning sensation during urination. In a small number of men, however, abscesses form in the prostate. These can result in fever, painful bowel movements, difficulty urinating, and general discomfort. In approximately 1 out of 5 men who remain untreated for longer than a month, the bacteria move down the vas deferens to infect one or both of the epididymal structures that lie along the back of each testis. In general, only one side is infected initially, usually the left. Even after successful treatment, gonococcal epididymitis leaves scar tissue, which can block the flow of sperm from the affected testis. Sterility does not usually result, because this complication typically affects only one testis. However, if treatment is still not carried out after epididymitis has occurred on one side, the infection can spread to the other testis, causing permanent sterility.

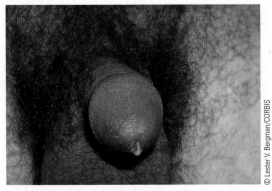

▌ **Figure 15.1** A cloudy discharge symptomatic of gonorrhea infection.

Early Symptoms in the Female Most women infected with gonorrhea are unaware of the early symptoms of this infection. The primary site of infection, the cervix, can become inflamed without producing any observable symptoms. Symptoms that may occur include a painful or burning sensation when urinating and/or increased vaginal discharge. However, because this discharge is rarely heavy, it commonly goes unnoticed. A woman who is aware of her vaginal secretions is more likely to note the infection during these early stages. Sometimes the discharge is irritating to the vulval tissues. However, when a woman seeks medical attention for an irritating discharge, her physician may fail to consider gonorrhea because many other infectious organisms produce this symptom. Also, many women who have gonorrhea also have trichomoniasis (discussed later in this chapter), and this condition can mask the presence of gonorrhea. Consequently, it is essential for any woman who thinks she may have gonorrhea to make certain that she is tested for the infection when she is examined. (A Pap smear is *not* a test for gonorrhea.)

Complications in the Female Serious complications result from the spread of this infection to the upper reproductive tract, where it often causes PID (Centers for Disease Control, 2009c). The symptoms of PID, discussed in the section on chlamydia infection, are often more severe when the infecting organism is *gonococcus* rather than *Chlamydia trachomatis*. Sterility and ectopic pregnancy are serious consequences occasionally associated with gonococcal PID. Another serious complication that can result from PID is the development of tough bands of scar tissue adhesions that may link several pelvic cavity structures (fallopian tubes, ovaries, uterus, etc.) to each other, to the abdominal walls, or to both. These adhesions can cause severe pain during coitus or when a woman is standing or walking.

Other Complications in Both Sexes In about 2% of adult men and women with gonorrhea, the bacteria enter the bloodstream and spread throughout the body to produce a variety of symptoms, including chills, fever, loss of appetite, skin lesions, and arthritic pain in the joints (Centers for Disease Control, 2009c; Martin et al., 2008). If arthritic symptoms develop, quick treatment is essential to avoid permanent joint damage. In rare cases the *gonococcus* organism can invade the heart, liver, spinal cord, and brain.

An infant can develop a gonococcal eye infection after passing through the birth canal of an infected woman (Workowski et al., 2010). In a few rare cases, adults have transmitted the bacteria to their own eyes by touching this region immediately after handling their genitals—one reason why it is important to wash with soap and water immediately after self-examination. ●

Oral contact with infected genitals can result in infection of the throat. Although this form of gonorrhea can cause a sore throat, most people experience no symptoms. Rectal gonorrhea can be caused by anal intercourse or, in a woman, by transmission of the bacteria from the vagina to the anal opening by means of menstrual blood or vaginal discharge. Rectal gonorrhea is often asymptomatic, particularly in females, but it might be accompanied by itching, bleeding, rectal discharge, and painful bowel movements.

Treatment

Because gonorrhea is often confused with other ailments, it is important to make the correct diagnosis. Because coexisting chlamydia infections often accompany gonorrhea, health practitioners often use a treatment strategy that is effective against both. For a number of years the treatment regimen recommended by the CDC involved the dual therapy of a single dose of a fluoroquinolone antibiotic, such as ciprofloxacin, plus a single dose of azithromycin (or doxycycline for 7 days). Unfortunately, in recent years there has been an alarming worldwide increase in strains of gonorrhea resistant to fluoroquinolone antibiotics (Dowell et al., 2012). Consequently, the CDC now recommends that health professionals stop using fluoroquinolones and substitute a cephalosporin medication (a different class of antibiotics, such as ceftriaxone) to treat gonorrhea infections.

Recent research has identified a new mutated strain of the gonococcus bacterium, HO41, that causes an infection that cannot be treated by available antibiotics, including cephalosporin-class antibiotics (Unemo et al., 2011). This alarming discovery suggests that a once easily treatable infection may become a global public health threat if this new drug-resistant strain becomes widespread (Bolan et al., 2012).

It is quite common for sexual partners of infected individuals to have also contracted gonorrhea. Consequently, all sexual partners exposed to a person with diagnosed gonorrhea should be examined, cultured, and, if necessary, treated with a drug regimen that covers both gonococcal and chlamydia infections (Katz, 2011).

Nongonococcal Urethritis

Any inflammation of the urethra that is not caused by gonorrhea is called **nongonococcal urethritis (NGU)**. It is believed that three microscopic bacterial organisms— *Chlamydia trachomatis*, *Ureaplasma urealyticum*, and *Mycoplasma genitalium*—are primary causes of NGU (Centers for Disease Control, 2009d). NGU can also result from invasion by other infectious agents, allergic reactions to vaginal secretions, or irritation from soaps, vaginal contraceptives, or deodorant sprays.

nongonococcal urethritis (NGU)
An inflammation of the urethral tube caused by organisms other than *gonococcus*.

Incidence and Transmission

NGU is quite common among men and in the United States male NGU may occur more frequently than gonorrhea in men. Although NGU generally produces urinary tract symptoms only in men, there is evidence that women harbor the organisms that can cause NGU. The most common forms of NGU are generally transmitted through coitus. That NGU rarely occurs in men who are not involved in sexual interaction supports this contention.

Symptoms and Complications

Men who contract NGU often manifest symptoms similar to those of gonorrhea infection, including discharge from the penis and a mild burning sensation during urination. Often the discharge is less pronounced than with gonorrhea; it may be evident only in the morning before urinating.

Women with NGU are generally unaware of the infection until they are informed that it has been diagnosed in a male partner. They frequently show no symptoms, although there may be some itching, a burning sensation during urination, and a mild discharge of pus from the vagina. A woman may unknowingly have the infection for a long time, during which she may pass it to sexual partners.

The symptoms of NGU generally disappear after 2 to 3 months without treatment. However, the infection may still be present. If left untreated in women, it can result in cervical inflammation or PID; in men it can spread to the prostate, epididymis, or both. In rare cases NGU can produce a form of arthritis.

Treatment

A single dose of azithromycin or a regimen of doxycycline for 7 days usually clears up NGU. All sexual partners of individuals diagnosed with NGU should be examined for the presence of an STI and treated if necessary.

Syphilis

syphilis
A sexually transmitted infection caused by a bacterium called *Treponema pallidum*.

Syphilis (SIH-fuh-lus) is an STI caused by a thin, corkscrewlike bacterium called *Treponema pallidum* (also commonly called a spirochete).

Incidence and Transmission

Syphilis rates declined steadily in the United States throughout the 1990s (Rosen, 2006). Unfortunately, syphilis rates have recently risen. This overall increased incidence of syphilis was largely attributable to an increase among men who have sex with men (MSM) (Mayer & Mimiaga, 2011).

Treponema pallidum requires a warm, moist environment for survival. It is transmitted almost exclusively from open lesions of infected individuals to the mucous membranes or skin abrasions of sexual partners through penile–vaginal, oral–genital, oral–anal, or genital–anal contacts.

An infected pregnant woman can also transmit *Treponema pallidum* to her unborn child through the placental blood system. The resulting infection can cause miscarriage, stillbirth, or *congenital syphilis*, which can result in death or extreme damage to infected newborns (Centers for Disease Control, 2010a; Hawkes et al., 2011). Worldwide more than 2 million pregnant women have active syphilis (Hawkes et al., 2011), and every year at least 500,000 children are born afflicted with congenital syphilis (Ramiandrisoa et al., 2011). If syphilis is successfully treated before the 4th month of pregnancy, the fetus will not be affected. Therefore pregnant women should be tested for syphilis sometime during their first 3 months of pregnancy. The CDC recommends that all pregnant women be tested for syphilis at the first prenatal visit.

Symptoms and Complications

If untreated, syphilis can progress through the primary, secondary, latent, and tertiary phases of development. We provide a brief description of each phase in the following paragraphs.

chancre
A raised, red, painless sore that is symptomatic of the primary phase of syphilis.

Primary Syphilis In its initial or primary phase, syphilis is generally manifested in the form of a single, painless sore called a **chancre** (SHANG-kur), which usually appears

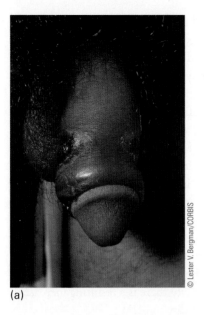
(a)

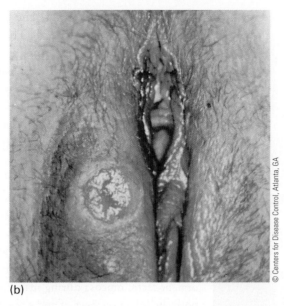
(b)

▌**Figure 15.2** The first stage of syphilis. A syphilitic chancre as it appears on (a) the penis and (b) the labia.

about 3 weeks after initial infection at the site where the spirochete organism entered the body (see ▌ Figure 15.2). In women this sore most commonly appears on the inner vaginal walls or cervix. It can also appear on the external genitals, particularly the labia. In men the chancre most often occurs on the glans of the penis, but it can also show up on the penile shaft or on the scrotum. Although most chancres are genital, the sores can occur in the mouth or rectum or on the anus or breast. People who have had oral sex with an infected individual might develop a sore on the lips or tongue. Anal intercourse can result in chancres appearing in the rectum or around the anus.

Since the chancre is typically painless, it often goes undiscovered when it occurs on internal structures, such as the rectum, vagina, or cervix. (Occasionally, chancres may be painful, and they may occur in multiple sites.) Even when the chancre is noticed, some people do not seek treatment. Unfortunately (from the long-term perspective), the chancre generally heals without treatment 3 to 6 weeks after it first appears. For the next few weeks, the infected person usually has no symptoms but can infect an unsuspecting partner. After about 6 weeks (although sometimes after as little as 2 weeks or as many as 6 months), the infection often progresses to the secondary stage in people with untreated primary syphilis.

Secondary Syphilis In the secondary phase, which usually emerges 2 to 8 weeks after exposure, a skin rash appears on the body, often on the palms of the hands and soles of the feet (see ▌ Figure 15.3). The rash can vary from barely noticeable to severe, with raised bumps that have a rubbery, hard consistency. Although the rash may look terrible, it typically does not hurt or itch. Besides a generalized rash, a person may experience flulike symptoms, such as fever, swollen lymph glands, fatigue, weight loss, and joint or bone pain. Even when not treated, these symptoms usually subside within a few weeks. Rather than being eliminated, however, the infection can then enter the potentially more dangerous latent phase (Centers for Disease Control, 2009e).

Latent Syphilis The latent stage can last for several years, during which time there may be no observable symptoms (Centers for Disease Control, 2009e). Nevertheless, the infecting organisms continue to multiply, preparing for the final stage of syphilitic infection. After 1 year of the latent stage, the infected individual is no longer contagious to sexual partners. However, a pregnant woman with syphilis in any stage can pass the infection to her fetus.

Tertiary Syphilis Approximately 15% of individuals who do not obtain effective treatment during the first three stages of syphilis enter the tertiary stage later in life (Centers

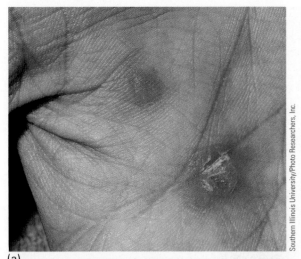

(a)

(b)

Figure 15.3 In the secondary phase of syphilis, a skin rash appears on the body, often on (a) the palms and (b) the feet.

Southern Illinois University/Photo Researchers, Inc.

© Biophoto Associates/Photo Researchers, Inc.

for Disease Control, 2009e). The final manifestations of syphilis can be severe, often resulting in death. They usually occur anywhere from 10 to 20 years after initial infection and include such conditions as heart failure, blindness, ruptured blood vessels, paralysis, skin ulcers, liver damage, and severe mental disturbance (Centers for Disease Control, 2009e). Treatment even at this late stage can be beneficial.

Genital sores (chancres) associated with the primary phase of syphilis infections increase the possibility of either transmitting or acquiring HIV infection through sexual activity. It is estimated that there is a two- to fivefold increased risk of becoming infected with HIV if exposed to this infectious virus when syphilitic sores are present (Centers for Disease Control, 2009e). Any sores, ulcers, or breaks in the skin (conditions that often accompany STIs) increase the possibility of either transmitting or becoming infected with HIV. Ulcerative sores bleed easily (blood is a major reservoir for HIV), and when they come into contact with genital, oral, or rectal mucosa during sexual activity there is a resulting increase in both the infectiousness of and susceptibility to HIV.

Treatment

Primary, secondary, or latent syphilis of less than 1 year's duration can be effectively treated with intramuscular injections of benzathine penicillin G. People who are allergic to penicillin can be treated with doxycycline, tetracycline, or ceftriaxone. Syphilis of more than 1 year's duration is treated with intramuscular injections of benzathine penicillin G once a week for 3 successive weeks. The CDC recommends follow-up at 6 and 12 months after initial diagnosis to determine the effectiveness of treatment. Recent research reveals significant risk factors for repeat syphilis infection, especially among MSM (Cohen et al., 2012).

All sex partners who have been exposed to a person with infectious syphilis should be tested and treated if necessary.

Viral Infections

Viruses are the cause of several common STIs. A virus is an organism that invades, reproduces, and lives within a cell, thereby disrupting normal cellular activity. Most viruses are transmitted through direct contact with infectious blood or other body fluids. We begin our discussion with herpes, the most common viral STI. Next, we describe genital warts caused by several varieties of viruses that have reached epidemic proportions in the U.S. population. We conclude with some information about viral hepatitis. AIDS, caused by HIV infection, is described in detail later in this chapter.

Herpes

herpes
An infection characterized by blisters on the skin in the regions of the genitals or mouth. It is caused by the *Herpes simplex* virus and is easily transmitted through sexual contact.

Herpes is caused by the *Herpes simplex* virus (HSV). Eight different herpes viruses infect humans, the most common being the varicella-zoster virus (VZV) that causes chicken pox, followed in frequency by *Herpes simplex* virus type 1 (HSV-1) and *Herpes simplex* virus type 2 (HSV-2). In the following discussion we confine our attention to HSV-1 and HSV-2 because these are the two herpes viruses that are widely transmitted through sexual contact. HSV-1 typically manifests itself as lesions or sores—called cold sores or fever blisters—in the mouth or on the lips (oral herpes). HSV-2 generally causes lesions on and around the genital areas (genital herpes).

Although genital and oral herpes are usually associated with different herpes viruses, oral–genital transmission is possible. HSV-1 can affect the genital area, and, conversely, HSV-2 can produce a sore in the mouth (Centers for Disease Control, 2009f). However, most infections of the genitals are of the HSV-2 variety, and most mouth infections are HSV-1 (Centers for Disease Control, 2009f; Looker et al., 2008).

Incidence and Transmission

Current estimates indicate that more than 100 million Americans have oral herpes, and at least 50 million (1 in 5 people over age 12) have genital herpes (Workowski et al., 2010). Worldwide genital herpes cases number in the hundreds of millions, and 24–25 million people are newly infected each year (Looker et al., 2008). Genital herpes infections in the United States are more common in women than in men, which may indicate that male-to-female transmission is more likely than female-to-male transmission (Centers for Disease Control, 2009f).

Genital herpes appears to be transmitted primarily by penile–vaginal, oral–genital, genital–anal, or oral–anal contact. Oral herpes can be transmitted by kissing or through oral–genital contact. A person who receives oral sex from a partner who has herpes in the mouth region can develop either type 1 or type 2 genital herpes.

When any herpes sores are present, the infected person is highly contagious. It is extremely important to avoid bringing the lesions into contact with someone else's body through touching, sexual interaction, or kissing.

Although it was once believed that herpes could be transmitted only when lesions were present, we now know that HSV can be transmitted even when there are no symptoms (Workowski et al., 2010). In fact, research strongly indicates that asymptomatic "viral shedding" (the emission of viable HSV onto body surfaces) is likely to occur at least some of the time in many people infected with HSV (Tronstein et al., 2011; Worcester, 2012). This asymptomatic viral shedding can result in transmission of the virus despite the absence of symptoms that suggest active infection. Many people who are infected with HSV are unaware of their infection, and the majority of infections are transmitted by these individuals (Mark et al., 2008).

Research has shown that herpes viruses do not pass through latex condoms. Thus condoms are effective in preventing transmission from a male whose only lesions occur on the glans or shaft of the penis. Condoms are helpful but less effective in preventing transmission from a female to a male, because vaginal secretions containing the virus can wash over the male's scrotal area. Nevertheless, using condoms consistently and correctly can minimize the risk of either acquiring or transmitting genital herpes.

What can infected people do to reduce the risk that they will transmit the virus to a sexual partner? Clearly, when lesions are present, individuals should avoid any kind of intimate or sexual activity that will expose a partner's body to viral shedding of HSV. However, as previously described, even when no sores or other symptoms are present, infected individuals are at risk for shedding the virus. The best strategy for people who are either infected themselves or involved with an infected partner is to consistently and correctly use condoms even when they or their partners are asymptomatic. ●

SEXUALHEALTH

Symptoms and Complications

The symptoms associated with HSV-1 and HSV-2 infections are quite similar.

Genital Herpes (Type 2) Symptoms The incubation period of genital herpes is 2 to 14 days, and the symptoms usually last 2 to 4 weeks (Centers for Disease Control, 2009f;

Looker et al., 2008). However, many individuals with genital herpes experience minimal or no recognizable symptoms (Centers for Disease Control, 2009f). When symptoms are present, they consist of one or more small painful red bumps, called *papules*, that usually appear in the genital region. In women the areas most commonly infected are the labia. The mons veneris, clitoris, vaginal opening, inner vaginal walls, and cervix can also be affected. In men the infected site is typically the glans or shaft of the penis. Men and women who have engaged in anal intercourse can develop eruptions in and around the anus.

Soon after their initial appearance, papules rapidly develop into tiny painful blisters filled with a clear fluid containing highly infectious virus particles. The body then attacks the virus with white blood cells, causing the blisters to fill with pus (see ▌Figure 15.4). Soon the blisters rupture to form wet, painful open sores surrounded by a red ring (health practitioners refer to this as the period of viral shedding). A person is highly contagious during this time. About 10 days after the first appearance of a papule, the open sore forms a crust and begins to heal—a process that can take as long as 10 more days. Sores on the cervix can continue to produce infectious material for as long as 10 days after labial sores have completely healed. Consequently, it is wise to avoid coitus for a 10-day period after all external sores have healed.

Other symptoms can accompany genital herpes, including swollen lymph nodes in the groin, fever, muscle aches, and headaches. In addition, urination may be accompanied by a burning sensation, and women may experience increased vaginal discharge.

Oral Herpes (Type 1) Symptoms Oral herpes is characterized by the formation of papules on the lips and sometimes on the inside of the mouth, on the tongue, and on the throat. These blisters tend to crust over and heal in 10 to 16 days. Other symptoms include fever, general muscle aches, swollen lymph nodes in the neck, flulike symptoms, increased salivation, and sometimes bleeding in the mouth.

Recurrence Even after complete healing, lesions can recur. Unfortunately, the herpes virus does not typically go away; instead, it retreats up the nerve fibers leading from the infected site (Colgan et al., 2003). Ultimately, the genital herpes virus finds a resting place in nerve cells adjacent to the lower spinal column, whereas the oral herpes virus becomes lodged in nerve cells in the back of the neck. The virus can remain dormant in these cells, without causing any apparent damage, perhaps for a person's entire lifetime. However, in many cases there will be periodic flare-ups as the virus retraces its path back down the nerve fibers leading to the genitals or lips.

Critical Thinking Question

Many individuals with genital herpes who have rare outbreaks of the infection worry about being rejected by prospective sexual partners if they disclose their condition. Do you believe that people who carefully monitor their health and take reasonable precautions can ethically enter into sexual relationships without revealing that they have genital herpes? Why or why not?

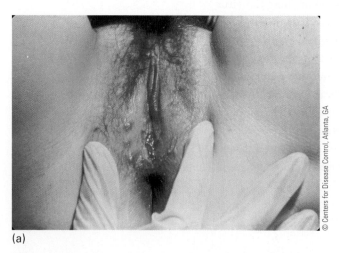

(a)

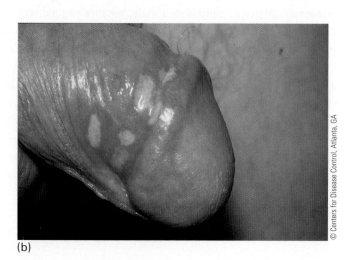

(b)

© Centers for Disease Control, Atlanta, GA

▌**Figure 15.4** Genital herpes blisters as they appear on (a) the labia and (b) the penis.

Although some people never experience a recurrence of herpes following the initial or primary infection, research suggests that most people who have undergone a primary episode of genital herpes infection experience at least one recurrence. Individuals who experience recurrences may do so frequently or only occasionally. Symptoms associated with recurrent attacks tend to be milder than primary episodes, and the infection tends to run its course more quickly.

Most people prone to recurrent herpes outbreaks experience some type of **prodromal symptoms** that warn of an impending eruption. These indications include itching, burning, throbbing, or "pins-and-needles" tingling at the sites commonly infected by herpes blisters, and sometimes pain in the legs, thighs, groin, or buttocks. Many health authorities believe that a person's degree of infectiousness increases during this stage and that it further escalates when the lesions appear. Consequently, a person should be particularly careful to avoid direct contact from the time he or she first experiences prodromal symptoms until the sores have completely healed. Even during an outbreak, it is possible to continue sexual intimacies with a partner, as long as infected skin does not come into contact with healthy skin. During this time, partners may wish to experiment with other kinds of sensual pleasuring, such as sensate focus (see Chapter 14), hugging, or manual stimulation.

A variety of factors can trigger reactivation of the herpes virus, including emotional stress, anxiety, depression, acidic food, ultraviolet light, fever, menstruation, poor nutrition, being overtired or run-down, and trauma to the affected skin region. Because triggering factors vary so widely, it is often difficult to associate a specific event with a recurrent herpes outbreak.

Some people may not experience a relapse of genital herpes until several years after the initial infection. Therefore, if you have been in what you believe is a sexually exclusive relationship and your partner shows symptoms or transmits the virus to you, it does not necessarily mean that she or he contracted the infection from someone else during the course of your relationship. Furthermore, as stated earlier, many people with genital herpes infections are asymptomatic or have mild symptoms that are often unrecognizable. Thus a first episode of symptomatic genital herpes may not be due to recent sexual contact with an infected person (Centers for Disease Control, 2009f).

Other Complications Although the sores are painful and bothersome, it is unlikely that men will experience major physical complications of herpes. Women, however, face two serious, although quite uncommon, complications: cancer of the cervix and infection of a newborn. Evidence suggests that the risk of developing cervical cancer is somewhat higher among women who have had genital herpes (Centers for Disease Control, 2006b). However, the role of genital herpes in cervical cancer is at most that of a cofactor, not that of a direct causative agent (Centers for Disease Control, 2006b). Fortunately, the great majority of women infected with herpes will never develop cancer of the cervix. Nonetheless, it is advisable for all women, particularly those who have had genital herpes, to obtain an annual cervical Pap smear. Some authorities recommend that women with genital herpes should have this test every 6 months.

A newborn can be infected with genital herpes while passing through the birth canal, and such an infection can cause severe damage or death (Looker et al., 2008; Workowski et al., 2010). It is believed that viral shedding from the cervix, vagina, or vulva plays the primary role in transmitting the infection perinatally from mother to infant. The risk of a pregnant mother transmitting genital herpes to her newborn is highest for women who are first infected during late pregnancy (Workowski et al., 2010). The CDC recommends that these women should consult with an infectious disease specialist to determine how to manage the impending birth.

prodromal symptoms
Symptoms that warn of an impending herpes eruption.

The presence of a genital herpes infection is associated with a two- to threefold increased risk of acquiring an HIV infection when exposed to HIV through sexual activity (Looker et al., 2008). The risk of transmission of HIV by a person infected with both HIV and HSV is estimated to increase fivefold on a per-sexual-act basis (Looker et al., 2008).

One additional serious complication can occur when a person transfers the virus to an eye after touching a virus-shedding sore. This can lead to a severe eye infection known as ocular herpes (Karpecki & Shechtman, 2011). The best way to prevent this complication is to avoid touching herpes sores. If you cannot avoid contact, thoroughly wash your hands with hot water and soap immediately after touching the lesions. There are effective treatments for ocular herpes, but they must be started quickly to avoid eye damage. ●

Many people who have recurrent herpes outbreaks are troubled with mild to severe psychological distress (Barnack-Tavlaris, 2011; Merin & Pachankis, 2011). In view of the physical discomfort associated with the infection, the unpredictability of recurrent outbreaks, and the lack of an effective cure (see next section), it is no small wonder that people who have herpes undergo considerable stress. We believe that becoming better informed about herpes may help to alleviate some of these emotional difficulties. In addition, talking with supportive partners might ease a person's psychological adjustment to recurrent genital herpes infections. Certainly, herpes is not the dread infection that some people believe it to be. In fact, many individuals have learned to cope effectively with it, as did the person in the following account:

> When I first discovered I had herpes several years ago, my first reaction was, "Oh no, my sex life is destroyed!" I was really depressed and angry with the person who gave me the infection. However, with time I learned I could live with it, and I even began to gain some control over it. Now, on those infrequent occasions when I have an outbreak, I know what to do to hurry up the healing process. (Authors' files)

Treatment

At the time of this writing, no medical treatment has been proven effective in curing either oral or genital herpes. However, medical researchers are pursuing an effective treatment on many fronts, with mounting optimism. Recent research suggests that efforts to develop a herpes vaccine may yield positive results sometime in the future (Belshe et al., 2012). Current treatment strategies are designed to prevent outbreaks or to reduce discomfort and to speed healing during an outbreak.

Three separate antiviral drugs are often highly effective in the management of herpes. Oral acyclovir taken several times daily is a common drug treatment for genital herpes. Two other antiviral agents, valacyclovir (Valtrex) and famciclovir (Famvir), taken orally, have also proven effective for management of genital herpes (Workowski et al., 2010).

Two antiviral treatment strategies are used to manage recurrent genital herpes infections. In *suppressive therapy* medication is taken daily to prevent recurrent outbreaks. Suppressive therapy often prevents HSV reactivation and development of herpes lesions (Workowski et al., 2010). Suppressive therapy also reduces asymptomatic viral shedding between outbreaks and decreases the risk of sexual transmission of HSV infections (Workowski et al., 2010). *Episodic treatment* involves treating herpes outbreaks when they occur with an antiviral agent. Episodic treatment has been shown to reduce the duration and severity of lesion pain and the time needed for total healing (Worcester, 2010). However, episodic treatment does not reduce the risk for transmitting HSV to a sexual partner (Workowski et al., 2010).

A number of other measures can provide relief from the discomfort associated with herpes. The following suggestions can be helpful. Because the effectiveness of these measures varies from person to person, we encourage people to experiment to find an approach that best meets their needs.

1. Keeping herpes blisters clean and dry will lessen the possibility of secondary infections, significantly shorten the period of viral shedding, and reduce the total time of lesion healing. Washing the area with warm water and soap two to three times daily is adequate for cleaning. After bathing, dry the area thoroughly by patting it gently with a soft cotton towel or by blowing it with a hair dryer set on cool. Because the moisture that occurs naturally in the genital area can slow the healing process, sprinkling the dried area liberally with cornstarch or baby powder can help. It is desirable to wear loose cotton clothing that does not trap moisture (cotton underwear absorbs moisture, but nylon traps it).

2. Two aspirin every 3 to 4 hours might help to reduce the pain and itching. Application of a local anesthetic, such as lidocaine jelly, can also help to reduce soreness. Ice packs applied directly to the lesions can also provide temporary relief (but avoid wetting the lesions as the ice melts). Keeping the area liberally powdered can also alleviate itching.

3. Some people have an intense burning sensation when they urinate if the urine comes into contact with herpes lesions. This discomfort can be reduced by pouring water over the genitals while voiding or by urinating in a bathtub filled with water. It might help to dilute the acid in the urine by drinking lots of fluids (but avoid liquids that make the urine more acidic, such as cranberry juice).

4. Because stress has been implicated as a triggering event in recurrent herpes, it is a good idea to try to reduce this negative influence. A variety of approaches may help reduce stress. These include relaxation techniques, yoga or meditation, and counseling about ways to cope with daily pressures.

5. If you are prone to repeated relapses of herpes, try recording events that occur immediately before an outbreak (either after the fact or as part of an ongoing journal). You may be able to recognize common precipitating events, such as fatigue, stress, or excessive sunlight, which you can then avoid in the future. ●

Genital Warts

Genital warts are caused by a virus called the *human papillomavirus* (HPV). Application of recently developed technology has led to the identification of more than 100 types of HPV, about half of which cause genital infections (Workowski et al., 2010).

genital warts
Viral warts that appear on the genitals and are primarily transmitted sexually.

Incidence and Transmission

The incidence of HPV infections has been increasing so rapidly in both sexes that this infection has reached epidemic proportions in recent years. HPV is now the most common viral STI in the United States (Navas, 2010). It is estimated that at least 15% of people in the United States are infected with HPV (Centers for Disease Control, 2009g). At least 50% of sexually active people will acquire an HPV infection at some point in their lives (Centers for Disease Control, 2009g).

HPV is primarily transmitted through vaginal, anal, oral, or oral–genital sexual interaction. Transmission of HPV between the hands and genitals may also occur (Hernandez et al., 2008). Condoms, which significantly reduce transmission of many bacterial and viral infections, provide some protection but are far from an ideal preventive measure for HPV because the virus is often present on skin not covered by a condom (Thomas, 2008).

HPV passed during oral sex is a common cause of throat cancer among American men (Girshman, 2011). About 60% of throat cancers in the United States are attributed to this virus, and the recent rise in the incidence of this cancer has occurred predominantly among men (Gillison, 2012; Girshman, 2011).

Subclinical or asymptomatic infections with HPV are common, and viral shedding and transmission of the virus can occur during asymptomatic periods of infection. In fact, HPV is most commonly transmitted by asymptomatic individuals who do not realize that they are infected (Centers for Disease Control, 2009g).

Symptoms and Complications

Most people who have genital HPV infections do not develop visible symptoms and thus are unaware that they are infected (Centers for Disease Control, 2009g). Visible warts, which have an average incubation period of about 3 months, may appear within weeks or months after sexual contact with an infected person.

In women genital warts most commonly appear on the bottom part of the vaginal opening. They can also occur on the perineum, the labia, the inner walls of the vagina, and the cervix. In men genital warts commonly occur on the glans, foreskin, or shaft of the penis (see ▌ Figure 15.5). Genital warts can also occur in the anus of either sex (Wieland, 2012). In moist areas (such as the vaginal opening and under the foreskin), genital warts are pink or red and soft, with a cauliflower-like appearance. On dry skin areas they are generally hard and yellow-gray.

If left untreated, genital warts may disappear, remain unchanged, or increase in size and number (Centers for Disease Control, 2009g). A healthy immune system often suppresses the virus, and most infected people with an effective immune response will become HPV-negative in 6–24 months after the initial positive test for the virus.

Genital warts are sometimes associated with serious complications. They can invade the urethra, causing urinary obstruction and bleeding. Research has also revealed an association between HPV infection and cancers of the cervix, vagina, vulva, urethra, penis, and anus (Giuliano et al., 2011; Kim, 2011). The types of HPV that cause genital warts are not the same as the types that can cause cancer (Centers for Disease Control, 2009g). Recent evidence indicates that HPV infections account for 85–90% of the attributable risk for the development of cervical cancer, which is the second most common cancer diagnosed in women worldwide and the leading cause of death from

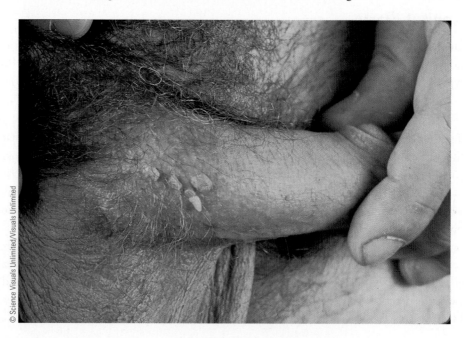

▌ **Figure 15.5** Genital warts on the penis.

© Science Visuals Unlimited/Visuals Unlimited

cancer among women in developing nations, where it kills about 250,000 women each year (Centers for Disease Control, 2009g; McNeil, 2011). However, there is actually little risk that a woman infected with HPV will develop cervical cancer unless the virus remains undetected and untreated (Centers for Disease Control, 2009g). This is the reason that regular Pap testing and appropriate follow-up treatment for precancerous lesions are essential to prevent most women from getting cervical cancer (Kahn & Hillard, 2006). A spokeswoman for the CDC recently stated that physicians often test young women for strains of HPV that are not associated with cervical cancer and thus needlessly subject women to unnecessary invasive tests (Saraiya in Neergaard, 2011).

Another rare but serious complication of HPV is that pregnant women infected with the virus can transmit it to their babies during birth (Rintala et al., 2005). Infected infants can develop a condition known as *respiratory papillomatosis*, which results from HPV infection of their upper respiratory tracts. Respiratory papillomatosis can have serious health consequences that produce lifelong distress and require multiple surgeries.

Treatment

No single treatment has been shown to be uniformly effective in removing warts or in preventing them from recurring. Current CDC guidelines suggest several fairly conservative approaches to HPV management that focus on the removal of visible warts. The most widely used treatments include cryotherapy (freezing) with liquid nitrogen or cryoprobe and topical applications of podofilox, imiquimod cream, or trichloroacetic acid. For large or persistent warts, cauterization by electric needle, vaporization by carbon dioxide laser, or surgical removal may be necessary. However, these more radical treatments can cause severe side effects. Even though there is no "cure" for HPV infections, genital warts often disappear on their own without treatment (Centers for Disease Control, 2009g). Consequently, some people elect to adopt a "wait and see" approach in lieu of immediate treatment.

In June 2006 Merck & Co., developer of a vaccine against four HPV types responsible for the majority of genital warts and cancers associated with HPV, obtained Food and Drug Administration (FDA) approval for their product Gardasil. In the same month, the Advisory Committee of Immunization Practices, appointed by the U.S. Department of Health and Human Services, voted unanimously that females ages 11–26 should be vaccinated with Gardasil (women older than 26 were not included in clinical trials) and that the vaccine should be available to girls as young as 9. Gardasil protects vaccine recipients against HPV types 16 and 18, two "high-risk" strains associated with the development of about 70% of cervical cancer cases (Centers for Disease Control, 2010d). The vaccine also blocks infection by two other strains of HPV (types 6 and 11), which are responsible for 90% of genital warts (Giuliano et al., 2011; Moon, 2011). Recent evidence also suggests that Gardasil could help reduce the incidence of oral cancer (cancer of the mouth or throat) caused by HPV, especially type 16 (Zelkowitz, 2009). The rate of oral cancer has risen steadily since 1973, and many health experts believe that this increase is related to the transmission of HPV via oral–genital contact (Zelkowitz, 2009).

In October 2009 the FDA licensed another HPV vaccine for use in females ages 9–26—Cervarix, produced by GlaxoSmithKline. This vaccine has also proven to be an effective prevention tool (Centers for Disease Control, 2010c). The Advisory Committee on Immunization Practices now recommends routine vaccination for females in the appropriate age range with either Gardasil or Cervarix.

Recently, the FDA also approved the use of Gardasil to prevent anal cancer in both males and females, ages 9–26 (Kuehn, 2011). In October 2009 the FDA licensed Gardasil as a tool for preventing HPV infections in males ages 9–26. A number of studies have demonstrated the effectiveness of Gardasil in males without accompanying serious adverse side effects (Giuliano et al., 2011; Kim, 2011).

Mandatory HPV vaccination for youth, especially for girls, has been the target of resistance from vocal political and religious organizations that oppose providing an STI prevention vaccine to teenagers and preteens. This is yet another example of how activist groups politicize public health issues related to sexual behavior, regardless of the harmful consequences of their actions, in seeking to exert control over our sexuality. The opposition to an HPV vaccine is mounted by the same groups that oppose over-the-counter sale of emergency contraception and comprehensive sex education in public schools because of the erroneous assumption that denying young people access to sexuality information, health protection, and birth control will prevent them from experiencing sexual intercourse before marriage.

The arguments for and against mandatory vaccination of American youth pose issues widely debated in both professional and nonprofessional circles. These viewpoints are outlined in the Sex and Politics box, "Arguments Against and For Mandatory HPV Vaccination."

Viral Hepatitis

Viral hepatitis (heh-puh-TIE-tus) is a disease in which liver function is impaired by a viral infection. There are three major types of viral hepatitis: hepatitis A, hepatitis B, and hepatitis C. Each of these forms of viral hepatitis is caused by a different virus.

Incidence and Transmission

As reflected in the annual rate of new hepatitis infections, hepatitis B is the most common form of viral hepatitis in the United States, followed in order of frequency by hepatitis A and hepatitis C (Centers for Disease Control, 2009h). Each of these three varieties of hepatitis infection has declined substantially in incidence over the last 20 years (Holtzman, 2008). Although all three types of hepatitis can be transmitted through sexual contact, types A and B are more likely to be transmitted sexually than type C. Hepatitis B is transmitted more often through sexual activity than is hepatitis A. Sexual transmission among adults accounts for most hepatitis B infections in the United States (Centers for Disease Control, 2009h). Hepatitis A is a relatively common infection of young homosexual men, especially those who have multiple sex partners and those who engage in anal intercourse or oral–anal contact (Centers for Disease Control, 2009h; Des Jarlais et al., 2003). Furthermore, both hepatitis A and hepatitis B are often transmitted by means of needle sharing among injection drug users (Centers for Disease Control, 2009h).

Hepatitis B can be transmitted through blood or blood products, semen, vaginal secretions, and saliva (Torpy et al., 2011). An infected mother can transmit a hepatitis B infection to her baby at birth (Centers for Disease Control, 2009h). The CDC recommends that pregnant women be tested for hepatitis B. Manual, oral, or penile stimulation of the anus is strongly associated with the spread of this viral agent. Hepatitis A seems to be spread primarily through the fecal–oral route. Consequently, epidemics often occur when infected handlers of food do not wash their hands properly after using the bathroom. Oral–anal sexual contact seems to be a primary mode for sexual transmission of hepatitis A (Centers for Disease Control, 2009h).

Recently, health officials in the United States have focused considerable attention on the most health-threatening of the hepatitis viruses, hepatitis C, which is an emerging communicable disease of epidemic proportions (Centers for Disease Control, 2010b; Edlin, 2011). Over the last few years, hepatitis C has become a major global

Critical Thinking Question

Should government agencies have the option of denying teenage women access to an HPV vaccine? Why or why not? What are the implications for society of politicizing and possibly blocking a chance to prevent cervical cancer?

viral hepatitis
An ailment in which liver function is impaired by a viral infection.

The controversy surrounding possible implementation of mandatory HPV vaccination for middle-school girls in the United States is grounded in political, religious, moral, economic, and sociocultural arguments (Gostin, 2011). One leading expert on the legality of mandatory HPV vaccination recently concluded that states have the constitutional authority to mandate such vaccinations (Dowling, 2008). Whether such laws will be adopted depends largely on the persuasiveness of nonlegal arguments.

Arguments Against Mandatory HPV Vaccination

Opponents of mandatory HPV vaccinations in public schools argue that parents, not government or school officials, should decide what is best for the protection of their children (Gostin, 2011). Why, they ask, should government be allowed to force people to undergo a medical solution to a potential health problem when HPV infection can be avoided through behavioral control?

Other arguments against mandatory HPV vaccination are based on medical evidence and economic factors. Gardasil protects against four types of HPV, "which together affect only about 3.5% of the female population" (Dowling, 2008, p. 74). This fact calls into question the practicality and necessity of requiring a costly vaccination that will benefit only a small number of women. The total cost of one vaccination series (3 shots given over a 6-month period) exceeds $300. Moreover, protection fades after 5 to 8 years, necessitating additional costly vaccination series (Tomljenovic & Shaw, 2012). The fact that Gardasil protects only against strains of HPV associated with 70% of cervical cancer cases suggests that the risk of developing this form of cancer later in life may not be proportional to the costs of required vaccination of all middle-school girls.

Other medically based arguments against mandatory HPV vaccination include concern that Gardasil has not been adequately tested to determine its long-term safety and efficacy and that HPV is not a highly contagious infection, like measles or chicken pox, that can be spread by casual contact. The majority of mandated vaccines in the United States protect against highly contagious diseases that cause serious and potentially widespread health problems. Some health officials suggest that at present it is not clear whether the risk of HPV-caused cervical cancer fits into this category. Gardasil has also been linked with a number of adverse side effects. However, health officials maintain that this vaccine is safe and appropriate for widespread use.

Arguments for Mandatory HPV Vaccination

Perhaps the most persuasive argument for mandatory HPV vaccination is clear evidence that the Gardasil vaccine is an important medical achievement that, if widely implemented, will result in a significant decrease in adverse health consequences, including death, for millions of American women (and men). Medical experts estimate that the "economic burden of HPV infections and their consequences cost[s] $5 billion per year in the United States alone" (Vamos et al., 2008, p. 305). Beyond the obvious monetary benefits of mandatory HPV vaccination, there are significant emotional and physical benefits associated with preventing the need for women to undergo invasive procedures to remove precancerous and cancerous cervical lesions, as well as the psychological stress women experience upon receiving word of an abnormal Pap smear. Moreover, a combination of HPV vaccination with routine Pap smear screening has the potential to largely eradicate cervical cancer in American women.

Mandatory HPV immunization for girls and perhaps for boys as well, at an age prior to the onset of sexual activity, is an ideal method for rapid and widespread implementation of a preventive health strategy for children regardless of socioeconomic status or race/ethnicity. Proponents of mandatory vaccination maintain that there can be little argument with the viewpoint that cervical cancer and other HPV-caused diseases are a significant enough health threat to classify a preventive measure effective against this threat as a public health necessity.

Medical and social scientists argue that while Gardasil has been shown to be safe in a well-designed clinical trial, there are widely publicized controversies surrounding HPV vaccination. These may prove beneficial to parent–child relationships by motivating parents to become more involved with their children regarding health decisions (Kowalczyk et al., 2012; London, 2011). Furthermore, recent research indicates that girls receiving HPV vaccinations continue to perceive a need for safer sexual behaviors after vaccination (Kowalczyk et al., 2012). Regardless of what actions parents advocate for their children (participating in or opting out of a school vaccination program or seeking immunization via a health-care provider outside the school setting), "[p]arents must assume a proactive posture with respect to their child's health care, an action for which parents or policy makers would be hard pressed to find a negative consequence" (Vamos et al., 2008, p. 307).

Arguments both against and in favor of mandatory HPV vaccinations have been voiced by activist groups, medical experts, and parents. Only time will tell how these arguments influence future decisions about implementing a mandatory HPV vaccination program in America's schools.

health problem, and it is now one of the most common chronic viral infections in North America. It is estimated that approximately 200 million people in the world have chronic hepatitis C infections—5 million of whom are in the United States (Centers for Disease Control, 2010b; Gravitz, 2011). People whose immune systems are deficient, such as HIV-infected individuals, are especially vulnerable to hepatitis C infections, which cause 12,000 deaths each year in the United States (Centers for Disease Control, 2010b).

Hepatitis C is transmitted most commonly through blood-contaminated needles shared by injection drug users (Centers for Disease Control, 2011b; Gravitz, 2011). Other, less common modes of transmission include transfusion of contaminated blood products, sexual contact, and perinatal transmission from an infected mother to her fetus or infant (Centers for Disease Control, 2009h). Whether transmission of hepatitis C through unprotected sexual intercourse is a significant factor in the spread of hepatitis C is debatable, but evidence indicates that some hepatitis C infections are sexually transmitted, especially among HIV-infected MSM (Centers for Disease Control, 2009h; Fierer et al., 2011; Montoya-Ferrer et al., 2011).

Symptoms and Complications

Symptoms of viral hepatitis vary from nonexistent to mild flulike symptoms (poor appetite, upset stomach, diarrhea, sore muscles, fatigue, headache) to an incapacitating illness characterized by high fever, vomiting, and severe abdominal pain. One of the most notable signs of viral hepatitis is a yellowing of the whites of the eyes; the skin of light-complexioned people can also take on a yellow, or jaundiced, look. Hospitalization is required only in severe cases. Chronic infections with hepatitis B or C are a major risk factor for developing liver cirrhosis, end-stage liver disease, and cancer of the liver, one of the most common cancers in the world (Centers for Disease Control, 2012c; Torpy et al., 2011).

Treatment

No specific therapy is known to be effective against hepatitis A. Treatment generally consists of bed rest and adequate fluid intake to prevent dehydration. The disease generally runs its course in a few weeks, although complete recovery can take several months in cases of severe infection. Infection with hepatitis B is typically treated in the same manner as hepatitis A, and it also generally runs its course in a few weeks. However, sometimes hepatitis B infections become chronic and persist for more than 6 months. An estimated 800,000 to 1.4 million Americans have a chronic hepatitis B infection (Centers for Disease Control, 2009h). These chronic infections can be treated with several antiviral drugs (Quan, 2008; Shamliyan et al., 2009).

Hepatitis C presents a more serious treatment problem. For most of the estimated 5 million Americans who have a hepatitis C infection, the disease is relatively mild, remains stable over several decades, and does not significantly erode the person's health (Centers for Disease Control, 2009h; Edlin, 2011). However, for about one quarter of those who develop the progressive form of the disease, active treatment is essential to avert severe complications and/or death (Centers for Disease Control, 2009h). By 2007 hepatitis C had superseded AIDS as a cause of death in the United States (Ly et al., 2012). Hepatitis C causes half of all liver cancers and is the most prevalent reason for liver transplants in the United States (Chung, 2012; Schlutter, 2011). A combination therapy with the antiviral drugs peglated interferon and ribavirin has been shown to be relatively effective in controlling some cases of chronic hepatitis C infection (Chung, 2008; Rodriguez-Torres et al., 2009). Recent research indicates that adding either of the drugs teleprevir or boceprevir to the peglated interferon/ribavirin protocol may significantly reduce the time necessary to successfully treat a chronic hepatitis C infection (Alter & Liang, 2012; Liu et al., 2012).

An effective and safe vaccine to prevent hepatitis B infection has been available since 1982, and in 1995 the U.S. Food and Drug Administration approved an effective and safe hepatitis A vaccine. Since the development and implementation of vaccinations for hepatitis A and B, the incidence of these infections in the United States has fallen dramatically to historic lows (Centers for Disease Control, 2010e; Ward, 2008). Unfortunately, no effective vaccine for hepatitis C exists, although efforts are under way to develop this prevention tool (Eisenstein, 2011).

Common Vaginal Infections

Several kinds of vaginal infections can be transmitted through sexual interaction. The infections we discuss in this section are also frequently contracted through nonsexual means. *Vaginitis* and *leukorrhea* are general terms applied to a variety of vaginal infections characterized by a whitish discharge. The secretion can also be yellow or green because of the presence of pus cells, and it often has a disagreeable odor. Additional symptoms of vaginitis include irritation and itching of the genital tissue, burning sensation during urination, and pain around the vaginal opening during intercourse.

Vaginal infections are common. Practically every woman experiences one or more of these infections during her lifetime. In fact, vaginitis is one of the most common reasons women consult health-care providers (Head, 2008). Under typical circumstances many of the organisms that cause vaginal infections are relatively harmless. In fact, some routinely live in the vagina and cause no trouble unless something alters the normal vaginal environment and allows them to overgrow. The vagina normally houses bacteria (*lactobacilli*) that help maintain a healthy vaginal environment. The pH of the vagina is usually sufficiently acidic to ward off most infections. However, certain conditions can alter the pH toward the alkaline side, which can leave a woman vulnerable to infection. Some factors that increase the likelihood of vaginal infection include antibiotic therapy, use of contraceptive pills, menstruation, pregnancy, wearing pantyhose and nylon underwear, and lowered resistance from stress or lack of sleep. Douching also increases the risk of vaginal infections, especially bacterial vaginosis (Centers for Disease Control, 2009i; Cottrell & Close, 2008). In spite of the negative health consequences associated with douching, evidence indicates that almost 36% of women of childbearing age in the United States engage in douching (Cottrell & Close, 2008).

Most women with vaginitis have an infection diagnosed as bacterial vaginosis, candidiasis, or trichomoniasis. Bacterial vaginosis is the most common of these infections.

Bacterial Vaginosis

Bacterial vaginosis (BV) is a vaginal infection caused by a replacement of the normal vaginal *lactobacilli* by an overgrowth of microorganisms, which can include anaerobic bacteria, *Mycoplasma* bacteria, and a bacterium known as *Gardnerella vaginalis*.

bacterial vaginosis (BV)
A vaginal infection caused by bacterial microorganisms; it is the most common form of vaginitis among U.S. women.

Incidence and Transmission

The presence of moderate levels of bacterial microorganisms in the vaginal environment is normal. However, under conditions of decreased levels of beneficial *lactobacilli*, an overgrowth of other vaginal microorganisms occurs. This can result in high concentrations of one or more of the bacterial microorganisms associated with BV (Marrazzo et al., 2011). BV is the most common vaginal infection in U.S. women (Centers for Disease Control, 2009i). Although the role of sexual transmission in BV is not fully understood, it is believed that coitus often provides a mode of transmission for the infection. BV occurs more frequently among sexually active women than among sexually inactive women (Doskoch, 2005). Furthermore, although BV is common among women in general, it is even more common among women with female sex partners (Gorgos et al., 2011). However, BV is not necessarily sexually transmitted, because this infection has been diagnosed in teenagers and women who have not experienced sexual intercourse (Coco & Vandenbosche, 2000).

Symptoms and Complications

Most women who are infected with BV manifest no overt symptoms of this infection (Centers for Disease Control, 2009i). However, when present, the most common symptom of bacterial vaginosis in women is a foul-smelling, thin discharge that resembles flour paste in consistency. The discharge is usually gray or white, but it can also be yellow or green. The disagreeable odor, often noticed first by an infected woman's sexual partner, is typically described as fishy or musty. This smell may be particularly noticeable after coitus because the alkaline seminal fluid reacts with the bacteria, causing the release of the chemicals that produce the smell. A small number of infected women experience irritation of the genital tissues and a mild burning sensation during urination. Recent evidence suggests a link between bacterial vaginosis and both PID and adverse pregnancy outcomes, including premature rupture of the amniotic sac and preterm labor (Centers for Disease Control, 2009i; Marrazzo et al., 2011).

Having a BV infection can both increase a woman's susceptibility to HIV infection if she is exposed to this virus and increase the probability that an HIV-infected woman will transmit HIV to her sexual partner(s) (Centers for Disease Control, 2009i).

Men may also harbor the infectious organisms that cause BV, often without manifesting detectable symptoms. However, some infected males develop inflammation of the foreskin and glans of the penis, **urethritis** (inflammation of the urethral tube), and **cystitis** (bladder infection).

urethritis
An inflammation of the urethral tube.

cystitis
An infection of the bladder.

Treatment

For many years the treatment of choice for bacterial vaginosis has been metronidazole (Flagyl) taken by mouth for 7 days. However, recent research indicates that intravaginal application of topical metronidazole gel or clindamycin cream is as effective as oral metronidazole (Workowski et al., 2010). Studies indicate that there is little or no proven benefit in treating male sex partners of women diagnosed with BV (Centers for Disease Control, 2009i). Female sex partners should be evaluated and treated if necessary.

Candidiasis

candidiasis
An inflammatory infection of the vaginal tissues caused by the yeastlike fungus *Candida albicans*.

Candidiasis (kan-duh-DIE-uh-sus), also commonly referred to as a yeast infection, is primarily caused by a yeastlike fungus called *Candida albicans*.

Incidence and Transmission

Candidiasis is the second most common vaginal infection in North America. An estimated 75% of women will have at least one genital candidiasis infection in their lifetime (Workowski et al., 2010). The microscopic *Candida albicans* organism is normally present in the vagina of many women; it also inhabits the mouth and large intestine of a large number of women and men. A disease state results only when certain conditions allow the yeast to overgrow in the vagina. This accelerated growth can result from pregnancy, use of oral contraceptives, or diabetes—conditions that increase the amount of sugar stored in vaginal cells (*Candida albicans* thrives in the presence of sugar) (Centers for Disease Control, 2009j). Another factor is the use of oral antibiotics or spermicidal jellies or creams, which reduce the number of *lactobacilli* (mentioned earlier as important for a healthy vaginal environment). This reduction permits *Candida albicans* to multiply rapidly.

If the yeast organism is not already present in the woman's vagina, it can be transmitted to this area in a variety of ways. It can be conveyed from the anus by wiping back to front or on the surface of a menstrual pad, or it can be transmitted through sexual interaction, because the organism can be harbored in various reservoirs in the male body, especially under the foreskin of an uncircumcised man (Ringdahl, 2000). The organism can also be passed from a partner's mouth to a woman's vagina during oral sex (Greer, 1998).

Symptoms

A woman with a yeast infection may notice that she has a white, clumpy discharge that looks something like cottage cheese. In addition, candidiasis is often associated with intense itching and soreness of the vaginal and vulval tissues, which typically become red and dry.

Treatment

A variety of treatments have proved effective in combating yeast infections. Traditional treatment strategies consist of vaginal suppositories or topical creams, such as clotrimazole, miconazole, butoconazole, or terconazole. Over-the-counter intravaginal preparations of clotrimazole and miconazole are now available for treatment of candidiasis; however, these medications are recommended only for women who have previously been medically diagnosed and treated and who have a recurrence of symptoms.

Two drugs taken by mouth, fluconazole and itraconazole, have also proven effective in treating candidiasis (Pitsouni et al., 2008). Because *Candida albicans* is a hardy organism, treatment should be continued for the prescribed length of time (usually several days to 2 weeks), even though the symptoms may disappear in 2 days.

Practical tips to help women reduce the risk of a yeast infection include decreasing sugar intake, adding yogurt or a daily *lactobacillus acidophilus* supplement to their diet, and avoiding glycerin-based lubricants that can fuel a yeast infection (Fink, 2006).

Trichomoniasis

Trichomoniasis (trih-kuh-muh-NIE-uh-sus) is caused by a one-celled protozoan parasite called *Trichomonas vaginalis*.

trichomoniasis
A form of vaginitis caused by the one-celled protozoan *Trichomonas vaginalis*.

Incidence and Transmission

Trichomoniasis is a common STI in both women and men. Between 7 and 8 million new cases of trichomoniasis occur each year in the United States (Centers for Disease Control, 2009k). The primary mode of transmission of this infection is through sexual contact. Women can acquire it from infected men via penile–vaginal intercourse and from infected women via vulva-to-vulva contact; however, men usually contract trichomoniasis only from infected women via coitus (Centers for Disease Control, 2009k).

Symptoms and Complications

The most common symptom of trichomoniasis infection in women is an abundant, frothy, white or yellow-green vaginal discharge with an unpleasant odor. The discharge can irritate the tissues of the vagina and vulva, causing them to become inflamed, itchy, and sore (Centers for Disease Control, 2009k). The infection is usually limited to the vagina and sometimes the cervix, but occasionally the organism invades the urethra, bladder, or Bartholin's glands. Inflammation of genital tissues caused by trichomoniasis can increase a woman's susceptibility to HIV infection and increase the probability that an HIV-infected woman will transmit HIV to her sex partner(s) (Centers for

Disease Control, 2009k). Untreated trichomoniasis infection in pregnant women is associated with premature rupture of the amniotic sac and preterm delivery (Centers for Disease Control, 2009k; Huppert, 2006). Trichomoniasis infections in men, usually asymptomatic, may be associated with an urge to urinate frequently, painful urination, or a slight urethral discharge.

Treatment

To avoid passing the protozoan back and forth, it is important that the sex partner(s) of an infected woman be treated, even if they are asymptomatic. If a male partner is not treated, the couple should use condoms to prevent reinfection. The recommended drug regimen for both sexes is a single 2-gram dose of metronidazole (Flagyl) or tinidazole taken by mouth. ●

Ectoparasitic Infections

ectoparasites
Parasitic organisms that live on the outer skin surfaces.

Ectoparasites are parasitic organisms that live on the outer skin surfaces of humans and other animals (*ecto* means "outer"). Two relatively common STIs are caused by ectoparasites: pubic lice and scabies.

Pubic Lice

pubic lice
Lice that primarily infest the pubic hair and are transmitted by sexual contact.

Pubic lice, more commonly called crabs, belong to a group of parasitic insects called biting lice. They are known technically as *Phthirus pubis*. Although tiny, adult lice are visible to the naked eye. They are yellowish-gray and under magnification resemble crabs, as ▮ Figure 15.6 shows. A pubic louse (the singular of lice) generally grips a pubic hair with its claws and sticks its head into the skin, where it feeds on blood from tiny blood vessels.

Incidence and Transmission

Pubic lice are quite common and are seen frequently in public health clinics and by private physicians. Pubic lice are especially prevalent among young (15- to 25-year-old) single people and are frequently associated with the presence of other sexually transmitted infections. Pubic lice are often transmitted during sexual contact when two people bring their pubic areas together (Centers for Disease Control, 2009b). The lice can live away from the body for 1 to 2 days, particularly if their stomachs are full of blood. They may drop off onto underclothes, bedsheets, sleeping bags, and so forth. Eggs deposited by the female louse on clothing or bedsheets can survive for several days. Thus it is possible to get pubic lice by sleeping in someone else's bed or by wearing his or her clothes. Furthermore, a successfully treated person can be reinfected by being exposed to her or his own unwashed sheets or underclothes. Pubic lice do not necessarily limit themselves to the genital areas. They can be transmitted, usually by the fingers, to the armpits or scalp.

Symptoms

Most people begin to suspect something is amiss when they start itching. Suspicions become stronger when scratching brings no relief. However, a few people seem to have great tolerance for the bite of a louse, experiencing little if any discomfort. Self-diagnosis is possible simply by locating a louse on a pubic hair.

▮ **Figure 15.6** A pubic louse, or "crab."

© E. Gray/SPL/Photo Researchers, Inc.

Treatment

Both prescription and over-the-counter medications (lotions and creams) are available for treatment of pubic lice (Centers for Disease Control, 2009b). These medications should be applied to all affected areas and washed off after a few minutes. It is advisable to apply the lotion or cream to all areas where there are concentrations of body hair—the genitals, armpits, scalp, and even eyebrows. These treatments should be repeated 7 to 10 days later if lice are still present. Be sure to wash all clothes and sheets that were used before treatment.

Scabies

Scabies is caused by a tortoise-shaped parasitic mite with four stubby legs called *Sarcoptes scabiei*. Unlike pubic lice, mites are too tiny to be seen by the naked eye. Scabies infestations are initiated by the female mite; after mating, she burrows beneath the skin to lay her eggs, which hatch shortly thereafter. Each hatched egg becomes a full-grown adult in 10 to 20 days. The adult mite forages for nourishment in the host's skin that is adjacent to the site of the original burrow. The average person with scabies is infested with 5 to 15 live adult female mites (Centers for Disease Control, 2009m).

scabies
An ectoparasitic infestation of tiny mites.

Incidence and Transmission

Although scabies is not among the infectious conditions reported to health organizations in the United States and elsewhere, the worldwide prevalence of this infection is estimated at about 300 million annual cases (Chosidow, 2006). Scabies is a highly contagious condition that can be transmitted by close physical contact, both sexual and nonsexual. The mites can also be transferred on clothing or bedding, where they can remain viable for up to 72 hours (Centers for Disease Control, 2009m). In addition to sexually active people, schoolchildren, nursing home residents, and indigent people are especially at risk for scabies infestations.

Symptoms

Symptoms of first-time scabies infections may not appear for up to 2 months after the person has been infested by the mites (Centers for Disease Control, 2009m). Small vesicles or pimplelike bumps occur in the area where the female mite tunnels into the skin. A red rash around the primary lesion indicates the area where hatched adult mites are feeding. Areas of infestation itch intensely, especially at night. Favorite sites of infestation typically include the webs and sides of fingers, wrists, abdomen, genitals, buttocks, and female breasts.

Treatment

Scabies is treated with a topical scabicide (lotion or cream product used to kill scabies) that is applied from the neck down to the toes. Several prescription scabicides are available; they are applied at bedtime and left on for 8 hours, then washed off with soap and water. A single application is usually effective, although some physicians advocate a second application 7–10 days later. It is recommended that all household members and close contacts of an infested person, including asymptomatic ones, be treated simultaneously. In addition, all clothing and bedding used by treated people should be washed in hot water or dry cleaned.

Acquired Immunodeficiency Syndrome (AIDS)

The **acquired immunodeficiency syndrome (AIDS)** epidemic is now recognized as the most serious disease pandemic of our time. An all-out research assault on this deadly disease, unprecedented in scope and extent, is being conducted throughout the world, and new findings are surfacing with startling rapidity.

acquired immunodeficiency syndrome (AIDS)
A catastrophic illness in which a virus (HIV) invades and destroys the ability of the immune system to fight disease.

At the end of the three decades since AIDS was first identified, researchers worldwide are pursuing ways to improve prevention and treatment of this disease while continuing to seek a cure (Dieffenbach & Fauci, 2011). We address these unprecedented efforts in the following pages.

AIDS results from infection with the **human immunodeficiency virus (HIV)**. HIV falls into a special category of viruses called *retroviruses*, so named because they reverse the usual order of reproduction within cells they infect, a process called *reverse transcription*.

Two forms of HIV have been linked with the development of AIDS: HIV-1 and HIV-2. HIV-1 was the first human immunodeficiency virus to be identified and is the one that causes the greatest number of AIDS cases in the United States and throughout the world (De Cock et al., 2011). HIV-2 occurs in some African countries along with HIV-1. HIV-1, the more virulent of the two forms, is a formidable enemy because it is constantly mutating and is present in multiple strains or subtypes (Osborn, 2008; Taylor et al., 2008). To simplify our discussion of AIDS, we refer to the infective agent simply as HIV.

A great deal of speculation about the origin of AIDS has occurred since the emergence of the global pandemic. It has been variously proposed that HIV came from residents of Africa or Haiti, mosquitoes, monkeys, pigs, or even from early testing of a polio vaccine in Africa in the 1950s. Recently published research appears to have solved the riddle of the origin of HIV/AIDS. Persuasive evidence that HIV was introduced to humans from chimpanzees was obtained by two international teams of scientists who traced the roots of HIV to a related virus in a subspecies of chimpanzees that reside in central and southwestern Africa (Gao et al., 1999; Keele et al., 2006). Genetic analysis revealed that this subspecies, *Pan troglodytes troglodytes*, harbors a simian immunodeficiency virus (SIV) that is the origin of HIV-1. Evidence suggests that SIV is quite ancient, at least 32,000 years old (Worobey et al., 2010). Scientists believe that SIV genetically converted to HIV either while it was still in a chimpanzee or after a human contracted SIV, perhaps through exposure to chimpanzee blood from hunting or handling the meat during food preparation (De Cock et al., 2011).

Armed with evidence implicating a specific subspecies of chimpanzees in the origin of HIV, another research team conducted tests that allowed them to estimate that HIV first evolved from the SIV carried by these chimpanzees sometime between 1915 and 1941, with 1931 being the most likely year (Korber et al., 2000). With such an early date of origin, why was HIV not identified as the AIDS-causing virus until 1983? Scientists believe that when SIV turned into a human killer, probably in the early 1930s, it likely remained confined to a small population in an isolated area, such as a village, until migration into large cities and jet travel spread the virus worldwide. Evidence that HIV existed well before its identification was provided by discovery of HIV in a frozen blood sample collected in 1959 from an adult male residing in Africa (De Cock et al., 2011; Zhu et al., 1998). Thus it now appears likely that HIV originated early in the 20th century by means of cross-species transmission from a subspecies of chimpanzees to humans, and then was spread worldwide much later, when Africa became less isolated.

HIV specifically targets and destroys the body's CD4 lymphocytes, also called T-helper cells or helper T-4 cells. In healthy people these cells coordinate the immune system's response to disease. The impairment of the immune system resulting from HIV infections leaves the body vulnerable to a variety of cancers and opportunistic infections (infections that take hold because of the reduced effectiveness of the immune system). Initially, HIV infection was diagnosed as AIDS only when the immune system became so seriously impaired that the person developed one or more severe, debilitating diseases, such as cancer or an unusual form of pneumonia caused by the protozoan *Pneumocystis carinii*. However, effective January 1, 1993, the CDC broadened this definition of AIDS to include any HIV infection in which the immune system is severely impaired. Now anyone who is infected with HIV and has a CD4 count of 200 cells or less per microliter of blood is considered to have AIDS, regardless of other symptoms. (Normal CD4 counts in healthy people not infected with HIV range from 600 to 1,200 cells per microliter of blood.)

Incidence

By January 2011 well over 1 million cumulative cases of AIDS had been reported in the United States, and almost 600,000 people had died of the disease since it was first diagnosed in 1981. The number of people in the United States living with HIV, approximately 1.2 million, continues to increase (Tasker, 2011; Torian et al., 2011). About 20% of people in the United States living with HIV are unaware of their HIV status (Centers for Disease Control, 2011f).

Each year about 2.6 million new HIV infections occur globally and almost 34 million people worldwide are infected (Dieffenbach & Fauci, 2011; Kelland, 2011). Before 2007, United Nations officials estimated that each year about 5 million new HIV infections occurred worldwide and that a total of about 40 million people were infected (UNAIDS, 2006). Recently, lower estimates of global HIV infection rates have been made based on a more accurate method for assessing worldwide HIV infection prevalence (Cheng, 2007). While the decline in global infection rates is due largely to revised numbers reflecting better methodology, there is mounting evidence that the HIV/AIDS pandemic is losing some of its global momentum (Brown, 2010). By the end of the first decade of the 21st century, the number of new HIV infections worldwide was nearly 20% lower than a decade earlier (Brown, 2010). The downward trend in the number of global HIV infections is the result of many influences, including a reduction of risky sexual behaviors, lower infectious risk among people undergoing antiretroviral drug treatment, and significant success in preventing mother-to-child HIV transmission (Brown, 2010). The decline in HIV/AIDS may also reflect "the epidemics' natural history, in which the annual number of new infections peaks and then declines as the disease saturates high-risk groups in the population" (Brown, 2010, p. 9).

In sub-Saharan Africa, national epidemics have stabilized or even declined slightly in several countries (Steinbrook, 2008). Nevertheless, in spite of these encouraging signs, we cannot lose sight of the fact that the pandemic continues to rage. To date, more than 25 million people worldwide have already died of AIDS, and the disease claims about 2 million lives each year (Friedrich, 2011a; Kelland, 2011). Global annual death rates caused by AIDS peaked in 2005 and decreased over the next several years, due in part to wider availability of antiretroviral drug therapy (Brown, 2010; Jaffe, 2008). Sub-Saharan Africa is estimated to be home to roughly two thirds of all people living with AIDS. The hardest hit nation, South Africa, is home to about one sixth of the world's HIV-infected people (De Cock et al., 2011).

The number of new AIDS cases reported annually in the United States grew rapidly throughout the early 1980s, increasing by about 85% each year, and reached a peak rate in the middle of the decade. Until recently, the CDC estimated that approximately 40,000 new HIV infections have occurred annually in the United States since the early 1990s through 2007. However, recent evidence indicates that federal officials have been underestimating the number of new HIV infections for more than a decade (Maugh, 2008). New laboratory-based procedures, which make possible improved estimation of HIV infection incidence, indicate that approximately 50,000 to 56,000 new infections have occurred each year during this period (Centers for Disease Control, 2010h; McNeil, 2011). Although the overall incidence of new HIV infections in the U.S. population has been stable for several years, the number of new cases among teenagers, women, and racial and ethnic minorities continues to rise (Guilamo-Ramos et al., 2011; Timpson et al., 2010).

Many people with AIDS were infected during their adolescent years (Balaji et al., 2008). Unfortunately, it is very uncommon for American adolescents to be tested for HIV. A recent nationwide survey found that only 12.7% of teenagers have been tested, with more females (14.7%) than males (10.9%) having had an HIV test (Centers for Disease Control, 2010h). The growing problem of HIV infection among adolescents has been attributed to a number of factors, including the following:

- Many teenagers have multiple sexual partners, increasing their exposure to infection.
- Many adolescents engage in sexual activity without using condoms.
- Access to condoms is generally more difficult for adolescents than for other age groups.
- Many adolescents do not use condoms correctly and consistently as revealed by the NSSHB (Reece et al., 2010b).
- Teenagers have high rates of other STIs, which are often associated with HIV infection.
- Substance abuse, which often increases risky behavior, is relatively widespread among adolescents (Freeman et al., 2011).
- Teenagers tend to be especially likely as a group to have feelings of invulnerability (see Chapter 12).
- On the other hand, a significant number of teenagers, nearly 15% according to a recent study, take chances and engage in risky behavior because of a strong sense of fatalism or belief they will die young (Borowsky et al., 2009).
- Homeless youth often engage in risky sexual behavior that increases their vulnerability to HIV infection (Rice et al., 2012).

MSM (men who have sex with men) and ethnic and racial minority groups in the United States account for a majority of the total number of AIDS cases reported since 1981 (Centers for Disease Control, 2011a; McCree et al., 2010). The higher AIDS rates among ethnic and racial minority groups might reflect, among other factors, (1) reduced access to health care, associated with disadvantaged socioeconomic status, (2) cultural or language barriers that limit access to information about strategies for preventing STIs, and (3) differences in HIV risk behaviors, especially higher rates of injection drug use.

Since AIDS first appeared in the United States, most cases have been directly or indirectly related to two risk-exposure categories: MSM and injection drug users. The prevalence of HIV infection in the United States remains highest among MSM, who account for 53–59% of HIV infections in the United States (Centers for Disease Control, 2011d; Oster et al., 2011). Reported AIDS cases among MSM declined sharply and then leveled off between the mid-1980s and the late 1990s (Adams et al., 2005). Unfortunately, the incidence rates of HIV infection among MSM are again moving upward (Centers for Disease Control, 2011d, 2011e; D. Smith et al., 2011). This resurgence of the HIV epidemic among MSM is especially prevalent among young MSM and among MSM of color (K. Jones et al., 2008; Oster et al., 2011; Mustanski, Newcomb et al., 2011).

In recent years an HIV/AIDS epidemic has emerged among MSM in countries in the Middle East and North Africa, especially Egypt, Sudan, and Tunisia (Friedrich, 2011a).

The number of HIV infections attributed to injection drug use has declined in recent years but still remains high at roughly 9% of new HIV infections occurring annually in the United States (Centers for Disease Control, 2012a).

In the United States about a third of all AIDS cases are attributable to heterosexual transmission (Maugh, 2008). Heterosexual contact has always been the primary form of HIV transmission worldwide, especially in Africa and Asia (Harris & Bolus, 2008; UNAIDS, 2006).

Over the last few years the number of women infected with HIV has steadily increased in the United States and worldwide (Harris & Bolus, 2008). In sub-Saharan Africa, women ages 15 to 24 are three to four times more likely to be infected with HIV than are young men their age (Underwood et al., 2011).

Research indicates that HIV is not as easily transmitted from women to men as it is from men to women (Shapiro & Ray, 2007). Thus the risk of becoming infected through heterosexual intercourse appears to be much greater for a female with an HIV-infected male partner than for a male with an infected female partner. One explanation for women's greater risk during heterosexual intercourse is that semen contains a higher concentration of HIV than vaginal fluids do, and the female mucosal surface is exposed to HIV in the ejaculate for a considerably longer time than a male's penis is exposed to HIV in vaginal secretions (Lamptey et al., 2006; Shapiro & Ray, 2007). In addition, a larger area of mucosal surface is exposed on the vulva and in the vagina than on the penis, and the female mucosal surface is subjected to greater potential trauma than is typically the case with the penis (Lamptey et al., 2006). Furthermore, some women engage in unprotected anal intercourse, a high-risk behavior because HIV transmission from an infected man to an uninfected woman is thought to be 10 times as likely with anal intercourse as with vaginal intercourse (Shapiro & Ray, 2007). In fact, receptive unprotected anal intercourse has been shown to be associated with the highest risk of HIV infection through sexual activity for both men and women (Jenness et al., 2011; Shapiro & Ray, 2007). Finally, adolescent women are especially biologically vulnerable to HIV infection because their immature reproductive tracts, especially the cervix, are highly susceptible to infection by STIs (Lamptey et al., 2006; Shapiro & Ray, 2007).

The global proportionate incidence of HIV/AIDS among women is considerably greater in Africa, Asia, and the Caribbean than in the United States. In sub-Saharan Africa—the epicenter of HIV/AIDS—about 57% of HIV infections among adults occur in women (Yount & Abraham, 2007). About 75–80% of HIV infections among African youth are of females (Tenkorang & Matick-Tyndale, 2008). It is estimated that among the 800,000 children infected with HIV each year (most in sub-Saharan African countries), about 90% of the infections result from mother-to-child transmission (Harris & Bolus, 2008; Stringer et al., 2008).

In developing nations, especially those in Africa, a majority of new HIV infections occur among 15- to 24-year-olds (Kim & Free, 2008). The terrible plight of Africa during these plague years is described in the following Sexuality and Diversity discussion.

SEXUALITY and DIVERSITY

AIDS in Africa: Death and Hope on a Ravaged Continent

To date, the vast majority of AIDS deaths have occurred in Africa, primarily in sub-Saharan nations, which contain about 10% of the global population but are home to approximately 70% of all people who are living with HIV/AIDS (Kelland, 2011). Of the millions of global AIDS orphans—children who have lost their parents to the disease—more than 90% reside in sub-Saharan Africa. Children in sub-Saharan African nations also often serve as the primary caregivers for parents living with HIV/AIDS (Skovdal, 2011).

For many years scientists and health professionals mistakenly assumed that the explosive spread of the pandemic in Africa, where HIV is transmitted primarily through heterosexual sex, was largely a function of risky sexual behavior reflected in a propensity of Africans to have sex at an early age and with a large number of partners. The falseness of this stereotypical notion about sexual behavior in Africa is revealed by numerous surveys indicating that sexual debut in Africa tends to occur in the late teens, just as it does in Europe and the United States, and that African men and women report similar, if not fewer, numbers of lifetime sexual partners than do heterosexuals in many Western nations (Epstein, 2007; Stephenson, 2010; Wellings et al., 2006). Why, then, are HIV infection rates so much higher in parts of Africa than in Western nations?

The answer to this question is perhaps best presented in a recent book written by Helen Epstein titled *The Invisible Cure: Africa, the West, and the Fight Against AIDS* (2007). Epstein, a molecular biologist, spent many years in Africa investigating the sky-high HIV infection rates in some regions of that continent. In her book she focuses on multiple, concurrent partnerships as the primary contributing factor to Africa's HIV/AIDS pandemic. In sub-Saharan African nations, a relatively high proportion of men and women are involved in simultaneous ongoing relationships with a small number of people—perhaps two or three—and these concurrent relationships might overlap for months or years. This pattern differs from the serial monogamy that is more common in Western cultures, and these "concurrent or simultaneous sexual partnerships are more dangerous than serial monogamy, because they link people up in a giant web of sexual relationships that creates ideal conditions for the rapid spread of HIV" (p. 55).

While relationship concurrency is clearly a major contributor to the HIV pandemic in sub-Saharan Africa, other factors also play an important role, not the least of which is a marked inclination among African youth to avoid using condoms during sexual intercourse. As pointed out elsewhere in this chapter, condoms are an important component of efforts to slow the HIV/AIDS pandemic in Africa. However, in many sub-Saharan nations, where young people account for about half of all new HIV infections, reported condom use among them remains low (Winskell et al., 2011).

The spread of HIV/AIDS in Africa is also strongly influenced by extremely limited health resources and government inaction (Dugger, 2008; Nullis, 2007). The absence of efficient health infrastructures has created major barriers to effective administration of antiretroviral drug treatment programs. This serious problem is further complicated by the reluctance of many African governments to recognize the seriousness of this pandemic and to mobilize whatever limited health resources are available to combat it. An especially disheartening example of government inaction or outright opposition to HIV/AIDS programs is provided by the nation of South Africa. For many years officials in this government, including former president Thabo Mbeki, refused to acknowledge that HIV causes AIDS (De Cock et al., 2011). Only recently, under a new government, has this nation finally begun to mobilize efforts to combat a disease that claims over 350,000 South African lives each year.

Cultural factors also play a significant role in perpetuating the African AIDS plague. African nations are male-dominated societies in which most women find themselves in relationships of economic dependency and sociocultural subordination to men (Higgins & Hirsch, 2007; Hindin & Muntifering, 2011). Women's lack of rights within relationships and their difficulties in negotiating safer sex with partners who dislike using condoms and typically refuse to acknowledge and discuss their other concurrent sexual relationships result in elevated vulnerability to HIV infection (Heisea et al., 2011; Onoya et al., 2011). Recent research conducted in 13 sub-Saharan African countries revealed that condom use by married couples is relatively uncommon (de Walgue & Kline, 2011). It is not uncommon for married African women, who are not engaged in extramarital sex, to be infected by their husbands, who are engaging in unprotected sex in outside relationships (Stephenson, 2010). Furthermore, the combination of poverty, economic inequity, and relationship power imbalances experienced by many African women often leads them to exchange sex for money, alcohol, gifts, and goods, a practice that significantly increases their risk of acquiring an HIV infection (Higgins & Hirsch, 2007; Watt et al., 2012). Research in Africa indicates that transactional sex can increase the risk of HIV infection in both sexes via involvement with multiple partners and inconsistent condom use (Watt et al., 2012).

Another cultural contributor to the spread of HIV in Africa is the practice of female genital cutting described in Chapter 3. The increased HIV risk associated with this practice is related to several factors, including possible HIV-tainted-blood contamination of cutting tools, increased risk among cut women of genital infections associated with increased susceptibility to HIV infection, and a stronger inclination to engage in anal intercourse, a high-risk behavior for acquiring HIV (Yount & Abraham, 2007).

Against such a grim background, can there be any hope for Africa's future? The answer is a cautious yes. Many government and nongovernment organizations (NGOs) are flooding Africa with disease specialists, financial resources, and affordable drugs to treat AIDS. Drug treatment–based programs have benefited from a dramatic decrease in the cost of antiretroviral drugs in recent years. The availability of generic versions of these medications, coupled with the willingness of Western pharmaceutical companies to provide them at "not for profit" prices, has, for example, dropped the cost of one widely used multiple-drug treatment regimen to 25 cents per day. In contrast, antiretroviral drugs can cost $20,000 or more a year for infected people in the United States (Tasker, 2011). While this increase in the affordability of treatment drugs in African nations is a marvelous improvement in the battle against HIV/AIDS, it is far from a panacea. For example, in Botswana, where antiretroviral drugs are widely available and where infection rates have stabilized and even declined slightly among some populations, the overall incidence of HIV infection is still "astonishingly high" (J. Cohen, 2008).

In recent years a number of educational programs focused on reducing HIV risk behaviors have been designed and implemented in developing countries, especially those located in sub-Saharan Africa. These innovative intervention methods use trained community members as *peer educators* to reach out in a grassroots educational effort that includes providing information and resources, a format for talking openly about sexual issues, and a supportive context for positive behavior changes. A major advantage of peer education is that this method places health-related knowledge in the hands of ordinary people, who act not only as peer educators but also as role models for positive behavior change. A number of studies have demonstrated that such grassroots programs increase the likelihood that people will engage in health-promoting behaviors (Campbell & Mzaidume, 2001; Crooks & Tucker, 2006; Wheeler, 2003).

A peer-educator–based HIV/AIDS intervention program was established some years ago in the Makindu region of southeastern Kenya, with planning and guidance provided by Bob Crooks and his wife, Sami Tucker, in collaboration with a number of Kenyan citizens and with the assistance of a German NGO. This program, partially funded by royalty revenues from this textbook, is described at the website *www.ithelps. org*. The involvement of Crooks and Tucker includes developing a research strategy to evaluate the impact of this grassroots program, designing and implementing a peer-educator–based educational strategy, and conducting 2-week training sessions for peer educator staff. Research evidence obtained via administration of anonymous pre- and postworkshop questionnaires has revealed improved awareness of HIV/AIDS risk behaviors and prevention strategies and significant increases in safer sexual behaviors among all categories of participants as a direct result of the Makindu program (Crooks & Tucker, 2006). In the fall of 2009 Crooks and Tucker launched a similar program in the South Coast region of Kenya.

Perhaps the best hope for Africa lies in the development of the ultimate weapon against any virus—an effective preventive vaccine. However, as discussed elsewhere in this chapter, progress on this front has been slow, and the likelihood of having such a vaccine soon is slight at best.

Transmission

HIV has been found in the semen, blood, vaginal secretions, saliva, urine, and breast milk of infected individuals. It also can occur in any other bodily fluids that contain blood, including cerebrospinal fluid and amniotic fluid. Blood, semen, and vaginal secretions are the three bodily fluids that most consistently contain high concentrations of the virus in infected people. Most commonly, HIV enters the body when bodily fluids are exchanged during unprotected vaginal or anal intercourse with an infected person. Transmission of HIV through sexual contact is estimated to be the cause of about 80% of worldwide HIV infections. HIV is also readily transmitted by means of blood-contaminated needles shared by injection drug users.

The virus can also be passed perinatally from an infected woman to her fetus before birth, to her infant during birth, or to her baby after birth through breast-feeding (Kumwenda et al., 2008; Osborn, 2008). Mother-to-child transmission (MTCT) is the primary way that children are infected with HIV.

The likelihood of transmitting HIV during sexual contact depends on both the viral dose and the route of HIV exposure. Viral dose is a direct effect of the **viral load**—how much virus is present in an infected person's blood. The viral load measurement widely used is the number of individual viruses in a milliliter of blood. In general, the greater the viral load, the higher the chance of transmitting the infection. As common sense would suggest, when a person is in a late stage of HIV/AIDS disease, with more advanced infection and thus greater viral load, he or she is highly infectious. However, many readers might be surprised to learn that evidence strongly indicates that in the initial period between exposure to HIV and the appearance of HIV antibodies in the blood—a period called *primary infection*, which usually lasts a few months—viral load can be extremely high, creating a state of heightened infectiousness (Harris & Bolus, 2008; Shapiro & Ray, 2007). This relatively brief peak in the transmissibility of HIV soon after a person is infected is especially troubling because most infected people are likely to remain unaware during these few months that they have been invaded by HIV. Some experts believe that transmission during primary infection accounts for a large portion of HIV infections worldwide (Cohen & Pilcher, 2005; Wawer et al., 2005).

The likelihood of infection during sexual activity is greater when HIV is transmitted directly into the blood (e.g., through small tears in the rectal tissues or vaginal walls) rather than onto a mucous membrane. Researchers have become increasingly aware that circumcision status affects a man's risk for contracting HIV. The foreskin of the uncircumcised penis is soft and prone to tiny lacerations that may allow HIV to enter the bloodstream more easily. In addition, the foreskin has high concentrations of CD4 and Langerhans cells, the immune cells typically targeted by HIV (Reynolds et al., 2004; Seppa, 2005). While health-care providers continue to debate the practice of circumcision on medical and ethical grounds, the case for circumcision as a means for reducing HIV transmission is building. Evidence supporting this position is discussed in the Spotlight on Research box, "Circumcision as a Strategy for Preventing HIV Infection."

Research also suggests that HIV can be transmitted during oral sex when the virus present in semen or vaginal secretions comes into contact with mucous membrane tissues in the mouth. Unfortunately, many people mistakenly consider oral sex to be a safe practice (Kaestle & Halpern, 2007). Current CDC recommendations for preventing HIV transmission call for using a condom during mouth-to-penis contact. However, it is rare for people to use condoms during oral sex (Torassa, 2000). If you engage in unprotected oral sex with partners whose HIV status is unknown, it would be wise to take certain precautions: Make sure that your gums are in good shape (oral sores or breaks in gum tissue provide HIV easier access to blood), avoid flossing immediately before or after sex (flossing can damage oral tissue and cause bleeding), and avoid taking

viral load
The amount of HIV present in an infected person's blood.

SEXUALHEALTH ▶

A number of health professionals and researchers have suggested that circumcision may significantly reduce the risk of HIV infection by removing an entry point for the virus—the thin foreskin with its high concentrations of cells that are easily infected by HIV. This contention is supported by several observational studies revealing that HIV infection is less prevalent in circumcised men than in uncircumcised men (Reynolds et al., 2004; WHO/UNAIDS, 2007). There is also strong empirical evidence from experimental clinical trials that circumcision provides some protection against HIV infection (Heisea et al., 2011). Three well-designed investigations, conducted in South Africa, Kenya, and Uganda, demonstrated that study participants who underwent circumcision experienced a 60%, 53%, and 51% reduction, respectively, in their risk of acquiring an HIV infection (Auvert et al., 2005; Bailey et al., 2007; Gray et al., 2007).

It is important to emphasize that circumcision does not in any way provide complete protection against HIV. Rather, it is best viewed as an additional strategy in the arsenal of tools used to prevent heterosexually acquired HIV infection in men (WHO/UNAIDS, 2007). Recent research indicates that circumcision may not provide protection from HIV transmission that occurs during insertive anal sex (Sanchez et al., 2011). Moreover, it appears that male circumcision may have no effect on the transmission of HIV from men to women (Berer, 2007; WHO/UNAIDS, 2007). Studies conducted in Uganda and Zimbabwe found no significant association between women's risk of acquiring an HIV infection and the circumcision status of their primary sexual partner (Turner et al., 2007). In addition, these investigations found no association between male circumcision and women's risk of acquiring chlamydia, gonorrhea, or trichomonal infections (Turner et al., 2007). There is, however, evidence that men who are circumcised are less vulnerable than uncircumcised men to infection by HPV (Auvert et al., 2008). A recent study of over 5,000 men found that circumcision significantly reduced the incidence of HPV and genital herpes infections as well as providing protection against HIV infection (Tobian et al., 2011).

The clear evidence that male circumcision for HIV prevention provides partial protection for HIV-negative men but not for their female partner(s) is highly problematic, as recently described by Marge Berer (2008), an expert in women's sexual and reproductive health and rights. Berer points out that while partners of circumcised men have an equal right to protection against HIV, the circumcised status of their male partners may in fact increase their vulnerability to HIV infection. For example, a circumcised man, falsely believing that he is not at risk for HIV infection, may choose not to practice safer sex, such as using condoms, thereby subjecting his partner to greater risk of infection. If a circumcised man "thinks he is protected, and he continues depositing semen in his partner's body unimpeded every time they have sex, then as I see it, his partner is in a worse position than before" (Berer, 2008, p. 172). A man who elects to be circumcised is able to achieve some protection for himself without any changes in his behavior. But for his sex partner(s) to achieve protection, safer sex is necessary. Thus, equity for partners of circumcised men is an issue that will be discussed and debated concurrently with the implementation of male circumcision programs in African nations in coming years.

Finally, two studies revealed potential obstacles to large-scale circumcision programs in Africa. In one study about one third of 1,007 young Kenyan men experienced complications (lacerations, scarring, etc.) after being circumcised (Bailey et al., 2008). The second study revealed that circumcision of all HIV-negative men in sub-Saharan Africa would be markedly less cost-effective than distributing free condoms to men who need them (McAllister et al., 2008). The authors of this report concluded that preventing one HIV infection via circumcision would cost almost $6,000—more than 100 times the cost of preventing a single infection with condoms.

ejaculated semen into your mouth. Furthermore, in light of the often substantial concentration of HIV in vaginal fluids, you might also be cautious about engaging in cunnilingus with a female partner who has not tested negative for HIV. Finally, even though there is some risk of HIV transmission via oral sex, the current consensus of experts is that unprotected oral sex is an effective risk reduction strategy compared to unprotected vaginal or anal penetration (Shapiro & Ray, 2007). ●

In the early 1980s, before the U.S. government required screening of donated blood for HIV, contaminated blood and blood products infected an estimated 25,000 transfusion recipients and people with blood-clotting disorders (such as hemophilia) in the United States (Graham, 1997). However, since early 1985, donated blood and blood products have been screened with extensive laboratory testing for the presence of HIV antibodies. "The risk of transfusion transmitted HIV infections has been almost eliminated by the use of questionnaires to exclude donors at higher risk for HIV infection and the use of highly sensitive laboratory screening to identify infected blood donations" (Centers for Disease Control, 2010f, p. 1335). There is no danger of being infected as a result of donating blood. Blood banks, the Red Cross, and other blood-collection centers use sterile equipment and a new disposable needle for each donor. Unfortunately, U.S. procedures for safeguarding the blood supply are not widely practiced globally. This problem is especially acute in some of the world's poorest nations, which also have high rates of blood-transmitted diseases, such as HIV and viral hepatitis (Lamptey et al., 2006).

Research indicates that a small percentage of people appear to be resistant to HIV infection and that about 1 in 300 untreated HIV-infected people do not progress to AIDS (Collins & Fauci, 2010; Lok, 2011). Evidence suggests that in some individuals this resistance has a genetic basis. Research in the laboratory of Stephen O'Brien (2003), a respected medical geneticist, has indicated that people who inherit two copies of a gene labeled CCR5-32, one from each parent, are resistant to HIV infection. CCR5 is a protein receptor on the surface of CD4 cells that acts as a docking station for HIV. People who are homozygous for the CCR5-32 gene—about 1% of White Americans—lack this docking station (HIV's doorway to cellular infection) and therefore are resistant to infection. This gene is much less common among African Americans, and the few copies of CCR5-32 among this population "derive exclusively from Caucasian gene flow to the African slaves and their descendants since their transport to America" (O'Brien, 2003, p. 215). This protective gene is completely absent in native African and native East Asian ethnic groups.

It is believed that the risk of transmitting HIV through saliva, tears, and urine is extremely low. Furthermore, no evidence indicates that the virus can be transmitted by casual contact, such as hugging, shaking hands, cooking or eating together, or other forms of casual contact with an infected person. All the research to date confirms that it is sexual contact with an infected person or sharing contaminated needles that places an individual at risk for HIV infection. Furthermore, certain high-risk behaviors increase the chance of infection. These behaviors include having multiple sexual partners, engaging in unprotected sex, having sexual contact with people known to be at high risk (such as injection drug users, sex workers, and people with multiple sexual partners), sharing drug injection equipment, and using noninjected drugs such as cocaine, marijuana, and alcohol, which can impair good decision making.

Symptoms and Complications

As with many other viruses, HIV often causes a brief flulike illness within a few weeks of initial infection. Symptoms include fevers, headaches, muscle aches, skin rashes, loss of appetite, diarrhea, fatigue, and swollen lymph glands (Harris & Bolus, 2008; Mosack et al., 2009). These initial reactions, which represent the body's defenses at work, tend to fade fairly rapidly. However, as the virus continues to deplete the immune system, other symptoms can occur, such as persistent or periodically repeating fevers, night sweats, weight loss, chronic fatigue, persistent diarrhea or bloody stools, easy bruising, persistent headaches, a chronic dry cough, and oral candidiasis. Candidiasis of the mouth and throat is the most common infection in HIV-infected people. Many of these physical manifestations also indicate common, everyday ailments that are by no means life threatening. However, observing that you have one or more of these symptoms that are persistent can alert you to seek a medical diagnosis of your ailment.

The late tennis great Arthur Ashe at a news conference announcing that he had AIDS as a result of receiving an HIV-tainted blood transfusion.

© Bettmann/CORBIS

HIV Antibody Tests

Within a few months of being infected with HIV, most people develop antibodies to the virus, in a process called *seroconversion*. Seroconversion typically occurs sometime between 25 days and 6 months after initial infection. HIV infection can be detected by standard blood tests for blood serum antibodies to HIV. Most HIV tests are now performed with a simplified diagnostic test kit that uses a finger-stick sample of blood and provides results that are 99.6% accurate in as little as 20 minutes. HIV antibodies can also be detected with a high degree of accuracy in urine and saliva samples (Wright & Katz, 2006). A survey of 128 U.S. college health centers found that HIV tests are widely available at campus clinics (Smith & Roberts, 2009). For more information about HIV tests and test sites, contact the CDC National Hotline at 1-800-232-4636 or go online to the website of the American Social Health Association.

Home testing for HIV, via the OraQuick HIV test, may soon be available. In May 2012, this test was approved by a 17-member FDA panel. The test, which utilizes a mouth swab, appears to be slightly less accurate than a professionally administered HIV test (Bacon, 2012).

Although quite uncommon, "silent" HIV infections can be present in some individuals for 3 years or more before being detected by standard serum antibody tests. More costly and more labor-intensive tests for the virus itself can be performed to detect a silent or latent infection. Once infected with HIV, a person should be considered contagious and capable of infecting others indefinitely, regardless of whether clinical signs of disease are present.

Many public health officials are advocating for greater use of a new blood test for genetic traces of HIV. The advantage of this procedure, compared to standard HIV tests, is that it can detect an HIV infection within 7 to 10 days of occurrence (Tuller, 2009). Identifying new HIV infections sooner may encourage infected people to seek counseling that will help them avoid transmitting the virus to other people, especially during the period of primary infection when they are highly infectious.

The development of better treatment strategies offers compelling reasons for people at risk to discover their HIV status as soon as possible. Presumably, once people become aware of their HIV-positive status, they will be much less likely to pass the infection on to others. This assumption was supported by a study which found that, of 615 men and women diagnosed with HIV infection, most adopted safer sexual behaviors after diagnosis, including regular use of condoms, less frequent or no sex, or engaging only in oral sex (Centers for Disease Control, 2000a). Another study found that a substantial majority of 1,363 HIV-infected men and women were using condoms during vaginal or anal intercourse with partners known to be HIV-negative and with partners of unknown HIV status (Centers for Disease Control, 2003).

Most HIV-infected people in the United States are not tested for HIV until they develop symptoms of disease, and most HIV infections are transmitted by people who are unaware of their status (Bowling, 2011; Koo et al., 2006). These alarming facts prompted the CDC to recommend, in September 2006, expanding HIV testing in the United States by including HIV screening in routine health-care services for people ages 13 to 64 and all pregnant women unless individuals specifically opt out (Bartlett et al., 2008; Bayer & Oppenheimer, 2011). The underlying goal of this recommendation is to promote early entry into medical care for HIV-infected people and facilitate behavior changes that inhibit transmission of the virus to others (Bartlett et al., 2008). The percentage of U.S. citizens ages 18 to 64 ever tested for HIV remained stable at approximately 40% from 2001 to 2006 and increased to 45% in 2009 (Centers for Disease Control, 2010h).

As discussed near the end of this chapter, we believe that all couples poised on the brink of a new sexual relationship should seriously consider undergoing medical examinations and laboratory testing designed to rule out HIV and other STIs before beginning any sexual activity that might put them at risk for infection. The following account expresses one man's experience in this matter:

> In the early stages of dating and getting to know one another, my future wife and I candidly discussed our prior relationship histories. Neither of us had been sexual with another for over a year, and we were both confident that we were free of diseases transmitted during sex. But since we were aware that the AIDS virus in an infected person's body may go undetected for years, we decided to be tested for the virus. We had our blood samples drawn at the same time, in the same room, and later shared our respective lab reports. Thankfully, as expected, we both tested negative. This process, while clearly reassuring, was also helpful in contributing to a sense of mutual trust and respect that has continued into our married years. (Authors' files)

Development of AIDS

As HIV continues to proliferate and invade healthy cells in an infected person's body, the immune system loses its capacity to defend the body against opportunistic infections. The incubation period for AIDS (i.e., the time between HIV infection and the onset of one or more severe, debilitating diseases associated with extreme impairment of the immune system) typically ranges from 8 to 10 years in adults. However, a small percentage of people infected with HIV remain symptom-free for much longer periods. Furthermore, as we will see, powerful new treatment strategies can dramatically slow the progress of HIV/AIDS in individuals who have access to these costly treatments.

People who experience progression to AIDS can develop a range of life-threatening complications. A common severe disease among HIV-infected people, and one that accounts for many AIDS deaths, is pneumonia caused by overgrowth of the protozoan *Pneumocystis carinii*, which normally inhabits the lungs of healthy people. Other opportunistic infections associated with HIV include tuberculosis, encephalitis (viral infection of the brain), severe fungal infections that cause a type of meningitis, salmonella illnesses (bacterial diseases), and toxoplasmosis (caused by a protozoan). Africa is currently plagued with an escalating tuberculosis epidemic fueled largely by the HIV/AIDS pandemic (Karim et al., 2011; Lawn, 2012). Worldwide tuberculosis is the most common infectious cause of death in HIV-infected people, and of the approximately 2 million annual deaths worldwide attributable to AIDS, about 25% are associated with this disease (Friedrich, 2011b; Török & Farrar, 2011). The body is also vulnerable to cancers, such as lymphomas (cancers of the lymph system), cervical cancer, and Kaposi's sarcoma, a common cancer in male AIDS patients that affects the skin and can also involve internal organs (Shiels et al., 2011).

Before the advent of much-improved antiretroviral treatments, once people living with AIDS developed life-threatening illnesses, such as pneumonia, tuberculosis, or cancer, the disease tended to run a fairly rapid course. Death usually occurred within 2 years for both men and women (Suligoi, 1997). Furthermore, most people who have developed AIDS since the beginning of the epidemic in the United States have already died. However, a significant decline in the rate of AIDS deaths began in 1996 (the first year that the death rate declined since the onset of the epidemic) and has continued to the present. This reversal in death trends was largely due to improvement in combination drug therapies, which we discuss in the next section. Even with this trend toward a lowering of the number of annual deaths from AIDS in the United States, an estimated 16,000 Americans died from AIDS in 2011 (Tasker, 2011).

A reduction in AIDS deaths is also occurring in other developed nations that have the resources to implement the more effective drug therapies. Unfortunately, this reversal in AIDS deaths is minimal or nonexistent in developing nations, especially those located in Africa, where HIV/AIDS continues to result in an unacceptable incidence of both infections and deaths. The high cost and difficulty of administering new and better therapies are barriers to the effective use of these treatments in poor, developing nations. Less than half of HIV-infected persons in the developing world receive antiretroviral drug therapy (Kelland, 2011). Drug therapy for infected people in the developing world is also negatively impacted by the recent downturn in the global economy, which resulted in a 10% drop in HIV/AIDS funding in 2010 compared to 2009 (Voelker, 2011).

Reduced accessibility to antiretroviral drugs is commensurate with a reduction in donor funds (Berkley, 2010). Significantly reduced donations to various African nations have resulted in funding cuts for HIV/AIDS treatment in many countries including South Africa, Kenya, Uganda, Zimbabwe, Congo, and Mozambique. The worldwide economic crisis has also resulted in decreased accessibility to antiretroviral medications in the United States. In 2010 long waiting lists for these drugs were the norm as many infected people lost health insurance along with their jobs. In addition, many states were forced to cut back on AIDS treatment programs due to the high cost of antiretroviral drugs.

Roger Ressmeyer/CORBIS

Kaposi's sarcoma, shown here with its distinctive skin lesions, is the most common cancer afflicting men with AIDS.

Treatment

No cure currently exists for HIV/AIDS. However, thousands of scientists are involved in an unprecedented worldwide effort to ultimately cure and/or prevent this horrific disease. This war is being waged on several fronts, including attempts to develop effective antiretroviral drugs that will kill or at least neutralize HIV and efforts to create a vaccine effective against HIV.

As we described earlier, HIV is classified as a retrovirus because, after invading a living cell, it works backward, using an enzyme called *reverse transcriptase*. This enzyme transcribes the viral RNA into DNA, which then acts to direct further synthesis of the lethal HIV RNA. HIV also encodes another enzyme, called a *protease* (protein digesting), that is equally critical to its reproduction. Once HIV invades a host CD4 cell, it eventually takes over the host cell's genetic material and manufacturing capacity, producing additional viruses to infect other cells. During this process, HIV kills the host cell and injects copies of its own lethal RNA into the blood to invade other healthy cells.

To date, treatment strategies have focused on drug interventions designed to block the proliferation and seeding of HIV throughout the immune system and other bodily tissues and organs. Up to the mid-1990s the main class of drugs used to combat HIV comprised products that inhibited the action of the reverse transcriptase enzyme. These reverse transcriptase (RT) inhibitors were designed to prevent the virus from copying its own genetic material and making more viruses. A major breakthrough in drug therapy took place in 1996 with the emergence of a new class of drugs that inhibit HIV's protease enzyme, which the virus uses to assemble new copies of itself. When a protease inhibitor (PI) drug was combined with two RT inhibitor drugs in early clinical trials, the combination was shown to dramatically reduce viral load in blood to minimal or undetectable levels in most patients (Louis et al., 1997; Wong et al., 1997).

Highly Active Antiretroviral Therapy

The use of a combination of three or more drugs to combat HIV has come to be known as **highly active antiretroviral therapy (HAART)**. Most clinicians commence treatment of HIV/AIDS with a combination of various RT and PI drugs. The availability of new antiretroviral drugs, including drugs in new classes, requires clinicians to constantly update and modify the HAART regimens used to combat HIV. Until recently it was common practice to begin HAART for any HIV-infected person whose CD4 count dropped below 200 or for anyone who manifested symptomatic disease (i.e., infections or cancers associated with HIV/AIDS). However, new data on treatment choices for infected people warranted an update of the International AIDS Society–USA guidelines for HAART. It is now suggested that treatment should be initiated before CD4 count declines to less than 350 (Hammer et al., 2008). The decision regarding when to begin therapy must be tailored to the individual patient based on the potential benefits and risks of early or delayed therapy.

HAART has proven to be an effective treatment regimen for many HIV/AIDS patients. Various studies have demonstrated that, when properly administered, HAART can inhibit HIV replication and frequently can reduce viral load to an undetectable level, improve immune function, and delay progression of the disease.

The excellent clinical results produced by HAART in the early years after it was implemented led to a surge of optimism that this advance in antiretroviral therapy might not only delay HIV/AIDS progression but also ultimately eradicate the virus. Unfortunately, as we will see, these early projections were overly optimistic.

A significant drawback of HAART that influences adherence is drug toxicity. Low compliance is often associated with adverse drug side effects, including anemia; insomnia; mouth ulcers; diarrhea; inflammation of the pancreas; respiratory difficulties; metabolic disturbances; increased cholesterol and triglyceride levels (major risk factors for cardiovascular diseases); gastrointestinal discomfort; liver damage; excess fat accumulation in areas such as the abdomen, upper back, and breasts; fat atrophy in the face, legs, and arms; and skin rashes (Lo et al., 2008; Mosack et al., 2009). These side effects can be so severe that affected people are unable to tolerate HAART. Fortunately, some of the HAART drug combinations introduced in recent years have fewer side effects than previously used combinations, making adherence less of an issue. Researchers have recently detected an especially troubling condition attributed to HAART called *immunosenescence*, a form of premature aging of the immune system that may occur among some people on this drug regimen. While the verdict is still out on this possible side effect, there are indications that prolonged use of antiretroviral medications may lead to loss of mental acuity and other age-related issues (Tasker, 2011).

Lack of adherence to HAART because of dosing complexities and/or drug toxicity side effects can lead to less than optimal therapy,

highly active antiretroviral therapy (HAART)
A strategy for treating HIV-infected people with a combination of antiretroviral drugs.

© Stephen Dunn/Allsport/Getty Images

In 1991 Earvin (Magic) Johnson, Los Angeles Lakers basketball All-Star, announced that he had been infected with HIV through heterosexual contact. By April 1997, HAART had reduced HIV to undetectable levels in his body.

outright treatment failure, and the development of drug-resistant strains of HIV (S. Boyer et al., 2011; Li et al., 2011). Recent improvements in medication dosing schedules (e.g., once or twice a day versus three times a day) and reductions in pill quantity (e.g., combining two or three drugs in one pill) have resulted in better adherence to HAART.

Despite the recent improvement in HAART regimens, evidence indicates that only about 28% of HIV-infected Americans are recipients of HAART treatment that produces optimal reduction in their viral load (Brown, 2011). This low percentage is primarily attributable to a large number of infected people who are unaware of their status or who cannot get or do not want treatment. Fortunately, about 77% of people receiving HAART have a fully suppressed viral load (Brown, 2011).

Another problem with HAART that surfaced in recent years further dampened the optimism and excitement associated with the early years of this treatment protocol. It is now clear that HAART does not eradicate HIV from latent or silent reservoirs in the brain, lymph nodes, intestines, bone marrow, and other tissues, cells, and organs where the virus may reside undetected and intact, even though blood plasma viral loads drop to minimal or undetectable levels (Carter et al., 2010; Fang, 2010; Sigal et al., 2011). Once treatment with the HAART regimen stops or is seriously compromised because a patient is too sick with toxic side effects or too confused by the complexity of dosing regimens, the virus sequestered in these lethal reservoirs typically comes roaring back, or it mutates, resulting in new strains of HIV that are less susceptible to the HAART drugs.

On a more positive note, HAART has been shown to reduce the likelihood of HIV transmission (Cohen et al., 2011; Hammer, 2011; Torian et al., 2011). A recent study indicates that treating HIV-infected people with HAART medications at an early stage of the disease process, when their immune systems are still relatively healthy, can reduce the likelihood of transmitting HIV to an uninfected partner by 96% (National Institute of Allergy and Infectious Diseases, 2011). However, an infected person can transmit the virus at any time after becoming infected, even while undergoing HAART (Shapiro & Ray, 2007). Many infected people transmit HIV to sexual partners before they are aware of their HIV-positive status and prior to beginning treatment.

Has the availability of HAART influenced HIV-negative people to change their sexual behaviors? Do people undergoing this treatment regimen change their sexual behaviors after beginning treatment? Evidence collected in the early years of HAART indicated that at least some HIV-negative gay and bisexual men increased their involvement in risky sex, perhaps because of the availability of this treatment regimen (Dilley et al., 1997; Kelly et al., 1998). More recent studies have confirmed a continuation of this trend toward increased sexual risk taking among gay and bisexual men as a result, at least in part, of improved treatment for HIV/AIDS (Brewer et al., 2006; Oster et al., 2011; Peterson & Bakeman, 2006).

Many persons who are aware that they are infected with HIV do refrain from engaging in risky sexual behavior (Shapiro & Ray, 2007). Two studies—one a 16-state sample of HIV-infected MSM and the other a representative sample of the adult U.S. population in care for HIV/AIDS—found that 31% of the MSM and 32% of the adult respondents in the broader study were engaging in "deliberate abstinence" by refraining from vaginal, anal, or oral intercourse over the previous 6 months to a year (Bogart et al., 2006).

Drug Therapy to Prevent Mother-to-Child Transmission of HIV

In 1994, research demonstrated that zidovudine, an RT inhibitor drug administered to both HIV-infected mothers and their newborns, reduced perinatal mother-to-child transmission (MTCT) by two thirds (Connor et al., 1994). In August 1994 the U.S. Public Health Service recommended zidovudine to reduce perinatal MTCT of HIV. Since 1994 the number of infants infected through MTCT has been almost

African children are often afflicted with HIV/AIDS as a result of mother-to-child transmission.

eliminated in the United States and Europe via widespread implementation of medical interventions (Lallemant et al., 2011). Sadly, this is not the case in Africa, where MTCT of HIV is still rampant and a majority of HIV-infected children do not receive antiretroviral therapy and half die before they reach age 2 (Lallemant et al., 2011).

The limited health systems of most African nations have stimulated a search for a less costly, more practical, and more effective short-course antiretroviral regimen. Studies in South Africa and Uganda found that infants who were provided with either (1) a single dose of the RT inhibitor drug nevirapine within 24 hours of birth or (2) a short-course regimen with this drug experienced excellent protection from HIV infection (Altman, 2002; Moodley et al., 2003). Because single-dose or short-course nevirapine therapy is dramatically less costly than the longer and more complex zidovudine regimen, many countries with limited resources are now utilizing this drug to reduce MTCT of HIV (Spensley et al., 2009).

Preventing perinatal MTCT does not eliminate the possibility of later transmission of the virus from a mother to a child through breast-feeding (Osborn, 2008). In sub-Saharan African countries, breast-feeding is usually essential for infant survival, because alternatives to breast milk are generally nonexistent or unaffordable. It is estimated that about 16% of untreated infants, whose mothers are HIV infected, will acquire MTCT of HIV if breast-feeding continues into the second year of life (Kumwenda et al., 2008). A recent investigation in Botswana revealed that HAART regimens were effective in suppressing viral loads during pregnancy and later during breast-feeding. The HAART regimen, commenced no later than the 34th week of gestation and continued through up to 6 months of breast-feeding, achieved a 1.1% rate of MTCT at 6 months, the lowest recorded in a breast-feeding population (Shapiro et al., 2010).

Health officials also hope that presenting alternatives to breast-feeding, such as breast-milk substitutes or early weaning, will help reduce the transmission of HIV through breast milk. Unfortunately, breast-milk transmission continues "in vast areas in which alternatives to breast-feeding are unavailable, unsafe, or both" (Osborn, 2008, p. 582).

The Search for a Vaccine

We close this section on treatment with an update on efforts to develop an effective vaccine for HIV. Development of a safe, effective, and affordable vaccine is a global public health priority and remains the best long-term hope for bringing the worldwide HIV/AIDS pandemic under control (Johnston & Fauci, 2011).

There are two broad categories of vaccines: (1) those that prevent initial infection by HIV (prophylactic vaccines) and (2) those that delay or prevent progression of disease in people already infected (therapeutic vaccines). Despite extensive efforts, researchers have failed to develop vaccines from either category that are broadly effective against HIV. The most promising vaccine trials conducted to date have all failed (Osborn, 2008). In July 2008, plans to conduct a large U.S.-based human trial of a government-developed HIV vaccine were canceled when federal health researchers realized that they had insufficient knowledge about how HIV vaccines interact with the immune system (Altman, 2008a). Discovery of an effective HIV vaccine remains elusive, and some HIV/AIDS specialists wonder whether an effective vaccine will ever be developed (De Cock et al., 2011; Johnston & Fauci, 2008).

A number of problems confront vaccine researchers, including the absence of an ideal animal model for research and the combined facts that HIV is extremely complicated, is present in multiple strains, and can change rapidly through genetic mutation (Johnston & Fauci, 2008; Osborn, 2008).

Some recent developments in HIV vaccine research do provide a basis for cautious optimism. A large study in Thailand provided evidence that a small percentage of vaccinated people exhibited immunity to HIV infection (Collins & Fauci, 2010). Several vaccine candidates are entering the development pipeline. Two recent studies with macaque and rhesus monkeys challenged with simian immunodeficiency virus (SIV) suggest that these animals may provide a viable study group for future vaccine research (R. Johnson, 2011; Liu et al., 2009).

Researchers are currently investigating the possibility that a mild-mannered virus carried by most people, cytomegalovirus (CMV), can be used to carry a few HIV genes to prime immune defenses against HIV (Hansen et al., 2011; Rojas-Burke, 2011). The advantage of using CMV as a carrier is that this virus persists indefinitely in humans without causing harm and thus may provide lifelong HIV immunity. How well modified CMV may effectively defend against HIV remains to be seen.

In spite of many setbacks in the search for a vaccine, many researchers "are optimistic that the tools of modern science will enable us to develop HIV vaccines that induce effective immune responses that . . . can prevent HIV infection" (Johnston & Fauci, 2011, p. 875).

For the sake of the world's population, especially in developing countries, we can only hope that effective, low-cost vaccines are available soon. Unfortunately, the time line for finding an effective HIV vaccine appears to stretch years into the future.

Prevention

The only certain way to avoid contracting HIV *sexually* is either to avoid all varieties of interpersonal sexual contact that place one at risk for infection or to be involved in a monogamous, mutually faithful relationship with one noninfected partner. If neither of these conditions is applicable, a wise person will act in a way that significantly reduces his or her risk of becoming infected with HIV.

SEXUAL HEALTH

Safer-sex practices that reduce the risk of contracting HIV/AIDS and other STIs are described in some detail in the last section of this chapter. Most of these preventive methods are directly applicable to HIV/AIDS. However, it is important to note that any strategies that reduce your risk of developing the other STIs previously discussed will also reduce your risk of HIV infection because of the known association between HIV/AIDS and other STIs.

Beyond the obvious safer-sex strategies of consistently and correctly using latex condoms and avoiding sex with multiple partners or with individuals at high risk for HIV, the following list provides suggestions particularly relevant to avoiding HIV infection. Note that several of these suggestions are less significant for two healthy people in a monogamous relationship who apply common sense in evaluating what is most likely to be risky for them.

1. If you use injected drugs, do not share needles or syringes.
2. Injection drug users may wish to check with local health departments to see if a syringe-exchange program (SEP) exists. These programs, which provide clean syringes or needles in exchange for used syringes or needles, have been shown to reduce the spread of HIV and other blood-borne infections among high-risk injection drug users (H. Cooper et al., 2011; Drach et al., 2011). In 2009, 189 SEPs were known to be operating in 36 states (Centers for Disease Control, 2010g). The U.S. federal government did not support SEPs until the onset of Obama's presidency (De Cock et al., 2011).
3. Avoid oral, vaginal, or anal contact with semen.

4. Avoid anal intercourse, because this is one of the riskiest of all sexual behaviors associated with HIV transmission (Ibanez et al., 2010; Jenness et al., 2011).

5. Do not engage in insertion of fingers or fists ("fisting") into the anus as an active or receptive partner. Fingernails can easily cause tears in the rectal tissues, thereby creating a route for HIV to penetrate the blood.

6. Avoid oral contact with the anus (a practice commonly referred to as rimming).

7. Avoid oral contact with vaginal fluids.

8. Do not allow a partner's urine to enter your mouth, anus, vagina, eyes, or open cuts or sores.

9. Avoid sexual intercourse during menstruation. HIV-infected women are at increased risk for transmitting their infection through intercourse while menstruating.

10. Do not share razor blades, toothbrushes, or other implements that could become contaminated with blood.

11. In view of the remote possibility that HIV may be transmitted by means of prolonged open-mouth wet kissing, it might be wise to avoid this activity. There is no risk of HIV transmission through closed-mouth kissing.

12. Avoid sexual contact with sex workers (male or female). Research indicates that sex workers have unusually high rates of HIV infection (Lamptey et al., 2006). ●

All these methods for preventing HIV infection focus on preventing exposure to the virus. Several years ago the U.S. Department of Health and Human Services issued guidelines for using antiretroviral drugs to prevent HIV infection after unanticipated sexual or injection-drug-use exposure. These guidelines indicate that a 28-day course of HAART commenced as soon as possible after exposure can significantly reduce the risk of infection (Centers for Disease Control, 2005). A number of health departments, clinics, and individual physicians in the United States are now providing postexposure prophylaxis (PEP) via HAART after unanticipated exposure to HIV. PEP has also been utilized as an HIV infection prevention strategy with South African children who have been raped (Collings et al., 2008). Some health professionals believe that preexposure prophylaxis (PrEP) via a daily pill may also be a viable option for preventing HIV infection. This possibility is discussed in the following paragraphs.

Is it possible that uninfected people could take a pill once daily to prevent HIV infection? Recent research suggests that PrEP with a once-daily ingestion of Truvada (a combination of two antiretroviral drugs) may accomplish this goal. In a study that included 2,494 gay men drawn from six countries, researchers found that men taking Truvada were 44% less likely to become infected with HIV than men taking a placebo. In addition, in men who took the pill every day, as indicated by blood tests, Truvada was more than 90% effective in preventing HIV infection (D. Smith et al., 2011). Some health professionals suggest that PrEP may prove especially advantageous for uninfected people whose primary partner is infected, for people who feel unable to insist on condom use, and for commercial sex workers who often experience unprotected exposure to HIV. Concern has also been expressed that people utilizing PrEP may become less concerned about HIV infections and thus less vigilant about protecting themselves via safer sexual behaviors (Hayden, 2011).

A recent study in Africa found that PrEP via Truvada did not help prevent HIV infection in women (Stephenson, 2011). However, other recent research that studied about 5,000 heterosexual couples in Kenya and Uganda demonstrated that a daily dose of antiretrovirals did significantly reduce transmission of HIV for both men and women (Maugh, 2011). We await further research to clarify the effectiveness of PrEP.

At present, the best hope for curtailing the spread of HIV/AIDS is through education and behavior change. Because neither an effective vaccine nor a drug-based cure seems likely to be available soon, the best strategy for significantly curtailing this pandemic is preventing exposure through education about effective prevention and risk-reduction strategies. A wide range of published studies of a variety of prevention strategies, directed at a broad range of target populations, has provided promising findings, indicating that intensive educational and behavioral interventions are often effective in reducing risky behaviors that increase vulnerability to HIV infection. The Obama administration recently increased HIV/AIDS prevention by establishing a national HIV/AIDS strategy that targets prevention efforts to those individuals most likely to be infected (Melby, 2012).

Many HIV/AIDS experts have stated that more emphasis needs to be placed on behavioral interventions that have been shown to help prevent the spread of HIV/AIDS (Altman, 2008b). These prevention strategies include increasing awareness of risk behaviors for HIV infection and promoting safer sex through condom use, having fewer sexual partners, delaying sexual debut, decreasing use of injection drugs, providing access to needle-exchange programs, and promoting male circumcision. Clearly, behavior-based HIV prevention interventions help slow the spread of HIV infections (Altman, 2008b; Jaffe, 2008; B. Johnson et al., 2011). In the absence of a cure or an effective vaccine, these efforts provide the best weapons in the worldwide war being waged against this devastating illness. An enduring frustration for the authors of this text and a multitude of researchers and health practitioners worldwide is the likelihood that "we will not know how the story of AIDS will finally end because the epidemic will outlast us" (De Cock et al., 2011, p. 1047).

Preventing Sexually Transmitted Infections

Many approaches to curtailing the spread of STIs have been advocated. These range from attempting to discourage sexual activity among young people to providing easy public access to information about the symptoms of STIs, along with free medical treatment. Unfortunately, the efforts of public health agencies have not been very successful in curbing the rapid spread of STIs. For this reason, it is doubly important to stress a variety of specific preventive measures that can be taken by an individual or a couple.

Clearly, abstinence from partner sex is one virtually surefire way to avoid an STI. Being infection-free and monogamous yourself and having a partner who is also infection-free and monogamous is another way to prevent contracting an STI. However, it is often difficult for people to assess the infection-risk status of prospective or current partners and, for that matter, to assess how committed their partners are to being monogamous.

Having a frank and open discussion before initial sexual interaction may seem difficult and embarrassing. However, in this era of epidemic health-damaging and life-threatening STIs, such discussions are essential to making sound judgments that may have profound ramifications for your physical and psychological well-being. Consequently, we address this issue early in our outline of prevention guidelines.

Prevention Guidelines

We discuss several methods of prevention—steps that can be taken before, during, or shortly after sexual contact to reduce the likelihood of contracting an STI. Many of these methods are effective against the transmission of a variety of infections. Several are applicable to oral–genital and anal–genital contacts in addition to genital–genital interaction.

None of the methods is 100% effective, but each method acts to significantly reduce the chances of infection. Furthermore—and this cannot be overemphasized—the use of preventive measures may help to curtail the booming spread of STIs. Because many infected people have sexual contact with one or more partners before realizing that they have an infection and seeking treatment, improved prevention rather than better treatment seems to hold the key to reducing these unpleasant effects of sexual expression.

Assess Your Risk Status and Your Partner's Risk Status

As a result of informed concern about acquiring an STI, you may understandably focus on assessing the risk status of a prospective sexual partner. However, in doing so, you may overlook the equally important need to evaluate your own risk status. If you previously engaged in sexual activity with others, is there any possibility that you may have contracted an STI from them? Have you been tested for STIs in general, not just for one specific infectious agent? Remember, many of the STIs discussed in this chapter produce little or no noticeable symptoms in an infected person. If you care enough to be sexually intimate with a new partner, is it not reasonable that you should also be open and willing to share information about your own sexual health?

Some experts maintain that one of the most important STI prevention messages to convey to people is to spend time, ideally several months or more, getting to know prospective sexual partners before engaging in genital sex. Unfortunately, research indicates that effective communication about risk factors and safer sexual behavior seems to be "more the exception than the rule in dating couples" (Buysse & Ickes, 1999, p. 121). Research has revealed that individuals who are beginning or are involved in romantic or intimate relationships are often reticent to discuss past sexual experiences (Anderson et al., 2011). We strongly encourage you to take time to develop a warm, caring relationship in which mutual empathy and trust are key ingredients. Use this time to convey to the other person any relevant information from your sexual history regarding your risk status—and to inquire about your partner's present or past behavior in the areas of sex and injection drug use. As discussed in Chapter 7, self-disclosure can be an effective strategy for getting a partner to open up. Thus you might begin your dialogue about these matters by discussing why you think that such an information exchange is vitally important in the AIDS era, and then share information about your own sexual history. Studies indicate that "reciprocal sexual self-disclosure contributes to greater relational and sexual satisfaction" (Anderson et al., 2011, p. 383).

Getting to know someone well enough to trust his or her answers to these important questions means taking the time to assess a person's honesty and integrity in a variety of situations. If you observe your prospective partner lying to friends, family members, or you about other matters, you may rightfully question the truthfulness of her or his responses to your risk-assessment queries.

Research suggests that we cannot always assume that potential sexual partners will accurately disclose their risk for STIs. Various studies have shown that people often engage in sexual deceptions with their partner(s) that may include failing to reveal the number (or identity or both) of previous sexual partners, other current sexual involvements, or their own STI status, or making false claims about testing negative for HIV/AIDS and other STIs. Several investigations reveal that it is not uncommon either to fail to disclose one's STI status or to lie about it in order to have sex (Anderson et al., 2011; Marelich et al., 2008; Newton & McCabe, 2005; Sullivan, 2005).

Obtain Prior Medical Examinations

Even when people are entirely candid about their own sexual histories, there is no way to ensure that their previous sexual partners were honest with them—or, for that matter, that they even asked previous partners about STI risk status. In view of these concerns, we strongly encourage couples who want to begin a sexual relationship to abstain from any activity that puts them at risk for STIs until both partners have had medical examinations and laboratory testing designed to rule out all STIs, including HIV. Taking this step not only reduces one's chance of contracting an infection but also contributes immeasurably to a sense of mutual trust and comfort with developing intimacy. If cost is an issue, contact your campus health service or a public health clinic in your area; both of these venues can provide examinations and laboratory testing free of charge or on a sliding fee scale commensurate with your financial status.

Use Condoms

It has been known for decades that condoms, when consistently and correctly used, help to prevent the transmission of many STIs (Reece et al., 2010b). The condom, one of the great underrated aids to sexual interaction, is the only current contraceptive method (other than abstinence) that protects against pregnancy and most STIs (Reece et al., 2010b). Male latex condoms, when used correctly and consistently, are effective in preventing the sexual transmission of HIV, and they reduce the risk of transmission of other STIs, such as chlamydia, gonorrhea, NGU, bacterial vaginosis, and trichomoniasis, that are also transmitted by fluids from mucosal surfaces. Condoms are less effective in preventing infections that are transmitted by skin-to-skin contact, such as syphilis, HSV, and HPV, and they have no value in combating pubic lice and scabies. Condoms made from sheep's membrane (also known as "natural skin" or "natural membrane") contain small pores that may permit passage of some STIs, including HIV, HSV, and hepatitis viruses.

The NSSHB reported that adults who used condoms during intercourse were just as likely to rate the sexual experience as positive in terms of pleasure as those who engaged in condomless intercourse (Reece et al., 2010b).

Unfortunately, the proven value of condoms in reducing the spread of HIV/AIDS in Africa was undermined by a change in U.S. policy during George W. Bush's administration. This change is discussed in the Sex and Politics box, "U.S. Policy During the Bush Administration Reduced Condom Promotion in Africa."

In March 2009, Pope Benedict XVI stated publicly during a visit to Africa that condoms have added to the problem of HIV/AIDS and that this pandemic should be tackled via abstinence rather than condom use. *Lancet*, a leading medical journal, called on the Pope to retract these inaccurate remarks that undermine HIV/AIDS prevention efforts in Africa (Staines, 2009). Fortunately, in November 2010 the Pope appeared to reverse his position on condoms by stating that "condoms are the lesser of two evils when used to curb the spread of AIDS, even if their use prevents pregnancy" (Simpson & Winfield, 2010, p. 1). This revision in the pontiff's position on condoms appears to reflect the Catholic Church's belief that staunch opposition to condoms as a birth control device cannot be justified when it puts lives at risk.

Laboratory studies indicate that the female condom (see Chapter 10) is an effective barrier to viruses, including HIV. If used correctly and consistently, the female condom can substantially reduce the risk of transmission of some STIs, and when the use of male condoms is not an option, we strongly encourage our readers to consider using a female condom. The female condom can be especially valuable to sexually active women who are at substantial risk for acquiring STIs from male partners who are unwilling to use male condoms consistently or at all.

Evidence indicates that vaginal spermicides containing nonoxynol-9 (N-9) are not effective in preventing transmission of chlamydia, gonorrhea, or HIV (Workowski et al., 2010). In fact, frequent use of N-9 has been associated with genital lesions in the

U.S. Policy During the Bush Administration Reduced Condom Promotion in Africa

Policy changes implemented by the U.S. government during the Bush administration made condom promotion in Africa controversial, resulting in a serious setback in efforts to bring the AIDS pandemic under control. Conservative U.S. government officials made clear the Bush administration's preference for abstinence-only approaches and registered strong misgivings about the moral and ethical advisability of providing condoms as part of AIDS prevention programs. In addition, U.S. officials removed scientifically accurate information about condom use effectiveness from the websites of several federal agencies and questioned whether condoms provide protection against STIs, including HIV (Kirby, 2008a; Masters et al., 2008).

To date, there is absolutely no evidence that abstinence-only programs have reduced HIV transmission anywhere in the world (Kirby, 2008a; Masters et al., 2008). Nevertheless, this unproven approach was exported to many sub-Saharan nations, especially Uganda, as part of President Bush's

Emergency Plan for AIDS Relief (PEPFAR) (Human Rights Watch, 2006; Jaffe, 2008).

A report by the U.S. Government Accountability Office revealed that the requirement to allocate a sizable portion of PEPFAR's funds to promote abstinence and fidelity significantly eroded other preventive efforts, including MTCT, prevention services for couples in which one person is HIV infected and the other is not infected, and promotion of comprehensive programs focused on high-risk groups such as sexually active youth (Brown, 2006; Steinbrook, 2008).

In 2011 the Obama administration issued new science-based guidance on U.S.-funded HIV/AIDS prevention programs overseas. These new directives essentially negated old prevention guidelines issued by the Bush administration that emphasized a narrow and largely ineffective focus on abstinence and being faithful. The new guidance "details a comprehensive approach to prevention including emphasis on combination prevention approaches" (Allana, 2011, p. 1).

---

vagina, which can increase vulnerability to HIV infection transmitted during vaginal intercourse (Van Damme, 2000). Furthermore, animal research has shown that N-9 can damage the cells lining the rectum, thus providing a portal of entry for HIV and other STI pathogens (Workowski et al., 2010). The CDC recommends against use of condoms lubricated with N-9 spermicide.

Available barrier methods for preventing STI transmission are often disadvantageous to women because they are either male controlled (the male condom) or require male cooperation (the female condom). Consequently, researchers are actively pursuing methods for STI prevention that can be controlled solely by women. These efforts are described in the following paragraphs.

Microbicides

Research efforts are currently under way to develop safe and effective topical gel or cream products or suppositories, called **microbicides**, that can be inserted into the vagina or rectum to prevent or minimize the risk of being infected with HIV and other STIs. These products would be applied before sexual intercourse, but they would not be a substitute for condoms. Rather, they would provide extra protection at low cost. In the developing world, where financial resources are limited and women are often unable to depend on male cooperation, microbicides would offer an especially beneficial option for STI prevention (Mahan et al., 2011).

Technically, the term *microbicide* means "a product that kills microbes." However, there are several ways that microbicide products could function to prevent STIs. Some microbicides would kill or destroy infection-causing organisms present in semen or vaginal secretions. Other microbicides under development would work not by destroying an infection-causing pathogen but by blocking its entry or fusion with target cells or by stopping its replication once inside target cells.

microbicide
A topical gel or cream product that women can use vaginally to prevent or minimize the risk of being infected with HIV or other STIs.

Correctly used condoms help prevent the transmission of many STIs, including HIV.

Several microbicide candidates are currently being studied in clinical trials with large study populations in developing countries that are at risk for infection by HIV and other STIs (Stadler & Saethre, 2011). The National Institutes of Health (2009) issued a report on a large-scale clinical trial of a microbicide known as PRO 2000 that was conducted with several thousand women in Africa and the United States. Although the findings of this study indicate that PRO 2000 may effectively protect women against HIV infection, more data are necessary to conclusively determine the effectiveness of this microbicide candidate.

The effectiveness of microbicide products is related to adherence to or consistency of use. This connection was revealed in the PRO 2000 study in which only about 60% of the enrolled subjects reported using the microbicide gel during every sexual act (Heisea et al., 2011).

Unfortunately, a recent research trial in Africa found that a vaginal gel microbicide containing the antiretroviral drug tenofovir was no more effective than a placebo gel in preventing HIV infection (Friedrich, 2012).

Some of the products under investigation have both spermicidal and antimicrobial capabilities. Health officials hope to eventually have effective products from both categories, because some users will want protection against both unwanted pregnancies and STIs, whereas others will seek only protection against infection. We hope that one or more of these much-needed products will be available soon.

Avoid Sexual Activity With Multiple Partners

You may wish to reevaluate the importance of sex with multiple partners in light of the clear and extensive evidence that having many sexual partners is one of the strongest predictors of becoming infected with HIV, HSV, chlamydia, HPV, and numerous other sexually transmitted infections. You might also elect not to have sex with individuals who you know or suspect have had multiple partners. People with multiple partners probably know each partner less well and thus may be less successful in avoiding people who engage in high-risk behaviors.

Inspect Your Partner's Genitals

Examining your partner's genitals before coital, oral, or anal contact might reveal the symptoms of an STI. Herpes blisters, vaginal and urethral discharges, and chancres and rashes associated with syphilis, genital warts, and gonorrhea may be seen. In most cases symptoms are more evident on a man. (If he is uncircumcised, be sure to retract the foreskin.) The presence of a discharge, an unpleasant odor, sores, blisters, a rash, warts, or anything else out of the ordinary should be viewed with some concern. "Milking" the penis is a particularly effective way to detect a suspicious discharge. This technique, sometimes called the "short-arm inspection," involves grasping the penis firmly and pulling the loose skin up and down the shaft several times, applying pressure on the base-to-head stroke. Then part the urinary opening to see if any cloudy discharge is present.

People frequently find it difficult to openly conduct such an inspection before sexual involvement. Sometimes the simple request "Let me undress you" can provide some opportunity to examine your partner's genitals. Sensate focus pleasuring, discussed in Chapter 14, could provide the opportunity for more-detailed visual exploration. Some people suggest a shower before sex, with an eye toward examining a partner. This may be helpful for noting visible sores, blisters, and so forth, but soap and water can also remove the visual and olfactory cues associated with a discharge.

If you note signs of infection, you may justifiably and wisely elect not to have sexual relations. Your intended partner may or may not be aware of his or her symptoms. Therefore it is important that you explain your concerns. Some people may decide to continue their sexual interaction after discovering possible symptoms of an STI; they would be wise, though, to restrict their activities to kissing, hugging, touching, and manual genital stimulation.

Obtain Routine Medical Evaluations

Many authorities recommend that sexually active people with more than one partner routinely visit their health-care practitioner or local public health clinic for periodic checkups, even when no symptoms of infection are evident. In view of the number of people, both women and men, who are symptomless carriers of STIs, this seems like good advice. How often to have such examinations is a matter of opinion. Our advice to people who are sexually active with several partners is that they should have checkups every 3 months and certainly no less often than twice a year.

Inform Your Partner(s) if You Have an STI

The high frequency of infections without symptoms makes it imperative for infected individuals to inform their sexual partner(s) once they are diagnosed with an STI. Partner notification, which is beneficial in reducing the spread of all STIs, is an especially imperative prevention tactic for curtailing the spread of HIV infections (Bird & Voisin, 2011; Obermeyer et al., 2011). Partner notification can be conducted by the infected person, by health-care providers, or by specially trained city, state, and federal employees called disease intervention specialists (DISs) (Kissinger et al., 2003). The Let's Talk About It box, "Telling a Partner," which appeared earlier in this chapter, offers suggestions that may be helpful to a person who elects to notify a partner about an STI infection. A potential benefit of partner notification conducted by a health-care provider or DIS is that informed people typically receive counseling about how to reduce the risk of exposure to STIs and are often provided with options for health-care services, including testing and treatment (Hoxworth et al., 2003).

A number of studies have found that partner notification often facilitates several desirable behavior changes, including increased condom use, reduction in number of sexual partners, and reduction in the incidence of STIs following notification (Niccolai et al., 2006; Semaan et al., 2004). Even though partner notification can be a powerful STI prevention strategy, we cannot assume that a sexual partner will be forthcoming about a diagnosed STI.

A survey of a national sample of 1,421 people receiving medical care for HIV infection found that 42% of gay or bisexual men, 19% of heterosexual men, and 17% of women participants reported engaging in sexual interaction without disclosing their HIV-positive status to their sex partners. This nondisclosure occurred primarily within nonexclusive partnerships (Ciccarone et al., 2003). In general, research indicates that even when people diagnosed with an STI inform a primary partner, other sexual contacts are likely to be left uninformed (Niccolai et al., 2006).

Summary

- About half of the STIs diagnosed annually in the United States occur among 15- to 24-year-olds.
- A number of factors probably contribute to the high incidence of STIs, including more people having unprotected (condomless) sex with multiple partners, the increased use of birth control pills, limited access to effective systems for prevention and treatment of STIs, inaccurate diagnosis and treatment, and the fact that many of these infections do not produce obvious symptoms, which results in people unknowingly infecting others.

Bacterial Infections

- Chlamydia infections are among the most prevalent and the most damaging of all STIs. Chlamydia is transmitted primarily through sexual contact. It can also be spread by fingers from one body site to another—for example, from the genitals to the eyes.
- There are two general types of genital chlamydia infections in females: infections of the lower reproductive tract, commonly manifested as urethritis or cervicitis; and invasive infections of the upper reproductive tract, expressed as PID (pelvic inflammatory disease).
- Most women with lower reproductive tract chlamydia infections have few or no symptoms. Symptoms of PID caused by chlamydia infection include disrupted menstrual periods, pelvic pain, elevated temperature, nausea, vomiting, and headache.
- Chlamydia salpingitis (infection of the fallopian tubes) is a major cause of infertility and ectopic pregnancy.
- Chlamydia infection also causes trachoma, the world's leading cause of preventable blindness.
- Recommended drugs for treating chlamydia infections include doxycycline and azithromycin.

- Gonorrhea is a common communicable bacterial infection that is transmitted through sexual contact. The infecting organism is a *gonococcus* bacterium.
- Early symptoms of gonorrhea infection are more likely to be manifested by men, who will probably experience a discharge from the penis and a burning sensation during urination. The early sign in women, often not detectable, is a mild vaginal discharge that may be irritating to vulval tissues.
- Complications of gonorrhea infection in men include prostate, bladder, and kidney involvement and, infrequently, gonococcal epididymitis, which can lead to sterility. In women gonorrhea can lead to PID, sterility, and abdominal adhesions.
- Recommended treatment for gonorrhea is the dual therapy of a single dose of a cephalosporin medication (e.g., ceftriaxone) plus a single dose of azithromycin (or doxycycline for 7 days).
- Nongonococcal urethritis (NGU) is a common infection of the urethral passage, typically seen in men. It is primarily caused by infectious organisms transmitted during coitus.
- Symptoms of NGU most apparent in men include penile discharge and a slight burning sensation during urination. Women may have a minor vaginal discharge and are thought to harbor the infecting organisms.
- Doxycycline or azithromycin therapy usually clears up NGU.
- Syphilis is less common but potentially more damaging than gonorrhea. It is almost always transmitted through sexual contact.
- If untreated, syphilis can progress through four phases: primary, characterized by the appearance of chancre sores; secondary, distinguished by the occurrence of a generalized skin rash; latent, a several-year period of no overt

symptoms; and tertiary, during which the infection can produce cardiovascular disease, blindness, paralysis, skin ulcers, liver damage, and severe mental pathological conditions.

- Syphilis can be treated with benzathine penicillin G at any stage of its development. People allergic to penicillin can be treated with doxycycline, tetracycline, or ceftriaxone.

Viral Infections

- Some of the most common herpes viruses are type 1, which generally produces sores on or in the mouth, and type 2, which generally infects the genital area. Type 1 can be found in the genital area, and type 2 can be found in the mouth area. Type 2 is transmitted primarily through sexual contact; type 1 can be passed by sexual contact or kissing.
- It has been estimated that more than 100 million Americans are afflicted with oral herpes and that 50 million people in the United States have genital herpes.
- The presence of painful sores is the primary symptom of herpes. A person is highly contagious during a herpes eruption, but evidence indicates that herpes can also be transmitted during asymptomatic periods.
- Genital herpes can predispose a woman to cervical cancer. It can also infect her newborn child, resulting in severe damage to or death of the child.
- Herpes has no known cure. Treatment is aimed at reducing pain and speeding the healing process. Acyclovir, valacyclovir, or famciclovir administered orally is effective in promoting healing during first episodes and, if taken continuously, in suppressing recurrent outbreaks.
- Genital and anal warts are an extremely common viral STI.
- Genital warts are primarily transmitted through vaginal, anal, or oral–genital sexual interaction.
- Research has revealed a strong association between genital warts and cancers of the cervix, vagina, vulva, urethra, penis, and anus.
- Genital warts are treated by freezing, applications of topical agents, cauterization, surgical removal, or vaporization by a carbon dioxide laser.
- Vaccines effective against several types of HPV were recently developed and approved by the FDA.
- Hepatitis A, hepatitis B, and hepatitis C are three major types of viral infections of the liver. All three types can be sexually transmitted.
- Hepatitis B can be transmitted through blood or blood products, semen, vaginal secretions, and saliva. Manual, oral, and/or penile stimulation of the anus are practices strongly associated with the spread of this viral agent.
- Oral–anal contact seems to be the primary mode of sexual transmission of hepatitis A.
- Hepatitis C is transmitted most commonly by means of injection drug use or less frequently through

contaminated blood products and sexual contact; perinatal mother-to-fetus or mother-to-infant transmission is also possible.

- The symptoms of viral hepatitis vary from mild to incapacitating illness. No specific therapy is available to treat hepatitis A. Chronic hepatitis B infections can be treated with a variety of antiviral drugs. Most people infected with A and B types recover in a few weeks with adequate bed rest.
- The most health-threatening of the hepatitis viruses, hepatitis C, is an emerging communicable disease of epidemic proportions.
- Hepatitis C accounts for the majority of deaths from complications of viral hepatitis. Combination therapy with antiviral drugs is relatively effective in controlling the severe complications associated with hepatitis C.

Common Vaginal Infections

- Bacterial vaginosis—typically caused by an overgrowth of anaerobic bacteria, *Mycoplasma* bacteria, or a bacterium known as *Gardnerella vaginalis*—is the most common cause of vaginitis (vaginal infection) in U.S. women. Male partners of infected women also harbor the infectious microorganisms, usually without clinical symptoms. Coitus often provides a mode of transmission for this infection.
- The most prominent symptom of bacterial vaginosis in women is a fishy- or musty-smelling, thin discharge that is like flour paste in consistency. Women can also experience irritation of the genital tissues.
- The treatment for bacterial vaginosis is metronidazole (Flagyl) taken by mouth or intravaginal applications of topical metronidazole gel or clindamycin cream.
- Candidiasis is a yeast infection that affects many women. The *Candida albicans* organism is commonly present in the vagina but causes problems only when overgrowth occurs. Pregnancy, diabetes, and the use of birth control pills or oral antibiotics are often associated with yeast infections. The organism can be transmitted through sexual or nonsexual means.
- Symptoms of yeast infections include a white clumpy discharge and intense itching of the vaginal and vulval tissues.
- Traditional treatment for candidiasis infection consists of vaginal suppositories or topical creams, such as clotrimazole, or orally administered fluconazole or itraconazole.
- Trichomoniasis is a common STI caused by a protozoan parasite called *Trichomonas vaginalis*. The primary mode of transmission of this infection is through sexual contact.
- Women infected with trichomoniasis and their male sexual partners can be successfully treated with one dose of metronidazole (Flagyl) or tinidazole.

Ectoparasitic Infections

- Ectoparasites are parasitic organisms that live on the outer skin of humans and other animals. Pubic lice and scabies are two relatively common STIs caused by ectoparasites.
- Pubic lice ("crabs") are tiny biting insects that feed on blood from small vessels in the pubic region. They can be transmitted through sexual contact or by using bedding or clothing contaminated by an infested individual.
- The primary symptom of a pubic lice infestation is severe itching that is not relieved by scratching. Sometimes pubic lice can be seen.
- Pubic lice are treated by application of prescription or over-the-counter lotions or creams to affected body areas.
- Scabies is caused by a tiny parasitic mite that forages for nourishment in its host's skin. Scabies is a highly contagious condition that can be transmitted by close sexual or non-sexual physical contact between people.
- The primary symptoms of scabies are small bumps and a red rash that itches intensely, especially at night. The bumps and rash indicate areas of infestation.
- A single application of a topical scabicide, applied from the neck to the toes, is usually an effective treatment.

Acquired Immunodeficiency Syndrome (AIDS)

- AIDS is caused by infection with a virus (HIV) that destroys the immune system, leaving the body vulnerable to a variety of opportunistic infections and cancers.
- It now appears likely that HIV originated early in the 20th century by means of cross-species transmission from a subspecies of African chimpanzees to humans. The virus then spread worldwide much later, when Africa became less isolated.
- More than 1 million people in the United States and 34 million people worldwide are infected with HIV.
- The number of new AIDS cases reported annually in the United States grew rapidly through the early 1980s and moderated in the late 1980s. This more moderate rate has continued to the present time.
- Even though the overall incidence of new HIV infections in the United States has remained relatively stable in recent years, the number of new cases among teenagers, women, racial and ethnic minorities, and MSM continues to rise.
- Even though the prevalence of HIV infection in the United States and the rest of the Western world remains highest among MSM, the proportion of reported AIDS cases among MSM declined sharply and then leveled off in the period from the mid-1980s to the late 1990s. In recent years the incidence of HIV infections among MSM has been increasing.
- In the United States, AIDS cases attributable to heterosexual transmission have declined slightly in recent years.

Heterosexual contact has always been the primary form of HIV transmission worldwide.

- HIV has been found in semen, blood, vaginal secretions, saliva, tears, urine, breast milk, and any other bodily fluids that can contain blood.
- Blood, semen, and vaginal fluids are the major vehicles for transmitting HIV, which appears to be passed primarily through sexual contact and through needle sharing among injection drug users.
- HIV can also be passed perinatally from an infected woman to her fetus or infant before or during birth, or by breast-feeding.
- *Viral load* refers to how much virus is present in an infected person's blood. In general, the greater the viral load, the higher the chance of transmitting the infection.
- HIV can be transmitted to the receptive partner during oral sex, when HIV comes into contact with mucous membrane tissues in the mouth. Evidence indicates that the risk of transmission of HIV via oral sex is minimal.
- The present possibility of being infected with HIV by means of transfusion of contaminated blood is remote. Furthermore, there is no danger of being infected as a result of donating blood.
- A small percentage of people appear to be resistant to HIV infection.
- The risk of transmitting HIV through saliva, tears, and urine appears to be low. There is no evidence that HIV can be transmitted by casual contact.
- High-risk behaviors that increase one's chances of becoming infected with HIV include engaging in unprotected (condomless) sex, having multiple sexual partners, having sexual contact with people known to be at high risk, and sharing injection equipment for drug use.
- HIV is not as easily transmitted from women to men as it is from men to women.
- HIV often causes a brief, flulike illness within a few weeks of initial infection. The initial illness tends to fade fairly rapidly. However, as the virus continues to deplete the immune system, other symptoms occur.
- Most people develop antibodies to HIV within months of being infected, but some silent infections can go undetected for 3 years or more.
- HIV infection can be detected by blood tests for blood serum antibodies to HIV.
- The incubation time for AIDS—defined as the time between infection with HIV and the onset of one or more severe, debilitating diseases—is estimated to range between 8 and 10 years.
- The symptoms of HIV/AIDS disease are many and varied, depending on the degree to which the immune system is compromised and the particular type of cancer or opportunistic infection that afflicts an infected person.

- A significant decline in the rate of AIDS deaths began in 1996. This reversal in death trends was due to improvement in combination drug therapies.
- There is still no cure for HIV/AIDS. However, when properly used, a combination of three or more antiretroviral drugs—a treatment approach known as highly active antiretroviral therapy (HAART)—can dramatically reduce viral load, improve immune function, and delay progression of the disease.
- HAART involves a complex protocol of drug dosing that can be difficult to adhere to. Furthermore, drug toxicity can result in adverse side effects that induce low compliance with the HAART protocol.
- HAART does not eradicate HIV from latent or silent reservoirs in various bodily tissues or organs.
- The availability of HAART has apparently influenced some people to increase their involvement in risky sex.
- The administration of nevirapine and/or zidovudine to newborns significantly reduces the incidence of mother-to-child transmission of HIV.
- Although progress has been made in developing HIV vaccines, many health officials believe that we may be years away from having an effective vaccine available.
- The best hope for curtailing the HIV/AIDS epidemic is through education and behavioral change.
- A person can significantly reduce her or his risk of becoming infected with HIV by following safer-sex strategies, which include using condoms and avoiding sex with multiple partners or with individuals who are at high risk for HIV infection.

Preventing Sexually Transmitted Infections

- Taking the time to carefully assess your risk status and your partner's risk status for transmitting STIs is perhaps the most important preventive strategy.
- Because it is often difficult to accurately assess risk status from conversations alone, couples are encouraged to undergo medical examinations and laboratory testing to rule out STIs before engaging in any sexual activity that puts them at risk for STIs.

- Condoms, when used correctly, offer good but not foolproof protection against the transmission of many STIs.
- Topical gel or cream products, called microbicides, may help prevent or minimize the risk of HIV infections.
- Avoid sex with multiple partners or with individuals who likely have had multiple partners.
- Inspecting a partner's genitals before sexual contact may be a way to detect symptoms of an STI.
- Sexually active people with multiple partners should routinely visit their health-care practitioner or local public health clinic for periodic checkups, even when no symptoms of infection are present.
- It is imperative for infected individuals to tell their sexual partner(s) once they are diagnosed as having an STI.

Media Resources

Log in to CengageBrain.com to access the resources your instructor requires.

Go to CengageBrain.com to access Psychology CourseMate, where you will find an interactive eBook, glossaries, flashcards, quizzes, videos, and more.

Also access links to chapter-related websites, including **American Social Health Association, JAMA HIV/AIDS Information Center, An Introduction to Sexually Transmitted Diseases, SaferSex.org, AIDSinfo, National Herpes Resource Center,** and **Centers for Disease Control and Prevention.**

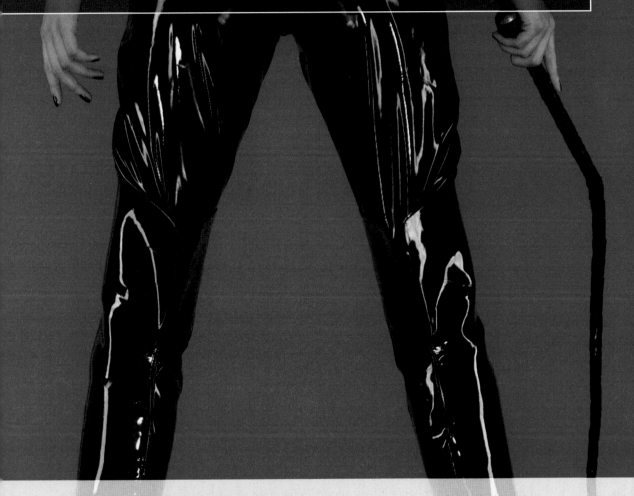

Atypical Sexual Behavior

16

What Constitutes Atypical Sexual Behavior?
What are the primary distinguishing characteristics of atypical sexual behaviors?

What impact do atypical sexual behaviors have on both a person who exhibits them and others to whom they may be directed?

Noncoercive Paraphilias
How do noncoercive paraphilias differ from coercive paraphilias?

How does fetishism develop?

How does transvestic fetishism differ from female impersonation, transsexualism, and homosexuality?

What factors might motivate people to engage in sadomasochistic behavior?

Coercive Paraphilias
What characteristics are common to individuals who engage in exhibitionism?

What are some helpful strategies for dealing with obscene phone calls?

Are there characteristics and causative factors common to people who engage in voyeurism?

Sexual Addiction: Fact, Fiction, or Misnomer?
Can people become addicted to sex?

Is there widespread support among professionals for the sexual addiction model?

Mike Diver/Stone/Getty Images

My last sexual partner was very much into golden showers. Having spent a little of my time watching G. G. Allen movies, I was well acquainted with the existence of water sports, but somehow it never occurred to me that I would like to partake in them. When my partner revealed his desire to drink my urine, I was taken off guard. I have been known to try some things I would deem a little atypical, so I gave it a shot. I was very nervous about the actual art of the procedure, though. Thoughts such as "What if he was joking—he would think I'm nuts" and "What if I completely miss" entered my head. It was nerve-racking and made it especially hard to pee. Eventually, my anxiety subsided and I was able to participate. His reaction was amazing to me. He began to masturbate feverishly and lapped up my urine ecstatically. I had never seen him so turned on. More surprising, though, was how much I enjoyed it. Although I cannot imagine being on the other end, it was really an empowering and enjoyable experience. (Authors' files)

This description of a rather unusual sexual experience, provided by a student in a sexuality class, may strike our readers as reflecting an abnormal or perhaps even deviant form of sexual behavior. However, we believe it is more realistic to consider this anecdote an account of uncommon or atypical sexual behavior. One note of caution: Because HIV has been found in the urine of infected persons, it is prudent to avoid contact with a partner's urine unless he or she is known to be HIV-negative and not infected with any other STIs. Now let us consider for a moment what constitutes atypical sexual behavior.

What Constitutes Atypical Sexual Behavior?

In this chapter, we focus on a number of sexual behaviors that have been variously labeled as deviant, perverted, aberrant, or abnormal. More recently, the less judgmental term **paraphilia** (pair-uh-FILL-ee-uh) has been used to describe these somewhat uncommon types of sexual expression. Literally meaning "beyond usual or typical love," this term stresses that such behaviors are usually not based on an affectionate or loving relationship but rather are expressions of behavior in which sexual arousal or response, or both, depends on some unusual, extraordinary, or even bizarre activity (American Psychiatric Association, 2000; Shindel & Moser, 2011). The term *paraphilia* is used in much of the psychological and psychiatric literature. However, in our own experience in dealing with and discussing variant sexual behaviors, the one common characteristic that stands out is that each behavior in its fully developed form is not typically expressed by most people in our society. Therefore we also categorize the behaviors discussed in this chapter as **atypical sexual behaviors**.

Several points should be noted about atypical sexual expression in general before we discuss specific behaviors. First, as with many other sexual expressions discussed in this book, the behaviors singled out in this chapter represent extreme points on a continuum. Atypical sexual behaviors exist in many gradations, ranging from mild, infrequently expressed tendencies to full-blown, regularly manifested behaviors. Although these behaviors are *atypical*, many of us may recognize some degree of such behaviors or feelings in ourselves—perhaps manifested at some point in our lives, or mostly repressed, or emerging only in private fantasies.

A second point has to do with the state of our knowledge about these behaviors. In most of the discussions that follow, the person who manifests the atypical behavior is assumed to be male, and evidence strongly indicates that in most reported cases

paraphilia
A term used to describe uncommon types of sexual expression.

atypical sexual behaviors
Behaviors not typically expressed by most people in our society.

of atypical or paraphilic behaviors, the agents of such acts are male (J. Miller, 2009). However, the tendency to assume that males are predominantly involved may be influenced by the somewhat biased nature of differential reporting and prosecution. Female exhibitionism, for example, is far less likely to be reported than is similar behavior in a male. Of the paraphilias discussed in this chapter, sexual masochism is the one most likely to be expressed by women (J. Miller, 2009). John Money (1981) suggested that atypical sexual behavior is decidedly more prevalent among males than females because male *erotosexual differentiation* (the development of sexual arousal in response to various kinds of images or stimuli) is more complex and subject to more errors than that of the female.

A third noteworthy point is that atypical behaviors often occur in clusters. That is, the occurrence of one paraphilia appears to increase the probability that others will also be manifested, simultaneously or sequentially (Bradford et al., 1992; Kafka, 2009). Research on men whose paraphilias resulted in medical or legal attention revealed that over half of the men reported engaging in more than one paraphilia and almost one in five reported experience with four or more paraphilias (Abel & Osborn, 2000). One hypothesis offered to account for this cluster effect is that engaging in one atypical behavior, such as exhibitionism, reduces the participant's inhibitions to the point that engaging in another paraphilia, such as voyeurism, becomes more likely (Stanley, 1993).

A final consideration is the effect of atypical behaviors both on the person who exhibits them and on the people to whom they may be directed. People who manifest atypical sexual behaviors often depend on these acts for sexual satisfaction. The behavior is frequently an end in itself. It is also possible that the unconventional behavior will alienate others. Consequently, these people often find it difficult to establish satisfying sexual and intimate relationships with partners. Instead, their sexual expression can assume a solitary, driven, even compulsive quality. Some of these behaviors do involve other people whose personal space is violated in a coercive, invasive fashion. In the following section, we consider the distinction between coercive and noncoercive paraphilias. ■ Table 16.1 summarizes the paraphilias discussed in this chapter.

Critical Thinking Question

Do you think that the disproportionate rate of atypical sexual behavior reported among men is due to biology or social/cultural conditioning? Explain.

At a Glance

■ TABLE 16.1 Summary of Several Paraphilias

Name	Description	Classification
Fetishism	Sexual arousal associated with focus on inanimate object or body part	Noncoercive
Transvestic fetishism	Sexual arousal derived from wearing clothing of other sex	Noncoercive
Sexual sadism	Association of sexual arousal with pain	Noncoercive
Sexual masochism	Sexual arousal through receiving physical or psychological pain	Noncoercive
Autoerotic asphyxia	Enhancement of sexual arousal by oxygen deprivation	Noncoercive
Klismophilia	Sexual pleasure associated with receiving enemas	Noncoercive
Coprophilia and Urophilia	Sexual arousal associated with contact with feces or urine, respectively	Noncoercive
Exhibitionism	Sexual arousal associated with exposing one's genitals to unwilling observer	Coercive
Obscene phone calls	Sexual arousal associated with obscene telephone conversation with unwilling recipient	Coercive
Voyeurism	Sexual arousal associated with observing naked bodies or sexual activities of people without their consent	Coercive
Frotteurism	Obtaining sexual pleasure by pressing or rubbing against another person in a crowded public place	Coercive
Zoophilia	Sexual contact between humans and animals	Coercive
Necrophilia	Sexual gratification obtained by viewing or having intercourse with a corpse	Coercive

Noncoercive Versus Coercive Paraphilias

A key distinguishing characteristic of paraphilias is whether they involve an element of coercion. Several of the paraphilias are strictly solo activities or involve the participation of consensual adults who agree to engage in, observe, or just put up with the particular variant behavior. Because coercion is not involved and a person's basic rights are not violated, such so-called noncoercive atypical behaviors are considered relatively benign or harmless by many. Clearly, the chapter opening account falls into this category. However, as we will see, these noncoercive behaviors occasionally engender potentially adverse consequences for people drawn into their sphere of influence.

Some paraphilias, such as voyeurism or exhibitionism, are definitely coercive or invasive, in that they involve unwilling recipients of the behavior. Furthermore, research suggests that such coercive acts can harm their targets, who may be psychologically traumatized by the experience. Such recipients may feel that they have been violated or that they are vulnerable to physical abuse, and they may develop fears that such unpleasant episodes will recur. This is one reason that many of these coercive paraphilias are illegal. On the other hand, many people who encounter such acts are not adversely affected. Because of this fact, and because many of these coercive behaviors do not involve physical or sexual contact with another person, many authorities view them as minor sex offenses (sometimes called nuisance offenses). However, evidence that some people progress from nuisance offenses to more serious forms of sexual abuse may lead to a reconsideration of whether these offenses are "minor" (Bradford et al., 1992; Fedora et al., 1992). We examine this issue in more detail later in this chapter.

In our discussion of both coercive and noncoercive paraphilias, we examine how each of these behaviors is expressed, common characteristics of people who exhibit the paraphilia, and various factors thought to contribute to the development of the behavior. More severe forms of sexual coercion, such as rape, incest, and child abuse, are discussed in Chapter 17.

Inanimate objects or a part of the human body, such as feet, can be sources of sexual arousal for some people.

Fuse/Jupiterimages

Noncoercive Paraphilias

In this section, we first discuss four fairly common types of noncoercive paraphilias: fetishism, transvestic fetishism, sexual sadism, and sexual masochism. We will also describe four less common varieties of noncoercive paraphilias.

Fetishism

fetishism
A sexual behavior in which a person obtains sexual excitement primarily or exclusively from an inanimate object or a particular part of the body.

Fetishism (FET-ish-iz-um) refers to sexual behavior in which an individual becomes sexually aroused by focusing on an inanimate object or a part of the human body. As with many other atypical behaviors, it is often difficult to draw the line between normal activities that might have fetishistic overtones and activities that are genuinely paraphilic. Many people are erotically aroused by the sight of women's lingerie and certain specific body parts, such as feet, legs, buttocks, thighs, and breasts. Many men and some women use articles of clothing and other paraphernalia as an accompaniment to masturbation or sexual activity with a partner. Only when a person becomes focused on these objects or body parts to the exclusion of everything else is the term *fetishism* truly applicable

(Lowenstein, 2002). In some instances, a person cannot experience sexual arousal and orgasm in the absence of the fetish object. In other situations where the attachment is not so strong, sexual response can occur in the absence of the object but often with diminished intensity. For some people fetish objects serve as substitutes for human contact and are dispensed with if a partner becomes available. Some common fetish objects include women's lingerie, shoes (particularly those with high heels), boots (often affiliated with themes of domination), hair, stockings (especially black mesh hose), and a variety of leather, silk, and rubber goods (American Psychiatric Association, 2000; Seligman & Hardenburg, 2000). Leather is an especially popular fetish object: leather coats, pants, corsets, and boots (Davis, 2011).

How does fetishism develop? One way is through incorporating the object or body part, often through fantasy, in a masturbation sequence in which the reinforcement of orgasm strengthens the fetishistic association (Juninger, 1997). Another possible explanation for the origins of some cases of fetishism looks to childhood. Some children learn to associate sexual arousal with objects (such as panties or shoes) that belong to an emotionally significant person, such as their mothers or older sisters (Freund & Blanchard, 1993). The process by which this occurs is sometimes called *symbolic transformation*. In this process, the object of the fetish becomes endowed with the power or essence of its owner, so that the child (usually a male) responds to this object as he might react to the actual person (Gebhard et al., 1965). If such a behavior pattern becomes sufficiently ingrained, the person will engage in little or no sexual interaction with other people during the developmental years and even as an adult may continue to substitute fetish objects for sexual contact with other humans.

Only rarely does fetishism develop into an offense that might harm someone. Occasionally, an individual may commit burglary to supply a fetish object, and burglary is the most frequent serious offense associated with fetishism (Lowenstein, 2002). Uncommonly, a person may do something bizarre, such as cut hair from an unwilling person. In extremely rare cases a man may murder and mutilate his victim, preserving certain body parts for fantasy masturbation activities.

Common fetish items include women's lingerie and shoes. People involved in fetishism can become aroused by these common inanimate objects.

Many people who engage in transvestic fetishism feel that cross-dressing is an appropriate and legitimate source of arousal and expression, rather than a disorder or impairment.

transvestic fetishism
A sexual behavior in which a person derives sexual arousal from wearing clothing of the other sex.

Transvestic Fetishism

Until recently, nontranssexual cross-dressers were generally labeled *transvestites*. This term is now considered appropriately applied only to people who put on the clothes of the other sex to achieve sexual arousal (Langstrom & Zucker, 2005). The sexual component of cross-dressing for these individuals distinguishes them from female impersonators who cross-dress to entertain, gay men who occasionally "go in drag" to attract men or as a kind of "camp" acting out, and transsexuals who, as we discussed in Chapter 5, cross-dress to obtain a partial sense of physical and emotional completeness rather than to achieve sexual arousal.

Transvestism comprises a range of behaviors. Some people prefer to don the entire garb of the other sex. This is often a solitary activity, occurring privately in their homes. Occasionally, a person may go out on the town while so attired, but this is unusual. In general, the cross-dressing is a momentary activity, producing sexual excitement that often culminates in gratification through masturbation or sex with a partner. In many cases of transvestism, a person becomes aroused by wearing only one garment, perhaps a pair of panties or a brassiere. Because this behavior has a strong element of fetishism (Freund et al., 1996), the American Psychiatric Association (2000) formalized the link between transvestism and fetishism by placing both conditions in the diagnostic category **transvestic fetishism**. A distinguishing feature of transvestic fetishism is that the clothing article is actually worn instead of just being viewed or fondled, as is the case with fetishism.

According to the American Psychiatric Association (2000), a diagnosis of transvestic fetishism is appropriately applied to heterosexual males who experience significant psychological distress or impaired functioning as a result of recurrent sexual fantasies, urges, or behavior involving cross-dressing that persist for at least 6 months.

Today, many members of the transgendered community, who are increasingly gaining a voice in both the professional literature and the popular media, contend that cross-dressing is often an appropriate and legitimate source of sexual arousal and expression rather than an indicator of disordered behavior or psychological impairment. Consequently, they reject the label of transvestic fetishism and its implication of abnormality.

The diagnostic criteria previously outlined specify that transvestic fetishism is the sole province of heterosexual males. Apparently, it is usually men who are attracted to transvestic fetishism. This seems true of all contemporary societies for which we have data. However, a few isolated cases of women cross-dressing for sexual pleasure also appear in the clinical literature (V. Bullough & Bullough, 1993; Stoller, 1982).

Several studies of both clinical and nonclinical populations suggest that transvestic fetishism occurs primarily among married men with predominantly heterosexual orientations (Bullough & Bullough, 1997; Doctor & Prince, 1997).

As with fetishism and some other atypical behaviors, the development of transvestic fetishism often reveals a pattern of conditioning. Reinforcement, in the form of arousal and orgasm, may accompany cross-dressing activities at an early point in the development of sexual interest, as illustrated in the following anecdote:

> When I was a kid, about 11 or 12, I was fascinated and excited by magazine pictures of women modeling undergarments. Masturbating while looking at these pictures was great. Later, I began to incorporate my mother's underthings in my little masturbation rituals, at first just touching them with my free hand, and later putting them on and parading before the mirror while I did my handjob. Now, as an adult, I have numerous sexual encounters with women that are quite satisfying without the dress-up part. But I still occasionally do the dress-up when I'm alone, and I still find it quite exciting. (Authors' files)

Sexual Sadism and Sexual Masochism

Sadism and masochism are often discussed under the common category **sadomasochistic** (SAY-doh-ma-suh-kis-tik) **(SM) behavior** because they are two variations of the same phenomenon: the association of sexual expression with pain. Furthermore, the dynamics of the two behaviors are similar and overlapping. Thus in the discussion that follows we will often refer to SM behavior or activities. However, a person who engages in one of these behaviors does not necessarily engage in the other, and thus sadism and masochism are actually distinct behaviors. The American Psychiatric Association (2000) underlines this distinction by listing these paraphilias as separate categories: **sexual sadism** and **sexual masochism**. Sexual masochism is the only paraphilia that is expressed by women with some frequency (American Psychiatric Association, 2000). (People who engage in SM often label these activities as bondage-domination-sadism-masochism, or BDSM; Gross, 2006.)

Labeling behavior as sexual sadism or sexual masochism is complicated because many people enjoy some form of aggressive interaction during sex play (such as "love bites") for which the label *sadomasochistic* seems inappropriate. Alfred Kinsey and his colleagues (1948, 1953) found that 22% of the males and 12% of the females in their sample responded erotically to stories with SM themes. In another study, approximately 25% of both sexes reported erotic response to receiving love bites during sexual interaction (Gross, 2006). Another survey of 975 men and women found that 25% reported occasionally engaging in a form of SM activity with a partner (Rubin, 1990). There are indications that ease of access to people with SM inclinations, facilitated by the Internet, has resulted in an increased number of people who are exploring their SM interests (Gross, 2006; Kleinplatz & Moser, 2004).

Although SM practices have the potential for being physically dangerous, most participants generally stay within mutually agreed-on limits, often confining their activities to mild or even symbolic SM acts with a trusted partner. In mild forms of sexual sadism the pain inflicted is often more symbolic than real. For example, a willing partner may be "beaten" with a feather or a soft object designed to resemble a club. Under these conditions the receiving partner's mere feigning of suffering is sufficient to induce sexual arousal in the individual inflicting the symbolic pain.

People with masochistic inclinations are aroused by such things as being whipped, cut, pierced with needles, bound, or spanked. The degree of pain that the person must experience to achieve sexual arousal varies from symbolic or very mild to, rarely, severe beatings or mutilations. Sexual masochism is also reflected in individuals who achieve sexual arousal as a result of "being held in contempt, humiliated, and forced to do menial, filthy, or degrading service" (Money, 1981, p. 83). The common notion that any kind of pain, physical or mental, will sexually arouse a person with masochistic inclinations is a misconception. The pain must be associated with a staged encounter whose express purpose is sexual gratification.

In yet another version of masochism, some individuals derive sexual pleasure from being bound, tied up, or otherwise restricted. This behavior, called **bondage**, usually takes place with a cooperative partner who binds or restrains the individual and sometimes administers *discipline*, such as spankings or whippings (Santilla et al., 2002). One survey of 975 heterosexual women and men revealed that bondage is a fairly common practice: One fourth of respondents reported engaging in some form of bondage during some of their sexual encounters (Rubin, 1990).

Many individuals who engage in SM activities do not confine their participation to exclusively sadistic or masochistic behaviors. Some alternate between the two roles, often out of necessity, because it may be difficult to find a partner who prefers only to inflict or to receive pain. Most of these people seem to prefer one or the other role, but some are equally comfortable in either role (Mosher & Levitt, 1987; Taylor & Ussher, 2001).

sadomasochistic (SM) behavior
The association of sexual expression with pain.

sexual sadism
The act of obtaining sexual arousal through giving physical or psychological pain.

sexual masochism
The act of obtaining sexual arousal through receiving physical or psychological pain.

bondage
A sexual behavior in which a person derives sexual pleasure from being bound, tied up, or otherwise restricted.

Some individuals derive sexual pleasure from the restrictions created by bondage attire and role-playing.

Research has indicated that individuals with sexual sadistic tendencies are less common than their masochistic counterparts (Sandnabba et al., 1999). This imbalance might reflect a general social script—certainly it is more virtuous to be punished than to carry out physical or mental aggression toward another. A person who needs severe pain as a prerequisite for sexual response may have difficulty finding a cooperative partner. Consequently, such individuals may resort to causing their own pain by burning or mutilation. Likewise, a person who needs to inflict intense pain to achieve sexual arousal may find it difficult to find a willing partner, even for a price. We occasionally read of sadistic assaults against unwilling victims: The classic lust murder is often of this nature (Money, 1990). In such instances orgasmic release may be achieved by the homicidal violence itself.

Many people in contemporary Western societies view sadomasochism in a highly negative light. This attitude is certainly understandable, particularly in people who regard sexual sharing as a loving, tender interaction between partners who wish to exchange pleasure. However, much of this negativity stems from a generalized perception of SM activities as perverse forms of sexual expression that involve severe pain, suffering, and degradation. It is commonly assumed that individuals caught up in such activities are often victims rather than willing participants.

One group of researchers disputed these assumptions, suggesting that the traditional medical model of sadomasochism as a pathological condition is based on a limited sample of individuals who come to clinicians' attention because of personality disorders or severe personality problems. As with some other atypical behaviors discussed in this chapter, these researchers argued that it is misleading to draw conclusions from such a sample. They conducted their own extensive fieldwork in nonclinical environments, interviewing a variety of sadomasochism participants and observing their behaviors in many different settings. Although some subjects' behaviors fit traditional perceptions, the researchers found that, for most participants, sadomasochism was simply a form of sexual enhancement involving elements of dominance and submission, role-playing, and consensuality, "which they voluntarily and mutually chose to explore" (Weinberg et al., 1984, p. 388). Another study of 164 men who were members of sadomasochism-oriented clubs revealed that these individuals were socially well adjusted and that sadomasochistic behavior occupied only a portion of their broader sexual lives (Sandnabba et al., 1999).

Many people who engage in SM activities are motivated by a desire to experience dominance or submission, or both, rather than pain (Weinberg, 1987, 1995). This desire is reflected in the following account, provided by a student in a sexuality class:

I fantasize about sadomasochism sometimes. I want to have wild animalistic sex under the control of my husband. I want him to "force" me to do things. Domination and mild pain would seem to fulfill the moment. I have read books and talked to people about the subject, and I am terrified at some of the things, but in the bounds of my trusting relationship I would not be afraid. It seems like a silly game, but it is so damned exciting to think about. Maybe someday it will happen. (Authors' files)

Studies of sexual behavior in other species reveal that many nonhuman animals engage in what might be labeled combative or pain-inflicting behavior before coitus (Gross, 2006). Some theorists have suggested that such activity has definite neurophysiological value, heightening accompaniments of sexual arousal such as blood pressure, muscle tension, and hyperventilation (Gebhard et al., 1965). For a variety of reasons (such as guilt, anxiety, or

Howard Kingsnorth/Stone/Getty Images

apathy), some people may need additional nonsexual stimuli to achieve sufficient arousal. It has also been suggested that resistance or tension between partners enhances sex and that sadomasochism is just a more extreme version of this common principle (Tripp, 1975).

Sadomasochism might also provide participants with an escape from the rigidly controlled, restrictive role they must play in their everyday public lives. This possibility helps explain why men who engage in SM activity are much more likely to play masochistic roles than are women (Baumeister, 1997). A related theory sees sexual masochism as an attempt to escape from high levels of self-awareness. Similar to some other behaviors (such as getting drunk) in which a person may attempt to lose himself or herself, masochistic activity blocks out unwanted thoughts and feelings, particularly those that induce anxiety, guilt, or feelings of inadequacy or insecurity (Baumeister, 1988).

Clinical case studies of people who engage in sadomasochism sometimes reveal early experiences that may have established a connection between sex and pain. For example, being punished for engaging in sexual activities (such as masturbation) might lead a child or an adolescent to associate sex with pain. A child might even experience sexual arousal while being punished—for example, getting an erection or lubricating when his or her pants are pulled down and a spanking is administered (spanking is a common SM activity).

Many people, perhaps the majority, who participate in SM behaviors do not depend on these activities to achieve sexual arousal and orgasm. SM interests often exist concurrently with more conventional sexual desires (Kleinplatz & Moser, 2004). Those who practice sadomasochism only occasionally find that at least some of its excitement and erotic allure stem from its being a marked departure from more conventional sexual practices. Other people who indulge in SM acts may have acquired strong negative feelings about sex, often believing it is sinful and immoral. For such people masochistic behavior provides a guilt-relieving mechanism: Either they get their pleasure simultaneously with punishment, or they first endure the punishment to entitle them to the pleasure. Similarly, people who indulge in sadism may be punishing partners for engaging in anything so evil. Furthermore, people who have strong feelings of personal or sexual inadequacy may resort to sadistic acts of domination over their partners to temporarily alleviate these feelings.

Other Noncoercive Paraphilias

In this section, we consider four additional varieties of noncoercive paraphilias that are generally uncommon or even rare. We begin our discussion by describing autoerotic asphyxia, a dangerous form of variant sexual behavior. We then offer a few brief comments about three other uncommon noncoercive paraphilias: klismaphilia, coprophilia, and urophilia.

Autoerotic Asphyxia

Autoerotic asphyxia (also called *hypoxyphilia* or *asphyxiophilia*) is a rare and life-threatening paraphilia in which an individual, almost always a male, seeks to reduce the supply of oxygen to the brain during a heightened state of sexual arousal (Hucker, 2009; Hucker et al., 2011). The oxygen deprivation is usually accomplished by applying pressure to the neck with a chain, leather belt, ligature, or rope noose (by means of hanging). Occasionally, a plastic bag or chest compression is used as the asphyxiating device. A person might engage in these oxygen-depriving activities while alone or with a partner. Available data indicate that the majority of people who express this paraphilia are White males (Sauvageau & Racette, 2006).

We can only theorize from limited data about what motivates such behavior. People who practice autoerotic asphyxia rarely disclose this activity to relatives, friends, or therapists, let alone discuss why they engage in such behavior (Garza-Leal & Landron,

autoerotic asphyxia
The enhancement of sexual excitement and orgasm by pressure-induced oxygen deprivation.

1991; Saunders, 1989). For some the goal seems to be to increase sexual arousal and to enhance the intensity of orgasm. In this situation the item used to induce oxygen deprivation (such as a rope) is typically tightened around the neck to produce heightened arousal during masturbation and is then released at the time of orgasm. Individuals often devise elaborate techniques that enable them to free themselves from the strangling device before losing consciousness.

The enhancement of sexual excitement by pressure-induced oxygen deprivation may bear some relationship to reports that orgasm is intensified by inhaling amyl nitrate ("poppers"), a drug used to treat heart pain. This substance is known to temporarily reduce brain oxygenation through peripheral dilation of the arteries that supply blood to the brain.

It has also been suggested that autoerotic asphyxia is a highly unusual variant of sexual masochism in which participants act out ritualized bondage themes (American Psychiatric Association, 2000; Cosgray et al., 1991). People who engage in this practice sometimes keep diaries of elaborate bondage fantasies and, in some cases, describe fantasies of being asphyxiated or harmed by others as they engage in this rare paraphilia.

One important fact about this seldom-seen paraphilia is quite clear: This is an extremely dangerous activity that often results in death (Cooper, 1996; Garos, 1994; Hucker, 2009). Accidental deaths sometimes occur because of equipment malfunction or mistakes, such as errors in the placement of the noose or ligature. Data from the United States, England, Australia, and Canada indicate that one to two deaths per 1 million people are caused by autoerotic asphyxiation each year (American Psychiatric Association, 2000; Hucker, 2009; Hucker et al., 2011). The Federal Bureau of Investigation estimates that deaths in the United States resulting from this activity may run as high as 1,000 per year.

Klismaphilia

klismaphilia
An unusual variant of sexual expression in which an individual obtains sexual pleasure from receiving enemas.

Klismaphilia (kliz-muh-FILL-ee-uh) is an unusual variant of sexual expression in which an individual obtains sexual pleasure from receiving enemas (Agnew, 2000). Less commonly, the erotic arousal is associated with giving enemas. The case histories of many individuals who express klismaphilia reveal that as infants or young children they were frequently given enemas by concerned and affectionate mothers. This association of loving attention with anal stimulation may eroticize the experience for some people so that as adults they may manifest a need to receive an enema as a substitute or prerequisite for genital intercourse.

Coprophilia and Urophilia

coprophilia
A sexual paraphilia in which a person obtains sexual arousal from contact with feces.

urophilia
A sexual paraphilia in which a person obtains sexual arousal from contact with urine.

Coprophilia (kah-pruh-FILL-ee-uh) and **urophilia** (yoo-roh-FILL-ee-uh) refer to activities in which people obtain sexual arousal from contact with feces and urine, respectively. Individuals who exhibit coprophilia achieve high levels of sexual excitement from watching someone defecate or by defecating on someone. In rare instances, they achieve arousal when someone defecates on them. Urophilia is expressed by urinating on someone or being urinated on. This activity, reflected in the chapter opening anecdote, has been referred to as "water sports" and "golden showers." There is no consensus about the origins of these highly unusual paraphilias.

Coercive Paraphilias

In this section, we first discuss three common forms of coercive paraphilic behaviors: exhibitionism, obscene phone calls, and voyeurism. Three other varieties of coercive paraphilias—frotteurism, zoophilia, and necrophilia—are also discussed.

Exhibitionism

Exhibitionism, often called indecent exposure, refers to behavior in which an individual (almost always male) exposes his genitals to an involuntary observer (usually an adult woman or a girl) (American Psychiatric Association, 2000; Marshall et al., 1991). Typically, a man who has exposed himself obtains sexual gratification by masturbating shortly thereafter, using mental images of the observer's reaction to increase his arousal. Some men, while having sex with a willing partner, fantasize about exposing themselves or replay mental images from previous episodes. Still others have orgasm triggered by the act of exposure, and some masturbate while exhibiting themselves (American Psychiatric Association, 2000; de Silva, 1999). The reinforcement of associating sexual arousal and orgasm with the actual act of exhibitionism or with mental fantasies of exposing oneself contributes significantly to the maintenance of exhibitionistic behavior (Blair & Lanyon, 1981). Exposure can occur in a variety of locations, most of which allow for easy escape. Subways, relatively deserted streets, parks, and cars with a door left open are common places for exhibitionism to occur. However, sometimes a private dwelling is the scene of an exposure, as revealed in the following account:

> One evening I was shocked to open the door of my apartment to a naked man. I looked long enough to see that he was underdressed for the occasion and then slammed the door in his face. He didn't come back. I'm sure my look of total horror was what he was after. But it is difficult to keep your composure when you open your door to a naked man. (Authors' files)

Certainly, many of us have exhibitionistic tendencies: We may go to nude beaches, parade before admiring lovers, or wear provocative clothes or scanty swimwear. However, such behavior is considered appropriate by a society that in many ways exploits and celebrates the erotically portrayed human body. That legally defined exhibitionistic behavior involves generally unwilling observers sets it apart from these more acceptable variations of exhibitionism.

Our knowledge of who displays this behavior is based largely on studies of arrested offenders—a sample that may be unrepresentative. This sampling problem is common to many forms of atypical behavior that are defined as criminal. From the available data, however limited, it appears that most people who exhibit themselves are men in their 20s or 30s, and over half are married or have been married (Murphy, 1997). They are often shy, nonassertive people who feel inadequate and insecure and suffer from problems with intimacy (Arndt, 1991; Marshall et al., 1991; Murphy & Page, 2008). Their sexual relationships are likely to have been unsatisfactory. Many were reared in atmospheres characterized by puritanical and shame-inducing attitudes toward sexuality.

A number of factors influence the development of exhibitionistic behavior. Many individuals have such powerful feelings of personal inadequacy that they are afraid to reach out to another person out of fear of rejection (Minor & Dwyer, 1997). Their exhibitionism is thus a limited attempt to somehow involve others, however fleetingly, in their sexual expression. Limiting contact to briefly opening a raincoat before dashing off minimizes the possibility of overt rejection. Some men who expose themselves may be looking for affirmation of their masculinity. Others, feeling isolated and unappreciated, may simply be seeking attention, which they desperately crave. A few feel anger and hostility toward people, particularly women, who have failed to notice them or who they believe have caused them emotional pain. Under these circumstances exposure can be a form of reprisal, designed to shock or frighten the people they see as the source of their discomfort. In addition, exhibitionism is not uncommon in emotionally disturbed,

exhibitionism
The act of exposing one's genitals to an unwilling observer.

Critical Thinking Question

People are typically much less concerned about female exhibitionism than they are about male exhibitionism. For example, if a woman observed a man undressing in front of a window, the man might be accused of being an exhibitionist. However, if the roles were reversed and the woman was undressing, the man would likely be labeled a voyeur. What do you think of this sex-based inconsistency in labeling these behaviors?

intellectually disabled, or mentally disoriented individuals. In these cases the behavior reflects a limited awareness of what society defines as appropriate actions, a breakdown in personal ethical controls, or both.

In contrast to the public image of an exhibitionist as a person who lurks about in the shadows, ready to grab hapless victims and drag them off to ravish them, most men who engage in exhibitionism limit this activity to exposing themselves (American Psychiatric Association, 2000). Yet the word *victim* is not entirely inappropriate, in that observers of such exhibitionistic episodes may be emotionally traumatized by the experience (Cox, 1988; Marshall et al., 1991). Some feel that they are in danger of being raped or otherwise harmed. A few, particularly young children, can develop negative feelings about genital anatomy from such an experience.

Investigators have noted that some people who expose themselves, probably a small minority, actually physically assault their victims (Brown, 2000). Furthermore, in some cases men who engage in exhibitionism may progress from exposing themselves to more serious offenses, such as rape and child molestation (Abel, 1981; Bradford et al., 1992).

What is an appropriate response if someone exposes himself to you? It is important to keep in mind that most people who express exhibitionist behavior want to elicit reactions of excitement, shock, fear, or terror. Although it may be difficult not to react in any of these ways, a better response is to calmly ignore the exhibitionist act and go about your business. Of course, it is also important to immediately distance yourself from the offender and to report such acts to the police or campus security as soon as possible. ●

Obscene Phone Calls

People who make obscene phone calls share characteristics with exhibitionists. Thus obscene phone calling (sometimes called *telephone scatologia*) is viewed by some professionals as a subtype of exhibitionism. People who make obscene phone calls typically experience sexual arousal when their victims react in a horrified or shocked manner, and many masturbate during or immediately after a "successful" phone exchange. These callers are typically male, and they often suffer from pervasive feelings of inadequacy and insecurity (Matek, 1988; Prince et al., 2002). Obscene phone calls are frequently the only way they can find to have sexual exchanges. However, when relating to the other sex, they frequently show greater anxiety and hostility than do people inclined toward exhibitionism, as revealed in the following account:

> One night I received a phone call from a man who sounded quite normal until he started his barrage of filth. Just as I was about to slam the phone down, he announced, "Don't hang up. I know where you live (address followed) and that you have two little girls. If you don't want to find them all mangled up, you will hear what I have to say. Furthermore, I expect you to be available for calls every night at this time." It was a nightmare. He called night after night. Sometimes he made me listen while he masturbated. Finally I couldn't take it any longer, and I contacted the police. Thank heavens, the calls eventually stopped. I was about to go crazy. (Authors' files)

Fortunately, a caller rarely follows up his verbal assault with a physical attack on his victim.

What is the best way to handle obscene phone calls? Information about how to deal with such calls is available from most local phone company offices. Because these offices are commonly besieged by such queries, you may need to be persistent in your request. A few tips are worth knowing; they may even make it unnecessary to seek outside help.

© Jutta Klee/Corbis

Exhibitionists often want to elicit reactions of excitement, shock, fear, or terror. The best response is to calmly ignore the act and casually go about your business.

First, quite often the caller has picked your name at random from a phone book or perhaps knows you from some other source and is just trying you out to see what kind of reaction he can get. Your initial response may be critical in determining his subsequent actions. He wants you to be horrified, shocked, or disgusted; thus the best response is usually not to react overtly. Slamming down the phone may reveal your emotional state and provide reinforcement to the caller. Simply set it down gently and go about your business. If the phone rings again immediately, ignore it. Chances are that he will seek out other, more responsive victims.

Other tactics may also be helpful. One, used successfully by a former student, is to feign deafness. "What is that you said? You must speak up. I'm hard of hearing, you know!" Setting down the phone with the explanation that you are going to another extension (which you never pick up) may be another practical solution. Finally, screening calls with an answering machine or caller ID might also prove helpful. The caller is likely to hang up in the absence of an emotionally responding person.

If you are persistently bothered by obscene phone calls, you may need to take additional steps. Your telephone company should cooperate in changing your number to an unlisted one at no charge. It is probably not a good idea to heed the common advice to blow a police whistle into the mouthpiece of the phone (which may be quite painful and even harmful to the caller's ear) because you may end up receiving the same treatment from your caller.

Call tracing, a service offered by many telephone companies, may assist you in dealing with repetitive obscene or threatening phone calls. After breaking connection with the caller, you enter a designated code, such as *star 57*. The telephone company then automatically traces the call. After a certain number of successful traces to the same number, a warning letter is sent to the offender indicating that he or she has been identified as engaging in unlawful behavior that must stop. The offender is warned that police intervention or civil legal action is an option if the behavior continues. Call tracing is clearly not effective when calls are placed from a public pay phone, and calls made from cellular phones cannot be traced. ●

Although your initial reaction to an obscene phone call may be horror, shock, or disgust, it is usually best not to respond emotionally. A caller who doesn't receive the desired response from you is less likely to call again.

Voyeurism

Voyeurism (voi-YUR-ih-zum) refers to deriving sexual pleasure from looking at the naked bodies or sexual activities of others, usually strangers, without their consent (American Psychiatric Association, 2000). Because a degree of voyeurism is socially acceptable (witness the popularity of sex sites on the Internet), it is sometimes difficult to determine when voyeuristic behavior becomes a problem (Arndt, 1991; Forsyth, 1996). To qualify as atypical sexual behavior, voyeurism must be preferred to sexual relations with another person or indulged in with some risk (or both). People who engage in this behavior are often most sexually aroused when the risk of discovery is high—which may explain why most are not attracted to such places as nudist camps and nude beaches, where looking is acceptable (Tollison & Adams, 1979).

Again, people inclined toward voyeurism often share characteristics with people who expose themselves (Arndt, 1991; Langevin et al., 1979). They may have poorly developed sociosexual skills, with strong feelings of inferiority and inadequacy, particularly as directed toward potential sexual partners (Kaplan & Krueger, 1997). As the common term *peeping Tom* implies, voyeurism is typically, although not exclusively, expressed by males (Davison & Neale, 1993). They tend to be young men, usually in their early 20s (Dwyer, 1988; Lavin, 2008). They rarely "peep" at someone they know, preferring strangers instead. Most individuals who engage in such activity are content merely to look, keeping their distance. However, in some instances such individuals go on to more serious offenses, such as burglary, arson, assault, and even rape (Abel & Osborn, 2000; Langevin, 2003).

voyeurism
The act of obtaining sexual gratification by observing undressed or sexually interacting people without their consent.

This behavior more typically includes peering into bedroom windows, stationing oneself by the entrance to women's bathrooms, and boring holes in the walls of public dressing rooms. Some men travel elaborate routes several nights a week for the occasional reward of a glimpse, through a window, of bare anatomy or, rarely, a scene of sexual interaction. A new form of voyeurism has emerged in which small, technologically advanced video cameras are used to surreptitiously invade the personal privacy of many unaware victims. It's perhaps best described as *video voyeurism*.

Small, affordable video cameras are increasingly being used to invade and record some of our most private moments. These images might then be displayed on the Internet or on someone's DVD player. High-tech video devices—hidden in such locations as smoke detectors, exit signs, ceiling fixtures, and gym bags—make it easy for unscrupulous individuals with either a penchant for peeping or an eye for a quick buck to victimize people by secretly recording them.

Both local and national media report on a proliferation of various forms of video voyeurism, which include hidden cameras or cell phones in such places as bathrooms ("bathroomcams"), shower facilities ("showercams"), locker rooms ("lockerroomcams"), and bedrooms ("bedroomcams") and under working women's desks ("upskirtcams"). Cell phones with video and still photography features have added another disconcerting dimension to the proliferation of video voyeurism. For example, a male school teacher in Florida was recently arrested and charged with using a cell phone, placed under a bathroom stall, to record images of minors and adults using the bathroom facilities (UPI Newstrack, 2011). In another similar case, an employee of an Illinois hardware business was charged with unauthorized videotaping via a video camera found in the store's bathroom (Nagle, 2011).

People who use "voyeurcams" do so either for their own sexual gratification or for financial gain. Technological advances in video equipment, together with the Internet, have allowed the emergence of a disturbing new financial market in which unethical entrepreneurs sell secret video invasions of privacy either for home DVD viewing or for viewing at pay-per-view websites. The number of both unauthorized and authorized occurrences of voyeuristic Internet video displays has exploded. The multiplicity of websites that appeal to video voyeurs are set up on a pay-per-view or subscription basis, and a person can log on to watch the activities of people, often attractive women, who may not know that they are being watched.

Unfortunately, many embarrassed and angry victims of video voyeurism have discovered that they have little legal recourse when secret videos are marketed by unscrupulous entrepreneurs based in foreign countries where the legal codes allow them to function without fear of legal reprisals. Currently all states, with the exception of Iowa, have some legal prohibitions pertaining to video voyeurism. However, vague legal wording, in conjunction with the dramatic increase in legal video surveillance since 9/11, has rendered these state laws difficult to interpret and enforce.

We hope that states will become increasingly effective in prosecuting high-tech video voyeurism and that the general public will become more aware of this serious form of personal privacy invasion. Furthermore, as we become more knowledgeable about the potential for this invasive process, we can be more aware and careful in situations where we might be victimized in this fashion. For example, when changing in a gym or health club, be on the lookout for clothes bags positioned so that they might allow secret video recording. A Missouri youth-group leader was recently convicted of producing and possessing child pornography obtained via secretly taping young boys in various settings (e.g., showers and bathroom facilities) with a video camera he had hidden inside a backpack (Mann, 2011).

It is difficult to isolate specific influences that trigger voyeuristic behavior, particularly because so many of us demonstrate voyeuristic tendencies in a somewhat more controlled fashion. The adolescent or young adult male who displays this behavior often feels great curiosity about sexual activity (as many of us do) but at the same time feels inadequate or insecure. His voyeurism, either while physically present or by means of hidden video cameras, becomes a vicarious fulfillment because he may be unable to engage in sexual activity without experiencing a great deal of anxiety. In some instances voyeuristic behavior is also reinforced by feelings of power and superiority over those who are secretly observed.

Other Coercive Paraphilias

We conclude our discussion of coercive paraphilias with a few brief comments about three additional varieties of these coercive or invasive forms of paraphilia. The first two, frotteurism and zoophilia, are fairly common. The third variant form, necrophilia, is a rare and extremely aberrant form of sexual expression.

Frotteurism

Frotteurism (frah-toor-IH-zum) is a fairly common coercive paraphilia that goes largely unnoticed. It involves an individual, usually a male, who obtains sexual pleasure by pressing or rubbing against a fully clothed female in a crowded public place, such as an elevator, a bus, a subway, a large sporting event, or an outdoor concert. The most common form of contact is between the man's clothed penis and a woman's buttocks or legs. Less commonly, he may use his hands to touch a woman's thighs, pubic region, breasts, or buttocks. This form of contact, called "toucherism," may seem to be inadvertent, and the woman who is touched may not notice or may pay little heed to the seemingly casual contact. On the other hand, she may feel victimized and angry (Freund et al., 1997).

A man who engages in frotteurism may achieve arousal and orgasm during the act. More commonly, he incorporates the mental images of his actions into masturbation fantasies at a later time. Men who engage in this activity have many of the characteristics manifested by those who practice exhibitionism. They are frequently plagued by feelings of social and sexual inadequacy. Their brief, furtive contacts with strangers in crowded places allow them to include others in their sexual expression in a safe, nonthreatening manner.

As with other paraphilias, it is difficult to estimate just how common this variety of coercive paraphilia is. One study of reportedly typical or normal college men found that 21% of the respondents had engaged in one or more frotteuristic acts (Templeman & Sinnett, 1991).

Zoophilia

Zoophilia (zoh-oh-FILL-ee-uh), sometimes called *bestiality*, involves sexual contact between humans and animals (American Psychiatric Association, 2000). You may wonder why we classify this as a coercive paraphilia, because such behavior does not involve coercing other people into acts that they would normally avoid. In many instances of zoophilia, it is reasonable to presume that the animals involved are also unwilling participants, and the acts performed are often both coercive and invasive. Consequently, assigning this paraphilia to the coercive category seems appropriate.

In Kinsey's sample populations, 8% of the males and almost 4% of the females reported having had sexual experiences with animals at some point in their lives. The frequency of such behavior among males was highest for those raised on farms (17% of these men reported experiencing orgasm as a result of animal contact). The animals most frequently involved in sex with humans are sheep, goats, donkeys, large fowl (ducks and geese), dogs, and cats. Males are most likely to have contact with farm animals and to engage in penile–vaginal intercourse or to have their genitals orally stimulated by the animals (Hunt, 1974;

Critical Thinking Question

Is it ethically acceptable to visit websites that offer video feeds from hidden cameras or unauthorized videos of people's private lives? Why or why not?

frotteurism
A fairly common paraphilia in which a person obtains sexual pleasure by pressing or rubbing against another person in a crowded public place.

zoophilia
A paraphilia in which a person has sexual contact with animals.

AP Photo/Laurent Rebours

Frotteurism is a fairly common paraphilia practiced in crowded public places, such as buses, subways, and outdoor concerts.

Kinsey et al., 1948; Miletski, 2002). Women are more likely to have contact with household pets, involving an animal in licking their genitals or masturbating a male dog. Less commonly, some women have trained a dog to mount them and engage in coitus (Gendel & Bonner, 1988; Kinsey et al., 1953).

Sexual contact with animals is commonly only a transitory experience of young people to whom a human sexual partner is inaccessible or forbidden (Money, 1981). Most adolescent males and females who experiment with zoophilia make a transition to adult sexual relations with human partners. True, or nontransitory, zoophilia exists only when sexual contact with animals is preferred, regardless of what other forms of sexual expression are available. Such behavior, which is rare, may be expressed only by people with deep-rooted psychological problems or distorted images of the other sex. For example, a man who has a pathological hatred of women may be attempting to express his contempt for them by choosing animals in preference to women as sexual partners. However, some men who engage in zoophilia do not appear to fit this profile. An anonymous Internet questionnaire study of 114 self-defined "zoophile" men found that while the majority of respondents indicated preferring animal sex to human sex, a desire for affection and pleasurable sex, and not hatred of women, were presented as the major reasons for sexual interest in animals (Williams & Weinberg, 2003).

Necrophilia

necrophilia
A rare sexual paraphilia in which a person obtains sexual gratification by viewing or having intercourse with a corpse.

Necrophilia (ne-kruh-FILL-ee-uh) is an extremely rare sexual variation in which a person obtains sexual gratification by viewing or having intercourse with a corpse. This paraphilia appears to occur exclusively among males, who may be driven to remove freshly buried bodies from cemeteries or to seek employment in morgues or funeral homes (Tollison & Adams, 1979). However, the vast majority of people who work in these settings do not have tendencies toward necrophilia.

There are a few cases on record of men with necrophilic preferences who kill someone to gain access to a corpse (Milner & Dopke, 1997). The notorious Jeffrey Dahmer, the Milwaukee man who murdered and mutilated his young male victims, is believed by some experts in criminal pathology to have been motivated by uncontrollable necrophilic urges. More commonly, the difficulties associated with gaining access to dead bodies lead some men with necrophilic preferences to limit their deviant behavior to contact with simulated corpses. Some prostitutes cater to this desire by powdering themselves to mimic the pallor of death, dressing in a shroud, and lying very still during intercourse. Any movement on their part may inhibit their customers' sexual arousal.

Men who engage in necrophilia almost always manifest severe emotional disorders (Goldman, 1992). They may see themselves as sexually and socially inept and may both hate and fear women. Consequently, the only "safe" woman may be one whose lifelessness epitomizes a nonthreatening, totally subjugated sexual partner (Rosman & Resnick, 1989; Stoller, 1977).

Sexual Addiction: Fact, Fiction, or Misnomer?

Both the professional literature and the popular media have directed considerable attention to a condition commonly referred to as sexual addiction. The idea that people can become dominated by insatiable sexual needs has been around for a long time, as exemplified by the terms *nymphomania*, applied to women, and *satyriasis* or *Don Juanism*, applied to men. Many professionals have traditionally reacted negatively to these labels, suggesting that they are disparaging terms likely to induce unnecessary guilt in individuals who enjoy an active sex life. Furthermore, it has been argued that one cannot assign a label implying excessive sexual activity when no clear criteria establish what constitutes "normal" levels of sexual involvement. The criteria often used to establish alleged subconditions of *hypersexuality*—nymphomania and satyriasis—are subjective and value laden. Therefore these terms are typically defined moralistically rather than scientifically, a fact that has generated harsh criticism from a number of professionals (Klein, 1991, 2003; Levine & Troiden, 1988). Psychotherapist Marty Klein (2003, 2012b) is especially critical of the sex addiction movement, which in his view both exploits people's fear of their own sexuality and pathologizes sexual behavior and impulses that are not unhealthy. Nevertheless, the concept of sexual addiction achieved a heightened legitimacy with the publication of Patrick Carnes's book *The Sexual Addiction* (1983), later retitled *Out of the Shadows: Understanding Sexual Addiction* (2001, 3rd ed.).

According to Carnes, many people who engage in some of the atypical or paraphilic behaviors described in this chapter (as well as extreme coercive behaviors, such as child molestation) are manifesting the outward symptoms of a psychological addiction in which feelings of depression, anxiety, loneliness, and worthlessness are temporarily relieved through a sexual high not unlike the high achieved by mood-altering chemicals such as alcohol and cocaine.

The concept of sexual addiction has generated considerable attention in the professional community. While Carnes and his supporters argue for acceptance of sexual addiction as a legitimate diagnostic category, detractors point to a continuing "tradition in the sex addiction literature of forgoing empirical research and presenting conjectures as fact" (Chivers, 2005, p. 476). Many sexologists do not believe that sexual addiction should be a distinct diagnostic category, because it is rare and lacking in distinction from other compulsive disorders, such as gambling and eating disorders, and because this label negates individual responsibility for "uncontrollable" sexual compulsions that victimize others (Levine & Troiden, 1988; Satel, 1993).

Despite the skepticism of many sexologists about including sexual addiction as a diagnostic category, "Americans are being diagnosed as sex addicts in record numbers" (C. Lee, 2011, p. 50). Recent media attention to two cases of alleged sexual addiction, one involving Tiger Woods and the other Dominique Strauss-Kahn, has focused the nation's attention on this type of behavior.

A number of professionals recognize that some people become involved in patterns of excessive sexual activity. Noteworthy in this group is sexologist Eli Coleman (1990, 1991, 2003), who prefers to describe these behaviors as symptomatic of sexual compulsion rather than addiction. According to Coleman, a person manifesting excessive sexual behaviors often suffers from feelings of shame, unworthiness, inadequacy, and loneliness. These negative feelings cause great psychological pain, and this pain then causes the person to search for a "fix," or an agent that has pain-numbing qualities, such as alcohol, certain foods, gambling, or, in this instance, sex. Indulging oneself in this fix produces only a brief respite from the psychological pain, which returns in full force, thus triggering a greater need to engage in such behaviors to obtain further temporary relief. Unfortunately, these repetitive compulsive acts soon tend to be self-defeating; that is, they compound feelings of shame and lead to intimacy dysfunction by interrupting the development of normal, healthy interpersonal functioning.

Other sexologists, notably John Bancroft and Zoran Vukadinovic (2004), believe that because of a lack of empirical research, the currently fashionable concepts of sexual addiction and compulsive sexual behavior are of uncertain scientific value. These authors suggest that until we have more data to evaluate the scientific validity of these concepts, it is preferable to use the more general descriptive term *out of control* to describe such problematic sexual behavior.

Critical Thinking Question

Which of the atypical sexual behaviors discussed in this chapter do you find the most unacceptable? Why?

We can expect that professionals in the field of sexuality will continue to debate for some time how to diagnose, describe, and explain problems of excessive or uncontrolled sexuality. Even as this discussion continues, professional treatment programs for compulsive or addictive sexual behaviors have emerged throughout the United States (more than 2,000 programs at last count), most modeled after the 12-step program of Alcoholics Anonymous (Kafka, 2009; National Council on Sexual Addiction and Compulsivity, 2002). Data pertaining to treatment outcomes for these programs are still too limited to allow evaluation of therapeutic effectiveness. Besides formal treatment programs, a number of community-based self-help organizations have surfaced throughout the United States. These groups include Sex Addicts Anonymous, Sexaholics Anonymous, Sexual Compulsives Anonymous, and Sex and Love Addicts Anonymous.

Because sex has become a highly sought-out topic among users of the Internet, some professionals have suggested that a new variety of sexual addiction or sexual compulsivity has emerged. The issue being debated is whether cybersex addiction and compulsivity is a harmless sexual outlet or problematic sexual behavior. We examine this issue in the final paragraphs of this chapter.

A prominent physician in our home state recently lost his position and staff privileges at a local hospital when it was discovered that he was using a hospital computer to visit sexually explicit Internet sites that specialize in child pornography. An investigation revealed that this individual spent an inordinate amount of time, both on the job and at home, compulsively surfing sexually oriented websites, especially those with explicit sexual content dealing with children. This case illustrates a variety of behavior, spawned by the Internet, that has raised the concern of a number of mental health specialists.

Sexually oriented Internet sites are among the most widely visited topical areas of the World Wide Web. Does the widespread incidence of "surfing for sex" indicate problematic behavior and warrant societal concern? Some suggest the opposite—that pursuing cybersex is a harmless recreational pursuit offering anonymous access to sexually oriented material that provides sexual outlets (such as chat room sex or masturbating to sexual images) that are safe from the dangers of STIs and other relationship risks (Waskul, 2004). In addition, the Internet can be useful to people who wish to explore sexual fantasies online in the safety and privacy of their homes (Quittner, 2003).

A less benign view of Internet sex emerges from a growing awareness that for a small but ever-increasing number of individuals who surf the Internet primarily for erotic stimulation and sexual outlets, the affordability, accessibility, and anonymity of the Internet are creating a new breed of sexual compulsives addicted to cybersex (M. Ross et al., 2011). Many of these individuals are using cybersex to the exclusion of personal relationships (Ayres & Haddock, 2009; Cooper, 2002, 2003; Dew & Chaney, 2004; Philaretou, 2005).

It is difficult to accurately estimate how many Internet users in the United States experience problems associated with visiting Web sex sites. A large majority of people who access the Internet for sexual purposes do not appear to experience adverse consequences (Waskul, 2004). However, some research indicates that 6–10% of Internet users do report being concerned about the possible negative consequences of their online sexual activities (Dew & Chaney, 2004). Furthermore, studies indicate that 1% of sex site surfers are so hooked on or addicted to cybersex that their capacity to function effectively in their everyday lives is severely damaged (Carnes, 2001; Cooper et al., 2000). Such individuals are likely to spend endless hours each day surfing sex sites, masturbating to sexually explicit images, or engaging in mutual online sex with someone contacted through a chat room.

The sexual excitement, stimulation, and orgasmic outlets provided by a virtually infinite variety of Internet sexual opportunities may lead to a compulsive pursuit of cyberspace sex that can have a devastating effect on a cybersex addict's life and family (Cooper, 2002; Woodward, 2003). Partners of these individuals report feeling ignored, abandoned, devalued, or betrayed as a result of their mate's compulsive pursuit of cybersex (Brody, 2000; Cooper, 2002). Some people devote so much time to forays into cybersex that they end up neglecting family members or job responsibilities, or both (Philaretou, 2005).

An additional hazard faced by some cybersex addicts and compulsives who pursue online sexual relationships is that they may progress to arranging off-line meetings that can have seriously adverse consequences, including exposure to STIs and sexual assault (Cooper, 2002; Genuis & Genuis, 2005).

Mental health professionals have expressed concern about teenage addiction to cybersex (Abelman, 2007; Fleming & Rickwood, 2004; Jancin, 2005). Some clinicians believe that teenagers, especially males, are becoming addicted to sex on the Internet. According to psychotherapist Ann Freeman, it is common to encounter youths who are addicted to masturbating to Web sex sites three or four times daily (in Jancin, 2005). Such excessive Internet-based sexual behavior may lead to social isolation, unhealthy sexual attitudes, loneliness, depression, and possible "stranger-danger" in the form of being tracked and lured by cybersex pedophile predators (Fleming & Rickwood, 2004; Jancin, 2005; Subrahmanyam & Greenfield, 2008). (See Chapter 17 for a discussion of pedophiles in cyberspace.)

We hope that future studies of cybersex will provide a clearer answer to the question, "Is compulsive exploration of online sex a relatively harmless sexual outlet or a potentially harmful variety of problematic sexual behavior?" For the present, a number of professionals have raised our awareness of the potentially adverse consequences of getting hooked on cybersex.

Summary

What Constitutes Atypical Sexual Behavior?

- Atypical, paraphilic sexual behavior involves a variety of sexual activities that, in their fully developed form, are statistically uncommon in the general population.
- Such behaviors exist in many gradations, ranging from mild, infrequently expressed tendencies to full-blown, regularly manifested behaviors.
- Paraphilias are usually expressed by males, are sometimes harmful to others, may be preludes to more serious sexual offenses, and tend to occur in clusters.

Noncoercive Paraphilias

- Noncoercive paraphilias are often solo activities or behaviors that involve the participation of adults who agree to engage in, observe, or just put up with the particular variant behavior.

- Fetishism, transvestic fetishism, sexual sadism, sexual masochism, autoerotic asphyxia, klismaphilia, coprophilia, and urophilia are all varieties of noncoercive paraphilias.
- Fetishism is a form of atypical sexual behavior in which an individual obtains arousal by focusing on an inanimate object or a part of the human body.
- Fetishism is often a product of conditioning, in which the fetish object becomes associated with sexual arousal through the reinforcement of masturbation-produced orgasm.
- Transvestic fetishism involves obtaining sexual excitement by cross-dressing. It is usually a solitary activity, expressed by a heterosexual male in the privacy of his own home.
- Sadomasochism can be defined as obtaining sexual arousal through receiving or giving physical or mental pain, or both.
- Most participants in sadomasochism view it as a form of sexual enhancement that they voluntarily and mutually choose to explore.

- People who engage in sadomasochistic behavior may be seeking additional nonsexual stimuli to achieve sufficient arousal. They may also be acting out of deeply rooted beliefs that sexual activity is sinful and immoral.
- For some participants, sadomasochism acts as an escape valve that allows them temporarily to step out of the rigid, restrictive roles they play in their everyday lives.
- Individuals who engage in sadomasochism sometimes describe early experiences that may have established a connection between sex and pain.
- Autoerotic asphyxia is a rare and life-threatening paraphilia in which an individual, almost always a male, seeks to enhance sexual excitement and orgasm by pressure-induced oxygen deprivation.
- Klismaphilia is a paraphilia that involves achieving sexual pleasure from receiving enemas.
- Coprophilia and urophilia are paraphilias in which a person obtains sexual arousal from contact with feces or urine, respectively.

Coercive Paraphilias

- Coercive paraphilias are invasive, in that they involve unwilling recipients of behavior such as voyeurism or exhibitionism. Coercive acts may harm their targets, who may be psychologically traumatized by the experience.
- Exhibitionism, obscene phone calls, voyeurism, frotteurism, zoophilia, and necrophilia are all varieties of coercive paraphilias.
- Exhibitionism is behavior in which an individual, almost always a male, exposes his genitals to an involuntary observer.
- People who exhibit themselves are usually young adult males who have strong feelings of inadequacy and insecurity. Sexual relationships, either past or present, are likely to be unsatisfactory.
- Gratification is usually obtained when the reaction to exhibitionism is shock, disgust, or fear. Physical assault is generally not associated with exhibitionism.
- The characteristics of individuals who make obscene phone calls are similar to those of exhibitionists.
- Although there may be an element of hostility in obscene phone calls, the caller rarely follows up his verbal assault with a physical attack on his victim.
- Voyeurism is obtaining sexual pleasure from looking at the exposed bodies or sexual activities of others, usually strangers.

- People inclined toward voyeurism, typically males, are often sociosexually underdeveloped, with strong feelings of inferiority and inadequacy.
- Video voyeurism is a form of voyeurism in which video cameras are used to surreptitiously invade the personal privacy of unaware victims.
- Frotteurism involves a person obtaining sexual pleasure by pressing or rubbing against another person in a crowded public place.
- Zoophilia involves sexual contact between humans and animals; it occurs most commonly as a transitory experience of young people to whom a sexual partner is inaccessible or forbidden.
- Necrophilia involves obtaining sexual gratification by viewing or having intercourse with a corpse.

Sexual Addiction: Fact, Fiction, or Misnomer?

- The concept of sexual addiction suggests that some people who engage in excessive sexual activity are manifesting symptoms of a psychological addiction, in which feelings of depression, anxiety, loneliness, and worthlessness are temporarily relieved through a sexual high.
- Many sexologists do not believe that sexual addiction should be a distinct diagnostic category, because it is rare and lacking in distinction from other compulsive disorders, such as gambling and eating disorders, and because this label negates individual responsibility for "uncontrollable" sexual compulsions that victimize others.

Media Resources

Log in to CengageBrain.com to access the resources your instructor requires.

Go to CengageBrain.com to access Psychology CourseMate, where you will find an interactive eBook, glossaries, flashcards, quizzes, videos, and more.

Also access links to chapter-related websites, including **Paraphilias, Tri-ESS,** and **Society for the Advancement of Sexual Health (SASH).**

Sexual Coercion

Rape
What are some major false beliefs about rape?

What sociocultural factors help explain the high incidence of rape in U.S. society?

Sexual Abuse of Children
What are some reasons that sexual abuse of children is so often unreported?

What can parents and other caregivers do to make children less vulnerable to sexual abuse?

Sexual Harassment
What kinds of sexual harassment occur in the workplace and in academia?

What are some options available to someone who is being sexually harassed?

AP Photo/Michael Manning

> I was sexually abused by my stepbrother throughout a great part of my child-hood. The abuse started the summer I was 10. He is three and a half years older than me, and he was my designated babysitter all summer. He usually wasn't violent. It was more coaxing and coercion, and threats of what would happen if I told. The strongest memories I have are of times when it was particularly physically painful. I put myself out of my body, and would just watch the ceiling fan go around and around. When I was 13 I saw a talk show on incest and then told a woman at my church what was happening to me, and it kind of all fell apart from there. As much as the thought of the whole experience is repulsive, what hurt the most is my parents calling it child's play in discussion with CPS [Child Protective Services]. My parents even had me believing at one point that I really had wanted it and was telling them about it for attention. Because of this reaction, I believed for a while that it was my fault and that I was dirty because of it. My stepbrother plea-bargained his case, and he was put on probation. I was taken out of the home and put in foster and group homes. I attempted suicide numerous times and was in four different psychiatric hospitals over about four years. I no longer have any contact with the "family." I am blessed to have been adopted into another loving family. My new dad is the one who saved me from hating all men forever. But I still have problems regarding sex. My boyfriend can't even hold me romantically. I have only stopped having flashbacks and nightmares fairly recently. I am in therapy for the umpteenth time, but this time it is really working. (Authors' files)

A person has been sexually victimized when she or he is deprived of free choice and is coerced or forced to comply with sexual acts under duress. Victims of coercive sexual acts often suffer grievous consequences, as revealed in the preceding account, provided by a 19-year-old college student. In this chapter, we focus on three particularly abusive and exploitative forms of sexual coercion: rape, the sexual abuse of children, and sexual harassment. All these behaviors involve strong elements of coercion, sometimes even violence.

Rape

Although the legal definition of **rape** varies from state to state, most state laws define rape as sexual intercourse occurring under actual or threatened forcible compulsion that overcomes the earnest resistance of the victim. This coercive act can range from violent assault by a stranger, an acquaintance, or a family member to a planned romantic date that degrades into an episode of coerced sex. What these acts have in common is a lack of empathy for the feelings of victims and a willingness to take advantage of and often harm them. Most writers and researchers on this topic distinguish at least three different types of rape. **Stranger rape** is rape by an unknown assailant. **Acquaintance rape**, or **date rape**, is committed by someone known to the victim. **Statutory rape** is intercourse with a person under the age of consent. (The age of consent varies by state and ranges from 14 to 18.) Statutory rape is considered to have occurred regardless of the apparent willingness of the underage partner.

Prevalence of Rape

Despite the fact that rape is a significant problem in our society, it has been difficult to obtain accurate statistics on its frequency. One reason is that many individuals do not report this crime. A recent study suggests that ethnic minority women may be especially

rape
Sexual intercourse that occurs without consent as a result of actual or threatened force.

stranger rape
Rape of a person by an unknown assailant.

acquaintance rape
Sexual assault by a friend, acquaintance, or date—that is, someone known to the victim.

date rape
Sexual assault by an acquaintance when on a date.

statutory rape
Intercourse with a person under the age of consent.

likely not to disclose or report sexual assault (Ullman et al., 2008). Estimates of the percentage of rapes that women victims report to police or other public agencies range from 11.9% (Hanson et al., 1999) to 28% (U.S. Department of Justice, 2001). This low percentage of reporting has led some writers to suggest that rape is the most underreported crime in the United States (Lonsway & Fitzgerald, 1994; Romeo, 2004).

According to the Federal Bureau of Investigation, 84,767 females nationwide reported being raped in 2010 (Goode, 2011). Based on the estimates of underreporting of rape we just stated, it is likely that the actual number of rapes occurring in 2010 ranged from about 303,000 to 712,000.

The FBI statistics on reported rape in 2010 noted in the previous paragraph include only rape perpetrated against a female forcibly and against her will. This definition of rape, unchanged since 1929, excludes victims of forced anal or oral sex, rape with an object, statutory rape, and male rape. In October 2011 the Uniform Crime Report Subcommittee of the FBI's Criminal Justice Information Services voted to expand its definition of rape. The new definition of rape defines the crime as penetration, no matter how slight, of the vagina or anus with any body part or object, or oral penetration by a sex organ of another person, without consent of the victim (WeNews Staff, 2011). This definition dramatically broadens the old, outdated definition of "forcible rape" and allows inclusion of many forms of rape victimization, including rape of males.

An exhaustive government survey of a nationally representative sample of 16,507 adults, the National Intimate Partner and Sexual Violence Survey, released in December 2011, found that almost one in five American women has been raped in her lifetime (Rabin, 2011). In this survey rape was defined as completed forced penetration, forced penetration facilitated by drugs or alcohol, or attempted forced penetration. While this definition expanded the old FBI definition, it excluded men and maintained an emphasis on rape as a "forced" act of sexual victimization. We can expect that FBI statistics on the annual number of rapes, determined under the new definition, will be revised sharply upward in future years. Research focused on college populations indicates that one in every four or five college women is victimized by attempted or completed rape (Crawford et al., 2008; Paulson, 2011; van der Voo & Smith, 2010).

Assaulted college women are often victimized again by a lack of institutional support and preparedness to handle allegations of sexual assault (van der Voo & Smith, 2010). Student victims of rape frequently describe a pervasive tendency to either subscribe to a "blame the victim" attitude or to characterize the assault as a "misunderstanding." An investigation by the Center for Public Integrity found that "students deemed responsible for sexual assault often face little or no consequences while the victims are frequently left in turmoil" (van der Voo & Smith, 2010, p. 1). Based on the widespread failure of colleges and universities to deal responsibly with the sexual assault of students, it is reasonable to suspect that the actual incidence of sexual victimization of college women is appreciably greater than the reported statistics indicate.

Victims of rape, whether students or nonstudents, do not report the crime for other reasons, including self-blame ("I shouldn't have had so much to drink"), fear of being blamed by others, concern for the rapist, fear of retaliation, and an attempt to block their recall of a traumatic experience (Miller et al., 2011; Romeo, 2004; Wolitzky-Taylor et al., 2011). A person who has been raped may feel vulnerable and frightened, and reliving the experience by telling about it can be understandably difficult. Also, mistrust of the police or legal system, fear of reprisal by the offender or his family, and concern about unwanted publicity may deter individuals from reporting rapes. And, as we discuss later in this chapter, a large proportion of rapes are committed by an acquaintance of the victim. Under these circumstances a woman's preconception of a "real" rape as a violent attack by a stranger may not match her experience of an acquaintance rape, and therefore she may not consider it reportable criminal behavior.

In the following pages, we look at a number of aspects of the act of rape, including the cultural context in which it occurs, the characteristics of perpetrators, and the characteristics of victims.

False Beliefs About Rape

An important factor in explaining the high incidence of rape in our society is the prevalence of misconceptions about this crime. False beliefs concerning rape, rapists, and rape victims abound (Heath et al., 2011; McMahon & Farmer, 2011). Many people believe that roughing up a woman is acceptable, that many women are sexually aroused by such activity, and that it is impossible to rape a healthy woman against her will (Gilbert et al., 1991; Malamuth et al., 1980). Research indicates that acceptance and endorsement of rape myths increase men's proclivity to commit rape (Bohner et al., 2006; Clarke & Stermac, 2011; Edwards et al., 2011). The effect of such rape myths is often "to deny and justify male sexual aggression against women" (Lonsway & Fitzgerald, 1994, p. 133). Another frequent effect is to place the blame on the victim. Many victims believe that the rape was basically their fault. Even when they were simply in the wrong place at the wrong time, a pervasive sense of personal guilt often remains. The following are some of the most common false beliefs about rape:

1. *False belief: "Women can't be raped if they really don't want to be."* The belief that women can always resist a rape attempt is false, for several reasons. First, men are usually physically larger and stronger than women. Second, female gender-role conditioning often trains a woman to be compliant and submissive. Such conditioning can limit the options a woman believes she has in resisting rape. Third, in many rapes, the rapist chooses the time and place. He has the element of surprise on his side. The fear and intimidation a woman usually experiences when attacked work to the assailant's advantage. His use of weapons, threats, or physical force further coerces her compliance.

2. *False belief: "Women say no when they mean yes."* Some rapists have distorted perceptions of their interactions with the women they rape—before, during, and even after the assault. They believe that women want to be coerced into sexual activity, even to the extent of being sexually abused (Muehlenhard & Rodgers, 1998). These distorted beliefs help the rapist justify his behavior: His act is not rape but, rather, "normal" sex play. Afterward, he may feel little or no guilt about his behavior because, in his own mind, it was not rape.

3. *False belief: "Many women 'cry rape.'"* False accusations of rape are uncommon, and they are even less frequently carried as far as prosecution. Nevertheless, false allegations of rape are sometimes made. The FBI estimates that fewer than 1 in 10 rape accusations is shown to be false (Gross, 2008). People may be motivated to fabricate a rape allegation by a need to create a "cover story" (e.g., a reason for becoming pregnant or contracting an STI), a desire for revenge or retribution directed toward the alleged rapist, an overwhelming need for attention, or an attempt to extort money from the accused (Gross, 2008). However, given the difficulties that exist in reporting and prosecuting a rape, few women (or men) could successfully proceed with an unfounded rape case.

4. *False belief: "All women want to be raped."* That some women have rape fantasies is sometimes used to support the idea that women want to be sexually assaulted. However, it is important to understand the distinction between an erotic fantasy and a conscious desire to be harmed. In a fantasy a person retains control. A fantasy carries no threat of physical harm or death; a rape does.

5. *False belief: "Rapists are 'obviously' mentally ill."* The mistaken idea that a potential rapist somehow "looks the part" is also prevalent. "This rape myth is particularly dangerous because potential victims may feel that they can identify a rapist (the crazed stranger) or that they are safe with someone they know" (Cowan, 2000, p. 809). As we discuss later, most rapes are committed by people who are not mentally ill and who are known to the victim.

6. *False belief: "The male sex drive is so high that men often cannot control their sexual urges."* The problem with this myth is that it shifts the responsibility from the perpetrator to the victim (Cowan, 2000). Women are seen as either the precipitator of the rape ("She should not have worn that dress") or as having been careless or naive ("What did she think would happen if she went back to his apartment with him?").

Critical Thinking Question

Which of these false beliefs about rape do you think is most dangerous and why?

Factors Associated With Rape

In an effort to understand the underlying causes of rape, researchers have looked at a number of psychosocial and sociobiological factors.

Psychosocial Basis of Rape

Many researchers and clinicians view rape more as a product of socialization processes that occur within the fabric of "normal" society than as a product of the individual rapist's pathological condition (Hill & Fischer, 2001; Hines, 2007; Simonson & Subich, 1999). Strong support for the view that rape is in many ways a cultural phenomenon was provided by the research of Peggy Reeves Sanday (1981), an anthropologist who compared the incidences of rape in 95 societies.

Sanday's research indicated that the frequency of rape in a given society is influenced by several factors. Foremost among these were the nature of the relations between the sexes, the status of women, and the attitudes that boys acquire during their developmental years. Sanday found that "rape-prone" societies tolerate and even glorify masculine violence, encouraging boys to be aggressive and competitive, and they view physical force as natural and exemplary. In these societies, men tend to have greater economic and political power than women, remaining aloof from "women's work," such as child rearing and household duties. These traits are especially pronounced in one markedly rape-prone society, South Africa, where a recent study found that 37% of men acknowledged they had raped a woman (Tay, 2010).

In contrast, relations between the sexes are quite different in societies where there is virtually no rape. Women and men in "rape-free" societies share power and authority and contribute equally to the community welfare. In addition, children of both sexes in these societies are raised to value nurturance and to avoid aggression and violence. With this cultural framework in mind, let us take a closer look at some of the aspects of male socialization in our own culture that contribute to the occurrence of rape and other forms of sexual coercion.

Women in Austin, Texas, protest against sexual assault. These women and others like them have helped challenge societal assumptions about rape.

© Bob Daemmrich/The Image Works

The high rate of rape in the United States is associated with widespread stereotypical gender roles. Males in our society are often taught that power, aggressiveness, and getting what one wants—by force, if necessary—are all part of the proper male role. Furthermore, they frequently learn that they should seek sex and expect to be successful—often with few qualms about using unethical means to achieve their goal. A recent study that investigated the attitudes of over 200 boys age 14 found that "believing that

Advertisements like this one are intended to educate men and women about rape.

rape is acceptable in some situations may account for adolescent boys' perpetration of forced sex on girls" (Manet & Herbe, 2011, p. 372).

It is not surprising, therefore, that many U.S. men view aggression as a legitimate means to obtain sexual access to women. Men whose peer groups openly legitimize and support these attitudes and behaviors are particularly likely to victimize women sexually (Sanday, 1996).

Impact of the Media

The media play a powerful role in transmitting cultural values and norms. Some novels, films, videos, Internet websites, and computer games perpetuate the notion that women want to be raped. Often, fictionalized rape scenes begin with a woman resisting her attacker, only to melt into passionate acceptance. In the rare cases where male-to-male rape is shown, as in the films *Deliverance* and *The Shawshank Redemption*, the violation and humiliation of rape are more likely to be realistically portrayed.

The mere act of viewing sexually explicit media, a practice indulged in by many American men (especially with the proliferation of Internet pornography), does not necessarily contribute to sexually aggressive behavior. In fact, one comprehensive review of available research studies assessing the effects of pornography concluded that "for the majority of American men, pornography exposure . . . is not associated with high levels of sexual aggression" (Malamuth et al., 2000, p. 85). Nevertheless, it does appear that exposure to violent pornography may have negative effects on men's attitudes and behaviors toward women (Simons et al., 2008).

A number of social scientists have suggested that sexually violent films, books, magazines, videos, and computer games contribute to some rapists' assaultive behaviors (Allen et al., 1995; Hall, 1996; Simons et al., 2008). Boeringer (1994) found that viewing pornography that depicted violent rape was strongly associated with judging oneself capable of sexual coercion and aggression and engaging in such coercive acts. Other research suggests that "exposure to media that combine arousing sexual images with violence may promote the development of deviant patterns of physiological sexual arousal" (Hall & Barongan, 1997, p. 5).

Is rape, then, a sexualization of violence? The evidence is equivocal. In two studies, the erectile responses of matched groups of rapists and nonrapists were measured as the men listened to audiotape descriptions of rape and of mutually consenting sexual activity. In both studies, rapists were more aroused by the sexual assault description than were nonrapists (Abel et al., 1977; Bernat et al., 1999). However, other research has failed to support this conclusion, finding little difference in the erectile responses of rapists and nonrapists in similar research designs (Eccles et al., 1994; Proulx et al., 1994). More research is needed to clarify these findings.

Characteristics of Rapists

Are rapists characterized by a single personality or behavioral pattern? Until recently, efforts to answer this question have been hindered by both a narrow conceptualization of rape and inadequate research methods. This was because our knowledge of the characteristics and motivations of rapists was based primarily on studies of men convicted of the crime—a sample group that probably represents less than 1% of rapists. Because convicted rapists are less educated, more inclined to commit other antisocial or criminal acts, and more alienated from society than are rapists who do not pass through the criminal justice system, we cannot say with certainty that men who rape without being prosecuted and convicted match the profile of convicted rapists.

We can say that many of the men incarcerated for rape have a strong proclivity toward violence, one that is often reflected in their acts of rape. This fact, along with certain assumptions about male-female relationships, has led a number of writers to argue that rape is not sexually motivated but is rather an act of power and domination (Brownmiller, 1975). This viewpoint prevailed for a number of years, during which the sexual component of rape and other assaults was de-emphasized. However, more recent research suggests that, although power and domination are often involved in sexual coercion, such coercion is also frequently motivated by a desire for sexual gratification. This view has been supported by several studies of the incidence and nature of sexual coercion among nonincarcerated males (Hickman & Muehlenhard, 1999; Senn et al., 1999).

It appears that a wide range of personality characteristics and motivations underlie sexual assault and how that assault is committed. Men who embrace traditional gender roles, particularly that of male dominance, are more likely to commit rape than are men who do not embrace traditional gender stereotypes (Ben-David & Schneider, 2005; Hartwick et al., 2007; Robinson et al., 2004). Anger toward women is a prominent attitude among some men who sexually assault women (Abbey & Jacques-Tiura, 2011; Anderson et al., 1997). Alcohol can also contribute to rapists' behavior; rapists often had been drinking just before assaulting their victims (Howard et al., 2008; Novik et al., 2011; Rapoza & Drake, 2009). Furthermore, alcohol-involved rapes are often associated with a high level of violence (Abbey et al., 2003; Young et al., 2008).

Many rapists have self-centered personalities, which may render them insensitive to others' feelings (Dean & Malamuth, 1997; Marshall, 1993). Research has provided strong evidence that men with a narcissistic personality trait may be especially inclined to commit rape and other acts of sexual coercion (Baumeister et al., 2002; Bushman et al., 2003). *Narcissism* is characterized by an inflated sense of self-importance, an unreasonable sense of entitlement, deficient empathy for others, and exploitative tendencies toward others. Research indicates that narcissists are also inclined to engage in aggressive retaliation against others for real or imagined slights (Baumeister et al., 2002; Bushman & Baumeister, 1998). In addition to these aggressive tendencies, narcissists' unreasonable sense of entitlement may influence them to view women as owing them sexual favors. Their lack of empathy for others would negate the impact of their victims' discomfort or suffering. Finally, their exaggerated sense of self-importance may facilitate their ability to rationalize their behavior and "convince themselves that their coercion victims had really desired sex or had expressed some form of consent" (Bushman et al., 2003, p. 1028).

Anger, power, and sexual gratification all play varying roles in rape. However, anger and a need to express power appear to predominate in stranger rape, whereas a desire for sexual gratification seems to predominate in acquaintance or date rape.

Characteristics of Female Rape Victims

Although females of all ages are raped, more than 50% of U.S. female rape victims reported that their first rape occurred before they were 18 years old, and 22% reported that their first rape occurred before they were 12 (see ▌ Figure 17.1). Women ages 16 to 24 are the most frequent victims of reported rape in the United States (U.S. Department of Justice, 2003). Being raped before the age of 18 greatly increases the chances that a woman will be raped again (Nishith et al., 2000; Tjaden & Thoennes, 1998). The younger the age of the rape victim, the more likely it is that the perpetrator is a relative or an acquaintance (U.S. Department of Justice, 2003). Research also

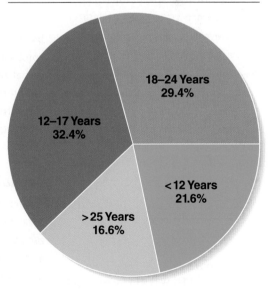

Women Victims' Age at Time of First Rape
(*n* = 1,323 women victims)

18–24 Years
29.4%

12–17 Years
32.4%

< 12 Years
21.6%

> 25 Years
16.6%

SOURCE: Tjaden & Thoennes (1998).

▌ **Figure 17.1** Age breakdown of women rape victims at time of first rape.

indicates that women who were victims of childhood sexual abuse are at increased risk for adult sexual revictimization by rapists (Reese-Weber & Smith, 2011).

Women involved in physically abusive relationships are especially vulnerable to being raped by their partners (Sormanti & Shibusawa, 2008). Evidence indicates that battered female victims of intimate partner violence (IPV) may be raped by their partners as frequently as several times per month (Sormanti & Shibusawa, 2008).

As noted earlier, the frequency of reported rape varies by culture. Asian and Pacific Islander women report being raped significantly less often than do White and African American women, Hispanic women report being raped less often than non-Hispanic women, and Native American and Alaska Native women report a much higher frequency of rape than any other group (Bryan, 2011; Tjaden & Thoennes, 1998). Recently published federal data reveal that one third of Native American women will be raped in their lifetimes (Bryan, 2011). Women who live in poverty are more frequent victims of all types of crimes including rape.

Acquaintance Rape and Sexual Coercion

Most rapes are committed by someone who is known to the victim—by an acquaintance or a friend—not (as popularly thought) by a stranger (deVaron, 2011; Ben-David & Schneider, 2005; P. McMahon, 2008). Research indicates that in approximately three out of four sexual assaults against women, the perpetrator is known by the victimized person (Romeo, 2004). A significant number of these acquaintance rapes occur in dating situations—hence the term *date rape*. Acquaintance rapes account for an estimated 90% of the rapes of women attending college in the United States (Crawford et al., 2008).

Considerable research has focused on the prevalence of sexual coercion in dating situations (Jenkins & Aube, 2002; Oswald & Russell, 2006; Shook et al., 2000). Until recently, much of this research examined women as victims and men as perpetrators of sexual coercion. Various studies have reported that 20–45% of teenage and adult women have been victims of coerced sexual activity, most commonly in dating or couple relationship situations (Brousseau et al., 2010; Rhynard et al., 1997; Shrier et al., 1998). However, women are not the only ones to experience sexual coercion. A number of studies have revealed that men also report experiencing some form of coercive sexual activity (Brousseau et al., 2010; Hartwick et al., 2007; Struckman-Johnson et al., 2003).

While sexual coercion in dating situations can be either verbal or physical, the verbal variety (e.g., threats to end a relationship or insistent arguing) is considerably more common. A study of college students found that 82% of participants reported using verbal sexual coercion and 21% acknowledged using physical sexual coercion against a dating partner in the past year (Shook et al., 2000). However, it is important to note that although many of the women in the studies previously cited were physically forced to engage in unwanted sex acts, physical force is considerably less likely to be used in the sexual coercion of men (Hartwick et al., 2007; Krahe et al., 2003).

Acquaintance Rape: The Role of Perceptions and Communication

Earlier in this chapter, we examined the relationship between sexual coercion and cultural expectations for males in our society. The socializing process that encourages men to be aggressive to get what they want is undoubtedly an important factor in rape and sexual coercion. As many have pointed out, in our society many males and females learn **sexual scripts** that encourage men to be aggressive and women to be passive (Dworkin & O'Sullivan, 2005). Yet some experts argue that in at least some cases of acquaintance rape, the picture is more complicated.

Consider the issue of men's misinterpretation of women's signals. Men often consider women's actions such as cuddling or kissing as indicating a desire to engage in

Critical Thinking Question

Some people perceive a woman who wears "suggestive clothing" and is then raped as somehow responsible for her own rape. In contrast, a man who dons an expensive suit, carries a lot of cash, and wears a Rolex watch is seldom, if ever, held responsible for being robbed on the street. What are your thoughts about this inconsistency in assigning the label *victim precipitation* to these two events? Is it ever appropriate to label a victim responsible for her or his own victimization?

sexual scripts
Culturally learned ways of behaving in sexual situations.

intercourse (Muehlenhard, 1988; Muehlenhard & Linton, 1987). However, a woman who feels like cuddling does not necessarily want to have sex, and she may express this to her date. Even if a woman clearly expresses her desire not to have sex, her date may read her actions as "token resistance," concluding that she really wants to have sex but does not want to appear "too easy" (Krahe et al., 2000; Osman, 2003).

In some cases this "reading" is entirely motivated by exploitative self-interest. But some women do say no when they mean yes. One study of 610 female undergraduates revealed that 39.3% had engaged in token resistance to sex at least once. Reasons for saying no when they really meant yes included not wanting to appear promiscuous, uncertainty about a partner's feelings, undesirable surroundings, game playing (wanting a partner to be more physically aggressive, to persuade her to have sex, etc.), and desiring to be in control (Muehlenhard & Hollabaugh, 1989). This kind of double message may actually promote rape by providing men with a rationale for ignoring sincere refusals. The researchers in this study concluded that if a man has had the experience of ignoring a woman's protests only to find that she actually did want to have sex, then "his belief that women's refusals are not to be taken seriously will be strengthened" (Muehlenhard & Hollabaugh, 1989, p. 878). He may thus proceed with his sexual advances despite further protests and genuine resistance from his date. Such a man may not even define his actions as rape.

The concept of token resistance underscores the fact that many sexual interactions are beset with problems of poor communication. The ambiguity and miscommunication that often characterize sexual encounters underscore the importance of building a foundation of clear communication, a topic addressed in Chapter 7.

Even men who believe their female partner when she says no may think that it is defensible to use force to obtain sex if they feel that they have been "led on." A number of studies have found that many men regard rape as justifiable, or at least hold the woman more responsible than themselves, if she leads a man on by such actions as dressing "suggestively" or going to his apartment (Muehlenhard et al., 1991; Workman & Freeburg, 1999). The implications of these findings for acquaintance rape prevention are discussed in the Your Sexual Health box, "Dealing With Rape and Attempted Rape."

Date Rape Drugs

In the early 1990s reports began to circulate about the increasing use of Rohypnol (roh-HIP-nol) to facilitate sexual conquest or to incapacitate victims who are then sexually molested or raped (Daly, 2011; Staten, 1997). Rohypnol, commonly known on the street as "roofies," is the brand name for flunitrazepam, a powerful tranquilizer that has a sedative effect 7 to 10 times more potent than that of Valium. In addition to producing a sedative effect in 20 to 30 minutes that can last for several hours, Rohypnol causes muscle relaxation and mild to pronounced amnesia (Romeo, 2004). Rohypnol is odorless and is excreted from the victim's system in a relatively short time, making discovery and prosecution of rapists who use this drug difficult. Many cases have emerged in which women were raped after their dates had given them the drug surreptitiously—hence the term *date rape drug*. When combined with alcohol, the drug's effects are greatly enhanced and can result in a dramatic "high," markedly reduced inhibitions, unconsciousness, and total amnesia concerning events that occur while a person is under its influence.

In an effort to counter the negative image of Rohypnol as a date rape drug, the manufacturer, Roche Pharmaceuticals, has changed the color and formulation of this drug. The result is a pill that is more difficult to dissolve and that produces a blue solution when dissolved (Olsen et al., 2005). In addition, recently developed laboratory procedures have made it easy to detect this reformulated drug in drinks spiked to accomplish date rape (Olsen et al., 2005).

Drugs slipped into the drinks of unsuspecting women may be used to facilitate sexual conquest or to incapacitate victims who are then sexually molested or raped.

Although rape is a society-wide problem, it is the rape victim who experiences the direct, personal violation. The suggestions offered in the following lists present strategies for reducing the risk of acquaintance rape and for avoiding stranger rape. However, following these suggestions offers no guarantee of avoiding rape. Even a woman who leads an extremely cautious and restricted life can be assaulted. Rape prevention consists primarily of making it as difficult as possible for a rapist to victimize you. Many of the following suggestions are commonsense measures against other crimes besides rape.

Reducing the Risk of Acquaintance Rape

1. The less you know about a person before meeting, the more important it is to be cautious. Thus, when dating someone for the first time, seriously consider doing so in a group situation or meeting your date at a public place. This will allow you to assess your date's behavior in a relatively safe environment.

2. Watch for indications that your date may be a dominating person who may try to control your behavior. A man who plans all activities and makes all decisions during a date may also be inclined to dominate in a private setting.

3. If the man drives and pays for all expenses, he may think he is justified in using force to get "what he paid for." If you cover some of the expenses, he may be less inclined to use this rationale to justify acting in a sexually coercive manner (Basrow & Minieri, 2011).

4. Avoid using alcohol or other drugs when you definitely do not wish to be sexually intimate with your date. Consumption of alcohol or other drugs, by both victim and perpetrator, is commonly associated with acquaintance rape (Novik et al., 2011; Rose et al., 2011). Caffeinated alcoholic beverages, such as Four Loko, have been linked to sexual assault cases on college campuses (Jalonick, 2010; Pang, 2010). Drug intoxication can both diminish your capacity to escape from an assault and reduce your date's reluctance to engage in assaultive behavior.

5. Avoid behavior that may be interpreted as "teasing." Clearly state what you do and do not wish to do in regard to sexual contact. For example, you might say, "I hope you do not misinterpret my inviting you back to my apartment. I definitely do not want to do anything more than relax, listen to some music, and talk." If you are interested in initiating an exploration of some kind of early physical contact, you might say, "Tonight I would like to hold you and kiss, but I would not be comfortable with anything else at this point in our relationship." Such direct communication can markedly reduce a man's inclinations to force unwanted sexual activity or to feel "led on" (Muehlenhard & Andrews, 1985; Muehlenhard et al., 1985).

6. If, despite direct communication about your intentions, your date behaves in a sexually coercive manner, you may use a "strategy of escalating forcefulness—direct refusal, vehement verbal refusal, and, if necessary, physical force" (Muehlenhard & Linton, 1987, p. 193). One study found that college students were most likely to label a scenario of date sex as rape if such activity was preceded by a clearly stated *no* (Sawyer et al., 1998). In another study, the response rated by men as most likely to get men to stop unwanted advances was for the woman to vehemently say, "This is rape, and I'm calling the cops" (Beal & Muehlenhard, 1987). If verbal protests are ineffective, reinforce your refusal with physical force, such as pushing, slapping, biting, kicking, or clawing your assailant. Men are more likely to perceive their actions as at least inappropriate, if not rape, when a woman protests not only verbally but also physically (Beal & Muehlenhard, 1987; Muehlenhard & Linton, 1987). Self-defense training can be beneficial in situations in which women are able to use physical force to protect themselves from assault (Orchowski et al., 2008).

Reducing the Risk of Stranger Rape

1. Do not advertise that you are a woman living alone. Use initials on your mailbox and in the phone book; even add a fictitious name.

2. Install and use secure locks on doors and windows, changing door locks after losing keys or moving into a

Many women take self-defense training to protect themselves from assault.

new residence. A peephole in your front door can be particularly helpful.

3. Do not open your door to strangers. If a repairman or public official is at your door, ask him to identify himself and call his office to verify that he is a reputable person on legitimate business.

4. When you are in situations in which strangers may be encountered, demonstrate self-confidence through your body language and speech to communicate that you will not be intimidated. Research reveals that rapists often tend to select as victims women who exhibit passivity and submissiveness (Richards et al., 1991).

5. Take a cell phone with you when you are out alone.

6. Lock your car when it is parked and while you are driving.

7. Avoid dark and deserted areas and be aware of your surroundings when you are walking. Such precautions can help if you need an opportunity to escape. Should a driver ask for directions when you are a pedestrian, avoid approaching his car. Instead, call out your reply from a safe distance.

8. Have house or car keys in hand before going to your door, and check the backseat before getting into your car.

9. Should your car break down, attach a white cloth to the antenna and lock yourself in. If someone other than a uniformed officer in an official car stops to offer help, ask this person to call the police or a garage but do not open your locked car door.

10. Never hitchhike or provide rides to hitchhikers or get into a car with a stranger.

11. Wherever you go, it can be helpful to carry a device for making a loud noise, such as a whistle or, even better, a pint-sized compressed-air horn (available in many sporting goods and boat supply stores). Sound the noise alarm at the first sign of danger.

Many cities have crime-prevention bureaus that provide further suggestions and home-safety inspections.

What to Do in Threatening Situations Involving Strangers

If you are approached by a man or men who may intend to rape you, you will have to decide what to do. *Each situation, assailant, and woman is unique. There are no absolute rules.*

1. Run away if you can.

2. Resist if you cannot run. Make it difficult for the rapist. On locating a potential victim, many men test her to see if she is easily intimidated. Resistance by the woman is often responsible for thwarting rape attempts (Heyden et al., 1999). Active and vociferous resistance—shouting, being rude, causing a scene, running away, fighting back—may deter the attack. This was the finding of a study of 150 rapes or attempted rapes: Women who used forceful verbal or physical resistance (screaming, hitting, kicking, biting, running,

and the like) were more likely to avoid being raped than women who tried pleading, crying, or offering no resistance (Zoucha-Jensen & Coyne, 1993).

3. Ordinary rules of behavior do not apply. Vomiting, screaming, or acting crazy—whatever you are willing to try—can be appropriate responses to an attempted rape.

4. Talking can be a way to stall and can give you a chance to devise an escape plan or another strategy. It can be helpful to get the attacker to start talking ("What has happened to make you so angry?"), to express some empathy ("It is really discouraging to lose a job"), or to negotiate ("Let's take time to talk about this"). Even when talking does not prevent an assault, it may reduce the degree of violence (Prentky et al., 1986).

5. Remain alert for an opportunity to escape. In some situations, it may be impossible to fight or elude an attacker initially. However, later on, you may have a chance to deter the attack and escape—for example, if the rapist becomes distracted or a passerby comes on the scene.

Self-defense classes are a resource for learning techniques of physical resistance that can injure the attacker or distract him long enough for you to escape.

What to Do if You Have Been Raped

If someone has raped you or tried to rape you, you will have to decide whether to report the attack to the police.

1. It is advisable to report a rape or even an unsuccessful rape attempt. The information you provide may prevent another woman from being raped.

2. When you report such an attack, any details you can remember about it may be helpful—the assaulter's physical characteristics, voice, clothes, car, even an unusual smell.

3. If you have been raped, you should call the police as soon as possible; do not bathe or change your clothes. Semen, hair, and material under fingernails or on your clothing may be useful in identifying the rapist.

4. It may be helpful to contact a rape crisis center, where qualified staff members can assist you in dealing with your trauma. Most large urban communities in the United States have such programs. If you cannot make the contact yourself, have a friend, family member, or the police make the call.

5. In addition to general counseling, there are effective treatment programs for women who have been raped. If your symptoms do not subside after a period of time, consider entering a treatment program. You do not have to continue to suffer.

6. Finally, it is important to remember that many women mistakenly blame themselves for the rape. However, being raped is not a crime; the crime has been committed by the man who raped you.

Other drugs, such as gamma hydroxybutyrate (GHB) and ketamine hydrochloride (Special K) have also been implicated in date rapes (Crawford et al., 2008; Elliott & Burgess, 2005). GHB was developed more than 40 years ago and was initially used as an anesthetic. Its mind-altering effects soon became well known, and it has become increasingly popular as a recreational drug—often with devastating results. GHB is a central nervous system depressant that can be especially lethal when combined with alcohol (Elliott & Burgess, 2005). Since 1990, emergency rooms have reported thousands of cases of GHB overdoses, some of which have resulted in death (Elliott & Burgess, 2005). GHB is odorless and tasteless, which makes it easy to administer to unsuspecting victims. GHB exits the body in 6 to 12 hours, which makes it an especially ideal drug for sexual predators, because a lack of toxicological evidence makes prosecution difficult.

SEXUALHEALTH ▶

It is important to be alert for potential victimization by means of a date rape drug. Do not accept a drink (alcohol, coffee, soda, etc.), especially an open-container beverage, from someone other than a trusted friend. Never leave your drink unattended. If you forget and do leave your drink unattended (for example, while dancing), pour it down the drain. If you experience one or more of the following symptoms after ingesting a beverage, it is possible that your drink was tainted: nausea, dizziness, slurred speech, movement impairment, or euphoria. If you find yourself in such a circumstance, call 911 or ask someone other than your date or companion to help you seek medical attention and, if possible, retain a sample of the beverage. ●

As a result of abuse and deaths associated with date rape drugs, the U.S. Congress has passed laws that strengthen the penalties for possessing Rohypnol, GHB, and other similar drugs and that significantly increase the prison sentences for rapists who use drugs to incapacitate victims. Recently published information indicates that an easy-to-use sensor, that when dipped into a beverage instantly detects the presence of a date rape drug, should be available soon (UPI NewsTrack, 2011a).

Wartime Rape

Although rape is most often a coercive interaction between two individuals, it has also been a strategy or policy of war throughout history (Mukamana & Brysiewicz, 2008). Records abound of the mass rape of women during war, from the time of ancient Greece to the more recent atrocities in Rwanda, Darfur, and the former Yugoslavia. In the 20th century hundreds of thousands of women have been victimized by wartime rape (Bergoffen, 2006; Polgreen, 2005; Van Zeijl, 2006). In the 1990s reports of mass rapes perpetrated by Serbian soldiers on thousands of Bosnian and Croatian women and girls increased the public's support for measures to label rape a war crime. Awareness was further heightened by reports that thousands of women and girls were raped during the 1994 war in Rwanda (Flanders, 1998; Mukamana & Brysiewicz, 2008). Rape has been employed as a weapon in the conflict in the Darfur region of Sudan (Polgreen, 2005). More recently reports have surfaced describing how hundreds of women have been raped by militiamen loyal to Moammar Gadhafi during the war in Libya (Fahim, 2011; Faul, 2011).

Accounts of the rape and sexual abuse of Jewish women during the Holocaust, a topic largely ignored for over 60 years, were presented in the book *Sexual Violence Against Jewish Women During the Holocaust*, coedited by Rochelle Saidel and Sonja Hedgepeth (2010). Thousands of Jewish women were raped, sexually abused, or subjected to threats of this abuse during the reign of the Third Reich. Many of the women abused in this deplorable fashion were subsequently killed by Nazi thugs (Cooper, 2011).

U.S. soldiers have also been guilty of wartime rape. Cases of gang rape of Vietnamese women appear in the records of courts-martial for American troops in Vietnam (Brownmiller, 1993). American soldiers have also been prosecuted for raping Iraqi women during the invasion of Iraq.

In 1996 the United Nations International Criminal Tribunal for the Former Yugoslavia ruled that wartime rape is a crime punishable by severe criminal sanctions (marking the first time that sexual assault was treated separately as a war crime). In 2001 this U.N. tribunal established "sexual enslavement" as a war crime and convicted several Bosnian Serbs for the multiple rapes of Muslim women enslaved in so-called rape camps. Convicted rapists received sentences ranging from 12 to 28 years (Comiteau, 2001). In recent years the Democratic Republic of Congo has become what United Nations officials label as the epicenter of rape as a weapon of war (Peterman et al., 2011). It is estimated that almost 2 million women have been raped in the Congo.

Why is rape so common during war? Wartime rape, in addition to being used as a means to dominate, humiliate, and control women, "can also be intended to disable an enemy by destroying the bonds of family and society" (Swiss & Giller, 1993, pp. 612–613). In wars instigated by ethnic conflict, as in the former Yugoslavia, Rwanda, and Darfur, mass rape is used as a military strategy to terrorize and demoralize a whole population, to destroy its cultural integrity, and sometimes to force entire communities to flee their houses, thereby achieving the goal of "ethnic cleansing" (Boustany, 2007; Eaton, 2004; Mukamana & Brysiewicz, 2008). Thus rape is an act of war that assaults not only the individual woman but also her family and her community.

The Sexuality and Diversity discussion on punishing women who have been raped provides insights into how societal reaction to rape, whether during wartime or otherwise, can add to the suffering of rape victims.

SEXUALITY and DIVERSITY
Punishing Women Who Have Been Raped

How would it feel to be raped by your enemies and then rejected by your family and friends for being sexually violated? Shortly after the war in Kosovo ended in 1999, reports surfaced in the press of the difficulties that Kosovar women who had been raped were having as they returned to their homes and families. Despite the tremendous suffering they had already endured from being sexually assaulted, if these women admitted that they had been raped, they risked being disowned by their families and friends. Instead of getting the support and compassion that they deserved, which have been shown to be helpful in healing the wounds caused by trauma, they had to keep their painful memories, thoughts, and feelings locked away from others or risk being shunned by their families and communities (Lorch & Mendenhall, 2000).

During the ongoing brutal war in the Democratic Republic of Congo, an estimated one in three Congolese women have been subjected to gang rape so violent that thousands suffer from vaginal fistula (rupture of the vaginal wall, which can cause urine and feces to leak uncontrollably). In some regions of the Congo, as many as 70% of females of all ages have been raped or sexually mutilated, or both, often while members of their families or communities were forced to watch the assault (Klapper, 2007; Persky, 2012; Soguel, 2008). Many of these victimized women, instead of receiving health care, have been abandoned by their husbands and ostracized by their communities (Longombe et al., 2008). Recent reports indicate that increasing numbers of men are also being raped by gangs of militiamen conducting a reign of terror in the Congo. These male victims of sexual brutality also become castaways in their communities, derisively referred to as "bush wives" (Gettleman, 2009). Sexual assaults of Congolese women are sometimes perpetrated by women (as many as 40% in a recent study), whereas the vast majority of male victims are assaulted by men (Johnson et al., 2010).

In a case that shocked people in Western nations and sparked an international outcry, a Saudi Arabian court sentenced a woman who had been gang-raped to 6 months in jail and a public lashing. The victim of this heinous crime was convicted of violating the nation's Islamic law against mixing of the sexes because she was accosted by her rapists while in a car with a man to whom she was not related. Eventually the Saudi monarch, King Abdullah, bending to criticism from the United States and other Western nations, elected to pardon the rape victim, who was 19 at the time of the attack (Shihri, 2007).

Unfortunately, these attitudes are not confined to Kosovo, the Congo, or Saudi Arabia. Research has shown that in the United States some men also tend to blame the victim of sexual abuse. In a study conducted among multiethnic groups in New York City, Cuban American men evaluated the teenage female *victim* of sexual abuse negatively (Rodriguez-Stednicki & Twaite, 1999). Another study found that Hispanic men in the United States tended to hold women more responsible for their rapes than did Caucasian men (Cowan, 2000). These cultural attitudes and behaviors have a profoundly negative effect on the victims of rape and sexual assault. In a study that evaluated 157 victims of violent crime, researchers found that shame and anger play an important role in determining whether victims will develop posttraumatic stress disorder and that shame especially plays a role in the severity of the victim's subsequent symptoms (Andrews et al., 2000). Thus it would appear that cultural values that blame women who have been raped (and those who uphold and apply them) can be a major contributing factor to these victims' continued suffering.

The Aftermath of Rape

Whether a person is raped by a stranger, an acquaintance, or a partner, the experience can be traumatic and can have long-term repercussions. Given the characteristics of rape—the physical violation and psychological trauma that it inflicts and our societal attitudes about it—it is understandable that many rape survivors suffer long-lasting emotional effects. Rape perpetrated by multiple offenders is often more violent and involves more severe forms of violation than does rape committed by a lone rapist (Woodhams et al., 2012).

Feelings of shame, anger, fear, guilt, depression, and powerlessness are common (Koss et al., 2002; Vandeusen & Carr, 2003). One reason that some women feel guilt and shame is that they are often seen, and see themselves, as being responsible—no matter what the circumstances—for not preventing unwanted sexual activity from taking place. Rape survivors may also exhibit a tendency toward subsequent victimization by further sexual assaults (Littleton et al., 2009; Reese-Weber & Smith, 2011). A recent study of several hundred college women found that some of these women were at greater risk for rape due to their use of substances (alcohol, marijuana, etc.) to reduce distress associated with previous trauma (sexual, physical, emotional abuse) (Messman-Moore et al., 2009).

In addition to the psychological impact of rape, physical symptoms such as nausea, headaches, gastrointestinal problems, genital injuries, and sleep disorders frequently occur (Hilden et al., 2005; Ullman & Brecklin, 2003). Approximately 32% of women and 16% of men who were raped after age 18 reported being physically injured during the assault (Tjaden & Thoennes, 1998). Rape survivors may associate sexual activity with the trauma of their assault. As a result, sexual activity may induce anxiety rather than desire or arousal (Koss et al., 2002, 2003).

When the emotional and physical reactions women experience following rape or attempted rape are severe, victims may be classified as suffering from **posttraumatic stress disorder (PTSD)**. PTSD, an official diagnostic category of the American Psychiatric Association (2000), refers to the long-term psychological distress that can develop after a person is subjected to a physically or psychologically traumatic event (or events). People who experience a profoundly disturbing incident, such as sexual assault, wartime combat, or a horrendous accident, often exhibit a range of

posttraumatic stress disorder (PTSD)
A psychological disorder caused by exposure to overwhelmingly painful events.

distressing symptoms as an aftermath of the occurrence. These reactions include disturbing dreams, nightmares, depression, anxiety, and feelings of extreme vulnerability. In addition, just as combat veterans may have flashbacks of traumatic war experiences, so too might a rape survivor have vivid flashbacks of the attack in which she reexperiences all the terror of the assault. Research indicates that rape produces one of the highest rates of PTSD among nonwartime traumatic events (Koss et al., 2002; Ullman et al., 2007).

Victims often find that supportive counseling, either individually or in groups, can help ease the trauma caused by rape (Romeo, 2004; Vandeusen & Carr, 2003). Research has shown that women who receive help soon after an assault experience less severe emotional repercussions than women whose treatment is delayed (Campbell, 2006). Most rape survivors find that it helps to talk about their assault and the emotional upheaval they are experiencing. Often the process of reviewing the event allows them to gain control over their painful feelings and to begin the process of healing. The Let's Talk About It box, "Helping a Partner or Friend Recover From Rape," suggests ways to communicate and interact with a rape victim.

Rape and Sexual Assault of Males

Health professionals who work with rape survivors know that men are raped. Although the vast majority of rape victims are women, men are also targets of sexual aggression, including rape (Coxell & King, 2010; Davies et al., 2006; Kassing et al., 2005). A 2007 survey conducted on American college campuses found that about 6% of college men are victims of attempted or completed sexual assault (Paulson, 2011). An exhaustive review of 120 studies of sexual victimization that collectively analyzed data from more than 100,000 respondents found incidence rates for completed and attempted male rape by female perpetrators of 3.3% and 5.5%, respectively (Spitzberg, 1999). The National Intimate Partner and Sexual Violence Survey of over 16,000 American adults found that up to 2% of men have been raped, many when they were under age 11 (Rabin, 2011). A recent Department of Justice report indicated that 3% of American men have been raped (Rabin, 2012).

Statistics on the frequency of male sexual victimization have been difficult to obtain for a variety of reasons, not the least of which is that men are even less likely than women to report that they have been raped (Choudhard et al., 2012; Davies et al., 2006; Kassing et al., 2005). It is estimated that only 1 in 10 male rapes are reported to the police (Kassing et al., 2005). One reason for this failure to report may be that men fear they will be judged harshly if they report abuse. At least one study supports this concern (Spencer & Tan, 1999). The investigators found that men who reported being sexually abused were viewed negatively, especially by other men. Victimized men may also anticipate that law enforcement personnel may not believe that a crime occurred or may believe that they somehow instigated or asked for the rape (Kassing et al., 2005; Walker et al., 2005). In addition, men who are socialized to be physically strong and able to protect themselves may believe that reporting their victimization will reflect weakness or personal blame (Kassing et al., 2005).

The sexual assault of men is rarely reported in the media or in the psychological and medical literature (Stermac et al., 1996). The result is that little research has been conducted on the issue of sexual aggression against men (Choudhard et al., 2012). In fact, only in the last decade or so have many states revised their criminal codes to include adult males as victims in the definition of rape.

Rapes of males may be perpetrated by heterosexual men, who often commit their crime with one or more cohorts (Frazier, 1993; Isely & Gehrenbeck-Shim, 1997). As in

The rape of a partner or friend can be a difficult experience for both partners and friends of rape survivors. To some degree, partners and close friends are also victimized by the assault. They may feel a range of emotions, including rage, disgust, and helplessness. They may also be confused and unsure about how to react to a lover's or friend's victimization. This confusion can prove painful for all concerned because reactions of partners and friends can profoundly affect a rape survivor's recovery. In the following list, we suggest ways to communicate and interact with a rape victim to help her recover from this traumatic experience. Some of these suggestions are adapted from two excellent books: *Sexual Solutions* (1980), by Michael Castleman, and *"Friends" Raping Friends: Could It Happen to You?* (1987), by Jean Hughes and Bernice Sandler. Although we will frequently refer to the victim as female, our recommendations are equally applicable to male rape survivors.

1. *Listen.* Probably the most important thing a person can do to help a rape victim begin recovering is to listen to her. A person comforting a rape survivor might understandably try to divert her attention from the terrible event. However, professionals who work with survivors of sexual assault have found that many victims need to talk repeatedly about the assault to come to terms with it. A partner or friend can help by encouraging her to discuss the rape as often as she can, in any way that she can.

2. *Let her know you believe her account of what happened.* A rape survivor needs to be believed by people she loves or feels close to. Consequently, it is essential to accept her version of the assault without questioning any of the facts. A simple statement, such as "What you describe is an intolerable violation, and I am so sorry that you had to endure such a dreadful experience," will convey both your acceptance of her account and your empathy with her pain.

3. *Let her know that it was not her fault and that she is not to blame.* Many victims of rape believe that they were somehow responsible for the attack ("I should not have invited him to my home," "I should have tried to fight him," or the like). Such impressions can lead to profound feelings of guilt. Self-blame is predictive of more severe PTSD symptoms and less successful recovery (Najdowski & Ullman, 2009). Try to head off these damaging self-recriminations by stating clearly and calmly, "I know that you are not to blame for what happened," or "You are the victim here and not responsible for what happened to you."

4. *Control your own emotions.* The last thing a rape survivor needs is the response of the partner who gets sidetracked by focusing attention on his or her own anger or imagined shortcomings ("I should have been along to protect you"). She has just been victimized by a violent man (or men), and being confronted with her own partner's or friends' outbursts will not help her regain control.

5. *Give comfort.* A rape victim is urgently in need of comfort, especially from someone she loves or cares about. She may want to be held, and the nurturing comfort of being encircled by the arms of someone she trusts may provide a powerful beginning to the process of healing. On the other hand, she also may not want to be touched at all. Respect that wish. Words can also be quite nurturing. Simply being told "I love you very much and will be here for you in any way that is right for you" may offer a great deal of welcome comfort.

6. *Allow the victim to make decisions.* A rape survivor may recover more quickly when she is able to decide for herself how to deal with the assault. Making her own decisions about what should be done after a rape is an important step in regaining control over her life after having been stripped of control by her attacker(s). Asking some open-ended questions (see Chapter 7) may help her regain control. Questions might include, "What kind of living arrangements for the next few days or weeks would you be comfortable with?" or "What can I do for you now?" Sometimes suggesting alternatives can be helpful. For example, while encouraging her to take some type of positive action, you might ask, "Would you like to call the police, go to a hospital, or call a rape hotline?" Remember, the decision is hers and one that needs to be respected and not questioned even if you do not agree with it.

7. *Offer shelter.* If she does not already live with you, offer to stay with her at her home, have her stay with you, or assist her in securing other living arrangements with which she is comfortable. Again, this is her choice to make.

8. *Continue to provide support.* In the days, weeks, and even months following the rape, partners and friends can continue to offer empathy, support, and reassurance to a rape survivor. They can encourage her to resume a normal life and be there for her when she feels particularly vulnerable, fearful, or angry. They can take time to listen, even if it means hearing the same things over and over again. If her assailant is prosecuted, she is likely to need support and understanding throughout the often arduous legal proceedings.

9. *Be patient about resuming sexual activity.* Resuming sexual activity after a rape may present problems for both the victim and her partner. Rape may precipitate

sexual difficulties for the woman; she may not want to be sexually intimate for quite a while. However, some women may desire relations very soon after the attack, perhaps for assurance that their lovers still care for them and do not consider them "tainted."

  a. Open-ended questions may help to fuel dialogue about resuming sexual sharing. Possibly helpful queries include "What are your thoughts and feelings about being sexual with me?" or "What kinds of concerns do you have about resuming our sexual activity?"

  b. Some women may prefer not to have intercourse for a while, opting instead for just closeness and affection. Deciding when and how to engage in intimate sharing is best left up to the woman. Her partner's support in this matter is important. Even when sexual intimacy resumes, it may be some time before she is able to relax and respond the way she did before the rape. A patient, sensitive partner can help her reach the point where she is again able to experience satisfying sexual intimacy.

10. *Consider counseling.* Sometimes a rape victim needs more help than lovers, friends, and families are able to provide, no matter how supportive they are. People close to her may recognize these needs and encourage her to seek professional help. Short- or long-term therapy may help a victim recover from the emotional trauma and reconstruct her life. Similarly, partners of sexually assaulted women may also need help coping with severe conflicts and deep feelings of rage and guilt.

rape of women, violence and power are often associated with the sexual assault of men. The possibility of being raped is a serious issue among male homosexuals because they are often the victims of such attacks. Although homosexual men are frequently raped by heterosexual men, the rapist is often a homosexual man who is a current or former sexual partner (Hickson et al., 1994; Walker et al., 2005).

Rape of inmates in penal institutions is a serious problem (Bell, 2006; Hensley et al., 2003; Richters et al., 2010). One comprehensive survey of almost 2,000 male inmates in seven prisons found that 21% had been sexually threatened or assaulted and 7% acknowledged being raped (Struckman-Johnson & Struckman-Johnson, 2000). Men who do the raping typically consider themselves heterosexual. When released, they usually resume sexual relations with women. The men who are raped often experience brutal gang assaults. Such a man may become the sexual partner of one particular dominant inmate for protection from others (Braen, 1980).

If a man is forced to penetrate someone's vagina, anus, or mouth with his penis, this is also classified as rape (McCabe & Wauchope, 2005). Accounts of men being sexually coerced by women who use threats of bodily harm have been reported with increasing frequency (Kassing et al., 2005). The idea that mature males can be raped by women has been widely rejected because it has been assumed that a man cannot function sexually in a state of extreme anxiety or fear. However, this common impression is not accurate. Alfred Kinsey and his associates were perhaps the earliest sex researchers to note that both sexes can function sexually in a variety of severe emotional states. Sexual response during sexual assault, particularly if orgasm occurs, may be a source of great confusion and anxiety for both female and male rape survivors.

Sexual assault of males also occurs during war. However, men as victims of wartime rape and sexual assault have received only scant media coverage and limited research attention. Among the few studies in this area are investigations of male sexual assault during wars in Greece (Lindholm et al., 1980), El Salvador (Agger & Jensen, 1994), and Croatia (Medical Center for Human Rights, 1995). The widespread belief that only females can be victimized by sexual assault has led many national legal systems to bury the issue of wartime male sexual assault under the more generalized categories of torture or abuse (Carlson, 1997). However, awareness that men also can be victimized was expanded when the International Criminal Tribunal for the Former Yugoslavia reported that many men were raped or otherwise sexually assaulted during the conflict in that region (Carlson, 1997).

Sexual Abuse of Children

The sexual (and physical and emotional) abuse of children in U.S. society and throughout the world is a problem of staggering proportions. Child sexual abuse can have long-lasting, painful effects. Consider the following:

> When I was 10, my mother remarried, and we moved into my stepfather's house. When I was 11 he started coming upstairs to say goodnight to me. The touching began soon after and lasted for years. I used to just lie there and pray that he would go away, but he never did. For a long time I thought it was my fault. I had trouble being in a sexual relationship because I felt so guilty, so dirty. I thought that if I didn't exist this never would have happened. I think my mother may have known, but she never did anything. She didn't want to upset things, because she was afraid of being alone again, of being poor. (Authors' files)

In this section, we look at the prevalence of child sexual abuse, the effects it has on many of its victims, what can be done to reduce the incidence of such abuse, and how to help those who have been abused. **Child sexual abuse** is defined as engagement by an adult in sexual contact of any kind with a child (inappropriate touching, oral–genital stimulation, coitus, etc.). Even if no overt violence or threats of violence occur, such interaction is considered coercive and illegal because a child is not considered mature enough to provide informed consent to sexual involvement. Informed consent implies the possession of adequate intellectual and emotional maturity to understand fully both the meaning and possible consequences of a particular action. Adults' exploitation of the naiveté of unsuspecting victims has become a serious problem for children who use the Internet, as discussed later in this chapter.

Mothers' fears about the vulnerability of their female children to sexual victimization can lead to extreme protective measures, as described in the following Sexuality and Diversity discussion.

child sexual abuse
An adult's engaging in sexual contact of any kind with a child, including inappropriate touching, oral–genital stimulation, and coitus.

SEXUALITY and DIVERSITY
Breast Ironing to Protect Girls From Sexual Victimization

In some areas of West and Central Africa, female relatives attempt to protect girls from sexual abuse and rape by means of "breast ironing." When girls begin to develop breasts, older women, usually mothers, massage and pound their daughters' newly forming breasts with heated, hard objects. This procedure causes the breast tissue to break down, and the young girls' breasts flatten and sag, changes that their mothers hope will hide the girls' sexual development. Breast ironing is very painful and often causes blisters, abscesses, and infections. Many girls who have been subjected to this painful procedure also have difficulty breast-feeding after giving birth. In areas where breast ironing is traditionally practiced, about one in four teenagers and an estimated 4 million women overall have had their breasts altered in this manner (Helfer, 2006; Ndonko & Ngo'o, 2006; Sa'ah, 2006).

Most researchers distinguish between nonrelative child sexual abuse, referred to as **pedophilia** or **child molestation**, and **incest**, which is sexual contact between two people who are related (one of whom is often a child). Incest includes sexual contact between siblings as well as sexual contact between children and their parents, grandparents, uncles, or aunts. Incest can occur between related adults, but more commonly it involves a child and

pedophilia or child molestation
Sexual contact between an adult and a child who are not related.

incest
Sexual contact between two people who are related (one of whom is often a child), other than husband and wife.

an adult relative (or an older sibling) perpetrator. Although its definition varies slightly from culture to culture, incest is one of the world's most widely prohibited sexual behaviors.

Each state has its own legal codes that determine whether sexual interaction between an adult and a younger person is considered child molestation (usually if the younger person is under age 12), statutory rape (usually ages 12 to 16 or 17), or a consenting sexual act. The age of consent in the United States tends to range from 16 to 18, but it can be as low as 14 or 15. The legal codes may appear ludicrous at times, particularly in cases of teenage interactions in which one partner is technically an adult and the other technically a minor, although only one or two years separate their ages.

Incest occurs at all socioeconomic levels and is illegal regardless of the ages of the participants. However, an incestuous relationship between consenting adult relatives is considerably less likely to precipitate legal action than one between an adult and a child.

Although it has been commonly assumed that father-daughter incest is most prevalent, studies have shown that brother-sister and first-cousin contacts are more common (Canavan et al., 1992). Sexual relations between brothers and sisters are seldom discovered, and when they are, they do not typically elicit the extreme reactions that father-daughter sexual contacts usually do. However, coercive sexual abuse by a sibling or a parent often has a devastating effect on the child victim.

The incestuous involvement of a father (or stepfather) with his daughter often begins without the child understanding its significance. It may start as playful activities involving wrestling, tickling, kissing, and touching. Over time the activities may expand to include touching of the breasts and genitals, perhaps followed by oral or manual stimulation and intercourse. In most cases, the father relies on his position of authority or on the pair's emotional closeness rather than on physical force to fulfill his desires. He may pressure his daughter into sexual activity by reassuring her that he is "teaching" her something important, by offering rewards, or by exploiting her need for love. Later, when she realizes that the behavior is not appropriate or when she finds her father's demands to be unpleasant and traumatizing, it may be difficult for her to escape. Occasionally, a daughter may value the relationship for the special recognition or privileges it brings her. The incestuous involvement may come to public attention when she gets angry with her father, often for nonsexual reasons, and "tells on him." Sometimes a mother may discover, to her horror, what has been transpiring between her husband and daughter. Other times, the mother may have been aware of the incest but allowed it to continue for reasons of her own. These may include shame, fear of reprisals, concern about having her family disrupted, or the fact that the incestuous activity allows her to avoid her husband's demands for sex.

Father-daughter sexual abuse is more likely to be reported to authorities than other varieties of incest. However, a child often does not report being victimized because of fear that the family may be disrupted—through imprisonment for the father, economic difficulties for the mother, and perhaps placement in foster homes for the victim and other siblings. Separation or divorce may result. Sometimes the victim herself is blamed. These potential consequences of revealing an incestuous relationship place tremendous pressures on the child to keep quiet. For these and other reasons, she may be extremely reluctant to tell anyone else in her family, let alone another adult such as a teacher or neighbor.

Characteristics of People Who Sexually Abuse Children

No classic profile of the pedophile offender has been identified, other than that most pedophiles are heterosexual males and are known to the victim (Murray, 2000; Salter et al., 2003). Child molesters cover the spectrum of social class, educational achievement, intelligence, occupation, religion, and ethnicity. Evidence suggests that many pedophile offenders, especially those who are prosecuted, are shy, lonely, poorly informed about sexuality, and moralistic or religious (Bauman et al., 1984; Hall & Hall, 2007).

Many are likely to have poor interpersonal and sexual relations with other adults and may feel socially inadequate and inferior (Dreznick, 2003; Minor & Dwyer, 1997). However, it is not uncommon to encounter pedophiles outside the legal system who are well educated, socially adept, civic-minded, and financially successful (Baur, 1995). They often pick their victims from among family friends, neighbors, or acquaintances (Murray, 2000). Relating to these children sexually may be a way of coping with powerful feelings of inadequacy that are likely to emerge in sociosexual relationships with other adults.

Other characteristics of some child molesters include alcoholism, severe marital problems, sexual difficulties, poor emotional adjustment, and various brain disorders (McKibben et al., 1994; Mendez & Shapira, 2011). Many of these offenders were sexually victimized themselves during their own childhood (Bouvier, 2003; Seto & Lalumiere, 2010).

Like pedophiles, perpetrators of incest are primarily males who cannot be easily identified or categorized by a classic profile. Rather, "they are a complex, heterogeneous group of individuals who look like everyone else" (Scheela & Stern, 1994, p. 91). However, the incest offender does tend to share some of the traits of many pedophiles. He tends to be economically disadvantaged, a heavy drinker, unemployed, devoutly religious, and emotionally immature (Rosenberg, 1988; Valliant et al., 2000). His behavior might result from general tendencies toward pedophilia, severe feelings of inadequacy in adult sexual relations, or rejection by a hostile spouse; his actions can also be an accompaniment to alcoholism or other psychological disturbances (Lee et al., 2002; Rosenberg, 1988). He also tends to have certain distorted ideas about adult-child sex. For example, he may think that a child who does not resist him desires sexual contact, that adult-child sex is an effective way for children to learn about sex, that a father's relationship with his daughter is enhanced by having sexual contact with her, and that a child does not report such contact because she enjoys it (Abel et al., 1984).

Prevalence of Child Sexual Abuse

Evidence indicates that it is exceedingly difficult for children who are sexually abused to reveal their victimization to others, especially adults. In spite of years of media revelations of abuse of children by members of the clergy, "the real shocker is remembering that most child sexual abuse victims aren't connected to churches, don't file lawsuits and never speak publicly at all" (Nielsen, 2010, E1).

One especially significant reason that child sexual abuse often is not reported is that adults who are legally required to report sexual abuse of children have little reason to fear punishment if they remain silent (Heath, 2011). "Examination of police and court records from across the USA found that a combination of infrequent enforcement and small penalties means adults often have little to fear from concealing abuse" (Heath, 2011, p. 1A). Most states prosecute no more than one or two adults each year for failing to report abuse (Heath, 2011). The recent sexual abuse scandal at Penn State University involving Jerry Sandusky, a former assistant coach of the Penn State football team, has unleashed increased scrutiny of mandatory abuse-reporting laws. It is hoped that more adults will take an active role in reporting child sexual abuse, if not as a moral choice then out of concern about possible prosecution.

Because child sexual abuse often goes unreported at the time it occurs, researchers have relied heavily on reports provided by adults regarding their childhood experiences of sexual abuse. The estimates of child abuse in U.S. society are startling. Various surveys indicate that the proportion of

Jerry Sandusky, a former assistant football coach at Penn State University, was convicted in July 2012 on 45 counts of child sexual abuse.

girls victimized ranges from 20% to 33%, whereas comparable figures for boys range from 9% to 16% (Finkelhor, 1993, 1994; Gorey & Leslie, 1997; Guidry, 1995). To date, the most comprehensive effort to estimate the prevalence of child sexual abuse was a 1997 meta-analysis in which data from 16 separate studies were combined and analyzed. Each of the investigations—14 U.S. and 2 Canadian studies—surveyed adult subjects who were asked to recall experiences of sexual abuse inflicted on them before they reached age 18. Combining these diverse samples yielded an aggregate sample of about 14,000 respondents. A summarization of all the studies indicated that approximately 22% of the women and 9% of the men reported being sexually abused as children (Gorey & Leslie, 1997).

We should also realize that, although the clinical literature has indicated that more girls than boys are victims of sexual abuse, the number of young boys who are sexually molested in the United States may be substantially higher than previously estimated (Denov, 2003a, 2003b). In fact, two surveys found that almost one fourth of male participants reported having experienced some form of sexual abuse by age 13 (Dilorio et al., 2002; Stander et al., 2002).

Mental health professionals have become increasingly aware that, although most sexual abusers of children are male, some children, both female and male, are sexually abused by women, often their mothers (Denov, 2003b; Hartwick et al., 2007; Strickland, 2008). The belief that women sometimes sexually victimize children has been slow to emerge, both because of the prevailing notion that such abuse is a male activity (Hartwick et al., 2007) and because "this subject is more of a taboo because female sexual abuse is more threatening—it undermines feelings about how women should relate to children" (Elliott, 1992, p. 12).

The preponderance of male perpetrators and male victims of child sexual abuse has become all too familiar via widespread media reports about clergy sexual abuse. This scandal has cost the Catholic Church in the United States over $2 billion in legal fees. In the authors' home state, the Oregon Province of the Catholic Church has filed for bankruptcy as a result of numerous sexual abuse lawsuits. Many other Catholic archdioceses and dioceses throughout the United States have filed for bankruptcy protection in recent years.

The Catholic Church in America recently announced the results of a study that allegedly provided information about the causes and context of sexual abuse of minors by Catholic priests (United States Conference of Catholic Bishops, 2011). Among the most egregious conclusions of this study was an attempt to shift blame for the sexual abuse of minors by priests to the culture of free love and social upheaval characteristic of America in the 1960s and 1970s (Roberts, 2011). In their misguided attempt to redirect blame from where it belongs, squarely on the shoulders of the perpetrators, the authors of the report concluded that the abuse of children had little or nothing to do with priestly traits. The document stated that "[a] very small percentage of priests who had allegations of abuse were motivated by pathological disorders such as pedophilia" (p. 5). This conclusion contrasts markedly to the definition of pedophilia in this textbook, which describes pedophilia as *sexual contact between an adult and a child who are not related*. The perpetrators were adult priests and most of the victims were minor children. Therefore, the denial of pedophilia in the report commissioned by Catholic bishops is clearly nonsensical.

The statistics on the prevalence of sexual abuse of children have aroused significant controversy. Some people claim that the statistics underestimate the problem, and others claim that they overestimate it. One of the most controversial types of reports has concerned the case of adults reporting so-called recovered memories of sexual abuse that they endured as children.

Recovered Memories of Childhood Sexual Abuse

The media have reported numerous cases in which alleged perpetrators of sexual abuse have been accused and convicted based on the testimony of adult women who "recover" memories of their childhood sexual abuse. This "recovery" has usually occurred during psychotherapy. But can a person repress memories of sexual abuse that may have occurred years or decades earlier and then suddenly or gradually "recover" them after exposure to certain triggering stimuli? Or can a "memory" of an event that never happened in childhood be suggested to an adult and then "remembered" as true? These questions lie at the heart of a debate among clinicians, researchers, and lawyers.

Skeptics of recovered memories claim that thousands of families and individuals have been devastated by the widespread inclination to accept claims of recovered memories at face value, in the absence of validating evidence. These skeptics offer as proof of their concern cases in which falsely accused and convicted individuals were later exonerated, either by the legal system or by victim recantation (Colangelo, 2007; Frazier, 2006; Gardner, 2006).

The possibility of being falsely accused of such a heinous crime is the substance of nightmares. But just how often are the accusations false; that is, what is the probability that recovered memories are imagined? To gain some perspective on this issue, let us briefly consider some of the evidence.

Support for the legitimacy of recovered memories has been provided by several studies. In one investigation, 129 adult women who had experienced childhood sexual abuse in the 1970s were identified and interviewed in the 1990s. Of this group, 38% did not recall the abuse that had been reported and documented 17 years earlier. The author of this investigation concluded that, if having no recall of child sexual abuse is a common occurrence for adult women, as indicated by the study's results, then "later recovery of child sexual abuse by some women should not be surprising" (L. Williams, 1994, p. 1174). In another study, 56% of 45 adult women survivors of childhood sexual abuse indicated that they had been amnesic about their abuse for varied lengths of time, and 16% reported remembering their abuse while receiving psychotherapy (Rodriguez et al., 1997). A survey of several hundred university students found that 20% of 111 victims of childhood sexual abuse reported that they had recovered memories of abuse (Melchert & Parker, 1997). Finally, a review of the research literature dealing with recovered memory reported finding 30 studies of adult survivors of child sexual abuse in which between 19% and 59% of the participants forgot and later recalled some or all of the abuse (Stoler et al., 2001).

On the other hand, several researchers have expressed skepticism about recovered memories of childhood sexual abuse. Some have argued that "repressed memories" are inadvertently planted in suggestible clients by overzealous or poorly trained psychotherapists who believe that most psychological problems stem from childhood sexual abuse (Colangelo, 2007; Gardner, 2006; Gross, 2004). Numerous studies have demonstrated the relative ease with which "memories" of events that never occurred can be created in the research laboratory (Brainerd & Reyna, 1998; Loftus et al., 1994; Porter et al., 1999). In one 11-week study, for instance, young children were asked at weekly intervals whether they had ever experienced five distinct events. Four of the events were real, and one—getting treated in the hospital for an injured finger—was fictitious. The children readily recognized the real events. However, more than one third also became gradually convinced over the course of the 11 weeks that one of their fingers had been injured. In some cases, they even "remembered" elaborate details about their injuries. Many continued to insist that these false memories were true even after being told otherwise (Ceci et al., 1994).

So where are we now on this controversial issue? A number of professional organizations, including the American Psychological Association, the American Psychiatric Association, and the American Medical Association, have all issued statements supporting the belief that memories can be recovered later in life. These professional organizations also acknowledge that a "memory" may be suggested and then remembered as true. In recent years the debate about recovered memories has subsided as mental health professionals have searched for common ground and ways to be more collaborative and less adversarial (Colangelo, 2007). Research evidence indicates that recovered memories may be fictitious at times and authentic at other times (Lindsay et al., 2009). There is now general agreement that traumatic memories are often processed differently than memories of ordinary events and that "recovered memories are possible while not necessarily accurate in their entirety" (Colangelo, 2007, p. 96). As professionals continue to discuss the issues surrounding recovered memories, it is important to remember that, despite the media spotlight on defendants who claim they have been falsely accused, sexual abuse of children is a fact, not a question. The recovered-memories debate must not turn back the clock to a time when victims of sexual abuse did not report their traumatic experiences out of fear of not being believed. In the same spirit, we must act responsibly to protect the innocent from wrongful accusations that stem from false memories.

Pedophiles in Cyberspace

Before the emergence of the Internet, pedophiles were largely isolated. Now, with several pedophile support groups online, child molesters can exchange child pornography, discuss their molestation experiences, validate each other's abusive acts, and secure reinforcement for the shared belief that sexual interaction between adults and children is acceptable (Lambert & O'Halloran, 2008; Malesky & Ennis, 2004). The Internet has also facilitated victimization of children by pedophiles, who, "hiding behind a veil of anonymity, roam cyberspace relatively undetected, posing all sorts of pretenses in their efforts to lure unsuspecting victims" (Philaretou, 2005, p. 181). These cyberspace predators can explore the bulletin boards on the Internet and cruise chat rooms designed for children and teenagers. These chat rooms provide rich hunting grounds for adults seeking unsuspecting kids in need of attention and kids with confused notions of sexuality.

While most of the pedophiles who are active in cyberspace are males, there is mounting evidence that almost one third of online pedophiles are female (Lambert & O'Halloran, 2008). Like male cyberspace predators, women "are using the Internet to express a sexual interest in children and they display similar characteristics to male individuals engaged in the same processes" (Lambert & O'Halloran, 2008, p. 284).

Typically, pedophiles first gain a child's trust by appearing to be genuinely empathic and interested in the child's problems and concerns. Then they may try to get their intended victim to agree to e-mail, postal mail, or phone contacts. Next they may send the child pornographic materials suggesting that adult–child sexual interaction is normal and appropriate. The final step is to arrange a meeting. One case in which this strategy was used involved a 32-year-old Seattle engineer, who used the Internet to lure a 13-year-old girl, whom he then repeatedly raped. He was sentenced in 2000 to a 23-year prison term. In New York State a 15-year-old boy's statement led police to a number of prominent local men who had been systematically abusing local boys, some as young as 13 (West, 2000). Many Internet sex crimes do not involve forcible sexual assault and more closely resemble statutory rape in which adult offenders use the Internet and face-to-face encounters to "meet, develop relationships with, and openly seduce underage teenagers" (Wolak et al., 2008, p. 111).

In September 1996 the U.S. Congress passed the Communications Decency Act (CDA), which prohibited the distribution of indecent materials to minors by computer. In July 1997 the Supreme Court overruled this legislation on constitutional grounds, concluding that the CDA would seriously erode the right of free speech (Levy, 1997). In 2002 the Supreme Court, in further defense of this right, struck down a section of the federal child pornography law that made it a crime to own or sell computer-created images of children engaged in sex ("virtual" child pornography). According to Justice Anthony Kennedy, making it a crime to show sexual images that only appear to be children would damage legitimate filmmakers, photographers, and advertisers (Savage, 2002). As a result of this decision, it is legal to display on the Internet both computer-generated images of children in sexual situations and depictions of minors by adult actors in sexual situations, provided that no real children are shown or "composited" into a sex scene.

Software filters may be more effective than legal prohibitions in limiting youthful access to Internet pornography. However, it is noteworthy that many U.S. households with children do not use such filters (Times Digest, 2009).

Some of the gateways to the Internet, such as America Online (AOL), have attempted to protect children from cyberspace predators by using "guards" to monitor kids-only chat rooms for inappropriate or suspicious dialogue. Unfortunately, these efforts are only minimally effective, because private messages cannot be screened. Knowledgeable cyberspace pedophiles are most likely to make conversations private before making inappropriate overtures. A decision by MySpace.com to apply technologies designed to block access of convicted sex offenders to this popular online hangout is an encouraging development in efforts to protect youth from cyberspace predators (Barnard, 2008). A number of states have recently established laws that prohibit sex offenders from visiting social networking sites such as Facebook and MySpace (Wynton, 2011).

It is becoming increasingly common for law enforcement officers to troll chat rooms looking for pedophiles who prey on youthful victims and for text messages, photos, and website posts that can serve as evidence (Younger, 2011). Classroom instruction on how to find and prosecute cyberspace predators has become more widespread as law enforcement officials seek to expand their arsenal of methods to combat sex offenders who lurk in cyberspace (Roman, 2011).

SEXUALHEALTH

Even if widely applied and effective laws or in-house procedures existed to curb cyberspace pedophilia, the responsibility for protecting children resides with parents. Just as most of us would not allow our children to play unsupervised in dangerous places, we should not allow them to cruise cyberspace or spend time in chat rooms without supervision. One potentially helpful strategy is to keep computers in a central location where children can be monitored more easily when they go online. However, parental monitoring of their children's cyberspace activities has become increasingly difficult in recent years with the availability of all kinds of mobile devices for surfing the Internet (Feldman, 2011). Parents should be clear that a child should never meet a cyberspace acquaintance in person without a parent or another responsible adult present. Finally, parents concerned about cyberspace pornography may wish to purchase Internet filtering software, such as NetNanny or Cybersitter, designed to block children's access to websites with obscene pictures or words. One recently developed social network protection system, SocialShield, provides parents with tools to help them protect their children's Internet safety. ●

Effects of Child Sexual Abuse

Much research suggests that child sexual abuse can be a severely traumatizing and emotionally damaging experience, with long-term negative consequences for many of the victims (Miner et al., 2006; Putman, 2009; Zwickl & Merriman, 2011). Clinical contact with adult survivors of child sexual abuse often reveals memories of a childhood filled with distress and confusion. Survivors speak of their loss of childhood innocence, the contamination and interruption of normal sexual development, and a profound sense of betrayal by a relative, family friend, priest or clergyperson, or community leader.

A number of factors influence the severity of a child victim's response to sexual abuse. The longer the molestation goes on, the worse the prognosis is for recovery from the trauma of the abuse (Brown et al., 2008; McLean & Gallop, 2003). Feelings of powerlessness and betrayal may be especially pronounced when physical force is used to perpetrate an act of child sexual abuse or when the victim has a close relationship to the offender. These two factors—physical force and victim-offender relationship—probably correlate most strongly with subsequent negative consequences for survivors of child sexual abuse (Brown et al., 2008; Hanson et al., 2001). Other factors known to influence how a child responds to sexual abuse include the age of the victim and perpetrator at the onset of the abuse, the victim's feelings of responsibility for the situation, and the number of perpetrators (Brown et al., 2008). The younger the child, the greater the discrepancy in age between victim and perpetrator, the stronger the feelings of responsibility, and the higher the number of perpetrators, the greater the severity of a child's response to sexual abuse.

Many victims of child sexual abuse have difficulty forming intimate adult relationships (Rumstein-McKean & Hunsley, 2001; Vandeusen & Carr, 2003). When relationships are established, they often lack emotional and sexual fulfillment (Feiring et al., 2009; Kristensen & Lau, 2011). For both sexes, a strong link exists between sexual abuse in childhood and sexual difficulties in adulthood (Camuso & Rellini, 2010; Zwickl & Merriman, 2011; Staples et al., 2011). Other common symptoms of sexual abuse survivors include low self-esteem, guilt, shame, a self-image of "badness" and low expectations for future happiness, depression, alienation, a lack of trust in others, revulsion at being touched, drug and alcohol abuse, obesity, elevated suicide rates, a predisposition to being repeatedly victimized in a variety of ways, and long-term medical problems, such as chronic pelvic pain and gastrointestinal disorders (Balsam et al., 2011; Putman, 2009; Reese-Weber & Smith, 2011).

Posttraumatic stress disorder, a common occurrence in adult women who have experienced rape, is also prevalent among many females who are sexually abused in childhood. About half of all victims of sexual abuse meet the criteria specified for PTSD (Frazier et al., 2009). Symptoms of PTSD in children include nightmares; psychic numbing (diminished responsiveness to the outside world); lack of interest in previously enjoyed activities; avoiding thoughts, feelings, or activities that produce memories of the abuse; irrational fears of being left by caregivers; excessive daydreaming; forgetfulness; and memory deficits (Frazier et al., 2009; Putman, 2009). Finally, studies reveal that adult survivors of child sexual abuse often exhibit detrimental parenting practices, such as the use of inconsistent or harsh discipline and inadequate supervision of their children (Martsolf & Draucker, 2008).

A variety of treatment approaches have emerged to help survivors of child sexual abuse resolve issues regarding these experiences and their emotional aftermath (Putnam, 2003; McPherson et al., 2012; Vandeusen & Carr, 2003). These treatment strategies range from individual therapy to group and couple-oriented approaches. Most metropolitan areas in the United States also have self-help support organizations for survivors of sexual abuse. (If you want more information about how to seek professional therapeutic assistance, we suggest reviewing the guidelines in Chapter 14.)

Preventing Child Sexual Abuse

Most child sexual abuse is perpetrated by someone known to the victim. Thus some health professionals suggest that many children can avoid being victimized if they are taught about their right to say no, the difference between "okay" and "not-okay" touches, and strategies for coping with an adult's attempt to coerce them into inappropriate intimate contact. A recent study of sex offenders revealed that children's saying no to the offender is an effective strategy for preventing child sexual abuse (Leclerc et al., 2011).

As indicated in Chapter 12, parents often avoid discussing sex with their children. Therefore it is probably unrealistic to expect better parent–child communication to significantly protect children. Furthermore, parents themselves are often the abusers. The following list, drawn from the writings of a number of child abuse specialists, offers suggestions for preventing child sexual abuse. They may be helpful to parents, educators, and other caregivers of children.

1. It is important to discuss sexual abuse prevention strategies with young children because victims are often younger than age 7. Be sure to include boys, because they too can be abused.

2. Avoid making a discussion of child sexual abuse unduly frightening. It is important that children be sufficiently concerned so that they will be on the lookout for potentially abusive adult behavior. However, they should also be confident in their ability to avoid such a situation.

3. Take time to carefully explain the differences between okay touches (pats, snuggles, and hugs) and not-okay touches that make a child feel uncomfortable or confused. Not-okay touches can be explained as touching under the panties or underpants or touching areas that bathing suits cover. Be sure to indicate that a child should not have to touch an adult in these areas even if the adult says it is all right. It is also a good idea to explain not-okay kisses (prolonged lip contact or tongue in mouth).

4. Encourage children to believe that they have rights—the right to control their bodies and the right to say no when they are being touched in a way that makes them uncomfortable.

5. Encourage children to tell someone right away if an adult has touched them in a way that is inappropriate or if an adult has made them do something with which they are uncomfortable. Emphasize that you will not be angry with them and that they will be okay when they tell, even if someone else has told them that they will get in trouble. Stress that no matter what happened, it was not their fault and they will not be blamed. Also, warn them that not all adults will believe them. Tell them to keep telling people until they find someone like you who will believe them.

6. Discuss with children some of the strategies that adults might use to get children to participate in sexual activities. For example, tell them to trust their own feelings when they think something is wrong, even if an adult who is a friend or relative says that it is okay and that he or she is "teaching" them something helpful. Given that many adults use the "this is our secret" strategy, it can be particularly helpful to explain the difference between a secret (something one is never to tell—a bad idea) and a surprise (a good idea because it is something one tells later to make someone happy).

7. Discuss strategies for getting away from uncomfortable or dangerous situations. Let children know that it is okay to scream, yell, run away, or get assistance from a friend or trusted adult.

8. Encourage children to state clearly to an adult who touches them inappropriately that they will tell a particular responsible adult about what went on. Interviews with perpetrators of child sexual abuse have revealed that many of them would be deterred from their abusive actions if a child said that she or he would tell a specific adult about the assault (Budin & Johnson, 1989; Daro, 1991).

9. Perhaps one of the most important things to incorporate in this prevention discussion, particularly for parents, is the message that private touching can be a loving and pleasurable experience, as they will discover when they grow older and meet someone they care for or love. Without some discussion of the positive aspects of sexuality, there is a risk that a child will develop a negative view of any kind of sexual contact between people, regardless of the nature of their relationship. ●

AP Photo/Merced Sun-Star, Marci Stenberg

Elementary school students light the "Candle of Hope," in recognition of National Child Abuse Prevention Month.

When the Child Tells

Research demonstrates that children who have been sexually abused often either delay disclosure of the abuse to a parent or another adult or do not tell at all (Goodman-Brown et al., 2003; Leander et al., 2007). A recent Swedish study found that sexually abused children are markedly more likely to disclose the abuse to a friend their own age than to an adult (Priebe & Svedin, 2008). Sexually abused boys may be less likely than abused girls to disclose the abuse, for reasons similar to those expressed by adult males who have been sexually assaulted (shame, fear of negative responses from others, etc.) (Sorsoli et al., 2008). Many children do not disclose their abuse to an adult until they have reached adulthood, if then (Berliner & Conte, 1995; Goodman-Brown et al., 2003). "Fears of retribution and abandonment, and feelings of complicity, embarrassment, guilt, and shame all conspire to silence children and inhibit their disclosures of abuse" (Goodman-Brown et al., 2003, p. 526).

As described previously, children suffer many adverse effects of sexual abuse. Their fears about potential consequences of revealing their victimization and their resultant hesitancy to reveal it further magnify their misery. Furthermore, the emotional trauma that a child experiences as a result of a sexual encounter with an adult may be intensified by excessive parental reactions (Davies, 1995). When telling a parent what happened, children may merely be relaying a sense of discomfort over something they do not fully understand. If parents react with extreme agitation, children are likely to respond with increased emotional negativity, developing a sense of being implicated in something terrible and often feeling extremely guilty about having participated in such an event. Children may feel guilty about such experiences even without parental displays of distress, because they sense the guilt of the person who molested them.

It is important that parents respond appropriately to instances of child abuse involving their child. Such acts should not be ignored! While remaining calm in the face of their child's revelation, parents should take great precautions to see that the child is not alone with the offender again. In many instances children are repeatedly molested by the same person, and they may come to feel a sense of obligation and guilt. It is essential to ensure that the child is protected from further experiences of this kind. Because it is also likely that the child will not have been the offender's only victim, it is essential to report the offender to the police to protect other children.

> **Critical Thinking Question**
>
> When children have been sexually abused, what steps should be taken to reduce the potentially adverse effects of the abuse?

Sexual Harassment

Whether in industry, the military, or academia, **sexual harassment** is widespread in U.S. society. Sexual harassment is more than just a demand for sexual favors. Sexual harassment can also occur when people's actions create a hostile or offensive working environment. One woman offered her experience:

> **sexual harassment**
> Unwelcome sexual advances, requests for sexual favors, and other verbal or physical conduct of a sexual nature in the workplace or academic setting.

I was the first woman they hired at that level. I was proud of what I had accomplished and looked forward to the challenges, but it has been much harder than I expected. I have been amazed and disgusted by the jokes and the unbelievable crude remarks that some men have made. People have sent me the most disgusting e-mails, and every day I get obscene messages on my voice mail. I spoke to my boss about this and told him how upsetting it was to me, but he told me that I needed to be a "team player" and that this was just the guys' way of welcoming me to the group. Maybe it shouldn't bother me as much as it does, but it is hurting my work. I'm having trouble concentrating, and I cringe every time I listen to my messages. (Authors' files)

Sexual harassment in the workplace is prohibited by Title VII of the 1964 Civil Rights Act. In 1980 the Equal Employment Opportunity Commission (EEOC) issued guidelines on sexual harassment. These guidelines make it clear that both verbal and physical harassment are illegal:

> Unwelcome sexual advances, requests for sexual favors, and other verbal or physical conduct of a sexual nature constitute sexual harassment when (1) submission to such conduct is made either explicitly or implicitly a term or condition of an individual's employment, (2) submission to or rejection of such conduct by an individual is used as a basis for employment decisions affecting such individual, or (3) such conduct has the purpose or effect of unreasonably interfering with an individual's work performance or creating an intimidating, hostile, or offensive working environment. (Equal Employment Opportunity Commission, 1980, pp. 74676–74677)

The EEOC guidelines describe two kinds of sexual harassment. One form, commonly labeled *quid pro quo*, is reflected in the first two situations described in the guidelines. Here, compliance with unwanted sexual advances is made a condition for securing a job or education benefits or for favorable treatment in employment or academic settings (such as receiving a promotion or high grades). Harassment is often evident in reprisals that follow refusals to comply.

A second form of sexual harassment, often referred to as a "hostile or offensive environment," is described in the third situation in the EEOC guidelines. This kind of sexual harassment is less clear but probably more common than the *quid pro quo* variety. Here, one or more supervisors, coworkers, teachers, or students engage in persistent, inappropriate behaviors that make the workplace or academic environment hostile, abusive, and generally unbearable. Unlike *quid pro quo* harassment, this second form does not necessarily involve power or authority differences. It may, however, involve attempts to defend status and position, because men often view the entrance of women into formerly male bastions of power and privilege as threatening (Dall'Ara & Maass, 1999).

Cases involving hostile or offensive environments have been the subject of considerable debate over what constitutes such an environment. Essentially, a hostile environment is seen as one in which a reasonable person in the same or similar circumstances would find the conduct of the harasser(s) to be intimidating, hostile, or abusive.

The reasonable-person interpretation is illustrated by a decision in which the U.S. Supreme Court ruled unanimously that a Tennessee woman was subjected to sexual harassment in the form of a hostile environment "that would seriously affect a reasonable person's psychological well-being" (Justice Sandra Day O'Connor, writing for the Court in *Harris v. Forklift Systems*, 92 U.S. 1168 [1993]). In this case the victim's male boss (the company president) (1) urged her to retrieve coins from his front pants pocket, (2) ridiculed the size of her buttocks, (3) described her as a "dumb-ass woman" in the presence of others, and (4) insinuated that she had won a large sales contract by providing sexual favors. The defendant's attorney unsuccessfully tried to pass off these behaviors as merely joking without any hostile intent. This case is noteworthy because it involved neither sexual blackmail nor unwanted touching. Nevertheless, the Supreme Court ruled that a reasonable person would find the offensive sexual speech intimidating and abusive.

Varieties and Incidence of Sexual Harassment on the Job

Twenty years after Anita Hill testified against Clarence Thomas on his nomination to the Supreme Court seared the issue of sexual harassment into the national consciousness, allegations of sexual misconduct by one-time 2012 GOP presidential candidate

Herman Cain has drawn fresh attention to this issue (Haq, 2011; Stout, 2011). Both the Hill/Thomas case and the more recent Herman Cain situation illustrate that sexual harassment related to the work environment can take many forms. It can start with such things as remarks of a sexual nature; sexist comments; unwelcome attention; violations of personal space; repeated unwelcome requests for a date; inappropriate, derogatory put-downs; leering and/or whistling; offensive and crude language; and displaying sexually oriented objects, materials, or pictures that create a hostile or offensive environment. In the expanding electronic environment of contemporary America, sexual harassment often involves e-mails, text messages, Facebook posts, and tweets (Greenwald, 2011). Some of these behaviors occupy a gray area because not all people would view them as genuine sexual harassment. However, they clearly become sexual harassment if they persist after the target of such acts has asked the offending person to stop.

At an intermediate level of severity, sexual harassment in the workplace can include inappropriate, graphic comments about a person's body or sexual competence, sexual propositions not directly linked to employment, verbal abuse of a sexual nature, and unwanted physical contact of a nonsexual nature. In its most severe manifestations, sexual harassment on the job can involve a boss or supervisor requiring sexual services from an employee as a condition for keeping a job or getting a promotion, unwanted physical contact or conduct of a sexual nature, and, less commonly, sexual assault.

Prevalence of Sexual Harassment in the Workplace

The annual number of sexual harassment complaints filed with the EEOC reached a peak at 15,889 in 1997. Claims dropped off in the 2000s, falling to 11,717 in 2010 (Haq, 2011). The drop in the number of annual claims may reflect improved efforts of American companies to provide effective workplace training on sexual harassment, or it may be a product of the economic downturn—harassed employees may be keeping quiet out of fear of jeopardizing their employment or career advancement (Haq, 2011; Stout, 2011). It is also possible that an increasing incidence of confidential settlements has resulted in fewer claims filed with the EEOC. For example, the National Restaurant Association, which Cain headed in the 1990s, entered into confidential and secret settlements with two women who had accused Cain of inappropriate and unwanted sexual advances (Haq, 2011).

Law professor Anita Hill, who testified during the confirmation hearings of Supreme Court Justice Clarence Thomas, triggered a national debate about sexual harassment in the workplace.

For whatever reason, we can be assured that many incidents of workplace sexual harassment go unreported. Some have estimated that only 5–15% of harassed people actually file complaints (Haq, 2011). An analysis of data derived from national surveys indicates that 40–70% of American women and 10–20% of men have experienced sexual harassment in the workplace (Equal Employment Opportunity Commission, 2009; Rospenda et al., 2009).

Sexual harassment is not limited to low-paying jobs or indeed to any particular segment of the employment force. It occurs in all professions and at every level. For example, over a decade ago the army's highest-ranking woman (a general) filed a complaint of sexual harassment that was substantiated by army investigators (Myers, 2000; Ricks & Suro, 2000). The level of sexual harassment in the U.S. military is quite high (Buchanan et al., 2008). Several studies have revealed high incidences of sexual harassment in medical settings as well. In one survey of 133 physicians, 73% of the female respondents and 22% of the men reported experiencing sexual harassment during their residency training (Komaromy et al., 1993). Other studies have revealed that 69–85% of nurses experience sexual harassment on the job (Valente & Bullough, 2004).

Same-Sex Sexual Harassment in the Workplace

Sexual harassment involving members of the same sex has become more of an issue, both in the workplace and in the U.S. courts. People who are victims of same-sex sexual harassment have generally found it difficult to obtain satisfactory legal judgments, regardless of their own sexual orientation. Until recently, this unfortunate situation was due in large part to the absence of a federal law specifically prohibiting same-sex sexual harassment and to many courts' narrow interpretation of Title VII as prohibiting sex discrimination only between men and women (Bible, 2006). The lack of a legal sanction against same-sex sexual harassment was finally addressed in late 2007, when the U.S. Congress passed a bill making it illegal for employers to engage in discrimination or harassment related to sexual orientation, gender identity, or gender expression. Nevertheless, even with the passage of this landmark legislation, attorneys representing victims of same-sex harassment frequently find themselves needing to prove that the accused acted out of "sexual interest." Proving this can be extremely difficult, because most defendants in these cases claim to be heterosexual. Furthermore, gay or lesbian plaintiffs may fear being "outed" or exposed, and plaintiffs who are not gay or lesbian may fear being thought of as such (Gover, 1996). Nevertheless, same-sex sexual harassment claims are increasing (Stout, 2011).

Effects of Workplace Sexual Harassment on the Victim

On-the-job sexual harassment can seriously erode a victim's financial status, job performance, career opportunities, psychological and physical health, and personal relationships (Berdahl & Aquino, 2009; Gradus et al., 2008). The financial ramifications of refusing to endure sexual harassment may be severe, especially for people in lower-level positions. Many victims, particularly if they are supporting families, cannot afford to be unemployed. Many find it exceedingly difficult to look for other jobs while maintaining their present job. If they are fired for resisting harassment, they may be unable to obtain unemployment compensation, and even if they do obtain compensation, it will probably provide only a fraction of their former income.

Various surveys report that the great majority of harassed workers (between 75% and 90%) report adverse psychological effects, including PTSD symptoms, eating disorders, crying spells, loss of self-esteem, and feelings of anger, humiliation, shame, embarrassment, nervousness, irritability, alienation, vulnerability, helplessness, and lack of motivation (Harned & Fitzgerald, 2002; Jorgenson & Wahl, 2000; Larsen & Fitzgerald, 2011).

Dealing With Sexual Harassment on the Job

If you face sexual harassment at work, you have a number of options. The suggestions in the following list provide guidelines for dealing with this abuse.

SEXUALHEALTH

1. If the harassment includes actual or attempted rape or assault, you can file criminal charges against the perpetrator.
2. If the harassment has stopped short of attempted rape or assault, consider confronting the person who is harassing you. State in clear terms that what he or she is doing is clearly sexual harassment, that you will not tolerate it, and that if it continues, you will file charges through appropriate channels. You may prefer to document what has occurred and your response to it in a letter directed to the harasser (keep a copy). In such a letter, you should include specific details of previous incidents of harassment, your unequivocal rejection of such inappropriate overtures, and your intent to take more serious action if they do not stop immediately.

3. If the offender does not stop the harassment after direct verbal or written confrontation, or both, it may be helpful to discuss your situation with your supervisor or the supervisor of the offender, or both.

4. If neither the harasser nor the supervisor responds appropriately to your concern, you may want to gather support from your coworkers. You may discover that you are not the only victim in your company. Discussing the offense with sympathetic women and men in your workplace may produce sufficient pressure to terminate the harassment. Be very sure of your facts, though, because such actions could result in a slander lawsuit.

5. If your attempts to deal with this problem within your company are unsuccessful or if you are fired, demoted, or refused promotion because of your efforts to end harassment, you can file an official complaint with your city or state Human Rights Commission or with the Fair Employment Practices Agency (the names may vary locally). You can also ask the local office of the federally funded EEOC to investigate the situation.

6. Finally, you may wish to pursue legal action to resolve your problem with sexual harassment. Lawsuits can be filed in federal courts under the Civil Rights Act. They can also be filed under city or state laws prohibiting employment discrimination. Moreover, a single lawsuit can be filed in a number of jurisdictions. A person who has been a victim of such harassment is most likely to receive a favorable court judgment if she or he has first tried to resolve the problem within the company before going to court. A number of legal decisions, including one made by the U.S. Supreme Court in 2004, have revealed that an employer may successfully defend against liability if a plaintiff does not seek relief from harassment by pursuing the employer's established sexual harassment grievance procedure (Mink, 2005). ●

When an employee files a sexual harassment claim with the EEOC, the employer or supervisor who is named in the claim may retaliate against the employee in a number of ways, such as by writing poor performance evaluations or transferring the employee to another position with less status, pay, or benefits. Such retaliatory actions are clear violations of Title VII, and retaliation charges are the fastest-growing body of claims processed by the EEOC, resulting in the recovery of $124 million in 2007 alone (Silverglate & Paskievitch, 2008).

U.S. businesses are becoming increasingly sensitive to the issue of sexual harassment in the workplace, in part because of the damage to morale and productivity caused by such behaviors but also because of court decisions that have awarded large sums of money to victims (Elkins et al., 2008; Patrick, 2011). Because Title VII imposes liability on companies for sexual harassment perpetrated by their employees, many corporations have implemented programs designed to educate employees about sexual harassment (Stout, 2011).

Nevertheless, despite these programs in business and in the military services, many women still keep silent when they have been harassed (Bruns & Bruns, 2005). They do so for many reasons, including a desire to protect their career (Becker, 2000) and the fear that formal reporting will not be helpful, may lead to retaliation, and could lead to their being negatively evaluated by others (Marin & Guadagno, 1999; Silverglate & Paskievitch, 2008).

Cyberstalking

Rapid technological advances have given rise to an intrusive form of harassment that occurs in cyberspace rather than a work environment. **Cyberstalking** refers to a

cyberstalking
Threatening behaviors or unwanted advances that use Web technologies as weapons for stalking and harassment.

process in which a person is harassed on the Internet. Almost 1 million Americans are victimized by cyberstalking each year, a majority of whom are women (Ginty, 2011). Cyberstalking encompasses threatening behaviors or unwanted advances that use Web technologies as weapons for stalking and harassment.

Cyberstalking can take many forms. Some people are victimized by former date partners who may post disparaging comments about them on social networking sites such as Facebook or MySpace or angry "tweets" on Twitter. Some cyberstalkers use blogs to stalk and denigrate their victims. For example, a California woman and founder of Survivors in Action reported that her abuser would create negative blogs about her and post messages on existing blog sites claiming that she was a "sluttty whore" (Ginty, 2011). An Oklahoma woman was victimized by a cyberstalker who posted threatening videos about her on YouTube (Ginty, 2011).

Cyberstalking is fueled by two major factors: the very rapid evolution of various technologies that create instantaneous large audiences and the nonchalance with which people use this technology to divulge personal details about their lives. In our discussion of Internet relationships in Chapter 7, we described how the anonymity of the Internet often allows people to express themselves with abandon. People communicating online often lose track of normal boundaries that are present in face-to-face relationships and thus may be more inclined to reveal intimate details that later can be used against them in episodes of cyberstalking. When a date goes wrong or after a nasty breakup, the jilted/rejected person can use these personal details to stalk and harass his or her victim in cyberspace.

Individuals can take several steps to reduce the possibility of being victimized by cyberstalking. These methods, outlined in an excellent article by Molly Ginty (2011), include creating passwords that are difficult to crack, being selective when admitting others to a person's location on a social networking site, not providing personal information on the Internet, and immediately alerting both police and the providers of Internet services and sites where stalking threats occur.

Sexual Harassment in Academic Settings

Sexual harassment also occurs in educational settings. College students often find themselves in the unpleasant situation of experiencing unwanted sexual advances from their professors. Both sexes are vulnerable to this form of harassment. However, it is most commonly male professors or instructors who harass female students (Bingham & Battey, 2005; Kelley & Parsons, 2000).

Academic sexual harassment differs somewhat from harassment that occurs in the workplace. For one thing, a student who encounters unwanted sexual advances often has the option of selecting a different instructor or adviser. In contrast, workers in an employment setting tend to have fewer alternatives for avoiding or escaping the harassment while still keeping their jobs. However, students can experience coercive pressures associated with the need to obtain a good grade, a letter of recommendation, or a desirable work or research opportunity. Furthermore, sexual harassment of students can result in poor school performance, altered or derailed academic careers, and a variety of psychological and physical symptoms comparable to those experienced by people harassed on the job (Bingham & Battey, 2005; Bruns & Bruns, 2005).

Students also tend to be more naive than workers about the implications of becoming sexually involved with someone who may be important to their successful pursuit of an education or a career. There is a real potential for inappropriate exploitation of youthful naiveté and awe regarding prestige and power. Furthermore, evidence has suggested that a student victim "might wonder whether her academic success has been due to her ability or her professor's sexual interest in her" (Satterfield & Muehlenhard, 1990, p. 1).

Many American higher-education institutions have established programs designed to educate faculty and administrators about sexual harassment (Franke, 2008). An increasing number of colleges and universities have also established policies prohibiting faculty from dating their students (Bruns & Bruns, 2005). The growing debate over professor–student liaisons, together with decisions to ban such relationships, is fueled largely by the belief that many relationships between faculty and students may seem consensual on the surface but actually are not. Rather, the power of professors or advisers or both to determine students' futures through grades and recommendations often creates pressure for students to comply to protect their class standing or future prospects.

Sexual harassment also occurs in high schools and even middle schools (Ormerod et al., 2008). A recent survey of almost 2,000 teens found that 56% of girls and 40% of boys reported being sexually harassed either in person or electronically (Anderson, 2012). In 1992 the U.S. Supreme Court ruled that school districts are liable for hostile sexual environments created by school employees and can be sued for damages. However, the Supreme Court has yet to extend this liability to sexual harassment perpetrated by peers. Nevertheless, many district courts have allowed students to litigate cases of peer harassment under Title IX, a 1972 civil rights law that prohibits federally funded schools from denying students opportunities based on their sex (Lichty et al., 2008; Scher, 1997). Furthermore, the U.S. Department of Education has published a manual of peer sexual harassment guidelines in which it is clearly stated that schools that do not take measures to remedy this form of harassment could lose federal funds (Scher, 1997).

Prevalence of Sexual Harassment in Academic Settings

Just how common is sexual harassment in educational settings? A survey of California high schools found that approximately 50% of the female respondents reported experiencing sexual harassment (Roscoe et al., 1994). Another survey of over 1,000 Canadian adolescent females in grades 7 through 12 found that more than 23% had experienced at least one event of sexual harassment in the previous 6 months (Bagley et al., 1997). A review of research suggests that the incidence of sexual harassment in American high schools, especially harassment by peers, is quite high—ranging in various studies from 37% to 87% (Lichty et al., 2008; Terrance et al., 2004). Sexual harassment in high schools and colleges is receiving considerable attention from school officials fueled in part by two Supreme Court decisions that found educational institutions liable for negligence in dealing with sexual harassment complaints (Terrance et al., 2004; Ramson, 2006).

In surveys of college and university populations, 20–40% of undergraduate women and 30–50% of graduate women report having been the target in one or more incidents of sexual harassment in their academic settings (Birdeau et al., 2005; Bruns & Bruns, 2005; Ramson, 2006). Because most studies of college populations have included only female students, we have less information about harassment of male students. However, research has revealed that between 9% and 29% of male undergraduates report having been sexually harassed (Kalof et al., 2001; Sundt, 1994). The number of male victims of sexual harassment in academic settings may be even higher, as indicated by an Internet survey of over 2,000 college students ages 18 to 24, in which almost two thirds of both male and female respondents reported being sexually harassed on campus (American Association of University Women, 2006).

Dealing With Sexual Harassment on Campus

What can you do if you experience sexual harassment on campus? Some students avoid or escape the harassment by dropping a class, finding another faculty adviser, or even leaving school. However, we advise someone who feels that she or he is being harassed to report it in order to curtail these inappropriate actions and to reduce the likelihood that other students will be victimized by the same person (it is common for people who harass students to have several targets). You may wish to speak to the offending individual's chairperson or dean. If you are not satisfied with that person's response, contact the campus officer or department that handles matters of civil rights or affirmative action. Although you may be concerned about grade discrimination or loss of position, federal affirmative action guidelines forbid discrimination against people who, in good conscience, file legitimate claims of sexual harassment. Furthermore, a professor guilty of such action will usually be closely monitored and will be less likely to continue to harass. ●

Summary

Rape

- The legal definition of rape varies from state to state, but most laws define rape as sexual intercourse that occurs under actual or threatened forcible compulsion that overcomes the earnest resistance of the victim.
- Although evidence strongly suggests that rape is widespread, it is difficult to obtain accurate statistics on the actual number of rapes and rape victims in the United States.
- Many false beliefs about rape tend to hold the victim responsible for the crime and excuse the attacker.
- Rape is often partly a product of socialization processes that occur in certain rape-prone societies. These processes glorify masculine violence, teach boys to be aggressive, and demean the role of women in the economic and political aspects of life.
- Males in U.S. society often acquire callous attitudes toward women that, when combined with a belief that "might makes right," provide a cultural foundation for rape and other acts of sexual coercion.
- Exposure to sexually violent media can contribute to more accepting attitudes toward rape, decrease one's sensitivity to the tragedy of rape, and perhaps even increase men's inclinations to be sexually aggressive toward women.
- No single personality or behavioral pattern characterizes rapists, and a wide range of individual differences exists among rapists.
- Incarcerated rapists have a strong proclivity toward violence. Men who embrace traditional gender roles are more likely to commit rape than are men who do not support such roles.

- Anger toward women is a prominent attitude among some rapists. Some rapists have self-centered, or narcissistic, personalities that may render them insensitive to the feelings of the people they victimize.
- More than 50% of U.S. female rape victims reported that their first rape occurred before they were 18 years old.
- Most rapes are acquaintance rapes, in which the perpetrator is known to the victim.
- Sexual coercion in dating situations is prevalent. Both sexes experience sexual coercion, but women are more likely than men to be physically forced into sexual activity they do not want.
- A variety of "date rape" drugs are widely used by unscrupulous individuals to facilitate sexual conquest or to incapacitate date partners.
- Rape has been a strategy of war throughout history. In addition to being used as a means to humiliate and control women, wartime rape is intended to destroy the bonds of family and society.
- Rape survivors often suffer severe emotional and physical difficulties that can lead to a diagnosis of posttraumatic stress disorder (PTSD).
- Rape victims often find that supportive counseling, either individually or in groups, can help ease the trauma caused by rape.
- Although the vast majority of rape victims are women, research indicates that as many as 3% of U.S. men have been raped.
- Males who are sexually assaulted often experience long-term adverse consequences similar to those reported by females who are sexually victimized.

Sexual Abuse of Children

- Child sexual abuse is sexual contact between an adult and a child. A distinction is generally made between nonrelative child sexual abuse, called pedophilia or child molestation, and incest, which involves sexual contact between an adult and a child relative.
- Most child sexual abusers are male relatives, friends, or neighbors of their victims.
- No classic profile of a pedophile exists, other than that most pedophiles are heterosexual males and known to the victim. Prosecuted offenders tend to be shy, lonely, conservative, and often moralistic or religious. They frequently have difficulty relating to other adults and tend to feel inadequate and inferior.
- Some pedophiles were sexually victimized themselves during childhood.
- It is difficult to estimate the frequency of incest and pedophilia in U.S. society. Estimates of the number of girls sexually victimized range from 20% to 33%, whereas comparable estimates for boys range from 9% to 16%.
- Research suggests that the number of boys who are sexually molested in the United States may be substantially higher than was previously reported.
- Considerable controversy exists over whether a person can repress memories of sexual abuse and then suddenly or gradually recover them after exposure to certain triggering stimuli.
- Cyberspace pedophilia is widespread, and the responsibility for protecting children, in the absence of other effective safeguards, resides primarily with parents.
- Child sexual abuse can be a traumatic and emotionally damaging experience, with long-term negative consequences for the victim.
- Survivors often experience a loss of childhood innocence, a disruption of their normal sexual development, and a profound sense of betrayal. Other damaging consequences include low self-esteem and difficulty establishing satisfying sexual and emotional relationships as adults.
- There are a number of treatment programs for survivors of child sexual abuse, ranging from individual therapy to group and couple-oriented approaches.
- It is important to talk to children about protecting themselves from sexual abuse. Children need to know the difference between okay and not-okay touching, the fact that they have rights, the fact that they can report abuse without fear of blame, and strategies for escaping uncomfortable situations.

Sexual Harassment

- Sexual harassment in the workplace or in an academic setting is any unwanted sexual attention from someone on the job or in academia that creates discomfort or interferes with the victim's job or education, or does both.
- Guidelines provided by the Equal Employment Opportunity Commission essentially describe two kinds of sexual harassment. In the *quid pro quo* variety, a worker or student believes that failure to comply with sexual advances will be detrimental to his or her professional or academic standing. In the second form, the actions of supervisors, coworkers, professors, or students make the workplace or academic setting a "hostile or offensive environment."
- Title VII of the 1964 Civil Rights Act prohibits sexual harassment. A company can be liable for such coercive actions by its employees.
- Estimates of the percentage of women sexually harassed on the job range from 40% to 70%. Comparable estimates for men range from 10% to 20%.
- Claims of same-sex sexual harassment, which is now prohibited by law, are increasing.
- Victims of sexual harassment may experience a variety of negative financial, emotional, and physical effects.
- Sexual harassment occurs on the Internet in the form of cyberstalking in which Web technologies are used as weapons for stalking and harassment.
- Sexual harassment also occurs in educational settings. Most commonly, perpetrators are male professors or instructors who harass female students.
- Surveys indicate that 20–40% of undergraduate women, 30–50% of graduate women, and 9–29% of male undergraduates report having been sexually harassed.

Media Resources

Log in to CengageBrain.com to access the resources your instructor requires.

Go to CengageBrain.com to access Psychology CourseMate, where you will find an interactive eBook, glossaries, flashcards, quizzes, videos, and more.

Also access links to chapter-related websites, including **Rape, Abuse, and Incest National Network; Facts About Sexual Harassment; Feminist Majority Foundation** (Sexual Harassment National Hotlines and Resources)**; A Parent's Guide to Internet Safety; American Academy of Pediatrics;** and **GetNetWise.**

18 Sex For Sale

Pornography

How is pornography defined, and what are different types of pornography?

Since the Middle Ages, what technological developments have made pornography more accessible to the general population?

How has pornography been used for social criticism?

How have obscenity and indecency been determined?

What is the current focus of the censorship/free speech controversy?

What are some indications of the "pornification" of mainstream culture?

What arguments can be made as to whether pornography is helpful or harmful to individuals and couples?

Prostitution and Sex Work

What are the different types of male and female prostitutes and sex workers?

To what kinds of locations do female sex tourists travel?

What percentage of sex workers enter the business before age 18?

What is the primary reason that people become sex workers?

What are the symptoms of PTSD?

How have the health and safety of sex workers in New Zealand changed following decriminalization?

Laurence Dutton/Getty Images

542

> I really don't appreciate pornography, it does nothing for me. I love naked women in person and in bed, but seeing them in porn is a pointless turn-on. Pornography is really degrading toward women, and it gives young people the wrong ideas about women. (Authors' files)
>
> I have found that when my partner and I watch porn I get extremely aroused and let myself go wild with my sexuality. One time I got so turned on that I took control of the evening by making him do everything I wanted, like being rough, domineering, or sensitive. We also tried different areas in the room, like the coffee table, recliner, and couch. It wore us out so bad that we fell asleep naked in the middle of the floor tangled in each other's embrace. I feel that my partner and I have really benefited from including porn in our sex. We have become so comfortable, close, and in love knowing that sex is a good thing. (Authors' files)

Throughout this text, we have explored many aspects of sexuality—from biology and behavior to sexual problems and their treatment. One topic we have not yet investigated is sex as business—the exchange of money for sexual stimulation. As we will see in this chapter, a great deal of controversy surrounds sex in the marketplace. In the following pages, we examine pornography and sex work in depth. We explore some of the social and legal issues surrounding these activities and the ways in which digital technology has changed the business of pornography and sex work. We look first at pornography.

Pornography

The term **pornography** refers to any written, visual, or spoken material depicting sexual activity or genital exposure that is intended to be sexually arousing. Pornography is usually considered *hard-core* when explicit images of genitals are shown, whereas *soft-core* stops short of revealing genitals. We can separate pornography into two additional categories. *Degrading pornography* objectifies and denigrates its subjects. Racial stereotypes presented in interracial pornography are one form of degradation (Cowan & Campbell, 1994). *Violent pornography* involves aggression and brutality; the violence might take the form of rape, beatings, dismemberment, and even murder. Violent and abusive fantasies are common in chat rooms; titles such as "Torture Females" or "Daughter Blows Dad" can easily be found (Michaels, 1997).

pornography
Sexually explicit material (e.g., images or text) intended to cause sexual arousal.

Erotica

A subtype of sexually explicit materials is **erotica**. Erotica can be either soft- or hard-core, but it is a distinct kind of pornography, regardless of how explicit the material is. The word *erotica* is rooted in *eros*, or "passionate love" (Steinem, 1998). Erotica consists of "depictions of sexuality which display mutuality, respect, affection, and a balance of power" (Stock, 1985, p. 13). Often, pornographic films directed by women are similar to those directed by men, but some women who have been involved in the making of sexually explicit materials have changed the themes of those materials (Sun et al., 2008; Milne, 2005). For example, Femme Productions' hard-core adult films emphasize sensuality and women's pleasure and assertiveness. Films such as *Nina Hartley's Guide to Better Cunnilingus* and *The Sluts and Goddesses Video Workshop* promote the development and expression of women's desire and arousal.

Is erotica appealing to women but not men? Not according to research on college students. The subjects, who were at least 21 years old, watched four video segments,

erotica
Respectful, affectionate depictions of sexuality.

Candida Royalle began producing porn videos designed for women and couples in the 1980s. *Stud Hunters* is a lighthearted look at the adult entertainment industry.

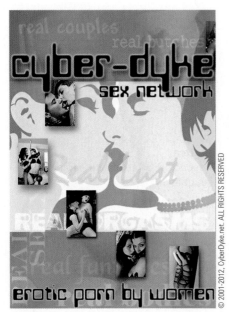

Cyber-dyke is a website by lesbian and bisexual women to create a network of high-quality erotic sites.

each of which represented different combinations of high versus low expressions of love and affection in conjunction with high versus moderate sexual explicitness (hard-core versus soft-core X-rated material). The study found that both male and female subjects rated most arousing the video that was both highly romantic, displaying love and affection, *and* highly sexually explicit. The researchers speculated that these results indicate that college-educated men and women have integrated love and affection with sexual arousal (Quackenbush et al., 1995). Another study of interviews with 150 men in the United States, Canada, and Europe found that men enjoyed pornography the most when men and women were equal participants or when men were recipients of female sexual assertion. For the men to enjoy watching the material, they consistently emphasized the importance of the women appearing to experience genuine pleasure (Loftus, 2002).

Variations in Straight, Gay, and Lesbian Pornographic Films

Sexually explicit films developed for heterosexual, gay, or lesbian consumers differ in some of their general characteristics. Much of straight porn is based on a formula of close-up views of various positions of intercourse and oral and anal sex. Two women having sex, threesomes, and group sex are often part of the formula. Women's bodies are the primary focus of the film. Most of the female porn stars have stereotypical underweight bodies with implant-enhanced large breasts. Eroticism of the male body is rare, and the male actors are often, sometimes at best, ordinary looking. The "money shot," a close-up of the man ejaculating outside of the woman's vagina or mouth, is a marker of straight porn (Paul, 2005).

The gay porn industry is comparable in size to the straight porn industry and shows the same range of low-cost to well-made films. Most of today's gay porn is made with well-groomed, muscular, good-looking men. Gay porn emphasizes eroticism of the male body and unfettered lust that ranges from aggressive to tender. Subgenres include more variation in body type. For example, "bear porn" features large men with extensive body hair (Blue, 2003).

Far fewer lesbian porn films are made, and they tend to be low-budget and unpolished compared with straight and gay porn. Most lesbian porn films feature real-life lovers. They realistically portray diverse and powerful lesbian sexual interaction instead of a performance for the viewer. A different style of beauty and sex is evident: A great variety of body types and a range of butch and femme styles pervade the films (Stites, 2007). Role-playing, talking, costuming, and sex toys take precedence over plot. Safersex practices are often included in the sexual activity (Blue, 2003).

To Each His or Her Own

Straight, gay, and lesbian porn are broad categories that do not begin to include the enormous variety of sexually explicit topics. Specialty pornography "is a mighty testament to the infinite variety of human imagination" (Hanus, 2006b, p. 59). It caters to the wide range of interests in bondage and discipline; sadomasochism fetishes; transgender, pregnant, old/mature, and interracial sex; orgies; pornographic Japanese animation; and almost any other imaginable topic.

The various categories of pornography previously described are useful as a working model to conceptualize different types of sexually explicit material, but we should stress that in real life, individual reactions to pornography have more variations than any specific category. "One person's pornography is another person's erotica, and one person's erotica can cause someone else to lose her lunch" (Kipnis, 1996, p. 64). And what may be harmless in one context (for instance, a couple using an erotic DVD to explore different ways of making love) may be potentially damaging in another context (such as a young child finding the DVD and watching it).

Child Pornography

Child pornography is excluded from the First Amendment protection of free speech. The production, sale, and distribution of sexual images of children under the age of 18 are illegal under numerous federal and state laws. Even offering to provide or requesting to obtain child pornography carries a mandatory 5-year prison sentence (Sherman, 2008). Federal law also prohibits the sale or distribution of images of adult women pretending to be under age 18.

Internet child pornography is a $20 billion-per-year industry that continues to expand throughout the world (Brockman, 2006). The Internet provides individuals drawn to child pornography with greatly increased access to illegal materials. The majority of child porn consumers who are apprehended are White males of all ages and educational and occupational backgrounds. Most have no prior criminal history or evidence of pedophilia (McGlone, 2011). Internet sting operations can be very successful and have resulted in many arrests of child pornographers and consumers of child pornography.

Sexting involves adolescents using primarily cell phones to take and send sexually explicit photos and text messages to other teens. In the last few years legislators in most states have been trying to determine how to respond to sexting. Under some states' laws, sexting is considered to be child pornography and sending or receiving it is a felony sex crime. Many states have amended these laws to allow minors to be charged with misdemeanor or lesser offenses and offer educational and diversion programs (J. Hoffman, 2011; Wolf & Ripley, 2012).

The Internet has exponentially expanded access to sexually explicit material. However, as we see in the following section, throughout history, advances in technology have both expanded access to and reduced control of sexual materials by the governing church or state.

Historical Overview

Pictorial and written representations of sexuality are not modern inventions; even prehistoric cave drawings depict sexual activity. The ancient Indian love manual *Kama Sutra*, dating from about 400 CE, summarized philosophies of sexuality and spirituality in its descriptions of specific sexual techniques. Ancient Greek and Roman societies extensively used sexual themes to decorate housewares and public architecture. Graphic representations of coitus in Japanese *schunga* paintings and woodcuts from the 1600s and 1700s are regarded as art masterpieces.

With the emergence of Christianity and the fall of the Roman Empire, the Roman Catholic Church became the most significant central authority in the West. During the Middle Ages, Catholic monks handwrote the books of the era, and the wealth of the Church enabled it to commission the majority of artworks. This power made it possible for the Church to control the production of both written materials and fine art, and naturally these works reflected the Catholic Church's

Ashmolean Museum, University of Oxford, UK/The Bridgeman Art Library

Homoerotic scene on 5th century BC Greek pottery. Ashmolean Museum, UK.

In 1973, *Deep Throat* was the first mainstream adult film to attract both men and women viewers.

restrictive attitudes toward sexuality. However, in 1450 Johannes Gutenberg's introduction of movable metal type in Europe ended the Church's monopoly on the written word. After the initial printings of the Bible, some presses became busy producing sexually explicit stories, which are credited with helping bring literacy to the masses. By the 1550s, books had veered so far from the Church's influence that Pope Paul IV established the Catholic Church's first list of prohibited books (Lane, 2000).

The next technology to expand pornography was photography, developed before the Civil War. With the advent of photography, sexual photographs proliferated so extensively that Congress passed the first U.S. law prohibiting the mailing of obscenity (Johnson, 1998). By the mid-1800s sexually explicit "advice literature," the burgeoning production of inexpensive pornographic novels, and the U.S. publication of the notorious English novel *Fanny Hill* prompted civic leaders to establish laws against publishing and selling pornographic materials. The champion of this cause was Anthony Comstock, who was appointed to the Society for the Suppression of Vice and as a special agent for the U.S. Post Office. Comstock claimed to have convicted more than 3,600 individuals and to have destroyed more than 160 tons of obscene literature. However, by the 1890s public approval of Comstock's actions had waned, and he was dismissed as old-fashioned and provincial. More importantly, the postal service's monopoly on the country's shipping was eliminated by the development of the railroad and automobile, private shipping companies, and the subsequent emergence of the airplane—all of which made the distribution of pornography much more difficult to control (Lane, 2000).

The transition of the pornography business from an underground enterprise to a multibillion-dollar industry began in 1953, with the publication of the first issue of *Playboy* magazine. The World War II generation bought 50,000 copies of the first issue, and the magazine's growing readership throughout the next decade made its publisher, Hugh Hefner, a multimillionaire. Another change involved sexually explicit movies. These films had been distributed only in the underground stag-film market until the 1973 film *Deep Throat*, which was the first adult film that drew mainstream audiences, including women, to X-rated movie houses. It generated $600 million in theater and video revenues. The success of *Deep Throat* launched the modern pornography industry and expanded the boundaries of sexual content in mainstream films. The increase in sexual explicitness also led to increased opposition by conservative political and religious groups that believed pornography was immoral, had a negative effect on adults, and increased crime around porn shops and adult movie theaters. Supreme Court decisions and government commissions attempted to determine legal questions regarding sexually explicit materials.

Freedom of Speech Versus Censorship

The U.S. Constitution's First Amendment guarantees freedom of speech and freedom of the press. Do these constitutional protections apply to sexually explicit materials? A 1957 Supreme Court decision declared that First Amendment guarantees of free speech did not apply categorically to "obscene" materials. This ruling has remained controversial to this day, beginning with the difficulty of clearly defining **obscenity**. Those who oppose limits on free speech believe that any such laws violate the First Amendment and infringe on freedom of personal expression and choice. Furthermore, they argue, censorship is then at the discretion of those with the most political power, who have the authority to interpret and rule on a wide variety of sexual images (Hudson & Graham, 2004). In fact, those outside of mainstream political power have at times employed pornography to challenge social norms and the hypocrisy of religion, politics, and the middle and upper classes (Beck, 1999; Kipnis, 1996; Penley, 1996). The Sex and Politics box, "Pornography as Social Criticism," discusses how sexually explicit materials are at times used for another purpose than sexual arousal.

obscenity
A term that implies a personal or societal judgment that something is offensive.

Critical Thinking Question

What examples have you seen of present-day pornography that challenge social and political hypocrisy?

Over the course of history, pornography has sometimes played the role of social critic. During the French Revolution, pornography, like the example shown in this box, helped incite the poor to rebel against the king and queen. Hundreds of pamphlets were printed and circulated that linked "degenerate" sexual activity with the material excesses and political corruption of royalty. The illustration shows a man of the lower classes servicing Queen Marie Antoinette's sexual appetites. This image challenged the king's ability to rule the country since he could not control his wife's sexual adventures (Beck, 1999).

The role of contemporary pornography in social and political criticism is also evident. *Hustler* magazine sometimes fuses nudity and vulgarity with attacks on political power, organized religion, and class privilege. For example, stark social and political criticism was evident in a photomontage titled "Farewell to Reagan: Ronnie's Last Bash." The faces of the political elite of that era were superimposed on top of naked bodies doing "obscene" things to one another. The accompanying text declares, "It's been eight great years—for the power elite, that is. . . . A radical tax plan that more than halved taxes for the rich while doubling the working man's load; . . . and we'll still get . . . sexual intimidation policies for years to come, particularly with conservative whores posing as Supreme Court justices" (Kipnis, 1996, pp. 152–153).

Another example is a relief sculpture erected in 2008 in a southern German town square. Five naked German politicians, including current Chancellor Angela Merkel, are laughing and holding one another's genitals. The sculptor, Peter Lenk, intended the sculpture to symbolize scandals involving politicians collaborating in the misuse of public money for political and corporate gain.

Another form of social criticism found in some pornography can be seen in the violation of conventional norms regarding what is "sexy." Sexually explicit materials featuring old people, such as "Promiscuous Granny," defy common views that older adults are asexual. Transgender pornography wreaks havoc with standard concepts of gender or sexual orientation in its portrayals of transgender individuals with breasts and penises engaging in sexual interaction with same-sex and other-sex partners.

Perhaps the most dramatic example of pornography's defiance of contemporary social norms is the subgenre of fat pornography. Large (between 200- and 500-pound) naked women in sexual situations are featured in an array of magazines and videos with titles such as *Life in the Fat Lane* and *Jumbo Jezebel*. Disbelief by many people that fat, fleshy bodies could be a turn-on shows how cultural conformity seems universally "normal." Actually, the amount of body fat considered most sexually appealing is historically and culturally relative. The 20th century's

From Porn 101: Eroticism, Pornography, and the First Amendment edited by James Elias, Veronica Diehl Elias, Gwen Brewer, Vern L. Bullough, Jeffrey J. Douglas, and Will Jarvis (Amherst, NY: Prometheus Books). Copyright © 1999 by James Elias, Veronica Diehl Elias, Gwen Brewer, Vern L. Bullough, Jeffrey J. Douglas, and Will Jarvis.

Pornography can be a form of political subversion, linking "degenerate" sexual activities to political corruption. This illustration shows a man of the lower classes servicing Queen Marie Antoinette's sexual appetites, implying that the king could not control his wife's sexual adventures or be certain of the paternity of his children. If he could not keep his own house in order, his ability to rule a country and its people could be challenged (Beck, 1999).

PATRICK SEEGER/dpa/Landov

The contemporary German sculptor, Peter Lenk, depicts politicians collaborating for their own benefit instead of for the public good.

preference for thinness contrasts with the previous 400 years' preference for hefty, rotund body types. Thinness was not sexually attractive during those years because it connoted lower-class poverty and ill health (Kipnis, 1996).

What Constitutes Obscenity?

The 1957 Supreme Court decision defined *obscenity* in order to implement censorship. It established the following three criteria for evaluating obscenity:

1. The dominant theme of the work as a whole must appeal to prurient interest in sex.
2. The work must be patently offensive to contemporary community standards.
3. The work must be without serious literary, artistic, political, or scientific value (*Roth v. United States*, 354 U.S. 476 [1957]).

Determining what materials are "obscene" and qualify for censorship has been plagued by ambiguity because the criteria are highly subjective. The subjectivity of these criteria is perhaps best reflected in Supreme Court Justice Potter Stewart's comment regarding obscenity: It is difficult to define intelligently, "but I know it when I see it" (*Jacobelis v. Ohio*, 379 U.S. 197 [1965]).

In addition, community standards for obscenity vary dramatically from one location to another. In small, rural communities, magazines such as *Playboy* have been banned, and the books *The Color Purple* and *Our Bodies, Ourselves* and *Ms.* magazine have been deemed obscene and consequently banned from high school libraries (Klein, 1999). Furthermore, the advent of cable TV, VCRs, DVDs, the Internet, and other wireless technologies has made "community standards" even more nebulous because people use these technologies in the privacy of their homes. In fact, some highly conservative communities have the highest rates of Internet access to pornography. For example, according to the FBI, Salt Lake City, Utah, ranked number one for Internet searches for adult-related content (Knox, 2006). A nationwide study of 2 years' worth of credit-card receipts from a major online provider of pornography found that states whose residents consume the most pornography tend to have more conservative and religious populations than states whose residents exhibit lower levels of consumption (Callaway, 2009).

The Japanese Hounen festival held in March, which celebrates fertility and renewal with a procession to the shrine of a female deity, would likely be considered unacceptably pornographic in the United States. A 13-foot-long, 885-pound phallus is the central focus of the celebration. Would your hometown allow this procession?

Everett Kennedy Brown/epa/CORBIS

The Commissions on Obscenity and Pornography

In addition to Supreme Court rulings regarding sexually explicit materials, since the late 1960s two presidential commissions have been appointed to study pornography. They came to very different conclusions. President Lyndon Johnson appointed the Commission on Obscenity and Pornography to study the effects of sexually explicit materials, and its report was published in 1970. It analyzed the effects of legalizing pornography in Denmark (which had occurred in 1967) and the findings of various studies done in the United States. The commission found that the increased availability of pornography after legalization did *not* result in an increase in sex offenses. Furthermore, research with college-student subjects in the United States found no significant, long-lasting changes in behavior after they were exposed to pornography. On that basis, this commission recommended repealing all laws prohibiting access to pornography for adults. However, both President Nixon and the U.S. Senate rejected these recommendations.

In 1986, President Ronald Reagan appointed another commission to study pornography, the U.S. Attorney General's Commission on Pornography (sometimes called the Meese Commission, after then attorney general Edwin Meese). It reached different conclusions and made radically different recommendations from those of the earlier commission. It claimed that pornography promoted promiscuity and that violent or degrading pornography caused sexually aggressive behavior toward women. It recommended prosecuting pornography vigorously and prohibiting "dial-a-porn" telephone services and sexual cable TV programs. However, leading researchers criticized the Meese Commission report for basing its recommendations on politics instead of science, because it did not produce adequate scientific evidence to support its conclusions (D'Amato, 2006). The recommendations were not implemented, except for one making possession of child pornography a felony (U.S. Attorney General's Commission on Pornography, 1986).

The Supreme Court continues to address issues of censorship, especially in response to technological developments. For example, in 1997, in *Reno v. American Civil Liberties Union et al.*, the Court gave free-speech protection to material on the Internet (except child pornography). The decision was based on the Court's opinion that the Internet is the most participatory form of communication ever developed and therefore is entitled to the "highest protection from governmental intrusion" (Beck, 1999, p. 83).

The Marriage of Technology and Sexually Explicit Materials

The ease of access and privacy afforded by cable television and the VCR, followed closely by the Internet and mobile wireless devices, has extended access to pornography to people who previously would not have gone to an adult movie theater or bookstore. This increase in availability may be especially true for women, who comprise one out of every three visitors to porn sites (Ropelato, 2012). A group of adult television networks has been developed exclusively for video-on-demand technology. Porn's appearance on cell phones, iPods, PDAs, and PSP game handhelds provides portable access to sexually explicit materials. Adult content on mobile devices became a multinational billion-dollar business in less than one year following its inception (Piccionelli, 2006; Ross, 2008).

Twenty-five percent of all search engine requests are for sexual imagery, and 4.2 million porn websites are available on the Internet (Ropelato, 2012; Young, 2008). The U.S. pornography industry released 13,588 hard-core porn video/DVDs in 2006, whereas Hollywood averages 400 feature films each year. In 2006 revenues from video/DVD sales were $3.62 billion, and Internet pornography generated $2.84 billion. These figures indicate that viewing pornography is a form of mainstream entertainment (Klein, 2012a). According to news and research organizations, worldwide pornography revenues in 2006 were over $97 billion, more than the revenues of Microsoft, Google, Amazon, eBay, Yahoo!, Apple, and Netflix combined (Ropelato, 2012). ▌Figure 18.1 indicates the countries where individuals spend the most for pornography.

However, beginning in 2006 YouTube-type sites with free porn have caused adult industry profits from films and pay websites to drop significantly (free sites make money by selling advertising space instead of charging for access). The proliferation of webcam sites where a viewer can video-chat with a live model also contributed to less use of film sites. Anyone with a camera and a web connection can set up a one-person operation (Alexander, 2008; Wallace, 2011). The adult industry also estimates that piracy of explicit material results in a $2 billion loss each year (Ross, 2008). By 2009 DVD sales had decreased by at least 25%, and pay-for-membership websites had a record low of new subscribers (Lucido, 2009).

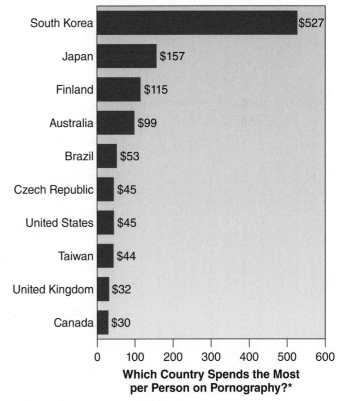

*rounded to the nearest dollar

▌**Figure 18.1** Dollars spent per person for pornography (Ropelato, 2012).

AP Photo/Keith Shimada

The "reality TV" show *Can You Be a Porn Star?* with hosts Tabitha Stevens and Mary Carey began airing on pay-per-view in early 2004, illustrating a trend toward mainstreaming of the porn industry.

The "Pornification" of U.S. Culture

Graphic sexual images have become so ubiquitous that many university literature, film, anthropology, law, and women's studies departments offer "porn curriculum" courses that delve into pornography issues (Cullen, 2006). The mainstreaming of aspects of pornography and sex work into U.S. culture is so prevalent that author Ariel Levy has described today's culture as "raunch culture" (Levy, 2005). For example, on her talk show, Oprah Winfrey featured a stripper instructor whose program has taught over 12,000 women how to strip and pole dance, and TV programs demonstrate and teach how to "lap dance" a man to orgasm. Hundreds of young women cheerfully strip and mimic pornographic poses for *Girls Gone Wild* videos that generate an estimated $40 million a year (Deveny, 2007). Preadolescent girls wear T-shirts with "PORN STAR" written in rhinestones on the front. Porn stars have hosted programs on cable TV, including the reality show *Can You Be a Porn Star?* (Paul, 2005).

Is Pornography Helpful?

One important issue is the impact of pornography on those who use it. Arguments have been advanced on both sides of the question of whether and how pornography is helpful or harmful. Pornography can provide an endless variety of sexual fantasy material for arousal during masturbation without the potential of being rejected, being criticized by a partner, becoming pregnant, or contracting an STI (Peter & Valkenburg, 2011). When individuals in a couple have significant differences in how frequently they want to be sexual, pornography can also facilitate sexual arousal for masturbation for the partner with the higher sex drive. Watching sexually explicit materials before sexual intimacy can help an individual who has difficulty getting in the mood for sex with a partner do so more easily.

Some couples find that watching mainstream pornography or erotica together has improved their sexual experiences. One study found that almost half of unmarried couples sometimes viewed sexually explicit materials together. Unmarried couples who only viewed sexually explicit materials with their partners reported more dedication and higher sexual satisfaction than those who viewed similar materials alone (Maddox et al., 2011). Studies have found that viewing pornography and engaging in online sexual activities helped individuals expand their previous sexual repertoire by being open to and exploring new sexual behaviors (Gowen, 2005; Grov et al., 2011). For example, a woman watching porn will see that it is common for porn actresses to stimulate their own clitorises during intercourse and may feel more comfortable doing this herself.

Individuals may also increase their communication about sex in their intimate relationships after revealing their sexual interests anonymously online (Grov et al., 2011): One study found that about 50% of women and 44% of men told their partners about sexual desires they had previously concealed after online sexual communication with others (Gowen, 2005).

Is Pornography Harmful?

In contrast with research discussed in the previous "Is Pornography Helpful?" section, other studies report correlations between Internet pornography use and diminished quality of relationships. One study of heterosexual college students found that higher use of pornography was associated with less sexual and relationship satisfaction (Morgan, 2011). A study of unmarried couples reported that individuals who viewed sexually explicit materials alone had lower relationship quality on measures of communication, relationship adjustment, commitment, sexual satisfaction, and fidelity compared to couples where individuals never viewed sexually explicit materials (Maddox et al., 2011). Divorce attorneys and marital therapists have seen a great increase in the number of couples for whom Internet pornography played a significant part in bringing them to counseling or divorce (Eberstadt, 2009; Hanus, 2006b).

A concern about exposure to pornography is that viewers will come to assume that what they see is "normal" and represents what sex *should* be like (Bowater, 2011; Lofgren-Martenson & Mansson, 2010). Ordinarily, the more often individuals see something, the more likely they are to view it as typical. A survey of heterosexual college students found that those who used sexually explicit materials most frequently also had a greater preference for the types of sexual practices typically presented in pornography (Morgan, 2011).

At the very least, typical scenarios in most of pornography are bad sex education and a very misleading guide to mutually pleasurable and satisfying sexual experiences (Castleman, 2008). The standard porn sexual style is impersonal, unfriendly, nonsensual, mechanical, and almost exclusively genitally focused. Oral sex to both men and women is portrayed as fast and rough. Women are instantly and continuously turned on and quickly want intercourse, but never experience orgasm. Commercial porn uses men whose penises are extra-large, and the men always have instant, continuous, long-lasting erections. Anal sex to women is aggressive, and the penis often goes directly from anus to vagina—almost a guarantee for vaginal and bladder infections. Viewers never see the actors use lubrication for vaginal or anal intercourse.

Researchers are also finding that young male adults—and adult males in general—are experiencing sexual problems related to extensive use of pornography. In some cases a man's arousal becomes dependent on the intense, varied sexual stimulation provided by pornography, and when he is sexual with a partner, he has difficulty experiencing or sustaining an erection. He may be unable to ejaculate and may resort to faking orgasm to conceal his difficulty (Robinson, 2011; Rothbart, 2011). Sex therapists have begun to see men who prefer to masturbate to pornography instead of having actual sex (Albright, 2008).

Another problem arises when individuals justify coercing their partners to engage in typical behaviors found in pornography (including, perhaps, ejaculating on a woman's face or body or having anal or group sex) (Morris, 2011; Paul, 2005). Research has found that in heterosexual relationships men are more likely than women to pressure their partners to engage in sexual behaviors they have seen in pornographic films (Albright, 2008). Further, because pornography portrays women as wildly responsive to anything men do, but real-life women do not react in such a manner, men may feel inadequate or cheated, and both men and women may doubt the normality of their own sexuality. For example, a woman may believe that there is something wrong with her when she does not experience anal sex as unrealistically pain-free and pleasurable as portrayed in porn (Castleman, 2008; Drey et al., 2009). These kinds of influences may help cause a relationship to deteriorate, as reflected in the following account:

> During my early and mid-twenties I spent a lot of time (and a fair bit of change) paying women with Web cam businesses to role-play sexual scenarios I liked to masturbate to. I considered it a healthy, safe, simple way to take care of my needs instead of counting on dating for sex. Then I met Jennifer and fell for her. After several months I started getting bored with our vanilla sex and asked her to do the "schoolgirl" role-play I'd liked via Web cam. She tried her best, but I was kind of pissed that she didn't do it "right," and I made her feel like she wasn't sexy enough for me. I hadn't figured out that I couldn't expect her to pull off a fantasy like the Web cam professionals. It's a trade-off, but I'd rather have sex with a woman who really cares about me than one who's a good actor. (Authors' files)

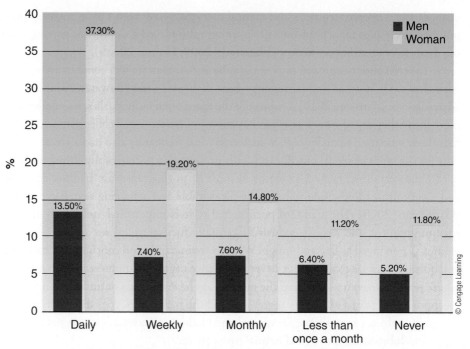

■ **Figure 18.2** Percentage of adolescents who believe their genitals should look like a porn star's genitals, correlated by frequency of pornography use.

Internet-related sexual difficulties occur in both adults and young people. However, the consequences of this dramatic social change will likely have a more significant impact on the sexual development of young people than on that of adults who came of age prior to the advent of the Internet. In the United States, 90% of young people have seen Internet porn by age 16. The average age of their first exposure was 11 years (Ropelato, 2012). Unlike the pre-Internet era, when a young person might see a *Playboy* magazine before his or her first kiss, significant numbers of young people in developed countries are exposed to a wide range of pornography on the Internet and other wireless technologies before they begin having sexual experiences with other young people.

Viewing pornography on the Internet can also negatively influence how people feel about their genitals. For example, ■ Figure 18.2 shows that the more often young people watch pornography, the more likely they are to believe that their own genitals should look like a porn star's penis or vulva. (Even 5.2% of male and 11.8% of female young adults who have never seen pornography believe that their genitals should look like a porn star's.) Young women are more likely than young men to believe that porn star vulvas are the "ideal," as demonstrated in the figure (Drey et al., 2009). Many of the young women who consider having plastic surgery to alter the shape of their labia do so for that reason, instead of appreciating the uniqueness of the shape and size of their labia (Gohman, 2009). In addition, after viewing pornography, heterosexual men and women are more likely to be critical of the woman's body in general (Albright, 2008).

prostitution
The exchange of sexual services for money.

sex worker
A person involved in prostitution and related activities, such as phone sex, nude dancing, erotic massage, Internet sex, and acting in porn movies.

Prostitution and Sex Work

Prostitution is the exchange of sexual services for money. Prostitution is typically thought of in terms of a woman selling sexual services to a man, although transactions between two males are also common. Payment for a man's services to a woman is less common. **Sex worker** is a term for a person involved in prostitution and related activities, such as phone sex, nude dancing, erotic massage, Internet sex, and acting in porn movies. Most people who are sex workers for more than a few months often move from one type of commercial sex work to another (Farley, 2004).

Relationships that involve exchanging sex for money also occur outside sex work. Advertising frequently portrays the "trade goods for sex" theme, and in 2000, one of the first reality-TV shows, *Who Wants to Marry a Multi-Millionaire?*, highlighted the prostitution-like aspects sometimes present in common male/female relationships (Peyser, 2000). A case could be made that the wife who is especially sexually pleasing before asking for extra money from her husband, or the woman who wants out of her marriage but stays in order to maintain her standard of living, plays out the dynamics of prostitution (Ridgeway, 1996).

History of Prostitution and Sex Work

Prostitution has existed throughout history and has been called the oldest profession. However, the importance and meaning of prostitution have varied in different times and societies. Evidence shows that men sold sexual services to other men as far back as the ancient Sumerian and Greek civilizations (Pandey, 2007). During some periods of ancient Greek history, certain types of prostitutes were valued for their intellectual, social, and sexual companionship. In other ancient societies, female prostitution was part of revered religious rituals in which sexual relations between prostitutes and men were seen as sacred acts. In medieval Europe prostitution was tolerated, and public baths provided opportunities for contact between customers and prostitutes. At times, some types of prostitution were a means for women to acquire status and power. For example, in Renaissance Italy *courtesans* provided social, intellectual, and sexual companionship to the most powerful men of the time. Courtesans often gained significant political influence through these relationships, while the men's upper-class wives were uneducated and sequestered in their homes. Courtesans were well-educated, charming, and witty women who were performers, artists, and writers (Valhouli, 2000). In Victorian

Imperia, a statue in the harbor of Konstanz, Germany, represents a 15th-century Italian courtesan. She holds a naked pope and king in each of her hands, representing her power over leaders of church and state. *Imperia* was created by sculptor Peter Lenk and installed in 1993.

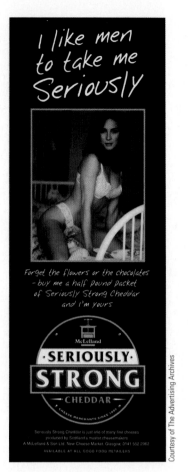

I like men to take me Seriously

Forget the flowers or the chocolates – buy me a half pound packet of Seriously Strong Cheddar and I'm yours

McLelland
SERIOUSLY STRONG
CHEDDAR
CHEESE MERCHANTS SINCE 1450

Seriously Strong Cheddar is just one of many fine cheeses produced by Scotland's master cheesemakers
A McLelland & Son Ltd, New Cheese Market, Glasgow, 0141 552 2962
AVAILABLE AT ALL GOOD FOOD RETAILERS

Courtesy of The Advertising Archives

Advertisements often demonstrate prostitution's sex-for-sale basis of relationships.

At a Glance

■ TABLE 18.1 Responses of Women Sex Workers to the Question "What Do You Need in Order to Leave Prostitution?" (in descending order of importance)

Job training
Home or safe place
Health care
Individual counseling
Legal assistance
Peer support
Drug/alcohol treatment
Self-defense training
Child care
Legalization of prostitution
Physical protection from pimp

SOURCE: Farley (2004).

brothel
A house in which a group of prostitutes work.

Great Britain, prostitution was viewed as a scandalous but necessary sexual and social outlet for men: It was a lesser evil for a middle-class man to have sexual relations with a prostitute than with another middle-class man's wife or daughter (Taylor, 1970).

Adult Male and Female Prostitutes

Adult sex workers vary from one another in characteristics such as public visibility, the amount of money they make, and social class. A critical distinction between sex workers is the degree to which they chose the work (Lieberman, 2011). Some sex workers pursue sex work in spite of having other viable options for a livelihood. However, most resort to sex work from economic incentive and necessity (Kempner, 2005; Shaver et al., 2011). For example, research has found that in the United States a majority of individuals became involved in sex work because they were unable to find work that paid a living wage (Hafer, 2011). Many had previously held babysitting, food service, and cleaning jobs (Thukral, 2008). Melissa Farley's comprehensive research on sex workers in nine countries (Canada, Colombia, Germany, Mexico, South Africa, Thailand, Turkey, the United States, and Zambia) found that the most common and compelling reason that individuals from both developed and developing countries enter sex work is to earn money. Most are in dire need of resources for survival needs: 75% were homeless when they became prostitutes (Farley, 2004). Others have been forced into sex work by pimps and traffickers, as we will discuss in detail in later sections.

Some sex workers work part-time and otherwise pursue conventional school, work, or social lifestyles. People who work as prostitutes on a temporary, part-time basis and have other occupational skills can leave sex work more easily than other prostitutes can. Many of these women and men have not identified themselves as "professionals." In contrast, the full-time sex worker who has identified herself or himself as part of the prostitute subculture (being arrested and having a criminal record facilitates this identification) typically has little education and few marketable skills. One study found that 89% of sex workers wanted to leave "the profession" (■ Table 18.1), but without other resources and economic opportunities, many find it difficult to become successfully independent of prostitution (Burnette et al., 2009; Farley, 2004; Thukral, 2008).

Female *streetwalkers* and male *hustlers* solicit straight and gay male customers, respectively, on the street or in bars. Hustlers extend their search for business into gay bathhouses, public parks, and restrooms. Streetwalkers and hustlers charge the least of all sex workers for their services. For example, in New York, a streetwalker charges an average of $75 for traditional intercourse, with a percentage going to the sex worker's pimp (Venkatesh, 2011). Hustlers rarely work for pimps, but streetwalkers usually do and must share a large portion of their earnings with them.

Hustlers and streetwalkers are most likely to be victims of abuse and robbery by customers or pimps (Valera et al., 2001). News stories frequently describe the discovery of a murdered prostitute or a hunt for a serial killer of sex workers. In addition, due to their visibility, streetwalkers and hustlers are easily subject to arrest. Most repeat the cycle of arrest, short jail sentences, and release many times throughout their careers.

A **brothel** is a house in which a group of female prostitutes work. Brothels were common in the United States during much of its history and are legal in some areas of Nevada today. A "madam" usually acts as the hostess and is usually the business manager of the brothel. Prostitutes who work in brothels where prostitution is illegal are somewhat more protected from arrest than are streetwalkers, because they are less visible to the police. In order to reduce street prostitution and offer greater safety to sex workers, the province of Ontario in Canada recently established that sex workers can legally work in brothels (Makin, 2012).

Massage parlors are often seen as a modern "quick service" version of brothels. Manual stimulation (a "local" or "hand finishing") or oral stimulation to orgasm is often arranged for a fee once the customer is in the massage room. In addition, the customer can often dictate in what state of dress or undress he would like his masseuse to be. Intercourse may occur as part of the "massage."

The types of sex workers who earn more than others are *call girls* and *call boys*, who provide services for men, and *gigolos*, who service women. Call girls, or escorts, often come from middle-class backgrounds and are sometimes educated, affluent women making a choice to enter sex work for money, autonomy, and job satisfaction (Hafer, 2011). Contacts are usually made by personal referral, through "escort services," or by independent ads on Internet sites, including Facebook. They commonly have several regular customers and frequently provide social and intellectual companionship as well as sexual services for their typically wealthy, middle-aged, and older customers (Blackmun, 1996). Regular customers are likely to give them goods, such as clothing, jewelry, and living accommodations. High-end escorts might have four to six regular clients, each of whom pays the escort a minimum of $20,000 a year (Venkatesh, 2011). Public visibility for these prostitutes is minimal, and their risk of arrest is much lower than that for the sex worker on the street.

One study found that call boys working through an escort agency had an average of six clients a month, client calls lasted about an hour, and oral sex was the most common sexual service they provided. Most of the escorts avoided anal sex. About 80% of the escorts disliked having sex with clients; the escorts preferred clients who were seeking nonsexual companionship for conversation, entertainment, or travel (Hagen, 2006).

Michael Goldman/Getty Images

Streetwalkers are at high risk for abuse by customers, pimps, and police.

The Internet and Sex Work

The Internet has transformed the world's oldest profession. Male and female sex workers are increasingly operating independently through individual websites. For example, by 2011 approximately 83% of sex workers in New York City advertised their services on Facebook (Venkatesh, 2011). The sex worker and customer negotiate through e-mail, which eliminates the need for part of the prostitute's fees to go to website companies, pimps, or brothels (Reynolds, 2006).

Whether working through a company or an individual website, sex workers on the Internet have far safer and less oppressive working conditions than other sex workers. While arrests of Internet sex workers are uncommon, the Internet does provide easy leads for arrest by police posing as customers (Linskey, 2006). The Internet has also created an easy and accessible venue for the commercial sexual exploitation of children (Saar, 2010), as discussed further in the next section.

Teenagers in Sex Work

The U.S. Department of Justice's Child Exploitation and Obscenity Section estimates that in the United States, the median age of entry into the sex industry is between 12 and 14 years of age (Lloyd, 2010). Statistics from the National Incident-Based Reporting System indicate that in the United States, of the total number of juvenile sex workers, male juvenile sex workers outnumber female juvenile sex workers by 61% to 39% (Finkelhor & Ormrod, 2004). Teenagers often become sex workers as a means of survival after they have run away from home. Approximately 100,000 children who leave their homes each year are sexually exploited as sex workers (Salario, 2011). Research indicates that approximately 95% have been victims of sexual abuse, and most have been rejected by their families, sometimes after parents found out their children are gay, lesbian, bisexual, or transgendered (Mok, 2006). Journalist Nicholas Kristof describes a common scenario:

> Typically, she's a 13-year-old girl of color from a troubled home who is on bad terms with her mother. Then her mom's boyfriend hits on her, and she runs away to the bus station, where the only person on the lookout for girls like her is a pimp. He buys her dinner, gives her a place to stay and next thing she knows she's earning him $1,550 a day (2011, p. 2).

Young women in this situation are routinely raped, beaten into submission, and utterly controlled by pimps who take the money they earn (Saar, 2010).

Many Americans perceive the teenage girls they may see on the streets as voluntarily selling sex, but most are exploited by pimps (Kristof, 2011). Pimps seek out young girls because they can charge higher prices and make more money than with adults (Loupe, 2011). Unfortunately, although many of the teens are too young to legally consent to sex, when apprehended by law enforcement, they will be charged with an act of prostitution and sent to a juvenile detention center or jail (Lloyd, 2010). Sixty-three percent of girls in the juvenile justice system are there due to prostitution (Saar, 2010). In 2008 New York passed the Safe Harbor for Exploited Youth Act, protecting them from prosecution and recognizing that underage prostituted girls are victims (Salario, 2011). Unfortunately, laws and programs to help prostituted teens heal from the trauma of sexual victimization and establish new lives are only in their infancy (Loupe, 2011).

While the awareness of sex trafficking in the United States has been limited, in recent years the problem of sex trafficking across the globe has received increasingly more attention, as discussed in the next section.

Worldwide Trafficking of Women and Children in Prostitution

The 60-year history of modern sex trafficking includes the brothels for U.S. troops that Japanese police officials and businessmen established at the end of World War II. Thousands of Japanese women provided cheap sex for 15–60 U.S. troops a day. The leadership of the U.S. occupation initially condoned the troops' use of the prostitutes and provided penicillin for the women and condoms for the servicemen. In the spring of 1946, however, General Douglas MacArthur shut the brothels down due to complaints from military chaplains, concern about bad publicity for the military, and the high rate of sexually transmitted infections among the troops (Talmadge, 2007). However, troops serving today in South Korea visit "camp towns" adjacent to U.S. military bases; these "towns" are filled with more than 1 million sex workers, primarily women brought in from Eastern Europe and the Philippines (Farr, 2004).

Sex traffickers are criminals who buy or kidnap women and children from underdeveloped and socially, economically, or politically unstable nations or entice them by promising legitimate employment. Traffickers range from mom-and-pop operations to networks of highly sophisticated, multinational crime groups, but organized crime is increasingly dominating global sex trafficking (Hodge, 2008). Corrupt individuals in legitimate positions of trust—police officers, border guards,

One of the posters developed by the Campaign to Rescue and Restore Victims of Human Trafficking to promote public awareness about, identification of, and assistance to victims of trafficking.

immigration officials, travel agents, and bankers—are also involved (Finnegan, 2008). The fact that one trafficked sex worker can earn between $75,000 and $250,000 a year for her "employer" provides enormous financial incentives to all involved (Farr, 2004). The worldwide exploitation of children and women through sex trafficking is estimated to generate $7 billion to $10 billion in profits each year (Cwikel & Hoban, 2005).

Instead of giving people the legitimate employment they have promised, traffickers sell them to others who force them into sex work, primarily in wealthier, more stable nations or in locales known for sex tourism (Farr, 2004). For example, after the fall of communism in Europe during the 1990s, traffickers falsely promised legitimate employment in Western Europe to Eastern European women facing poverty in their home countries (Thompson, 2008). Some women are lured into prostitution by promises of marriage in a foreign country. Traffickers also rely on kidnapping. Due to the chaos caused by the U.S. occupation of Iraq, for example, by 2011 criminal trafficking gangs had abducted an estimated 5,000 Iraqi women and girls (Naili, 2011b). Iraqi women and children who fled Iraq to escape the U.S. war also face the fear of being sold into prostitution by male relatives who are desperate for money (Soguel, 2010).

Traffickers also buy children from parents when the children are more of a financial burden than the family can manage. Orphans whose parents died of AIDS or were killed in the ethnic and tribal wars of Africa and Eastern Europe are highly vulnerable to exploitation (Hodge, 2008; Rios, 1996). Younger and younger children are sought for prostitution because customers regard them as more likely to be free of HIV. It is estimated that in Nepal each year about 7,000 girls as young as 9 years old are sold to "employers" who promise them good jobs; they end up in brothels in Mumbai, India, where HIV-positive men have sex with them, believing that having sex with a virgin will cure them (Kottler, 2008). Once the girls are infected, they are often sent back home. Consequently, sex trafficking plays a major role in the spread of HIV and other sexually transmitted infections across South Asia (Silverman et al., 2008).

It is impossible to know how many women and children are trafficked across the world. The U.S. State Department estimates that 2 million children are subjected to prostitution across the globe (Spitzer, 2011). Destination countries tend to be wealthy and/or industrialized nations. A CIA–State Department report estimated that within the United States alone, 50,000 women and children from more than 40 different countries of origin are essentially slaves in the sex industry, and more are imported each year. In tourist and convention cities across the nation, it is estimated that one third of street prostitutes are children (Hodge, 2008; Leuchtag, 2003). Cities where major sports and entertainment events occur, such as the Super Bowl, bring a surge in trafficked sex workers (Goldberg, 2011b).

The harm to women and children who have been trafficked is severe. Studies of women from various countries who have been trafficked found that the slave-like existence of confinement, abuse, and systematic rape these women endured over months or years resulted in continued psychological and physical problems even after they found a way out of being trafficked (Zimmerman et al., 2011). The women often blamed themselves for failing to recognize deceptive recruitment tactics. During transit, women faced the risk of arrest and death from dangerous modes of

CHOR SOKUNTHEA/Reuters/Landov

These young prostitutes in Phnom Penh, Cambodia, must endure the hardships of a life they probably would not have chosen for themselves if they had other work to support their families.

transport and border crossings. Traffickers confiscated their identity papers and threatened to kill them or their families back home if they tried to escape. They were deprived of food, held in solitary confinement, and forced to use drugs to coerce their compliance. Over 96% were physically or sexually assaulted, and 100% were coerced into sex acts, including unprotected sex, anal and oral sex, and gang rape. Most had to service 10 to 25 clients a night; some had as many as 40 to 50. Twenty-five percent had at least one unintended pregnancy and abortion. Nearly 40% had suicidal thoughts during or after their ordeal (Tsutsumi et al., 2008; Van Hook et al., 2006; Zimmerman et al., 2003).

Poverty provides traffickers with unlimited opportunities to exploit vulnerable individuals (Footner, 2008; Gjermeni et al., 2008). Women's organizations and other human rights groups have consistently advocated for women's educational and economic empowerment to eradicate the connection between poverty and sexual exploitation. Private organizations in many countries have developed programs to assist women escaping from trafficking (Katongo, 2012). In 2011 Google donated $11.5 million to help leading organizations combat human trafficking (Horn, 2011).

The United States made human trafficking a federal crime in the Trafficking Victims Protection Act of 2000, which defines human sex trafficking as a commercial sex act involving a minor or induced by force, fraud, or coercion (Spitzer, 2011). Prior to that law, no comprehensive federal law existed to protect victims of trafficking. However, many states continue to charge prostituted children and send them to juvenile detention centers.

The Personal Costs of Sex Work

Sex workers have very diverse working conditions and experiences (Weitzer, 2007). Decriminalization and legalization of sex work significantly improves the health and safety of sex workers, but most sex workers across the world operate under the disadvantages of criminal legal statutes. Sex workers can develop physical and mental health problems as a result of violence, chronic stress, exposure to sexually transmitted diseases, and a lack of control over their working conditions (Ward & Day, 2006; Wong et al., 2006). At the worst, women in the sex trade are murdered by their customers (Pelisek, 2011). The research in this section pertains to countries where prostitution is not decriminalized.

Two thirds of the sex workers in a nine-country study met diagnostic criteria for posttraumatic stress disorder (PTSD), which develops when an individual experiences overwhelming trauma. Some of the symptoms include recurrent nightmares, emotional numbness or fear, difficulty sleeping and concentrating, and flashbacks (feelings of reliving the original traumatic experience). According to this research, it is a misconception that sex workers enter the business to support their drug habits. Various studies have reported that prostitution precedes drug and alcohol abuse for 39–60% of individuals. Sex workers often began to abuse drugs and alcohol to try to cope with overwhelming negative feelings while working (Farley, 2004).

HIV/AIDS is another danger sex workers and their customers face. There is strong evidence that the number of infected prostitutes correlates with the HIV prevalence in a country (Talbott, 2007). Customers often pressure sex workers not to use condoms, and those in the United States who face the greatest pressures not to use condoms are younger than 18, are under the influence of drugs or alcohol, service customers in cars or public spaces, are the most desperate for money, and are in the country illegally (Akarro, 2008; Shannon et al., 2009). A study in Mexico found that prostitutes receive a premium of between 23% and 46% for unprotected sex—an increase from over $14,000 to $51,000 in income per year (Gertler et al., 2005). Programs that provide safe sex education or give female condoms to sex workers have seen an increase in the numbers of sex workers practicing safe sex (Hoke et al., 2007).

Customers of Sex Workers

Sex workers exist because there is a demand for their services. In the United States, "John" is the label for the men of all backgrounds, ages, races, religions, and socioeconomic status who buy sex. One study found that most men buying sex were married or with a partner and ranged in age from 20 to 75, with an average age of 41 (Bennetts, 2011). How many men have sex with prostitutes? A study of a representative sample of men around the world found that about 10% of them had exchanged money for sex in the last 12 months (Carael et al., 2006). In the United States, 93% of the men who used prostitutes had contact with a prostitute at least once a month (Freund et al., 1991).

What appeals to men about paying for sex? Sex in exchange for money gives a customer sexual contact without any emotional involvement or future commitment; it eliminates the risk of rejection and offers an opportunity to engage in sexual activities that the customer does not perform with a partner (Califia, 2002; Watson & Vidal, 2011). Some Johns seek the feeling of power from aggressive sex (Bennetts, 2011). Research has found that men purchase sex at a higher rate in regions where women's sexuality is tightly controlled: Prostitution rates are highest in Africa and China. The researchers concluded that gender equality would significantly reduce prostitution (Wellings et al., 2006).

Women are far less likely than men to pay for sex. However, female sex tourism has increased. Single, divorced, and married White women, primarily from Europe and North America, travel to third-world locales for liaisons with "beach boys," who provide flattery, companionship, and sex for money or gifts. African American women are most likely to travel as sex tourists to Jamaica, and Japanese women usually go to Bali (Hari, 2006). One female sex tourist stated, "In England, men our age aren't remotely interested. . . . Here, the men make us feel like gorgeous, sexy women again" (Knight, 2006, p. 2).

The female sex tourists and the men they hire often hold a benign view of their commercial relationship. One researcher found that the men often imagine they receive gifts of appreciation for helping these women, and female sex tourists believe they are helping the men and the local economy by giving them money and gifts (Hari, 2006).

© Peter Dench/In Pictures/Corbis

Jamaica is one of the countries to which women "sex tourists" travel for their vacations to find local men for companionship and sex.

Glorification of Pimps in the United States

Rachel Lloyd is an anti-trafficking advocate and founder of GEMS, the nation's largest service provider to commercial sexually exploited and trafficked girls and young women. Pimps sell women to other men for sex, and Lloyd describes how pimping and "the adult men who seduce, kidnap, torture, brainwash then sell girls for sex" have become a status business identity in the United States. Rappers glamorize pimping, and corporate sponsors further popularize being a pimp. For example, in 2003, rapper 50 Cent released his song "P.I.M.P" and Reebok gave him a $50 million advertising contract. Rapper Snoop Dogg bragged about his pimping career and was described as "America's Most Lovable Pimp" when featured on the December 2006 issue of *Rolling Stone*. His corporate endorsement deals include Boost Mobile cell phones, Orbit gum, and a commercial for Chrysler. The entertainment industry also contributes to glorifying pimps. In 2006 "It's Hard Out Here for a Pimp" by Three 6 Mafia won the Academy Award for Best Song. In reality, compared to other criminal behaviors, pimping is not particularly "hard" or risky and is usually a more profitable crime than selling drugs (Kristof, 2011; Saar, 2010).

Rachel Lloyd identifies pimps as essentially traffickers of girls and young women and states, "Frankly, it's hard out here for a 13-year-old girl who's under the control of an adult man who beats her daily, tattoos, brands his name on her body to mark her as his property, who controls her every movement and forces her to have sex nightly with dozens of adult men and then takes her money. If that's not trafficking and slavery I don't know what is" (Lloyd, 2010).

Legal Status and Sex Work

The legal status and the principles underlying the laws pertaining to the buying and selling of sexual services vary from place to place (Shaver, 2009). In most countries, including the United States, prostitution is considered an immoral activity and is illegal under criminal laws, except for some areas in Nevada. (Weitzer, 2007). In Sweden and some other Nordic countries, prostitution is viewed as a social ill and a form of violence against women (Månsson, 2009). Therefore, the purchase, not the sale, of sexual services is a crime: Sex workers are not arrested, but their customers may be and can receive up to 6 months in jail if convicted. Also, assisting others to purchase sexual services—procuring customers or running a brothel—is illegal under criminal law (Månsson, 2009).

In the United States a shift to prosecuting buyers of sexual services is developing (Burleigh, 2012). In Illinois men arrested for soliciting sex must pay a fine up to $1,000. Across the United States about 40 education programs emphasize the consequences and human rights issues of sex work and sex trafficking for men arrested for soliciting. Some locations publish the names and photos of men arrested for solicitation in newspapers as an attempt to deter men from purchasing sex (Salario, 2011).

In a few places, including some areas of Nevada, the Netherlands, and Germany, prostitution has been legalized but continues to be regulated under criminal laws. With legalization, sex work is usually viewed as morally repugnant, but an inevitable activity between consenting adults. Some advantages accrue for prostitutes under legalization when regulations for worker benefits include pensions, sick leave, and unemployment benefits and when brothel regulations emphasize safety and better working conditions (Weitzer, 2007). Generating tax revenues is a benefit for governments that legalize prostitution. For example, the tax revenues from legalized prostitution in the Netherlands are estimated to be $57 million per year (Global Agenda, 2003).

In contrast, New Zealand, New South Wales, and parts of Australia have decriminalized sex work, in large part due to public health concerns and the advocacy of sex worker organizations. The ministry of health, police, other governmental organizations, and citizens consulted in order to develop decriminalization standards. The basis for decriminalization is the tenet that sex work is a private matter between consenting adults. Therefore, the appropriate role of government is to establish policies to protect public health and to improve the health and safety of sex workers. Under decriminalization in New Zealand, sex work is no longer a crime but is governed by regulations that promote public health and working conditions of sex workers. Sex workers now have the same employment, legal, health, and safety rights and responsibilities that other workers have. When a sex worker wants to leave sex work for another occupation, she is not burdened by a criminal record that makes finding new work very difficult. She is also able to take advantage of education and training provided for sex workers who want out of the industry. However, prostitution of anyone under 18 years of age, coercing someone into prostitution, and sex trafficking are still illegal under criminal law.

New Zealand completed a 5-year follow-up study of the impact on public health and the welfare of sex workers since the decriminalization in 2003 (Gillian et al., 2009). The report clarified the benefits of decriminalization. First, sex workers had a high level of condom use and safe sex practices, which supports both the sex worker and public health by reducing the incidence of sexually transmitted infections. Regulations require sex workers and customers to use condoms during sex, with a $2,000 fine for noncompliance. A sex worker was able to go to court and successfully sue a customer who secretly slipped off his condom prior to intercourse with her. Sex workers, whether working on the street or in brothels, reported having a greater ability to control their work environment to increase their safety. They were more able to refuse individual clients and to decline to engage in specific activities. They could work on well-lit streets and could utilize police as a resource for their protection instead of fearing arrest or harassment. They could declare their income and pay taxes and be involved in political activism for sex workers without fear of revealing their occupation. One aspect of sex work did not change: The social stigma of sex work remained the same. However, some sex workers were able to maintain a psychological distance between their sex work and their personal lives and to feel less stigmatization (Abel, 2011).

In spite of concerns raised by some prior to decriminalization in New Zealand, no overall increase in the number of sex workers or underage sex workers occurred (Gillian et al., 2009). The research findings about decriminalization of sex work in New Zealand indicate quite strongly that the most significant risks to the health and safety of sex workers are caused by sex work's criminal status rather than by the work itself. Based partially on New Zealand's experience, the Canadian government declared anti-prostitution laws unconstitutional in 2010 (Ansari, 2012). A report compiled from interviews with public health advocates, 450 sex workers, and 40 law enforcement officials recommended that sex work be decriminalized in order to protect the social, psychological, and physical rights of sex workers (Shaver et al, 2011).

Summary

Pornography

- Pornography is broadly defined as sexually explicit material (e.g., images or text) intended to cause sexual arousal.
- Characteristics of erotica include mutual affection, respect, and pleasure.
- Pornographic materials developed for straight men, straight women, gays, and lesbians have unique characteristics to appeal to each group.
- The Internet has both increased the availability of child pornography and improved the ability to find and prosecute child pornographers.
- Soon after the development of the printing press, photography, film, cable television, the VCR, the Internet, and wireless technologies, they were used to produce pornography.
- The Supreme Court, in attempting to determine what is "obscene," established these criteria: The dominant theme of the work as a whole must appeal to prurient interest, be offensive to contemporary community standards, and be without serious literary, artistic, political, or scientific value.
- The U.S. Constitution's First Amendment guarantees of freedom of speech and freedom of the press do not apply categorically to obscene materials.
- The increased availability and legalization of pornography in Denmark were not followed by an increase in reported sex offenses.
- The 1970 report of the Commission on Obscenity and Pornography recommended that laws prohibiting access to pornography to adults should be repealed, but the recommendations were rejected. The controversial 1986 report of the Attorney General's Commission on Pornography did not produce adequate evidence to support its conclusions.
- Whether sexually explicit materials are helpful or harmful to individuals and couples has arguments on each side.

Prostitution and Sex Work

- Prostitution refers to the exchange of sexual services for money.
- Research indicates that about 10% of men have exchanged money for sex in the last year.
- Female sex tourism has become common in some third-world locations.
- Streetwalkers, male hustlers, women in brothels or massage parlors, and call girls, call boys, and gigolos are general categories of sex workers.
- Almost half of sex workers enter the business before they are 18 years old.
- The Internet is transforming sex work, providing more autonomy and safety to some sex workers.
- The legal status of commercial sex varies, and the activity can be illegal, legal, or decriminalized.
- Economic incentive and necessity are the usual compelling reasons for individuals to do sex work.
- Decriminalization of sex work in New Zealand has improved the health and safety of sex workers and has made it easier for women to leave sex work.

- A high percentage of sex workers develop posttraumatic stress disorder as a result of the chronic stress, danger, and violence inherent in commercial sex work.
- Sex workers often receive more money if they agree to unprotected sex.
- Trafficking of women and children is a worldwide problem, and traffickers prey on people who are vulnerable because of poverty, war, and political instability.

Media Resources

Log in to CengageBrain.com to access the resources your instructor requires.

Go to CengageBrain.com to access Psychology CourseMate, where you will find an interactive eBook, glossaries, flashcards, quizzes, videos, and more.

Also access links to chapter-related websites, including **Prostitution Research and Education**.

Glossary

Acquaintance rape Sexual assault by a friend, acquaintance, or date—that is, someone known to the victim.

Acquired immunodeficiency syndrome (AIDS) A catastrophic illness in which a virus (HIV) invades and destroys the ability of the immune system to fight disease.

Afterbirth The placenta and amniotic sac following their expulsion through the vagina after childbirth.

Amenorrhea The absence of menstruation.

Anaphrodisiac A substance that inhibits sexual desire and behavior.

Androgen insensitivity syndrome (AIS) A condition resulting from a genetic defect that causes chromosomally normal males to be insensitive to the action of testosterone and other androgens. These individuals develop female external genitals of normal appearance.

Androgens A class of hormones that promote the development of male genitals and secondary sex characteristics and influence sexual motivation in both sexes. These hormones are produced by the adrenal glands in males and females and by the testes in males.

Androgyny A blending of typical male and female behaviors in one individual.

Anilingus Oral stimulation of the anus.

Aphrodisiac A substance that allegedly arouses sexual desire and increases the capacity for sexual activity.

Artificial insemination A medical procedure in which semen is placed in a woman's vagina, cervix, or uterus.

Asexuality A lack of sexual attraction to either sex.

Assisted reproductive technology (ART) The techniques of extrauterine conception.

Attachment Intense emotional tie between two individuals, such as an infant and a parent or adult lovers.

Atypical sexual behaviors Behaviors not typically expressed by most people in our society.

Autoerotic asphyxia The enhancement of sexual excitement and orgasm by pressure-induced oxygen deprivation.

Autosomes The 22 pairs of human chromosomes that do not significantly influence sex differentiation.

Backup methods Contraceptive methods used simultaneously with another method to support it.

Bacterial vaginosis (BV) A vaginal infection caused by bacterial microorganisms; it is the most common form of vaginitis among U.S. women.

Bartholin's glands Two small glands slightly inside the vaginal opening that secrete a few drops of fluid during sexual arousal.

Basal body temperature method A birth control method based on body temperature changes before and after ovulation.

Bisexuality Sexual attraction to both men and women.

Blastocyst Multicellular descendant of the united egg and sperm that implants on the wall of the uterus.

Bondage A sexual behavior in which a person derives sexual pleasure from being bound, tied up, or otherwise restricted.

Brothel A house in which a group of prostitutes work.

Calendar method A birth control method based on abstinence from intercourse during calendar-estimated fertile days.

Candidiasis An inflammatory infection of the vaginal tissues caused by the yeastlike fungus *Candida albicans*.

Case study A nonexperimental research method that examines either a single subject or a small group of subjects individually and in depth.

Castration Surgical removal of the testes.

Cavernous bodies The structures in the shaft of the clitoris or penis that engorge with blood during sexual arousal.

Celibacy Historically defined as the state of being unmarried; currently defined as abstention from sexual behavior.

Cerebral cortex Outer layer of the cerebral hemispheres that is responsible for higher mental processes.

Cerebral hemispheres The two sides (right and left) of the cerebrum.

Cerebrum The largest part of the brain, consisting of two cerebral hemispheres.

Cervix The small end of the uterus, located at the back of the vagina.

Cesarean section (C-section) A childbirth procedure in which the infant is removed through an incision in the abdomen and uterus.

Chancre A raised, red, painless sore that is symptomatic of the primary phase of syphilis.

Child sexual abuse An adult's engaging in sexual contact of any kind with a child, including inappropriate touching, oral–genital stimulation, and coitus.

Chlamydia Urogenital infection caused by the bacterium *Chlamydia trachomatis*.

Circumcision Surgical removal of the foreskin of the penis.

Climacteric Physiological changes that occur during the transition period from fertility to infertility in both sexes.

Clitoris A highly sensitive structure of the female external genitals, the only function of which is sexual pleasure.

Cohabitation Living together and having a sexual relationship without being married.

Colostrum A thin fluid secreted by the breasts during later stages of pregnancy and the first few days after delivery.

Combined genital and subjective sexual arousal disorder Absent or diminished subjective and physical sexual arousal.

Coming out The process of becoming aware of and disclosing one's homosexual identity.

Commitment The thinking component of Sternberg's triangular love theory.

Companionate love A type of love characterized by friendly affection and deep attachment based on extensive familiarity with the loved one.

Complete celibacy An expression of sexuality in which an individual does not engage in either masturbation or interpersonal sexual contact.

Condom A sheath that fits over the penis and is used for protection against unwanted pregnancy and sexually transmitted infections.

Conjunctivitis Inflammation of the mucous membrane that lines the inner surface of the eyelid and the exposed surface of the eyeball.

Consensual extramarital relationship A sexual relationship that occurs outside the marriage bond with the consent of one's spouse.

Constant-dose combination pill Birth control pill that contains a constant daily dose of estrogen.

Conversion therapy/sexual reorientation therapy Therapy to help homosexual men and women change their sexual orientation.

Coprophilia A sexual paraphilia in which a person obtains sexual arousal from contact with feces.

Corona The rim of the penile glans.

Corpus callosum The broad band of nerve fibers that connects the left and right cerebral hemispheres.

Corpus luteum A yellowish body that forms on the ovary at the site of the ruptured follicle and secretes progesterone.

Cowper's glands Two pea-sized glands located alongside the base of the urethra in the male that secrete an alkaline fluid during sexual arousal.

Crura The innermost tips of the cavernous bodies that connect to the pubic bones.

Cryptorchidism A condition in which the testes fail to descend from the abdominal cavity to the scrotal sac.

Cunnilingus Oral stimulation of the vulva.

Cyberstalking Threatening behavior or unwanted advances that utilize Web technologies as weapons for stalking and harassment.

Cystitis An infection of the bladder.

Date rape Sexual assault by an acquaintance when on a date.

Demographic bias A kind of sampling bias in which certain segments of society (such as White, middle-class, white-collar workers) are disproportionately represented in a study population.

Dependent variable In an experimental research design, an outcome or a resulting behavior that the experimenter observes and records but does not control.

DHT-deficient male A chromosomally normal (XY) male who develops external genitalia resembling those of a female as a result of a genetic defect that prevents the prenatal conversion of testosterone into dihydrotestosterone (DHT).

Dilation and evacuation (D and E) An abortion procedure in which a curette and suction equipment are used.

Direct observation A method of research in which subjects are observed as they go about their activities.

Domestic partnership An unmarried couple living in the same household in a committed relationship.

Dopamine A neurotransmitter that facilitates sexual arousal and activity.

Douching Rinsing out the vagina with plain water or a variety of solutions. It is usually unnecessary for hygiene, and douching too often can result in vaginal irritation.

Dysmenorrhea Pain or discomfort before or during menstruation.

Dyspareunia Pain or discomfort during sexual intercourse.

Ectoparasites Parasitic organisms that live on the outer skin surfaces.

Ectopic pregnancy A pregnancy that occurs when a fertilized ovum implants outside the uterus, most commonly in a fallopian tube.

Effacement Flattening and thinning of the cervix that occurs before and during childbirth.

Either/or question A question that allows statement of a preference.

Ejaculation The process by which semen is expelled from the body through the penis.

Ejaculatory ducts Two short ducts located within the prostate gland.

Elective abortion Medical procedure performed to terminate pregnancy.

Emergency contraception Hormone pills or an IUD that can be used after unprotected intercourse to prevent pregnancy.

Emission phase The first stage of male orgasm, in which the seminal fluid is gathered in the urethral bulb.

Endometriosis A condition in which uterine tissue grows on various parts of the abdominal cavity.

Endometrium The tissue that lines the inside of the uterine wall.

Epididymis The structure along the back of each testis in which sperm maturation occurs.

Episiotomy An incision in the perineum that is sometimes made during childbirth.

Erectile disorder (ED) Consistent or recurring lack of an erection sufficiently rigid for penetrative sex, for a period of at least 3 months.

Erection The process by which the penis or clitoris engorges with blood and increases in size.

Erogenous zones Areas of the body that are particularly responsive to sexual stimulation.

Erotica Respectful, affectionate depictions of sexuality.

Estrogens A class of hormones that produce female secondary sex characteristics and affect the menstrual cycle.

Excitement phase Masters and Johnson's term for the first phase of the sexual response cycle, in which engorgement of the sexual organs and increases in muscle tension, heart rate, and blood pressure occur.

Exhibitionism The act of exposing one's genitals to an unwilling observer.

Experimental research Research conducted in precisely controlled laboratory conditions so that subjects' reactions can be reliably measured.

Expulsion phase The second stage of male orgasm, during which the semen is expelled from the penis by muscular contractions.

Failure rate The number of women out of 100 who become pregnant by the end of 1 year of using a particular contraceptive.

Fallopian tubes Two tubes, extending from the sides of the uterus, in which the egg and sperm travel.

Fellatio Oral stimulation of the penis.

Female genital sexual arousal disorder Persistent inability to attain or maintain the lubrication-swelling response.

Female orgasmic disorder The absence, marked delay, or diminished intensity of orgasm.

Female subjective sexual arousal disorder Absent or diminished awareness of physical arousal.

Fertility awareness methods Birth control methods that use the signs of cyclic fertility to prevent or plan conception.

Fetal alcohol syndrome (FAS) Syndrome in infants caused by heavy maternal prenatal alcohol use; characterized by congenital heart defects, damage to the brain and nervous system, numerous physical malformations of the fetus, and below-normal IQ.

Fetally androgenized female A chromosomally normal (XX) female who, as a result of excessive exposure to androgens during prenatal sex differentiation, develops external genitalia resembling those of a male.

Fetishism A sexual behavior in which a person obtains sexual excitement primarily or exclusively from an inanimate object or a particular part of the body.

Fimbriae Fringelike ends of the fallopian tubes, into which the released ovum enters.

First-stage labor The initial stage of childbirth in which regular contractions begin and the cervix dilates.

Follicle-stimulating hormone (FSH) A pituitary hormone secreted by a female during the secretory phase of the menstrual cycle. FSH stimulates the development of ovarian follicles. In males it stimulates sperm production.

Foreskin A covering of skin over the penile glans.

Frenulum A highly sensitive thin strip of skin that connects the glans to the shaft on the underside of the penis.

"Friends with benefits" relationships (FWBRs) Sexual interaction between friends who do not define their relationship as romantic.

Frotteurism A fairly common paraphilia in which a person obtains sexual pleasure by pressing or rubbing against another person in a crowded public place.

Gamete intrafallopian transfer (GIFT) Procedure in which the sperm and ovum are placed directly in a fallopian tube.

Gay A homosexual person, typically a homosexual male.

Gay-affirmative therapy Therapy to help homosexual clients cope with negative societal attitudes.

Gender The psychological and sociocultural characteristics associated with our sex.

Gender assumptions Assumptions about how people are likely to behave based on their maleness or femaleness.

Gender dysphoria Unhappiness with one's biological sex or gender role.

Gender identity How one psychologically perceives oneself as either male or female.

Gender nonconformity A lack of conformity to stereotypical masculine and feminine behaviors.

Gender role A collection of attitudes and behaviors that a specific culture considers normal and appropriate for people of a particular biological sex.

Genital retraction syndrome (GRS) Unusual, culture-bound phenomenon in which a male believes his penis is shrinking and retracting into his body.

Genital warts Viral warts that appear on the genitals and are primarily transmitted sexually.

Genito-pelvic pain/Penetration disorder Pain with partial vaginal entry, during intercourse, and after intercourse.

Giving permission Providing reassurance to one's partner that it is okay to talk about specific feelings or needs.

Glans The head of the clitoris or penis, which is richly endowed with nerve endings.

Gonadotropins Pituitary hormones that stimulate activity in the gonads (testes and ovaries).

Gonads The male and female sex glands: ovaries and testes.

Gonorrhea A sexually transmitted infection that initially causes inflammation of mucous membranes.

Grafenberg spot (G-spot) Glands and ducts in the anterior wall of the vagina. Some women experience sexual pleasure, arousal, orgasm, and an ejaculation of fluids from stimulation of the Grafenberg spot.

Gynecology The medical practice specializing in women's health and in diseases of the female reproductive and sexual organs.

Herpes An infection characterized by blisters on the skin in the regions of the genitals or mouth. It is caused by the *Herpes simplex* virus and is easily transmitted through sexual contact.

Heteroflexibility Individuals who are primarily heterosexual and have some degree of sexual interest and/or experience with the same sex.

Highly active antiretroviral therapy (HAART) A strategy for treating HIV-infected people with a combination of antiretroviral drugs.

Homoflexibility Individuals who are primarily homosexual and have some degree of sexual interest and/or experience with the other sex.

Homophobia Irrational fears of homosexuality, the fear of the possibility of homosexuality in oneself, or loathing toward one's own homosexuality.

Hook-ups Short-term, loveless sexual liaisons that occur during a brief interval.

Hormone therapy (HT) The use of supplemental hormones during and after menopause or following surgical removal of the ovaries.

Human chorionic gonadotropin (HCG) A hormone that is detectable in the urine of a pregnant woman within 1 month of conception.

Human immunodeficiency virus (HIV) The immune-system-destroying virus that causes AIDS.

Hymen Tissue that partially covers the vaginal opening.

Hypoactive sexual desire disorder (HSDD) Lack of interest prior to and during sexual activity.

Hypogonadism Impaired hormone production in the testes that results in testosterone deficiency.

Hypothalamus A small structure in the central core of the brain that controls the pituitary gland and regulates motivated behavior and emotional expression.

Hysterectomy Surgical removal of the uterus.

In vitro fertilization (IVF) Procedure in which mature eggs are removed from a woman's ovary and fertilized by sperm in a laboratory dish.

Incest Sexual contact between two people who are related (one of whom is often a child), other than husband and wife.

Independent variable In an experimental research design, a condition or component that is under the control of the researcher, who manipulates or determines its value.

Intersexed A term applied to people who possess biological attributes of both sexes.

Interstitial cells Cells located between the seminiferous tubules that are the major source of androgen in males.

Intimacy The emotional component of Sternberg's triangular love theory.

Intracytoplasmic sperm injection (ICSI) Procedure in which a single sperm is injected into an egg.

Intrauterine device (IUD) A small, plastic device that is inserted into the uterus for contraception.

Introitus The opening to the vagina.

Intromission Insertion of the penis into the vagina.

Kegel exercises A series of exercises that strengthen the muscles underlying the external female or male genitals.

Klinefelter's syndrome A condition characterized by the presence of two X chromosomes and one Y chromosome (XXY) in which affected individuals have undersized external male genitals.

Klismaphilia An unusual variant of sexual expression in which an individual obtains sexual pleasure from receiving enemas.

Koro A widely used term for the genital retraction syndrome.

Labia majora The outer lips of the vulva.

Labia minora The inner lips of the vulva, one on each side of the vaginal opening.

Late-term abortion (intact dilation and evacuation) An abortion done between 20 and 24 weeks when serious health risks to the woman or severe fetal abnormalities exist.

Limbic system A subcortical brain system composed of several interrelated structures that influences the sexual behavior of humans and other animals.

Lochia A reddish uterine discharge that occurs after childbirth.

Luteinizing hormone (LH) The hormone secreted by the pituitary gland that stimulates ovulation in the female. In males it is called the interstitial cell hormone (ISCH) and stimulates production of androgens by the testes.

Male orgasmic disorder The inability of a man to ejaculate during sexual stimulation from his partner.

Mammary glands Glands in the female breast that produce milk.

Mammography A highly sensitive X-ray test for the detection of breast cancer.

Mastectomy Surgical removal of the breast(s).

Masturbation Stimulation of one's own genitals to create sexual pleasure.

Matriarchal society A society in which women carry the family name through the generations, and women govern the economic and social affairs of the community.

Medical abortion The use of medications to end a pregnancy of 7 weeks or less.

Menarche The initial onset of menstrual periods in a young woman.

Menopause Cessation of menstruation as a result of the aging process or surgical removal of the ovaries.

Menstrual phase The phase of the menstrual cycle during which menstruation occurs.

Menstruation The sloughing off of the built-up uterine lining that takes place if conception has not occurred.

Mere exposure effect A phenomenon in which repeated exposure to novel stimuli tends to increase an individual's liking for such stimuli.

Microbicide A topical gel or cream product that women can use vaginally to prevent or minimize the risk of being infected with HIV or other STIs.

Mons veneris A triangular mound over the pubic bone above the vulva.

Mucosa Collective term for the mucous membranes; moist tissue that lines certain body areas such as the penile urethra, vagina, and mouth.

Mucus method A birth control method based on determining the time of ovulation by means of the cyclical changes of the cervical mucus.

Multi-person-sex (MPS) Adolescent sexual interaction involving multiple simultaneous partners that may be either consensual or forced.

Multiple orgasms More than one orgasm experienced within a short time period.

Mutual empathy The underlying knowledge that each partner in a relationship cares for the other and knows that the care is reciprocated.

Myometrium The smooth muscle layer of the uterine wall.

Myotonia Muscle tension.

Necrophilia A rare sexual paraphilia in which a person obtains sexual gratification by viewing or having intercourse with a corpse.

Neuropeptide hormones Chemicals produced in the brain that influence sexuality and other behavioral functions.

Nocturnal emission Involuntary ejaculation during sleep; also known as a wet dream.

Nocturnal orgasm Involuntary orgasm during sleep.

Noncoital sex Physical contact, including kissing, touching, and manual or oral–genital stimulation, but excluding coitus.

Nonconsensual extramarital sex Sexual interaction in which a married person engages in an outside sexual relationship without the consent (or presumably, the knowledge) of his or her spouse.

Nongonococcal urethritis (NGU) An inflammation of the urethral tube caused by organisms other than *gonococcus*.

Nonmonogamy Sexual interaction outside of a couple relationship.

Nonresponse The refusal to participate in a research study.

Obscenity A term that implies a personal or societal judgment that something is offensive.

Oophorectomy Surgical removal of the ovaries.

Open marriage A marriage in which spouses, with each other's permission, have intimate relationships with other people as well as with the marital partner.

Open-ended question A question that allows a respondent to share any feelings or information she or he thinks is relevant.

Orchidectomy The surgical procedure for removing the testes.

Orgasm A series of muscular contractions of the pelvic floor muscles occurring at the peak of sexual arousal.

Os The opening in the cervix that leads to the interior of the uterus.

Outercourse Noncoital forms of sexual intimacy.

Ovaries Female gonads that produce ova and sex hormones.

Ovulation The release of a mature ovum from the ovary.

Ovum The female reproductive cell.

Oxytocin A neuropeptide produced in the hypothalamus that influences sexual response and interpersonal attraction.

Pap smear A screening test for cancer of the cervix.

Paraphilia A term used to describe uncommon types of sexual expression.

Partial celibacy An expression of sexuality in which an individual does not engage in interpersonal sexual contact but continues to engage in masturbation.

Passing Presenting a false image of being heterosexual.

Passion The motivational component of Sternberg's triangular love theory.

Passionate love State of extreme absorption in another person. Also known as romantic love.

Pedophilia or child molestation Sexual contact between an adult and a child who are not related.

Pelvic inflammatory disease (PID) An infection in the uterus and pelvic cavity.

Penis A male sexual organ consisting of the internal root and the external shaft and glans.

Perimenopause The time period before menopause when estrogen is decreasing.

Perimetrium The thin membrane covering the outside of the uterus.

Perineum The area between the vagina and anus of the female and the scrotum and anus of the male.

Persistent genital arousal disorder (PGAD) Spontaneous, intrusive, and unwanted genital arousal.

Peyronie's disease Abnormal fibrous tissue and calcium deposits in the penis.

Pheromones Certain odors produced by the body that relate to reproductive functions.

Phimosis A condition characterized by an extremely tight penile foreskin.

Physical attractiveness Physical beauty, which is a powerful factor in attracting lovers to each other.

Placenta A disk-shaped organ attached to the uterine wall and connected to the fetus by the umbilical cord. Nutrients, oxygen, and waste products pass between mother and fetus through the cell walls of the placenta.

Plateau phase Masters and Johnson's term for the second phase of the sexual response cycle, in which muscle tension, heart rate, blood pressure, and vasocongestion increase.

Polyamory Multiple consensual sexual relationships of trios, groups of couples, and intentionally created families that emphasize emotional commitment.

Pornography Sexually explicit material (e.g., images or text) intended to cause sexual arousal.

Postpartum depression (PPD) Symptoms of depression and obsessive thoughts of hurting the baby.

Postpartum period The first several weeks after childbirth.

Posttraumatic stress disorder (PTSD) A psychological disorder caused by exposure to overwhelmingly painful events.

Premature ejaculation (PE) A pattern of ejaculations within one minute and an inability to delay ejaculation, resulting in a man's impairing his or his partner's pleasure.

Premenstrual dysphoric disorder (PMDD) Premenstrual symptoms severe enough to significantly disrupt a woman's functioning.

Premenstrual syndrome (PMS) Symptoms of physical discomfort and emotional irritability that occur 2 to 12 days before menstruation.

Prepared childbirth Birth following an education process that can involve information, exercises, breathing, and working with a labor coach.

Prepuce The foreskin or fold of skin over the clitoris.

Primary erogenous zones Areas of the body that contain dense concentrations of nerve endings.

Prodromal symptoms Symptoms that warn of an impending herpes eruption.

Progestational compounds A class of hormones, including progesterone, that are produced by the ovaries.

Progestin-only pill Contraceptive pill that contains a small dose of progestin and no estrogen.

Proliferative phase The phase of the menstrual cycle during which the ovarian follicles mature.

Prostaglandins Hormones that induce uterine contractions. They are sometimes used to induce contractions and fetal expulsion for second-trimester abortions.

Prostate gland A gland located at the base of the bladder that produces about 30% of the seminal fluid released during ejaculation.

Prostitution The exchange of sexual services for money.

Proximity The geographic nearness of one person to another, which is an important factor in interpersonal attraction.

Psychosocial Refers to a combination of psychological and social factors.

Puberty A period of rapid physical changes in early adolescence during which the reproductive organs mature.

Pubic lice Lice that primarily infest the pubic hair and are transmitted by sexual contact.

Random sample A randomly chosen subset of a population.

Rape Sexual intercourse that occurs without consent as a result of actual or threatened force.

Reciprocity The principle that when we are recipients of expressions of liking or loving, we tend to respond in kind.

Refractory period The period of time following orgasm in the male, during which he cannot experience another orgasm.

Representative sample A type of limited research sample that provides an accurate representation of a larger target population of interest.

Resolution phase The fourth phase of the sexual response cycle, as outlined by Masters and Johnson, in which the sexual systems return to their nonexcited state.

Retrograde ejaculation The process by which semen is expelled into the bladder instead of out of the penis.

Root The portion of the penis that extends internally into the pelvic cavity.

Rugae The folds of tissue in the vagina.

Sadomasochistic (SM) behavior The association of sexual expression with pain.

Scabies An ectoparasitic infestation of tiny mites.

Scrotum The pouch of skin of the external male genitals that encloses the testes.

Seasonale Birth control pill that reduces menstrual periods to four times a year.

Secondary erogenous zones Areas of the body that have become erotically sensitive through learning and experience.

Secondary sex characteristics The physical characteristics other than genital development that indicate sexual maturity, such as body hair, breasts, and deepened voice.

Second-stage labor The middle stage of labor, in which the infant descends through the vaginal canal.

Secretory phase The phase of the menstrual cycle during which the corpus luteum develops and secretes progesterone.

Self-selection The bias introduced into research study results because of participants' willingness to respond.

Semen or seminal fluid A viscous fluid ejaculated through the penis that contains sperm and fluids from the prostate, seminal vesicles, and Cowper's glands.

Seminal vesicles Small glands adjacent to the terminals of the vas deferens that secrete an alkaline fluid (conducive to sperm motility) that constitutes the greatest portion of the volume of seminal fluid released during ejaculation.

Seminiferous tubules Thin, coiled structures in the testes in which sperm are produced.

Sensate focus A process of touching and communication used to enhance sexual pleasure and to reduce performance pressure.

Serotonin A neurotransmitter that inhibits sexual arousal and activity.

Sex Biological maleness and femaleness.

Sex chromosomes A single set of chromosomes that influences biological sex determination.

Sex flush A pink or red rash that can appear on the chest or breasts during sexual arousal.

Sex worker A person involved in prostitution and related activities, such as phone sex, nude dancing, erotic massage, Internet sex, and acting in porn movies.

Sexology The study of sexuality.

Sexting Sending sexually suggestive photos or text messages via the Internet, cell phones, or other electronic devices.

Sexual aversion disorder Extreme and irrational fear of sexual activity.

Sexual fluidity Variability in same-sex and other-sex attraction and involvement at different times and in different situations throughout the life span.

Sexual harassment Unwelcome sexual advances, requests for sexual favors, and other verbal or physical conduct of a sexual nature in the workplace or academic setting.

Sexual intelligence Sexual intelligence involves self-understanding, interpersonal sexual skills, scientific knowledge, and consideration of the cultural context of sexuality.

Sexual masochism The act of obtaining sexual arousal through receiving physical or psychological pain.

Sexual orientation Sexual attraction to one's own sex (homosexual), to the other sex (heterosexual), or to both sexes (bisexual), or lack of sexual interest in either sex (asexual).

Sexual sadism The act of obtaining sexual arousal through giving physical or psychological pain.

Sexual scripts Culturally learned ways of behaving in sexual situations.

Sexually transmitted infections (STIs) Infections that are transmitted by sexual contact.

Shaft The length of the clitoris or penis between the glans and the body.

Similarity The similarity of beliefs, interests, and values, which is a factor in attracting people to one another.

Smegma A cheesy substance of glandular secretions and skin cells that sometimes accumulates under the foreskin of the penis or hood of the clitoris.

Socialization The process by which our society conveys behavioral expectations to the individual.

Speculum An instrument used to open the vaginal walls during a gynecological exam.

Sperm The male reproductive cell.

Spermatic cord A cord attached to the testis that contains the vas deferens, blood vessels, nerves, and cremasteric muscle fibers.

Spongy body A cylinder that forms a bulb at the base of the penis, extends up into the penile shaft, and forms the penile glans.

Spontaneous abortion (miscarriage) The spontaneous expulsion of the fetus from the uterus early in pregnancy, before it can survive on its own.

Standard days method A birth control method that requires couples to avoid unprotected intercourse for a 12-day period in the middle of the menstrual cycle.

Statutory rape Intercourse with a person under the age of consent.

Stereotype A generalized notion of what a person is like based only on that person's sex, race, religion, ethnic background, or similar criteria.

Steroid hormones The sex hormones and the hormones of the adrenal cortex.

Stop-start technique A treatment technique for premature ejaculation, consisting of stimulating the penis to the point of impending orgasm and then stopping until the preejaculatory sensations subside.

Stranger rape Rape of a person by an unknown assailant.

Suction curettage A procedure in which the cervical os is dilated by using graduated metal dilators or a laminaria; then a small plastic tube, attached to a vacuum aspirator, is inserted into the uterus, drawing the fetal tissue, placenta, and built-up uterine lining out of the uterus.

Surrogate mother A woman who is artificially inseminated by the male partner in a childless couple, carries the pregnancy to term, delivers the child, and gives it to the couple for adoption.

Survey A research method in which a sample of people are questioned about their behaviors and/or attitudes.

Swinging The exchange of marital partners for sexual interaction.

Syphilis A sexually transmitted infection caused by a bacterium called *Treponema pallidum*.

Testes Male gonads inside the scrotum that produce sperm and sex hormones.

Third-stage labor The last stage of childbirth, in which the placenta separates from the uterine wall and comes out of the vagina.

Toxic shock syndrome (TSS) A disease that occurs most commonly in menstruating women and that can cause a person to go into shock.

Trachoma A chronic, contagious form of conjunctivitis caused by chlamydia infections.

Transcervical sterilization A method of female sterilization using a tiny coil that is inserted through the vagina, cervix, and uterus into the fallopian tubes.

Transgendered A term applied to people whose appearance and/or behaviors do not conform to traditional gender roles.

Transsexual A person whose gender identity is opposite to his or her biological sex.

Transvestic fetishism A sexual behavior in which a person derives sexual arousal from wearing clothing of the other sex.

Tribadism Rubbing one's genitals against another's body or genitals.

Trichomoniasis A form of vaginitis caused by the one-celled protozoan *Trichomonas vaginalis*.

Triphasic pill Birth control pill that varies the dosages of estrogen and progestin during the menstrual cycle.

Tubal sterilization Female sterilization accomplished by severing or tying the fallopian tubes.

Turner's syndrome A rare condition, characterized by the presence of one unmatched X chromosome (XO), in which affected individuals have normal female external genitals but their internal reproductive structures do not develop fully.

Urethra The tube through which urine passes from the bladder.

Urethritis An inflammation of the urethral tube.

Urology The medical specialty dealing with reproductive health and genital diseases of the male and urinary tract diseases in both sexes.

Urophilia A sexual paraphilia in which a person obtains sexual arousal from contact with urine.

Uterus A pear-shaped organ inside the female pelvis, within which the fetus develops.

Vagina A stretchable canal in the female that opens at the vulva and extends about 3 to 5 inches into the pelvis.

Vaginal spermicides Foam, cream, jelly, suppositories, and film that contain a chemical that kills sperm.

Vaginismus Involuntary spasmodic contractions of the muscles of the outer third of the vagina.

Vaginitis Inflammation of the vaginal walls caused by a variety of vaginal infections.

Varicocele A damaged or enlarged vein in the testis or vas deferens.

Vas deferens A sperm-carrying tube that begins at the testis and ends at the urethra.

Vasectomy Male sterilization procedure that involves removing a section from each vas deferens.

Vasocongestion The engorgement of blood vessels in particular body parts in response to sexual arousal.

Vernix caseosa A waxy, protective substance on the fetus's skin.

Vestibular bulbs Two bulbs, one on each side of the vaginal opening, that engorge with blood during sexual arousal.

Vestibule The area of the vulva inside the labia minora.

Vestibulodynia A small area at the entrance of the vagina that causes severe pain.

Viral hepatitis An ailment in which liver function is impaired by a viral infection.

Viral load The amount of HIV present in an infected person's blood.

Voyeurism The act of obtaining sexual gratification by observing undressed or sexually interacting people without their consent.

Vulva The external genitals of the female, including the pubic hair, mons veneris, labia majora, labia minora, clitoris, and urinary and vaginal openings.

Yes/no question A question that asks for a one-word answer (yes or no) and thus provides little opportunity for discussing an issue.

Zoophilia A paraphilia in which a person has sexual contact with animals.

Zygote The single cell resulting from the union of sperm and egg cells.

Zygote intrafallopian transfer (ZIFT) Procedure in which an egg is fertilized in the laboratory and then placed in a fallopian tube.

References

Aaronson, L. (2005, September/October). The mend of the affair. *Psychology Today*, 48.

Aaronson, L. (2006, March/April). An upside to infertility? *Psychology Today*, 38.

Abbey, A. (2011). Alcohol and dating risk factors for sexual assault: Double standards are still alive and well entrenched. *Psychology of Women Quarterly, 35*, 362–368.

Abbey, A., Clinton-Sherrod, A., McAuslan, P., Zawacki, T., & Buck, P. (2003). The relationship between the quantity of alcohol consumed and the severity of sexual assaults committed by college men. *Journal of Interpersonal Violence, 18*, 813–833.

Abbey, A., & Jacques-Tiura, A. (2011). Sexual assault perpetrators' tactics: Associations with their personal characteristics and aspects of the incident. *Journal of Interpersonal Violence, 26*, 2866–2889.

Abbott, E. (2000). *A history of celibacy: From Athena to Elizabeth I, Leonardo da Vinci, Gandhi and Cher.* New York: Simon and Schuster.

Abdel-Meguid, T. (2012). Predictors of sperm recovery and azoospermia relapse in men with nonobstructive azoospermia after varicocele repair. *Journal of Urology, 187*, 222–226.

Abel, G. (1981, October 15). *The evaluation and treatment of sexual offenders and their victims.* Paper presented at St. Vincent Hospital and Medical Center, Portland, OR.

Abel, G. (2011). Different stage, different performance: The protective strategy of role play on emotional health in sex work. *Social Science and Medicine, 72*, 1177–1184.

Abel, G., Barlow, D., Blanchard, E., & Guild, D. (1977). The components of rapists' sexual arousal. *Archives of General Psychiatry, 34*, 895–903.

Abel, G., Becker, J., & Cunningham-Ratder, J. (1984). Complications, consent, and cognitions in sex between children and adults. *International Journal of Law and Psychiatry, 7*, 89–103.

Abel, G., & Osborn, C. (2000). The paraphilias. In M. Gelder, J. Lopez-Ibor, & N. Andreasen (Eds.), *New Oxford textbook of psychiatry.* Oxford: Oxford University Press.

Abelman, R. (2007). Fighting the war on indecency: Mediating TV, Internet, and videogame usage among achieving and underachieving gifted children. *Roeper Review, 29*, 100–112.

Abidde, S. (2008). The missing or shrinking organ? No, it is genital retraction syndrome. Retrieved October 30, 2008, from http://www.niger.ansinamerica.com/articles/2645/1/The-Missing-or-Shrinking-Organ-No-It-Is-Genital-Retraction-Syndrome/Page1.html

Abraham, L. (2011, November 16). Teaching good sex. Retrieved from http://www.nytimes.com/2011/11/20/magazine/teaching-good-sex.html

Absi-Semaan, N., Crombie, G., & Freeman, C. (1993). Masculinity and femininity in middle childhood: Developmental and factor analysis. *Sex Roles, 28*, 187–202.

Acevedo, B., & Aron, A. (2009). Does a long-term relationship kill romantic love? *Review of General Psychology, 13*, 59–65.

Achermann, J., Eugster, E., & Shulman, D. (2011). Ambiguous genitalia. *Journal of Clinical Endocrinology and Metabolism, 96*, 33–38.

Acker, M., & Davis, M. (1992). Intimacy, passion, and commitment in adult romantic relationships: A test of the triangular theory of love. *Journal of Social and Personal Relationships, 9*, 21–50.

Ackerman, M., Montague, D., & Morganstern, S. (1994, March). Impotence: Help for erectile dysfunction. *Patient Care, 22*–56.

Adams, B. (2003, November 11). Keeping it up. *Advocate*, 38–40.

Adams, B., Husbands, W., Murray, J., & Maxwell, J. (2005). AIDS optimism, condom fatigue, or self-esteem? Explaining unsafe sex among gay and bisexual men. *Journal of Sex Research, 42*, 238–248.

Addiego, F., Belzer, E., Comolli, J., et al. (1981). Female ejaculation: A case study. *Journal of Sex Research, 17*, 13–21.

Addis, I., Van Den Eeden, S., Wassel-Fyr, C., & Vittinghoff, E. (2006). Sexual activity and function in middle-aged and older women. *Obstetrics and Gynecology, 107*, 755–764.

Adeniyi, A., et al. (2007). Yohimbine in the treatment of orgasmic dysfunction. *Asian Journal of Andrology, 9*, 403–407.

Afifi, W., & Faulkner, S. (2000). On being "just friends": The frequency and impact of sexual activity in cross-sex friendships. *Journal of Social and Personal Relationships, 17*, 205–222.

Agbayani-Siewert, P. (2004). Assumptions of Asian American similarity: The case of Filipino and Chinese students. *Social Work, 49*, 39–51.

Agence France-Presse. (2011, December 20). 675 "honour killing" victims in Pakistan. Retrieved from http://tribune.com.pk/story/309279/675-honour-killing-victims-in-pakistan-hrcp

Agger, I., & Jensen, S. (1994). Sexuality as a tool of political repression. In H. Riguelme (Ed.), *Era in twilight: Psychocultural situation under state terrorism in Latin America.* Bilbao, Spain: Instituto Horizonte.

Aggleton, P. (2007). "Just a snip"?: A social history of male circumcision. *Reproductive Health Matters, 15*, 15–21.

Agnew, J. (2000). Klismaphilia. *Venereology, 13*, 75–79.

Ahmad, S., & Bhugra, D. (2010). Homophobia: An updated review of the literature. *Sexual and Relationship Therapy, 25*, 447–455.

Ahmed, A., & Ellsworth, P. (2012). To circ or not: A reappraisal. *Urologic Nursing, 32*, 10–19.

Ahrold, T., et al. (2011). The relationship among sexual attitudes, sexual fantasy, and religiosity. *Archives of Sexual Behavior, 40*, 619–630.

Ainsworth, M. (1979). Infant–mother attachment. *American Psychologist, 34*, 932–937.

Ainsworth, M. (1989). Attachments beyond infancy. *American Psychologist, 44*, 709–716.

Ainsworth, M., Blehar, M., Waters, E., & Walls, S. (1978). *Patterns of attachment: A psychological study of the strange situation.* Hillsdale, NJ: Erlbaum.

Akarro, R. (2008). Some factors associated with condom use among bar maids in Tanzania. *Journal of Biosocial Science, 13*, 284–297.

Akers, A., et al. (2011). Interventions to improve parental communication about sex: A systematic review. *Pediatrics, 127,* 494–510.

Akert, J. (2003). A new generation of contraceptives. *RN, 66,* 54–61.

Albert, B. (2004). With One Voice 2004: America's adults and teens sound off about teen pregnancy. Washington, DC: National Campaign to Prevent Teen Pregnancy. Retrieved February 4, 2009, from http://www.teenpregnancy.org/resources/data/pdf/wov2004.pdf

Albright, J. (2008). Sex in America online: An exploration of sex, marital status, and sexual identity in Internet sex seeking and its impacts. *Journal of Sex Research, 45,* 175–186.

Aldridge, L., Daniels, J., & Jukic, A. (2006). Mammograms and healthcare access among U.S. Hispanic and non-Hispanic women 40 years and older. *Family and Community Health, 29,* 80–89.

Alexander, B. (2006, August 17). Will technology revolutionize boinking? Retrieved August 21, 2006, from http://www.msnbc.msn.com/id/14292504/print/1/displaymode/1098/

Alexander, B. (2008, December 3). Women on top: Female execs rise in porn biz. Retrieved December 12, 2008, from http://www.msnbc.mxn.com/id/28022805/print/1/displaymode/1098

Alexander, J., Dennerstein, L., Burger, H., & Graziottin, A. (2006). Testosterone and libido in surgically and naturally menopausal women. *Women's Health, 2,* 459–477.

Alexander, M., & Rosen, R. (2008). Spinal cord injuries and orgasm: A review. *Journal of Sex and Marital Therapy, 34,* 308–324.

Alford, S., & Hauser, D. (2011). Adolescent sexual health in Europe and the U.S. Retrieved from http://www.advocatesforyouth.org/publications/419-adolescent-sexual-health-in-europe-and-the-u.s.

Ali, A. (2006). *The caged virgin: An emancipation proclamation for women and Islam.* New York: Free Press.

Ali, L. (2008, July 7 & 14). True or false? Having kids makes you happy. *Newsweek,* 62–63.

Ali, L., & Miller, L. (2004, July 12). The secret lives of wives. *Newsweek,* 47–54.

Al-Krenawi, A., & Slonim-Nevo, V. (2008). The psychosocial profile of Bedouin Arab women in polygamous and monogamous marriages. *Families in Society, 89,* 139–149.

Al-Krenawi, A., & Wiesel-Lev, R. (1999). Attitudes toward and perceived psychosocial impact of female circumcision as practiced among the Bedouin-Arabs of the Negev. *Family Process, 38,* 431–443.

Allameh, A., et al. (2011). Circulating sex hormones play no role in the association between sexual activity and the risk of prostate cancer. *Journal of Sexual Medicine, 8,* 905–913.

Allana, D. (2011). Evidence drives new U.S. HIV prevention guidance. *Center for Health and Gender Equity,* September 13, 1–2.

Allen, E., & Rhoades, G. (2008). Not all affairs are created equal: Emotional involvement with an extradyadic partner. *Journal of Sex and Marital Therapy, 34,* 51–65.

Allen, J. (2011, October 27). Ovarian cancer risk slashed by the pill. Retrieved from http://abcnews.go.com/Health/WomensHealth/ovarian-cancer-risk-slashed-pill/story?id=14821039

Allen, L., & Gorski, R. (1990). Sex difference in the bed nucleus of the stria terminalis of the human brain. *Journal of Comparative Neurology, 302,* 697–706.

Allen, M., D'Alessio, D., & Brezgel, K. (1995). A meta-analysis summarizing the effects of pornography II: Aggression after exposure. *Human Communications Research, 22,* 258–283.

Allen, R., & Forcier, M. (2011). Adolescent sexuality and the use of contraceptives. *SRM: Sexuality, Reproduction and Menopause, 9.*

Allers, K. (2011, August 26). When "breast is best" is not enough. Retrieved from http://www.womensenews.org/story/reprductive-health/110825/when-breast-best-not-enough

Allgeier, E. (1981). The influence of androgynous identification on heterosexual relations. *Sex Roles, 7,* 321–330.

Al-Mograbi, E. (2011, November 1). Palestinian women's radio crosses boundaries. Retrieved from http://www.womensenews.org/story/media-stories/111031

Alo, O., & Babatunde, G. (2011). Intergenerational attitude change regarding female genital cutting in Yoruba-speaking ethnic group of southwest Nigeria: A qualitative and quantitative enquiry. *Electronic Journal of Human Sexuality, 14,* 1–10. Retrieved July 6, 2011, from http://www.ejhs.org/volume14/FGC.htm

Alonzo, D. (2003, April). *Dancing in the autumn light: Gay men, sexuality, and the mid-life transition.* Paper presented at the Western Region Annual Conference of the Society for the Scientific Study of Sexuality, Los Angeles, CA.

Alperstein, L. (2001, May 2–6). *For two: Some basic perspectives and skills for couples therapy.* Paper presented at the 33rd Annual Conference of the American Association of Sex Educators, Counselors, and Therapists, San Francisco, CA.

Alston, J. (2010, November 1). The bully pulpit. *Newsweek,* 56.

Alston, C. (2012). *Hotwifing: Whether to Try It, Ways to Go about It How to Handle It.* Austin, TX: Bold Type Press.

Alter, H., & Liang, T. (2012). Hepatitis C: The end of the beginning and possibly the beginning of the end. *Annals of Internal Medicine, 156,* 317–318.

Althof, S. (2000). Erectile dysfunction: Psychotherapy with men and couples. In S. Leiblum & R. Rosen (Eds.), *Principles and practice of sex therapy.* New York: Guilford Press.

Althof, S. (2006). The psychology of premature ejaculation: Therapies and consequences. *Journal of Sexual Medicine, 3,* 324–331.

Althof, S., Dean, J., Derogatis, L., & Rosen, R. (2005). Current perspectives on the clinical assessment and diagnosis of female sexual dysfunction and clinical studies of potential therapies: A statement of concern. *Journal of Sexual Medicine, 2,* 146–153.

Althof, S., Rowland, D., McNulty, P., & Rothman, M. (2006, November). *Evaluation of the impact of premature ejaculation on a man's self-esteem, confidence, and overall relationship.* Paper presented at the Sexual Medicine Society of North America Fall Meeting, New York, NY.

Altman, C. (1999). Gay and lesbian seniors: Unique challenges of coming out in later life. *SIECUS Report, 27,* 14–17.

Altman, L. (2002, July 14). Inexpensive drug prevents HIV in newborns, study shows. *Oregonian,* p. A20.

Altman, L. (2008a, November 27). HIV vaccine human trial canceled. *Oregonian,* p. A20.

Altman, L. (2008b, August 6). AIDS experts urge focus on prevention. *Oregonian,* p. A5.

Amato, P. (2001). What children learn from divorce. *Population Today, 29,* 1.

Amato, P., & Previti, D. (2003). People's reasons for divorcing: Gender, social class, the life course, and adjustment. *Journal of Family Issues, 24,* 602–626.

American Academy of Pediatrics. (2001). Sexuality, contraception, and the media. Retrieved January 29, 2001, from http://www.aap.org/policy/re0038.html

American Academy of Pediatrics. (2006). Adolescent pregnancy: Current trends and issues. Retrieved February 2, 2006, from http://www.Pediatrics.org

American Association of University Women. (2006). Drawing the line: Sexual harassment on campus. Retrieved March 3, 2010, from http://www.aauw.org/

American Cancer Society. (2009, May 13). Detailed guide: Cervical cancer—How is cervical cancer diagnosed? Retrieved May 22, 2009, from http://www.cancer.org/docroot/CRI/content/CRI_2_4_3x_How_is_cervical_cancer_diagnosed_8.asp

American Cancer Society. (2010). *Breast cancer facts and figures 2009–2010*. Atlanta: Author.

American Life League. (2004). *Why do we oppose Planned Parenthood*. Stafford, VA: Author.

American Life League. (2011). Birth control. Retrieved from http://www.all.org/nav/index/headingOQ/cat/Mzc

American Psychiatric Association. (2000). *Diagnostic and statistical manual of mental disorders* (4th ed., text rev.). Washington, DC: Author.

American Psychological Association. (2008). *Report of the APA Task Force on Mental Health and Abortion: Executive summary*. Washington, DC: Author.

American Psychological Association. (2009). Resolution on appropriate affirmative responses to sexual orientation distress and change efforts. Retrieved from http://www.apa.org/pi/lgbc/publications/resolution-resp.html

American Psychological Association. (2012). Guidelines for psychological practice with lesbian, gay, and bisexual clients. *American Psychologist, 67*, 10–42.

American Society for Aesthetic Plastic Surgery. (2009). Breast augmentation statistics for 2008. Retrieved from http://acesspro.org/plastic-surgery/breast-augmentation-statistics-for-2008

American Society for Reproductive Medicine. (2008). *Patient fact sheet: Diagnostic testing for male factor infertility*. Birmingham, AL: Author.

Amnesty International. (2011, November 30). Iranian women fight controversial "polygamy" bill. Retrieved from http://www.amnesty.org/en/news/Iranian-women-fight-controversial-polygamy-bill-2011-11-30

Amodio, D., & Showers, C. (2005). "Similarity breeds liking" revisited: The moderating role of commitment. *Journal of Social and Personal Relationships, 22*, 817–836.

Anand, M. (1991). *The art of sexual ecstasy*. Los Angeles: Tarcher.

Ananth, C., & Vintzileos, A. (2011). Trends in cesarean delivery at preterm gestation and association with perinatal mortality. *American Journal of Obstetrics and Gynecology, 204*, 505.e1–505e8.

Anderson, E. (2011). Updating the outcome: Gay athletes, straight teams, and coming out in educationally based sports teams. *Gender and Society, 25*, 250–268.

Anderson, J. (2012). National study finds widespread sexual harassment of students in grades 7 to 12. Retrieved January 20, 2012, from http://www.nytimes.com/2011/11/07/education/widespread-sexual-harassment-in-grades-7-to-12-found-in-study.html

Anderson, K., Cooper, H., & Okamura, L. (1997). Individual differences and attitudes toward rape: A meta-analytic review. *Personality and Social Psychology Bulletin, 23*, 295–315.

Anderson, M., Kunkel, A., & Dennis, M. (2011). "Let's (not) talk about that": Bridging the past sexual experiences taboo to build healthy romantic relationships. *Journal of Sex Research, 48*, 381–391.

Anderson-Hunt, M., & Dennerstein, L. (1994). Increased female sexual response after oxytocin. *British Medical Journal, 309*, 929.

Andrews, B., Brewin, C., Rose, S., & Kirk, M. (2000). Predicting PTSD symptoms in victims of violent crime: The role of shame, anger, and childhood abuse. *Journal of Abnormal Psychology, 109*, 69–73.

Andrews, G. (2006, February 10). Treating menopausal women. *Practice Nurse, 1*.

Andruff, H., & Wentland, J. (2012). Looking back: The experience of first sexual intercourse and current sexual adjustment in young heterosexual adults. *Journal of Sex Research, 49*, 27–36.

Anghelescu, I. (2008, November 20). "Conscience rule" creates quandary for hospitals. Retrieved December 12, 2008, from http:www.womensenews.org/article.cfm?aid=3828

Angier, N. (1999). *Woman: An intimate geography*. Boston: Houghton Mifflin.

Ansari, S. (2012, January 24). Aboriginal groups warily watch Canada brothel law. Retrieved from http://www.womensenews.org/print/8931

Antonarakis, E., & Eisenberger, M. (2011). Expanding treatment options for metastatic prostate cancer. *New England Journal of Medicine, 364*, 2055–2058.

Apantaku-Olajide, T., Gibbons, P., & Higgins, A. (2011). Drug-induced sexual dysfunction and mental health patients' attitude to psychotropic medications. *Sexual and Relationship Therapy, 26*, 145–155.

Apel, S. (2011). Why compensating surrogate mothers is the right thing to do. *Hastings Center Report, 41*, 1.

Apfelbaum, B. (2000). Retarded ejaculation: A much misunderstood syndrome. In S. Leiblum & R. Rosen (Eds.), *Principles and practice of sex therapy*. New York: Guilford Press.

Apodaca, T., & Moser, N. (2011). The use and abuse of prescription medication to facilitate or enhance sexual behavior among adolescents. *Nature, 89*, 22–24.

Aponte, R., & Machado, M. (2006). Marital aspects associated with sexual satisfaction. *Journal of Sexual Medicine, 3*, 382–452.

Ards, A. (2000, June/July). Dating and mating. *Ms., 10*.

Arevalo, M., Jenning, V., & Sinai, I. (2002). Efficacy of a new method of family planning: The standard days method. *Contraception, 65*, 333–338.

Argiolas, A. (1999). Neuropeptides and sexual behavior. *Neuroscience Biobehavioral Review, 23*, 1127–1142.

Arndt, W. (1991). *Gender disorders and the paraphilias*. Madison, CT: International Universities Press.

Arnon, S., Shamai, S., & Ilatov, Z. (2008). Socialization agents and activities of young adolescents. *Adolescence, 43*, 373–397.

Arnow, B., Desmond, J., Banner, L., Glover, G., et al. (2002). Brain activation and sexual arousal in healthy, heterosexual males. *Brain, 125*, 1014–1023.

Artyk, N. (2008). Muslim feminists confront a world of obstacles. Retrieved December 9, 2008, from http://www.womensenews.org/article.cfm?aid=3412

Arusha, I. (2008, January 19). Women and polygamy: A controversial issue. Retrieved January 28, 2008, from http://allafrica.com/stories/printable/200801210535.html

Asexual Visibility and Education Network. (2009). Overview. Retrieved January 13, 2009, from http://www.asexuality.org/home/overview.html

Ashby, S., Arcari, C., & Edmonson, M. (2006). Television viewing and risk of sexual initiation by young adolescents. *Archives of Pediatric Adolescent Medicine, 160*, 375–380.

Aspelmeier, J., & Kerns, K. (2003). Love and school: Attachment/exploration dynamics in college. *Journal of Social and Personal Relationships, 20*, 5–30.

Athanasiou, R., Shaver, P., & Tavris, C. (1970, July). Sex. *Psychology Today*, 39–52.

Atkins, D., Yi, J., Baucom, D., & Christensen, A. (2005). Infidelity in couples seeking marital therapy. *Journal of Family Psychology, 19*, 470–473.

Aubin, S., Heiman, J., Berger, R., Murally, V., & Yung-Wen, L. (2009). Comparing sildenafil alone vs. sildenafil plus brief couple sex therapy on erectile dysfunction and couples' sexual and marital quality of life: A pilot study. *Journal of Sex and Marital Therapy, 35*, 122–143.

Austoni, E., & Guarneri, G. (1999). Penile elongation and thickening: A myth? Is there a cosmetic or medical indication? *Andrologia, 31*(Suppl. 1), 45–51.

Auvert, B., Sobngwi-Tambekou, J., Puren, A., et al. (2008, August). *Effect of male circumcision on human papillomavirus, neisseria gonorrhoeae and trichomonas vaginalis infections in men: Results from a randomized controlled trial.* Paper presented at the 17th International AIDS Conference, Mexico City, Mexico. Retrieved November 9, 2008, from http://www.aids2008.org/Pag/Abstracts.aspx?SID=288&AID=15881

Auvert, B., Taljaard, D., et al. (2005, July). *Impact of male circumcision on the female-to-male transmission of HIV: Results of the intervention trial: ANRS 1265.* Paper presented at the IAS Conference on HIV Pathogenesis and Treatment, Rio de Janeiro, Brazil.

Avis, N., Stellato, R., & Crawford, S. (2001). Is there a menopausal syndrome? Menopausal status and symptoms across racial/ethnic groups. *Social Science and Medicine, 52,* 345–356.

Ayres, M., & Haddock, S. (2009). Therapists' approaches in working with heterosexual couples struggling with male partners' online sexual behaviors. *Sexual Addiction and Compulsivity, 16,* 55–78.

Aziz, Y., & Gurgen, F. (2009). Marital satisfaction, sexual problems, and the possible difficulties on sex therapy in traditional Islamic culture. *Journal of Sex and Marital Therapy, 35,* 68–75.

Baba, S., et al. (2011). Risk factors of early spontaneous abortions among Japanese: A matched case-control study. *Human Reproduction, 26,* 466–472.

Baber, R. (2011). Breast cancer in postmenopausal women after hormone therapy. *Journal of the American Medical Association, 305,* 466.

Backus, F., & Mahalik, J. (2011). The masculinity of Mr. Right: Feminist identity and heterosexual women's ideal romantic partners. *Psychology of Women Quarterly, 35,* 318–326.

Bacon, C., Mittleman, M., Kawachi, I., & Giovannucci, E. (2006). A prospective study of risk factors for erectile dysfunction. *Journal of Urology, 176,* 217–221.

Bacon, J. (2012, May 16). Home tests for HIV may be on horizon. *USA Today,* p. 7a.

Badgett, L. & Herman, J. (2011, November 9). Patterns of relationship recognition by same-sex couples in the United States. Retrieved from http://williamsinstitute.law.ucla.edu/research/marriage-and-couples-rights/patterns-of-relationship-recognition-by-same-sex-couples-in-the-united-states/

Bagley, C., Bolitho, F., & Bertrand, L. (1997). Sexual assault in school, mental health and suicidal behaviors in adolescent women in Canada. *Adolescence, 32,* 361–366.

Bahrick, A. (2008). Persistence of sexual dysfunction side effects after discontinuation of antidepressant medications: Emerging evidence. *Open Psychology, 1,* 42–50.

Bailey, J., et al. (1991). A study of male sexual orientation. *Archives of General Psychiatry, 48,* 1089–1096.

Bailey, J., et al. (1993). Heritable factors influence sexual orientation in women. *Archives of General Psychiatry, 50,* 217–223.

Bailey, J., Dunne, M., & Martin, N. (2000). Genetic and environmental influences on sexual orientation and its correlates in an Australian twin sample. *Journal of Personality and Social Psychology, 78,* 524–536.

Bailey, J., & Triea, K. (2007). What many transgender activists don't want you to know: And why you should know it anyway. *Perspectives in Biology and Medicine, 50,* 52–65.

Bailey, J., Willerman, L., & Parks, C. (1991). A test of the maternal stress theory of human male homosexuality. *Archives of Sexual Behavior, 20,* 277–293.

Bailey, R., Egesah, O., & Rosenberg, S. (2008). Male circumcision for HIV prevention: A prospective study of complications in clinical and traditional settings in Bungoma, Kenya. *Bulletin of the World Health Organization, 86,* 669–677.

Bailey, R., Moses, S., Parker, C., et al. (2007). Male circumcision for HIV prevention in young men in Kisumu, Kenya: A randomized controlled trial. *Lancet, 369,* 643–656.

Baines, S. (2006, January 26). Articles of faith. Retrieved May 24, 2006, from http://www.advocate.com/print_article_ektid24859.asp

Balaji, A., Lowry, R., Brener, N., et al. (2008). Trends in HIV- and STD-related risk behaviors among high school students—United States, 1991–2007. *Morbidity and Mortality Weekly Report, 57,* 817–822.

Baldaro-Verde, J., Catania, L., & Puppo, V. (2007, April 15–19). *Pleasure and orgasm in women with female genital mutilation.* Paper presented at the 18th Congress of the World Association for Sexual Health, Sydney, Australia.

Ball, H. (2005). Extensive genital cutting elevates risk of infertility among Sudanese women. *International Family Planning Perspectives, 31,* 154–156.

Ball, H. (2011). Chlamydia and gonorrhea infection may be associated with poor birth outcomes. *Perspectives on Sexual and Reproductive Health, 43,* 132–133.

Balon, R. (2008). The DSM criteria of sexual dysfunction: Need for a change. *Journal of Sex and Marital Therapy, 34,* 186–197.

Balon, R., & Segraves, R. (2008). Survey of treatment practices for sexual dysfunction(s) associated with anti-depressants. *Journal of Sex and Marital Therapy, 34,* 353–365.

Balsam, K., et al. (2011). Sexual revictimization and mental health: A comparison of lesbians, gay men, and heterosexual women. *Journal of Interpersonal Violence, 26,* 1798–1814.

Balsam, K., Beauchaine, T., Rothblum, E., & Solomon, S. (2008). Three-year follow-up of same-sex couples who had civil unions in Vermont, same-sex couples not in civil unions, and heterosexual married couples. *Developmental Psychology, 44,* 102–116.

Bancroft, J. (2002). The medicalization of female sexual dysfunction: The need for caution. *Archives of Sexual Behavior, 31,* 451–455.

Bancroft, J. (Ed.) (2003). *Sexual development in childhood.* Bloomington: Indiana University Press.

Bancroft, J., & Graham, C. (2011). The varied nature of women's sexuality: Unresolved issues and a theoretical approach. *Hormones and Behavior, 59,* 717–729.

Bancroft, J., Herbenick, D., & Reynolds, M. (2003). Masturbation as a marker of sexual development. In J. Bancroft (Ed.), *Sexual development in childhood.* Bloomington: Indiana University Press.

Bancroft, J., Loftus, J., & Long, J. (2003). Distress about sex: A national survey of women in heterosexual relationships. *Archives of Sexual Behavior, 32,* 193–209.

Bancroft, J., Long, J., & McCabe, J. (2011). Sexual well-being: A comparison of U.S. Black and White women in heterosexual relationships. *Archives of Sexual Behavior, 40,* 725–740.

Bancroft, J., & Vukadinovic, Z. (2004). Sexual addiction, sexual compulsivity, sexual impulsivity, or what? Toward a theoretical model. *Journal of Sex Research, 41,* 225–234.

Banerjee, N. (2006, June 19). Episcopal Church picks woman as leader. *Oregonian,* pp. A1, A6.

Barbach, L. (1975). *For yourself: The fulfillment of female sexuality.* Garden City, NY: Doubleday.

Barbach, L. (1982). *For each other: Sharing intimacy.* New York: Anchor Press/Doubleday.

Barbaree, H., Marshall, W., & Lanthier, R. (1979). Deviant sexual arousal in rapists. *Behavior Research and Therapy, 17,* 215–222.

Barclay, L. (2010). Commentary on the National Survey of Sexual Health and Behavior (NSSHB). *Journal of Sexual Medicine, 7*(Suppl. 5), 253–254.

Bardoni, B., Zanaria, E., Guioli, S., et al. (1994). A dosage sensitive locus at chromosome Xp21 is involved in male to female sex reversal. *Nature Genetics, 7,* 497–501.

Baredis, D., et al. (2011). An assessment of positive illusions of the physical attractiveness of romantic partners. *Journal of Social and Personal Relationships, 298,* 706–719.

Barfield, R., Wilson, C., & McDonald, P. (1975). Sexual behavior: Extreme reduction of postejaculatory refractory period by midbrain lesions in male rats. *Science, 189,* 147–149.

Barker, R. (1987). *The green-eyed marriage: Surviving jealous relationships.* New York: Free Press.

Barnack-Tavlaris, J. (2011). Psychological adjustment among women living with genital herpes. *Journal of Health Psychology, 16,* 12–21.

Barnard, A. (2008, January 15). MySpace agrees to lead fight to stop sex predators. *New York Times,* p. B3.

Barnard, C. (2011). AIDS at 30 holds special peril for under-30s. Retrieved June 12, 2011, from http://www.womensenews.org/story/hivaids/110603/aids-at-30-holds-special-peril-under-30s#

Barnett, R., & Rivers, C. (2012). Female's 'stereotype threat' brain deaths U.S. STEM. Retrieved May 25, 2012, from http://www.womensenews.

Barnhart, K., Furman, I., & Devoto, L. (1995). Attitudes and practice of couples regarding sexual relations during the menses and spotting. *Contraception, 51,* 93–98.

Baron, R., Markman, G., & Bollinger, M. (2006). Exporting social psychology: Effects of attractiveness on perceptions of entrepreneurs, their ideas for new products, and their financial success. *Journal of Applied Social Psychology, 36,* 467–492.

Barot, S. (2009). Reclaiming the lead: Restoring U.S. leadership in global sexual and reproductive health policy. *Guttmacher Policy Review, 12,* 1–15.

Barot, S. (2011). Unsafe abortion: The missing link in global efforts to improve maternal health. *Guttmacher Policy Review, 14,* 24–38.

Barrett, G., Pendry, E., & Peacock, J. (2000). Women's sexual health after childbirth. *British Journal of Gynecology, 107,* 186–195.

Bartels, A., & Zeki, S. (2004). The neural correlates of maternal and romantic love. *Neuroimage, 21,* 1155–1166.

Bartlett, J., Branson, B., Fenton, K., et al. (2008). Opt-out testing for human immunodeficiency virus in the United States. *Journal of the American Medical Association, 300,* 945–951.

Basoff, E., & Glass, G. (1982). The relationship between sex roles and mental health: A meta-analysis of twenty-six studies. *Counseling Psychologist, 10,* 105–112.

Basow, S., & Rubenfeld, K. (2003). Troubles talk: Effects of gender and gender-typing. *Sex Roles, 48,* 183–187.

Basrow, S., & Minieri, A. (2011). "You owe me": Effects of date cost, who pays, participant gender, and rape myth beliefs on perceptions of rape. *Journal of Interpersonal Violence, 26,* 479–497.

Basson, R. (2002). A model of women's sexual arousal. *Journal of Sex and Marital Therapy, 28,* 1–10.

Basson, R. (2009, January). Persistent genital arousal disorder. Retrieved May 19, 2009, from http://www.merck.com/mmpe/sec18/ch251/ch251g.html

Basson, R., Leiblum, S., Brotto, L., & Derogatis, L. (2004). Revised definitions of women's sexual dysfunction. *Journal of Sexual Medicine, 1,* 40–48.

Basson, R., Leiblum, S., Brotto, L., Derogatis, L., Fourcroy, J., et al. (2003). Definitions of women's sexual dysfunction reconsidered: Advocating expansion and revision. *Journal of Psychosomatic Obstetrics and Gynecology, 24,* 221–229.

Bastian, L., Smith, C., & Nanda, K. (2003). Is this woman perimenopausal? *Journal of the American Medical Association, 289,* 895–901.

Bates, B. (2010). Surrogacy faces challenges in U.S., other nations. *OB GYN News, 45,* 38–39.

Battaglia, C., Nappi, R., Mancini, F., Cianciosi, A., & Persico, N. (2008). Menstrual cycle–related morphometric and vascular modifications of the clitoris. *Journal of Sexual Medicine, 5,* 2853–2861.

Bauman, R., Kasper, C., & Alford, J. (1984). The child sex abusers. *Corrective and Social Psychiatry, 30,* 76–81.

Baumeister, R. (1988). Masochism as escape from self. *Journal of Sex Research, 25,* 28–59.

Baumeister, R. (1997). The enigmatic appeal of sexual masochism: Why people desire pain, bondage, and humiliation in sex. *Journal of Social and Clinical Psychology, 16,* 133–150.

Baumeister, R., Catanese, K., & Wallace, H. (2002). Conquest by force: A narcissistic reactance theory of rape and sexual coercion. *Review of General Psychology, 6,* 92–135.

Baumeister, R., & Leary, M. (1995). The need to belong: Desire for interpersonal attachments as a fundamental human motivation. *Psychological Bulletin, 11,* 497–529.

Baumgardner, J. (2007, October 9). Lesbian after marriage. *Advocate,* 40–43.

Baumgardner, J. (2008, February 26). Objects of suspicion. *Advocate,* 24–27.

Bauminger, N., Finzi-Dottan, R., et al. (2008). Intimacy in adolescent friendship: The roles of attachment, coherence, and self-disclosure. *Journal of Social and Personal Relationships, 25,* 409–428.

Baur, K. (1995). Socioeconomic and personality traits of nonadjudicated child sex offenders in a clinical practice. Unpublished.

Bayer, R., & Oppenheimer, G. (2011). Routine HIV screening—What counts in evidence-based policy. *New England Journal of Medicine, 365,* 1265–1268.

Beach, F. (Ed.) (1978). *Human sexuality in four perspectives.* Baltimore: Johns Hopkins University Press.

Beal, G., & Muehlenhard, C. (1987, November). *Getting sexually aggressive men to stop their advances: Information for rape prevention programs.* Paper presented at the Annual Meeting of the Association for Advancement of Behavior Therapy, Boston, MA.

Beck, C. (2006). Postpartum depression: It isn't just the blues. *American Journal of Nursing, 106,* 40–49.

Beck, M. (1999). The pornographic tradition: Formative influences in sixteenth- to nineteenth-century European literature. In J. Elias, V. Elias, V. Bullough, et al. (Eds.), *Porn 101: Eroticism, pornography, and the First Amendment.* Amherst, NY: Prometheus Books.

Becker, E. (2000, May 12). Women in military say silence on harassment protects careers. *New York Times,* p. A1.

Becker, J., Berkley, K., et al. (2008). *Sex differences in the brain: From genes to behavior.* New York: Oxford University Press.

Becker, J., & Kaplan, M. (1991). Rape victims: Issues, theories, and treatment. *Annual Review of Sex Research, 2,* 267–272.

Becker, J., Skinner, L., Abel, G., & Axelrod, R. (1986). Level of postassault sexual functioning in rape and incest victims. *Archives of Sexual Behavior, 15,* 37–49.

Beckman, N., Waern, M., & Skoog, I. (2006). Determinants of sexuality in 70-year-olds. *Journal of Sex Research, 43,* 876.

Beech, H. (2005, December). Sex, please—We're young and Chinese. *Time,* 61.

Begala, P. (2012, January 1). The GOP's suicidal tendency. *Newsweek*, 6.

Begley, S. (2001, January 22). Brave new monkey. *Newsweek*, 50–52.

Begley, S. (2010, July 2). The anti-lesbian drug. Retrieved from http://www.newsweek.com/2010/07/02/the-anti-lesbian-drug

Beil, L. (2009, March). Single, pregnant and panicked. *Self*, 174–179.

Beji, N. (2003). The effect of pelvic floor training on sexual function. *Nursing Standard*, 16, 33–36.

Beksinska, M., et al. (2011). Female condom technology: New products and regulatory issues. *Contraception*, 83, 316–321.

Bell, A., & Weinberg, M. (1978). *Homosexualities: A study of diversity among men and women*. New York: Simon and Schuster.

Bell, A., Weinberg, M., & Hammersmith, S. (1981). *Sexual preference: Its development in men and women*. Bloomington: Indiana University Press.

Bell, D. (2006, July 10). "They deserve it." *Nation*, pp. 18–24.

Bell, H., Thanel, F., & Huntington, M. (2012). Infertility: Help for couples starts with you. *Journal of Family Practice*, 61, 82–88.

Bellizzi, K., & Blank, T. (2006). Predicting posttraumatic growth in breast cancer survivors. *Health Psychology*, 25, 47–56.

Belluck, P. (2011, July 23). Scientific advances on contraceptive for men. Retrieved from http://www.nytimes.com/2011/07/24/health/research/24contraception.html

Belshe, R., et al. (2012). Efficacy results of a trial of a herpes simplex vaccine. *New England Journal of Medicine*, 366, 34–43.

Belzer, E., Whipple, B., & Moger, W. (1984). A female ejaculation. *Journal of Sex Research*, 20, 403–406.

Bem, S. (1975). Sex role adaptability: One consequence of psychological androgyny. *Journal of Personality and Social Psychology*, 31, 634–643.

Bem, S. (1993). *The lenses of gender*. New Haven, CT: Yale University Press.

Benda, W. (2008, May). Compound fractures: The battle between Wyeth Pharmaceuticals and the compounding industry over bioidentical hormones. *Townsend Letter*, 100–103.

Bendavid, E., Avila, P., & Miller, G. (2011, September 27). United States aid policy and induced abortion in sub-Saharan Africa. Retrieved from http://www.who.int/bulletin/volumes/89/12/11-091660/en/

Ben-David, S., & Schneider, O. (2005). Rape perceptions, gender role attitudes, and victim-perpetrator acquaintance. *Sex Roles: A Journal of Research*, 53, 385–399.

Bennett, J., & Ellison, J. (2010, June 21). "I don't": The case against marriage. *Newsweek*, 42–44.

Bennett, W. (1996, June 3). Leave marriage alone. *Newsweek*, 27.

Bennetts, L. (2011, July 25). The John next door. *Newsweek*, 60–63.

Bennion, J. (2005, July 19). Rough cut: The women's kingdom. Retrieved June 28, 2006, from http://www.pbs.org/frontlineworld/rough/2005/07/introduction_togen.html

Benotsch, E., Kalichman, S., & Cage, M. (2002). Men who have sex partners via the Internet: Prevalence, predictors, and implications for HIV prevention. *Archives of Sexual Behavior*, 31, 177–183.

Benson, E. (2003). The science of sexual arousal. *Monitor on Psychology*, 34, 50–52.

Benson, R. (1985). Vacuum cleaner injury to penis: A common urologic problem? *Urology*, 25, 41–44.

Bentz, E., et al. (2008). A polymorphism of the CYP17 gene related to sex steroid metabolism is associated with female-to-male but not male-to-female transsexualism. *Fertility and Sterility*, 90, 56–59.

Benuto, L., & Meana, M. (2008). Acculturation and sexuality: Investigating gender differences in erotic plasticity. *Journal of Sex Research*, 45, 217–224.

Ben-Ze'ev, A. (2003). Privacy, emotional closeness, and openness in cyberspace. *Computers in Human Behavior*, 19, 451–467.

Ben-Ze'ev, A. (2004). *Love online: Emotions on the Internet*. Cambridge, UK: Cambridge University Press.

Berdahl, J., & Aquino, K. (2009). Sexual behavior at work: Fun or folly? *Journal of Applied Psychology*, 94, 34–47.

Berenson, A., Odom, S., Breitkopf, C., & Rahman, M. (2008). Physiologic and psychologic symptoms associated with use of injectable contraception and 20 mg oral contraceptive pills. *American Journal of Obstetrics and Gynecology*, 199, 351–362.

Berenson, A., & Rahman, M. (2009). Changes in weight, total fat, percent body fat, and central-to-peripheral fat ratio associated with injectable and oral contraceptive use. *American Journal of Obstetrics and Gynecology*, 200, 328–406.

Berer, M. (2007). Male circumcision for HIV prevention: Perspectives on gender and sexuality. *Reproductive Health Matters*, 15, 45–48.

Berer, M. (2008). Male circumcision for HIV prevention: What about protecting men's partners? *Reproductive Health Matters*, 16, 171–175.

Berga, S., & McCord, J. (2005). Circulating androgen levels and self-reported sexual function in women. *OB/GYN Clinical Alert*, August 1.

Berger, R. (1996). *Gay and gray: The older homosexual man*. New York: Haworth Press.

Bergeron, S. (2009, June 21–25). *The treatment of dyspareunia in women*. Paper presented at the 19th WAS World Congress for Sexual Health, Göteborg, Sweden.

Bergman, M. (2006, May 25). Americans marrying older, living alone more, see households shrinking, Census Bureau reports. Retrieved July 15, 2009, from http://www.census.gov/Press-Release/www/releases/archives/families_households/006840

Bergoffen, D. (2006). From genocide to justice: Women's bodies as a legal writing pad. *Feminist Studies*, 32, 11–37.

Bergstrom, R., Neighbors, C., & Malheim, J. (2009). Media comparisons and threats to body image: Seeking evidence of self-affirmation. *Journal of Social and Clinical Psychology*, 28, 264–280.

Berkley, S. (2010, December 1). Medical gains hit financial roadblocks. *Honolulu Star Advertiser*, pp. A14, A15.

Berkman, C., Turner, S., & Cooper, M. (2000). Sexual contact with clients: Assessment of social workers' attitudes and educational preparation. *Social Work*, 45, 223–235.

Berliner, L., & Conte, J. (1995). The effects of disclosure and intervention on sexually abused children. *Child Abuse and Neglect*, 27, 525–540.

Berman, J., & Berman, L. (2005). *For women only: A revolutionary guide to overcoming sexual dysfunction and reclaiming your sex life*. New York: Henry Holt.

Berman, L. (2004). *The health benefits of sexual aids and devices*. Evanston, IL: Northwestern University.

Bernat, J., Calhoun, K., & Adams, H. (1999). Sexually aggressive and nonaggressive men: Sexual arousal and judgments in response to acquaintance rape and consensual analogues. *Journal of Abnormal Psychology*, 108, 662–673.

Bernstein, E., & Schaffner, L. (2005). *Regulating sex: The politics of intimacy and identity*. New York: Routledge.

Berridge, C., & Romich, J. (2011). Raising him to pull his own weight: Boys' household work in single-mother households. *Journal of Family Issues*, 32, 38–45.

Bettelheim, R. (March 6, 2012). The war on sex: The contraception controversy's hidden agenda. Retrieved from http://www.huffingtonpost.com/ruth-bettelheim/the-war-on-sex-the-contra_b_1324716.html

Bhatti, F. (2005, July 10–15). *The role of non-availability of sex education on the prevalence of sexual dysfunction in conservative Muslim society like Pakistan.* Paper presented at the World Congress of Sexology, Montreal, Canada.

Bible, J. (2006). Disorder in the courts: Proving same-sex sex discrimination in Title VII cases via "gender stereotyping." *Employee Relations Law Journal, 31,* 42–72.

Biederman, P. (2003, April 17). For gays, secrecy in love, war. Retrieved April 22, 2003, from http://www.sldn.org/templates/press/record.html?record=882

Bierce, A. (1943). *The devil's dictionary.* New York: World.

Bingham, S., & Battey, K. (2005). Communication of social support to sexual harassment victims: Professors' responses to a student's narrative of unwanted sexual attention. *Communication Studies, 56,* 131–155.

Bingham, S., Luben, R., Welch, A., & Wareham, N. (2003). Are imprecise methods obscuring a relation between fat and breast cancer? *Lancet, 362,* 212–214.

Bird, J., & Voisin, D. (2011). A conceptual model of HIV disclosure in casual sexual encounters among men who have sex with men. *Health Psychology, 18,* 365–373.

Birdeau, D., Somers, C., & Lenihan, G. (2005). Effects of educational strategies on college students' identification of sexual harassment. *Education, 125,* 496–510.

Bissonauth, W., Shatenstein, B., & Ghadirian, P. (2008). Nutrition and breast cancer among sporadic cases and gene mutation carriers: An overview. *Cancer Detection and Prevention.* doi:10.1016/j.cdp.2008.01.005

Bivona, J., & Critelli, J. (2009). The nature of women's rape fantasies: An analysis of prevalence, frequency, and contents. *Journal of Sex Research, 46,* 33–45.

Black, A. (1994). Perverting the diagnosis: The lesbian and the scientific basis of stigma. *Historical Reflections, 20,* 201–216.

Blackburn, R., Cunkelman, J., & Zlidar, V. (2000). Oral contraceptives: An update. *Population Reports, 28,* 1–39.

Blackmun, M. (1996, June 16). Escort services: Look all you want but don't touch. *Oregonian,* pp. D1, D4.

Blair, C., & Lanyon, R. (1981). Exhibitionism: Etiology and treatment. *Psychological Bulletin, 89,* 439–463.

Blanchard, R. (1991). Clinical observations and systematic studies of autogynephilia. *Journal of Sex and Marital Therapy, 17,* 235–251.

Blanchard, R. (1995). Early history of the concept of autogynephilia. *Archives of Sexual Behavior, 34,* 439–446.

Blank, H. (2007). *Virgin: The untouched history.* New York: Bloomsbury U.S.A.

Bleakley, A., Hennessy, M., & Fishbein, M. (2011). A model of adolescents seeking sexual content in their media choices. *Journal of Sex Research, 48,* 309–315.

Blee, K., & Tickamyer, A. (1995). Racial differences in men's attitudes about women's gender roles. *Journal of Marriage and Family, 57,* 21–30.

Bloche, M. (2004). Health care disparities: Science, politics, and race. *New England Journal of Medicine, 350,* 1568–1570.

Block, S. (2006). *Rape and sexual power in early America.* Chapel Hill: University of North Carolina Press.

Blue, V. (2003). *The ultimate guide to adult videos: How to watch adult videos and make your sex life sizzle.* San Francisco, CA: Cleis Press.

Blue, V. (2007). *The smart girl's guide to the G-spot.* San Francisco, CA: Cleis Press.

Blumenthal, H., et al. (2011). Elevated social anxiety among early maturing girls. *Developmental Psychology, 47,* 1133–1140.

Blumenthal, P., Gemzell-Danielsson, K., & Marintcheva-Petrova, M. (2008). Tolerability and clinical safety of Implanon. *European Journal of Contraception and Reproductive Health Care, 13,* 29–36.

Blythe, M., Fortenberry, D., Temkit, M., & Tu, W. (2006). Incidence and correlates of unwanted sex in relationships of middle and late adolescent women. *Archives of Pediatric and Adolescent Medicine, 160,* 591–595.

Bockting, W. (2005). Biological reductionism meets gender diversity in human sexuality. *Journal of Sex Research, 42,* 267–270.

Bockting, W., et al. (2011). Care of transsexual persons. *New England Journal of Medicine, 364,* 2559–2560.

Boekhout, B., Hendrick, S., & Hendrick, C. (1999). Relationship infidelity: A loss of perspective. *Journal of Personal and Interpersonal Loss, 4,* 97–124.

Boeringer, S. (1994). Pornography and sexual aggression: Association of violent and nonviolent depictions with rape and rape proclivity. *Deviant Behavior: An Interdisciplinary Journal, 15,* 289–304.

Bogaert, A. (2004). Asexuality: Prevalence and associated factors in a national probability sample. *Journal of Sex Research, 41,* 279–288.

Bogaert, A. (2005). Sibling sex ratio and sexual orientation in men and women: New tests in two national probability samples. *Archives of Sexual Behavior, 34,* 111–117.

Bogaert, A., Friesen, C., & Klentrou, P. (2002). Age of puberty and sexual orientation in a national probability sample. *Archives of Sexual Behavior, 31,* 73–81.

Bogart, L., Collins, R., Kanovse, D., et al. (2006). Patterns and correlates of deliberate abstinence among men and women with HIV/AIDS. *American Journal of Public Health, 96,* 1078–1084.

Bogren, L. (1991). Changes in sexuality in women and men during pregnancy. *Archives of Sexual Behavior, 20,* 35–46.

Bohner, G., Siebler, F., & Schmelcher, J. (2006). Social norms and the likelihood of raping: Perceived rape myth acceptance of others affects men's rape proclivity. *Personality and Social Psychology Bulletin, 32,* 286–297.

Bolan, G., et al. (2012). The emerging threat of untreatable gonococcal infections. *New England Journal of Medicine, 366,* 485–487.

Bolin, A. (1997). Transforming transvestism and transsexualism: Polarity, politics, and gender. In B. Bullough, V. Bullough, and J. Elias (Eds.), *Gender blending.* New York: Prometheus Books.

Bolton, S., & Sareen, J. (2011). Sexual orientation and its relation to mental disorders and suicide attempts: Findings from a nationally representative sample. *Canadian Journal of Psychiatry, 56,* 35–43.

Bolus, J. (1994). Teaching teens about condoms. *Registered Nurse,* March, 44–47.

Bond, J. (2006, October 10). Deadly homophobia. *Advocate,* 4.

Bonet, L., Bimbi, D., & Tomassilli, J. (2006). Behind closed doors: An exploration of specialized sexual behaviors in urban women who have sex with women. *Journal of Sex Research,* February.

Bonierbale, M., Clement, A., Loundou, A., & Simeoni, M. (2006). A new evaluation of concept and its measurement: "Male sexual anticipating cognitions." *Journal of Sexual Medicine, 3,* 96–103.

Boonstra, H., Gold, R., Richards, C., & Finer, L. (2006). *Abortion in women's lives.* New York: Guttmacher Institute.

Boonstra, H., & Sonfield, A. (2000). Rights without access: Revisiting public funding of abortion for poor women. *Guttmacher Report, 3,* 1–5.

Borg, C., deJong, P., & Schultz, W. (2011). Vaginismus and dyspaurenia: Relationship with general and sex-related moral standards. *Journal of Sexual Medicine, 8,* 223–231.

Bornstein, R. (1989). Exposure and effect: Overview and meta-analysis of research, 1968–1987. *Psychological Bulletin, 106*, 265–289.

Borowsky, I., Ireland, M., & Resnick, M. (2009). Health status and behavioral outcomes for youth who anticipate a high likelihood of early death. *Pediatrics, 124*, e81–e88.

Bos, H., & van Balen, F. (2008). Children in planned lesbian families: Stigmatization, psychological adjustment and protective factors. *Culture, Health and Sexuality, 10*, 221–236.

Bos, H., van Balen, F., Gartrell, N., Peyser, H., & Sandfort, T. (2008). Children in planned lesbian families: A cross-cultural comparison between the United States and the Netherlands. *American Journal of Orthopsychiatry, 78*, 211–219.

Boschert, S. (2004). Majority of circumcisions are performed without analgesia. *Family Practice News, 34*, 63.

Boss, S., & Maltz, W. (2001). *Private thoughts: Exploring the power of women's sexual fantasies*. Novato, CA: New World Library.

Boston Women's Health Book Collective. (1971). *Our bodies, ourselves*. Boston, MA: New England Free Press.

Boswell, J. (1980). *Christianity, social tolerance, and homosexuality*. Chicago: University of Chicago Press.

Botros, S., Abramov, Y., Miller, J., & Sand, P. (2006). Effect of parity on sexual function. *Obstetrics and Gynecology, 107*, 765–770.

Boulet, S., Yang, Q., Mai, C., & Kirby, R. (2008). Trends in the postfortification prevalence of spina bifida and anencephaly in the United States. *Clinical and Molecular Teratology, 82*, 527–532.

Bourdeau, B., Thomas, V., & Long, J. (2008). Latino sexual styles: Developing a nuanced understanding of risk. *Journal of Sex Research, 45*, 71–81.

Boustany, N. (2007, July 4). Militants use rape as integral weapon in Darfur. *Oregonian*, p. A5.

Bouvier, P. (2003). Child sexual abuse: Vicious circles of fate or paths to resilience? *Lancet, 361*, 446.

Bowater, D. (2011, December 16). Pornography is replacing sex education. Retrieved from http://.telegraph.co.uk/news/8961010/Pornography-is-replacing-sex-education.html

Bowen, A. (2005). Internet sexuality research with rural men who have sex with men: Can we recruit and retain them? *Journal of Sex Research, 42*, 317–323.

Bowling, L. (2011). HIV prevention efforts mired in patient denial, physician discomfort. *AIDS Alert*, February 1.

Bowman, J. (2008). Gender-role orientation and relational closeness: Self-disclosure behavior in same-sex male friendships. *Journal of Men's Studies, 16*, 316–330.

Boyd, R. (2009, January 14). New estimates for IVF live birth rates. Retrieved April 22, 2009, from http://www.webmd.com/infertility-and-reproduction/news/20090114/new-estimates-for-ivf

Boyer, S., et al. (2011). Non-adherence to antiretroviral treatment and unplanned treatment interruption among people living with HIV/AIDS in Cameroon. *Social Science and Medicine, 72*, 1383–1392.

Boynton, P. (2003). "I'm just a girl who can't say no"? Women, consent, and sex research. *Journal of Sex and Marital Therapy, 29*(Suppl.), 23–32.

Bradford, J. (1998). Treatment of men with paraphilia. *New England Journal of Medicine, 338*, 464–465.

Bradford, J., Boulet, J., & Pawlak, A. (1992). The paraphilias: A multiplicity of deviant behaviors. *Canadian Journal of Psychiatry, 37*, 104–107.

Bradley, H., et al. (2012). Prevalence of *Neisseria gonorrhoeae* infections among men and women entering the National Job Training Programs—United States, 2004–2009. *Sexually Transmitted Diseases, 39*, 49–54.

Bradley, S., Oliver, G., Chernick, A., & Zucker, K. (1998). Experiment of nurture: Ablatio penis at 2 months, sex reassignment at 7 months, and a psychosexual follow-up in young adulthood. *Pediatrics, 102*, E91–E95.

Bradley, S., & Zucker, K. (1997). Gender identity disorder: A review of the past 10 years. *Journal of the American Academy of Child and Adolescent Psychology, 36*, 872–880.

Bradshaw, C. (1994). Asian and Asian American women: Historical and political considerations in psychotherapy. In L. Comas-Diaz & B. Greene (Eds.), *Women of color*. New York: Guilford Press.

Brady, S., & Halpern-Felsher, B. (2007). Adolescents' reported consequences of having oral sex versus vaginal sex. *Pediatrics, 119*, 29–236.

Braen, G. (1980). Examination of the accused: The heterosexual and homosexual rapist. In C. Warner (Ed.), *Rape and sexual assault*. Germantown, MD: Aspen Systems.

Brainerd, C., & Reyna, V. (1998). When things that were never experienced are easier to "remember" than things that were. *Psychological Science, 9*, 484–489.

Brakman, A. (2011). Teen topic: Emergency contraception changes may benefit teens. *Contraceptive Technology Update*, February 1.

Brandes, M., et al. (2011). Unexplained infertility: Overall ongoing pregnancy rate and mode of conception. *Human Reproduction, 26*, 360–368.

Brehm, S., Miller, R., Perlman, D., & Campbell, S. (2002). *Intimate relationships*. Boston: McGraw-Hill.

Bremer, J. (1959). *Asexualization*. New York: Macmillan.

Brewer, D., Golden, M., & Handsfield, H. (2006). Unsafe sexual behavior and correlates of risk in a probability sample of men who have sex with men in the era of highly active antiretroviral therapy. *Sexually Transmitted Diseases, 33*, 250–255.

Brewer G., & Hendrie, C. (2011). Evidence to suggest that copulatory vocalizations in women are not a reflexive consequence of orgasm. *Archives of Sexual Behavior, 40*, 559–564.

Brewster, A. (2012). Commentary: How I talk about sex with my kids. Retrieved May 22, 2012, from *http://commonhealth.wbur.org/2012/05/sex-talk-kids*.

Briddell, D., & Wilson, G. (1976). Effects of alcohol and expectancy set on male sexual arousal. *Journal of Abnormal Psychology, 85*, 225–234.

Bridges, A. (2006, July 19). FDA approves contraceptive implant. *Oregonian*, p. A4.

Bringle, R., & Buunk, B. (1991). Extradyadic relationships and sexual jealousy. In K. McKinney & S. Sprecher (Eds.), *Sexuality in close relationships*. Hillsdale, NJ: Erlbaum.

Brinker, N. (2009, December 29). Debating mammograms. *Newsweek*, 20.

Brinton, L., Sherman, M., & Carreon, J. (2008). Recent trends in breast cancer among younger women in the United States. *Journal of the National Cancer Institute, 100*, 1643–1648.

Britton, G., & Lumpkin, M. (1984). Battle to imprint for the 21st century. *Reading Teacher, 37*, 724–733.

Brockman, J. (2006, April 5). Child sex as Internet fare, through eyes of a victim. *New York Times*, p. A20.

Brody, J. (2000, May 16). Cybersex gives birth to a psychological disorder. *New York Times*, pp. F7, F12.

Brooks, J., & Watkins, M. (1989). Recognition memory and the mere exposure effect. *Journal of Experimental Psychology: Learning, Memory, and Cognition, 15*, 968–976.

Brossman, S. (2008). Penile cancer. Retrieved October 31, 2008, from http://www.emedicine.com/med/topic3046.htm

Brotto, L., Chik, H., Ryder, A., & Gorzalka, B. (2005). Acculturation and sexual function in Asian women. *Archives of Sexual Behavior, 34,* 613–627.

Brotto, L., & Yule, M. (2011). Physiological and subjective sexual arousal in self-identified asexual women. *Archives of Sexual Behavior, 40,* 699–712.

Brousseau, M., et al. (2010). Sexual coercion victimization and perpetration in heterosexual couples: A dyadic investigation. *Archives of Sexual Behavior, 40,* 363–372.

Brown, A. (2011). Relationships, community, and identity in the new virtual society. *Futurist, 45,* 29–33.

Brown, D. (2006, April 5). GAO faults Bush's AIDS-abstinence emphasis. *Oregonian,* p. A2.

Brown, D. (2010, November 24). Annual report: Progress made against AIDS. *Oregonian,* p. A9.

Brown, D. (2011, December 1). Only 28% of Americans with HIV get best treatment. *Oregonian,* p. A4.

Brown, E. (2008, May 14). New vaginal ring offers nonhormonal contraception. Retrieved May 19, 2008, from http://www.docguide.com/news/content.nsf/NewsPrint/852571020057CCF685257449D

Brown, J., & L'Engle, K. (2008). X-rated: Sexual attitudes and behaviors associated with U.S. early adolescents' exposure to sexually explicit media. *Journal of Geriatric Psychiatry and Neurology,* December 10.

Brown, M., Perry, A., Cheesman, A., & Pring, T. (2000). Pitch change in male-to-female transsexuals: Has phonosurgery a role to play? *International Journal of Language and Communications Disorders, 35,* 129–136.

Brown, R. (2000). Understanding the disorders of sexual preference. *Practitioner, 244,* 438–442.

Brown, S., Brack, G., & Mullis, F. (2008). Traumatic symptoms in sexually abused children: Implications for school counselors. *Professional School Counseling, 11,* 368–379.

Brown, S., Calibuso, M., & Roedl, A. L. (2011). Women's sexuality, well-being, and the menstrual cycle: Methodological issues and their interrelationships. *Archives of Sexual Behavior, 40,* 755–756.

Brown, T., & Fee, E. (2003). Alfred Kinsey: A pioneer of sex research. *American Journal of Public Health, 93,* 896–897.

Brownmiller, S. (1975). *Against our will: Men, women, and rape.* New York: Simon and Schuster.

Brownmiller, S. (1993, January 4). Making female bodies the battlefield. *Newsweek,* 37.

Bruce-Jones, E., & Itaborahy, L. (2011). *State sponsored homophobia.* Brussels, Belgium: International Lesbian, Gay, Bisexual, Trans and Intersex Association.

Bruns, D., & Bruns, J. (2005). Sexual harassment in higher education. *Academic Exchange Quarterly, 9,* 201–204.

Bryan, S. (2011, October 24). New law combats tribal violence. *Oregonian,* p. A6.

Bryant, S., & Demian, N. (1998). Terms of same-sex endearment. *SIECUS Report, 26*(4), 10–13.

Buchanan, N., Settles, I., & Wood, K. (2008). Comparing sexual harassment subtypes among Black and White women by military rank: Double jeopardy, the Jezebel, and the cult of true womanhood. *Psychology of Women Quarterly, 32,* 347–361.

Budin, L., & Johnson, C. (1989). Sex abuse prevention programs: Offenders' attitudes about their efficacy. *Child Abuse and Neglect, 13,* 77–87.

Buffie, W. (2011). Public health implications of same-sex marriage. *American Journal of Public Health, 101,* 986–990.

Bulcroft, R., Carmady, D., & Bulcroft, K. (1996). Patterns of parental independence giving to adolescents: Variations by race, age, and gender of child. *Journal of Marriage and Family, 58,* 866–883.

Bullough, B., & Bullough, V. (1997). Are transvestites necessarily heterosexual? *Archives of Sexual Behavior, 26,* 1–12.

Bullough, V. (2001). Religion, sex, and science: Some historical quandaries. *Journal of Sex Education and Therapy, 26,* 254–258.

Bullough, V., & Bullough, B. (1993). *Cross dressing, sex and gender.* Philadelphia: University of Pennsylvania Press.

Bulun, S. (2009). Endometriosis. *New England Journal of Medicine, 360,* 268–279.

Burdge, B. (2007). Bending gender, ending gender: Theoretical foundations for social work practice with the transgender community. *Social Work, 52,* 243–250.

Bureau of Labor Statistics. (2012). Labor force statistics from the Current Population Survey. Retrieved January 2, 2008, from http://www.stats.bls.gov

Burkett, A., & Hewitt, G. (2005). Progestin only contraceptives and their use in adolescents: Clinical options and medical indications. *Adolescent Medicine, 16,* 553–567.

Burleigh, N. (2012, March 19). This little piggy paid for sex. *New York Observer,* pp. A1–A2.

Burn, S., O'Neil, A., & Nederend, S. (1996). Childhood tomboyism and adult androgyny. *Sex Roles, 34,* 419–428.

Burnette, M., Schneider, R., Timko, C., & Ilgen, M. (2009). Impact of substance-use disorder treatment on women involved in prostitution: Substance use, mental health, and prostitution one year after treatment. *Journal of Studies on Alcohol and Drugs, 70,* 32–41.

Burr, C. (1996, July 23). Gimme shelter. *Advocate,* 37–38.

Burri, A., Cherkas, L., & Spector, T. (2009). Emotional intelligence and its association with orgasmic frequency in women. *Journal of Sexual Medicine,* April 28.

Burri, A., Rahman, Q., & Spector, T. (2011). Genetic and environmental risk factors for sexual distress and its association with female sexual dysfunction. *Psychological Medicine, 41,* 2435–2445.

Bushman, B., & Baumeister, R. (1998). Threatened egoism, narcissism, self-esteem, and direct and displaced aggression: Does self-love or self-hate lead to violence? *Journal of Personality and Social Psychology, 43,* 372–384.

Bushman, B., Bonacci, A., Dijk, M., & Baumeister, R. (2003). Narcissism, sexual refusal, and aggression: Testing a narcissistic reactance model of sexual aggression. *Journal of Personality and Social Psychology, 84,* 1027–1040.

Buss, D. (1994). *The evolution of desire: Strategies of human mating.* New York: Basic Books.

Buss, D. (1999). *Evolutionary psychology: The new science of the mind.* Boston: Allyn and Bacon.

Buss, D. (2000). *The dangerous passion: Why jealousy is as necessary as love and sex.* New York: Free Press.

Butzer, B., & Campbell, L. (2008). Adult attachment, sexual satisfaction, and relationship satisfaction: A study of married couples. *Personal Relationships, 15,* 141–154.

Buysse, A., & Ickes, W. (1999). Communication patterns in laboratory discussions of safer sex between dating versus nondating partners. *Journal of Sex Research, 36,* 121–134.

Byers, E., & Demmons, S. (1999). Sexual satisfaction and sexual self-disclosure within dating relationships. *Journal of Sex Research, 36,* 180–189.

Byers, S. (2011). Beyond the birds and the bees and was it good for you? Thirty years of research on sexual communication. *Canadian Psychology, 52,* 20–28.

Byrd, J., Hyde, J., DeLamater, J., & Plant, E. (1998). Sexuality during pregnancy and the year postpartum. *Journal of Family Practice, 47,* 305–308.

Cado, S., & Leitenberg, H. (1990). Guilt reactions to sexual fantasies during intercourse. *Archives of Sexual Behavior, 19,* 49–71.

Cain, S. (2000). Breast cancer genetics and the role of tamoxifen in prevention. *Journal of the American Academy of Nurse Practitioners, 12,* 21–28.

Caldwell, J. (2003, March 25). The trouble with "gay." Retrieved May 6, 2003, from http://www.advocate.com/html/ stories/886/ 886_sogay.asp

Caldwell, J. (2005, April 12). Sheath that scalpel: The only way to be sure of an intersex baby's gender is to wait until you can ask them, researchers say. *Advocate,* 44.

Califia, P. (2002). Whoring in utopia. In A. Soble (Ed.), *The philosophy of sex: Contemporary readings.* Lanham, MD: Rowman and Littlefield.

Callaway, E. (2009, February 28). Porn in the USA: Conservatives are biggest consumers. Retrieved March 1, 2009, from http://abcnews.go.com/ print?id=6977202

Calzo, J., et al. (2011). Retrospective recall of sexual orientation identity development among gay, lesbian, and bisexual adults. *Developmental Psychology, 47,* 1658–1673.

Campbell, A. (2008). The morning after the night before: Affective reactions to one-night stands among mated and unmated women and men. *Human Nature.* doi:10.1007/s12110-008-9036-2

Campbell, C., & Mzaidume, Z. (2001). Grassroots participation, peer education, and HIV prevention by sex workers in South Africa. *American Journal of Public Health, 91,* 1978–1986.

Campbell, D., Lake, M., Falk, M., & Backstrand, J. (2006). A randomized control trial of continuous support in labor by a lay doula. *Journal of Obstetric, Gynecologic, and Neonatal Nursing, 35,* 456.

Campbell, N., & Schubert, C. (2007). Spontaneous orgasms with Duloxetine and Citalopram in an elderly woman. *Journal of the American Geriatrics Society, 55,* 521–522.

Campbell, R. (2006). Rape survivors' experiences with the legal and medical systems: Do rape victim advocates make a difference? *Violence Against Women, 12,* 30–45.

Campbell, S., Cropsey, K., & Matthews, C. (2007). Intrauterine device use in a high-risk population. *American Journal of Obstetrics and Gynecology, 197,* 193–197.

Campos, S. (2008, February 24). Anterior motives: A G shot on the G spot. *New York Times Magazine,* p. L172.

Camuso, J., & Rellini, A. (2010). Sexual fantasies and sexual arousal in women with a history of childhood sexual abuse. *Sexual and Relationship Therapy, 25,* 275–288.

Canavan, M., Meyer, W., & Higgs, D. (1992). The female experience of sibling incest. *Journal of Marital and Family Therapy, 18,* 129–142.

Cantor, J. (2012). To improve maternity care in the United States, think midwives. *Contraception, 85,* 128–129.

Capellen, J., Bell, S., & Althof, S. (2006). Comparison between sildenafil-treated subjects with erectile dysfunction and control subjects on the self-esteem and relationship questionnaire. *Journal of Sexual Medicine, 3,* 274–282.

Caplan, A. (2008, July 24). New IVF dilemmas make old fears seem quaint. Retrieved November 11, 2008, from http://www/ msnbc .msn.com/id/25837220

Carael, M., Slaymaker, E., Lyerla, R., & Sarkar, S. (2006). Clients of sex workers in different regions of the world: Hard to count. *Sexually Transmitted Infections,* 82(Suppl. 3), iii26–iii33.

Cardenas, K., & Frisch, K. (2003). Comprehensive breast cancer screening. *Postgraduate Medicine, 113,* 34–46.

Cardinalli, A. (2011). *Pashtun sexuality.* Human Terrain Team (HTT) AF-6 Research Update and Findings.

Carlson, E. (1997). Sexual assault on men in war. *Lancet, 349,* 129.

Carnes, P. (1983). *The sexual addiction.* Minneapolis: Compcare Publications.

Carnes, P. (2001). *Out of the shadows: Understanding sexual addiction* (3rd ed.). Center City, MN: Hazelden.

Carollo, K. (2011, June 21). Equal opportunity cheating: Women and men cheat at same rate. Retrieved from http://abcnews.go.com/ Health/women-cheating-men-study/ story?id=13885519

Carr, C. (2006). Saddle safety. *Time Bonus Section,* A4.

Carrobles, J., & Gamez, M. (2007, April 15–19). *Effect of mode of female orgasm induction on perception of vaginal contractions.* Paper presented at the 18th Congress of the World Association for Sexual Health, Sydney, Australia.

Carroll, R. (1999). Outcomes of treatment for gender dysphoria. *Journal of Sex Education and Therapy, 24,* 128–136.

Carson, C. (2003). Penile prostheses: Are they still relevant? *British Journal of Urology International, 91,* 176–177.

Carson, C., & Wyllie, M. (2010). Improved ejaculatory latency, control and sexual satisfaction when PSD502 is applied topically in men with premature ejaculation: Results of a phase III, double-blind, placebo-controlled study. *Journal of Sexual Medicine,* June 25 (e-pub).

Carter, C., et al. (2010). HIV-1 infects multipotent progenitor cells causing cell death and establishing latent cellular reservoirs. *Nature Medicine, 16,* 446–451.

Carter, J. (2005). *Our endangered values: America's moral crisis.* Waterville, ME: Thorndike Press.

Casabe, A., et al. (2011). Risk factors of Peyronie's disease: What does our clinical experience show? *Journal of Sexual Medicine, 8,* 518–523.

Castleman, M. (1980). *Sexual solutions.* New York: Simon and Schuster.

Castleman, M. (1997, July–August). Recipes for lust. *Psychology Today,* 50–56.

Castleman, M. (2008). *Great sex: A man's guide to the secret principles of total body sex.* Emmaus, PA: Rodale Books.

Catania, J. (1999). A framework for conceptualizing reporting bias and its antecedents in interviews assessing human sexuality. *Journal of Sex Research, 36,* 25–38.

Caufriez, A. (1997). The pubertal spurt: Effects of sex steroid on growth hormone and insulin-like growth factor I. *European Journal of Obstetrics and Gynecology and Biology, 71,* 215–217.

Cavazos-Rehg, P., et al. (2011). Substance use and the risk for sexual intercourse with and without a history of teenage pregnancy among adolescent females. *Journal of Studies on Alcohol and Drugs, 72,* 194–198.

Cavazos-Rehg, P., et al. (2012). Associations between sexuality education in schools and adolescent birthrates. *Archives of Pediatric and Adolescent Medicine, 166,* 134–140.

Ceci, S., Loftus, E., Leichtman, M., & Bruck, M. (1994). The role of source misattributions in the creation of false beliefs among preschoolers. *International Journal of Clinical and Experimental Hypnosis, 42,* 304–320.

Ceci, S., & Williams, W. (2011). Understanding current causes of women's underrepresentation in science. *Proceedings of the National Academy of Sciences, 108,* 3157–3162.

Cela-Conde, C., Ayala, F., et al. (2009). Sex-related similarities and differences in the neural correlates of beauty. *Proceedings of the National Academy of Sciences, 106,* 3847–3852.

Center for Health and Gender Equity. (2009, February 22). Consequences for women's health and democracy. Retrieved February 20, 2009, from http://www .genderhealth.org/ GlobalGagRule.php

Center for Health and Gender Equity. (2011). *Female condoms and U.S. foreign assistance: An unfinished imperative for women's health.* Washington, DC: Author.

Centers for Disease Control. (1996). Youth risk behavior surveillance: United States, 1995. *Morbidity and Mortality Weekly Report, 45*(SS-4), 1–84.

Centers for Disease Control. (1998). Trends in sexual risk behaviors among high school students: United States, 1991–1997. *Morbidity and Mortality Weekly Report, 47,* 749–752.

Centers for Disease Control. (2000a). Adoption of protective behavior among persons with recent HIV infection and diagnosis: Alabama, New Jersey, and Tennessee, 1997–1998. *Morbidity and Mortality Weekly Report, 49,* 512–515.

Centers for Disease Control. (2000b). Youth risk behavior surveillance: United States, 1999. *Morbidity and Mortality Weekly Report, 49,* 1–79.

Centers for Disease Control. (2002). Youth risk behavior surveillance: United States, 2001. *Morbidity and Mortality Weekly Report, 51,* 1–62.

Centers for Disease Control. (2003). Advancing HIV prevention: New strategies for a changing epidemic—United States, 2003. *Morbidity and Mortality Weekly Report, 52,* 329–332.

Centers for Disease Control. (2005). Antiretroviral postexposure prophylaxis after sexual, injection-drug use, or other nonoccupational exposure to HIV in the United States: Recommendations from the U.S. Department of Health and Human Services. *Morbidity and Mortality Weekly Report, 54*(RR-2), 1–20.

Centers for Disease Control. (2006a). Youth risk behavior surveillance: United States, 2005. *Morbidity and Mortality Weekly Report, 55,* 1–108.

Centers for Disease Control. (2006b). *Genital herpes—CDC Fact Sheet.* Retrieved January 17, 2006, from http://www.cdc.gov/std/Herpes/STDFact-Herpes.htm

Centers for Disease Control. (2008). Youth risk behavior surveillance: United States, 2007. *Morbidity and Mortality Weekly Report, 57,* 1–131.

Centers for Disease Control. (2009a, January 5). Women need 400 micrograms of folic acid every day. Retrieved May 2, 2009, from http://www.ckc.gov/Features/FolicAcid/

Centers for Disease Control. (2009b). *Chlamydia—CDC fact sheet.* Retrieved February 6, 2009, from http://www.cdc.gov/std/Chlamydia/STDFact-chlamydia.htm

Centers for Disease Control. (2009c). *Gonorrhea—CDC fact sheet.* Retrieved February 6, 2009, from http://www.cdc.gov/std/Gonorrhea/STDFact-gonorrhea.htm

Centers for Disease Control. (2009d). Diseases characterized by urethritis and cervicitis. Retrieved February 6, 2009, from http://cdc.gov/stdtreatment/2006/urethritis-and-cervicitis.htm

Centers for Disease Control. (2009e). *Syphilis—CDC fact sheet.* Retrieved February 6, 2009, from http://www.cdc.gov/std/Syphilis/STDFact-Syphilis.htm

Centers for Disease Control. (2009f). *Genital herpes—CDC fact sheet.* Retrieved February 6, 2009, from http://www.cdc/gov/std/Herpes/STDFact-Herpes.htm

Centers for Disease Control. (2009g). *Genital HPV infection—CDC fact sheet.* Retrieved February 6, 2009, from http://www.cdc/gov.std/HPV/STDFact-HPV.htm

Centers for Disease Control. (2009h). *Viral hepatitis.* Retrieved February 6, 2009, from http://www.cdc.gov/hepatitis/Resources/PublicEdMaterials.htm

Centers for Disease Control. (2009i). *Bacterial vaginosis—CDC fact sheet.* Retrieved February 6, 2009, from http://www.cdc/gov.std/bv/STDFact-Bacterial-Vaginosis.htm

Centers for Disease Control. (2009j). *Candidiasis.* Retrieved February 6, 2009, from http://www.cdc.gov/nczved/dfbmd/disease_listing/candidiasis_gi.html

Centers for Disease Control. (2009k). *Trichomoniasis—CDC fact sheet.* Retrieved February 6, 2009, from http://www.cdc.gov/std/Trichomoniasis/STDFact-Trichomoniasis.htm

Centers for Disease Control. (2009l). *Pubic "crab" lice.* Retrieved February 6, 2009, from http://www.cdc.gov/lice/Pubic/Factsheet.html

Centers for Disease Control. (2009m). *Scabies.* Retrieved February 6, 2009, from http://www.cdc.gov/scabies/Factsheet.html

Centers for Disease Control. (2010a). Congenital syphilis—United States, 2003–2008. *Morbidity and Mortality Weekly Report, 59,* 413–417.

Centers for Disease Control. (2010b). Evaluation of acute hepatitis C infections surveillance—United States, 2008. *Morbidity and Mortality Weekly Report, 59,* 1407–1410.

Centers for Disease Control. (2010c). FDA licensure of bivalent human papillomavirus vaccine (HPV2, Cervarix) for use in females and updated HPV vaccination recommendations from the Advisory Committee on Immunization Practices (ACIP). *Morbidity and Mortality Weekly Report, 59,* 626–629.

Centers for Disease Control. (2010d). FDA licensure of quadrivalent human papillomavirus vaccine (HPV4, Gardasil) for use in males and guidance from the Advisory Committee on Immunization Practices (ACIP). *Morbidity and Mortality Weekly Report, 59,* 630–632.

Centers for Disease Control. (2010e). Hepatitis A vaccination coverage among U.S. children aged 12–23 months—Immunization information system sentinel sites, 2006–2009. *Morbidity and Mortality Weekly Report, 59,* 776–779.

Centers for Disease Control. (2010f). HIV transmission through transfusion—Missouri and Colorado, 2008. *Morbidity and Mortality Weekly Report, 59,* 1335–1339.

Centers for Disease Control. (2010g). Syringe exchange programs—United States, 2008. *Morbidity and Mortality Weekly Report, 59,* 1488–1491.

Centers for Disease Control. (2010h). Vital signs: HIV testing and diagnosis among adults—United States, 2001–2009. *Morbidity and Mortality Weekly Report, 59,* 1550–1555.

Centers for Disease Control. (2010i). Youth risk behavior surveillance—United States, 2009. *Morbidity and Mortality Weekly Report, 59,* 1–146.

Centers for Disease Control. (2011a). Disparities in diagnoses of HIV infection between African Americans and other racial/ethnic populations—37 states, 2005–2008. *Morbidity and Mortality Weekly Report, 60,* 93–96.

Centers for Disease Control. (2011b). Hepatitis awareness month—May 2011. *Morbidity and Mortality Weekly Report, 60,* 537.

Centers for Disease Control. (2011c). Hepatitis C virus infection among adolescents and young adults—Massachusetts, 2002–2009. *Morbidity and Mortality Weekly Report, 60,* 537–541.

Centers for Disease Control. (2011d). HIV testing among men who have sex with men, 21 cities, United States, 2008. *Morbidity and Mortality Weekly Report, 60,* 694–700.

Centers for Disease Control. (2011e). Interim guidance: Pre-exposure prophylaxis for the prevention of HIV infection in men who have sex with men. *Morbidity and Mortality Weekly Report, 60,* 65–68.

Centers for Disease Control. (2011f). Results of the expanded HIV testing initiative—25 jurisdictions, United States, 2007–2010. *Morbidity and Mortality Weekly Report, 60,* 805–810.

Centers for Disease Control. (2011g). Vital signs: Teen pregnancy—United States, 1991–2009. *Morbidity and Mortality Weekly Report, 60,* 414–420.

Centers for Disease Control. (2012a). HIV infection and HIV-associated behaviors among injecting drug users—20 cities, United States, 2009. *Morbidity and Mortality Weekly Report, 61,* 133–138.

Centers for Disease Control. (2012b). Pre-pregnancy contraceptive use among teens with unintended pregnancies resulting in live births. *Morbidity and Mortality Weekly Report, 61,* 25–29.

Centers for Disease Control. (2012c). Surveillance for chronic hepatitis B virus infection, New York City, June 2008–November 2009. *Morbidity and Mortality Weekly Report, 61,* 6–9.

Cerny, J., & Janssen, E. (2011). Patterns of sexual arousal in homosexual, bisexual, and heterosexual men. *Archives of Sexual Behavior, 40,* 687–697.

Cespedes, Y., & Huey, S. (2008). Depression in Latino adolescents: A cultural discrepancy perspective. *Cultural Diversity and Ethnic Minority Psychology, 14,* 168–172.

Chalker, R. (2002). *The clitoral truth: The world at your fingertips.* New York: Seven Stories Press.

Chambers, W. (2007). Oral sex: Varied behaviors and perceptions in a college population. *Journal of Sex Research, 44,* 28–43.

Chandra, A., Martino, S., Collins, R., et al. (2008). Does watching sex on television predict teen pregnancy? Findings from a national longitudinal survey of youth. *Pediatrics, 122,* 1047–1054.

Chandra, A., et al. (2011, March 3). Sexual behavior, sexual attraction, and sexual identity in the United States: Data from the 2006–2008 National Survey of Family Growth (National Health Statistics Reports, No. 36). Washington, DC: U.S. Department of Health and Human Services.

Chappell, K., & Davis, K. (1998). Attachment, partner choice, and perception of romantic partners: An experimental test of the attachment–security hypothesis. *Personal Relationships, 5,* 327–342.

Cheever, S. (2011, May 23). The princess and the terminator. *Newsweek,* 10.

Chen, W., et al. (2012). Moderate alcohol consumption during adult life, drinking patterns, and breast cancer risk. *Journal of the American Medical Association, 306,* 1884–1890.

Cheng, M. (2007, November 20). Global AIDS cases drop, but only after officials revise data. *Oregonian,* p. A5.

Cheng, Y., & Landale, N. (2011). Adolescent overweight, social relationships and the transition to first sex: Gender and racial variations. *Perspectives on Sexual and Reproductive Health, 43,* 6–15.

Chiang, H. (2009, February 12). Homosexual behavior in the United States, 1988–2004: Quantitative empirical support for the social construction theory of sexuality. Retrieved March 17, 2009, from http://www.ejhs.org/Volume12/Homosexuality.htm

Chivers, M. (2005). Clinical management of sex addiction [Book review]. *Archives of Sexual Behavior, 34,* 476–478.

Chivers, M., Gieger, G., Latty, E., & Bailey, J. (2005). A sex difference in the specificity of sexual arousal. *Psychological Science, 15,* 736–744.

Chivers, M., et al. (2010). Agreement of self-reported and genital measures of sexual arousal in men and women: A meta-analysis. *Archives of Sexual Behavior, 39,* 861–873.

Chivers, M., et al. (2011). The relationship between sexual functioning and depressive symptomatology in postpartum women: A pilot study. *Journal of Sexual Medicine, 8,* 792–799.

Chlebowski, R., et al. (2010). Estrogen plus progestin and breast cancer incidence and mortality in postmenopausal women. *New England Journal of Medicine, 304,* 1684–1692.

Chosidow, D. (2006). Scabies. *New England Journal of Medicine, 354,* 1718–1727.

Choudhary, E., et al. (2012). Epidemiological characteristics of male sexual assault in a criminological database. *Journal of Interpersonal Violence, 27,* 523–546.

Chrisler, J., Johnston, I., Champagne, N., & Preston, K. (1994). Menstrual joy. *Psychology of Women Quarterly, 18,* 375–387.

Chrisler, J., & Levy, K. (1990). The media construct a menstrual monster: A content analysis of PMS articles in the popular press. *Women and Health, 16*(2), 89–104.

Chu, L., & Benoit, R. (2011). Estimating the trade-off between survival and morbidity resulting from prostate cancer screening. *Journal of Urology, 185,* e19–e20.

Chumlea, W., Schubert, M., Roche, A., et al. (2003). Age at menarche and racial comparisons in U.S. girls. *Pediatrics, 111,* 110–113.

Chung, P. (2006, July 14). Government to expand childbirth incentives. Retrieved July 24, 2006, from http://times.hankooki.com/service/print/Print.php?po=times.hankooki.com/lpage/natio/20

Chung, R. (2008). Acute hepatitis C: To treat or not to treat. *Consultant, 48,* 664.

Chung, R. (2012). A watershed moment in the treatment of hepatitis C. *New England Journal of Medicine, 366,* 273–275.

Chung, W., De Vries, G., & Schaab, D. (2002). Sexual differentiation of the bed nucleus of the stria terminalis in humans may extend into adulthood. *Journal of Neurosciences, 22,* 1027–1033.

Ciccarone, D., Kanouse, D., Collins, R., et al. (2003). Sex without disclosure of positive HIV serostatus in a U.S. probability sample of persons receiving medical care for HIV infection. *American Journal of Public Health, 93,* 949–954.

Cihan, A., Demir, O., Demir, T., & Aslan, G. (2009). The relationship between premature ejaculation and hyperthyroidism. *Journal of Urology, 181,* 1273–1280.

Clanton, G., & Smith, L. (1977). *Jealousy.* Englewood Cliffs, NJ: Prentice Hall.

Clark, J. (2005, January–February). The big turnoff: Stymied by politics and Viagra, sex research goes limp. *Psychology Today,* 17–18.

Clarke, A., & Stermac, L. (2011). The influence of stereotypical beliefs, participant gender, and survivor weight on sexual assault responses. *Journal of Interpersonal Violence, 28,* 2285–2305.

Clarnette, T., Sugita, Y., & Hutson, J. (1997). Genital anomalies in human and animal models reveal the mechanisms and hormones governing testicular descent. *British Journal of Urology, 79,* 99–112.

Clements, M. (1994, August 7). Sex in America today. *Parade,* 4–6.

Cloud, J. (2005, October 10). The battle over gay teens. *Time,* 43–51.

CNN. (2011, April 9–10). CNN Opinion Research Poll. CNN Opinion Research Corporation. Retrieved from http://i2.cdn.turner.com/cnn/2011/images/04/19/rel6h.pdf

CNN HEALTH Library (2008). Penis-enlargement scams: You're more normal than you think. Retrieved October 28, 2008, from http://www.cnn.com/HEALTH/LIBRARY/MC/0026.html

Coady, D., & Fish, N. (2011, December 10). Painful sex not in our heads but right docs scarce. Retrieved from http://www.womensenews.org/story/books/111209/painful-sex-not-in-our-heads-right-docs-scarce

Coco, A., & Vandenbosche, M. (2000). Infectious vaginitis. *Postgraduate Medicine, 107,* 63–74.

Coeytaux, F., Darnovsky, M., & Fogel, S. (2011). Assisted reproduction and choice in the biotech age: Recommendations for a way forward [Editorial]. *Contraception, 83,* 1–4.

Cohen, J. (2008). Botswana's success comes at a steep cost. *Science, 321*, 526–529.

Cohen, M., & Pilcher, C. (2005). Amplified HIV transmission and new approaches to HIV prevention. *Journal of Infectious Diseases, 191*, 1391–1393.

Cohen, M., et al. (2011). Prevention of HIV-1 infection with early antiretroviral therapy. *New England Journal of Medicine, 365*, 1934–1935.

Cohen, N. (2012a). *Delirium: How the sexual counterrevolution is polarizing America.* Berkeley, CA: Counterpoint.

Cohen, N. (2012b, January 11). Republicans push pro-zygote extremism over the top. Retrieved from http://www.womensenews.org/print/8916

Cohen, S. (2010). Hope for change amidst changing political realities: A status report on U.S. sexual and reproductive health policy. *Guttmacher Policy Review, 13*, 22–24.

Cohen, S., et al. (2012). Repeat syphilis among men who have sex with men in California, 2002–2006: Implications for syphilis elimination efforts. *American Journal of Public Health, 102*, e1–e8.

Cohen-Kettenis, P. (2005). Gender change in 46,XY persons with 5[alpha]-reductase-2 deficiency and 17[beta]-hydroxysteroid dehydrogenase-3 deficiency. *Archives of Sexual Behavior, 34*, 399–410.

Cohen-Kettenis, P., & Gooren, L. (1999). Transsexualism: A review of etiology, diagnosis, and treatment. *Journal of Psychosomatic Research, 46*, 315–333.

Cohn, B., Wolff, M., Cirillo, P., & Sholtz, R. (2007). DDT and breast cancer in young women: New data on the significance of age at exposure. *Environmental Health Perspective, 115*, 1406–1414.

Colangelo, J. (2007). Recovered memory debate revisited: Practice implications for mental health counselors. *Journal of Mental Health Counseling, 29*, 93–120.

Colapinto, J. (2000). *As nature made him: The boy who was raised as a girl.* New York: HarperCollins.

Cole, C., & Cole, A. (1999). Marriage enrichment and prevention really works: Interpersonal competence training to maintain and enhance relationships. *Family Relations: Interdisciplinary Journal of Applied Family Studies, 48*, 273–275.

Cole, D. (1987, July). It might have been: Mourning the unborn. *Psychology Today*, 64–65.

Cole, J. (1992). Commonalities and differences. In M. Andersen & P. Collins (Eds.), *Race, class, and gender.* Belmont, CA: Wadsworth.

Cole, S., Denny, D., Eyler, A., & Samons, S. (2000). Issues of transgender. In L. Szuchman & F. Muscarella (Eds.), *Psychological perspectives on human sexuality.* New York: Wiley.

Coleman, E. (1990). The obsessive-compulsive model for describing compulsive sexual behavior. *American Journal of Preventive Psychiatry and Neurology, 2*, 9–14.

Coleman, E. (1991). Compulsive sexual behavior: New concepts and treatments. *Journal of Psychology and Human Sexuality, 4*, 37–51.

Coleman, E. (1999). Revolution. *Contemporary Sexuality*, September, 1–4.

Coleman, E. (2003). Compulsive sexual behavior: What to call it, how to treat it? *SIECUS Report, 31*, 12–16.

Coleman, E. (2007, April 15–19). *Development of sexual identity, barriers to intimacy, and the promotion of sexual health.* Paper presented at the 18th Congress of the World Association for Sexual Health, Sydney, Australia.

Coley, R., & Chase-Lansdale, P. (1998). Adolescent pregnancy and parenthood. *American Psychologist, 53*, 152–166.

Colgan, R., Michocki, R., Greisman, L., & Moore, T. (2003). Antiviral drugs in the immunocompetent host. Part I. Treatment of hepatitis, cytomegalovirus, and herpes infections. *American Family Physician, 67*, 757–762.

Colino, S. (1991, February). Sex and the expectant mother. *Parenting*, 111.

Colino, S. (2006, March). Your period: What's normal, what's not; Changes in your cycle can be nothing—or signal a serious health problem. Here's how to tell the difference. *Shape*, 88–92.

Collett-Solberg, P. (2011). Update in growth hormone therapy of children. *Journal of Clinical Endocrinology and Metabolism, 96*, 573–579.

Collings, S., Bugwandeen, S., & Wiles, W. (2008). HIV past-exposure prophylaxis for child rape survivors in KwaZulu-Natal, South Africa: Who qualifies and who complies? *Child Abuse and Neglect, 32*, 477–483.

Collins, D. (2002). Scarring after penile augmentation. *Contemporary Urology, 14*, 12.

Collins, F., & Fauci, A. (2010, May 23). AIDS in 2010: How we are living with HIV. *Parade*, 10–12.

Collins, G. (2011, February 17). Mrs. Bush, abstinence and Texas. *New York Times*, p. A31.

Collins, N., Ford, M., Guichard, A., & Allard, L. (2006). Working models of attachment and attribution processes in intimate relationships. *Personality and Social Psychology Bulletin, 32*, 201–219.

Colliver, V. (2011, October 8). Prostate cancer test advice creates confusion. *San Francisco Chronicle*, p. A1.

Colucci, J. (2006, May 9). Eight years of great laughs. *Advocate*, 57.

Comfort, A. (1972). *The joy of sex.* New York: Crown.

Comiteau, L. (2001, February 23). "Sexual enslavement" established as a war crime. *USA Today*, p. A10.

Conde-Agudelo, A., Rosas-Bermudex, A., & Kafury-Goeta, A. (2006). Birth spacing and risk of adverse perinatal outcomes. *Journal of the American Medical Association, 295*, 1809–1823.

Condon, S. (2012, January 31). White House defends birth control coverage policy as conservatives push back. Retrieved from http://www.cbsnews.com/2102-503544_162-57369110.html

Conley, M. (2012, March 15). New guidelines discourage yearly pap tests. Retrieved from http://abcnews.go.com/blogs/health/2012/03/15/new-guidelines-discourage-yearly-pap-tests/

Conley, T. (2011). Perceived proposer personality characteristics and gender differences in acceptance of casual sex offers. *Journal of Personality and Social Psychology, 100*, 309–329.

Conner, S. (2009, March 3). How the smell of rotten eggs makes men randy. Retrieved May 19, 2009, from http://www.independent.co.uk/news/science/how-the-smell-of-rotten-eggs-makes-men-randy

Connor, E., Sperling, R., & Gelber, R. (1994). Reduction of maternal-infant transmission of human immunodeficiency virus type 1 with zidovudine treatment. *New England Journal of Medicine, 331*, 1173–1180.

Constantine, N., Jerman, P., & Huang, A. (2007). California parents' preferences and beliefs regarding school-based sex education policy. *Perspectives on Sexual and Reproductive Health, 39*, 167–175.

Contemporary Sexuality. (2002). Pediatricians group backs gay parents. *Contemporary Sexuality, 36*, 10.

Cook, L., Kamb, M., & Weiss, N. (1997). Perineal powder exposure and the risk of ovarian cancer. *American Journal of Epidemiology, 145*, 459–465.

Coontz, S. (2005, July 5). The heterosexual revolution. *New York Times*, p. A17.

Coontz, S. (2006, June 5). Three "rules" that don't apply. *Newsweek*, 49.

Coontz, S. (2011). *A strange stirring: The feminine mystique and American women at the dawn of the 1960s.* New York: Basic Books.

Coontz, S. (2012). Mating games: Changing rules for sex and marriage. *Chistian Century, 129,* 22–24.

Cooper, A. (1996). Autoerotic asphyxiation: Three case reports. *Journal of Sex and Marital Therapy, 22,* 47–53.

Cooper, A. (2003, December). *Cybersex addictions: How to identify and treat the effects of aberrant online sexual pursuits.* Paper presented at the American Society of Professional Education, Portland, OR.

Cooper, A. (Ed.) (2002). *Sex and the Internet.* Philadelphia: Brunner-Routledge.

Cooper, A. (2004). Online sexual activity in the new millennium. *Contemporary Sexuality, 38,* i–vii.

Cooper, A., Boies, S., Maheu, M., & Greenfield, D. (2000). Sexuality and the Internet: The next sexual revolution. In L. Szuchman & F. Muscarella (Eds.), *Psychological perspectives on human sexuality.* New York: Wiley.

Cooper, A., Scherer, C., Boies, S., & Gordon, B. (1999). Sexuality on the Internet: From sexual exploration to pathological expression. *Professional Psychology: Research and Practice, 30,* 154–164.

Cooper, C. (2008). Georgia charts setbacks for reproductive freedom. Retrieved August 5, 2008, from Women's eNews.

Cooper, C. (2011). Holocaust women's rape breaks decades of taboo. Retrieved June 12, 2011, from http://www.womensnews. org/story/our_history/110529/holocaust-women's-rape-breaks-decades-taboo

Cooper, G. (2006). Viagra's false promise. *Psychotherapy Networker,* March/April, 21.

Cooper, H., et al. (2011). Spatial access to syringe exchange programs and pharmacies selling over-the-counter syringes as predictors of drug injectors use of sterile syringes. *American Journal of Public Health, 101,* 1118–1125.

Cooper, M., et al. (2011). Motivational pursuits in the context of human sexual relationships. *Journal of Personality, 79,* 1031–1066.

Coppus, S., et al. (2011). *Chlamydia trachomatic IgG seropositivity is associated* with lower natural conception rates in ovulatory subfertile women without visible tubal pathology. *Human Reproduction, 26,* 3061–3067.

Corona, B., Ricca, V., Bandini, E., et al. (2009). Selective serotonin reuptake inhibitor-induced sexual dysfunction. *Journal of Sexual Medicine, 6,* 1259–1269.

Corona, G., Petrone, L., Mannucci, E., & Forti, G. (2006). Difficulties in achieving versus maintaining erection: Organic, psychogenic and relational determinants. *Journal of Sexual Medicine, 3*(Suppl. 3), 224–286.

Corona, G., Rastrelli, G., & Maggi, M. (2011). Update in testosterone therapy for men. *Journal of Sexual Medicine, 8,* 639–654.

Correa, S., Petchesky, R., & Parker, R. (2008). *Sexuality, health and human rights.* New York: Routledge.

Cortez-Gonzales, J., & Glina, S. (2009). Have phosphodiesterase-5 inhibitors changed the indications for penile implants? *British Journal of Urology International, 103,* 1518–1521.

Cosgray, R., Hanna, V., Fawley, R., & Money, M. (1991). Death from auto-erotic asphyxiation in long-term psychiatric setting. *Perspectives in Psychiatric Care, 27,* 21–24.

Cottrell, B. (2003). Vaginal douching. *Journal of Obstetrical, Gynecological, and Neonatal Nursing, 32,* 12–18.

Cottrell, B., & Close, F. (2008). Vaginal douching among university women in the southeastern United States. *Journal of American College Health, 56,* 415–421.

Coutts, E., & Jann, B. (2011). Sensitive questions in online surveys: Experimental results for the randomized response technique (RRT) and the unmatched count technique. *Sociological Methods and Research, 40,* 169–193.

Courtois, C. (2000a). The aftermath of child sexual abuse: The treatment of complex posttraumatic stress reactions. In L. Szuchman & F. Muscarella (Eds.), *Psychological perspectives on human sexuality.* New York: Wiley.

Courtois, C. (2000b). The sexual after-effect of incest/child sexual abuse. *SIECUS Report, 29,* 11–16.

Coutino, S. (2007). An evolutionary perspective of friendship selection. *College Student Journal, 41,* 1163–1167.

Cowan, G. (2000). Beliefs about the causes of four types of rape. *Sex Roles, 42,* 807–823.

Cowan, G., & Campbell, R. (1994). Racism and sexism in interracial pornography. *Psychology of Women Quarterly, 18,* 323–338.

Cowan, P., & Cowan C. (1992). *When partners become parents.* New York: HarperCollins.

Cox, D. (1988). Incidence and nature of male genital exposure behavior as reported by college women. *Journal of Sex Research, 24,* 227–234.

Coxell, A., & King, M. (2010). Adult male rape and sexual assault: Prevalence, revictimization and the tonic immobility response. *Sexual and Relationship Therapy, 25,* 372–379.

Crabb, P., & Marciano, D. (2011). Representations of material culture and gender in award-winning children's books: A 20-year follow-up. *Journal of Research in Childhood Education, 25,* 390–398.

Cramer, R., Lipinski, R., Meteer, J., & Housda, J. (2008). Sex differences in subjective distress to unfaithfulness: Testing competing evolutionary and violation of infidelity expectations hypotheses. *Journal of Social Psychology, 148,* 389–405.

Crary, D. (2007, July 1). Sharing chores, sex outrank kids for wedded bliss. *Oregonian,* p. A7.

Crary, D. (2009, August 6). Psychologists reject gay-to-straight therapy. *Oregonian,* p. A4.

Crary, D. (2010, October 10). Bullying opens political minefield. *Oregonian,* p. A8.

Crary, D. (2012, March 4). Costs, not rules, hinder abortion, experts say. *Sunday Oregonian,* p. A4.

Crawford, E., Wright, M., & Birchmeier, Z. (2008). Drug-facilitated sexual assault: College women's risk perception and behavioral choices. *Journal of American College Health, 57,* 261–272.

Crenshaw, T. (1996). *The alchemy of love and lust.* New York: Putnam.

Crenshaw, T., & Goldberg, J. (1996). *Sexual pharmacology: Drugs that affect sexual function.* New York: Norton.

Critelli, J., & Bivona, J. (2008). Women's erotic rape fantasies: An evaluation of theory and research. *Journal of Sex Research, 45,* 57–71.

Crooks, R., & Tucker, S. (2006). A peer-educator–based HIV/AIDS prevention program in Kenya. Unpublished.

Crosby, R., & Danner, R. (2008). Adolescents' sexually transmitted diseases protective attitudes predict sexually transmitted disease acquisition in early adulthood. *Journal of School Health, 78,* 310–313.

Cui, J. (2006). China's cracked closet. *Foreign Policy,* May/June, 90–92.

Cullen, L. (2006, April 3). Sex in the syllabus. *Time,* 80–81.

Cullen, L., & Masters, C. (2008, January 28). We just clicked. *Time,* 85–89.

Cunningham, G., & Toma, S. (2011). Why is androgen replacement in males controversial? *Journal of Clinical Endocrinology and Metabolism, 96,* 38–52.

Curtis, C. (2005, March 2). U.S. House bill aims to repeal "don't ask." Retrieved February 25, 2006, from http://www. planetout.com/news/article-print. html?2005/03/02/1

Cutler, W. (1999). Human sex-attractant pheromones: Discovery, research, development, and application in sex therapy. *Psychiatric Annals, 29,* 54–59.

Cwikel, J., & Hoban, E. (2005). Contentious issues in research on trafficked women working in the sex industry: Study design, ethics, and methodology. *Journal of Sex Research, 42,* 306–317.

Czuczka, D. (2000). The twentieth century: An American sexual history. *SIECUS Report, 28*, 15–18.

D'Amato, A. (2006). *Porn up, rape down.* Chicago, IL: Northwestern Law School.

D'Emilio, J., & Freedman, E. (1988). *Intimate matters.* New York: Harper and Row.

Dalgaard, M. (2012). A genome-wide associations study of men with symptoms of testicular dysgenesis syndrome and its network biology interpretation. *Medical Genetics, 49*, 58–65.

Dall'Ara, E., & Maass, A. (1999). Studying sexual harassment in the laboratory: Are egalitarian women at higher risk? *Sex Roles, 41*, 681–704.

Dall'Era, M., Hosang, N., et al. (2009). Sociodemographic predictors of prostate cancer risk category at diagnosis: Unique patterns of significant and insignificant disease. *Journal of Urology, 181*, 1622–1627.

Daly, A. (2011, November). Has your drink been spiked? NEED to know drugs in drinks. *Cosmopolitan,* 162.

Daly, M., Wilson, M., & Weghorst, S. (1982). Male sexual jealousy. *Ethology and Sociobiology, 3*, 11–27.

Dandona, P., & Dhindsa, S. (2011). Update: Hypogonadotropic hypogonadism in type 2 diabetes and obesity. *Journal of Clinical Endocrinology and Metabolism, 96*, 2643–2651.

Daniluk, J. (1998). *Women's sexuality across the life span: Challenging myths, creating meanings.* New York: Guilford Press.

Dao, J. (2011, July 21). Same-sex marriage advocates focus on military. *Oregonian,* p. A8.

Dariotis, J., et al. (2011). Racial and ethnic disparities in sexual risk behavior and STDs among young men's transition to adulthood. *Perspectives on Sexual and Reproductive Health, 43*, 51–59.

Darling, C., Davidson, J., & Conway-Welch, C. (1990). Female ejaculation: Perceived origins, the Grafenberg spot/area, and sexual responsiveness. *Archives of Sexual Behavior, 19*, 29–47.

Daro, D. (1991). Child sexual abuse prevention: Separating fact from fiction. *Child Abuse and Neglect, 15*, 1–4.

Darroch, J., Sedgh, G., & Ball, H. (2011). *Contraceptive technologies: responding to women's needs.* New York: Guttmacher Institute.

Davidson, J., & Chutka, D. (2008). Benign prostatic hyperplasia: Treat or wait? Questionnaire with "bother score" can help you decide. *Journal of Family Practice, 57*, 454–463.

Davidson, J., Moore, N., Earle, J., & Davis, J. (2008). Sexual attitudes and behavior at four universities: Do region, race,

and/or religion matter? *Adolescence, 43*, 189–220.

Davies, A. (2011, June). What your bedside table is missing. *Cosmopolitan,* 134–136.

Davies, M. (1995). Parental distress and ability to cope following disclosure of extrafamilial sexual abuse. *Child Abuse and Neglect, 19*, 399–408.

Davies, M., Pollard, P., & Archer, J. (2006). Effects of perpetrator gender and victim sexuality on blame toward male victims of sexual assault. *Journal of Social Psychology, 146*, 275–291.

Davis, A. (2002). Don't let nobody bother yo' principle: The sexual economy of American slavery. In S. Harley and the Black Women and Work Collective (Eds.), *Sister circle: Black women and work.* New Brunswick, NJ: Rutgers University Press.

Davis, B., & Noble, M. (1991). Putting an end to chronic testicular pain. *Medical Aspects of Human Sexuality,* April, 26–34.

Davis, K., & Latty-Mann, H. (1987). Love styles and relationship quality: A contribution to validation. *Journal of Social and Personal Relationships, 4*, 409–428.

Davis, P. (2011, February 14). Three-day fetish fair attracts thousands to Providence. *Providence Journal.*

Davis, S. (1999). The therapeutic use of androgens in women. *Journal of Steroid Biochemistry and Molecular Biology, 69*, 177–184.

Davis, S. (2000). Testosterone and sexual desire in women. *Journal of Sex Education and Therapy, 25*, 25–32.

Davis, S. (2007, April 15–19). *Androgens and female sexual dysfunction.* Paper presented at the 18th Congress of the World Association for Sexual Health, Sydney, Australia.

Davis, S., et al. (2008). Testosterone for low libido in postmenopausal women not taking estrogen. *New England Journal of Medicine, 359*, 2005–2017.

Davis, S., Binik, Y., & Carrier, S. (2009). Sexual dysfunction and pelvic pain in men: A male sexual pain disorder? *Journal of Sex and Marital Therapy, 35*, 182–205.

Davison, G., & Neale, J. (1993). *Abnormal psychology* (6th ed.). New York: Wiley.

Dayal, M., & Zarek, S. (2008, November 11). Preimplantation genetic diagnosis. Retrieved May 2, 2009, from http://emedicine.medscspe.com/article/273415-overview

Dean, K., & Malamuth, N. (1997). Characteristics of men who aggress sexually and men who imagine aggressing: Risk and moderating variables. *Journal of Personality and Social Psychology, 72*, 449–455.

Deans, R., et al. (2011) Why are women referred for female genital cosmetic

surgery? *Medical Journal of Australia, 195*, 99–107.

Deardorff, J., Tschann, J., Flores, E., & Ozer, E. (2010). Sexual values and risky sexual behaviors among Latino youths. *Perspectives on Sexual and Reproductive Health, 42*, 23–33.

De Bro, S., Campbell, S., & Peplau, L. (1994). Influencing a partner to use a condom. *Psychology of Women Quarterly, 18*, 165–182.

Deckers, P., & Ricci, A., Jr. (1992). Pain and lumps in the female breast. *Hospital Practice,* February 28, 67–94.

De Cock, K., Jaffe, H., & Curran, J. (2011). Reflections on 30 years of AIDS. *Emerging Infectious Diseases, 17*, 1044–1049.

De Cuypere, G., T'sjoen, G., Beerten, R., et al. (2005). Sexual and physical health after sex reassignment surgery. *Archives of Sexual Behavior, 34*, 679–690.

DeForge, D., & Blackmer, J. (2005, July 10–15). *Male sexuality following spinal cord injury: A systematic review.* Paper presented at the World Congress of Sexology, Montreal, Canada.

Degler, C. (1980). *At odds: Women and the family in America from the Revolution to the present.* Oxford: Oxford University Press.

De Jong, D. (2009). The role of attention in sexual arousal: Implications for treatment of sexual dysfunction. *Journal of Sex Research, 46*, 237–248.

De Lacoste, M., Adesanya, T., & Woodward, D. (1990). Measures of gender differences in the human brain and their relationship to brain weight. *Biological Psychiatry, 28*, 931–942.

DeLamater, J., & Friedrich, W. (2002). Human sexual development. *Journal of Sex Research, 39*, 10–14.

DeLamater, J., & Sill, M. (2005). Sexual desire in later life. *Journal of Sex Research, 42*, 138–150.

Delaney, J., Lupton, M., & Toth, E. (1976). *The curse: A cultural history of menstruation.* New York: Dutton.

Deliganis, A., Maravilla, K., Heiman, J., et al. (2000). Dynamic MR imaging of the female genitalia using Angiomark: Initial experience evaluating the female sexual response [Abstract]. *Radiology, 214*, 611. Originally presented as an RSNA Hot Topic presentation, Chicago, November 1999.

DeLuzio, C. (2011). Theoretical issues in the study of asexuality. *Archives of Sexual Behavior, 40*, 713–723.

Démare, D., Briere, J., & Lips, H. (1988). Violent pornography and self-reported likelihood of sexual aggression. *Journal of Research in Personality, 22*, 140–153.

DeMoranville, V. (2008). Semen analysis. Retrieved November 1, 2008, from http://www.healthline.com/galecontent/semen-analysis-1

Dempsey, A., Johnson, S., & Westhoff, C. (2011). Predicting oral contraceptive continuation using the transtheoretical model of health behavior change. *Perspectives on Sexual and Reproductive Health, 43*, 23–29.

Dempsey, C. (1994). Health and social issues of gay, lesbian, and bisexual adolescents. *Families in Society*, March, 160–167.

Dennerstein, L., & Goldstein, I. (2005). Postmenopausal female sexual dysfunction: At a crossroads. Retrieved April 15, 2006, from http://www.blackwell-synergy.com/doi/full/10.1111/j.1743-6109.2005.00127.x

Dennerstein, L., Hayes, R., Sand, M., & Lehert, P. (2009). Attitudes toward and frequency of partner interactions among women reporting decreased sexual desire. *Journal of Sexual Medicine*, April 23.

Denov, M. (2003a). *Perspectives on female sexual offending: A culture of denial.* Brookfield, VT: Ashgate.

Denov, M. (2003b). To a safer place: Victims of sexual abuse by females and their disclosures to professionals. *Child Abuse and Neglect, 27*, 47–61.

DePaulo, B. (2012, January/February). Are you single at heart? *Psychology Today*, 54–55.

Derlego, V., Metts, S., Petronia, S., & Margulis, S. (1993). *Self-disclosure.* Newbury Park, CA: Sage.

De Rosa, C., et al. (2010). Sexual intercourse and oral sex among public middle school students: Prevalence and correlates. *Perspectives on Sexual and Reproductive Health, 42.*

de Silva, W. (1999). Sexual variations. *British Medical Journal, 318*, 654–656.

Des Jarlais, D., Diaz, T., Perlis, T., et al. (2003). Variability in the incidence of human immunodeficiency virus, hepatitis B virus, and hepatitis C virus infection among young injecting drug users in New York City. *American Journal of Epidemiology, 157*, 467–471.

Dessens, A., Cohen-Kettenis, P., Mellenbergh, G., et al. (1999). Prenatal exposure to anticonvulsants and psychosexual development. *Archives of Sexual Behavior, 28*, 31–44.

Dessens, A., Slijper, F., & Drop, S. (2005). Gender dysphoria and gender change in chromosomal females with congenital hyperplasia. *Archives of Sexual Behavior, 34*, 389–397.

deVaron, T. (2011, June 28). At colleges plagued by date rape, why "no" still means "yes." *Christian Science Monitor* (e-pub).

Deveny, K. (2003, June 30). We're not in the mood. *Newsweek*, 40–46.

Deveny, K. (2007, February 12). Girls gone bad? *Newsweek*, 41–47.

Devi, K. (1977). *The Eastern way of love: Tantric sex and erotic mysticism.* New York: Simon and Schuster.

De Villers, L., & Turgeon, H. (2005). The uses and benefits of "sensate focus" exercises. *Contemporary Sexuality, 39*, i–vii.

de Visser, R., & McDonald, D. (2007). Swings and roundabouts—jealousy in heterosexual couples. *British Journal of Social Psychology, 46*, 459–476.

DeVita-Raeburn, E. (2006, January/February). Lust for the long haul. *Psychology Today*, 1–5.

Devroey, P., Aboulghar, M., Garcia-Velasco, J., & Griesinger, G. (2009). Improving the patient's experience of IVF/ICSI: A proposal for an ovarian stimulation protocol with GnRH antagonist co-treatment. *Human Reproduction, 24*, 764–774.

Dew, B., & Chaney, M. (2004). Sexual addiction and the Internet: Implications for gay men. *Journal of Addictions and Offender Counseling, 24*, 101–114.

de Walgue, D., & Kline, R. (2011). Variations in condom use by type of partner. *Studies of Family Planning, 42*, 1–10.

DeWall, C., et al. (2011). So far away from one's partner, yet so close to romantic alternatives: Avoidant attachment, interest in alternatives, and infidelity. *Journal of Personality and Social Psychology, 101*, 1302–1316.

Diabetes Care. (2009). An overview on the types of diabetic neuropathy. Retrieved May 23, 2009, from http://diabetescareinfo.com/2009/02/an-overview-on-the-types-of-diabetic-neuropathy/

Diamond, L. (2008a). *Sexual fluidity: Understanding women's love and desire.* Cambridge, MA: Harvard University Press.

Diamond, L. (2008b). Female bisexuality from adolescence to adulthood: Results from a 10-year longitudinal study. *Developmental Psychology, 44*, 5–14.

Diamond L., & Wallen, K. (2011). Sexual minority women's sexual motivation around the time of ovulation. *Archives of Sexual Behavior, 40*, 237–246.

Diamond, M. (1991). Hormonal effects on the development of cerebral lateralization. *Psychoneuroendocrinology, 16*, 121–129.

Diamond, M. (1997). Sexual identity and sexual orientation in children with traumatized or ambiguous genitalia. *Journal of Sex Research, 34*, 199–211.

Diamond, M. (1998). Intersexuality: Recommendations for management. *Archives of Sexual Behavior, 27*, 634–641.

Diamond, M., & Sigmundson, H. (1997). Sex reassignment at birth: Long-term review and clinical implications. *Archives of Pediatric and Adolescent Medicine, 151*, 298–304.

Diamond, R., Kezur, D., Meyers, M., Scharf, C., & Weinshel, M. (1999). *Couple therapy for infertility.* New York: Guilford Press.

Diaz, A., Bhandari, S., et al. (2008). Characteristics of children with premature pubarche in the New York metropolitan area. *Hormone Research, 70*, 150–154.

DiBlasio, N. (2012). Roommate in Rutgers webcam case gets 30 days. *USA Today*, May 22, p. 5A.

Dickerman, J. (2007). Circumcision in the time of HIV: When is there enough evidence to revise the American Academy of Pediatrics policy on circumcision? *Pediatrics, 119*, 1006–1007.

Dieffenbach, C., & Fauci, A. (2011). Thirty years of HIV and AIDS: Future challenges and opportunities. *Annals of Internal Medicine, 154*, 766–771.

DiFulvio, G. (2011). Sexual minority youth, social connections and resilience: From personal struggle to collective identity. *Social Science and Medicine, 72*, 1611–1617.

Dilley, J., Woods, W., & McFarland, W. (1997). Are advances in treatment changing views about high-risk sex? *New England Journal of Medicine, 337*, 501–502.

Dilorio, C., Hartwell, T., & Hanson, N. (2002). Childhood sexual abuse and risk behaviors among men at high risk for HIV infection. *American Journal of Public Health, 92*, 214–219.

Dirks, T. (2006). Timeline of influential milestones and turning points in film history. Retrieved October 13, 2006, from http://www.filmsite.org/milestone-spre1900s.html

Djinovic, R. (2011). Penile corporoplasty in Peyronies' disease: Which technique, which graft? *Current Opinion in Urology, 6*, 470–477.

Doan, A., & Williams, J. (2008). *The politics of virginity: Abstinence in sex education.* Westport, CT: Praeger.

Doctor, R., & Prince, V. (1997). Transvestism: A survey of 1,032 cross-dressers. *Archives of Sexual Behavior, 26*, 589–605.

Dodson, B. (1974). *Liberating masturbation.* New York: Betty Dodson.

Doheny, K. (2009, April 22). New view in debate on breast self-exams. Retrieved from http://www.webmd.com/breast-cancer/news/20090422/new-view-in-debate-on-breast-self-exams

Dokoupil, T. (2009, January 19). The lost shepherd. *Newsweek*, 53–54.

Dolezal, C., et al. (2011). A comparison of audio computer-assisted self-interviews to face-to-face interviews of sexual behavior among perinatally HIV-exposed youth. *Archives of Sexual Behavior, May 21*, 1–10.

Dolgoff, S. (2008). The best (and worst) moments in women's health. *Health*, September, 138–141.

Donaldson, R., & Meana, M. (2011). Early dyspareunia experience in young women: Confusion, consequences, and help-seeking barriers. *Journal of Sexual Medicine, 8*, 814–823.

Donaldson, Z., & Young, L. (2008). Oxytocin, vasopressin, and the neurogenics of sociability. *Science, 322*, 900–904.

Donnelly, P., & White, C. (2000). Testicular dysfunction in men with primary hypothyroidism: Reversal of hypogonadotrophic hypogonadism with replacement thyroxine. *Clinical Endocrinology, 52*, 197–201.

Donnerstein, E., & Linz, D. (1984, January). Sexual violence in the media: A warning. *Psychology Today*, 14–15.

Doskoch, P. (2005). Evidence supporting the notion that bacterial vaginosis can be transmitted sexually continues to accumulate. *Perspectives on Sexual and Reproductive Health, 37*, 206.

Doskoch, P. (2011). Many men 75 and older consider sex important and remain sexually active. *Perspectives on Sexual and Reproductive Health, 43*, 67–68.

Doss, B., Rhoades, G., & Scott, S. (2009). The effect of the transition to parenthood on relationship quality: An 8-year prospective study. *Journal of Personality and Social Psychology, 96*, 601–619.

Douglas, C., Verna, P., Goktepe, K., & Nixon, L. (2005). United States: Men coerce women into vaginal cosmetic surgery. *Off Our Backs, 35*, 9.

Douglas, K. (1999). *Sexuality and the Black church: A womanist perspective*. Maryknoll, NY: Orbis Books.

Douglas, T. (2006, August 14). The new world is on the ascent. *Education News*, 27.

Douglass, M., & Lin, J. (2010). Erectile dysfunction and premature ejaculation: Underlying causes and available treatments. *Formulary, 45*, 17–27.

Dow, M., Hart, D., & Forrest, C. (1983). Hormonal treatments of unresponsiveness in post-menopausal women: A comparative study. *British Journal of Obstetrics and Gynecology, 90*, 361–366.

Dowell, D., et al. (2012). Changes in fluoroquinolone use for gonorrhea following publication of revised treatment guidelines. *American Journal of Public Health, 102*, 148–155.

Dowling, T. (2008). Mandating a human papillomavirus vaccine: An investigation into whether such legislation is constitutional and prudent. *American Journal of Law and Medicine, 34*, 65–84.

Downs, V., & Javidi, M. (1990). Linking communication motives to loneliness in the lives of older adults: An empirical test of interpersonal needs and gratifications. *Journal of Applied Communication Research, 18*, 32–48.

Doyle, A. (2006, October 12). Homosexual animals exhibit opens. Retrieved November 8, 2006, from http://www.news.com.au/story/0,23599,20571062-1702,00.html

Doyle, J., & Paludi, M. (1991). *Sex and gender* (2nd ed.). Dubuque, IA: Brown and Benchmark.

Drach, L., et al. (2011). Should we move from syringe exchange to distribution? *American Journal of Public Health, 101*, 389–390.

Dragowski, E., et al. (2011). Childhood gender identity . . . disorder? Developmental, cultural, and diagnostic concerns. *Journal of Counseling and Development, 89*, 360–366.

Dreger, A. (2003). Notes on the treatment of intersex. Retrieved February 19, 2003, from http://www.isna.org

Dreger, A., Feder, E., & Tamar-Mattis, A. (2010, June 29). Preventing homosexuality (and uppity women) in the womb? Retrieved from http://www.thehastingscenter.org/Bioethicsforum?Post.aspx?id=4754&blogid=140&utm

Dreier, H. (2011). Jewish groups oppose circumcision ban in US city. Retrieved March 5, 2011, from http://news.yahoo.com/s/afp/ushealthnewsreligioncircumcision

Drey, M., Pastoetter, J., & Pryce, A. (2009). Sex-Study 2008: Sexual behavior in Germany. DGSS and City University London in Collaboration with ProSieben. Duesseldorf–London, forthcoming.

Dreznick, M. (2003). Heterosocial competence of rapists and child molesters: A meta-analysis. *Journal of Sex Research, 40*, 170–178.

Drigotas, S., Rusbult, C., & Verette, J. (1999). Level of commitment, mutuality of commitment, and couple well-being. *Personal Relationships, 6*, 389–409.

Drysdale, K. (2010, March 3). Healing it to a single crease. Retrieved from http://hungrybeast.abc.net.au/blog/kdrysdale/healing-it-single-crease

Dubé, E. (2000). The role of sexual behavior in the identification process of gay and bisexual males. *Journal of Sex Research, 37*, 123–132.

Duberstein, L., Lindberg, R., & Santelli, J. (2008). Non-coital sexual activities among adolescents. *Journal of Adolescent Health, 42*, 44–45.

Duffy, J., Warren, K., & Walsh, M. (2001). Classroom interactions: Gender of teacher, gender of student and classroom subject. *Sex Roles, 45*, 579–593.

Dugger, C. (2008, November 27). South African AIDS policies cost lives. *Oregonian*, p. A20.

Duncan, S. (2011). A legal response is necessary for self-produced child pornography: A legislator's checklist for drafting bill. *Oregon Law Review, 89*, 645–668.

Dunn, M., & Cutler, N. (2000). Sexual issues in older adults. *AIDS Patient Care and STDs, 14*, 67–69.

Dunn, M., & Trost, J. (1989). Male multiple orgasms: A descriptive study. *Archives of Sexual Behavior, 18*, 377–388.

Durex. (2006). 2005 global sex survey results. Retrieved July 3, 2006, from www.durex.com/gss

Durex. (2008). Sexual well-being global survey 2007/2008. Retrieved April 4, 2009, from http://wwwdurexworld.com/en-US/SexualWellbeingSurvey/pages/default.aspx

Dush, C., & Taylor, M. (2012). Trajectories of marital conflict across the life course: Predictors and interactions with marital happiness trajectories. *Journal of Family Issues, 33*, 341–368.

Dworkin, S., & O'Sullivan, L. (2005). Actual versus desired initiation patterns among a sample of college men: Tapping disjunctures within traditional male sexual scripts. *Journal of Sex Research, 42*, 150–158.

Dwyer, M. (1988). Exhibitionism/voyeurism. *Journal of Social Work and Human Sexuality, 7*, 101–112.

Dzokoto, V., & Adams, G. (2005). Understanding genital-shrinkage epidemics in West Africa: Koro, juju, or mass psychological illness? *Culture, Medicine, and Psychiatry, 29*, 53–78.

Eardley, I., Collins, O., Hackett, G., & Edwards, D. (2006). Partners of heterosexual men with erectile dysfunction, treated with vardenafil, feel themselves to be sexually more desirable. *Journal of Sexual Medicine, 3*(Suppl. 3), 224–286.

Eastwick, P., Finkel, P., & Eli, J. (2008). Sex differences in mate preferences revisited: Do people know what they initially desire in a romantic partner? *Journal of Personality and Social Psychology, 9*, 245–264.

Eaton, S. (2004). Sierra Leone: The proving ground for prosecuting rape as a war crime. *Georgetown Journal of International Law, 35*, 873–919.

Eberstadt, M. (2009). Is pornography the new tobacco? *Policy Review, 154*, 3–19.

Eccles, A., Marshall, W., & Barbaree, H. (1994). Differentiating rapists and non-rapists using the rape index. *Behaviour Research and Therapy, 32*, 539–546.

Eccles, J., Barber, E., & Jozefowicz, D. (1999). Linking gender to educational, occupational, and recreational choices: Applying the Eccles et al. model of achievement-related choices. In W. Swann & J. Langlois (Eds.), *Sexism and stereotypes in modern society: The gender science of Janet Taylor Spence*. Washington, DC: American Psychological Association.

Ecker, N. (1993). Culture and sexual scripts out of Africa. *SIECUS Report, 22,* 16.

Edlin, B. (2011). Test and treat this silent killer. *Nature, 474,* S18–S19.

Edwards, J. (2008). Diagnosis and management of benign prostatic hyperplasia. *American Family Physician, 77,* 1403–1405.

Edwards, K., et al. (2012). Rape myths: history, individual and institutional-level presence and implications for change. *Sex Roles, 65,* 761–773.

Egan, N. (2012, March 19). Are sperm donors' kids at risk? *People,* 110.

Eggener, S., Mueller, S., et al. (2009). A multi-institutional evaluation of active surveillance for low-risk prostate cancer. *Journal of Urology, 181,* 1635–1641.

Eheman, C., Peipins, L., Wynn, M., & Ryerson, B. (2006). Development of a public health research program for ovarian cancer. *Journal of Women's Health, 15,* 339–345.

Eibach, R., & Mock, S. (2011). Idealizing parenthood to rationalize parental investments. *Psychological Science, 22,* 203–208.

Ein-Dor, T., & Hirschberger, G. (2012). Sexual healing: Daily diary evidence that sex relieves stress for men and women in satisfying relationships. *Journal of Social and Personal Relationships, 29,* 126–139.

Einstein, G. (2008). From body to brain: Considering the neurobiological effects of female genital cutting. *Perspectives in Biology and Medicine, 51,* 84–98.

Eisenstein, M. (2011). Vaccines: A moving target. *Nature, 474,* S16–S17.

Eisner, T., Conner, J., & Carrel, J. (1990). Systemic retention of ingested cantharidin by frogs. *Chemoecology, 1,* 57–62.

Eitzen, D., & Zinn, M. (2000). *Social problems* (8th ed.). Boston: Allyn and Bacon.

Eke, N., & Nkanginieme, K. (2006). Female genital mutilation and obstetric outcome. *Lancet, 367,* 1799–1800.

Elder, S. (2005, March/April). The lock box. *Psychology Today,* 42–46.

Elders, J. (2010). Sex for health and pleasure throughout a lifetime. *Journal of Sexual Medicine, 7,* 248–249.

Elias, J., & Gebhard, P. (1969). Sexuality and sexual learning in childhood. *Phi Delta Kappan, 50,* 401–405.

Eliot, L. (2009). *Pink brain, blue brain: How small differences grow into troublesome gaps—and what we can do about it.* Boston: Houghton Mifflin Harcourt.

Elkind, D. (1967). Egocentrism in adolescence. *Child Development, 38,* 1025–1034.

Elkins, T., Phillips, J., & Ward, S. (2008). Organizational sexual harassment investigations: Observers' perceptions of fairness. *Journal of Managerial Issues, 20,* 88–108.

Elliott, D. (2012). Can we better predict and treat urinary incontinence after prostatectomy? *Journal of Urology, 187,* 789–790.

Elliott, L., & Brantley, C. (1997). *Sex on campus.* New York: Random House.

Elliott, M. (1992). Tip of the iceberg? *Social Work Today,* March, 12–13.

Elliott, S., & Burgess, V. (2005). The presence of gamma-hydroxybutyric acid (GHB) and gamma-butyrolactone (GBL) in alcoholic and nonalcoholic beverages. *Forensic Science International, 151,* 289–292.

Ellis, L., Robb, B., & Burke, D. (2005). Sexual orientation in United States and Canadian college students. *Archives of Sexual Behavior, 34,* 569–582.

Ellison, C. (2000). *Women's sexualities.* Oakland, CA: New Harbinger Publications.

El-Noshokaty, A. (2006). Sex and the city. Retrieved September 26, 2006, from http://weekly.ahram.org.eg/print/2006/813/lil.htm

Elton, C. (2010, May/June). Learning to lust. *Psychology Today,* 70–77.

England, P. (2010). The gender revolution: Uneven and stalled. *Gender and Society, 24,* 149–166.

Ensler, E. (2006, June). Belly, dancing. *O: The Oprah Magazine,* 47.

Epp, S. (1997). The diagnosis and treatment of athletic amenorrhea. *Physician Assistant,* March, 129–144.

Epstein, H. (2007). *The invisible cure: Africa, the West, and the fight against AIDS.* New York: Farrar, Straus and Giroux/Macmillan.

Epstein, R. (2006). Do gays have a choice? *Scientific American Mind,* February/March, 51–57.

Equal Employment Opportunity Commission. (1980). Guidelines on discrimination because of sex. *Federal Register, 45,* 74676–74677.

Equal Employment Opportunity Commission. (2009). *Sexual harassment charges EEOC and FEPHS combined.* Retrieved February 7, 2009, from http://www.eeoc.gov/stat/harass.html

Ertelt, S. (2011, August 8). Members of Congress back Indiana Planned Parenthood de-funding. Retrieved from http://aclj.org/planned-parenthood/lifenews-members-congress-back-indiana-planned-parenthood-defunding

Escobar-Chaves, S., Tortolero, S., Markham, C., & Low, B. (2005). Impact of the media on adolescent sexual attitudes and behaviors. *Pediatrics, 116,* 303–326.

Espelage, D., Aragon, S., Birkett, M., & Koenig, B. (2008). Homophobic teasing, psychological outcomes, and sexual orientation among high school students: What influence do parents and schools have? *School Psychology Review, 37,* 202–216.

Essen, B., Blomkvist, A., Helstrom, L., & Johnsdotter, S. (2010). The experience and responses of Swedish health professionals to patients requesting virginity restoration. *Reproductive Health Matters, 18,* 38–39.

Estrada, F., et al. (2011). Machismo and Mexican American men: An empirical understanding using a gay sample. *Journal of Counseling Psychology, 58,* 358–367.

Evans, M. (2009, March 2). The truth about multiple births. *Newsweek,* 14.

Evans, M., et al. (2011). Circumcision in boys and girls: Why the double standard? *British Medical Journal, 342,* 978.

Evans, N. (2006). *State of evidence.* San Francisco: Breast Cancer Fund.

Ewing, M. (2011, September 30). Abortion suicide link fails a court test. Retrieved from http://www.womensenews.org/pring8789

Eyal, K., & Kunkel, D. (2008). The effects of sex in television drama shows on emerging adults' sexual attitudes and moral judgments. *Journal of Broadcasting and Electronic Media, 52,* 161–183.

Fahim, K. (2011, June 20). Claims of wartime rape unsettle and divide Libyans. *New York Times,* p. A11.

Fahs, B. (2011). *Performing sex: The making and unmaking of women's erotic lives.* Albany: The State University of New York Press.

Fan, M. (2006, September 20). On China's airwaves, a discourse on sex ed: Radio show caters to young audience. Retrieved September 26, 2006, from http://www.boston.com/news/world/asia/articles/2006/09/20/on_chinas_airwaves_a_discourse_on_sex_ed

Fang, B. (2007, Spring). The Talibanization of Iraq. *Ms.,* 46–51.

Fang, J. (2010). Hiding place for HIV revealed. Retrieved October 15, 2010, from http://www.nature.com/news/2010/100306/fall/news.2010.109.html

Farley, M. (2004). *Prostitution, trafficking, and traumatic stress.* New York: Haworth Maltreatment and Trauma Press.

Farr, K. (2004). *Sex trafficking: The global market in women and children.* New York: W. H. Freedman.

Farr, L. (2000, June). The danger zone. *W*, 100–104.

Faul, M. (2011, May 29). Libyan women report rapes. *Oregonian*, p. A11.

Fausto-Sterling, A. (1993). The five sexes: Why male and female are not enough. *Sciences*, *33*, 20–24.

Fausto-Sterling, A. (2000). *Sexing the body: Gender politics and the construction of sexuality*. New York: Basic Books.

FDA. (2011, May 31). Birth control pills containing drospirenone: Possible increase of blood clots. Retrieved from http://www.fda.gov/Safety/MedWatch/SafetyInformation/SafetyAlertsforHumanMedicalProducts

Federman, D. (2006). The biology of human sex differences. *New England Journal of Medicine*, *354*, 1507–1514.

Fedora, O., Reddon, J., Morrison, J., & Fedora, S. (1992). Sadism and other paraphilias in normal controls and aggressive and nonaggressive sex offenders. *Archives of Sexual Behavior*, *21*, 1–15.

Feeney, J., & Noller, P. (1996). *Adult attachment*. Thousand Oaks, CA: Sage.

Fei, C., McLaughlin, J., Lipworth, L., & Olsen, J. (2009, January 28). Maternal levels of perflourinated chemicals and subfecundity. Retrieved April 21, 2009, from http://humrep.oxfordjournals.org/cgi/contents/abstract/den490v1

Feiring, C., Simon, V., et al. (2009). Childhood sexual abuse, stigmatization, internalizing symptoms, and the development of sexual difficulties and dating aggression. *Journal of Consulting and Clinical Psychology*, *77*, 127–137.

Feldman, C. (2011, February 21). Social networks carry risks at any age. *Oregonian*, p. B7.

Fenigstein, A., & Preston, M. (2007). The desired number of sexual partners as a function of gender, sexual risks, and the meaning of "ideal." *Journal of Sex Research*, *44*, 89–95.

Fentiman, I., Fourquet, F., & Hortobagyi, G. (2006). Male breast cancer. *Lancet*, *367*, 595–605.

Ferber, L. (2006, July 18). Queering the comics. *Advocate*, 51.

Ferguson, D., Hosmane, B., & Heiman, J. (2010). Randomized, placebo-controlled, double-blind, parallel design trial of the efficacy and safety of Zestra. *Journal of Sex and Marital Therapy*, *36*, 66–86.

Ferguson, D., Steidle, C., Singh, G., Alexander, S., et al. (2003). Randomized, placebo-controlled, double-blind, crossover design trial of the efficacy and safety of Zestra for women in women with and without female sexual arousal disorder. *Journal of Sex and Marital Therapy*, *29*, 33–44.

Ferguson, N. (2011, March 14). Men without women: The ominous rise of Asia's bachelor generation. *Newsweek*, 15.

Fernandes, E. (2008, December). The swinging paradigm: An evaluation of the marital and sexual satisfaction of swingers. Retrieved March 17, 2009, from http://www.ejhs.org/Volum12/Swinging.htm

Feroli, K., & Burstein, G. (2003). Adolescent sexually transmitted diseases. *American Journal of Maternal/Child Nursing*, *28*, 113–118.

Fetters, A. (2011, December). The new full-frontal: Has pubic hair in America gone extinct? Retrieved from http://www.theatlantic.com/health/print/2011/12the-new-full-frontal-has-pubic-hair-in-america-gone-extinct?

Fields, J., & Casper, L. (2001). *America's families and living arrangements: March 2000*. Washington, DC: U.S. Census Bureau.

Fierer, D., et al. (2011). Sexual transmission of hepatitis C virus among HIV-infected men who have sex with men—New York City, 2005–2010. *Morbidity and Mortality Weekly Report*, *60*, 945–950.

Fifer, W., Ten Fingers, S., Youngman, M., et al. (2009). Effects of alcohol and smoking during pregnancy on infant autonomic control. *Developmental Psychobiology*, *51*, 234–242.

Fillion, K. (1996, February). This is the sexual revolution? *Saturday Night*, 36–41.

Fine, R. (2008, November 7–9). *Multidisciplinary approach for prostate cancer awareness*. Paper presented at the 18th Deutsche Gesellschaft für Sozialwissenschaftliche Sexualforschung Conference, "Sexuality and the Media," Munich, Germany.

Finer, L., & Zolna, M. (2011). Unintended pregnancy in the United States: Incidence and disparities, 2006. *Contraception*, *84*, 478–485.

Finger, W. (2000). Avoiding sexual exploitation: Guidelines for therapists. *SIECUS Report*, *28*, 12–13.

Finger, W., Lund, M., & Slagle, M. (1997). Medications that may contribute to sexual disorders. *Journal of Family Practice*, *44*, 33–43.

Finger, W., Quillen, J., & Slagle, M. (2000, May 10–14). *They can't all be viagra: Medications causing sexual dysfunctions*. Paper presented at the 32nd Annual Conference of the American Association of Sex Educators, Counselors, and Therapists, Atlanta, Georgia.

Fingerhut, A. (2011). Straight allies: What predicts heterosexuals' alliance with the LGBT community? *Journal of Applied Social Psychology*, *41*, 2230–2248.

Fingerhut, A., Riggle, E., & Rostosky, S. (2011). Same-sex marriage: The social and psychological implications of policy and debates. *Journal of Social Issues*, *67*, 225–241.

Fink, J. (2006). Practical tips for women who suffer from yeast infections. *RN*, *69*, 52.

Fink, P. (2012). The sex abuse scandal at Penn State is making pedophiles part of the national conversation. How should psychiatrists process this case as it unfolds? *Clinical Psychiatry News*, *40*, 6–7.

Finkelhor, D. (1993). Epidemiological factors in the clinical identification of child sexual abuse. *Child Abuse and Neglect*, *17*, 67–70.

Finkelhor, D. (1994). The international epidemiology of child sexual abuse. *Child Abuse and Neglect*, *18*, 409–417.

Finkelhor, D., & Ormrod, R. (2004). Prostitution of juveniles: Patterns from NIBRS. *Juvenile Justice Bulletin*, June, 1–2.

Finnegan, W. (2008, May 5). The counter-traffickers. *New Yorker*, 42–59.

Fischer, J., & Heesacker, M. (1995). Men's and women's preferences regarding sex-related and nurturing traits in dating partners. *Journal of College Student Development*, *36*, 260–269.

Fischetti, M. (2011a, February 14). Your brain in love. *Scientific American*, 17.

Fischetti, M. (2011b). Passionate love in the brain as revealed by MRI scans. *Scientific American*, *14*, 2.

Fisher, L. (2010). *Sex, romance, and relationships: AARP survey of midlife and older adults*. Washington, DC: AARP.

Fisher, M., Ulrich, T., & Voracek, M. (2008). The influence of relationship status, mate seeking, and sex on intrasexual competition. *Journal of Social Psychology*, *148*, 493–508.

Fisher, W., Branscombe, N., & Lemery, C. (1983). The bigger the better? Arousal and attributional responses to erotic stimuli that depict different size penises. *Journal of Sex Research*, *19*, 377–396.

Fisher, W., Rosen, R., Sand, M., & Eardley, I. (2006). Prevalence of premature ejaculation among men with erectile dysfunction in the men's attitudes to life events and sexuality (MALES) study. *Journal of Sexual Medicine*, *3*(Suppl. 3), 176–198.

Flam, F. (2008, February 7). Carnal knowledge: They give pleasure; science asks why. *Philadelphia Inquirer*.

Flanders, L. (1998, March/April). Rwanda's living casualties. *Ms.*, 27–30.

Fleming, M., & Kleinbart, E. (2001). Breast cancer and sexuality. *Journal of Sex Education and Therapy*, *26*, 215–224.

Fleming, M., & Pace, J. (2001). Sexuality and chronic pain. *Journal of Sex Education and Therapy*, *26*, 204–214.

Fleming, M., & Rickwood, D. (2004). Teens in cyberspace: Do they encounter friend or foe? *Youth Studies Australia, 23*, 46–52.

Flory, N., Bissonnette, F., Amsel, R., & Binik, Y. (2006). The psychosocial outcomes of total and subtotal hysterectomy: A randomized controlled trial. *Journal of Sexual Medicine, 3*, 483–491.

Floyd, K. (2006). *Communicating affection: Interpersonal behavior and social context.* Cambridge, England: Cambridge University Press.

Floyd, K., Mikkelson, A., Tafoya, M., et al. (2007). Human affection exchange: XIV. Relational affection predicts resting heart rate and free cortisol secretion during acute stress. *Behavioral Medicine, 32*, 151–155.

Floyd, K., & Morman, M. (2000). Affection received from fathers as a predictor of men's affection with their own sons: Tests of the modeling and compensation hypotheses. *Community Monograph, 67*, 347–361.

Foderaro, L. (2011, April 21). Roommate faces hate-crime charges in Rutgers spying-suicide case. *New York Times*, p. A19.

Foehr, U. (2006). *Media multitasking among American youth.* Menlo Park, CA: Henry J. Kaiser Family Foundation.

Foldes, P., & Silvestre, C. (2007, April 15–19). *Surgical repair of the clitoris after ritual genital mutilation: Results on 453 cases.* Paper presented at the 18th Congress of the World Association for Sexual Health, Sydney, Australia.

Foley, D. (2006). Spice up your love life. *Prevention, 58*, 172.

Foley, D., & Nechas, L. (1995). *Before you hit the pillow, talk.* New York: Bantam Books.

Foley, S. (2003). Women in sex therapy: Developing a sexual identity. *Contemporary Sexuality, 37*, 7–13.

Fone, B. (2000). *Homophobia: A history.* New York: Metropolitan Books.

Food and Drug Administration. (1997). FDA statement on generic Premarin. Retrieved May 5, 2003, from http://www.fda.gov/cder/cepressrelease.htm

Footner, A. (2008, January 8). Paraguay's traffic hub imperils female teens. Retrieved January 8, 2008, from Women's eNews.

Forbes, G., Adams-Curtis, L., White, K., & Holmgren, K. (2003). The role of hostile and benevolent sexism in women's and men's perceptions of the menstruating woman. *Psychology of Women Quarterly, 27*, 58–63.

Ford, C., & Beach, F. (1951). *Patterns of sexual behavior.* New York: Harper and Row.

Forrest, J., & Singh, S. (1990). The sexual and reproductive behavior of American women, 1982–1988. *Family Planning Perspectives, 22*, 206–214.

Forsyth, C. (1996). The structuring of vicarious sex. *Deviant Behavior: An Interdisciplinary Journal, 17*, 279–295.

Fortenberry, D., et al. (2010). Sexual behaviors and condom use at last vaginal intercourse: A national sample of adolescents ages 14 to 17 years. *Journal of Sexual Medicine, 7*, 305–314.

Fox, R., Burton, D., & Lawson, D. (2006, June/July). *The effect of spiritual attitudes on hypoactive sexual desire disorder.* Paper presented at the Gumbo Sexualité Upriver: Spicing Up Education and Therapy (AASECT 38th Annual Conference), St. Louis, MO.

Fox, T. (1995). *Sexuality and Catholicism.* New York: George Braziller.

Francis, A. (2008). Family and sexual orientation: The family-demographic correlates of homosexuality in men and women. *Journal of Sex Research, 45*, 371–378.

Frank, J., Mistretta, P., & Will, J. (2008). Diagnosis and treatment of female sexual dysfunction. *American Family Physician, 77*, 635–650.

Franke, A. (2008). New lessons in dealing with sexual harassment. *Chronicle of Higher Education, 55*.

Frank-Hermann, P., Heil, J., Gnoth, C., Toledo, E., & Baur, S. (2007). The effectiveness of a fertility awareness–based method to avoid pregnancy in relation to a couple's sexual behavior during the fertile time. *Human Reproduction, 22*, 1310–1319.

Franklin, R., & Dotger, S. (2011). Sex education knowledge differences between freshman and senior college undergraduates. *College Student Journal, 45*, 199–213.

Frankowski, B. (2004). Sexual orientation and adolescents. *Pediatrics, 113*, 1827–1832.

Fraser, L. (1999, September 6). Why more men are going under the knife. *Ottawa Citizen*, p. A10.

Fraunfelder, F. (2000). Treating your patients with breast cancer. *British Medical Journal, 320*, 457–459.

Frayser, S. (1994). Defining normal childhood sexuality: An anthropological approach. *Annual Review of Sex Research, 5*, 173–217.

Frazier, K. (2006). Memory wars and monster stories. *Skeptical Inquirer, 30*, 4.

Frazier, K., West-Olatunji, C., Juste, S., & Goodman, R. (2009). Transgenerational trauma and child sexual abuse: Reconceptualizing cases involving young survivors of CSA. *Journal of Mental Health Counseling, 31*, 22–33.

Frazier, P. (1993). A comparative study of male and female victims seen at hospital-based rape crises programs. *Journal of Interpersonal Violence, 8*, 65–79.

Freedland, S., et al. (2011). Screening, risk assessment, and the approach to therapy in patients with prostate cancer. *Cancer, 117*, 1123–1135.

Freeman, P., et al. (2011). Methamphetamine use and risk for HIV among young men who have sex with men in 8 U.S. cities. *Archives of Pediatric and Adolescent Medicine, 165*, 736–740.

French, D., & Dishion, T. (2003). Predictors of early initiation of sexual intercourse among high-risk adolescents. *Journal of Early Adolescence, 23*, 295–315.

Freud, S. (2000). *Three essays on the theory of sexuality.* New York: Basic Books Classics. (Original work published 1905).

Freund, K., & Blanchard, R. (1993). Erotic target location errors in male gender dysphorics, paedophiles, and fetishists. *British Journal of Psychiatry, 162*, 558–563.

Freund, K., Seto, M., & Kuban, M. (1996). Two types of fetishism. *Behaviour Research and Therapy, 34*, 687–694.

Freund, K., Seto, M., & Kuban, M. (1997). Frotteurism and the theory of courtship disorder. In D. Laws & W. O'Donohue (Eds.), *Sexual deviance: Theory, assessment, and treatment.* New York: Guilford Press.

Freund, M., Lee, N., & Leonard, T. (1991). Sexual behavior of clients with street prostitutes in Camden, N.J. *Journal of Sex Research, 28*, 579–591.

Friday, N. (1980). *Men in love.* New York: Delacorte.

Friedan, B. (1994). *The fountain of age.* New York: Simon and Schuster.

Friedrich, M. (2011a). Emerging HIV epidemic. *Journal of the American Medical Association, 306*, 1191.

Friedrich, M. (2011b). TB prevention and HIV. *Journal of the American Medical Association, 305*, 243–244.

Friedrich, M. (2012). HIV trial modification. *Journal of the American Medical Association, 307*, 243.

Friedrich, W., Fisher, J., Broughton, D., Houston, M., & Shafran, C. (1998). Normative sexual behavior in children: A contemporary sample. *Pediatrics, 101*, 1–13. Retrieved May 30, 2000, from http://www.pediatrics.org/cgi/content/full/101/4/e9

Friedrich, W., Grambsch, P., Broughton, D., Kuiper, J., & Beilke, R. (1991). Normative sexual behavior in children. *Pediatrics, 88*, 456–464.

Friess, S. (2003, March 24). Jews oy, two boys? *Newsweek*, 8.

Frisch, M., et al. (2011). Associations of unhealthy lifestyle factors with sexual inactivity and sexual dysfunctions in Denmark. *Journal of Sexual Medicine, 8,* 1903–1916.

Fritz, M., & Speroff, L. (2010). *Clinical gynecologic endocrinology and infertility* (8th ed.). New York: Lippincott, Williams & Wilkins.

Frohlich, P., & Meston, C. (2005). Tactile sensitivity in women with sexual arousal disorder. *Archives of Sexual Behavior, 34,* 207–218.

Fromm, E. (1965). *The ability to love.* New York: Farrar, Straus and Giroux.

Frost, D. (2011). Similarities and differences in the pursuit of intimacy among sexual minority and heterosexual individuals: A personal projects analysis. *Journal of Social Issues, 67,* 282–301.

Frost, D., & Meyer, I. (2009). Internalized homophobia and relationship quality among lesbians, gay men, and bisexuals. *Journal of Counseling Psychology, 56,* 97–109.

Frost, J., & Darroch, J. (2008). Factors associated with contraceptive choice and inconsistent method use, United States, 2004. *Perspectives on Sexual and Reproductive Health, 40,* 94–104.

Fu, H., Darroch, J., Hass, T., & Ranjit, N. (1999). Contraceptive failure rates: New estimates from the 1995 National Survey of Family Growth. *Family Planning Perspectives, 31,* 56–63.

Fugere, M., Escoto, C., Cousins, A., et al. (2008). Sexual attitudes and double standards: A literature review focusing on participant gender and ethnic background. *Sexuality and Culture, 12,* 169–182.

Fugh-Berman, A. (2008). Hormones for hot flashes: Is "natural" better? *Women's Health Activist, 33,* 11–13.

Fugl-Meyer, K., Oberg, K., Lundberg, P., & Lewin, B. (2006). On orgasm, sexual techniques, and erotic perceptions in 18- to 74-year-old Swedish women. *Journal of Sexual Medicine, 3,* 56–68.

Furman, W., & Shaffer, L. (2011). Romantic partners, friends with benefits, and casual acquaintances as sexual partners. *Journal of Sex Research, 48,* 554–564.

Gaboury, J. (2005). A personal perspective: Saying "I don't." *SIECUS Report, 33,* 29–31.

Gaby, A. (2005, December). Vitamin E relieves menstrual pain. *Townsend Letter for Doctors and Patients,* 46.

Gaby, A. (2011, February/March). Cranberry for chronic nonbacterial prostatitis. *Townsend Letter,* 331–332.

Galbally, M., et al. (2011). The role of oxytocin in mother-infant relations: A systematic review of human studies. *Harvard Review of Psychiatry, 19,* 1–14.

Galewitz, P. (2000). New birth control method approved. Retrieved October 6, 2000, from http://www.salon.com/mwt/wire/2000/10/06/birth_control/index.html

Galhardo, A., et al. (2011). The impact of shame and self-judgment on psychopathology in infertile patients. *Human Reproduction, 26,* 2408–2414.

Galinsky, A., & Sonenstein, F. (2011). The association between developmental assets and sexual enjoyment among emerging adults. *Journal of Adolescent Health, 48,* 610–615.

Gallo, L., & Smith, T. (2001). Attachment style in marriage: Adjustment and responses to interaction. *Journal of Social and Personal Relationships, 18,* 263–289.

Gange, S. (1999). When is adult circumcision necessary? Retrieved September 20, 1999, from http://www.cnn.com/HEALTH/men/circumcision.adult/index.html

Gangestad, S., Thornhill, R., & Garver-Apgar, C. (2010). Fertility in the cycle predicts women's interest in sexual opportunism. *Evolution and Human Behavior, 31,* 400–411.

Ganong, L., & Coleman, M. (1987). Sex, sex roles, and family love. *Journal of Genetic Psychology, 148,* 45–52.

Gao, F., Bailes, E., Robertson, D., et al. (1999). Origin of HIV-1 in chimpanzee *Pan troglodytes troglodytes. Nature, 397,* 436–441.

Garcia, L. (1982). Sex-role orientation and stereotypes about male-female sexuality. *Sex Roles, 8,* 863–876.

Garcia, L., & Markey, C. (2007). Matching in sexual experience for married, cohabitating, and dating couples. *Journal of Sex Research, 44,* 250–255.

Gardner, M. (2006). The memory wars: Part I. *Skeptical Inquirer, 30,* 28–31.

Garlough, C. (2008). The risks of acknowledgement: Performing the sex-selection identification and abortion debate. *Women's Studies in Communication, 31,* 368–395.

Garnick, M., & Rose, S. (2008, January 21). Very personal medicine. *Newsweek,* 69.

Garos, S. (1994). Autoerotic asphyxiation: A challenge to death educators and counselors. *Omega: Journal of Death and Dying, 28,* 85–99.

Gartell, N., Bos, H. & Goldberg, N. (2011). Adolescents of the U.S. National Longitudinal Lesbian Family Study: Sexual orientation, sexual behavior, and sexual risk exposure. *Archives of Sexual Behavior, 40,* 1199–1209.

Garza-Leal, J., & Landron, F. (1991). Autoerotic asphyxial death initially

misinterpreted as suicide and review of the literature. *Journal of Forensic Science, 36,* 1753–1759.

Gaspari, L. (2011). Prenatal environmental risk factors for genital malformations in a population of 1,442 French newborns. *Human Reproduction, 26,* 3155–3159.

Gastaud, F., et al. (2007). Impaired sexual and reproductive outcomes in women with classical forms of congenital adrenal hyperplasia. *Journal of Clinical Endocrinology and Metabolism, 92,* 1391–1396.

Gates, G., Badgett, L., & Ho, D. (2008, July). Marriage, registration and dissolution by same-sex couples. Retrieved January 1, 2009, from http://www.law.ucla.edu/williamsinstitute/homne/html

Gates, G., & Cooke, A. (2011). *United States census snapshot: 2011.* Los Angeles, CA: Williams Institute.

Gazzar, B. (2008, February 21). Spain sizes up fashion world's measuring stick. Retrieved February 22, 2008, from Women's eNews.

Geary, S., & Moon, Y. (2006). The human embryo in vitro: Recent progress. *Journal of Reproductive Medicine, 51,* 293–302.

Gebhard, P. (1971). Human sexual behavior: A summary statement. In D. Marshall & R. Suggs (Eds.), *Human sexual behavior: Variations in the ethnographic spectrum.* Englewood Cliffs, NJ: Prentice Hall.

Gebhard, P., Gagnon, J., Pomery, W., & Christenson, C. (1965). *Sex offenders: An analysis of types.* New York: Harper and Row.

Geer, J., & Manguno-Mire, G. (1997). Gender differences in cognitive processes in sexuality. *Annual Review of Sex Research, 7,* 90–124.

Gelfand, M. (2000). The role of androgen replacement therapy for postmenopausal women. *Contemporary Obstetrics and Gynecology,* February, 107–116.

Gelperin, N. (2005, May). *Oral sex and teens: The new third base?* Paper presented at What's New and What Works: Pioneering Solutions for Today's Sexual Issues (AAS-ECT 37th Annual Conference), Portland, OR.

Gendel, E., & Bonner, E. (1988). Gender identity disorders and paraphilias. In H. Goldman (Ed.), *Review of general psychiatry.* Norwalk, CT: Appleton and Lange.

Genevie, L., & Margolies, E. (1987). *The motherhood report: How women feel about being mothers.* New York: Macmillan.

Genuis, S., & Genuis, S. (2005). Implications of cyberspace communication. *Southern Medical Journal, 98,* 451–455.

George, A., Waxman, A., Scott, C., & Kimmel, S. (2006, May). *"Hooking up" and its clinical implications.* Paper presented at the American College of Obstetricians and Gynecologists 54th Annual Clinical Meeting.

Gerritsen, J., van der Made, F., Bloemers, J., et al. (2009). The clitoral photoplethysmograph: A new way of assessing genital arousal in women. *Journal of Sexual Medicine*, March 30.

Gertler, P., Shah, M., & Bertozzi, S. (2005). Risky business: The market for unprotected commercial sex. *Journal of Political Economy, 113,* 518–551.

Gettleman, J. (2009, August 9). Men raping men is latest atrocity in grisly Congo conflict. *Oregonian,* p. A11.

Ghanem, H. (2011). Common sexual complaints in conservative societies: Unconsummated marriages and small penis. *Journal of Sexual Medicine, 8,* 87.

Ghent, B. (2003, March 18). A new day in Washington. *Advocate,* 18.

Giaquinto, S., Buzzelli, S., Di Francesco, L., & Nolfe, G. (2003). Evaluation of sexual changes after stroke. *Journal of Clinical Psychiatry, 64,* 302–307.

Giargiari, T., Mahaffey, A., Craighead, W., & Hutchison, K. (2005). Appetitive responses to sexual stimuli are attenuated in individuals with low levels of sexual desire. *Archives of Sexual Behavior, 34,* 547–557.

Gibbons, A. (1991). The brain as a "sexual organ." *Science, 253,* 957–959.

Gibbons, M. (2011, September 14). States attack Planned Parenthood on funding, regs. Retrieved from http://www .womensenews.org/print8770

Gibbs, N. (2008, March 3). Wanted: Someone to play god. *Time,* 68.

Gilbert, B., Heesacker, M., & Gannon, L. (1991). Changing the sexual aggression-supportive attitudes of men: A psychoeducational intervention. *Journal of Counseling Psychology, 38,* 197–203.

Gildersleeve, K., et al. (2012). Body odor attractiveness as a cue of impending ovulation in women: Evidence from a study using hormone-confirmed ovulation. *Hormones and Behavior, 61,* 157–166.

Gillespie, L. (2012). Large companies push progressive benefits forward: One-third of major employers offer transgendered employees coverage for gender-reassignment surgery. *Employee Benefits News, 26,* 16.

Gillian, A., Fitzgerald, L., & Brunton, C. (2009, June 21–25). *Decriminalization of sex work: The New Zealand experience.* Paper presented at the 19th WAS World Congress for Sexual Health, Göteborg, Sweden.

Gillison, M., et al. (2012). Prevalence of oral HPV infection in the United States,

2009–2010. *Journal of the American Medical Association, 307,* 693–703. doi:10.1001

Ginsburg, K., Wolf, N., & Fidel, P. (1997). Potential effects of midcycle cervical mucus on mediators of immune reactivity. *Fertility and Sterility, 67,* 46–56.

Ginty, M. (2007, March 30). U.S. girls' early puberty attracts research flurry. Retrieved April 9, 2007, from Women's eNews.

Ginty, M. (2008, June 24). Tough economy tightens surrogacy market. Retrieved June 24, 2008, from Women's eNews.

Ginty, M. (2011). Cyberstalking turns Web technologies into weapons. Retrieved May 2, 2011, from http://www.womensenews .org/story/crime-policylegislation/ 110501/cyberstalking-turns-web-technologies-weapons

Girman, A., Lee, R., & Kligler, B. (2003). An integrative medicine approach to premenstrual syndrome. *American Journal of Obstetrics and Gynecology, 188,* S56–S63.

Girshman, P. (2011). Virus passed during anal sex tops tobacco as throat cancer cause. Retrieved February 25, 2011, from http://www.npr.org/blogs/ health/2011/2/22/133968901/virus-passed-during-oral-sex-tops-tobacco-as-throat-cancer-cause

Giuliano, A., et al. (2011). Efficacy of quadrivalent HPV vaccine against HPV infection and disease in males. *New England Journal of Medicine, 364,* 401–411.

Gjermeni, E., Van Hook, M., & Gjipali, S. (2008). Trafficking of children in Albania: Patterns of recruitment and reintegration. *Child Abuse and Neglect, 10,* 941–948.

GLAAD. (2011, September). Where we are on TV report: 2011–2012 season. Retrieved from http://www.glaad.org/ publications/whereweareontv11

Glaude, B., et al. (1990). Sexual orientation and spatial ability in men and women. *Psychobiology, 18,* 101–108.

Glazer, A., Wolf, A., & Gorby, N. (2011). Postpartum contraception: Needs vs. reality. *Contraception, 83,* 238–241.

Gleason, J., et al. (2011). Regular nonsteroidal anti-inflammatory drug use and erectile dysfunction. *Journal of Urology, 184,* 1388–1393.

Glei, D. (1999). Measuring contraceptive use patterns among teenage and adult women. *Family Planning Perspectives, 31,* 73–80.

Glennon, L. (1999). *The 20th century: An illustrated history of our lives and times.* North Dighton, MA: JG Press.

Glick, L. (2005). *Marked in your flesh: Circumcision from ancient Judea to modern America.* Oxford, England: Oxford University Press.

Glick, P., & Fiske, S. (2001). An ambivalent alliance: Hostile and benevolent sexism as

complementary justifications for gender inequality. *American Psychologist,* February, 109–118.

Glina, S. (2006). What to say to the couple regarding their future sex life at the time of working out the treatment strategy? *Journal of Sexual Medicine, 3*(Suppl. 2), 85.

Global Agenda. (2003). Sex for sale, legally: Prostitution, the oldest profession, goes legit. *Global Agenda,* July 11.

Global Sex Survey. (2005). Frequency of sex. Retrieved December 29, 2008, from http://www.durex.com/cm/gss2005Content.asp?intQuid

Global Study of Sexual Attitudes and Behaviors. (2002). *Global Study of Sexual Attitudes and Behaviors.* Retrieved December 11, 2003, from http://www.pfizerglobalstudy.com/study-results.asp

Goad, K. (2006). Big-earning wives, and the men who love them. Retrieved August 12, 2006, from http://lifestyle.msn.com/ Relationships/CouplesandMarriage

Goddard, A. (2011, April 19). Sex, church and nation state. Retrieved from http://amyjogoddard.com/ sex-church-nation-state-569

Godeau, E., Gabhainn, S., Vignes, C., et al. (2008). Contraceptive use by 15-year-old students at their last sexual intercourse. *Archives of Pediatric Adolescent Medicine, 162,* 66–73.

Gohman, J. (2009, June/July). The vagina dialogues. *Bust,* 49–53.

Gold, R., & Sonfield, A. (2011). Publicly funded contraceptive care: A proven investment. *Contraception, 84,* 437–439.

Gold, R., Sonfield, A., Richards, C., & Frost, J. (2009). *Next steps for America's family planning program: Leveraging the potential of Medicaid and Title X in an evolving health care system.* New York: Guttmacher Institute.

Goldberg, A., & Smith, J. (2011). Stigma, social context and mental health: Lesbian and gay couples across the transition to adoptive parenthood. *Journal of Counseling Psychology, 58,* 139–150.

Goldberg, M. (2006). *Kingdom coming: The rise of Christian nationalism.* New York: W. W. Norton.

Goldberg, M. (2011a, September 26). Marry—or else. *Newsweek,* 48–50.

Goldberg, M. (2011b, February 7). The super bowl of sex trafficking. *Newsweek,* 7.

Golden, N., Seigel, W., & Fisher, M. (2001). Emergency contraception: Pediatricians' knowledge, attitudes, and opinions. *Pediatrics, 107,* 287–292.

Goldfinger, C., Pukall, C., Gentilcore-Saulnier, E., et al. (2009). A prospective study of pelvic floor physical therapy: Pain and psychosexual outcomes in provoked vestibulodynia. *Journal of Sexual Medicine,* April 28 (e-pub).

Goldman, H. (1992). *Review of general psychiatry.* Norwalk, CT: Appleton and Lange.

Goldman, R., & Goldman, J. (1982). *Children's sexual thinking: A comparative study of children aged 5 to 15 years in Australia, North America, Britain, and Sweden.* London: Routledge & Kegan Paul.

Goldschmidt, D. (2012, January 10). North Carolina task force recommends $50,000 for sterilization victims. Retrieved from http://inamerica.blogs.cnn.com/2012/01/10/north-carolina-to-decide-how-much-to-compensate-victims

Goldstein, A., Klingman, D., Christopher, K., & Johnson, C. (2006). Surgical treatment of vulvar vestibulitis syndrome: Outcome assessment derived from a postoperative questionnaire. *Journal of Sexual Medicine, 3,* 923–931.

Goleman, D. (2006). *Social intelligence.* New York: Bantam Dell.

Gonzales, G. (2001). Function of seminal vesicles and their role on male fertility. *Asian Journal of Andrology,* December, 251–258.

Goode, E. (2011, October 2). Critics of report charge rape definition narrow. *Oregonian,* p. A8.

Goodman, D. (2001, May 2–6). *Communicating with strangers . . . or, How to become more culturally competent sex educators and counselors.* Paper presented at the 33rd Annual Conference of the American Association of Sex Educators, Counselors, and Therapists, San Francisco, CA.

Goodman-Brown, T., Edelstein, R., Goodman, G., Jones, D., & Gordon, D. (2003). Why children tell: A model of children's disclosure of sexual abuse. *Child Abuse and Neglect, 27,* 525–540.

Goodrum, J. (2000). A transgender primer. Retrieved February 16, 2000, from http://www.ntac.org/tg101.html

Goodson, P., Suther, S., Pruitt, B., & Wilson, K. (2003). Defining abstinence: Views of directors, instructors, and participants in abstinence-only-until-marriage programs in Texas. *Journal of School Health, 73,* 91–96.

Goodstein, L. (2011, May 11). Presbyterians approve ordination of gays. *Oregonian,* p. 5.

Goodwin, P., et al. (2010). *Marriage and cohabitation in the United States: A statistical portrait based on cycle 6 (2002) of the National Survey of Family Growth.* Hyattsville, MD: National Center for Health Statistics.

Gordon, C., & Pitts, S. (2012). Approach to the adolescent requesting contraception.

Journal of Clinical Endocrinology and Metabolism, 97, 9–15.

Gordon, L. (2011). Proposed city measure banning circumcision of boys under 18. *ABA Journal, 97,* 12–13.

Gordon, S., & Gordon, J. (1989). *Raising a child conservatively in a sexually permissive world.* New York: Simon and Schuster.

Gorey, K., & Leslie, D. (1997). The prevalence of child sexual abuse: Integrative review adjustment for potential response and measurement biases. *Child Abuse and Neglect, 21,* 391–398.

Gorgos, L., et al. (2011). Sexually transmitted infections among women who have sex with women. *Clinical Infectious Diseases, 53,* 584–591.

Gostin, L. (2011). Mandatory HPV vaccination and political debate. *Journal of the American Medical Association, 306,* 1699–1700.

Gotthardt, M. (2003, November/December). Lust and found. *AARP,* 28–31.

Gottlieb, S., et al. (2011). Screening and treatment to prevent sequelae in women with *Chlamydia trachomatis* genital infection: How much do we know? *Journal of Infectious Diseases, 201*(Suppl. 5), S156–S167.

Gottman, J. (1994). *Why marriages succeed or fail.* New York: Simon and Schuster.

Gottman, J., Coan, J., Carrere, S., & Swanson, C. (1998). Predicting marital happiness and stability from newlywed interactions. *Journal of Marriage and Family, 60,* 5–22.

Gottman, J., Murray, J., Swanson, C., Tyson, R., & Swanson, K. (2003). *The mathematics of marriage: Dynamic linear models.* Cambridge, MA: MIT Press.

Gottman, J., & Silver, N. (2000). *The seven principles for making marriage work.* New York: Crown.

Gottman, J., Swanson, C., & Murray, J. (1999). The mathematics of marital conflict: Dynamic mathematical nonlinear modeling of newly-wed marital interaction. *Journal of Family Psychology, 13,* 3–19.

Gottman, J. M., Levenson, R.W., Gross, J., et al. (2004). Correlates of gay and lesbian couples' relationship satisfaction and relationship dissolution. *Journal of Homosexuality, 45*(1), 23–43.

Gover, T. (1996, November 26). Occupational hazards. *Advocate,* 36–38.

Gowen, L. (2005). Normative use of online sexual activities. *Oregon Psychologist,* November/December, 5–6.

Gradus, J., Street, A., Kelly, K., & Stafford, J. (2008). Sexual harassment experiences and harmful alcohol use in a military sample: Differences in gender and the

mediating role of depression. *Journal of Studies on Alcohol and Drugs, 69,* 348–351.

Grady, W., Klepinger, D., & Nelson-Wally, A. (2000). Contraceptive characteristics: The perceptions and priorities of men and women. *Family Planning Perspectives, 31,* 168–175.

Graedon, J., & Graedon, T. (2008, October 22). Depression medications can prompt sex difficulty. *Oregonian,* p. C4.

Graesslin, O., & Korver, T. (2008). The contraceptive efficacy of Implanon: A review of clinical trials and marketing experience. *European Journal of Contraception and Reproductive Health Care, 13,* 4–12.

Graf, N., & Schwartz, C. (2011). The uneven pace of change in heterosexual romantic relationships. *Gender and Society, 25,* 101–107.

Grafenberg, E. (1950). The role of the urethra in female orgasm. *International Journal of Sexology, 3,* 145–148.

Graham, J. (2011). Measuring love in romantic relationships: A meta-analysis. *Journal of Social and Personal Relationships, 28,* 748–771.

Graham, N. (1997). Epidemiology of acquired immunodeficiency syndrome: Advancing to an endemic era. *American Journal of Medicine, 102*(Suppl. 4A), 2–8.

Grant, T., Huggins, J., Sampson, P., et al. (2009). Alcohol use before and during pregnancy in western Washington, 1989–2004. *American Journal of Obstetrics and Gynecology, 200,* 278–286.

Gravitz, L. (2011). A smoldering public-health crisis. *Nature, 474,* 52–54.

Gray, R., Kigozi, G., Serwadda, D., et al. (2007). Male circumcision for HIV prevention in men in Rakai, Uganda: A randomized controlled trial. *Lancet, 369,* 657–666.

Green, L., Fein, D., Modahl, C., et al. (2001). Oxytocin and autistic disorder: Alterations in peptide forms. *Biological Psychiatry, 50,* 609–613.

Green, R. (1974). *Sexual identity conflict in children and adults.* New York: Basic Books.

Greene, K., & Faulkner, S. (2005). Gender, belief in the sexual double standard, and sexual talk in heterosexual dating relationships. *Sex Roles: A Journal of Research, 53,* 239–251.

Greenstein, A., Plymate, S., & Katz, G. (1995). Visually stimulated erection in castrated men. *Journal of Urology, 153,* 650–652.

Greenwald, E., & Leitenberg, H. (1989). Long-term effects of sexual experiences with siblings and nonsiblings during childhood. *Archives of Sexual Behavior, 18,* 389–400.

Greenwald, J. (2011). Harassment remains major workplace problem: Informal environments, social media fuel problems. *Business Insurance, 45,* 3.

Greer, P. (1998). Vaginal thrush: Diagnosis and treatment options. *Nursing Times, 94,* 50–52.

Greil, A., et al. (2011). Variation in distress among women with infertility: Evidence from a population-based sample. *Human Reproduction, 26,* 2101–2112.

Gretz, H., Bradley, W., Zakashansky, K., & Nezhat, F. (2008). Patient clinical factors influencing use of hysterectomy in New York, 2001–2005. *American Journal of Obstetrics and Gynecology, 199,* 349.e1–349.e5.

Gribble, J., Lundgren, R., Velasquez, C., & Anastasi, E. (2008). Being strategic about contraceptive introduction: The experience of the standard days method. *Contraception, 77,* 147–154.

Grimes, D., & Schulz, K. (2011). Nonspecific side effects of oral contraceptives: Nocebo or noise? *Contraception, 83,* 5–9.

Grisell, T. (1988). Brief report. *Indiana Medical Journal, 81,* 252.

Gross, B. (2004). Sleeping dogs—dreams and repressed memories. *Annals of the American Psychotherapy Association, 7,* 43–44.

Gross, B. (2006). The pleasure of pain. *Forensic Examiner, 15,* 56–61.

Gross, B. (2008). False rape allegations: An assault on justice. *Annals of the American Psychotherapy Association, 11,* 45–49.

Gross, L. (2001). *Up from invisibility: Lesbians, gay men, and the media in America.* New York: Columbia University Press.

Gross, M. (2003). The second wave will drown us. *American Journal of Public Health, 93,* 872–881.

Grossbard, J., Lee, C., Neighbors, C., et al. (2007). Alcohol and risky sex in athletes and nonathletes: What roles do sex motives play? *Journal of American College Health, 68,* 566–574.

Grossman, C. (2011). United Church of Christ goes Father-free in updated bylaws. Retrieved July 5, 2011, from http://www.content.usatoday.com/communities/Religion/index

Grov, C., et al. (2011). Perceived consequences of casual online sexual activities on heterosexual relationships: A U.S. online survey. *Archives of Sexual Behavior, 40,* 429–239.

Gruszecki, L., Forchuk, C., & Fisher, W. (2005). Factors associated with common sexual concerns in women: New findings from the Canadian contraception study. *Canadian Journal of Human Sexuality, 14,* 1–14.

Gryboski, M. (2012, May 9). The war on sex: The contraception controversy's hidden agenda. Retrieved http://www.huffingtonpost.com/ruth-bettelheim/the-war-on-sex-the-contra_b1324716.html.

Gu, G., Cornea, A., & Simerly, R. (2003). Sexual differentiation of projections from the principal nucleus of the bed nuclei of the stria terminalis. *Journal of Comparative Neurology, 460,* 542–562.

Guidry, H. (1995). Childhood sexual abuse: Role of the family physician. *American Family Physician, 51,* 407–414.

Guilamo-Ramos, U., et al. (2012). A comparative study of interventions for delaying the initiation of sexual intercourse among Latino and Black youth. *Perspectives on Sexual and Reproductive Health, 43,* 247–254.

Gullette, M. (2011, August 21). Sex can also get better, not worse, with age. Retrieved from http://www.womensenews.org/story/books/110820/sex-can-also-get-better-not-worse-age

Gurevich, R. (2011, August 16). How much does IVF cost? Retrieved from http://infertility.about.com/od/ivf/f/ivf_cost.htm

Gurney, K. (2007). Sex and the surgeon's knife: The family courts' dilemma … informed consent and the specter of iatrogenic harm to children with intersex characteristics. *American Journal of Law and Medicine, 33,* 625–661.

Guttmacher Institute. (2006). *Top 10 ways sexual and reproductive health suffered in 2004.* Retrieved February 2, 2006, from http://www.guttmacher.org

Guttmacher Institute. (2008a). *Facts on contraceptive use.* New York: Guttmacher Institute.

Guttmacher Institute. (2008b, July). *Facts on induced abortion in the United States.* Retrieved on March 6, 2009, from http://www.guttmacher.org/pubs/fb_induced_abortion.html

Guttmacher Institute. (2008c, October). *Facts on induced abortion worldwide.* Retrieved March 6, 2009, from http://www.guttmacher.org/pubs/fb_IAW.html

Guttmacher Institute (2009b). *State policies in brief: Bans on "partial birth" abortion.* New York: Guttmacher Institute.

Guttmacher Institute. (2011a, May). *Facts on induced abortion in the United States.* Retrieved from http://www.guttmacher.org/pubs/fb_induced-abortion.html.

Guttmacher Institute. (2011b). *State policies in brief: Insurance coverage of contraceptives.* New York: Guttmacher Institute.

Guttmacher Institute. (2011c). *State policies in brief: Refusing to provide health services.* New York: Guttmacher Institute.

Guttmacher Institute. (2011d, July 13). *States enact record number of abortion restrictions in first half of 2011.* Retrieved from http://www.guttmacher.org/media/inthenews/print/2011/07/13/index.html

Guttmacher Institute. (2012a, January). *Facts on induced abortion worldwide.* Retrieved from http://www.guttmacher.org/pubs/fb_IAW.html

Guttmacher Institute. (2012b). *State policies in Brief: Requirements for ultrasound.* Washington, DC: Guttmacher Institute.

Guy-Sheftall, B. (2003). African American women: The legacy of Black feminism. In R. Morgan (Ed.), *Sisterhood is forever.* New York: Washington Square Press.

Haansbaek, T. (2006). Partner to a rape victim: How is he doing? *Journal of Sex Research, 43,* 18–19.

Hafer, J. (2011, May 21). *Affluent, educated women may choose sexual prostitution.* Retrieved from http://newswire.uark.edu/article.aspx?id=16181

Haffner, D. (1993). Toward a new paradigm of adolescent sexual health. *SIECUS Report, 21,* 26–30.

Hagan, P., & Knott, P. (1998). Diagnosing and treating polycystic ovary syndrome. *Practitioner, 242,* 98–106.

Hagen, R. (2006, August 15). At your service. *Advocate,* 26.

Hahn, J., & Blass, T. (1997). Dating partner preferences: A function of similarity of love styles. *Journal of Social Behavior and Personality, 12,* 595–610.

Hahn-Holbrook, J., et al. (2011). Maternal defense: Breast-feeding increases aggression by reducing stress. *Psychological Science, 22,* 1288–1295.

Halarnkar, S. (2011, January 27). India's silent genocide. *Hindustan Times,* p. 10.

Halbreich, U., et al. (2012). Continuous oral levonorgestrel/ethinyl estradiol for treating premenstrual dysphoric disorder. *Contraception, 85,* 19–27.

Hall, B. (2006, January 17). Pro-Bush, pro-equality. Retrieved May 24, 2006, from http://www.advocate.com/exclusive_detail_ektid24536.asp

Hall, G. (1996). *Theory-based assessment, treatment, and prevention of sexual aggression.* New York: Oxford University Press.

Hall, G., & Barongan, C. (1997). Prevention of sexual aggression: Sociocultural risk and protective factors. *American Psychologist, 52,* 5–14.

Hall, H. (2007). Bioidentical hormones: Estrogen is bad. No, it's good. *Skeptic, 13,* 6–8.

Hall, H. (2009, January 6). South Dakota's abortion script: The hijacking of informed consent. Retrieved April 12, 2009, from http://www.sciencebasedmedicine.org/?p=329

Hall, J. (2009, February 22). Giving mothers and babies a healthy start breast-feeding rates: Culpeper Regional Hospital's emphasis on breast-feeding has earned it the title, baby friendly. *Free Lance-Star*, p. C2.

Hall, J., & Kimura, D. (1995). Sexual orientation and performance on sexually dimorphic motor tasks. *Archives of Sexual Behavior, 24*, 395–407.

Hall, K. (2008). Childhood sexual abuse and adult sexual problems: A new view of assessment and treatment. *Feminism and Psychology, 18*, 546–556.

Hall, R., & Hall, R. (2007). A profile of pedophilia: Definition, characteristics of offenders, recidivism, treatment outcomes, and forensic issues. *Mayo Clinic Proceedings, 82*, 457–481.

Halliwell, E., Malson, H., & Tishner, I. (2011). Are contemporary media images which seem to display women as sexually empowered actually harmful to women? *Psychology of Women Quarterly, 35*, 38–45.

Halpern, D., & LaMay, M. (2000). The smarter sex: A critical review of sex differences in intelligence. *Educational Psychology Review, 12*, 229–246.

Halpern-Felsher, B., Cornell, J., Kropp, R., & Tschann, J. (2006). Oral versus vaginal sex among adolescents: Perceptions, attitudes, and behavior. *Pediatrics, 44*, 115, 845–851, 1023–1024.

Halpern-Felsher, B., Kropp, B., Boyer, C., Tschann, J., & Ellen, J. (2004). Adolescents' self-efficacy to communicate about sex: Its role in condom attitudes, commitment, and use. *Adolescence, 39*, 443–456.

Hamilton, E. (1978). *Sex, with love*. Boston: Beacon Press.

Hamilton, T. (2002). *Skin flutes and velvet gloves*. New York: St. Martin's Press.

Hammer, S. (2011). Antiretroviral treatment as prevention. *New England Journal of Medicine, 365*, 561–562.

Hammer, S., Eron, J., Reiss, P., et al. (2008). Antiretroviral treatment of adult HIV infection: 2008 recommendations of the International AIDS Society–USA Panel. *Journal of the American Medical Association, 300*, 555–570.

Hammond, C. (2006). Time to change. *Obstetrics and Gynecology, 107*, 549.

Hammond, L., et al. (2011). "It feels good": Australian young women's attitudes to oral sex. *Youth Studies Australia, 30*, 15–17.

Hampton, T. (2012). Breast cancer symposium highlights risk, recurrence, and research trials. *Journal of the American Medical Association, 306*, 1884–1890.

Hannaford, P., Selvaraj, S., Elleitt, A., et al. (2007). Cancer risk among users of oral contraceptives. *British Medical Journal, 32*, 104–121.

Hannon, K. (2009, February 1). Planning ahead for a fertile future: Pregnancy may last nine months, but the road to having a child starts years earlier. *U.S. News & World Report*, 59.

Hanrahan, S. (1994). Historical review of menstrual toxic shock syndrome. *Women and Health, 21*, 141–157.

Hans, J., Gillen, M., & Akande, K. (2010). Sex redefined: The reclassification of oral–genital contact. *Perspectives on Sexual and Reproductive Health, 42*, 74–78.

Hansen, S., et al. (2011). Profound early control of highly pathogenic SIV by an effector memory T-cell vaccine. *Nature, 473*, 523–527.

Hanson, R., Resnick, H., Saunders, B., Kilpatrick, D., & Best, C. (1999). Factors related to the reporting of childhood rape. *Child Abuse and Neglect, 23*, 559–569.

Hanson, R., Saunders, B., Kilpatrick, D., Resnick, H., et al. (2001). Impact of childhood rape and aggravated assault on mental health. *American Journal of Orthopsychiatry, 71*, 108–118.

Hanus, J. (2006a). Monomaniacal monogamy. *Utne Reader*, March/April, 55.

Hanus, J. (2006b). The culture of pornography is shaping our lives, for better and for worse. *Utne Reader*, September/October, 58–60.

Haq, H. (2011). Two decades after Anita Hill: How workplaces are handling sexual harassment. *Christian Science Monitor*, November 14.

Hare, L., Bernard, P., Sanchez, F., et al. (2009). Androgen receptor repeat length polymorphism associated with male-to-female transsexualism. *Biological Psychiatry, 65*, 93–96.

Hari, J. (2006, July 13). What we can learn from female sex tourists. *Independent* (London), p. C7.

Harley, V., Jackson, D., Hextall, P., et al. (1992). DNA binding activity of recombinant *SRY* from normal males and XY females. *Science, 255*, 453–456.

Harlow, H., & Harlow, M. (1962). The effects of rearing conditions on behavior. *Bulletin of the Menninger Clinic, 26*, 13–24.

Harmon, A. (2010, June/July). A woman of faith. *Advocate*, 28–30.

Harned, M., & Fitzgerald, L. (2002). Understanding a link between sexual harassment and eating disorder symptoms: A mediational analysis. *Journal of Consulting and Clinical Psychology, 70*, 1170–1181.

Harris Poll (2006). *Large majority support more access to birth control information.*

Retrieved February 2, 2006, from www.harrisinteractive.com/news/NewsID=1064

Harris, A., & Bolus, N. (2008). HIV/AIDS: An update. *Radiologic Technology, 79*, 243–255.

Harris, G. (2010, August 13). FDA approves 5-day emergency contraceptive. Retrieved from http://www.mytimes.com/2010/08/14/health/policy/14pill.html?

Harris, L. (2010, August). The opposite of sex: Neither gay nor straight, men and women in a growing new movement are calling themselves asexual. Legit? Or naive? *Marie Claire*, 81–83.

Harrison, A., et al. (2012). Prepregnancy contraceptive use among teens with unintended pregnancies resulting in live births. *Morbidity and Mortality Weekly Report, 61*, 25–29.

Harrison-Hohner, J. (2010, April 22). Is there a new approach to birth control in your future? Retrieved from http://blogs.webmd.com/womens-health/2010/04/is-there-a-new-approach-to-birth-control-in-your-future

Harte, C., & Meston, C. (2008a). Acute effects of nicotine on physiological and subjective sexual arousal in nonsmoking men: A randomized, double-blind, placebo-controlled trial. *Journal of Sexual Medicine, 5*, 110–121.

Harte, C., & Meston, C. (2008b). The inhibitory effects of nicotine on physiological sexual arousal in nonsmoking women: Results from a randomized, double-blind, placebo-controlled, cross-over trial. *Journal of Sexual Medicine, 5*, 1184–1197.

Harte, C., & Meston, C. (2011). Recreational use of erectile dysfunction medications in undergraduate men in the United States: Characteristics and associated risk factors. *Archives of Sexual Behavior, 40*, 289–300.

Hartwick, C., Desmarais, S., & Hennig, K. (2007). Characteristics of male and female victims of sexual coercion. *Canadian Journal of Human Sexuality, 16*, 31–44.

Harvard Health Publications. (2006, March). *Life after 50: A Harvard study of male sexuality.* Retrieved August 9, 2006, from http://health.msn.com/centers/mensexualhealth/articlepage.aspx?cp-documentid=100127818

Harvard Women's Health Watch. (2012, January). *Sex and the older woman.* Retrieved from http://www.health.harvard.edu/newsletters/harvard_womens_health_watch/2012/January

Haselton, M., & Gildersleeve, K. (2011). Can men detect ovulation? *Current*

Directions in Psychological Science, 20, 87–92.

Hass, A. (1979). *Teenage sexuality.* New York: Macmillan.

Hatcher, R. (2003). *A pocket guide to managing contraception.* Tiger, GA: Bridging the Gap Foundation.

Hatcher, R. (2006). Why is the IUD number one? *Contraceptive Technology Update,* February 1.

Hatcher, R., & Guillebaud, J. (1998). The pill: Combined oral contraceptives. In R. Hatcher, J. Trussell, F. Stewart, et al. (Eds.), *Contraceptive technology.* New York: Ardent Media.

Hatfield, E., & Sprecher, S. (1986). Measuring passionate love in intimate relationships. *Journal of Adolescence, 9,* 383–410.

Hatfield, E., et al. (2012). A brief history of social scientists' attempts to measure love. *Journal of Social and Personal Relationships, 29,* 143–164.

Hatzenbuehler, M. (2011). The social environment and suicide attempts in lesbian, gay, and bisexual youth. *Pediatrics, 127,* 896–903.

Haught, N. (2008, July 17). Circumcision: A painful decision. *Oregonian,* p. E1.

Haught, N. (2009, September 2). Popular Bible revised gender issues. *Oregonian,* p. A1.

Hausknecht, R. (2003). Mifepristone and misoprostol for early medical abortion: 18 months experience in the United States. *Contraception, 67,* 463–465.

Hawkes, S., et al. (2011). Effectiveness of interventions to improve screening for syphilis in pregnancy: A systematic review and meta-analysis. *Lancet Infectious Diseases, 11,* 684–691.

Hayden, E. (2011). HIV drug-prevention strategy carries risks. *Nature, 476,* 260–261.

Hayes, R., Dennerstein, L., Bennett, C., & Sidat, M. (2008). Risk factors for female sexual dysfunction in the general population: Exploring factors associated with low sexual function and sexual distress. *Journal of Sexual Medicine, 5,* 1681–1693.

Hazan, C., & Shaver, P. (1987). Love conceptualized as attachment process. *Journal of Personality and Social Psychology, 52,* 511–524.

Hazell, L., Cornelius, V., Wilton, L., & Shakir, S. (2009). The safety profile of tadalafil as prescribed in general practice in England. *British Journal of Urology International, 103,* 506–514.

Head, K. (2008). Natural approaches to prevention and treatment of infections of the lower urinary tract. *Alternative Medicine Review, 13,* 227–245.

Healy, B. (2003, August 11). Whose breasts, anyway? *U.S. News & World Report,* 50.

Heath, B. (2011, December 16). Silent abuses. *USA Today,* p. A1.

Heath, N., et al. (2011). Silent survivors: Rape myth acceptance in incarcerated women's narratives of disclosure and reporting of rape. *Psychology of Women Quarterly, 35,* 596–601.

Heath, R. (1972). Pleasure and brain activity in man. *Journal of Nervous and Mental Disease, 154,* 3–18.

Heavy, S. (2009, March 11). U.S. FDA approves new, cheaper female condom. Retrieved March 11, 2009, from http://www.reuters.com/articlePrint?articleId=USN10547381

Heck, J., Sell, R., & Gorin S. (2006). Health care access among individuals involved in same-sex relationships. *American Journal of Public Health, 96,* 1111–1118.

Hedayat, N. (2011, October 3). What is it like to be a child bride? Retrieved from http://www.bbc.co.uk/news/magazine-15082550

Heim, N. (1981). Sexual behavior of castrated sex offenders. *Archives of Sexual Behavior, 10,* 11–19.

Heiman, J. (2008). Treating low sexual desire: New findings for testosterone in women. *New England Journal of Medicine, 359,* 2047–2049.

Heiman, J. (2009, June). *Researching women's sexual health: A social responsibility.* Paper presented at the 19th WAS World Congress for Sexual Health, Göteborg, Sweden.

Heiman, J., et al. (2011). Sexual satisfaction and relationship happiness in midlife and older couples in five countries. *Archives of Sexual Behavior, 40,* 741–753.

Heinlein, R. (1961). *Stranger in a strange land.* New York: Putnam.

Heisea, L., et al. (2011). Apples and oranges? Interpreting success in HIV prevention trials. *Contraception, 83,* 10–15.

Helfer, A. (2006). Cameroon GTZ active in the fight against mutilation of teenage girls. Retrieved October 17, 2006, from http://gtz.de/en/aktuell/16442.htm

Helfing, K. (2008, May 23). Dealing with war's less-visible wounds. *Oregonian,* p. A4.

Helien, A., Casabe, A., & Bechara, A. (2005, December). *Male anorgasmia: Contributions to its treatment.* Paper presented at the 8th Congress of the Latin American Society for Sexual and Impotence Research, Cairns, Australia.

Hellstrom, W. (2010). Available and future therapies for premature ejaculation. *Drugs Today, 46,* 502–521.

Hellstrom, W., Nehra, A., Shabsigh, R., & Sharlip, I. (2006, November). *Premature ejaculation: The most common male sexual dysfunction.* Paper presented at the Sexual Medicine Society of North America Fall Meeting, New York, NY.

Henderson, M. (2007, October 17). Sex every day is prescription for improving sperm quality. Retrieved on October 21, 2007, from http://www.timesonline.co.uk/tol/life_and_style/health/article2665688.ece

Hendrick, C., & Hendrick, S. (1986). A theory and method of love. *Journal of Personality and Social Psychology, 50,* 392–402.

Hendrick, C., & Hendrick, S. (2003). Romantic love: Measuring Cupid's arrow. In S. Lopez and C. Snyder (Eds.), *Positive psychological assessment: A handbook of models and measures.* Washington, DC: American Psychological Association.

Hendrick, C., Hendrick, S., & Adler, N. (1988). Romantic relationships: Love, satisfaction, and staying together. *Journal of Personality and Social Psychology, 54,* 980–988.

Hendrick, S., & Hendrick, C. (1992). *Liking, loving, and relating* (2nd ed.). Pacific Grove, CA: Brooks/Cole.

Hendrick, S., & Hendrick, C. (1995). Gender differences and similarities in sex and love. *Personal Relationships, 2,* 5–65.

Heng, B. (2009). Stringent regulation of oocyte donation in China. *Human Reproduction, 24,* 14–16.

Henneman, T. (2003, September 2). New York public. *Advocate,* 38.

Hensley, C., Tewksbury, R., & Castle, T. (2003). Characteristics of prison sexual assault targets in Oklahoma's male correctional facilities. *Journal of Interpersonal Violence, 18,* 595–606.

Herbenick, D., et al. (2010a). An event-level analysis of the sexual characteristics and composition among adults ages 18–59: Results from a national probability sample in the United States. *Journal of Sexual Medicine, 7*(Suppl. 5), 346–361.

Herbenick, D., et al. (2010b). Sexual behavior in the United States: Results from a national probability sample of men and women ages 14–94. *Journal of Sexual Medicine, 7*(Suppl. 5), 255–265.

Herbenick, D., et al. (2011a). Beliefs about women's vibrator use: Results from a nationally representative probability survey in the United States. *Journal of Sex and Marital Therapy, 37,* 329–345.

Herbenick, D., et al. (2011b). The female genital self-image scale (FGSIS): Results from a nationally representative probability sample of women in the United States. *Journal of Sexual Medicine, 8,* 158–166.

Herek, G. (2011). Anti-equity marriage amendments and sexual stigma. *Journal of Social Issues, 67,* 413–426.

Herek, G., & Capitanio, J. (1999). Sex differences in how heterosexuals think about lesbians and gay men: Evidence from survey context effects. *Journal of Sex Research, 36,* 348–360.

Herek, G., Cogan, J., & Gillis, J. (1999). Psychological sequelae of hate-crime victimization among lesbian, gay, and bisexual adults. *Journal of Consulting and Clinical Psychology, 67,* 945–951.

Herek, G., Gillis, R., & Gogan, J. (2009). Internalized stigma among sexual minority adults: Insights from a social psychological perspective. *Journal of Counseling Psychology, 56,* 32–43.

Herman, M., & Campbell, M. (2012). I wouldn't, but you can: Attitudes toward interracial relationships. *Social Science Research, 41,* 343–358.

Hernandez, B., Wilkens, L., Zhu, X., et al. (2008). Transmission of human papillomavirus in heterosexual couples. *Emerging Infectious Diseases, 14,* 888–894.

Herper, M. (2011, December 14). Placebo is the real "female Viagra." Retrieved from http://www.forbes.com/sites/matthewherper/2011/12/14/placebo-is-the-real-female-viagra/

Hertzberg, H. (2008, December 1). Eight is enough. *New Yorker,* 27–28.

Hesketh, R., & Xing, A. (2006). Abnormal sex ratios in human populations: Causes and consequences. *Proceedings of the National Academy of Sciences, 103,* 13271–13275.

Hess, A. (2011). The politics of virginity: Abstinence in sex education. *Social Forces, 89,* 1080–1082.

Hess, J., & Coffelt, T. (2011). Verbal communication about sex in marriage: Patterns of language use and its connection with relational outcomes. *Journal of Sex Research.* doi:10.1080/00224499.2011.619282

Hetzner, A. (2010, March 17). Girls close math with boys, keep their edge in reading. *Oregonian,* p. A3.

Heyden, M., Anger, B., Tiel, T., & Ellner, T. (1999). Fighting back works: The case for advocating and teaching self-defense against rape. *Journal of Physical Education, Recreation, and Dance, 70,* 31–34.

Hickman, S., & Muehlenhard, C. (1999). "By the semi-mystical appearance of a condom": How young women and men communicate sexual consent in heterosexual situations. *Journal of Sex Research, 36,* 258–272.

Hickson, F., Davies, P., Hunt, A., et al. (1994). Gay men as victims of nonconsensual sex. *Archives of Sexual Behavior, 23,* 281–294.

Higa, G. (2000). Altering the estrogenic milieu of breast cancer with a focus on the new aromatase inhibitors. *Pharmacotherapy, 20,* 280–291.

Higgins, J., et al. (2011). Sexual satisfaction and sexual health among university students in the United States. *American Journal of Public Health, 101,* 1643–1654.

Higgins, J., & Hirsch, J. (2007). The pleasure deficit: Revisiting the "sexuality connection" in reproductive health. *Perspectives on Sexual and Reproductive Health, 39,* 240–247.

Higgins, J., Hirsch, J., & Trussell, J. (2008). Pleasure, prophylaxis and procreation: A qualitative analysis of intermittent contraceptive use and unintended pregnancy. *Perspectives on Sexual and Reproductive Health, 40,* 130–137.

Hilden, M., Schei, B., & Sidenius, K. (2005). Genitoanal injury in adult female victims of sexual assault. *Forensic Science International, 154,* 200–205.

Hill, E., et al. (2011). Gynecologic and breast cancer survivors' sexual health care needs. *Cancer, 117,* 2643–2651.

Hill, M., & Fischer, A. (2001). Does entitlement mediate the link between masculinity and rape-related variables? *Journal of Counseling Psychology, 48,* 39–50.

Hindin, M., & Muntifering, C. (2011). Women's autonomy and timing of most recent sexual intercourse in sub-Saharan Africa: A multi-country analysis. *Journal of Sex Research, 48,* 511–519.

Hines, D. (2007). Predictors of sexual coercion against women and men: A multinational study of university students. *Archives of Sexual Behavior, 36,* 403–422.

Hines, M. (2004). *Brain gender.* New York: Oxford University Press.

Hines, M., Ahmed, S., & Hughes, I. (2003). Psychological outcomes and gender-related development in complete androgen insensitivity syndrome. *Archives of Sexual Behavior, 32,* 93–101.

Hirokawa, K., Yagi, A., & Miyata, Y. (2004). An experimental examination of the effects of sex and masculinity/femininity on psychological, physiological, and behavioral responses during communication situations. *Sex Roles: A Journal of Research, 51,* 91–99.

Hitti, M. (2006). Most men unsatisfied with penis enlargement results. Retrieved October 27, 2008, from http://www.foxnews.com/story/0,2933,185156,00.html

Hodge, D. (2008). Sexual trafficking in the United States: A domestic problem with transnational dimensions. *Social Work, 53,* 143–152.

Hodge, D., & Nadir, A. (2008). Culturally competent practice with Muslims. *Social Work, 53,* 31–41.

Hoffman, C., Jeffers, S., Carter, J., & Duthely, L. (2007). Pregnancy at or beyond age 40 years is associated with an increased risk of fetal death and other adverse outcomes. *American Journal of Obstetrics and Gynecology, 196,* 11–13.

Hoffman, J. (2011, March 27). States struggle with minors' sexting. *New York Times.*

Hoffman, M. (2009, March 2). Hydrogen sulfide: Potential help for ED. Retrieved May 19, 2009, from http://www.webmd.com/erectile-dysfunction/news/20090302/hydrogen-sulfide-potential-help-for-ED

Hoffman, R. (2011). Screening for prostate cancer. *New England Journal of Medicine, 365,* 2013–2019.

Hoke, T., Feldblum, P., Van Damme, K., Nasution, M., & Grey, T. (2007). Temporal trends in sexually transmitted infection prevalence and condom use following introduction of the female condom to Madagascar sex workers. *International Journal of STD and AIDS, 18,* 461–466.

Hollander, D. (2006). Skills-oriented counseling holds promise for increasing women's use of barrier methods. *Perspectives on Sexual and Reproductive Health, 38,* 58–59.

Hollander, D. (2008a). Computer-assisted surveys may expand understanding of STD risks and incidence. *Perspectives on Sexual and Reproductive Health, 40,* 183–184.

Hollander, D. (2008b). No cut might make the cut. *Perspectives on Sexual and Reproductive Health, 40,* 4–11.

Hollander, D. (2008c). The measure of the man. *Perspectives on Sexual and Reproductive Health, 40,* 4–5.

Holmberg, D., & Blair, K. (2008). Sexual desire, communication, satisfaction, and preferences of men and women in same-sex versus mixed-sex relationships. *Journal of Sex Research, 46,* 57–66.

Holmes, S. (2003). Tadalafil: A new treatment for erectile dysfunction. *British Journal of Urology International, 92,* 466–468.

Holstege, G., Georgiadis, J., Paans, A., et al. (2003). Brain activation during human male ejaculation. *Journal of Neuroscience, 23,* 9185–9193.

Holtzman, D. (2008). Viral hepatitis prevention: New challenges, new directions. *American Journal of Public Health, 98,* 782–783.

Hope, J. (2012, April 16). Women in chance sex encounters can receive the morning-after pill by courier from next week. Retrieved from http://www.dailymail.co.uk/health/article-2130556

Hormone Foundation. (2011). What is amenorrhea? *Journal of Clinical Endocrinology and Metabolism, 96,* 35A.

Horn, L. (2011, December 14). Google donates $11.5 million to fight slavery, human trafficking. Retrieved from http://www.pcmag.com/article/print/291707

Horton, M. (2005). Circumcision shouldn't hurt. *Fit Pregnancy, 12,* 25.

Horvath, K., Rosser, S., & Remafedi, G. (2008). Sexual risk taking among young Internet-using men who have sex with men. *American Journal of Public Health, 98,* 1059–1067.

Hoskote, S., et al. (2012). Prostate cancer risk and vitamin E. *Journal of the American Medical Association, 307,* 454–458.

Hotchkiss, A., Ankley, G., et al. (2008). Of mice and men (and mosquitofish): Antigens and androgens in the environment. *Bioscience, 58,* 1037–1050.

Houssami, N., Abrahan, L., Miglioretti, D. , & Sickles, E. (2011). Accuracy and outcomes of screening mammography in women with a personal history of early-stage breast cancer. *Journal of the American Medical Association, 305,* 790–799.

Hovde, E. (2011, February 14). Some tempted to "friend" past boundaries. *Oregonian,* p. D1.

Howard, D., Griffin, M., & Boekeloo, B. (2008). Prevalence and psychosocial correlates of alcohol-related sexual assault among university students. *Adolescence, 43,* 733–750.

Howes, R. (2011, July/August). A match made on earth. *Psychotherapy Networker,* 67–68.

Howey, N., & Samuels, E. (2000). *Out of the ordinary: Essays on growing up with gay, lesbian, and transgender parents.* New York: St. Martin's Press.

Hoxworth, T., Spencer, N., Peterman, T., et al. (2003). Changes in partnerships and HIV risk behavior after partner notification. *Sexually Transmitted Diseases, 30,* 83–88.

Hoyer, J., Uhmann, S., Fambow, J., & Jacobi, F. (2009). Reduction of sexual dysfunction: By-product of cognitive-behavioral therapy for psychological disorders? *Sexual and Relationship Therapy, 24,* 64–73.

Hsiao, W. (2012). Nomograms to predict patency after microsurgical vasectomy reversal. *Journal of Urology, 187,* 607–612.

Huang, P., et al. (2011). He says, she says: Gender and cohabitation. *Journal of Social Issues, 32,* 876–905.

Hucker, S. (2009). Hypoxyphilia/auto-erotic asphyxia. Retrieved February 9, 2009, from http://www.forens.cpsych.atry.ca/paraphilia/aea.htm

Hucker, S., et al. (2011). Hypoxyphilia. *Archives of Sexual Behavior, 40,* 1323–1326.

Hudepohl, D. (2011, October 9). Fighting for women. *Parade,* p. 16.

Hudson, J., Prestage, G., & Weerakoon, G. (2007, April). *The married men have sex with men study: An outline of findings.* Paper presented at the 18th Congress of the World Association for Sexual Health, Sydney, Australia.

Hudson, M., & Graham, C. (2004, May 11). Censorship: The big chill. *Advocate,* 48–53.

Hudson, W. (1992). *The WALMYR assessment scales scoring manual.* Tallahassee, FL: WALMYR Publishing.

Hughes, J., & Sandler, B. (1987). *"Friends" raping friends: Could it happen to you?* Washington, DC: Association of American Colleges.

Hughes, M., Morrison, K., & Asada, K. (2005). What's love got to do with it? Exploring the impact of maintenance rules, love attitudes, and network support on friends with benefits relationships. *Journal of Sex Research, 42,* 113–118.

Hull, E., Lorrain, D., Du, J., et al. (1999). Hormone–neurotransmitter interactions in the control of sexual behavior. *Behavioral Brain Research, 105,* 105–116.

Human Rights Campaign. (2011). *Adoption laws: State by state.* Retrieved from http://www.hrc.org/issues/parenting/adoptions/8464.htm

Human Rights Watch. (2006). *The less they know, the better: Abstinence-only HIV/AIDS programs in Uganda.* Retrieved July 18, 2006, from http://hrw.org/reports/2005/uganda0305/

Humphrey, J. (2011). Curb your crazy cramps: Those monthly menstrual pains are enough to make anyone cranky. *Shape, 30,* 87.

Humphreys, T., & Newby, J. (2007). Initiating new behaviors in heterosexual relationships. *Canadian Journal of Human Sexuality, 16,* 77–88.

Hunt, M., & Jung, P. (2009). "Good sex" and religion: A feminist overview. *Journal of Sex Research, 46,* 156–167.

Hunt, M. (1974). *Sexual behavior in the 1970s.* Chicago, IL: Playboy Press.

Hunter, L. (2011, June 16). C-section jump allied with higher medical bills. Retrieved from http://www.womensenews.org/print/8659

Huppert, J. (2006). New detection methods for trichomoniasis may help curb more serious STIs. *Patient Care,* May, 32–36.

Hurlbert, D., & Whittaker, K. (1991). The role of masturbation in marital and sexual satisfaction: A comparative study of female masturbators and nonmasturbators. *Journal of Sex Education and Therapy, 17,* 272–282.

Hutchinson, K., Kip, K., & Ness, R. (2007). Vaginal douching and development of bacterial vaginosis among women with normal and abnormal vaginal microflora. *Sexually Transmitted Diseases, 34,* 671–675.

Hutchinson, M., & Cederbaum, J. (2011). Talking to daddy's little girl about sex: Daughters' reports of sexual communication and support from fathers. *Journal of Family Issues, 32,* 550–572.

Hutchinson, M., & Cooney, T. (1998). Patterns of parent-teen sexual risk communication: Implications for intervention. *Family Relations, 47,* 185–194.

Hutti, M. (2003). New and emerging contraceptive methods. *Association of Women's Health, Obstetric, and Neonatal Nurses Lifelines, 7,* 32–39.

Huxley, C., Clarke, V., & Halliwell, E. (2011). "It's a comparison thing, isn't it?": Lesbian and bisexual women's accounts of how partner relationships shape their feelings about their body and appearance. *Psychology of Women Quarterly, 35,* 415–427.

Hvistendahl, M. (2011). *Unnatural selection: Choosing boys over girls, and the consequences of a world full of men.* New York: PublicAffairs.

Hyde, J. (2006). *Half the human experience: The psychology of women* (7th ed.). Boston, MA: Houghton Mifflin.

Hymowitz, K. (2011). The national adultery ritual: Against all odds, America still demands male marital fidelity. *Commentary, 132,* 40–45.

Iasenza, S. (2000). Lesbian sexuality post-Stonewall to post-modernism: Putting the "lesbian bed death" concept to bed. *Journal of Sex Education and Therapy, 25,* 59–69.

Ibanez, G., et al. (2010). Correlates of heterosexual anal intercourse among substance-using club-goers. *Archives of Sexual Behavior, 39,* 959–967.

Iervolino, A., Hines, M., Golombok, S., et al. (2005). Genetic and environmental influences on sex-typed behavior during preschool years. *Child Development, 76,* 826–840.

Imperato-McGinley, J., Peterson, R., Gautier, T., & Sturla, E. (1979). Androgens and the evolution of male-gender identity among male pseudohermaphrodites with 5-alpha-reductase deficiency. *New England Journal of Medicine, 300,* 1233–1237.

Incrocci, L. (2006). The effect of cancer on sexual function. *Journal of Sexual Medicine, 3*(Suppl. 2), 73.

International Center for Research on Women. (2009). *Child marriage by the numbers.* Washington, DC: Author.

International Collaboration of Epidemiological Studies of Cervical Cancer. (2007). Cervical cancer and hormonal contraceptives. *Lancet, 370,* 1609–1621.

International Male Contraception Coalition. (2011, July 27). What are experimental male contraceptives? Retrieved from http://malecontraceptives.org/methods/index.php

Internet World Stats. (2011). Internet world users by language. Retrieved from www.internetworldstats.com/stats7.htm

Intersex Society of North America. (2006). *Frequency: How common are intersex conditions?* Retrieved January 4, 2006, from http://www.isna.org/faq/frequency.html

Iovine, V. (1997). *The girlfriends' guide to pregnancy.* New York: Perigee.

Ipas. (2007). *The global gag rule harms democracy, women, and U.S. interests abroad.* Chapel Hill, NC: Author.

Isely, P., & Gehrenbeck-Shim, D. (1997). Sexual assault of men in the community. *Journal of Community Psychology, 25,* 159–166.

Ishak, W., et al. (2011). Oxytocin role in enhancing well-being: A literature review. *Journal of Affective Disorders, 130,* 1–9.

Ishii-Kuntz, M. (1997a). Chinese American families. In M. DeGenova (Ed.), *Families in cultural context: Strengths and challenges in diversity.* Mountain View, CA: Mayfield.

Ishii-Kuntz, M. (1997b). Japanese American families. In M. DeGenova (Ed.), *Families in cultural context: Strengths and challenges in diversity.* Mountain View, CA: Mayfield.

Ito, T., Trant, A., & Polan, M. (2001). A double-blind placebo-controlled study of ArginMax, a nutritional supplement for enhancement of female sexual function. *Journal of Sex and Marital Therapy, 27,* 541–549.

Iuliano, A., Speizer, I., Santelli, J., & Kendall, C. (2006). Reasons for contraceptive nonuse at first sex and unintended pregnancy. *American Journal of Health Behavior, 30,* 92–102.

Jadva, V. (2010). Infants' preferences for toys, colors, and shapes: Sex differences and similarities. *Archives of Sexual Behavior, 39,* 1261–1273.

Jaeger, M. (2011). "A thing of beauty is a joy forever"? Returns to physical attractiveness over the life course. *Social Forces, 89,* 983–1003.

Jaffe, H. (2008)). Universal access to HIV/AIDS treatment. *Journal of the American Medical Association, 300,* 573–575.

Jakobsen, J., & Pellegrini, A. (2003). *Love the sin: Sexual regulation and the limits of religious tolerance.* New York: New York University Press.

Jalonick, M. (2010, November 18). A state of wide-awake drunk. *Star Advertiser,* p. A3.

Jancin, B. (2005). Teen addiction to cybersex called pervasive. *Family Practice News, 35,* 36–37.

Jandt, F., & Hundley, H. (2007). Intercultural dimensions of communicating masculinities. *Journal of Men's Studies, 15,* 216–231.

Janiszewski, P., Janssen, I., & Ross, R. (2009). Abdominal obesity and physical inactivity are associated with erectile dysfunction independent of body mass index. *Journal of Sexual Medicine,* April 28 (e-pub).

Jannini, E., et al. (2011). Is testosterone a friend or foe of the prostate? *Journal of Sexual Medicine, 8,* 946–955.

Janssen, D. (2007). First stirrings: Cultural notes on orgasm, ejaculation and wet dreams. *Journal of Sex Research, 44,* 122–134.

Janssen, D. (2008). Growing up sexually in Oceania. Retrieved October 24, 2008, from http://www.huberlin.de/sexology/GESLUND/ARCHI/GUS/PACIFICSOLD.htm

Janssen, P., Bakker, S., Rethelyi, J., et al. (2009). Serotonin transporter promoter region (5-HTTLPR) polymorphism is associated with the intravaginal ejaculation latency time in Dutch men with lifelong premature ejaculation. *Journal of Sexual Medicine, 6,* 276–284.

Janssens, K., et al. (2011). Can buy me love: Mate attraction goals lead to perceptual readiness for status products. *Journal of Experimental Social Psychology, 47,* 254–258.

Jarrell, A. (2000, April 16). Model maturity. *Sunday Oregonian,* p. L13.

Jayson, S. (2012, March 22). Nearly 4 in 10 women have never married. *USA Today,* p. 1A.

Jefferson, D. (2005, February 28). Party, play—and pay. *Newsweek,* 38–39.

Jeffery, C. (2006, January/February). Why women can't win for trying. *Mother Jones,* 22–23.

Jehl, D. (1998, October 4). Western masterpieces locked away from Iranian view. *Oregonian,* p. A7.

Jenkins, S., & Aube, J. (2002). Gender differences and gender-related constructs in dating aggression. *Personality and Social Psychology Bulletin, 28,* 1106–1118.

Jenness, S., et al. (2011). Unprotected anal intercourse and sexually transmitted diseases in high-risk heterosexual women. *American Journal of Public Health, 101,* 745–750.

Jennings, V., Lamprecht, V., & Kowal, D. (1998). Fertility awareness methods. In R. Hatcher, J. Trussell, F. Stewart, et al. (Eds.), *Contraceptive technology.* New York: Ardent Media.

Jensen, J., Burke, A., Barnhart, K., et al. (2008). Effects of switching from oral to transdermal or transvaginal contraception on markers of thrombosis. *Contraception, 78,* 451–458.

Jervis, R. (2012, January 30). Priests decry birth control order. *USA Today,* p. 3A.

Joannides, P. (1996). *The guide to getting it on!* Walport, OR: Goofy Foot Press.

Joensen, U., Bossi, R., Leffers, H., & Jensen, A. (2009). Do perfluoroalkyl compounds impair human semen quality? *Environmental Health Perspectives, 117,* 923–927.

Joffe, C. (2009). *Dispatches from the abortion wars: The costs of fanaticism to doctors, patients, and the rest of us.* Boston, MA: Beacon Press.

Johnsdotter, S., & Essén, B. (2010). Genitals and ethnicity: The politics of genital modifications. *Reproductive Health Matters, 18,* 29–37.

Johnson, B., et al. (2011). Interventions to reduce sexual risk for human immunodeficiency virus in adolescents. *Archives of Pediatrics and Adolescent Medicine, 165,* 77–84.

Johnson, H., et al. (2011). Sexually transmitted infections and adverse pregnancy outcomes among women attending inner city public sexually transmitted diseases clinics. *Sexually Transmitted Diseases, 38,* 167–171.

Johnson, K. (2002). Time, patience needed to find right testosterone level with HRT. *Family Practice News, 32,* 31.

Johnson, K., et al. (2010). Association of sexual violence and human rights violations with physical and mental health in territories of the Eastern Democratic Republic of Congo. *Journal of the American Medical Association, 304,* 553–562.

Johnson, P. (1998). Pornography drives technology: Why not censor the Internet? In R. Baird & S. Rosenbaum (Eds.), *Pornography: Private right or public menace?* Amherst, NY: Prometheus Books.

Johnson, R. (2011). Vaccinology: Persistence pays off. *Nature, 473,* 456–457.

Johnson, S. (2011, April 22). Black women's maternal risks go unquestioned. Retrieved from http://www.womensenews.org/story/reproductive-health/110421

Johnston, M., & Fauci, A. (2008). An HIV vaccine—challenges and prospects. *New England Journal of Medicine, 359,* 888–890.

Johnston, M., & Fauci, A. (2011). HIV vaccine development—Improving on natural immunity. *New England Journal of Medicine, 365,* 873–875.

Jones, C., Chan, C., & Farine, D. (2011). Primer: Sex in pregnancy. *Canadian Medical Association Journal, 183,* 815–818.

Jones, H., et al. (2011). Testosterone replacement in hypogonadal men with type 2 diabetes and/or metabolic syndrome. *Diabetes Care, 34,* 828–837.

Jones, J. (2011, May 25). Support for legal gay relations hits new high. Retrieved from http://gallup.com/poll/147785/Support-Legal-Gay-Relations-Hits-New-High.aspx?version=

Jones, K., Gray, P., et al. (2008). Evaluation of an HIV prevention intervention adapted for Black men who have sex with men. *American Journal of Public Health, 98,* 1043–1050.

Jones, R. (2003). The height of vanity: In China, height equals more than beauty. *Marie Claire, 10,* 92–98.

Jones, R., & Biddlecom, L. (2011). The more things change . . . : The relative importance of the Internet as a source of contraceptive information for teens. *Sexuality Research and Social Policy, 8,* 27–37.

Jones, R., & Dreweke, J. (2011). *Countering conventional wisdom: New evidence on religion and contraceptive use.* New York: Guttmacher Institute.

Jones, R., & Finer, L. (2011, December 16). Who has second-trimester abortions in the United States? doi:10.1016/j.contraception.2011.10.012

Jones, R., Frowirth, L., & Moore, A. (2008). "I would want to give my child, like, everything in the world." *Journal of Family Issues, 29,* 79–99.

Jones, R., & Henshaw, S. (2002). Mifepristone for early medical abortion: Experiences in France, Great Britain, and Sweden. *Perspectives on Sexual and Reproductive Health, 34,* 154–161.

Jones, R., & Kavanaugh, M. (2011). Changes in abortion rates between 2000 and 2008 and lifetime incidence of abortion. *Obstetrics and Gynecology, 117,* 1358–1367.

Jones, R., & Kooistra, K. (2011). Abortion incidence and access to services in the United States, 2008. *Perspectives on Sexual and Reproductive Health, 43,* 41–50.

Jones, R., Moore, A., & Frowirth, L. (2010). Perceptions of male knowledge and support among U.S. women obtaining abortions. *Women's Health Issues, 21,* 117–123.

Jones, S., & Yarhouse, M. (2011). A longitudinal study of attempted religiously mediated sexual orientation change. *Journal of Sex and Marital Therapy, 37,* 404–427.

Jones, W., Chernovetz, M., & Hansson, R. (1978). The enigma of androgyny: Differential implications for males and females. *Journal of Consulting and Clinical Psychology, 46,* 298–313.

Jong, E. (2003, June 30). The zipless fallacy. *Newsweek,* 48.

Jordan, R., et al. (2011). Developing treatments for female sexual dysfunction. *Clinical Pharmacology and Therapeutics, 89,* 137–141.

Jordan-Young, R. (2010). *Brainstorm: The flaws in the science of sex differences.* Cambridge, MA: Harvard University Press.

Jorgenson, L., & Wahl, K. (2000). Psychiatrists as expert witnesses in sexual harassment cases under *Daubert* and *Kumho. Psychiatric Annals, 30,* 390–396.

Joseph, R. (1991). A case analysis in human sexuality: Counseling to a man with severe cerebral palsy. *Sexuality and Disability, 9*(2), 149–159.

Joyce, T. (2011). The supply-side economics of abortion. *New England Journal of Medicine, 365,* 1466–1469.

Joyce, T., Kaestner, R., & Colman, S. (2006). Changes in abortions and births and the Texas parental notification law. *New England Journal of Medicine, 354,* 1031–1038.

Juarez, V. (2006, February 20). www.findlovehere.com. *Newsweek,* 60.

Juninger, J. (1997). Fetishism: Assessment and treatment. In D. Laws & W. O'Donohue (Eds.), *Sexual deviance: Theory, assessment, and treatment.* New York: Guilford Press.

Kaare, M. (2009). Do mitochondrial mutations cause recurrent miscarriage? *Molecular Human Reproduction, 15,* 295–300.

Kabir, A. (2005). Racial differences in cesareans: An analysis of U.S. 2001 national inpatient sample data. *Obstetrics and Gynecology, 105,* 710–718.

Kaelin, C., Fuller, A., & Coltrera, F. (2006, April 24). New hopes, longer life. *Newsweek,* 65.

Kaestle, C., & Allen, K. (2011). The role of masturbation in healthy sexual development: Perceptions of young adults. *Archives of Sexual Behavior, 40,* 983–994.

Kaestle, C., & Halpern, C. (2007). What's love got to do with it? Sexual behaviors of opposite-sex couples through emerging adulthood. *Perspectives on Sexual and Reproductive Health, 39,* 134–140.

Kaestle, C., Morisky, D., & Wiley, D. (2002). Sexual intercourse and age difference between adolescent females and their romantic partners. *Perspectives on Sexual and Reproductive Health, 34,* 304–309.

Kafka, M. (2009). Paraphilias and paraphilia-related disorders. Retrieved February 10, 2009, from http://www.health.am/sex/more/paraphilias_related_disorders/

Kaftanovskaya, E., et al. (2011). Suppression of insulin-like 3 receptor reveals the role of beta-catennin and notch signaling in gubernaculum development. *Molecular Endocrinology, 25,* 170–183.

Kagan-Krieger, S. (1998). Women with Turner syndrome: A maturational and developmental perspective. *Journal of Adult Development, 5,* 125–135.

Kahn, J., Brett, B., & Holmes, J. (2011). Concerns with men's academic motivation in higher education: An exploratory investigation of the role of masculinity. *Journal of Men's Studies, 19,* 65–83.

Kahn, J., & Hillard, P. (2006). Progress in preventing cervical cancer and other HPV-related diseases. *Contemporary Pediatrics, 23,* 56–63.

Kaiser, C. (2003, October 14). Throwing the backlash off balance. *Advocate,* 96.

Kaiser, C. (2004, March 30). Civil marriage, civil rights. *Advocate,* 72.

Kaiser Family Foundation. (2003, February). Seventeen magazine and Kaiser Family Foundation release new survey of teens about gender roles. Retrieved June 12, 2003, from http://www.kff.org/content/2003/3301

Kaiser Family Foundation. (2006). Sex on TV. Retrieved February 15, 2006, from http://www.kff.org/entmedia/entmedia/0905nr.cfm

Kaiser Family Foundation. (2011, January). *Sexual health of adolescents and young adults in the United States.* Menlo Park, CA: Henry J. Kaiser Foundation.

Kalb, C. (2003, February 3). Farewell to "Aunt Flo." *Newsweek,* 48.

Kalb, C. (2006, February 20). Marriage: Act II. *Newsweek,* 62–63.

Kalb, C., & Springen, K. (2006, April 24). The war on HPV. *Newsweek,* 61–64.

Kalfoglou, A., Scott, J., & Hudson, K. (2008). Attitudes about preconception sex selection: A focus group study with Americans. *Human Reproduction, 23,* 2731–2736.

Kalof, L., Eby, K., Matheson, J., & Kroska, R. (2001). The influence of race and gender on student self-reports of sexual harassment by college professors. *Gender and Society, 15,* 282–302.

Kaminetsky, J., et al. (2011). A phase IV prospective evaluation of the safety and efficacy of extended release testosterone pellets for the treatment of male hypogonadism. *Journal of Sexual Medicine, 8,* 1186–1196.

Kane, E. (2006). "No way my boys are going to be like that!" Parents' responses to children's gender nonconformity. *Gender and Society, 20,* 149–176.

Kapinus, C. (2005). The effect of parental marital quality on young adults' attitudes toward divorce. *Sociological Perspectives, 48,* 319–335.

Kaplan, H. (1974). *The new sex therapy: Active treatment of sexual dysfunction*. New York: Brunner/Mazel.

Kaplan, H. (1979). *Disorders of sexual desire*. New York: Brunner/Mazel.

Kaplan, M., & Krueger, R. (1997). Voyeurism: Psychopathology and theory. In D. Laws & W. O'Donohue (Eds.), *Sexual deviance: Theory, assessment, and treatment*. New York: Guilford Press.

Karama, S., Lecours, A., Leroux, J., Blurgovin, P., et al. (2002). Areas of brain activation in males and females during viewing of erotic film excerpts. *Human Brain Mapping, 16*, 1–13.

Kari, L., et al. (2011). Generation of targeted *Chlamydia trachomatis* null mutants. *Proceedings of the National Academy of Sciences, 108*, 7189–7193.

Karim, S., et al. (2011). Integration of antiretroviral therapy with tuberculosis. *New England Journal of Medicine, 365*, 1492–1501.

Karney, B., & Bradbury, T. (1995). The longitudinal course of marital quality and stability: A review of theory, method, and research. *Psychological Review, 118*, 3–34.

Karpecki, P., & Shechtman, D. (2008). Take chlamydia seriously: Adult inclusive conjunctivitis is often caused by a concomitant chlamydia infection. *Review of Optometry, 145*, 93–94.

Karpecki, P., & Shechtman, D. (2011). New treatments for ocular HSV. *Review of Optometry, 148*, 113–114.

Karpel, A. (2011, August). Monogamish. *Advocate*, 21–25.

Karras, N. (2003). *Petals*. San Diego, CA: Chrystal River Publishing.

Kaschak, E., & Tiefer, L. (Eds.). (2002). *A new view of women's sexual problems*. Binghamton, NY: Haworth Press.

Kasl, C. (1999). *If the Buddha dated: Handbook for finding love on a spiritual path*. New York: Penguin/Arkana.

Kassabian, V. (2003). Sexual function in patients treated for benign prostatic hyperplasia. *Lancet, 361*, 60–62.

Kassing, L., Beesley, D., & Frey, L. (2005). Gender role conflict, homophobia, age, and education as predictors of male rape myth acceptance. *Journal of Mental Health Counseling, 27*, 311–328.

Kates, T. (2008, March 7). UVA research creates post-vasectomy test. *Daily Progress*, p. B2.

Katongo, C. (2012, January 16). Zambian sex workers offered "transformation." Retrieved from http://www.womensenews.org/story/hivaids/120115/zambian-sex-workers-offered-transformation

Katz, A. (2011). Drug resistance demands dual therapy. *Journal of Family Practice, 60*, 320.

Katz, J. (1976). *Gay American history*. New York: Avon Books.

Keegan, K., Dall'Era, M., & Durbin, B. (2011). A simulator study of the costs of active surveillance compared to immediate treatment for prostate cancer. *Journal of Urology, 185*, e127.

Keele, B., Van Heuverswyn, F., Li, Y., et al. (2006). Chimpanzee reservoirs of pandemic and nonpandemic HIV-1. Retrieved June 22, 2006, from http://www.sciencexpress.org

Keister, D., & Neal, R. (2008). Managing BPH: When to consider surgery. *American Family Physician, 77*, 1375.

Kelland, K. (2011). HIV numbers hit new high as AIDS drugs save lives. Retrieved December 6, 2011, from http://news.yahoo.com/life-saving-aids-drugs-push-hiv-numbers-high-0914/0745.html

Keller, J. (2002). Blatant stereotype threat and women's math performance. *Sex Roles, 47*, 193–198.

Kellett, J. (2000). Older adult sexuality. In L. Szuchman & F. Muscarella (Eds.), *Psychological perspectives on human sexuality*. New York: Wiley.

Kelley, M., & Parsons, B. (2000). Sexual harassment in the 1990s. *Journal of Higher Education, 71*, 548.

Kellog-Spadt, S. (2006, June/July). *Innovative treatments for vulvar and sexual pain*. Paper presented at the Gumbo Sexualité Upriver: Spicing Up Education and Therapy (AASECT 38th Annual Conference), St. Louis, MO.

Kelly, J., Hoffman, R., Rompa, D., & Gray, M. (1998). Protease inhibitor combination therapies and perceptions of gay men regarding AIDS severity and the need to maintain safer sex. *AIDS, 12*, F91–F95.

Kelly, M. (2008). Lock them up and throw away the key: The preventive detention of sex offenders in the United States and Germany. *Georgetown Journal of International Law, 39*, 551–572.

Kelly, M., Strassberg, D., & Kircher, J. (1990). Attitudinal and experiential correlates of anorgasmia. *Archives of Sexual Behavior, 19*, 165–181.

Kelsberg, G., Bishop, R., & Morton, J. (2006). When should a child with an undescended testis be referred to a urologist? *Journal of Family Practice, 55*, 336–337.

Kempner, M. (2005). Sex workers: A glimpse into public health perspectives. *SIECUS Report, 33*, 2.

Kennedy, K., & Trussell, J. (1998). Postpartum contraception and lactation. In R. Hatcher, J. Trussell, F. Stewart, et al. (Eds.), *Contraceptive technology*. New York: Ardent Media.

Kent, C., Chaw, J., Wong, W., et al. (2005). Prevalence of rectal, urethral, and pharyngeal chlamydia and gonorrhea detected in two clinical settings among men who have sex with men. *Clinical Infectious Diseases, 41*, 67–74.

Kerns, J., & Darney, P. (2011). Vaginal ring contraception. *Contraception, 83*, 107–115.

Keskin, U., et al. (2011). Differences in prevalence of sexual dysfunction between primary and secondary infertile women. *Fertility and Sterility, 96*, 1213–1217.

Kessel, M., & Hopper, J. (2011, November 7). Victims speak out about North Carolina sterilization program, which targeted women, young girls and Blacks. Retrieved from rockcenter.msnbc.msn.com/_news/2011/11/07/8640744-victims-speak-out

Khalife, N. (2011, December 16). Yemen could seize moment to ban child marriage. Retrieved from http://www.womensenews.org/pring/8882

Khan, H. (2011, November 4). Mississippi's "personhood" amendment a challenge for moderate conservatives. Retrieved from http://abcnews.go.com/blogs/politics/2011/11mississippis-personhood-amendment-a-challenge-for-moderate-conservatives

Khan, M., Masood, M., Mukhtar, Z., & Rasool, A. (2007, April). *Concepts of sexology in progressive Islamic ideology*. Paper presented at the 18th Congress of the World Association for Sexual Health, Sydney, Australia.

Khoosal, D., Grover, P., & Terry, T. (2011). Satisfaction with a gender realignment service. *Sexual and Relationship Therapy, 26*, 72–83.

Kiel, R., & Nashelsky, J. (2003). Does cranberry juice prevent or treat urinary tract infection? *Journal of Family Practice, 52*, 154–155.

Kilbourn, C., & Richards, C. (2001). Abnormal uterine bleeding. *Postgraduate Medicine, 109*, 137–150.

Kim, C., & Free, C. (2008). Recent evaluations of the peer-led approach in sexual health education: A systematic review. *Perspectives on Sexual and Reproductive Health, 40*, 144–151.

Kim, C., et al. (2011). Longitudinal influences of friends and parents upon unprotected vaginal intercourse in adolescents. *Contraception, 83*, 138–144.

Kim, E., & Lipshultz, L. (1997). Advances in the treatment of organic erectile dysfunction. *Hospital Practice*, April 15, 101–120.

Kim, J. (2011). Weighing the benefits and costs of HPV vaccination of young men. *New England Journal of Medicine, 364,* 393–395.

Kim, J., Sorsoli, C., Collins, K., et al. (2007). From sex to sexuality: Exposing the heterosexual script on primetime network television. *Journal of Sex Research, 44,* 145–157.

Kimlicka, T., Cross, H., & Tarnai, J. (1983). A comparison of androgynous, feminine, masculine, and undifferentiated women on self-esteem, body satisfaction, and sexual satisfaction. *Psychology of Women Quarterly, 1,* 291–294.

Kimport, K., Foster, K., & Weitz, T. (2011). Social sources of women's emotional difficulty after abortion: Lessons from women's abortion narratives. *Perspectives on Sexual and Reproductive Health, 43,* 103–109.

Kingsberg, S. (2002). The impact of aging on sexual function in women and their partners. *Archives of Sexual Behavior, 31,* 431–437.

Kingsbury, K. (2007a, October 15). Matching treatments to patients. *Time,* 47.

Kingsbury, K. (2007b, October 15). The changing face of breast cancer. *Time,* 34–48.

Kinsey, A., Pomeroy, W., & Martin, C. (1948). *Sexual behavior in the human male.* Philadelphia: Saunders.

Kinsey, A., Pomeroy, W., Martin, C., & Gebhard, P. (1953). *Sexual behavior in the human female.* Philadelphia: Saunders.

Kipnis, L. (1996). *Bound and gagged: Pornography and the politics of fantasy in America.* New York: Grove Press.

Kirby, D. (2002). The impact of schools and school programs upon adolescent sexual behavior. *Journal of Sex Research, 39,* 27–33.

Kirby, D. (2008). Emerging answers 2007: Research findings on programs to reduce teen pregnancy and sexually transmitted diseases. Retrieved November 21, 2008, from http://www.thenationalcampaign .org/EA2007/EA2007_full.pdf

Kirchick, J. (2009, January 13). The new religious right. *Advocate,* 40–43.

Kirchmeyer, C. (1996). Gender roles in decision-making in demographically diverse groups: A case for reviving androgyny. *Sex Roles, 34,* 649–663.

Kirkpatrick, L., & Davis, K. (1994). Attachment style, gender, and relationship stability: A longitudinal analysis. *Journal of Personality and Social Psychology, 66,* 502–512.

Kissinger, P., Niccolai, L., Magnus, M., et al. (2003). Partner notification for HIV and syphilis. *Sexually Transmitted Diseases, 30,* 75–82.

Kissinger, P., Trim, S., Williams, E., et al. (1997). An evaluation of initiatives to improve family planning use by African-American adolescents. *Journal of the National Medical Association, 89,* 110–114.

Kissling, E. (2002, January). *On the rag on screen: Menarche in film and television.* Retrieved May 25, 2003, from http://www.findarticles.com/cf_0/m2294/2002_Jan/90333581/p1/article.jhtml

Kissling, F. (2009, May 31). Abortion provider George Tiller murdered at church. Retrieved June 1, 2009, from http://www.religiondispatches.org/dialogs/print/?id=1590

Kite, M., & Whitley, B. (1998b). Heterosexuals' attitudes toward homosexuality. In G. Herek (Ed.), *Stigma and sexual orientation: Understanding prejudice against lesbians, gay men, and bisexuals.* Thousand Oaks, CA: Sage.

Klapper, B. (2007, July 31). Congo's women suffer abuse far beyond rape. *Oregonian,* p. A6.

Klausner, J., & Morris, B. (2012). Benefits of male circumcision. *Journal of the American Medical Association, 307,* 455–456.

Klein, J. (2005). Adolescent pregnancy: Current trends and issues. *Pediatrics, 116,* 281–286.

Klein, M. (1991). Why there's no such thing as sexual addiction and why it really matters. In R. Francoeur (Ed.), *Taking sides: Clashing views of controversial issues in human sexuality* (3rd ed.). Guilford, CT: Dushkin.

Klein, M. (1999). Censorship and the fear of sexuality. In J. Elias, V. Elias, V. Bullough, et al. (Eds.), *Porn 101: Eroticism, pornography, and the First Amendment.* Amherst, NY: Prometheus Books.

Klein, M. (2003). Sex addiction: A dangerous clinical concept. *SIECUS Report, 31,* 8–11.

Klein, M. (2012a). *Sexual intelligence: What we really want from sex and how to get it.* New York: HarperCollins.

Klein, M. (2012b). Why "sexual addiction" is not a useful diagnosis—and why it matters. Retrieved May 25, 2012, from http://www.SexualIntelligence.org

Kleinplatz, P., & Moser, C. (2004). Toward clinical guidelines for working with BDSM clients. *Contemporary Sexuality, 38,* 1, 4.

Kliff, S. (2010, April 26). Remember Roe! *Newsweek,* 38–40.

Kliff, S. (2007, July 30). A stem-cell surprise. *Newsweek,* 46–48.

Kluger, J. (2004, January 19). The power of love. *Time,* 62–65.

Knickmeyer, R., et al. (2011). Turner syndrome and sexual differentiation of the brain: Implications for understanding male-biased neurodevelopmental disorder. *Journal of Neurodevelopmental Disorders, 3,* 293–306.

Knight, K. (2006). Men for sale? Retrieved August 16, 2006, from http://www.dailymail.co.uk/pages/test/print.hrml?in_article_id= 400187&in_page_id=1879

Knox, D., Breed, R., & Zusman, M. (2007). College men and jealousy. *College Student Journal, 41,* 494–498.

Knox, D., Zusman, M., & McNeely, A. (2008). University students' beliefs about sex: Men vs. women. *College Student Journal, 42,* 181–185.

Knox, K. (2006, November 11). Report finds adult-themed searches rank high in Utah. Retrieved November 26, 2006, from http://www.freespeechcoalition.com/FSCprint.asp?coid=9777

Knox, S., Jackson, T., & Javins, B. (2011) Implications of early menopause in women exposed to perfluorocarbons. *Journal of Clinical Endocrinology and Metabolism, 96,* 1747–1753.

Knudson, G., Brotto, L., & Inskip, J. (2007, April). *Understanding asexuality: Sexual characteristics and personality profiles of asexual men and women.* Paper presented at the 18th Congress of the World Association for Sexual Health, Sydney, Australia.

Knudson-Martin, C., & Silverstein, R. (2009). Suffering in silence: A qualitative metadata-analysis of postpartum depression. *Journal of Marital and Family Therapy, 35,* 145–158.

Koch-Straube, U. (1982). Attitude toward sexuality in old age. *Zeitschrift für Gerontologie, 15,* 220–227.

Koehler, J., Zangwill, W., & Lotz, L. (2000, May). *Integrating the power of EMDR into sex therapy.* Paper presented at the 32nd Annual Conference of the American Association of Sex Educators, Counselors, and Therapists, Atlanta, GA.

Kohl, J. (2002). *The scent of Eros: Mysteries of odor in human sexuality.* Lincoln, NE: iUniverse.

Kollin, C., Hesser, U., Ritzen, M., & Karpe, B. (2006). Testicular growth from birth to two years of age, and the effect of orchidopexy at age nine months: A randomized controlled study. *Acta Paediatrica, 95,* 318–324.

Kols, A., & Lande, R. (2008). Vasectomy: Reaching out to new users. *Population Reports, 6,* 1–23.

Komaromy, M., Bindman, A., Haber, R., & Sande, M. (1993). Sexual harassment in medical training. *New England Journal of Medicine, 328,* 322–326.

Komisaruk, B., Beyer-Flores, C., & Whipple, B. (2006). *The science of orgasm.* Baltimore, MD: Johns Hopkins University Press.

Koo, D., Begier, E., Henn, M., et al. (2006). HIV counseling and testing: Less targeting, more testing. *American Journal of Public Health, 96,* 962–963.

Korber, B., Muldoon, M., Theiler, J., et al. (2000). Timing the ancestor of the HIV-1 pandemic strains. *Science, 288,* 1789–1796.

Koren, G. (2009). In utero drug exposure and the media. *Ob.Gyn. News, 44,* 11–12.

Korenman, S., & Viosca, S. (1992). Use of a vacuum tumescence device in the management of impotence in men with a history of penile implant or severe pelvic disease. *Journal of the American Geriatrics Society, 40,* 61–64.

Kosnik, A., Carroll, W., Cunningham, A., et al. (1977). *Human sexuality: New directions in American Catholic thought.* New York: Paulist Press.

Koss, M., Bailey, J., Yuan, N., et al. (2003). Depression and PTSD in survivors of male violence: Research and training initiatives to facilitate recovery. *Psychology of Women Quarterly, 27,* 130–142.

Koss, M., Figueredo, A., & Prince, R. (2002). Cognitive mediation of rape's mental, physical, and social health impact: Tests of four models in cross-sectional data. *Journal of Consulting and Clinical Psychology, 70,* 926–941.

Kost, K., Finer, L., & Singh, S. (2012). Variation in state unintended pregnancy rates in the United States. *Perspectives on Sexual and Reproductive Health, 44,* 57–64.

Kotb, H. (2008, November). *Sexuality and media in Arabic countries.* Paper presented at the 18th Deutsche Gesellschaft für Sozialwissenschaftliche Sexualforschung Conference, "Sexuality and the Media," Munich, Germany.

Kottler, J. (2008). From intention to action. *Psychotherapy Networker,* November/December, 43–47.

Koukounas, E., & McCabe, M. (1997). Sexual and emotional variables influencing sexual response to erotica. *Behavior Research and Therapy, 35,* 221–231.

Kovach, G., & Murr, A. (2008, April 10). Trouble in the hills. Retrieved April 12, 2008, from http://www.newsweek.com/id/131379

Kovacs, A., & Osvath, P. (2006). Genital retraction syndrome in Korean woman: A case of Koro in Hungary. Retrieved January 7, 2006, from http://www.Medscape/abstract/9697166

Kowalczyk, T., et al. (2012). Adolescent perceptions of risk and need for safer sexual behaviors after first human papillomavirus vaccination. *Archives of Adolescent Medicine, 166,* 82–88.

Kozhimannil, K., et al. (2011). Racial and ethnic disparities in postpartum depression care among low-income women. *Psychiatric Services, 62,* 619–625.

Krahe, B., Scheinberger-Olwig, R., & Kolpin, S. (2000). Ambiguous communication of sexual intentions as a risk marker of sexual aggression. *Sex Roles, 42,* 313–337.

Krahe, B., Waizenhofer, E., & Moller, I. (2003). Women's sexual aggression against men: Prevalence and predictors. *Sex Roles, 49,* 219–232.

Kreahling, L. (2005, February 1). The perils of needles to the body. *New York Times,* p. F5.

Kreider, H. (2010). *Increase in opposite sex cohabiting couples from 2009 to 2010.* Washington, DC: U.S. Census Bureau.

Kreinin, T., Rodriquez, M., & Edwards, M. (2001). Adolescents would prefer parents as primary sexuality educators. *SIECUS Report Supplement,* December/January, 1.

Kripke, C. (2006). Cyclic vs. continuous or extended-cycle combined contraceptives. *American Family Physician, 73,* 803.

Kristensen, E., & Lau, M. (2011). Sexual function in women with a history of intrafamilial childhood sexual abuse. *Sexual and Relationship Therapy, 26,* 229–241.

Kristof, N. (2011, April 23). What about American girls sold on the streets? Retrieved from http://www.nytimes.com/2011/04/24/opinion/24kristof.html?

Kristof, N. (2012, March 3). When states abuse women. Retrieved from http://www.nytimes.com/2012/03/04/opinion/sunday/kristof-when-states-abuse-women.html

Kroll, K., & Klein E. (1992). *Enabling romance.* New York: Harmony Books.

Kruger, T., Haake, P., Hartmann, U., et al. (2002). Orgasm-induced prolactin secretion: Feedback control of sexual drive? *Neuroscience and Biobehavioral Reviews, 26,* 3144.

Krujiver, F., Zhou, J., Pool, C., et al. (2000). Male-to-female transsexuals have female neuron member in a limbic nucleus. *Journal of Clinical Endocrinology, 85,* 2034–2040.

Krychman, M. (2011). Vaginal estrogens for the treatment of dyspareunia. *Journal of Sexual Medicine, 8,* 666–674.

Kuehn, B. (2011). New HPV vaccine indication. *Journal of the American Medical Association, 305,* 770–771.

Kuipers, H. (1998). Anabolic steroids: Side effects. *Encyclopedia of Sports Medicine and Science,* March 7.

Kulczycki, A. (2011). Abortion in Latin America: Changes in practice, growing conflict, and recent policy developments. *Studies in Family Planning, 42,* 199–220.

Kumwenda, N., Hoover, D., Mofenson, L., et al. (2008). Extended antiretroviral prophylaxis to reduce breast-milk HIV-1 transmissions. *New England Journal of Medicine, 359,* 119–129.

Kunst, J. (2011). *Unprotected texts: The Bible's surprising contradictions about sex and desire.* New York: HarperOne.

Kurdek, L. (1995a). Developmental changes in relationship quality in gay and lesbian cohabiting couples. *Developmental Psychology, 31,* 86–94.

Kurdek, L. (1995b). Lesbian and gay couples. In A. D'Augelli & C. Patterson (Eds.), *Lesbian, gay, and bisexual identities over the lifespan.* New York: Oxford University Press.

Kuriansky, J. (1996). Sexuality and television advertising: An historical perspective. *SIECUS Report, 24,* 13–15.

Kuriansky, J., & Simonson, H. (2005, May). *What is tantra?* Paper presented at What's New and What Works: Pioneering Solutions for Today's Sexual Issues (AASECT 37th Annual Conference), Portland, OR.

Kurtz-Costes, B., Rowley, S., Harris-Britt, A., & Woods, T. (2008). Gender stereotypes about mathematics and science and self-perceptions of ability in late childhood and early adolescence. *Merrill-Palmer Quarterly, 54,* 386–409.

Kuyper, L., et al. (2011). Doing more good than harm? The effects of participation in sex research on young people in the Netherlands. *Archives of Sexual Behavior,* June 17, 1–10.

Kuyper, L., & Fokkema, T. (2011a). Loneliness among older lesbian, gay and bisexual adults: The role of minority stress. *Archives of Sexual Behavior, 39,* 1171–1180.

Kuyper, L., & Fokkema, T. (2011b). Minority stress and mental health among Dutch LGBs: Examination of differences between sex and sexual orientation. *Journal of Counseling Psychology, 58,* 222–233.

Laan, E. (2008). What makes women experience desire? *Feminism and Psychology, 18,* 505–514.

Laan, E. (2009, June). The use of drugs and technical aids to help experiencing orgasm in women. Paper presented at the 19th WAS World Congress for Sexual Health, Göteborg, Sweden.

Laan, E., & Everaerd, W. (1996). Determinants of female sexual arousal: Psychophysiological theory and data. *Annual Review of Sex Research, 6,* 32–76.

Lacey, R., Reifman, A., Scott, J., Harris, S., & Fitzpatrick, J. (2004). Sexual-moral attitudes, love styles, and mate selection. *Journal of Sex Research, 41,* 121–128.

LaCroix, A., et al. (2011). Health outcomes after stopping conjugated equine estrogens among postmenopausal women with prior hysterectomy. *Journal of the American Medical Association, 305*, 1305–1314.

Lagana, L. (1999). Psychological correlates of contraceptive practices during late adolescence. *Adolescence, 34*, 463–482.

Laino, C. (2008, December 12). Gene test better predicts breast cancer risk. Retrieved from http://www.webmd .com/breast-cancer/news/20081212/ gene-test-better-predicts-breast-cancer

Lallemant, M., et al. (2011). Pediatric HIV—A neglected disease? *New England Journal of Medicine, 365*, 581–583.

Lalumiere, M., Blanchard, R., & Zucker, K. (2000). Sexual orientation and handedness in men and women: A meta-analysis. *Psychological Bulletin, 126*, 575–592.

Lamb, D., Catanzaro, S., & Moorman, A. (2003). Psychologists reflect on their sexual relationships with clients, supervisees, and students: Occurrence, impact, rationales, and collegial intervention. *Professional Psychology: Research and Practice, 34*, 102–107.

Lambert, S., & O'Halloran, E. (2008). Deductive thematic analysis of a female paedophilia website. *Psychiatry, Psychology and the Law, 15*, 284–300.

Lambert, T., Kahn, A., & Apple, K. (2003). Pluralistic ignorance and hooking up. *Journal of Sex Research, 40*, 129–133.

Lammers, C., Ireland, M., Resnick, M., & Blum, R. (2000). Influences on adolescents' decisions to postpone onset of sexual intercourse: A survival analysis of virginity among youths ages 13 to 18 years. *Journal of Adolescent Health, 26*, 42–48.

Lammers, J., et al. (2011). Power increases infidelity among men and women. *Psychological Science, 22*, 1191–1197.

Lamptey, P., Johnson, J., & Khan, M. (2006). The global challenge of HIV and AIDS. *Population Bulletin, 61*, 3–24.

Landsberg, M. (2002, October 6). First openly gay member will serve in Israeli parliament. *Sunday Oregonian*, p. A16.

Lane, F. (2000). *Obscene profits: The entrepreneurs of pornography in the cyber age.* New York: Routledge.

Langevin, R. (2003). A study of the psychosexual characteristics of sex killers: Can we identify them before it is too late? *International Journal of Offender Therapy and Comparative Criminology, 47*, 366–382.

Langevin, R., Paitich, D., & Ramsay, G. (1979). Experimental studies of the etiology of genital exhibitionism. *Archives of Sexual Behavior, 8*, 307–331.

Langstrom, N., & Zucker, K. (2005). Transvestic fetishism in the general population: Prevalence and correlates. *Journal of Sex and Marital Therapy, 31*, 87–95.

Lannutti, P. (2011). Security, recognition, and misgivings: Exploring older same-sex couples' experiences of legally recognized same-sex marriage. *Journal of Social and Personal Relationships, 28*, 64–82.

Larimore, W., & Stanford, J. (2000). Post-fertilization effects of oral contraceptives and their relationship to informed consent. *Archives of Family Medicine, 9*, 126–133.

Larsen, E. (2007, March/April). Drugs, knives, and midwives. *Utne Reader*, 61–63.

Larsen, S., & Fitzgerald, L. (2011). PTSD symptoms and sexual harassment: The role of attributions and perceived control. *Journal of Interpersonal Violence, 26*, 2555–2567.

Larsson, I., & Svedin, C. (2002). Sexual experiences in childhood: Young adults' recollections. *Archives of Sexual Behavior, 31*, 263–273.

LaSala, M. (2007). Parental influence, gay youths, and safer sex. *Health and Social Work, 32*, 49–55.

Lash, M., & Armstrong, A. (2009). Impact of obesity on women's health. *Fertility and Sterility, 91*, 1712–1716.

Latty-Mann, H., & Davis, K. (1996). Attachment theory and partner choice: Preference and actuality. *Journal of Social and Personal Relationships, 13*, 5–23.

Lauer, J., & Lauer, R. (1985, June). Marriages made to last. *Psychology Today*, 22–26.

Laumann, E., Gagnon, J., Michael, R., & Michaels, S. (1994). *The social organization of sexuality: Sexual practices in the United States.* Chicago: University of Chicago Press.

Laumann, E., Masi, C., & Zuckerman, E. (1997). Circumcision in the United States: Prevalence, prophylactic effects, and sexual practice. *Journal of the American Medical Association, 277*, 1052–1057.

Laumann, E., Paik, A., Glasser, D., & Kang, J. (2006). A cross-national study of subjective sexual well-being among older women and men: Findings from the global study of sexual attitudes and behaviors. *Archives of Sexual Behavior, 35*, 143–159.

Laumann, E., Paik, A., & Rosen, R. (1999). Sexual dysfunction in the United States. *Journal of the American Medical Association, 281*, 537–544.

Laurent, B. (1995). Intersexuality: A plea for honesty and emotional support. *AHP Perspective*, November/December, 8–9, 28.

Lauzen, M., Dozier, D., & Horan, N. (2008). Constructing gender stereotypes through social roles in prime-time television. *Journal of Broadcasting and Electronic Media, 52*, 200–214.

Lavie-Ajayi, M., & Joffe, H. (2009). Social representations of female orgasm. *Journal of Health Psychology, 14*, 98–107.

Lavin, M. (2008). Voyeurism: Psychopathology and theory. In D. Laws & W. O'Donohue (Eds.), *Sexual deviance: Theory, assessment, and treatment* (2nd ed.). New York: Guilford Press.

Lawn, S. (2012). Timing of antiretroviral therapy for HIV-1-associated tuberculosis. *New England Journal of Medicine, 366*, 474–476.

Lawrence, A. (2003). Factors associated with satisfaction or regret following male-to-female sex reassignment surgery. *Archives of Sexual Behavior, 32*, 299–316.

Lawrence, A. (2005). Sexuality before and after male-to-female sex reassignment surgery. *Archives of Sexual Behavior, 34*, 147–166.

Lawrence, A. (2007). Becoming what we love: Autogynephilic transsexualism conceptualized as an expression of romantic love. *Perspectives in Biology and Medicine, 50*, 506–520.

Lawrence, R., et al. (2011a). Adolescents, contraception and confidentiality: A national survey of obstetrician-gynecologists. *Contraception, 84*, 259–265.

Lawrence, R., et al. (2011b). Factors influencing physicians' advice about female sterilization in USA: A national survey. *Human Reproduction, 26*, 106–111.

Lazar, K. (2011, July 25). Gay Massachusetts teens more likely than peers to be homeless. Retrieved from http://www.boston .com?Boston/whitecoatnotes/2011/07/ gay-mass-teens-more-likely-than-peers-to-be-homeless

Lazzarini, Z. (2008). South Dakota's abortion script: Threatening the physician-patient relationship. *New England Journal of Medicine, 359*, 2189–2191.

Leadbeater, B., & Way, N. (1995). *Urban adolescent girls: Resisting stereotypes.* New York: University Press.

Leander, L., Christianson, S., & Granhag, P. (2007). A sexual abuse case: Children's memories and reports. *Psychiatry, Psychology, and Law, 14*, 120–129.

Leaper, C., Anderson, K., & Sanders, P. (1998). Moderators of gender effects on parents' talk to their children: A meta-analysis. *Developmental Psychology, 34*, 3–27.

Leclerc, B., et al. (2011). Victim resistance in child sexual abuse: A look into the efficacy of self-protection strategies based on offender's experience. *Journal of Interpersonal Violence, 26*, 1868–1883.

Lederman, R., Chan, W., & Roberts-Gray, C. (2008). Parent-Adolescent Relationship Education (PARE): Program delivery to reduce risks for adolescent pregnancy and STDs. *Behavioral Medicine, 33,* 137–143.

Lee, A., & Scheurer, V. (1983). Psychological androgyny and aspects of self-image in women and men. *Sex Roles, 9,* 289–306.

Lee, C. (2011, December 5). This man is addicted to sex. *Newsweek,* 50.

Lee, D. (2011). Confessions of a single, female pastor. *Marie Claire, 18,* 87–88.

Lee, J. (1974). The styles of loving. *Psychology Today, 8,* 43–51.

Lee, J. (1988). Love-styles. In R. Sternberg & M. Barnes (Eds.), *The psychology of love.* New Haven, CT: Yale University Press.

Lee, J. (1998). Ideologies of lovestyle and sexstyle. In V. de Munck (Ed.), *Romantic love and sexual behavior.* Westport, CT: Praeger.

Lee, J., et al. (2002). Developmental risk factors for sexual offending. *Child Abuse and Neglect, 26,* 73–92.

Lee, M. (2011, October 14). Designer vagina surgery: Snip, stitch, kerching. Retrieved from www.guardian.co.uk/lifeandstyle/2011/oct/14/designer-vagina-surgery

Lee, M. (2009, March 18). U.S. endorses UN gay rights text. Retrieved March 23, 2009, from http://news.yahoo.com/s/ap20090318/ap_on_go_pr_wh/obama_gay_rights

Lee, M., Morgan, M., & Rapkin, A. (2011). Clitoral and vulvar vestibular sensation in women taking 20 mcg ethinyl estradiol combined oral contraceptives: A preliminary study. *Journal of Sexual Medicine, 8,* 213–218.

Lee-St. John, J., & Gallatin, J. (2008, December 22). Permanent birth control. *Time,* 70.

Legate, N., Ryan, R., & Weinstein, N. (2012). Is coming out always a "good thing"? Exploring the relations of autonomy support, outness, and wellness for lesbian, gay, and bisexual individuals. *Social Psychological and Personality Science, 3,* 145–152.

Lehmann-Haupt, R. (2009, May 11). Why I froze my eggs. *Newsweek,* 50–52.

Lehmiller, J., et al. (2011). Sex differences in approaching friends with benefits relationships. *Journal of Sex Research, 48,* 275–284.

Lehr, S., Demi, A., Dilorio, C., & Facteau, J. (2005). Predictors of father-son communication about sexuality. *Journal of Sex Research, 42,* 119–129.

Leibenluft, E. (1996). Sex is complex. *American Journal of Psychiatry, 15,* 969–972.

Leiblum, S. (2000). Vaginismus: A most perplexing problem. In S. Leiblum & R. Rosen (Eds.), *Principles and practice of sex therapy.* New York: Guilford Press.

Leiblum, S., & Bachmann, G. (1988). The sexuality of the climacteric woman. In B. Eskin (Ed.), *The menopause: Comprehensive management.* New York: Yearbook Medical Publications.

Leiblum, S., & Goldmeier, D. (2008). Persistent genital arousal disorder in women: Case reports of association with antidepressant usage and withdrawal. *Journal of Sex and Marital Therapy, 34,* 150–159.

Leitenberg, H., & Henning, K. (1995). Sexual fantasy. *Psychological Bulletin, 117*(3), 469–496.

Leitzmann, M., Moore, S., Peters, T., & Lacey, J. (2008). Prospective study of physical activity and risk of postmenopausal breast cancer. *Breast Cancer Research, 53,* 10–15.

Leland, J. (2000a, May 29). The science of women and sex. *Newsweek,* 46–53.

Leland, J. (2000b, March 20). Shades of gay. *Newsweek,* 46–49.

Leland, J., & Beals, G. (1997, May 5). In living color. *Newsweek,* 58–60.

Leprout, R., & Van Cauter, E. (2011). Effects of 1 week sleep deprivation on testosterone levels in young healthy men. *Journal of the American Medical Association, 305,* 2173–2174.

Lepowsky, M. (1994). *Fruit of the motherland: Gender in an egalitarian society.* New York: Columbia University Press.

Letourneau, E., Schewe, P., & Frueh, B. (1997). Preliminary evaluation of sexual problems in combat veterans with PTSD. *Journal of Traumatic Stress, 10,* 125–132.

Leuchtag, A. (2003, January/February). Human rights, sex trafficking, and prostitution. *Humanist,* 10–15.

Levant, R. (1997). *Men and emotions: A psychoeducational approach.* New York: Newbridge Communications.

Leventhal-Alexander, J. (2005, July). Female sexual dysfunction and menopause. Paper presented at the 17th World Congress of Sexology, Montreal, Canada.

Lever, J. (1994, August 23). Sexual revelations. *Advocate,* 17–24.

Lever, J., Frederick, D., & Peplau, L. (2006). Does size matter? Men's and women's views on penis size across the lifespan. *Psychology of Men and Masculinity, 7,* 127.

Levin, R. (2002). The physiology of sexual arousal in the human female: A recreational and procreational synthesis. *Archives of Sexual Behavior, 31,* 405–411.

Levin, R. (2003a). Do women gain anything from coitus apart from pregnancy? Changes in the human female genital tract activated by coitus. *Journal of Sex and Marital Therapy, 29*(Suppl.), 59–69.

Levin, R. (2003b). Is prolactin the biological "off switch" for human sexual arousal? *Sexual and Relationship Therapy, 18,* 237–243.

Levin, R., & Meston, C. (2006). Nipple/breast stimulation and sexual arousal in young men and women. *Journal of Sexual Medicine, 3,* 450–454.

Levine, M., & Troiden, R. (1988). The myth of sexual compulsivity. *Journal of Sex Research, 25,* 347–363.

Levine, R., Sato, S., Hashomoto, T., & Verman, J. (1995). Love and marriage in eleven cultures. *Journal of Cross-Cultural Psychology, 26,* 554–571.

Levine, S. (2007, April). *Seeing beneath the sexual desire disorders by understanding the nature of sexual desire and psychological intimacy.* Paper presented at the 18th Congress of the World Association for Sexual Health, Sydney, Australia.

Levy, A. (2005). *Female chauvinist pigs: Women and the rise of raunch culture.* New York: Free Press.

Levy, A., Crowley, T., & Gingell, C. (2000). Nonsurgical management of erectile dysfunction. *Clinical Endocrinology, 52,* 253–260.

Levy, J. (2001). HIV and AIDS in people over 50. *SIECUS Report, 30,* 10–15.

Levy, J. (2010, May/June). Between gay and straight. *Psychotherapy Networker,* 59–62.

Levy, S. (1997, July 7). On the Net, anything goes. *Newsweek,* 28–30.

Lew, M. (2004). Adult male survivors of sexual abuse: Sexual issues in treatment and recovery. *Contemporary Sexuality, 38,* i–v.

Leye, E., Powell, R., Nienhuis, G., & Claeys, P. (2006). Health care in Europe for women with genital mutilation. *Health Care for Women International, 27,* 362–378.

Li, C., Kayes, O., Kell, P., et al. (2006). Penile suspensory ligament division for penile augmentation: Indications and results. *European Urology, 49,* 729–733.

Li, J., et al. (2011). Low-frequency HIV-1 drug resistance mutations and risk of NNRT1-based antiretroviral treatment failure. *Journal of the American Medical Association, 305,* 1327–1335.

Li, T., & Fung, H. (2011). The dynamic goal theory of marital satisfaction. *Review of General Psychology, 15,* 246–254.

Li, Y., Baer, D., Friedman, G., Udaltsova, N., & Klatsky, A. (2007, September). *Wine, liquor, beer, and risk of breast cancer.* Paper presented at the European Cancer Conference, Barcelona, Spain.

Liao, L., Michala, L., & Creighton, S. (2010). Labial surgery for well women: A review of the literature. *British Journal of Gynecology, 117,* 20–25.

Liao, Z., et al. (2010). Transcription factor Stat5a/b as a therapeutic target protein for prostate cancer. *International Journal of Biochemistry and Cell Biology, 42,* 186–192.

Lichty, L., Torres, J., Valenti, M., & Buchanan, N. (2008). Sexual harassment policies in K–12 schools: Examining accessibility to students and content. *Journal of School Health, 78,* 607–614.

Lieberman, A. (2011, April 21). U.S. sex workers hail nation's new stance. Retrieved from http://www.womensenews.org/story/prostitution-and-trafficking/110420

Liebowitz, M. (1983). *The chemistry of love.* Boston: Little, Brown.

Lief, H., & Hubschman, L. (1993). Orgasm in the postoperative transsexual. *Archives of Sexual Behavior, 22,* 145–155.

Lindau, S., Schumm, P., Laumann, E., et al. (2007). A study of sexuality and health among older adults in the United States. *New England Journal of Medicine, 357,* 762–774.

Lindberg, S., Hyde, J., & Hirsch, L. (2008). Gender and mother-child interaction during mathematics homework: The importance of individual differences. *Merrill-Palmer Quarterly, 54,* 232–255.

Lindholm, J., Lunde, I., Rasmussen, O., & Wagner, G. (1980). Gonadal and sexual functions in tortured Greek men. *Danish Medical Bulletin, 27,* 243–245.

Lindsay, S., Merckelbuch, H., et al. (2009). Cognitive mechanisms of recovered memory. *Psychological Science, 20.*

Linskey, A. (2006, August 9). Police target Internet-advertised prostitution. *Baltimore Sun.*

Lippa, R. (2003). Handedness, sexual orientation, and gender-related personality traits in men and women. *Archives of Sexual Behavior, 32,* 103–115.

Lippa, R. (2006). Is high sex drive associated with increased sexual attraction to both sexes? It depends on whether you're male or female. *Psychological Science, 17,* 46–52.

Lippa, R. (2008). Sex differences in sex drive, sociosexuality, and height across 53 nations: Testing evolutionary and social structural theories. Retrieved October 8, 2008, from http://www.majorityrights.com/images/uploads/sex_differences_BBC.pdf

Lips, H. (1997). *Sex and gender* (2nd ed.). Mountain View, CA: Mayfield.

Lisotta, C. (2007, June 19). Coming home. *Advocate,* 25.

Lithwick, D. (2009, February 23). Teens, nude photos and the law. *Newsweek,* 18.

Littlefield, A. (2011, September 7). Sexual pleasure called key to HIV-gel efficacy. Retrieved from http://www.womensenews.org/print/8760

Littleton, H., Axsom, D., & Grills-Taquechel, A. (2009). Sexual assault victims' acknowledgement status and revictimization. *Psychology of Women Quarterly, 33,* 34–42.

Liu, C. (2003). Does quality of marital sex decline with duration? *Archives of Sexual Behavior, 32,* 55–60.

Liu, J., O'Brien, D., et al. (2009). Immune control of an SIV challenge by a T-cell-based vaccine in rhesus monkeys. *Nature, 457,* 87–91.

Liu, S., et al. (2012). New protease inhibitors for the treatment of chronic hepatitis C: A cost-effectiveness analysis. *Annals of Internal Medicine, 156,* 279-290.

Lloyd, R. (2010, January 11). Corporate sponsored pimping plays role in US human trafficking. Retrieved from http://www.thegrio.com/opinion/corporate-sponsored-pimping-plays-role-in-US-human-trafficking

Lo, J., Min, S., Canavan, B., et al. (2008). Low-dose physiological growth hormone in patients with HIV and abdominal fat accumulation. *Journal of the American Medical Association, 300,* 509–519.

Lofgren-Martenson, L., & Mansson, S. (2010). Lust, love, and live: A qualitative study of Swedish adolescents' perceptions and experiences with pornography. *Journal of Sex Research, 47,* 568–580.

Loftus, D. (2002). *Watching sex.* New York: Thunder's Mouth Press.

Loftus, E., Polonsky, S., & Fullilove, M. (1994). Memories of childhood sexual abuse: Remembering and repressing. *Psychology of Women Quarterly, 18,* 67–84.

Lok, C. (2011). Vaccines: His best shot. *Nature, 473,* 419–424.

London, S. (2011). HPV vaccine chat: Urge parents to talk about sex. *Pediatric News, 45,* 16.

Lonee-Hoffmann, R., & Schei, B. (2007, April). *Sexual experience of partners after subtotal compared to total hysterectomy.* Paper presented at the 18th Congress of the World Association for Sexual Health, Sydney, Australia.

Long, V. (2002). Contraceptives choices: New options in the U.S. market. *SIECUS Report, 31,* 13–18.

Longombe, A., Claude, K., & Ruminjo, J. (2008). Fistula and traumatic genital injury from sexual violence in a conflict setting in Eastern Congo: Case studies. *Reproductive Health Matters, 16,* 132–141.

Lonsway, K., & Fitzgerald, L. (1994). Rape myths. *Psychology of Women Quarterly, 18,* 133–164.

Looker, K., Garnett, G., & Schmid, G. (2008). An estimate of the global prevalence and incidence of herpes simplex virus type 2 infection. *Bulletin of the World Health Organization, 85,* 805–812.

Looy, H., & Bouma, H. (2005). The nature of gender: Gender identity in persons who are intersexed or transgendered. *Journal of Psychology and Theology, 33,* 166–178.

LoPiccolo, J. (2000, May). Post-modern sex therapy: An integrated approach. Paper presented at the 32nd Annual Conference of the American Association of Sex Educators, Counselors, and Therapists, Atlanta, GA.

Lorber, J. (1995). Gender is determined by social practices. In D. Bender & B. Leone (Eds.), *Human sexuality: Opposing viewpoints.* San Diego, CA: Greenhaven Press.

Lorch, D., & Mendenhall, P. (2000, August). A war's hidden tragedy. *Newsweek,* 35–36.

Louis, M., Wasserheit, J., & Gayle, H. (1997). Janus considers the HIV pandemic: Harnessing recent advances to enhance AIDS prevention [Editorial]. *American Journal of Public Health, 87,* 10–12.

Loulan, J. (1984). *Lesbian sex.* San Francisco, CA: Spinsters Ink.

Loupe, D. (2011, May 23). Georgia law turns focus on sex-trafficked girls. Retrieved from http://www.womensenews.org/content/admin/georgia-law-turns-focus-on-sex-trafficked-girls

Love, P. (2001). *The truth about love.* New York: Simon and Schuster.

Love, S., & Rochman, S. (2006, Spring). Going natural: Are "bio-identical" hormones better than synthetics for menopausal relief? *Ms.,* 63–64.

Lowenstein, L. (2002). Fetishes and their associated behavior. *Sexuality and Disability, 20,* 135–147.

Lowenthal, M. (2010, September 20). A taste of Nanjing China. *Advocate,* 22.

Lown, J., & Dolan, E. (1988). Financial challenges in re-marriage. *Lifestyles: Family and Economic Issues, 9,* 73–88.

Lucido, J. (2009, May). Porn panic. *Advocate,* 52–57.

Lue, T., Basson, R., Rosen, R., & Giuliano, F. (2004). *Second international consultation on sexual medicine: Sexual dysfunctions in men and women.* Paris: Health Publications.

Lue, T., Giuliano, F., Montorsi, F., & Rosen, R. (2004). Summary of the recommendations on sexual dysfunctions in men. *Journal of Sexual Medicine, 1,* 6–23.

Lundgren, E., Tuvemo, T., & Gustafsson, J. (2011). Short adult stature and overweight are associated with poor intellectual performance in subjects born preterm. *Hormone Research in Pediatrics, 75,* 138–145.

Luongo, M. (2007). *Gay travels in the Muslim world.* Kirkwood, NY: Harrington Park Press.

Lurie, L., Wilkens, L., Thompson, P., et al. (2008). Combined oral contraceptive use and epithelial ovarian cancer risk: Time related effects. *Epidemiology, 19,* 237–243.

Lutfey, K., Link, C., & McKinlay, F. (2006, November). *Prevalence and predictors of female sexual dysfunction: Results from the Boston Area Community Health (BACH) Survey.* Paper presented at the Sexual Medicine Society of North America Fall Meeting, New York.

Luzzi, G., & Schaeffer, A. (2007). Chronic prostatitis. *New England Journal of Medicine, 356,* 423–424.

Ly, K., et al. (2012). The increasing burden of the mortality from viral hepatitis in the United States between 1999 and 2007. *Annals of Internal Medicine, 156,* 271–278.

Lyman, F. (2006, Fall). The geography of breast cancer. *Ms.,* 47–51.

Lyons, H., et al. (2011). Idenity, peer relationships, and adolescent girls' sexual behavior: An exploration of the contemporary double standard. *Journal of Sex Research, 48,* 37–49.

Maccio, E. (2010). Influence of family, religion, and social conformity on client participation in sexual reorientation therapy. *Journal of Psychology and Theology, 2010,* 284–286.

Maccoby, E. (1998). *The two sexes: Growing up apart, coming together.* Cambridge: Harvard University Press.

MacDorman, M., & Kirmeyer, S. (2009, April). The challenge of fetal mortality. Retrieved April 21, 2009, from http://www.cdc.gtov/nchs/data/databriefs/db16.htm

MacKay, A., Berg, C., King, J., & Duran, C. (2006). Pregnancy-related mortality among women with multifetal pregnancies. *Obstetrics and Gynecology, 107,* 563–568.

Mackeen, D. (2007, May 10). The ups and downs (and all-arounds) of your mones! Retrieved December 23, 2008, from https://www.drerika.com/newsmaker/files/657035189786902/blog05100071.html

Macklon, N., & Fauser, B. (1999). Aspects of ovarian follicle development throughout life. *Hormone Research, 52,* 161–170.

MacNeil, S., & Byers, S. (2009). Role of sexual self-disclosure in the sexual satisfaction of long-term heterosexual couples. *Journal of Sex Research, 46,* 3–14.

Maddox, A., Rhoades, G., & Markman, H. (2011). Viewing sexually-explicit materials alone or together: Associations with relationship quality. *Archives of Sexual Behavior, 40,* 441–448.

Mah, K., & Binik, Y. (2002). Do all orgasms feel alike? Evaluating a two-dimensional model of orgasm experience across gender and sexual context. *Journal of Sex Research, 39,* 104–113.

Mahaffey, A., Bryan, A., & Hutchison, K. (2005). Sex differences in affective responses to homoerotic stimuli: Evidence for an unconscious bias among heterosexual men, but not heterosexual women. *Archives of Sexual Behavior, 34,* 537–546.

Mahaffey, A., et al. (2011). In search of the defensive function of sexual prejudice: Exploring antigay bias through shorter and longer lead startle eye blink. *Journal of Applied Social Psychology, 41,* 27–44.

Mahan, E., Morrow, K., & Hayes, J. (2011). Quantitative perceptual differences among over-the-counter vaginal products using standardized methodology: Implications for microbicide development. *Contraception, 84,* 184–193.

Maheshwari, A., Hamilton, M., & Bhattacharya, S. (2008). Effect of female age on the diagnostic categories of infertility. *Human Reproduction, 23,* 538–542.

Mahoney, C. (2007, April). *Sexuality, infertility and fertility treatments.* Paper presented at the 18th Congress of the World Association for Sexual Health, Sydney, Australia.

Mahoney, S. (2003, November/December). Seeking love: The 50-plus dating game has never been hotter. *AARP,* 57–66.

Maisel, N., Gable, S., & Strachman, A. (2008). Responsive behaviors in good times and bad. *Personal Relationships, 15,* 317–338.

Majewska, M. (1996). Sex differences in brain morphology and pharmacodynamics. In M. Jensvold & U. Halbreich (Eds.), *Psychopharmacology and women: Sex, gender, and hormones.* Washington, DC: American Psychiatric Press.

Makadon, H. (2006). Improving health care for the lesbian and gay communities. *New England Journal of Medicine, 354,* 895–897.

Maki, P., Drogos, L., Rubin, L., Banuvar, S., Shulman, L., & Geller, S. (2008). Objective hot flashes are negatively related to verbal memory performance in midlife women. *Menopause, 15,* 848–856.

Makin, K. (2012, March 26). Ontario's top court legalizes brothels in bid to protect prostitutes. Retrieved from http://www.theglobeandmail.com/news/national/ontarios-top-court-legalizes-brothels

Makinen, J., et al. (2011). Androgen replacement therapy in late-onset hypogonadism: Current concepts and controversies—A mini-review. *Gerontology, 57,* 193–202.

Malamuth, N., Addison, T., & Koss, M. (2000). Pornography and sexual aggression: Are there reliable effects and can we understand them? In J. Heiman & C. Davis (Eds.), *Annual review of sex research.* Mason City, IA: Society for the Scientific Study of Sexuality.

Malamuth, N., & Check, J. (1981). The effects of mass media exposure on acceptance of violence against women: A field experiment. *Journal of Research in Personality, 15,* 436–446.

Malamuth, N., Haber, S., & Feshback, S. (1980). Testing hypotheses regarding rape: Exposure to sexual violence, sex differences, and the normality of rapists. *Journal of Research in Personality, 14,* 121–137.

Malcolm, J. (2008). Heterosexually married men who have sex with men: Marital separation and psychological adjustment. *Journal of Sex Research, 45,* 350–357.

Malesky, L., & Ennis, L. (2004). Supportive distortions: An analysis of posts on a pedophile Internet message board. *Journal of Addictions and Offender Counseling, 24,* 92–100.

Mallis, D., Moisidis, K., Kirana, P., & Papaharitou, S. (2006). Moderate and severe erectile dysfunction equally affects life satisfaction. *Journal of Sexual Medicine, 3,* 442–449.

Maltz, W. (2001). *The sexual healing journey: A guide for survivors of sexual abuse.* New York: Quill.

Maltz, W. (2003). Treating the sexual intimacy concerns of sexual abuse. *Contemporary Sexuality, 37,* i–vii.

Maltz, W., & Boss, S. (1997). *In the garden of desire.* New York: Broadway Books.

Mandoki, M., Sumner, G., Hoffman, R., & Riconda, D. (1991). A review of Klinefelter's syndrome in children and adolescents. *Journal of the American Academy of Child and Adolescent Psychiatry, 30,* 167–172.

Manet, P., & Herbe, D. (2011). Does knowledge about sexuality prevent adolescents from developing rape-supportive beliefs? *Journal of Sex Research, 48,* 372–381.

Manganello, J., Franzini, A., & Jordan, A. (2008). Sampling television programs for content analysis of sex on TV: How many episodes are enough? *Journal of Sex Research, 45,* 9–8.

Manier, B. (2008, November 18). France strikes down court ruling on virginity. Retrieved November 11, 2008, from Women's eNews.

Manji, I. (2006, May 23). My Islam. *Advocate,* 33.

Manlove, J., & Terry-Humen, E. (2007). Contraceptive use patterns within females' first sexual relationships: The role of relationships, partners, and methods. *Journal of Sex Research, 44,* 3–16.

Manlove, J., Ryan, S., & Franzetta, K. (2004). Contraceptive use and consistency in U.S. teenagers' most recent sexual relationships. *Perspectives on Sexual and Reproductive Health, 36,* 265–275.

Manlove, J., Ryan, S., & Franzetta, K. (2007). Contraceptive use patterns across teens' sexual relationships: The role of relationships, partners, and sexual histories. *Demography, 44,* 603–621.

Mannino, D., Klevens, R., & Flanders, W. (1994). Cigarette smoking: An independent risk factor for impotence? *American Journal of Epidemiology, 140,* 1003–1008.

Mansfield, P., Voda, A., & Koch, P. (1995). Predictors of sexual response changes in heterosexual midlife women. *Health Values: The Journal of Health Behavior, Education, and Promotion, 19,* 10–20.

Mansour, D., et al. (2011). Fertility after discontinuation of contraception: A comprehensive review of the literature. *Contraception, 84,* 465–477.

Mansour, D., Korver, T., Marintcheva-Petrova, M., & Fraser, I. (2008). The effects of Implanon on menstrual bleeding patterns. *European Journal of Contraception and Reproductive Health Care, 13,* 13–28.

Månsson, S.-A. (2009, June). *Nordic prostitution policies at a crossroad.* Paper presented at the 19th WAS World Congress for Sexual Health, Göteborg, Sweden.

Maravilla, K., Cao, Y., Garland, P., et al. (2000, November). Reproducibility of serial MR measurement of female sexual arousal response. RSNA Hot Topic presentation, Chicago, IL. Abstract available in *Radiology, 218* (2000), 610.

Maravilla, K., Heiman, J., Garland, P., et al. (2003). Dynamic MR imaging of the sexual arousal response in women. *Journal of Sex and Marital Therapy, 29*(Suppl.), 71–76.

Marchina, E., Gambera, A., et al. (2009). Identification of a new mutation in the SRY gene in a 46,XY woman with Swyer syndrome. *Fertility and Sterility, 91,* e7–e11.

Marcus, D., & Miller, R. (2003). Sex differences in judgments of physical attractiveness: A social relations analysis. *Personality and Social Psychology Bulletin, 29,* 325–335.

Marcus, R. (2009, December 7). Abortion's new battleground. *Newsweek,* 48–50.

Marelich, W., Lundquist, J., Painter, K., & Mechanic, M. (2008). Sexual deception as a social-exchange process: Development of a behavior-based sexual deception scale. *Journal of Sex Research, 45,* 27–35.

Margolis, L. (2000). Ethical principles for analyzing dilemmas in sex research. *Health Education and Behavior, 27,* 24–27.

Marin, A., & Guadagno, R. (1999). Perceptions of sexual harassment as a function of labeling and reporting. *Sex Roles, 41,* 921–940.

Mark, H., Nanda, J., Roberts, J., et al. (2008). Serologic screening for herpes simplex virus among university students: A pilot study. *Journal of American College Health, 57,* 291–296.

Mark, K., Janssen, E., & Milhausen, R. (2011). Infidelity in heterosexual couples: Demographic, interpersonal, and personality-related predictors of extradyadic sex. *Archives of Sexual Behavior.* doi:10.1007/s10508-011-9771-z

Markle, G. (2008). "Can women have sex like a man?" Sexual scripts in *Sex and the City. Sexuality and Culture,12,* 45–57.

Markowitz, J., Donovan, J., DeVane, C., & Ruan, R. (2003). Effect of St. John's wort on drug metabolism by induction of cytochrome P450 3A4 enzyme. *Journal of the American Medical Association, 290,* 1500–1504.

Marr, J., Niknian, M., Schulman, L., et al. (2011). Premenstrual dysphoric disorder symptom cluster improvement by cycle with the combined oral contraceptive ethinylestradiol 20 mcg plus drospirenone 3 mg administered in a 24/4 regime. *Contraception, 84,* 81–86.

Marrazzo, J., et al. (2011). Interpreting the epidemiology and natural history of bacterial vaginosis: Are we still confused? *Anaerobe, 17,* 186–190.

Marshall, K. (2009, March 24). Unkind cuts. Retrieved from http://newsweek.washingtonpost.com/onfaith/georgetown/2009/03/unkind_cuts.html

Marshall, W. (1993). A revised approach to the treatment of men who sexually assault adult females. In G. Hall, R. Hirschman, J. Graham, & M. Zaragoza (Eds.), *Sexual aggression: Issues in etiology, assessment, and treatment.* Washington, DC: Taylor and Francis.

Marshall, W., Eccles, A., & Barbaree, H. (1991). The treatment of exhibitionists: A focus on sexual deviance versus cognitive and relationship features. *Behaviour Research and Therapy, 29,* 129–135.

Martin, J., et al. (2012). Three decades of twin births in the United States, 1980–2009 (NCHS Data Brief, no. 80). Hyattsville, MD: National Center for Health Statistics.

Martin, J., Hamilton, B., Sutton, P., et al. (2009). Births: Final data for 2006. *National Vital Statistics Report, 57,* 1–120.

Martin, M. (2009, March). Divide and conquer. *Advocate,* 18.

Martin, M., Perez, F., Moreno, A., et al. (2008). *Neisseria gonorrhoeae* meningitis in pregnant adolescents. *Emerging Infectious Diseases, 14,* 672–674.

Martinez, G., Chandra, A., Abma, J., Jones, J., & Mosher, W. (2006). Fertility, contraception, and fatherhood: Data on men and women from cycle 6 (2002) of the National Survey of Family Growth. *Vital and Health Statistics, 23, 26.*

Martinez, G., Copen, C. E., & Abma, J. C. (2011).Teenagers in the United States: Sexual activity, contraceptive use, and childbearing, 2006–2010. National Survey of Family Growth. National Center for Health Statistics. *Vital Health Statistics, 23*(31).

Martino, S., Collins, R., Elliott, M., et al. (2006). Exposure to degrading versus nondegrading music lyrics and sexual behavior among youth. *Pediatrics, 118,* 782–791.

Martinson, F. (1994). *The sexual life of children.* Westport, CT: Bergin and Garvey.

Martsolf, D., & Draucker, C. (2008). The legacy of childhood sexual abuse and family adversity. *Journal of Nursing Scholarship, 40,* 333–340.

Marvan, M., Cortes-Iniestra, S., & Gonzalez, R. (2005). Beliefs about and attitudes toward menstruation among young and middle-aged Mexicans. *Sex Roles: A Journal of Research, 53,* 273–280.

Marvan, M., Ramirez-Esparza, D., Cortes-Iniestra, S., & Chrisler, J. (2006). Development of a new scale to measure beliefs about and attitudes toward menstruation (BATM): Data from Mexico and the United States. *Health Care for Women International, 27,* 453–473.

Marx, J., & Hopper, F. (2005). Faith-based versus fact-based social policy: The case of teenage pregnancy prevention. *Social Work, 50,* 280–282.

Mashek, D., et al. (2011). Wanting less closeness in romantic relationships. *Basic and Applied Social Psychology, 33,* 333–345.

Mass, R., Holldorfer, M., Moll, B., Bauer, R., & Wolf, K. (2009). Why we haven't died out yet: Changes in women's mimic reactions to visual erotic stimuli during their menstrual cycles. *Hormones and Behavior, 55,* 267–271.

Masters, N., Beadnell, B., Morrison, D., et al. (2008). The opposite of sex? Adolescents' thoughts about abstinence and sex, and their sexual behavior. *Perspectives on Sexual and Reproductive Health, 40,* 87–93.

Masters, W., & Johnson, V. (1961). Orgasm, anatomy of the female. In A. Ellis & A. Abarbonel (Eds.), *Encyclopedia of sexual behavior* (Vol. 2). New York: Hawthorn.

Masters, W., & Johnson, V. (1966). *Human sexual response.* Boston: Little, Brown.

Masters, W., & Johnson, V. (1970). *Human sexual inadequacy.* Boston: Little, Brown.

Masters, W., & Johnson, V. (1976). *The pleasure bond.* New York: Bantam Books.

Match.com (2012, February 2). Second annual comprehensive study on singles.

Retrieved from http://match.mediaroom.com/index.php?s=43&item=116

Matek, O. (1988). Obscene phone callers. *Journal of Social Work and Human Sexuality, 7*, 113–130.

Mather, C. (2005). Accusations of genital theft: A case from Northern Ghana. *Culture, Medicine, and Psychiatry, 29*, 33–52.

Mathes, E., & Verstrate, C. (1993). Jealous aggression: Who is the target, the beloved or the rival? *Psychological Reports, 72*, 1071–1074.

Mathews, G., Fane, B., et al. (2009). Personality and congenital adrenal hyperplasia: Possible effects of prenatal androgen exposure. *Hormones and Behavior, 55*, 285–291.

Mathieu, C., Courtois, F., & Noreau, L. (2006). Sexual activities, desire, and sensations in paraplegic and tetraplegic men and women. *Journal of Sex Research, 43*, 21–22.

Maugh, T. (2008, August 3). U.S. AIDS cases underestimated. *Oregonian*, p. A4.

Maugh, T. (2011, July 14). Pills can block HIV infections, studies show. *Oregonian*, p. A4.

May, E. (2010). *America and the pill: A history of promise, peril, and liberation*. New York: Basic Books.

May, R. (1969). *Love and will*. New York: Norton.

Mayer, K., & Mimiaga, M. (2011). Resurgent syphilis in the United States: Urgent need to address an evolving epidemic. *Annals of Internal Medicine, 155*, 92–93.

Maynard, E., et al. (2009). Women's experiences with anal sex: Motivations and implications for STD prevention. *Perspectives on Sexual and Reproductive Health, 41*, 142–150.

Mayo Clinic. (2008). Retrograde ejaculation. Retrieved November 1, 2008, from http://www.mayoclinic.com/health/retrograde ejaculation/DS00913

Mazur, T. (2005). Gender dysphoria and gender change in androgen insensitivity or micropenis. *Archives of Sexual Behavior, 34*, 411–421.

McAllister, R., et al. (2008). The cost to circumcise Africa. *International Journal of Men's Health, 7*, 307–316.

McBride, K., & Fortenberry, D. (2010). Heterosexual anal sexuality and anal sex behaviors: A review. *Journal of Sex Research, 47*, 123–137.

McCabe, J., et al. (2011). Gender in twentieth-century children's books: Patterns of disparity in titles and central characters. *Gender and Society, 25*, 197–226.

McCabe, M. (1999). The interrelationship between intimacy, relationship functioning, and sexuality among men and women in committed relationships. *Canadian Journal of Human Sexuality, 8*, 31–39.

McCabe, M., et al. (2011). The impact of oral ED medication on female partners' relationship satisfaction. *Journal of Sexual Medicine, 8*, 479–483.

McCabe, M., & Goldhammer, D. (2012). Demographic and psychological factors related to sexual desire among heterosexual women in a relationship. *Journal of Sex Research, 49*, 78–87.

McCabe, M., & Wauchope, M. (2005). Behavioral characteristics of men accused of rape: Evidence for different types of rapists. *Archives of Sexual Behavior, 34*, 241–253.

McCarthy, B. (2001, May). *Primary and secondary prevention of sexual problems and dysfunction*. Paper presented at the 33rd Annual Conference of the American Association of Sex Educators, Counselors, and Therapists, San Francisco, CA.

McCarthy, B., & McDonald, D. (2009). Assessment, treatment, and relapse prevention: Male hypoactive sexual desire disorder. *Journal of Sex and Marital Therapy, 35*, 58–67.

Mccarthy, M., et al. (2011). A lumpers versus splitters approach to sexual differentiation of the brain. *Frontiers of Neuroendocrinology, 32*, 114–123.

McClelland, S. (2010). Intimate justice: A critical analysis of sexual satisfaction. *Social and Personality Psychology Compass, 4*, 663–680.

McCormick, C., & Whitelson, S. (1991). A cognitive profile of homosexual men compared to heterosexual men and women. *Psychoneuroendocrinology, 16*, 459–473.

McCree, D., Jones, K., & O'Leary, A. (Eds.). (2010). *African Americans and HIV/AIDS: Understanding and addressing the epidemic*. New York: Springer.

McCrory, C., & Layte, R. (2011). The effect of breastfeeding on children's educational test scores at nine years of age: Results of an Irish cohort study. *Social Science and Medicine, 72*, 1515–1521.

McEwen, B. (1997). Meeting report: Is there a neurobiology of love? *Molecular Psychiatry, 2*, 15–16.

McEwen, B. (2001). Estrogen effects on the brain: Multiple sites and molecular mechanisms. *Journal of Applied Physiology, 91*, 2785–2801.

McGee, E., & Shevlin, M. (2009). Effect of humor on interpersonal attraction and mate selection. *Journal of Psychology, 143*, 67–77.

McGinn, D. (2006, June 5). Marriage by the numbers. *Newsweek*, 40–48.

McGinn, S., & Skipp, C. (2002, June 3). Does Gran get it on? *Newsweek*, 10.

McGinty, K., Knox, D., & Zusman, M. (2007). Friends with benefits: Women want "friends," men want "benefits." *College Student Journal, 41*, 1128–1131.

McGlone, T. (2011, January 16). As child porn activity grows, efforts to trap offenders do too. *Virginian-Pilot*.

McKay, A. (2005). Sexuality and substance use: The impact of tobacco, alcohol, and selected recreational drugs on sexual function. *Canadian Journal of Human Sexuality, 14*, 47–56.

McKibben, A., Proulx, J., & Lusignan, R. (1994). Relationships between conflict, affect, and deviant sexual behaviors in rapists and pedophiles. *Behavior Research and Therapy, 32*, 571–575.

McLaren, A. (1990). *A history of contraception: From antiquity to the present day*. Cambridge, MA: Basil Blackwell.

McLaren, C., & Ringe, A. (2006). Curious mental illnesses around the world. Retrieved January 7, 2006, from http://www.stayfreemagazine.org/archives/21/mental_illness.html

McLean, L., & Gallop, R. (2003). Implications of childhood sexual abuse for adult borderline personality disorder and complex posttraumatic stress disorder. *American Journal of Psychiatry, 160*, 369–371.

McMahon, C. (2008, April). Pharmacotherapy for premature ejaculation. Paper presented at the 18th Congress of the World Association for Sexual Health, Sydney, Australia.

McMahon, C., et al. (2011a). Age at first birth, mode of conception and psychological well-being in pregnancy. *Human Reproduction, 26*, 1389–1398.

McMahon, C., et al. (2011b). Efficacy and safety of dapoxetine for the treatment of premature ejaculation: Integrated analysis of results from five phase 3 trials. *Journal of Sexual Medicine, 8*, 524–539.

McMahon, P. (2008). Sexual violence on the college campus: A template for compliance with federal policy. *Journal of American College Health, 57*, 361–365.

McMahon, S., & Farmer, L. (2011). An updated measure for measuring subtle rape myths. *Social Work Research, 35*, 71–81.

McNeil, D. (2011, January 18). Prevention: Male circumcision may help protect sexual partners against cervical cancer. *New York Times*, p. D6.

McNeill, B., Prieto, L., Niemann, Y., et al. (2001). Current directions in Chicana/o psychology. *Counseling Psychologist, 29*, 5–17.

McNicholas, T., Dean, J., Mulder, H., Carnegie, C., & Jones, N. (2003). Andrology. *British Journal of Urology International, 91*, 69–74.

McPherson, P., et al. (2012). Barriers to successful treatment completion in child sexual abuse survivors. *Journal of Interpersonal Violence, 27,* 23–39.

Mcquillan, J., Greil, A., Shreffler, K., & Tichenor, V. (2008). The importance of motherhood among women in the contemporary United States. *Gender and Society, 22,* 477–496.

Meacham, J. (2009, January 21). Who we are now. *Newsweek,* 38–42.

Mead, M. (1963). *Sex and temperament in three primitive societies.* New York: Morrow.

Meana, M., & Nunnink, S. (2006). Gender differences in the content of cognitive distraction during sex. *Journal of Sex Research, 43,* 59–68.

Mechcatie, E. (2009). DNA-based test for HPV types 16, 18 approved. *OB.GYN. News, 44,* 32–41.

Media Project. (2008, December 2). Making differences one scene at a time. Retrieved December 17, 2008, from http://www .themediaproject.com/news/shows/index .htm

Medical Center for Human Rights. (1995). *Characteristics of sexual abuse of men during war in the Republic of Croatia and Bosnia.* Zagreb, Croatia: Author.

Megan, K. (2008, May 8). Head of polyamory group discusses multiple partners. *Hartford Courant,* p. B2.

Melby, T. (2002). Pain and (possibly) a loss of pleasure. *Contemporary Sexuality, 36,* 7–12.

Melby, T. (2011). Hello PBF. *Contemporary Sexuality, 45,* 1–6.

Melby, T. (2012). Three major accomplishments of Obama administration. *Contemporary Sexuality, 46,* 1–5.

Melchert, T., & Parker, R. (1997). Different forms of childhood abuse and memory. *Child Abuse and Neglect, 21,* 125–135.

Meldrum, K., & Rink, R. (2005). Nonspecific penile anomalies: Practical management in infants and children. *Contemporary Urology, 17,* 13–20.

Melhado, L. (2011). U.S. pregnancy-related mortality ratio for 1998–2005 higher than for any other period in past 20 years. *Perspectives on Sexual and Reproductive Health, 43,* 66. doi:10.1363/4306611_1

Meltzer, D. (2005). Complications of body piercing. *American Family Physician, 72,* 2029.

Menard, A., & Kleinplatz, P. (2008). Twenty-one moves guaranteed to make his thighs go up in flames: Depictions of "Great Sex" in popular magazines. *Sexuality and Culture, 12,* 1–20.

Mendez, M., & Shapira, J. (2011). Pedophilic behavior from brain disease. *Journal of Sexual Medicine, 8,* 1092–1100.

Menvielle, E. (2004). Parents struggling with their child's gender issues. *Brown University Child and Adolescent Behavior Letter, 20,* 1–3.

Merek, G., & Gonzalez-Rivera, M. (2006). Attitudes toward homosexuality among U.S. residents of Mexican descent. *Journal of Sex Research, 43,* 122–136.

Merin, A., & Pachankis, J. (2011). The psychological impact of genital herpes stigma. *Journal of Health Psychology, 16,* 80–90.

Merki-Feld, G., Imthurn, B., & Seifert, B. (2008). Effects of the progestagen-only contraceptive implant Implanon on cardiovascular risk factors. *Clinical Endocrinology, 68,* 355–360.

Merkin, D. (2006, January 1). Our vaginas, ourselves. *New York Times Magazine,* p. 13.

Meschke, L., Bartholomae, S., & Zentall, S. (2000). Adolescent sexuality and parent–adolescent processes: Promoting healthy teen choices. *Family Relations, 49,* 143–154.

Messenger, J. (1971). Sex and repression in an Irish folk community. In D. Marshall & R. Suggs (Eds.), *Human sexual behavior: Variations in the ethnographic spectrum.* Englewood Cliffs, NJ: Prentice Hall.

Messman-Moore, T., Ward, R., & Brown, A. (2009). Substance use and PTSD symptoms impact the likelihood of rape and revictimization in college women. *Journal of Interpersonal Violence, 24,* 499–521.

Meston, C. (2000). The psychophysiological assessment of female sexual function. *Journal of Sex Education and Therapy, 25,* 6–16.

Meston, C., & Buss, D. (2007). Why humans have sex. *Archives of Sexual Behavior, 36,* 477–507.

Meston, C., Rellini, A., & Heiman, J. (2006). Women's history of sexual abuse, their sexuality, and sexual self-schemas. *Journal of Consulting Clinical Psychology, 74,* 229–236.

Meston, C., & Worcel, M. (2002). The effects of yohimbine plus L-arginine glutamate on sexual arousal in postmenopausal women with sexual arousal disorder. *Archives of Sexual Behavior, 31,* 323–332.

Metcalfe, K., Finch, A., & Poll, A. (2008, November). *Family history of breast cancer increases risk regardless of BRCA status.* Paper presented at the Amerian Association for Cancer Research's Seventh Annual International Conference, Washington, DC.

Metz, M., & McCarthy, B. (2008, July/ August). Eros and aging. *Psychotherapy Networker,* 55–58.

Mevel, P. (2011, September 22). French court hands down first "burqa ban" fines. Retrieved from http://af.reuters .com/articlePrint?articleId=AFTRE78L 2QK20110922

Meyer, S., & Schwitzer, A. (1999). Stages of identity development among college students with minority sexual orientations. *Journal of College Student Psychotherapy, 13,* 41–65.

Meyer-Bahlburg, H. (2005). Introduction: Gender dysphoria and gender change in persons with intersexuality. *Archives of Sexual Behavior, 34,* 371–373.

Meyer-Bahlburg, H., et al. (1995). Prenatal estrogens and the development of homosexual orientation. *Developmental Psychology, 31,* 12–21.

Meyer-Bahlburg, H., Gruen, R., New, M., et al. (1996). Gender change from female to male in classical congenital adrenal hyperplasia. *Hormones and Behavior, 30,* 319–322.

Meyerhoff, M. (2004). An androgynous generation? *Pediatrics for Parents, 21,* 8–9.

Mezin, Z. (2006, January 29). France's birth rate booms but marriage loses favor. *Oregonian,* p. A17.

Michael, R., Gagnon, J., Laumann, E., & Kolata, G. (1994). *Sex in America.* Boston: Little, Brown.

Michaels, D. (1997, March/April). Cyberrape: How virtual is it? *Ms.,* 68–72.

Michaels, M., & Johnson, P. (2006). *The essence of tantric sexuality.* Woodbury, MN: Llewellyn Publications.

Midanik, L., & Greenfield, T. (2008). Interactive voice response versus computer-assisted telephone interviewing (CATI) surveys and sensitive questions: The 2005 National Alcohol Survey. *Journal of Studies on Alcohol and Drugs, 69,* 580–588.

Migeon, C., Wisniewski, A., Gearhart, J., et al. (2002). Ambiguous genitalia with perineoscrotal hypospadias in 46,XY individuals: Long-term medical, surgical, and psychosexual outcome. *Pediatrics, 110,* 616–621.

Miklaszewski, J., & Kube, C. (2011, July 21). Panetta to OK end of military's gay ban. Retrieved from http://www.msnbc .msn.com/cleanprint/CleanPringProxy .aspx?unique=1311307819937

Miletski, H. (2002). *Understanding bestiality and zoophilia.* Bethesda, MD: East-West Publishing.

Miller, A., et al. (2011). Stigma-threat motivated nondisclosure of sexual assault and sexual victimization: A prospective analysis. *Psychology of Women Quarterly, 35,* 119–128.

Miller, G., Tybur, J., & Jordan, B. (2007). Ovulatory cycle effects on tip earnings by lap dancers: Economic evidence for human estrus? *Evolution and Human Behavior, 28,* 375–381.

Miller, J. (2009). Paraphilias. Retrieved February 10, 2009, from http://www.athealth.com/Consumer/disorders/Paraphilias.html

Miller, L. (2001). Continuous administration of 100 µg levonorgestrel and 20 µg ethinyl estradiol for elimination of menses: A randomized trial. *Obstetrics and Gynecology, 97,* 16S.

Miller, L. (2007, July 30). Islam U.S.A. *Newsweek,* 25–28.

Miller, L. (2008, April 21). Why this pope doesn't connect. *Newsweek,* 41.

Miller, L. (2011). College student knowledge and attitudes toward emergency contraception. *Contraception, 83,* 68–73.

Miller, R. (2008). Legacy denied: African American gay men, AIDS, and the Black church. *Social Work, 52,* 51–59.

Miller, S., & Maner, J. (2011). Ovulation as a male mating prime: Subtle signs of women's fertility influence men's mating cognition and behavior. *Journal of Personality and Social Psychology, 100,* 295–308.

Miller, T. (2000). Diagnostic evaluation of erectile dysfunction. *American Family Physician, 61,* 95–104.

Milne, C. (2005). *Naked ambition: Women pornographers and how they are changing the sex industry.* Berkeley, CA: Pub Group West.

Milner, J., & Dopke, C. (1997). Paraphilia not otherwise specified: Psychopathology and theory. In D. Laws & W. O'Donohue (Eds.), *Sexual deviance: Theory, assessment, and treatment.* New York: Guilford Press.

Milow, V. (1983). Menstrual education: Past, present, and future. In S. Golub (Ed.), *Menarche.* Lexington, MA: Lexington Books.

Miner, M., Flitter, J., & Robinson, B. (2006). Association of sexual revictimization with sexuality and psychological function. *Journal of Interpersonal Violence, 21,* 503–524.

Mink, G. (2005, Fall). Stop sexual harassment now! *Ms.,* 36–37.

Minor, M., & Dwyer, S. (1997). The psychosocial development of sex offenders: Differences between exhibitionists, child molesters, and incest offenders. *International Journal of Offenders Therapy and Comparative Criminology, 41,* 36–44.

Mishail, A., Marshall, S., Schulsinger, D., & Sheynkin, Y. (2009). Impact of a second semen analysis on treatment decision making in the infertile man with varicocele. *Sterility and Fertility, 91,* 1619–1966.

Mitchell, A., et al. (2011). Medication use during pregnancy, with particular focus on prescription drugs: 1976–2008. *American Journal of Obstetrics and Gynecology, 205,* 51.e1–51.e8.

Mitchell, K., & Ybarra, M. (2009). Social networking sites: Finding a balance between their risks and benefits. *Archives of Pediatrics and Adolescent Medicine, 163,* 87–89.

Mock, S., & Eiback, R. (2011). Stability and change in sexual orientation identity over a 10-year period in adulthood. *Archives of Sexual Behavior,* May 17 (e-pub).

Mohr, J., & Daly, C. (2008). Sexual minority stress and changes in relationship quality in same-sex couples. *Journal of Social and Personal Relationships, 25,* 989–1007.

Mok, F. (2006, August 29). A haven for homeless youths. *Advocate,* 26–27.

Moller, L., Hymel, S., & Rubin, K. (1992). Sex typing in play and popularity in middle childhood. *Sex Roles, 26,* 331–335.

Mona, L., & Gardos, P. (2000). Disabled sexual partners. In L. Szuchman & F. Muscarella (Eds.), *Psychological perspectives on human sexuality.* New York: Wiley.

Money, J. (1963). Cytogenetic and psychosexual incongruities with a note on space-form blindness. *American Journal of Psychiatry, 119,* 820–827.

Money, J. (1965). Psychosocial differentiation. In J. Money (Ed.), *Sex research: New developments.* New York: Holt, Rinehart and Winston.

Money, J. (1968). *Sex errors of the body: Dilemmas, education, counseling.* Baltimore, MD: Johns Hopkins University Press.

Money, J. (1981). Paraphilias: Phyletic origins of erotosexual dysfunction. *International Journal of Mental Health, 10,* 75–109.

Money, J. (1990). Forensic sexology: Paraphilic serial rape (biastophilia) and lust murder (erotophonophilia). *American Journal of Psychotherapy, 44,* 26–37.

Money, J. (1994a). The concept of gender identity disorder in childhood and adolescence after 39 years. *Journal of Sex and Marital Therapy, 20,* 163–177.

Money, J. (1994b). *Sex errors of the body and related syndromes: A guide to counseling children, adolescents, and their families* (2nd ed.). Baltimore, MD: Brookes.

Money, J., & Ehrhardt, A. (1972). Prenatal hormonal exposure: Possible effects on behavior in man. In R. Michael (Ed.), *Endocrinology and human behavior.* London: Oxford University Press.

Money, J., Lehne, G., & Pierre-Jerome, F. (1984). Micropenis: Adult follow-up and comparison of size against new norms. *Journal of Sex and Marital Therapy, 10,* 105–116.

Mongeau, P., Ramirez, A., & Vorrell, M. (2003, February). Friends with benefits: Initial exploration of sexual, non-romantic relationships. Paper presented at the annual meeting of the Western Communication Association, Salt Lake City, UT.

Montesi, J., et al. (2011). The specific importance of communicating about sex to couples' sexual and overall relationship satisfaction. *Journal of Social and Personal Relationships, 28,* 591–609.

Montgomery, C., Lees, S., Stadler, J., Morar, N., & Ssali, A. (2008). The role of partnership dynamics in determining the acceptability of condoms and microbicides. *AIDS Care, 20,* 733–740.

Montoya-Ferrer, A., et al. (2011). Acute hepatitis C outbreak among HIV-infected men, Madrid, Spain. *Emerging Infectious Diseases, 17,* 560–562.

Moodley, D., Moodley, J., Coovadia, H., et al. (2003). A multicenter randomized controlled trial of nevirapine versus a combination of zidovudine and lamivudine to reduce intrapartum and early postpartum mother-to-child transmission of human immunodeficiency virus type 1. *Journal of Infectious Diseases, 187,* 725–735.

Moon, M. (2011). Quadrivalent HPV vaccine found effective in males. *Family Practice News, 41,* 44–45.

Moore, K. (2010, September 27). Why Cosmo Magazine makes me want to blow my brains out. Retrieved from http://sexreally.com/the-blog/why-cosmo-magazine-makes-me-want-blow-my-brains-out

Morales, A. (2003). The andropause: Bare facts for urologists. *British Journal of Urology International, 91,* 311–313.

Moran, R. (2001). *Interracial intimacy: The regulation of race and romance.* Chicago: University of Chicago Press.

Morehouse, R. (2001, May). *Using the crucible approach to enhance women's sexual potential.* Paper presented at the 33rd Annual Conference of the American Association of Sex Educators, Counselors, and Therapists, San Francisco, CA.

Morey, A. (2012). Penile fracture: Long-term results of surgical and conservative management. *Journal of Urology, 187,* 937.

Morgan, E. (2011). Associations between young adults' use of sexually explicit materials and their sexual preferences, behaviors, and satisfaction. *Journal of Sex Research, 48,* 520–530.

Morgan, T. (2007). Turner syndrome: Diagnosis and management. *American Family Physician, 76,* 405.

Morin, J. (1981). *Anal pleasure and health.* Burlingame, CA: Down There Press.

Morris, A. (2011, January 30). They know what boys want. Retrieved from http://nymag.com/print/?news/features/70977

Morrison, M., & Morrison, T. (2011). Sexual orientation bias toward gay men and lesbian women: Modern homonegative attitudes and their association with discriminatory behavioral intentions. *Journal of Applied Social Psychology, 41,* 2573–2599.

Morry, M., Kito, M., & Ortiz, L. (2011). The attraction-similarity model and dating couples: Projection, perceived similarity, and psychological benefits. *Personal Relationships, 18,* 125–143.

Mosack, K., Winhardt, L., Kelly, J., et al. (2009). Influence of coping, social support, and depression on subjective health status among HIV-positive adults with different sexual identities. *Behavioral Medicine, 34,* 33–44.

Moses, J. (2009, February 11). Are parents driven to design their babies? Retrieved February 13, 2009, from http://www.the-hastingscenter.org/Bioethicsforum/Post.aspx?id=3196

Mosher, C., & Levitt, E. (1987). An exploratory-descriptive study of a sadomasochistically oriented sample. *Journal of Sex Research, 23,* 322–337.

Mosher, C., & Tomkins, S. (1988). Scripting the macho man: Hypermasculine socialization and enculturation. *Journal of Sex Research, 25,* 60–84.

Mosher, W., & Jones, J. (2010). Use of contraception in the United States: 1982–2008. *Vital Health Statistics, 23,* 29.

Moskowitz, D. (2006). A comprehensive review of the safety and efficacy of bioidentical hormones for the management of menopause and related health risks. *Alternative Medicine Review,11,* 208–224.

Mott, F., & Haurin, R. (1988). Linkages between sexual activity and alcohol and drug use among American adolescents. *Family Planning Perspectives, 20,* 128–137.

Movement Advancement Project. (2011). The momentum report: 2011 edition. Denver, CO: Author.

Moyer-Guse, E., Chung, A., & Jain, P. (2011). Identification with characters and discussion of taboo topics after exposure to an entertainment narrative about sexual health. *Journal of Communication, 61,* 387–406.

Muehlenhard, C. (1988). Misinterpreting dating behaviors and the risk of date rape. *Journal of Social and Clinical Psychology, 6,* 20–37.

Muehlenhard, C., & Andrews, S. (1985, November). *Open communication about sex: Will it reduce risk factors related to rape?* Paper presented at the Annual Meeting of the Association for Advancement of Behavior Therapy, Houston, TX.

Muehlenhard, C., Felts, A., & Andrews, S. (1985, June). *Men's attitudes toward the justifiability of date rape: Intervening variables and possible solutions.* Paper presented at the Midcontinent Meeting of the Society for the Scientific Study of Sex, Chicago, IL.

Muehlenhard, C., Goggins, M., Jones, J., & Satterfield, A. (1991). Sexual violence and coercion in close relationships. In K. McKinney & S. Sprecher (Eds.), *Sexuality in close relationships.* Hillsdale, NJ: Erlbaum.

Muehlenhard, C., & Hollabaugh, L. (1989). Do women sometimes say no when they mean yes? The prevalence and correlates of women's token resistance to sex. *Journal of Personality and Social Psychology, 54,* 872–879.

Muehlenhard, C., & Linton, M. (1987). Date rape and sexual aggression in dating situations: Incidence and risk factors. *Journal of Consulting Psychology, 34,* 186–196.

Muehlenhard, C., & Rodgers, C. (1998). Token resistance to sex: New perspectives on an old stereotype. *Psychology of Women Quarterly, 22,* 443–463.

Muehlenhard, C., & Shippee, S. (2010). Men's and women's reports of pretending orgasm. *Journal of Sex Research, 47,* 552–568.

Mugge, J. (2011). *Abortion after the first trimester in the United States.* New York: Planned Parenthood Federation of America.

Mukamana, D., & Brysiewicz, P. (2008). The lived experience of genocide rape survivors in Rwanda. *Journal of Nursing Scholarship, 40,* 379–385.

Munarriz, R., Maitland, S., Garcia, S., Talkakoub, L., & Goldstein, I. (2003). A prospective duplex Doppler ultrasonographic study in women with sexual arousal disorder to objectively assess genital engorgement induced by EROS therapy. *Journal of Sex and Marital Therapy, 29,* 85–94.

Munk-Olsen, T., et al., (2011). Induced first-trimester abortion and risk of mental disorders. *New England Journal of Medicine, 364,* 332–339.

Murnen, S., & Stockton, M. (1997). Gender and self-reported sexual arousal in response to sexual stimuli: A meta-analytic review. *Sex Roles, 37,* 135–154.

Murphy, D., & Page, I. (2008). Exhibitionism: Psychopathology and theory. In D. Laws & W. O'Donohue (Eds.), *Sexual deviance: Theory, assessment, and treatment* (2nd ed.). New York: Guilford Press.

Murphy, T. (2008). Brief history of a recurring nightmare. *Gay and Lesbian Review Worldwide, 15,* 17–24.

Murphy, T. (2011). Surrogate health care decisions and same-sex relationships. *Hastings Center Report, 41,* 24–27.

Murphy, W. (1997). Exhibitionism: Psychopathology and theory. In D. Laws & W. O'Donohue (Eds.), *Sexual deviance: Theory, assessment, and treatment.* New York: Guilford Press.

Murray, J., (2000). Psychological profile of pedophiles and child molesters. *Journal of Psychology, 134,* 211–224.

Murray, L. (1992, August). Love and longevity. *Longevity, 64.*

Murray, T. (2009, February 20). The new old age: Lost in translation. Retrieved February 20, 2009, from http://www.thehastingscenter.org/Bioethicsforum?Post.aspx?id=330

Murry, V. (1996). An ecological analysis of coital timing among middle-class African American adolescent females. *Journal of Adolescent Research, 11,* 261–279.

Murstein, B., & Tuerkheim, A. (1998). Gender differences in love, sex, and motivation for sex. *Psychological Reports, 82,* 425–450.

Mustanski, B. (2001). Getting wired: Exploiting the Internet for the collection of valid sexuality data. *Journal of Sex Research, 38,* 292–302.

Mustanski, B., Lyons, T., & Garcia, S. (2011). Internet use and sexual health of young men who have sex with men: A mixed-methods study. *Archives of Sexual Behavior, 40,* 289–300.

Mustanski, B., Newcomb, M. E., & Clerkin, E. M. (2011). Relationship characteristics and sexual risk-taking in young men who have sex with men. *Health Psychology, 30,* 597–605.

Myers, S. (2000, March 31). Female general in army alleges sex harassment. *New York Times,* p. A1.

Nagle, M. (2011, March 30). Store fires employee accused of voyeurism. *Jacksonville Journal-Courier.*

Naili, H. (2011a, December 27). Interfaith women don veil as common heritage. Retrieved from http://www.womensenews.org/print/8898

Naili, H. (2011b, November 9). Study details sex-traffic in post-Saddam Iraq. Retrieved from http://www.womensenews.org/print/8835

Najdowski, C., & Ullman, S. (2009). PTSD symptoms and self-rated recovery among adult sexual assault survivors: The effects of traumatic life events and psychosocial variables. *Psychology of Women Quarterly, 33,* 43–53.

Nanda, K., et al. (2011). Discontinuation of oral contraceptives and depot medroxyprogesterone acetate among women with and without HIV in Uganda, Zimbabwe and Thailand. *Contraception, 83,* 542–548.

Napolitane, C. (1997). *Living and loving after divorce.* New York: Signet.

Nappi, R., et al. (2011). Hypoactive sexual desire disorder: Can we treat it with drugs? *Sexual and Relationship Therapy, 25,* 264–274.

Nash, E. (2012, January 5). Losing ground on women's rights: In 2011, sex ed, contraception, abortion rights all under siege. Retrieved from http://www.rhreality-check.org/article/2012/01/05.losing-ground-on-womens-rights-in-2011-sex-ed-contraception-abortion-rights-under-siege.html?

Nasserzadeh, S. (2009, June). *Psychosexual therapy in the context of three major world religions—Islam.* Paper presented at the 19th WAS World Congress for Sexual Health, Göteborg, Sweden.

National Abortion Rights Action League. (2009, April 27). Abortion. Retrieved April 27, 2009, from http://naral.org/issues/abortion

National Campaign to Prevent Teen and Unplanned Pregnancy. (2008, December 4). Sex and tech: Results from a survey of teens and young adults. Retrieved December 10, 2008, from http://www.thenationalcampaign.org/sextech/PDF/SexTech_Summary.pdf

National Campaign to Prevent Teen and Unplanned Pregnancy. (2011, February). *Policy brief: Title X plays a critical role in preventing unplanned pregnancy.* Washington, DC: Author, pp. 1–3.

National Cancer Institute. (2006). Inflammatory breast cancer: Questions and answers. Retrieved from http://www.cancer.gov/cancertopics/factsheet/Sites-Types/IBC

National Cancer Institute. (2010). Cancer advances in focus. Retrieved from http://www.cnacer.gov/cancertopics/factsheet/cancer-advances-in-focus/breast

National Cancer Institute. (2011a). Breast cancer home page. Retrieved from http://www.cancer.gov/cancertopics/types/breast

National Cancer Institute. (2011b). Clinical trial results. Retrieved from http://www.cancer.gov/clinicaltrials/results/summary/2011/WHI10511

National Center for Health Statistics. (2011, October 12). *Report on teen sexual activity and contraceptive use in the United States, 2006–2010.* Hyattsville, MD: Author, 1–3.

National Conference of State Legislatures. (2011a, February). Pharmacist conscience clauses: Laws and information. Retrieved from http://www.ncsl.org/Default.aspx?TabId=14380

National Conference of State Legislatures. (2011b, July 14). Same-sex marriage, civil unions and domestic partnerships. Retrieved from http://www.ncsl.org/IssuesResearch/HumanServices/SameSexMarriage

National Council on Sexual Addiction and Compulsivity. (2002). Information statement: Women sex addicts. *Sexual Addiction and Compulsivity, 9,* 293–295.

National Gay and Lesbian Task Force. (2003, April 23). National Gay and Lesbian Task Force slams Santorum's "gutter language" comparing homosexuality to pedophilia, bestiality. Retrieved April 26, 2003, from http://www.ngltf.org/news/printed.cfm?releaseID=534

National Gay and Lesbian Task Force. (2011). *Relationship recognition for same-sex couples in the U.S.* Washington, DC: Author.

National Gay and Lesbian Task Force. (2012). *State nondiscrimination laws in the U.S.* Washington, DC: Author.

National Institute of Allergy and Infectious Diseases. (2011, May 12). Treating HIV-infected people with antiretrovirals protects partners from infection. *NIH News,* 1–2.

National Institutes of Health. (2009). Anti-HIV gel shows promise in large-scale study in women. Retrieved February 18, 2009, from http://www3.naid.gov/news/newsrelease/2009/HPTN_U35_gel.htm

National Pro-Life Alliance. (2009). *NPLA's mission.* Annandale, VA: National Pro-Life Alliance.

Navas, M. (2010, September 1). New HPV vaccine available for boys. *Oregonian,* p. A1.

Ndonko, F., & Ngo'o, G. (2006). Study on breast modeling in Cameroon. Retrieved October 25, 2006, from http://www.tantines.org/campaign_fichiers/slide0002.htm

Nedrow, A., Miller, J., Walker, M., & Nygren, P. (2006). Complementary and alternative therapies for the management of menopause-related symptoms. *Archives of Internal Medicine, 166,* 1453–1465.

Neergaard, L. (2011, June 22). Doctors not following guidelines on HPV tests, study finds. *Oregonian,* p. C2.

Neff, L. (2004, March 20). Gay in the navy. *Advocate,* 32–33.

Negy, C., & Eisenman, R. (2005). A comparison of African American and White college students' affective and attitudinal reactions to lesbian, gay, and bisexual individuals: An exploratory study. *Journal of Sex Research, 42,* 291–299.

Nelson, A. (2006). Extended-regimen contraception: Effects on menstrual symptoms and quality of life. *Journal of Family Practice, 55,* S1–S9.

Nelson, A., & Purdon, C. (2011). Non-erotic thoughts, attentional focus, and sexual problems in a community sample. *Archives of Sexual Behavior, 40,* 395–406.

Nelson, T. (2010, July/August). The new monogamy. *Psychotherapy Networker,* 20–25.

Nelson, R. (2008, November 26). AACR FCPR 2008: Family history increases breast cancer risk. Retrieved December 20, 2008, from http://www.medscape.com/viewarticle584292_print

Neukom, J., et al. (2011). Dedicated providers of long-acting reversible contraception: New approach in Zambia. *Contraception, 83,* 447–452.

Newman, A. (2011, April 15). A younger group for feminine products. *New York Times,* p. B3.

Newman, R. (2008). It starts in the womb: Helping parents understand infant sexuality. *Electronic Journal of Human Sexuality, 11,* 1–12.

Newton, D., & McCabe, M. (2005). The impact of stigma on couples managing a sexually transmitted infection. *Sexual and Relationship Therapy, 20,* 51–63.

Newton, D., & McCabe, M. (2008). Effects of sexually transmitted infection status, relationship status, and disclosure status on sexual self-concept. *Journal of Sex Research, 45,* 187–192.

NHS Choices (2009, February 19). Testicular cancer. *Nursing Times.*

Niccolai, L., Ethier, K., Kershaw, T., Lewis, J., & Ickovics, J. (2003). Pregnant adolescents at risk: Sexual behaviors and sexually transmitted disease prevalence. *American Journal of Obstetrics and Gynecology, 188,* 63–70.

Niccolai, L., King, E., D'Entremont, D., & Pritchett, N. (2006). Disclosure of HIV serostatus to sex partners: A new approach to measurement. *Sexually Transmitted Diseases, 33,* 102–105.

Nichols, M. (1989). Sex therapy with lesbians, gay men, and bisexuals. In S. Leiblum & R. Rosen (Eds.), *Principles and practice of sex therapy.* New York: Guilford Press.

Nichols, M. (2000). Therapy with sexual minorities. In S. Leiblum & R. Rosen (Eds.), *Principles and practice of sex therapy.* New York: Guilford Press.

Niedowski, E. (2006, August 6). From Russia with love. Retrieved August 7, 2006, from http://baltimoresun.com/news/opinion/ideas/balid.births06aug06,1,4659161,print.stor

Nielsen, S. (2010, June 20). Most child sex abuse never sees the light. *Oregonian,* pp. D1, D2.

Nieschlag, E., & Henke, A. (2005). Hopes for male contraception. *Lancet, 365,* 554.

Nishi, M., et al. (2011). The role of SRY mutations in the etiology of gonadal-dysgenesis in patients with 45,X/46,XY disorder of sex development and variants. *Hormone Research in Paediatrics, 75,* 26–31.

Nishith, P., Mechanic, M., & Resnick, P. (2000). Prior interpersonal trauma: The contribution to current PTSD symptoms in female rape victims. *Journal of Abnormal Psychology, 109,* 20–25.

Nixin, D. (2003). *Are penises going the way of the dodo?* Retrieved March 13, 2003, from http://www.mamimonline.com/grit/articles/article_3715.html

Nobre, P., & Pinto-Gouveia, J. (2006). Dysfunctional sexual beliefs as vulnerability factors for sexual dysfunction. *Journal of Sex Research, 43,* 68–76.

Nolan, B. (2011). Gay marriage divides evangelicals along generation gap. Retrieved from http://www.huffingtonpost.com/2011/09/07/gay-marriage-evangelicals

Nordenberg, T. (2008). The facts about aphrodisiacs. Retrieved November 11, 2008, from http://www.cfsan.fda.gov/~dms/fdaphrod.html

Nordlund, M. (2009, June). *Shakespeare and the nature of love.* Paper presented at the 19th WAS World Congress for Sexual Health, Göteborg, Sweden.

Nordqvist, C. (2011, June 21). Intrauterine devices safe and effective. Retrieved from http://www.medicalnewstoday.com/printerfriendlynews.php?newsid+229212

North American Registry of Midwives. (2008, January 25). The midwife model. *St. Louis Post-Dispatch.*

Norton, J. (2009, April 10). Benefits of breast-feeding touted. *Pueblo Chieftain,* p. B3.

Nour, N. (2000). Female circumcision and genital mutilation: A practical and sensitive approach. *Contemporary OB/GYN,* March, 50–55.

Novik, M., et al. (2011). Drinking motivations and experiences of unwanted sexual advances among undergraduate students. *Journal of Interpersonal Violence, 26,* 34–49.

Nowak, N., et al. (2011). The relationship between second to fourth digital ratio, spatial cognition, and virtual navigation. *Archives of Sexual Behavior, 40,* 575–585.

Nullis, C. (2007, May 25). Shortage of doctors fails AIDS work. *Oregonian,* p. A13.

Nusbaum, M., Lenahan, P., & Sadovsky, R. (2005). Sexual health in aging men and women: Addressing the physiologic and psychological sexual changes that occur with age. *Geriatrics, 60,* 18–28.

Nussbaum, E. (2000, January). A question of gender. *Discover,* 92–99.

Obermeyer, C., Baijah, P., & Pegurri, E. (2011). Facilitating HIV disclosure across diverse settings: A review. *American Journal of Public Health, 101,* 1011–1023.

O'Brien, P., Wyatt, K., & Dimmock, P. (2000). Premenstrual syndrome is real and treatable. *Practitioner, 244,* 185–189.

O'Brien, S. (2003). *Tears of the cheetah and other tales from the genetic frontier.* New York: St. Martin's Press.

O'Donnell, L., Stueve, A., Wilson-Simmons, R., et al. (2006). Heterosexual risk behaviors among urban adolescents. *Journal of Early Adolescence, 26,* 87–109.

O'Donnell, S., Meyer, I., & Schwartz, S. (2011). Increased risk of suicide attempts among Black and Latino lesbians, gay men, and bisexuals. *American Journal of Public Health, 101,* 1055–1059.

O'Keeffe, G., & Clarke-Pearson, K. (2011). Clinical report—The impact of social media on children, adolescents, and families. *Pediatrics, 127,* 800–804.

O'Neill, P. (2000, July 9). The Adonis complex. *Sunday Oregonian,* p. L11.

O'Sullivan, L., Cheng, M., Harris, K., & Brooks-Gunn, J. (2007). I wanna hold your hand: The progression of social, romantic and sexual events in adolescent relationships. *Perspectives on Sexual and Reproductive Health, 39,* 100–107.

Oattles, M., & Offman, A. (2007). Global self-esteem and sexual self-esteem as predictors of sexual communication in intimate relationships. *Canadian Journal of Human Sexuality, 16,* 489–500.

Ochs, E., & Binik, Y. (1999). The use of couple data to determine the reliability of self-reported sexual behavior. *Journal of Sex Research, 36,* 374–384.

O'Connell, H. (2007, April). "What's in a name . . ." Paper presented at the 18th Congress of the World Association for Sexual Health, Sydney, Australia.

O'Conner, D., et al. (2011). The relationship between sex hormones and sexual function in middle-aged and older European men. *Journal of Clinical Endocrinology and Metabolism, 96,* 1577–1587.

Ofman, U. (2000). Guest editor's note. *Journal of Sex Education and Therapy, 25,* 3–5.

Ogden, J. (1989). Visuospatial and other "right-hemispheric" functions after long recovery periods in left-hemispherectomized subjects. *Neuropsychologia, 27,* 765–776.

Ogden, J., & Lindridge, L. (2008). The impact of breast scarring on perceptions of attractiveness. *Journal of Health Psychology, 13,* 303–310.

Ogodo, O. (2009, January 7). Second chance against FGM. Retrieved January 7, 2009, from http://www.islamonline.net/servlet/Satellite?c=Article_C&cid=1165994389008

Okazaki, S. (2002). Influences of culture on Asian Americans' sexuality. *Journal of Sex Research, 39,* 34–41.

O'Leary, K., et al. (2012). Is long-term love more than a rare phenomenon? If so, what are its correlates? *Social Psychological and Personality Science, 3,* 241–249.

Olsen, V., Gustavsen, I., Bramness, J., Hasvold, I., Karinen R., et al. (2005). The concentrations, appearance and taste of nine sedating drugs dissolved in four different beverages. *Forensic Science International, 151,* 171–174.

Olson, J., Forbes, C., & Belzer, M. (2011). Management of the transgender adolescent. *Archives of Pediatrics and Adolescent Medicine, 165,* 171–176.

Olson, T. (2010, January 18). The conservative case for gay marriage. *Newsweek,* 48–50.

Olsson, S., & Moller, A. (2003). On the incidence and sex ratio of transsexualism in Sweden. *Archives of Sexual Behavior, 32,* 381–386.

Olujobi, G. (2009, July 2). Designer vaginas: Is female circumcision coming out of the closet? Retrieved from http://www.truthdig.com/report/item/20090702_designer_vaginas_is_female_circumcision_coming_out_of_the_closet/

Onoya, D., et al. (2011). Psychosocial correlates of condom use consistency among Isixhosa-speaking women living with HIV in the Western Cape Province of South Africa. *Journal of Health Psychology, 16,* 1208–1220.

Orchowski, L., Gidycz, C., & Raffle, H. (2008). Evaluation of a sexual assault risk reduction and self-defense program: A prospective analysis of a revised protocol. *Psychology of Women Quarterly, 32,* 204–218.

Ormerod, A., Collingsworth, L., & Perry, L. (2008). Critical climate: Relations among sexual harassment, climate, and outcomes for high school girls and boys. *Psychology of Women Quarterly, 32,* 113–125.

O'Shaughnessy, M., et al. (2011). Intensity modulated radiotherapy replaces 3-dimensional external beam as the preferred radiotherapy modality in prostate cancer. *Journal of Urology, 185,* e34.

Osborn, J. (2008). The past, present, and future of AIDS. *Journal of the American Medical Association, 300,* 581–583.

Osman, A., & Al-Sawaf, M. (1995). Cross-cultural aspects of sexual anxieties and the associated dysfunction. *Journal of Sex Education and Therapy, 21,* 174–181.

Osman, S. (2003). Predicting men's rape perceptions based on the belief that "no" really means "yes." *Journal of Applied Social Psychology, 33,* 683–692.

Østbye, T., Kolotkin, R. L., He, H., et al. (2011). Sexual functioning among obese adults enrolling in a weight loss study. *Journal of Sex and Marital Therapy, 37*(3), 224–235.

Oster, A., et al. (2011). HIV risk among young African American men who have sex with men. *American Journal of Public Health, 101,* 137–143.

Ostling, R. (2000, October 29). Schism threatens Southern Baptists. *Sunday Oregonian,* p. A3.

Ostrovsky, G. (2011, July 22). VIBERECT device FDA cleared for erectile dysfunction. Retrieved from http://medgadget.com/2011/07/viberect-device-fda-cleared-for-erectile-dysfunction.html/

Oswald, D., & Russell, B. (2006). Perceptions of sexual coercion in heterosexual dating relationships: The role of aggressor gender and tactics. *Journal of Sex Research, 43,* 87–96.

Otis, M., Rostosky, S., Riggle, E., & Hamrin, R. (2006). Stress and relationship quality in same-sex couples. *Journal of Social and Personal Relationships, 23,* 81–99.

Ott, M., Adler, N., Millstein, S., Tschann, J., & Ellen, J. (2002). The trade-off between hormonal contraceptives and condoms among adolescents. *Perspectives on Sexual and Reproductive Health, 34,* 6–14.

Ott, M., et al. (2011). Stability and change in self-reported sexual orientation identity in young people. *Archives of Sexual Behavior, 40,* 519–532.

Overbeck, G., Vollebergh, W., Engels, R., & Meeus, W. (2003). Parental attachment and romantic relationships: Associations with emotional disturbance during late adolescence. *Journal of Counseling Psychology, 50,* 28–39.

Owen, J., et al. (2011). Short-term prospective study of hooking up among college students. *Archives of Sexual Behavior, 40,* 331–341.

Owen, J., & Fincham, F. (2011). Young adults' emotional reactions after hooking up encounters. *Archives of Sexual Behavior, 40,* 321–330.

Owen, L. (1993). *Her blood is gold.* San Francisco: HarperCollins.

Oz, M., & Roizen, M. (2010, November 3). Hormone therapy a smart idea for many women. *Oregonian,* p. C3.

Pace, B. (2000). Urinary tract infections. *Journal of the American Medical Association, 283,* 1646.

Padilla, Y., Crisp, C., & Rew, D. (2010). Parental acceptance and illegal drug use among gay, lesbian, and bisexual adolescents: Results from a national survey. *Social Work, 55,* 265–275.

Page, S., et al. (2011). Dutasteride reduces prostate size and prostate specific antigen in older hypogonadal men with prostatic hyperplasia undergoing testosterone replacement therapy. *Journal of Urology, 186,* 191–197.

Palmer, J., Rao, R., Adams-Campbell, L., & Rosenberg, L. (1999). Correlates of hysterectomy among African-American women. *American Journal of Epidemiology, 150,* 1309–1315.

Palmer, J., Rosenberg, L., Wise, L., & Horton, N. (2003). Onset of natural menopause in African American women. *American Journal of Public Health, 93,* 299–306.

Pandey, U. (2007, April). *Male sex work: Implications for HIV/AIDS in India.* Paper presented at the 18th Congress of the World Association for Sexual Health, Sydney, Australia.

Pang, G. (2010, November 13). Drink linked to UH attacks. *Star Advertiser,* pp. A1, A9.

Panzer, C., Guay, A., & Goldstein, I. (2006). Do oral contraceptives produce irreversible effects on women's sexuality? A reply. *Journal of Sexual Medicine, 3,* 568–570.

Pappas, S. (2012, April 9). Does the vaginal orgasm exist? Experts debate. Retrieved from http://www.livescience.com/19579-vaginal-orgasm-debate.html

Paredes, R., & Baum, M. (1997). Role of the medial preoptic area/anterior hypothalamus in the control of masculine sexual behavior. *Annual Review of Sex Research, 8,* 68–101.

Parish, W., Laumann, E., & Mojola, S. (2007). Sexual behavior in China: Trends and comparisons. *Population and Developmental Review, 14,* 729–738.

Park, L., Sanchez, D., & Brynildsen, K. (2011). Maladaptive responses to relationship dissolution: The role of relationship contingent self-worth. *Journal of Applied Social Psychology, 41,* 1749–1773.

Parker, C., & Dearnaley, D. (2003). Hormonal therapy as an adjuvant to radical radiotherapy for locally advanced prostate cancer. *British Journal of Urology International, 91,* 6–8.

Parker-Pope, T. (2011, June 14). Digital flirting: Easy to do, and easy to get caught. *New York Times,* p. D5.

Parkes, A., et al. (2011). Is parenting associated with teenagers' early sexual risk-taking, autonomy and relationship with sexual partners? *Perspectives on Sexual and Reproductive Health, 43,* 30–40.

Parks, C. (1999). Lesbian identity development: An examination of differences across generations. *American Journal of Orthopsychiatry, 69,* 347–361.

Parks, K., Pardi, A., & Bradizza, C. (2006). Collecting data on alcohol use and alcohol-related victimization: A comparison of telephone and Web-based survey methods. *Journal of Studies on Alcohol, 67,* 318–324.

Parry, J. (2006). Controversial new vaccine to prevent cervical cancer. *Bulletin of the World Health Organization, 84,* 86–88.

Parsons, J. (1983). Sexual socialization and gender roles in childhood. In E. Allgeier & N. McCormick (Eds.), *Changing boundaries: Gender roles and sexual behavior.* Palo Alto, CA: Mayfield.

Pathela, P. (2011). Same-sex teen behavior much higher than thought. *AIDS Alert, 26,* 29–30.

Pathfinder International. (2006, July). Creating partnerships to prevent early marriage in the Amhara region. *Pathfinder International.*

Patrick, M., Maggs, J., & Abar, C. (2007). Reasons to have sex, personal goals, and sexual behavior during the transition to college. *Journal of Sex Research, 44,* 240–249.

Patrick, R. (2011, June 9). Women awarded $95 million over sex harassment in Fairview Heights stores. *St. Louis Post-Dispatch.*

Patterson, C. (1995). Sexual orientation and human development: An overview. *Developmental Psychology, 31,* 3–11.

Patz, A. (2000, January/February). Will your marriage last? *Psychology Today,* 58–65.

Paukku, M., Kilpikari, R., Puolakkainen, M., et al. (2003). Criteria for selective screening for *Chlamydia trachomatis. Sexually Transmitted Diseases, 30,* 120–123.

Paul, L., & Galloway, J. (1994). Sexual jealousy: Gender differences in response to partner and rival. *Aggressive Behavior, 20,* 203–211.

Paul, P. (2005). *Pornified: How pornography is transforming our lives, our relationships, and our families.* New York: Times Books.

Pauls, R., Mutema, G., Segal, J., et al. (2006). A prospective study examining the anatomic distribution of nerve density in the human vagina. *Journal of Sexual Medicine, 3,* 979–987.

Paulson, A. (2011, April 4). White House targets sexual assault on campus. *Christian Science Monitor.*

Pear, R. (2012, January 20). Obama reaffirms insurers must cover contraception. Retrieved from http://www.nytimes.com/2012/01/21/health/policy/administration-rules-insurers-must-cover-contraception

Pearlman, S. (2005). When mothers learn a daughter is a lesbian: Then and now. *Journal of Lesbian Studies, 9*, 117–137.

Pearson, C. (2011). You heard it here first: Hysterectomy for benign conditions isn't so benign after all. *Women's Health Activist, 36*, 6–11.

Pearson, H. (2000). So that's why you can't fit into your jeans. *New Scientist*, April 8, 6.

Pearson, M., et al. (2012). Pathways to early coital debut for adolescent girls: A recursive partitioning analysis. *Journal of Sex Research, 49*, 13-28.

Peipert, J., et al. (2011). Adherence to dual-method contraceptive use. *Contraception, 84*, 252–258.

Pelisek, C. (2011, April 25). Terror on Long Island. *Newsweek*, 38–40.

Penhollow, T., & Young, M. (2008, October 15). Predictors of sexual satisfaction: The role of body image and fitness. Retrieved March 17, 2009, from http://www.ejhs.org

Penley, C. (1996). From NASA to the 700 Club (with a detour through Hollywood): Cultural studies in the public sphere. In C. Nelson & D. Gaonkar (Eds.), *Disciplinarity and dissent in cultural studies*. New York: Routledge.

Penson, D. (2011). Is this as good as it gets? *Journal of the American Medical Association, 305*, 197–198.

Perel, E. (2006) *Mating in captivity: Reconciling the erotic and the domestic*. New York: Harper.

Perelman, M. (2001). Integrating sildenafil and sex therapy: Unconsummated marriage secondary to erectile dysfunction and retarded ejaculation. *Journal of Sex Education and Therapy, 26*, 13–21.

Perlman, F., & McKee, M. (2009). Trends in family planning in Russia, 1994–2003. *Perspectives on Sexuality and Reproductive Health, 41*, 40–50.

Persky, A. (2012). The capital of rape: fighting widespread sexual violence in the Democratic Republic of the Congo. *ABA Journal, 98*, 59–61.

Peter, J., & Valkenburg, P. (2011). The use of sexually explicit Internet material and its antecedents: A longitudinal comparison of adolescents and adults. *Archives of Sexual Behavior, 40*(5), 1015–1025 (e-pub July 10, 2010).

Peterman, A., Palermo, T., & Bredenkamp, C. (2011). Estimates and determinants of sexual violence against women in the Democratic Republic of Congo. *American Journal of Public Health, 101*, 1060–1067.

Petersen, J., & Hyde, J. (2011). Gender differences in sexual attitudes and behaviors: A review of meta-analytic results and large datasets. *Journal of Sex Research, 48*, 149–165.

Peterson, H. (2008). Sterilization. *Obstetrics and Gynecology, 111*, 189–203.

Peterson, J., & Bakeman, R. (2006). Impact of beliefs about HIV treatment and peer condom norms on risky sexual behavior among gay and bisexual men. *Journal of Community Psychology, 34*, 37–46.

Petitti, D., & Reingold, A. (1988). Tampon characteristics and menstrual toxic shock syndrome. *Journal of the American Medical Association, 259*, 686–687.

Pettaway, C. (2008). What to know about penile cancer. Retrieved October 31, 2008, from http://www.cancerwise.org/june_2004/display.cfm?id=66fa5f82-1b18-4fa2-beaf-11e6f4b1cf86&method=displayfull&color=green

Pew Forum on Religion and Public Life. (2011, June 4). The future of the global Muslim population. Retrieved from http://www.pewforum.org/The-Future-of-the-Global-Muslim-Population.aspx

Pew Research Center. (2006, March 14). Guess who's coming to dinner: 22% of Americans have a relative in a mixed-race marriage. Retrieved August 7, 2006, from http://pewresearch.org/social/pack.php?PackID=4

Pew Research Center. (2009a, July 15). Are we happy yet? Is marriage bliss? Retrieved July 15, 2009, from http://pewresearch.org/pubs/?ChartID=17

Peyser, M. (2000, February 28). Prime time "I do's." *Newsweek*, 48.

Peyser, M. (2006, December 26, 2005/January 2). The spouses of "Big Love." *Newsweek*, 91.

Philaretou, A. (2005). Sexuality and the Internet. *Journal of Sex Research, 42*, 180–181.

Phillips, K. (2006). *American theocracy: The peril and politics of radical religion, oil, and borrowed money in the 21st century*. New York: Viking Press.

Piaggio, G., Kapp, N., & von Hertzen, H. (2011). Effect on pregnancy rates of the delay in the administration of levonorgestrel for emergency contraception: A combined analysis of four WHO trials. *Contraception, 84*, 35–39.

Picardi, A., et al. (2011). A twin study of attachment style in young adults. *Journal of Personality, 79*, 965–992.

Piccionelli, G. (2006). Midterm porn politics: 1. Retrieved September 17, 2006, from http://www.xbiz.com/articles/16336/Piccionelli

Picker, L. (2005, April 25). And now, the hard part. *Newsweek*, 46–50.

Pikkarainen, E., Lehtonen-Veromaa, M., & Mottonen, T. (2008). Estrogen-progestin contraceptive use during adolescence prevents bone mass acquisition. *Contraception, 6*, 236–243.

Pines, A., Sturdee, D., Birkhauser, M., de Villers, T., Naftolin, F., & Gompel, A. (2008, March). HRT in the early menopause: Scientific evidence and common perceptions. Summary of the First IMS Global Summit on Menopause-Related Issues.

Pinker, S. (2011). *The better angels of our nature: Why violence has declined*. New York: Viking.

Pinkerton, J., & Zion, A. (2006). Vasomotor symptoms in menopause: Where we've been and where we're going. *Journal of Women's Health, 15*, 135–143.

Pisco, J., et al. (2011, March 15). Paper presented at the 36th Annual Scientific Meeting of the Society of Interventional Radiology, Chicago, IL.

Pitsouni, E., Iavazzo, C., & Falagas, M. (2008). Itraconazole vs. fluconazole for the treatment of uncomplicated acute vaginal and vulvovaginal candidiasis in nonpregnant women: A meta-analysis of randomized controlled trials. *American Journal of Obstetrics and Gynecology, 198*, 153–160.

Pittman, F. (1990). *Private lies: Infidelity and the betrayal of intimacy*. New York: W. W. Norton.

Pitts, S., & Emans, S. (2008). Controversies in contraception. *Current Opinion in Pediatrics, 20*, 383–389.

Planned Parenthood Federation of America. (2002). *Masturbation: From stigma to sexual health* [White paper]. New York: Katherine Dexter McCormick Library.

Planned Parenthood Federation of America. (2003). Masturbation: From myth to sexual health. *Contemporary Sexuality, 37*, i–vii.

Planned Parenthood Federation of America. (2008, February 8). Birth control. Retrieved April 1, 2009, from http://www.plannedparenthood.org/health-topics/birth-control-4211.htm

Plato, C. (2008). Come out, come out, wherever you are! For bisexuals the lovely lifelong process of coming out is often twice as long—a double life sentence, if you will. *Curve, 18*, 62–72.

Plaud, J., Gaither, G., Hegstad, H., & Rowan, L. (1999). Volunteer bias in human psychophysiological sexual arousal research: To whom do our research results apply? *Journal of Sex Research, 36,* 171–179.

Pluta, R., & Golub, R. (2011). BRCA genes and breast cancer. *Journal of the American Medical Association, 305,* 2244.

Pluta, R., et al. (2012). Prostatitis. *Journal of the American Medical Association, 307,* 527–531.

Pokoradi, A., Iversen, L., & Hannaford, P. (2011). Factors associated with age of onset and type of menopause in a cohort of UK women. *American Journal of Obstetrics and Gynecology, 205,* 34.e1–34.e13.

Polgreen, L. (2005, February 18). Casualties of Sudan's war: Rape is a weapon in the fight over land and ethnicity in Darfur. *Oregonian,* p. A19.

Polinsky, M. (1995). Functional status of long-term breast cancer survivors: Demonstrating chronicity. *Health and Social Work, 19*(3), 165–173.

PolitiFact. (2010). McConnell claims stimulus includes "$219,000 to study the sex lives of female college freshmen." Retrieved October 13, 2010, from http://www.politifact.com/truth-o-meter/statements/2010/

Pollitt, K. (2006). Virginity or death. Retrieved June 4, 2006, from http://www.thenation.com/doc/20050530/pollitt

Pomeroy, W. (1965). Why we tolerate lesbians. *Sexology,* May, 652–654.

Population Council, New York. (2005). Emergency contraception's mode of action clarified. *SIECUS Report, 33,* 20–22.

Porter, P. (2008). "Westernizing" women's risks? Breast cancer in lower-income countries. *New England Journal of Medicine, 358,* 213–216.

Porter, S., Yuille, J., & Lehman, D. (1999). The nature of real, implanted, and fabricated childhood emotion events: Implications for the recovered memory debate. *Law and Human Behavior, 23,* 517–537.

Potdar, R., & Koenig, M. (2005). Does audio-CASI improve reports of risky behavior? Evidence from a randomized field trial among young urban men in India. *Studies in Family Planning, 36,* 107–116.

Poteat, V. (2008). Contextual and moderating effects of the peer group climate on use of homophobic epithets. *School Psychology Review, 37,* 188–201.

Poteat, V., et al. (2011). The effects of general and homophobic victimization on adolescents' psychosocial and educational concerns: The importance of intersecting identities and parental support. *Journal of Counseling Psychology, 58,* 597–609.

Potter, J., & Ship, A. (2001). Survivors of breast cancer. *New England Journal of Medicine, 344,* 309–314.

Potter, L., Oakley, D., & de Leon-Wong, E. (1996). Measuring compliance among oral contraceptive users. *Family Planning Perspectives, 28,* 154–158.

Poulin, C., & Rutter, V. (2011, April 8). How color-blind is love? Interracial dating facts and puzzles: A fact sheet from the Council on Contemporary Families. Retrieved from http://www.contemporaryfamilies.org/conference/14thannualconference.html

Power, C. (2006, August). A generation of women wiped out? *Glamour,* 172–175.

Powers, M., Adekeye, T., & Volny, R. (2011). Chlamydia screening: What about men? *American Journal of Public Health, 101,* 583–584.

Prause, N., Staley, C., & Finn, P. (2011). The effects of acute ethanol consumption on sexual response and sexual risk-taking intent. *Archives of Sexual Behavior, 40,* 373–384.

Prentky, R., Burgess, A., & Carter, D. (1986). Victim responses by rapist type: An empirical and clinical analysis. *Journal of Interpersonal Violence, 1,* 73–98.

Prescott, J. (1975, April). Body pleasure and the origins of violence. *Futurist,* 64–74.

Prescott, J. (1989). Affectional bonding for the prevention of violent behaviors: Neurological, psychological, and religious/spiritual determinants. In L. Hertzberg (Ed.), *Violent behavior: Vol. 1. Assessment and intervention.* New York: PMA Publishing.

Preston, P. (2005). Nonverbal communication: Do you really say what you mean? *Journal of Healthcare Management, 50,* 83–86.

Price, S. (2008). Women and reproductive loss: Client-worker dialogues designed to break the silence. *Social Work, 53,* 367–375.

Priebe, G., & Svedin, G. (2008). Child sexual abuse is largely hidden from the adult society: An epidemiological study of adolescents' disclosures. *Child Abuse and Neglect, 32,* 1095–1108.

Primack, B., Douglas, E., Fine, M., & Dalton, M. (2009). Exposure to sexual lyrics and sexual experience among urban adolescents. *American Journal of Preventative Medicine, 36,* 317–323.

Prince, M., Kafka, M., Commons, M., et al. (2002). Telephone scatologia—Comorbidity with other paraphilias and paraphilia-related disorders. *International Journal of Law and Psychiatry, 25,* 37–49.

Proctor, F., Wagner, N., & Butler, J. (1974). The differentiation of male and female orgasm: An experimental study. In N. Wagner (Ed.), *Perspectives on human sexuality.* New York: Behavioral Publications.

Propst, A., & Laufer, M. (1999). Diagnosing and treating adolescent endometriosis. *Contemporary OB/GYN,* December, 52–59.

Proulx, J., Aubut, J., McKibben, A., & Cote, M. (1994). Penile responses of rapists and nonrapists to rape stimuli involving physical violence or humiliation. *Archives of Sexual Behavior, 23,* 295–310.

Puente, S., & Cohen, D. (2003). Jealousy and the meaning (or nonmeaning) of violence. *Personality and Social Psychology Bulletin, 29,* 449–460.

Puentes, J., Knox, D., & Zusman, M. (2008). Participants in "friends with benefits" relationships. *College Student Journal, 42,* 176–180.

Pujois, Y., Meston, C., & Seal, B. (2010). The association between sexual satisfaction and body image in women. *Journal of Sexual Medicine, 7,* 905–916.

Purdon, C., & Watson, C. (2011). Non-erotic thoughts and sexual functioning. *Archives of Sexual Behavior, 40,* 891–902.

Puri, S., et al. (2011). A qualitative study of son preference and fetal sex selection among Indian immigrants in the United States. *Social Science and Medicine, 72,* 1169–1176.

Putman, S. (2009). The monsters in my head: Posttraumatic stress disorder and the child survivor of sexual abuse. *Journal of Counseling and Development, 87,* 80–89.

Putnam, F. (2003). Ten-year research update review: Child sexual abuse. *Journal of the American Academy of Child and Adolescent Psychiatry, 42,* 269–278.

Pyke, K., & Johnson, D. (2003). Asian American women and racialized femininities: "Doing" gender across cultural worlds. *Gender and Society, 17,* 33–53.

Quackenbush, D., Strassberg, D., & Turner, C. (1995). Gender effects of romantic themes in erotica. *Archives of Sexual Behavior, 24,* 21–35.

Quan, D. (2008). Pharmacotherapy of hepatitis B infection: A brief review. *Nephrology Nursing Journal, 35,* 507–601.

Quindlen, A. (2003, January 27). Out of the time warp. *Newsweek,* 26.

Quindlen, A. (2005, July 11). Now available: Middle ground. *Newsweek,* 74.

Quindlen, A. (2009a, April 13). The end of an error. *Newsweek,* 60.

Quindlen, A. (2009b, February 16). On their own terms. *Newsweek,* 60.

Quinta, G., & Nobre, P. (2011). Personality traits and psychopathology on male sexual dysfunction: An empirical study. *Journal of Sexual Medicine, 8,* 461–469.

Quittner, J. (2003, February 4). Addicted to dot.com sex. *Advocate,* 34–36.

Raasch, C. (2012, April 6). Abortion restrictions gain steam. *USA Today,* p. 3A.

Rabin, R. (2007a, June 4). At-home tests evaluate fertility of him, her. *Oregonian,* p. A2.

Rabin, R. (2007b, March 7). Men and the biological clock. *Oregonian,* p. C1.

Rabin, R. (2010, August 18). Drop seen in male circumcision rate. *Oregonian.*

Rabin, R. (2011, December 15). 1 in 5 women hurt by rape. *Oregonian,* pp. A1, A8.

Rabin, R. (2012). Men struggle for rape awareness. *New York Times,* January, 24, D1.

Rabock, J., Mellon, J., & Starka, L. (1979). Klinefelter's syndrome: Sexual development and activity. *Archives of Sexual Behavior, 8,* 333–340.

Radlove, S. (1983). Sexual response and gender roles. In E. Allgeier & N. McCormick (Eds.), *Changing boundaries: Gender roles and sexual behavior.* Mountain View, CA: Mayfield.

Rako, S. (1996). *The hormone of desire.* New York: Harmony Books.

Rako, S. (1999). Testosterone deficiency and supplementation for women: Matters of sexuality and health. *Psychiatric Annals, 29,* 23–26.

Rako, S., & Friebely, J. (2004). Pheromonal influences on sociosexual behavior in postmenopausal women. *Journal of Sex Research, 41,* 372–380.

Ramakrishnan, K., & Scheid, D. (2006). Ectopic pregnancy: Forget the "classic presentation" if you want to catch it sooner. *Journal of Family Practice, 55,* 388–395.

Ramiandrisoa, J., et al. (2011). Congenital syphilis, Reunion Island, 2010. *Emerging Infectious Diseases, 17,* 2082–2083.

Ramson, A. (2006). Sexual harassment education on campus: Communication using media. *Community College Review, 33,* 38–54.

Ranjit, N., Bankole, A., & Darroch, J. (2001). Contraceptive failure in the first two years of use: Differences across socioeconomic subgroups. *Family Planning Perspectives, 33,* 19–27.

Rapoza, K., & Drake, J. (2009). Relationships of hazardous alcohol use, alcohol expectancies, and emotional commitment to male sexual coercion and aggression in dating couples. *Journal of Studies on Alcohol and Drugs, 70,* 55–63.

Rasheed, A., White, C., & Shaikh, N. (1997). The incidence of post-vasectomy chronic testicular pain and the role of

nerve stripping (denervation) of the spermatic cord in its management. *British Journal of Urology, 79,* 269–270.

Rasmussen, K., & Geraghty, S. (2011). The quiet revolution: Breastfeeding transformed with the use of breast pumps. *American Journal of Public Health, 101,* 1356–1359.

Ravnborg, T., et al. (2011). Prenatal and adult exposures to smoking are associated with adverse effects on reproductive hormones, semen quality, final height, and body mass index. *Human Reproduction, 26,* 1000–1011.

Ray, A., & Gold, S. (1996). Gender roles, aggression, and alcohol use in dating relationships. *Journal of Sex Research, 33,* 47–55.

Ray, C. (2011, March 8). Control yourself! Science Desk Q & A bladder control exercises. *New York Times,* p. D2.

Ray, D. (2012). *Sex and God: How religion distorts sexuality.* Bonner Springs, KS: IPC Press.

Raz, R., Gennesin, Y., & Wasser, J. (2000). Recurrent urinary tract infections in postmenopausal women. *Clinical Infectious Diseases, 30,* 152–156.

Reading, B. (2012, March 27). Growth in world contraceptive use stalling: 215 million women's needs still unmet. Retrieved from http://www.treehugger.com/health/growth-world-contraceptive-use-stalling

Real, T. (2002). *How can I get through to you? Reconnecting men and women.* New York: Scribner.

Reamer, F. (2003). Boundary issues in social work: Managing dual relationships. *Social Work, 48,* 121–133.

Reece, M., et al. (2010a). Background and considerations on the National Survey of Sexual Health and Behavior (NSSHB) from the investigators. *Journal of Sexual Medicine, 7,* 243–245.

Reece, M., et al. (2010b). Condom use rates in a national probability sample of males and females ages 14 to 94 in the United States. *Journal of Sexual Medicine, 7*(Suppl. 5), 266–276.

Reece, M., Herbenick, D., Fortenberry, J. D., et al. (2010). *The National Survey of Sexual Health and Behavior (NSSHB).* Center for Health Promotion. Retrieved May 22, 2011, from http://www.nationalsexstudy.indiana.edu/

Reece, M., Herbenick, D., Sanders, S., et al. (2009). Prevalence and characteristics of vibrator use by men in the United States. *Journal of Sexual Medicine,* April 24 (e-pub).

Reed, S., et al. (2007). Night sweats, sleep disturbance, and depression associated with diminished libido in late menopausal

transition and early postmenopause. *American Journal of Obstetrics and Gynecology, 196,* 593.e1–593.e7.

Reeder, H. (1996). The subjective experience of love through adult life. *International Journal of Aging and Human Development, 43,* 325–340.

Reefhuis, J., Honein, M., & Schieve, L. (2008). Assisted reproductive technology and major structural birth defects in the United States. *Human Reproduction, 24,* 360–366.

Rees, P., Fowler, C., & Maas, C. (2007). Sexual function in men and women with neurological disorders. *Lancet, 369,* 512–525.

Rees, R. (2008). Clinical review: Peyronie's disease. *General Practice,* April 4, 27.

Reese-Weber, M., & Smith, D. (2011). Outcomes of child sexual abuse as predictors of later sexual victimization. *Journal of Interpersonal Violence, 26,* 1884–1905.

Regan, P. (1998). Of lust and love: Beliefs about the role of sexual desire in romantic relationships. *Personal Relationships, 5,* 139–157.

Regan, P., & Berscheid, E. (1995). Gender differences about the causes of male and female sexual desire. *Personal Relationships, 2,* 345–358.

Regehr, C., & Glancy, G. (1995). Sexual exploitation of patients: Issues for colleagues. *American Journal of Orthopsychiatry, 65*(2), 194–202.

Regnerus, M., & Luchies, L. (2006). The parent-child relationship and opportunities for adolescents' first sex. *Journal of Family Issues, 27,* 159–183.

Reid, P., & Bing, V. (2000). Sexual roles of girls and women: An ethnocultural lifespan perspective. In C. Travis & J. White (Eds.), *Sexuality, society, and feminism.* Washington, DC: American Psychological Association.

Reinberg, S. (2006). Testosterone offers women benefits, risks: Higher levels may boost sexual function, but increase heart trouble, studies find. Retrieved July 10, 2006, from http://health.msn.com/healthnews/articlepage.aspx?cp-documentid=100138390

Reiner, W. (1997a). Sex assignment in the neonate with intersex or inadequate genitalia. *Archives of Pediatric and Adolescent Medicine, 151,* 1044–1045.

Reiner, W. (1997b). To be male or female: That is the question. *Archives of Pediatric and Adolescent Medicine, 151,* 224–225.

Reiner, W. (2000, May). *Gender and "sex reassignment."* Paper presented at the Lawson Wilkins Pediatric Endocrine Society meeting, Boston, MA. Retrieved August 19, 2000, from http:// mayohealth.org/mayo/headline/htm/hw000516.htm

Reinisch, J., & Beasley, R. (1990). *The Kinsey Institute's new report on sex*. New York: St. Martin's Press.

Reitan, E. (2011). Gay suicide and the ethic of love: A progressive Christian response. *Humanist, 71,* 24–26.

Reiter, R., & Milburn, A. (1994). Exploring effective treatment for chronic pelvic pain. *Contemporary OB/GYN,* March, 84–103.

Reitsamer, R., Glueck, S., Peintinger, E., & Gschwandtner, E. (2007, April). *Sexual function in breast cancer patients*. Paper presented at the 18th Congress of the World Association for Sexual Health, Sydney, Australia.

Rellini, A., et al. (2011). The effect of pre-existing affect on the sexual responses of women with and without a history of childhood sexual abuse. *Archives of Sexual Behavior.* doi:10.1007/s10508-011-9772-y

Rellini, A., & Meston, C. (2011). Sexual self-schemas, sexual dysfunction, and the sexual responses of women with a history of childhood sexual abuse. *Archives of Sexual Behavior, 40,* 351–362.

Rempel, J., & Baumgartner, B. (2003). The relationship between attitudes towards menstruation and sexual attitudes, desires, and behavior in women. *Archives of Sexual Behavior, 32,* 155–163.

Renshaw, D. (1987). Painful intercourse associated with cerebral palsy. *Journal of the American Medical Association, 257,* 2086.

Reynolds, J. (2006, July 9). Sex, secrets and cyberspace: Area prostitution flourishes via Web. *Monterey County Herald.*

Reynolds, J. (2009, March 13). Preventing the next fertility clinic scandal. Retrieved March 23, 2009, from http://www.thehastingscenter.org/Bioethicsforum/Post.aspx?id=3240

Reynolds, S., Shepherd, M., Risbud, A., et al. (2004). Male circumcision and risk of HIV-1 and other sexually transmitted infections in India. *Lancet, 363,* 1039–1040.

Rhoades, G., Stanley, S., & Markman, H. (2009). Couples' reasons for cohabitation. *Journal of Family Issues, 30,* 233–258.

Rhodes, S., Bowie, D., & Hergenrather, K. (2003). Collecting behavioral data using the World Wide Web: Considerations for researchers. *Journal of Epidemiology and Community Health, 57,* 68–73.

Rholes, W., Simpson, J., & Friedman, M. (2006). Avoidant attachment and the experience of parenting. *Personality and Social Psychology Bulletin, 32,* 275–285.

Rhynard, J., Krebs, M., & Glover, J. (1997). Sexual assault in dating relationships. *Journal of School Health, 67,* 89–93.

Ribner, D. (2009, , June). *Psychosexual therapy in the context of three major world religions—Judiasm.* Paper presented at the 19th WAS World Congress for Sexual Health, Göteborg, Sweden.

Rice, E., et al. (2012). Position-specific HIV risk in a large network of homeless youth. *American Journal of Public Health, 102,* 141–147.

Richard, D. (2002). Tantra 101. *Contemporary Sexuality, 36,* 1, 4–7.

Richards, L., Rollerson, B., & Phillips, J. (1991). Perceptions of submissiveness: Implications for victimization. *Journal of Psychology, 125,* 407–411.

Richardson, D., Wood, K., & Goldmeier, D. (2006). A qualitative pilot study of Islamic men with lifelong premature (rapid) ejaculation. *Journal of Sexual Medicine, 3,* 337–343.

Richie, J. (2011). Screening for testicular cancer: An evidence review for the U.S. Preventive Services Task Force. *Journal of Urology, 186,* 111.

Richter, S., Leibovitch, I., & Alkalay, R. (2006). An ejaculation and orgasmic disorder in men after penile implant surgery. *Journal of Sexual Medicine, 3*(Suppl. 3), 224–286.

Richters, J., Visser, R., Rissel, C., & Smith, A. (2006). Sexual practices at last heterosexual encounter and occurrence of orgasm in a national survey. *Journal of Sex Research, 43,* 217–210.

Richters, J., et al. (2010). Consensual sex between men and sexual violence in Australian prisons, *Archives of Sexual Behavior,* September 2 (e-pub), 1–8.

Rickert, V., Sanghvi, R., & Wiemann, C. (2002). Is lack of sexual assertiveness among adolescent and young adult women a cause for concern? *Perspectives on Sexual and Reproductive Health, 34,* 178–183.

Ricks, T., & Suro, R. (2000, May 11). Army confirms harassment charge by top woman general. *Oregonian,* p. A8.

Rideout, V. (2008). *Television as a health educator: A case study of Grey's Anatomy.* Menlo Park, CA: Kaiser Family Foundation.

Rideout, V., Foehr, U., & Roberts, D. (2010). Generation M2: Media in the lives of 8- to 18-year-olds. Menlo Park, CA: Henry J. Kaiser Family Foundation. Retrieved from http://www.kff.org/entmedia/8010.cfm

Ridgeway, J. (1996). *Inside the sex industry.* New York: Powerhouse Books.

Rieger, G., Linsenmeier, J., Gygax, L., & Bailey, J. (2008). Sexual orientation and childhood gender nonconformity: Evidence from home videos. *Developmental Psychology, 44,* 46–58.

Rieger, G., & Savin-Williams, R. (2011). Gender nonconformity, sexual orientation, and psychological well-being. *Archives of Sexual Behavior,* February 25 (e-pub).

Rienzo, B., Button, J., Sheu, J., & Li, Y. (2006). The politics of sexual orientation issues in American schools. *Journal of School Health, 76,* 93–97.

Rierdan, J., Koff, E., & Stubbs, M. (1998). Gender, depression and body image in early adolescence. *Journal of Early Adolescence, 8,* 109–117.

Riggio, H., & Weiser, D. (2008). Attitudes toward marriage: Embeddedness and outcomes in personal relationships. *Personal Relationships, 15,* 123–140.

Riggs, S., Cusimano, A., & Benson, K. (2011). Childhood emotional abuse and attachment processes in the dyadic adjustment of dating couples. *Journal of Counseling Psychology, 58,* 126–138.

Riley, A. (2010). Double blind trial of yohimbine hydrochloride in the treatment of erection inadequacy: An update. *Sexual and Relationship Therapy, 25,* 392–396.

Riley, A., & Riley, E. (2000). Controlled studies on women presenting with sexual drive disorder. I. Endocrine status. *Journal of Sex and Marital Therapy, 26,* 269–283.

Ring, T. (2012, February). Making history at home. *Advocate.*

Ringdahl, E. (2000). Treatment of recurrent vulvovaginal candidiasis. *American Family Physician, 61,* 3306–3312.

Rintala, M., Grenman, S., Jarvenkyla, M., Syrjanen, K., & Syrjanen, S. (2005). High-risk types of human papillomavirus (HPV) DNA in oral and genital mucosa of infants during their first 3 years of life: Experience from the Finnish HPV family study. *Clinical Infectious Diseases, 41,* 1728–1733.

Rios, D. (1996, November 17). The gone girls. *Oregonian,* pp. E1–E3.

Ritter, J. (2003). More choices available for birth control. Retrieved April 11, 2003, from http://www.suntimes.com/output/news/cst-nws-birth06.html

Ritts, V. (2003). Infusing culture into psychopathology. Retrieved March 13, 2003, from http://www.stlcc.cc.mo.us/mc/users/vritts/psypath.htm

Rivers, I., & Noret, N. (2008). Well-being among same-sex- and opposite-sex-attracted youth at school. *School Psychology Review, 37,* 174–187.

Rivkees, S., et al. (2011). A highly sensitive, high-throughput assay for the detection of Turner's syndrome. *Journal of Clinical Endocrinology and Metabolism, 96,* 699–705.

Robbins, C., et al. (2011). Prevalence, frequency, and associations of masturbation with partnered sexual behaviors among

U.S. adolescents. *Archives of Pediatric Adolescent Medicine, 165,* 1087–1093.

Robbins-Cherry, S., et al. (2011). The experiences of men living with inhibited ejaculation. *Sexual and Relationship Therapy, 26,* 242–253.

Roberts, S., et al. (2011). Reducing the incidence of twins from IVF treatments: Predictive modeling from a retrospective cohort. *Human Reproduction, 26,* 569–575.

Roberts, T. (2011). Critics point to John Jay study's limitations. *National Catholic Reporter, 47,* 17–18.

Robertson, G. (2011, October 21). Judge blocks ultrasound viewing rules in NC's new abortion law. Retrieved from http://www.therepublic.com/view/story/43c77756d2b94b56bfla9512e42a871f/NC

Robertson, W. (2011, January 11). Starting the conversation. Retrieved from http://www.showoffbooks.com/features/wrennarobertson/starting/conversation-wrenna-robertson

Robinson, D., Gibson-Beverly, G., & Schwartz, J. (2004). Sorority and fraternity membership and religious behaviors: Relation to gender attitudes. *Sex Roles: A Journal of Research, 50,* 871–877.

Robinson, M. (2011, July 11). Porn-induced sexual dysfunction is a growing problem. Retrieved from http://www.psychologytoday.com/print/67790

Robnett, B., & Feliciano, C. (2011). Patterns of racial-ethnic exclusion by Internet daters. *Social Forces, 89,* 807–828.

Rochman, B. (2012, March 19). Blue Ivy League. *Time,* 53.

Rodriguez, N., Ryan, S., Vande Kemp, H., & Foy, D. (1997). Posttraumatic stress disorder in adult female survivors of childhood sexual abuse: A comparison study. *Journal of Consulting and Clinical Psychology, 65,* 53–59.

Rodriguez-Stednicki, O., & Twaite, J. (1999). Attitudes toward victims of child abuse among adults from four ethnic/cultural groups. *Journal of Child Sexual Abuse, 8,* 1–24.

Rodriguez-Torres, M., Jeffers, L., et al. (2009). Peginterferon alpha-2a and ribavirin in Latino and non-Latino Whites with Hepatitis C. *New England Journal of Medicine, 360,* 257–267.

Roffman, D. (2005). Lakoff for sexuality educators: The power and magic of "framing." *SIECUS Report, 33,* 20–25.

Rogers, C. (1951). *Client-centered therapy: Its current practice, implications, and theory.* Boston: Houghton Mifflin.

Rogol, A. (2010). Considerations for androgen therapy in children and adolescents with Klinefelter syndrome. *Pediatric Endocrinology Reviews, 8*(Suppl.), 145–150.

Roisman, G., Clausell, E., Holland, A., Fortuna, K., & Elieff, C. (2008). Adult romantic relationships as contexts of human development: A multimethod comparison of same-sex couples with opposite-sex dating, engaged, and married dyads. *Developmental Psychology, 44,* 91–101.

Rojas-Burke, J. (2011, May 12). OHSU takes new aim at HIV. *Oregonian,* pp. A1, A4.

Roman, D. (2011, March 17). Detecting cyberspace predators. *Times Union.*

Romano, A. (2006, April 24). Walking a new beat. *Newsweek,* 48.

Romano, A. (2009, February 23). Our model marriage. *Newsweek,* 59.

Romeo, F. (2004). Acquaintance rape on college and university campuses. *College Student Journal, 38,* 61–65.

Romo, R. (2012, January 25). Ecuadorian clinics allegedly use abuse to "cure" homosexuality. Retrieved from http://articles.cnn.com/2012-0125/americas/world_americas-ecuador-homosexual-abuse

Root, A., Dana, K., & Lippe, B. (2011). Treatment of growth hormone-deficient infants with recombinant human growth hormone to near-adult height: Patterns of growth. *Hormone Research in Paediatrics, 75,* 276–283.

Ropelato, J. (2012). Internet pornography statistics. Retrieved from http://internet-filter-review.toptenreviews.com/internet-pornography-statistics.html

Rosario, V. (2011). Of genes, genitals, and gender. *Gay and Lesbian Review Worldwide, 18,* 9–13.

Roscoe, B., Strouse, J., & Goodwin, M. (1994). Sexual harassment: Early adolescents' self-reports of experiences and acceptance. *Adolescence, 115,* 515–523.

Rose, L., et al. (2011). Nonconsensual sexual experiences and alcohol consumption among women entering college. *Journal of Interpersonal Violence, 26,* 399–413.

Rosen, R., & Ashton, A. (1993). Prosexual drugs: Empirical status of the "new aphrodisiacs." *Archives of Sexual Behavior, 22,* 521–541.

Rosen, R., & Beck, J. (1988). *Patterns of sexual arousal.* New York: Guilford Press.

Rosen, T. (2006). Sexually transmitted diseases 2006: A dermatologist's view. *Cleveland Clinic Journal of Medicine, 73,* 537–550.

Rosenbaum, J. (2009). Patient teenagers? A comparison of the sexual behavior of virginity pledgers and matched non-pledgers. *Pediatrics, 123,* e110–e120.

Rosenbaum, T. (2011). Addressing anxiety in vivo in physiotherapy treatment of women with severe vaginismus. *Journal of Sex and Marital Therapy, 37,* 89–93.

Rosenberg, D. (2001, January 15). A place of their own. *Newsweek,* 54–55.

Rosenberg, J. (2008). Prevalence of female genital cutting in Egypt. *International Family Planning Perspectives, 34,* 60–61.

Rosenberg, M. (1988, May). Adult behaviors that reflect childhood incest. *Medical Aspects of Human Sexuality,* 114–124.

Rosenberg, M., Hazzard, M., Tallman, C., & Ohl, D. (2006, November). *Evaluation of the prevalence and impact of premature ejaculation in a community practice using the men's sexual health questionnaire.* Paper presented at the Sexual Medicine Society of North America Fall Meeting, New York, NY.

Rosenberger, J., et al. (2012). Sex toy use by gay and bisexual men in the United States. *Archives of Sexual Behavior, 41,* 449–458.

Rosenbloom, S. (2007, October 28). What did you call it? *New York Times.* Retrieved from http://www.nytimes.com/2007/10/28/fashion/28vajayjay.html?

Rosenblum, S. (2011, November 14). The laws of attraction when looking for romance online: Dating sites offer a trove of data about what we really look for in a mate. *International Herald Tribune.*

Rosengarten, A. (2007, April). *The right touch: Enabling sensual touching.* Paper presented at the 18th Congress of the World Association for Sexual Health, Sydney, Australia.

Rosenshein, B. (2007, October). Preventing menopause. *Townsend Letter,* 75–80.

Rosenthal, D., Smith, A., & de Visser, R. (1999). Personal and social factors influencing age at first intercourse. *Archives of Sexual Behavior, 28,* 319–333.

Rosenthal, E. (2006, June 2). Study finds genital cutting can be deadly. *New York Times,* p. F4.

Rosenzweig, J., & Daily, D. (1989). Dyadic adjustment/sexual satisfaction in women and men as a function of psychological sex role self-perception. *Journal of Sex and Marital Therapy, 15,* 42–56.

Rosler, A., & Witztum, E. (1998). Treatment of men with paraphilia with a long-acting analogue of gonadotropin releasing hormone. *New England Journal of Medicine, 338,* 416–422.

Rosman, J., & Resnick, P. (1989). Sexual attraction to corpses: A psychiatric review of necrophilia. *Bulletin of the American Academy of Psychiatry and the Law, 17,* 153–163.

Rospenda, K., et al. (2009). Prevalence and mental health correlates of harassment and discrimination in the workplace: Results from a national study. *Journal of Interpersonal Violence, 24,* 819–843.

Ross, J., et al. (2011). Growth hormone plus childhood low-dose estrogen in Turner's syndrome. *New England Journal of Medicine, 364,* 1230–1234.

Ross, M. (2005). Typing, doing, and being: Sexuality and the Internet. *Journal of Sex Research, 42,* 342–353.

Ross, M., Mansson, S., & Daneback, K. (2011). Prevalence, severity, and correlates of problematic sexual Internet use in Swedish men and women. *Archives of Sexual Behavior,* May 12, 1–8.

Ross, M., Rosser, S., McCurdy, S., & Feldman, J. (2007). The advantages and limitations of seeking sex online: A comparison of reasons given for online and offline sexual liaisons by men who have sex with men. *Journal of Sex Research, 44,* 59–71.

Ross, R. (2008). *State of the industry report 2007–2008.* Canoga Park, CA: Free Speech Coalition.

Rothbart, D. (2011, January 30). He's just not that into anyone. Retrieved from http://nymag.com/print/?news/features/70976

Rothbaum, B., & Jackson, J. (1990). Religious influence on menstrual attitudes and symptoms. *Women and Health, 16*(1), 63–77.

Rothblum, E. (2000). Comments on "Lesbians' sexual activities and efforts to reduce risks for sexually transmitted diseases." *Journal of the Gay and Lesbian Medical Association, 4,* 39.

Rothblum, E., Balsam, K., & Solomon, S. (2011). The longest "legal" U.S. same-sex couples reflect on their relationships. *Journal of Social Issues, 67,* 302–315.

Rotheram, M., & Weiner, N. (1983). Androgyny, stress, and satisfaction. *Sex Roles, 9,* 151–158.

Rothman, E., et al. (2011). Multi-person sex among a sample of adolescent female urban health clinic patients. *Journal of Urban Health,* December 9, doi:10.1007/s11524-011-9630-1

Routh, L. (2000, May). *Inside the mind of a woman: Neuropsychiatric disorders and the impact of hormones throughout the female lifecycle.* Paper presented at a workshop given by the Amen Clinic for Behavioral Medicine, Fairfield, CA.

Rowe, M. (2009, October). The new Cuban revolution. *Advocate,* 62–63.

Rowland, D., Strassberg, D., de Gouveia Brazao, C., & Slob, A. (2000). Ejaculatory latency and control in men with premature ejaculation: An analysis across sexual activities using multiple sources of information. *Journal of Psychosomatic Research, 48,* 69–77.

Rubin, J., Provenzano, F., & Luria, Z. (1974). The eye of the beholder: Parents' views on sex of newborns. *American Journal of Orthopsychiatry, 44,* 512–519.

Rubin, L. (1990). *Erotic wars.* New York: Farrar, Straus and Giroux.

Rubin, R. (2009, February 3). Octuplet birth raises questions. *USA Today,* p. 5D.

Rubin, R. (2010, May 7–9). The pill turns 50. *USA Today,* p. 1A.

Rubin, Z. (1970). Measurement of romantic love. *Journal of Personality and Social Psychology, 16,* 265–273.

Rubin, Z. (1973). *Liking and loving.* New York: Holt, Rinehart and Winston.

Rubinsky, H., Eckerman, D., Rubinsky, E., & Hoover, C. (1987). Early-phase physiological response patterns to psychosexual stimuli: Comparisons of male and female patterns. *Archives of Sexual Behavior, 16,* 45–55.

Rudski, J., Bernstein, L., & Mitchell, J. (2011, May). Effects of menstrual cycle phase on ratings of implicitly erotic art. *Archives of Sexual Behavior,* doi:10.1007/s10508-011-9756-y

Rumstein-McKean, O., & Hunsley, J. (2001). Interpersonal and family functioning of female survivors of childhood sexual abuse. *Clinical Psychology Review, 21,* 471–490.

Ruowei, L. (2002). Prevalence of exclusive breastfeeding among U.S. infants. *American Journal of Public Health, 92,* 1107–1110.

Russell, G., & Richards, J. (2003). Stressor and resilience factors for lesbians, gay men, and bisexuals confronting antigay politics. *American Journal of Community Psychology, 31,* 313–327.

Russell, S., & Toomey, R. (2012). Men's sexual orientation and suicide: Evidence for U.S. adolescent specific risk. *Social Science and Medicine, 74,* 523-529.

Ryan, C., & Futterman, D. (1997). Lesbian and gay youth: Care and counseling. *Adolescent Medicine: State of the Art Reviews, 8,* 221.

Ryan, C., & Futterman, D. (2001). Social and developmental challenges for lesbian, gay, and bisexual youth. *SIECUS Report, 29,* 5–6.

Ryan, C., Hueebner, D., Diaz, R., & Sanchez, J. (2009). Family rejection as a predictor of negative health outcomes in White and Latino lesbian, gay and bisexual young adults. *Pediatrics, 123,* 346–352.

Ryan, C., & Jetha, C. (2010). *Sex at dawn.* New York: HarperCollins.

Ryan, G. (2000). Childhood sexuality: A decade of study. Part I. Research and curriculum development. *Child Abuse and Neglect, 24,* 33–48.

Ryan, G., Miyoshi, T., & Krugman, R. (1988). *Early childhood experience of professionals working in child abuse.* Paper presented at the 17th Annual Symposium on Child Sexual Abuse and Neglect, Keystone, CO.

Ryan, S., Franzetta, K., Manlove, J., & Holcombe, B. (2007). Adolescents' discussions about contraception or STDs with partners before first sex. *Perspectives on Sexual and Reproductive Health, 39,* 149–157.

Ryan, S., Franzetta, K., Manlove, J., & Schelar, E. (2008). Older sexual partners during adolescence: Links to reproductive health outcomes in young adulthood. *Perspectives on Sexual and Reproductive Health, 40,* 17–26.

Ryan-Berg, J. (2011). Organic erectile dysfunction. *Clinician Reviews, 21,* 23–28.

Saad, L. (2011, August 8). Plenty of common ground found in abortion debate. Retrieved from http://www.gallup.com/poll/148880/Plenty-Common-Ground-Found-Abortion-Debate

Sa'ah, R. (2006). Cameroon girls battle "breast ironing." Retrieved June 26, 2006, from http://www.news.bbc.co.uk/2/hi/africa/ 5107360.stm

Saar, M. (2010, April 20). Girl slavery in America. Retrieved from http://www.rebeccaproject.org/index.php?opinion=com

Saario, T., Jacklin, C., & Tittle, C. (1973). Sex role stereotyping in public schools. *Harvard Educational Review, 43,* 386–416.

Sadovsky, R. (2005). Androgen therapy for effects of aging in older men. *American Family Physician, 72,* 170–171.

Sadovsky, R., & Nusbaum, M. (2006). Sexual health inquiry and support is a primary care priority. *Journal of Sexual Medicine, 3,* 3–11.

Saewyc, E., Poon, C., et al. (2008). Stigma management? The links between enacted stigma and teen pregnancy trends among gay, lesbian, and bisexual students in British Columbia. *Canadian Journal of Human Sexuality, 17,* 123–139.

Safren, S., & Heimberg, R. (1999). Depression, hopelessness, suicidality, and related factors in sexual minority and heterosexual adolescents. *Journal of Consulting and Clinical Psychology, 67,* 859–866.

Saidel, R., & Hedgepeth, S. (2010). *Sexual violence against Jewish women during the Holocaust.* Waltham, MA: Brandeis University Press.

Saigal, C., Wessells, H., Pace, J., & Schonlau, M. (2006). Predictors and prevalence of erectile dysfunction in a racially diverse population. *Archives of Internal Medicine, 166,* 207–212.

Salagierski, M., & Schalken, J. (2012). Molecular diagnosis of prostate cancer: PCA3 and TMPRSS2:ERG. *Journal of Urology, 187,* 795–801.

Salam, M. (2012, February 1). Egypt's Muslim Brotherhood says won't require veil, to uphold freedoms. Retrieved from http://bikyamasr.com/55650/egypts-muslim-brotherhood-says-wont-require-veil-to-uphold-freedoms/

Salario, A. (2011, April 18). Anti-sex trade turns to focus on men who buy sex. Retrieved from http://www.womens enews.org/pring/8582

Salber, P. (2010, July 11). Want to look pretty "down there"? Retrieved from http://www.thedoctorweighsin.com/want-to-look-pretty-down-there/

Saleem, A., & Pasha, G. (2008). Women's reproductive autonomy and barriers to contraceptive use in Pakistan. *European Journal of Contraception and Reproductive Health Care, 13,* 83–89.

Salem, R. (2006). New attention to the IUD. *Population Reports,* Series B, No. 7. Baltimore, MD: Johns Hopkins Bloomberg School of Public Health, The INFO Project, February, 47–56.

Salovey, P., & Rodin, J. (1985, September). The heart of jealousy. *Psychology Today,* 22–29.

Salter, D., McMillan, D., Richards, M., et al. (2003). Development of sexually abusive behavior in sexually victimized males: A longitudinal study. *Lancet, 361,* 471–476.

Samantha, J., MacDonald, G., & Atsushsi, S. (2011). Conflicting pressures on romantic commitment for anxiously attached individuals. *Journal of Personality, 79,* 51–74.

Samuels, H. (1997). The relationships among selected demographics and conventional and unconventional sexual behaviors among Black and White heterosexual men. *Journal of Sex Research, 34,* 85–92.

Samuels, L. (2008, September 8). Stay in the closet, or else. *Newsweek,* 8.

Sanchez, D., Kiefer, A., & Ybarra, O. (2006). Sexual submissiveness in women: Costs for sexual autonomy and arousal. *Personality and Social Psychology Bulletin, 32,* 512–524.

Sanchez, J., et al. (2011). Male circumcision and risk of HIV acquisition among men who have sex with men. *AIDS, 25,* 519–523.

Sand, D., Fisher, W., Rosen, R., Eardley, I., & Nadel, N. (2005, July). *ED, constructs of masculinity, and quality of life in the multinational MALES study.* Paper presented at the 17th World Congress of Sexology, Montreal, Canada.

Sanday, P. (1981). The sociocultural context of rape: A cross-cultural study. *Journal of Social Issues, 37,* 5–27.

Sanday, P. (1996). *A woman scorned: Acquaintance rape on trial.* New York: Doubleday.

Sandelowski, M. (1994). Separate but less unequal: Fetal ultrasonography and the transformation of expectant mother/fatherhood. *Gender and Society, 8,* 230–245.

Sanders, G. (2000). Men together: Working with gay couples in contemporary times. In P. Papp (Ed.), *Couples on the fault line.* New York: Guilford Press.

Sanders, S., Graham, C., & Janssen, E. (2003). *Factors affecting sexual arousal in women.* Retrieved March 8, 2003, from http://www.kinseyinstitute.org/research/focus_group.html

Sandnabba, N., Santtila, P., & Nordling, N. (1999). Sexual behavior and social adaptation among sadomasochistically oriented males. *Journal of Sex Research, 36,* 273–282.

Sandnabba, N., Santtila, P., Wannas, M., & Krook, K. (2003). Age and gender specific sexual behaviors in children. *Child Abuse and Neglect, 27,* 579–605.

Sandstrom, E., & Fugl-Meyer, K. (2007, April). *Retarded ejaculation: When the orgasm just becomes a target and never the destination of a pleasure journey.* Paper presented at the 18th Congress of the World Association for Sexual Health, Sydney, Australia.

Santelli, J. (2008). Medical accuracy in sexuality education: Ideology and scientific process. *American Journal of Public Health, 98,* 1786–1792.

Santhya, K., et al. (2010). Associations between early marriage and young women's marital and reproductive health outcomes: Evidence from India. *International Perspectives on Sexual and Reproductive Health, 36*(3), 132–139.

Santilla, P., Sandnabba, K., Alison, L., & Nordling, N. (2002). Investigating the underlying structure in sadomasochistically oriented behavior. *Archives of Sexual Behavior, 31,* 185–196.

Satel, S. (1993). The diagnostic limits of addiction. *Journal of Clinical Psychiatry, 54,* 237.

Satterfield, A., & Muehlenhard, C. (1990, November). *Flirtation in the classroom: Negative consequences on women's perceptions of their ability.* Paper presented at the annual meeting of the Society for the Scientific Study of Sex, Minneapolis, MN.

Saunders, E. (1989). Life-threatening autoerotic behavior: A challenge for sex educators and therapists. *Journal of Sex Education and Therapy, 15,* 77–81.

Sauvageau, A., & Racette, S. (2006). Autoerotic deaths in the literature from 1954 to 2004: A review. *Journal of Forensic Sciences, 51,* 140–146.

Savage, C., & Stolberg, S. (2011, February 23). In shift, U.S. says marriage act blocks gay rights. Retrieved from http://www.nytimes.com/2011/02/24/us/24marriage

Savage, D. (2002, April 17). Justices void law on child sex images. *Oregonian,* pp. A1, A7.

Savage, D., & Miller, T. (Eds.). (2011). *It gets better: Coming out, overcoming bullying, and creating a life worth living.* New York: Dutton.

Savic, I., Berglund, H., & Lindstrom, P. (2005). Brain responses to putative pheromones in homosexual men. *Proceedings of the National Academy of Sciences, 102,* 7356–7361.

Savic, I., & Lindstrom, P. (2008). PET and MRI show differences in cerebral asymmetry and functional connectivity between homosexual and heterosexual subjects. Retrieved September 18, 2008, from http://www.pnas.org/content/105/27/9403

Savin-Williams, R. (2005). *The new gay teenager.* Cambridge, MA: Harvard University Press.

Sawyer, R., Pinciaro, P., & Jessell, J. (1998). Effects of coercion and verbal consent on university students' perception of date rape. *American Journal of Health Behavior, 22,* 46–53.

Sbarra, D. (2006). Predicting the onset of emotional recovery following nonmarital relationship dissolution: Survival analyses of sadness and anger. *Personality and Social Psychology Bulletin, 32,* 298–312.

Schaalma, H., Abraham, C., Gillmore, R., & Kok, G. (2004). Sex education as health promotion: What does it take? *Archives of Sexual Behavior, 33,* 259–269.

Schachner, D., Shaver, P., & Gillath, O. (2008). Attachment style and long-term singlehood. *Personal Relationships, 15,* 479–491.

Schagen, S., et al. (2011). Sibling sex ratio and birth order in early-onset gender dysphoric adolescents. *Archives of Sexual Behavior,* June 15 (e-pub).

Scharma, P., Malhotra, C., Taneja, D., & Saha, R. (2008). Problems related to menstruation among adolescent girls. *Indian Journal of Pediatrics, 75,* 125–129.

Schatz, C., & Robb-Nicholson, C. (2006, April 24). Anatomy of a hot flash. *Newsweek,* 73.

Scheela, R., & Stern, P. (1994). Falling apart: A process integral to the remodeling of male incest offenders. *Archives of Psychiatric Nursing, 8,* 91–100.

Scheidler, A. (2006). The deception of contraception: League takes the lead exposing the abortion-birth control link. Retrieved July 8, 2006, from http://www.prolifeaction.org/news/2006v25n2/contraception.htm

Scher, H. (1997, March/April). The drive to stop harassment in schools. *Ms.,* 22.

Schick, V., Calabrese, S., Rima, B., & Zucker, A. (2010). Genital appearance dissatisfaction: Implications for women's genital image self-consciousness, sexual esteem, sexual satisfaction, and sexual risk. *Psychology of Women's Quarterly, 34,* 394–404.

Schlutter, J. (2011). Therapeutics—New drugs hit the target. *Nature, 474,* S5–S7.

Schmidt, L., et al. (2012). Demographic and medical consequences of the postponement of parenthood. *Human Reproduction, 18,* 29–43.

Schmitt, D. (2003). Universal sex differences in the desire for sexual variety: Tests from 52 nations, 6 continents, and 13 islands. *Journal of Personality and Social Psychology, 85,* 85–104.

Schmitt, D., Realo, A., Voracek, M., & Alik, J. (2008). Why can't a man be more like a woman? Sex differences in Big Five personality traits across 55 cultures. *Journal of Personality and Social Psychology, 94,* 168–182.

Schmitt, D., Shackelford, T., Duntley, J., Tooke, W., & Buss, D. (2001). The desire for sexual variety as a key to understanding basic human mating strategies. *Personal Relationships, 8,* 425–455.

Schnarch, D. (1993, March/April). Inside the sexual crucible. *Networker,* 40–48.

Schoen, E., Anderson, G., Bohon, C., Hinman, F., Poland, R., & Wakeman, E.

(1989). Report of the Task Force on Circumcision. *Pediatrics, 84,* 388–391.

Schoen, J. (2006). *Choice and coercion: Birth control, sterilization, and abortion in public health and welfare.* Chapel Hill: University of North Carolina Press.

Schoen, R., & Cheng, Y. (2006). Partner choice and the differential retreat from marriage. *Journal of Marriage and Family, 68,* 1–10.

Schoofs, M. (1997, June 24). Berlin. *Advocate,* 115–116.

Schooler, D., & Ward, M. (2006). Average Joes: Men's relationships with media, real bodies, and sexuality. *Psychology of Men and Masculinity, 7,* 27–41.

Schooler, D., Ward, L., Merriweather, A., & Caruthers, A. (2005). Cycles of shame: Menstrual shame, body shame, and sexual decision-making. *Journal of Sex Research, 42,* 324–335.

Schover, L. (2000). Sexual problems in chronic illness. In S. Leiblum & R. Rosen (Eds.), *Principles and practice of sex therapy.* New York: Guilford Press.

Schover, L., & Jensen, S. (1988). *Sexuality and chronic illness.* New York: Guilford Press.

Schredl, M., Ciric, P., Gotz, S., & Wittmann, L. (2004). Typical dreams: Stability and gender differences. *Journal of Psychology, 138,* 485–495.

Schroder, M., & Carroll, R. (1999). New women: Sexological outcomes of male-to-female gender reassignment surgery. *Journal of Sex Education and Therapy, 24,* 137–146.

Schrodt, P. (2011). Stepparents' and nonresidential parents' relational satisfaction as a function of coparental communication in stepfamilies. *Journal of Social and Personal Relationships, 28,* 983–1004.

Schroer, K. (2008). When size matters: Genital retraction syndrome in cultural perspective. Retrieved October 30, 2008, from http://www.focusanthro.org/essays0506/schroer0506.htm

Schubach, G. (1996). *Urethral expulsions during sensual arousal and bladder catheterization in seven human females* (Ed.D. thesis). Institute for Advanced Study of Human Sexuality, San Francisco, CA.

Schwartz, G., & Russek, J. (1998). Family love and lifelong health? A challenge for clinical psychology. In D. Routh and R. DeRubein (Eds.), *The science of clinical psychology: Accomplishments and future directions.* Washington, DC: American Psychological Association.

Schwartz, P. (2006, April). *Revitalizing sexuality for mental and physical health.* Paper

presented at the Women's Health Conference, Portland, OR.

Schwartz, R. (2003, May/June). Pathways to sexual intimacy. *Psychotherapy Networker,* 36–43.

Schwarz, M. (2007, August 21). Genital surgery helps Burkina's mutilated women. Retrieved January 7, 2009, from http://www.reuters.com/articlePrint?articleId=USL269289777

Sciolino, E., & Mekhennet, S. (2008a, June 11). In Europe, debate over Islam and virginity. Retrieved June 22, 2008, from http://www.nytimes.com/2008/06/11/world/europe/11virgin.html

Sciolino, E., & Mekhennet, S. (2008b, June 11). Muslim women and virginity: Two worlds collide. *New York Times,* p. A1.

Scott, C., & Cortez, A. (2011). No longer his and hers, but ours: Examining sexual arousal in response to erotic stories designed for both sexes. *Journal of Sex and Marital Therapy, 37,* 165–75.

Scott, L. (2006). An alternative to surgery in treating ectopic pregnancy. *Nursing Times, 102,* 24–26.

Scott, M., et al. (2011). Risky adolescent sexual behavior and reproductive health in young adulthood. *Perspectives on Sexual and Reproductive Health, 43,* 110–118.

Seager, I. (2011, October 24). Adoption by gay and lesbian couples tripled in the last decade. Retrieved from http://ww.glaad.org/blog/adoption-gay-and-lesbian-couples-tripled-last-decade

Seal, B., & Meston, C. (2007). The impact of body awareness on sexual arousal in women with sexual dysfunction. *Journal of Sexual Medicine, 4,* 990–1000.

Seal, D., Bloom, F., & Somlai, A. (2000). Dilemmas in conducting qualitative sex research in applied field settings. *Health Education and Behavior, 27,* 10–23.

Seaman, B., & Seaman, G. (1978). *Women and the crisis in sex hormones.* New York: Bantam Books.

Seepersad, S., Choi, M., & Shin, N. (2008). How does culture influence the degree of romantic loneliness and closeness? *Journal of Psychology, 142,* 209–216.

Seftel, A. (2012). Testosterone gel replacement improves sexual function in depressed men taking serotonergic antidepressants: A randomized, placebo-controlled clinical trial. *Journal of Urology, 187,* 235–236.

Segal, N., & Stohs, J. (2007). Resemblance for age at menarche in female twins reared apart and together. *Human Biology, 79,* 623–634.

Segraves, R., & Segraves, K. (1995). Human sexuality and aging. *Journal of Sex Education and Therapy, 21,* 88–102.

Seibert, C., Barbouche, E., Fagan, J., & Myint, E. (2003). Prescribing oral contraceptives for women older than 35 years of age. *Annals of Internal Medicine, 138,* 54–64.

Seligman, L., & Hardenburg, S. (2000). Assessment and treatment of paraphilias. *Journal of Counseling and Development, 78,* 107–113.

Semaan, S., Klovdahl, A., & Aral, S. (2004). Protecting the privacy, confidentiality, relationships, and medical safety of sex partners in partner notification and management studies. *Journal of Research Administration, 35,* 39–53.

Semans, J. (1956). Premature ejaculation: A new approach. *Southern Medical Journal, 49,* 353–358.

Senn, C., Desmarais, S., Verberg, N., & Wood, E. (1999). Predicting coercive sexual behavior across the lifespan in a random sample of Canadian men. *Journal of Social and Personal Relationships, 17,* 95–113.

Senn, T., et al. (2011). Age of partner at first adolescent intercourse and adult sexual risk behavior among women. *Journal of Women's Health, 26,* 61–66.

Seppa, N. (2005). Defense mechanism: Circumcision averts some HIV infections. *Science News, 168,* 275.

Serefoglu, E., et al. (2011). Prevalence of the complaint of ejaculating prematurely and the four premature ejaculation syndromes. *Journal of Sexual Medicine, 8,* 540–548.

Seto, M., & Lalumiere, M. (2010). What is so special about male adolescent sexual offending? A review and test of explanations through meta-analyses. *Psychological Bulletin, 136,* 526–575.

Setoodeh, R. (2008, July 28). Young, gay and murdered. *Newsweek,* 41–45.

Sevcikova, A., & Daneback, K. (2011). Anyone who wants sex? Seeking sex partners on sex-oriented contact websites. *Sexual and Relationship Therapy, 26,* 170–181.

Shaeer, O. (2011). Trans-corporal incision of Peyronie's plaques. *Journal of Sexual Medicine, 8,* 589–593.

Shafer, E., & Malhotra, N. (2011). The effect of a child's sex on support for traditional gender roles. *Social Forces, 90,* 209–221.

Shafii, T., Stovel, K., & Holmes, K. (2007). Association between condom use at sexual debut and subsequent sexual trajectories.

American Journal of Public Health, 97, 97–103.

Shah, J., & Fisch, H. (2006). Managing the vasectomy patient: From preoperative counseling through postoperative follow-up. *Contemporary Urology, 18,* 40–45.

Shah, K., & Montoya, C. (2007). Do testosterone injections increase libido for elderly hypogonadal patients? *Family Practice, 56,* 301–303.

Shah, N., & Breedlove, S. (2007). Behavioural neurobiology: Females can also be from Mars. *Nature, 448,* 999–1000.

Shah, P., Aliwalas, L., & Shah, V. (2006). Breast-feeding or breast milk for procedural pain in neonates. *Cockrane Database of Systematic Reviews* 2006, Issue 3. Art. No. CD004950. doi:101002/14651858. CD004950.pub2

Shah, S. (2011, July 9). Homosexuality permitted in 113 countries, illegal in 76. Retrieved from http://www.thenews.compk/TodaysPrintDetail.aspx?ID=56851&Cat=2&dt=7/9/2011

Shamliyan, T., MacDonald, R., et al. (2009). Antiviral therapy for adults with chronic hepatitis B: A systematic review for a National Institutes of Health Consensus Development Conference. *Annals of Internal Medicine, 150,* 111–124.

Shamloul, R., & Bella, A. (2011). Impact of cannabis use on male sexual health. *Journal of Sexual Medicine, 8,* 971–975.

Shannon, K., Strathdee, S., Shoveller, J., Rusch, M., Kerr, T., & Tyndall, M. (2009). Structural and environmental barriers to condom use negotiation with clients among female sex workers: Implications for HIV-prevention strategies and policy. *American Journal of Public Health, 99,* 659–665.

Shapiro, K., & Ray, S. (2007). Sexual health for people living with HIV. *Reproductive Health Matters, 15,* 67–92.

Shapiro, R., et al. (2010). Antiretroviral regimens in pregnancy and breast-feeding in Botswana. *New England Journal of Medicine, 362,* 2282–2294.

Shaughnessy, K., et al. (2010). Online sexual activity experience of heterosexual students: Gender similarities and differences. *Archives of Sexual Behavior, 40,* 419–427.

Shaver, F. (2009, June). *The criminal toleration of sex work: Canadian opportunities for positive action.* Paper presented at the 19th WAS World Congress for Sexual Health, Göteborg, Sweden.

Shaver, F., Lewis, J., & Maticka-Tyndale, E. (2011). Rising to the challenge: Addressing the concerns of people working in the

sex industry. *Canadian Review of Sociology, 48,* 47–65.

Shaver, P., Hazan, C., & Bradshaw, D. (1988). Love as attachment: The integration of three behavioral systems. In R. Sternberg & M. Barnes (Eds.), *The psychology of love.* New Haven, CT: Yale University Press.

Shaw, J. (2008). Diagnosis and treatment of testicular cancer. *American Family Physician, 77,* 469–480.

Shaw, T., & Garber, B. (2011). Coloplast Titan inflatable penile prosthesis with one-touch release pump. *Journal of Sexual Medicine, 8,* 310–314.

Shearer, B., Mulvihill, B., Klerman, L., et al. (2002). Association of early childbearing and low cognitive ability. *Perspectives on Sexual and Reproductive Health, 34,* 236–243.

Sheeran, P. (1987). *Women, society, the state, and abortion: A structuralist analysis.* New York: Praeger.

Sheets, V., Fredendall, L., & Claypool, H. (1997). Jealousy evocation, partner reassurance, and relationship stability: An exploration of the potential benefits of jealousy. *Evolution and Human Behavior, 18,* 387–402.

Shell-Duncan, B., et al. (2011). Dynamics of change in the practice of female genital cutting in Senegambia: Testing predictions of social convention theory. *Social Science and Medicine, 73,* 1275–1283.

Shelton, J. D. (2010). Masturbation: Breaking the silence. *International Perspectives on Sexual and Reproductive Health, 36,* 157–158.

Sheppard, K. (2011). Then they came for your birth control. Retrieved from http://motherjones.com/print/143621

Sherfey, M. (1972). *The nature and evolution of female sexuality.* New York: Random House.

Sherkat, D., et al. (2011). Religion, politics, and support for same-sex marriage in the United States, 1988–2008. *Social Science Research, 40,* 167–180.

Sherman, M. (2008, May 20). Court sides with limits on Internet child porn. *Oregonian,* p. A1.

Shernoff, M. (2006). The heart of a virtual hunter. *Gay and Lesbian Review Worldwide, 13,* 20–23.

Shiels, M., et al. (2011). Proportions of Kaposi sarcoma, selected non-Hodgkin lymphomas, and cervical cancer in the United States occurring in persons with AIDS, 1980–2007. *Journal of the American Medical Association, 305*(14), 1450–1459.

Shih, G., Turok, D., & Parker, W. (2011). Vasectomy: The other (better) form of sterilization. *Contraception, 83,* 310–315.

Shihri, A. (2007, December 18). Saudi king pardons rape victim sentenced to prison. *Oregonian,* p. A6.

Shimonaka, Y., Nakazato, K., Kawaai, C., & Sato, S. (1997). Androgyny and successful adaptation across the life span among Japanese adults. *Journal of Genetic Psychology, 158,* 389–400.

Shindel, A., & Moser, C. (2011). Why are the paraphilias mental disorders? *Journal of Sexual Medicine, 8,* 927–929.

Shook, N., Gerrity, D., Jurich, J., & Segrist, A. (2000). Courtship violence among college students: A comparison of verbally and physically abusive couples. *Journal of Family Violence, 15,* 1–22.

Shortridge, E., & Miller, K. (2007). Contraindications to oral contraceptive use among women in the United States, 1999–2001. *Contraception, 75,* 355–360.

Shrestha, A., et al. (2011). Smoking and alcohol use during pregnancy and age of menarche in daughters. *Human Reproduction, 26,* 259–265.

Shrier, L., Pierce, J., Emans, S., & DuRant, R. (1998). Gender differences in risk behaviors associated with forced or pressured sex. *Archives of Pediatric and Adolescent Medicine, 152,* 57–63.

Shtarkshall, R. (2005, July). *Conducting sex therapy in a cross-cultural environment: When the paradigm of the therapy and the worldview of the clients mismatch.* Paper presented at the World Congress of Sexology, Montreal, Canada.

Shtarkshall, R., Santelli, J., & Hirsch, J. (2007). Sex education and sexual socialization: Roles for educators and parents. *Perspectives on Sexual and Reproductive Health, 39,* 116–119.

Shulman, J., Gotta, G., & Green, R. (2012). Will marriage matter? Effects of marriage anticipated by same-sex couples. *Journal of Family Issues, 33,* 158–181.

Shuntich, R., Loh, D., & Katz, D. (1998). Some relationships among affection, aggression, and alcohol abuse in the family setting. *Perceptual Motor Skills, 86,* 1051–1060.

Sigal, A., et al. (2011). Cell-to-cell spread of HIV permits ongoing replication despite antiretroviral therapy. *Nature, 477,* 95–98.

Signorile, M. (1995). *Outing yourself.* New York: Fireside.

Signorile, M. (2009, April). Of pastors and politicians. *Advocate,* 48–52.

Signorile, M. (2011, January). The bully pulpit. *Advocate,* 22–23.

Silverberg, C. (2008a). Spontaneous orgasms: A rare sexual side effect of antidepressants. Retrieved November 29, 2008, from http://www.sexuality.about .com/od/sexualsideeffects/a/orgasm_ spontane.htm?=1

Silverberg, C. (2008b). Morning erections: Definition, causes, and problems with morning erections. Retrieved November 1, 2008, from http://www.about.com/od/ malesexualanatomy/a/morning_ erection .htm?r=qI

Silverglate, S., & Paskievitch, B. (2008). Don't get mad, get even: Practical strategies for dealing with retaliation claims by the plaintiff-employee. *Defense Counsel Journal, 75,* 388–399.

Silverman, J., et al. (2011). Coercive forms of sexual risk and associated violence perpetrated by male partners of female adolescents. *Perspectives on Sexual and Reproductive Health, 43,* 60–65.

Silverman, J., Decker, M., Jhumka, G., Dharmadhikari, A., Seage, G., & Raj, A. (2008). Syphilis and hepatitis B co-infection among HIV-infected, sex-trafficked women and girls, Nepal. *Emerging Infectious Diseases, 14,* 932–935.

Silvertsen, C. (2000). Court: Discard embryos. Retrieved June 2, 2000, from http://abcnews.go.com/sections/us/ DailyNews/embryos000602.html

Simon, H. (2010, January 1). On call: Inhibited ejaculation. *Harvard Men's Health Watch.*

Simon, S. (2012, March 5). States slash birth control subsidies as federal debate rages. Retrieved from http://www.reuters.com/assets/ print?aid=USTRE8240ZM2012035

Simons, D., Wurtele, S., & Durham, R. (2008). Developmental experiences of child sexual abusers and rapists. *Child Abuse and Neglect, 32,* 549–560.

Simonson, K., & Subich, L. (1999). Rape perceptions as a function of gender-role traditionality and victim-perpetrator association. *Sex Roles, 40,* 617–633.

Simpson, V., & Winfield, N. (2010, November 24). Pope finds condoms "lesser evil" in HIV fight. *Oregonian,* pp. A1, A9.

Sinclair, D., & Kligman, E. (2005). Do antiaging approaches promote longevity? *Patient Care, 39,* 10–17.

Sinderbrand, R. (2005, March 28). A shameful little secret: North Carolina confronts its history of forced sterilization. *Newsweek,* 33.

Singer, L. (2002). Cognitive and motor outcomes of cocaine-exposed infants. *Journal of the American Medical Association, 287,* 1952–1960.

Singh, S., & Darroch, J. (2000). Adolescent pregnancy and childbearing levels and trends in developed countries. *Family Planning Perspectives, 32,* 14–23.

Singh, V., Saunders, C., Wylie, L., & Bourke, A. (2008). New diagnostic techniques for breast cancer detection. *Future Oncology, 4,* 501–503.

Sinnott, J. (1986). *Sex roles and aging: Theory and research from a systems perspective.* Basel, Switzerland: Karger.

Sipe, A. (1990). *A secret world: Sexuality and the search for celibacy.* New York: Brunner/ Mazel.

Skolnick, A. (1992). *The intimate environment: Exploring marriage and the family.* New York: HarperCollins.

Skovdal, M. (2011). Picturing the coping strategies of caregiving children in Western Kenya: From images to action. *American Journal of Public Health, 101,* 452–453.

Slaetan, W. (2009, February 22). This is the way the culture wars end. *New York Times,* 11.

Slatkoff, S., et al. (2011). PSA testing, when it's useful and when it's not: Routine PSA testing leads to more diagnoses of prostate cancer, but does not save lives. *Journal of Family Practice, 60,* 357–360.

Slijper, F., Drop, S., Molenaar, J., & Keizer-Schrama, S. (1998). Long-term psychological evaluation of intersex children. *Archives of Sexual Behavior, 27,* 125–143.

Smeltzer, S., & Kelley, C. (1997). Multiple sclerosis. In M. Sipski & C. Alexander (Eds.), *Sexual function in people with disability and chronic illness.* Gaithersburg, MD: Aspen Publishers.

Smith, A., et al. (2011). Sexual and relationship satisfaction among heterosexual men and women: The importance of desired frequency of sex. *Journal of Sex and Marital Therapy, 37,* 104–115.

Smith, D., et al. (2011). Interim guidance: Pre-exposure prophylaxis for the prevention of HIV infection in men who have sex with men. *Morbidity and Mortality Weekly Report, 60,* 65–68.

Smith, D., & Over, R. (1987). Correlates of fantasy-induced and film-induced male sexual arousal. *Archives of Sexual Behavior, 16,* 395–409.

Smith, J., Hawkinson, K., & Paull, K. (2011). Spoiled milk: An experimental examination of bias against mothers who breastfeed. *Personality and Social Psychology Bulletin, 37,* 867–878.

Smith, K., & Pukall, C. (2011). A systematic review of relationship adjustment and sexual satisfaction among women with provoked vestibulodynia. *Journal of Sex Research, 48,* 166–192.

Smith, M. (2011, October). Not your mother's birth control, same troubles. Paper presented at the 139th American Public Health Association Annual Meeting, Washington, DC.

Smith, P., & Roberts, C. (2009). American College Health Association annual Pap test and sexually transmitted infection survey: 2006. *Journal of American College Health, 57,* 389–395.

Smith, R., Aboitiz, F., Schroter, C., et al. (2005). Relative size versus controlling for size: Interpretation of ratios in research on sexual dimorphism in the human corpus callosum. *Current Anthropology, 46,* 249–273.

Smith, T. (2011, April). *Cross-national differences in attitudes towards homosexuality* (GSS Cross-national Report No. 31). NORC/University of Chicago. Retrieved from http://williamsinstitute.law.ucla.edu/wp-content/uploads/Smith-Cross National-NORC-May-2011.pdf

Smith, W. (2005). Reducing teen pregnancy. *Issues in Science and Technology, 21,* 18–19.

Snabes, M., & Simes, S. (2009). Approved hormonal treatments for HSDD: An unmet medical need. *Journal of Sexual Medicine,* April 24 (e-pub).

Soguel, D. (2008). Mass stigma scars Congo's rape survivors. Retrieved October 11, 2008, from http://www.womensenews.org

Soguel, D. (2010, October 12). In Syria, Iraqi refugee daughters risk being sold. Retrieved from http://womensenews.org/story/war/101011/in-syria-iraqi-refugee-daughters-risk-being-sold

Solinger, R. (2005). *Pregnancy and power: A short history of reproductive politics in America.* New York: New York University Press.

Solmonese, J. (2005, December 15). Fairness at Ford and beyond. Retrieved May 24, 2006, from http://www.advocate.com/print_article_ektid23468.asp

Solomini, C. (1991, May). Cures for yeast infections. *New Woman,* 129.

Somers, C., & Surmann, A. (2004). Adolescents' preferences for source of sex education. *Child Study Journal, 34,* 47–59.

Sonenstein, F., Pleck, J., & Ku, L. (1991). Levels of sexual activity among adolescent males in the United States. *Family Planning Perspectives, 23,* 162–167.

Song, A., & Halpern-Felsher, B. (2011). Predictive relationships between adolescent oral and vaginal sex. *Archives of Pediatrics and Adolescent Medicine, 165,* 243–249.

Song, Y., Hwang, K., et al. (2009). Innervation of vagina: Microdissection and immunohistochemical study. *Journal of Sex and Marital Therapy, 35,* 144–153.

Sontag, S. (1972, September 23). The double standard of aging. *Saturday Review,* 29–38.

Sorenson, R. (1973). *Adolescent sexuality in contemporary America.* New York: World.

Sormanti, M., & Shibusawa, T. (2008). Intimate partner violence among midlife and older women: A descriptive analysis of women seeking medical services. *Health and Social Work, 33,* 33–41.

Sorrells, M., Snyder, J., Reiss, M., et al. (2007). Fine-touch pressure thresholds in the adult penis. *British Journal of Urology, 99,* 864–869.

Sorsoli, L., Kia-Keating, M., & Grossman, F. (2008). "I keep that hush-hush": Male survivors of sexual abuse and the challenges of disclosure. *Journal of Counseling Psychology, 55,* 333–345.

Span, S., & Vidal, L. (2003). Cross-cultural differences in female university students' attitudes toward homosexuals: A preliminary study. *Psychological Reports, 92,* 565–572.

Spencer, T., & Tan, J. (1999). Undergraduate students' reactions to analogue male disclosure of sexual abuse. *Journal of Child Sexual Abuse, 8,* 73–90.

Spensley, A., Sripipatana, T., et al. (2009). Preventing mother-to-child transmission of HIV in resource-limited settings. *American Journal of Public Health, 99,* 631–637.

Speroff, L., & Fritz, M. (2005). *Clinical gynecologic endocrinology and infertility* (7th ed.). Philadelphia: Lippincott Williams and Wilkins.

Spitzberg, B. (1999). An analysis of empirical estimates of sexual aggression, victimization, and perpetration. *Violence and Victims, 14,* 241–260.

Spitzer, J. (2011, October 6). Trailblazing state law on human-traffic bogs down. Retrieved from http://www.womens enews.org/print/8795

Spivey, A. (2010). Light at night and breast cancer risk worldwide. *Environmental Health Perspective, 118,* 525–535.

Splete, H. (2011). U.S. teen birth rates tumble to record lows. *OB.GYN. News, 46,* 12.

Sprague, B., Trentham-Dietz, A., & Egan, K. (2008). Proportion of invasive breast cancer attributable to risk factors modifiable

after menopause. *American Journal of Epidemiology, 168,* 404–411.

Sprecher, S. (1998). Insiders' perspectives on reasons for attraction to a close other. *Social Psychology Quarterly, 61,* 287–300.

Sprecher, S. (2002). Sexual satisfaction in premarital relationships: Associations with satisfaction, love, commitment, and stability. *Journal of Sex Research, 39,* 190–196.

Sprecher, S., & Fehr, B. (2011). Dispositional attachment and relationship-specific attachment as predictors of compassionate love for a partner. *Journal of Social and Personal Relationships, 28,* 558–574.

Sprecher, S., Harris, G., & Meyers, A. (2008). Perceptions of sources of sex education and targets of communication: Sociodemographic and cohort effects. *Journal of Sex Research, 45,* 17–26.

Sprecher, S., & McKinney, K. (1993). *Sexuality.* Newbury Park, CA: Sage.

Sprecher, S., Metts, S., Burleson, B., Hatfield, E., & Thompson, A. (1995). Domains of expressive interaction in intimate relationships: Associations with satisfaction and commitment. *Family Relations, 44,* 203–210.

Sprecher, S., & Regan, P. (1998). Passionate and companionate love in courting and young married couples. *Sociological Inquiry, 68,* 163–185.

Sprecher, S., Sullivan, Q., & Hatfield, E. (1994). Mate selection preferences: Gender differences examined in a national sample. *Journal of Personality and Social Psychology, 66,* 1074–1080.

Springen, K. (2003, January 13). New year, new breasts? *Newsweek,* 65–66.

Springen, K. (2005, February 7). The miscarriage maze. *Newsweek,* 63.

Springen, K. (2007, June 11). Indecent exposure? *Newsweek,* 49.

Springen, K. (2008, February 25). Get your sperm moving. *Newsweek,* 59.

Spruyt, A., Steiner, M., Joanis, C., et al. (1998). Identifying condom users at risk for breakage and slippage: Findings from three international sites. *American Journal of Public Health, 88,* 239–244.

Sreekumar, A., Poisson, L., et al. (2009). Metabolomic profiles delineate potential role for sarcosine in prostate cancer progression. *Nature, 457,* 910–914.

Stadler, J., & Saethre, E. (2011). Blockage and flow: Intimate experiences of condoms and microbicides in a South African clinical trial. *Culture, Health, and Sexuality, 13,* 31–44.

Staines, R. (2009). *Lancet* calls for pope to retract comments about condoms and HIV/AIDS. *Lancet, 373,* 1054.

Stander, V., Olson, C., & Merrill, L. (2002). Self-definition as a survivor of childhood sexual abuse among navy recruits. *Journal of Consulting and Clinical Psychology, 70,* 369–377.

Stanford, J. (2012, March 14). Rick Perry's war on Texas women. Retrieved from http://www.huffingtonpost.com/jason-stanford/rick-perry-women_b_1340720.html

Stanicic, A., & Jokic-Begic, N. (2010). Psychophysical characteristics of the premenstrual period. *Collegium Antropologicum, 34,* 1421–1425.

Stanley, D. (1993). To what extent is the practice of autoerotic asphyxia related to other paraphilias? In K. Haas & A. Haas (Eds.), *Understanding sexuality.* St. Louis: Mosby.

Staples, J., et al. (2011). Avoiding experiences: Sexual dysfunction in women with a history of sexual abuse in childhood and adolescence. *Archives of Sexual Behavior,* June 11, 1–10.

Stark, C. (2005). Behavioral effects of stimulation of the medial amygdala in the male rat are modified by prior experience. *Journal of General Psychology, 132,* 207–224.

Staropoli, C., Flaws, J., Bush, T., & Moulton, A. (1997). *Cigarette smoking and frequency of menopausal hot flashes.* Abstract for the 30th Annual Meeting of the Society for Epidemiologic Research, Edmonton, Alberta, Canada, 71.

Starr, B., & Weiner, M. (1981). *The Starr Weiner report on sex and sexuality in the mature years.* New York: Stein and Day.

Staten, C. (1997). "Roofies": The new "date rape" drug of choice. *Emergency Net News,* October 21.

Steele, J. (1999). Teenage sexuality and media practice: Factoring in the influences of family, friends, and school. *Journal of Sex Research, 36,* 331–341.

Steer, A., & Tiggemann, M. (2008). The role of self-objectification in women's sexual functioning. *Journal of Social and Clinical Psychology, 27,* 205–225.

Steggall, M., Fowler, C., & Pryce, A. (2008). Combination therapy for premature ejaculation: Results of a small-scale study. *Sexual and Relationship Therapy, 23,* 365–376.

Stein, D., Baer, M., & Bruemmer, N. (2008). Sexual and emotional health in men. *Annals of the American Psychotherapy Association, 11,* 20–26.

Stein, E. (1999). *The mismeasure of desire.* Oxford: Oxford University Press.

Stein, R. (2011, October 7). Task force discounts PSA test for cancer. *Oregonian,* pp. A1, A6.

Steinberg, B. (2010, December 8). Now safe for TV: Female desire. Retrieved from http://adage.com/print?article_id=147517

Steinberg, J., & Finer, L. (2011). Examining the association of abortion history and current mental health: A reanalysis of the National Comorbidity survey using a common-risk-factors model. *Social Science and Medicine, 72,* 72–82.

Steinbrook, R. (2008). The AIDS epidemic—A progress report from Mexico City. *New England Journal of Medicine, 359,* 885–887.

Steinem, G. (1998). Erotic and pornography: A clear and present difference. In R. Baird & S. Rosenbaum (Eds.), *Pornography: Private right or public menace?* Amherst, NY: Prometheus Books.

Steiner, M., Pearlstein, T., Cohen, L., & Endicott, J. (2006). Expert guidelines for the treatment of severe PMS, PMDD, and comorbidities: The role of SSRIs. *Journal of Women's Health, 15,* 57–69.

Stener-Victorin, E., Waldenstrom, U., & Tagnfors, U. (2000). Effects of electro-acupuncture on anovulation in women with polycystic ovary syndrome. *Acta Obstetricia et Gynecologica Scandinavica, 79,* 180–188.

Stephen, T., & Harrison, T. (1985). A longitudinal comparison of couples with sex-typical and non-sex-typical orientation to intimacy. *Sex Roles, 12,* 195–206.

Stephenson, J. (2011). Study halted: No benefit seen from antiretroviral pill in preventing HIV in women. *Journal of the American Medical Association, 305,* 1952.

Stephenson, R. (2010). Community-level gender equity and extramarital sexual risk-taking among married men in eight African countries. *International Perspectives on Sexual and Reproductive Health, 36,* 178–188.

Stermac, L., Sheridan, P., Davidson, A., & Dunn, S. (1996). Sexual assault of adult males. *Journal of Interpersonal Violence, 11,* 52–64.

Sternberg, R. (1986). A triangular theory of love. *Psychological Review, 93,* 119–135.

Sternberg, R. (1988). Triangulating love. In R. Sternberg & M. Barnes (Eds.), *The psychology of love.* New Haven, CT: Yale University Press.

Steuber, K., & Solomon, D. (2008). Relational uncertainty, partner interference and infertility. *Journal of Social and Personal Relationships, 25,* 831–855.

Stevens, A. (2008, July 16). White House defines contraception as abortion. Retrieved November 22, 2008, from http://www.womensenews.org/article.cfm/dyn/aid/3672

Stewart, D. (2011). Depression during pregnancy. *New England Journal of Medicine, 365,* 1605–1611.

Stewart, G. (1998). Intrauterine devices (IUDs). In R. Hatcher, J. Trussell, F. Stewart, et al. (Eds.), *Contraceptive technology.* New York: Ardent Media.

Stewart, G., & Carignan, C. (1998). Female and male sterilization. In R. Hatcher, J. Trussell, F. Stewart, et al. (Eds.), *Contraceptive technology.* New York: Ardent Media.

Stier, D., Leventhal, J., Berg, A., Johnson, L., & Mezger, J. (1993). Are children born to young mothers at increased risk of maltreatment? *Pediatrics, 91,* 642–648.

Stites, J. (2007, August). Dyke porn's new mastermind. *Advocate,* 22.

Stock, W. (1985, September). *The effect of pornography on women.* Paper presented at a hearing of the Attorney General's Commission on Pornography, Houston, TX.

Stockdale, C., Sauter, M., & Alazaraki, M. (2011, August 30). Oklahoma tops list of highest divorce rate. Retrieved from http://www.msnbc.msn.com/cleanprint/CleanPrintProxy.aspx?unique=1314715480078

Stoler, L., Quina, K., DePrince, A., & Freyd, J. (2001). Recovered memories. In J. Worrell (Ed.), *Encyclopedia of women and gender* (Vol. 2). San Diego, CA: Academic Press.

Stoller, R. (1977). Sexual deviations. In F. Beach (Ed.), *Human sexuality in four perspectives.* Baltimore, MD: Johns Hopkins University Press.

Stoller, R. (1982). Transvestism in women. *Archives of Sexual Behavior, 11,* 99–115.

Stoller, R., & Herdt, G. (1985). Theories of origins of male homosexuality: A cross-cultural look. *Archives of General Psychiatry, 42,* 399–404.

Stone, J., Ferrara, L., Kamrath, J., & Getrajdam, J. (2008). Contemporary outcomes with the latest 1000 cases of multifetal pregnancy reduction. *American Journal of Obstetrics and Gynecology, 199,* 406–408.

Stone, N., & Ingham, R. (2002). Factors affecting British teenagers' contraceptive use at first intercourse: The importance of partner communication. *Perspectives on Sexual and Reproductive Health, 34,* 191–197.

Stoop, D., Nekkebroeck, J., & Devroey, P. (2011). A survey on the intentions and attitudes towards oocyte cryopreservation for non-medical reasons among women of reproductive age. *Human Reproduction, 26,* 655–661.

Stotland, N. (1998). *Abortion facts and feelings.* Washington, DC: American Psychiatric Press.

Stout, H. (2011, November 6). Less "he said, she said" in sex harassment cases. *New York Times,* p. 10.

Strassberg, D. (2007, April). *Dealing with premature ejaculation.* Paper presented at the 18th Congress of the World Association for Sexual Health, Sydney, Australia.

Straus, J. (2006). *Unhooked generation: The truth about why we're still single.* New York: Hyperion.

Strauss, J. (2011). Contextual influences on women's health concerns and attitudes toward menopause. *Health and Social Work, 36,* 121–127.

Streib, L. (2011, September 26). The worst places to be a woman. *Newsweek,* 30–32.

Striar, S., & Bartlik, B. (2000). Stimulation of the libido: The use of erotica in sex therapy. *Psychiatric Annals, 29,* 60–62.

Strickland, S. (2008). Female sex offenders. *Journal of Interpersonal Violence, 23,* 474–489.

Stringer, E., Chi, B., Chintu, N., et al. (2008). Monitoring effectiveness of programmes to prevent mother-to-child HIV transmission in lower-income countries. *Bulletin of the World Health Organization, 86,* 57–62.

Struckman-Johnson, C., & Struckman-Johnson, D. (2000). Sexual coercion rates in seven midwestern prison facilities for men. *Prison Journal, 80,* 379–390.

Struckman-Johnson, C., Struckman-Johnson, D., & Anderson, P. (2003). Tactics of sexual coercion: When men and women won't take no for an answer. *Journal of Sex Research, 40,* 76–86.

Stuart, F., Hammond, C., & Pett, M. (1998). Inhibited sexual desire in women. *Archives of Sexual Behavior, 16,* 91–106.

Stubbs, K. (1992). *Sacred orgasms.* Berkeley, CA: Secret Garden.

Stulhofer, A., & Ajdukovi?, D. (2011). Should we take anodyspareunia seriously? A descriptive analysis of pain during receptive anal intercourse in young heterosexual women. *Journal of Sex and Marital Therapy, 37,* 346–358.

Sturdee, D., Sitruk-Ware, R., de Villiers, T., & Pines, A. (2008, August 22). WISDOM study: Reconfirming improved quality of life in all HRT users. Press statement issued on behalf of the International Menopause Society.

Subrahmanyam, K., & Greenfield, P. (2008). Online communication and adolescent relationships. *Future of Children, 18,* 119–146.

Suligoi, B. (1997). The natural history of human immuno-deficiency virus infection among women as compared with men. *Sexually Transmitted Diseases, 24,* 77–83.

Sullivan, A. (1996, June 3). Let gays marry. *Newsweek,* 26.

Sullivan, A. (2011, July 25). Why gay marriage is good for straight America. *Newsweek,* 12–14.

Sullivan, M. (2005). Abstinence pledges don't protect against STDs. *Family Practice, 35,* 24.

Sun, C., Bridges, A., Wosnitzer, R., Scharrer, E., & Liberman, R. (2008). A comparison of male and female directors in popular pornography: What happens when women are at the helm? *Psychology of Women Quarterly, 32,* 312–325.

Sundt, M. (1994). *Identifying the attitudes and beliefs that accompany sexual harassment* (Doctoral dissertation). University of California, Los Angeles.

Sung, T., Chen, P., Lee, L., Lin, Y., & Hsieh, G. (2007). Increased standardized incidence ratio of breast cancer in female electronics workers. *BMC Public Health, 7,* 102.

Sungur, M. (2007, April). *Management of sexual disorders: Does being Muslim make any difference?* Paper presented at the 18th Congress of the World Association for Sexual Health, Sydney, Australia.

Susman, J. (2011). The perils of PSA screening: Prostate-specific antigen. *Journal of Family Practice, 60,* 319–320.

Swaab, D., Gooren, L., & Hoffman, M. (1995). Brain research, gender, and sexual orientation. *Journal of Homosexuality, 28,* 283–301.

Swami, V., & Furnham, A. (2008). *The psychology of physical attraction.* New York: Routledge.

Swiss, S., & Giller, J. (1993). Rape as a crime of war. *Journal of the American Medical Association, 270,* 612–615.

Symons, J., et al. (2011). Quality of life changes following radical prostatectomy: A prospective comparison of robotic and open techniques. *Journal of Urology, 185,* e63–e64.

Sytsma, M., & Taylor, D. (2008). Fake an orgasm? *Marriage Partnership, 25,* 45–46.

Szabo, L. (2012). The AIDS epidemic: Is it the beginning of the end? *USA Today,* July 18, A1.

Szalavitz, M. (2012, March 26). Plan B: 1 in 5 pharmacists may deny eligible teens access to emergency contraception. Retrieved from http://healthland.time. com/2012/03/26/plan-b-1-in-5-pharmacists-may-deny-eligible-teens-access-to-emergency-contraception

Szymanski, D., & Gupta, A. (2009). Examining the relationship beween multiple internalized oppressions and African American lesbian, gay, bisexual, and questioning persons' self-esteem and psychological distress. *Journal of Counseling Psychology, 56,* 110–118.

Tabak, B., et al. (2011). Oxytocin indexes relational distress following interpersonal harms in women. *Psychoneuroendocrinology, 36,* 115–122.

Tag-Eldin, M., Gadallah, M., Al-Tayeb, M., et al. (2008). Prevalence of female genital cutting among Egyptian girls. *Bulletin of the World Health Organization, 86,* 269–276.

Talbott, J. (2007). Size matters: The number of prostitutes and the global HIV/AIDS pandemic. *PLoS One, 6,* e543.

Talmadge, E. (2007, April 25). GIs frequented Japan's "comfort women." Retrieved June 6, 2009, from http://www.washingtonpost.com/wp-dyn/content/article/2007/04/25/AR2007042501801.html

Tamar-Mattis, A. (2011). Leave intersex out of the DSM-V. *Hastings Center Report, 41,* 1–3.

Tamimi, I. (2011, August 22). Child bride in Jordan puts daughter on same path. Retrieved from http://www.comensenews.org/story/marriagedivorde/110821

Tang, N., Zhou, B., Wang, B., & Yu, R. (2009). Coffee consumption and risk of breast cancer: A meta-analysis. *American Journal of Obstetrics and Gynecology, 200,* 290e1–290e9.

Taormino, T. (2011). *The secrets of great G-spot orgasms and female ejaculation.* Beverly, MA: Quiver.

Tarkovsky, S. (2006, March 19). Sperm taste: 10 simple tips for better tasting semen. Retrieved January 1, 2009, from http://ezinearticles.com/?Sperm-Taste-10-Simple-Tips-For-Better-Tasting-Semen

Task Force on Circumcision. (1999). Circumcision policy statement. *Pediatrics, 103,* 686–693.

Tasker, F. (2011, June 5). Thirty years of HIV: Toll falls, cases dip. *Oregonian,* pp. A1, A8.

Tauber, M., Smith, K., & Fields-Meyer, T. (2005). Abstinence: Can sex wait? *People Weekly, 63,* 94–95.

Tavernise, S. (2011, May 26). Married couples are no longer a majority, census finds. Retrieved from http://www.nytimes.com/2011/05/26/us/26marry.html?_r=1

Tavris, C. (2005). Brains, biology, science, and skepticism: On thinking about sex differences (again). *Skeptical Inquirer, 29,* 11–12.

Tay, N. (2010, November 28). 37% of S. African men admit to rape in study. *Oregonian,* p. A12.

Taylor, B., Sobieszczyk, M., et al. (2008). The challenge of HIV-1 subtype diversity. *New England Journal of Medicine, 358,* 1590–1602.

Taylor, E., & Sharkey, L. (2003). *The big bang.* New York: Plume.

Taylor, G., & Ussher, J. (2001). Making sense of S & M: A discourse analytic account. *Sexualities, 4,* 293–314.

Taylor, H., & Manson, J. (2011). Update in hormone therapy use in menopause. *Journal of Clinical Endocrinology and Metabolism, 96,* 255–264.

Taylor, J. (1971). Introduction. In R. Haber & C. Eden (Eds.), *Holy living* (Rev. ed.). New York: Adler.

Taylor, J. (1995, September). The long, hard days of Dr. Dick. *Esquire,* 120–123.

Taylor, L. (2005). All for him: Articles about sex in American lad magazines. *Sex Roles: A Journal of Research, 52,* 153–164.

Taylor, L., et al. (2011). "Out of my league": A real-world test of the matching hypothesis. *Personality and Social Psychology Bulletin, 37,* 942–954.

Taylor, R. (1970). *Sex in history.* New York: Harper and Row.

Teich, M. (2006, March/April). Love but don't touch. *Psychology Today,* 81–86.

Templeman, T., & Sinnett, R. (1991). Patterns of sexual arousal and history in a "normal" sample of young men. *Archives of Sexual Behavior, 20,* 137–150.

Templeton, A., & Grimes, D. (2011). A request for abortion. *New England Journal of Medicine, 365,* 2198–2204.

Tenkorang, E., & Matick-Tyndale, E. (2008). Factors influencing the timing of first sexual intercourse among young people in Nzanza, Kenya. *International Family Planning Perspectives, 34.*

Terada, N., Kulkami, P., & Getzenberg, R. (2011). CRY61 is a potential serum marker for identifying non-organ-confined prostate cancer. *Journal of Urology, 185,* e54.

Terrance, C., Logan, A., & Peters, D. (2004). Perceptions of peer sexual harassment among high school students. *Sex Roles: A Journal of Research, 51,* 479–490.

Terry, G. (2007, April). *Sex, celibacy and masculinities.* Paper presented at the 18th Congress of the World Association for Sexual Health, Sydney, Australia.

Thanasiu, P. (2004). Childhood sexuality: Discerning healthy from abnormal sexual behaviors. *Journal of Mental Health Counseling, 26,* 309–319.

Thomas, J. (2009). Abortion or pill access is associated with lower birthrates among minors. *Perspectives on Sexual and Reproductive Health, 41,* 65–75.

Thomas, S. (2012, March 3). The gray divorcés. Retrieved from http://online.wsj.com/article/SB10001424052970203753704577255230471480276.html

Thomas, T. (2008). The new papillomavirus (HPV) vaccine: Pros and cons for pediatric and adolescent health. *Pediatric Nursing, 34,* 429–431.

Thompson, E. (2008, March 17). Slavery in our times. *Newsweek,* 64.

Thompson, K., et al. (2011). Contraceptive policies affect post-abortion provision of long-acting reversible contraception. *Contraception, 83,* 41–47.

Thorup, J., et al. (2011). The challenge of early surgery for cryptorchidism. *Scandinavian Journal of Urology and Nephrology, 45,* 184–189.

Throckmorton, W. (2011, October 27). The Jones and Yarhouse study: What does it mean? Retrieved from http://wthrockmorton.com/2011/10/27/the-jones-amd-yarhouse-study-what-does-it-mean/

Thukral, J. (2008). Sex workers need safety, not prosecutors. Retrieved March 16, 2008, from Women's eNews.

Thunyarat, A., et al. (2011). Management of chronic prostatitis/chronic pelvic pain: A systematic review and network meta-analysis. *Journal of the American Medical Association, 305,* 78–86.

Tiefer, L. (1995). *Sex is not a natural act and other essays.* Boulder, CO: Westview Press.

Tiefer, L. (2011). New View Campaign. Retrieved December 13, 2011, from http://www.newviewcampaign.org

Tierney, J. (2008, October 3). Gender gap research shakes up theories. *Oregonian,* p. E2.

Times Digest. (2009, January 22). Justices let stand Internet decision, p. 3.

Timm, T., & Kelley, M. (2011). The effects of differentiation of self, adult attachment, and sexual communication on sexual and marital satisfaction: A path analysis. *Journal of Sex and Marital Therapy, 37,* 206–223.

Timpson, S., et al. (2010). Sexual activity in HIV-positive American crack cocaine smokers. *Archives of Sexual Behavior, 39,* 1353–1358.

Tjaden, P., & Thoennes, N. (1998). *Prevalence, incidence, and consequences of violence against women: Findings from the National Violence Against Women Survey.* Washington, DC: National Institutes of Justice.

Tobey, J., et al. (2011). Demographic differences in adolescents' sexual attitudes and behaviors, parent communication about sex, and school sex education. *Electronic Journal of Human Sexuality, 14,* 1–9.

Tobian, A., et al. (2011). Male circumcision for the prevention of HSV-2 and HPV infections and syphilis. *New England Journal of Medicine, 360,* 1298–1309.

Tobian, A., & Gray, R. (2012). Benefits of male circumcision—Reply. *Journal of the American Medical Association, 307,* 457.

Tollison, C., & Adams, H. (1979). *Sexual disorders: Treatment, theory, research.* New York: Gardner.

Tom Tong, S., & Walther, J. B. (2011). Just say "no thanks": Romantic rejection in computer-mediated communication. *Journal of Social and Personal Relationships, 28,* 488–508.

Tomlinson, F., Raphael, H., & Mehta, R. (2006). Is androgen replacement therapy for hypogonadal men in the form of a transdermal gel (Tesogel) acceptable to patients attending a men's sexual health clinic, compared with older applications? *Journal of Sexual Medicine, 3*(Suppl. 3), 199–223.

Tomljenovic, L., & Shaw, C. (2012). Mandatory HPV vaccination. *Journal of the American Medical Association, 307,* 253–254.

Tone, A. (2002). The contraceptive conundrum. *SIECUS Report, 31,* 4–8.

Török, E., & Farrar, J. (2011). When to start antiretroviral therapy in HIV-associated tuberculosis. *New England Journal of Medicine, 365,* 1538–1540.

Torassa, U. (2000). S.F. study: HIV spread through oral sex. Retrieved February 1, 2000, from http://www.examiner.com/oral.html

Torian, L., et al. (2011). HIV surveillance—United States, 1981–2008. *Morbidity and Mortality Weekly Report, 60,* 689–693.

Torpy, J. (2003). Perimenopause: Beginning of menopause. *Journal of the American Medical Association, 289,* 940.

Torpy, J., Burke, A., & Golub, R. (2011). Hepatitis B. *Journal of the American Medical Association, 305,* 1500.

Touhara, K., & Vosshall, L. (2009). Sensing odorants and pheromones with chemosensory receptors. *Annual Review of Physiology, 71,* 307–332.

Traish, A., et al. (2011). Adverse side effects of 5-reductase inhibitors therapy: Persistent diminished libido and erectile dysfunction and depression in a subset of patients. *Journal of Sexual Medicine, 8,* 844–872.

Treas, J., & Giesen, D. (2000). Sexual infidelity among married and cohabiting Americans. *Journal of Marriage and Family, 62,* 48–60.

Treger, S., & Sprecher, S. (2011). The influences of sociosexuality and attachment style on reactions to emotional versus sexual infidelity. *Journal of Sex Research, 48,* 413–422.

Trepka, M., Kim, S., Pekovic, V., et al. (2008). High-risk sexual behavior among students of a minority-serving university in a community with a high HIV/AIDS prevalence. *Journal of American College Health, 57,* 77–84.

Trevor, C. (2002). Number of controversies decline as schools adopt conservative policies. *SIECUS Report, 30,* 4–17.

Tripoli, T., et al. (2011). Evaluation of quality of life and sexual satisfaction in women suffering from chronic pelvic pain with or without endometriosis. *Journal of Sexual Medicine, 8,* 974–503.

Tripp, C. (1975). *The homosexual matrix.* New York: McGraw-Hill.

Troiden, R. (1988). *Gay and lesbian identity: A sociological analysis.* New York: General Hall.

Trompeter, S., et al. (2012). Sexual activity and satisfaction in healthy community-dwelling older women. *American Journal of Medicine, 125,* 37–43.

Tronstein, E., et al. (2011). Genital shedding of herpes simplex virus among symptomatic and asymptomatic persons with HSV-2 infection. *Journal of the American Medical Association, 305,* 1441–1449.

Troy, A., Lewis-Smith, J., & Laurenceau, J. (2006). Interracial and intraracial romantic relationships: The search for differences in satisfaction, conflict, and attachment style. *Journal of Social and Personal Relationships, 23,* 65–80.

Trudel, G., Boyer, R., Villeneuve, V., Anderson, A., Pilon, G., & Bounader, J. (2008). The Marital Life and Aging Well Program: Effects of a group preventive intervention on the marital and sexual functioning of retired couples. *Sexual and Relationship Therapy, 23,* 5–23.

Truitt, W., & Coolen, L. (2002). Identification of a potential ejaculation generator in the spinal cord. *Science, 297,* 1566–1599.

Trussell, J., Lalla, A., Doan, Q., et al. (2009). Cost effectiveness of contraceptives in the United States. *Contraception, 79,* 5–14.

Tsai, C., Shepherd, B., & Vermund, S. (2009). Does douching increase risk for sexually transmitted infections? A prospective study in high-risk adolescents. *American Journal of Obstetrics and Gynecology, 200,* 38.e1–38.e8.

T'Sjoen, G., et al. (2010). Male gender identity in complete androgen insensitivity syndrome. *Archives of Sexual Behavior, 40,* 635–638.

Tsutsumi, A., Izutsu, T., Poudyal, A., Kato, S., & Marui, E. (2008). Mental health of female survivors of human trafficking in Nepal. *Social Science and Medicine, 66,* 1841–1847.

Tucker, C. (2011). Teen pregnancy news story earns national award for the *Nation's Health. Nation's Health, 41,* 5.

Tucker, M. (2004). Sexual desire, activity up with testosterone patch. *Family Practice News, 34,* 44.

Tucker, M. (2010). Go minimally invasive for most hysterectomies: Taking a vaginal or laparoscopic approach is best, except in a few specific, defined circumstances. *Family Practice News, 40,* 77–81.

Tucker, M. (2012, January/February). New center embraces LGBT seniors. *AARP the Magazine,* 9.

Tuiten, A., Van Honk, J., Koppeschaar, H., et al. (2000). Time course of effects of testosterone administration on sexual arousal in women. *Archives of General Psychiatry, 57,* 149–153.

Tuller, D. (2009, May 1). AIDS experts pushing for new test, strategy. *Oregonian,* p. A3.

Tumlinson, K., et al. (2011). The promise of affordable implants: Is cost recovery possible in Kenya? *Contraception, 83,* 88–93.

Tummino, A. (2006). FDA's plan B ruling doesn't end battle for access. *Women's eNews,* October 25.

Turner, A., Morrison, C., Padian, N., et al. (2007). Male circumcision and women's risk of incident chlamydial, gonococcal, and trichomonal infections. *Sexually Transmitted Diseases, 35,* 689–695.

Turner, H. (1999). Participation bias in AIDS-related telephone surveys: Results from the National AIDS Behavior Study (NABS) nonresponse study. *Journal of Sex Research, 52,* 58.

Turner, M. (2010, March 1). U.K. aims to shield kids from sexuality. *Hollywood Reporter,* pp. 6–11.

Ullman, S., & Brecklin, L. (2003). Sexual assault history and health-related outcomes in a national sample of women. *Psychology of Women Quarterly, 27,* 46–57.

Ullman, S., et al. (2007. Structural models of the relations of assault, severity, social support, avoidance coping, self-blame, and PTSD among sexual assault survivors. *Psychology of Women Quarterly, 31,* 23–27.

Ullman, S., Starzynski, L., et al. (2008). Exploring the relationships of women's sexual assault disclosure, social reactions, and problem drinking. *Journal of Interpersonal Violence, 23,* 1235–1257.

Umberson, D., Williams, K., Powers, D., & Liu, H. (2006). You make me sick: Marital quality and health over the life course. *Journal of Health and Social Behavior, 47,* 1–16.

UN Department of Public Information. (2010, September). We can end poverty: 2015 millennium development goals. New York: United Nations.

UN Office for the Coordination of Humanitarian Affairs. (2006, July 31). Pakistan: Over a thousand women freed under change in law. Retrieved July 31, 2006, from http://www.irinnews.org/print .asp?ReportID=54498

UNAIDS. (2006). *AIDS epidemic update: December 2005.* Retrieved January 16, 2006, from http://www.unaids.org/ Epi2005/doc/EPIupdate2005_html_en/ epi05_03

Underwood, C., et al. (2011). Structural determinants of adolescent girls' vulnerability to HIV: Views from community members in Botswana, Malawi, and Mozambique. *Social Science and Medicine, 73,* 343–350.

Unemo, M., et al. (2011, July). *New untreatable strain of gonorrhea found.* Paper presented at the 19th Conference of the International Society for Sexually Transmitted Disease Research, Quebec City, Canada.

United States Conference of Catholic Bishops. (2011). *The causes and context of sexual abuse of minors by Catholic priests in the United States, 1950–2010.* Retrieved May 21, 2011, from http://www.usccb.org/mr/ causes-and-context-of-sexual-abuse-of-minors-by-catholic-priests-in-the-united-states-1950-2010.pdf

UPI NewsTrack. (2011a, August 9). Date rape drug detector developed. UPI.com (e-pub).

UPI NewsTrack. (2011b, January 14). Teacher charged with bathroom voyeurism. UPI.com (e-pub).

Urman, B., & Yakin, K. (2006). Ovulatory disorders and infertility. *Journal of Reproductive Medicine, 51,* 267–282.

U.S. Attorney General's Commission on Pornography. (1986). *Final report of the Attorney General's Commission on Pornography.* Washington, DC: U.S. Justice Department.

U.S. Census Bureau. (2002). *Statistical abstract of the United States: 2002.* Washington, DC: U.S. Government Printing Office.

U.S. Census Bureau. (2006, May 25). Americans marrying older, living alone more, see households shrinking, Census Bureau reports. Retrieved August 10, 2006, from http://www.census.gov/ Press-Release/www/releases/archives/ families_households

U.S. Census Bureau. (2010, June). *Current population survey.* Retrieved November 19, 2011, from http://www.census.gov/hhes/ fertility/data/cps/2010.html

U.S. Department of Justice. (2001). *Criminal victimization in the United States: 1999 statistical tables* (NCJ 184938). Washington, DC: U.S. Government Printing Office.

U.S. Department of Justice, Bureau of Justice Statistics. (2003). *Criminal victimization, 2002.* Washington, DC: U.S. Department of Justice.

U.S. Preventive Services Task Force. (2008). Screening for prostate cancer: U.S. Preventive Services Task Force recommendation statement. *Annals of Internal Medicine, 149,* 185–189.

Usher-Seriki, K., Bynum, M., & Callands, T. (2008). Mother-daughter communication about sex and sexual intercourse among middle- to upper-class African American girls. *Journal of Family Issues, 29,* 901–917.

Valente, S., & Bullough, V. (2004). Sexual harassment of nurses in the workplace. *Journal of Nursing Care Quality, 19,* 234–241.

Valera, R., Sawyer, R., & Schiraldi, G. (2001). Perceived health needs of inner-city street prostitutes: A preliminary study. *American Journal of Health and Behavior, 25,* 50–59.

Valhouli, C. (2000, November 15). Courtesan power. Retrieved June 1, 2009, from http://archive.salon.com/ses/feature/2000/11/15/courtesan_1/print.html

Valliant, P., Gauthier, T., Pottier, D., & Kosmyna, R. (2000). Moral reasoning, interpersonal skills, and cognitions of rapists, child molesters, and incest offenders. *Psychological Reports, 86,* 67–75.

Vamos, C., McDermott, R., & Daley, E. (2008). The HPV vaccine: Framing the arguments for and against mandatory vaccination of all middle school girls. *Journal of School Health, 78,* 302–309.

Van Damme, L. (2000, July). *Advances in topical microbicides.* Paper presented at the 13th International AIDS Conference, Durban, South Africa.

Vandello, J., & Cohen, D. (2003). Male honor and female fidelity: Implicit cultural scripts that perpetuate domestic violence. *Journal of Personality and Social Psychology, 84,* 997–1010.

Van den Boogaard, N., et al. (2011). Patients' and professionals' barriers and facilitators of tailored expectant management in subfertile couples with a good prognosis of a natural conception. *Human Reproduction, 26,* 2122–2128.

Vanderdrift, L., et al. (2012). Commitment in friends with benefits relationships: Implications for relational and safe-sex outcomes. *Personal Relationships, 19,* 1–13.

Van der Voo, L., & Smith, C. (2010, June 20). Assaulted and abandoned. *Oregonian,* pp. D1, D2.

Vandeusen, K., & Carr, J. (2003). Recovery from sexual assault: An innovative two-stage group therapy model. *International Journal of Group Psychotherapy, 53,* 201–223.

Van Ecke, Y. (2007). Attachment style and dysfunctional career thoughts: How attachment style can affect the career counseling process. *Career Development Quarterly, 55,* 339–350.

Van Gelderen, L., et al. (2012). Stigmatization associated with growing up in a lesbian-parented family: What do adolescents experience and how do they deal with it? *Children and Youth Services Review.* doi:10.1016/j.childyouth.2012.01.048

Van Hook, M., Gjermeni, E., & Haxhiymeri, E. (2006). Sexual trafficking of women. *International Social Work, 49,* 29–40.

Van Howe, R. (1998). Circumcision and infectious diseases revisited. *Pediatric Infectious Diseases Journal, 17,* 1–6.

Van Howe, R., & Svoboda, J. (2008). Neonatal pain relief and the Helsinki declaration. *Journal of Law, Medicine, and Ethics, 36,* 808–823.

Van Lankveld, J. (2009). Self-help therapies for sexual dysfunction. *Journal of Sex Research, 46,* 143–155.

Van Lankveld, J., ter Kuile, M., de Groot, H., & Melles, R. (2006). Cognitive-behavioral therapy for women with lifelong vaginismus: A randomized waiting-list controlled trial of efficacy. *Journal of Consulting and Clinical Psychology, 74,* 168–178.

Vannier, S., & O'Sullivan, L. (2010, September 2). Communicating interest in sex: Verbal and nonverbal initiation of sexual activity in adults' romantic dating relationships. *Archives of Sex Research,* 1–9.

Van Straaten, I., et al. (2009). Meeting your match: How attractiveness similarity affects approach behavior in mixed-sex dyads. *Personality and Social Psychology Bulletin, 35,* 685–697.

Van Voorhis, R., & Wagner, M. (2002). Among the missing: Content on lesbian and gay people in social work journals. *Social Work, 47,* 345–354.

Van Wyk, P. (1984). Psychosocial development of heterosexual, bisexual, and homosexual behavior. *Archives of Sexual Behavior, 13,* 505–544.

Van Zeijl, F. (2006, Winter). The agony of Darfur. *Ms.,* 24–26.

Vardi, Y., McMahon, C., Waldinger, M., & Rubio-Aurioles, E. (2008). Are premature ejaculation symptoms curable? *Journal of Sexual Medicine, 5,* 1546–1551.

Vargas-Cooper, N. (2012, February 26). The billion-dollar battle over premenstrual disorder. *Salon.* Retrieved from http://www .salon.com/2012/02/26/the_billion_ dollar_battle_over_premenstrual_disorder

Vary, A. (2006, June 20). Is gay over? *Advocate,* 98–102.

Vasconcellos, D., Vion-Dury, K., & Kuntz, D. (2006). Sexuality and well-being among older women: A cross-cultural approach. *Journal of Sex Research, 43,* 9–11.

Vasquez, M. (1994). Latinas. In L. Comas-Diaz & B. Greene (Eds.), *Women of color.* New York: Guilford Press.

Vaughn, G. (2003). *Koro: A natural history of penis panics.* Retrieved March 13, 2003, from http://www.koro5hin.org/story

Vejar, C., Madison-Colmore, O., & Ter Maat, M. (2006). Understanding the transition from career to full-time motherhood: A qualitative study. *American Journal of Family Therapy, 34,* 17–31.

Vekshin, A. (2011, June 19). Circumcision referendum raises hate concerns. *Oregonian,* p. A8.

Veneman, A. (2009, April 13). Statement by UNICEF executive director Ann M. Veneman on child marriage. Retrieved May 11, 2009, from http://www.unicef.org/ media/media_49363.html

Venkatesh, S. (2011, January 13) How tech tools transformed New York's sex trade. Retrieved from http://www.wired.com/ magazine/2011/01/ff_sextrade/all/1

Vennemann, M., Bajanowski, D., & Brinkmann, B. (2009). Does breastfeeding reduce the risk of sudden infant death syndrome? *Pediatrics, 123,* 406–410.

Verheyden, B., Bitton, A., Toumeguere, T., & Roos, E. (2007, April). *Effectiveness and patient satisfaction with 6 months tadalafil treatment: Results from the Detect Study.* Paper presented at the 18th Congress of the World Association for Sexual Health, Sydney, Australia.

Verloop, J., Rookus, M., van der Kooy, K., & van Leeuwen, F. (2000). Physical activity and breast cancer risk in women aged 20–54 years. *Journal of the National Cancer Institute, 92,* 128–135.

Versteeg, K., Knopf, J., et al. (2009). Teenagers wanting medical advice: Is MySpace the answer? *Archives of Pediatrics and Adolescent Medicine, 163,* 91–92.

Voelker, R. (2011). HIV/AIDS funding dropped by 10% in 2010. *Journal of the American Medical Association, 306,* 1642–1643.

Vogel, J. (2006, October). *Understanding the controversy: Hormone testing and bioidentical hormones.* Paper presented at Proceedings from the Postgraduate Course (17th Annual Meeting of the North American Menopause Society), Nashville, TN.

Volsky, I. (2011, October 19). Rick Santorum pledges to defund contraception: "It's not okay, it's a license to do things." Retrieved from http://thinkprogress.org/health/2011/10/19/34800i7/rick-santorum-pledges-to-defund-contraception

Wade, N. (2011, January 11). Depth of kindness hormone appears to know some bounds. *New York Times,* p. D1.

Wadhawan, R., et al. (2011). Neurodevelopmental outcomes of triplets or higher-order extremely low birth weight infants. *Pediatrics, 127,* 654–660.

Waldinger, M. (2008). Premature ejaculation: Different pathophysiologies and etiologies determine its treatment. *Journal of Sex and Marital Therapy, 34,* 1–13.

Waldinger, M., & Schweitzer, D. (2006). Changing paradigms from a historical DSM-III and DSM-IV view toward an evidence-based definition of premature ejaculation. Part II. Proposals for DSM-V and ICD-11. *Journal of Sexual Medicine, 3,* 693–705.

Waldinger, M., & Schweitzer, D. (2009). Persistent genital arousal disorder in 18 Dutch women: Part II. A syndrome clustered with restless legs and overactive bladder. *Journal of Sexual Medicine, 6,* 482–512.

Waldinger, M., van Gils, A., Ottervanger, P., Wandenbroucke, W., & Tavy, D. (2009). Persistent genital arousal disorder in 18 Dutch women: Part I. MRI, EEG, and transvaginal ultrasonography investigations. *Journal of Sexual Medicine, 6,* 474–481.

Waldman, A. (2012, February 15). All the rage. Retrieved from http://www.nytimes.com/2012/02/19/t-magazine/womens-fashion/all-the-rage.html?

Wales, S., & Todd, K. (2001, May). *Sexuality and intimacy across the lifespan.* Paper presented at the 33rd Annual Conference of the American Association of Sex Educators, Counselors, and Therapists, San Francisco, CA.

Walfish, S., & Myerson, M. (1980). Sex role identity and attitudes toward sexuality. *Archives of Sexual Behavior, 9,* 199–203.

Walker, J. (2008, November). *Religion and its effects on sexuality.* Paper presented at the 18th Deutsche Gesellschaft für Sozialwissenschaftliche Sexualforschung Conference, "Sexuality and the Media," Munich, Germany.

Walker, J., Archer, J., & Davies, M. (2005). Effects of rape on men: A descriptive analysis. *Archives of Sexual Behavior, 34,* 69–80.

Wallace, B. (2011, January 30). The geek-kings of smut. Retrieved from http://nymag.com/print/?/news/features/70985/

Wallen, K., et al. (2011). Female sexual arousal: Genital anatomy and orgasm in intercourse. *Hormones and Behavior, 59,* 780–792.

Wallis, M., Daneback, K., Mansson, S., Tikkahen, R., & Cooper, A. (2003). Characteristics of men and women who complete or exit from an on-line Internet sexuality questionnaire: A study of instrument dropout bias. *Journal of Sex Research, 40,* 396–402.

Walsh, A. (1991). *The science of love: Understanding love and its effects on mind and body.* Buffalo, NY: Prometheus Books.

Walsh, J., & Ward, M. (2010). Magazine reading and involvement and young adults' sexual health knowledge, efficacy, and behaviors. *Journal of Sex Research, 47,* 285–316.

Walsh, T., Frezieres, R., & Peacock, K. (2004). Contraceptive effectiveness of male condoms high. *Reproductive Health Matters, 13,* 184–185.

Walter, M. (2012). Human experiments: First do no harm. *Nature, 482,* 148–152.

Wang, L., et al. (2011). Reversible contraceptive effect of the oviduct plug with nickel-titanium shape memory alloy and silicone rubber in rabbits. *Contraception, 83,* 373–377.

Wang, S. (2011, May 10). The tricky chemistry of attraction. *Wall Street Journal,* pp. D1, D6.

Wang, W. (2012, February 16). The rise of intermarriage: Rates, characteristics vary by race and gender. Retrieved from http://www.pewsocialtrends.org/2012/02/16/the-rise-of-intermarriage/?src=prc-headline

Warbelow, S. (2008). The speech divide: GLBT students struggle for visibility and safety. *Human Rights, 35,* 20–22.

Ward, H., & Day, S. (2006). What happens to women who sell sex? Report of a unique occupational cohort. Retrieved June 26, 2006, from http://sti.bmjjournals.com/cgi/content/abstract/sti.2006.020982v1

Ward, J. (2008). Time for renewed commitment to viral hepatitis prevention. *American Journal of Public Health, 98,* 779–781.

Warner, T., et al. (2011). Everybody's doin it (right?). Neighborhood norms and sexual activity in adolescence. *Social Science Research, 40,* 1676–1690.

Waskul, D. (Ed.). (2004). *Net.SeXXX: Readings on sex, pornography, and the Internet.* New York: Peter Lang.

Wassersug, R., & Johnson, T. (2007). Modern-day eunuchs: Motivations for and consequences of contemporary castration. *Perspectives in Biology and Medicine, 50,* 544–556.

Watson, R., & Vidal, M. (2011). "Do you see other men who do this?" Reflections upon working with men who visit commercial sex workers in a National Health Service sexual health clinic. *Sexual and Relationship Therapy, 26,* 61–67.

Watt, M., et al. (2012). "Because he has bought for her, he wants to sleep with her": Alcohol as a currency for sexual exchange in South Africa drinking venues. *Social Science and Medicine, 74,* 1005–1012.

Wawer, M., Gray, R., Sewankambo, N., et al. (2005). Rates of HIV-1 transmission per coital act, by stage of HIV-1 infection, Rakai, Uganda. *Journal of Infectious Diseases, 191,* 1403–1409.

Weber, A. (1998). Losing, leaving, and letting go: Coping with nonmarital breakups. In B. Spitzberg & W. Cupah (Eds.), *The dark side of close relationships.* Mahwah, NJ: Erlbaum.

Wegner, D., Lane, J., & Dimitri, S. (1994). The allure of secret relationships. *Journal of Personality and Social Psychology, 66,* 287–300.

Wehrfritz, G. (1996, April 1). Joining the party. *Newsweek, 46,* 48.

Weinberg, M., Williams, C., & Moser, C. (1984). The social constituents of sadomasochism. *Social Problems, 31,* 379–389.

Weinberg, T. (1987). Sadomasochism in the United States: A review of recent sociological literature. *Journal of Sex Research, 23,* 50–69.

Weinberg, T. (1995). *S & M: Studies in dominance and submission*. New York: Prometheus Books.

Weiss, J. (2001). Treating vaginismus: Patient without partner. *Journal of Sex Education and Therapy, 26,* 28–33.

Weitzer, R. (2007). The social construction of sex trafficking: Ideology and institutionalization of a moral crusade. *Politics and Society, 35*–45.

Wellings, K., Collumbien, M., Slaymaker, E., et al. (2006). Sexual behavior in context: A global perspective. *Lancet, 368,* 1706–1728.

Wendling, P. (2007). Vulvovaginal plastic surgery gains popularity. *Internal Medicine News, 40,* 30–31.

Wendling, P. (2011). Recurrent PID ups risk of adverse long-term outcomes. *Family Practice News, 41,* 34.

WeNews Staff. (2011). Cheers. Retrieved October 24, 2011, from http://www.womensnews.org/breaking-news

Wessells, H., et al. (2011). Effect of intensive glycemic therapy on erectile function in men with type 1 diabetes. *Journal of Urology, 185,* 1828–1834.

Wessells, H., Lue, T., & McAninch, J. (1996). Complications of penile lengthening and augmentation seen at one referral center. *Journal of Urology, 155,* 1617–1620.

West, D. (2000, July 12). Aftermath of incest pedophilia case: Guilt and a new awareness danger. *New York Times,* p. B5.

Westhoff, C., Heartwell, S., & Edwards, S. (2007). Oral contraceptive discontinuation: Do side effects matter. *American Journal of Obstetrics and Gynecology, 196,* 412–419.

Westwood, M. (2007). Adolescence: Hormones rule OK? *Biological Sciences Review, 19,* 2–6.

Wheeler, M. (1991). Physical changes of puberty. *Endocrinology and Metabolism Clinics of North America, 20,* 1–14.

Wheeler, M. (2003). *AIDS education through Imams.* Retrieved January 2, 2003, from http://www.unaids.org/publications/documents/sectors/religion/imamscse.pdf

Whipple, B. (2000). Beyond the G spot. *Scandinavian Journal of Sexology, 3,* 35–42.

Whipple, B., & Komisaruk, B. (1999). Beyond the G spot: Recent research on female sexuality. *Psychiatric Annals, 29,* 34–37.

Whipple, B., & Komisaruk, B. (2006). Where in the brain is a woman's sexual response? Laboratory studies including brain imaging during orgasm. *Journal of Sex Research, 43,* 29–30.

Whisman, M., & Snyder, D. (2007). Sexual infidelity in a national survey of American women: Differences in prevalence and correlates as a function of method of assessment. *Journal of Family Psychology, 21,* 147–154.

Whitaker, D., & Miller, K. (2000). Parent-adolescent discussions about sex and condoms: Impact on peer influence of sexual risk behavior. *Journal of Adolescent Research, 15,* 251–273.

Whitaker, D., Miller, K., May, D., & Levin, M. (1999). Teenage partners' communication about sexual risk and condom use: The importance of parent-teenager discussions. *Family Planning Perspectives, 31,* 117–121.

Whitchurch, E., Wilson, T., & Gilbert, D. (2011). "He loves me, he loves me not . . .": Uncertainty can increase romantic attraction. *Psychological Science, 22,* 172–175.

White, G., & Helbick, R. (1988). Understanding and treating jealousy. In R. Brown & J. Fields (Eds.), *Treatment of sexual problems in individuals and couples therapy.* Boston: PMA Publishing.

White, J. (2003, May/June). Who do you love? *Utne Reader,* 24–26.

White, R. (2012, January 11). It's not just the economy, stupid. Retrieved from http://www.thehastingscenter.org/Bioethicsforum/Post.aspx?id=5704&blogid=140&utm

Whittaker, P., et al. (2010). Withdrawal attitudes and experiences: A qualitative perspective among young urban adults. *Perspectives on Sexual and Reproductive Health, 42*(2).

Whittelsey, F. (2007, September 10). EU's hormone patch stirs uneasy debate in U.S. Retrieved September 10, 2007, from Women's eNews.

WHO/UNAIDS. (2007). Male circumcision for HIV prevention: Research implications for policy and programming. *Reproductive Health Matters, 15,* 11–14.

Wiederman, M. (2000). Women's body image self-consciousness during physical intimacy with a partner. *Journal of Sex Research, 37,* 60–68.

Wiederman, M. (2001). *Understanding sexuality research.* Belmont, CA: Wadsworth.

Wiegratz, I., Kutschera, E., Lee, J., et al. (2003). Effect of four different oral contraceptives on various sex hormones and serum-binding globulins. *Contraception, 67,* 25–32.

Wieland, U. (2012). HPV vaccine against anal intraepithelial neoplasia. *New England Journal of Medicine, 366,* 378–379.

Wiesner-Hanks, M. (2000). *Christianity and sexuality in the early modern world.* London: Routledge.

Wiest, W. (1977). Semantic differential profiles of orgasm and other experiences among men and women. *Sex Roles, 3,* 399–403.

Wiest, W., Harrison, J., Johanson, C., Laubsch, B., & Whitley, A. (1995, February 25). Paper presented at the meeting of the Oregon Academy of Sciences, Reed College, Portland, OR.

Wikstrom, A., et al. (2011). Klinefelter syndrome. *Clinical Endocrinology and Metabolism, 25,* 239–250.

Wilcox, C., & Robinson, C. (2011). *Onward Christian soldiers? The religious right in American politics* (4th ed.). Boulder, CO: Westview Press.

Wildman, S. (2001, January 16). Continental divide. *Advocate,* 47–48.

Wilhelm, D., Palmer, S., & Koopman, P. (2007). Sex determination and gonadal development in mammals. *Physiological Reviews, 87,* 1–27.

Wilkes, D. (2006). Clinical: GP involvement in fertility treatment. *GP,* January 20, 30.

Willford, J., Leech, S., & Day, N. (2006). Moderate prenatal alcohol exposure and cognitive status of children at age 10. *Alcoholism: Clinical and Experimental Research, 30,* 1051–1059.

Williams, A. (2008, October 5). Hopelessly devoted to you, you, and you. *New York Times,* p. 9L.

Williams, C., & Weinberg, M. (2003). Zoophilia in men: A study of sexual interest in animals. *Archives of Sexual Behavior, 32,* 523–535.

Williams, D., & D'Alessandro, J. (1994). A comparison of three measures of androgyny and their relationship to psychological adjustment. *Journal of Social Behavior and Personality, 9,* 469–480.

Williams, J., & Best, D. (1990). *Measuring sex stereotypes: A multinational study.* Newbury Park, CA: Sage.

Williams, J., Zenilman, J., Nanda, J., & Mark, H. (2008). Recruitment strategies and motivations for sexually transmitted disease testing among college students. *Journal of American College Health, 57,* 357–360.

Williams, L. (1994). Recall of childhood trauma: A prospective study of women's memories of child sexual abuse. *Journal of Consulting and Clinical Psychology, 62,* 1167–1176.

Williams, S. (2000, April 24). A new smoking peril. *Newsweek,* 78.

Williams, Z., Litscher, E., Darie, C., & Wassarman, P. (2006). Rational design of pregnancy vaccine. *Obstetrics and Gynecology, 107*(Suppl.), 14S–15S.

Willoughby, B., Malik, N., & Lindahl, K. (2006). Parental reactions to their sons' sexual orientation disclosures: The roles of family cohesion, adaptability, and parenting style. *Psychology of Men and Masculinity, 7*, 14–26.

Willoughby, B., & Vitas, J. (2011). Sexual desire discrepancy: The effect of individual differences in desired and actual sexual frequency on dating couples. *Archives of Sexual Behavior*, May 14 (e-pub).

Wilson, B., & Lawson, D. (1976). Effects of alcohol on sexual arousal in women. *Journal of Abnormal Psychology, 85*, 489–497.

Wilson, E., & Koo, H. (2008). Associations between low-income women's relationship characteristics and their contraceptive use. *Perspectives on Sexual and Reproductive Health, 40*, 171–179.

Wilson, J. (2003). *Biological foundations of human behavior.* Belmont, CA: Wadsworth/Thomson Learning.

Wilson, M., Kastrinakis, M., D'Angelo, L., & Getson, P. (1994). Attitudes, knowledge, and behavior regarding condom use in urban black adolescent males. *Adolescence, 29*, 13–26.

Wimpissinger, F., et al. (2009). Magnetic resonance imaging of female prostate pathology. *Journal of Sexual Medicine, 6*, 1704–1711.

Wind, R. (2006, May 4). A tale of two Americas for women. Retrieved May 10, 2006, from http://www.guttmacher.org/media/mr/2006/05/05/index.html

Winer, R., Hughes, J., Feng, Q., & O'Reilly, S. (2006). Condom use and the risk of genital human papillomavirus infection in young women. *New England Journal of Medicine, 354*, 2645–2654.

Winik, L. (2008, October 5). The truth about teen pregnancy. *Parade Magazine, 6.*

Winskell, K., Obyerodhyambo, D., & Stephenson, R. (2011). Making sense of condoms: Social representations in young people's HIV-related narratives from six African countries. *Social Science and Medicine, 72*, 953–961.

Winters, S. (1999). Current status of testosterone replacement therapy in men. *Archives of Family Medicine, 8*, 257–263.

Wischmann, T., Scherg, H., Strowitzki, T., & Verres, R. (2009). Psychosocial characteristics of women and men attending infertility counseling. *Human Reproduction, 24*, 378–385.

Wise, N. (2006, June/July). *Polyamory and other forms of negotiated non-monogamy: A crash course for the curious.* Paper presented at the Gumbo Sexualité Upriver: Spicing Up Education and Therapy (AASECT 38th Annual Conference), St. Louis, MO.

Wisniewski, A., Prendeville, M., & Dobs, A. (2005). Handedness, functional cerebral hemispheric lateralization, and cognition in male-to-female transsexuals receiving cross-sex hormone treatment. *Archives of Sexual Behavior, 34*, 167–172.

Witting, K., Santtila, P., & Alanko, K. (2008). Female sexual function and its associations with number of children, pregnancy, and relationship satisfaction. *Journal of Sex and Marital Therapy, 34*, 89–106.

Witting, K., Santtila, P., & Varjonen, M. (2008). Female sexual dysfunction, sexual distress, and compatibility with partner. *Journal of Sexual Medicine, 5*, 2587–2599.

Wolak, J., Finkelhor, D., et al. (2008). Online "predators" and their victims: Myths, realities, and implications for prevention and treatment. *American Psychologist, 63*, 111–128.

Wolf, J., & Ripley, W. (2012, February 4). 4 students' phones seized in sexting investigation. Retrieved from http://www.9news.com/cleanpring/?unique=1329882381390

Wolfers, J. (2010, October 24). The economy is hurting marriage rates? Not so fast . . . *Sunday Oregonian*, p. E2.

Wolfson, E. (2005). Ending marriage discrimination: America in a civil rights moment. *SIECUS Report, 33*, 13–18.

Wolitzky-Taylor, K., et al. (2011). Is reporting of rape on the rise? A comparison of women with reported versus unreported rape experiences in the National Women's Study—Replication. *Journal of Interpersonal Violence, 26*, 807–832.

Women on Words and Images. (1972). *Dick and Jane as victims.* Princeton, NJ: Author.

Wong, E. (2010, May 23). Chinese swinger's prison sentence raises privacy issues. *Sunday Oregonian*, p. A9.

Wong, J., Gunthard, H., Havlir, D., et al. (1997, January). *Reduction of HIV in blood and lymph nodes after potent antiretroviral therapy.* Paper presented at the 4th Conference on Retroviruses and Other Opportunistic Infections, Washington, DC.

Wong, W., Holroyd, E., Gray, A., & Ling, D. (2006). Female street sex workers in Hong Kong: Moving beyond sexual health. *Journal of Women's Health, 15*, 390–399.

Woo, J., Brotto, L., & Gorzalka, B. (2011). The role of sex guilt in the relationship between culture and women's sexual desire. *Archives of Sexual Behavior, 40*, 385–394.

Wood, A., Drazen, J., & Greene, M. (2012). The politics of emergency contraception. *New England Journal of Medicine, 366*, 101–102.

Wood, G., & Ruddock, E. (1918). *Vitalogy.* Chicago: Vitalogy Association.

Wood, H., & Elder, J. (2009). Cryptorchidism and testicular cancer: Separating fact from fiction. *Journal of Urology, 181*, 452–461.

Wood, K., Becker, J., & Thompson, K. (1996). Body image dissatisfaction in preadolescent children. *Journal of Applied Developmental Psychology, 17*, 85–100.

Woodhams, J., et al. (2012). Leadership in multiple perpetrator stranger rape. *Journal of Interpersonal Violence, 27*, 728–752.

Woodward, S. (2003, September 7). Him, her—and the Internet. *Oregonian*, pp. L1, L8.

Woolf, L. (2001). Gay and lesbian aging. *SIECUS Report, 30*, 16–21.

Worcester, S. (2012). Viral shedding persists despite HSV-2 therapy. *Skin and Allergy News, 43*, 32–33.

Worden, M., & Worden, B. (1998). *The gender dance in couples therapy.* Pacific Grove, CA: Brooks/Cole.

Workman, J., & Freeburg, E. (1999). An examination of date rape, victim dress, and perceiver variables within the context of attribution theory. *Sex Roles, 41*, 261–277.

Workowski, K., et al. (2010). Sexually transmitted diseases treatment guidelines, 2010. *Morbidity and Mortality Weekly Report, 59*, 1–110.

World Health Organization. (2009). *Maternal mortality in 2005: Estimates developed by WHO, UNICEF, UNFPA and the World Bank.* Geneva: Author.

Worobey, M., Telfer, P., Souqviere, S., et al. (2010). Island biogeography reveals the deep history of SIV. *Science, 329*, 1487.

Worthman, C. (1999). Faster, farther, higher: Biology and the discourses on human sexuality. In D. Suggs & A. Miracle (Eds.), *Culture, biology, and sexuality.* Athens: University of Georgia Press.

Wright, A., & Katz, I. (2006). Home testing for HIV. *New England Journal of Medicine, 354*, 437–440.

Wright, K. (2011, March/April). How to take feedback. *Psychology Today*, pp. 55–62.

Wright, R., Frost, C., & Turok, D. (2012). A qualitative exploration of emergency contraception users' willingness to select the copper IUD. *Contraception, 86*, 32–35.

Wyand, F., & Arrindell, D. (2005). Understanding human papillomavirus and cervical cancer. *SIECUS Report, 33,* 13–15.

Wyatt, G. (1997). *Stolen women: Reclaiming our sexuality, taking back our lives.* New York: Wiley.

Wyatt, T. (2003). *Pheromones and animal behavior: Communication by smell and taste.* New York: Cambridge University Press.

Wylie, M., & Hellstrom, W. (2011). The link between penile hypersensitivity and premature ejaculation. *British Journal of Urology, 107,* 452–457.

Wynton, J. (2011). MySpace, yourspace, but not theirspace: The constitutionality of banning sex offenders from social networking sites. *Duke Law Journal, 60,* 1859–1903.

Wysocki, D., & Childers, C. (2011). "Let my fingers do the talking": Sexting and infidelity in cyberspace. *Sexuality and Culture.* doi:10.1007/s12119-011-9091-4

Yang, M., Fullwood, E., Goldstein, J., & Mink, J. (2005). Masturbation in infancy and early childhood presenting as a movement disorder: 12 cases and a review of the literature. *Pediatrics, 116,* 1427–1452.

Yarab, P., & Allgeier, E. (1998). Don't even think about it: The role of sexual fantasies as perceived unfaithfulness in heterosexual dating relationships. *Journal of Sex Education and Therapy, 23,* 246–254.

Yared, R. (2004, May). AIDS rate surges in people 50+. *AARP Bulletin,* 2.

Yarian, D., & Anders, S. (2006, June/July). *Tantra and sex therapy: Convergence of ancient wisdom and modern sexology—A didactic and experiential workshop.* Paper presented at the Gumbo Sexualité Upriver: Spicing Up Education and Therapy (AASECT 38th Annual Conference), St. Louis, MO.

Yates, A., & Wolman, W. (1991). Aphrodisiacs: Myth and reality. *Medical Aspects of Human Sexuality,* December, 58–64.

Yekenkurul, S. (2007, April). *Benefits of Tantric sacred sexuality.* Paper presented at the 18th Congress of the World Association for Sexual Health, Sydney, Australia.

Ying, Y., & Han, M. (2008). Cultural orientation in Southeast Asian and American young adults. *Cultural Diversity and Ethnic Minority Psychology, 14,* 138–146.

Yoshida, K., & Busby, D. (2012). Intergenerational transmission effects on relationship satisfaction: A cross-cultural study. *Journal of Family Issues, 33,* 202–222.

Yost, M., & Thomas, G. (2012). Gender and binegativity: Men's and women's attitudes toward male and female bisexuals. *Archives of Sexual Behavior, 41,* 691–702.

Young, A. (2008). The state is still in the bedroom of the nation: The control and regulation of sexuality in Canadian criminal law. *Canadian Journal of Human Sexuality, 17,* 203–218.

Young, A., Grey, M., Abbey, A., et al. (2008). Alcohol-related sexual assault victimization among adolescents: Prevalence, characteristics, and correlates. *Journal of Studies on Alcohol and Drugs, 69,* 39–48.

Young, L. (2009). Being human: Love—Neuroscience reveals all. *Nature, 457,* 148–149.

Younger, J. (2011, March 6). Authorities increasingly patrol alleys of MySpace, chat rooms to track crime. *Arizona Daily Star.*

Yount, K., & Abraham, B. (2007). Female genital cutting and HIV/AIDS among Kenyan women. *Studies in Family Planning, 38,* 73–88.

Yuan, W., Basso, O., & Sorensen, H. (2001). Maternal prenatal lifestyle factors and infectious disease in early childhood: A follow-up study of hospitalization within a Danish birth cohort. *Pediatrics, 107,* 357–362.

Yuan, W., Steffensen, F., & Nielsen, G. (2000). A population-based cohort study of birth and neonatal outcome in older primipara. *International Journal of Gynecology and Obstetrics, 68,* 113–118.

Yunzal-Butler, C., Sackoff, J., & Li, W. (2011). Medication abortions among New York City residents, 2001–2008. *Perspectives on Sexual and Reproductive Health, 43*(4), 218–223.

Yuxin, P., Petula, S., & Lun, N. (2007). Studies on women's sexuality in China since 1980: A critical review. *Journal of Sex Research, 44,* 202–211.

Zafar, A. (2010). The year without sex. Retrieved July 2, 2010, from http://www.theatlantic.com/culture/print/2010/06/the-year-without-sex/58592/

Zak, A., & McDonald, C. (1997). Satisfaction and trust in intimate relationships: Do lesbians and heterosexual women differ? *Psychological Reports, 80,* 904–906.

Zakaib, G. (2011). Science gender gap probed. *Nature, 470,* 153.

Zambrana, R., & Scrimshaw, S. (1997). Maternal psychosocial factors associated with substance use in Mexican-origin and African American low-income pregnant women. *Pediatric Nursing, 23*(3), 253–254.

Zaviacic, M., & Whipple, B. (1993). Update on the female prostate and the phenomenon of female ejaculation. *Journal of Sex Research, 30,* 148–151.

Zayas, V., et al. (2011). Roots of adult attachment: Maternal caregiving at 18 months predicts adult peer and partner attachment. *Social Psychology and Personality Science, 2,* 289–297.

Zeger, M., et al. (2011). Prospective study confirms oxandrolone-associated improvement in height in growth hormone-treated adolescent girls with Turner's syndrome. *Hormone Research in Pediatrics, 75,* 38–46.

Zeliadt, S., et al. (2011, May). *Costs and sequela following PSA testing among healthy insured men in the U.S.* Paper presented at the Annual Meeting of the American Urological Association, Washington, DC.

Zelkowitz, R. (2009). HPV casts a wider shadow. *Science, 323,* 580–581.

Zelnick, M., & Kantner, J. (1977). Sexual and contraceptive experiences of young unmarried women in the United States, 1976 and 1971. *Family Planning Perspectives, 9,* 55–71.

Zelnick, M., & Kantner, J. (1980). Sexual activity, contraceptive use, and pregnancy among metropolitan-area teenagers: 1971–1979. *Family Planning Perspectives, 12,* 230–237.

Zenilman, J. (2006). The state of condom use education in a Texas community: Is this the future? *Sexually Transmitted Diseases, 33,* 5.

Zhang, X., & Jin, B. (2007). The role of seminal vesicles in male reproduction and sexual function. *Zhonghua Nan Ke Xue,* December, 1113–1116.

Zhang, X., et al. (2011). Trends in in-hospital newborn male circumcision—United States, 1999–2010. *Morbidity and Mortality Weekly Report, 60,* 1167–1168.

Zhang, Y., Miller, L., & Harrison, K. (2008). The relationship between exposure to sexual music videos and young adults' sexual attitudes. *Journal of Broadcasting and Electronic Media, 52,* 368–387.

Zhou, J., Hofman, M., Gooren, L., & Swaab, D. (1995). A sex difference in the human brain and its relation to transsexuality. *Nature, 378,* 68–70.

Zhu, T., Korber, B., Nahmias, A., Hooper, E., Sharp, P., & Ho, D. (1998). An African HIV-1 sequence from 1959 and implications for the origin of the epidemic. *Nature, 391,* 594–597.

Zhu, Y., et al. (2011). New N staging system of penile cancer provides a better reflection of prognosis. *Journal of Urology, 186,* 518–523.

Zielinski, L. (2006, Winter). Jane Doe's choice. *Ms.,* 69–71.

Zilbergeld, B. (1978). *Male sexuality: A guide to sexual fulfillment.* Boston: Little, Brown.

Zilbergeld, B. (1992). *The new male sexuality.* New York: Bantam Books.

Zimmerman, C., Hossain, M., & Watts, C. (2011). Human trafficking and health: A conceptual model to inform policy, intervention and research. *Social Science and Medicine, 73*, 327–335.

Zimmerman, C., Yun, K., Shvab, I., & Watts, C. (2003). *The health risks and consequences of trafficking in women and adolescents: Findings from a European study.* London: London School of Hygiene and Tropical Medicine (LSHTM).

Zimmerman, R., Cupp, P., Donohew, L., et al. (2008). Effects of a school-based, theory-driven HIV and pregnancy prevention curriculum. *Perspectives on Sexual and Reproductive Health, 40*, 42–51.

Zimmerman, R., Noar, S., Feist-Prince, S., et al. (2007). Longitudinal test of a multiple domain model of adolescent condom use. *Journal of Sex Research, 44*, 380–394.

Zlidar, V. (2000). Helping women use the pill. *Population Reports, 28*, 1–28.

Zohdy, W., Ghazi, S., & Arafa, M. (2011). Impact of varicocelectomy on gonadal and erectile functions in men with hypogonadism and infertility. *Journal of Sexual Medicine, 8*, 885–893.

Zoucha-Jensen, J., & Coyne, A. (1993). The effects of resistance strategies on rape. *American Journal of Public Health, 83*, 1633–1634.

Zuloaga, D., Puts, D., et al. (2008). The role of androgen receptors in the masculinization of brain and behavior: What we've learned from the testicular feminization mutation. *Hormones and Behavior, 53*, 613–626.

Zwickl, S., & Merriman, G. (2011). The association between childhood sexual abuse and adult female sexual difficulties. *Sexual and Relationship Therapy, 26*, 16–32.

Author Index

Subject Index

Note: Page numbers with *f* indicate figures; those with *t* indicate tables.

Biting lice, 458
Black sexuality during slavery, 15–16
Blastocyst, 68, 329, 329f
Blindness, 410
Bloody show, 336
Bondage, 493, 494
The Book of Virtues (Bennett), 266
Books, gender roles and, 138
Brain
  chemicals, 186
    sex differentiation of, 117–119, 117f
    sexual arousal and, 146, 148–150
Brazil, cosmetic surgery in, 415
Breaking the bag of waters, 336
Breast cancer, 82–84
  breast self-exam, 79–80, 79f
  inflammatory, 80
  reconstructive breast surgery, 83
  risk factors for, 82–83, 82t
  screening, 80–81
  treatments, 83
Breast-feeding, 338–339
Breast ironing, 524
Breast lumps, 81–82
Breasts, 77–84, 78f
  breast cancer, 82–84
  breast lumps, 81–82
  breast self-exam, 79–80, 79f
  nipple, 78
  size and shape of, variations in, 78–79
Breast self-examination (BSE), 79–80, 79f
Bris, 88–89
British Broadcasting Corporation (BBC)
  Internet survey, 174
Brokeback Mountain, 268, 270
Brothel, 554–555
Buck v. Bell, 304
Bulbourethral glands, 95f, 96
Bush, Laura, 267
Butt-enhancing cosmetic surgery, 415
"By default" myth, 254

Cain, Herman, 535
Calendar (or rhythm) method, 285t, 286t, 303
Calvin, John, 14
Camp towns, 556
Cancer, 408
Candida albicans, 456–457
Candidiasis, 436t, 456–457
  incidence and transmission, 456–457
  symptoms, 457
  treatment, 457
Cantharides as aphrodisiac, 155
Can You Be a Porn Star?, 550
Carey, Mary, 550
Casanova, Giovanni, 279
Case studies, 31–33, 32t
Castration, 89, 158

Catholics, 6
Catholics for Choice, 326
Cavernous bodies, penile, 87, 88f
CCR5-32 gene, 468
CD4 lymphocytes, 460–461
Celibacy, 12, 226–227
Cell phones, sexual self-expression and, 25
Censorship, freedom of speech *vs.*, 546
Center for Genetics and Society, 318
Center for Reproductive Rights, 363
Centers for Disease Control and Prevention
  (CDC), 339, 435
Cerebral cortex, 117f, 118, 148, 148f
Cerebral hemispheres, 117, 117f, 118
Cerebral palsy (CP), 410
Cerebrum, 117f, 118
Cervical barrier devices, 297–299, 298f
Cervical cancer, 76, 77
Cervical cap, 285t, 286t, 297–299, 298f
Cervix, 62
Cesarean section (C-section), 336–337
Chancre, 442–443, 443f, 444
Cheating, 386, 387
Chemical balance of vagina, 61–62
Chemistry of love, 186–187
The Chemistry of Love (Liebowitz), 186
Chicago, Judy, 50
Childbirth, 335–337
  contemporary, 335–336
  multiple births, 315, 317, 319
  stages of, 336–337, 337f
Childbirth, after, 338–340
  breast-feeding, 338–339
  sexual interaction after childbirth,
    339–340
Child Exploitation and Obscenity
  Section, 555
Childhood sexuality, 344–348
  masturbation, 345, 346–347
  negative childhood learning, 411
  sex play, 347–348
  sexual behavior during, 343–348, 346t
Child marriage, 378–380
Child molestation, 524–525
Child pornography, 545
Children, trafficking in prostitution,
  556–558
Child sexual abuse, 524–533
  abusers, characteristics of, 525–526
  breast ironing, 524
  children who reveal abuse, 533
  cyberspace pedophiles, 529–530
  defined, 524
  effects of, 530–531
  incest, 524–525
  pedophilia or child molestation, 524–525
  prevalence of, 526–527
  preventing, 531–532
  recovered memories of, 528–529

China
  abortion in, 9
  contraception in, 281
  cosmetic surgery in, 415
  HIV and, 9
  sex education programs in, 21–22
  sexuality and, 8–9
China Sex Museum, 9
Chlamydia, 435t, 438–439, 439f
  incidence and transmission, 438
  symptoms and complications, 438–439
  treatment, 439
Chlamydia trachomatis, 438, 439, 440, 441
Cho, Margaret, 6
Christian traditions, sexuality and, 6, 12–13
Chromosomal sex, 113f, 114
Chronic illness, 407, 408–409
  cancer, 408
  diabetes, 408
  enhancement strategies, 411
  multiple sclerosis, 408–409
  strokes, 409
Cialis, 155, 426
Cilia, 95
Cingulate gyrus, 148, 148f
Circumcision, 102–104, 102f
  criminalizing in San Francisco, 103
  cultural beliefs and practices, 88–89, 89f
Civil Rights Act of 1964, 265
Clementi, Tyler, 361
Client-Centered Therapy (Rogers), 205
Climacteric, 71–72
Clinton, Bill, 10, 26, 265, 267
Clitoridectomy, 55
Clitoris, 54–55, 54f, 116f, 117t
Cloacal exstrophy, 126–127
Cocaine
  as aphrodisiac, 155, 156t
  sexual difficulties and, 408t
Coercive paraphilias, 496–502
  exhibitionism, 497–498
  frotteurism, 501
  necrophilia, 502
  vs. noncoercive, 490
  obscene phone calls, 498–499
  summary of, 489t
  voyeurism, 499–501
  zoophilia, 501–502
Cohabitation, 375–376, 375f
Coitus and coital positions, 243
  college students on favorite position, 243t
  face-to-face, side-lying intercourse
    position, 244, 245f
  man-above, face-face intercourse
    position, 244f
  rear-entry intercourse position, 246f
  tailgate position, 244, 245f
  Tantric sex, 245–246
  woman-above intercourse position, 244f